standard catalog of®

PONTIAC

1926-2002 **2nd Edition**

John Gunnell

Published by

**krause
publications**

700 E. State Street • Iola, WI 54990-0001
Telephone: 715/445-2214

Please call or write for our free catalog.
Our toll-free number to place an order or obtain a free catalog is 800-258-0929.

Library of Congress Catalog Number: 95-79461
ISBN: 0-87349-263-3

Printed in the United States of America

On The Cover:

Back Cover: 1955 Pontiac Star Chief Custom two-door Safari. (OCW)
Front Cover: 1927 Pontiac. (OCW)
 1955 Pontiac Star Chief two-door hardtop. (OCW)
 1995 Pontiac Grand Prix 300 GXP. (OCW)
Title Page: 1988 Pontiac Fiero Formula. (OCW)

CONTENTS

1936 Pontiac Deluxe Six cabriolet. (OCW)

1967 Pontiac Firebird coupe. (OCW)

1949 Pontiac Chieftain Deluxe Eight two-door convertible. (OCW)

1985 Pontiac Bonneville Brougham four-door sedan. (P)

FOREWORD

The concept behind Krause Publications' Standard Catalog of® series is to compile massive amounts of information about motor vehicles and present it in a standard format which the hobbyist, collector, or professional dealer can use to answer some commonly asked questions. These questions include: What year, make, and model is the vehicle? What did it sell for when new? Is it original or modified? How rare is it? What is special about it? How much is it worth today? Illustrations in the catalogs provide some answers, while the data charts and text present others.

The standardized format presents the following data: (1) a description of the vehicle; (2) where available, a list of standard factory equipment; (3) vehicle and/or engine identification codes and advice on how to interpret these; (4) a chart containing model codes, type descriptions, original retail price, original shipping weight, and available production totals; (5) engine specifications; (6) a concise description of chassis features; (7) technical information regarding the drivetrain and running gear; (8) option lists or a description of accessories seen on vehicles in original period photos; (9) a "thumbnail" history of the vehicle and/or manufacturer; and (10) a price guide for vehicles up to 1994 located at the end of the book featuring data from the *Old Cars Price Guide*.

Chester L. Krause of Krause Publications is responsible for the basic concept of creating the *Standard Catalog of American Cars* series. Automotive historian David V. Brownell undertook preliminary work on the concept while editing *Old Cars Weekly* in the 1970s. John A. Gunnell edited the first of the *Standard Catalogs of American Cars*. Standard Catalogs are not history books, encyclopedias, or repair manuals for motor vehicle enthusiasts. They are intended to be collector's guides, much like the popular spotter's guides, buyer's digests, and pricing guides, but utilize a large size, broad scope, and deluxe format. They represent the accumulated efforts of many talented individuals including automotive historians, enthusiasts who lend their expertise, editors, and a production team that transforms piles of facts, figures, and photos into a finished book.

All of the catalogs published to date reflect this unique balance between professional researchers and the materials compiled by hobbyists that possess specialized knowledge regarding their favorite marques. A continuing goal for all future Standard Catalogs is to coordinate efforts so that each section in the book will represent both the skilled prose of a professional writer and the in-depth knowledge, expertise, and enthusiasm of the hobbyist. All automotive enthusiasts are potential contributors to the series, and are encouraged to maintain an ongoing file of new research, corrections to the current Standard Catalog edition, and additional photos that can be used to refine, update, and expand future editions. (All materials received will be returned!)

The long-range goal of Krause Publications is to publish a series of catalogs that are as near to perfect as possible. The feedback and participation of hobby experts is critical to the achievement of this goal. We intend to provide enthusiasts with hours of enjoyable reading, dependable guides in the search for vehicle acquisitions, and essential references when journeying to car shows, wrecking yards, and swap meets. Our diligent efforts combined with the accumulated knowledge of experts will make this goal a reality.

To submit information for future editions, contact:
Krause Publications
Automotive Books
700 E. State St.
IOLA, WI 54990-0001
(800) 258-0929
www.krause.com

To receive a free products catalog, contact:
Krause Publications
Products Catalog
700 E. State St.
IOLA, WI 54990-0001
(800) 258-0929
www.krause.com

1923 Oakland Model 6-44 roadster. (JAG)

1957 Pontiac Star Chief two-door Custom Safari station wagon. (JL)

ABBREVIATIONS

ABS	Antilock Braking System	ETS	Enhanced Traction System	OHV	overhead valve
AC	air Conditioning	FI	fuel injection	Nov.	November
APV	all purpose vehicle	Ft	foot/feet	P	passenger(s)
Aug.	August	FWD	front wheel drive	PMD	Pontiac Motor Div.
Auto	automatic transmission	Gal.	Gallons	PRNDL	park-reverse-nuetral-drive-low
AWD	all wheel drive	GP	Grand Prix	R	reverse (3F/1R)
Bonn.	Bonneville	Hi-fi	high-fidelity	RWB	regular wheelbase
BOP	Buick-Pontiac-Oldsmobile	H.O.	High-output	Rds	roadster
Bus.	business	HP	horsepower	RDS	radio data system
Cabr.	cabriolet	HT	hardtop	Rpm	revolutions per minute
CD	compact disc	HUD	heads-up display	R/S	rumbleseat
CID	cubic inch displacement	HVAC	heating, ventilation and air conditioning system	RWD	rear wheel drive
Co.	company			RWL	raised white letter (tire)
CPC	Chevrolet-Pontiac-GM of Canada	I-4	Inline four-cylinder engine	RWOL	raised white outline letter (tire)
Cpe	coupe	I-6	Inline six-cylinder engine	Safari	station wagon
cu. in.	cubic inch	I-8	Inline eight-cylinder engine	SBR	steel belted radial (tires)
Cus.	custom	I.D.	identification	Sed	sedan
D	door (2d, 4d)	In.	inch(es)	Sept.	September
Dec.	December	Jan.	January	SD	Super Deluxe
Del.	deluxe	L	L-head engine	SFI	sequential fuel injection
Div	division	L-4	Same as I-4	SLA	short/long arm suspension
DOHC	double overhead cam	L-6	Flathead six-cylinder engine	Spl	special
DRL	daytime running lamps	L-8	Flathead eight-cylinder engine	Spt	sport
EFI	electronic fuel injection	Lan	landau	Sta Wag	station wagon (Safari)
ETC	electronic transmission control	LCD	liquid crystal display	Std	standard
EWB	extended wheelbase	Lbs.-ft.	foot-pounds	SUV	sport utility vehicle
F	forward (3F/1R)	LWB	long wheelbase	SWB	short wheelbase
PGMC	Pontiac-GMC Div.	MFI	multiport fuel injection	T & B	Truck & Bus (factory)
In.	inch(es)	Mich.	Michigan	THM	Turbo-Hydra-Matic transmission
Cabr.	Cabriolet	MPG	miles per gallon	Trg	touring
Cat	Catalina	MPH	miles per hour	US	United States
CFI	Crossfire fuel injection	MPV	multi purpose vehicle	V	V-shaped
Co.	company	MVSS	Motor Vehicle Safety Standard	VV	Vision & Ventilation
Conv	convertible	NACC	National Automobile Chamber of Commerce	V-6	six-cylinder V-block engine
Cpe.	Coupe			V-8	eight-cylinder V-block engine
Cu. in.	cubic inches	NASCAR	National Association of Stock Car Auto Racing	Wag	wagon
Cyl.	Cylinder			3F/1R	three forward/one reverse
Del.	Deluxe	NHP	net horsepower	4F/1R	four forward/one reverse
DIC	Driver Information Center	No.	number		
DIV	Division	Nos.	numbers		
EBD	electronic brakeforce distribution	Oct.	October		
EGR	exhaust gas recirculation	OHC	overhead cam		

Factory prices are in dollars
Factory weights are in lbs.
No periods used in abbreviations used in tables

PHOTO CREDITS

AA	Applegate & Applegate	JG	Jesse Gunnell
CP	Crestline Publishing	JH	Jerry Heasley
HAC	Henry Austin Clark, Jr.	OCW	*Old Cars Weekly*, Krause Publications Collection
IMSC	Indianapolis Motor Speedway Corp.	PGMC	Pontiac-GMC Division, General Motors
JAC	John A. Conde	RK	Ron Kowalke
JAG	John A. Gunnell Collection		

HOW TO USE THIS CATALOG

APPEARANCE AND EQUIPMENT: Word descriptions help identify trucks down to details such as styling features, trim and interior appointments. Standard equipment lists usually begin with low-priced base models. Then, subsequent data blocks cover higher-priced lines of the same year.

VEHICLE I.D. NUMBERS: This edition features expanded data explaining the basic serial numbering system used by each postwar vehicle manufacturer. This data reveals where, when and in what order your vehicle was built. There is much more information on assembly plant, body style and original engine codes.

SPECIFICATIONS CHART: The first chart column gives series or model numbers for trucks. The second column gives body type. The third column tells factory price. The fourth column gives GVW. The fifth column gives the vehicle's original shipping weight. The sixth column provides model year production totals (if available) or makes reference to additional notes found below the specifications chart. When the same vehicle came with different engines or trim levels at different prices and weights, slashes (/) are used to separate the low price or weight from the high one. In some cases, model numbers are also presented this way. In rare cases where data is non-applicable or not available the abbreviation "N.A." appears.

BASE ENGINE DATA: According to make of vehicle, engine data will be found either below the data block for each series or immediately following the specifications chart for the last vehicle-line. Displacement, bore and stroke and horsepower ratings are listed, plus a lot more data where available. This edition has more complete engine listings for many models. In other cases, extra-cost engines are listed in the "options" section.

VEHICLE DIMENSIONS: The main data compiled here consists of wheelbase, overall length and tire size. Front and rear tread widths are given for most trucks through the early 1960s and some later models. Overall width and height appears in some cases, too.

OPTIONAL EQUIPMENT LISTS: This section includes data blocks listing all types of options and accessories. A great deal of attention has been focused on cataloging both the availability and the original factory retail prices of optional equipment. Because of size and space limitations, a degree of selectivity has been applied by concentrating on those optional features of greatest interest to collectors. Important option packages have been covered and detailed as accurately as possible in the given amount of space. When available, options prices are listed.

HISTORICAL FOOTNOTES: Trucks are already recognized as an important part of America's automotive heritage. Revealing statistics; important dates and places; personality profiles; performance milestones; and other historical facts are highlighted in this "automotive trivia" section.

SEE PRICING SECTION IN BACK OF BOOK.

DELUXE - SERIES 8BA - EIGHT: The Pontiac Deluxe Eight had the company's longest wheelbase. The extra length was taken up in the hood and runningboards. Fenders varied slightly in the manner in which they overlapped the cowl, but were actually the same with the attachment holes drilled differently. The words "Pontiac 8" appeared on the grille and the hood ornament was a distinctive, circular design instead of the oblong loop style used on sixes. Standard sedan equipment included front and rear arm rests, twin assist straps, oriental grain interior moldings and a dash mounted clock. The eight had "Knee-Action" front suspension, a pressurized cooling system, automatic choke and a new type of clutch.

I.D. DATA: [Series 6BB] Serial numbers were located on top of frame just ahead of steering gear. Starting: 6BB-1001. Ending: 6BB-91362. Pacific Coast numbers were C-1001 to C-1400. Bench seat cars had an "AB" prefix instead of "BB". Engine numbers located on left side of crankcase and on front left corner of cylinder block. Starting: 6-84001. Ending: 6-219182. [Series 6BA] Serial numbers were in the same location. Starting: 6BA-1001. Ending: 6BA-41352. Pacific Coast numbers were C-1001 to C-1300. Engine numbers were in the same location. Starting: 6-84001. Ending: 6-219182. [Series 8BA] Serial numbers were in the same location. Starting: 8BA-1001. Ending: 8BA-38371. Pacific Coast numbers were C-1001 to C-1260. Engine numbers were in the same locations. Starting: 8-44001. Ending: 8-82040.

Model No.	Body Type & Seating	Price	Weight	Prod. Total
8BA	2-dr. Cpe.-2P	730	3250	Note 1
8BA	2-dr. Spt. Cpe.-2/4P	785	3285	Note 1
8BA	2-dr. Cabr.-2/4P	855	3335	Note 1
8BA	2-dr. Sed.-5P	770	3390	Note 1
8BA	2-dr. Tr. Sed.-5P	795	3390	Note 1
8BA	4-dr. Sed.-5P	815	3415	Note 1
8BA	4-dr. Tr. Sed.-5P	840	3420	Note 1

Note 1: Total series production was 38,755.

ENGINE: [Series 6BB] Inline. L-head. Six. Cast iron block. Bore & Stroke: 3-3/8 in. x 3-7/8 in. Displacement: 208 cu. in. Compression Ratio: 6.2:1. Brake hp: 81 @ 3600 rpm. Net hp: 27.34. Main bearings: Four. Valve litters: Solid. Carb.: Carter one-barrel model 340S. [Series 6BA] Inline. L-head. Six. Cast iron block. Bore & Stroke: 3-3/8 in. x 3-7/8 in. Displacement: 208 cu. in. Compression Ratio: 6.2: 1. Brake hp: 81 @ 3600 rpm. Net hp: 27.34. Main bearings: Four. Valve lifters: Solid. Carb.: Carter one-barrel model 342S. [Series 8BA] Inline. L-head. Eight. Cast iron block. Bore & Stroke: 3-1/4 in. x 3-1/2 in. Displacement: 232.3 cu. in. Compression Ratio: 6.5:1. Brake hp: 87 @ 3800 rpm. Net hp: 33.8. Main bearings: Five. Valve lifters: Solid. Carb.: Carter one-barrel model 322S.

CHASSIS: [Series 6BB] Wheelbase: 112 in. Overall Length: 189-3/4 in. Height: 67-9/16 in. Tires: 16 x 6.00. [Series 6AB] Wheelbase: 112 in. Overall Length: 189-3/4 in. Height: 67-9/16 in. Tires: 16 x 6.00. [Series 8AB] Wheelbase: 116-5/8 in. Overall Length: 194-5/16 in. Height: 67-9/16 in. Tires: 16 x 6.50.

TECHNICAL: Manual synchromesh transmission. Speeds: 3F/IR. Floor mounted controls. Ventilated dry disc clutch. Semi-floating rear axle. Overall Ratio: (std.) 4.55:1; (mountain) 4.85:1; (plains) 4.11:1. Four-wheel hydraulic brakes. Steel spoke wheels.

OPTIONS: Front bumper. Rear bumper. Dual sidemount. Sidemount cover(s). Fender skirts. Set of four bumper guards (3.95). Air Chief Radio (62.50). Air Mate Radio (47.95). Outdraft heater (7.50). Deluxe heater (12.25). Clock (10.00). Cigar lighter (1.50). Radio antenna package (3.00). Seat covers (Santoy). Spotlight(s). R.H. taillight (3.45). Dual horn kit (12.50). Triplex air cleaner (6.50). Set of five wire wheel discs (11.25). Set of five wheel trim rings (8.50). Glove compartment smoker set and clock (13.50). Pull-wind clock (3.95). Safety light (15.95). License frame set (2.45). Luggage set (19.75). R.H. inside visor (2.00).

HISTORICAL: Introduced: September 25, 1935. Innovations: Larger bore eight. Improved clutch. Improved cooling system on eight. New front suspension with King pins mounted in floating bronze bearings. Automatic choke on deluxe models. Model year production: 176,270. The president of Pontiac was Harry Klingler. Pontiac held sixth rank in U.S. auto sales for 1936. The new models were called "The Most Beautiful Thing on Wheels."

THE HISTORY OF OAKLAND AND PONTIAC

The Oakland was the idea of two men: Edward M. Murphy, who was anxious to move his Pontiac Buggy Co. into the automotive age, and Alanson P. Brush, who created the design of early Cadillacs. They met around 1906, by which time Brush had set himself up in business as an engineering consultant in Detroit.

Brush showed Murphy his design for a small two-cylinder car that Cadillac had rejected. Its vertical engine rotated counterclockwise and its planetary transmission was unusual for a lack of braking bands. Brush used clutches running in oil instead. Murphy bought this automotive idea, which he decided should carry the same name—Oakland—as his horse-drawn vehicles. During the summer of 1907, Murphy organized the Oakland Motor Car Co.

1908-1919

The first Oakland was ready by auto-show time in January 1908, although Brush was no longer in Pontiac. Having found another automotive pioneer, named Frank Briscoe, with available funds, Brush was back in Detroit building his single-cylinder Brush runabout.

Lackluster sales of less than 300 Oaklands in 1908 must have convinced Murphy that Cadillac had been right in rejecting the Brush-designed twin. For 1909, a line of 40-hp four-cylinder cars with sliding-gear transmissions was introduced. Tragically, at the age of 44, Edward M. Murphy died suddenly in September 1908. Five months prior to his passing, Murphy had met with another former buggy man, William C. Durant. Soon afterwards, Oakland became part of Durant's General Motors empire.

Oakland manufactured four-cylinder cars exclusively in 1910 and sales of 3,000-5,000 cars a year became the norm. "The Car with a Conscience" was Oakland's slogan and the marque acquitted itself admirably in motor sports, particularly in reliability runs and hill climbs. The brand won no less than 25 hill climbs including those at Giant's Despair and Dead Horse Hill.

Oakland's first six-cylinder model—a big 334-cid 60-hp car on a 130-in. wheelbase—arrived in 1913, together with self-starter, electric lights, and an eye-catching rounded V-shaped radiator for all Oaklands. Almost 9,000 cars were sold that year. Production increased to nearly 12,000 in 1915 and more than doubled the following year following, when the Oakland range included fours, sixes, and a new V-8.

World War I exigencies resulted in the V-8's discontinuation in 1918. The company's efforts then focused on its six-cylinder model, which would be produced without noticeable change into the 1920s. It was during this period that Billy Durant was undergoing his second and last departure from General Motors. With the arrival of Alfred P. Sloan, Jr., all divisions of the corporation were given a fresh look.

1920-1929

An examination of Oakland's affairs revealed a haphazard production schedule (maybe 50 cars built one day, only 10 the next) and a loss of quality (some cars had to be repaired even before leaving the factory). Fred W. Warner—a Durant man—resigned as Oakland's general manager in 1921. George W. Hannum, who began his career at Autocar in 1907, succeeded Warner. Hannum had worked in various GM-related companies before arriving in the city of Pontiac. An official statement from General Motors indicated that Oakland would continue its present line "with gradual improvements."

The big news for Oakland arrived in a 1924 model with a new L-head engine, four-wheel brakes, centralized controls, automatic spark advance, and Duco nitro-cellulose lacquer. Oakland's choice of color in pioneering the new finish was a shade of blue that allowed the company to promote its car as the "True Blue Oakland Six." It could be had for as little as $995.

Unfortunately, insofar as being "true blue" as a GM man, George Hannum wasn't. The GM-decreed slot for the Oakland among the corporation cars was between the top-of-the-line Chevrolet and the bread-and-butter Buick. Among other flagrancies, the Oakland was too heavy for its slot, which was not entirely Hannum's fault since the car's chassis was eight years old. He was, however, guilty of occasionally not considering sales demand when shipping Oaklands to dealers. In spite of a healthy annual production of over 35,000 cars in both 1923 and 1924, Hannum was eased out of Oakland.

By early 1925, Hannum's place was taken by Alfred R. Glancy, a likable fellow who joined Oakland the previous year as assistant general manager. Although Hannum had first bruited the concept of the car in the early 1920s, it was Al Glancy who would introduce the Pontiac, in 1926, as a quality six designed to sell for the price of a four. This new "companion car" to Oakland was a runaway success and, undoubtedly, an impetus to the later marketing of the Marquette by Buick and the Viking by Oldsmobile. Pontiac became one of the few companion cars to survive the rigors of competition. For years—until Saturn came along—it held the distinction of being the only line introduced by General Motors after formation of the corporation to survive into modern times.

Oaklands for 1927 were called "Greater Oakland Sixes," with "All-American Six" becoming a designation for the Oakland senior models that summer. The cars were restyled for 1929.

1930-1939

In 1930, there was an 85-hp V-8 under the hood of the Oakland, but calendar year production was just 24,443 cars. In October 1930, Buick's Irving J. Reuter moved into Al Glancy's job at Oakland. For 1931, the cars featured a new synchromesh transmission with silent second gear. Fewer than 9,000 cars were produced that year. With the effects of the Great Depression now weighing heavy, Irving Reuter announced the demise of the Oakland name. Its V-8 series would be revamped into a 1932 Pontiac model. During 1932, the name Oakland Motor Car Co. was changed to Pontiac Motor Co.

Soon after the introduction of Pontiac, it was evident that the original factory site, near the center of the city of Pontiac, was too small, so 246 acres were acquired on the northern edge of the city for a new plant. The new facility was known as the "Daylight Plant" because the extensive use of glass skylights provided natural illumination. It was considered a miracle in the construction industry that within 90 days after ground was broken cars were being produced in the new plant. A new Fisher Body Div. plant was built nearby and connected to the Daylight Plant by an overhead closed bridge. This was a convenience not available to many manufacturers, who had to truck in their bodies.

In 1933, Harry J. Klinger was named general manager of Pontiac. It was decided to put a "six" back in the line, but retain an eight as well. The new engine was not a V-8, like Oaklands and 1932 Pontiacs had, but an L-head inline eight. The 1935 Pontiacs became the first to bear "Silver Streak" identification. Sales then doubled, requiring further factory expansion. Pontiac's selling of the "big car" image proved successful in 1935 and no drastic changes were made in the 1936 line. Both the sixes and the eights grew larger for 1937 as Pontiac switched from the small Chevrolet "A" body to the "B" body shared with Buicks, Oldsmobiles and LaSalles. All-steel construction was another important advance. In 1938, a young designer named Virgil Exner crafted a handsome new front end for the 1937 bodies, but a sagging economy held sales to 103,314 cars. Three all-new cars were offered for 1939, with a new smaller model called the Quality Six returning to using the Chevrolet body on a 115-in. wheelbase. A column-mounted gearshift was another new feature.

1940-1949

Pontiac continued with the A-bodied Quality Six and B-bodied Deluxe Six and Deluxe Eight in 1940, and added a Torpedo Eight series that shared its GM C-body with large Buicks, Oldsmobiles, and Cadillacs. Sales hit an impressive 239,477 units for the calendar year, more than doubling those of just three years earlier. To follow up the rising trend, Pontiac produced 330,061 units of its 1941 models, thus becoming the largest producer in its price class and the fifth largest in the nation. After an outstanding World War II production record, Pontiac returned to passenger car production in 1945. For the next three years it produced warmed-over 1942 models with bolted-on front fender extensions to provide a big-car look. Then, in 1949, an all-new postwar design evolved with slab sides and lower lines.

To satisfy growing demand, a vast expansion program was launched to increase productivity and capacity by 50 percent. Pontiac's iron foundry was greatly enlarged. The layout of the engine plant was altered to provide for more machines and heavier production. A new building was erected for increased production of rear axles and for heat-treating of steel forgings to make them tougher and more durable. Pontiac's electroplating system—one of the largest automatic setups in the new warehouse for handling past-model parts—was put into service.

1950-1959

Pontiac's 1950 models had minor updates to the new postwar body, but a two-door hardtop called the Catalina generated the most excitement. The inline eight was increased to 268 cid and 108 hp to try to keep up with the overhead valve V-8s that other automakers were releasing. Late in 1951, Harry J. Klinger became vice president in charge of vehicle production for GM and Arnold Lenz was appointed general manager of Pontiac. Lenz served as general manager until his tragic death in a car-train crash during 1952. R.M. Critchfield then succeeded Lenz as general manager. Under his guidance Pontiac embarked on its most extensive enlargement and modernization program since 1927. A new car-finish building was completed and the engine plant was completely modernized to produce 1955 V-8 engines in record volumes. Production for 1955 established a new high of 581,860 cars.

A new era started for Pontiac in 1956 when Semon E. (Bunkie) Knudsen took over the reins as general manager. Knudsen was the son of William S. Knudsen, a former GM president. Knudsen, 43-years-old at the time, was the youngest GM general manager. He proceeded without fanfare to make over the Pontiac image. Innovative models included a fuel-injected 1957 Bonneville convertible and the 1957 Transcontinental station wagon which combined sportiness with four-door utility value. With a revamped engineering group headed by E.M. "Pete" Estes, new Pontiacs were methodically developed. Starting with the 1959 models, an image of a youthful car, with appeal across the broad spectrum of new car buyers, emerged.

1960-1969

In the fall of 1960, following intensive research, development, and testing, Pontiac introduced the completely new Tempest series. Unique in concept and fresh in styling, the Tempest became an immediate success and was recognized as the outstanding engineering achievement of the year. When Knudsen moved to Chevrolet as general manager in 1961, Estes took over at Pontiac. Under his direction the division continued to grow in sales volume and facilities.

With the addition of the Tempest, Pontiac Motor Div. moved into third place in sales in 1961. Long regarded as the hot spot in automobile sales, third place has a reputation of being hard to keep. Several car manufacturers have occupied the position over the years only to lose out to another make. Pontiac continued its dominance of third place all during the 1960s, as sales records were shattered.

The division also moved ahead in plant construction and, in 1964, three new projects were announced. All were completed the

following year and added some 1-1/2 million square feet to Pontiac's home production facilities. These included a 180,000-sq.-ft. addition to the foundry for new core-making machines, water-cooled cupolas and a new finishing room to make Pontiac's foundry the most modern in the industry. Also added was a service parts warehouse containing 1,070,000 sq. ft. under one roof to consolidate storage of service parts. A one-story storage and shipping building, 800 feet long and 330 feet wide, to expedite shipments to other Pontiac assembly plants, was completed in 1964.

Estes followed Knudsen's footsteps to Chevrolet as general manager in 1965 and John Z. DeLorean was named to Pontiac's top position, moving up from chief engineer of the division. Before the introduction of its 1966 models, Pontiac announced a completely new overhead camshaft (OHC) engine as standard equipment on all 1966 Tempest models. This was the first time such an engine had been used in an American passenger car.

In January 1967, Pontiac unveiled the Firebird. Aimed at the youthful sports car market, it was offered with the so-called "OHC-6" and with a 400-cid V-8 engine. 1968 was another milestone year for Pontiac. Production and sales records were shattered as 943,253 cars were produced for an all-time high. Pontiac's GTO was chosen "Car of the Year" by *Motor Trend* magazine for "being so successful in confirming the correlations between safety, styling and performance." The presentation of the "Golden Calipers" trophy marked the fourth time Pontiac had won the *Motor Trend* award, more than any other manufacturer. Contributing to the GTO's success was the innovative energy-absorbing Endura front bumper developed by Pontiac engineering. Hailed as an industry first and projected as a pacesetter for others to copy, the car and bumper attracted nationwide publicity. Sales boomed in 1968 and, for the first time, the specialty cars like the Tempest, Grand Prix and Firebird, brought in more customers than the traditional line. When the final tallies were in, 910,977 Pontiacs had been sold.

The 1969 Grand Prix was a phenomenal success, as its sales more than tripled over the previous model year to 105,000. *Car Life* magazine awarded the Grand Prix its "Car of the Year" award. In February 1969, F. James McDonald returned to Pontiac as general manager, replacing DeLorean who moved up to Chevrolet in the same capacity. McDonald had served as Pontiac's works manager from 1965-1968 and returned after spending one year to the day at Chevrolet, as its director of manufacturing operations.

1970-1975

The division's new 300,000-sq.-ft., ultra-modern administration building opened in early 1970. The five-level structure headquartered the general manager and the sales, accounting, data processing, purchasing and public relations departments.

In March 1971, Pontiac entered the compact car market with the low-priced, stylish Ventura II. Built on a 111-in. wheelbase, the Ventura II was offered in two- and four-door models. In April 1971, Pontiac dedicated a new multi-million dollar vehicle emissions control and carburetor testing facility. The two-story, 43,000-sq.-ft. building was being used by Pontiac engineers working on the development of vehicle emissions controls of components in the power train and the fuel system. The 1971 calendar year saw Pontiac take firm hold on third place in the auto industry's sales race. Pontiac dealers sold 710,352 cars to capture the hotly contested third spot in sales for the 10th time in the last 11 years.

For 1972, Pontiac featured a new energy-absorbing bumper on all full-size cars. The system consisted of two telescoping steel boxes that contained urethane positioned between the bumper and the frame of the car. Since the urethane blocks were not damaged by an impact, the bumper could be struck numerous times during the life of the car and continue to absorb energy. On Oct. 1, 1972, Martin J. Caserio became general manager of Pontiac, replacing McDonald, who was named Chevrolet general manager. Caserio had been general manager of the GMC Truck & Coach Div. since 1966.

The 1973 Pontiac lineup was highlighted by a totally redesigned intermediate series, topped by a stunning-looking Grand Am. This fine road touring car featured a "soft nose" front end made of flexible rubber-like urethane for protection. Pontiac sales of 854,343 for the 1973 model year were the second-best in history.

The 1974 Pontiac lineup featured significant engineering improvements in energy absorbing bumpers and a new Radial Tuned Suspension (RTS) package. By 1974, the major construction was completed on a multi-million dollar program to clean up smoke emissions from the Pontiac casting plant. Five modern arc-melt furnaces and four electric induction-molding furnaces with the latest dust collecting units were installed. Two remaining coke-fired cupolas had modern emission control equipment installed, making them as clean as the electric furnaces.

Introduction of the sub-compact Astre, bold restyling of the compact Ventura and extensive use of Radial Tuned Suspension with steel-belted radial tires, highlighted introduction of the 1975 Pontiacs. Rectangular headlamps were utilized on the Bonneville and Grand Ville Brougham for the first time. On Oct. 1, 1975, Alex C. Mair was appointed general manager of Pontiac, succeeding Caserio, who became General Motors' vice president and group executive in charge of the automotive components electrical group. Mair had been general manager of the GMC Truck & Coach Div. since 1972 and previously had been director of engineering for the Chevrolet Motor Div.

1976-1979

Pontiac's Golden Anniversary model lineup for 1976 included a new sporty car—the Sunbird—and a new top-of-the-line entry called the Bonneville Brougham. The use of rectangular headlamps was expanded to include the intermediate LeMans, the Grand Prix and the new Sunbird. The new models showed the positive results of Pontiac engineers' continuing efforts to improve fuel economy.

Pontiac's 1977 model lineup was headlined by the introduction of completely redesigned full-size cars, plus two new engines. Catalina, Bonneville, Bonneville Brougham, Catalina Safari and Grand Safari models all were redesigned to be shorter and lighter than their predecessors. They continued to offer as much or more interior and luggage compartment space as earlier models. The new engines—a 2.5-liter (151-cid) cast-iron L-4 and a 4.9-liter (301-cid) V-8—were designed from the outset to provide improved durability and reliability as well as outstanding fuel economy.

Pontiac introduced a new car midyear in 1977. The Phoenix was added to the Pontiac lineup as the top-of-the-line compact car. It and the Pontiac Ventura were the only American compact cars to offer a four-cylinder engine. Among other features, the Phoenix offered the first U.S. headlamps completely designed under the metric measurement system.

The complete redesign of the mid-sized LeMans and Grand LeMans and personal luxury Grand Prix, the return of the Grand Am and continuing engineering and fuel economy improvements, were the highlights of Pontiac's 1978 model lineup. The LeMans, Grand LeMans and Grand Prix were all shorter and lighter than their predecessors, providing significant increases in fuel economy while retaining traditional levels of roominess and comfort. New front and rear design treatments and several new interior trims were offered in the 1978 full-size Pontiacs. The Grand Am was re-introduced with distinctive features that included a soft, flexible rubber front-end panel. The Phoenix replaced the Ventura and the Sunbird replaced the Astre as Pontiac's compact and subcompact cars, respectively, for the 1978 model year. In April 1978, the completely modernized manufacturing office building was dedicated. Occupying the new building were the following staffs: Industrial Engineering, Manufacturing, Reliability, Plant Engineering and Production Engineering.

Pontiac Motor Div. sold more new cars—871,391—during the 1978 model year than in any previous model year in its history. Firebirds, led by the performance-oriented Trans Am, continued to be among the most popular cars in the auto industry, setting an all-time model year sales record of 175,607. Pontiac's sporty little Sunbird also set a sales record.

On Nov. 6, 1978, Robert C. Stempel became Pontiac general manager. He succeeded Alex Mair, who was named vice president and group executive in charge of the Technical Staffs Group at the GM Technical Center in Warren, Mich. Stempel had formerly been Director of Engineering for Chevrolet Motor Division.

The 1979 Pontiac lineup was highlighted by new Firebird styling, and for the Sunbird, a new four-cylinder engine with a "crossflow" cylinder head that improved performance. The 1979 model year was the first full year since the 1930s that Pontiac offered genuine wire wheels on certain models. Four-wheel power disc brakes were introduced as an option for Firebird Formula and Trans Am models. The Grand Safari wagon was renamed the Bonneville Safari to more closely identify it with the Pontiac family of cars. Pontiac's 400-cid V-8 was discontinued for all Catalina and Bonneville models in an effort to increase average fuel economy and help General Motors meet stringent federal fuel economy standards.

Pontiac introduced its first front-wheel-drive car in April 1979, with a totally redesigned "efficiency-sized" Phoenix. Available as a two-door coupe and five-door hatchback sedan, the Phoenix came in base, luxury LJ, and sporty SJ editions. A transverse 2.5-liter (151-cid) four-cylinder L-4 crossflow engine was standard in the Phoenix, with an optional 2.8-liter (173-cid) 60-degree transverse V-6 engine available. The 1980 Phoenix was smaller and more tightly packaged on the outside, but larger in many respects on the inside, compared to the 1979 Phoenix.

1980-1984

The remainder of Pontiac's 1980 model line—introduced in October 1979—included major styling changes to full-size Pontiacs and a revised engine lineup that promised more fuel efficiency while maintaining good performance. A GM 4.9-liter (301-cid) four-barrel turbocharged engine, produced by Pontiac Motor Div., was introduced as a federal option for Firebird Trans Am and Formula models. A GM 4.3-liter (265-cid) V-8 engine—also produced by Pontiac—was introduced. It was essentially a downsized version of the Pontiac-produced 4.9-liter (301-cid) V-8. A white Limited Edition Pontiac Turbo Trans Am was chosen as the official pace car for the 64th running of the Indianapolis 500 race, May 25, 1980.

In August 1980, William E. Hoglund, who had been comptroller of General Motors, returned to Pontiac as general manager. He replaced Robert Stempel who was appointed managing director for Adam Opel AG in Germany. A major design change for Grand Prix and a new General Motors Computer Command Control system for all Pontiac car lines (except those with a diesel engine) highlighted Pontiac's 1981 product lineup. The 1980 Sunbird was carried over through the end of the 1980 calendar year.

The 1981-1/2 Pontiac T1000 made its debut at the Chicago Auto Show in February. Targeted at the price-conscious family buyer in need of inexpensive entry-level transportation, the T1000 was available as a three- or five-door hatchback. In May, Pontiac's J2000 was introduced as a totally new, efficient, and functional front-wheel-drive subcompact. Built on a 101.2-in. wheelbase, the J2000 was available as a two-door coupe, four-door sedan, three-door hatchback or four-door station wagon. Its standard power train was a 1.8-liter (112-cid) L-4 engine with a two-barrel carburetor linked to a four-speed manual transaxle. Pontiac J2000s were promoted as appealing to both traditional and "new value" buyers as a car that combined functionality with a blend of flair and excitement.

Pontiac Motor Div. produced over 700,000 four-cylinder engines during the 1981 model year. During the summer of 1981, the division opened a new engine facility in Plant 55, where it produced additional GM 2.5-liter four-cylinder engines. Pontiac was one of the first in the industry to use microwave measurement for accurately timing these engines. Other technological innovations used in the 712,000-sq.-ft., $200 million plant included a functional check that performed several tests, a signature analysis torque rate system, and a computerized Management Information System.

The world-famous Bonneville nameplate adorned a more fuel-efficient luxury car in Pontiac's 1982 fall product introductions. The Pontiac-produced 1982 GM 2.5-liter four-cylinder engine underwent major technological improvements, including elimination of the conventional carburetor. It also offered improved drivability and fuel economy through advanced technology including electronic fuel injection. All-new ultra-aerodynamic Firebirds and contemporary five-passenger front-wheel-drive Pontiac 6000 models joined the 1982 Pontiac lineup in January

Available in three distinct models—the sporty base coupe, the performance-oriented Trans Am, and the new sophisticated luxury SE—each Firebird had its own specific identity. The base engine was a 2.5-liter EFI engine, while the SE had a 2.8-liter V-6 and the Trans Am was powered by a 5.0-liter four-barrel V-8. All models had a standard four-speed manual transmission. Extensive wind tunnel testing on the Firebird resulted in an excellent drag coefficient that made it one of the most aerodynamic cars ever produced.

Although the Pontiac 6000 was based on the General Motors X-car platform and power train, it was a completely different car inside, outside, and underneath with ride and handling characteristics that made it internationally competitive. Available in first level and LE series as a spacious four-door sedan or contemporary two-door coupe, the Pontiac 6000 was powered by a fuel-injected 2.5-liter four-cylinder engine with three-speed automatic transmission as standard equipment. The dramatic wedge shape of the 6000 was the result of many hours of aerodynamic tuning of the surface, body contours, and details, making the 6000 one of the most aerodynamic sedans available in America.

In April 1982, Pontiac offered a new overhead cam, fuel-injected four-cylinder engine for its subcompact J2000 models with an automatic transmission. The OHC fuel-injected engine provided exceptional smoothness with responsive, fuel-efficient performance.

The 1983 model lineup saw the introduction of the new Pontiac STE as a high-styled, world-class performance sedan. The STE was designed to compete head-on with the best import sedans in the special touring market. The standard engine was a 130-hp high-output 2.8-liter two-barrel V-6. Also in 1983, Pontiac re-introduced the full-sized Parisienne to its model lineup after a two-year absence.

1984 was a banner year for Pontiac and the division took a major step up, as the *performance* division of General Motors, with the introduction of a revolutionary two-seat sports car called the Fiero. It was the first production car in the world to utilize a "space-frame chassis" with separate reinforced "Enduraflex" plastic body panels. Pontiac's first two-seater was built on a 93.4-in. wheelbase and powered by a 92-hp 2.5-liter four-cylinder engine. The Fiero was a tremendous success during its first year in the market with sales of nearly 100,000 units—which nearly doubled the sales of the previous best selling two-seater in the U.S. Pontiac also announced, in 1984, that it was adding an exciting turbocharged 1.8 liter-engine to its 2000/Sunbird lineup. The impressive turbo churned out 150 hp at 5600 rpm.

In January of 1984, GM announced the formation of two new car groups: the C-P-C Group (Chevrolet, Pontiac, GM Canada) and the B-O-C Group (Buick, Oldsmobile, Cadillac). As a part of the C-P-C group, Pontiac was charged with developing a product line for the late-1980s that would appeal to the entry-level youth market with exciting, fun-to-drive, performance-oriented sporty vehicles. In July, GM announced that the idle Pontiac Motor Home Plant 8, which had built Pontiacs since the 1920s, would be re-activated to build several models of GM rear-wheel-drive midsize passenger cars.

Also in July, Pontiac general manager William E. Hoglund was promoted to group executive in charge of the GM Operating Staffs Group. He was later named president of Saturn Corp. J. Michael Losh became the 14th general manager of Pontiac replacing Hoglund. Losh had been managing director of General Motors de Mexico. Calendar year 1984 was Pontiac's best sales year in the previous five, as dealers sold 704,684 new cars. The number one nameplate in the Pontiac lineup for 1984 was the Sunbird, which had sales of 126,916 units.

1985-1989

In 1985, hot in the tracks of the successful Fiero, STE, and Sunbird Turbo, Pontiac introduced the newest in a series of bold image cars, the driver-oriented Grand Am. Available only as a two-door coupe, the Grand Am was designed to compete head-to-head with the upscale imports and to appeal to the "new values" consumer of the 1980s. Engines offered were the new electronic-fuel-injected (EFI) 2.5-liter four-cylinder or the performance-oriented 125-hp multiport-fuel-injected (MFI) 3.0-liter V-6. The 1985 model year saw Pontiac dealers sell 785,617 cars, the best performance since 1979. The 6000 was the division's top seller, with deliveries of 156,995 units.

The 1986 Pontiac product lineup was highlighted by the addition of several new expressive "Drivers Cars" such as the Grand Am SE, the Sunbird GT, and in early 1986, the bold new Fiero GT. These new models helped Pontiac to achieve the biggest market share gain of any GM division in 1986. Sales reached 840,137 cars, with

the Grand Am almost doubling its sales to 190,994 units, from 98,567 the previous year.

Early in the model year for Pontiac's 1987 lineup, the Bonneville was converted to GM's front-wheel-drive H-body platform at the Willow Run, Mich., plant. Also, with the spring 1987 arrival of the new South Korean import, the LeMans (as a 1988 model), Pontiac was able to offer a much-needed, entry-level subcompact and revive a proven name. Pontiac sales totaled 715,536 units in 1987. They were led by the Grand Am, which had 216,065 sales.

In October 1987, production began on the 1988 Grand Prix, which was built at the new GM assembly plant in Fairfax, Kan. The new front-drive Grand Prix, based on the W-platform, reached sales of 76,723 units and helped Pontiac to a record of 740,928 units sold in 1988. The Grand Am was again Pontiac's top seller with 221,438 sales. Bonneville's new SSE model came with the new 3.8-liter V-6 as its standard powerplant. The Fiero line had a new Formula model. It featured fully independent suspension, which was offered on all Fieros for 1988, the final year the car was produced.

In calendar year 1989, Pontiac offered GM's first all-wheel-drive car, the 6000 STE. Also new were limited editions of the Trans Am 20th Anniversary model and the McLaren Turbo Grand Prix. Only 1,500 of the 20th Anniversary Trans Ams were built. A 3.8-liter turbocharged engine rated at 250 hp powered them. A small run of 2,000 McLaren Turbo Grand Prixs was also assembled. Domestic sales hit 675,422 cars, again led by the Grand Am. John G. Middlebrook replaced J. Michael Losh and became the 15th general manager of Pontiac Motor Div.

1990-1994

Pontiac launched the 1990s with its foray into the minivan market via the Trans Sport. This APV (all-purpose vehicle) was constructed of composite materials on a space frame substructure. It could be ordered with seating for five, six or seven passengers. The popular Firebird—offered in the spring of 1990—also took on a new look for 1991. It received an exterior overhaul to improve aerodynamics and also got more muscle under its hood. The popular 1991 Grand Am's sales hit 170,622 cars in 1991. In Lordstown, Ohio, autoworkers stayed busy building Pontiac's second best-selling model, the Sunbird. The 1991 Sunbird's new features included a 3.1-liter V-6. Production of Sunbird LE convertibles rose to 18,611, up from 13,197 in 1990. The Grand Prix had some of the most exciting changes in 1991. A GTP model replaced the Turbo Coupe. It looked like the turbocharged model, but had an all-new 210-hp Twin Dual Cam V-6. New features for 6000s were few. Bonneville innovations for 1991 included a new brake-transmission interlock; London/Empress cloth trims for SEs (optional on LEs); 15-in. bolt-on LE wheel covers and P215/65R-15 tires for LEs. New features for 1991 Trans Sports included stainless-steel exhaust, a roof luggage carrier, larger outside mirrors, and a self-aligning steering wheel. The SE also offered a new 2+3+2 seating option. PMD made 18,319 Trans Sports in a factory in Tarrytown, N.Y.

Priced from $7,899-$9,810, the 1992 LeMans had a new sport-tuned exhaust system, amber section taillights, revised engine calibration, and new Bright Yellow paint for the coupe. The base LE was re-badged as the SE. Sunbird features included multipoint fuel injection, more horsepower for the four, and standard anti-lock brakes. Sunbird GTs added dual-exhausts, 15-in., machine-faced aluminum wheels, tinted glass, and a spoiler. Pontiac's popular Grand Am offered SE and GT coupes and sedans with new aerodynamic exteriors. Functional changes included a 2.3-liter Quad 4 engine and a 3.3-liter V-6. The 1992 Firebirds had what Pontiac called "structural enhancements," plus new non-asbestos brake pads and new colors were added. AM/FM cassette radio graphics were redesigned and a new Beige interior bowed. This was the Firebird's 25th anniversary, but no special commemorative model was released. Antilock brakes became standard on the Grand Prix GT, GTP, and STE. The Bonneville turned 35. It had major interior and exterior changes, plus a Sport package. The 1992 Trans Sport featured a new antilock braking system.

An acoustics package made 1993 Sunbirds quieter. A Sport Appearance package for SE coupes, a glass convertible rear window, a low-oil-level sensor on 2.0-liter fours, several colors, and a trunk cargo net were new. The fourth-generation Firebird arrived in

1993 with Firebird, Firebird Formula, and Trans Am coupes. All had a 68-degree windshield, new aluminum wheels and tires, composite body panels, new instruments, new suspensions, and a standard 3.4-liter V-6. A new 5.7-liter V-8 was standard in Formula and Trans Am models, which also got a six-speed manual transmission. Advanced four-wheel antilock brakes were standard with four-wheel disc brakes and on Formulas and Trans Ams. New Grand Prix features included an optional "second-gear start" transmission with 3.1-liter V-6s, a Ruby Red interior, a Sport Appearance package for the LE sedan, a four-speed electronic automatic transmission option (with 3.1-liter V-6s), standard automatic door locks, and provisions for installation of a cell phone. Pontiac dropped the Trans Sport GT. With John Middlebrook continuing on as general manager, Pontiac Motor Div. generated 6.39 percent of U.S. sales.

Despite bitterly cold weather across the country, sales of new Pontiacs for calendar year 1994 rose nearly eight percent. Pontiac dropped three Sunbirds (SE sedan, SE convertible, and GT coupe), three Grand Prixs (LE sedan, STE sedan, and GT coupe), and the Bonneville SSEi sedan. Pontiac added a Sunbird LE ragtop. The Grand Am remained Pontiac's sales leader. The 1994 Firebirds didn't change much. A convertible returned in each series—Firebird, Formula, and Trans Am. The Trans Am ragtop came as a GT. New features included Dark Aqua Metallic color, floodlit interiors, visor straps, Delco 2001 series radios, CD players, and a 5.7-liter sequential-fuel-injected (SFI) V-8. Grand Prix changes included a "Special Edition Coupe" package, a GTP Performance Package for the coupe, and a GT Performance package for the sedan. Pontiac replaced the Bonneville SSEi with an SSEi supercharger package. The Trans Sport got a standard driver's side air bag and integral child seats as a new option.

On Jan. 27, 1994, Pontiac announced a special model to honor the silver anniversary of the Trans Am. This 25th Anniversary Edition Trans Am included Bright White exterior finish, a bright blue center line stripe, anniversary logos and door badges, lightweight 16-in. aluminum wheels painted Bright White, and white Prado leather seats with blue 25th Anniversary embroidery. Buyers received a special 25th Anniversary portfolio when they picked up a car. As a special nod to Trans Am history, PMD headquarters announced that it would build a very limited number of 25th Anniversary Trans Am GT convertibles to honor the eight famous T/A ragtops made when the sports-performance model was first released in mid-1969.

1995-1999

The Sunfire subcompact replaced the Sunbird in 1995. It had new styling, engineering, and technology. Standard engines were a 2.2-liter OHV four for SEs and a 2.3-liter DOHC 16-valve Quad 4 for GTs. A GT coupe entered production in May 1995, along with a convertible. Pontiac's lone rear-wheel-drive model was offered as a coupe or convertible in three series: Firebird, Formula, and Trans Am. The Canadian-built F-cars had several changes like traction control with V-8s and either manual or automatic transmission, three new exterior colors, and two new leather interiors. Also new were 16-in., five-spoke aluminum wheels, speed-rated tires, a power antenna, a four-spoke Sport steering wheel, and a remote CD changer. New-for-1995 Grand Prix features included variable-effort steering with the GT or GTP packages, a standard brake/transmission interlock, a new floor console, and a modified suspension. A new Sports Luxury Edition (SLE) package was available to upgrade the 1995 Bonneville SE. Traction control and a brake/transmission shift interlock were standard on 1995 Trans Sports. Calendar year sales were 566,826 cars, plus 32,297 Trans Sports.

A 1996 sales brochure described the Grand Prix as "the sports car for grown-ups." Nearly 20 percent of all GM cars being built were Pontiacs and the Grand Am was among the top 10 selling American cars. The smooth-lined Sunfire returned and its Quad 4 performance engine was replaced by a new 2.4-liter 150-hp Twin-Cam powerplant. Traction control was included with four-speed automatics, which were now available with the base 2.2-liter engine. Daytime running lights (DRLs) were now standard. A 3800 Series II 200-hp V-6 was the new standard engine for 1996 Firebirds. An optional WS6 Ram Air Performance and Handling package was available on Formula and Trans Am coupes with the 5.7-liter V-8. The Grand Am was the ninth best-selling car in America. Its exterior was revamped

with new fascias, headlamps, and taillights. The Bonneville got an optional 240-hp supercharged 3800 Series II V-6 with 240 hp. The 1996 Trans Sport offered standard front air conditioning. This was the final year of its production in Tarrytown. Roy S. Roberts became general manager of Pontiac-GMC Division.

The Grand Prix had an all-new Wide Track stance and revised model lineup for 1997. There was an SE sedan, a GT coupe, a GT sedan, and a GTP Performance package with a supercharged 240-hp V-6. Sunfire coupes were now being made at an assembly plant in Ramos Arizpe, Mexico. Grand Am SE and GT coupes and sedans returned with minimal changes. Firebird models and engines carried over from 1996, but new options were added. A Ram Air Performance and Handling package was offered for convertibles. The mid-1996 Sport and Appearance package for V-6 Firebirds included ground effects, fog lamps, and dual exhausts with cast aluminum extensions. New for the Bonneville was an ETC four-speed automatic transmission with the supercharged engine, an adjustable "heads-up" display, a Delco/Bose premium sound system, Magnasteer variable effort power steering, remote keyless entry, and electronic load leveling. An all-new steel-bodied, eight-passenger Trans Sport MPV, made in Doraville, Ga., replaced the plastic-bodied 1996 model. PMD also offered a Montana package with sport utility vehicle (SUV) styling cues, extra-traction tires, and a traction-control system.

For 1998, the Pontiac Sunfire's 2.2-liter engine was enhanced with roller rocker arms, a new intake manifold, combustion chamber improvements, and a new cylinder head design. The 1998 Grand Am was largely unchanged. The hot Firebird offered five models since the Formula convertible was dropped. Formulas and Trans Ams received a new, all-aluminum 5.7-liter 305-hp V-8 with a six-speed manual transmission. A Ram Air package provided 320 hp. Styling was freshened with a front fascia that incorporated a new headlamp design and the taillights were updated, too. V-8s with four-speed automatic transmissions had a larger torque converter and all Firebirds got standard four-wheel disc brakes. A midyear Formula option was an AutoCross package with a beefed-up suspension. The all-new-for-'97 "Wide-Track" Grand Prix was slightly refined for 1998. The Bonneville SE and SSE sedans mirrored the previous models, except that the optional supercharged 3.8-liter V-6 was no longer available on SE sedans. The 1998 Trans Sport MPV got standard side-impact air bags for front passengers. In late 1997 and early 1998, Pontiac-GMC Div. moved its offices into GM's new World Headquarters Building in Detroit's Renaissance Center.

Pontiac made sweeping changes in four of its six series in 1999. The Bonneville was the only Pontiac line that cloned last year's offerings. A new Sunfire GT convertible was introduced. New Grand Am SE coupe and sedan models came out in the spring of 1998 as 1999 Pontiacs. The Firebird section of the 1999 Pontiac sales catalog was the same as in the 1998 catalog, but a new 30th Anniversary Limited Edition Trans Am added a little distinction to the year's offerings. The 1999 Grand Prix SE and GT models got a standard Enhanced Traction System. The non-turbo 3.8-liter V-6 went up to 200 hp. An all-new 2000 Bonneville was already being promoted in 1999, so the series that returned was essentially a carryover from the previous year. Promoted as "A new state of excitement," the Trans Sport became the Montana in 1999. New options included a Sport Performance Group and a Vision package featuring a drop-down rear seat with an LCD color monitor, video cassette player, and CD player. During 1999, Lynn Myers took over as general manager of Pontiac-GMC Division.

2000-2002

When 2000 arrived, Pontiac Motor Div. was poised to lead GM into the new millennium. The Aztek, which began as a concept car that represented a cross between a car and a SUV, didn't wait long after the Y2K threat evaporated to become a reality. With controversial styling, the Aztek was very much aimed at the youth market that Pontiac harvested so successfully in the 1950s. Standard equipment included a "VERSATRAK" on-demand all-wheel-drive system, a rear cargo sliding tray with pop-up storage compartments, a removable front console/cooler, a Pioneer premium 10-speaker sound system with rear-cargo-area controls, and lightweight, removable second-row flip/fold modular bench seats. The 2000 Bonneville debuted in the fall with SE, SLE, and SSEi sedans. The SSEi's 240-hp supercharged engine was good for under-seven-second 0-to-60 times.

The new Bonneville's "attitude" was showcased at the Bonneville Salt Flats in Utah during the 2000 Speedweek event there. A factory-backed "assault on the Salt" racing promotion was designed to show that the Bonneville nameplate was in touch with its 1957 high-performance roots. It included a Bonneville racer with a supercharged 3.8-liter V-6 that put out more than *twice* the production SSEi's 240 hp. It was said to have "well over 500 hp." During the six days of racing, Bonneville veteran Mike Cook drove the car to a 150-mph preliminary run, followed by an easy 189-mph pass, before engine and computer problems set in. The Bonneville was slowly repaired and managed a top run of 195 mph before time ran out.

In the little-changed Firebird line, Formula and Trans Am models were available with new 17-in. wheels as part of a Ram Air package. A five-speed manual transmission was standard on all 2000 Grand Am SEs in combination with a 2.4-liter DOHC four. The Grand Prix's millennium restyling included a new front air deflector designed to help reduce aerodynamic drag and further improve performance. A limited edition Grand Prix paced the Daytona 500 for the 11th time. Only 2,000 Grand Prix GTP Daytona 500 Pace Car replicas were made. The Y2K Montana featured an upgraded electrical system and instrument cluster, and improved antilock braking system. Sunfire SE and GT coupes feature restyled front and rear fascias, while GT models added sporty dual-exhaust outlets and unique front-end styling.

For 2001, Pontiac continued to offer Aztek, Grand Am, Firebird, Grand Prix, Bonneville, and Montana car lines. The big changes for the year were in the Aztek, Montana, and Grand Prix series. The Aztek—billed as the "World's First Sport Recreation Vehicle"—came in base and GT models that combined riveting design, exciting performance, athletic handling, and outstanding versatility and flexibility. An all-wheel-drive version was new and started appearing in showrooms late in 2000 or very early in 2001. The Montana received a fresh new look for 2001 with a redesigned front grille and fascia and a new rear fascia. A factory-installed luggage rack was standard equipment and allowed owners to carry more cargo or luggage. Black body finish was also new for the Pontiac minivan. Extended-wheelbase Montanas now offered a Rear Parking aid system with four ultrasonic sensors and an optional fully integrated rear-seat entertainment system called MontanaVision. The wider-is-better Grand Prix was refined with a freshened SE exterior and the introduction of Special Edition GT and GTP option packages based on the 2000 Daytona Pace Car.

For 2002, Pontiac marketed Aztek, Bonneville, Firebird, Grand Am, Grand Prix, Montana, and Sunfire models and planned to bring an all-new vehicle called the Vibe to market. PMD also kicked off a new marketing campaign themed, "Pontiac Excitement. Pass It On." It was based on real people experiencing real excitement in a Pontiac Grand Am or Grand Prix. The campaign debuted during the Emmy Awards on Oct. 7, 2001. "Think of it as reality TV meets marketing," said general manager Lynn Myers. "These are real people and we'll give them the keys to a Pontiac for a week so we can film what happens and share their experience with Pontiac Excitement before they pass on the keys to someone else." The drivers' adventures were quickly documented in TV commercials or on the Web site.

The controversial Pontiac Aztek entered 2002 with a new look, more standard features, and lower prices of $19,995 for the front-drive version and $22,995 for the Versatrak all-wheel drive model. "We have given Aztek a fresh new look for 2002, while keeping up with the competitive marketplace and giving consumers a better value and more for their money," Aztek brand manager Jim Vurpillat told the press. On Sept. 25, 2001, General Motors announced that it would stop selling the Firebird (along with the Chevrolet Camaro) after 2002 due to slow sales. In addition, a $3,000-plus 35th anniversary package would be offered to help spur Firebird sales, which were down 28 percent through August 2001. The plant that builds Firebirds and Camaros, in Ste. Therese, Quebec Canada, was slated to close in the fall of 2002.

Following is a list of general managers for Oakland Motor Car Company and Pontiac Motor Div.:

OAKLAND MOTOR CAR COMPANY:

1907-08	Edward M. Murphy
1909-10	Lee Dunlap
1911-14	George P. Daniels
1915	Charles W. Nash
1916-20	Fred W. Warner
1921-23	George H. Hannum
1924-30	Alfred R. Glancy
1931	Irving J. Reuter

PONTIAC MOTOR DIVISION:

1932-33	William S. Knudsen/P. O. Tanner
1933-51	Harry J. Klinger
1951-52	Arnold Lenz
1952-56	Robert M. Critchfield
1956-61	Semon E. Knudsen
1961-65	Elliott M. Estes
1965-69	John Z. DeLorean
1969-72	F. James McDonald
1972-75	Martin J. Caserio
1975-78	Alex C. Mair
1978-80	Robert C. Stempel
1980-84	William E. Hoglund
1984-89	J. Michael Losh
	John G. Middlebrook
	Roy S. Roberts
	Lynn Myers

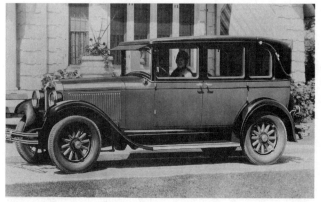

1928 Oakland All-American landau sedan. (OCW)

1964 Pontiac Tempest LeMans GTO two-door convertible. (OCW)

Pontiac Oakland Club International Caters to Pontiac Owners and Pontiac History Buffs Worldwide

By Larry Kummer

The Pontiac-Oakland Club International (POCI) is devoted exclusively to Pontiac and Oakland automobiles. POCI, through its various services and publications, promotes the preservation and restoration of Pontiacs and Oaklands. Members of the club do not have to own one of these fine automobiles to join POCI, but it helps if you really love them. Membership allows access to a vast pool of information, parts, and automotive resources.

Reflecting Pontiac's leadership in the performance-car market, POCI enjoys strong support from the high-performance segment of the car-collecting hobby. Whether you are restoring a fuel-injected 1957 Bonneville, a 1962 Super-Duty Catalina, a 1969 GTO "The Judge," or a Trans Am with an H.O. V-8, or building an earthshaking drag-racing machine, or a one-of-a-kind street rod, POCI can help. The club offers something for everyone, from the antique-auto "purest" to the customizer.

POCI members receive a subscription to a 72-page monthly magazine called *Smoke Signals*. The large, colorful magazine contains articles relating to Pontiac and Oakland automobiles, technical data, restoration tips, classified advertising, and more. Readers can find stories about other members and their cars, along with high-performance tips and news about local chapter activities across the United States, Canada and the world.

The classified ads in *Smoke Signals* offer POCI members the largest all Pontiac and Oakland marketplace anywhere. Ads from members offer vehicles wanted or for sale, as well as parts, original service literature, and promotional items. Free classified advertising privileges are extended to club members only. Paid commercial advertising is also available to help keep POCI members current on all the latest parts and services offered in the collector-car industry.

The POCI Web site, at www.poci.org, is an inter-active forum through which members can immediately realize many of the great benefits POCI has to offer. Within a few quick computer mouse

An unrestored 1948 Pontiac Streamliner was a hit at the club's 1977 convention in san Diego, Calif. (POCI photo)

clicks, members can gain technical information in the Technical Forum, view parts for sale in the On-Line Want Ads, find out upcoming local events in the Chapter News Section, and interact with other members via POCI's "real-time" chat room.

The *POCI Membership Roster* is published annually and includes each member and associate member's name, address and phone number (at member's discretion) along with a list of Pontiac or Oakland cars they own. It's a valuable tool for locating other members and a must when traveling nearby other member's homes.

POCI maintains one of the largest libraries of Pontiac and Oakland information available today. Its services are open to all members. The library is one of the ways membership dues are used to

Pontiac shared space with banquet tables inside a hotel in Orlando, Fla., during an early POCI convention held there. (POCI photo)

This tram carried POCI members on tours of the Pontiac motor Div. engine plant during the 1975 meet at the automaker's headquarters in Pontiac, Mich. (John Gunnell photo)

Byron "Joe" Stout III had several "stretched" Pontiacs in his collection and brought this 1963 Bonneville-based Superior combination car to the 1982 POCI convention in Minneapolis. (John Gunnell photo)

POCI has always welcomed Pontiacs of all years. This 1975 Grand Ville convertible picked up a trophy at the 1975 convention in Medina, Ohio. (John Gunnell photo)

POCI member Jim Pauling's 1948 Pontiac Torpedo sedan was used in a motion picture flmed years ago in England. (POCI photo)

further the preservation of Pontiac automobiles and their history. Duplicate items are periodically offered for sale to members, with the proceeds going towards the purchase of additional items to further enhance the collection.

POCI's Technical Advisor program has been a great help to members since the formation of the club in the early 1970s. It continues to grow and offer more services as the membership expands and covers more areas of expertise. The technical advisors are board-approved members who possess knowledge in a particular area. These men and women volunteer their time to assist fellow members with their questions and needs. Any problems, from authentic paint and upholstery, to mechanical rebuilds and performance problems, can be addressed by POCI's staff of technical advisors.

Local and regional chapters are the backbone of POCI. These far-flung "arms" of the club host a wide variety of activities and offer members a means of group participation in car shows, meets, tours, rallies, and many other family oriented activities located near their homes. Members are strongly urged to join a local chapter. POCI also provides "specialty" chapters to serve members interested in a particular type of Pontiac or Oakland across regional boundaries.

An annual POCI International Convention is held each year in a different part of the country. The convention attracts hundreds of members and their cars from all over. The convention is held annually in various locations throughout the U.S., but draws visitors from overseas as well.

POCI is a strong, active, concerned organization. Much of the current interest in Pontiac and Oakland automobiles is due to the Pontiac-Oakland Club. In nearly 30 years of operation, it has grown into a worldwide group of devoted Pontiac and Oakland enthusiasts numbering nearly 11,000 strong. Contact the club at: POCI, PO Box 9569, Bradenton, FL 34206 or call (941) 750-9234.

This 1939 Pontiac street rod owned by Fred Menger showed up the the club's convention in Minneapolis, Minn., in 1982. It has been to many other of the annual gatherings, too. (John Gunnell photo)

Graham Weber, of Great Britain, has been a long-time POCI member and club officer. He is seen here with his 1938 Pontiac six-cylinder coupe. (POCI photo)

PONTIAC HISTORIC SERVICES

By John Gunnell

Pontiac enthusiasts interested in finding out more about the history of their car have two great sources of information available. Pontiac Historic Services (PHS) will perform historical research services for owners of 1961-97 Pontiacs for a small fee. For those with late-model Pontiacs, the Pontiac Customer Assistance Center is very helpful. Call (800) 762-2737 to find out about this free service for owners of 1998-2001 Pontiacs.

Pontiac Historic Services is an independent business that works hand-in-hand with Pontiac Motor Division. It was created by Jim Mattison, a noted Pontiac historian and car enthusiast. In addition to handling concept car logistics for Pontiac, PHS provides Pontiac collectors with two main services: a vehicle identification number (VIN) and an information packet about their cars and copies of factory-original window stickers. The VIN and Information Packet cost was $35 ($45 by fax) when Krause Publications visited PHS recently. The window stickers cost $28.

Each VIN and Information Packet is put together for each car researched according to its VIN. The packets include an official factory photo of the particular model Pontiac, a copy of the dealer order form for that car, a copy of the factory invoice, a copy of the original press release, and other information such as AMA (Automobile Manufacturers Assoc.) specifications sheets, production numbers, engine production numbers, and production breakdowns by engine and transmission.

Documents like these can come in very handy when a collector is authenticating the originality or rarity of a vehicle. They can also help potential Pontiac buyers check the car out.

Pontiac Historic Services supplies a standard ordering form that car owners must complete and mail or fax to the company. The form can be downloaded from the Pontiac Historic Services Web site, but online ordering is not available. Checks, money orders, or Visa or MasterCard credit cards can be used to order by mail at the standard price, or by fax for the $10 higher fee.

Jim Mattison retains the Pontiac historical files once housed in the company's public relations department. Believe it or not, the desk that Jim Mattison uses once belonged to Pontiac's famous general manager "Bunkie" Knudesen. (John Gunnell photo)

Dayna Hart, of Pontiac-GMC Public Relations, works as a laison between PMD and Pontiac Historical Services. (John Gunnell photo)

Krause Publications has known of the existence of Pontiac Historic Services for several years, but had not used its services since our staff members owned pre-1961 Pontiacs. Our recent visit convinced us that the company has an impressive collection of materials. In fact, I was very impressed when I saw file cabinets full of Pontiac Motor Division records that I had not seen since the early 1980s when I researched my first book on Pontiac-Oakland history called *75 Years of Pontiac-Oakland*. Many of the materials in that collection were gathered together in the 1970s by my old friend John Harwood.

Having good files and using them properly are two quite different things, and before I wrote this article publicizing Pontiac Historic Services, I wanted some first-hand reports from someone who had used the service. While poking around the Internet, I came across the Web site www.gtasourcepage.com which detailed how the Pontiac Historic Services had been used to research a 1988 Pontiac Trans Am GTA.

"Through the activities of PHS, virtually any Pontiac owner can now know all the information that the factory had on their car when it was new," says the Web site. "For those of us collectors and enthusiasts who really love our cars, it is an invaluable service indeed."

To get additional information about PHS, write to: Jim Mattison, president, Pontiac Historic Services, P.O. Box 884, Sterling Heights, MI 48311-0884. You can also visit www.phs-online.com or email 1gmman@home.com.

OAKLAND
1908-1931

1908 OAKLAND

1908 Oakland Model B touring. (HAC)

OAKLAND — TWO-CYLINDER — The Oakland was the idea of two men: Edward M. Murphy, who was anxious to move his Pontiac Buggy Co. into the automotive age, and Alanson P. Brush, who was responsible for early Cadillac designs. They met around 1906, by which time Brush had set himself up in business as an engineering consultant in Detroit. Brush showed Murphy his design for a small two-cylinder car that Cadillac had rejected. Its vertical engine rotated counterclockwise and its planetary transmission was unusual for a lack of braking bands. Brush used clutches running in oil instead. Murphy bought this automotive idea, which he decided should carry the same name—Oakland—as his horse-drawn vehicles. During the summer of 1907, Murphy organized the Oakland Motor Car Co. The first Oakland was ready by auto-show time in January 1908, although Brush was no longer in Pontiac. Having found another automotive pioneer, named Frank Briscoe, with available funds, Brush was back in Detroit building his single-cylinder Brush runabout. Standard equipment included a wood frame, oil lamps, generator, brass horn, 10-spoke wheels in front (all)/12-spoke wheels in rear (all), and right-hand steering.

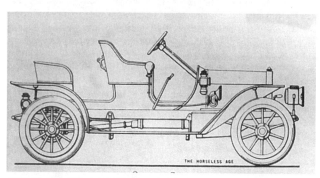

1908 Oakland Model C Tourabout. (JAG)

Model Number	Body/Style Number	Body Type & Seating	Factory Price	Shipping Weight	Production Total
A	—	3P Runabout	1,375	1,600	Note 1
B	—	5P Touring	1,400	1,650	Note 1
C	—	4P Tourabout	—	—	Note 1
D	—	Taxicab	1,850	1,800	Note 1
E	—	Landaulette	—	—	Note 1

NOTE 1: Estimated production for all Oakland models in 1908 was 200-278 cars.

ENGINE: Used in 1908 and 1909 production. (Serial number 1-300) KMC engine: Vertical. Two-cylinder. Bore & stroke: 4-1/2 x 5 in. Displacement: 159.1 cid. Horsepower: 20. Water-cooled. (Serial number 300-750) GMC engine: Vertical. Two-cylinder. Bore & stroke: 4-1/2 x 5 in. Displacement: 159.1 cid. Horsepower: 20. Water-cooled.

TECHNICAL: Planetary transmission with two speeds forward, one reverse. Direct drive on high. Multiple disc clutch. Shaft drive to live rear axle. Tubular front axle (early production only).

CHASSIS: Wheelbase: 96 in. Semi-elliptic front springs 36 x 2 in. Full elliptic rear springs 38 x 2 in. 32-in. wheels (front on two-point ball-bearing; rear on roller bearings). 3-1/2-in. tires.

OPTION: Folding top ($75).

HISTORICAL: One of two remaining 1908 Oaklands, a Model B touring, is part of the collection of the Indianapolis Motor Speedway Museum in Speedway, Ind.

1909 OAKLAND

1909 Oakland Model 40G four-passenger touring roadster. (JAG)

OAKLAND — TWO-CYLINDER/FOUR-CYLINDER — For 1909, a line of 40-hp four-cylinder cars with sliding-gear transmissions was introduced. Tragically, at the age of 44, Edward M. Murphy died suddenly in September 1908. Five months prior to his passing, Murphy met with another former buggy man named William C. Durant. Soon afterwards, Oakland became part of Durant's General Motors empire. Standard equipment included: wood frame, spare tire carrier, running board-mounted tool boxes, lamps, generator, brass horn, 12-spoke wheels front and rear (all), right-hand steering.

1909 Oakland Model 40 five-passenger touring. (OCW)

1909 Oakland Model 40F five-passenger touring. (JAG)

HP Series Number	Model Number	Body Type & Seating	Factory Price	Shipping Weight	Production Total
SERIES 20 (2-cyl.)					
20	20-A	3P Runabout	1,250	1,700	Note 1
20	20-B	5P Touring	1,250	1,740	Note 1
20	20-C	4P Touring Rds	1,250	1,740	Note 1
SERIES 40 (4-cyl.)					
40	40-E	3P Runabout	1,600	2,025	Note 1
40	40-F	5P Touring	1,600	2,100	Note 1
40	40-G	4P Touring Rds	1,600	2,100	Note 1
40	40-H	Toy Tonneau	1,600	—	Note 1

NOTE 1: Estimated production for all Oakland models in 1909 was 1,035 cars of which approximately 700 were 40 Series and the rest were 20 Series.

ENGINE [40 Series]: Four-cylinder, Bore & stroke: 4-1/2 x 5 in. Displacement: 318.1 cid. Horsepower: 40. Water-cooled.

ENGINE [20 Series]: Used in 1908 and 1909 production. (Serial number 1-300) KMC engine: Vertical. Two-cylinder. Bore & stroke: 4-1/2 x 5 in. Displacement: 159.1 cid. Horsepower: 16. Water-cooled. (Serial number 300-750) GMC engine: Vertical. Two-cylinder. Bore & stroke: 4-1/2 x 5 in. Displacement: 159.1 cid. Horsepower: 20. Water-cooled.

TECHNICAL: [40 Series] Sliding transmission. Shaft drive. [20 Series] Planetary transmission with two speeds forward, one reverse. Direct drive on high. Multiple disc clutch. Shaft drive to live rear axle.

CHASSIS: [40 Series] Wheelbase: 112 in., 4-in. tires. [20 Series] Wheelbase: 100 in., 3-1/2-in. tires.

OPTIONS: Folding top ($75). Storage batteries ($15). Tire cover ($3.50). Prestolite tank ($18-$35). Stewart speedometer ($25). Windshield ($35). Tire chains ($10-$11).

HISTORICAL: On April 9, 1909, Oakland joined Buick and Oldsmobile as part of the General Motors Corp.

1910 OAKLAND

1910 Oakland Model 24 touring. (HAC)

OAKLAND — FOUR-CYLINDER — Oakland manufactured four-cylinder cars exclusively in 1910 and sales of 3,000-5,000 cars a year became the norm. "The Car with a Conscience" was Oakland's slogan and the marque acquitted itself admirably in motor sports, particularly in reliability runs and hill climbs. The brand won no less than 25 hill climbs including those at Giant's Despair and Dead Horse Hill. Standard equipment included: headlamps, a taillight, door handles, brass horn, 12-spoke wheels front and rear (all), right-hand steering.

HP Series Number	Model Number	Body Type & Seating	Factory Price	Shipping Weight	Production Total
SERIES (4-cyl.)					
30	24	2P Runabout	1,000	1,600	Note 1
30	25	5P Touring	1,250	1,800	Note 1
40	K	5P Touring	1,700	2,250	Note 1
40	M	2P Roadster	1,700	—	Note 1

NOTE 1: Estimated calendar year production for all Oakland models in 1910 was 4,049 cars.

ENGINE [30 Series]: Four-cylinder. Bore & stroke: 4 x 4 in. Displacement: 201.1 cid. Horsepower: 30. Water-cooled.

ENGINE [40 Series]: Four-cylinder. Bore & stroke: 4-1/2 x 5 in. Displacement: 318.1 cid. Horsepower: 40. Water-cooled.

TECHNICAL: [30 Series] Force-feed lubrication with pump, jump spark ignition with magneto, bronze and steel multiple disc clutch with cork inserts. [40 Series] Sliding transmission. Shaft drive. Brakes: (all) lined expanding and contracting units on rear wheel drums.

CHASSIS: [30 Series] Wheelbase: 100 in., 3-1/2-in. tires, wheels mounted on ball and roller bearings. [40 Series] Wheelbase: 112 in., 4-in. tires.

1910 Oakland touring. (OCW)

OPTIONS: Folding top. Full side and front curtains. Brass cowl lamps.

HISTORICAL: 40 Series Oaklands were assigned serial numbers 3000 to 5000 while 30 Series cars were given serial numbers A-1000 to A-4500.

1911 OAKLAND

1911 Oakland Model 24 30-hp runabout. (JAG)

OAKLAND — FOUR-CYLINDER — Oakland offered two four-cylinder lines in 1911. The model designations were based on their National Automobile Chamber of Commerce (NACC) horsepower ratings. Standard equipment on the 30 Series included a pressed steel frame, gas headlights, oil sidelights, and right-hand steering. The 40 Series models featured a pressed steel frame, gas headlights, oil sidelights, a taillight, a horn, a robe rail, a gas generator, tools, an air pump, jack, a tire repair kit, and right-hand steering.

HP Series Number	Model Number	Body Type & Seating	Factory Price	Shipping Weight	Production Total
SERIES 30 (4-cyl.)					
30	24	2P Runabout	1,000	—	Note 1

Note: A closed-bodied two-passenger coupe body fitted to the Model 24 Runabout chassis was also available. This version of the Model 24 sold for $1,500.

30	25	5P Touring	1,150	—	Note 1

Note: A Torpedo Touring model of the Model 25 was also available for $1,200.

30	33	5P Touring	1,200	—	Note 1
SERIES 40 (4-cyl.)					
40	K Special	5P Touring	1,600	—	Note 1
40	K	5P Touring	1,500	—	Note 1
40	M	2P Roadster	1,550	—	Note 1

NOTE 1: Estimated calendar year production for all Oakland models in 1911 was 3,386 cars.

ENGINE [30 Series]: L-head four-cylinder. Bore & stroke: 4 x 4 in. Displacement: 201.1 cid. Horsepower: 30. Water-cooled.

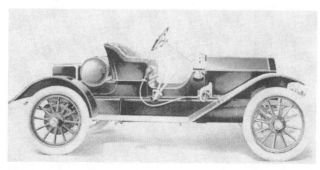

1911 Oakland Model M 40-hp roadster. (JAG)

1911 Oakland Model 30 five-passenger touring. (JAG)

ENGINE [40 Series]: L-head four-cylinder. Bore & stroke: 4-1/2 x 5 in. Displacement: 318.1 cid. Horsepower: 40. Water-cooled.

TECHNICAL: Both series: Force-feed lubrication with pump, jump spark ignition with magneto, selective, sliding-gear transmission working through multiple disc clutch. Brakes: foot or outboard lever-operated expanding and contracting units on rear wheel drums.

CHASSIS: [30 Series] Wheelbase: 100 in. except Model 24 Runabout with 96 in., 3-1/2-in. tires, 37-in. front semi-elliptic springs, 42-in. rear full-elliptic springs. [40 Series] Wheelbase: 112 in., 4-in. tires, 36-in. front semi-elliptic springs, 39-in. rear full-elliptic springs. Both series: Dropped I-beam front axle, strut rods added to rear suspension.

OPTIONS: Folding top. Speedometer. Spare tire carrier.

HISTORICAL: George P. Daniels, former president of General Motors Corp., became Oakland's third general manager and held this post through 1914.

1912 OAKLAND

1912 Oakland Model 40 sociable roadster. (HAC)

OAKLAND — FOUR — Common features of all 1912 Oaklands included drop-forged I-beam front axles, inside controls, water cooling with centrifugal pump and belt-driven fan, enclosed drive shafts, front semi-elliptic springs, three-quarter elliptic rear springs, worm-and-nut steering gear, artillery wheels with quick demountable rims, splash system lubrication, and a 56-in. tread. A restyled line of cars that appeared at the New York Auto Salon in early January had black painted radiators, decorative trim moldings, beveled or "lipped" front fender edges, new headlights (painted black) and higher mounted side lamps. Standard equipment included: Inside controls, acetylene tanks (replaced tool boxes mounted on right-hand running boards at midyear), gas headlights, oil sidelights, taillight, horn, tire repair kit, and right-hand steering.

Model Number	Body/Style Number	Body Type & Seating	Factory Price	Shipping Weight	Production Total
SERIES 30 (4-cyl.)					
30	—	2P Roadster	1,200	2,400	Note 1
30	—	5P Touring	1,250	2,600	Note 1
SERIES 40 (4-cyl.)					
40	—	5P Touring	1,450	2,900	Note 1
40	—	3P Coupe	1,900	3,150	Note 1
40	—	3P Roadster	1,450	2,275	Note 1

Model Number	Body/Style Number	Body Type & Seating	Factory Price	Shipping Weight	Production Total
SERIES 45 (4-cyl.)					
45	—	7P Touring	2,100	3,650	Note 1
45	—	4P Touring	2,250	—	Note 1
45	—	Limousine	3,000	4,150	Note 1

NOTE 1: Estimated model year production for all Oakland models in 1912 was 4,366 cars, while calendar year production was estimated to be 5,838 cars.

ENGINE [Model 30]: L-head four-cylinder. Bore & stroke: 4 x 4 in. Displacement: 201.1 cid. Horsepower: 30. Water-cooled.

ENGINE [Model 40]: Four-cylinder. Bore & stroke: 4-1/8 x 4-3/4 in. Displacement: 253.9 cid. Horsepower: 40. Water-cooled.

ENGINE [Model 45]: Four-cylinder. Bore & stroke: 4-1/2 x 5-1/4 in. Displacement: 334 cid. Horsepower: 45. Water-cooled.

TECHNICAL: [All models] worm and nut steering gear; artillery-type wheels with quick-demountable rims; splash system lubrication; water cooling with centrifugal pump and belt-driven fan; magneto ignition; three-speed, selective, sliding-gear transmission (except Model 30 "Oriole 33" that used transmission utilizing multiple disc clutch carried over from 1911 Model 33); enclosed drive shafts.

CHASSIS: [Model 30] Wheelbase: 100 in. for roadster-bodied cars, 106 in. for other coachwork, 3-1/2-in. tires, semi-floating rear axle. [Model 40] Wheelbase: 112 in., 4-in. tires, semi-floating rear axle. [Model 45] Wheelbase: 120 in., 4-1/2-in. tires, full-floating rear axle. All: Drop-forged I-beam front axles, front semi-elliptic springs, rear three-quarter-elliptic springs.

OPTIONS: Folding top. Windshield. Right side mounted spare tire carrier.

HISTORICAL: Oakland automobiles underwent numerous design changes during the 1912 models production run as well as having models drop in and out of sales catalogs depicting that year's offerings. At least 22 distinct automobiles can be found pictured in sales literature promoting 1912 Oaklands. One model that appeared briefly in 1912 was the Model 30 Model "26" that was similar to the Model 30 "Oriole 33," which was basically a carry-over of the 1911 Model 33. Oakland ranked eighth in sales within the industry.

1913 OAKLAND

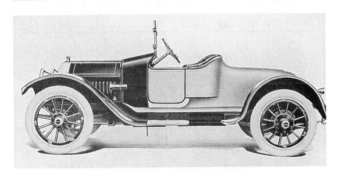

1913 Oakland Model 42 sociable roadster. (HAC)

OAKLAND — FOUR/SIX — The big news from Oakland Motor Car Co. in 1913 was the six-cylinder 60-hp Greyhound line. New coachwork features for models introduced in 1913 included rounded V-shaped radiators with German silver tops, flush-sided panels with concealed door handles and hinges, a sleek low-angle cowl dash, nickel trimming and extra-heavy upholstery. Other models were carried over from 1912. Standard equipment features included a double-drop steel frame on 6-60 and 42 Models and a single-drop steel frame on 40 and 35 Models. Model 35s offered both right-hand and left-hand steering. Air or electric self starter systems were offered on the 6-60 line. Also offered as standard equipment on the Greyhound line were electric headlights, side lights, a tail lamp, a Klaxon horn, a complete tool kit, a tire repair outfit, a pump and a jack. Aluminum steps were used in place of running boards on 6-60 and 42 Models. All models had artillery-spoke wheels with demountable rims.

1913 Oakland touring. (JAG)

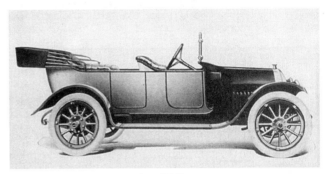

1913 Oakland Model 35 touring. (JAG)

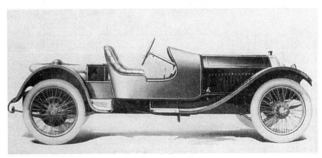

1913 Oakland Model 6-60 roadster. (JAG)

Model Number	Body/Style Number	Body Type & Seating	Factory Price	Shipping Weight	Production Total
SERIES 35 (4-cyl.)					
—	35	3P Roadster	1,000	2,760	Note 1
—	35	5P Touring	1,075	2,660	Note 1

Model 35 Note: Both Torpedo-bodied Speedster and Runabout versions based on the Model 35 chassis were also available.

Model Number	Body/Style Number	Body Type & Seating	Factory Price	Shipping Weight	Production Total
SERIES 40 (4-cyl.)					
—	40	5P Touring	1,450		2,900 Note 1
SERIES 42 (4-cyl.)					
—	42	4P Coupe	2,500	3,700	Note 1
—	42	3P Roadster	1,750	—	Note 1
—	42	5P Touring	1,750	3,600	Note 1
—	45	Limousine	3,000	4,150	Note 1
GREYHOUND SERIES 60 (6-cyl.)					
Greyhound	6-60	2P Roadster	2,550	4,235	Note 1
Greyhound	6-60	4P Touring	2,550	4,160	Note 1
Greyhound	6-60	7P Touring	2,550	4,235	Note 1

NOTE 1: Calendar year production for Oakland in 1913 was recorded as 7,030 cars.

ENGINE [Model 35]: L-head four-cylinder. Bore & stroke: 3-1/2 x 5 in. Displacement: 192.4 cid. Horsepower: 30. Water-cooled.

ENGINE [Model 40]: Four-cylinder. Bore & stroke: 4-1/8 x 4-3/4 in. Displacement: 253.9 cid. Horsepower: 40. Water-cooled.

ENGINE [Model 42]: Four-cylinder. Bore & stroke: 4-1/8 x 4-3/4 in. Displacement: 253.9 cid. Horsepower: 40. Water-cooled.

ENGINE [Model 45]: Four-cylinder. Bore & stroke: 4-1/2 x 5-1/4 in. Displacement: 334 cid. Horsepower: 45. Water-cooled.

ENGINE [Model 6-60]: Six-cylinder. Bore & stroke: 4-1/8 x 4-3/4 in. Displacement: 380.9 cid. Horsepower: 60. Water-cooled.

TECHNICAL: [Model 35] Spiral timing gears; force-feed lubrication through a camshaft-driven oil pump. [Model 40/42] 4.0:1 final gear ratio; gear-driven engine accessories. [Model 6-60] Silent Coventry chain system to drive magneto; water pump; and camshaft. 3.5:1 final gear ratio. Delco system with electric lighting and ignition combined with air self-starter or electric self-starter.

CHASSIS: [Model 35] Wheelbase: 112 in., 3-1/2-in. tires, semi-floating rear axle. [Model 40] Wheelbase: 114 in., semi-floating rear axle. [Model 42] Wheelbase: 116 in., 4-in. tires, full-floating rear axle. [Model 45] Wheelbase: 120 in., 4-1/2- in. tires, full-floating rear axle. [Model 6-60] Wheelbase: 130 in., 4-1/2-in. tires, underslung rear springs, open shaft drive via a rear parallel torque arm system.

OPTIONS: Folding top. Windshield. Delco system on 6-60 optional on Model 42.

HISTORICAL: As in the previous year, Oakland sales literature offered many different models, 14 for 1913. The new Model 35 was the sales leader for Oakland in this year.

1914 OAKLAND

1914 Oakland Model 36 touring. (HAC)

OAKLAND — FOUR/SIX — References sources conflict a bit as to exactly what models comprised the "1914 Oakland" line at any given point in the year. What is clear is that four types of cars were sold at various times during the season. Standard equipment varied as follows: [Model 36] Full running boards, single-drop channel steel frame, right-hand steering, loop-type handles on "suicide" doors on Cabriolet Coupe as well as fold-down top with detachable side window frames, locking stowage compartment on Roadsters. [Model 43] Full running boards, double-drop channel steel frame, Center Door Sedan also featured loop-type door handles as well as forward door pillar-mounted coach lamps, silk window curtains, interior dome lamp, flip-out windshield glass. [Model 6-48] Roadster featured tool box and spare tire carried on rear deck, steering wheel-mounted spark and throttle control, toe board-mounted foot accelerator. [Model 6-60] Centrifugal pump on magneto shaft used to circulate coolant.

Model Number	Body/Style Number	Body Type & Seating	Factory Price	Shipping Weight	Production Total
LIGHT FOUR SERIES (4-cyl.)					
Light Four	36	2P Cabriolet Coupe	1,585	—	Note 1
Light Four	36	3P Roadster	1,150	2,760	Note 1
Light Four	36	5P Touring	1,200	2,660	Note 1

Model 36 Notes: A two-passenger roadster-bodied Model 36 was also available in 1914 for $1,100. Also, some sources list the Model 36 three-passenger Roadster as a carry-over Model 35 from 1935.

Model Number	Body/Style Number	Body Type & Seating	Factory Price	Shipping Weight	Production Total
BIG FOUR SERIES (4-cyl.)					
Big Four	43	4P Coupe	2,500	—	Note 1
Big Four	43	4P Sedan	2,600	—	Note 1
Big Four	43	5P Touring	1,785	—	Note 1
LIGHT SIX SERIES (6-cyl.)					
Light Six	6-48	2P Speedster	1,785	—	Note 1
Light Six	6-48	2P Roadster	1,785	—	Note 1
Light Six	6-48	5P Touring	1,785	3,350	Note 1
BIG SIX SERIES (6-cyl.)					
Big Six	6-60	2P Raceabout	2,450	—	Note 1
Big Six	6-60	4P Touring	2,450	4,235	Note 1
Big Six	6-60	5P Touring	2,450	4,160	Note 1
Big Six	6-60	7P Touring	2,450	4,235	Note 1

Model 6-60 Notes: Some sources list the final 950 Model 6-60s built as Model 6-61s. The 6-60/6-61 evolved at midyear 1914 into the Model 6-62, which was available only as a seven-passenger touring for $2,500. Also, some sources list a 6-60 Roadster as part of the Big Six lineup.

NOTE 1: Calendar year production for all Oaklands in 1914 was recorded as 6,105 cars.

ENGINE [Model 36]: Four-cylinder. Bore & stroke: 3-1/2 x 5 in. Displacement: 192.4 cid. Horsepower: 35. Water-cooled.

ENGINE [Model 43]: Four-cylinder. Bore & stroke: 4-1/4 x 5-1/4 in. Displacement: 297.8 cid. Horsepower: 48. Water-cooled.

ENGINE [Model 6-48]: Six-cylinder. Bore & stroke: 3-1/2 x 5 in. Displacement: 288.9 cid. Horsepower: 48. Water-cooled.

ENGINE [Model 6-60]: Six-cylinder. Bore & stroke: 4-1/8 x 4-3/4 in. Displacement: 380.9 cid. Horsepower: 60. Water-cooled, four-bearing crankshaft with babbitt bearings.

TECHNICAL: [Model 36] Spiral timing gears; force-feed lubrication through a camshaft-driven oil pump. 4.0:1 final gear ratio. [Model 43] 4.0:1 final gear ratio (3.5:1 and 3.7:1 optional); gearbox offered three forward speeds and one reverse operated off a cone-type clutch, both enclosed in an extension off the crankcase. [Model 6-48] 3.5:1 final gear ratio; same gearbox and clutch system as Model 43; worm and nut steering. [Model 6-60] Motor-clutch-transmission formed three-point suspended unit drivetrain.

CHASSIS: [Model 36] Wheelbase: 112 in., 4-in. tires, semi-floating rear axle on roller bearings, semi-elliptic front springs and three-quarter elliptic rear springs. Brakes: 12-in. drum on rear only. [Model 43] Wheelbase: 116 in., 4-1/2-in. tires. [Model 6-48] Wheelbase: 123-1/2 in., 4-in. tires. Brakes: 14-in. drum on rear only, semi-elliptic front springs and three-quarter elliptic rear springs. [Model 6-60] Wheelbase: 130 in., full-floating rear axle, 4-1/2-in. tires. (Midyear 6-62 replacement for Model 6-60 had a longer, 138-in. wheelbase and 5-in. tires.) Brakes: dual set of internal expanding brakes acting on 16 -in. drums on rear only.

OPTIONS: Wire wheels for Model 6-48 Roadster and Speedster, spare tire for Model 43 (fifth rim was standard equipment).

HISTORICAL: An estimated 100 of the Model 6-62 seven-passenger touring were built. The 7.32-liter (446.6 cid.) engine in the 6-62 was the biggest engine ever installed in an Oakland chassis.

1915 OAKLAND

1915 Oakland Model 37 touring. (HAC)

OAKLAND — FOUR/SIX — Oakland created a five-car lineup for 1915. It was based entirely on the Light Four and Light Six chassis. Left-hand steering was now used on all Oakland models. Standard equipment included a one-man top equipped with storm-proof side curtains, full running boards, a Stewart speedometer, a tail-light, headlights with a dimmer switch, a shroud light, and an electric horn. The Model 37 speedster featured low-cut side panels, twin bucket seats, a folding windshield, a toolbox, and two spare

20

1915 Oakland Model 37 roadster. (JAG)

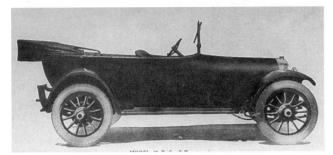
1915 Oakland Model 6-49 touring. (JAG)

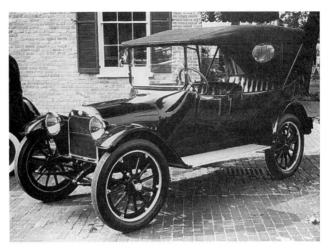
1916 Oakland touring. (OCW)

tires on a platform behind seats. The Model 6-49 also included a motor-driven tire pump.

Model Number	Body/Style Number	Body Type & Seating	Factory Price	Shipping Weight	Production Total
LIGHT FOUR SERIES (4-cyl.)					
Light Four	37	2P Speedster	1100	2450	Note 1
Light Four	37	2P Roadster	1150	2530	Note 1
Light Four	37	5P Touring	1200	2660	Note 1
LIGHT SIX SERIES (6-cyl.)					
Light Six	6-49	2P Convertible Rds	1685	—	Note 1
Light Six	6-49	5P Touring	1685	3470	Note 1

Model 6-49 Note: Some sources list a Speedster as being available, but no specifics on this model are available.

NOTE 1: Calendar year production for all Oaklands in 1915 totaled 11,952 cars.

ENGINE [Model 37]: Four-cylinder. Bore & stroke: 3-1/2 x 5 in. Displacement: 192.4 cid. Horsepower: 30. Water-cooled.

ENGINE [Model 6-49]: Six-cylinder. Bore & stroke: 3-1/2 x 5 in. Displacement: 288.9 cid. Horsepower: 30. Water-cooled.

TECHNICAL: [Model 37] Wedge-connection brake rods that eliminated bearing use; tubular propeller shaft; self-cleaning brake lever rockers. [Model 6-49] Delco electrical system featuring low-tension magneto; storage battery and dry cells; three-speed-sliding selective gear transmission; and leather-faced cone clutch. Both Models: Oakland-Stewart vacuum-gravity fuel-feed system.

CHASSIS: [Model 37] Wheelbase: 112 in., 4-in. tires (Non-Skid tires mounted on rear), Hotchkiss drive rear axle. [Model 6-49] Wheelbase: 123-1/2 in., 4-1/2-in. tires, full-floating rear axle, underslung springs front and rear.

HISTORICAL: General Motors President Charles Nash was listed as general manager of Oakland in 1915. Serial numbers for Model 37s ran from 370000 to 373599 while Model 6-49 serial numbers ran from 490000 to 490500. Oakland's first V-8 engine was introduced late in 1915 for use in a 1916 model Oakland.

1916 OAKLAND

OAKLAND — FOUR/SIX — For 1916 Oakland offered a Light Four called the Model 38 that was much like the previous Model 37 and

an all-new Light Six Model 32. Late in the fall of 1915, the company also introduced the Model 50 as a 1916 model. This huge, powerful and expensive offering came only as a big seven-passenger touring car with dual-cowl styling. Standard Oakland equipment included a single-wire electrical system operated at six volts and a one-man folding top. The Model 38 featured a ventilating windshield, an ammeter, and a Stewart speedometer. The Model 50 added two folding auxiliary seats.

Model Number	Body/Style Number	Body Type & Seating	Factory Price	Shipping Weight	Production Total
LIGHT FOUR SERIES (4-cyl.)					
Light Four	38	Speedster	1,050	2,440	Note 1
Light Four	38	Roadster	1,050	2,460	Note 1
Light Four	38	5P Touring	1,050	2,575	Note 1
LIGHT SIX SERIES (6-cyl.)					
Light Six	32	2P Roadster	795	2,115	Note 1
Light Six	32	5P Touring	795	2,185	Note 1

Model 32 Note: Midyear 1916 the Model 32 became the Model 32-B with no production changes to the car.

	Body/Style Number	Body Type & Seating	Factory Price	Shipping Weight	Production Total
V-8 SERIES (8-cyl.)					
-	50	7P Dual Cowl Tour	1,585	3,515	Note 1

NOTE 1: Calendar year production for all Oaklands in 1916 totaled 25,675 cars.

ENGINE [Model 38]: Four-cylinder. Bore & stroke: 3-1/2 x 5 in. Displacement: 192.4 cid. Horsepower: 30. Water-cooled.

ENGINE [Model 32]: Flathead six-cylinder. Bore & stroke: 2-13/16 x 4-3/4 in. Displacement: 177 cid. Horsepower: 30-35. Water-cooled.

ENGINE [Model 50]: V-8. Bore & stroke: 3-1/2 x 4-1/2-in. Displacement: 346.3 cid. Horsepower: 71 at 2600 rpm. This V-8 engine featured aluminum pistons and a counterbalanced crankshaft.

TECHNICAL: [Model 38] More compact unit powerplant due to downsized clutch. [Model 32] Three-speed selective-type transmission with cone clutch. [Model 50] Three-point unit suspended drive.

CHASSIS: [Model 38] Wheelbase: 112 in., 4 in. tires (Non-Skid tires mounted on rear). [Model 32] Wheelbase: 110 in., 3-1/2-in. tires (Non-Skid tires mounted on rear). [Model 50] Wheelbase: 127 in., 4-1/2-in. tires, overslung half-elliptic front springs and underslung three-quarter rear springs, pressed steel full-floating rear axle. Brakes: 14-in. drum.

HISTORICAL: Fred W. Warner was appointed general manager of Oakland in 1916. Serial numbers for Model 38s ran from 380000 to 384001 while Model 32 serial numbers ran from 320000 to 347110. Serial numbers for Oakland's first V-8 engined Model 50 ran from 500000 to 502000.

1917 OAKLAND

OAKLAND — SIX/V-8 — In December 1916 *MoToR* magazine announced that "detail refinements in the Oakland Six" had been

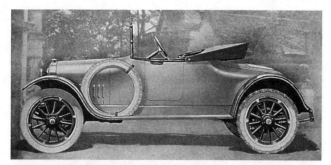
1917 Oakland Model 34 roadster. (HAC)

made. The result was the Model 34. Standard equipment on the Model 34 included a dash light to monitor oil flow and a driver's side mounted spare tire. The Model 50 was carried over unchanged from 1916.

Model Number	Body/Style Number	Body Type & Seating	Factory Price	Shipping Weight	Production Total
OAKLAND SIX SERIES (6-cyl.)					
Oakland Six	34	2P Roadster	795	2,230	Note 1
Oakland Six	34	5P Touring	795	2,330	Note 1
Oakland Six	34	Convertible Sedan	1,020	2,450	Note 1
Oakland Six	34	Convertible Coupe	995	2,350	Note 1
OAKLAND V-8 SERIES (8-cyl.)					
Oakland Eight	50	7P Dual Cowl Trg	1,585	3,515	Note 1

NOTE 1: Calendar year production for all Oaklands in 1917 totaled 33,171 cars.

ENGINE [Model 34]: OHV flathead six-cylinder. Bore & stroke: 2-13/16 x 4-3/4 in. Displacement: 177 cid. Horsepower: 41 at 2500 rpm. Water-cooled.

ENGINE [Model 50]: V-8. Bore & stroke: 3-1/2 x 4-1/2 in. Displacement: 346.3 cid. Horsepower: 71 at 2600 rpm. This V-8 engine featured aluminum pistons and a counterbalanced crankshaft.

TECHNICAL: [Model 34] Circulating splash system engine oiling, cooling via pump mounted on fan shaft operated off fan belt. [Model 50] Unchanged from 1916.

CHASSIS: [Model 34] Wheelbase: 112 in., 4-in. tires (Non-Skid tires mounted on rear), semi-elliptic rear springs. [Model 50] Wheelbase: 127 in., 4-1/2-in. tires, overslung half-elliptic front springs and under-slung three-quarter rear springs, pressed steel full-floating rear axle. Brakes: 14-in. drum.

HISTORICAL: On Aug. 1, 1917, the Oakland Motor Car Co. became the Oakland Motor Div. due to General Motors changing from a holding company to an operating company. Model 34 serial numbers ran from 134 to 3000034.

1918 OAKLAND

1918 Oakland Model 34-B roadster. (OCW)

OAKLAND — SIX — Better engine manifolding and a new cooling fan were the chief merits of the 1918 Oakland Model 34-B. New

1918 Oakland Model 34-B Sensible Six roadster. (JAG)

features found in the engine included aluminum pistons and redesigned connecting rods. Standard equipment included a one-man folding top with detachable side curtains, a footrest for easy operation of accelerator pedal, and an oil-pan-mounted oil gauge. The dashboard instrumentation included amp, oil pressure and fuel-level gauges, as well as an odometer and trip odometer. A power tire pump was also featured.

Model Number	Body/Style Number	Body Type & Seating	Factory Price	Shipping Weight	Production Total
SENSIBLE SIX SERIES (6-cyl.)					
Sensible Six	34-B	2P Roadster	1,185	2,070	Note 1
Sensible Six	34-B	5P Touring	1,185	2,130	Note 1
Sensible Six	34-B	Sedan	1,760	2,650	Note 1
Sensible Six	34-B	Coupe	1,760	2,350	Note 1
Sensible Six	34-B	Roadster Coupe	1,210	2,175	Note 1
Sensible Six	34-B	5P Touring Sedan	1,250	2,290	Note 1

1918 Oakland Model 34-B Sensible Six touring sedan. (JAG)

1918 Oakland Model 34-B Sensible Six unit-body coupe. (JAG)

1918 Oakland Model 34-B Sensible Six touring. (JAG)

1918 Oakland Model 34-B Sensible Six convertible roadster. (JAG)

5P Touring Sedan Note: Some sources list this model as being replaced midyear 1918 by a "Removable Post Sedan" priced at $1,685. This model was the equivalent of a 1950s four-door hardtop. It did not survive into the 1919 model run.

NOTE 1: Estimated calendar year production for Oakland in 1918 totaled 27,757 cars.

ENGINE: Model 111 Northway OHV six-cylinder. Bore & stroke: 2-13/16 x 4-3/4 in. Displacement: 177 cid. Horsepower: 44. Water-cooled.

TECHNICAL: Jacox irreversible screw-and-double half-nut steering gear; tubular propeller shaft; Northway cone-type clutch in unit with a three-speed selective sliding gear transmission; heating box induction system that utilized exhaust gases to preheat incoming mixture; cup-and-cone ball bearings on wheel spindles; Remy two-unit starting and lighting system; Prestolite three-cell, six-volt battery; bi-plane-type fan in unit with water pump driven by camshaft-activated V-belt; Oakland-Stewart vacuum fuel delivery system. Fuel tank: 13 gal.

CHASSIS: Wheelbase: 112 in., 4-in. tires (Non-Skid tires mounted on rear), 35-in. semi-elliptic front springs and 51-in. underslung semi-elliptic rear springs, Hotchkiss drive and full-floating rear axle. Brakes: 12-in. external contracting and internal expanding brakes with bands faced with wire-woven asbestos. Frame: Channel section pressed steel 4-1/2 in. deep, 2 in. wide, and 1/8 in. thick with five crossmembers; frame width: 40-3/4 in. rear, 28 in. front. Turning circle: 38 ft.

OPTIONS: Wire spoke wheels ($75).

HISTORICAL: Due to the material shortages caused by World War I, the Model 34-B was the exclusive Oakland offering from September 1917 to June 1, 1920.

1919 OAKLAND

OAKLAND — SIX — There is no concrete date when the Model 34-B Oakland changed from a 1918 model to a 1919 model. As in 1918, standard equipment included a one-man folding top with detachable side curtains, a footrest for easy operation of accelerator pedal, and an oil-pan-mounted oil gauge. The dashboard

1919 Oakland Model 34-B Sensible Six sedan. (JAG)

instrumentation included amp, oil pressure and fuel-level gauges, as well as an odometer and trip odometer. A power tire pump was also featured.

Model Number	Body/Style Number	Body Type & Seating	Factory Price	Shipping Weight	Production Total
SENSIBLE SIX SERIES (6-cyl.)					
Sensible Six	34-B	2P Roadster	1,075	2,070	Note 1
Sensible Six	34-B	5P Touring	1,075	2,130	Note 1
Sensible Six	34-B	Sedan	1,650	2,650	Note 1
Sensible Six	34-B	Coupe	1,650	2,350	Note 1

NOTE 1: Estimated calendar year production for Oakland in 1919 totaled 52,124 cars.

ENGINE: Model 111 Northway OHV six-cylinder. Bore & stroke: 2-13/16 x 4-3/4 in. Displacement: 177 cid. Horsepower: 44 at 2600 rpm. Water-cooled.

TECHNICAL: Jacox irreversible screw-and-double half-nut steering gear; tubular propeller shaft; Northway cone-type clutch in unit with a three-speed selective sliding gear transmission; heating box induction system that utilized exhaust gases to preheat incoming mixture; cup-and-cone ball bearings on wheel spindles; Remy two-unit starting and lighting system; Prestolite three-cell; six-volt battery; bi-plane-type fan in unit with water pump driven by camshaft-activated V-belt; and Oakland-Stewart vacuum fuel delivery system. Fuel tank: 13 gal.

CHASSIS: Wheelbase: 112 in., 4-in. tires (Non-Skid tires mounted on rear), 35-in. semi-elliptic front springs and 51-in. underslung semi-elliptic rear springs, Hotchkiss drive and full-floating rear axle. Brakes: 12 in. external contracting and internal expanding brakes with bands faced with wire-woven asbestos. Frame: Channel section pressed steel 4-1/2 in. deep, 2 in. wide, and 1/8 in. thick with five crossmembers; frame width: 40-3/4 in. rear, 28 in. front. Turning circle: 38 ft.

OPTIONS: Wire spoke wheels ($75).

HISTORICAL: Oakland climbed to rank sixth in industry sales charts.

1919 Oakland touring. (OCW)

1920 OAKLAND

1920 Oakland Model 34-C Sensible Six touring. (JAG)

OAKLAND – MODEL 34-C - SIX: The most obvious change in 1920 Oaklands was a three-inch linger wheelbase. Being larger, the new Oaklands weighed more and required some technical changes. These included revised steering knuckles and a new frame with an increased depth of section. Regular equipment features included a windshield, an electric horn, an ammeter, a power tire pump, a speedometer, and demountable wheel rims. Open cars were finished with the body in Dark Brewster Green and Black running gear. Closed body styles were Blue with Black running gear.

Model Number	Body/Style Number	Body Type & Seating	Factory Price	Shipping Weight	Production Total
SENSIBLE SIX SERIES (6-cyl.)					
Sensible Six	34-C	3P Roadster	1,165	2,070	Note 1
Sensible Six	34-C	5P Touring	1,235	2,330	Note 1
Sensible Six	34-C	5P Sedan	1,835	2,733	Note 1
Sensible Six	34-C	4P Coupe	1,835	2,550	Note 1

NOTE 1: Oakland production in 1920 is recorded as 35,356 cars.

ENGINE: OHV six-cylinder. Bore & stroke: 2-13/16 x 4-3/4 in. Displacement: 177 cid. Horsepower: 44 at 2600 rpm. Water-cooled.

TECHNICAL: Worm-and-nut design steering gear; cone-type clutch in unit with a three-speed selective sliding gear transmission; heating box induction system that utilized exhaust gases to preheat incoming mixture; positive force-feed engine lubrication via a gear-driven oil pump and drilled crankshaft; three-blade, bi-plane-type cooling fan; Oakland-Stewart vacuum fuel delivery system. Fuel tank: 12-1/2 gal.

CHASSIS: Wheelbase: 115 in., 4-in. tires (Non-Skid tires mounted on rear), semi-elliptic springs front and rear, full-floating rear axle, external contracting and internal expanding brakes. Frame: Channel section pressed steel 6-1/2 in. deep.

OPTIONS: Wire spoke wheels ($75).

HISTORICAL: George H. Hannum was appointed president and general manager of Oakland in 1920. The 1920 Model 34-C serial numbers ended at 152356-34 (the last 1920 model was built on Jan. 6, 1921).

1921 OAKLAND

OAKLAND — MODEL 34-C — SIX — According to the *1921 Handbook* published by the Association of Licensed Automobile Manufacturers (ALAM) Oakland body styles remained the same for the new year, while prices increased rather steeply. Higher weights were registered by the 1921 roadster and touring car, but the closed models weighed the same. This indicates that the added poundage was due to equipment changes for ragtops, rather than any basic redesign affecting all models. Standard features included an electric horn, an ammeter, a power tire pump, a speedometer, and demountable wheel rims.

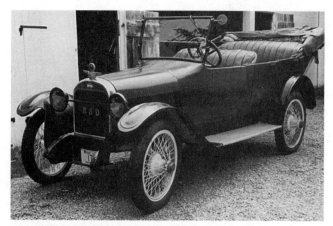

1921 Oakland Model 34-C touring. (OCW)

Model Number	Body/Style Number	Body Type & Seating	Factory Price	Shipping Weight	Production Total
SENSIBLE SIX SERIES (6-cyl.)					
Sensible Six	34-C	3P Roadster	1,395	2,070	Note 1
Sensible Six	34-C	5P Touring	1,395	2,421	Note 1
Sensible Six	34-C	5P Sedan	2,065	2,733	Note 1
Sensible Six	34-C	4P Coupe	2,065	2,550	Note 1

NOTE 1: Oakland production in 1921 totaled 5,444 cars.

ENGINE: OHV six-cylinder. Bore & stroke: 2-13/16 x 4-3/4 in. Displacement: 177 cid. Horsepower: 44 at 2600 rpm. Water-cooled.

TECHNICAL: Remy two-unit electrical system with thermostatic generator control (provided automatic adjustment of the charging rate for warm or cold weather); worm-and-nut design steering gear; cone-type clutch in unit with a three-speed selective sliding gear transmission; heating box induction system that utilized exhaust gases to preheat incoming mixture; positive force-feed engine lubrication via a gear-driven oil pump and drilled crankshaft; three-blade, bi-plane-type cooling fan; and Oakland-Stewart vacuum fuel delivery system. Fuel tank: 12-1/2 gal.

CHASSIS: Wheelbase: 115 in., 4-in. tires (Non-Skid tires mounted on rear), semi-elliptic springs front and rear, full-floating rear axle, external contracting and internal expanding brakes. Frame: Channel section pressed steel 6-1/2 in. deep. Final gear ratio: 4.50:1.

OPTIONS: Wire spoke wheels ($75).

HISTORICAL: The 1921 Model 34-C serial numbers ran from 152357-34 (built Jan. 7, 1921) to 159700-34 (the last 1921 model was built on July 27, 1921).

1922 OAKLAND

1922 Oakland Model 34-C sedan. (HAC)

OAKLAND — MODEL 34-D — SIX — The first 1922 Oaklands, appearing on the assembly line in August of 1921, were refined versions of the Model 34-C with better fit and finish and one all-new body type, the Sports Touring model. The latter car had a high radiator, low body lines, rich Maroon finish with black fenders, genuine Brown Spanish leather upholstery, a walnut instrument board, wire wheels and cord tires. Standard equipment on basic models included a speedometer, an ammeter, an oil pressure gauge, demountable wheel rims, and a power tire pump.

Model Number	Body/Style Number	Body Type & Seating	Factory Price	Shipping Weight	Production Total
SENSIBLE SIX SERIES (6-cyl.)					
Sensible Six	34-D	2P Roadster	—	2,495	Note 1
Sensible Six	34-D	5P Touring	1,395	2,620	Note 1
Sensible Six	34-D	5P Sedan	2,065	2,733	Note 1
Sensible Six	34-D	4P Coupe	2,065	2,620	Note 1
Sensible Six	34-D	4P Sports Touring	1,265	2,565	Note 1

Model 34-D Note: A chassis-only version of the Model 34-D was also available.

NOTE 1: Oakland Model 34-D production in 1922 totaled 7,849 cars.

ENGINE: OHV six-cylinder. Bore & stroke: 2-13/16 x 4-3/4 in. Displacement: 177 cid. Horsepower: 44 at 2600 rpm. Water-cooled.

TECHNICAL: Remy two-unit electrical system with thermostatic generator control (provided automatic adjustment of the charging rate for warm or cold weather); worm-and-nut design steering gear; cone-type clutch in unit with a three-speed selective sliding gear transmission; heating box induction system that utilized exhaust gases to pre-heat incoming mixture; positive force-feed engine lubrication via a submerged gear pump and drilled crankshaft; and an Oakland-Stewart vacuum fuel delivery system. Fuel tank: 12-1/2 gal.

CHASSIS: Wheelbase: 115 in., 4-in. tires (Non-Skid tires mounted on rear), 36-in. semi-elliptic front springs and 51-in. semi-elliptic rear springs, full-floating rear axle. Frame: Channel section pressed steel 6-1/2 in. deep.

HISTORICAL: The 1922 production of Oaklands had the Model 34-D produced from August 1921 to Dec. 31, 1921. Serial numbers for the Model 34-D ran from 159701-34 to 167550-34. At that point, the Model 34-D was dropped and the Model 6-44 was produced, also as a 1922 Model. Records show that 10,250 1922 Model 6-44s were produced with serial numbers that ran from 1-44 to 10250-44.

1923 OAKLAND

1923 Oakland Model 6-44 five-passenger sedan. (AA)

OAKLAND — MODEL 6-44 — SIX — A new Sports Roadster was included in the 1923 Oakland lineup. It had many of the special features of last year's Sports Touring car. Both sporty models switched from standard wire wheels to standard disc wheels. The former four-place coupe became a five-passenger model and curved brackets were added to either side of its "cadet" sun visor. The dashboard on all 1923 models was changed to relocate the choke mechanism and to group all gauges into one circular-shaped housing. Standard features included drum-type headlights; a choke control; a steering wheel-mounted, wire-operated spark and gas lever control box; a speedometer; an ammeter; an oil pressure gauge; hinged front seats for easier rear seat access; demountable wheel rims (Sports Touring and Sports Roadster both had solid disc rims); and a power tire pump.

Model Number	Body/Style Number	Body Type & Seating	Factory Price	Shipping Weight	Production Total
SENSIBLE SIX SERIES (6-cyl.)					
Sensible Six	6-44	2P Roadster	975	2,530	Note 1

1923 Oakland Model 6-44 roadster. (JAG)

Model Number	Body/Style Number	Body Type & Seating	Factory Price	Shipping Weight	Production Total
Sensible Six	6-44	5P Touring	995	2,675	Note 1
Sensible Six	6-44	5P Sedan	1,545	3,060	Note 1
Sensible Six	6-44	5P Coupe	1,445	2,970	Note 1
Sensible Six	6-44	2P Coupe	1,185	2,645	Note 1
Sensible Six	6-44	4P Sports Touring	1,165	2,680	Note 1
Sensible Six	6-44	2P Sports Roadster	2,610		Note 1

NOTE 1: Oakland Model 6-44 production in 1923 totaled 30,901 cars.

ENGINE: OHV six-cylinder. Bore & stroke: 2-13/16 x 4-3/4 in. Displacement: 177 cid. Horsepower: 44 at 2600 rpm. Water-cooled.

TECHNICAL: Oil dip lubrication for clutch bearing; positive force-feed engine lubrication via a submerged gear pump and drilled crankshaft; and Oakland-Stewart vacuum fuel delivery system. Fuel tank: 12 gal.

CHASSIS: Wheelbase: 115 in., 4-in. tires (Non-Skid tires mounted on rear), 36-in. semi-elliptic front springs and 51-in. semi-elliptic rear springs, Alemite lubrication system for chassis. Brakes: 12-in. external contracting and internal expanding brakes. Frame: Channel section pressed steel 6-1/2 in. deep. Final gear ratio: 4.66:1.

HISTORICAL: The Model 6-44 was produced from January 1922 to June 15, 1923. The first 10,250 Model 6-44s produced were considered early/1922 versions. Model 6-44s with serial numbers that ranged from 10251-44 to 41152-44 were recorded as 1923 models.

1924 OAKLAND

1924 Oakland Model 6-54 touring. (AA)

OAKLAND — MODEL 6-54A — SIX — The body lines of the all-new 1924 Oaklands were generally more rounded than in the past few years. Shorter running boards were seen. The cars had a new L-head engine and were among the first of their price class to feature four-wheel brakes. Duco satin finish proxylin enamel was a major Oakland advance this year. The new nitro-cellulose lacquer cut the time required to paint and dry an Oakland body from 336 hours to 13-1/2 hours. Although this paint was made available in many colors, the 1924 Oaklands that pioneered it came only in Blue and became known as "True Blue Oakland" models. Standard equipment included steel disc wheels, a rear-mounted spare tire carrier, permanent tops, a speedometer, an ammeter, an oil gauge, a windshield cleaner, a cowl ventilator, tools and a jack and roller shades. Sports Touring and Sports Roadster featured bumpers, a motometer with wing cap, windshield wings, a dash gasoline gauge, nickeled lamp rims, a sun visor, and a rearview mirror.

Model Number	Body/Style Number	Body Type & Seating	Factory Price	Shipping Weight	Production Total
OAKLAND SIX SERIES (6-cyl.)					
Oakland Six	6-54A	3P Roadster	995	2,420	Note 1
Oakland Six	6-54A	5P Touring	995	2,845	Note 1
Oakland Six	6-54A	5P Sedan	1,445	2,860	Note 1
Oakland Six	6-54A	4P Coupe	1,395	2,720	Note 1
Oakland Six	6-54A	3P Business Coupe	1,195	2,620	Note 1
Oakland Six	6-54A	4P Sports Touring	1,195	2,550	Note 1
Oakland Six	6-54A	3P Sports Roadster	1,195	2,510	Note 1

NOTE 1: Oakland Model 6-54A model-year production (Aug. 23, 1923, to July 29, 1924) totaled 37,080 cars.

ENGINE: L-head six-cylinder. Bore & stroke: 2-13/16 x 4-3/4 in. Displacement: 177 cid. Horsepower: 44 at 2600 rpm. Water-cooled.

TECHNICAL: Automatic spark advance, three-speed selective sliding gear transmission, force-feed lubrication, screw and split-nut steering.

CHASSIS: Wheelbase: 113 in., 4-in. tires (Non-Skid tires mounted on rear), semi-elliptic front and rear springs. Brakes: Four-wheel mechanical brakes.

OPTIONS: Glass enclosures ($60 for Touring model, $40 for Sport Touring model).

HISTORICAL: All 1924 Oaklands were finished in Duco satin finish proxylin "enamel," which was essentially a nitro-cellulose lacquer solution.

1925 OAKLAND

1925 Oakland Model 6-54 Landau sedan. (AA)

OAKLAND — MODEL 6-54B — SIX — Changes and improvements in the Oakland for 1925 included larger cylinder bores, a higher compression ratio, a new Stromberg carburetor, the use of balloon tires, and new styling features. All closed-body cars had a new Fisher Vision & Ventilating (V.V.) windshield with automatic wipers. The sun visors on these cars now wrapped over at the sides, eliminating the old exposed-brackets look. The bar between the headlights disappeared and open cars had permanent tops, close-fitting side curtains, and the windshield molded in rubber. Glass enclosures were available at slight extra cost. Standard equipment included a theft-proof ignition lock, steel disc wheels and balloon cord tires (except Special Sedan equipped with artillery-type, wood-spoke wheels and balloon tires), automatic windshield wipers, door locks, permanent tops, a rear-mounted spare tire carrier, a cowl ventilator, a speedometer, an ammeter, an oil gauge, an odometer, tools, a tire pump, a jack, and roller shades. The Special Touring and Special Roadster featured a front bumper, rear fender guards, a motometer with wing cap, windshield wings and nickel-plated head, cowl, and tail lamps.

Model Number	Body/Style Number	Body Type & Seating	Factory Price	Shipping Weight	Production Total
OAKLAND SIX SERIES (6-cyl.)					
Oakland Six	6-54B	3P Roadster	1,095	2,420	Note 1
Oakland Six	6-54B	5P Touring	1,095	2,845	Note 1

Model Number	Body/Style Number	Body Type & Seating	Factory Price	Shipping Weight	Production Total
Oakland Six	6-54B	5P Sedan	1,545	2,860	Note 1
Oakland Six	6-54B	4P Coupe	1,495	2,720	Note 1
Oakland Six	6-54B	3P Landau Coupe	1,295	2,620	Note 1
Oakland Six	6-54B	5P Landau Sedan	1,645	2,885	Note 1
Oakland Six	6-54B	4P Special Touring	1,195	2,550	Note 1
Oakland Six	6-54B	3P Special Rds	1,195	2,510	Note 1
Oakland Six	6-54B	5P Special Sedan	1,375	—	Note 1
Oakland Six	6-54B	5P Coach	1,215	2,745	Note 1

NOTE 1: Oakland Model 6-54B model-year production (July 17, 1924, to May 29, 1925) totaled 27,423 cars.

ENGINE: L-head six-cylinder. Bore & stroke: 2-7/8 x 4-3/4 in. Displacement: 177 cid. Compression ratio: 5.0:1. Horsepower: 44 at 2600 rpm. Water-cooled.

TECHNICAL: Interchangeable bronze-backed engine bearings; single-plate self-ventilated clutch; silent chain cam drive; full pressure engine lubrication system; full automatic spark control; exhaust-heated manifold with provision for winter and summer adjustment; three-speed selective sliding gear transmission; parking brake on transmission; worm and half-nut steering gear; and steering knuckles supported by ball thrust bearings.

CHASSIS: Wheelbase: 113 in., 31 x 4.95 balloon cord tires, semi-elliptic front and rear springs, semi-floating rear axle using spiral bevel drive gears. Brakes: 12-3/8-in. external contracting brakes on all four wheels. Final gear ratio: 4.7:1.

HISTORICAL: A.R. Glancy was promoted from vice president and assistant general manager to Oakland's president and general manager in 1925 (ironically, in 1903, Glancy wrote a thesis to prove the automobile had no future). All Oaklands this year had Fisher bodies finished in permanent Duco colors.

1926 OAKLAND

1926 Oakland Greater Six Landau sedan. (JAG)

1926 Oakland Greater Six roadster. (OCW)

OAKLAND — MODEL 6-54 — SIX — Closed-body Oaklands had new styling with attractive twin belt moldings, a new headlight design, and a tie-bar linking the lights in front of the radiator. In late autumn, the rear windows on the Landau sedan were converted from an oval design to a "D" shape. In February 1926, a handsome long-deck Sports Roadster was added to the line. Its equipment included step-up fenders, a rumbleseat, a golf bag compartment, windshield wings, front bumpers, rear fender guards, and other deluxe features. Standard equipment on basic models included an air cleaner, an oil filter, wood-spoke artillery wheels, a speedometer, an oil pressure gauge, automatic windshield wipers, door locks, window lifts, tools, a tire pump, and a jack.

Model Number	Body/Style Number	Body Type & Seating	Factory Price	Shipping Weight	Production Total
OAKLAND SIX SERIES (6-cyl.)					
Oakland Six	6-54C	2P Roadster	975	2,425	Note 1
Oakland Six	6-54C	5P Touring	1,025	2,500	Note 1
Oakland Six	6-54C	5P Sedan	1,195	2,765	Note 1
Oakland Six	6-54C	3P Landau Coupe	1,125	2,615	Note 1
Oakland Six	6-54C	5P Landau Sedan	1,295	2,885	Note 1
Oakland Six	6-54C	2P Sport Roadster	1,175	2,550	Note 1
Oakland Six	6-54C	5P Coach	1,215	2,640	Note 1

NOTE 1: Oakland Model 6-54C model-year production (July 2, 1925, to June 17, 1926) totaled 58,827 cars.

ENGINE: L-head six-cylinder. Bore & Stroke: 2-7/8 x 4-3/4 in. Displacement: 185 cid. Compression ratio: 5.0:1. Horsepower: 44 at 2600 rpm. Water-cooled.

TECHNICAL: Harmonic balancer built into crankshaft; full-pressure oiling system.

CHASSIS: Wheelbase: 113 in., 30 x 5.25 balloon cord tires, semi-elliptic front and rear springs. Brakes: 12-3/8-in. external contracting brakes on all four wheels.

OPTION: Steel disc wheels.

HISTORICAL: Under the umbrella of the Oakland Motor Div., production of 1926 Pontiacs began on Dec. 28, 1925, the first year models consisting of a five-passenger coach and a two-passenger coupe. In June of 1926, approval was given to build the new "Daylight Plant" for the assembly of 1,000 Pontiacs and 600 Oaklands per day.

1927 OAKLAND

1927 Oakland Greater Six sport phaeton. (AA)

1927 Oakland Model 6-54D 2-dr. sedan. (OCW)

OAKLAND — MODEL 6-54D — GREATER SIX — While unchanged in major features, the 1927 Oaklands had 77 "important refinements" the company said. New "crowned" front fenders were

1927 Oakland Model 6-54D sport roadster. (OCW)

1927 Oakland Model 6-54D Landau sedan. (OCW)

broader and met the wider and thicker running boards in a more graceful sweep. The running boards were trimmed with screw-less moldings. A Stewart-bodied five-passenger Sport Phaeton with distinctive styling replaced the touring car. Basic standard equipment included a dimmer pedal to operate Guide Tilt-Ray double filament headlamps, a shift lever ball, and a steering wheel rim. The Sport Phaeton and Sport Roadster included plate glass windshield wings, a front bumper, rear guards, a windshield wiper, a rearview mirror, and nickeled headlamps.

Model Number	Body/Style Number	Body Type & Seating	Factory Price	Shipping Weight	Production Total
GREATER OAKLAND SIX SERIES (6-cyl.)					
Greater Oakland 6	6-54D	5P Sedan	1,195	2,765	Note 1
Greater Oakland 6	6-54D	3P Landau Coupe	1,125	2,615	Note 1
Greater Oakland 6	6-54D	5P Landau Sedan	1,295	2,885	Note 1
Greater Oakland 6	6-54D	2P Sport Roadster	1,175	2,600	Note 1
Greater Oakland 6	6-54D	5P Sport Phaeton	1,095	2,500	Note 1
Greater Oakland 6	6-54D	5P Coach	1,215	2,640	Note 1

NOTE 1: Oakland Model 6-54D model-year production (June 7, 1926, to May 24, 1927) totaled 44,658 cars.

ENGINE: L-head six-cylinder. Bore & stroke: 2-7/8 x 4-3/4 in. Displacement: 185 cid. Horsepower: 45 at 2600 rpm. Water-cooled (10-1/2 quart cooling capacity).

TECHNICAL: Harmonic balancer fitted with coil springs; chrome-vanadium steel spring leaves; lightweight undercut transmission gears; rubber joint inserted in driveshaft behind front universal joint to isolate rear end noise; rubber engine-to-chassis mounting.

CHASSIS: Wheelbase: 113 in., 30 x 5.25 balloon cord tires, semi-elliptic front and rear springs. Brakes: 12-3/8-in. external contracting brakes on all four wheels.

HISTORICAL: Oakland's 1927 Model 6-54D production began with serial number 120801-54 and ended with serial number 167943-54. Between July 29, 1926, and Jan. 9, 1927, a Greater Oakland Six Landau sedan with a clear viewing panel over the engine compartment was run nonstop on a treadmill as a public display in Detroit. Done to promote the stamina and performance of the Model 6-54D, the car reached 100,000 miles after six months and was still running strong.

1928 OAKLAND

1928 Oakland All-American landau sedan. (OCW)

OAKLAND — MODEL 212 ALL-AMERICAN — SIX — The all-new OaklAND All-American Six had a new 212-cid L-head engine and a longer 117-in. wheelbase. Seven body styles were offered. The general appearance of all models was enhanced by the use of lower, longer bodies, new fenders, longer hoods, and rear panel design revisions. The radiator, lamp rims, and hood latches were chrome plated. A spare tire was now standard on all Oakland models. Also featured were a Fisher Vision & Ventilating windshield, a rearview mirror, a single stop and backing lamp, a dash gasoline gauge, sun

1928 Oakland All-American Six four-door sedan. (AA)

1928 Oakland All-American Six roadster. (JAG)

1928 Oakland All-American Six landau sedan. (OCW)

visors (closed models only), a chrome radiator shell, chrome lamp rims, and chrome hood latches. The Sport Phaeton and Sport Roadster had a trunk rack.

Model Number	Body/Style Number	Body Type & Seating	Factory Price	Shipping Weight	Production Total
OAKLAND ALL-AMERICAN SIX SERIES (6-cyl.)					
AA6	212	5P Sedan	1,145	2,980	Note 1
AA6	212	5P Sedan (2d)	1,045	2,840	Note 1
AA6	212	3P Landau Coupe	1,045	2,805	Note 1
AA6	212	5P Landau Sedan	1,265	—	Note 1
AA6	212	2P Sport Roadster	1,075	2,730	Note 1
AA6	212	5P Sport Phaeton	1,075	2,740	Note 1
AA6	212	3P Sport Cabriolet	1,145	2,825	Note 1

NOTE 1: Oakland first edition/1928 Model 212 model year production (June 22, 1927, to June 25, 1928) totaled 60,121 cars.

ENGINES: L-head six-cylinder. Bore & stroke: 3-1/4 x 4-1/4 in. Displacement: 212 cid. Horsepower: 60 at 2800 rpm. Compression ratio: 4.9:1. Water-cooled.

TECHNICAL: General Motors Research (GMR) cylinder head incorporated a convex baffle over pistons to reduce detonation and permit a higher compression ratio; four bearing crankshaft forged with integral counterweight setup and torsional damper; side-engine block-mounted distributor; pioneering use of fuel pump and fuel filter (replaced vacuum tank system).

CHASSIS: Wheelbase: 117 in., 29 x 5.50 tires mounted on 19-in. wood-spoke artillery style wheels. Brakes: External, four-wheel brakes with 12-3/8 in. drums measuring 1-7/8 in. wide. Final gear ratio: 4.41:1.

OPTIONS: All 1928 Oaklands had frames drilled for the installation of optional Delco-Remy-Lovejoy shock absorbers. Sport Roadster: sidemount tire covers, six-wheel equipment and wire spoke wheels.

HISTORICAL: 1928 would be the final year that Oakland would experience increased sales.

1929 OAKLAND

1929 Oakland All-American Six convertible cabriolet. (JAG)

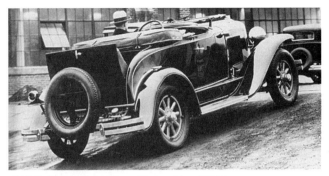

1929 Oakland All-American Six roadster. (JAG)

OAKLAND — ALL-AMERICAN — SIX — Highlighting the second series of Oakland All-American Six models were new body designs with higher hood lines and belt lines, lower rooflines, cadet visors, and wider fenders. A unique horseshoe-shaped radiator shell was split by a vertical center bar. The attractive hood had five sets of vertical louvers. A single belt molding extended entirely around the bodies from the radiator. All models except the roadster and phaeton, which were built by Stewart, had Fisher bodies. Standard features included a cadet visor, an automatic windshield wiper, and a rearview mirror.

Model Number	Body/Style Number	Body Type & Seating	Factory Price	Shipping Weight	Production Total
OAKLAND ALL-AMERICAN SIX SERIES (6-cyl.)					
AA6	212	5P Sedan	1,245	3,305	Note 1
AA6	212	5P Sedan (2d)	1,145	3,185	Note 1
AA6	212	5P Special Sedan	1,320	3,305	Note 1
AA6	212	5P Landaulet Sed	1,375	3,275	Note 1
AA6	212	5P Brougham Sed	1,195	3,285	Note 1
AA6	212	3P Coupe	1,145	3,090	Note 1
AA6	212	2P Sport Roadster	1,145	2,920	Note 1
AA6	212	5P Sport Phaeton	1,145	2,990	Note 1
AA6	212	3P Conv Cabriolet	1,265	3,145	Note 1

NOTE 1: Oakland second edition/1929 Model 212 model year production (Sept. 24, 1928, to Oct. 9, 1929) totaled 50,693 cars.

ENGINE: L-head six-cylinder. Bore & stroke: 3-3/8 x 4-1/4 in. Displacement: 228 cid. Horsepower: 68 at 3000 rpm. Water-cooled.

TECHNICAL: Four-point rubber engine mountings; frame cross members beefed up to accommodate weightier bodies.

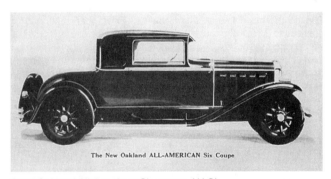

The New Oakland ALL-AMERICAN Six Coupe

1929 Oakland All-American Six coupe. (JAG)

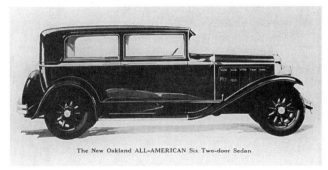

The New Oakland ALL-AMERICAN Six Two-door Sedan

1929 Oakland All-American Six two-door sedan. (JAG)

1929 Oakland All-American Six four-door sedan. (JAG)

Sport Roadster

1929 Oakland All-American Six sport roadster. (JAG)

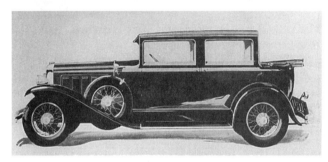

1929 Oakland All-American Six convertible landau sedan. (JAG)

CHASSIS: Wheelbase: 117 in. Brakes: Midland Steeldraulic four-wheel brakes. Final gear ratio: From 4.42:1 to 4.73:1.

OPTIONS: Lovejoy shock absorbers. Six wire wheels with wide-faced hubcaps. Chrome-plated sidemount clamps. Tire cover for rear-mounted spare.

HISTORICAL: On Jan. 24, 1929, Oakland chief engineer Ben Anibal filed U.S. patent number 1897783 for his V-design, eight-cylinder engine that would become the 1930-31 Oakland engine. On March 8, 1929, the one-millionth Oakland was built. At the conclusion of 1929, Oakland ranked 21st in industry sales among 33 automakers.

1930 OAKLAND

1930 Oakland Model 101 coupe. (JAG)

OAKLAND — SERIES 101 — V-8 — The 1930 Oakland 101 was the first eight that the company had built since 1917. It was based on a 117-in. wheelbase and sported lower, longer-looking Fisher bodies. Standard equipment included front and rear bumpers and guards (at slightly higher prices), safety indicator lamps atop the

1930 Oakland Model 101 roadster. (JAC)

1930 Oakland Model 101 phaeton. (JAG)

front fenders, a vibrator horn mounted on the front fender tie bar, a cadet windshield visor, an automatic windshield wiper, a non-glare rearview mirror, an adjustable driver's seat, natural finish Jaxon wood-spoke wheels, and Lovejoy hydraulic shock absorbers.

Model Number	Body/Style Number	Body Type & Seating	Factory Price	Shipping Weight	Production Total
SERIES 101 (V-8)					
Oakland V-8	101	5P Sedan	995	3,205	Note 1
Oakland V-8	101	5P Sedan (2d)	895	3,095	Note 1
Oakland V-8	101	5P Custom Sedan	1,045	3,210	Note 1
Oakland V-8	101	3P Coupe	895	3,010	Note 1
Oakland V-8	101	2P Sport Roadster	895	2,770	Note 1
Oakland V-8	101	5P Sport Phaeton	945	2,910	Note 1
Oakland V-8	101	3P Sport Coupe	965	3,075	Note 1

NOTE 1: Oakland Model 101 model year production (December 1929 to October 1930) totaled 21,943 cars.

ENGINE: V-8. Bore & stroke: 3-7/16 x 3-3/8 in. Displacement: 251 cid. Horsepower: 85. Compression ratio: 5.0:1. Water-cooled.

TECHNICAL: Three main bearing engine crankshaft of 180 degree; single-plane design; horizontally positioned valves operated directly by rocker arms working from a centrally located, chain driven camshaft; four-point engine mountings with rubber insulators at the rear and laminated springs at the front corners, plus a special synchronizer (one end of this device was attached to the frame while the other end passed into the block where it was actuated by revolutions of the camshaft); 9-5/8-in. single plate clutch; three-speed transmission.

CHASSIS: Wheelbase: 117 in., 28 x 5.50-in. tires. Brakes: Self-energizing internal four-wheel brakes. Final gear ratio: 4.42:1 (optional ratios of 3.9:1 and 5.2:1 were available).

OPTIONS: Six wire wheels and chrome-plated sidemount trim rings; front fenders with tire wells.

HISTORICAL: On Oct. 15, 1930, Irving J. Reuter moved from the presidency of Olds Motor Works to become general manager of Oakland Motor Div. Oakland car number 273501 was the first V-8 built by the automaker since 1917. Due to the stock market crash of October 1929, Oakland's 1930 industry sales would drop by one-third compared to the previous year.

1931 OAKLAND

OAKLAND — SERIES 301 — V-8 — Longer and lower Fisher bodies with a single, wide belt molding were carried on the 1931 Oakland

1931 Oakland Model 301 sedan. (JAC)

chassis. They were similar to Pontiac bodies, but the wheelbase was five inches longer than that of the Pontiac. Styling features included V-type radiators with chrome-plated grilles, once-piece full-crown fenders, a curved headlight tie bar and fender-top indicator lights. Standard equipment included single-bar front and rear bumpers and guards (at slightly higher prices), a vibrator horn mounted on the front fender tie bar, a cadet visor, an automatic windshield wiper, a non-glare rearview mirror, an adjustable driver's seat, natural finish Jaxon wood spoke wheels and Lovejoy hydraulic shock absorbers.

Model Number	Body/Style Number	Body Type & Seating	Factory Price	Shipping Weight	Production Total
SERIES 301 (V-8)					
Oakland V-8	301	5P Sedan	995	3,138	Note 1
Oakland V-8	301	5P Sedan (2d)	895	3,173	Note 1
Oakland V-8	301	5P Custom Sedan	1,055	3,138	Note 1
Oakland V-8	301	3P Coupe	895	3,088	Note 1
Oakland V-8	301	3P Sport Coupe	975	3,153	Note 1
Oakland V-8	301	3P Conv Coupe	995	3,105	Note 1

NOTE 1: Oakland Model 301 model-year production (ending Oct. 8, 1931) totaled 13,408 cars.

ENGINE: V-8. Bore & stroke: 3-7/16 x 3-3/8 in. Displacement: 251 cid. Horsepower: 85 at 3400 rpm. Compression ratio: 5.0:1. Water-cooled.

TECHNICAL: New synchromesh transmission, new chassis frame with 2-1/8-in. thick flange widths and 5-1/2 in. depth of channel.

CHASSIS: Wheelbase: 117 in. Tires; 28 x 5.50 in. mounted on 45-spoke Motor Wheel Corp. wire wheels with semi-drop base rims. Brakes: 13-in. diameter drum brakes. Final gear ratio: 4.55:1 (revised to 3.90:1 after June 1931).

HISTORICAL: After dismal sales of the 1931 Model 301 and the lingering effects of the Great Depression, in midyear 1932 the Oakland Motor Div. was no more, being absorbed by the Pontiac Motor Co. In fact, as early as the beginning of the year at the New York Auto Show, only models with the Pontiac nameplate were shown, some being Oaklands with the names switched.

1931 Oakland Model 101 custom sedan. (JAG)

PONTIAC
1926-2002

1926 PONTIAC

1926 Pontiac landau sedan. (JAG)

PONTIAC — SERIES 6-27 — SIX — Fisher bodies with double beading, plate glass windows, Vision & Ventilating windshield and automatic windshield wipers. Coupe has landau bars on roof and safety lock on right-hand door. Coach has foot rest, carpeting and dome lamp. Triple-steppe front fenders on both models. Drum-style headlamps and wraparound-type sun visors. Honeycomb radiator with Indian head mascot. Cowl lamps standard. Coupe finished in light Sage Green with Faerie Red striping. Coach finished in Arizona Gray. Black fenders on both.

I.D. DATA: Car number stamped on brass plate on rear frame cross-member. Starting: P-1. Ending: 84262-27. Engine number on block above water pump. All cars built in Pontiac, Mich.

Model Number	Body Style Number	Body Type & Seating	Factory Price	Shipping Weight	Production Total
SERIES 6-27 (6-cyl.)					
6-27	6650	2d Coach-5P	825	2,335	Note 1
6-27	6640	2d Coupe-5P	825	2,270	Note 1

Note 1: Body style breakouts not available. About 42,000 early 1926 models believed built. A total of 204,553 of these cars were built between Dec. 28, 1925 and Oct. 31, 1927.

ENGINE: L-head. Inline, (split-head). Six. Cast-iron block. Bore & stroke: 3-1/4 x 3-3/4 in. Displacement: 186.5 cid. Compression

1926 Pontiac roadster. (JAG)

1926 Pontiac landau coupe. (JAG)

1926 Pontiac coach. (JAG)

Ratio: 4.8:1. Brake horsepower: 40 at 2400 rpm. NACC horsepower: 25.35. Main bearings: Three. Valve lifters: Solid. Carburetor: Carter one-barrel.

CHASSIS: Wheelbase: 110 in. Overall Length: 151-1/4 in. Front/Rear tread: 56/56 in. Tires: 29 x 4.75.

TECHNICAL: Manual transmission. Speeds: 3F/IR. Floor shift controls. Ventilated single dry disc clutch. Shaft drive. Semi-floating rear axle. Overall ratio: 4.18:1. Mechanical brakes on two (rear) wheels. Wood-spoke wheels. Rim size: 20 in.

OPTIONS: Front bumper. Rear fender guards. Heater. Special colors. Rear mount spare tire (spare rim standard).

HISTORICAL: Introduced Jan. 3, 1926. First Pontiac built by Oakland as a small "companion" car. First series 6-27 models were built Dec. 28, 1925, through February 1, 1927. A total of 76,742 cars were sold in the nameplate's first 12 months.

1926-1/2 PONTIAC

PONTIAC — SERIES 6-27 — SIX — The 1926-1/2 Pontiacs, built after August 1926, were sold as early 1927 models. They had some small changes from the original 1926 models. A Landau Sedan was introduced at this time. It had a leather covered top with dummy landau bars. The coupe and coach could now be had in other colors and with different color striping. In October 1926, a 3/4-ton Pontiac Deluxe Delivery truck was added. In November 1926, Deluxe versions of the coupe and Landau Sedan were introduced. They had nickel-plated bumpers and fender guards, mohair upholstery and a foot operated headlight dimmer switch. A new type of sun visor with exposed brackets was first seen on these Deluxe cars.

I.D. DATA: Car number stamped on brass plate on rear frame crossmember. Starting: 41716-25. Engine numbers on block above water pump. All cars built in Pontiac, Mich.

Model Number	Body Style Number	Body Type & Seating	Factory Price	Shipping Weight	Production Total
SERIES 6-27 (6-cyl.)					
6-27	6650	2d Coach-5p	825	2,335	Note 1
6-27	6640	2d Coupe-2P	825	2,270	Note 1
6-27	7160	4d Lan Sed-5P	895	2,455	Note 1
6-27	7160D	4d Del Lan Sed-5P	975	2,565	Note 1
6-27	6640D	2d Del Coupe 2/4P	895	2,380	Note 1

Note 1: Body style breakouts are not available. Approximately 34,700 cars were built.

ENGINE: L-head. Inline, (split-head). Six. Cast-iron block. Bore & stroke: 3-1/4 x 3-3/4 in. Displacement: 186.5 cid. Compression Ratio: 4.8:1. Brake horsepower: 40 at 2400 rpm. NACC horsepower: 25.35. Main bearings: Three. Valve lifters: Solid. Carburetor: Carter one-barrel.

CHASSIS: Wheelbase: 110 in. Overall Length: 151-1/4 in. Front/Rear Tread: 56/56 in. Tires: 29 x 4.75.

TECHNICAL: Manual transmission. Speeds: 3F/1R. Floor shift controls. Ventilated single dry disc clutch. Shaft drive. Semi-floating rear axle. Overall ratio: 4.18:1. Mechanical brakes on two (rear) wheels. Wood-spoke wheels. Rim size: 20 in.

OPTIONS: Front bumper (std. on Deluxe). Rear fender guards (std. on Deluxe). Heater. Rear mounted spare tire (spare rim standard).

HISTORICAL: Introduced August 1926. New colors: coupe in blue with red stripe; coach in blue or gray with orange stripe; Landau sedan in green with red stripe. Deluxe models finished in Peter Pan Blue with matching fenders. Company president is A.R. Glancy. For more information on Deluxe delivery truck see Krause Publications *Standard Catalog of® American Light-Duty Trucks, 3rd Edition.*

1927 PONTIAC

1927 Pontiac landau sedan. (JAG)

NEW-FINER — SERIES 6-27 — SIX — These were Pontiac's true 1927 models, which were built and sold from January 1927 to July 1927. Smooth, full-crown front fenders were introduced. Flat sun visors with exposed sides were used on all models. A Sport Roadster with a Stewart body was introduced. The Deluxe Coupe was replaced by a Sport Cabriolet (closed coupe) with rumbleseat.

I.D. DATA: Car number stamped on a brass plate on rear frame cross-member. Starting numbers continued from 1926-1/2 series. Ending: 144999 (approximate). Engine number on block above water pump. All cars built in Pontiac, Mich.

1927 Pontiac deluxe delivery. (JAG)

1927 Pontiac deluxe delivery. (JAG)

Model Number	Body Style Number	Body Type & Seating	Factory Price	Shipping Weight	Production Total
SERIES 6-27 (6-cyl.)					
6-27	7430	2d Coupe-2P	775	2,270	Note 1
6-27	7460	2d Sport Cabr-2/4P	835	2,401	Note 1
6-27	7440	2d Coach-5P	775	2,335	Note 1
6-27	7450	2d Lan Sedan-5P	895	2,455	Note 1
6-27	7450D	4d Del Lan Sed-5P	975	2,565	Note 1

Note 1: Body style breakouts not available. Approximately 68,300 cars were built.

ENGINE: L-head. Inline, (split-head). Six. Cast-iron block. Bore & stroke: 3-1/4 x 3-3/4 in. Displacement: 186.5 cid. Compression Ratio: 4.8:1. Brake horsepower: 40 at 2400 rpm. NACC horsepower: 25.35. Main bearings: Three. Valve lifters: Solid. Carburetor: Carter one-barrel.

CHASSIS: Wheelbase: 110 in. Overall Length: 151-1/4 in. Front/Rear Tread: 56/56 in. Tires: 29 x 4.75.

TECHNICAL: Manual transmission. Speeds: 3F/1R. Floor shift controls. Improved type ventilated single dry disc clutch. Shaft drive. Semi-floating rear axle. Overall ratio: 4.18:1. Mechanical brakes on two (rear) wheels. Wood-spoke wheels. Rim size: 20 in.

OPTIONS: Front bumper (standard on Deluxe). Rear fender guards (standard on Deluxe). Single sidemount tires on Sport models only. Heater.

HISTORICAL: Introduced January 1927. New body styles include first open Pontiac. Improved clutch. Larger cooling system capacity. Foot operated tilt-beam headlights standard. President of Pontiac is A.R. Glancy.

1927-1/2 PONTIAC

PONTIAC — NEW-FINER SERIES 6-27 — SIX — The 1927-1/2 Pontiacs were virtually identical to the true 1927 models, but were sold as 1928 models. The only changes in these cars were the use of a smaller (11-gallon) gas tank, plus a few new exterior paint colors. They had lower prices and slight adjustments in shipping weight.

I.D. DATA: Serial numbers were on the right side of the rear frame cross-member or on the frame under the left front fender. Starting: 145000-27. Ending: 204000-27. Motor numbers were on the left side of the crankcase or near the left front corner of the block. Starting: P56250. Ending: P220000 (approximate). All cars built in Pontiac, Mich.

Model Number	Body Style Number	Body Type & Seating	Factory Price	Shipping Weight	Production Total
SERIES 6-27 (6-cyl.)					
6-27	ROAD	2d R/S Rds-2/4P	745	2160	Note 1
6-27	7430	2d Coupe-2P	745	2275	Note 1
6-27	7460	2d R/S Cabr-2/4P	795	2345	Note 1
6-27	7440	2d Sedan-5P	745	2275	Note 1
6-27	7450D	4d Del Sedan-5P	925	2510	Note 1
6-27	7450	4d Lan Sedan-5P	845	2460	Note 1

Note 1: Body style breakouts not available. Approximately 59,000 cars were built from July-October 1927.

ENGINE: L-head. Inline, (split-head). Six. Cast-iron block. Bore & stroke: 3-1/4 x 3-3/4 in. Displacement: 186.5 cid. Compression Ratio: 4.8:1. Brake horsepower: 40 at 2400 rpm. NACC horsepower: 25.35. Main bearings: Three. Valve lifters: Solid. Carburetor: Carter one-barrel.

CHASSIS: Wheelbase: 110 in. Overall Length: 151-1/4 inches. Front/Rear Tread: 56/56 in. Tires: 29 x 4.75.

TECHNICAL: Manual transmission. Speeds: 3F/1R. Floor shift controls. Improved type ventilated dry disc clutch. Shaft drive. Semi-floating rear axle. Overall ratio: 4.18:1. Mechanical brakes on two (rear) wheels. Wood-spoked wheels. Rim size: 20 in.

OPTIONS: Front bumper (standard on Deluxe). Rear fender guards (standard on Deluxe). Single sidemounts on Sport models only. Heater.

HISTORICAL: Introduced July 1927. Interchangeable bronze backed bearings. Automatic spark control. Indirectly lighted dashboard. Last Pontiacs to use vacuum tank. A.R. Glancy was president of Oakland.

1928 PONTIAC

1928 Pontiac Model 6-28 two-door sedan. (OCW)

PONTIAC — NEW SERIES 6-28 — SIX — The true 1928 Pontiacs had a higher, deeper, narrower radiator shell and lower, more sweeping body lines. A cross-flow radiator was introduced. There was a new, raised panel along the top of the hood. Deep crowned front fenders with beaded edges were used. The Deluxe Landau Sedan was renamed the Sport Sedan. A four-door Sport Phaeton with a Stewart body was introduced. Many technical changes were seen in the engine, drive train and running gear. The Indian chief on the hood became an Indian brave. New headlights were used. The Sport Cabriolet was now called Sport Coupe.

I.D. DATA: Serial numbers were on the right side of the rear frame cross-member or on the frame under the left front fender. Starting: 204001-28. Ending: 334005-28. Motor numbers were on the left side of the crankcase or near the left front corner of the block. Starting: P220001. Ending: P376340 (approximate). All cars built in Pontiac, Mich.

1928 Pontiac Model 6-28 coupe. (OCW)

1928 Pontiac Model 6-28 sport phaeton. (JAG)

Model Number	Body Style Number	Body Type & Seating	Factory Price	Shipping Weight	Production Total
SERIES 6-28 (6-cyl.)					
6-28	ROAD	2d R/S Rds-2/4P	745	2,270	Note 1
6-28	PHAE	4d Sport Phae-5P	775	2,390	Note 1
6-28	8250	2d Coupe-2P	745	2,435	Note 1
6-28	8260	2d Sport Coupe-4P	795	2,455	Note 1
6-28	8240	2d Sedan-5P	745	2,520	Note 1
6-28	8820	4d Sedan-5P	825	2,595	Note 1
6-28	8230	4d Sport Sedan-5P	875	2,640	Note 1

Note 1: Body style breakouts not available. Approximately 130,000 cars were built.

ENGINE: L-head. Inline. (GMR cylinder head). Six. Cast-iron block. Bore & stroke: 3-1/4 x 3-3/4. Displacement: 186.5 cid. Compression Ratio: 4.9:1. NACC horsepower: 25.3. Main bearings: Three. Valve lifters: Solid. Carburetor: Carter one-barrel.

CHASSIS: Wheelbase: 110 in. Tires: 29 x 5.00.

TECHNICAL: Manual transmission. Speeds: 3F/1R. Floor shift controls. New dry disc clutch. Shaft drive (torque tube). Semi-floating rear axle. Overall ratio: 4.18:1. Four-wheel mechanical brakes. 12-spoke wood artillery wheels.

OPTIONS: Front bumper (standard on Deluxe). Rear bumper (standard on Deluxe). Single sidemount. Heater. Disc wheels. Wind wings (open cars).

HISTORICAL: Introduced January 1928. New Carter updraft carburetor. Larger intake manifold. New Oakland type muffler. Improved steering gear. New frame and front axle. Blossom coincidental ignition lock. New thermostat, steering wheel and dash-mounted gas gauge. Higher compression GMR cylinder head. Internal front wheel brakes. AC fuel filter and fuel pump. New "Daylight" factory opens in Pontiac, Mich. A.R. Glancy remained as president of Oakland.

1928 Pontiac Model 6-28 rumbleseat roadster. (JAC)

1928 Pontiac Model 6-28 deluxe delivery. (JAG)

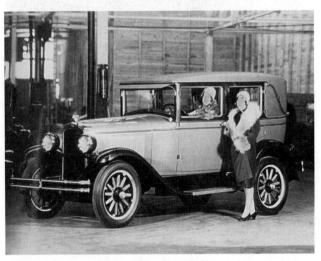

1928 Pontiac Model 6-28 sport sedan. (JAG)

1928 Pontiac Model 6-28 sport sedan. (JAG)

1928 Pontiac Model 6-28 four-door sedan. (JAG)

1928-1/2 PONTIAC

1928-1/2 Pontiac coupe. (CP)

PONTIAC — NEW SERIES 6-28 — SIX — New Series 6-28 Pontiacs built after June 1928 were sold as 1929 models. They were identical to the true 1928 models except for minor technical alterations. A Marvel carburetor, heavier 10-spoke Jaxon wood-spoke artillery wheels and a new rear axle ratio were the major changes. An increase in horsepower was noted on specifications sheets.

I.D. DATA: Serial numbers were on the rear frame cross-member or under the left front fender. Starting: 334006. Ending: 410100. Engine numbers were on left side of crankcase or near left front corner of block. Starting: P376341. Ending: P461000 (approximate). All cars built at Pontiac, Mich.

Model Number	Body Style Number	Body Type & Seating	Factory Price	Shipping Weight	Production Total
SERIES 6-28 (6-cyl.)					
6-28	ROAD	2d R/S Rds-2/4P	745	2,270	Note 1
6-28	PHAE	4d Phaeton-5P	775	2,390	Note 1
6-28	8250	2d Coupe-2P	745	2,435	Note 1
6-28	8260	2d Sport Cpe-2/4P	795	2,455	Note 1
6-28	8240	2d Sedan-5P	745	2,520	Note 1
6-28	8820	4d Sedan-5P	825	2,595	Note 1
6-28	8230	4d Sport Sedan-5P	875	2,640	Note 1

Note 1: Body style breakouts not available. Approximately 80,000 series 6-28 Pontiacs were sold as 1929 models.

ENGINE: L-head. Inline. Six. Cast-iron block. Bore & stroke: 3-1/4 x 3-3/4 in. Displacement: 186.5 cid. Compression Ratio: 4.9:1. Brake horsepower: 48 at 2850 rpm. NACC horsepower: 25.35. Main bearings: Three. Valve lifters: Solid. Carburetor: Marvel one-barrel.

CHASSIS: Wheelbase: 110 in. Tires: 29 x 5.00.

TECHNICAL: Manual transmission. Speeds: 3F/1R. Floor shift controls. Dry disc clutch. Shaft drive (Torque tube). Semi-floating rear axle. Overall ratio: 4.36:1. Four-wheel mechanical brakes. Jaxon 10-spoke wood artillery wheels.

OPTIONS: Front bumper (standard on Deluxe). Rear bumper (standard on Deluxe). Single sidemount. Heater. Disc wheels. Wind wings (open cars).

HISTORICAL: Introduced June 1928. First year with Marvel carburetor. New, heavier wheels. Instruments grouped in metal case in center. A.R. Glancy president of Oakland.

1929 PONTIAC

1929 Pontiac Model 6-29 sedan with Richard Dix. (JAC)

PONTIAC — NEW-BIG SIX — SERIES 6-29 — SIX — The true 1929 Pontiacs had new styling derived from the British Vauxhall. The radiator grille had a vertical center divider. A corrugated apron covered the gas tank in the rear. Larger, bullet-shaped headlights were seen. Wider hood sills and more deeply crowned fenders were used. The bodies gained a handsome, concave belt molding. From January to April, a handsome hood with horizontal louvers was employed. Because of heat warpage problems, a vertically louvered hood was used thereafter. Interiors were upgraded. Closed cars had oval rear windows. The new Landaulet featured a collapsible rear roof section. A bigger, more powerful engine was one of many technical changes. Pontiac introduced its first Convertible Cabriolet this year. (Earlier models called Cabriolets were really Sports Coupes). Standard equipment on all models included an automatic windshield wiper, rear view mirror, dash gasoline gauge and combination transmission and ignition lock.

I.D. DATA: Serial numbers were on the right side of rear crossmember or under left front fender. Starting: 410101. Ending: 530874. Engine numbers were on the left side of crankcase or near left front corner of block. Starting: P376341. Ending: P461000 (approximate). All cars built in Pontiac, Mich.

Model Number	Body Style Number	Body Type & Seating	Factory Price	Shipping Weight	Production Total
SERIES 6-29 (6-cyl.)					
6-29	ROAD	2d R/S Rds-2/4P	775	2,342	Note 1

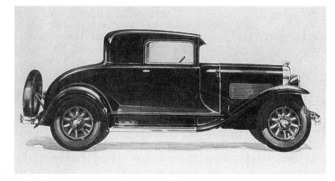

1929 Pontiac Model 6-29 coupe. (CP)

Model Number	Body Style Number	Body Type & Seating	Factory Price	Shipping Weight	Production Total
6-29	PHAE	4d Phaeton-5P	825	2,407	Note 1
6-29	8950	2d Coupe-2P	745	2,532	Note 1
6-29	8960	2d Cabr Conv-2/4P	845	2,537	Note 1
6-29	8940	2d Sedan-5P	745	2,595	Note 1
6-29	8920	4d Sedan-5P	845	2,717	Note 1
6-29	8930	4d Landaulette-5P	895	2,702	Note 1

Note 1: Body style breakouts are not available. Approximately 120,000 New Big Sixes were made as 1929 models.

ENGINE: L-head. Inline Six. Cast-iron block. Bore & stroke: 3-5/16 x 3-7/8. Displacement: 200 cid. Compression Ratio: 4.9:1. Brake horsepower: 60 at 3000 rpm. NACC horsepower: 26.3. Main bearings: Three. Valve lifters: Solid. Carburetor: Marvel one-barrel.

CHASSIS: Wheelbase: 110 in. Overall Length: 169 in. Tires: 29 x 5.00.

TECHNICAL: Improved manual transmission. Speeds: 3F/1R. Floor shift controls. Dry disc clutch. Hotchkiss drive. Semi-floating axle. Four-wheel mechanical brakes. Wood-spoke wheels.

OPTIONS: Front bumper. Rear bumper. Single sidemount. Dual sidemount. Leather sidemount cover(s). Heater. Spotlight. Pedestal mirrors. Wind wings (open cars). Running lamps. Spare tire cover. Lovejoy shock absorbers.

HISTORICAL: Introduced January 1929. Twenty percent more powerful engine. Counterweighted crankshaft. Self-energizing brakes. Adjustable front seats. Improved transmission. Larger carburetor. Wider intake manifold. Larger valves with increased lift. First true Pontiac convertible. A.R. Glancy president of the company.

1929 Pontiac Model 6-29 roadster. (OCW)

The SPORT ROADSTER

1929 Pontiac Model 6-29 roadster. (JAG)

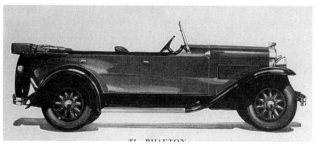

1929 Pontiac Model 6-29 phaeton. (JAG)

1929 Pontiac Model 6-29 convertible cabriolet. (JAG)

1929 Pontiac Model 6-29 four-door sedan. (CP)

1929 Pontiac Model 6-29 two-door sedan. (CP)

1929 Pontiac Model 6-29 landaulette. (CP)

1929 Pontiac Model 6-29 four-door sedan. (CP)

1929 Pontiac Model 6-29 four-door sedan. (CP)

1929-1/2 PONTIAC

PONTIAC — BIG SIX — 6-29A — SIX — This would be the last season for carrying over a mid-year series into the next model year. Pontiacs with serial numbers above 530875-29 were considered 1930 automobiles. There were no specifications changes in these cars, but several models were dropped. Cut from the line were the Convertible Cabriolet and Landaulette Sedan.

I.D. DATA: Serial numbers were on the right side of rear cross-member or under left front fender. Starting: 530875. Ending: 591500. Engine numbers were on the left side of crankcase or near left front corner of block. Starting: 608157. Ending: 673500. All cars built at Pontiac, Mich.

Model Number	Body Style Number	Body Type & Seating	Factory Price	Shipping Weight	Production Total
SERIES 6-29A (6-cyl.)					
6-29A	ROAD	2d R/S Rds-2/4P	775	2,342	Note 1
6-29A	APHAE	4d Phaeton-5P	825	2,407	Note 1
6-29A	A8950	2d Coupe-2P	745	2,532	Note 1
6-29A	A8940	2d Sedan-5P	745	2,595	Note 1
6-29A	A8920	4d Sedan-5P	845	2,717	Note 1

Note 1: Body style breakouts are not available. Approximately 60,625 cars were built in the 6-29A series (August 1929-Oct. 31, 1929).

ENGINE: L-head. Inline. Six. Cast-iron block. Bore & stroke: 3-5/16 x 3-7/8 in. Displacement: 200 cid. Compression Ratio: 4.9:1. Brake horsepower: 60 at 3000 rpm. NACC horsepower: 26.3. Main bearings: Three. Valve lifters: Solid. Carburetor: Marvel one-barrel.

CHASSIS: Wheelbase: 110 in. Overall Length: 169 in. Tires: 29 x 5.00.

TECHNICAL: Improved manual transmission. Speeds: 3F/1R. Floor shift controls. Dry disc clutch. Hotchkiss drive. Semi-floating rear axle. Overall ratio: 4.42:1. Four-wheel mechanical brakes. Wood-spoke wheels.

OPTIONS: Front bumper. Rear bumper. Single sidemount. Leather sidemount cover(s). Heater. Spotlight. Pedestal mirrors. Wind wings (open cars). Running lamps. Spare tire cover. Lovejoy shock absorbers.

HISTORICAL: Introduced August 1929. A.R. Glancy continued as president of Oakland.

1930 Pontiac Series 6-30B sport roadster. (HAC)

1930 Pontiac Series 6-30B two-door sport coupe. (JAG)

PONTIAC — BIG SIX — 6-30B — SIX — A sloping windshield characterized the "real" 1930 Pontiac's new looks. Horizontal lines were emphasized by a half-oval belt molding that extended entirely around the car and over the hood to the radiator. The hood had 31 thin, vertical louvers. The vertical cowl feature line was straightened. A host of technical advances were led by improvements to the engine mounting and suspension systems. A Custom Sedan and Sport Coupe were new body styles. Closed cars had oval rear windows again. Plated headlamp buckets were used on Sport and Custom models. Closed models had cadet style sun visors.

I.D. DATA: Serial numbers on right side of rear cross-member or under left front fender. Starting: 591501. Ending: 649000. Engine numbers on left side of crankcase or left front corner of block. Starting: 673501. Ending: 744000 (approximate). All cars built at Pontiac, Mich.

Model Number	Body Style Number	Body Type & Seating	Factory Price	Shipping Weight	Production Total
SERIES 6-30B (6-cyl.)					
6-30B	ROAD	2d Spt Rds-2/4P	765	2,345	Note 1
6-30B	PHAE	4d Phaeton-5P	795	2,410	Note 1
6-30B	30307	2d Coupe-2P	745	2,518	Note 1
6-30B	30308	2d Spt Coupe-2/4P	825	2,590	Note 1
6-30B	30301	2d Sedan-5P	775	2,630	Note 1
6-30B	30302	4d Sedan-5P	825	2,680	Note 1
6-30B	30309	4d Custom Sed-5P	875	2,720	Note 1

Note 1: Body style breakouts not available. Series production total was 62,888 cars in 1930 model year.

ENGINE: Inline. L-head. Six. Cast-iron block. Bore & stroke: 3-5/16 x 3-7/8 in. Displacement: 200 cid. Compression Ratio: 4.9:1. Brake horsepower: 60 at 3000 rpm. NACC horsepower: 26.3. Main bearings: Three. Valve lifters: Solid. Carburetor: Marvel one-barrel.

CHASSIS: Wheelbase: 110 in. Overall Length: 167 in. Tires: 29 x 5.00.

TECHNICAL: Manual transmission. Speeds: 3F/1R. Floor shift controls. Dry disc clutch. Hotchkiss drive. Overall ratio: 4.42:1. Four-wheel mechanical brakes. Wood-spoke wheels. Rim size: 19 in.

OPTIONS: Front bumper. Rear bumper. Single sidemount. Dual sidemount. Sidemount cover(s). Radio. Heater. Spotlight. Wind wings (open cars). Wire-spoke wheels.

HISTORICAL: Introduced January 1930. Brake drums increased to 12 in. Metric spark plugs. Four-point, rubber-cushioned engine mounting. Coil lock ignition. Manual gear starter. Ribbing added to base of engine block. Four-wheel hand-brake. Lovejoy shock absorbers standard. Model year production: 62,888. A.R. Glancy company president.

1931 Pontiac Series 401 two-door sport coupe. (AA)

PONTIAC — FINE SIX — SERIES 401 — SIX — For 1931 Pontiac featured a longer wheelbase and new bodies. A V-shaped chrome plated radiator with a wire grille was used. Headlamps were chrome plated on all models and mounted on a curved tie bar. One-piece full crown fenders carried parking lights on top. Hoods were secured by a single handle lock on each side. The splash apron on the rear extended from fender to fender. Aluminum moldings decorated the molded runningboard mats. Single-bar bumpers were considered "standard" at slight extra cost. Wire wheels became standard equipment in midyear. Technical refinements to the engine and chassis and running gear changes were among technical improvements. A new convertible coupe replaced the roadster and phaeton.

1930 Pontiac Series 6-30B four-door sedan. (OCW)

1931 Pontiac Series 401 four-door sedan. (OCW)

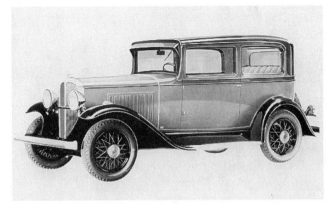

1931 Pontiac Series 401 two-door sedan. (OCW)

I.D. DATA: Serial numbers on right side of rear cross-member or under left front fender. Starting: 649001. Ending: 729000. Engine numbers on left side of crankcase or left front corner of block. Starting: 744001. Ending: 835000. All cars built at Pontiac, Mich.

Series Number	Body Style Number	Body Type & Seating	Factory Price	Shipping Weight	Production Total
SERIES 401					
401	31307	2d Coupe-2P	675	2,558	Note 1
401	31308	2d Spt Coupe-2/4P	715	2,618	Note 1
401	31318	2d Conv Cpe-2/4P	745	2,598	Note 1
401	31301	2d Sedan-5P	675	2,653	Note 1
401	31309	4d Sedan-5P	745	2,733	Note 1
401	31319	4d Custom Sed-5P	785	2,743	Note 1

Note 1: Body style breakouts not available. Model year production total of Series 401 Pontiacs was 84,708 cars.

ENGINE: L-head. Inline. Six. Cast-iron block. Bore & stroke: 3-5/16 x 3-7/8 in. Displacement: 200 cid. Brake horsepower: 60 at 3000 rpm. NACC horsepower: 26.3. Main bearings: Three. Valve lifters: Solid. Carburetor: Marvel one-barrel.

CHASSIS: Wheelbase: 112 in. Tires: 29 x 5.00.

TECHNICAL: Manual transmission. Speeds: 3F/1R. Floor shift controls. Dry disc clutch. Hotchkiss drive. Semi-floating rear axle. Overall ratio: 4.55:1. Four-wheel mechanical brakes. Wire-spoke wheels (Kelsey-Hayes). Rim size: 19 in.

OPTIONS: Front bumper. Rear bumper. Dual sidemount. Sidemount cover(s). Radio. Heater. Clock. Spotlight. Pedestal mirrors. Trunk rack. Touring trunk. Wood-spoke wheels. Dual windshield wipers. Trippe lights.

HISTORICAL: Introduced January 1931. Steeldraulic brakes. Full-pressure lubrication. New AC intake silencer. Improved engine mounting. Heavier, sturdier frame. Inlox spring bushings. Stronger rear axle with Hyatt roller pinion bearings. Redesigned brake toggles. This was the last year for Oakland.

1932 PONTIAC

1932 Pontiac Series 402 two-door sedan. (CP)

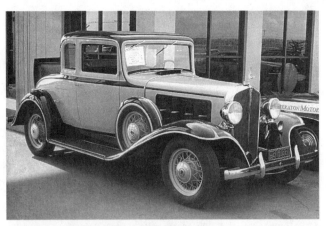

1932 Pontiac Series 302 sport coupe. (OCW)

1932 Pontiac Series 302 sport coupe. (OCW)

PONTIAC — SERIES 402 — SIX — The Oakland became the Pontiac V-8 in 1932. Pontiac also offered a separate six-cylinder line. The new sixes had a longer wheelbase and longer, roomier bodies. They featured a slanted windshield without an outside sun visor. A new V-shaped radiator with vertical grille bars was used. The sides of the hood had four ventilator doors. Dual horns and front fender lights were standard on Custom models. The six-cylinder hood ornament had an Indian head within a circle.

PONTIAC V-8 — SERIES 302 — EIGHT — The 1932 Pontiac V-8s were a continuation of the 1931 Oakland with a new name and updated styling. They used a V-type radiator shell with built-in grille. A slanting windshield was seen. Sun visors were moved

1932 Pontiac Series 302 four-door custom sedan. (JAG)

1932 Pontiac Series 402 two-door convertible coupe. (JAG)

1932 Pontiac Series 402 four-door sedan. (JAG)

from outside to inside. Door-type hood ventilators appeared. All models had new radiator emblems, dual horns, and front fender lights. A bird with raised wings was the V-8 hood ornament.

I.D. DATA: Serial numbers were on the right side of rear cross-member or under left front fender. Starting: 729001. Ending: 763983. Engine numbers on left side of crankcase or near left front corner of block. [series 402] Starting: 835001. Ending: 879565 (approximate). [Series 302] Starting: 310001. Ending: 316282. All cars built in Pontiac, Mich.

Series Number	Body Style Number	Body Type & Seating	Factory Price	Shipping Weight	Production Total
SERIES 402 (6-Cyl.)					
402	32317	2d Coupe-2P	635	2,689	Note 1
402	32308	2d Spt Coupe-2/4P	715	2,734	Note 1
402	32318	2d Conv Cpe-2/4P	765	2,694	Note 1
402	32301	2d Sedan-5P	645	2,794	Note 1
402	32309	4d Sedan-5P	725	2,884	Note 1
402	32319	4d Custom Sed-5P	795	2,889	Note 1
SERIES 302 (V-8)					
302	32367	2d Coupe-2P	845	3,069	Note 2
302	32358	2d Spt Coupe-2/4P	925	3,129	Note 2
302	32368	2d Conv Cpe-2/4P	945	3,089	Note 2
302	32351	2d Sedan-5P	845	3,149	Note 2
302	32359	4d Sedan-5P	945	3,224	Note 2
302	32369	4d Custom Sed-5P	1,025	3,259	Note 2

Note 1: Body style breakouts not available. Total series production was 35,059 units.

Note 2: Body style breakouts not available. Total series production was 6,281 units.

ENGINE [Series 402]: L-head. Inline. Six. Cast-iron block. Bore & stroke: 3-5/16 x 3-7/8 in. Displacement: 200 cid. Compression Ratio: 5.1:1. Brake horsepower: 65 at 3200 rpm. N.A.C.C. horsepower: 26.3. Main bearings: Three. Valve lifters: Solid. Carburetor: Marvel one-barrel.

ENGINE [Series 302]: L-head. V-block. Eight. Cast-iron block. Bore & stroke: 3-7/16 x 3-3/8 in. Displacement: 251 cid. Compression Ratio: 5.2:1. Brake horsepower: 85 at 3200 rpm. NACC horsepower: 37.8. Main bearings: Three. Valve lifters: Solid. Carburetor: Marvel one-barrel.

CHASSIS: [Series 402]: Wheelbase 114 in. Tires: 18 x 5.25. [Series 302]: Wheelbase 117 in. Tires: 17 x 6.00.

TECHNICAL: [Series 402]: Synchromesh transmission (Muncie). Speeds: 3F/1R. Floor shift controls. Dry disc clutch. Hotchkiss drive.

1932 Pontiac Series 402 two-door sport coupe. (JAG)

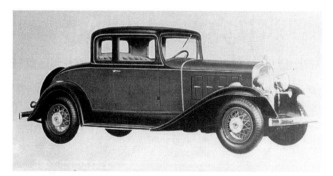
1932 Pontiac Series 402 two-door sport coupe. (JAG)

1932 Pontiac Series 402 four-door custom sedan. (JAG)

1932 Pontiac Series 302 two-door sport coupe. (JAG)

1932 Pontiac Series 302 two-door convertible coupe. (JAG)

Semi-floating rear axle. Overall ratio: 4.55:1. Four-wheel mechanical brakes. Kelsey-Hayes wire spoke wheels. Freewheeling standard. [Series 302]: Synchromesh transmission (Muncie). Speeds: 3F/1R. Floor shift controls. Dry disc clutch. Hotchkiss drive. Semi-floating rear axle. Overall ratio: 4.22:1. Four-wheel mechanical brakes. Wire spoke wheels.

OPTIONS: Front bumper. Rear bumper. Dual sidemount. Sidemount cover(s) (fabric or metal). Radio. Heater. Clock. Cigar lighter. Radio antenna (under runningboard). Spotlight. Trippe lights. Tandem windshield wipers. Dual horns (std. on Custom). Dual taillights (std. on Custom). Pedestal mirrors. Trunk rack. Touring trunk. Rear view mirror.

HISTORICAL: Production of six began Dec. 8, 1931. Production of V-8 began Dec. 22, 1931. Interchangeable steel-backed bearings. Floorboard mounted handbrake. Valve guides with tapered holes. First Pontiac eight and first V-8. Manually operated "Ride Control." Synchromesh transmission with silent second gear. Free wheeling. Smaller tires. Improved cooling. Calendar year registrations: 47,926 cars. Model year production: 41,340 cars. Irving J. Reuter and F.O. Tanner shared general manager position at Oakland Motor Co. in early 1932. Pontiac became part of the new B-O-P (Buick-Olds-Pontiac) General Motors division. The name Pontiac Motors was adopted around June 1932.

1933 PONTIAC

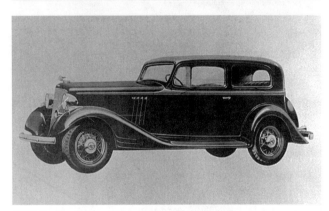

1933 Pontiac Series 601 two-door sedan. (JAG)

PONTIAC — ECONOMY EIGHT — SERIES 601 — The 1933 Pontiacs had a new straight eight plus many styling and technical changes. A new Fisher body with beaver tail rear styling was used. There was a slanting, V-type radiator with vertical bars. The hood had four wide, slanting louvers back towards the cowl. Valanced front fenders gave a streamlined look. There was an airplane type instrument panel on the left and glove compartment on the right of the dash. Pontiacs were made in five different assembly plants. The hood ornament was a brave's head in a circle with a round base.

1933 Pontiac Series 601 four-door sedan. (JAG)

1933 Pontiac Series 601 two-door roadster. (OCW)

I.D. DATA: Serial numbers were in the previous locations. Pontiac, Mich., numbers: 770001 to 838455. Oakland, Calif., numbers: C3001 to C5678. Atlanta, Ga., numbers: A1001 to A3195. Tarrytown, N.Y., numbers: T1001 to T10,600. St. Louis, Mo., numbers S1001 to S4996. Engine numbers were in the same location. Pontiac, Mich., numbers: 885001 to 987400. (Numbers for other factories not available).

Series Number	Body Style Number	Body Type & Seating	Factory Price	Shipping Weight	Production Total
SERIES 601 (8-cyl.)					
601	ROAD	2d Roadster-2/4P	585	2,675	Note 1
601	33317	2d Coupe-2P	635	2,865	Note 1
601	33328	2d Sport Cpe-2/4P	670	2,930	Note 1
601	33318	2d Conv Cpe-2/4P	695	2,905	Note 1
601	33301	2d Sedan-5P	635	2,945	Note 1
601	33331	2d Trg Sedan-5P	675	2,995	Note 1
601	33309	4d Sedan-5P	695	3,020	Note 1

Note 1: Body style breakouts not available. Series production total: 90,198 units.

ENGINE: Inline. L-head. Eight. Cast-iron block. Bore & stroke: 3-3/16 x 3-1/2 in. Displacement: 223.4 cid. Compression Ratio: 5.7:1. Brake horsepower: 77 at 3600 rpm. NACC horsepower: 32.52. Main bearings: Five. Valve lifters: Solid. Carburetor: Carter one-barrel.

CHASSIS: Wheelbase: 115 in. Overall Length: 181.5 in. Height: 67-3/4 in. Tires: 17 x 5.50.

TECHNICAL: Muncie Synchromesh transmission. Speeds: 3F/1R. Floor shift. Single plate clutch. Torque tube drive. Semi-floating rear axle. Overall ratio: 4.44 1. Four-wheel mechanical brakes. K-H 40-spoke wire wheels. Rim Size: 17 x 3.62 in. Freewheeling standard.

OPTIONS: Front bumper. Rear bumper. Dual sidemounts. Sidemount cover(s). Bumper guards. Radio. Heater. Clock. Cigar lighter. Radio antenna (under runningboard). Spotlight. Disc wheels. Jumbo tires. Trunk rack. Touring trunk. Rear tire cover. Mud guards. Rear view mirror.

HISTORICAL: Entered production Dec. 7, 1932. Closed production Oct. 6, 1933. Individually controlled No-Draft ventilation system. Safety glass in windshield and vent windows. New, stronger frame.

Twelve Flxible-Pontiac funeral cars built this year. Roadster reintroduced for one final season. Model year production: 90,198 units. Late in the year the B-0-P program was dissolved and Harry J. Klinger was appointed Pontiac general manager.

1934 PONTIAC

1934 Pontiac Series 603 two-door convertible cabriolet. (OCW)

1934 Pontiac Series 603 four-door touring sedan. (AA)

PONTIAC — SERIES 603 — EIGHT — Larger Fisher bodies were used for 1934. Deep skirted fenders were seen. Longer, bullet-shaped headlamp buckets appeared. The cowl ventilator opened towards the rear. Horizontal grille type hood louvers were new. Hoods were seven inches longer. Cars with standard equipment had hood ornaments with a brave's head in a circle on a teardrop base. Cars with Deluxe equipment had an Indian maiden hood ornament.

I.D. DATA: Serial numbers were in the previous locations. Pontiac, Mich., numbers were 83850 and up. Engine numbers were in the previous locations. Numbers were 987401 and up.

Series Number	Body Style Number	Body Type & Seating	Factory Price	Shipping Weight	Production Total
SERIES 603 (8-cyl.)					
603	34317	2d Coupe-2P	675	3,185	Note 1
603	34328	2d Spt Coupe-2/4P	725	3,260	Note 1
603	34318	2d Cabriolet-2/4P	765	3,225	Note 1

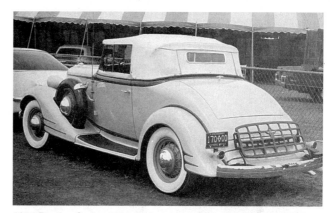

1934 Pontiac Series 603 two-door convertible cabriolet. (OCW)

Series Number	Body Style Number	Body Type & Seating	Factory Price	Shipping Weight	Production Total
603	34301	2d Sedan-5P	705	3,280	Note 1
603	34331	2d Trg Sedan-5P	745	3,300	Note 1
603	34309	4d Sedan-5P	765	3,350	Note 1
603	34319	4d Trg Sedan-5P	805	3,405	Note 1

Note 1: Body style breakouts not available. Series production was 78,859 units.

ENGINE: L-head. Inline. Eight. Cast-iron block. Bore & stroke: 3-3/16 x 3-1/2 in. Displacement: 223.4 cid. Compression Ratio: 6.2:1. Brake Horsepower: 84 at 3800 rpm. NACC Horsepower: 32.51. Main bearings: Five. Valve lifters: Solid. Carburetor: Carter one-barrel.

CHASSIS: Wheelbase: 117-1/4 in. Overall Length: 187-1/4 in. Height: 68-7/16 in. Tires: 17 x 6.00.

TECHNICAL: Synchromesh transmission. Speeds: 3F/1R. Floor shift controls. Single plate clutch. Torque tube drive. Semi-floating rear axle. Overall ratio: 4.55: 1. Four-wheel mechanical brakes. Wire-spoke wheels.

OPTIONS: Front bumper. Dual sidemount. Sidemount cover(s). Bumper guards. Radio (Air Chief). Heater. Clock. Cigar lighter. Radio antenna. Seat covers. Spotlight. Touring trunk. Spare tire cover. Trunk rack. Standup sedan trunk. Trippe lights. Supertone horn. Right-hand sun visor. Ash receiver set. Right-hand tail lamp. Luggage sets. Twin windshield wipers. License plate frame.

HISTORICAL: Production began Jan. 1, 1934. 1934 Pontiac convertible was Indy 500 "Official Speedway" car. Stock Pontiac hit 93 mph at Muroc Dry Lake speed trial. Improved intake manifolding.

1934 Pontiac Series 603 two-door sport coupe. (JAG)

1934 Pontiac Series 603 two-door convertible cabriolet. (IMSC)

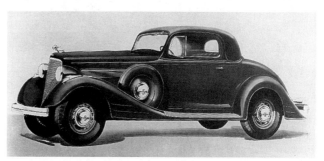

1934 Pontiac Series 603 two-door coupe. (OCW)

1934 Pontiac Series 603 two-door sedan. (OCW)

1934 Pontiac Series 603 two-door sport coupe. (JAG)

1934 Pontiac Series 603 two-door sedan. (OCW)

1934 Pontiac Series 603 Miller-Meteor funeral car. (JAG)

"Knee-Action" front suspension introduced. Multi-beam headlights. Roomier bodies. New G.M.R. high-compression head. Gaselector added to distributor. Gas mileage (in tests): 19-24 miles per gallon. Harry J. Klingler general manager.

1935 PONTIAC

1935 Pontiac Eight two-door sedan. (OCW)

PONTIAC — STANDARD — SERIES 701-B — SIX — Pontiacs came in Standard and Deluxe six and Improved eight car-lines this year. The Standard six models had transmissions with non-synchromesh first gears, solid I-beam front axles and headlamp beam indicators on the instrument dial. They did not have parking lamps on the front fenders. A single tail lamp was standard and fenders only came with black finish. The year's new styling featured a waterfall grille and "Silver Streak" trim moldings on the hood. More rounded grille shells and fenders were seen. The hood ornament on sixes was a brave's head in a circle. The headamps were mounted on pedestals between fenders and grilles.

PONTIAC — DELUXE — SERIES 701-A — SIX — The Deluxe sixes had the same wheelbase and engine as standard models. They had "Knee-Action" front suspension and all-synchromesh transmissions. Multi-beam headlights were used. Streamlined parking lights sat atop the front fenders. Single taillights were regular equipment, but dual taillights were a common option. Styling changes were the same as standard models had.

PONTIAC — IMPROVED — SERIES 605 — EIGHT — The eight-cylinder Pontiac chassis had a 4-5/8 inch longer wheelbase. While the main body was identical to that used by sixes, the front end sheet metal was longer. Styling changes were the same as on other car-lines. An Indian maiden hood ornament was used. Dual taillights were standard equipment, along with twin windshield wipers and fender safety lamps. "Pontiac Eight" grille badges were used. The rear windows on four-door sedans and two-door touring sedans featured ventipanes.

I.D. DATA: [Series 701-B] Serial numbers on a plate or right side of frame center of right front wheel. Starting: P6AB-1001. Ending: P6AB-46752. Engine numbers in previous location. Starting Engine No.: 6-1001 and up. [Series 701-B] Serial and engine number locations were the same as on the Standard six models. Starting serial no.: 6AA-100. Ending serial no.: 6AA-32187. Engine nos.: 6-1001 and up. [Series 605] Serial and engine number locations were as on

1935 Pontiac Eight sport coupe. (JAG)

1935 Pontiac Eight two-door sedan. (OCW)

Standard Six. Starting serial no.: 8AA-1001. Ending serial no.: 8AA-42561. Engine nos.: 8-1001 and up.

Series Number	Body Style Number	Body Type & Seating	Factory Price	Shipping Weight	Production Total
SERIES 701-B STANDARD SIX (6-cyl.)					
701-B	2107AB	2d Coupe-2P	615	3,065	Note 1
701-B	2111AB	2d Touring Sed -5P	695	3,195	Note 1
701-B	2101AB	2d Sedan-5P	665	3,195	Note 1
701-B	2119AB	4d Touring Sed-5P	745	3,245	Note 1
701-B	2109AB	4d Sedan-5P	715	3,245	Note 1
SERIES 701-A DELUXE SIX (6-cyl.)					
701-A	2107AA	2d Coupe-2P	675	3,125	Note 2
701-A	2157AA	2d Sport Cpe-2/4P	725	3,150	Note 2
701-A	2167AA	2d Cabriolet-2/4P	775	3,180	Note 2
701-A	2111AA	2d Touring Sed -5P	745	3,245	Note 2
701-A	2101AA	2d Sedan-5P	715	3,245	Note 2
701-A	2119AA	4d Touring Sed -5P	795	3,300	Note 2
701-A	2109AA	4d Sedan-5P	765	3,300	Note 2
SERIES 605 DELUXE EIGHT (8-cyl.)					
605	2007	2d Coupe-2P	730	3,260	Note 3
605	2057	2d Sport Cpe 2/4P	780	3,290	Note 3
605	2067	2d Cabriolet-2/4P	840	3,305	Note 3
605	2011	2d Touring Sed -5P	805	3,400	Note 3
605	2001	2d Sedan-5P	775	3,400	Note 3
605	2019	4d Touring Sed -5P	860	3,450	Note 3
605	2009	4d Sedan-5P	830	3,450	Note 3

Note 1: Body style breakouts not available. Series production: 49,302 units.

Note 2: Body style breakouts not available. Series production: 36,032 units.

Note 3: Body style breakouts not available. Series production: 44,134 units.

1935 Pontiac Six four-door sedan. (JAG)

1935 Pontiac Six cabriolet. (OCW)

1935 Pontiac Six cabriolet. (JAG)

ENGINE [Series 701-B]: L-head. Inline. Six. Cast-iron block. Bore & stroke: 3-3.8 x 3-7/8 in. Displacement: 208 cid. Compression Ratio: 6.2:1. Brake Horsepower: 80 at 3600 rpm. NACC Horsepower: 27.34. Main bearings: Four. Valve lifters: Solid. Carburetor: Carter one-barrel (manual choke).

ENGINE [Series 701-A]: L-head. Inline. Six. Cast-iron block. Bore & stroke: 3-3/8 x 3-7/8 in. Displacement: 208 cid. Compression Ratio: 6.2:1. Brake Horsepower: 80 at 3600 rpm. NACC Horsepower: 27.34. Main bearings: Four. Valve lifters: Solid. Carburetor: Carter one-barrel (manual choke).

1935 Pontiac Six four-door touring sedan. (OCW)

1935 Pontiac Deluxe Six two-door sedan. (JAG)

1935 Pontiac Eight FIxible funeral car. (JAG)

ENGINE [Base Eight]: L-head. Inline. Eight. Cast-iron block. Bore & stroke: 3-3/16 x 3-1/2 in. Displacement: 223.4 cid. Compression Ratio: 6.2:1. Brake Horsepower: 84 at 3800 rpm. NACC Horsepower: 32.51. Main bearings: Five. Valve lifters: Solid. Carburetor: Carter one-barrel.

CHASSIS: [Series 701-B]: Wheelbase: 112 in. Overall Length: 189 in. Tires: 16 x 6.00. [Series 701-A]: Wheelbase: 112 in. Overall Length: 189 in. Tires: 16 x 6.00. [Series 605]: Wheelbase: 116-5/8 in. Overall Length: 193-5/8 in. Tires: 16 x 6.50.

TECHNICAL: [Series 701-B]: Manual transmission (non-synchromesh first). Speeds: 3F/1R. Floor shift controls. Single plate clutch. Torque tube drive. Semi-floating rear axle. Overall ratio: 4.44:1. Hydraulic brakes. Steel spoke wheels. [Series 701-A]: All-synchromesh. Speeds: 3F/1R. Floor shift controls. Single plate clutch. Torque tube drive. Semi floating rear axle. Overall ratio: 4.44: 1. Hydraulic brakes. Wire-spoke wheels. [Series 605]: All-synchromesh. Speeds: 3F/1R. Floor shift controls. Dry plate clutch. Torque tube drive. Semi-floating rear axle. Overall ratio: 4.55: 1. Hydraulic brakes. Wire-spoke wheels.

OPTIONS: Antifreeze ($3.15). Right-hand tail lamp ($3.45). Dual horn kit ($12.50). Triplex air cleaner ($6.50). Wheel disc ($2.30). Five wheel discs ($1.25). Five wheel trim rings ($8.50). Four bumper guards ($3.95). Outdraft heater ($7.50). Deluxe heater ($12.25). Heater ports package ($4.00). Air Chief radio ($62.50). Air Mate radio ($47.95). Radio antenna package ($3). Glove box smoker set & watch ($13.50). Dash watch ($10). 30-hour mirror watch ($3.95). Safety light ($15.95). License frame ($2.45). Luggage set ($19.75). Rear mat ($1.75). Visor vanity mirror ($1). Right-hand inside visor ($2). Dual sidemounts (not available on standard six).

HISTORICAL: Date of Introduction: December 29, 1934. Innovations: "suicide" front door hinging. Hydraulic brakes. Micro polished engine bearings. Improved double-drop "KY" frame. Model year production: 129,463 units. Company president was Harry J. Klinger.

1936 PONTIAC

1936 Pontiac Eight four-door touring sedan. (AA)

MASTER — SERIES 6BB — SIX — The 1936 Pontiac had a new, waterfall grille with a thinner shell, fewer "silver streaks" and the

1936 Pontiac Deluxe Eight cabriolet. (JAG)

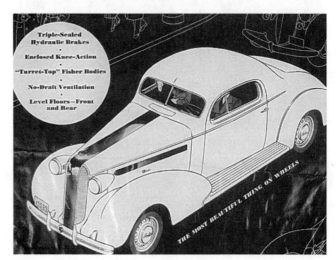

1936 Pontiac Deluxe Eight coupe. (JAG)

outer sections finished in body color. The horizontal hood louvers came to a point at the front this year. Longer, slimmer headlamps were mounted on the sides of the hood. The fenders no longer had "speed lines" sculpted into them. The Master Six could most easily be identified by its solid front axle. It also had a non-locking glove box, taupe mohair or brown pattern broadcloth upholstery and black bakelite door handle and instrument panel hardware. Two-door sedans at first came only with bucket front seats, and a bench seat option was introduced at midyear. Standard equipment included Delco-Remy ignition, hydraulic brakes, cross-flow cooling, and foot-operated starter buttons. Flush mounted taillights were used on some Master Sixes built early in the model year.

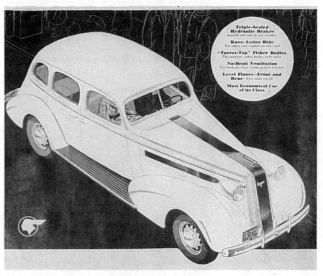

1936 Pontiac Eight four-door sedan. (JAG)

1936 Pontiac Deluxe Six cabriolet. (OCW)

1936 Pontiac Six coupe. (JAG)

DELUXE — SERIES 6BA — SIX — The Deluxe Six was virtually identical to the Master Six, except that it had "Knee Action" independent front suspension. Upholstery in closed cars was taupe mohair or modified tweed pattern taupe woolen cloth. Deluxe sixes also had translucent dash knobs and door handle knobs. Additional standard equipment in this series included a larger gas tank, higher capacity six-volt battery, and automatic choke.

DELUXE — SERIES 8BA — EIGHT — The Pontiac Deluxe Eight had the company's longest wheelbase. The extra length was taken up in the hood and runningboards. Fenders varied slightly in the manner in which they overlapped the cowl, but were actually the same with the attachment holes drilled differently. The words "Pontiac 8" appeared on the grille and the hood ornament was a distinctive, circular design instead of the oblong loop style used on sixes. Standard sedan equipment included front and rear armrests, twin

1936 Pontiac Eight two-door sedan. (OCW)

the latest developments

1936 Pontiac Six Superior funeral car. (OCW)

1936 Pontiac Six four-door touring sedan. (OCW)

assist straps, oriental grain interior moldings, and a dash-mounted clock. The eight had "Knee-Action" front suspension, a pressurized cooling system, automatic choke, and a new type of clutch.

I.D. DATA: [Series 6BB] Serial numbers were located on top of frame just ahead of steering gear. Starting: 6BB-1001. Ending: 6BB-91362. Pacific Coast numbers were C-1001 to C-1400. Bench seat cars had an "AB" prefix instead of "BB." Engine numbers located on left side of crankcase and on front left corner of cylinder block. Starting: 6-84001. Ending: 6-219182. [Series 6BA] Serial numbers were in the same location. Starting: 6BA-1001. Ending: 6BA-41352. Pacific Coast numbers were C-1001 to C-1300. Engine numbers were in the same location. Starting: 6-84001. Ending: 6-219182. [Series 8BA] Serial numbers were in the same location. Starting: 8BA-1001. Ending: 8BA-38371. Pacific Coast numbers were C-1001 to C-1260. Engine numbers were in the same locations. Starting: 8-44001. Ending: 8-82040.

Series Number	Body Style Number	Body Type & Seating	Factory Price	Shipping Weight	Production Total
MASTER SIX SERIES (6-cyl.)					
6BB	—	2d Coupe-2P	615	3,085	Note 1
6BB	—	2d Sport Cpe-2/4P	675	3,120	Note 1
6BB	—	2d Cabriolet-2/4P	760	3,125	Note 1
6BB	—	2d Sedan-5P	675	3,195	Note 1
6BB	—	2d Touring Sed-5P	700	3,195	Note 1
6BB	—	4d Sedan-5P	720	3,235	Note 1
6BB	—	4d Touring Sed-5P	745	3,245	Note 1
DELUXE SIX SERIES (6-cyl.)					
6BA	—	2d Coupe-2P	665	3,130	Note 2
6BA	—	2d Sport Cpe -2/4P	720	3,165	Note 2
6BA	—	2d Cabriolet-2/4P	810	3,200	Note 2
6BA	—	2d Sedan-5P	720	3,265	Note 2
6BA	—	2d Touring Sed-5P	745	3,270	Note 2
6BA	—	4d Sedan-5P	770	3,300	Note 2
6BA	—	4d Touring Sed-5P	795	3,300	Note 2
DELUXE EIGHT SERIES (8-cyl.)					
8BA	—	2d Coupe-2P	730	3,250	Note 3
8BA	—	2d Sport Cpe -2/4P	785	3,285	Note 3
8BA	—	2d Cabriolet-2/4P	855	3,335	Note 3
8BA	—	2d Sedan-5P	*770*	3,390	Note 3
8BA	—	2d Touring Sed-5P	795	3,390	Note 3
8BA	—	4d Sedan-5P	815	3,415	Note 3
8BA	—	4d Touring Sed-5P	840	3,420	Note 3

Note 1: Series production was 93,475 units.

Note 2: Total series production was 44,040 units.

Note 3: Total series production was 38,755 units.

ENGINE [Series 6BB]: Inline. L-head. Six. Cast-iron block. Bore & stroke: 3-3/8 in. x 3-7/8 in. Displacement: 208 cid. Compression Ratio: 6.2:1. Brake Horsepower: 81 at 3600 rpm. Net Horsepower:

27.34. Main bearings: Four. Valve lifters: Solid. Carburetor: Carter one-barrel model 340S.

ENGINE [Series 6BA]: Inline. L-head. Six. Cast-iron block. Bore & stroke: 3-3/8 in. x 3-7/8 in. Displacement: 208 cid. Compression Ratio: 6.2: 1. Brake Horsepower: 81 at 3600 rpm. Net Horsepower: 27.34. Main bearings: Four. Valve lifters: Solid. Caburetor: Carter one-barrel model 342S.

ENGINE [Series 8BA]: Inline. L-head. Eight. Cast-iron block. Bore & stroke: 3-1/4 in. x 3-1/2 in. Displacement: 232.3 cid. Compression Ratio: 6.5:1. Brake Horsepower: 87 at 3800 rpm. Net Horsepower: 33.8. Main bearings: Five. Valve lifters: Solid. Carburetor: Carter one-barrel model 322S.

CHASSIS: [Series 6BB] Wheelbase: 112 in. Overall Length: 189-3/4 in. Height: 67-9/16 in. Tires: 16 x 6.00. [Series 6AB] Wheelbase: 112 in. Overall Length: 189-3/4 in. Height: 67-9/16 in. Tires: 16 x 6.00. [Series 8AB] Wheelbase: 116-5/8 in. Overall Length: 194-5/16 in. Height: 67-9/16 in. Tires: 16 x 6.50.

TECHNICAL: Manual synchromesh transmission. Speeds: 3F/IR. Floor mounted controls. Ventilated dry disc clutch. Semi-floating rear axle. Overall Ratio: (std.) 4.55:1; (mountain) 4.85:1; (plains) 4.11:1. Four-wheel hydraulic brakes. Steel spoke wheels.

OPTIONS: Front bumper. Rear bumper. Dual sidemount. Sidemount cover(s). Fender skirts. Set of four bumper guards ($3.95). Air Chief Radio ($62.50). Air Mate Radio ($47.95). Outdraft heater ($7.50). Deluxe heater ($12.25). Clock ($10). Cigar lighter ($1.50). Radio antenna package ($3). Seat covers (Santoy). Spotlight(s). Right-hand taillight ($3.45). Dual horn kit ($12.50). Triplex air cleaner ($6.50). Set of five wire wheel discs ($11.25). Set of five wheel trim rings ($8.50). Glove compartment smoker set and clock ($13.50). Pull-wind clock ($3.95). Safety light ($15.95). License frame set ($2.45). Luggage set ($19.75). Right-hand inside visor ($2.00).

HISTORICAL: Introduced: Sept. 25, 1935. Innovations: Larger bore eight. Improved clutch. Improved cooling system on eight. New front suspension with King pins mounted in floating bronze bearings. Automatic choke on deluxe models. Model year production: 176,270 units. Pontiac held sixth rank in U.S. auto sales for 1936. The president of Pontiac was Harry Klingler. The new models were called "The Most Beautiful Thing on Wheels."

1937 PONTIAC

1937 Pontiac Eight convertible sedan. (OCW)

PONTIAC — DELUXE — SERIES 26 — SIX — The 1937 Pontiacs had longer, one-piece solid bodies with Turret tops. The hoodline was higher and the radiator grille was narrower. Silver Streak moldings ran down the center of the hood and over the grille in waterfall fashion. The side grilles had chrome horizontal bars grouped into four lower segments and a narrower upper segment that continued down the sides of the hood. New, one-piece front fenders with a split-pear shape were used. Longer headlamp buckets were mounted on pedestals attached to the fender catwalks. A wider windshield with a rakish 39-degree slant gave a more modern appearance. The six-cylinder hood ornament was a flat, solid Indian head.

1937 Pontiac Eight convertible sedan. (OCW)

1937 Pontiac Eight convertible sedan. (OCW)

PONTIAC — DELUXE — SERIES 28 — EIGHT — Pontiac Eights were longer cars. They had longer hoods and fenders. Styling was similar to the Pontiac Sixes. The winged nose badge and trunk emblem said "Pontiac Eight." The hood ornament was a flat brave's head that projected above the hood moldings and served as a hood latch handle.

I.D. DATA: [Series 26] Serial numbers on top of frame ahead of steering gear (visible upon raising hood). Starting: 6CA-1001. Ending: 6CA-154827 (Pontiac, Mich.). Cars built at Southgate, Calif., had serial number prefix "C". Cars built at Linden, N.J., had prefix "L". Engine numbers on front left corner of block. Starting: 6-220001. Ending: 6-399286. [Series 28] Serial numbers on top of frame ahead of steering gear. Starting: 8CA-1001. Ending: 8CA-49442. California cars had a "C" prefix. New Jersey cars had an "L" prefix. Engine numbers on front left corner of block. Starting: 8-830001. Ending: 8-139968.

Series Number	Body Style Number	Body Type & Seating	Factory Price	Shipping Weight	Production Total
DELUXE 6 SERIES 26 (6-cyl.)					
26	27	2d Spt Coupe2/4P	853	3165	Note 1
26	67	2d Cabriolet-2/4P	945	3250	Note 1
26	01	2d Sedan-5P	830	3240	Note 1
26	11	2d Trg Sedan-5P	855	3240	Note 1
26	09	4d Sedan-5P	881	3265	Note 1
26	19	4d Trg Sedan-5P	906	3275	Note 1
26	49	4d Conv Sedan-5P	1197	3375	Note 1
26	STAWAG	4d Sta Wag-7P	992	3340	Note 1

1937 Pontiac Deluxe Eight four-door touring sedan. (HAC)

1937 Pontiac Deluxe Eight coupe. (OCW)

1937 Pontiac Deluxe Six four-door touring sedan. (JAG)

1937 Pontiac Deluxe Six cabriolet. (OCW)

Series Number	Body Style Number	Body Type & Seating	Factory Price	Shipping Weight	Production Total
DELUXE 8 SERIES 28 (8-cyl.)					
28	27B	2d Coupe-2P	857	3,305	Note 2
28	27	2d Sport Cpe-2/4P	913	3,305	Note 2
28	67	2d Cabriolet-2/4P	985	3,360	Note 2

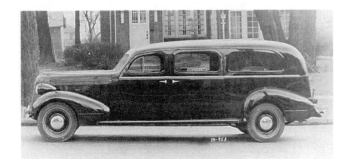

1937 Pontiac Miller-Meteor limousine funeral car. (JAG)

1937 Pontiac Deluxe Six Superior Guardian ambulance. (OCW)

1937 Pontiac Deluxe Six Superior Rosehill funeral service car. (OCW)

1937 Pontiac Deluxe Eight Superior Graceland funeral car. (OCW)

Series Number	Body Style Number	Body Type & Seating	Factory Price	Shipping Weight	Production Total
28	01	2d Sedan-5P	893	3,385	Note 2
28	11	2d Touring Sed-5P	919	3,380	Note 2
28	09	4d Sedan-5P	939	3,410	Note 2
28	19	4d Touring Sed-5P	965	3,400	Note 2
28	49	4d Conv Sedan-5P	1,235	3,505	Note 2

Note 1: Body style breakouts not available. Series production total was 179,244 cars.

Note 2: Body style breakouts not available. Series production total was 56,945 cars.

ENGINE [Series 26]: L-head. Inline. Six. Cast-iron block. Bore & stroke: 3-7/16 x 4 in. Displacement: 222.7 cid. Compression Ratio: 6.2:1. Brake Horsepower: 85 at 3520 rpm. NACC Horsepower: 28.3. Main bearings: Four. Valve lifters: Solid. Carburetor: Carter one-barrel.

ENGINE [Series 28]: L-head. Inline. Eight. Cast-iron block. Bore & stroke: 3-1/4 x 3-3/4 in. Displacement: 248.9 cid. Compression Ratio: 6.2:1. Brake Horsepower: 100 at 3800 rpm. NACC Horsepower: 33.8. Main bearings: Five. Valve lifters: Solid. Carburetor: Carter one-barrel.

1937 Pontiac Deluxe Six Superior Oakridge funeral car. (OCW)

CHASSIS: [Series 26] Wheelbase: 117 in. Overall Length: 193.06 in. Height: 67 in. Tires: 16 x 6.00. [Series 28] Wheelbase: 122 in. Overall Length 198.06 in. Height: 67 in. Tires: 16 x 6.50.

TECHNICAL: [Series 26] Synchromesh transmission. Speeds: 3F/1R. Floor shift controls. Dry disc clutch. Hotchkiss drive. Semi-floating axle. Overall ratio: 4.37:1. Four-wheel hydraulic brakes. Steel disc wheels. [Series 28] Synchromesh transmission. Speeds: 3F/1R. Floor shift controls. Dry disc clutch. Hotchkiss drive. Semi-floating axle. Overall ratio: 4.37:1. Four-wheel hydraulic brakes. Steel disc wheels.

OPTIONS: Deluxe radio. Master radio. Deluxe heater. Master heater. Running board antennas (dual). Antifreeze. Tenite shift ball. Commercial pickup box (coupes). Locking gas cap. Tour top luggage carrier. Santoy seat covers. Electric dash clock. Pull wind headboard clock. Battery charger. Wheel discs. Dual safety defroster. Electric fan defroster. Electric windshield defroster. Tailpipe extension. License frames. Master guard. License jewel unit. Fog lamp. Right-hand tail lamp. Safety light. Cigar lighter. Fender marker. Luggage mat. Wheel moldings. Rain deflector. Peep mirror. Outside rearview mirror. Visor mirror. Fuel pump vacuum booster. Ash receiver. Rear luggage compartment strap. Insect screen. Frost shields. Right-hand sun visor. Flexible steering wheel. Sidemount tires. Metal sidemount tire covers. Three-passenger gearshift lever. Oil bath air cleaner.

HISTORICAL: Introduced: November 1936. All-steel bodies. First Pontiac station wagon. New 19:1 steering gear ratio. Larger GM B-bodies. Stronger X-member frames. Two-piece propellor shaft. Hotchkiss drive reintroduced. Calendar year production: 235,322. Model year production: 236,189. Best sales year in Pontiac history to date. Advertised as "America's finest low-priced car," Pontiac claimed its products cost only 15 cents more per day to own than low-priced models. Company manager was Harry J. Klingler.

1938 PONTIAC

1938 Pontiac Six station wagon. (AA)

1938 Pontiac Six station wagon. (JAG)

1938 Pontiac Six four-door sedan. (JAG)

1938 Pontiac Eight two-door sedan. (JAG)

DELUXE — SERIES 26 — SIX — The 1938 Pontiac used the same body as previous models. Wide, horizontal bars characterized the new grille design. On sixes there was a "6" emblem at bottom center. Chrome ribs ran along the top of the hood and down the center of the radiator grille. There were vertical hood louvers with the Pontiac name between chrome bars near the radiator on the Six. The six-cylinder hood ornament was a long, low Indian head.

PONTIAC — DELUXE — SERIES 28 — EIGHT — Pontiac Eight again had slightly longer front end sheet metal. Styling was similar to the Pontiac Six. Emblem at bottom center of grille bore "8" designation. Trunk emblem read Pontiac Eight. Louvers on the side of the hood had an extra chrome bar in middle and no Pontiac name. Eight-cylinder hood ornament was a short Indian head with fin-like feathers.

I.D. DATA: [Series 26] Serial numbers on top of frame ahead of steering gear (visible upon raising hood), Starting: 6DA-1616 or C-60A-1001. Ending: 6DA60416 or C-6DA-1615 (Pontiac, Mich.) Cars built at Southgate, Calif., were numbered C6DA-2001 to C6DA-8155. Cars built at Linden, N.J., had an "L" prefix. Engine numbers

1938 Pontiac Eight four-door touring sedan. (JAG)

1938 Pontiac Deluxe Eight four-door touring sedan. (JAG)

1938 Pontiac Deluxe Six cabriolet. (JAG)

on front left corner of block. Starting: 6-399501. Ending: 6-486022. [Series 28] Serial numbers on top of frame ahead of steering gear. Starting: 8DA-1001. Ending: 8DA-15729. California cars had a "C" prefix. New Jersey cars had an "L" prefix. Engine numbers on front left corner of block. Starting: 8-140001. Ending: 8-159441.

Series Number	Body Style Number	Body Type & Seating	Factory Price	Shipping Weight	Production Total
DELUXE SIX SERIES 26 (6-cyl.)					
26	27B	2d Coupe-2P	835	3,190	Note 1
26	27	2d Sport Cpe-2/4P	891	3,200	Note 1
26	67	2d Cabriolet-2/4P	993	3,285	Note 1
26	01	2d Sedan-5P	865	3,265	Note 1
26	11	2d Touring Sed-5P	891	3,265	Note 1
26	09	4d Sedan-5P	916	3,295	Note 1
26	19	4d Touring Sed-5P	942	3,280	Note 1
26	49	4d Conv Sedan-5P	1,310	3,410	Note 1
26	STA WAG	4d Sta Wagon-7P	1,110	3,420	Note 1
DELUXE EIGHT SERIES 28 (8cyl.)					
28	27B	2d Coupe-2P	898	3,320	Note 2
28	27	2d Sport Cpe -2/4P	955	3,325	Note 2
28	67	2d Cabriolet-2/4P	1,057	3,390	Note 2
28	01	2d Sedan-5P	934	3,395	Note 2
28	11	2d Touring Sed-5P	960	3,385	Note 2
28	09	4d Sedan-5P	980	3,415	Note 2
28	19	4d Touring Sed-5P	1,006	3,410	Note 2
28	49	4d Conv Sedan-5P	1,353	3,530	Note 2

Note 1: No body style breakouts. Series production total was 77,713 cars.

1938 Pontiac Deluxe Six convertible sedan. (JAG)

Note 2: No body style breakouts. Total series production was 97,139 cars.

ENGINE [Series 26]: L-head. Inline. Six. Cast-iron block. Bore & stroke: 3-7/16 x 4 in. Displacement: 222.7 cid. Compression Ratio: 6.2:1. Brake horsepower: 85 at 3520 rpm. NACC horsepower: 28.3. Main bearings: Four. Valve lifters: Solid. Carburetor: Carter one-barrel.

ENGINE [Series 28]: L-head. Inline. Eight. Cast-iron block. Bore & stroke: 3-1/4 x 3-3/4 in. Displacement: 248.9 cid. Compression Ratio: 6.2:1. Brake horsepower: 100 at 3700 rpm. NACC horsepower: 33.8. Main bearings: Five. Valve lifters: Solid. Carburetor: Carter: one-barrel.

CHASSIS: [Series 26] Wheelbase: 117 in. Overall Length: 192 in. Height: 67 in. Tires: 16 x 6.00. [Series 28] Wheelbase: 122 in. Overall Length: 196.63 in. Height: 67 in. Tires: 16 x 6.50.

TECHNICAL: [Series 26] Synchromesh transmission. Speeds: 3F/IR. Floor shift controls (standard). Dry disc clutch. Hotchkiss Drive. Semi-floating rear axle. Overall ratio: 4.37:1. Four wheel hydraulic brakes. Steel disc wheels. Column gearshift $10 extra. [Series 28] Synchromesh transmission. Speeds: 3F/IR. Floor shift controls (standard). Dry disc clutch. Hotchkiss Drive. Semi-floating rear axle. Overall ratio: 4.37:1. Four wheel hydraulic brakes. Steel disc wheels. Column gearshift $10 extra.

OPTIONS: Deluxe radio ($58.25). Master radio ($44.70). Dual running board antenna ($5.25). Overhead antenna ($5.25). Deluxe heater ($17.95). Master heater ($12.75). Defroster ($7.90). Tenite shift ball ($.50). Commercial pickup box ($25). Seat covers (set): front ($5.95); front & rear ($10.95). Battery charger ($8.50). Dash electric clock ($11.65). Header board windup clock ($4). Single wheel disc ($2.30). Electric windshield defroster ($3). Tailpipe extension ($1). Pair, license frames ($2.45). Front master guard ($2.25). Rear master guard ($3.90). Dual horns ($10.95). Jewel license unit ($4.68). Fog lamp ($5). Right-hand tail lamp ($4.95). Cigar lighter ($2.25). Fender marker ($1.25). Rear mats in sedan ($2.25); in coupes ($3.75). Peep mirror ($1.50). Visor mirror ($1). Rear view mirror ($2.95). Wheel molding ($1.58). Fuel pump vacuum booster ($12). Ash receiver ($1.25). Single sun visor ($2.40). Flexible steering wheel ($1.50). Sidemounts (price not available).

HISTORICAL: Introduced: October 1937. Improved transmission synchronizers. Quieter gearshift yoke design. Toggle action helper spring added to clutch. Larger generator. Larger water pump with ball bearings. Battery moved under hood. Improved front suspension.

1938 Pontiac Deluxe Six coupe. (JAG)

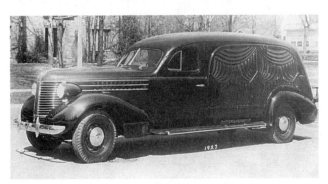

1938 Pontiac Eight Superior carved-side hearse. (JAG)

Calendar year production: 95,128 units. Model year production: 97,139 units. Advertised as a "better looking, better built, better buy." Pontiac offered buyers a factory delivery program allowing them to save shipping costs. The president of Pontiac was Harry J. Klingler.

1939 PONTIAC

1939 Pontiac Six four-door touring sedan. (AA)

1939 Pontiac Six two-door convertible. (OCW)

1939 Pontiac Deluxe Eight station wagon. (OCW)

1939 Pontiac Deluxe Eight two-door touring sedan. (OCW)

PONTIAC — QUALITY 115 — SERIES 25 — SIX — The 1939 Pontiac Quality Six was a new type of economy class model. It employed the Chevrolet A-body shell with Pontiac front-end sheet metal, making it a small car with a big car look. All 1939 Pontiacs had a new, streamlined appearance. The thin, rounded nose was brightened by Silver Streak moldings running to the bumper line. There were four groups of four horizontal, louver type grille bars on either side of the Silver Streaks. Each lower group of louvers were shorter. Separate, twin side grilles had multiple vertical bars over high front fender splash aprons. The headlights rested directly on the front fender catwalks. Horizontal louvers were placed on the hood sides near the cowl. The Quality Six came only with conventional running boards.

PONTIAC — DELUXE 120 — SERIES 26 — SIX — The 1939 Pontiac Deluxe Six models used the larger GM A-body. They were longer and wider, but lower than Quality Six models. Front-end styling changes were similar for both lines. The Deluxe bodies had larger windshields, wider back windows, V-shaped window openings, and bright metal beltline trim. They could be ordered with conventional runningboards or streamlined "body skirts."

PONTIAC — SERIES 28 — EIGHT — The 1939 Pontiac Deluxe Eight models used the same body as the Deluxe "120" six models. The Indian head hood ornaments on eight-cylinder cars had a fin-like feather design, compared to the straight-back feather design used on six-cylinder models. A "Pontiac Eight" emblem was affixed to the rear deck. There was also a fancier trim plate around the circular badge on the front bumper.

I.D. DATA: [Series 25] Serial numbers on front cross-member behind radiator. Starting: P6EA-1001. Ending: P6EA-43679 (Pontiac, Mich.) Cars built at Southgate, Calif., had a "C" prefix. Cars built in Linden, N.J., had an "L" prefix. Engine numbers on front left corner of block. Starting: 6-486201. Ending: 6-595763. [Series 26] Serial numbers on

1939 Pontiac Deluxe Six coupe. (OCW)

1939 Pontiac Deluxe Six sport coupe. (OCW)

1939 Pontiac Deluxe Eight sport coupe. (JAC)

1939 Pontiac Deluxe Six sport coupe. (JAG)

front cross-member behind radiator. Starting: P6EB-1001. Ending: P6EB-41263 (Pontiac, Mich.) California cars had a "C" prefix. New Jersey cars had an "L" prefix. Engine numbers on front left corner of block. Starting: 6-486201. Ending: 6-595763. [Series 28] Serial numbers on front cross-member behind radiator. Starting: P8EA-1001. Ending: P8EA-27627 (Pontiac, Mich.). California cars had a "C" prefix. New Jersey cars had an "L" prefix. Engine numbers on front left corner of block. Starting: 8-159601. Ending: 8-194380.

Series Number	Body Style Number	Body Type & Seating	Factory Price	Shipping Weight	Production Total
SERIES 25 QUALITY SIX (6-cyl.)					
25	27B	2d Coupe-3P	758	2,875	Note 1
25	27	2d Sport Cpe-5P	809	2,920	Note 1
25	11	2d Touring Sed-5P	820	2,965	Note 1
25	19	4d Touring Sed-6P	866	3,000	Note 1
25	Sta Wagon	4d Sta Wagon-8P	990	3,175	Note 1
SERIES 26 DELUXE SIX (6-cyl.)					
26	27B	2d Coupe-3P	814	3,020	Note 2
26	27	2d Sport Cpe-5P	865	3,055	Note 2
26	67	2d Conv Coupe-5P	993	3,155	Note 2
26	11	2d Touring Sed-6P	871	3,115	Note 2
26	19	4d Touring Sed-6P	922	3,165	Note 2
SERIES 28 DELUXE EIGHT (8-cyl.)					
28	27B	2d Coupe-3P	862	3,115	Note 3
28	27	2d Sport Cpe-5P	912	3,165	Note 3
28	67	2d Conv Coupe-5P	1,046	3,250	Note 3
28	11	2d Touring Sed-5P	919	3,225	Note 3
28	19	4d Touring Sed-5P	970	3,265	Note 3

Note 1: No body style breakouts. Total series production was 55,736 cars.

Note 2: No body style breakouts. Total series production was 53,830 cars.

Note 3: No body style breakouts. Total series production was 34,774 cars.

1939 Pontiac Six four-door touring sedan. (JAG)

ENGINE [Series 25]: L-head. Inline. Six. Cast-iron block. Bore & stroke: 3-7/16 x 4 in. Displacement: 222.7 cid. Compression Ratio: 6.2:1. Brake horsepower: 85 at 3520 rpm. NACC horsepower: 28.3. Main bearings: Four. Valve lifters: Solid. Carburetor: Carter one-barrel.

ENGINE [Series 26]: L-head. Inline. Six. Cast-iron block. Bore & stroke: 3-7/16 x 4 in. Displacement: 222.7 cid. Compression Ratio: 6.2:1. Brake horsepower: 85 at 3520 rpm. NACC horsepower: 28.3. Main bearings: Four. Valve lifters: Solid. Carburetor: Carter one-barrel.

ENGINE [Series 28]: L-head. Inline. Eight. Cast-iron block. Bore & stroke: 3-1/4 x 3-3/4 in. Displacement: 248.9 cid. Compression Ratio: 6.2:1. Brake horsepower: 100 at 3700 rpm. NACC horsepower: 33.8. Main bearings: Five. Valve lifters: Solid. Carburetor: Carter one-barrel.

CHASSIS: [Series 25] Wheelbase: 115 in. Overall Length: 190 in. Tires: 16 x 6.00. [Series 26] Wheelbase: 120 in. Overall Length: 196.25 in. Tires: 16 x 6.00. [Series 28] Wheelbase: 120 in. Overall Length: 196.25 in. Tires: 16 x 6.50.

TECHNICAL: [Series 25] Synchromesh transmission. Speeds: 3F/IR. Column gear shift controls. Dry disc clutch. Hotchkiss drive. Semi-floating rear axle. Overall ratio: 4.1:1. Four-wheel hydraulic brakes. Steel disc wheels. [Series 26] Synchromesh transmission. Speeds: 3F/IR. Column gear shift controls. Dry disc clutch. Hotchkiss drive. Semi-floating rear axle. Overall ratio: 4.1:1. Four-wheel hydraulic brakes. Steel disc wheels. [Series 28] Synchromesh transmission. Speeds: 3F/IR. Column gear shift controls. Dry disc clutch. Hotchkiss drive. Semi-floating rear axle. Overall ratio: 4.1:1. Four-wheel hydraulic brakes. Steel disc wheels.

OPTIONS: Master radio (Quality Six only). Deluxe radio. Dual horns. Right-hand taillight. Fender skirts. Bumper guards. Constant-action wiper pump. Deluxe heater. Electric clock. Wind-up clock. Cigar lighter. Master cowl antenna. Runningboard antenna. Seat covers. Whitewall tires. Spotlight. Exhaust deflector. License plate frame. Weather Chief heater and defroster. Special runningboard. Flexible steering wheel. Ash receiver. Wheel covers. Wheel trim moldings. Oil bath air cleaner. Oil filter. Fog lamps. Sunshine roof.

HISTORICAL: Introduced October 1938. Redesigned clutch. Variable rate Duflex springs. Revised transmission. Improved long-life muffler. Column-mounted Safety Gearshift standardized. Three-passenger front seating. No-Rol device optional. Calendar year registrations: 212,403 cars. Calendar year production: 170,726 cars. Model year production: 144,340 cars. Advertised as "America's Finest Low-Priced Car." A "see through" 1939 Pontiac Deluxe Six four-door touring sedan with Plexiglass body panels was built for exhibition at the 1939 New York World's Fair. The president of Pontiac was Harry J. Klingler.

1940 PONTIAC

PONTIAC — SPECIAL — SERIES 25 — SIX — Characteristics of 1940 Pontiacs included larger and more streamlined bodies; more massive front fenders with built-in headlight fairings; lower floors; and "alligator" type hoods trimmed with three sets of slanting louvers. The 1940 grilles had horizontal bars, arranged in top point formation. The grilles were placed on either side of the "Silver Streak"

1940 Pontiac Deluxe Eight four-door touring sedan. (OCW)

1940 Pontiac Deluxe Six two-door touring sedan. (OCW)

center rail that carried a Pontiac nameplate and chevron emblem below. The Special Six models employed the small GM A-body. Distinguishing styling characteristics of the series included six-window four-door sedans; exposed lower front door hinges; key hole-type door handles; and gas filler caps on the right rear fenders. They came only with conventional runningboards. The six-cylinder hood ornament was a chrome-plated, solid Indian head that also served as a hood latch mechanism. The Special Six had a more rounded rear deck. The Special Six station wagon came standard with a single, side-mounted spare tire.

PONTIAC — DELUXE — SERIES 26 — SIX — Deluxe Six models used the larger GM B-body. Front sheet metal styling was the same as for the Special Six models. Concealed hinges were used in all places except lower front doors. The door handles had weather sealed keyholes. Gas filler doors were on the left rear fenders. Buyers could order optional body skirts in place of conventional running boards. The hood ornament was the same used on Special Six models. Deluxe Sixes had a squared-off rear deck.

PONTIAC — DELUXE — SERIES 28 — EIGHT — The Deluxe Eight models used the same bodies as Deluxe Six models. An "8" emblem was affixed to the front chevron-shaped trim plate. A Pontiac Eight nameplate was on the rear deck. The eight-cylinder hood ornament had a plastic Indian head mounted in a metal base.

PONTIAC — TORPEDO — SERIES 29 — EIGHT — New this year was the Torpedo Eight using the extra-large GM C-body. These cars had larger windows, wider seats, front and rear ventipanes on four-door sedans, and long, gracefully streamlined rear decks. Concealed hinges were used on all doors. The doors were extra-wide. The hood ornament was the same as on Deluxe eights. Front-end

1940 Pontiac Deluxe Eight two-door cabriolet. (JAC)

1940 Pontiac Torpedo Eight four-door sedan. (AA)

sheet metal looked like that on other Pontiacs. Eight-cylinder badges were used front and rear. The door locks had weather sealed keyholes. Gas filler tubes were enclosed under "flip-up" lids on the left rear fenders. The window openings were trimmed with bright metal moldings.

I.D. DATA: [Series 25] Serial numbers on front crossmember behind radiator. Starting: P6HA-1001. Ending: P6HA-84545 (Pontiac, Mich.) Cars built in Southgate, Calif., had a "C" prefix. Cars built in Linden, N.J., had an "L" prefix. Engine numbers on front left corner of block. Starting: 6-595801. Ending: 6-761162. [Series 26] Serial numbers on front crossmember behind radiator. Starting: P6HB-1001. Ending: P6HB-44296 (Pontiac, Mich.) California cars had a "C" prefix. New Jersey cars had an "L" prefix. Engine numbers on front left corner of block. Starting: 6-595801. Ending: 6-761162. [Series 28] Serial numbers on front crossmember behind radiator. Starting: P8HA-1001. Ending: P8HA-16817 (Pontiac, Mich.). California cars had a "C" prefix. New Jersey cars had an "L" prefix. Engine numbers on front left corner of block. Starting: 8-194401. Ending: 8-246073. [Series 29] Serial numbers on front crossmember behind radiator. Starting: P8HB-1001. Ending: P8HB-24376. (Pontiac, Mich.), California cars had a "C" prefix. New Jersey cars had an "L" prefix. Engine numbers on front left corner of block. Starting: 8-194401. Ending: 8-246073.

Series Number	Body Style Number	Body Type & Seating	Factory Price	Shipping Weight	Production Total
SERIES 25 SPECIAL SIX (6-cyl.)					
25	27B	2d Coupe-3P	783	3,060	Note 1
25	27	2d Sport Cpe-4P	819	3,045	Note 1
25	11	2d Touring Sed-5P	830	3,095	Note 1
25	19	4d Touring Sed-5P	876	3,125	Note 1
25	STA WAG	4d Sta Wagon-8P	1,015	3,295	Note 1
SERIES 26 DELUXE SIX (6-cyl.)					
26	27B	2d Coupe-3P	835	3,115	Note 2
26	27	2d Sport Cpe-4P	876	3,105	Note 2
26	67	2d Cabriolet-4P	1,003	3,190	Note 2
26	11	2d Touring Sed-5P	881	3,170	Note 2
26	19	4d Touring Sed-5P	932	3,210	Note 2
SERIES 28 DELUXE EIGHT (8-cyl.)					
28	27B	2d Coupe-3P	875	3,180	Note 3
28	27	2d Sport Cpe-4P	913	3,195	Note 3
28	67	2d Cabriolet-4P	1,046	3,280	Note 3
28	11	2d Touring Sed-5P	919	3,250	Note 3
28	19	4d Touring Sed-5P	970	3,300	Note 3
SERIES 29 TORPEDO EIGHT (8-cyl.)					
29	27C	2d Sport Cpe-4P	1,016	3,390	Note 4
29	19	4d Touring Sed-5P	1,072	3,475	Note 4

Note 1: No body style breakouts. Total series production was 106,892 cars.

1940 Pontiac Torpedo Eight four-door touring sedan. (OCW)

1940 Pontiac Deluxe Eight station wagon. (OCW)

1940 Pontiac Deluxe Six sport coupe. (OCW)

Note 2: No body style breakouts. Total series production was 58,452 cars.

Note 3: No body style breakouts. Total series production was 20,433 cars.

Note 4: No body style breakouts. Total series production was 31,224 cars.

ENGINE [Series 25]: L-head. Inline. Six. Cast-iron block. Bore & stroke: 3-7/16 x 4 in. Displacement: 222.7 cid. Compression Ratio: 6.5:1. Brake horsepower: 100 at 3700 rpm. NACC horsepower: 28.3. Main bearings: Four. Valve lifters: Solid. Carburetor: Carter one-barrel.

ENGINE [Series 26]: L-head. Inline. Six. Cast-iron block. Bore & stroke: 3-7/16 x 4 in. Displacement: 222.7 cid. Compression Ratio: 6.5:1. Brake horsepower: 100 at 3700 rpm. NACC horsepower: 28.3. Main bearings: Four. Valve lifters: Solid. Carburetor: Carter one-barrel.

ENGINE [Series 28]: L-head. Inline. Eight. Cast-iron block. Bore & stroke: 3-1/4 in. x 3-3/4 in. Displacement: 248.9 cid. Compression Ratio: 6.5:1. Brake horsepower: 103 at 3700 rpm. NACC horsepower: 33.8. Main bearings: Five. Valve lifters: Solid. Carburetor: Carter two-barrel. Torque: 175 lbs.-ft. at 1600 rpm.

1940 Pontiac Deluxe Six sport coupe. (JAG)

1940 Pontiac Special Six four-door touring sedan. (JAG)

1940 Pontiac Torpedo four-door sedan. (JAG)

ENGINE [Series 29]: L-head. In-line. Eight. Cast-iron block. Bore & stroke: 3-1/4 in. x 3-3/4 in. Displacement: 248.9 cid. Compression Ratio: 6.5:1. Brake horsepower: 103 at 3700 rpm. NACC horsepower: 33.8. Main bearings: Five. Valve lifters: Solid. Carburetor: Carter two-barrel. Torque: 175 lbs.-ft. at 1600 rpm.

CHASSIS: [Series 25] Wheelbase: 116.5 in. Overall Length: 198.75 in. Height: 66.75 in. Front tread: 58 in. Rear tread: 59 in. Tires: 16 x 6.00. [Series 26] Wheelbase: 120.25 in. Overall Length: 199.75 in. Height: 66 in. Front tread: 58 in. Rear tread: 59 in. Tires: 6.00 x 16. [Series 28] Wheelbase: 120.25 in. Overall Length: 200 in. Height: 66-3/8 in. Front tread: 58 in. Rear tread: 59 in. Tires: 16 x 6.50. [Series 29] Wheelbase: 121-1/2 in. Overall Length: 207-1/2 in. Height: 65 in. Front tread: 58 in. Rear tread: 59 in. Tires: 16 x 6.50.

1940 Pontiac convertible. (OCW)

1940 Pontiac Deluxe Eight Superior limousine coach. (JAG)

TECHNICAL: [All] Synchromesh transmission. Speeds: 3F/IR. Steering column gearshift. Inland single disc clutch. Hotchkiss drive. Semi-floating rear axle. Overall ratio: 4.3:1. Duo-servo four-wheel hydraulic brakes. Steel disc wheels. Rim size: 4.5 in. Drive train options: Hill-Holder.

OPTIONS: Vacuum booster fuel pump. Cigar lighter. Electric clock. Deluxe six-tube electric tuning radio. Automatic tuning six-tube radio. Automatic tuning five-tube radio. Portable radio. Master dash heater. Weather Chief dash heater. Auto furnace. Defroster. Fresh air intake. Deluxe steering wheel. White sidewall tire. Glove box light. Trunk light. Directional signals. Vacuum radio antenna. Master grille guards. Fender skirts. Body skirts (except Special Sixes). Wheel discs. Wheel trim rings. Rear view mirror. Cowl antenna.

HISTORICAL: Introduced: August 1939. Center armrest in Torpedo sedan. Sealed beam headlights. Safety roll front seat backs. New anti-skid tires. Improved Safety Shift gear control. Tilting and adjustable front seats. New, high-compression cylinder head. New gasoline filter. Calendar year production: 249,303 cars. Calendar year registrations: 235,815 cars. Model year production: 217,001 cars. A plexiglass bodied "see through" Pontiac appeared at the New York World's Fair again. This may have been a new show car, or the 1939 model with a new front end. The "see through" Pontiac survives today in the collection of an Indiana hobbyist. The president of Pontiac was H.J. Klingler.

1941 PONTIAC

1941 Pontiac Torpedo four-door sedan. (AA)

PONTIAC — DELUXE TORPEDO — JA LINE — SIX/EIGHT — A wide grille with horizontal bars was used on 1941 Pontiacs. The parking lights were built into the grille. Headlamps were fully recessed into the new, wider fenders. Speed-line ribbing was molded into the sides of both front and rear fenders. Deluxe Sixes were in Series 25. Deluxe Eights were in Series 27. The sixes had shorter hood ornaments, a "6" badge on the hood and Pontiac lettering on the side. The eights had larger hood ornaments, an "8" badge on the hood and Pontiac Eight lettering on the side. All 1941 Pontiacs were nicknamed "Torpedos." Deluxe Torpedos used the small GM A-body shell with notchback styling. Streamlined body skirts replaced conventional running

1941 Pontiac Custom Torpedo four-door station wagon. (AA)

1941 Pontiac Custom Torpedo four-door station wagon. (OCW)

1941 Pontiac Torpedo two-door convertible. (OCW)

boards on all models. The Metropolitan Sedan had four-window styling and was added to the line at midyear.

PONTIAC — STREAMLINER TORPEDO — JB LINE — SIX/ EIGHT — Sleek, fastback styling characterized Pontiac's 1941 Streamliner Torpedo models. Their rooflines swept from the windshield to the rear bumper in one, smooth curve. The front-end sheet metal was of the same design used on Deluxe Torpedos and trim differences between Sixes and Eights were also the same. Beige corded wool cloth upholstery was featured. Streamliners utilized GM's larger B-body. There was also a Super Streamliner sub-series. Supers had the same body styling and trim, but featured two-tone worsted wool cloth upholstery with pin stripes. They also added sponge rubber seat cushions, electric clocks, deluxe flexible steering wheels and divan type seats with folding center armrests. Streamliners (and Customs) had concealed interior steps.

PONTIAC — CUSTOM TORPEDO — JC LINE — SIX/EIGHT — The extra-large GM C-body was used for 1941 Pontiac Custom Torpedos. This line included a notchback sedan and coupe, plus the standard and Deluxe wood-bodied station wagons. Annual styling changes were the same seen for other lines, as were trim variations between Sixes and Eights. Station wagon bodies were built by Hercules and Ionia. The Ionia bodies had a more rounded rear end treatment. Standard station wagons had imitation leather upholstery while Deluxe types had genuine leather cushions.

1941 Pontiac Streamliner Torpedo sedan-coupe. (OCW)

1941 Pontiac Custom Torpedo sedan-coupe. (OCW)

1941 Pontiac Torpedo four-door sedan. (OCW)

I.D. DATA: [Series 25/27 Deluxe Torpedo] Serial numbers on left side of dash. Starting: [Six] P6JA-1001/[Eight] P8JA-1001. Ending: [Six] P6JA-80460/[Eight] P8JA-27219. These codes apply to cars built at Pontiac, Mich. Cars built at Southgate, Calif., had a "C" prefix. Cars built at Linden, N.J., had an "L" prefix. Engine numbers on front left corner of block. Starting: [Six] 6-761501/[Eight] 8-246501. Ending: [Six] 6-971768/[Eight] 8-368240. [Series 26/28 Streamliner Torpedo] Serial numbers on left side of dash. Starting: (six) P6JB-1001/(eight) P8JB-1001. Ending: (six) P6JB-62545/(eight) P8JB-52428. These codes apply to cars built at Pontiac, Mich. California cars had a "C" prefix. New Jersey cars had an "L" prefix. Engine numbers on front left corner of block. Numbers were the same given for Deluxe Torpedo engines. [Series 24/29 Custom Torpedo] Serial numbers on left side of dash. Starting: (six) P6JC-1001/(eight) P8JC-1001. Ending: (six) P6JC-6345/(eight) P8JC-12576. These codes apply to cars built at Pontiac, Mich. California cars had a "C" prefix. New Jersey cars had an "L" prefix. Engine numbers on front left corner of block. Numbers were the same given for Deluxe Torpedo engines.

Series Number	Body Style Number	Body Type & Seating	Factory Price	Shipping Weight	Production Total
SERIES 25 DELUXE TORPEDO SIX (6-cyl.)					
25	27B	2d Bus Coupe-3P	828	3,145	Note 1
25	27	2d Sed Coupe-5P	864	3,180	Note 1
25	67	2d Conv Coupe-5P	1,023	3,335	Note 1

1941 Pontiac Torpedo four-door sedan. (JAG)

Series Number	Body Style Number	Body Type & Seating	Factory Price	Shipping Weight	Production Total
25	11	2d Sedan-5P	874	3,190	Note 1
25	19	4d Sedan-5P	921	3,235	Note 1
25	69	4d Metro Sedan-5P	921	3,230	Note 1
SERIES 27 DELUXE TORPEDO EIGHT (8-cyl.)					
27	27B	2d Bus Coupe-3P	853	3,220	Note 2
27	27	2d Sed Coupe-5P	889	3,250	Note 2
27	67	2d Conv Coupe-5P	1,048	3,390	Note 2
27	11	2d Sedan-5P	899	3,250	Note 2
27	19	4d Sedan-5P	946	3,285	Note 2
27	69	4d Metro Sedan-5P	946	3,295	Note 2
SERIES 26 STREAMLINER TORPEDO SIX (6-cyl.)					
26	27	2d Sed Coupe-5P	923	3,305	Note 3
26	09	4d Sedan-5P	980	3,365	Note 3
SERIES 26 SUPER STREAMLINER TORPEDO SIX (6-cyl.)					
26	27D	2d Sed Coupe-5P	969	3,320	Note 3
26	09D	4d Sedan-5P	1,026	3,400	Note3
SERIES 28 STREAMLINER TORPEDO EIGHT (8-cyl.)					
28	27	2d Sed Coupe-5P	948	3,370	Note 4
28	09	4d Sedan-5P	1,005	3,425	Note 4
SERIES 28 SUPER STREAMLINER TORPEDO EIGHT (8-cyl.)					
28	27D	2d Sed Coupe-5P	994	3,385	Note 4
28	09D	4d Sedan-5P	1,51	3,460	Note 4
SERIES 24 CUSTOM TORPEDO SIX (6-cyl.)					
24	27	2d Sed Coupe-5P	995	3,260	Note 5
24	19	4d Sedan-5P	1,052	3,355	Note 5
24	STA WAG	4d Sta Wag-8P	1,175	3,650	Note 5
24	STA WAG	4d Del Sta Wag-8P	1,225	3,665	Note 5
SERIES 29 CUSTOM TORPEDO EIGHT (8-cyl.)					
29	27	2d Sed Coupe-5P	1,020	3,325	Note 6
29	19	4d Sedan-5P	1,077	3,430	Note 6
29	STA WAG	4d Sta Wag-8P	1,200	3,715	Note 6
29	STA WAG	4d Del Sta Wag-8P	1,250	3,730	Note 6

Note 1: No body style breakouts. Total series production was 117,976 cars.

Note 2: No body style breakouts. Total series production was 37,823 cars.

Note 3: No body style breakouts. Total production of Streamliner and Super Streamliner Sixes was 82,527 cars.

Note 4: No body style breakouts. Total production of Streamliner and Super Streamliner Eights was 66,287 cars.

Note 5: No body style breakouts. Total series production (six) was 8,257 cars.

Note 6: No body style breakouts. Total series production (eight) was 17,191 cars.

ENGINE [All six-cylinder]: L head. Inline. Six. Cast-iron block. Bore & stroke: 3-9/16 in. x 4 in. Displacement: 239.2 cid. Compression Ratio: 6.5:1 (7.2:1 optional). Brake horsepower: 90 at 3200 rpm. NACC horsepower: 30.4. Main bearings: Four. Valve lifters: Solid. Carburetor: Carter one-barrel. Torque: 175 lbs.-ft. at 1400 rpm.

ENGINE [All eight-cylinder]: L-head. Inline. Eight. Cast-iron block. Bore & stroke: 3-1/4 in. x 3-3/4 in. Displacement: 248.9 cid. Compression Ratio: 6.5:1 (7.2:1 optional). Brake horsepower: 103 at 3500 rpm. NACC horsepower: 33.8. Main bearings: Five. Valve lifters: Solid. Carburetor: Carter two-barrel. Torque: 190 lbs.-ft. at 2200 rpm.

CHASSIS: [Series 25/27] Wheelbase: 191 in. Overall Length: 201-1/2 in. Height: 66 in. Front tread: 58 in. Rear tread: 61-1/2 in. Tires: 16 x 6.00. [Series 26/28] Wheelbase: 122 in. Overall Length: 207-1/2 in. Height: 65-3/4 in. Front tread: 58 in. Rear tread: 61-1/2 in. Tires: 16 x 6.50. [Series 24/29] Wheelbase: 122 in. Overall Length: 201 in. Height: 65 in. Front tread: 58 in. Rear tread: 61-1/2 in. Tires: 16 x 6.50.

TECHNICAL: [Series 25/27] Synchromesh transmission. Speeds: 3F/1R. Column shift control. Inland single disc clutch. Hotchkiss drive. Semi-floating rear axle. Overall ratio: 4.1:1. Duo servo hydraulic brakes on four wheels. Steel disc wheels. Rim size: 4-1/2 in. Drivetrain options: No-Rol device to keep car from rolling backwards on hill. [Series 26/28] Synchromesh transmission. Speeds: 3F/1R. Column shift control. Inland single disc clutch. Hotchkiss drive. Semi-floating rear axle. Overall ratio: 4.1:1. Duo servo hydraulic brakes on four wheels. Steel disc wheels. Rim size: 4-1/2 in. Drivetrain options: No-Rol device to keep car from rolling backwards on hill. [Series 24/29] Synchromesh transmission. Speeds: 3F/1R. Column shift control. Inland single disc clutch. Hotchkiss drive. Semi-floating rear axle. Overall ratio: 4.1:1. Duo servo hydraulic brakes on four wheels. Steel disc wheels. Rim size: 4-1/2 in. Drivetrain options: No-Rol device to keep car from rolling backwards on hill.

1941 Pontiac Torpedo Superior funeral coach. (JAG)

OPTIONS: Exhaust deflector. Wheel trim rings. Bumper wing tips. White sidewall tires. Fender skirts. Master grille guards. Deluxe seven-tube radio. Weather Chief heater. Electric clock (standard in Super and Custom). Cigar lighter. Mast radio antenna (standard with radio). Spotlight. Wide running boards (Custom Torpedo only). Vacuum radio antenna. Master five-tube radio. Safety-flex steering wheel (standard in Super and Custom). Safe Sight Airight defroster control. Electric visor vanity mirror. Back window sun baffle. Nonglare rear view mirror. Directional signals. Constant action wiper pump. Glove box light. Luggage compartment light. Chrome fog lamp. Deluxe safety light. Rear bumper hinge guard.

HISTORICAL: Introduced September 1940. New clutch pedal booster. Adjustable sun visors. Power operated convertible top. New bridge type frames. Improved multi-seal brakes. New, built-in, permanent oil cleaner. Dual rear lamps had automatic stop signal feature. New semi-automatic safety shift. Calendar year registrations: 286,123 cars. Calendar year production: 282,087 cars. Model year production: 330,061 cars. Pontiac became the best-selling car in the middle-price class in 1941. The president of Pontiac was H.J. Klingler.

1942 PONTIAC

1942 Pontiac Chieftain Eight station wagon. (AA)

PONTIAC — TORPEDO — KA LINE — SIX/EIGHT — All 1942 Pontiacs looked lower, heavier, and wider. Extension caps on the front doors lengthened the forward fender lines. The hood extended back to the front doors, eliminating the cowl. The grille, bumper and

1942 Pontiac Torpedo Six Metro sedan. (OCW)

1942 Pontiac Torpedo Eight business coupe. (JAG)

1942 Pontiac Torpedo Six two-door sedan. (OCW)

hood were widened and headlamps were farther apart. Long, horizontal parking lamps sat just above the vertical side grilles. The horseshoe shaped center grille had horizontal bars and a circular emblem in the middle of the upper main surround molding. Torpedos used the GM A-body and featured notch back styling. After December 15, 1941, wartime "blackout" trim was used, All parts previously chrome plated were finished in Duco Gun-Metal Gray. The word Pontiac appeared on the hood side molding of six-cylinder models, while the moldings on eight-cylinder cars said Pontiac Eight.

PONTIAC — STREAMLINER — KB LINE — SIX/EIGHT — Streamliner styling changes were the same as Torpedo changes. Streamliners used the larger GM B-body and had fastback rooflines (except station wagons). The 1941 Super models with folding rear seat center armrests were called Chieftains in 1942. The hood side moldings on Sixes and Eights carried different wording.

I.D. DATA: [Torpedo] Serial numbers on left side of dash. Starting: (six) P6KA-1001/(eight) P8KA-1001. Ending: (six) P6KA-25802/ (eight) P8KA-13146. Above numbers for cars built in Pontiac, Mich. Cars built in Southgate, Calif., had a "C" prefix. Cars built in Linden, N.J., had an "L" prefix. Engine numbers on front left corner of block. Starting: same as serial numbers. Ending: same as serial numbers. [Streamliner] Serial numbers on left side of dash. Starting: (six) P6KB-1001/(eight) P8KB-1001. Ending: (six) P6KB-11115/(eight) P8KB-22928. (Pontiac, Mich.). California cars had a "C" prefix. New Jersey cars had an "L" prefix. Engine numbers on front left corner of block. Starting: same as serial numbers. Ending: same as serial numbers.

1942 Pontiac Streamliner Eight two-door sedan-coupe. (OCW)

1942 Pontiac Torpedo Six four-door sedan. (JAG)

Series Number	Body Style Number	Body Type & Seating	Factory Price	Shipping Weight	Production Total
SERIES 25 TORPEDO SIX (6-cyl.)					
25	27B	2d Coupe-3P	895	3,210	Note 1
25	07	2d Sed Coupe-5P	950	3,255	Note 1
25	27	2d Spt Coupe-5P	935	3,260	Note 1
25	67	2d Conv Coupe-5P	1,165	3,535	Note 1
25	11	2d Sedan-5P	940	3,265	Note 1
25	19	4d Sedan-5P	985	3,305	Note 1
25	69	4d Metro Sedan-5P	985	3,295	Note 1
SERIES 27 TORPEDO EIGHT (8-cyl.)					
27	27B	2d Coupe-3P	920	3,270	Note 2
27	07	2d Sed Coupe-5P	975	3,320	Note 2
27	27	2d Spt Coupe-5P	960	3,320	Note 2
27	67	2d Conv Coupe-5P	1,190	3,605	Note 2
27	11	2d Sedan-5P	965	3,325	Note 2
27	19	4d Sedan-5P	1,010	3,360	Note 2
25	69	4d Metro Sedan-5P	1,010	3,355	Note 2
SERIES 26 STREAMLINER SIX (6-cyl.)					
26	07	2d Sed Coupe-5P	980	3,355	Note 3
26	09	4d Sedan-5P	1,035	3,415	Note 3
26	STA WAG	4d Sta Wagon-8P	1,265	3,810	Note 3
SERIES 26 CHIEFTAIN SIX (6-cyl.)					
26	07D	2d Sed Coupe-5P	1,030	3,400	Note 3
26	09D	4d Sedan-5P	1,085	3,460	Note 3
26	STA WAG	4d Sta Wagon-8P	1,315	3,785	Note 3
SERIES 28 STREAMLINER EIGHT (8-cyl.)					
28	07	2d Sed Coupe-5P	1,005	3,430	Note 4
28	09	4d Sedan-5P	1,060	3,485	Note 4
28	STA WAG	4d Sta Wagon-8P	1,290	3,885	Note 4
SERIES 28 CHIEFTAIN EIGHT (8-cyl.)					
28	07D	2d Sed Coupe-5P	1,055	3,460	Note 4
28	09D	4d Sedan-5P	1,110	3,515	Note 4
28	STA WAG	4d Sta Wagon-8P	1,340	3,865	Note 4

Note 1: No body style breakouts. Total series production (six) was 29,886 cars.

Note 2: No body style breakouts. Total series production (eight) was 14,421 cars.

Note 3: No body style breakouts. Total series production (six) was 12,742 cars (includes 2,458 Chieftains).

Note 4: No body style breakouts. Total series production (eight) was 26,506 cars. (Includes 11,041 Chieftains).

ENGINE [All sixes]: L-head. Inline. Six. Cast-iron block. Bore & stroke: 3-9/16 in. x 4 in. Displacement: 239.2 cid. Compression Ratio: 6.5:1 (7.5:1 optional). Brake horsepower: 90 at 3200 rpm. N.A.C.C horsepower: 30.4. Main bearings: Four. Valve lifters: Solid. Carburetor: Carter one-barrel. Torque: 175 lbs.-ft. at 1400 rpm.

ENGINE [All eights]: L-head. Inline. Eight. Cast-iron block. Bore & stroke: 3-1/4 in. x 3-3/4 in. Displacement: 248.9 cid. Compression Ratio: 6.5:1 (7.5:1 optional). Brake horsepower: 103 at 3500 rpm. NACC horsepower: 33.8. Main bearings: Five. Valve lifters: Solid. Carburetor: Carter two-barrel. Torque: 190 lbs.-ft. at 2200 rpm.

CHASSIS: [Series 25/27] Wheelbase: 119 in. Overall Length: 204-1/2 in. Height: 66 in. Front tread: 58 in. Rear tread: 61-1/2 in. Tires: 16 x 6.00. [Series 26/28] Wheelbase: 122 in. Overall Length: 210-1/4 in. Height: 65-1/4 in. Front tread: 58 in. Rear tread: 61-1/2 in. Tires: 16 x 6.50.

TECHNICAL: [Series 25/27] Synchromesh transmission. Speeds: 3F/1R. Column gear shift controls. Single disc clutch. Hotchkiss drive. Semi-floating rear axle. Overall ratio: 4.1:1. Duo-servo hydraulic brakes on four wheels. Steel disc wheels. Rim size: 4-1/2 in. Drive train options: No-Rol Economy (3.9) or Mountain (4.55) axles. [Series 26/28] Synchromesh transmission. Speeds: 3F/1R. Column gear shift controls. Single disc clutch. Hotchkiss drive. Semi-floating rear axle. Overall ratio: 4.3: 1. Duo-servo hydraulic

brakes on four wheels. Steel disc wheels. Rim size: 4-1/2 in. Drive train options: No-Rol Economy (3.9) or Mountain (4.55) axles.

OPTIONS: Master grille guard. Bumper wing tip guards. Wheel trim rings. Oil bath air cleaner. Electric clock (standard in Chieftains). Safety-flex steering wheel (standard in Chieftains). Five-tube radio. Seven-tube radio. Mast antenna (standard with radio package). Vacuum antenna. Rear view mirror. Weather chief header. Fender skirts. Seat covers.

HISTORICAL: Introduced: September 1941. Steering wheel with center horn button. Bigger front brakes. Oil cleaner redesigned and improved. Triple-sealed brakes. Duplex rear springs improved to eliminate squeaks. Rheostat dash panel lighting. Calendar year production: 15,404 cars. Model year production: 85,555 cars. Production halted February 10, 1942, because of U.S. entry into World War II. In January 1942, Pontiac became first U.S. automaker to win U.S. Navy "E" pennant for production excellence. Company president was H.J. Klingler.

1946 PONTIAC

1946 Pontiac Torpedo Eight two-door sedan. (OCW)

TORPEDO SERIES — (SIX) SERIES 25 — (EIGHT) SERIES 27 — Torpedos comprised Pontiac's short wheelbase (A-Body) line. Buyers could order any Torpedo on either the six- or eight-cylinder chassis ($27-$30 extra for Eights). There was no difference in Series 25 or Series 27 features, except for engine identifying trim. Styling highlights of all Pontiacs were: wraparound bumpers, a massive 14-blade grille, new nameplates, and concealed safe-light parking lamps. An Indian head mascot with upward curved feathers, short moldings atop front fenders, absence of belt moldings, and painted pin stripes on the fender "speed line" ribs distinguished Torpedos. Lettering on hood emblems and badges placed forward of the "speed lines" identified eights. Closed-body Torpedos came with gray tan cloth trims and convertibles were done in cloth combined with black, tan, green, blue, or red leather.

1946 Pontiac Streamliner Eight four-door station wagon. (OCW)

1946 Pontiac Streamliner Eight sedan-coupe. (OCW)

STREAMLINER SERIES — (SIX) SERIES 26 — (EIGHT) SERIES 28

STREAMLINER SERIES — (SIX) SERIES 26 — (EIGHT) SERIES 28 — Streamliners represented Pontiac's B-Body line. The first postwar Pontiac available (September 13, 1945) was the Streamliner Sedan-Coupe, which remained the sole product for a time. Straight-back Indian head hood ornaments, chrome beltline moldings, and bright moldings on the "speed line" fender ribs identified Streamliners. They also had longer front fender crown moldings and were generally larger in size. Interior trims on passenger cars were in gray striped cloth. Station wagons had three seats in standard trim; two seats in Deluxe trim, Sedan imitation leather upholstery, and passenger car style interior hardware.

I.D. DATA: VIN located on left side of firewall under hood. First symbol indicated the assembly plant: P=Pontiac, Mich.; C=California (Southgate); L=Linden, N.J.; K=Kansas City, Kan. Second symbol indicated engine type: 6=six-cylinder; 8=eight-cylinder. Next two symbols were series code appearing as last two characters in first column of charts below. Following this came the sequential production number, which began with 1001 at each assembly plant. Engine serial number on raised pad on front left side of block. VINs matched the engine serial number. The 1946 numbers for each series were: [TORPEDO SIXES]: (Mich.) P6LA-1001 to P6LA-17381; (Calif.) C6LA-1001 to C6LA-3314; (Kan.) K6LA-1001 to K6LA-2520; (N.J.) L6LA-1001 to L6LA4721. [TORPEDO EIGHTS] (Mich.) P8LA-1001 to P8LA-13652; (Calif.) C8LA-1001 to C8LA-2786; (Kan.) K8LA-1001 to K8LA-2520; (N.J.) L8LA-1001 to L8LA-3738. [STREAMLINER SIXES]: (Mich.) P6LB-1001 to P6LB35238; (Calif.) C6LB-1001 to C6 LB3696; (Kan.) K6LB-1001 to K6LB-2299; (N.J.) L6LB-1001 to L6LB-5357. [STREAMLINER EIGHTS]: (Mich.) P8LB-1001 to P8LB-39764; (Calif.) C8LB-1001 to C8LB-4257;

1946 Pontiac Torpedo Eight convertible. (OCW)

1946 Pontiac Streamliner Eight sedan-coupe. (OCW)

1946 Pontiac Streamliner Eight four-door sedan. (OCW)

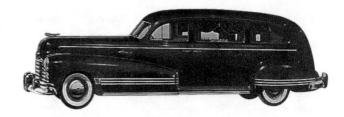

1946 Superior-Pontiac Streamliner Eight funeral coach. (JAG)

(Kans.) K8LB-1001 to K8LB-2590; (N.J.) L8LB-1001 to L8LB-6618. Another code located on the firewall tag on Pontiacs is the Fisher Body/style number. It consists of a prefix indicating model year (46=1946) and suffix indicating series number and body type. These numbers appear in the second column of the charts below. Pontiac parts suppliers use these numbers to aid proper parts applications so they are important.

Model Number	Body/Style Number	Body Type & Seating	Factory Price	Shipping Weight	Production Total
TORPEDO SIX (6-cyl.)					
25	27B	2d Coupe-3P	1,307	3,261	Note 1
25	07	2d Sed Coupe-5P	1,399	3,326	Note 1
25	27	2d Sport Cpe-5P	1,353	3,311	Note 1
25	67	2d Convertible-5P	1,631	3,591	Note 1
25	11	2d Sedan-5P	1,368	3,326	Note 1
25	19	4d Sedan-5P	1,427	3,361	Note 1
TORPEDO EIGHT (8-cyl.)					
27	27B	2d Coupe-3P	1,335	3,331	Note 2
27	07	2d Sed Coupe-5P	1,428	3,391	Note 2
27	27	2d Sport Cpe-5P	1,381	3,376	Note 2
27	67	2d Convertible-5P	1,658	3,651	Note 2
27	11	2d Sedan-5P	1,395	3,396	Note 2
27	19	4d Sedan-5P	1,455	3,436	Note 2
STREAMLINER SIX (6-cyl.)					
26	07	2d Sed Coupe-5P	1,438	3,435	Note 3
26	09	4d Sedan-5P	1,510	3,490	Note 3
26	STA WAG	4d Std Sta Wag-8P	1,942	3,790	Note 3
26	STA WAG	4d Del Sta Wag-6P	2,019	3,735	Note 3
STREAMLINER EIGHT (8-cyl.)					
28	07	2d Sed Coupe-5P	1,468	3,495	Note 4
28	09	4d Sedan-5P	1,538	3,550	Note 4
28	STA WAG	4d Std Sta Wag-8P	1,970	3,870	Note 4
28	STA WAG	4d Del Sta Wag-6P	2,047	3,805	Note 4

Note 1: 26,636 Torpedo sixes built; no body style breakouts available.

Note 2: 18,273 Torpedo eights built; no body style breakouts available.

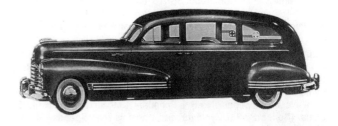

1946 Superior-Pontiac Streamliner Eight ambulance. (JAG)

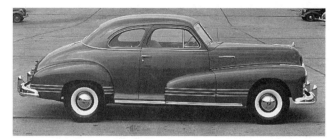
1946 Pontiac Club coupe. (OCW)

Note 3: 43,430 Streamliner sixes built; no body style breakouts.

Note 4: 49,301 Streamliner eights built; no body style breakouts.

ENGINE [SIX]: Six-cylinder. Inline. L-head. Cast iron block. Displacement: 239.2 cid. Bore & stroke: 3-9/16 x 4 in. Compression Ratio: (standard) 6.5:1, (optional) 7.5:1. Brake horsepower: 90 at 3200 rpm. Four main bearings. Solid valve lifters. Carburetor: Carter WAI-537-S one-barrel.

ENGINE [EIGHT]: Eight-cylinder. Inline. L-head. Cast iron block. Displacement: 248.9 cid. Bore & stroke: 3-1/4 x 3-3/4 in. Compression Ratio: See Torpedo six. Brake horsepower: 103 at 3500 rpm. Five main bearings. Solid valve lifters. Carburetor: Carter WDO548-S two-barrel.

CHASSIS: [TORPEDO] Wheelbase: 119 in. Overall length: 204.5 in. Front tread: 58 in. Rear tread: 61-1/2 in. Tire size: 6.00 x 16. [STREAMLINER] Wheelbase: 122 in. Overall length: (passenger cars) 210-1/4 in., (wagons) 215-5/8 in. Front tread: 58 in. Rear tread: 61-1/2 in. Tires: 6.50 x 16.

OPTIONS: Rear windshield wiper. Windshield washer. White sidewall discs. Fog lights. Safety light. Weather Chief heater (dash type). Defroster (dash type). Venti-Heat underseat heater and defroster. Five-tube Master radio. Seven-tube Air Mate radio. Eight-tube Air King radio. Mast antenna. Rear fender panels (Torpedo). Rear fender panels with moldings (Streamliner). Sponge rubber cushions (per body style). Kool Kushin. Luggage compartment light. Lock package. Electric visor vanity mirror. E-Z-I non-glare rearview mirror. Non-electric visor vanity mirror. Hand brake lamp. Umbrella holder. Santoy seat covers (per body style). Bumper guards, wheel rim rings, electric clock, exhaust deflector, and various lights available in standard accessory packages. All 1946 Pontiacs had three-speed manual transmission with column shifting. Performance options were limited to 3.9:1 (economy) and 4.55:1 (mountain) rear axle gear ratios, a 7.5:1 "high-compression" cylinder head and automatic No-Rol device.

HISTORICAL: The first postwar Pontiac was built Sept. 13, 1945. The full model line was back in production by June 10, 1946. Calendar year production was 131,538 cars. Model year production was 137,640 cars. George Delaney became the company's chief engineer this season, replacing Ben Anibal, who worked on the development of the first 1926 Pontiacs. The three-passenger coupe was called a business coupe. The convertible was called a Convertible Sedan-Coupe. General Motors two-door fastbacks were also referred to as "Sport Dynamic" coupes. The early postwar Pontiacs sometimes had the words "Silver Streak" on the hoods, but the proper model names are Streamliner and Torpedo. Silver Streak is *not* an official model name. Harry J. Klingler was general manager of Pontiac Motor Div. (PMD).

1947 PONTIAC

TORPED0 SERIES — (SIX) SERIES 25 — (EIGHT) SERIES 27 — The Torpedos comprised the same line as in 1946. A "Silver Streak" styling theme was continued, now with five bands of chrome on hoods. All Pontiacs had new grilles with four broad, gently bowed horizontal bars. Hoods and fenders were protected by an inverted steer's horn-shaped bar incorporating a die cast plate with Indian-head relief. Torpedos carried no beltline or speedline moldings and had short strips of chrome on the front fender crowns. All 1947 Pontiacs had identical hood ornaments. Interiors were similar to 1946,

1947 Pontiac Torpedo Eight convertible. (OCW)

1947 Pontiac Streamliner Eight sedan-coupe. (OCW)

but due to material shortages some convertibles were built with red, blue, or black imitation leather upholstery in combination with tan Bedford cloth. Only the Torpedo sedan-coupe had fastback styling with individual-loop chrome moldings on the side windows.

STREAMLINER SERIES — (SIX) SERIES 26 — (EIGHT) SERIES 28 — Streamliners also stayed basically the same as 1946, except for grille and trim variations. Interiors for coupes and sedans were redesigned with Berwick beige panels for dashboard and windows. Windshield, door, and garnish moldings were finished in Autumn Brown with dado-stripe border moldings. All coupes and sedans in this series were fastbacks with full-loop-around window moldings.

I.D. DATA: VIN located on left side of firewall under hood. First symbol indicated the assembly plant: P=Pontiac, Mich.; C=California (South Gate); L=Linden, N.J.; W=Wilmington, Del.; K=Kansas City, Kan.; A=Atlanta, Ga. Second symbol indicated engine type: 6=six-cylinder; 8=eight-cylinder. Next two symbols were series code appearing as last two characters in first column of charts below. Following this came the sequential production number, which began with 1001 at each assembly plant. Engine serial number on raised pad on front left side of block. VINs matched the engine serial number. The 1947 numbers for each series were: [TORPEDO SIXES]:

1947 Pontiac Streamliner Eight sedan-coupe. (OCW)

1947 Pontiac two-door fastback. (OCW)

1947 Pontiac Streamliner Eight station wagon. (OCW)

1947 Pontiac Torpedo four-door sedan. (OCW)

Model Number	Body/Style Number	Body Type & Seating	Factory Price	Shipping Weight	Production Total
27	07	2d Sed Coupe-5P	1,350	3,370	Note 2
27	27	2d Sport Coupe-5P	1,306	3,360	Note 2
27	67	2d Convertible-5P	1,640	3,635	Note 2
27	11	2d Sedan-5P	1,320	3,370	Note 2
27	19	4d Sedan-5P	1,376	3,405	Note 2
STREAMLINER SIX (6-cyl.)					
26	07	2d Sed Coupe-5P	1,359	3,400	Note 3
26	09	4d Sedan-5P	1,407	3,405	Note 3
26	STA WAG	4d Std Sta Wag-8P	1,992	3,775	Note 3
26	STA WAG	4d DeL Sta Wag-6P	2,066	3,715	Note 3
STREAMLINER EIGHT (8-cyl.)					
28	07	2d Sed Coupe-5P	1,404	3,455	Note 4
28	09	4d Sedan-5p	1,452	3,515	Note 4
28	STA WAG	4d Std Sta Wag-8P	2,037	3,845	Note 4
28	STA WAG	4d DeL Sta Wag-6P	2,111	3,790	Note 4

NOTE 1: 67,125 Torpedo Sixes built; no body style breakouts available.

NOTE 2: 34,815 Torpedo Eights built; no body style breakouts available.

NOTE 3: 42,336 Streamliner sixes built; no body style breakouts available.

NOTE 4: 86,324 Streamliner eights built; no body style breakouts available.

ENGINE [SIX]: Six-cylinder. Inline. L-head. Cast-iron block. Displacement: 239.2 cid. Bore & stroke: 3-9/16 x 4 in. Compression Ratio: (standard) 6.5:1, (optional) 7.5:1. Brake horsepower: 90 at 3200 rpm. Four main bearings. Solid valve lifters. Carburetor: Carter WAI-537-S one-barrel.

ENGINE [EIGHT]: Eight-cylinder. Inline. L-head. Cast-iron block. Displacement: 248.9 cid. Bore & stroke: 3-1/4 x 3-3/4 in. Compression Ratio: See Torpedo six. Brake horsepower: 103 at 3500 rpm. Five main bearings. Solid valve lifters. Carburetor: Carter WCD two-barrel models 630S or 630SB.

CHASSIS: [TORPEDO] Wheelbase: 119 in. Overall length: 204.5 in. Front tread: 58 in. Rear tread: 61-1/2 in. Tire size: 6.00 x 16. [STREAMLINER] Wheelbase: 122 inches. Overall length: (passenger cars) 210-1/4 in., (wagons) 215-5/8 in. Front tread: 58 in. Rear tread: 61-1/2 in. Tires: 6.50 x 16.

OPTIONS: Rear windshield wiper. Windshield washer. White sidewall discs. Fog lights. Safety light. Weather Chief heater (dash type). Defroster (dash type). Venti-Heat under seat heater and defroster. Five-tube Master radio. Seven-tube Air Mate radio. Eight-tube Air King radio. Mast antenna. Rear fender panels (Torpedo). Rear fender panels with moldings (Streamliner). Sponge rubber cushions (per body style). Kool Kushin. Luggage compartment light. Lock package. Electric visor vanity mirror. E-Z-I non-glare rearview mirror. Non-electric visor vanity mirror. Hand brake lamp. Umbrella holder. Santoy seat covers (per body style). Bumper guards, wheel rim rings, electric clock, exhaust deflector, and various lights available in standard accessory packages. All 1946 Pontiacs had three-speed manual transmission with column shifting. Performance options were limited to 3.9:1 (economy) and 4.55:1 (mountain) rear axle gear ratios, a 7.5:1 "high-compression" cylinder head and automatic No-Rol device.

HISTORICAL: Production of 1947 Pontiacs began Dec. 19, 1946. Calendar year output came to 223,015 units. Model year assemblies totaled 230,600 cars. A Pontiac prototype with a rear-mounted straight eight-cylinder engine was constructed in 1947. Aluminum replacement fenders for 1942-1948 models were made available later and at least one modern collector has discovered such fenders on his car. Body styles 47-2567 and 47-2767 were now called convertible coupes. Body styles 47-2507, 47-2707, 47-2607, and 47-2807 were Sport Dynamic coupes and are commonly known as fastbacks today. Body styles 47-2609 and 47-2809 were Sport Dynamic four-door sedans, also with fastback styling.

1948 PONTIAC

TORPEDO SERIES — (SIX) SERIES 25 — (EIGHT) SERIES 27 — There were no radical appearance changes in Torpedos, except for adoption of new Pontiac styling including triple "Silver Streaks," a horizontal grille theme with vertical shafts, and round taillights. The

(Mich.) P6MA-1001 to P6MA-37322; (N.J.) L6MA-1001 to L6MA-13895; (Kan.) K6MA-1001 to K6MA-8096; (Del.) W6MA-1001 to W6MA-1850; (Calif.) C6MA-1001 to C6MA-7794. [TORPEDO EIGHTS] (Mich.) P8MA-1001 to P8MA-22682; (N.J.) L8MA-1001 to L8MA-7387; (Kan.) K8MA-1001 to K8MA-4165; (Del.) W8MA-1001 to W8MA-1431; (Calif.) C8MA-1001 to C8MA-4150. [STREAMLINER SIXES] (Mich.) P6MB-1001 to P6MB-27844; (N.J.) L6MB-1001 to L6MB-7877; (Kan.) K6MB-1001 to K6MB-4569; (Del.) W6MB-1001 to W6MB-3976; (Calif.) C6MB-1001 to C6-MB-3976; (Ga.) A6MB-1001 to A6MB-1080. [STREAMLINER EIGHTS] (Mich.) P8MB-1001 to P8MB-56382; (N.J.) L8MB-1001 to L8MB-15246; (Kan.) K8MB-1001 to K8MB-9184; (Del.) W8MB-1001 to W8MB-1954; (Calif.) C8MB-1001 to C8MB-8197; (Ga.) A8MB-1001 to A8MB-1145. Another code located on the firewall tag on Pontiacs is the Fisher Body/style number. It consists of a prefix indicating model year (47=1947) and suffix indicating series number and body type. These numbers appear in the second column of the charts below. Pontiac parts suppliers use these numbers to aid proper parts applications so they are important.

Model Number	Body/Style Number	Body Type & Seating	Factory Price	Shipping Weight	Production Total
TORPEDO SIX (6-cyl.)					
25	27B	2d Coupe-3P	1,217	3,245	Note 1
25	07	2d Sed Coupe-5P	1,305	3,300	Note 1
25	27	2d Sport Coupe-5P	1,261	3,295	Note 1
25	67	2d Convertible-5P	1,595	3,560	Note 1
25	11	2d Sedan-5P	1,275	3,295	Note 1
25	19	4d Sedan-5P	1,331	3,320	Note 1
TORPEDO EIGHT (8-cyl.)					
27	27B	2d Coupe-3P	1,262	3,310	Note 2

1948 Pontiac Torpedo Deluxe Six four-door sedan. (OCW)

word "Silver Streak" was carried on the sides of the hood with eights having an "8" placed between the two words. The model lineup was expanded by offering several body styles with Deluxe trims. Characterizing standard models were plain fenders and rubber gravel guards. Deluxes had fender moldings, bright metal gravel guards and chrome-plated wheel discs. Gray tan cloth continued as trim on standard Torpedos, but Deluxe types with closed bodies used tan and dark blue pattern cloth combinations. Convertibles came with genuine colonial grain leather or imitation leather upholstery and had instrument boards lacquered in body color.

STREAMLINER SERIES — (SIX) SERIES 36 — (EIGHT) SERIES 28 — Streamliners were again larger and more expensive. All Streamliners, two-door and four-door fastbacks (B-Body) and the station wagon, now came standard or Deluxe. As on Torpedos, Deluxe models were distinguished by spear moldings on front fenders, bright gravel guards and chrome plated wheel discs on all cars except wagons. Deluxe interiors had two-tone trims with pillow-and-tuft seatbacks, quarter-sawed mahogany dash and window trim, electric glove box door clocks, Deluxe steering wheels, and other rich appointments. Standard wagons had tan imitation leather seats and Deluxe wagons had red upholstery of the same type.

I.D. DATA: VIN located on left side of firewall under hood. Serial numbers took the form ( )[ ]P{ }-1001 to ( )[ ]P{ }-ending number. First symbol ( ) indicated the assembly plant: P=Pontiac, Mich.; C=California (South Gate); L=Linden, N.J.; W=Wilmington, Del.; K=Kansas City, Kan.; A=Atlanta, Ga.; F=Framingham, Mass. Second symbol [ ] indicated engine type: 6=inline six-cylinder; 8=inline eight-cylinder. Third symbol indicated model year: P=1948. Fourth symbol { } contains a letter indicating series: A=Torpedo; B=Streamliner. Remaining symbols are the sequential unit production number for each car line at each assembly plant. Beginning number at each plant is 1001. Ending numbers for 1948 were: [TORPEDO SIX] (Mich.) 25366; (Calif.) 5150; (N.J.) 5301; (Del.) 4375; (Kan.) 5303; (Ga.) 3429 and (Mass.) 3454. [TORPEDO EIGHT] (Mich.) 18933; (Calif.) 4368; (N.J.) 5471; (Del.) 3854; (Kan.) 4134; (Ga.) 2820; (Mass.) 2720. [STREAMLINER SIX] (Mich.) 18146; (Calif.) 4765; (N.J.) 4350; (Del.) 3772; (Kan.) 5556; (Ga.) 2926 and (Mass.) 2951. [STREAMLINER EIGHT] (Mich.) 61682; (Calif.) 13302; (N.J.) 12359; (Del.) 10616; (Kan.) 16561; (Ga.) 7603) and (Mass.) 7776. Engine serial number on raised pad on front left side of block. VINs matched the engine serial number. Fisher Body/style number on plate under hood on left of firewall can be very helpful for identification of model and ordering parts. A prefix to the main number indicates model year, 48=1948. The first two symbols in the main number indicate series 25, 26, 27, or 28. The next two symbols indicate the body style. Some numbers have an alphabetical suffix indicating trim level, such as D=Deluxe. These numbers appear in

1948 Pontiac Torpedo Deluxe Eight two-door convertible. (OCW)

body/style number column of charts below adjacent to corresponding body style listing.

Model Number	Body/Style Number	Body Type & Seating	Factory Price	Shipping Weight	Production Total
TORPEDO SIX (6-cyl.)					
6PA	48-2527B	2d Bus Coupe-3P	1,500	3,230	See Notes
6PA	48-2527(D)	2d Sport Coupe-5P	1,552/1,641	3,220/3,230	See Notes
6PA	48-2507(D)	2d Sed Coupe-5P	1,614/1,704	3,275/3,275	See Notes
6PA	48-2567(D)	2d Convertible-5P	1,935/2,025	3,525/3,530	See Notes
6PA	48-2511	2d Sedan-5P	1,583	3,280	See Notes
6PA	48-2519(D)	4d Sedan-5P	1,641/1,731	3,320/3,340	See Notes
TORPEDO EIGHT (8-cyl.)					
8PA	48-2727B	2d Bus Cpe-3P	1,548	3,296	See Notes
8PA	48-2727(D)	2d Sport Coupe-5P	1,599/1,689	3,295/3,305	See Notes
8PA	48-2707(D)	2d Sed Coupe-5P	1,661/1,751	3,340/3,340	See Notes
8PA	48-2767(D)	2d Convertible-5P	1,982/2,072	3,595/3,600	See Notes

1948 Pontiac Streamliner Eight four-door station wagon. (OCW)

1948 Pontiac Streamliner Eight four-door sedan. (JAG)

1948 Pontiac Streamliner Eight two-door sedan-coupe. (OCW)

Model Number	Body/Style Number	Body Type & Seating	Factory Price	Shipping Weight	Production Total
8PA	48-2711	2d Sedan-5P	1,630	3,360	See Notes
8PA	48-2719(D)	4d Sedan-5P	1,689/1,778	3,395/3,395	See Notes
STREAMLINER SIX (6-cyl.)					
6PB	48-2607(D)	2d Sed Coupe-5P	1,677/1,766	3,365/3,370	See Notes
6PB	48-2609(D)	4d Sedan-5P	1,727/1,817	3,450/3,455	See Notes
6PB	STA WAG (D)	4d Sta Wagon-6/8P	2,364/2,442	3,755/3,695	See Notes
STREAMLINER EIGHT (8-cyl.)					
8PB	48-2807(D)	2d Sed Coupe-5P	1,724/1,814	3,425/3,455	See Notes
8PB	48-2809(D)	4d Sedan-5P	1,755/1,864	3,525/,65	See Notes
8PB	STA WAG (D)	4d Sta Wagon-6/8P	2,412/2,490	3,820/3,765	See Notes

NOTE 1: 25,325 Torpedo sixes with Hydra-Matic built.

NOTE 2: 13,937 Torpedo sixes with synchromesh built.

NOTE 3: 49,262 total Torpedo sixes built; no body style breakouts available.

NOTE 4: Data above slash for standard/below slash for Deluxe.

NOTE 5: 24,294 Torpedo eights with Hydra-Matic built.

NOTE 6: 11,006 Torpedo eights with synchromesh built.

NOTE 7: 35,360 total Torpedo eights built; no body style breakouts available.

NOTE 8: "D" suffix indicates car came as both standard and Deluxe.

NOTE 9: Data above slash for standard/below slash for Deluxe.

NOTE 10: Factory info conflicts (i.e. standard convertible probably not made).

NOTE 11: 23,858 Streamliner sixes with Hydra-Matic built.

NOTE 12: 13,834 Streamliner sixes with Synchromesh built.

NOTE 13: 37,742 total Streamliner sixes built; no body style breakouts.

NOTE 14: 98,469 Streamliner eights built with Hydra-Matic.

NOTE 15: 24,646 Streamliner eights built with synchromesh.

NOTE 16: 123,115 total Streamliner eights built; no breakouts per body style.

NOTE 17: "D" suffix indicates car came as both standard and Deluxe sub-series.

NOTE 18: Data above slash for standard/below slash for Deluxe.

NOTE 19: Station wagon seating: Deluxe=6-passenger; Standard=8-passenger.

ENGINE [SIX]: Six-cylinder. Inline. L-head. Cast-iron block. Displacement: 239.2 cid. Bore & stroke: 3-9/16 x 4 in. Compression Ratio: (standard) 6.5:1, (optional) 7.5:1. Brake hp: (standard) 90 at 3400 rpm, (optional) 93 at 3400 rpm. Four main bearings. Solid valve lifters. Carburetor: Carter WA1-537-S one-barrel.

ENGINE [EIGHT]: Eight-cylinder. Inline. L-head. Cast-iron block. Displacement: 248.9 cid. Bore & stroke: 3-1/4 x 3-3/4 in. Compression Ratio: Same as on six-cylinder. Brake hp: (standard head) 104 at 3800 rpm, (optional "high head") 106 at 3800 rpm. Five main bearings. Solid valve lifters. Carburetor: Carter WCD-630-S two-barrel.

CHASSIS: [TORPEDO] Wheelbase: 119 in. Overall length: 204.5 in. Front tread: 58 in. Rear tread: 61-1/2 in. Tire size: 6.00 x 16 tube type. [STREAMLINER] Wheelbase: 122 in. Overall length: (cars) 204.5 in., (wagons) 215-5/8 in. Front tread: 58 in. Rear tread: 61-1/2 in. Tire size: 6.50 x 16 tube type.

OPTIONS: Rear windshield wiper. Windshield washer. White sidewall discs. Fog lights. Safety light. Weather Chief heater (dash type). Defroster (dash type). Venti-Heat underseat heater and defroster. Five-tube Master radio. Seven-tube Air Mate radio. Eight-tube Air King radio. Mast antenna. Rear fender panels (Torpedo). Rear fender panels with moldings (Streamliner). Sponge rubber cushions (per body style). Kool Kushin. Luggage compartment light. Lock package. Electric clock vanity mirror. E-Z-I non-glare rearview mirror. Non-electric visor vanity mirror. Handbrake lamp. Umbrella holder. Santoy seat covers (per body style). Bumper guards, wheel rim rings, electric clock, exhaust deflector, and various lights available in standard accessory packages. All 1948 Pontiacs had three-speed manual transmission with column shifting as standard equipment. A new option was Hydra-Matic Drive ($185). Performance options were limited to 3.9:1 (economy) and 4.55:1 (mountain) rear axle gear ratios, a 7.5:1 "high-compression" cylinder head, and automatic No-Rol device.

HISTORICAL: The 1948 Pontiacs entered production on Dec. 29, 1947. Model year output came to 245,419 cars, which gave Pontiac a 6.56 percent share of the domestic automobile marketplace.

Calendar year production peaked at 253,469 cars, making Pontiac America's fifth ranked automaker.

1949 PONTIAC

1949 Pontiac Chieftain Eight four-door sedan. (OCW)

STREAMLINER LINE — (SIX) SERIES 25 — (EIGHT) SERIES 27 — The 1949 Pontiacs featured low, sleek envelope bodies. Streamliner coupes and sedans utilized the fastback B-body shell. Station wagons were also incorporated in this line. All these cars came as standards or Deluxes. All station wagons and other standard models had small hubcaps. Standard coupes, sedans, and wagons were characterized by an absence of beltline trim along with use of rubber gravel guards and painted headlight rims. Deluxes had belt moldings, chrome gravel guards, and bright plated headlight doors. Silver Streak styling was seen again. Silver Streak lettering was placed above front fender spears on Deluxes and high on the fenders of standards. Eights had the number '8' between the two words. Most standard models had gray striped pattern cloth upholstery. Most Deluxes used dark gray broadcloth trims. Convertibles and wagons were trimmed as before, except imitation leather was used only on standard wagons.

CHIEFTAIN LINE — (SIX) SERIES 25 — (EIGHT) SERIES 27 — Chieftains were characterized by notchback body styling and all models in the line used the General Motors A-body shell. The only dimensional difference between the new Streamliners and Chieftains was that the latter were approximately 3/4-in. higher than

1949 Pontiac Streamliner Eight four-door sedan. (OCW)

1949 Pontiac Chieftain Deluxe Eight four-door sedan. (OCW)

1949 Pontiac Chieftain Deluxe Eight two-door convertible. (OCW)

1949 Pontiac Chieftain Deluxe Eight two-door sport coupe. (OCW)

comparable B-body styles. Lengths and widths were identical for all models in both lines, except station wagons. Trim variations between sixes and eights or standards and Deluxes were the same as on Streamliners.

I.D. DATA: VIN located on tag on left front door post. Matching engine serial number located on raised pad on front left side of cylinder block. Serial numbers took the form ( )-[ ]R{ }-1001 to ( )-[ ]P{ }-ending number. First symbol ( ) indicated the assembly plant: P=Pontiac, Mich.; C=California (South Gate); L=Linden, N.J.; W=Wilmington, Del.; K=Kansas City, Kan.; A=Atlanta, Ga.; F=Framingham, Mass. Second symbol [ ] indicated engine type: 6=inline six-cylinder; 8=inline eight-cylinder. Third symbol indicated model year: R=1949. Fourth symbol { } changed to a letter indicating type of transmission: S=synchromesh; H=Hydra-Matic. Remaining symbols are the sequential unit production number for each car line at each assembly plant. Beginning number at each plant is 1001. Ending numbers for 1949 were: [SERIES 25 SIX with synchromesh] (Mich.) 17919; (Calif.) 4767; (N.J.) 4657; (Del.) 4077; (Kan.) 7406; (Ga.) 3404 and (Mass.) 3613. [SERIES 25 SIX with/Hydra-Matic] (Mich.) 12,320; (Calif.) 4142; (N.J.) 3998; (Del.) 3425; (Kan.) 5887; (Ga.) 2903; (Mass.) 3012. [SERIES 27 EIGHT with synchromesh] (Mich.) 26,054; (Calif.) 7209; (N.J.) 7398; (Del.) 6200; (Kan.) 10608; (Ga.) 4975 and (Mass.) 5188. [SERIES 27 EIGHT with Hydra-Matic] (Mich.) 68,436; (Calif.) 19,959; (N.J.) 19,989; (Del.) 16,062; (Kan.) 30,890; (Ga.) 12,657 and (Mass.) 13,336. Fisher Body/style number on plate under hood on left of

1949 Pontiac Chieftain Deluxe Eight two-door sport coupe. (OCW)

1949 Pontiac Chieftain Deluxe Eight sedan delivery and Pontiac General Manager Harry J. Klinger. (OCW)

firewall can be helpful for identification of model and ordering parts. A prefix to the main number indicates model year, 49=1949. The first two symbols in the main number indicate series 25 or 27. The next two symbols indicate the body style. Some numbers have an alphabetical suffix indicating trim level, such as D=Deluxe. These numbers appear in body/style number column of charts below adjacent to corresponding body style listing.

Model Number	Body/Style Number	Body Type & Seating	Factory Price	Shipping Weight	Production Total
STREAMLINER SIX (6-cyl.)					
6R	2508(D)	4d Sedan-5P	1,740/1,835	3,385/3,415	See Notes
6R	2507(D)	2d Sedan Cpe-5P	1,689/1,784	3,360/3,375	See Notes
6R	2561(D)	4d Wood Wag-6/8P	2,543/2,622	3,745/3,730	See Notes
6R	2562(D)	4d Metal Wag-6/8P	2,543/2,622	3,650/3,580	See Notes
STREAMLINER EIGHT (8-cyl.)					
8R	2508(D)	4d Sedan-5P	1,808/1,903	3,470/3,500	See Notes
8R	2507(D)	2d Sedan Cpe-5P	1,758/1,853	3,435/3,445	See Notes
8R	2561(D)	4d Wood Wag-6/8P	2,611/2,690	3,835/3,800	See Notes
8R	2562(D)	4d Metal Wag-6/8P	2,611/2,690	3,690/3,640	See Notes
CHIEFTAIN SIX (6-cyl.)					
6R	2569(D)	4d Sedan-5P	1,761/1,856	3,385/3,415	See Notes
6R	2511(D)	2d Sedan-5P	1,710/1,805	3,355/3,360	See Notes
6R	2527(D)	2d Sedan Cpe-5P	1,710/1,805	3,330/3,345	See Notes
6R	2527B	2d Bus Coupe-3P	1,587	3,280	See Notes
6R	2567DTX	2d Del Conv-5P	2,183	3,600	See Notes
CHIEFTAIN EIGHT (8-cyl.)					
8R	2569(D)	4d Sedan-5P	1,829/1,924	3,475/3,480	See Notes
8R	2511(D)	2d Sedan-5P	1,779/1,874	3,430/3,430	See Notes
8R	2527(D)	2d Sedan Cpe-5P	1,779/1,874	3,390/3,415	See Notes
8R	2427B	2d Bus Coupe-3P	1,656	3,355	See Notes
8R	2567DTX	2d Del Conv-5P	2,206	3,670	See Notes

NOTE 1: See Historical Footnotes for series production total.

NOTE 2: Data above slash for standard/below slash for Deluxe.

NOTE 3: See Historical Footnotes for series production total.

NOTE 4: Data above slash for standard/below slash for Deluxe.

NOTE 5: See Standard Catalog of American Light-Duty Trucks for sedan delivery.

NOTE 6: See Historical Footnotes for series production total.

NOTE 7: Data above slash for standard/below slash for Deluxe.

NOTE 8: See Historical Footnotes for series production total.

NOTE 9: Data above slash for standard/below slash for Deluxe.

ENGINE [Six]: Six-cylinder. Inline. L-head. Cast-iron block. Displacement: 239.2 cid. Bore & stroke: 3-9/16 x 4 in. Compression Ratio: (standard) 6.5:1 (optional) 7.5:1. Brake horsepower: (standard) 90 at 3400 rpm, (optional) 93 at 3400 rpm. Four main bearings. Solid valve lifters. Carburetor: Carter WA1-537-S one-barrel.

ENGINE [Eight]: Eight-cylinder. Inline. L-head. Cast-iron block. Displacement: 248.9 cid. Bore & stroke: 4-1/4 x 4-3/4 in. Compression Ratio: Same as sixes. Brake horsepower: (standard) 103 at 3800 rpm, (optional) 106 at 3800 rpm. Five main bearings. Solid valve lifters. Carburetor: Carter WCD two-barrel model 6305B.

CHASSIS: Wheelbase: 120 in. all lines. Overall Length: (all cars) 202-1/2 in.; (station wagons) 203.8 in. Front tread: 58 in. Rear tread: 59 in. Tires: (standard) 7.10 x 15 (special equipment) 7.60 x 15. Tube type.

OPTIONS: Seven-tube Chieftain radio. Mast antenna. No-Blo wind deflectors. Car cushions. Venti-Seat underseat heater. Venti-Shades. Windshield Sun Visor. Traffic light viewer. Polaroid visor. Rear fender panels (skirts). License frames. Illuminated hood ornament. Wheel trim rings. Steel wheel discs. White sidewall discs. Deluxe steering wheel. Remington Auto-Home shaver. Visor vanity mirror. Tissue dispenser. Direction signals. Compass. Rear window wiper. Windshield washers. Deluxe electric clock. Glove compartment light. Leather utility pocket. Luggage compartment light. Seat covers. Safti-Jack, Outside rearview mirror. Back-up lights. Safety spotlight. Fog lights. No-Rol. Bumper guards. Grille guard. Exhaust deflector. Venetian blinds. No-Mar gas filler trim. Fuel door lock. Scuff pads. Multi-purpose lamp. Underhood trouble lamp. Jack bag. Tool kit. A three-speed Synchromesh gearbox with column shift was standard on all models. Hydra-Matic four-speed automatic transmission was available at $159 extra. Rear axle ratios: (standard) 4.1:1, (economy) 3.9:1, (mountain) 4.3:1, (Hydra-Matic) 3.63:1.

HISTORICAL: Calendar year production was 333,957 cars. Model year production was 304,819 cars. The latter included a total of 69,654 Streamliner and Chieftain sixes (29,515 with Hydra-Matic and 40,139 with synchromesh) and 235,165 Streamliner and Chieftain eights (174,449 with Hydra-Matic and 60,716 with synchromesh). Pontiac sold 21.2 percent of the U.S. cars in its price class. Hydra-Matic Drive was installed in 78 percent of all Pontiacs made for the year. During 1949, the company built the three millionth Pontiac made since the marque was introduced in 1926. Prototypes of a new "Catalina" two-door hardtop Sports Coupe were seen this year. Note that Pontiac Motor Division now kept production records by chassis series (six or eight), without regard to car-line (Streamliner or Chieftain). This practice was followed through 1954 and there are no breakouts by car-line of body style available until model year 1955. Standard station wagons continued to feature eight-passenger seating, while Deluxe wagons came with six-passenger seating. Body styles 2527 and 2527D are often called Club Coupes and feature direct-action (non-cranking) rear quarter window operation. These styles resemble the two-door sedan, but have shorter roofs and longer rear decks.

1950 PONTIAC

1950 Pontiac Chieftain Deluxe Eight convertible. (OCW)

STREAMLINER — (SIX) SERIES 25 — (EIGHT) SERIES 27 — The 1950 Pontiacs utilized the popular 1949 envelope bodies with revisions to trim and appointments. The horizontal center grille bar now wrapped around the corners of the body. Deluxe models had a chrome body strip, chrome wheel rings, chrome headlight rings, and stainless steel gravel guards. Eights had an "8" between the words Silver Streak on the fenders. Streamliners (except station wagons and sedan delivery trucks) had sloping fastback styling.

CHIEFTAIN LINE — (SIX) SERIES 25 — (EIGHT) SERIES 27 — Chieftains were built off the A-body shell with trim distinctions for Deluxe models and eights the same as on Streamliners. A new Chieftain body style was the Catalina two-door hardtop. It was classified as a Super Deluxe model within the Deluxe sub-series. It

1950 Pontiac Chieftan Deluxe Catalina Sport Coupe (OCW)

1950 Pontiac Streamliner Eight four-door metal station wagon. (OCW)

came finished only in San Pedro Ivory, Sierra Rust or two-tone combinations of these colors. The interior was done in Rust and Ivory leather combinations.

I.D. DATA: VIN located on tag on left front door post. Matching engine serial number located on raised pad on front left side of cylinder block. Serial numbers took the form ( )-[ ]T{ }-1001 to ( )-[ ]T{ }-ending number. First symbol ( ) indicated the assembly plant: P=Pontiac, Mich.; C=California (South Gate); L=Linden, N.J.; W=Wilmington, Del.; K=Kansas City, Kan.; A=Atlanta, Ga.; F=Framingham, Mass. Second symbol [ ] indicated engine type: 6=inline six-cylinder; 8=inline eight-cylinder. Third symbol indicated model year: T=1950. Fourth symbol { } changed to a letter indicating type of transmission: S=synchromesh; H=Hydra-Matic. Remaining symbols are the sequential unit production number for each car-line at each assembly plant. Beginning number at each plant is 1001. Ending numbers for 1950 were: [Series 25 six with synchromesh] (Mich.) 47948; (Calif.) 5571; (N.J.) 8011; (Del.) 74745; (Kan.) 14626; (Ga.) 4925 and (Mass.) 8048. [Series 25 six with/Hydra-Matic] (Mich.) 15001; (Calif.) 2553; (N.J.) 2999; (Del.) 2534; (Kan.) 3696; (Ga.) 1960; (Mass.) 2575. [Series 27 eight with synchromesh] (Mich.) 3815; (Calif.) 4746; (N.J.) 4619; (Del.) 5558; (Kan.) 11497; (Ga.) 5257 and (Mass.) 4070. [Series 27 eight with Hydra-Matic] (Mich.) 128647; (Calif.) 29630; (N.J.) 19508; (Del.) 17360; (Kan.) 42698; (Ga.) 14851 and (Mass.) 117242. Fisher Body style number on plate under hood on left of firewall can be helpful for identification of model and ordering parts. A prefix to the main number indicates

1950 Pontiac Chieftain Deluxe Eight four-door sedan. (OCW)

1950 Pontiac Chieftain Deluxe Eight two-door sedan. (OCW)

1950 Pontiac Streamliner Six two-door sedan coupe. (OCW)

1950 Pontiac Streamliner Eight four-door sedan. (OCW)

1950 Pontiac Chieftain Deluxe Eight convertible. (OCW)

model-year, 50=1950. The first two symbols in the main number indicate series 25 or 27. The next two symbols indicate the body style. Some numbers have an alphabetical suffix indicating trim level, such as B=Business and D=Deluxe. These numbers appear in Body/Style Number column of charts below adjacent to corresponding body style listing.

Model Number	Body Style Number	Body Type & Seating	Factory Price	Shipping Weight	Production Total
STREAMLINER SIX (6-cyl.)					
25	08(D)	4d Sedan-6P	1,724/1,745	3,414/3,499	Note 1
25	07(D)	2d Sedan Coupe-6P	1,673/1,768	3,379/3,399	Note 1
25	62(D)	4d Sta Wagon-8/6P	2,264/2,343	3,714/3,649	Note 1
STREAMLINER EIGHT (8-cyl.)					
25	08(D)	4d Sedan-6P	1,792/1,887	3,499/3,509	Note 1
25	07(D)	2d Sedan Coupe-6P	1,742/1,837	3,464/3,469	Note 1
25	62(D)	4d Sta Wagon-8/6P	2,332/2,411	3,799/3,739	Note 1
CHIEFTAIN SIX (6-cyl.)					
25	69(D)	4d Sedan-6P	1,745/1,840	3,409/3414	Note 1
25	11(D)	2d Sedan-6P	1,694/1,789	3,384/3,389	Note 1

Model Number	Body Style Number	Body Type & Seating	Factory Price	Shipping Weight	Production Total
25	27(D)	2d Sedan Coupe-6P	1,694/1,789	3,359/3,364	Note 1
25	37SD	2d Catalina HT-6P	2,000	3,469	Note 1
25	67DTX	2d Convertible-6P	2,122	3,624	Note 1
25	27B	2d Bus Coupe-3P	1,571	3,319	Note 1
CHIEFTAIN EIGHT (8-cyl.)					
25	69(D)	4d Sedan-6P	1,813/1,908	3,494/3,499	Note 1
25	11(D)	2d Sedan-6P	1,763/1,858	3,454/3,464	Note 1
25	27(D)	2d Sedan Coupe-6P	1,763/1,858	3,444/3,454	Note 1
25	37SD	2d Catalina HT-6P	2,069	3,549	Note 1
25	67DTX	2d Convertible-6P	2,190	3,704	Note 1

NOTE 1: See Historical Footnotes for series production total.

NOTE 2: Data above slash for standard/below slash for Deluxe.

ENGINE [Six]: Six-cylinder. Inline. L-head. Cast-iron block. Displacement: 239.2 cid. Bore & stroke: 3-9/16 x 4 in. Compression Ratio: (standard) 6.5:1; (optional) 7.5:1. Brake horsepower: (standard) 90 at 3400 rpm; (optional) 93 at 3400 rpm. Four main bearings. Solid valve lifters. Carburetor: Carter WA1-719-S one-barrel.

ENGINE [Eight]: Eight-cylinder. Inline. L-head. Cast-iron block. Displacement: 268.2 cid. Bore & stroke: 3-3/8 x 3-3/4 in. Compression Ratio: (standard); 6.5:1 (optional) 7.5:1. Brake horsepower: (standard) 108 at 3600 rpm; (optional) 113 at 3600 rpm. Five main bearings. Solid valve lifters. Carburetor: Carter WCD-719-S two-barrel.

1950 Pontiac Chieftain Eight Super Deluxe Catalina. (OCW)

1950 Pontiac Streamliner Deluxe Eight two-door sedan-coupe. (OCW)

1950 Pontiac Streamliner Six sedan delivery. (OCW)

CHASSIS: Wheelbase: 120 in. all lines. Overall length: (all cars) 202-1/2 in.; (wagons) 203.8 in. Front tread: 58 in. Rear tread: 59 in. Tires: (standard) 7.10 x 15 (special equipment) 7.60 x 15. Tube type.

OPTIONS: Seven-tube Chieftain radio. Mast antenna. No-Blo wind deflectors. Car cushions. Venti-Seat underseat heater. Venti-Shades. Windshield sun visor. Traffic light viewer. Polaroid visor. Rear fender panels (skirts). License frames. Illuminated hood ornament. Wheel trim rings. Steel wheel discs. White sidewall discs. Deluxe steering wheel. Remington Auto-Home shaver. Visor vanity mirror. Tissue dispenser. Direction signals. Compass. Rear window wiper. Windshield washers. Deluxe electric clock. Glove compartment light. Leather utility pocket. Luggage compartment light. Seat covers. Safti-Jack. Outside rearview mirror. Back-up lights. Safety spotlight. Fog lights. No-Rol. Bumper guards. Grille guard. Exhaust deflector. Venetian blinds. No-Mar gas filler trim. Fuel door lock. Scuff pads. Multi-purpose lamp. Underhood trouble lamp. Jack bag. Tool kit. A three-speed synchromesh gearbox with column shift was standard on all models. Hydra-Matic four-speed automatic transmission was available at $159 extra. Rear axle ratios: (standard) 4.1:1, (economy) 3.9:1, (mountain) 4.3:1, (Hydra-Matic) 3.63:1.

HISTORICAL: Production of 1950 Pontiacs began Nov. 10, 1949. Calendar year assemblies were a strong 467,655 units. Model year output was also strong at 446,426 cars. The latter included a total of 115,542 Streamliner and Chieftain sixes (24,930 with Hydra-Matic and 90,612 with synchromesh) and a total of 330,887 Streamliner and Chieftain eights (263,188 with Hydra-Matic and 67,699 with synchromesh).

1951 PONTIAC

1951 Pontiac Chieftain Deluxe Eight four-door sedan. (OCW)

1951 Pontiac Chieftain Six two-door sedan. (OCW)

1951 Pontiac Chieftain Six two-door sedan-coupe. (OCW)

1951 Pontiac Chieftain Eight Super Deluxe Catalina. (OCW)

STREAMLINER LINE — (SIX) SERIES 25 — (EIGHT) — SERIES 27 — The 1951 "Silver Anniversary" Pontiacs reflected 25 years of advanced engineering. A wing-shaped grille was seen and a Silver Streak theme continued. Streamliners again used the B-body shell with sloping fastbacks on coupes. Deluxe models had chrome body strips, bright gravel guards and headlight rings. Belt line moldings on all Deluxe passenger cars (not station wagons), had a dip behind the doors. Standard belt moldings were straight. A script plate reading Pontiac was used on series 25 sixes and on series 27 eights a different script read Pontiac eight.

CHIEFTAIN LINE — (SIX) SERIES 25 — (EIGHT) SERIES 27 — Chieftains had notchback A-body styling. Trim variations distinguishing standards and Deluxes, or sixes and eights were the same as on Streamliners. Convertibles came as Deluxes only. Catalina hardtops came only as Deluxes or Super Deluxes, the latter forming a separate Super sub-series. Deluxe Catalinas (style 2537D) had interiors similar to other Deluxes, but the interior trim on Super Deluxe Catalinas (style 2537SD) came in a Blue and Ivory leather/cloth combination or optional all-leather (in the same colors). Super Deluxe Catalinas can be distinguished externally by horizontally grooved trim plates on their rear roof pillars. The three-passenger business coupe was available only in standard trim.

I.D. DATA: VIN located on tag on left front door post. Matching engine serial number located on raised pad on front left side of cylinder block. Serial numbers took the form ( )-[ ]U{ }-1001 to ( )-[ ]U{ }-ending number. First symbol ( ) indicated the assembly plant: P=Pontiac, Mich.;

1951 Pontiac Streamliner Eight four-door station wagon. (OCW)

1951 Pontiac Streamliner Six sedan delivery. (OCW)

1951 Pontiac Streamliner Six sedan delivery. (JAG)

C=California (South Gate); L=Linden, N.J.; W=Wilmington, Del.; K=Kansas City, Kan.; A=Atlanta, Ga.; F=Framingham, Mass. Second symbol [ ] indicated engine type: 6=inline six-cylinder; 8=inline eight-cylinder. Third symbol indicated model year: U=1951. Fourth symbol { } changed to a letter indicating type of transmission: S=synchromesh; H=Hydra-Matic. Remaining symbols are the sequential unit production number for each car line at each assembly plant. Beginning number at each plant is 1001. Ending numbers for 1951 were: [Series 25 six with synchromesh] (Mich.) 24,016; (Calif.) 3519; (N.J.) 4133; (Del.) 4175; (Kan.) 6567; (Ga.) 3282 and (Mass.) 3181. [Series 25 six with/Hydra-Matic] (Mich.) 6543; (Calif.) 1473; (N.J.) 1592; (Del.) 1562; (Kan.) 1954; (Ga.) 1416; (Mass.) 1323. [Series 27 eight with synchromesh] (Mich.) 31,777; (Calif.) 6224; (N.J.) 5984; (Del.) 6068; (Kan.) 11,644; (Ga.) 5406 and (Mass.) 4177. [Series 27 eight with Hydra-Matic] (Mich.) 119,780; (Calif.) 20,125; (N.J.) 22,197; (Del.) 23,140; (Kan.) 40,060; (Ga.) 18,117 and (Mass.) 14,080. Fisher Body style number on plate under hood on left of firewall can be helpful for identification of model and ordering parts. A prefix to the main number indicates model year, 51=1951. The first two symbols in the main number indicate series 25 or 27. The next two symbols indicate the body style. Some numbers have an alphabetical suffix indicating trim level, such as B=Business; D=Deluxe; and SD=Super Deluxe. These numbers appear in body/style number column of charts below adjacent to corresponding body style listings.

Model Number	Body Style Number	Body Type & Seating	Factory Price	Shipping Weight	Production Total
STREAMLINER SIX					
24	07(D)	2d Sed Coupe-6P	1,824/1927	3,248/3,263	Note 1
24	62(D)	4d Sta Wagon-8/6P	2,470/2556	3,603/3,523	Note 1
STREAMLINER EIGHT					
25	07(D)	2d Sed Coupe-6P	1,900/2,003	3,343/3,348	Note 1
25	62(D)	4d Sta Wagon-8/6P	2,544/2,629	3,698/3,628	Note 1

1951 Pontiac-Acme limousine hearse. (JAG)

1951 Pontiac-Barnette hearse. (JAG)

Model Number	Body Style Number	Body Type & Seating	Factory Price	Shipping Weight	Production Total
CHIEFTAIN SIX					
25	69(D)	4d Sedan-6P	1,903/2,006	3,073	Note 1
25	11(D)	2d Sedan-6P	1,848/1,951	3,043	Note 1
25	27(D)	2d Sed Coupe-6P	1848/1951	3128	Note 1
25	27B	2d Bus Coupe-3P	1,713	3,193	Note 1
CHIEFTAIN DELUXE SIX					
25	37D	2d Catalina HT-6P	2,182	3,343	Note 1
25	67DTX	2d Convertible-6P	2,314	3,488	Note 1
CHIEFTAIN SUPER DELUXE SIX					
25	37SD	2d Catalina HT-6P	2,244	3,353	Note 1
CHIEFTAIN EIGHT					
25	69(D)	4d Sedan-6P	1,977/2,081	3,363/3,373	Note 1
25	11(D)	2d Sedan-6P	1,922/2,026	3,328/3,333	Note 1
25	27(D)	2d Sedan Coupe-6p	1,922/2,026	3,303/3,318	Note 1
25	27B	2d Bus Coupe-3P	1,787	3,273	Note 1
CHIEFTAIN DELUXE EIGHT					
25	37D	2d Catalina HT-6P	2,257	3,428	Note 1
25	67DTX	2d Convertible-6P	2,388	3,568	Note 1
CHIEFTAIN SUPER DELUXE EIGHT					
25	37SD	2d Catalina HT-6P	2,320	3,433	Note 1

NOTE 1: See Historical section for series production total.

NOTE 2: Data above slash for standard/below slash for Deluxe.

ENGINE [Six]: Six-cylinder. Inline. L-head. Cast-iron block. Displacement: 239.2 cid. Bore & stroke: 3-9/16 x 4 in. Compression Ratio: (standard) 6.5:1; (optional) 7.5:1. Brake horsepower: (standard) 96 at 3400 rpm; (optional) 100 at 3400 rpm. Four main bearings. Solid valve lifters. Carburetor: Rochester BC one-barrel.

ENGINE [Eight]: Eight-cylinder. Inline. L-head. Cast-iron block. Displacement: 268.4 cid. Bore & stroke: 3-3/8 x 3-3/4 in. Compression Ratio: (standard) 6.5:1; (optional) 7.5:1. Brake horsepower: (standard) 116 at 3600 rpm; (optional) 120 at 3600 rpm. Five main bearings. Solid valve lifters. Carburetor: (synchromesh) Carter WCD 719S or WCD 719SA; (Hydra-Matic) Carter WCD 720S or WCD 720SA.

CHASSIS: Wheelbase: 120 in. all lines. Overall length: (all cars) 202-1/2 in.; (wagons) 203.8 in. Front tread: 58 in. Rear tread: 59 in. Tires: (standard) 7.10 x 15 (special equipment) 7.60 x 15. Tube type.

OPTIONS: Seven-tube Chieftain radio. Mast antenna. No-Blo wind deflectors. Car cushions. Venti-Seat underseat heater. Venti-Shades. Windshield sun visor. Traffic light viewer. Poloroid visor. Rear fender panels (skirts). License frames. Illuminated hood ornament. Wheel trim rings. Steel wheel discs. White sidewall discs. Deluxe steering wheel. Remington Auto-Home shaver. Visor vanity mirror. Tissue dispenser. Direction signals. Compass. Rear window wiper. Windshield washers. Deluxe electric clock. Glove compartment light. Leather utility pocket. Luggage compartment light. Seat

1951 Pontiac Chieftain Deluxe Eight two-door sedan. (OCW)

1951 Pontiac Chieftain station wagon. (OCW)

covers. Safti-Jack. Outside rearview mirror. Back-up lights. Safety spotlight. Fog lights. No-Rol. Bumper guards. Grille guard. Exhaust deflector. Venetian blinds. No-Mar gas filler trim. Fuel door lock. Scuff pads. Multi-purpose lamp. Underhood trouble lamp. Jack bag. Tool kit. A three-speed synchromesh gearbox with column shift was standard on all models. Hydra-Matic four-speed automatic transmission was available at $159 extra. Rear axle ratios: (standard) 4.1:1, (economy) 3.9:1, (mountain) 4.3:1, (Hydra-Matic) 3.63:1.

HISTORICAL: Production start-up took place November 27, 1950. The 1951 models were introduced Dec. 11, 1950, and commemorated the company's 25th anniversary year. Arnold Lenz became the general manager of Pontiac Motor Division, but his tenure would be cut short by a tragic accident in 1952. Pontiac made 343,795 cars during the calendar-year. Model-year production came to 343,795 units. This included a total of 53,748 Streamliner and Chieftain sixes (10,195 with Hydra-Matic and 43,553 with synchromesh) and a total of 316,411 Streamliner and Chieftain eights (251,987 with Hydra-Matic and 64,424 with synchromesh). On an industry-wide basis for the calendar year, Pontiac built 6.7 percent of America's convertibles; 9.6 percent of domestic hardtops; and 4.7 percent of domestic station wagons. In the final count, car output was down 26 percent from 1950, but still second-best in Pontiac history. Body styles 2507 and 2507D Streamliner sedan-coupes were discontinued in April 1951. Pontiac's dropping of the fastback Streamliner series marked one of the closing chapters in a styling trend for a while. However, the Pontiac fastback would return in the mid-1960s. In 1951, Pontiac's headquarters operations in Pontiac, Mich., sourced 169,087 of 343,795 Pontiacs built or 49.2 percent of production. The Pontiac factory facilities included 5,800,000 square feet of floor area, of which 1,743,443 square feet were added since World War II. Main operations headquartered in Pontiac included car assembly, sheet metal works, an axle plant, a foundry, and an engine factory. Engine blocks made in Pontiac were also furnished to other General Motors divisions. The company also produced the amphibious Otter, a continuous-track military vehicle used in the Korean War. Despite the defense operations, employment at Pontiac, Mich., was reduced from 16,000 workers at the end of 1950 to 12,500 in December 1951.

1952 PONTIAC

1952 Pontiac Chieftain Eight four-door station wagon. (OCW)

1952 CHIEFTAIN LINE — (SIX) SERIES 25 — (EIGHT) SERIES 27
— The fastback Streamliner line was discontinued and station wagons

1952 Pontiac Chieftain Deluxe Eight two-door convertible. (OCW)

joined the A-body notchback styles in the Chieftain line. Grilles were similar to 1951, but all models had four black oblong indentations in the upper grille blade, under a new Pontiac nameplate. Dual sweep spear body moldings, stainless steel gravel guards, and chrome wheel rings and headlight rings characterized Deluxe models. Standard models had Dark Gray check pattern cloth door trim and solid Gray wool cloth seats. Deluxe models were trimmed in rich wool diamond-pattern cloth with a button-back look. Convertibles and Deluxe Catalina hardtops had leather and cloth trims. Super Deluxe Catalinas had two-tone green top grain cowhide seats with leather and cloth trim optional. The Super Deluxe Catalina hardtop also carried special horizontally grooved trim plates on the rear roof pillar for outward identification. Standard station wagons featured seats in rust imitation leather. Deluxe station wagons offered a choice of Gray Bedford cord cloth with genuine leather in tan, red, green, blue, or black.

I.D. DATA: VIN located on tag on left front door post. Matching engine serial number located on raised pad on front left side of cylinder block. Serial numbers took the form ( )-[ ]W{ }-1001 to ( )-[ ]W{ }-ending number. First symbol ( ) indicated the assembly plant: P=Pontiac, Mich.; C=California (South Gate); L=Linden, N.J.; W=Wilmington, Del.; K=Kansas City, Kan.; A=Atlanta, Ga.; F=Framingham, Mass. Second symbol [ ] indicated engine type: 6=inline six-cylinder; 8=inline eight-cylinder. Third symbol indicated model year: W=1952. Fourth symbol { } is a letter indicating type of transmission: S=synchromesh; H=Hydra-Matic. Remaining symbols are the sequential unit production number for each car line at each assembly plant. Beginning number at each plant is 1001. Ending numbers for 1952 were: [Series 25 six with synchromesh] (Mich.) 10,041; (Calif.) 1723; (N.J.) 1986; (Del.) 1967; (Kan.) 2745; (Ga.) 1669 and (Mass.) 1551. [Series 25 six with/ Hydra-Matic] (Mich.) 3457; (Calif.) 1883; (N.J.) 1210; (Del.) 1223; (Kan.) 1406; (Ga.) 1165; (Mass.) 1103. [Series 27 eight with synchromesh] (Mich.) 16,833; (Calif.) 3440; (N.J.) 3920; (Del.) 3736; (Kan.) 6109; (Ga.) 3444 and (Mass.) 2312. [Series 27 eight with Hydra-Matic] (Mich.) 89,530; (Calif.) 20,083; (N.J.) 23,732; (Del.) 22,776; (Kan.) 39,194; (Ga.) 18,358 and (Mass.) 10,897. Fisher Body/style number on plate under hood on left of firewall can be helpful for identification of model and ordering parts. A prefix to the main number indicates model-year, 52=1952. The first two symbols in the main number indicate series 25 or 27. The next two symbols indicate the body style. Some numbers have an alphabetical suffix indicating trim level, such as D=Deluxe and SD=Super Deluxe. These numbers appear in body/style number column of charts below adjacent to corresponding body style listings.

1952 Pontiac Chieftain Deluxe Eight two-door sedan. (OCW)

1952 Pontiac Chieftain Eight four-door station wagon. (OCW)

1952 Pontiac Custom Catalina Eight two-door hardtop. (OCW)

Model Number	Body Style Number	Body Type & Seating	Factory Price	Shipping Weight	Production Total
CHIEFTAIN SIX					
6W	2569(D)	4d Sedan-6P	2,014/2,119	3,278/3,278	Note 1
6W	2511(D)	2d Sedan-6P	1,956/2,060	3,253/3,253	Note 1
6W	2563(D)	4d Sta Wagon-8/6P	2,615/2,699	3,593/3,528	Note 1
CHIEFTAIN DELUXE SIX					
6W	2537D	2d Catalina HT-6P	2,304	3,358	Note 1
6W	2567DTX	2d Convertible-6P	2,444	3,478	Note 1
CHIEFTAIN SUPER DELUXE SIX					
6W	2537SD	2d Catalina HT-6P	2,370	3,368	Note 1
CHIEFTAIN EIGHT					
8W	2569(D)	4d Sedan-6P	2,090/2,194	3,378/3,378	Note 1
8W	2511(D)	2d Sedan-6P	2,031/2,136	3,333/3,333	Note 1
8W	2562(D)	4d Sta Wagon-8/6P	2,689/2,772	2,688/3,633	Note 1
CHIEFTAIN DELUXE EIGHT					
8W	2537D	2d Catalina HT-6P	2,380	3,443	Note 1
8W	2567DTX	2d Convertible-6P	2,518	3,558	Note 1
CHIEFTAIN SUPER EIGHT					
8W	2537SD	2d Catalina HT-6P	2,446	3,448	Note 1

NOTE 1: See Historical Footnotes for series production total.

NOTE 2: Data above slash for standard/below slash for Deluxe.

NOTE 3: When (D) appears model came in both standard and Deluxe.

ENGINE [Six]: Six-cylinder. Inline. L-head. Cast-iron block. Displacement: 239.2 cid. Bore & stroke: 3-9/16 x 4 in. Compression Ratio: (synchromesh) 6.8:1; (Hydra-Matic) 7.7:1. Brake horsepower: (synchromesh) 100 at 3400 rpm; (Hydra-Matic) 102 at 3400 rpm. Four main bearings. Solid valve lifters. Carburetor: Rochester BC one-barrel.

1952 Pontiac Chieftain Eight two-door sedan delivery. (OCW)

1952 Pontiac Chieftain Deluxe Eight four-door sedan. (OCW)

ENGINE [Eight]: Eight-cylinder. Inline. L-head. Cast-iron block. Displacement: 268.4 cid. Bore & stroke: 3-3/8 x 3-3/4 in. Compression Ratios: (synchromesh) 6.8:1; (Hydra-Matic) 7.7:1. Brake horsepower: (synchromesh) 118 at 3600 rpm; (Hydra-Matic) 122 at 3600 rpm. Five main bearings. Solid valve lifters. Carburetor: Carter WCD 720S or WCD 720SA two-barrel.

CHASSIS: Wheelbase: 120 in. Overall Length: (cars) 202.5 in. (station wagons) 203.9 in. Front tread: 58 in. Rear tread: 59 in. Tires: (standard) 7.10 x 15 (special equipment) 7.60 x 15. Tube type.

OPTIONS: Seven-tube Chieftain radio. Mast antenna. No-Blo wind deflectors. Car cushions. Venti-Seat underseat heater. Venti-Shades. Windshield sun visor. Traffic light viewer. Polaroid visor. Rear fender panels (skirts). License frames. Illuminated hood ornament. Wheel trim rings. Steel wheel discs. White sidewall discs. Deluxe steering wheel. Remington Auto-Home shaver. Visor vanity mirror. Tissue dispenser. Direction signals. Compass. Rear window wiper. Windshield washers. Deluxe electric clock. Glove compartment light. Leather utility pocket. Luggage compartment light. Seat covers. Safti-Jack. Outside rearview mirror. Back-up lights. Safety spotlight. Fog lights. No-Rol. Bumper guards. Grille guard. Exhaust deflector. Venetian blinds. No-Mar gas filler trim. Fuel door lock. Scuff pads. Multi-purpose lamp. Underhood trouble lamp. Jack bag. Tool kit. A three-speed synchromesh gearbox with column shift was standard on all models. Hydra-Matic four-speed automatic transmission was available at $159 extra. Rear axle ratios: (standard) 4.1:1, (economy) 3.9:1, (mountain) 4.3:1, (Hydra-Matic) 3.08:1.

HISTORICAL: Production of 1952 Pontiacs began in November 1951. The new cars were introduced Dec. 3, 1951. Production was 277,156 cars for the calendar-year giving Pontiac fifth rank in the American auto industry. This was, however, a 19.4 percent decrease from 1951, which followed the general industry trend. Sedan Delivery truck production was held down under NPA Korean War guidelines that favored production of heavy-duty trucks. Only 984 Pontiac Sedan Deliveries were manufactured. Pontiac escaped a complete shutdown during a steel shortage in 1952, although production hit rock bottom in July. The division quickly got up steam after the strike ended, and achieved full utilization of resources in October when 32,843 cars were built. Model-year production included a total of 19,809 Series 25 Chieftain sixes (15,582 with Hydra-Matic and 4227 with synchromesh) and a total of 251,564 Series 27 Chieftain eights (218,602 with Hydra-Matic and 32,962 with synchromesh). Combined model-year assemblies were 271,373. Registration gains in five states—Arizona, Arkansas, Louisiana, Minnesota, and South Carolina—helped Pontiac capture 6.4 percent of 1952 U.S. new-car sales. Seven other states retained their same percentage. Michigan, Pontiac's home state, reported the highest state percentage (7.4), but New York claimed the highest number sold (23,156). In total 1952 car output, Pontiac accounted for 6.39 percent of industry production, against 6.44 percent in 1951. This gave it a secure hold on fifth place. Catalina Hardtops accounted for 19 percent of 1952 volume, edging up from 13 percent in 1951. Hydra-Matic Drive was used in 84 percent of all Pontiacs. Defense work went into high gear in 1952, with strong production on major contracts for all-aluminum amphibious cargo carriers (Otters), 4.5-in. rockets, and twin Bofors-type dual 40-mm cannon—plus a secret project launched late in the fall. With the defense work, Pontiac employment rose from 1951's low of 12,500 workers to more than 17,500. At year's end, Pontiac dealers had practically no new-cars in inventory and many orders for 1953 models. Also at the close of 1952, Pontiac entered its 60th year as a vehicle builder and its 45th in the automotive field—first under the Oakland designation and since 1926 with the Pontiac name. Arnold Lenz was general manager of Pontiac Motor Division. E.R. Pettengill was the administrative assistant to the general manager. L.W. Ward was general sales manager. George A. Delaney was chief engineer. Pontiac general manager Arnold Lenz was killed in a car-train crash at a Lapeer, Mich., railroad crossing. *Motor Trend* road tested the 1952 Pontiac Chieftain Deluxe sedan recording a 21-second quarter-mile run and top speed of 95.24 mph. Fuel economy was 16.4 mpg in overall driving.

1953 PONTIAC

1953 Pontiac Chieftain Deluxe Eight four-door sedan. (OCW)

CHIEFTAIN LINE — (SIX) SERIES 25 — (EIGHT) SERIES 27 — The 1953 Pontiacs were new from bumper to bumper. Changes included one-piece windshields; wraparound rear windows; new hood ornaments; ignition key starting; stepped-up rear fenders; more massive chrome headlight doors on all models; new grille styling that encircled parking lamps; and "panorama view" instrument panels. Standard models were now called Specials and came with small hubcaps, rubber gravel guards, straight upper beltline trim, and short arrow-shaped side trim. Deluxe Chieftains had long "dual streak" body moldings, stainless steel gravel guards with rear fender extensions, dipping belt moldings, and chrome full wheel discs. Eights had an '8' emblem between twin "Silver Streaks" on deck lids. Cars finished in Caravan Blue, Spruce Green, Marathon Gray, and Black had red Pontiac nameplates in front, while those done in other colors had black nameplates. The Custom Catalina hardtop was outwardly distinguished by horizontally grooved decorative trim plates at the rear

1953 Pontiac Chieftain Deluxe Eight two-door convertible. (OCW)

1953 Pontiac Custom Catalina Eight two-door hardtop. (OCW)

1953 Pontiac Chieftain Eight two-door sedan delivery. (OCW)

roof pillar edge. This car was available only in Laurel Green, Milano Ivory, or two-tone combinations of these hues. A nylon and leather interior of harmonizing tones was featured and an all-leather option was available and frequently ordered.

I.D. DATA: VIN located on tag on left front door post. Matching engine serial number located on raised pad on front left side of cylinder block. Serial numbers took the form ( )-[ ]X{ }-1001 to ( )-[ ]X{ }-ending number. First symbol ( ) indicated the assembly plant: P=Pontiac, Mich.; C=California (South Gate); L=Linden, N.J.; W=Wilmington, Del.; K=Kansas City, Kan.; A=Atlanta, Ga.; F=Framingham, Mass. Second symbol [ ] indicated engine type: 6=inline six-cylinder; 8=inline eight-cylinder. Third symbol indicated model year: X=1953. Fourth symbol { } is a letter indicating type of transmission: S=synchromesh; H=Hydra-Matic; P=Powerglide. Remaining symbols are the sequential unit production number for each car line at each assembly plant. Beginning number at each plant is 1001. Ending numbers for 1953 were: [SERIES 25 SIX with synchromesh] (Mich.) 18,925; (Calif.) 3115; (N.J.) 3799; (Del.) 3496; (Kan.) 4543; (Ga.) 2888 and (Mass.) 2691. [SERIES 25 SIX with/Hydra-Matic] (Mich.) 3872; (Calif.) 1227;

1953 Pontiac Chieftain Eight four-door station wagon. (OCW)

1953 Pontiac Chieftain Deluxe Eight two-door convertible. (OCW)

1953 Pontiac-Superior ambulance. (JAG)

(N.J.) 1163; (Del.) 1180; (Kan.) 1305; (Ga.) 1138; (Mass.) 1058. [SERIES 25 SIX with Powerglide] (Mich.) 1384. [SERIES 27 EIGHT with synchromesh] (Mich.) 35,914; (Calif.) 4469; (N.J.) 8264; (Del.) 6368; (Kan.) 9013; (Ga.) 6391 and (Mass.) 5041. [SERIES 27 EIGHT with Hydra-Matic] (Mich.) 117,860; (Calif.) 28,700; (N.J.) 30,873; (Del.) 28,720; (Kan.) 48,580; (Ga.) 25,799 and (Mass.) 19,391. [SERIES 27 EIGHT with Powerglide] (Mich.) 9950. Fisher Body/style number on plate under hood on left of firewall can be helpful for identification of model and ordering parts. A prefix to the main number indicates model year, 53=1953. The first two symbols in the main number indicate series 25 or 27. The next two symbols indicate the body style. Some numbers have an alphabetical suffix indicating trim level, such as D=Deluxe and SD=Super Deluxe. These numbers appear in body/style number column of charts below adjacent to corresponding body style listings.

Model Number	Body Style Number	Body Type & Seating	Factory Price	Shipping Weight	Production Total
CHIEFTAIN SPECIAL/CHIEFTAIN DELUXE SIX					
6X	2569W(D)	4d Sedan-6P	2,015/2,119	3,391/3,396	NA
6X	2511W(D)	2d Sedan-6P	1,956/2,060	3,341/3,356	NA
6X	2537D	2d Del Catalina-6P	2,304	3,416	NA
6X	2567DTX	2d Del Conv-6P	2,444	3,546	NA
6X	2563DF	4d Del Sta Wag-6P	2,590	3,636	NA
6X	2562(F)	4d Spl Sta Wag-8/6	2,450/2,505	3,633/3,606	NA
CHIEFTAIN CUSTOM SIX					
6X	2537SD	2d Cus Catalina-6P	2,370	3,416	NA

1953 Pontiac-Star Chief convertible prototype. (OCW)

1953 Pontiac-Superior funeral car. (JAG)

Model Number	Body Style Number	Body Type & Seating	Factory Price	Shipping Weight	Production Total
CHIEFTAIN SPECIAL/CHIEFTAIN DELUXE EIGHT					
8X	2569W(D)	4d Sedan-6P	2,090/2,194	3,456/3,471	NA
8X	2511W(D)	2d Sedan-6P	2,031/2,136	3,421/3,436	NA
8X	2537D	2d Del Catalina-6P	2,380	3,496	NA
8X	2567DTX	2d Del Conv-6P	2,515	3,626	NA
8X	2562DF	4-Del Sta Wag-6P	2,664	3,716	NA
8X	2562(F)	4d Spl Sta Wag-8/6	2,525/2,580	3,713/3,686	NA
CHIEFTAIN CUSTOM EIGHT					
8X	2537SD	2d Cus Catalina-6P	2446	3,496	NA

NOTE 1: See Historical Footnotes for series production total.

NOTE 2: Data above slash for standard/below slash for Deluxe.

NOTE 3: (D) indicates available in both Special and Deluxe sub-series.

Notes on model nomenclature: Body style suffix 'SD' indicates Super Deluxe trim. The term Catalina was Pontiac's nomenclature for pillarless hardtop styling. Body style 2562, the Special station wagon, came standard with three seats. Body style 2562F was the Special station wagon with two seats, the second of the folding type. Body style 2537SD, T Body Style numbers were embossed on the firewall data plate and preceded by the prefix '53' to designate the model year.

ENGINE [Six]: Six-cylinder. Inline. L-head. Cast-iron block. Displacement: 239.2 cid. Bore & stroke: 3-9/16 x 4 in. Compression Ratio: (synchromesh) 7.0:1; (Hydra-Matic) 7.7:1. Brake horsepower: (synchromesh) 115 at 3800 rpm; (Hydra-Matic) 118 at 3800 rpm. Four main bearings. Solid valve lifters. Carburetor: Carter WCD-2010-S two-barrel.

ENGINE [Eight]: Eight-cylinder. Inline. L-head. Cast-iron block. Displacement: 268.4 cid. Bore & stroke: 3-3/8 x 3-3/4 in. Compression Ratios: (synchromesh) 6.8:1; (Hydra-Matic) 7.7:1. Brake horsepower: (synchromesh) 118 at 3600 rpm; (Hydra-Matic) 122 at 3600 rpm. Five main bearings. Solid valve lifters. Carburetors: (synchromesh) Carter WCD 719S or 719SA; (Hydra-Matic) Carter WCD 720S or 720SA two-barrel.

CHASSIS: [All] Wheelbase: 122 in. Overall Length: (passenger cars) 202-11/16 in.; (station wagons) 205.3 in. Front tread: 58.5 in. Rear tread: 59.05 in. Tires: (passenger cars) 7.10 x 15 four-ply; (regular equipment station wagons and sedan deliveries/optional passenger cars) 7.10 x 15 six-ply; (optional passenger cars only) 7.60 x 15 four-ply. Pontiac promoted new "Tru-Arc" safety steering and "Curve Control" front suspension in 1953.

OPTIONS: Power steering ($134). Wood grain Di-Noc exterior trim ($80 all station wagons). Venti-heat underseat heater and defroster. Chieftain seven-tube radio. Directional signals. Autronic Eye. Back-up lamps. Non-glare rearview mirror. Rear fender panels (skirts came

1953 Pontiac-station wagon. (OCW)

with steel underscore on Deluxes). Exhaust deflector. No-Mar fuel guard door trim. Deluxe steering wheel (standard on Deluxes). Illuminated hood ornament. Windshield sun visor. Traffic light viewer. Latex foam seat cushions. Windshield washers. Outside rearview mirror. Visor vanity mirror. Glove box lamp. Trunk lamp. Underhood lamp. Lighted ashtray. Hand brake signal. Grille guard. Wing guards. E-Z-Eye glass. Dual fog lamps. Rear seat speaker. Electric antenna. Safety spot lamp. Chrome trim rings. Safti-jack. Oil bath air cleaner. (Dealer installed options): Seat covers. Hand spot lamp. Ventishades. Fold-away umbrella. Draft deflectors; Rear window wiper. Tissue dispenser. Magna Tray. Fuel door lock. Illuminated compass. Color tipon. Road reflector flares. Thermaster refrigerator. Thermaster bottle. Auto-Home Remington electric shaver. Continental tire extension. Simulated wire wheel discs. A three-speed synchromesh gearbox with column-mounted gearshift was standard on all models. Dual-Range four-speed Hydra-Matic drive was available at $178 extra. Two-speed Powerglide automatic transmission (by Chevrolet) was installed in Pontiacs built at Pontiac, Mich., from Sept. 8, 1953, to Nov. 19, 1953, after an August 12 fire at GM's Livonia, Mich., Hydra-Matic factory. Rear axle ratios: (six) 4.1:1; (Eight) 3.9:1; (six/mountain) 4.3:1, (eight/mountain) 4.1:1; (Hydra-Matic) 3.08:1. The high-compression Hydra-Matic cylinder head was available, as an option, on cars with synchromesh.

HISTORICAL: A total of 38,914 Chieftain sixes were built. Of these, 33,705 had synchromesh; 4,507 had Hydra-Matic and 702 had Powerglide attachments. A total of 379,705 Chieftain eights were built. Of these, 68,565 had synchromesh; 293,343 had Hydra-Matic and 17,797 had Powerglide attachments. Production lines started cranking out 1953 Pontiacs on November 17 of the previous year and they were introduced to the public Dec. 6, 1952. Model year output came to 418,619 units. The calendar year counted production of 414,011 cars. This maintained Pontiac's rank as the fifth largest American automaker another season. After the devastating fire August 12 at the Hydra-Matic transmission plant in Livonia, Mich., cars were made for a time at the Pontiac, Mich., factory, with Chevrolet Powerglide transmissions installed. Following the untimely death of Arnold Lenz, Robert Critchfield became general manager of Pontiac Motor Div. Plans to install V-8s in 1953 Pontiacs were set back by Lenz's fatal accident and flathead straight eights continued to be used. However, the 1953 Pontiac chassis is designed to accommodate the 1955-style V-8.

1954 PONTIAC

1954 Pontiac Chieftain Deluxe Eight four-door sedan. (OCW)

CHIEFTAIN LINE — (SIX) SERIES 25 — (EIGHT) SERIES 27 — In 1954 the Chieftains represented Pontiac's least costly line of A-body models on a 122-in. wheelbase and had styling changes common to all Pontiacs. Included were a grille with an oval centerpiece; new hood ornament and nameplate; and thinner "Silver Streaks." Chieftain Specials had straight upper beltline moldings; small stainless steel gravel guards; four "Silver Streaks" on the deck lid; and short front fender spears. Chieftain Deluxes had broad, full-length "sweepspears" that blended into the gravel guards; the gravel guards had rear fender extensions and the upper beltline trim "dipped" down. There were also four deck lid streaks. The Chieftain Custom series included

1954 Pontiac Chieftain Deluxe Eight four-door sedan. (JAG)

1954 Pontiac Star Chief Eight Custom Catalina two-door hardtop. (OCW)

1954 Pontiac Star Chief Eight Custom Catalina two-door hardtop. (OCW)

the 'Super Deluxe' Catalina hardtop, which was outwardly distinguished by decorative edge plates on the roof pillars. Custom Catalina hardtops also have special plated interior roof bows. Interior trims ranged from two-tone pattern cloth-and-elascofab combinations on standard models to all-leather options on Catalinas, convertibles and Deluxe station wagons. A new B-O-P assembly plant in Arlington, Texas, began operations this year.

STAR CHIEF LINE — (EIGHT) SERIES 28 — A brand new long wheelbase Star Chief line was created by adding an 11-inch frame extension towards the rear of the GM A-body platform and fitting longer rear sheet metal. Two "28" sub-series, Deluxe and Custom, were provided. Both came only with eight-cylinder power. All Star Chiefs had five "Silver Streaks" on the deck lid, special visored taillight doors with rear fender extensions, longer sweep spears and three small stylized stars on rear fender fins. Deluxe trims were regular equipment, but the "Super Deluxe" Custom Sedan and Custom Catalina were further distinguished by extra-rich cloth-and-leather upholstery inside and distinctive roof trim outside. The Star Chief Custom Catalina hardtops also have special plated interior roof bows.

I.D. DATA: VIN located on tag on left front door post. Matching engine serial number located on raised pad on front left side of cylinder block. Serial numbers took the form ( )-[ ]X{ }-1001 to ( )-[

1954 Pontiac Chieftain Deluxe Eight Catalina two-door hardtop. (JAG)

1954 Pontiac Star Chief Deluxe Eight convertible. (JAG)

]X{ }-ending number. First symbol ( ) indicated the assembly plant: P=Pontiac, Mich.; C=California (South Gate); L=Linden, N.J.; W=Wilmington, Del.; K=Kansas City, Kan.; A=Atlanta, Ga.; F=Framingham, Mass.; T=Arlington, Texas. Second symbol [ ] indicated engine type: 6=inline six-cylinder; 8=inline eight-cylinder. Third symbol indicated model year: Z=1954. Fourth symbol { } is a letter indicating type of transmission: S=synchromesh; H=Hydra-Matic or (Star Chief only) C=conventional (synchromesh); A=automatic (Hydra-Matic). Remaining symbols are the sequential unit production number for each car line at each assembly plant. Beginning number at each plant is 1001. Ending numbers for 1954 were: [SERIES 25 SIX with synchromesh] (Mich.) 12,141; (Calif.) 1799; (N.J.) 2429; (Dela.) 2233; (Kan.) 2622; (Ga.) 1866 and (Mass.) 2033; (Texas) 1399. [SERIES 25 SIX with/Hydra-Matic] (Mich.) 2858; (Calif.) 1076; (N.J.) 1090; (Del.) 1096; (Kan.) 1117; (Ga.) 1067; (Mass.) 1053.; (Texas) 1023. [SERIES 27 EIGHT with synchromesh] (Mich.) 16612; (Calif.) 2351; (N.J.) 3471; (Del.) 3032; (Kan.) 3890; (Ga.) 3265; (Mass.) 3146; (Texas) 2043. [SERIES 27 EIGHT with Hydra-Matic] (Mich.) 60,891; (Calif.) 8698; (N.J.) 16,002; (Del.) 10,002; (Kan.) 12,490; (Ga.) 7477; (Mass.) 7854; (Texas) 4330. [SERIES 28 with synchromesh] (Mich.) 1371; (Calif.) 1015; (N.J.) 1046; (Del.) 1049; (Kan.) 1036; (Ga.) 1010; (Mass.) 1035; (Texas) 1008. [SERIES 28 with Hydra-Matic] (Mich.) 60,543; (Calif.) 8165; (N.J.) 13,680; (Del.) 8629; (Kan.) 12,117; (Ga.) 8076; (Mass.) 6382; (Texas) 4925. Fisher Body/style number on plate under hood on left of firewall can be helpful for identification of model and ordering parts. A prefix to the main number indicates model year, 54=1954. The first two symbols in the main number indicate series 25, 27, or 28 Star Chief. The next two symbols indicate the body style. Some numbers have an alphabetical suffix indicating trim level, such as D=Deluxe and SD=Super Deluxe. These numbers appear in body/style number column of charts below adjacent to corresponding body style listings.

1954 Pontiac Star Chief Eight Custom Catalina two-door hardtop. (OCW)

Model Number	Body Style Number	Body Type & Seating	Factory Price	Shipping Weight	Production Total
CHIEFTAIN SIX SPECIAL/DELUXE					
6Z	2569W(D)	4d Sedan-6P	2,027/2,131	3,391/3,406	NA
6Z	2511W(D)	2d Sedan-6P	1,968/2,072	3,331/3,351	NA
6Z	2537D	2d Del Cat HT-6P	2,316	3,421	NA
6Z	2562DF	4d Del Sta Wag-6P	2,504	3,646	NA
6Z	2562(F)	4d Spl Sta Wag-8/6	2,364/2,419	3,691/3,601	NA
CHIEFTAIN CUSTOM SIX					
6Z	2537SD	2d Cus Cat HT-6P	2,582	3,421	NA
CHIEFTAIN EIGHT SPECIAL/DELUXE					
8Z	2569W(D)	4d Sedan-6P	2,102/2,206	3,451/3,466	NA
8Z	2511W(D)	2d Sedan-6P	2,043/2,148	3,396/3,416	NA
8Z	2537D	2d Del Cat HT-6P	2,392	3,491	NA
8Z	2562DF	4d Del Sta Wag-6P	2,579	3,716	NA
8Z	2562(F)	4d Spl Sta Wag-8/6	2,439/2,494	3,771/3,676	NA
CHIEFTAIN CUSTOM EIGHT					
8Z	2537SD	2d Cus Cat HT-6P	2,458	3,491	NA
STAR CHIEF DELUXE (LONG-DECK)					
8Z	2869WD	4d Sedan-6P	2,301	3,536	NA
8Z	2867DTX	2d Convertible-6P	2,630	3,776	NA
STAR CHIEF CUSTOM (LONG-DECK)					
8Z	2869WSD	4d Sedan-6P	2,394	3,526	NA
8Z	2837SD	2d Cus Cat HT-6P	2,557	3,551	NA

NOTE 1: See Historical Footnotes for series production total.

NOTE 2: Data above slash for standard/below slash for Deluxe.

NOTE 3: (D) indicates model is available in Special and Deluxe sub-series.

NOTE 4: (F) indicates folding second seat in station wagons.

ENGINE [Six]: Six-cylinder. Inline. L-head. Cast-iron block. Displacement: 239.2 cid. Bore & stroke: 3-9/16 x 4 in. Compression Ratio: (synchromesh) 7.0:1; (Hydra-Matic) 7.7:1. Brake horsepower: (synchromesh) 115 at 3800 rpm; (Hydra-Matic) 118 at 3800 rpm. Four main bearings. Solid valve lifters. Carburetor: Carter WCD-2010-S two-barrel.

ENGINE [Eight]: Eight-cylinder. Inline. L-head. Cast-iron block. Displacement: 268.4 cid. Bore & stroke: 3-3/8 x 3-3/4 in. Compression Ratios: (synchromesh) 6.8:1; (Hydra-Matic) 7.7:1. Brake horsepower: (synchromesh) 122 at 3800 rpm; (Hydra-Matic) 127 at 3800 rpm. Five main bearings. Solid valve lifters. Carburetors: (synchromesh) Carter WCD 719SA used in early production; WCD 720SA used on most; (Hydra-Matic) Carter WCD 2122S.

CHASSIS: Wheelbase: (Chieftains) 122 in.; (Star Chiefs) 124 in. Overall Length: (Chieftain passenger cars) 202-11/16 in.; (Chieftain station wagons) 205.3 in.; (Star Chiefs) 213.7 in. Front tread: (All) 58.5 in. Rear tread: (All) 59.05 in. Tires: (passenger cars) 7.10 x 15 four-ply; (station wagons) 7.10 x 15 six-ply; (optional passenger cars only) 7.60 x 15 four-ply.

OPTIONS: Power steering ($134). Wood grain Di-Noc exterior trim ($80 all station wagons). Venti-heat underseat heater and defroster. Chieftain 7-tube radio. Directional signals. Autronic Eye. Back-up lamps. Non-glare rearview mirror. Rear fender panels (skirts came with steel underscore on Deluxes). Exhaust deflector. No-Mar fuel guard door trim. Deluxe steering wheel (standard on Deluxes). Illuminated

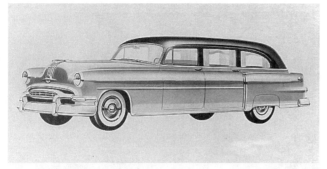

1954 Pontiac Meteor funeral car. (JAG)

hood ornament. Windshield sun visor. Traffic light viewer. Latex foam seat cushions. Windshield washers. Outside rearview mirror. Visor vanity mirror. Glove box lamp. Trunk lamp. Underhood lamp. Lighted ashtray. Hand brake signal. Grille guard. Wing guards. E-Z-Eye glass. Dual fog lamps. Rear seat speaker. Electric antenna. Safety spot lamp. Chrome trim rings. Safti-jack. Oil bath air cleaner. (Dealer installed options): Seat covers. Hand spot lamp. Venti-shades. Fold-away umbrella. Draft deflectors; Rear window wiper. Tissue dispenser. Magna Tray. Fuel door lock. Illuminated compass. Color tipon. Road reflector flares. Thermaster refrigerator. Thermaster bottle. Auto-Home Remington electric shaver. Continental tire extension. Simulated wire wheel discs. Power brakes ($36). Air-conditioning. Electric window lifts. Padded dashboard. Door edge guards. Door handle guards. Arctic windshield wipers. Dash panel courtesy lamps. Wide brake pedals. Reduced ratio power steering. Grille bug screen. Comfort-Control 300-position manual seat. Remote control outside mirrors. Deluxe steering wheel for Special station wagons. A three-speed synchromesh gearbox with column-mounted gearshift was standard on all models. Dual-Range four-speed Hydra-Matic drive was available at $178 extra. Rear axle ratios: (six) 4.1:1; (eight) 3.9:1; (Star Chief with Hydra-Matic) 3.23:1 (six/mountain) 4.3:1, (eight/mountain) 4.1:1; (Hydra-Matic) 3.08:1. The high-compression Hydra-Matic cylinder head was available, as an option, on cars with synchromesh.

HISTORICAL: Production began Dec. 1, 1953. The 1954 models were introduced Dec. 18, 1953. Calendar year production was 370,887 cars. Model year production was 287,744 cars. The only model year production breakouts available are: [Chieftain] A total of 22,670 Chieftain sixes were built. Of these 19,666 had synchromesh and 3,004 had Hydra-Matic attachments. A total of 149,986 Chieftain eights were built. Of these, 29,906 had synchromesh and 120,080 had Hydra-Matic attachments. [Star Chief] A total of 115,088 Star Chiefs were built. Of these, 571 had synchromesh and 114,517 had Hydra-Matic attachments. The new Buick-Olds-Pontiac (BOP) assembly plant in Arlington, Texas, opened on June 3, 1953. A Catalina hardtop built on June 18, 1954, was the company's five millionth automobile produced. The sedan delivery was not cataloged this year although rumors persist that four were built in early production.

1955 PONTIAC

1955 Pontiac Chieftain 860 Colony station wagon. (OCW)

1955 Pontiac Chieftain 870 two-door sedan. (OCW)

1955 Pontiac Chieftain 870 four-door sedan. (OCW)

CHIEFTAIN LINE — (V-8) — SERIES 27 — Completely new bodies and chassis were featured on all 1955 Pontiacs. Changes from 1954 included a massive, divided bumper grille; revised body moldings; split Silver Streak bands; twin streaks atop rear fenders; swept style front wheel cutouts; and wraparound windshields. Chieftains were divided into three sub-series. One was a unique station wagon. This Custom Safari had two-door hardtop styling and Star Chief trim and appointments on the smaller Series 27 chassis. The two-door Custom

1955 Pontiac Star Chief two-door convertible. (OCW)

1955 Pontiac Star Chief Custom two-door Safari. (OCW)

1955 Pontiac Star Chief Custom two-door Safari. (OCW)

1955 Pontiac Star Chief Custom Catalina two-door hardtop. (OCW)

Safari was announced Jan. 31, 1955. These Safaris feature two-door hardtop styling with slanting tailgates, width-wise grooved roofs, Pontiac rear fenders, and luxury interior appointments. Except for this offering, which was really considered a Star Chief, Chieftains featured constant width slanting vertical slash moldings. Chieftain 860s had small hubcaps; painted taillight housings, and no upper beltline moldings. Chieftain 870s had full wheel discs, chrome taillight rings, and upper beltline trim.

1955 Pontiac Star Chief two-door convertible. (JAG)

1955 Pontiac Star Chief four-door sedan. (JAG)

1955 Pontiac Memphis Coach Co. Memphibian ambulance. (JAG)

STAR CHIEF LINE — (V-8) — SERIES 28 — Completely new A-body styling with an 11-inch rear frame extension characterized the 1955 Star Chiefs. All models featured tapered slanting vertical slash moldings, which were also used on the Series 27 two-door Star Chief Custom Safari. Star Chiefs, including the Safari, had three stylized star emblems on front fenders and doors. The Catalina coupe and the convertible had wide fluted lower rear fender extensions. The Custom four-door sedan had stainless steel moldings encircling the side windows. Full wheel discs were regular equipment on all Star Chiefs.

I.D. DATA: VIN located on left front door hinge pillar. Matching engine serial number on pad on front of right-hand cylinder bank. Serial numbers took the form ( )-[ ]55{ }-1001 to ( )-[ ]55{ }-ending number. The first symbol ( ) was a letter indicating assembly plant: P=Pontiac, Mich.; T=Arlington, Texas; A=Atlanta, Ga.; F=Framingham, Mass.; K=Kansas City, Kan.; L=Linden, N.J.; C=South Gate, Calif.; W=Wilmington, Del. The second symbol [ ] indicated series: 7=Series 27; 8=Series 28. The third and fourth symbols indicated model year: 55=1955. The fifth symbol indicated transmission: S=synchromesh; H=Hydra-Matic. The following symbols were the sequential unit production number starting at 1001 for each series at each assembly plant. Ending numbers for 1955 were: [SERIES 27 with synchromesh] (Mich.) 26879; (Texas) 3331; (Ga.) 6802; (Mass.) 4714; (Kan.) 5868; (N.J.) 6536; (Calif.) 4572; (Del.) 5564. [SERIES 27 with Hydra-Matic] (Mich.) 12,6714; (Texas) 14,339; (Ga.) 26,027; (Mass.) 15,847; (Kan.) 30,873; (N.J.) 33,154; (Calif.) 31,707; (Del.) 24,851. [SERIES 28 with synchromesh] (Mich.) 1696; (Texas) 1026; (Ga.) 1018; (Mass.) 1085; (Kan.) 1061; (N.J.) 1134; (Calif.) 1061; (Del.) 1075. [SERIES 28 with Hydra-Matic] (Mich.) 85,247; (Texas) 10,511; (Ga.) 17,315; (Mass.) 10,484; (Kan.) 20,584; (N.J.) 24,173; (Calif.) 20,372; (Del.) 17,278. Fisher Body/style number on plate under hood on left of firewall can be helpful for identification of model and ordering parts. A prefix to the main number indicates model year, 55=1955. The first two symbols in the main number indicate series 27 or 28 Star Chief. The next two symbols indicate the body style. Some numbers have an alphabetical suffix indicating trim level, such as D=Deluxe and SD=Super Deluxe. These numbers appear in body/style number column of charts below adjacent to corresponding body style listings.

Model Number	Body Style Number	Body Type & Seating	Factory Price	Shipping Weight	Production Total
CHIEFTAIN 860 (SPECIAL)					
860-27	2519	4-dr Sedan-6P	2,164	3,621	65,155
860-27	2511	2-dr Sedan-6P	2,105	3,586	58,654
860-27	2562	4-dr Sedan-6P	2,518	3,736	6,091
860-27	2563F	2-dr Sta Wagon-6P	2,434	3,736	8,618
CHIEFTAIN 870 (DELUXE)					
870-27	2519D	4-dr Sedan-6P	2,268	3,621	91,187
870-27	2511D	2-dr Sedan-6P	2,209	3,586	28,950
870-27	2537D	2-dr Del Cat HT-6P	2,335	3,631	72,608
870-27	2563DF	4-dr Sta Wagon-6P	2,603	3,786	19,439
STAR CHIEF CUSTOM SAFARI (SERIES 27)					
27	2764DF	2-dr Sta Wagon-6P	2,962	3,746	3,760
STAR CHIEF (SERIES 28)					
28	2819D	4-dr Sedan-6P	2,362	3,666	44,800
28	2867DTX	2-dr Convertible-6P	2,691	3,901	19,762
STAR CHIEF CUSTOM (SERIES 28)					
28	2819SD	4-dr Sedan-6P	2,455	3,666	35,153
28	2837SD	2-dr Cat HT-6P	2,499	3,676	99,929

NOTE 1: 354,466 Chieftain 860s and 870s were built.

NOTE 2: 57,730 had synchromesh and 296,736 had Hydra-Matic.

NOTE 3: Two Series 27 chassis were converted into hearses or ambulances.

NOTE 4: 199,624 Series 28 Star Chiefs were built.

NOTE 5: 1156 had synchromesh and 198,468 had Hydra-Matic.

NOTE 6: 280 Series 28 chassis were converted into hearses or ambulances.

ENGINE [Synchromesh V-8]: Overhead valves. Cast-iron block. Displacement: 287.2 cid. Bore & stroke: 3-3/4 x 3-1/4 in. Compression Ratio: 7.4:1. Brake horsepower: 173 at 4400 rpm. Five main bearings. Hydraulic valve lifters. Carburetors: Carter WGD models 2182S, 2182SA, 2182SB, 2207S, or 2207SB two-barrel. Also, Rochester 2GC two-barrel.

ENGINE [Hydra-Matic V-8]: Overhead valves. Cast-iron block. Displacement: 287.2 cid. Bore & stroke: 3-3/4 x 3-1/4 in. Compression Ratio: 8.0:1. Brake horsepower: 180 at 4600 rpm. Five main bearings. Hydraulic valve lifters. Carburetors: Carter WGD models 2182S, 2182SA, 2182SB, 2207S, or 2207SB two-barrel. Also, Rochester 2GC two-barrel.

CHASSIS: Wheelbase: (Series 27) 122 in.; (Series 28) 124 in. Overall Length: (Series 27 passenger cars) 203.2 in.; (Series 27 station wagons) 202.9 in.; (Series 28) 210.2 in. Front tread: (All) 58.66 in. Rear tread: (All) 59.05 in. Tires: (passenger cars) 7.10 x 15; (station wagons) 7.60 x 15, tubeless type. The use of 7.60 x 15 tires was recommended for Star Chiefs.

OPTIONS: Power steering ($108). Power brakes ($36). Fender skirts ($11). Power windows ($97). Four-way power seat ($40). Venti-heat underseat heater and defroster. Chieftain seven-tube radio. Directional signals. Autronic Eye. Back-up lamps. Non-glare rearview mirror. Exhaust deflector. No-Mar fuel guard door trim. Deluxe steering wheel (standard on Deluxes). Illuminated hood ornament. Windshield sun visor. Traffic light viewer. Latex foam seat cushions. Windshield washers. Outside rearview mirror. Visor vanity mirror. Glove box lamp. Trunk lamp. Underhood lamp. Lighted ashtray. Handbrake signal. Grille guard. Wing guards. E-Z-Eye glass. Dual fog lamps. Rear seat speaker. Electric antenna. Safety spot lamp. Chrome trim rings. Saftijack. Oil bath air cleaner. (Dealer installed options): Seat covers. Hand spot lamp. Venti-shades. Fold-away umbrella. Draft deflectors; Rear window wiper. Tissue dispenser. Magna Tray. Fuel door lock. Illuminated compass. Color tipon. Road reflector flares. Thermaster refrigerator. Thermaster bottle. Auto-Home Remington electric shaver. Continental tire extension. Simulated wire wheel discs. Power brakes ($36). Air-conditioning. Electric window lifts. Padded dashboard. Door edge guards. Door handle guards. Arctic windshield wipers. Dash panel courtesy lamps. Wide brake pedals. Reduced ratio power steering. Grille bug screen. Comfort-Control 300-position manual seat. Remote control outside mirrors. Deluxe steering wheel for Special station wagons. A three-speed synchromesh gearbox with column-mounted gearshift was standard on all models. Dual-Range four-speed Hydra-Matic drive was available at $178 extra. Available after March 1, 1955, for $35 was an optional engine "power-pack." It consisted of a Rochester 4GC four-barrel carburetor providing a boost of 20 hp over standard V-8s or a maximum of 200 hp on Hydra-Matic equipped cars. Carter WCFB model 2268S and 2283S four-barrel carburetors were also used on some 1955 Pontiacs as optional equipment. A variety of rear axle gear ratios was available.

HISTORICAL: Production of 1955 Pontiacs started Oct. 4, 1954. They were introduced to the public 15 days later, with the Star Chief Custom two-door Safari bowing the following January 31. Calendar year production of 581,860 cars made Pontiac America's sixth ranked manufacturer. Hydra-Matic transmission was in 90.6 percent of these cars. Model year production was 554,090 units. The new engine introduced in 1955 was Pontiac's *first* overhead valve V-8, although it was the *second* V-8 for the company, as the first had been used in 1932 models. An all-time monthly production record was recorded in December 1955. Chieftain station wagons for 1955 utilized Chevrolet station wagon rear fender styling. Styles number 2562 and 2562DF had distinctive rear ventipanes. The two-door Chieftain station wagon, style number 2563F, was sometimes called the Colony wagon.

1956 PONTIAC

CHIEFTAIN LINE — (V-8) — SE RIES 27 — New Pontiac styling for 1956 featured combination bumper grilles with enclosed circular

1956 Pontiac Chieftain 870 four-door station wagon. (OCW)

parking lights and round, bomb-type bumper guards. All models had reversed vertically slanting slash accent moldings and sweep spear body rub trim. On Chieftains the slash accents were of constant width. There were reflectorized oval embossments on rear fenders with gull-wing and circle medallions on the deck lid. Special level Chieftain 860s lacked upper belt moldings, wore small hubcaps, and had plain taillight rings. Deluxe level Chieftain 870 models (except station wagons) had visored taillight rings, full wheel discs, and upper beltline trim. The two-door Custom Safari was continued as a Star Chief on the Chieftain chassis, now with the base four-barrel Star Chief engine. An 860 Catalina Coupe was new as were 860 and 870 four-door hardtops, the latter pair designated as Catalina Sedans. In some factory literature Chieftain 870s are called Super Chiefs.

STAR CHIEF LINE — (V-8) — SERIES 28 — All Star Chiefs were distinguished by tapered diagonal accent slash moldings on front doors and three stylized star emblems on front fenders and doors. Catalinas and convertibles had wide fluted lower rear fender extensions. The Custom Catalina sedan had stainless steel window surround moldings and all Custom Star Chiefs used hooded taillight rings.

I.D. DATA: VIN located on left front door hinge pillar. Matching engine serial number on pad on front of right-hand cylinder bank. Serial numbers took the form ( )-[ ]56{ }-1001 to ( )-[ ]56{ }-ending number. The first symbol ( ) was a letter indicating assembly plant: P=Pontiac, Mich.; T=Arlington, Texas; A=Atlanta, Ga.; F=Framingham, Mass.; K=Kansas City, Kan.; L=Linden, N.J.; C=South Gate, Calif.; W=Wilmington, Del. The second symbol [ ] indicated series: 7=Series 27; 8=Series 28. The third and fourth symbols indicated model year: 56=1956. The fifth symbol indicated transmission: S=synchromesh; H=Hydra-Matic. The following symbols were the sequential unit production number starting at

1956 Pontiac Custom Star Chief Safari two-door station wagon. (OCW)

1956 Pontiac 860 two-door sedan. (OCW)

1956 Pontiac Star Chief Custom Catalina four-door hardtop. (OCW)

1001 for each series at each assembly plant. Ending numbers for 1956 were: [SERIES 27 with synchromesh] (Mich.) 12,447; (Texas) 2383; (Ga.) 3633; (Mass.) 3050; (Kan.) 3526; (N.J.) 3089; (Calif.) 3117; (Del.) 3139. [SERIES 27 with Hydra-Matic] (Mich.) 97,877; (Texas) 14,815; (Ga.) 22,073; (Mass.) 13,307; (Kan.) 27,978; (N.J.) 26,487; (Calif.) 33,138; (Del.) 26,575. [SERIES 28 with synchromesh] (Mich.) 1259; (Texas) 1016; (Ga.) 1013; (Mass.) 1038; (Kan.) 1022; (N.J.) 1052; (Calif.) 1014; (Del.) 1026. [SERIES 28 with Hydra-Matic] (Mich.) 47,697; (Texas) 8896; (Ga.) 11,452; (Mass.) 6999; (Kan.) 13,124; (N.J.) 13,766; (Calif.) 15,590; (Del.) 13,092. Fisher Body/style number on plate under hood on left of firewall can be helpful for identification of model and ordering parts. A prefix to the main number indicates model year, 56=1956. The first two symbols in the main number indicate series 27 or 28 Star Chief. The next two symbols indicate the body style. Some numbers have an alphabetical suffix indicating trim level, such as D=Deluxe and SD=Super Deluxe. These numbers appear in body/style number column of charts below adjacent to corresponding body style listings.

Model Number	Body Style Number	Body Type & Seating	Factory Price	Shipping Weight	Production Total
CHIEFTAIN 860 (SPECIAL)					
860-27	2719	4d Sedan-6P	2,294	3,617	41,987
860-27	2739	4d Catalina HT-6P	2,439	3,682	35,201
860-27	2711	2d Sedan-6P	2,236	3,557	41,908
860-27	2737	2d Catalina HT-6P	2,366	3,617	46,335
860-27	2763	2d Sta Wagon-6P	2,564	3,717	6,099
860-27	2762FC	4d Sta Wagon-6P	2,648	3,812	12,702
CHIEFTAIN 870 (DE LUXE)					
870-27	2719D	4d Sedan-6P	2,409	3,617	22,082
870-27	2739D	4d Catalina HT-6P	2,530	3,682	25,372
870-27	2737D	2d Catalina HT-6P	2,476	3,617	24,744
870-27	2763DF	4d Sta Wagon-6P	2,744	3,762	21,674
STAR CHIEF CUSTOM SAFARI (SERIES 27)					
27	2764DF	2d Sta Wagon-6P	3,124	3,762	4,042
STAR CHIEF (SERIES 28)					
28	819D	4d Sedan-6P	2,523	3,697	18,346
28	2867DTX	2d Convertible-6P	2,853	3,917	13,510
STAR CHIEF CUSTOM (SERIES 28)					
28	2839SD	4d Catalina HT-6P	2,731	3,767	48,035
28	2837SD	2d Catalina HT-6P	2,661	3,687	43,392

1956 Pontiac Star Chief four-door sedan. (JAG)

1956 Pontiac Star Chief convertible. (OCW)

1956 Pontiac Star Chief Catalina two-door hardtop. (OCW)

NOTE 1: 184,232 Chieftain 860s were built.

NOTE 2: 24,117 Chieftain 860s had synchromesh and 160,115 had Hydra-Matic.

NOTE 3: 93,872 Chieftain 870s (or Super Chiefs) were built.

NOTE 4: 3,289 Chieftain 870s had synchromesh and 90,583 had Hydra-Matic.

NOTE 5: 10 Custom Safaris had synchromesh and 4,032 had Hydra-Matic.

NOTE 6: 123,584 Series 28 Star Chiefs were built.

NOTE 7: 440 had synchromesh and 123,144 had Hydra-Matic.

NOTE 8: Does not include two-door Star Chief Custom Safari.

NOTE 9: 301 vehicles converted into professional vehicles.

ENGINE [Chieftain synchromesh]: V-8: Overhead valves. Cast-iron block. Displacement: 316.6 cid. Bore & stroke: 3.94 x 3.25 in. Compression Ratio: 7.9:1. Brake horsepower: 192 at 4400 rpm. Five main bearings. Hydraulic valve lifters. Carburetor: Rochester 2GC two-barrel with black tag number 8696. The two-door Custom Safari came standard with a Star Chief four-barrel V-8.

ENGINE [Chieftain Hydra-Matic]: V-8: Overhead valves. Cast-iron block. Displacement: 316.6 cid. Bore & stroke: 3.94 x 3.25 in. Compression Ratio: 8.9:1. Brake horsepower: 205 at 4800 rpm. Five main bearings. Hydraulic valve lifters. Carburetor: Rochester 2GC two-barrel with brass tag number 8695. The two-door Custom Safari came standard with a Star Chief four-barrel V-8.

ENGINE [Star Chief synchromesh]: V-8: Overhead valve. Cast-iron block. Displacement: 316.6 cid. Bore & stroke: 3.94 x 3.25 in. Compression ratio: 7.9:1. Brake horsepower: 216 at 4800 rpm. Five main bearings. Hydraulic valve lifters. Carburetor: Rochester 4GC four-barrel with black tag number 7900. Some cars were also equipped with Carter WCFB model 2364S four-barrels.

ENGINE [Star Chief]: V-8: Overhead valve. Cast-iron block. Displacement: 316.6 cid. Bore & stroke: 3.94 x 3.25 in. Compression ratio: 8.9:1. Brake horsepower: 227 at 4800 rpm. Five main bearings. Hydraulic valve lifters. Carburetor: Rochester 4GC four-barrel with brass tag number 8697. Some cars were also equipped with Carter WCFB model 2364S four-barrels.

CHASSIS: Wheelbase: (Series 27) 122 in.; (Series 28) 124 in. Overall Length: (Series 27 passenger cars) 205.6 in.; (Series 27 Chieftain station wagons) 206 in.; (Series 27 Safari) 206.7 in.; (Series 28) 212.6 in. Front tread: (All) 58.66 in. Rear tread: (All) 59.05 in. Tires: (Passenger cars) 7.10 x 15; (station wagons) 7.60 x 15, tubeless.

OPTIONS: Power brakes ($38). Power windows ($97). Power steering ($108). Six-Way power seat ($93). Radios ($90 or $118). Seat belts ($11 per passenger). Air-conditioning ($431). Hydra-Matic attachments were now considered "standard," but cost extra. The D-56 Dual-Range type ($188) was used in Chieftains in both the 860

77

and 870 sub-series. A new Strato-Flight Hydra-Matic ($205) was employed in two-door Star Chief Custom Safaris and all Series 28 models. A three-speed synchromesh gearbox with column-mounted shift was the base price transmission. In March 1956, an "extra horsepower" V-8 was released. It also displaced 317 cid, but came with 10.0:1 compression heads, dual four-barrel Rochester carburetors (part no. 7009820) and additional high-performance components. The output of this engine was rated 285 hp at 5100 rpm. Pontiac experts have estimated that 200 cars were equipped with this motor. Standard rear axle gear ratios were as follows: (synchromesh) 3.64:1; (Hydra-Matic) 3.23:1. Additional ratios were also available. Dual exhausts were optional on all Pontiacs except the Chieftain 860 three-seat station wagon (not available) and cars with "extra hp" V-8s (standard). Four-barrel carburetion was optional for Chieftain 860 and 870 models.

HISTORICAL: Production of 1956 models started Oct. 3, 1955. They were introduced Oct. 21, 1955. Calendar year output was 332,268 cars. Model year output was 405,730 cars. Pontiac remained the sixth largest American automaker. On Aug. 3, 1956, the six millionth Pontiac was built. The 227-hp 1956 Star Chief four-door sedan was good for 0-to-60 mph in 11.4 seconds and an 18.1 second quarter-mile. Semon "Bunkie" Knudsen took over as Pontiac general manager on July 1, 1956.

1957 PONTIAC

1957 Pontiac Chieftain two-door sedan. (OCW)

CHIEFTAIN LINE — (V-8) — SERIES 27 — Pontiac introduced new "Star Flight" styling. General features were missile-shaped side trim, flatter tailfins, extended rear fenders with V-shaped tips, lower hoods, a more massive bumper grille, longer horizontal taillights and 14-in. wheels. The budget-priced line was now called the Chieftain. The Super Chief name totally replaced the old Chieftain 870 designation for cars on the small wheelbase with Deluxe trim. The two-door Star Chief Custom Safari remained on the Series 27 platform and again had a four-barrel V-8 as its base engine. Chieftains had small hubcaps, three stars on rear fenders, and Chieftain front fender scripts. Super Chiefs had full wheel discs, upper belt moldings, three stars on rear fenders, and Super Chief front fender scripts. The distinctive Custom Safari had Star Chief trims and a companion four-door Custom Safari Transcontinental station wagon was announced in late December 1956.

STAR CHIEF LINE — (V-8) — SERIES 28 — Star Chiefs were identified by suitable front fender scripts, four stars on rear fenders, chrome semi-cylindrical trim at the back of missile-shaped inserts, and full wheel discs. The Custom (Super Deluxe) Sedan was reinstated and distinguished by off-shoulder interior styling patterns. A unique, limited-edition Custom Bonneville Convertible was announced in early December 1956 and released on Jan. 11, 1957. This car was in the Custom Star Chief sub-series. Released only on a one-to-a-dealer basis, Bonneville availability was limited to 630 production examples and two prototypes. The

1957 Pontiac Chieftain four-door sedan. (JAG)

pre-production prototypes had four bucket seats and small trim differences. A fuel-injected V-8 was used in all of these cars.

I.D. DATA: VIN located on left front door hinge pillar. Matching engine serial number on pad on front of right-hand cylinder bank. Serial numbers took the form ( )-[ ]57{ }-1001 to ( )-[ ]57{ }-ending number. The first symbol ( ) was a letter indicating assembly plant: P=Pontiac, Mich.; T=Arlington, Texas; A=Atlanta, Ga.; F=Framingham, Mass.; K=Kansas City, Kan.; L=Linden, N.J.; C=South Gate, Calif.; W=Wilmington, Del. The second symbol [ ] indicated series: 7=Series 27; 8=Series 28. The third and fourth symbols indicated model year: 57=1957. The fifth symbol indicated transmission: S=synchromesh; H=Hydra-Matic. The following symbols were the sequential unit production number starting at 1001 for each series at each assembly plant. Ending numbers for 1957 were: [SERIES 27 with synchromesh] (Mich.) 7722; (Texas) 1656; (Ga.) 2041; (Mass.) 2040; (Kan.) 2301; (N.J.) 2223; (Calif.) 1765; (Del.) 1970. [SERIES 27 with Hydra-Matic] (Mich.) 94,357; (Texas) 10,608; (Ga.) 18,541; (Mass.) 11,045; (Kan.) 24,194; (N.J.) 21,243; (Calif.) 22,055; (Del.) 22,332. [SERIES 28 with synchromesh] (Mich.) 1212; (Texas) 1004; (Ga.) 1005; (Mass.) 1010; (Kan.) 1019; (N.J.) 1028; (Calif.) 1016; (Del.) 1015. [SERIES 28 with Hydra-Matic] (Mich.) 45,497; (Texas) 6679; (Ga.) 9462; (Mass.) 5007; (Kan.) 11,022; (N.J.) 11,067; (Calif.) 11,387; (Del.) 10,558. Fisher Body/style number on plate under hood on left of firewall can be very helpful for identification of model and ordering parts. A prefix to the main number indicates model year, 57=1957. The first two symbols in the main number indicate series 27 or 28 Star Chief. The next two symbols indicate the body style. Some numbers have an alphabetical suffix indicating trim level, such as D=Deluxe and SD=Super Deluxe. These

1957 Pontiac Super Chief Catalina two-door hardtop. (OCW)

1957 Pontiac Star Chief Custom Bonneville convertible. (OCW)

1957 Pontiac Chieftain Catalina two-door hardtop. (RK)

1957 Pontiac Chieftain Catalina two-door hardtop. (OCW)

1957 Pontiac Super Chief Catalina four-door hardtop. (OCW)

1957 Pontiac Super Chief Safari four-door station wagon. (OCW)

1957 Pontiac Star Chief Custom Catalina two-door hardtop. (OCW)

1957 Pontiac Star Chief two-door Custom Safari station wagon. (JL)

numbers appear in Body/style number column of charts below adjacent to corresponding body style listings.

Model Number	Body Style Number	Body Type & Seating	Factory Price	Shipping Weight	Production Total
CHIEFTAIN					
27	2719	4d Sedan-6P	2,527	3,670	35,671
27	2739	4d Catalina HT-6P	2,614	3,745	40,074
27	2711	2d Sedan-6P	2,463	3,625	21,343
27	2737	2d Catalina HT-6P	2,529	3,665	51,017
27	2762FC	4d Sta Wagon-9P	2,898	3,945	11,536
27	2763F	2d Sta Wagon-6P	2,841	3,800	2,934
SUPER CHIEF					
27	2719D	4d Sedan-6P	2,664	3,695	15,153
27	2739D	4d Catalina HT-6P	2,793	3,750	19,758
27	2737D	2d Catalina HT-6P	2,735	3,680	15,494
27	2762DF	4d Sta Wagon-6P	3,021	3,875	14,095
STAR CHIEF CUSTOM SAFARI (SERIES 27)					
27	2764DF	2d Sta Wagon-6P	3,636	3,955	1,292
27	2762SDF	4d Sta Wagon-6P	3,481	3,860	1,894
STAR CHIEF (SERIES 28)					
28	2819D	4d Sedan-6P	2,839	3,740	3,774
28	2867DTX	2d Convertible-6P	3,105	3,970	12,789
STAR CHIEF CUSTOM (SERIES 28)					
28	2819SD	4d Sedan-6P	2,896	3,755	8,874
28	2839SD	4d Catalina HT-6P	2,975	3,820	44,283
28	2837SD	2d Catalina HT-6P	2,901	3,750	32,862
28	2867SDX	2d Bonn Conv-6P	5,782	4,285	630

NOTE 1: All Pontiac station wagons used the Safari name starting in 1957.

NOTE 2: 162,575 Chieftains were built.

NOTE 3: 12,867 Chieftains had synchromesh and 149,708 had Hydra-Matic.

NOTE 4: 64,692 Super Chiefs were built.

NOTE 5: 1063 had Super Chiefs had synchromesh and 63,629 had Hydra-Matic.

NOTE 6: 3186 Star Chief Custom Safaris were built.

NOTE 7: Four Custom Safaris had synchromesh and 3182 had Hydra-Matic.

NOTE 8: 192 Super Chiefs were used for hearse and ambulance conversions.

NOTE 9: 103,588 Series 28 Star Chiefs were built.

NOTE 10: 309 Star Chiefs had synchromesh and 103,279 had Hydra-Matic.

NOTE 11: Totals do not include Series 27 two- or four-door Custom Safaris.

1957 Pontiac Star Chief two-door Custom Safari station wagon. (JL)

1957 Pontiac Star Chief four-door sedan. (OCW)

1957 Pontiac Star Chief two-door convertible. (RK)

NOTE 12: 376 Star Chief chassis were built for professional car conversions.

ENGINE [Chieftain synchromesh]: V-8. Overhead valves. Cast-iron block. Displacement: 347 cid. Bore & stroke: 3.94 x 3.56 in. Compression Ratio: 8.5:1. Brake horsepower: 227 at 4600 rpm. Five main bearings. Hydraulic valve lifters. Carburetor: Rochester 2GC two-barrel.

ENGINE [Chieftain Hydra-Matic]: V-8. Overhead valves. Cast-iron block. Displacement: 347 cid. Bore & stroke: 3.94 x 3.56 in. Compression Ratio: 10.0:1. Brake horsepower: 252 at 4600 rpm. Five main bearings. Hydraulic valve lifters. Carburetor: Rochester 2GC two-barrel.

ENGINE [Custom Safari/Super Chief/Star Chief synchromesh]: V-8. Overhead valves. Cast-iron block. Displacement: 347 cid. Bore & stroke: 3.94 x 3.56 in. Compression Ratio: 8.5:1. Brake horsepower: 244 at 4800 rpm. Five main bearings. Hydraulic valve lifters. Carburetor: (Early production) Rochester 4GC four-barrel; (Late production) A Carter AFB four-barrel was used in mixed production with the Rochester 4GC type.

ENGINE [Custom Safari/Super Chief/Star Chief Hydra-Matic]: V-8. Overhead valves. Cast-iron block. Displacement: 347 cid. Bore & stroke: 3.94 x 3.56 in. Compression Ratio: 10.0:1. Brake horsepower: 270 at 4800 rpm. Five main bearings. Hydraulic valve lifters. Carburetor: (Early production) Rochester 4GC four-barrel; (Late production) A Carter AFB four-barrel was used in mixed production with the Rochester 4GC type.

ENGINE [Bonneville fuel-injection]: V-8. Overhead valves. Cast-iron block. Displacement: 347 cid. Bore & stroke: 3.94 x 3.56 in. Compression Ratio: 10.25:1. Brake horsepower: (estimated) 315 at 4800 rpm. Five main bearings. Hydraulic valve lifters. Induction: Rochester mechanical fuel-injection.

ENGINE [Tri-Power Hydra-Matic]: V-8. Displacement: 347 cid. Bore & stroke: 3.94 x 3.56 in. Compression ratio: 10.0:1. Brake horsepower: 290 hp at 5000 rpm. Carburetion: 3 x 2V Rochester carburetors. Hydraulic valve lifters. Single-breaker ignition. Released in December 1956.

ENGINE [NASCAR Tri-Power synchromesh]: V-8. Displacement: 347 cid. Bore & stroke: 3.94 x 3.56 in. Compression ratio: 10.0:1. Brake horsepower: 317 hp at 5200 rpm. Carburetion: 3 x 2V Rochester carburetors. Hydraulic valve lifters. Dual-breaker ignition. Released in December 1956.

ENGINE [NASCAR Tri-Power Hydra-Matic]: V-8. Displacement: 347 cid. Bore & stroke: 3.94 x 3.56 in. Compression ratio: 10.0:1. Brake horsepower: 317 hp at 5200 rpm. Carburetion: 3 x 2V Rochester carburetors. Hydraulic valve lifters. Single-breaker ignition. Released in December 1956.

CHASSIS: Wheelbase: (Series 27) 122 in.; (Series 28) 124 in. Overall Length: (Series 27 passenger cars) 206.8 in.; (Series 27 station wagons) 207.7 in.; (Series 28) 213.8 in. Front tread: 59.0 in. Rear tread: 59.4 in. Tires: (Chieftain with synchromesh) 7.50 x 14; (station wagons and Bonneville) 8.50 x 14; (others) 8.00 x 14.

OPTIONS: Power steering ($108). Power brakes ($39). Eight-way power seat ($97). Six-way manual seat ($41). Power windows ($102). Radios ($99 and $125). Heater and defroster ($91). Air conditioning ($431). Tinted glass ($34). Lamp group ($23.10). Mirror group ($12.35). Power Sweep Contour electric wiper/washer ($25.25). Deluxe steering wheel and padded dash ($31.70). Electric clock ($10.50). White sidewall tires ($58.70). Deluxe carpet floor mat ($11). Cowl vent chrome trim and Custom wheel discs ($21.80). Deluxe basic group ($255.50). Hydra-Matic attachments were again considered "standard," but cost extra. Strato-Flight Hydra-Matic ($231) was used in all lines. A three-speed synchromesh gearbox with column-shift was the base price transmission. Four-barrel carburetion was optional in Chieftains. Dual exhausts were $24 extra. Rear axle ratios: (synchromesh) 3.42:1; (Hydra-Matic) 3.08:1. In December 1956, a 3.23:1 axle was made standard for Hydra-Matic equipped cars and the 3.08:1 axle was made a Plains ratio option for all cars except Safari models.

HISTORICAL: Production of 1957 models started Oct. 17, 1956. They were introduced Nov. 19, 1956. Model year output was 334,041 cars. Calendar year output was 343,298 cars. Pontiac held a 5.4 percent share of the U.S. market and was ranked the sixth largest automaker. First news of the Bonneville convertible was released Dec. 2, 1956, the same day the Tri-Power carburetor options were announced. The four-door Custom Star Chief Safari Transcontinental wagon and the Bonneville convertible were both introduced on Jan. 11, 1957. The 1957 Pontiac Super Chief two-door Sedan with the 290-hp V-8 was capable of doing 0-to-60 mph in 8.5 seconds and the quarter-mile in 16.8 seconds. E.M. "Pete" Estes became the chief engineer of Pontiac this year.

1958 PONTIAC

1958 Pontiac Chieftain two-door sedan. (OCW)

CHIEFTAIN LINE — (V-8) — SERIES 25 AND SERIES 27 — The 1958 Pontiacs featured all new styling and chassis engineering that was hailed as a bold advance over the past. General appearance characteristics included honeycomb grilles; a longer, lower silhouette; quad headlamps and tail lamps; recessed floors; and concave rear fender panels. Chieftains could be identified by the script model nameplates at the front of concave insert panels on the rear doors or fenders and three stars on the rear fenders. Small hubcaps were

1957 Pontiac Star Chief two-door convertible. (OCW)

standard on all Chieftains, but many were sold with optional full wheel discs. Tail lamps without trim rings were seen on Chieftains, except the convertible. The ragtop was in a separate series sharing a unique ribbed rear deck lid with the Bonneville convertible. Princess pattern Lustrex upholstery with Morrokide imitation leather trim was seen inside Chieftains, except the convertible, which had special Seville-finish Morrokide seats in "off shoulder" combination patterns.

SUPER CHIEF LINE — (V-8) — SERIES 28 — In 1958 the Super Chief nameplate was used to designate three cars on the long wheelbase (Star Chief) chassis with two-barrel (Chieftain) V-8s as base engines. Identification features included full wheel discs, tail lamps with chrome rings, and rear fender coves decorated with Super Chief

1958 Pontiac Chieftain Catalina two-door hardtop. (OCW)

script and four stars. Deluxe steering wheels were used. The four-door sedan was upholstered in a blend of Palisades pattern Lustrex with Plaza pattern bolsters. Catalina buyers could choose either all-Morrokide or Morrokide and Lustrex trims at the same price.

STAR CHIEF LINE — (V-8) — SERIES 27 AND SERIES 28 — Pontiac's "something really special" cars were four Super Deluxe level Star Chiefs. A distinctive four-door Custom Safari station wagon was on the shorter Chieftain platform, while other models had the 124-in. wheelbase shared with Super Chiefs. Identification features included Star Chief front fender script plates; four stars within the concave insert panels; tail lamp trim rings; and funnel-shaped decorative scoops at the front of the insert panels. These scoops were embellished with golden rectangular 'V' badges and triple windsplit moldings. Chrome wheel discs were regular equipment outside, while a Deluxe steering wheel and electric clock were found inside. Upholstery trims were tri-dimensional Prado pattern Lustrex in the Catalina sedan, with all-leather optional at no extra cost on both Catalinas. A roof rack, horizontal tailgate moldings and distinct Safari gate scripts were featured on the Custom Safari and all Star Chiefs boasted "Stardust" carpeting. Jeweltone Lucite acrylic lacquer paint finish was standard and exclusive on Star Chiefs and Bonnevilles.

BONNEVILLE LINE — (V-8) — SERIES 25 — Bonneville became a line name instead of a single model designation in 1958. A convertible and sport coupe were offered. Base powerplants in Bonnevilles were the Star Chief V-8s and both cars were on the Chieftain wheelbase, but with the same longer, ribbed rear deck lid used on the Series 25 Chieftain convertible. This made the bodies slightly longer than Series 27 types. Identification features included Bonneville front fender scripts; Bonneville block letters on hoods and decks; four bright metal chevrons on the lower front fender sides; four stars on the rear fender panels; and rocket-shaped, ribbed semi-cylindrical moldings at the front of the concave inserts. Standard equipment included a deluxe steering wheel, chrome wheel discs and special upholstery.

I.D. DATA: VIN located on left front door hinge pillar. Matching engine serial number on pad on front of right-hand cylinder bank.

1958 Pontiac Chieftain two-door convertible. (OCW)

1958 Pontiac Star Chief Catalina four-door hardtop. (OCW)

1958 Pontiac Super Chief four-door sedan. (OCW)

Serial numbers took the form ( )-[ ]58{ }-1001 to ( )-[ ]58{ }-ending number. The first symbol ( ) was a letter indicating assembly plant: P=Pontiac, Mich.; T=Arlington, Texas; A=Atlanta, Ga.; F=Framingham, Mass.; K=Kansas City, Kan.; L=Linden, N.J.; C=South Gate, Calif.; W=Wilmington, Del. The second symbol [ ] indicated series: 7=Series 27; 8=Series 28; 5=Series 25 Bonneville. The third and fourth symbols indicated model year: 58=1958. The fifth symbol indicated transmission: S=synchromesh; H=Hydra-Matic. The following symbols were the sequential unit production number starting at 1001 for each series at each assembly plant. Ending numbers for 1958 were: [SERIES 27 with synchromesh] (Mich.) 4036; (Texas) 1429; (Ga.) 1508; (Mass.) 1296; (Kan.) 2003; (N.J.) 1568; (Calif.) 1592; (Del.) 1427. [SERIES 27 with Hydra-Matic] (Mich.) 43,381; (Texas) 7317; (Ga.) 11,942; (Mass.) 6113; (Kan.) 17,504; (N.J.) 14,411; (Calif.) 12585; (Del.) 12,574. [SERIES 28 with synchromesh] (Mich.) 1159; (Texas) 1006; (Ga.) 1008; (Mass.) 1011; (Kan.) 1016; (N.J.) 1026; (Calif.) 1018; (Del.) 1015. [SERIES 28 with Hydra-Matic] (Mich.) 25986; (Texas) 5695; (Ga.) 8672; (Mass.) 4130; (Kan.) 10785; (N.J.) 8446; (Calif.) 8168; (Del.) 8157. [BONNEVILLE SERIES 25 with synchromesh] (Ga.) 1003; (Calif.) 1021; (Mass.) 1005; (Kan.) 1023; (N.J.) 1020; (Mich.) 1163; (Texas) 1016; (Del.) 1015. [BONNEVILLE SERIES 25 with Hydra-Matic] (Ga.) 2543; (Calif.) 3324; (Mass.) 1969; (Kan.) 2640; (N.J.) 3180; (Mich.) 9141; (Texas) 1677; (Del.) 2858. Fisher Body/style number on plate under hood on left of firewall can be helpful for identification of model and ordering parts. A prefix to the main number indicates model year, 58=1958. The first two symbols in the main number indicate series 27 or 28 Star Chief or 25 Bonneville. The next two symbols indicate the body style. Some numbers have an alphabetical suffix indicating trim level, such as D=Deluxe and SD=Super Deluxe. These numbers appear in Body/style number column of charts below adjacent to corresponding body style listings.

Model Number	Body Style Number	Body Type & Seating	Factory Price	Shipping Weight	Production Total
CHIEFTAIN (SERIES 27)					
27	2749	4d Sedan-6P	2,638	3,815	44,999
27	2739	4d Catalina HT-6P	2,792	3,900	17,946
27	2741	2d Sedan-6P	2,573	3,755	17,394
27	2731	2d Catalina HT-6P	2,707	3,765	26,003
27	2793	4d Sta Wagon-6P	3,019	4,140	9,701
27	2794	2d Sta Wagon-9P	3,088	4,185	5,417

1958 Pontiac Super Chief Catalina two-door hardtop. (OCW)

1958 Pontiac Super Chief Catalina two-door hardtop. (OCW)

1958 Pontiac Super Chief Catalina four-door hardtop. (OCW)

1958 Pontiac Super Chief Catalina four-door hardtop. (OCW)

Model Number	Body Style Number	Body Type & Seating	Factory Price	Shipping Weight	Production Total
CHIEFTAIN (SERIES 25)					
25	2567	2d Convertible-5P	3,019	3,965	7,359
SUPER CHIEF (SERIES 28 DELUXE)					
28	2849D	4d Sedan-6P	2,834	3,865	12,006
28	2839D	4d Catalina HT-6P	2,961	3,925	7,886
28	2831D	2d Catalina HT-6P	2,880	3,805	7,236
STAR CHIEF (SERIES 28 SUPER DELUXE)					
28	2849SD	4d Cus Sedan-6P	3,071	3,915	10,547
28	2839SD	4d Catalina HT-6P	3,210	3,965	21,455
28	2831SD	2d Catalina HT-6P	3,122	3,850	13,888
STAR CHIEF CUSTOM SAFARI					
27	2793SD	4d Cus Sta Wag-6P	3,350	4,180	2,905
BONNEVILLE (SERIES 25 SUPER DELUXE)					
25	2547SD	Cus Sport Cpe-5P	3,481	3,825	9,144
25	2567SD	Cus Convertible-5P	3,586	4,040	3,096

Note 1: Pontiac experts believe that 200 Bonnevilles carried the optional fuel-injection V-8.

ENGINE [Chieftain/Super Chief synchromesh]: Base V-8. Overhead valves. Cast-iron block. Displacement: 370 cid. Bore & stroke: 4.06 x 3.56 in. Compression Ratio: 8.6:1. Brake horsepower: 240 at 4500 rpm. Five main bearings. Hydraulic valve lifters. Carburetor: (early) Rochester 2GC two-barrel; (late) same with air bypass idle.

1958 Pontiac Star Chief Custom Safari four-door station wagon. (OCW)

1958 Pontiac Star Chief Catalina two-door hardtop. (OCW)

1958 Pontiac Chieftain four-door station wagon. (OCW)

1958 Pontiac Bonneville Custom two-door convertible. (OCW)

ENGINE [Chieftain/Super Chief Hydra-Matic]: Base V-8. Overhead valves. Cast-iron block. Displacement: 370 cid. Bore & stroke: 4.06 x 3.56 in. Compression Ratio: 10.0:1. Brake horsepower: 270 at 4600 rpm. Five main bearings. Hydraulic valve lifters. Carburetor: (early) Rochester 2GC two-barrel; (late) same with air bypass idle.

ENGINE [Star Chief/Bonneville synchromesh]: Base V-8. Overhead valves. Cast-iron block. Displacement: 370 cid. Bore & stroke: 4.06 x 3.56 in. Compression Ratio: 8.6:1. Brake horsepower: 255 at 4500 rpm. Five main bearings. Hydraulic valve lifters. Carburetor: (Regular production) Carter AFB four-barrel; (Special) 500 cars were built with Rochester 4GC four-barrel carburetors late in the year. These were available only in four sales zones and were likely 'PM' optioned cars assembled for NASCAR certification.

ENGINE [Star Chief/Bonneville Hydra-Matic]: Base V-8. Overhead valves. Cast-iron block. Displacement: 370 cid. Bore & stroke: 4.06 x 3.56 in. Compression Ratio: 10.0:1. Brake horsepower: 285 at 4600

1958 Pontiac Bonneville Custom two-door convertible. (OCW)

1958 Pontiac Star Chief Barnette hearse with Tri-Power. (JAG)

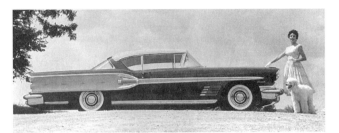

1958 Pontiac Bonneville Custom two-door hardtop. (OCW)

rpm. Five main bearings. Hydraulic valve lifters. Carburetor: (Regular production) Carter AFB four-barrel; (Special) 500 cars were built with Rochester 4GC four-barrel carburetors late in the year. These were available only in four sales zones and were likely 'PM' optioned cars assembled for NASCAR certification.

ENGINE [Standard Tri-Power]: V-8. Overhead valves. Cast-iron block. Displacement: 370 cid. Bore & stroke: 4.06 x 3.56 in. Compression Ratio: 10.5:1. Brake horsepower: 300 at 4600 rpm. Five main bearings. Hydraulic valve lifters. Carburetor: Three (3) Rochester two-barrel. ($84 for Chieftain/Super Chief and $93.50 for Star Chief/Bonneville).

ENGINE [Fuel-injection]: V-8. Overhead valves. Cast-iron block. Displacement: 370 cid. Bore & stroke: 4.06 x 3.56 in. Compression Ratio: 10.5:1. Brake horsepower: 310 at 4800 rpm. Five main bearings. Hydraulic valve lifters. Induction: Rochester fuel injection. ($500 on any Pontiac model)

ENGINE [NASCAR extra-horsepower Tempest 395-A Code PK]: V-8. Overhead valves. Cast-iron block. Displacement: 370 cid. Bore & stroke: 4.06 x 3.56 in. Compression Ratio: 10.5:1. Brake horsepower: 315 at 5000 rpm. Five main bearings. Hydraulic valve lifters. High-lift camshaft. Carburetor: Four-barrel. (Released in March 1958 at $254 for Chieftain/Super Chief and $233 for Star Chief/Bonneville).

ENGINE [NASCAR extra-horsepower Tempest 395-A Code PM]: V-8. Overhead valves. Cast-iron block. Displacement: 370 cid. Bore & stroke: 4.06 x 3.56 in. Compression Ratio: 10.5:1. Brake horsepower: 330 at 5200 rpm. Five main bearings. Hydraulic valve lifters. High-lift camshaft. Low-restriction dual exhausts. Carburetor: Three (3) Rochester two-barrel. ($331 for Chieftain/Super Chief and $320 for Star Chief/Bonneville).

CHASSIS: Wheelbase: (Series 25 and 27) 122 in.; (Series 28) 124 in. Overall Length: (Series 25) 211.7 in.; (Series 27) 210.5 in.;

1958 Pontiac Bonneville Custom two-door hardtop. (OCW)

Standard Catalog of ® Pontiac, 2nd Edition

(Series 28) 124 in. Front tread: 58.8 in. Rear tread: 59.4 in. Tires: (coupes and sedans) 8.00 x 14 in.; (station wagons and all with air conditioning) 8.50 x 14 in.

OPTIONS: Power steering ($108). Power brakes ($38). Power windows ($108). Power seat ($77). Deluxe radio ($102). Deluxe Electromatic radio ($161). Power antenna ($30). Rear seat speaker ($13.75, $18.90 and $21 on Safari/Bonneville, Star Chief and Chieftain/Super Chief, respectively). Heater and defroster ($96). Dual exhaust ($31). White sidewall tires 8.00 x 14, four-ply ($65). Two-tone paint in standard colors ($27). E-Z Eye Glass ($38). Electric clock ($20). Windshield washer ($14). Electric contour wipers ($14). Oil filter ($10). Padded dash ($19). Foam seat ($13). Deluxe steering wheel ($14). Outside rearview mirror ($7). Wheel discs ($18). Brake-on light ($6). Air conditioning ($430). Air suspension ($175). Bonneville bucket seats ($84). Transmission and axle options: A three-speed synchromesh gearbox with column-mounted gearshift was the base price transmission. Four-speed StratoFlight Hydra-Matic was $231.34 extra. In late production a Borg-Warner heavy-duty police gearbox was optional. At least one car, built for racing at Daytona Beach, left the factory with a floor-mounted four-speed manual transmission. Transmission attachment data was now recorded by series. A total of 19,599 cars were built in Series 25. Of these, 210 had synchromesh and 19,389 had Hydra-Matic attachments. A total of 124,685 cars were built in Series 27. Of these, 6,943 had synchromesh and 117,742 had Hydra-Matic attachments. A total of 73,019 cars were built in Series 28. Of these, 258 had synchromesh and 72,761 had Hydra-Matic attachments. The difference between output of individual models and total series production was 321 cars, which indicates the number of Pontiac chassis delivered for professional car conversions this year. Of these, 320 were Series 27 chassis and one was a Series 28 chassis. Rear axle options included Safe-T-Track differential and the following gear ratios: (Hydra-Matic) 3.23:1; (optional Hydra-Matic) 3.08:1; (synchromesh) 3.42:1; (optional synchromesh) 3.64:1; (dealer installed) 3.90:1 and 4.10:1. Power plant options: The four-barrel V-8 could be installed as an option in Chieftains and Super Chiefs.

HISTORICAL: Model year production was 217,303 units for a 5.1 percent share of market. Calendar year output was 219,823 cars. To celebrate General Motors' 50th anniversary, a special "Golden Jubilee" trim and paint scheme was announced in November. This color was coded "Z" with DuPont stock number 2865L. Special "Golden Jubilee" ornamentation was applied to a limited number of cars, all of which are believed to have been Star Chief Custom four-door sedans. The number made is not known. Cars with optional fuel injection had "fuel-injection" call-outs on the front fenders. Cars with Tri-Power engines had a different type of front fender call-out. A Tri-Power Bonneville convertible was selected as the Official Pace Car for the Indianapolis 500 Mile

1958 Pontiac Chieftain four-door sedan. (OCW)

1958 Pontiac Chieftain four-door sedan. (OCW)

Race in May 1958. The 1958 Bonneville hardtop with the 300-hp engine was road tested by a magazine. Zero-to-60 mph took 7.6 seconds and the quarter-mile took 16 seconds.

1959 PONTIAC

1959 Pontiac Star Chief two-door Sport Sedan. (OCW)

CATALINA SERIES — (V-8) — SERIES 21 — Major styling changes for 1959 Pontiacs included lower, longer bodies with more interior room, a new twin grille theme, twin-fin rear fenders, 'V' contour hood, increased glass area, and flat, rear over-hanging roofs on four-door Vista hardtops. The Chieftain line was renamed, adopting Catalina as its new series name. Identification features included Catalina script on rear fins, plain deck lids, and body sides trimmed by clean sweep spear moldings with undecorated projectile flares. Standard equipment included directional signals, electric wipers, dual sun visors, dome lamps, cigarette lighter, dual headlamps, front and rear ashtrays, coat hooks, instrument panel Snak Bar, dual horns, tubeless tires, bumper jack, and wheel lug wrench.

CUSTOM STAR CHIEF SERIES — (V-8) — SERIES 24 — The Super Chief disappeared and 1959 Custom Star Chiefs were large-sized Pontiacs utilizing the base Catalina engines. There were Star Chief emblems on the fins, four stylized stars on the projectile flares, sweep spear body side moldings, and a narrow deck lid ornament to aid with identification. Regular equipment included all standard Catalina features, plus two-speed electric wipers, deluxe steering wheel, electric clock, deluxe chrome wheel covers, and loop-pile Lurex-flexed carpeting.

BONNEVILLE CUSTOM LINE — (V-8) — SERIES 27 AND SERIES 28 — The Bonneville Customs were the prestige offering. They were big, powerful Pontiacs with high-level trim and appointments and four-barrel V-8s. Bonnevilles were set apart by golden

1959 Pontiac Bonneville two-door convertible. (OCW)

1959 Pontiac Star Chief four-door sedan. (OCW)

scripts on the right-hand grille; rear fins and deck lid; four groups of short, horizontal louvers on the projectile-shaped rearfenderflares;

1959 Pontiac Catalina four-door Vista hardtop. (OCW)

1959 Pontiac Catalina two-door convertible. (OCW)

1959 Pontiac Catalina two-door hardtop. (OCW)

1959 Pontiac Catalina two-door hardtop. (OCW)

1959 Pontiac Bonneville four-door Vista hardtop. (OCW)

1959 Pontiac Bonneville two-door hardtop. (JAG)

and crest medallions on the deck lid and doors. Regular equipment included all Star Chief features plus padded dashboard, inside door safety reflectors, rear seat foam cushions, dash courtesy lights, and padded assist rails for passengers.

I.D. DATA: VIN located on left front door hinge pillar. Matching engine serial number on pad on front of right-hand cylinder bank. Assembly plant codes: P=Pontiac, Mich.; T=Arlington, Texas; A=Atlanta, Ga.; F=Framingham, Mass.; K=Kansas City, Kan.; L=Linden, N.J.; C=South Gate, Calif.; W=Wilmington, Del. [CATALINA] Serial numbers took the following form - 159WI001 and up. The first character (1) indicating Series 21; the second and third characters (59) indicating model year; the fourth character (W) indicating factory. Serial numbers at each factory began with 1001 and transmission type was no longer indicated. [STAR CHIEF] Serial numbers took the same general form as Catalina I.D. numbers, but with a '4' as the first character to designate Series 24. [BONNEVILLE CUSTOM] Serial numbers for Bonneville passenger cars began with an '8' and for Custom Safaris with a "7" representing the series the cars were in.

Model Number	Body Style Number	Body Type & Seating	Factory Price	Shipping Weight	Production Total
CATALINA					
21	2119	4d Sedan-6P	2,704	3,955	72,377
21	2139	4d Vista HT-6P	2,844	4,005	45,012
21	2111	2d Sport Sedan-6P	2,633	3,870	26,102
21	2137	2d Hardtop-6P	2,768	3,900	38,309
21	2167	2d Convertible-5P	3,080	3,970	14,515
21	2135	4d Sta Wagon-6P	3,101	4,345	21,162
21	2145	4d Sta Wagon-9P	3,209	4,405	14,084
CUSTOM STAR CHIEF					
24	2419	4d Sedan-6P	3,005	4,005	27,872
24	2439	4d Vista HT-6P	3,138	4,035	30,689
24	2411	2d Sport Sedan-6P	2,934	3,930	10,254
27	2735	4d Sta Wagon-6P	3,532	4,370	4,673
BONNEVILLE CUSTOM (SERIES 28)					
28	2839	4d Vista HT-6P	3,333	4,085	38,696
28	2837	2d Hardtop-6P	3,257	3,985	27,769
28	2867	2d Convertible-6P	3,478	4,070	11,426

NOTE 1: 231,561 Catalinas were built.

NOTE 2: 9939 Catalinas had synchromesh and 221,622 had Hydra-Matic.

NOTE 3: 68,815 Custom Star Chiefs were built.

NOTE 4: 333 Custom Star Chiefs had synchromesh and 68,482 had Hydra-Matic.

NOTE 5: 4,673 Bonneville Custom Safari station wagons (Series 27) were built.

1959 Pontiac Bonneville two-door hardtop. (JAG)

1959 Pontiac Bonneville four-door station wagon.

NOTE 6: 16 Custom Safaris had synchromesh and 4,657 had Hydra-Matic.

NOTE 7: 78,271 Bonnevilles (Series 28) were built.

NOTE 8: 673 Bonneville Customs (Series 28) with synchromesh and 77,596 with Hydra-Matic.

NOTE 9: 380 (124-in. wheelbase cars) used for hearse/ambulance conversions.

ENGINE [Catalina/Custom Star Chief synchromesh]: V-8. Overhead valves. Cast-iron block. Displacement: 389 cid. Bore & stroke: 4.06 x 3.75 in. Compression ratio: 8.6:1. Brake horsepower: 245 at 4200 rpm. Five main bearings. Hydraulic valve lifters. Carburetor: Rochester model no. 7015910 two-barrel.

ENGINE [Catalina/Custom Star Chief Hydra-Matic]: V-8. Overhead valves. Cast-iron block. Displacement: 389 cid. Bore & stroke: 4.06 x 3.75 in. Compression ratio: 10.0:1. Brake horsepower: 280 at 4400 rpm. Five main bearings. Hydraulic valve lifters. Carburetor: Rochester model no. 7015909 two-barrel.

ENGINE [Bonneville Custom synchromesh]: V-8. Overhead valves. Cast-iron block. Displacement: 389 cid. Bore & stroke: 4.06 x 3.75 in. Compression ratio: 8.6:1. Brake horsepower: 260 at 4200 rpm. Five main bearings. Hydraulic valve lifters. Carburetor: Carter AFB-2820S (no. 532301) four-barrel. The four-barrel Bonneville V-8 was available in Catalinas and Star Chiefs at $20 extra.

ENGINE [Bonneville Custom Hydra-Matic]: V-8. Overhead valves. Cast-iron block. Displacement: 389 cid. Bore & stroke: 4.06 x 3.75 in. Compression ratio: 10.0:1. Brake horsepower: 300 at 4600 rpm. Five main bearings. Hydraulic valve lifters. Carburetor: Carter AFB-2820S (no. 532302) four-barrel. The four-barrel Bonneville V-8 was available in Catalinas and Star Chiefs at $20 extra.

ENGINE [Tempest 420E]: V-8. Overhead valves. Cast-iron block. Displacement: 389 cid. Bore & stroke: 4.06 x 3.75 in. Compression ratio: 8.6:1. Brake horsepower: 215 at 3600 rpm. Five main bearings. Hydraulic valve lifters. Carburetor: Rochester model no. 7015958 two-barrel. The Tempest 420E option was available as a super-economy offering that was available for no extra charge in any Pontiac. It had an especially fuel-efficient camshaft.

ENGINE [Standard Tri-Power]: V-8. Overhead valves. Cast-iron block. Displacement: 389 cid. Bore & stroke: 4.06 x 3.75 in. Compression ratio: 10.0:1. Brake horsepower: 315 at 4600 rpm. Five main bearings. Hydraulic valve lifters. Carburetor: Three Rochester two-barrels. Tri-Power on the standard Hydra-Matic block was $73 for Bonnevilles and $81 for other series.

ENGINE [NASCAR Four-barrel]: V-8. Overhead valves. Cast-iron block. Displacement: 389 cid. Bore & stroke: 4.06 x 3.75 in. Compression ratio: 10.5:1. Brake horsepower: 330 at 4800 rpm. Five main bearings. Hydraulic valve lifters. Carburetor: Four-barrel. Dual exhausts, normally a $26 option, were standard with this engine.

ENGINE [NASCAR Tri-Power]: V-8. Overhead valves. Cast-iron block. Displacement: 389 cid. Bore & stroke: 4.06 x 3.75 in. Compression ratio: 10.5:1. Brake horsepower: 345 at 4800 rpm. Five main bearings. Hydraulic valve lifters. Carburetor: Three Rochester two-barrels. Dual exhausts, normally a $26 option, were standard with this engine.

CHASSIS: Wheelbase: (Series 21 and 27) 122 in.; (Series 24 and 28) 124 in. Overall Length: (Catalina passenger cars) 213.7 in.; (Star Chief and Bonneville passenger cars) 220.7 in.; (All station wagons) 214.3 in. Front tread: 63.7 in. Rear tread: 64 in. Pontiac promoted "Wide Track Drive" this year. Tires: (passenger cars) 8.00 x 14; (station wagons and all with air conditioning) 8.50 x 14.

OPTIONS: Push-button radio ($74). Wonder Bar radio ($100). Sportable radio ($104). Electric antenna ($20). Rear seat speaker ($11). Fresh air heater and defroster ($74). Air-conditioning ($355). Tinted glass ($35). Back-up lights ($9). Windshield washers ($11). Deluxe steering wheel in Catalina ($12). Parking brake signal ($4). Padded dash ($16). Two-speed power brakes ($35). Power windows (four-door) $85; (two-door) $48. Power tailgate window ($27). Six-way power seat ($81). Ever-Level air ride ($155). Oil filter ($8). Heavy-duty air cleaner ($6). Clear plastic seat covers ($30). 8.00 x 14 white sidewall tires ($34). 8.50 x 14 white sidewall tires ($37). Two-tone paint ($11). Front foam seat cushion ($9). Bonneville convertible bucket seats ($84). Catalina decor trim ($45). Lamp group ($23). Safety group ($34). Mirror group ($10). Custom wheel covers ($26). Full wheel discs on Catalina ($14). Outside rearview mirror ($5). Tilt mirror ($4). Undercoating ($15). Antifreeze ($7). Tissue dispenser ($6). Safety belts ($12). A three-speed manual gearbox with column-mounted gearshift was standard on all models. Four-speed Super Hydra-Matic (Strato-Flight) transmission was $180 extra. Rear axle ratios were approximately the same as 1958. Safe-T-Track non-slip differential was $42 extra. A number of optional V-8s were offered, all on the 389-cid block.

HISTORICAL: Production start-up took place Sept. 11, 1958. Introductions were made one month later. Model year output was 383,320 units for a 6.9 percent market share. Calendar year production included 388,856 cars for fourth place in the industry. One or two El Camino type car-based pickup trucks were built from the 1959 Catalina chassis as prototypes. One of these vehicles was used as a "yard car" at the Pontiac factory in Pontiac, Mich., for many years. Reports of a second "El Catalina" in the West have surfaced from time to time. Pontiac introduced its famous eight-lug aluminum wheels on Aug. 27, 1959, though it's likely that they were intended for 1960 sale. *Motor Trend* magazine selected the 1959 Pontiac as its "Car of the Year." Pontiacs were victorious in many 1959 stock car races, including the Daytona 500 and Darlington 500, with drivers such as Fireball Roberts behind the wheel. The hot "Wide-Tracks" also captured the National Hot Rod Association's "Top Eliminator" title and earned the checkered flag at Pikes Peak. The 280-hp 1959 Catalina two-door hardtop (or Sport Coupe) was tested at 8.8 seconds for 0-to-60 mph and 16.9 seconds for the quarter-mile. Catalina was no longer a body style designation. Vista was now Pontiac's nomenclature for pillarless hardtop styling. The Sport Coupe was a two-door hardtop. The Sport Sedan was the two-door pillared sedan. Nine-passenger station wagons now used a rear-facing third seat of foldaway design. Station wagons were still called Safaris and all Safaris had four-door bodies. Tail lamps used on all station wagons and Catalinas were short horizontal-oval types without trim rings. Tail lamps used on Custom Star Chiefs and Bonneville Customs were long horizontal types with dual trim rings. The 1959 Bonneville Custom was picked as "Best Buy in the $2,000-$3,000 Class" by *Car Life* magazine.

1960 PONTIAC

1960 Pontiac Catalina four-door Safari station wagon. (OCW)

CATALINA SERIES — (V-8) — SERIES 21 — Pontiac's major styling changes for 1960 included undivided-horizontal bar grilles, straight full-length side trim moldings and a new deck lid which was nearly flush with the tops of the fenders. Catalinas had plain belt line moldings, Catalina front fender scripts, and Pontiac block letters on the belt

1960 Pontiac Catalina four-door Safari station wagon. (OCW)

1960 Pontiac Star Chief two-door sedan. (OCW)

latch panel. Standard features included turn signals, oil filter, five tubeless tires, and courtesy lamps on convertibles.

VENTURA SERIES — (V-8) — SERIES 23 — The Ventura was a Custom trim level Pontiac on the short wheelbase. Identifying cars in this series were plain belt moldings, Ventura front fender scripts, and the model name, in block letters, on the trunk latch panel. Venturas had all Catalina features plus a custom steering wheel, electric clock, Deluxe wheel discs, full carpeting, triple-tone Morrokide seats, right-hand ash trays, and special decor moldings.

STAR CHIEF SERIES — (V-8) SERIES 24 — Built off the long wheelbase with the Catalina two-barrel V-8 for base power, Star Chiefs had the same regular equipment as Venturas, plus dual-speed wipers. Distinguishing touches included Star Chief front fender scripts and four stylized stars at the rear of the lower beltline moldings.

BONNEVILLE LINE — (V-8) SERIES 27 AND SERIES 28 — Pontiac's top line could be told by distinctive front fender scripts, Bonneville lettering on the deck latch panel, beltline moldings ending in three dashes of chrome at the rear, and a V-shaped crest on the lower front fenders. Bonnevilles incorporated rear foam seat cushions, padded dashboards with walnut inserts, courtesy lamps, and four-barrel V-8s, in addition to everything found in lower-priced Pontiacs. All-Morrokide seats were standard and genuine cowhide leather was available as an option.

I.D. DATA: The VIN is located on a plate attached to left front door post. First symbol identifies series: 21=Catalina; 23=Ventura; 24=Star Chief; 27=Bonneville Safari; 28=Bonneville. Second and third symbols indicate model year: 60=1960. Fourth symbol identifies assembly plant: P=Pontiac, Mich.; S=South Gate, Calif.; L=Linden, N.J.; W=Wilmington, Del.; K=Kansas City, Kan.; D=Doraville, Ga.; A=Arlington, Texas; E=Euclid, Ohio. Remaining

1960 Pontiac Catalina two-door convertible. (OCW)

1960 Pontiac Bonneville two-door hardtop. (OCW)

1960 Pontiac Bonneville two-door hardtop. (OCW)

symbols are the unit's sequential production number starting with 1001 at each factory. Body/style number plate on left side of cowl below hood indicates manufacturer and various codes. Body/style number prefixed by model year code (60=1960). First two symbols in main body/style number are the series code, last two symbols are the body style code. These four numbers appear in second column of charts below. Trim, paint and some accessory codes may also be shown on the body/style number plate. Pontiac engines are stamped with a production code and motor serial number matching the VIN. Production code on pad on front of right-hand cylinder bank has an alphanumerical stamping identifying the engine. All 1960 V-8s were 389 cid. Engine codes included: A1 (283 hp); A2 (215 hp); B1 (303 hp); B2 (281 hp); C1 (318 hp/Tri-Power); C4 (318 hp/Tri-Power); E3 (215 hp); F1 (330 hp); F4 (330 hp); M1 (345 hp/Tri-Power); M4 (345 hp/Tri-Power).

Model Number	Body Style Number	Body Type & Seating	Factory Price	Shipping Weight	Production Total
CATALINA					
21	2119	4d Sedan-6P	2,702	3,935	72,650
21	2139	4d Vista HT -6P	2,842	3,990	32,710
21	2111	2d Sport Sedan-6P	2,631	3,850	25,504
21	2137	2d Hardtop-6P	2,766	3,835	27,496
21	2167	2d Convertible-6P	3,078	3,940	17,172
21	2145	4d Sta Wagon-9P	3,207	4,365	14,149
21	2135	4d Sta Wagon-6P	3,099	4,310	21,253
VENTURA					
23	2339	4d Vista HT-6P	3,047	3,990	28,700
23	2337	2d Hardtop-6P	2,971	3,865	27,577
STAR CHIEF					
24	2419	4d Sedan-6P	3,003	3,995	23,038
24	2439	4d Vista HT-6P	3,136	4,040	14,856
24	2411	2d Sport Sedan-6P	2,932	3,910	5,797
BONNEVILLE CUSTOM (SERIES 27)					
27	2735	4d Sta Wagon-6p	3,532	4,370	5,163
BONNEVILLE (SERIES 28)					
28	2839	4d Vista HT-6P	3,333	4,085	39,037
28	2837	2d Hardtop-6P	3,257	3,985	24,015
28	2867	2d Convertible-5P	3,478	4,070	17,062

NOTE 1: 210,934 Catalinas were built.

1960 Pontiac Catalina four-door Vista hardtop. (OCW)

1960 Pontiac Ventura four-door Vista hardtop. (OCW)

1960 Pontiac Catalina four-door Vista hardtop. (OCW)

NOTE 2: 10,831 Catalinas had synchromesh and 200,101 had Hydra-Matic.

NOTE 3: Some "AmbleWagons" on the standard Safari chassis may have been sold.

NOTE 4: 56,277 Venturas were built.

NOTE 5: 2,381 Venturas had synchromesh and 53,896 had Hydra-Matic.

NOTE 6: 43,691 Star Chiefs were built.

NOTE 7: 166 Star Chiefs had synchromesh and 43,525 had Hydra-Matic.

NOTE 8: 5,163 Bonneville Custom Safaris were built.

NOTE 9: 12 Safaris had synchromesh and 5,151 had Hydra-Matic.

NOTE 10: 80,651 Series 28 Bonnevilles were built.

NOTE 11: 1,111 Series 28 Bonnevilles had synchromesh; 79,540 had Hydra-Matic.

NOTE 12: 537 Bonneville chassis were sold to hearse/ambulance makers.

ENGINE [Catalina/Ventura/Star Chief synchromesh]: V-8. Overhead valves. Cast-iron block. Displacement: 389 cid. Bore & stroke: 4.06 x 3.75 in. Compression ratio: 8.6:1. Brake horsepower: 245 at 4200 rpm. Five main bearings. Hydraulic valve lifters. Carburetor: Rochester 2GC two-barrel. Engine code: A2 (245 hp).

ENGINE [Catalina/Custom Star Chief Hydra-Matic]: V-8. Overhead valves. Cast-iron block. Displacement: 389 cid. Bore & stroke: 4.06 x 3.75 in. Compression ratio: 10.0:1. Brake horsepower: 283 at 4400 rpm. Five main bearings. Hydraulic valve lifters. Carburetor: Rochester 2GC two-barrel. Engine code: A1 (283 hp).

ENGINE [Bonneville synchromesh]: V-8. Overhead valves. Cast-iron block. Displacement: 389 cid. Bore & stroke: 4.06 x 3.75 in. Compression ratio: 8.6:1. Brake horsepower: 281 at 4400 rpm. Five main bearings. Hydraulic valve lifters. Carburetor: Carter AFB-2975S four-barrel. The Bonneville four-barrel carburetor was $23.94 extra in other lines. Engine code: B2.

1960 Pontiac Catalina two-door convertible. (OCW)

1960 Pontiac Bonneville Vista hardtop. (OCW)

ENGINE [Bonneville Hydra-Matic]: V-8. Overhead valves. Cast-iron block. Displacement: 389 cid. Bore & stroke: 4.06 x 3.75 in. Compression ratio: 10.0:1. Brake horsepower: 303 at 4600 rpm. Five main bearings. Hydraulic valve lifters. Carburetor: Carter AFB four-barrel. The Bonneville four-barrel carburetor was $23.94 extra in other lines. Engine code: B1 (303 hp).

ENGINE [Tempest 420E]: V-8. Overhead valves. Cast-iron block. Displacement: 389 cid. Bore & stroke: 4.06 x 3.75 in. Compression ratio: 8.6:1. Brake horsepower: 215 at 3600 rpm. Five main bearings. Hydraulic valve lifters. Carburetor: Rochester model no. 7015073 two-barrel. The Tempest 420E option was available as a super-economy offering that was available for no extra charge in any Pontiac with Hydra-Matic only. It had an especially fuel efficient camshaft. Engine code: E3 (215 hp).

ENGINE [Standard Tri-Power with synchromesh]: V-8. Overhead valves. Cast-iron block. Displacement: 389 cid. Bore & stroke: 4.06 x 3.75 in. Compression ratio: 10.0:1. Brake horsepower: 315 at 4600 rpm. Five main bearings. Hydraulic valve lifters. Carburetor: Three Rochester two-barrels. Tri-Power on the standard Hydra-Matic block was $73 for Bonnevilles and $81 for other series. Price for this option was $89/$99/$132/$142 depending on the engine/transmission combination. Engine code: C1 (315 hp/Tri-Power).

ENGINE [Standard Tri-Power with Hydra-Matic]: V-8. Overhead valves. Cast-iron block. Displacement: 389 cid. Bore & stroke: 4.06 x 3.75 in. Compression ratio: 10.0:1. Brake horsepower: 318 at 4600 rpm. Five main bearings. Hydraulic valve lifters. Carburetor: Three Rochester two-barrels. Tri-Power on the standard Hydra-Matic block was $73 for Bonnevilles and $81 for other series. Price for this option was $89/$99/$132/$142 depending on the engine/transmission combination. Engine code: C4 (318 hp/Tri-Power).

ENGINE [Tempest 425 NASCAR Four-barrel]: V-8. Overhead valves. Cast-iron block. Displacement: 389 cid. Bore & stroke: 4.06 x 3.75 in. Compression ratio: 10.75:1. Brake horsepower: 333 at 4600 rpm. Five main bearings. Hydraulic valve lifters. Carburetor: Four-barrel. Dual exhausts were standard with this engine. Prices for this engine were $230/$251/$273/$279 depending upon model and transmission. Engine code: F1 (333 hp).

ENGINE [Tempest 425 NASCAR Tri-Power]: V-8. Overhead valves. Cast-iron block. Displacement: 389 cid. Bore & stroke: 4.06 x 3.75 in. Compression ratio: 10.75:1. Brake horsepower: 348 at 4600 rpm. Five main bearings. Hydraulic valve lifters. Carburetor: Three Rochester two-barrels. Dual exhausts were standard with this engine. Prices for this engine were $316/$326/$359/$369 depending upon model and transmission. Engine code: M1 (348 hp/Tri-Power); M4 (348 hp/Tri-Power).

CHASSIS: Wheelbase: (Series 21, 23, and 27) 123 in.; (Series 24 and 28) 124 in. Overall Length: (Catalina, Ventura, and Bonneville Custom Safari) 213.7 in.; (All others) 220.7 in. Front tread: 63.7 in. Rear tread: 64 in. Tires: (Passenger cars) 8.00 x 14; (station wagons and all with air-conditioning) 8.50 x 14.

OPTIONS: Air-conditioning ($430). Electric antenna ($30). Aluminum hubs and drums ($107). E-Z-Eye glass ($43). Circ-L-Aire heater defroster ($43). Direct Aire heater defroster ($94). Sportable radio ($129). Wonder Bar radio ($125). Super Deluxe radio ($89). Rear seat speaker ($14). Luggage carrier ($99). Padded dash ($19). Bucket seats ($100). Safeguard speedometer ($15). Magi-Cruise ($13). Custom wheel discs ($17-$32); Deluxe wheel discs ($16). Windshield washer ($13). Continental spare tire and cover ($258). Underhood utility lamp ($12). Remote control mirror ($15). Power windows ($58 two-door or $106 four-door). Power steering ($108). Power brakes ($43). Custom steering wheel ($15). A column-shift

three-speed manual transmission was standard. Super Hydra-Matic (Strato-Flight) transmission was $231.34 extra. A four-speed manual floor-mounted transmission became available in midyear, though not as a regular production option (RPO). Most went into professionally-driven NASCAR race cars. The unit was basically the same one used by Corvettes and Chevrolets and retailed for $188.30 from Chevrolet. The Pontiac price is probably the same. A variety of rear axle ratios were available. Safe-T-Track differential was $43 extra and optional dual exhausts cost $31.

HISTORICAL: Production began Aug. 31, 1959. Introductions were Oct. 1, 1959. Calendar year output was 450,206 cars (including early 1961 Tempests) for 6.6 percent market share. Model year production was 396,716. Four NASCAR Grand Nationals and three other stock car races were won by Pontiacs. Jim Wangers drove a 1960 Pontiac to the NHRA "Top Eliminator" title. Mickey Thompson installed four Pontiac engines in his Challenger I World Land Speed Record car and drove it 363.67 mph. The 333-hp Catalina two-door hardtop was timed at 7.8 seconds for 0-to-60 mph and 16 seconds for the quarter-mile. Safari remained Pontiac's nomenclature for a station wagon. All 1960 Safaris were four-door types and nine-passenger (three-seat) versions had power tailgate windows and rear-facing folding seats. The term Vista meant four-door pillarless hardtop. The term Sport Sedan meant two-door pillared coupe. Safaris had distinctive single tail lamps and rear decor trim. Starlight two-toning was $40 in regular colors or $52 in special colors. AmbleWagons were low-cost professional cars built off a standard Pontiac station wagon chassis by the Automotive Conversion Corp., Troy, Mich.

1961 PONTIAC

1961 Pontiac Catalina two-door convertible. (OCW)

CATALINA SERIES — (V-8) — SERIES 23 — Downsizing was seen at Pontiac this year. Thanks to a new perimeter frame design the bodies on standard sized cars were smaller and lighter in weight. Major design differences included a return to the twin grille styling theme, sculptured side panels, taller rooflines and squared-off bodies with small tailfins added. Catalinas also had horizontal-oval tail lamps and small hubcaps were standard. Base equipment on Catalinas included turn signals, oil filter, cigarette lighter, sun visors, electric windshield wipers and five tubeless black sidewall tires.

1961 Pontiac Catalina two-door hardtop. (OCW)

1961 Pontiac Star Chief four-door sedan. (OCW)

VENTURA SERIES — (V-8) — SERIES 25 — The Ventura continued as a Catalina-sized car with Custom level trim inside and out. Identification included chrome outline moldings for side spears, Ventura script inside the spear on the door, and bright metal roof drip moldings. Venturas carried two round tail lamps and full Deluxe wheel discs. Interiors were trimmed in three-tone Jeweltone Morrokide. Standard equipment included custom steering wheel, electric clock, and right-hand ashtray, plus all features seen on Catalinas.

STAR CHIEF SERIES — (V-8) — SERIES 26 — Star Chiefs could be outwardly identified by chrome outline moldings on the concave portion of the side spears which encircled a Star Chief script on the front door, thin horizontal moldings on the convex section of the spear, three chrome stars stacked on the side of the fins, and triple taillights on each side. Standard equipment was comprised of all features found in Venturas, plus two-speed wipers. Interiors were furnished in Jacquard woven cloth with metallic highlights accented by Jeweltone Morrokide.

BONNEVILLE SERIES — (V-8) — SERIES 28 — Cars in Pontiac's top series were distinguished by golden Bonneville nameplates on the left-hand grille, bright metal moldings on side spears, Bonneville block letters on the convex portion of the spears where front fenders and doors met, and triple tail lamps set into bright metal housings. Everything included on Star Chiefs was considered standard. Rear foam cushions, padded instrument panels, and courtesy lamps were added. Upholstery ranged from nylon and Morrokide combinations on closed cars to all-Morrokide on convertibles, with full genuine leather trims optional.

BONNEVILLE CUSTOM SERIES — (V-8) — SERIES 27 — Comprising a separate series by itself was the Bonneville Custom Safari station wagon. It was built off the Catalina platform, but featured Bonneville power and appointments. The majority of trim and equipment was similar to that on other Bonnevilles, but the four-door station wagon had unique "Safari" rear fender scripts, vertical tail lamps, and a circular keyhole ornament on the tailgate.

TEMPEST — (4-CYL) — SERIES 21 — A radically new compact named the Tempest was introduced as a Pontiac entry in the growing small-car marketplace. In appearance the Tempest was pure Pontiac with twin grilles, sculptured body panels, V-contour hood, and body side wind splits. It was technically innovative and featured an integral body and frame, flexible "rope" drive shaft, torque tube drive, independent rear suspension, rear-mounted transaxle, and a four-cylinder base power plant created by cutting a 389 cid V-8 in half. Standard equipment included electric wipers, turn signals, dual sun visors, and five tubeless black sidewall tires. A four-door sedan and Safari station wagon were first to appear. The sedan and station wagon models were joined by a pair of two-door hardtops (or Sport Coupes) later in the year. One of these was a deluxe model with bucket seats that was named the LeMans.

1961 Pontiac Tempest four-door sedan. (OCW)

I.D. DATA: VIN on left front door post. First symbol tells series: 21=Tempest; 23=Catalina; 25=Ventura; 26=Star Chief; 27=Bonneville Safari; 28=Bonneville. Second and third symbols tell year: 61=1961. Fourth symbol tells assembly plant: P=Pontiac, Mich.; S=South Gate, Calif.; L=Linden, N.J.; W=Wilmington, Del.; K=Kansas City, Kan.; D=Doraville, Ga.; A=Arlington, Texas; E=Euclid, Ohio. Fifth through last symbols are the sequential numbers starting at 1001 for each assembly plant. Body/style number plate under hood tells manufacturer, Fisher style number, assembly plant, trim code, paint code, accessory codes. Style number consists of 61 (for 1961) prefix and four symbols that appear in second column of charts below. First two symbols indicate series; second two symbols indicate body type. VIN appears on front of engine at right-hand cylinder bank along with an alphanumerical engine production code. Engine production codes included: [195-cid/110-hp four] DA/DS; [195-cid/120-hp four] OSY; [195-cid/155-hp four] XS/YS/XA; [195-cid/140-hp four] OA; [215-cid/155-hp aluminum V-8] YA. [389-cid/215-hp V-8] A2/G4; [389-cid/230-hp V-8] E3/W3/E7/W7/; [389-cid/235-hp V-8] P4/B4/H4 [389-cid/267-hp V-8] S1/S5; [389-cid/287-hp V-8] A1/A5; [389-cid/303-hp V-8] B1/T1/PO/B5/T5/. [389-cid/318-hp H.O. Tri-Power V-8] C4/RC4/CO/RCO/19/R19; [389-cid/333-hp V-8] F4/FO/RMO/U9; [389-cid/348-hp H.O. Tri-Power V-8] M4/RM4/MO/V9; [389-cid/363-hp Super-Duty Tri-Power V-8] RMP. [421-cid/373-hp Super-Duty V-8] 11-5.

Model Number	Body Style Number	Body Type & Seating	Factory Price	Shipping Weight	Production Total
CATALINA					
23	2369	4d Sedan-6P	2,702	3,725	38,638
23	2339	4d Vista HT-6P	2,842	3,785	17,589
23	2311	2d Sport Sedan-6P	2,631	3,650	9,846
23	2337	2d Hardtop-6P	2,766	3,680	14,524
23	2367	2d Convertible-5P	3,078	3,805	12,379
23	2345	4d Sta Wagon-9P	3,207	4,175	7,783
23	2335	4d Sta Wagon-6P	3,099	4,135	12,595
VENTURA					
25	2539	4d Vista HT-6P	3,047	3,795	13,912
25	2537	2d Hardtop-6P	2,971	3,685	13,297
STAR CHIEF					
26	2669	4d Sedan-6P	3,003	3,840	16,024
26	2639	4d Vista HT-6P	3,136	3,870	13,557
BONNEVILLE					
28	2839	4d Vista HT-6P	3,331	3,895	30,830
28	2837	2d Hardtop-6P	3,255	3,810	16,906
28	2867	2d Convertible-5P	3,476	3,905	18,264

1961 Pontiac Bonneville two-door convertible. (OCW)

1961 Pontiac Tempest LeMans two-door. (OCW)

Standard Catalog of ® Pontiac, 2nd Edition

1961 Pontiac Tempest four-door station wagon. (OCW)

Model Number	Body Style Number	Body Type & Seating	Factory Price	Shipping Weight	Production Total
BONNEVILLE CUSTOM					
27	2735	4d Sta Wagon-6P	3,530	4,185	3,323
TEMPEST					
21	2119	4d Sedan-6P	2,702	2,800	22,557
21	2127	2d Hardtop-6P	2,113	2785	7,432
21	2135	4d Sta Wagon-6P	2,438	2,980	7,404
TEMPEST (WITH CUSTOM TRIM PACKAGE)					
21	2119	4d Sedan-6P	2,884	2,800	40,082
21	2127	2d LeMans HT-6P	2,297	2,795	7,455
21	2135	4d Sta Wagon-6P	2,611	2,980	15,853

NOTE 1: 113,354 Catalinas were built.

NOTE 2: 6,337 had synchromesh and 107,017 had Hydra-Matic.

NOTE 3: 27,209 Venturas were built.

NOTE 4: 1,940 had synchromesh and 25,269 had Hydra-Matic.

NOTE 5: 29,581 Star Chief chassis were made.

NOTE 6: 130 had synchromesh and 29,451 had Hydra-Matic.

NOTE 7: A total of 66,385 Bonnevilles were built.

NOTE 8: 1,480 had synchromesh and 64,905 had Hydra-Matic.

NOTE 9: About 385 Bonneville chassis went to professional car makers.

NOTE 10: 3,323 Custom Safaris were built.

NOTE 11: 18 had synchromesh and 3,305 had Hydra-Matic.

NOTE 12: 98,779 Tempest with four-cylinder engines were built.

NOTE 13: 26,737 Tempest fours had synchromesh and 72,042 had Hydra-Matic.

NOTE 14: 2,004 Tempests were built with optional (Buick) aluminum V-8s.

NOTE 15: Three Tempest V-8s had synchromesh and 2,001 had Hydra-Matic.

PONTIAC ENGINES

ENGINE [Catalina/Ventura/Star Chief with synchromesh]: Base V-8. Overhead valves. Cast-iron block. Displacement: 389 cid. Bore & stroke: 4.06 x 3.75 in. Compression ratio: 8.6:1. Brake horsepower: 215 at 3600 rpm. Five main bearings. Hydraulic valve lifters. Carburetor: Rochester Number 7019060 two-barrel.

ENGINE [Catalina/Ventura/Star Chief with Hydra-Matic]: Base V-8. Overhead valves. Cast-iron block. Displacement: 389 cid. Bore & stroke: 4.06 x 3.75 in. Compression ratio: 10.25:1. Brake horsepower: 267 at 4200 rpm. Five main bearings. Hydraulic valve lifters. Carburetor: Rochester Number 7019060 two-barrel.

ENGINE [Bonneville/Bonneville Custom with synchromesh]: Base V-8. Overhead valves. Cast-iron block. Displacement: 389 cid. Bore & stroke: 4.06 x 3.75 in. Compression ratio: 8.6:1. Brake horsepower: 235 at 3600 rpm. Five main bearings. Hydraulic valve lifters. Carburetor: Carter AFB3123S four-barrel. Optional all other Pontiacs with synchromesh.

ENGINE [Bonneville/Bonneville Custom with Hydra-Matic]: Base V-8. Overhead valves. Cast-iron block. Displacement: 389 cid. Bore & stroke: 4.06 x 3.75 in. Compression ratio: 10.25:1. Brake horsepower: 303 at 4600 rpm. Five main bearings. Hydraulic valve lifters. Carburetor: Carter AFB3123S four-barrel.

ENGINE [Optional all Pontiacs with Hydra-Matic]: V-8. Overhead valves. Cast-iron block. Displacement: 389 cid. Bore & stroke: 4.06 x 3.75 in. Compression ratio: 8.6:1. Brake horsepower: 230 at 4000 rpm. Five main bearings. Hydraulic valve lifters. Carburetor: Rochester two-barrel.

ENGINE [Optional in Star Chiefs with Hydra-Matic]: V-8. Overhead valves. Cast-iron block. Displacement: 389 cid. Bore & stroke: 4.06 x 3.75 in. Compression ratio: 10.25:1. Brake horsepower: 283 at 4400 rpm. Five main bearings. Hydraulic valve lifters. Carburetor: Rochester two-barrel.

ENGINE [Optional in Catalina with Hydra-Matic]: V-8. Overhead valves. Cast-iron block. Displacement: 389 cid. Bore & stroke: 4.06 x 3.75 in. Compression ratio: 10.25:1. Brake horsepower: 287 at 4400 rpm. Five main bearings. Hydraulic valve lifters. Carburetor: Four-barrel.

ENGINE [Tri-Power Tempest '425A' optional for all Pontiacs with any transmission]: V-8. Overhead valves. Cast-iron block. Displacement: 389 cid. Bore & stroke: 4.06 x 3.75 in. Compression ratio: 10.75:1. Brake horsepower: 318 at 4600 rpm. Five main bearings. Hydraulic valve lifters. Carburetor: Three Rochester two-barrels.

ENGINE [Tempest '425A' four-barrel optional for all Pontiacs with any transmission]: V-8. Overhead valves. Cast-iron block. Displacement: 389 cid. Bore & stroke: 4.06 x 3.75 in. Compression ratio: 10.75:1. Brake horsepower: 333 at 4800 rpm. Five main bearings. Hydraulic valve lifters. Carburetor: four-barrel.

ENGINE: [Tri-Power Tempest '425A' optional for all Pontiacs with any transmission]: V-8. Overhead valves. Cast-iron block. Displacement: 389 cid. Bore & stroke: 4.06 x 3.75 in. Compression ratio: 10.75:1. Brake horsepower: 348 at 4800 rpm. Five main bearings. Hydraulic valve lifters. Carburetor: Three Rochester two-barrels.

ENGINE: [Super-Duty: available only in Catalina two-door; off-road use only]: V-8. Overhead valves. Cast-iron block. Displacement: 421 cid. Bore & stroke: 4.094 x 4.00 in. 421 cid. Compression ratio: 11:1 Brake horsepower: 405 at 5600 rpm. Five main bearings. Solid valve lifters. Carburetion: two four-barrels.

TEMPEST ENGINES

ENGINE [Tempest "Indy Four" with synchromesh]: Inline. Four-cylinder. Overhead valves. Cast-iron block. Displacement: 194.5 cid. Bore & stroke: 4.06 x 3.75 in. Compression ratio: 8.6:1. Brake horsepower: 110 at 3800 rpm rpm. Five main bearings. Hydraulic valve lifters. Carburetor: Rochester Number one-barrel.

ENGINE [Tempest "Indy Four"]: Inline. Four-cylinder. Overhead valves. Cast-iron block. Displacement: 194.5 cid. Bore & stroke: 4.06 x 3.75 in. Compression ratio: 10.25:1. Brake horsepower: 120 at 3800 rpm. Five main bearings. Hydraulic valve lifters. Carburetor: Rochester one-barrel.

ENGINE [Tempest "Indy Four"]: Inline. Four-cylinder. Overhead valves. Cast-iron block. Displacement: 194.5 cid. Bore & stroke: 4.06 x 3.75 in. Compression ratio: 10.25:1. Brake horsepower: 140 at 4400 rpm. Five main bearings. Hydraulic valve lifters. Carburetor: Rochester one-barrel.

ENGINE [Tempest "Indy Four"]: Inline. Four-cylinder. Overhead valves. Cast-iron block. Displacement: 194.5 cid. Bore & stroke: 4.06 x 3.75 in. Compression ratio: 10.25:1. Brake horsepower: 155 at 4800 rpm. Hydraulic valve lifters. Carburetor: Rochester four-barrel.

ENGINE [Tempest "Indy Four" Economy]: Inline. Four-cylinder. Overhead valves. Cast-iron block. Displacement: 194.5 cid. Bore &

1961 Pontiac Bonneville two-door hardtop. (OCW)

stroke: 4.06 x 3.75 in. Compression ratio: 8.6:1. Brake horsepower: 115 at 4000 rpm. Hydraulic valve lifters. Carburetor: One-barrel.

ENGINE [Base V-8]: Overhead valves. Cast-iron block. Displacement: 215 cid. Bore & stroke: 3.50 x 2.80 in. 215.5 cid. Compression ratio: 8.8:1. Brake horsepower: 155 at 4600 rpm. Hydraulic valve lifters. Carburetion: Rochester four-barrel.

CHASSIS: Wheelbase: (Series 23, 25, and 27) 119 in.; (Series 26 and 28) 123 in.; (Series 21) 112 in. Overall Length: (Series 23 and 25) 210 in.; (Series 27 and Series 23 Safaris) 209.7 in.; (Series 26 and 28) 217 in.; (Tempest) 189.3 in. Front tread: (Pontiac) 62.5 in.; (Tempest) 56.8 in. Rear tread: (Pontiac) 62.5 in.; (Tempest) 56.8 in. Tires: (Pontiac) 8.00 x 14; (Pontiac Safaris) 8.50 x 14; (Tempests) 6.00 x 15.

OPTIONS: [PONTIAC] Air-conditioning ($430). Electric antenna ($30). Guide-Matic headlamp control ($43). Power brakes ($43). Six-way power seat ($97). Power windows ($104). Safeguard speedometer ($19). Magic-Cruise ($16). Aluminum hubs and drums ($107). Bucket seats ($116). Heavy-duty springs ($19). E-Z Eye glass ($43). Luggage carrier ($99). Power tailgate ($32) and more. A three-speed manual transmission was standard. Four-speed Super Hydra-Matic was $231.34 extra. A four-speed manual gearbox with floor shift was $306.66 extra on full-sized cars. Rear axle ratios: (synchromesh) 3.23:1; (Hydra-Matic) 2.87:1. Other ratios were available. Safe-T-Track differential was $43 extra. The four-barrel induction system was $24 extra on all cars except Bonnevilles. Tri-Power induction was priced $110 to $168 depending upon model and transmission. The four-barrel Tempest '425A' high-performance engine was priced $230 to $293 depending upon model and transmission. The Tri-Power Tempest '425A' high-performance engine was priced $338 to $396 depending upon model and transmission. **[TEMPEST]** Basic group ($167-$172); Power tailgate window ($54). Deluxe wheel discs ($16). Windshield washer ($13). Power steering ($75). Bumper guards ($16). Back-up lights ($11-$12). Cool-Pack air-conditioner ($318). Interior decor group ($70-$75). Lower exterior decor group ($13). Upper exterior decor group ($40). Protection group ($40-$42). A three-speed manual transmission was standard. A two-speed Tempes-Torque automatic transmission with dashboard-mounted "spoon" lever control was $172 extra. Engine options included a high-output one-barrel edition of the four with 140 hp at 4400 rpm; a four-barrel edition of the four with 155 hp at 4800 rpm and a 215 cid/155 hp V-8 with 8.8:1 compression, two-barrel carburetor, and 155 hp at 4600 rpm ($216 extra).

HISTORICAL: Production start-up: Sept. 1, 1960. Introduction: Oct. 6, 1960. Model year assemblies were 340,635. Calendar year output was 360,336 Pontiacs and Tempests. Pontiac had a 6.3 percent market share. The term Vista means four-door hardtop. The term Sport Sedan means two-door pillared coupe. The term Safari means station wagon. Bucket seats available only in body style 2867. Pontiac took 21 of 52 NASCAR Grand Nationals. Two road tests were done on Pontiacs with the 348 hp V-8. The first featured a Ventura hardtop that went 0-to-60 mph in 8.2 seconds and did the quarter-mile in 15.5 seconds. The second featured a Catalina S/S drag racing car based on the two-door hardtop. It went from 0-to-60 mph in 4.6 seconds and did the quarter-mile in 13.7 seconds. Bunkie Knudsen was the general manager of Pontiac Motor Division.

1962 PONTIAC

1962 Pontiac Catalina four-door Vista hardtop. (OCW)

CATALINA SERIES — (V-8) — SERIES 23 — Standard Pontiacs grew about an inch-and-a-half for 1962. Styling revisions included a

1962 Pontiac Catalina two-door convertible. (OCW)

V-shaped twin grille, full-length side sculpturing and new rear end styling with curved tail lamps. Vista sedans no longer sported the "flat-top" look and Sport Coupes had multi-plane roofs with a "convertible-like" appearance. Ventura trim became an add-on package for two Catalinas. Regular equipment on Catalinas included turn signals, oil filter, cigarette lighter, sun visors, heater and defroster, windshield wiper, and five tubeless tires. Nine-passenger Catalina Safaris had power tailgate windows. Outwardly the cars came with small hubcaps, unaccented side spears, and Catalina front fender scripts.

STAR CHIEF SERIES — (V-8) — SERIES 26 — Star Chiefs were distinguished by full-length body rub moldings and three slanting stars on the rear fins. Standard equipment included all Catalina features, plus custom steering wheel; electric clock; Deluxe wheel discs; right-hand ashtray and decor molding; dual speed wipers; and special upholstery. Interior trims included Pyramid Pattern cloth and Morrokide combinations or all-Morrokide.

BONNEVILLE SERIES — (V-8) — SERIES 28 — Trim on Bonneville included chrome side spear moldings with ribbed bands in the concave portion, elongated V-shaped rear fender medallions, ribbed trim moldings on the deck lid latch panel, Bonneville block letters on the front fenders and deck lid latch panel, and series identification on the left-hand radiator grille. Standard equipment included all items found on Star Chiefs plus rear foam cushions, padded dashes, and courtesy lamps. Upholstery was of fine woven Morrokide or optional all-leather. High-wing bucket seats were optional in convertibles.

BONNEVILLE CUSTOM SERIES — (V-8) — SERIES 27 — The Custom Safari again formed a separate series. It was the heaviest and most expensive Pontiac. Pleated Morrokide upholstery in two-tones was featured, as well as a concealed luggage locker.

GRAND PRIX SERIES — (V-8) SERIES 29 — The new Grand Prix replaced the Ventura model, although Ventura-Catalinas were still available as a trim option. The "GP" was identified by clean side styling with a checkered flag badge in the concave section of side spears; rocker panel molding; an anodized grille insert and nosepiece; and special rear end styling. The from-the-factory equipment list included all Bonneville features (except courtesy lamps), plus solid color Morrokide upholstery, bucket seats, and center console with tachometer.

TEMPEST — (4-CYL) — SERIES 21 — Styling changes for Tempests included a new wider-spaced split grille theme with a third grille section (incorporating a V-shaped emblem) placed in the center and the addition of bolt-in bright metal fins at the rear. There were five basic models, but two were called Customs and could be optioned with the LeMans trim package. Standard equipment

1962 Pontiac Star Chief four-door sedan. (OCW)

1962 Pontiac Bonneville two-door hardtop. (OCW)

included heater and defroster, electric wipers, turn signals, left-hand visors, and five tubeless black sidewall tires. Those delivered in Custom trim level had twin sun visors, cigarette lighters, Deluxe steering wheel, custom upholstery, and special exterior trim. The Custom Convertible sported courtesy lamps.

I.D. DATA: VIN on left front door post. First symbol tells series: 21=Tempest; 23=Catalina; 26=Star Chief; 27=Bonneville Safari; 28=Bonneville; 29=Grand Prix. Second and third symbols tell year: 62=1962. Fourth symbol tells assembly plant: P=Pontiac, Mich.; S=South Gate, Calif.; L=Linden, N.J.; W=Wilmington, Del.; K=Kansas City, Kan.; D=Doraville, Ga.; A=Arlington, Texas. The remaining symbols in VIN are the sequential production number beginning at 1001 for each factory. Body/style number plate under hood tells manufacturer, Fisher style number, assembly plant, trim code, paint code, accessory codes. Style number consists of 62 (for 1962) prefix and four symbols that appear in second column of charts below. First two symbols indicate series; second two symbols indicate body type. VIN appears on front of engine at right-hand cylinder bank along with an alphanumerical engine production code. Engine production codes included: [195-cid/110-hp four] 89Z/85Z; [195-cid/115-hp four] 79Y; [195-cid/120-hp four] 86Z; [195-cid/140-hp four] 76Y; [195-cid/166-hp four] 77Y/87Z; [215/185-hp aluminum V-8] 91Z/97Z. [389-cid/215-hp V-8] O1A/O3B. [389-cid/230-hp V-8] 20L/21L/40R/41R. [389-cid/235-hp V-8] O2B. [389-cid/267-hp V-8] 15H/17H. [389-cid/283-hp V-8] 35M/37M. [389-cid/303-hp V-8] 16J/16K/18K/39N/36P/38P. [389-cid/318-hp H.O. Tri-Power V-8] 10B/27J/49N. [389-cid/333-hp V-8] O8B/25/47NJ. [389-cid/348-hp H.O. Tri-Power V-8] 11B/28J/50N. [421-cid/405-hp Super-Duty V-8].

Model Number	Body Style Number	Body Type & Seating	Factory Price	Shipping Weight	Production Total
CATALINA					
23	2389	4d Sedan-6P	2,796	3,765	68,124
23	2389	4d Vista HT-6P	2,936	3,825	29,251
23	2311	2d Sedan-6P	2,725	3,705	14,263
23	2347	2d Hardtop-6P	2,860	3,730	46,024
23	2367	2d Convertible-5P	3,172	3,855	16,877
23	2345	4d Sta Wagon-9P	3,301	4,220	10,716
23	2335	4d Sta Wagon-6P	3,193	4,180	19,399
STAR CHIEF					
26	2669	4d Sedan-6P	3,097	3,875	27,760
26	2639	4d Vista HT-6P	3,230	3,925	13,882
BONNEVILLE					
28	2839	4d Vista HT-6P	3,425	4,005	44,015
28	2847	2d Hardtop-6P	3,349	3,900	31,629
28	2867	2d Convertible-5P	3,570	4,005	21,582
BONNEVILLE CUSTOM					
27	2735	4d Sta Wagon-6P	3,624	4,255	4,527
GRAND PRIX					
29	2947	2d Hardtop-5P	3,490	3,835	30,195
TEMPEST					
21	2119	4d Sedan-6P	2,240	2,815	16,057 (21,373)
21	2127	2d Coupe-6P	2,186	2,785	15,473
21	2117	2d Hardtop-6P	2,294	2,800	12,319
21	2167	2d Convertible-5P	2,564	2,955	5,076
21	2135	4d Sta Wagon-6P	2,511	2,995	6,504 (11,170)
TEMPEST CUSTOM (LEMANS OPTION)					
21	2117	2d Hardtop-6P	2,418	—	39,662
21	2167	2d Convertible-5P	2,742	—	15,599

NOTE 1: 204,654 Catalinas were built.

NOTE 2: 13,104 had synchromesh and 191,550 had Hydra-Matic.

NOTE 3: A total of 41,642 Star Chiefs were built.

NOTE 4: 196 had synchromesh and 41,446 had Hydra-Matic.

NOTE 5: 97,772 Series 28 Bonnevilles were built.

NOTE 6: 1,874 Series 28 Bonnevilles had synchromesh; 95,848 had Hydra-Matic.

NOTE 7: 496 Series 28 chassis were provided to professional car builders.

NOTE 8: 4,527 Series 27 Bonneville Custom station wagons were built.

NOTE 9: 35 had synchromesh and 4,492 had Hydra-Matic.

NOTE 10: 30,195 GPs were built.

NOTE 11: 3,939 had synchromesh and 26,556 had Hydra-Matic.

NOTE 12: 141,535 Tempest fours were built.

NOTE 13: 28,867 Tempest fours had synchromesh; 112,668 had Tempes-Torque.

NOTE 14: 1,658 Tempest V-8s were built.

NOTE 15: 86 Tempest V-8s had synchromesh and 1,572 had Tempes-Torque automatic.

NOTE 16: Figures in parenthesis are production of Tempests with Deluxe package.

NOTE 17: Sport Coupe and convertible came Custom-only; no Deluxe option.

PONTIAC ENGINES

ENGINE [Catalina/Star Chief with synchromesh]: Base V-8. Overhead valves. Cast-iron block. Displacement: 389 cid. Bore & stroke: 4.06 x 3.75 in. Compression ratio: 8.6:1. Brake horsepower: 215 at 3600 rpm. Five main bearings. Hydraulic valve lifters. Carburetor: Rochester Number two-barrel.

ENGINE [Catalina with Hydra-Matic]: Base V-8. Overhead valves. Cast-iron block. Displacement: 389 cid. Bore & stroke: 4.06 x 3.75 in. Compression ratio: 10.25:1. Brake horsepower: 267 at 4200 rpm. Five main bearings. Hydraulic valve lifters. Carburetor: Rochester two-barrel.

ENGINE [Star Chiefs with Hydra-Matic]: V-8. Overhead valves. Cast-iron block. Displacement: 389 cid. Bore & stroke: 4.06 x 3.75 in. Compression ratios: 10.25:1. Brake horsepower: 283 at 4400 rpm. Five main bearings. Hydraulic valve lifters. Carburetor: Rochester two-barrel.

ENGINE [Bonneville/Grand Prix with synchromesh]: Base V-8. Overhead valves. Cast-iron block. Displacement: 389 cid. Bore & stroke: 4.06 x 3.75 in. Compression ratios: 8.6:1. Brake horsepower: 235 at 3600 rpm. Five main bearings. Hydraulic valve lifters. Carburetor: Carter AFB3123S four-barrel. Optional all other Pontiacs with synchromesh.

ENGINE [Bonneville/Bonneville Custom with Hydra-Matic]: Base V-8. Overhead valves. Cast-iron block. Displacement: 389 cid. Bore & stroke: 4.06 x 3.75 in. Compression ratios: 10.25:1. Brake horsepower: 303 at 4600 rpm. Five main bearings. Hydraulic valve lifters. Carburetor: Carter AFB3123S four-barrel.

ENGINE [Optional all Pontiacs with Hydra-Matic]: V-8. Overhead valves. Cast-iron block. Displacement: 389 cid. Bore & stroke: 4.06 x 3.75 in. Compression ratios: 8.6:1. Brake horsepower: 230 at 4000 rpm. Five main bearings. Hydraulic valve lifters. Carburetor: Rochester two-barrel.

ENGINE [Tri-Power Tempest '425A' optional for all Pontiacs with any transmission]: V-8. Overhead valves. Cast-iron block. Displacement: 389 cid. Bore & stroke: 4.06 x 3.75 in. Compression ratios: 10.75:1. Brake horsepower: 318 at 4600 rpm. Five main bearings. Hydraulic valve lifters. Carburetor: Three Rochester two-barrels.

ENGINE [Tempest '425A' four-barrel optional for all Pontiacs with any transmission]: V-8. Overhead valves. Cast-iron block. Displacement: 389 cid. Bore & stroke: 4.06 x 3.75 in. Compression ratios: 10.75:1. Brake horsepower: 333 at 4800 rpm. Five main bearings. Hydraulic valve lifters. Carburetor: four-barrel.

1962 Pontiac Bonneville two-door hardtop. (OCW)

1962 Pontiac Bonneville two-door hardtop. (OCW)

1962 Pontiac Tempest Safari four-door station wagon. (OCW)

ENGINE [Tri-Power Tempest '425A' optional for all Pontiacs with any transmission]: V-8. Overhead valves. Cast-iron block. Displacement: 389 cid. Bore & stroke: 4.06 x 3.75 in. Compression ratios: 10.75:1. Brake horsepower: 348 at 4800 rpm. Five main bearings. Hydraulic valve lifters. Carburetor: Three Rochester two-barrels.

ENGINE [Super-Duty 389: available only in Catalina two-door; off-road use only]: V-8. Overhead valves. Cast-iron block. Displacement: 389 cid. Bore & stroke: 4.06 x 3.75 in. Compression ratios: 10.75:1. Brake horsepower: 385 at 5200 rpm. Five main bearings. Hydraulic valve lifters. Carburetor: four-barrel.

ENGINE [Super-Duty 421: available only in Catalina two-door; off-road use only]: V-8. Overhead valves. Cast-iron block. Displacement: 421 cid. Bore & stroke: 4.094 x 4.00 in. 421 cid. Compression ratio: 11:1. Brake horsepower: 405 at 5600 rpm. Five main bearings. Solid valve lifters. Carburetion: two four-barrels.

TEMPEST ENGINES

ENGINE [Tempest "Indy Four" with synchromesh]: Inline. Four-cylinder. Overhead valves. Cast-iron block. Displacement: 194.5 cid. Bore & stroke: 4.06 x 3.75 in. Compression ratio: 8.6:1. Brake horsepower: 110 at 3800 rpm rpm. Five main bearings. Hydraulic valve lifters. Carburetor: Rochester Number one-barrel.

ENGINE [Tempest "Indy Four"]: Inline. Four-cylinder. Overhead valves. Cast-iron block. Displacement: 194.5 cid. Bore & stroke: 4.06 x 3.75 in. Compression ratio: 10.25:1. Brake horsepower: 120 at 3800 rpm. Five main bearings. Hydraulic valve lifters. Carburetor: Rochester one-barrel.

ENGINE [Tempest "Indy Four"]: Inline. Four-cylinder. Overhead valves. Cast-iron block. Displacement: 194.5 cid. Bore & stroke: 4.06 x 3.75 in. Compression ratio: 10.25:1. Brake horsepower: 140 at 3800 rpm. Five main bearings. Hydraulic valve lifters. Carburetor: Rochester one-barrel.

ENGINE [Tempest "Indy Four"]: Inline. Four-cylinder. Overhead valves. Cast-iron block. Displacement: 194.5 cid. Bore & stroke: 4.06 x 3.75 in. Compression ratio: 10.25:1. Brake horsepower: 166 at 3800 rpm. Hydraulic valve lifters. Carburetor: Rochester four-barrel.

ENGINE [Tempest "Indy Four" Economy]: Inline. Four-cylinder. Overhead valves. Cast-iron block. Displacement: 194.5 cid. Bore & stroke: 4.06 x 3.75 in. Compression ratio: 8.6:1. Brake horsepower: 115 at 4000 rpm. Hydraulic valve lifters. Carburetor: One-barrel.

ENGINE [Base V-8]: Overhead valves. Cast-iron block. Displacement: 215 cid. Bore & stroke: 3.50 x 2.80 in. 215.5 cid. Compression ratio: 10.25:1. Brake horsepower: 185 at 4800 rpm. Hydraulic valve lifters. Carburetor: Rochester four-barrel.

CHASSIS: Wheelbase: (Series 23 Safari and Series 27) 119 in.; (Series 23 and 29) 120 in.; (Series 26 and 28) 123 in.; (Series 21) 112 in. Overall Length: (Series 23 and Safari and Series 27) 212.3 in.; (Series 23 and 29) 211.6 in.; (Series 26 and 28) 218.6 in. Front tread: (Pontiac) 62.5 in.; (Tempest) 56.8 in. Rear tread: (Pontiac) 62.5 in.; (Tempest) 56.8 in. Tires: (Pontiac) 8.00 x 14; (Tempest) 6.00 x 15.

OPTIONS: [PONTIAC] Guidematic headlamp control ($43). Bucket seats for body style 2867 ($116). Console for Body Style 2867 with bucket seats ($161). Padded dash ($16). Power bench seat ($97). Power bucket seat ($28). Power brakes ($43). Power steering ($108). Magi-Cruise ($16). Ventura trim for Body Styles 2339 and 2347 ($118.) Aluminum hubs and drums ($108-$122). Two-speed wipers ($5). Windshield washers ($13). Power tailgate window ($31). Power windows ($18). Split-back Safari seat ($116). A three-speed manual transmission was standard. Super Hydra-Matic was $231.34 extra. Four-speed synchromesh with floor shift was $231.34 extra. Dual exhausts were standard with the Trophy "425A" V-8s and $30.88 extra on others. Safe-T-Track differential was $42 extra. Four-barrel carburetion was standard on Bonneville and Grand Prix and $24 extra on others. Tri-Power induction was $116-$174 extra depending on model and transmission. The four-barrel "425A" V-8 was $199-$294 extra depending on model and transmission. The Tri-Power "425A" V-8 was $312-$401 extra depending on model and transmission. Approximately 1,514 cars were built with 421 cid Super-Duty V-8s. This motor represented a stroked version of the Trophy V-8 block with two four-barrel carburetors. Such engines developed 405 hp at 5600 rpm and cost $2,250 extra. Seven rear axle gear ratios were provided, the 3.64:1 and 3.90:1 on special order only. **[TEMPEST]** Air conditioner ($319). Back-up lights ($11-$13). Bumper guards ($16). Electric clock ($16). Tinted windshield ($20). Padded dash ($4). Remote control mirror ($12). Power steering ($75). Power tailgate window ($54). Manual radio ($54). Push-button radio ($62). Upper decor group ($19-$34). Lower decor group ($34). Interior decor group ($70-$75). Exterior decor group combo ($54-$67). Code 088 LeMans option group: (Custom Convertible) $178; (Custom Sports Coupe) $124. A three-speed manual transmission was standard. Two-speed Tempes-Torque automatic or four-speed synchromesh were $172.80 extra. Four-barrel carburetion on the "Indy Four" (166 hp at 4800 rpm) was $38.74 extra. The two-barrel aluminum Buick V-8 (185 hp at 4800 rpm) was $261.36 extra. A 3.55:1 rear axle was standard and 3.31:1 was optional.

HISTORICAL: Production started Aug. 15, 1961. Introductions took place Sept. 21, 1961. The model year saw 521,933 assemblies. In the calendar year, 547,350 cars were made, putting Pontiac in third place in vehicle production in the United States. Pontiacs took 14 of 18 United States Auto Club stock car races and 22 of 53 NASCAR events. Joe Weatherly won the driving championship in a Pontiac. Jim Wanger's 1962 Catalina Super-Duty hardtop was tested in a car buff magazine. The 405-hp "Poncho" went from 0-to-60 mph in 5.4 seconds and did the quarter-mile in 13.9 at 107 mph. A Catalina with a special 370-hp "Royal Bobcat" package from Royal Pontiac

1962 Pontiac Grand Prix two-door hardtop. (OCW)

1962 Pontiac Tempest two-door convertible. (OCW)

1962 Pontiac Bonneville Superior limousine. (OCW)

(Royal Oak, Mich.) ran 0-to-60 mph in 6.5 seconds and did the quarter-mile in 14.5. Carol Cox took the NHRA Winternationals with a 13.06 quarter-mile performance in a Catalina S/SA drag car. Vista means four-door hardtop. Safari means station wagon. Body styles 2117 and 2167 came only as Tempest Custom or Tempest Custom with LeMans option. Bucket seats, center console, and floor mounted gearshift control were standard on Body Style 2947. Bunkie Knudsen moved to Chevrolet and E.M. "Pete" Estes took over as the new general manager of Pontiac Motor Div.

1963 PONTIAC

1963 Pontiac Catalina four-door sedan. (OCW)

CATALINA — (V-8) — SERIES 23 — Styling and luxury were emphasized by Pontiac in 1963 and GM banned factory competition efforts. Styling was totally new with clean, square lines, angled roofs, upward curving tail lamps, recessed split grilles and non-panoramic windshields. Catalinas wore small hubcaps, plain full-length body moldings and Catalina front fender scripts. Turn signals, oil filters, cigarette lighter, sun visors, heater and defroster, electric wipers, and five tubeless tires were standard equipment. Safaris had oversize 8.50 x 14 tires and the nine-passenger model had a power tailgate window.

STAR CHIEF — (V-8) — SERIES 26 — Star Chiefs had full-length body moldings, Deluxe wheel discs, star emblems on the rear roof pillar, and Star Chief front fender scripts. Rocker panel moldings were also seen. Standard equipment included all Catalina features plus custom steering wheel, electric clock, dual-speed wipers, and special upholstery.

BONNEVILLE — (V-8) — SERIES 28 — Bonnevilles came with all Star Chief features plus rear foam cushions, padded instrument

1963 Pontiac Catalina four-door station wagon. (OCW)

1963 Pontiac Grand Prix. (OCW)

panels, and courtesy lamps. They were outwardly identified by broad, ribbed moldings on the front fenders and doors, rear fin badges, left-hand grille nameplates, rocker panel moldings, and block-lettered horizontal decor panels on the deck lid latch panel that carried the Bonneville name.

GRAND PRIX — (V-8) — SERIES 29 — The Grand Prix was restyled from bumper to bumper. It had a clean look with no side trim, a grille emphasizing negative space with bright accents and enclosed parking lamps, grilled-over tail lamps mounted on the deck lid, and a concave rear window treatment. Standard equipment included the full list of Bonneville items, plus special solid color Morrokide upholstery, wood-grained steering wheel and dash trim, bucket type front seats, and a center console with a vacuum gage. The Grand Prix badges were now mounted on the sides of the rear fenders and rocker panel moldings were employed.

TEMPEST — (4-CYL) — SERIES 21 — The term "senior compact" was often used to describe the new Tempests. They had the same wheelbase and technical features as earlier Tempests, but they were two inches wider and five inches longer. Design changes included a slight "coke bottle" shape, more angular rooflines, creased side panels, longer trunks, split grille styling, wider wheel openings, and dual vertically-stacked tail lamps. Standard equipment included heater and defroster, electric wipers, turn signals, left-hand sun visors, and five black tubeless tires. Oversize 6.50 x 15 tires were uses on V-8 equipped Tempests and Safaris.

TEMPEST LEMANS — (V-8) — SERIES 22 — The LeMans nameplate was listed as a separate series. Standard equipment on LeMans included dual sun visors, deluxe steering wheel, custom interior, bucket seats, console, and power convertible top. Identification features included model badges on front fenders, partially blacked-out grilles, horizontal taillights, and a horizontal decor panel on the deck latch panel.

I.D. DATA: VIN on left front door post. First symbol tells series: 21=Tempest; 22=LeMans; 23=Catalina; 26=Star Chief; 28=Bonneville;

1963 Pontiac Bonneville two-door convertible. (OCW)

29=Grand Prix. Second and third symbols tell year: 63=1963. Fourth symbol tells assembly plant: P=Pontiac, Mich.; S=South Gate, Calif.; L=Linden, N.J.; W=Wilmington, Del.; K=Kansas City, Kan.; D=Doraville, Ga.; A=Arlington, Texas. Following symbols are sequential production number starting with 1001 at each assembly plant. Body/style number plate under hood tells manufacturer, Fisher style number, assembly plant, trim code, paint code, accessory codes. Style number consists of 63 (for 1963) prefix and four symbols that appear in second column of charts below. First two symbols indicate series; second two symbols indicate body type. VIN appears on front of engine at right-hand cylinder bank along with an alphanumerical engine production code. Engine production codes included: [195-cid/115-hp four] 89Z/85Z/79Y. [195-cid/120-hp four] 86Z/83Z. [195-cid/140-hp four] 76Y. [195-cid/166-hp four] 77Y/84Z/87Z. [326-cid/260-hp V-8] 68X/71X/60O/69O. [326-cid/280-hp V-8] 70X/59O. [389-cid/215-hp V-8] O1A/O3B. [389-cid/230-hp V-8] 20L/21L/40R/41R. [389-cid/235-hp V-8] O2B/O4B. [389-cid/267-hp V-8] 15H/17H. [389-cid/283-hp V-8] 35M/37M. [389-cid/303-hp V-8] O6B/16K/18K/36P/38P. [389-cid/313-hp H.O. Tri-Power V-8] O7B/48N/26G. [421-cid/320-hp V-8] 22B/43N/34J. [421-cid/353-hp V-8] O8B/47Q/25G. [421-cid/370-hp H.O. Tri-Power V-8] 11B/28G/50Q. [421-cid/405-hp Super-Duty V-8] 12-5. [421-cid/420-hp Super-Duty V-8] 13-5.

Model Number	Body Style Number	Body Type & Seating	Factory Price	Shipping Weight	Production Total
CATALINA					
23	2311	2d Sedan-6P	2,725	3,685	14,091
23	2369	4d Sedan-6P	2,795	3,755	79,961
23	2347	2d Hardtop-6P	2,859	3,725	60,795
23	2339	4d Vista HT-6P	2,935	3,815	31,256
23	2367	2d Convertible-5P	3,300	3,835	18,249
23	2335	4d Sta Wagon-6P	3,171	4,175	18,446
23	2345	4d Sta Wagon-9P	3,193	4,230	11,751
STAR CHIEF					
26	2669	4d Sedan-6P	3,096	3,885	28,309
26	2639	4d Vista HT-6P	3,229	3,915	12,448
BONNEVILLE					
28	2847	2d Hardtop-6P	3,348	3,895	30,995
28	2839	4d Vista HT-6P	3,423	3,985	49,929
28	2867	2d Convertible-5P	3,568	3,970	23,459
28	2835	4d Safari-6P	3,623	4,245	5,156
GRAND PRIX					
29	2957	2d Hardtop-5P	3,490	3,915	72,959
TEMPEST					
21	2127	2d Coupe-6P	2,188	2,810	13,307
21	2117	2d Hardtop-6P	2,294	2,820	(13,157)
21	2119	4d Sedan-6P	2,241	2,815	12,808 (15,413)
21	2167	2d Cus Conv-5P	2,554	2,955	5,012
21	2135	4d Sta Wagon-6P	2,512	2,995	4,203 (5,932)
TEMPEST LEMANS					
22	2217	2d Hardtop-6P	2,418	2,865	45,701
22	2267	2d Cus Conv-5P	2,742	3,035	15,957

NOTE 1: 234,549 Catalinas were built.

1963 Pontiac Bonneville two-door hardtop. (OCW)

1963 Pontiac Tempest LeMans Custom Convertible. (OCW)

1963 Pontiac Grand Prix two-door hardtop. (OCW)

NOTE 2: 16,811 Catalinas had synchromesh and 217,738 had Hydra-Matic.

NOTE 3: 40,757 Star Chiefs were built.

NOTE 4: 175 Star Chiefs had synchromesh and 40,582 had Hydra-Matic.

NOTE 5: 110,316 Bonnevilles were built.

NOTE 6: 1,819 Bonnevilles had synchromesh and 108,497 had Hydra-Matic attachments.

NOTE 7: 777 Bonneville chassis were provided for professional car builders.

NOTE 8: 72,959 Grand Prixs were built.

NOTE 9: 5,157 Grand Prixs had synchromesh and 67,802 had Hydra-Matic.

NOTE 10: 69,831 Series 21 Tempests were built.

NOTE 11: 16,657 Tempests had synchromesh and 53,174 had Tempes-Torque automatic transmission.

NOTE 12: Figures in parenthesis are Tempests with optional deluxe trim.

NOTE 13: Production of body style 63-2117 is not broken out separately.

NOTE 14: 61,659 LeMans were built.

NOTE 15: 18,034 LeMans had synchromesh and 43,625 had Tempes-Torque.

NOTE 16: 23,227 LeMans Sport Coupes and 8,744 LeMans convertibles had four-cylinder engines.

NOTE 17: All other LeMans were V-8 powered.

PONTIAC ENGINES

ENGINE [Base V-8 Catalina/Star Chief with synchromesh]: Overhead valves. Cast-iron block. Displacement: 389 cid. Bore & stroke: 4.06 x 3.75 in. Compression ratio: 8.6:1. Brake horsepower: 215 at 3600 rpm. Five main bearings. Hydraulic valve lifters. Carburetor: Rochester model 7023066 two-barrel.

ENGINE [Base V-8 Catalina with Hydra-Matic]: Overhead valves. Cast-iron block. Displacement: 389 cid. Bore & stroke: 4.06 x 3.75 in. Compression ratio: 10.25:1. Brake horsepower: 267 at 4200 rpm. Five main bearings. Hydraulic valve lifters. Carburetor: Rochester model 7023066 two-barrel.

ENGINE [Base V-8 Star Chiefs with Hydra-Matic]: Overhead valves. Cast-iron block. Displacement: 389 cid. Bore & stroke: 4.06 x 3.75 in. Compression ratio: 10.25:1. Brake horsepower: 283 at 4400 rpm. Five main bearings. Hydraulic valve lifters. Carburetor: Rochester two-barrel.

1963 Pontiac Catalina two-door convertible. (OCW)

1963 Pontiac Tempest LeMans two-door hardtop. (OCW)

ENGINE [Base V-8 Bonneville/Grand Prix with synchromesh]: Overhead valves. Cast-iron block. Displacement: 389 cid. Bore & stroke: 4.06 x 3.75 in. Compression ratio: 8.6:1. Brake horsepower: 235 at 3600 rpm. Five main bearings. Hydraulic valve lifters. Carburetor: Carter AFB four-barrel. Optional all other Pontiacs with synchromesh.

ENGINE [Base V-8 Bonneville/Grand Prix with Hydra-Matic]: Overhead valves. Cast-iron block. Displacement: 389 cid. Bore & stroke: 4.06 x 3.75 in. Compression ratio: 10.25:1. Brake horsepower: 303 at 4600 rpm. Five main bearings. Hydraulic valve lifters. Carburetor: Carter AFB four-barrel.

ENGINE [Optional V-8 all Pontiacs with Hydra-Matic]: Overhead valves. Cast-iron block. Displacement: 389 cid. Bore & stroke: 4.06 x 3.75 in. Compression ratio: 8.6:1. Brake horsepower: 230 at 4000 rpm. Five main bearings. Hydraulic valve lifters. Carburetor: Rochester two-barrel.

ENGINE [Base V-8 (Tri-Power Tempest "425A"); Optional for all Pontiacs with any transmission]: Overhead valves. Cast-iron block. Displacement: 389 cid. Bore & stroke: 4.06 x 3.75 in. Compression ratio: 10.75:1. Brake horsepower: 313 at 4600 rpm. Five main bearings. Hydraulic valve lifters. Carburetor: Three Rochester two-barrels.

ENGINE [421 H.O.: optional all "B" body models]: V-8. Overhead valves. Cast-iron block. Displacement: 421 cid. Bore & stroke: 4.094 x 4.00 in. 421-cid. Compression ratio: 10.75:1. Brake horsepower: 353 at 5000 rpm. Five main bearings. Solid valve lifters. Carburetion: Four-barrel.

ENGINE [421 H.O.: optional all "B" body models]: V-8. Overhead valves. Cast-iron block. Displacement: 421 cid. Bore & stroke: 4.094 x 4.00 in. 421-cid. Compression ratio: 10.75:1. Brake horsepower: 370 at 5200 rpm. Five main bearings. Solid valve lifters. Carburetion: Three two-barrels.

ENGINE [Super-Duty 421: available only in Catalina two-door; off-road use only]: V-8. Overhead valves. Cast-iron block. Displacement: 421 cid. Bore & stroke: 4.094 x 4.00 in. 421-cid. Compression ratio: 12.0:1. Brake horsepower: 390 at 5800 rpm. Five main bearings. Solid valve lifters. Carburetion: Four-barrel.

ENGINE [Super-Duty 421: available only in Catalina two-door; off-road use only]: V-8. Overhead valves. Cast-iron block. Displacement: 421 cid. Bore & stroke: 4.094 x 4.00 in. 421-cid. Compression ratio: 12.0:1. Brake horsepower: 405 at 5600 rpm. Five main bearings. Solid valve lifters. Carburetion: two four-barrels.

ENGINE [Super-Duty 421: available only in Catalina two-door; off-road use only]: V-8. Overhead valves. Cast-iron block. Displacement: 421 cid. Bore & stroke: 4.094 x 4.00 in. 421-cid. Compression ratio: 13.0:1. Brake horsepower: 410 at 5600 rpm. Five main bearings. Solid valve lifters. Carburetion: two four-barrels.

TEMPEST ENGINES

ENGINE [Tempest "Indy Four" with synchromesh]: Inline. Four-cylinder. Overhead valves. Cast-iron block. Displacement: 194.5 cid. Bore & stroke: 4.06 x 3.75 in. Compression ratio: 8.6:1. Brake horsepower: 115 at 4000 rpm. Five main bearings. Hydraulic valve lifters. Carburetor: Rochester Number one-barrel.

ENGINE [Tempest "Indy Four"]: Inline. Four-cylinder. Overhead valves. Cast-iron block. Displacement: 194.5 cid. Bore & stroke: 4.06 x 3.75 in. Compression ratio: 10.25:1. Brake horsepower: 120 at 3800 rpm. Five main bearings. Hydraulic valve lifters. Carburetor: Rochester one-barrel.

ENGINE [Tempest "Indy Four"]: Inline. Four-cylinder. Overhead valves. Cast-iron block. Displacement: 194.5 cid. Bore & stroke: 4.06 x 3.75 in. Compression ratio: 10.25:1. Brake horsepower: 140 at 3800

1963 Pontiac Bonneville Superior Embassy limousine. (JAG)

rpm. Five main bearings. Hydraulic valve lifters. Carburetor: Rochester one-barrel.

ENGINE [Tempest "Indy Four"]: Inline. Four-cylinder. Overhead valves. Cast-iron block. Displacement: 194.5 cid. Bore & stroke: 4.06 x 3.75 in. Compression ratio: 10.25:1. Brake horsepower: 166 at 3800 rpm. Hydraulic valve lifters. Carburetor: Rochester four-barrel.

ENGINE [Base V-8]: Overhead valves. Cast-iron block. Displacement: 325.8 cid. Bore & stroke: 3.718 x 3.75 in. Compression ratio: 10.25:1. Brake horsepower: 260 at 4800 rpm. Hydraulic valve lifters. Carburetion: Rochester two-barrel.

CHASSIS: Wheelbase: (All Pontiac Safaris) 119 in.; (Series 23 and 29) 120 in.; (Series 26 and 28) 123 in.; (Tempests) 112 in. Overall Length: (All Pontiac Safaris) 212.8 in.; (Series 23 and 29) 211.9 in.; (Series 26 and 28) 218.9 in.; (All Tempests) 194.3 in. Front tread: (Pontiac) 64 in.; (Tempest) 57.3 in. Rear tread: (Pontiac) 64 in.; (Tempest) 58 in. Standard tires: (Pontiac) 8.00 x 14; (Tempest) 6.00 x 15.

OPTIONS: [PONTIAC] Air-conditioning ($430). Console including tachometer ($161). Instrument gage cluster ($21-$59). Luggage carrier ($94). Remote control mirror ($12). Power brakes ($57). Power seat ($96). Power tilt left-hand bucket seat ($71). Tachometer ($54). Cordova top ($86). Ventura trim on body styles 2339, 2347 and 2369 ($118). Sports wheelcovers ($30-46). Aluminum hubs and drums ($122-$138). A three-speed manual transmission was standard. A heavy-duty thee-speed manual gearbox was $48 extra on Catalinas and Bonnevilles. A four-speed manual gearbox with floor shift was $231 extra. Super Hydra-Matic was also $231 extra. Dual exhausts were standard with "425A" V-8s and $31 extra on others. Safe-T-Track differential was $43 more. Four-barrel carburetion was standard on Bonneville and Grand Prix and $35 extra on others. Tri-Power induction was $126 on Catalinas and Star Chiefs and $116 on Grand Prix and Bonnevilles. This engine, with 10.25:1 compression, now gave 313 hp at 4600 rpm. The "421" engines, with 10.75:1 compression heads, were now called H.O. motors. The four-barrel edition was priced $291-$343 extra depending upon model and transmission. It produced 353 hp at 5000 rpm. The Tri-Power 421 H.O. engine was priced $404-$445 extra depending on model and transmission. It produced 370 hp at 5200 rpm. A variety of axle ratios were available. [TEMPEST] Air-conditioner ($319). LeMans console shift ($48). Padded dash ($16). Power convertible top ($54). Power tilt left bucket seat ($67). Power steering ($75). Power tailgate window ($54). Push-button radio ($62). Bucket seats ($134). Custom steering wheel

1963 Pontiac Bonneville Superior combination car. (JAG)

($6-$9). Deluxe steering wheel with ring ($4). Tachometer ($54). Cordova top ($75). Two-speed wipers and washer ($17). A three-speed manual transmission was standard. Two-speed Tempes-Torque automatic was $173 extra. A four-speed manual gearbox with floor shift was priced $189. Four-barrel carburetion on the "Indy Four" was $39 extra. A new V-8 was available at $167 over base price. Based on a standard Pontiac V-8 with bore size reduced, this engine displaced 326 cid. (5.3 liters). Bore & stroke measured 3.72 x 3.75 in. With a two-barrel carburetor and 10.25:1 compression it produced 260 hp at 4800 rpm. A heavy-duty clutch was available for the one-barrel and four-barrel versions of the "Indy Four" at prices of $27 and $66, respectively. Standard axle ratio for Tempest was 3.55:1 and optional was 3.31:1.

HISTORICAL: Production began Sept. 4, 1962. Introductions were on Oct. 4, 1962. Model year output was 590,071 for an 8.9 percent share of market. Calendar year output was 625,268, making Pontiac the third largest auto producer. Pontiac had four NASCAR wins and startled the drag racing world with the release of "Swiss Cheese" Catalina factory lightweight racing cars. The name came from the fact that their frames were drilled to decrease the weight. The 370-hp 1963 Grand Prix was good for 0-to-60 mph in 6.6 seconds and did the quarter-mile in 15.1 seconds. Vista means four-door hardtop. Safari means station wagon. Sports Sedan was sometimes used to identify two-door pillared coupes. Body style 2957 had a distinctive roofline not shared with other lines. Bucket seats were now available for Catalina coupes and convertibles with the Ventura option, plus Bonnevilles including the Custom Safari station wagon. The following "Super-Duty 421" vehicles were built in 1963: 13 Catalina and Grand Prix four-barrels; 59 Catalinas and Grand Prix with two four-barrel carburetors; five unspecified models (believed to be Catalinas with aluminum front ends) with dual four-barrel induction and 11 Tempests with the dual-quad engine.

1964 PONTIAC

1964 Pontiac Catalina 2 + 2 two-door hardtop. (OCW)

CATALINA — (V-8) — SERIES 23 — Full-size Pontiacs got a facelift for 1964. They looked shorter, but were about an inch longer overall. Trim identification features seen on Catalinas included three-quarter length side moldings running from the front wheel opening back, Catalina front fender scripts and series medallions on the rear fender. Standard equipment was about the same as a year earlier. Full wheel

1964 Pontiac Catalina 2 + 2 two-door convertible. (OCW)

1964 Pontiac Catalina four-door sedan. (OCW)

discs and rocker moldings were options seen on many Catalinas. The Catalina 2 + 2 option package was available on style numbers 2347 and 2367 at approximately $291. The Ventura trim package was available as an interior decor option for Catalina style numbers 2339, 2347, and 2367 at approximately $118.

STAR CHIEF — (V-8) — SERIES 26 — Star Chiefs had Deluxe steering wheels and wheelcovers as standard equipment, as well as two-speed wipers and electric clocks. Trim features included Catalina-like side spears, front fender model scripts, and three stylized stars stacked on rear fenders.

BONNEVILLE — (V-8) — SERIES 28 — Bonnevilles had no body side moldings. Identifiers included V-shaped front fender badges, ribbed lower body beauty moldings (on rocker panels) with front and rear fender extensions and Bonneville block lettering on the rear fender sides. Courtesy lamps, padded dashboards and rear foam seat cushions were standard, plus all items found on the Star Chief equipment list. A Bonneville Brougham trim package was available for style number 2839 and included special interior trim and roof pillar nameplates.

GRAND PRIX — (V-8) — SERIES 29 — The Grand Prix was identified by model lettering and badges behind the front wheel cutout, rectangular front parking lamps, more deeply recessed grilles, and GP lettering on the left-hand grille. Concave rear window treatments, grilled-over tail lamps and wood-grained trim for dashboards and steering wheels were seen. Standard equipment included dual exhausts, bucket seats, center console, and front foam seat cushions.

TEMPEST — (6-CYL) — SERIES 20 — Tempests were enlarged again and had separate frame construction with conventional drive train engineering. A six-cylinder engine, assembled by Pontiac Motor Div. from Chevrolet-produced components, was the base power plant. There were three lines. Identifying Series 20 base Tempests were small hubcaps, the absence of upper belt line moldings, and triple windsplits behind front wheel openings. Cars with optional V-8 power were dressed with front fender badges.

TEMPEST CUSTOM — (6 CYL) — SERIES 21 — Tempest Customs had the same general styling features as base Tempests, but could be easily identified by the bright upper beltline moldings accenting the "Coke bottle" shape. There were also Tempest Custom nameplates on the rear fenders. Extra standard equipment included carpeting, deluxe steering wheel, and courtesy lamps on convertibles.

1964 Pontiac Bonneville two-door convertible. (OCW)

1964 Pontiac Grand Prix two-door hardtop. (OCW)

1964 Pontiac Tempest LeMans two-door hardtop. (OCW)

TEMPEST LEMANS — (6-CYL) — SERIES 22 — LeMans series Tempests had distinct styling touches such as LeMans nameplates on the rear fender sides, ribbed decor plates for the deck lid latch panel, model badges on the deck lid, simulated slanting louvers ahead of rear wheel cutouts and LeMans script plates for the dashboard. Bucket seats were standard on all models. The famous Grand Turismo Omologato (GTO) option package was released for LeMans models this year. The idea behind this package was to circumvent a corporate high-performance ban by providing the 389-cid V-8 as an option in the most luxurious Pontiac intermediate. GTOs featured special appearance items in place of some regular LeMans styling touches.

I.D. DATA: VIN on left front door post. First symbol tells engine type: 6=six-cylinder; 8=V-8. Second symbol indicates series: 0=Tempest; 1=Tempest Custom; 2=LeMans; 3=Catalina; 6=Star Chief; 8=Bonneville; 9=Grand Prix. Third symbol tells year: 64=1964. Fourth symbol tells assembly plant: P=Pontiac, Mich.; S=South Gate, Calif.; L=Linden, N.J.; K=Kansas City, Kan., GMAD plant; D=Doraville, Ga.; A=Arlington, Texas; F=Fremont, Ohio; B=Baltimore, Md.; M=Kansas City, Kan. Chevrolet assembly plant. Following symbols are sequential production numbers starting with 1001 at each assembly plant. Body/style number plate under hood tells manufacturer, Fisher style number, assembly plant, trim code, paint code, accessory codes. Style number consists of 64 (for 1964) prefix and four symbols that appear in second column of charts below. First two symbols indicate series; second two symbols indicate body type. VIN appears on front of engine at right-hand cylinder bank along with an alpha-numerical engine production code. Engine production codes included: [215-cid/140-hp six] 80Z/81Z/85Z/83Y/88Y/ 89Y. [326-cid/250-hp V-8] 92X/96O. [326-cid/280-hp V-8] 94X/97O. [389-cid/215-hp V-8] O1A/O2B/O3B. [389-cid/230-hp V-8] O4L/O5L/ O8R/O9R. [389-cid/239-hp V-8] O3B/O4B. [389-cid/235-hp] 22B. [389-cid/240-hp V-8] 13H. [389-cid/257-hp V-8] 19M. [389-cid/267-hp V-8] 11H/12H. [389-cid/276-hp V-8] 30P. [389-cid/283-hp V-8] 10A/17M/18M. [389-cid/303-hp V-8] 25K/26K/27P/28P. [389-cid/ 306-hp V-8] 23B/29N/ [389-cid/330-hp H.O. Tri-Power V-8] 32B/ 33G/34N. [421-cid/320-hp V-8] 35B/38S/43N. [421-cid/350-hp H.O.

Tri-Power V-8] 44B/47S/49N. [421-cid/370-hp H.O. Tri-Power V-8] 45B/46G/50Q. [389-cid/325-hp four-barrel GTO V-8] 78X with synchromesh; 79J with Hydra-Matic. [389-cid/348-hp GTO Tri-Power V-8] 76X with synchromesh; 77J with Hydra-Matic. (Note: Some Pontiac experts claim that a few GTOs were built with factory-installed and/or dealer-installed 421 V-8s.)

Model Number	Body Style Number	Body Type & Seating	Factory Price	Shipping Weight	Production Total
CATALINA					
23	2369	4d Sedan-6P	2,806	3,770	84,457
23	2339	4d Hardtop-6P	2,945	3,835	33,849
23	2311	2d Sedan-6P	2,735	3,695	12,480
23	2347	2d Hardtop-6P	2,869	3,750	74,793
23	2367	2d Convertible-5P	3,181	3,825	18,693
23	2345	4d Sta Wagon-9P	3,311	4,235	13,140
23	2335	4d Sta Wagon-6P	3,203	4,190	20,356
STAR CHIEF					
26	2669	4d Sedan-6P	3,107	3,885	26,453
26	2639	4d Hardtop-6P	3,239	3,945	11,200
BONNEVILLE					
28	2839	4d Hardtop-6P	3,433	3,995	57,630
28	2847	2d Hardtop-6P	3,358	3,920	34,769
28	2867	2d Convertible-5P	3,578	3,985	22,016
28	2835	4d Sta Wagon-6P	3,633	4,275	5,844
GRAND PRIX					
29	2957	2d Hardtop-5P	3,99	3,930	63,810
TEMPEST					
20	2069	4d Sedan-6P	2,313	2,970	15,516 (3,911)
20	2027	2d Hardtop-6P	2,259	2,930	17,169 (4,596)
20	2035	4d Sta Wagon-6P	2,605	3,245	4,597 (2,237)
TEMPEST CUSTOM					
21	2169	4d Sedan-6P	2,399	2,990	15,851 (14,097)
21	2167	2d Convertible-5P	2,641	3,075	4,465 (3,522)
21	2127	2d Hardtop-6P	2,345	2,955	12,598 (13,235)
21	2135	4d Sta Wagon-6P	2,691	3,260	4,254 (6,442)
TEMPEST LEMANS					
22	2227	2d Cpe-5P	2,491	2,975	11,136 (20,181)
22	2237	2d Hardtop-5P	2,556	2,995	7,409 (23,901)
22	2267	2d Convertible-5P	2,796	3,125	5,786 (11,773)
TEMPEST LEMANS (WITH GTO OPTION)					
22	2227	2d Coupe-5P	2,852	3,106	7,384
22	2237	2d Hardtop-5P	2,963	3,126	18,422
22	2267	2d Convertible-5P	3,081	3,360	6,644

NOTE 1: 257,768 Catalinas were built.

NOTE 2: 15,194 had synchromesh and 242,574 had Hydra-Matic.

1964 Pontiac Tempest Custom two-door convertible. (OCW)

1964 Pontiac Tempest LeMans two-door hardtop. (OCW)

Standard Catalog of ® Pontiac, 2nd Edition

1964 Pontiac Tempest LeMans GTO two-door hardtop. (OCW)

1964 Pontiac Catalina two-door hardtop. (OCW)

1964 Pontiac Tempest LeMans GTO two-door convertible. (OCW)

1964 Pontiac Bonneville two-door hardtop. (OCW)

NOTE 3: 7,998 cars had the 2 + 2 option package.

NOTE 4: 37,653 Star Chiefs were built.

NOTE 5: 132 had synchromesh and 37,521 had Hydra-Matic.

NOTE 6: 115,060 Bonnevilles (123-in. wheelbase) were built.

NOTE 7: 1,470 cars (123-in. wheelbase) had synchromesh and 113,590 had Hydra-Matic.

NOTE 8: 5,844 Bonneville (119-in. wheelbase) were built.

NOTE 9: 42 cars (119-in. wheelbase) had synchromesh and 5,802 had Hydra-Matic.

NOTE 10: 645 Bonneville (123-in. wheelbase) chassis provided for conversions.

NOTE 11: 63,810 Grand Prix were built.

NOTE 12: 3,124 had synchromesh and 60,686 had Hydra-Matic.

NOTE 13: No brackets=Tempest six production; brackets=Tempest V-8 production.

PONTIAC ENGINES

ENGINE [Catalina/Star Chief with synchromesh]: Base V-8. Overhead valves. Cast-iron block. Displacement: 389 cid. Bore & stroke: 4.06 x 3.75 in. Compression ratio: 8.6:1. Brake horsepower: 235 at 3600 rpm. Five main bearings. Hydraulic valve lifters. Carburetor: Carter AFB four-barrel. Optional all other Pontiacs with synchromesh.

ENGINE [Catalina with Hydra-Matic]: Base V-8. Overhead valves. Cast-iron block. Displacement: 389 cid. Bore & stroke: 4.06 x 3.75 in. Compression ratio: 10.25:1. Brake horsepower: 267 at 4200 rpm. Five main bearings. Hydraulic valve lifters. Carburetor: Rochester model 7023066 two-barrel.

ENGINE [Star Chiefs with Hydra-Matic]: V-8. Overhead valves. Cast-iron block. Displacement: 389 cid. Bore & stroke: 4.06 x 3.75 in. Compression ratio: 10.25:1. Brake horsepower: 283 at 4400 rpm. Five main bearings. Hydraulic valve lifters. Carburetor: Rochester two-barrel.

ENGINE [Bonneville/Grand Prix with synchromesh]: Base V-8. Overhead valves. Cast-iron block. Displacement: 389 cid. Bore & stroke: 4.06 x 3.75 in. Compression ratio: 8.6:1. Brake horsepower: 255 at 4000 rpm. Five main bearings. Hydraulic valve lifters. Carburetor: Carter AFB four-barrel. Optional all other Pontiacs with synchromesh.

ENGINE [Bonneville with Hydra-Matic]: Base V-8. Overhead valves. Cast-iron block. Displacement: 389 cid. Bore & stroke: 4.06 x 3.75 in. Compression ratio: 10.25:1. Brake horsepower: 306 at 4600 rpm. Five main bearings. Hydraulic valve lifters. Carburetor: Carter AFB model 3674S four-barrel.

ENGINE [Grand Prix with Hydra-Matic]: Base V-8. Overhead valves. Cast-iron block. Displacement: 389 cid. Bore & stroke: 4.06 x 3.75 in. Compression ratio: 10.25:1. Brake horsepower: 303 at 4600 rpm. Five main bearings. Hydraulic valve lifters. Carburetor: Carter AFB model 3674S four-barrel. Same as Bonneville Hydra-Matic V-8, but horsepower slightly lower due to use of HM 61-10 "Slim Jim" transmission in Grand Prix.

1964 Pontiac Tempest LeMans two-door convertible. (OCW)

1964 Pontiac Bonneville Safari four-door station wagon. (OCW)

Standard Catalog of ® Pontiac, 2nd Edition

ENGINE [Optional all Pontiacs with Hydra-Matic]: V-8. Overhead valves. Cast-iron block. Displacement: 389 cid. Bore & stroke: 4.06 x 3.75 in. Compression ratio: 8.6:1. Brake horsepower: 230 at 4000 rpm. Five main bearings. Hydraulic valve lifters. Carburetor: Rochester two-barrel.

ENGINE [Tri-Power V-8; optional for all Pontiacs with any transmission]: V-8. Overhead valves. Cast-iron block. Displacement: 389 cid. Bore & stroke: 4.06 x 3.75 in. Compression ratio: 10.75:1. Brake horsepower: 330 at 4600 rpm. Five main bearings. Hydraulic valve lifters. Carburetor: Three Rochester two-barrels.

ENGINE [421 H.O.: optional all "B" body models]: V-8. Overhead valves. Cast-iron block. Displacement: 421 cid. Bore & stroke: 4.094 x 4.00 in. 421 cid. Compression ratio: 10.5:1 Brake horsepower: 320 at 4400 rpm. Five main bearings. Solid valve lifters. Carburetion: Four-barrel.

ENGINE [421 H.O.: optional all "B" body models]: V-8. Overhead valves. Cast-iron block. Displacement: 421 cid. Bore & stroke: 4.094 x 4.00 in. 421 cid. Compression ratio: 10.75:1 Brake horsepower: 370 at 5200 rpm. Five main bearings. Solid valve lifters. Carburetion: Three two-barrels.

ENGINE [421 H.O.: optional all "B" body models]: V-8. Overhead valves. Cast-iron block. Displacement: 421 cid. Bore & stroke: 4.094 x 4.00 in. 421 cid. Compression ratio: 10.75:1. Brake horsepower: 350 at 4600 rpm. Five main bearings. Solid valve lifters. Carburetion: Three two-barrels.

TEMPEST ENGINES

ENGINE [Tempest Six]: Inline. Six-cylinder. Overhead valves. Cast-iron block. Displacement: 215 cid. Bore & stroke: 3.75 x 3.25 in. Compression ratio: 8.6:1. Brake horsepower: 140 at 4200 rpm rpm. Seven main bearings. Hydraulic valve lifters. Carburetor: Rochester one-barrel.

ENGINE [Base V-8]: Overhead valves. Cast-iron block. Displacement: 325.8 cid. Bore & stroke: 3.718 x 3.75 in. Compression ratio: 10.25:1. Brake horsepower: 250 at 4600 rpm. Hydraulic valve lifters. Carburetion: Rochester two-barrel.

ENGINE [Base V-8]: Overhead valves. Cast-iron block. Displacement: 325.8 cid. Bore & stroke: 3.718 x 3.75 in. Compression ratio: 10.25:1. Brake horsepower: 280 at 4800 rpm. Hydraulic valve lifters. Carburetion: Rochester four-barrel. Optional in Tempest and LeMans models.

LEMANS GTO ENGINES

ENGINE [Standard GTO]: V-8. Overhead valves. Cast-iron block. Displacement: 389 cid. Bore & stroke: 4.06 x 3.75 in. Compression ratio: 10.75:1. Brake horsepower: 325 at 4800 rpm. Five main bearings. Hydraulic valve lifters. Carburetor: Four-barrel.

ENGINE [Optional GTO only]: V-8. Overhead valves. Cast-iron block. Displacement: 389 cid. Bore & stroke: 4.06 x 3.75 in. Compression ratio: 10.75:1. Brake horsepower: 348 at 4600 rpm. Five main bearings. Hydraulic valve lifters. Carburetor: Three Rochester two-barrels.

CHASSIS: Wheelbase: (All Pontiac Safaris) 119 in.; (Series 23 and 29 passenger cars) 120 in.; (Series 26 and 28 passenger cars) 123 in.; (All Tempests) 115 in. Overall Length: (All Pontiac Safaris) 213.8 in.; (Series 23 and 29 passenger cars) 213 in.; (Series 26 and 28 passenger cars) 220 in.; (All Tempests) 203 in. Front track: (Pontiac) 62.5 in. (Tempest) 58 in. Rear track: (Pontiac) 64 in.; (Tempest) 58 in. Standard tires: (Pontiac) 8.00 x 14; (Tempest) 6.50 x 14.

OPTIONS: [PONTIAC] Air-conditioning ($430). Console including tachometer ($161). Instrument gage cluster ($21-$59). Luggage carrier ($94). Remote control mirror ($12). Power brakes ($57). Power seat ($96). Power tilt left-hand bucket seat ($71). Tachometer ($54). Cordova top ($86). Ventura trim on body styles 2339, 2347 and 2369 ($118). Sports wheel covers ($30-$46). Aluminum hubs and drums ($122-$138). Three-speed manual transmission was standard. Hydra-Matic was optional. A four-speed manual transmission with floor shift was optional. The four-barrel V-8 was optional in Catalinas and Star Chiefs. The economy version of the 389 cid V-8 was a no-cost option giving 230 hp at 4000 rpm with Hydra-Matic only. Tri-Power on the 389 V-8 was available with 10.75:1 compression heads in two forms. The first gave 330 hp at 4600 rpm; the second gave 348 hp at 4900 rpm. Tri-Power 421 cid V-8s, also with 10.75:1 heads, came in two variations. The first gave 350 hp at 4600 rpm; the second gave 370 hp at 3800 rpm. [TEMPEST] Air-conditioner ($319). LeMans console shift ($48). Padded dash ($16). Power Convertible top ($54). Power tilt left bucket seat ($67). Power steering ($75). Power tailgate window ($54). Push-button radio ($62). Bucket seats ($134). Custom steering wheel ($6-$9). Deluxe steering wheel with ring ($4). Tachometer ($54). Cordova top ($75). Two-speed wipers and washer ($17). Three-speed manual transmission was standard. Automatic transmission was optional. A four-speed manual transmission was optional. A 326 cubic V-8 was optional in Tempest, Tempest Custom, and Tempest LeMans lines for cars without the GTO option. With synchromesh and 8.6:1 heads this motor gave 250 hp at 4600 rpm. With Hydra-Matic and 10.5:1 heads this motor gave 280 hp at 4800 rpm. The 389 cid V-8 was available exclusively in the GTO. It came with 10.75:1 compression and two different induction setups. The standard version had four-barrel carburetion and gave 325 hp at 4,800 rpm. Tri-Power was optional on the same block and produced 348 hp at 4900 rpm. The GTO could also be ordered with a heavy-duty three-speed manual gearbox or a Muncie close-ratio four-speed manual box with Hurst linkage. GTO option package included 389 cid high-performance V-8; special GTO nameplates for the grille, fenders, deck lid, and glove box door; simulated engine-turned aluminum dash panel inserts; and dual simulated air scoops on the hood. Many special GTO accessories were available.

HISTORICAL: Production started Sept. 3, 1963. Pontiac introductions were held Oct. 3, 1963. Model year output of 715,261 cars was good for a 9.1 percent share of market. Calendar year output of 693,634 vehicles maintained Pontiac Motor Div.'s third rank in the industry. The Catalina 2 + 2 and GTO options were introduced for performance buyers this season. Victor Borge and the Smothers Brothers were among famous people who helped promote Pontiac sales. Pete Estes remained general manager of the division. At least three high-performance Pontiacs were road tested by contemporary magazines. The 325-hp GTO convertible went 0-to-60 mph in 7.7 seconds and did the quarter-mile in 15.8 seconds at 93 mph. Its top speed was 115 mph. The 348-hp GTO hardtop went 0-to-60 mph in 6.6 seconds and did the quarter-mile in 14.8 seconds. The 1964 Catalina 2 + 2 with the 370-hp Tri-Power "421" did 0-to-60 mph in 7.2 seconds and covered the quarter-mile in 16.1 seconds. The term Sport Coupe was now commonly used to identify the pillarless two-door hardtop body. The term Vista was phased out and Safari nomenclature was still used to identify station wagons.

1964 Pontiac Bonneville Superior airport limousine. (OCW)

1965 PONTIAC

1965 Pontiac Catalina four-door sedan. (OCW)

CATALINA — (V-8) — SERIES 252 — Styling changes for full-size 1965 Pontiacs included larger bodies; twin air-slot grilles; vertically stacked barrel-shaped headlamps under cut-back front fenders that formed visors over them; V-shaped hoods with a prominent center bulge; curved side glass; and symmetrical Venturi contours with fin-shaped creases along the lower body sides. Catalinas had thin moldings along the lower body crease; V-shaped front fender badges; and Catalina rear fender scripts. Coupes and convertibles with the optional 2 + 2 Sports package were trimmed with "421" engine badges on front fenders, 2 + 2 numbering on rear fenders, and deck lid, and simulated louvers behind the front wheel cutouts. Catalinas with the Ventura package also had special trims. Standard equipment for all Catalinas included turn signals; oil filter; cigarette lighter; front foam seat cushions; sun visors; heater and defroster; electric windshield wipers; front seat belt; and five tubeless black sidewall tires. Safaris came standard with oversized 8.55 x 14 tires. The nine-passenger Safari had a power tailgate window.

STAR CHIEF — (V-8) — SERIES 256 — External decorations on Star Chief included stylized stars on the rear roof pillar, Star Chief script on the rear fender, and wider chrome moldings along the fin-shaped body crease. All features found in Catalinas were standard equipment, and extras included deluxe wheel discs and steering wheels, electric clock, dual-speed wipers, and special upholstery.

BONNEVILLE — (V-8) — SERIES 262 — Bonneville identification features included Bonneville lettering on the left-hand side of the hood and on the rear fenders, elongated V-shaped badges behind front wheel cutouts and wide stainless steel accent panels along the lower body under the fin-shaped crease. Standard equipment was everything found on Star Chief plus padded instrument panel, front and rear armrests, padded assist grip, courtesy lamps, and cloth and vinyl upholstery combinations. An undetermined number of four-door hardtops had the Brougham option package that included Ponchartrain cloth and Morrokide upholstery, a cordova top and "Brougham by Fisher" roof pillar badges. Bonneville passenger cars wore fender skirts.

GRAND PRIX — (V-8) — SERIES 266 — The Grand Prix hardtop sports coupe was the most distinctive of all 1965 full-sized Pontiacs. For special identification it had an air slot grille with a unique, vertically divided, aluminized insert that incorporated rectangular parking lamps. The fin-shaped crease along the lower body was trimmed with a wide stainless steel molding. The letters "GP" appeared on the left-hand lip of the hood and Grand Prix lettering was placed on the front fenders behind the wheel opening. A badge for further identification was placed on the sides of the rear fenders. As on Bonneville passenger cars, the Grand Prix wore fender skirts. Standard equipment included all features found on Bonneville, plus monotone Morrokide upholstery. Buyers had a choice of special front bench seats or bucket seats with a console and tachometer. A glove box lamp was also included.

1965 Pontiac Catalina 2 + 2 two-door hardtop. (OCW)

1965 Pontiac Star Chief four-door sedan. (OCW)

1965 Pontiac Bonneville two-door convertible. (OCW)

TEMPEST — (6-CYL) — SERIES 233 — Design refinements characterized the three Tempest lines for 1965 and included vertically stacked headlamps, larger wheel openings, crisper side body sculpturing, and more deeply recessed grilles. Base models in the 233 Series were identified by the absence of upper beltline moldings and plainer interior trims. Vinyl rubber floor mats were used. Standard equipment included heater and defroster, electric wipers, seat belts, turn signals, and five black tubeless tires. Safari station wagons came with 7.35 x 14 oversized tires as regular equipment.

TEMPEST CUSTOM — (6-CYL) — SERIES 235 — Tempest Custom models had bright upper beltline moldings to accent the venturi-shaped body styling. Standard extras included carpeting and deluxe steering wheel. The Custom convertible had courtesy lamps.

TEMPEST LEMANS — (6-CYL) — SERIES 237 — Special identifying features seen on the Tempest LeMans models included grilled-over tail lamps, LeMans front fender nameplates, LeMans lettering on the sides of rear fenders, and simulated louvers behind front wheel cutouts (two-door models only). All features found on Tempest Customs were considered standard equipment, as well as vinyl interior trim, custom foam front seat cushions, front bucket seats on two-door styles, and power-operated folding tops on LeMans convertibles. Cars equipped with GTO equipment had standard V-8 power. The GTO was not yet in a separate series, although special identification features on GTOs replaced some items regularly seen on LeMans Tempests. This included GTO lettering for the left-hand grille, rear fender sides, and deck lid; a single hood scoop; and elongated V-shaped badges behind the front wheel openings.

I.D. DATA: VIN on left front door post. First symbol indicates GM division: 2=Pontiac. Second and third symbols indicate series: 33=Tempest; 35=Tempest Custom; 37=LeMans; 52=Catalina;

1965 Pontiac Bonneville Brougham four-door hardtop. (JAG)

1965 Pontiac Grand Prix two-door hardtop sport coupe, V-8. (OCW)

1965 Pontiac Tempest LeMans two-door hardtop. (OCW)

56=Star Chief; 62=Bonneville; 66=Grand Prix. Fourth and fifth symbols indicate body style and appear as last two symbols in body/style number column of charts below. Sixth symbol indicates model year: 5=1965. Seventh symbol tells assembly plant: P=Pontiac, Mich.; C=South Gate, Calif.; E=Linden, N.J.; X=Kansas City, Kan.; D=Doraville, Ga.; R=Arlington, Texas; Z=Fremont, Calif.; B=Baltimore, Md.; K=Kansas City, Mo.; U=Lordstown, Ohio. Following symbols are sequential production numbers starting with 100001 at each assembly plant. Body/style number plate under hood tells manufacturer, Fisher style number, assembly plant, trim code, paint code, accessory codes. Style number consists of 65 (for 1965) prefix and four symbols that appear in second column of charts below. First two symbols indicate series; second two symbols indicate body type. VIN appears on front of engine at right-hand cylinder bank along with an alpha-numerical engine production codes included: [215-cid/125-hp six] ZD/ZE. [215-cid/140-hp six ZK/ZL/ZM/ZN/ZR/ZS. [326-cid/250-hp V-8] WP/YN6O. [326-cid/285-hp V-8] WR/YP. [389-cid/256-hp V-8] WA/WB/YA/YB. [389-cid/260-hp V-8] XA/XB. [389-cid/276-hp V-8] WDB/O4B. [389-cid/290-hp] WC/YC/YD. [389-cid/293-hp V-8] XC. [389-cid/325-hp V-8] YE/YF. [389-cid/333-hp V-8] WE. [389-cid/338-hp Tri-Power V-8] WF/YG. [421-cid/338-hp V-8] WG/YH. [421-cid/356-hp Tri-Power V-8] YJ/WH. [421-cid/376-hp Tri-Power V-8] WJ/YK. [389-cid/335-hp four-barrel GTO V-8] WT with synchromesh; YS with Hydra-Matic. [389-cid/360-hp GTO Tri-Power V-8] WS with synchromesh; YR with Hydra-Matic.

Model Number	Body Style Number	Body Type & Seating	Factory Price	Shipping Weight	Production Total
CATALINA (SERIES 252)					
252	25269	4d Sedan-6P	2,748	3,772	78,853
252	25239	4d Hardtop-6P	2,885	3,843	34,814
252	25211	2d Sedan-6P	2,678	3,702	9,526
252	25237	2d Hardtop-6P	2,809	3,748	92,009
252	25267	2d Convertible-6P	3,103	3,795	18,347
252	25245	4d Sta Wagon-9P	3,241	4,244	15,110
252	25235	4d Sta Wagon-6P	3,136	4,211	22,399
STAR CHIEF (SERIES 256)					
256	25669	4d Sedan-6P	3,042	3,858	22,183
256	25639	4d Hardtop-6p	3,171	3,917	9,132
BONNEVILLE (SERIES 262)					
262	26239	4d Hardtop-6P	3,362	3,993	62,480

1965 Pontiac Tempest LeMans GTO two-door convertible. (OCW)

Model Number	Body Style Number	Body Type & Seating	Factory Price	Shipping Weight	Production Total
262	26237	2d Hardtop-6P	3,288	3,909	44,030
262	26267	2d Convertible-6P	3,520	3,935	21,050
262	26235	4d Sta Wagon-6P	3,557	4,282	6,460
GRAND PRIX (SERIES 266)					
266	26657	2d Hardtop Cpe-5P	3,426	4,282	57,881
TEMPEST (SERIES 233)					
233	23369	4d Sedan-6P	2,263	2,963	15,705
233	23327	2d Coupe-6P	2,211	2,943	18,198
233	23335	4d Sta Wagon-6P	2,549	3,237	5,622
TEMPEST CUSTOM (SERIES 235)					
235	23569	4d Sedan-6P	2,496	3,021	25,242
235	23527	2d Coupe-6P	2,295	2,965	18,367
235	23537	2d Hardtop-6P	2,359	2,983	21,906
235	23567	2d Convertible-6P	2,584	3,064	8,346
235	23535	4d Sta Wagon-6P	2,633	3,250	10,792
TEMPEST LEMANS (SERIES 237)					
237	23769	4d Sedan-6P	2,496	3,021	14,227
237	23727	2d Coupe-5P	2,437	2,996	18,881
237	23737	2d Hardtop-5P	2,501	3,014	60,548
237	23767	2d Convertible-5P	2,736	3,107	13,897
TEMPEST LEMANS (SERIES 237 WITH GTO OPTION)					
237	23727	2d Coupe-5P	2,787	3,478	8,319
237	23737	2d Hardtop-5P	2,855	3,478	55,722
237	3767	2d Convertible-5P	3,093	3,700	11,311

NOTE 1: 271,058 Catalinas were built.

NOTE 2: 14,817 had synchromesh and 256,241 had Hydra-Matic.

NOTE 3: Figures include 11,521 cars with W51 Catalina 2 + 2 option.

NOTE 4: 5,316 Catalina 2 + 2 had synchromesh and 6,205 had Hydra-Matic.

NOTE 5: No body style breakouts are available for the 2 + 2 option.

NOTE 6: No record of the number of Ventura options sold.

NOTE 7: 31,315 Star Chiefs were built.

NOTE 8: 97 had synchromesh and 31,214 had Hydra-Matic.

NOTE 9: 134,663 Bonnevilles and Bonneville station wagons were built.

NOTE 10: 1,449 had synchromesh and 133,214 had Hydra-Matic.

NOTE 11: 643 Bonnevilles chassis were provided for conversions.

NOTE 12: 57,881 Grand Prix were built.

NOTE 13: 1,973 had synchromesh and 55,908 had Hydra-Matic attachments.

NOTE 14: 39,525 Tempests were built.

NOTE 15: 9,255 had synchromesh and 30,270 had automatic attachments.

1965 Pontiac Tempest LeMans GTO two-door hardtop. (OCW)

1965 Pontiac Catalina two-door convertible. (JAG)

1965 Pontiac Catalina 2 + 2 two-door convertible. (OCW)

1965 Pontiac Bonneville Safari four-door station wagon. (JAG)

NOTE 16: 84,653 Tempest Customs were built.

NOTE 17: 10,630 had synchromesh and 74,023 had automatic attachments.

NOTE 18: 182,905 LeMans Tempests were built including cars with the GTO option.

NOTE 19: 75,756 had synchromesh attachments and 107,149 had automatic.

NOTE 20: 75,352 GTOs are included in these totals.

NOTE 21: 56,378 had synchromesh and 18,974 had automatic.

NOTE 22: Four-speed gearboxes were in 18.8 percent of all 1965 Tempests.

PONTIAC ENGINES

ENGINE [Catalina/Star Chief with synchromesh]: Base V-8. Overhead valves. Cast-iron block. Displacement: 389 cid. Bore & stroke: 4.06 x 3.75 in. Compression ratio: 8.6:1. Brake horsepower: 256 at 4600 rpm. Five main bearings. Hydraulic valve lifters. Carburetor: Rochester model 7025071 two-barrel. (Economy option for Bonneville/Grand Prix with synchromesh.)

ENGINE [Catalina/Star Chief with Hydra-Matic]: Base V-8. Overhead valves. Cast-iron block. Displacement: 389 cid. Bore & stroke: 4.06 x 3.75 in. Compression ratio: 10.25:1. Brake horsepower: 290 at 4600 rpm. Five main bearings. Hydraulic valve lifters. Carburetor: Rochester model 7025060 two-barrel. (Economy option for Bonneville/Grand Prix with Hydra-Matic.)

ENGINE [Bonneville/Grand Prix with synchromesh]: Base V-8. Overhead valves. Cast-iron block. Displacement: 389 cid. Bore & stroke: 4.06 x 3.75 in. Compression ratio: 8.6:1. Brake horsepower: 325 at 4800 rpm. Five main bearings. Hydraulic valve lifters. Carburetor: Carter AFB model 3895S four-barrel. Optional Catalina/Star Chief with synchromesh.

1965 Pontiac Bonneville two-door hardtop. (OCW)

1965 Pontiac Superior Embassy limousine. (JAG)

ENGINE [Bonneville/Grand Prix with Hydra-Matic]: Base V-8. Overhead valves. Cast-iron block. Displacement: 389 cid. Bore & stroke: 4.06 x 3.75 in. Compression ratio: 10.5:1. Brake horsepower: 333 at 5000 rpm. Five main bearings. Hydraulic valve lifters. Carburetor: Carter AFB model 3895S four-barrel. Optional Catalina/Star Chief with Hydra-Matic.

ENGINE [Bonneville with Hydra-Matic]: Base V-8. Overhead valves. Cast-iron block. Displacement: 389 cid. Bore & stroke: 4.06 x 3.75 in. Compression ratio: 10.25:1. Brake horsepower: 306 at 4600 rpm. Five main bearings. Hydraulic valve lifters. Carburetor: Carter AFB model 3674S four-barrel.

ENGINE [Grand Prix with Hydra-Matic]: Base V-8. Overhead valves. Cast-iron block. Displacement: 389 cid. Bore & stroke: 4.06 x 3.75 in. Compression ratio: 10.25:1. Brake horsepower: 303 at 4600 rpm. Five main bearings. Hydraulic valve lifters. Carburetor: Carter AFB model 3674S four-barrel. Same as Bonneville Hydra-Matic V-8, but horsepower slightly lower due to use of HM 61-10 "Slim Jim" transmission in Grand Prix.

ENGINE [Optional Catalina/Star Chief]: V-8. Overhead valves. Cast-iron block. Displacement: 389 cid. Bore & stroke: 4.06 x 3.75 in. Compression ratio: 10.5:1. Brake horsepower: 325 at 4800 rpm. Five main bearings. Hydraulic valve lifters. Carburetor: Carter AFB model 3895S four-barrel.

ENGINE [421 H.O.: optional all "B" body models]: V-8. Overhead valves. Cast-iron block. Displacement: 421 cid. Bore & stroke: 4.094 x 4.00 in. 421 cid. Compression ratio: 10.5:1. Brake horsepower: 338 at 4600 rpm. Five main bearings. Solid valve lifters. Carburetor: Carter AFB model 3895S four-barrel.

ENGINE [421 H.O.: optional Catalina/Star Chief]: V-8. Overhead valves. Cast-iron block. Displacement: 421 cid. Bore & stroke: 4.094 x 4.00 in. 421 cid. Compression ratio: 10.75:1. Brake horsepower: 376 at 5000 rpm. Five main bearings. Solid valve lifters. Carburetor: three Rochester model 7024078 two-barrels.

ENGINE [421 H.O.: optional all "B" body models]: V-8. Overhead valves. Cast-iron block. Displacement: 421 cid. Bore & stroke: 4.094 x 4.00 in. 421 cid. Compression ratio: 10.75:1. Brake horsepower: 356 at 4800 rpm. Five main bearings. Solid valve lifters. Carburetor: three Rochester model 7024078 two-barrels.

TEMPEST ENGINES

ENGINE [Tempest Six]: Inline. Six-cylinder. Overhead valves. Cast-iron block. Displacement: 215 cid. Bore & stroke: 3.75 x 3.25 in. Compression ratio: 8.6:1. Brake horsepower: 140 at 4200 rpm.

1965 Pontiac Superior ambulance. (JAG)

Seven main bearings. Hydraulic valve lifters. Carburetor: Rochester model 7025167 one-barrel.

ENGINE [Base V-8]: Overhead valves. Cast-iron block. Displacement: 325.8 cid. Bore & stroke: 3.718 x 3.75 in. Compression ratio: 9.2:1. Brake horsepower: 250 at 4600 rpm. Hydraulic valve lifters. Carburetion: Rochester model 7025071 two-barrel.

ENGINE [Base V-8]: Overhead valves. Cast-iron block. Displacement: 325.8 cid. Bore & stroke: 3.718 x 3.75 in. Compression ratio: 10.5:1. Brake horsepower: 285 at 5000 rpm. Hydraulic valve lifters. Carburetion: Carter AFB model 3899S four-barrel.

LEMANS GTO ENGINES

ENGINE [Standard GTO]: V-8. Overhead valves. Cast-iron block. Displacement: 389 cid. Bore & stroke: 4.06 x 3.75 in. Compression ratio: 10.75:1. Brake horsepower: 335 at 5000 rpm. Five main bearings. Hydraulic valve lifters. Carburetor: Carter AFB model 3895S four-barrel.

ENGINE [Optional GTO only]: V-8. Overhead valves. Cast-iron block. Displacement: 389 cid. Bore & stroke: 4.06 x 3.75 in. Compression ratio: 10.75:1. Brake horsepower: 360 at 5200 rpm. Five main bearings. Hydraulic valve lifters. Carburetor: Three Rochester model 7024178 two-barrels.

CHASSIS: Wheelbase: (All Pontiac Safaris) 121 in.; (Series 252 and 266 passenger cars) 121 in.; (Series 256 and 262 passenger cars) 124 in.; (All Tempests) 115 in. Overall Length: (All Pontiac Safaris) 217.9 in.; (Series 252 and 266 passenger cars) 214.6 in.; (Series 256 and 262 passenger cars) 221.7 in.; (Tempest Safaris) 204.4 in.; (Tempest passenger cars) 206.2 in. Front tread: (Pontiacs) 62.5 in.; (Tempests) 58 in. Rear tread: (Pontiacs) 64 in. (Tempests) 58 in. Standard tires: (Pontiacs) 8.25 x 14; (Tempest) 6.95 x 14; (GTO) 7.75 x 14.

OPTIONS: [PONTIAC] Bonneville Brougham option for style number 26239 ($161). Front bucket seats for Bonneville style numbers 26237 and 26267 ($116). Console ($108). Remote control deck lid ($11). Electro Cruise and fuel warning ($96). Tinted glass ($43). Tinted windshield ($29). Instrument gauge cluster ($21-38). Safari luggage carrier ($86). Glare-proof tilt mirror ($4). Remote control rearview mirror ($12). Power brakes ($43). Power door locks ($46-$70). Six-way power seat ($97). Power windows ($106). Power tilt bucket seats L.H. ($71). AM/FM manual radio ($151). Push-button AM radio ($89). Split-back Safari seat ($38). Front bucket seats for Catalina two-door hardtop and convertible with special trims ($204). Super-Lift shock absorbers ($40). Sports option 2 + 2 package for style number 25237 ($419). Sports option 2 + 2 package for style number 25267 ($397). Tachometer, except on cars with four-speed and console ($54). Cordova top ($97-$108). Safari cordova top ($135). Ventura trim package for style numbers 25237, 25239, and 25269 ($118). Wire wheel discs ($20-$71). Aluminum hubs and drums ($120-$138). A three-speed manual transmission was standard. Turbo-Hydra-Matic transmission and four-speed manual transmission were $231 extra. A heavy-duty clutch was $9 extra on Catalinas with certain engines. Safe-T-Track differential was $43 extra. Dual exhausts were $31 extra, but standard on Grand Prix. The four-barrel V-8 with heavy-duty clutch was $44 extra for Catalinas and Star Chiefs. A Tri-Power 389 cid V-8 with 10.75:1 compression and 338 hp at 4800 rpm was $134-$174 extra on model and transmission. A four-barrel 421 cid V-8 with 10.5:1 compression and 338 hp at 4600 rpm was $108-$174 extra depending on model and was standard in cars with the 2 + 2 Sports Option. A Tri-Power 421 cid V-8 with 10.75:1 compression and 356 hp at 4800 rpm was $241-$307 extra depending upon model. The Tri-Power H.O. V-8 of 421 cid with 10.75:1 compression was $344-$410 extra depending on model. It produced 376 hp at 5500 rpm. A two-barrel premium fuel version of the 389 cid V-8 was $21 extra in Catalinas and Star Chiefs with three-speed manual transmission. Transistor ignition was $75 extra on air-conditioned cars and $65 extra on others. A transistorized regulator was $11 extra. Various rear axle ratios were available. **[TEMPEST]** Air-conditioner ($346). Carpets ($19). Electric clock ($19). Remote control deck lid ($11). GTO option for style numbers 23727, 23737, and 23767 ($296). Handling & ride package ($16). Parking brake signal ($3). Safari luggage carrier ($65). Panel cluster and tachometer rally gauge ($86). AM/FM push-button radio ($137). Safeguard speedometer ($16). Super-Life shock absorbers ($40). Custom sports steering wheel ($39-$43). Tilt steering with power assist only ($43). Power steering ($97). Power brakes ($43). Cordova tops ($72-$86). Wire wheel discs ($54-$71). Custom wheel discs ($20-$37). Rally wheels ($36-53). Two-speed wipers and washers ($17) and much more. A three-speed manual transmission was standard. A four-speed manual transmission was $188 extra. Two different two-speed automatic gearboxes were available. With six-cylinder power the first automatic was $188 extra; with V-8s the second was $199 extra. Transistor ignition was priced the same as on full-sized cars. Dual exhausts were standard with the GTO option and $31 extra on other cars. Safe-T-Grip differential was $38 extra. A two-barrel 326-cid V-8 with 9.2 compression and 250 hp at 4600 rpm was $108 extra on all Tempests. With four-barrel induction and 10.5:1 compression heads, this engine produced 285 hp at 5500 rpm and was $173 extra on all Tempests. A four-barrel 389-cid V-8 with 335 hp at 5000 rpm was standard with the GTO option. A Tri-Power 389-cid V-8 with 10.75:1 compression and 360 hp at 5200 rpm was $116 extra in GTOs only. A variety of rear axle ratios were available.

HISTORICAL: Production started Aug. 24, 1964. Introductions were done on Sept. 24, 1964. The one-millionth Tempest was built late in the year. Calendar year output was 860,652 cars. Model year output was 802,000 cars. On April 13, 1965, the 10 millionth Pontiac was made. It was a gold Catalina. The 335-hp GTO convertible went 0-to-60 mph in 7.2 seconds and did the quarter-mile in 16.1 seconds. The 1965 Catalina 2 + 2 hardtop with the 338 hp "421" did 0-to-60 mph in 7.4 seconds and the quarter-mile in 15.8 seconds. The 1965 Catalina 2 + 2 hardtop with the 376-hp "421" was even faster. It could do 0-to-60 mph in 7.2 seconds and the quarter-mile took 15.5 seconds. Pontiac fans could get a GTO record and poster for 25-cents, which is a collector's item today. The term Safari was used to denote station wagons. In the Tempest series a Sport Coupe was a pillared two-door sedan. Pete Estes moved to Chevrolet and John Z. DeLorean became the general manager of Pontiac Motor Division.

1966 PONTIAC

1966 Pontiac Catalina 2 + 2 two-door hardtop. (OCW)

CATALINA — (V-8) — SERIES 252 — Styling changes for full-sized 1966 Pontiacs were subtle ones. New plastic grilles were adopted and headlamp extension caps gave a more integrated frontal appearance. Catalinas now had thin full-length horizontal belt moldings, instead of body crease trim. An identifying script was placed on the front fenders behind the wheel openings. A rear fender badge was also seen. Standard equipment was the same as the previous year. Cars with the Ventura option had special upholstery and fender lettering.

1966 Pontiac Catalina Vista Sedan four-door hardtop. (OCW)

CATALINA 2 + 2 — (V-8) — SERIES 254 — The Catalina 2 + 2 models were in a separate series for 1966. They could be easily identified by appearance items such as a twin lens tail lamp treatment, 2 + 2 badges on the deck lid and rear fenders, vertical air slots behind the doors, and "Pontiac 421" front fender emblems. Standard equipment included a four-barrel 421-cid V-8 with 338 hp, low-restriction exhausts, chromed air cleaner and valve covers, and three-speed Hurst linkage transmission. Heavy-duty suspension, carpeting, bucket seats, Sports Custom steering wheel, and non-glare inside rearview mirror were standard. Available axle ratios included 3.08, 3.23, and 3.42.

STAR CHIEF EXECUTIVE — (V-8) — SERIES 256 — For identification, models in the 256 Series had "Executive" lettering behind front wheel openings. They wore thin horizontal body rub moldings, stylized rear fender stars, and Jeweltone monochromatic Morrokide upholstery. Star Chief Executives incorporated all Catalina equipment, plus deluxe wheel discs and steering wheel, electric clock, and dual-speed wipers.

BONNEVILLE — (V-8) — SERIES 262 — Bonnevilles could easily be distinguished by their broad accent panels below the lower body crease, Bonneville block lettering on the left-hand grille and behind the front wheel openings, and by their standard fender skirts. Regular equipment on closed cars included cloth upholstery, padded dashboards, and front rear armrests. The convertible had deeply piped Morrokide covered seats. The Brougham option package added tufted Plaza pattern cloth upholstery and model identification badges for the rear roof pillars, but cordova tops were optional, even on Broughams.

GRAND PRIX — (V-8) — SERIES 266 — Grand Prix were distinguished by wire mesh grilles enclosing rectangular parking lamps, GP identification on front fenders, and elongated V-shaped emblems on the ribbed lower beauty panels. A monochromatic interior of deeply piped Morrokide was featured. Standard equipment was the same as in 1965, except Strato Bucket seats were new. Fender skirts were seen again.

STANDARD TEMPEST — (6-CYL) — SERIES 233 — Tempests were completely restyled with smoother bodies, rounder contours, wider wheel openings, recessed split grilles, and stacked headlamps. Each of four series now had completely distinctive ornamentation. An undetermined number of cars in each series were built with a sporty-looking Sprint option package. The really big news was under the hood, where a unique overhead camshaft six-cylinder engine was now employed as the base power plant for all models, except GTOs. Standard Tempest trim appointments included wind split moldings behind front wheel openings, Tempest rear fender scripts, and nylon-faced fabric upholstery with Jeweltone Morrokide accents.

TEMPEST CUSTOM — (6-CYL) — SERIES 235 — Tempest Custom trimmings included thin moldings accenting the smooth new "Coke bottle" shape and Tempest Custom script/badge identification on the rear fenders. Deluxe steering wheels and carpets were extra standard features. Convertibles sported courtesy lamps and Morrokide trims.

TEMPEST LEMANS — (6-CYL) — SERIES 237 — LeMans models had special trim features that set them apart. They included simulated louvers on the forward edge of front fenders, elongated V-shaped emblems behind front wheel openings, and LeMans lettering on the rear fender sides. A new "shadow box" roofline was seen on the two-door hardtop coupe. Standard equipment included Morrokide-and-cloth trim combinations in four-door hardtops and all-Morrokide in others. Convertibles, hardtops, and Sport Coupes (two-door sedans) came with the choice of bucket or notch back front seats with folding armrest. All LeMans had carpeting; front foam seat cushions; lamps for ashtray; cigarette lighter; glove box; and a power top on convertibles.

TEMPEST GTO — (V-8) — SERIES 242 — GTO line was now a separate series with distinctive trim on the new Tempest sheet metal. A wire mesh grille insert without horizontal divider bars was used. The grille incorporated rectangular parking lamps and a GTO nameplate on the left-hand side. A single scoop appeared on the hood; elongated V-shaped badges were mounted behind the front wheel openings; GTO lettering appeared on the deck lid and rear fenders; the upper beltline contour was pin striped; and horizontal twin-slot tail lamps were used. Standard equipment included all

1966 Pontiac Tempest GTO two-door hardtop. (OCW)

LeMans items, plus a special 389-cid four-barrel V-8; walnut grain dash panel inserts; dual exhausts; heavy-duty shock absorbers, springs, and stabilizer bar; and 7.75 x 14 redline or whitewall tires.

I.D. DATA: VIN on left front door post. First symbol indicates GM division: 2=Pontiac. Second and third symbols indicate series: 33=Tempest; 35=Tempest Custom; 37=LeMans; 52=Catalina; 56=Star Chief; 62=Bonneville; 66=Grand Prix. Fourth and fifth symbols indicate body style and appear as last two symbols in body/style number column of charts below. Sixth symbol indicates model year: 6=1966. Seventh symbol tells assembly plant: P=Pontiac, Mich.; C=South Gate, Calif.; E=Linden, N.J.; X=Kansas City, Kan.; D=Doraville, Ga.; R=Arlington, Texas; Z=Fremont, Calif.; B=Baltimore, Md.; K=Kansas City, Mo.; U=Lordstown, Ohio. Following symbols are sequential production number starting with 100001 at each assembly plant. Body/style number plate under hood tells manufacturer, Fisher style number, assembly plant, trim code, paint code, accessory codes. Style number consists of 66 (for 1966) prefix and four symbols that appear in second column of charts below. First two symbols indicate series; second two symbols indicate body type. VIN appears on front of engine at right-hand cylinder bank along with an alpha-numerical engine production code. Engine production codes included: [230-cid/155-hp OHC six] ZF/ZG. [230-cid/165-hp OHC six] ZK/ZS/ZN/ZM. [230-cid/207-hp OHC six] ZD/ZE. [326-cid/250-hp V-8] WP/WX/YN/XF. [326-cid/285-hp V-8] WR/YP/XG. [389-cid/256-hp V-8] WA/WB/YA. [389-cid/260-hp V-8] XA/XB. [389-cid/290-hp] WC/YC/YD/YU/YV. [389-cid/293-hp V-8] XC. [389-cid/325-hp V-8] YE/YF/YL/YW/YX. [389-cid/333-hp V-8] WE. [421-cid/338-hp V-8] WK/YZ/YT/WG/YH. [421-cid/356-hp Tri-Power V-8] YJ/YM/WH. [421-cid/376-hp Tri-Power V-8] WJ/YK. [389-cid/335-hp four-barrel GTO V-8] WT/WW with synchromesh; YS/XE with Hydra-Matic. [389-cid/360-hp GTO Tri-Power V-8] WS/WV with synchromesh; XS/YR with Hydra-Matic.

Model Number	Body Style Number	Body Type & Seating	Factory Price	Shipping Weight	Production Total
CATALINA (SERIES 252)					
252	25269	4d Sedan-6P	2,831	3,785	80,483
252	25239	4d Hardtop-6P	2,968	3,910	38,005
252	25211	2d Sedan-6P	2,762	3,715	7,925
252	25237	2d Hardtop-6P	2,893	3,835	79,013
252	25267	2d Convertible-6P	3,219	3,860	14,837
252	25245	4d Sta Wagon-9P	3,38	4,315	12,965

1966 Pontiac Tempest two-door coupe. (JAG)

1966 Pontiac Star Chief Executive four-door sedan. (OCW)

1966 Pontiac Bonneville two-door convertible. (OCW)

Model Number	Body Style Number	Body Type & Seating	Factory Price	Shipping Weight	Production Total
252	25235	4d Sta Wagon-6P	3,217	4,250	21,082
CATALINA 2 + 2 (SERIES 254)					
254	25437	2d Hardtop-5P	3,298	4,005	N/A
254	25467	2d Convertible-5P	3,602	4,030	N/A
STAR CHIEF EXECUTIVE (SERIES 256)					
256	25669	4d Sedan-6P	3,114	3,920	24,489
256	25639	4d Hardtop-6P	3,244	3,980	10,583
256	25637	2d Hardtop-6P	3,170	3,920	10,140
BONNEVILLE (SERIES 262)					
262	26239	4d Hardtop-6P	3,428	4,070	68,646
262	26237	2d Hardtop-6P	3,354	4,020	42,004
262	26267	2d Convertible-6P	3,586	4,015	16,229
262	26245	4d Sta Wagon-9P	3,747	4,390	8,452
GRAND PRIX (SERIES 266)					
266	26657	2d Hardtop-5P	3,492	4,015	36,757
STANDARD TEMPEST (SERIES 233)					
233	23369	4d Sedan-6P	2,331	3,075	17,392
233	233307	2d Coupe-6P	2,278	3,040	22,266
233	23335	4d Sta Wagon-6P	2,624	3,340	4,095

1966 Pontiac Grand Prix two-door hardtop. (OCW)

1966 Pontiac Tempest Custom two-door Sprint Coupe. (OCW)

1966 Pontiac GTO two-door hardtop. (OCW)

1966 Pontiac Tempest Custom two-door hardtop. (JAG)

Model Number	Body Style Number	Body Type & Seating	Factory Price	Shipping Weight	Production Total
TEMPEST CUSTOM (SERIES 235)					
235	23569	4d Sedan-6P	2,415	3,100	23,988
235	23539	4d Hardtop-6P	2,547	3,195	10,996
235	23507	2d Coupe-6P	2,362	3,060	17,182
235	23517	2d Hardtop-6P	2,426	3,075	31,32
235	23567	2d Convertible-6P	2,655	3,170	5,557
235	23535	4d Sta Wagon-6p	2,709	3,355	7,614
TEMPEST LEMANS (SERIES 237)					
237	23739	4d Hardtop-6P	2,701		3,19513,89
237	23707	2d Coupe-6p	2,505	3,090	16,654
237	23717	2d Hardtop-6P	2,568	3,125	78,109
237	23767	2d Convertible-6P	2,806	3,220	13,080

1966 Pontiac Tempest Custom two-door convertible. (JAG)

1966 Pontiac Tempest LeMans four-door hardtop. (JAG)

Standard Catalog of ® Pontiac, 2ⁿᵈ Edition

1966 Pontiac Tempest LeMans two-door convertible. (OCW)

1966 Pontiac Tempest LeMans two-door coupe. (OCW)

Model Number	Body Style Number	Body Type & Seating	Factory Price	Shipping Weight	Production Total
TEMPEST GTO (SERIES 242)					
242	24207	2d Coupe-5P	2,783	3,445	10,363
242	24217	2d Hardtop-5P	2,847	3,465	73,78
242	24267	2d Convertible-5P	3,082	3,555	12,798

NOTE 1: 247,927 Catalinas were built.

NOTE 2: 5,003 Catalinas had synchromesh and 242,924 had Hydra-Matic.

NOTE 3: 6,383 Catalina 2 + 2s were built.

NOTE 4: 2,208 Catalina 2 + 2s had synchromesh and 4,175 had Hydra-Matic.

NOTE 5: Body style breakouts were not recorded for this series.

NOTE 6: 45,212 Star Chief Executives were built.

NOTE 7: 134 Star Chief Executives had synchromesh and 45,078 had Hydra-Matic.

NOTE 8: 135,954 Bonnevilles were built.

NOTE 9: 729 Bonnevilles had synchromesh and 35,840 had Hydra-Matic.

NOTE 10: 553 Bonneville chassis were provided for conversions.

NOTE 11: 36,757 Grand Prix were built.

NOTE 12: 917 Grand Prix had synchromesh and 35,840 had Hydra-Matic.

NOTE 13: 43,753 standard Tempests were built.

NOTE 14: 10,610 had standard Tempests synchromesh and 33,143 had automatic.

NOTE 15: 96,659 Tempest Customs were built.

NOTE 16: 13,566 Tempest Customs had synchromesh and 83,093 had automatic.

NOTE 17: 121,740 LeMans were built.

1966 Pontiac Superior Embassy limousine. (JAG)

NOTE 18: 22,862 LeMans had synchromesh and 98,878 had automatic attachments.

PONTIAC ENGINES

ENGINE [Catalina/Star Chief Executive with synchromesh]: Base V-8. Overhead valves. Cast-iron block. Displacement: 389 cid. Bore & stroke: 4.06 x 3.75 in. Compression ratio: 8.6:1. Brake horsepower: 256 at 4600 rpm. Five main bearings. Hydraulic valve lifters. Carburetor: Rochester model 7026066 two-barrel. (Economy option for Bonneville/Grand Prix with synchromesh.)

ENGINE [Catalina/Star Chief Executive with Hydra-Matic]: Base V-8. Overhead valves. Cast-iron block. Displacement: 389 cid. Bore & stroke: 4.06 x 3.75 in. Compression ratio: 10.5:1. Brake horsepower: 290 at 4600 rpm. Five main bearings. Hydraulic valve lifters. Carburetor: Rochester model 7026066 two-barrel. (Economy option for Bonneville/Grand Prix with synchromesh.)

ENGINE [Bonneville/Grand Prix with synchromesh]: Base V-8. Overhead valves. Cast-iron block. Displacement: 389 cid. Bore & stroke: 4.06 x 3.75 in. Compression ratio: 8.6:1. Brake horsepower: 325 at 4800 rpm. Five main bearings. Hydraulic valve lifters. Carburetor: Carter AFB model 4033S four-barrel.

ENGINE [Bonneville/Grand Prix with Hydra-Matic]: Base V-8. Overhead valves. Cast-iron block. Displacement: 389 cid. Bore & stroke: 4.06 x 3.75 in. Compression ratio: 10.5:1. Brake horsepower: 333 at 5000 rpm. Five main bearings. Hydraulic valve lifters. Carburetor: Carter AFB model 4033S four-barrel.

ENGINE [Optional Catalina/Star Chief Executive]: V-8. Overhead valves. Cast-iron block. Displacement: 389 cid. Bore & stroke: 4.06 x 3.75 in. Compression ratio: 10.75:1. Brake horsepower: 360 at 5200 rpm. Five main bearings. Hydraulic valve lifters. Carburetor: Three Rochester model 7025178 two-barrels.

ENGINE [Standard Catalina 2 + 2]: V-8. Overhead valves. Cast-iron block. Displacement: 421 cid. Bore & stroke: 4.094 x 4.00 in. Compression ratio: 10.5:1. Brake horsepower: 338 at 4600 rpm. Five main bearings. Solid valve lifters. Carburetor: Carter AFB model 4033S four-barrel.

ENGINE [421 H.O.: optional Bonneville/Grand Prix/Catalina/2 + 2]: V-8. Overhead valves. Cast-iron block. Displacement: 421 cid. Bore & stroke: 4.094 x 4.00 in. Compression ratio: 10.75:1. Brake horsepower: 376 at 5000 rpm. Five main bearings. Solid valve lifters. Carburetor: Three Rochester model 7024078 two-barrels.

1966 Pontiac Tempest GTO two-door convertible. (OCW)

1966 Pontiac Superior combination car. (JAG)

ENGINE [421 H.O.: optional Bonneville/Grand Prix/Catalina/2 + 2]: V-8. Overhead valves. Cast-iron block. Displacement: 421 cid. Bore & stroke: 4.094 x 4.00 in. Compression ratio: 10.75:1. Brake horsepower: 356 at 4800 rpm. Five main bearings. Solid valve lifters. Carburetor: Three Rochester model 7024078 two-barrels.

TEMPEST ENGINES

ENGINE [Tempest Six]: Inline. Six-cylinder. Overhead valves. Overhead camshaft. Cast-iron block. Displacement: 230 cid. Bore & stroke: 3.75 x 3.25 in. Compression ratio: 9.0:1. Brake horsepower: 165 at 4700 rpm rpm. Hydraulic valve lifters. Carburetor: Rochester model 7026167 one-barrel.

ENGINE [Tempest Sprint Six]: Inline. Six-cylinder. Overhead valves. Overhead camshaft. Cast-iron block. Displacement: 230 cid. Bore & stroke: 3.75 x 3.25 in. Compression ratio: 10.5:1. Brake horsepower: 207 at 4200 rpm rpm. Hydraulic valve lifters. Carburetor: Rochester four-barrel.

ENGINE [Base V-8]: Overhead valves. Cast-iron block. Displacement: 325.8 cid. Bore & stroke: 3.718 x 3.75 in. Compression ratio: 9.2:1. Brake horsepower: 250 at 4600 rpm. Hydraulic valve lifters. Carburetion: Rochester model 7025071 two-barrel.

ENGINE [Base V-8]: Overhead valves. Cast-iron block. Displacement: 325.8 cid. Bore & stroke: 3.718 x 3.75 in. Compression ratio: 10.5:1. Brake horsepower: 285 at 5000 rpm. Hydraulic valve lifters. Carburetion: Carter AFB moderl 3899S four-barrel.

LEMANS GTO ENGINES

ENGINE [Standard GTO]: V-8. Overhead valves. Cast-iron block. Displacement: 389 cid. Bore & stroke: 4.06 x 3.75 in. Compression ratio: 10.75:1. Brake horsepower: 335 at 5000 rpm. Five main bearings. Hydraulic valve lifters. Carburetor: Carter AFB model 4033S four-barrel.

ENGINE [Optional GTO only]: V-8. Overhead valves. Cast-iron block. Displacement: 389 cid. Bore & stroke: 4.06 x 3.75 in. Compression ratio: 10.75:1. Brake horsepower: 360 at 5200 rpm. Five main bearings. Hydraulic valve lifters. Carburetor: Three Rochester model 7024178 two-barrels.

CHASSIS: Wheelbase: (Pontiac Safaris) 121 in.; (series 252 and 266, passenger cars) 121 in.; (series 256 and 262 passenger cars) 124 in.; (Tempests) 115 in. Overall Length: (Pontiac Safaris) 218.1 in.; (series 252 and 266 passenger cars) 214.8 in.; (series 256 and 262 passenger cars) 221.8 in.; (2 + 2) 214.8 in.; (Tempest Safari) 203.6 in.; (Tempest and GTO passenger cars) 206.4 in. Front tread: (Pontiac) 63 in.; (Tempest) 58 in. Rear tread: (Pontiac) 64 in.; (Tempest) 58 in. Standard tires: (Pontiac) 8.25 x 14; (Tempest convertible and hardtop) 7.35 x 14; (other Tempests) 6.95 x 14. Oversized tires for all Safaris are noted above.

OPTIONS: [PONTIAC] Bonneville Brougham option for style number 26239 ($161). Front bucket seats for Bonneville style numbers 26237 and 26267 ($105). Console ($108). Remote control deck lid ($11). Electro Cruise and fuel warning ($96). Tinted glass ($43). Tinted windshield ($29). Instrument gauge cluster ($21-38). Safari luggage carrier ($86). Glare-proof tilt mirror ($4). Remote control rearview mirror ($12). Power brakes ($43). Power door locks ($46-$70). Six-way power seat ($97). Power windows ($106). Power tilt bucket seats L.H. ($71). AM/FM manual radio ($151). Push-button AM radio ($89). Split-back Safari seat ($38). Front bucket seats for Catalina two-door hardtop and convertible with special trims ($204). Super-Lift shock absorbers ($40). Sports option 2 + 2 package for style number 25237 ($419). Sports option 2 + 2 package for style

number 25267 ($397). White sidewall tires ($29). Tilt steering wheel ($43); Power steering ($97). Air-conditioning ($300). Heavy-duty suspension ($16). Manual AM radio ($89). Tachometer, except on cars with four-speed and console ($54). Cordova top ($97-$108). Safari cordova top ($135). Ventura trim package for style numbers 25237, 25239, and 25269 ($118). Wire wheel discs ($20-$71). Aluminum hubs and drums ($120-$138). A three-speed manual transmission was standard. Super Hydra-Matic transmission and four-speed manual transmission were $230 extra. A heavy-duty clutch was $9 extra on Catalinas with certain engines. Safe-T-Track differential was $43 extra. Dual exhausts were $31 extra, but standard on Grand Prix. The four-barrel V-8 with heavy-duty clutch was $44 extra for Catalinas and Star Chiefs. A Tri-Power 389 cid V-8 with 10.75:1 compression and 338 hp at 4800 rpm was $134-$174 extra depending on model and transmission. A four-barrel 421 cid V-8 with 10.5:1 compression and 338 hp at 4600 rpm was $108-$174 extra depending on model and was standard in cars with the 2 + 2 Sports Option. A Tri-Power 421 cid V-8 with 10.75:1 compression and 356 hp at 4800 rpm was $241-$307 extra depending upon model. The Tri-Power H.O. V-8 of 421 cid with 10.75:1 compression was $344-$410 extra depending on model. It produced 376 hp at 5500 rpm. A two-barrel premium fuel version of the 389 cid V-8 was $21 extra in Catalinas and Star Chiefs with three-speed manual transmission. Transistor ignition was $75 extra on air-conditioned cars and $65 extra on others. A transistorized regulator was $11 extra. Various rear axle ratios were available. [TEMPEST] Power steering ($95). Air-conditioning ($343). Sprint option package ($127). Standard white sidewall tires ($41). Ride and Handling package ($16). Rally wheel rims ($40). Custom steering wheel ($29). Safe-T-Track ($37). The 338-hp version of the 389-cid V-8 with 10.75:1 compression and Tri-Power was dropped. Tempest and GTO V-8 options were the same as in 1965. The new overhead camshaft six-cylinder Tempest engine was the only significantly changed power train option. This engine came in two forms.

HISTORICAL: Production began Sept. 13, 1965, and model introductions took place Oct. 7, 1965. Model year output was 831,331 units. Calendar year production was 866,385 units. The big news of the year was the introduction of the overhead cam six. Also, Pontiac earned an over 10 percent share of market for the first time ever. In magazine road tests, the 335-hp GTO coupe was found to go 0-to-60 mph in 6.8 seconds and down the quarter-mile in 15.4 seconds. The 360-hp GTO convertible had the same 0-to-60 mph time and did the quarter-mile in 15.5 seconds at 93 mph. The 207-hp Tempest Sprint could go 0-to-60 mph in 8.2 seconds and do the quarter-mile in 16.7 seconds at 82 mph. The term Safari and station wagon were synonymous. Style number 26657 had distinct roofline styling. The Brougham option was available for Bonneville four-door hardtops. The term Vista was sometimes used to describe full-sized four-door hardtops. The Ventura option was available for Catalina hardtops, convertibles, and Vistas. The term Sport Coupe was used to describe two-door Tempest pillared sedans, not hardtops. Two-door Tempests with the Sprint option had horizontal racing stripes between the wheel openings.

1967 PONTIAC

1967 Pontiac Catalina Ventura two-door hardtop. (OCW)

CATALINA — (V-8) — SERIES 252 — Integral bumper-grilles, "wasp waist" body styling, angular wedge-shaped front fender tips

1966 Pontiac Superior funeral car. (JAG)

1967 Pontiac Catalina 2 + 2 two-door hardtop. (OCW)

and recessed windshield wipers characterized full-sized Pontiacs for 1967. A crisp horizontal beltline crease and flare sculpturing between the doors and rear wheel openings were other new design traits. All standard GM safety features were found in Catalinas, plus wood-grain trimmed dashboards and nylon blend carpeting. Small hubcaps were regular equipment and there were Pontiac letters on the left-hand grille and the word Catalina on the sides of fenders. Tail lamps were mainly horizontal with a single long lens that curved downwards at each side. Cars with Ventura or 2 + 2 options were trimmed differently.

EXECUTIVE — (V-8) — SERIES 256 — The Star Chief name was dropped. Executives had the same equipment as Catalinas, plus electric clocks, deluxe wheel covers, deluxe steering wheels, decor moldings and special ornamentation. Trim features included V-shaped deck lid emblems and Executive front fender side lettering. Only wagons with external wood-grained paneling were called Safaris and the Executive Safari was born.

BONNEVILLE — (V-8) — SERIES 262 — As usual, the word Bonneville appeared on the left-hand grille on cars in Pontiac's luxury class series. Similar lettering was on the rear fender below the beltline crease. Taillights were of the same overall shape as on Catalinas and Executives, but three individual lenses were seen. Fender skirts were featured along with rocker panel and rear panel accent moldings. Standard equipment included all items found on Executives plus notch back front seats with center armrests, burl style dashboard trim and a four-barrel V-8. Station wagons had rear folding seats, courtesy lamps, power tailgate windows, and load area carpeting.

GRAND PRIX — (V-8) — SERIES 266 — The Grand Prix was set apart this year by distinct styling touches and a new convertible body style. For identification there were GP letters on the left-hand grille, Grand Prix rear fender lettering, hide-away headlights, front parking lamps hidden behind slits in the fender, and straight horizontal twin-slot tail lamps. Fender skirts and lower body accent moldings were seen as well. Grand Prix featured all standard GM safety equipment, plus a 350-hp V-8, front Strato Bucket seats and a console. The hardtop coupe did not have vent windows. Convertibles had GP initials leaded into the vent window glass.

TEMPEST — (6-CYL) — SERIES 233 — All Tempests were mildly face-lifted with grille and rear panel treatments varying by series. The base models had new molded plastic grille bars arranged vertically, in groups of four, with wide spaces between them. Three block-shaped tail lamp lenses set into rectangular frames were seen. The Tempest name appeared behind the front wheel opening and the rear fender had three horizontal slits on

1967 Pontiac Executive Safari station wagon. (OCW)

1967 Pontiac Bonneville two-door hardtop. (OCW)

1967 Pontiac Grand Prix two-door convertible. (OCW)

1967 Pontiac Tempest Safari four-door station wagon. (OCW)

1967 Pontiac Tempest four-door hardtop. (OCW)

the side that housed side markers. All GM safety features were standard, plus vinyl floor mats, cigar lighters, armrests, heater and defroster, five black sidewall tubeless tires, and standard type steering wheel.

TEMPEST CUSTOM — (6-CYL) — SERIES 235 — Standard equipment on Tempest Custom models included special interior trim, carpeting, Deluxe steering wheel, and courtesy lamps on convertibles. There were no horizontal slits on the rear fender sides and the nameplate behind the front wheel opening carried Tempest Custom lettering. Upper beltline and wheel opening decor moldings were used.

TEMPEST LEMANS — (6-CYL) — SERIES 237 and 239 — When the name LeMans appeared on the back fenders, Tempest buyers got carpeting, front foam seat cushions, and lamps for the ashtray,

1967 Pontiac Tempest LeMans two-door hardtop. (OCW)

cigar lighter, and glove box as standard equipment. Buyers of two-door models in this line found three vertical air slots on rear fenders and had a choice of bucket or notch-back bench seats with armrests. The four-door hardtop came with cloth-and-Morrokide trim and short slanting chrome slashes on the rear roof pillar. Other styles had all-Morrokide upholstery. A special station wagon with wood-grained exterior paneling was called the Series 239 Tempest Safari and was generally finished in LeMans level-trim appointments.

TEMPEST GTO — (V-8) — SERIES 242 — On GTOs the trim along the center grille divider now went from one side of the car to the other, with a dip around the center divider. V-shaped fender badges behind the front wheel opening were eliminated. Like the Grand Prix, the GTO had twin pin stripes along the upper beltline region. Body side accent moldings were slightly revised. Rectangular front grille parking lamps were still used in front and the taillights now took the form of four thin rectangles at each side. All LeMans features were standard, plus walnut-grain dash inserts, heavy-duty shocks, springs and stabilizer bars, red line or white sidewall tires, dual exhausts, and a 335-hp four-barrel 400-cid V-8.

FIREBIRD — (6-CYL) — SERIES 223 — The first Firebird was made at Lordstown, Ohio, in early January 1967. The new car line was officially released February 23, 1967. External features included sculptured body styling, twin grilles of a bumper-integral design, front vent windows, and three vertical air slots on the leading edge of rear body panels. Bucket seats were standard. Two body styles were offered and came with any of the Tempest or GTO power trains. However, the two body styles were marketed in five "model-options" created by adding regular production options (RPOs) in specific combinations. Production records were not kept according to the RPO packages, but by the number of sixes and V-8s built with standard or deluxe appointments. The model-option such as Sprint, H.O., and 400 are described in the optional equipment section below.

I.D. DATA: VIN on left front door post. First symbol indicates GM division: 2=Pontiac. Second and third symbols indicate series: 23=Firebird; 33=Tempest; 35=Tempest Custom; 37=LeMans; 39=Tempest Safari; 42=GTO; 52=Catalina; 56=Star Chief; 62=Bonneville; 66=Grand Prix. Fourth and fifth symbols indicate body style and appear as last two symbols in body/style number column of charts below. Sixth symbol indicates model year: 7=1967. Seventh symbol tells assembly plant: P=Pontiac, Mich.; C=South Gate, Calif.; E=Linden, N.J.; X=Kansas City, Kan.; R=Arlington, Texas; Z=Fremont, Calif.; B=Baltimore, Md.; K=Kansas City, Mo.; U=Framingham, Mass.; V=Lordstown, Ohio. Following symbols are

1967 Pontiac GTO two-door hardtop. (OCW)

1967 Pontiac Firebird two-door convertible. (OCW)

sequential production number starting with 100001 at each assembly plant. Body/style number plate under hood tells manufacturer, Fisher style number, assembly plant, trim code, paint code, accessory codes. Style number consists of 67 (for 1967) prefix and four symbols that appear in second column of charts below. First two symbols indicate series; second two symbols indicate body type. VIN appears on front of engine at right-hand cylinder bank along with an alpha-numerical engine production code. Engine production codes included: [230-cid/155-hp ohc six] ZF/ZG. [230-cid/165-hp ohc six] ZK/ZS/ZN/ZM. [230-cid/215-hp ohc six] ZD/ZE/ZR/ZL. [326-cid/250-hp V-8] WP/WX/YN/XF/WH/WC/YJ/XL. [326-cid/285-hp V-8] WK/WO/WR/YM/YP/XG/XO/XR. [400-cid/260-hp V-8] YB. [400-cid/265-hp V-8] WA/YA/YB/WB. [400-cid/290-hp] YC/YD. [400-cid/293-hp V-8] XC. [400-cid/325-hp V-8] YE/YF/YT/WI/WQ/WZ/WU/XN. [400-cid/333-hp V-8] WE/WD/XZ/XY/XH. [400-cid/350-hp V-8] XZ/XY/XJ. [428-cid/360-hp V-8] WG/WK/XD/Y2/YH/YY/YZ/YT. [428-cid/376-hp V-8] WJ/WL/XK/YK. [400-cid/255-hp two-barrel GTO V-8; automatic only] XL/XM. [400-cid/335-hp four-barrel special GTO V-8] WT/WW with synchromesh; YS with Turbo-Hydra-Matic. [400-cid/360-hp GTO special V-8] WS/WV with synchromesh; XP/XS/YR/YZ with Hydra-Matic.

Model Number	Body Style Number	Body Type & Seating	Factory Price	Shipping Weight	Production Total
CATALINA (SERIES 252)					
252	25269	4d Sedan-6P	2,866	3,825	80,551
252	25239	4d Hardtop-6	3,020	3,960	37,256
252	25211	2d Sedan-6P	2,807	3,735	5,633
252	25287	2d Hardtop-6P	2,951	3,860	77,932
252	25267	2d Convertible-6P	3,276	3,910	10,033
252	25245	4d Sta Wagon-9P	3,374	4,340	11,040
252	25235	4d Sta Wagon-6P	3,252	4,275	18,305
EXECUTIVE (SERIES 256)					
256	25669	4d Sedan-6P	3,165	3,955	19,861
256	25639	4d Hardtop-6P	3,296	4,020	8,699
256	25687	2d Hardtop-6P	3,227	3,925	6,931
256	25645	4d Sta Wagon-9P	3,722	4,370	5,593
256	25635	4d Sta Wagon-6P	3,600	4,290	5,903
BONNEVILLE (SERIES 262)					
262	26239	4d Hardtop-6P	3,517	4,110	56,307
262	26287	2d Hardtop-6P	3,227	3,925	31,016
262	26267	2d Convertible-6P	3,680	4,010	8,902
262	26245	4d Sta Wagon-9P	3,819	4,415	6,771
GRAND PRIX (SERIES 266)					
266	26657	2d Hardtop-5P	3,549	4,005	37,125
266	26667	2d Convertible-5P	3,813	4,040	5,856
STANDARD TEMPEST (SERIES 233)					
233	23369	4d Sedan-6P	2,388	3,140	13,136
233	23307	2d Coupe-6P	2,341	3,110	17,978
233	23335	4d Sta Wagon-6P	2,666	3,370	3,495
TEMPEST CUSTOM (SERIES 235)					
235	23569	4d Sedan-6P	2,482	3,145	17,445
235	23539	4d Hardtop-6P	2,608	3,240	5,493
235	23507	2d Coupe-6P	2,434	3,130	12,469
235	23517	2d Hardtop-6P	2,494	3,140	30,512
235	23567	2d Convertible-6P	2,723	3,240	4,082
235	23535	4d Sta Wagon-6P	2,760	3,370	5,324
TEMPEST LEMANS (SERIES 237)					
237	23739	4d Hardtop-6P	2,771	3,265	8,424
237	23707	2d Coupe-5P	2,586	3,155	10,693
237	23717	2d Hardtop-5P	2,648	3,155	75,965
237	23767	2d Convertible-5P	2,881	3,250	9,820
TEMPEST SAFARI (SERIES 239)					
239	23935	4d Sta Wagon-6P	2,936	3,390	4,511
TEMPEST GTO (SERIES 242)					
242	24207	2d Coupe-5P	2,871	3,425	7,029
242	24217	2d Hardtop-5P	2,935	3,430	65,176
242	24267	2d Convertible-5P	3,165	3,515	9,517

1967 Pontiac Catalina Ventura two-door hardtop. (OCW)

1967 Pontiac Catalina Safari four-door station wagon. (JAG)

Model Number	Body Style Number	Body Type & Seating	Factory Price	Shipping Weight	Production Total
FIREBIRD (SERIES 223)					
223	22337	2d Hardtop-5P	2,666	2,955	67,032
223	22367	2d Convertible-5P	2,903	3,247	15,528

NOTE 1: 211,405 Catalinas were built.

NOTE 2: 3,653 had synchromesh and 207,752 had Turbo-Hydra-Matic.

NOTE 3: 1,768 Catalinas had 2 + 2 option with no body style break-out available.

NOTE 4: 35,491 Executive passenger cars were built.

NOTE 5: 84 Executive passenger cars had synchromesh and 35,407 had Turbo-Hydra-Matic.

NOTE 6: 11,496 Executive station wagons were also built.

NOTE 7: 38 Executive wagons had synchromesh and 11,458 had Turbo-Hydra-Matic.

NOTE 8: 96,708 Bonneville passenger cars were built.

NOTE 9: 278 Bonneville passenger cars had synchromesh and 96,430 had Turbo-Hydra-Matic.

NOTE 10: 6,771 Bonneville station wagons were built.

1967 Pontiac Bonneville two-door convertible. (OCW)

1967 Pontiac Bonneville four-door hardtop. (OCW)

1967 Pontiac Tempest Safari four-door station wagon. (OCW)

NOTE 11: 29 Bonneville wagons had synchromesh and 6,742 had Turbo-Hydra-Matic.

NOTE 12: 483 Bonneville chassis sold to professional car converters.

NOTE 13: A total of 42,981 Grand Prix were built.

NOTE 14: 760 Grand Prix had synchromesh and 42,221 had Turbo-Hydra-Matic.

NOTE 15: A total of 34,609 standard Tempests were built.

NOTE 16: 7,154 standard Tempests had synchromesh and 27,455 had automatic.

NOTE 17: A total of 75,325 Tempest Customs were built.

NOTE 18: 8,302 Tempest Customs had synchromesh and 67,023 had automatic.

NOTE 19: 104,902 LeMans passenger cars were built.

NOTE 20: 14,770 LeMans passenger cars had synchromesh and 90,132 had automatic.

NOTE 21: 129 Tempest Safari wagons had synchromesh and 4,382 had automatic.

NOTE 22: 81,722 GTOs were built.

NOTE 23: 39,128 GTOs had synchromesh and 42,594 had automatic.

Note 24: Prices/weights for base Firebird with 165-hp ohc six and synchromesh.

PRODUCTION NOTES:

	Synchromesh	Automatic	Total
Standard ohc six Firebirds	5,258	5,597	10,855
Standard V-8 Firebirds	8,224	15,301	23,525
Deluxe ohc six Firebirds	2,963	3,846	6,809
Deluxe V-8 Firebirds	11,526	29,845	41,371
Totals	27,971	54,589	82,560

PONTIAC ENGINES

ENGINE [Catalina/Executive with synchromesh]: V-8. Overhead valves. Cast-iron block. Displacement: 400 cid. Bore & stroke: 4.125 x 3.746 in. Compression ratio: 8.6:1. Brake horsepower: 265 at 4600 rpm. Five main bearings. Hydraulic valve lifters. Carburetor: Rochester model 7027066 two-barrel.

ENGINE [Catalina/Executive with Hydra-Matic]: V-8. Overhead valves. Cast-iron block. Displacement: 400 cid. Bore & stroke: 4.125 x

1967 Pontiac Tempest two-door coupe. (OCW)

1967 Pontiac Tempest Safari four-door station wagon. (JAG)

3.746 in. Compression ratio: 10.5:1. Brake horsepower: 290 at 4600 rpm. Five main bearings. Hydraulic valve lifters. Carburetor: Rochester model 7027066 two-barrel.

ENGINE [Bonneville with synchromesh]: V-8. Overhead valves. Cast-iron block. Displacement: 400 cid. Bore & stroke: 4.125 x 3.746 in. Compression ratio: 8.6:1. Brake horsepower: 325 at 4800 rpm. Five main bearings. Hydraulic valve lifters. Carburetor: Carter AFB four-barrel.

ENGINE [Bonneville with Hydra-Matic]: V-8. Overhead valves. Cast-iron block. Displacement: 400 cid. Bore & stroke: 4.125 x 3.746 in. Compression ratio: 10.5:1. Brake horsepower: 333 at 5000 rpm. Five main bearings. Hydraulic valve lifters. Carburetor: Carter AFB-4243S four-barrel.

ENGINE [Grand Prix with Hydra-Matic]: V-8. Overhead valves. Cast-iron block. Displacement: 400 cid. Bore & stroke: 4.125 x 3.746 in. Compression ratio: 10.5:1. Brake horsepower: 350 at 5000 rpm. Five main bearings. Hydraulic valve lifters. High-lift camshaft. Carburetor: Carter AFB-4243S four-barrel.

ENGINE [Optional Grand Prix/Bonneville with synchromesh]: V-8. Overhead valves. Cast-iron block. Displacement: 400 cid. Bore & stroke: 4.125 x 3.746 in. Compression ratio: 8.6:1. Brake horsepower: 265 at 4600 rpm. Five main bearings. Hydraulic valve lifters. Carburetor: Carter AFB four-barrel.

ENGINE [Base V-8]: Overhead valves. Cast-iron block. Displacement: 428 cid. Bore & stroke: 4.125 x 4.00 in. Compression ratio: 10.5:1. Brake horsepower: 360 at 4600 rpm. Five main bearings. Hydraulic valve lifters. Carburetor: Carter AFB four-barrel.

1967 Pontiac Tempest LeMans two-door convertible. (JAG)

1967 Pontiac Tempest GTO two-door convertible. (OCW)

ENGINE [Base V-8]: Overhead valves. Cast-iron block. Displacement: 428 cid. Bore & stroke: 4.125 x 4.00 in. Compression ratio: 10.75:1. Brake horsepower: 376 at 5100 rpm. Five main bearings. Hydraulic valve lifters. Carburetor: Carter AFB four-barrel.

TEMPEST ENGINES

ENGINE [OHC Six]: Inline. Six-cylinder. Overhead valves. Overhead camshaft. Cast-iron block. Displacement: 230 cid. Bore & stroke: 3.85 x 3.25 in. Compression ratio: 9.0:1. Brake horsepower: 165 at 4700 rpm. Hydraulic valve lifters. Carburetor: Rochester model 7027167 one-barrel.

ENGINE [OHC Sprint Six]: Inline. Six-cylinder. Overhead valves. Overhead camshaft. Cast-iron block. Displacement: 230 cid. Bore & stroke: 3.85 x 3.25 in. Compression ratio: 10.5:1. Brake horsepower: 215 at 5200 rpm. Hydraulic valve lifters. Carburetor: Rochester four-barrel.

ENGINE [Base V-8]: Overhead valves. Cast-iron block. Displacement: 326 cid. Bore & stroke: 3.718 x 3.75 in. Compression ratio: 9.2:1. Brake horsepower: 250 at 4600 rpm. Hydraulic valve lifters. Carburetor: Rochester model 7025071 two-barrel.

ENGINE [Base V-8]: Overhead valves. Cast-iron block. Displacement: 326 cid. Bore & stroke: 3.718 x 3.75 in. Compression ratio: 10.5:1. Brake horsepower: 285 at 5000 rpm. Hydraulic valve lifters. Carburetor: Four-barrel.

LEMANS GTO ENGINES

ENGINE [Base V-8]: Overhead valves. Cast-iron block. Displacement: 400 cid. Bore & stroke: 4.125 x 3.746 in. Compression ratio: 8.6:1. Brake horsepower: 255 at 4600 rpm. Five main bearings. Hydraulic valve lifters. Carburetor: Four-barrel.

ENGINE [Base V-8]: Overhead valves. Cast-iron block. Displacement: 400 cid. Bore & stroke: 4.125 x 3.746 in. Compression ratio: 10.75:1. Brake horsepower: 335 at 5000 rpm. Five main bearings. Hydraulic valve lifters. Carburetor: Rochester model 7027071 four-barrel.

ENGINE [Base V-8]: Overhead valves. Cast-iron block. Displacement: 400 cid. Bore & stroke: 4.125 x 3.746 in. Compression ratio: 10.75:1. Brake horsepower: 360 at 5100 rpm. Five main bearings. Hydraulic valve lifters. Carburetor: Four-barrel.

FIREBIRD ENGINES

ENGINE [OHC Six]: Inline. Six-cylinder. Overhead valves. Overhead camshaft. Cast-iron block. Displacement: 230 cid. Bore & stroke: 3.85

1967 Pontiac Bonneville Brougham four-door hardtop. (OCW)

Standard Catalog of ® Pontiac, 2nd Edition

1967 Pontiac Firebird coupe. (OCW)

x 3.25 in. Compression ratio: 9.0:1. Brake horsepower: 165 at 4700 rpm. Hydraulic valve lifters. Carburetor: Rochester model 7027167 one-barrel.

ENGINE [Tempest OHC Sprint Six]: Inline. Six-cylinder. Overhead valves. Overhead camshaft. Cast-iron block. Displacement: 230 cid. Bore & stroke: 3.85 x 3.25 in. Compression ratio: 10.5:1. Brake horsepower: 215 at 5200 rpm. Hydraulic valve lifters. Carburetor: Rochester four-barrel.

ENGINE [Base V-8]: Overhead valves. Cast-iron block. Displacement: 326 cid. Bore & stroke: 3.718 x 3.75 in. Compression ratio: 9.2:1. Brake horsepower: 250 at 4600 rpm. Hydraulic valve lifters. Carburetion: Rochester model 7025071 two-barrel.

ENGINE [Base V-8]: Overhead valves. Cast-iron block. Displacement: 326 cid. Bore & stroke: 3.718 x 3.75 in. Compression ratio: 10.5:1. Brake horsepower: 285 at 5000 rpm. Hydraulic valve lifters. Carburetion: Four-barrel.

ENGINE [Base V-8]: Overhead valves. Cast-iron block. Displacement: 400 cid. Bore & stroke: 4.125 x 3.746 in. Compression ratio: 10.75:1. Brake horsepower: 335 at 5000 rpm. Five main bearings. Hydraulic valve lifters. Carburetor: Rochester model 7027071 four-barrel.

ENGINE [Base V-8]: Overhead valves. Cast-iron block. Displacement: 400 cid. Bore & stroke: 4.125 x 3.746 in. Compression ratio: 10.75:1. Brake horsepower: 325 at 4800 rpm. Five main bearings. Hydraulic valve lifters. Carburetor: Four-barrel.

CHASSIS: Wheelbase: (Pontiac station wagons) 121 in.; (Series 252 and 266 passenger cars) 121 in.; (Series 256 and 262 passenger cars) 124 in.; (Tempests) 115 in.; (Firebirds) 108 in. Overall Length: (Pontiac station wagons) 218.4 in.; (Series 252 and 266 passenger cars) 215.6 in.; (Series 256 and 262 passenger cars) 222.6 in.; (Tempest station wagons) 203.4 in.; (Tempest and GTO passenger cars) 206.6 in.; (Firebirds) 188.4 in. Front tread: (Pontiac) 63 in.; (Tempest) 58 in.; (Firebird) 60 in. Rear tread: (Pontiac) 64 in.; (Tempest) 59 in.; (Firebird) 60 in. Standard tires: (two-door and four-door Catalina sedans) 8.25 x 14; (other full-size Pontiacs) 8.55 x 14; (Tempest) 7.75 x 14; (Firebird) E70 x 14; (GTO) F70 x 14.

OPTIONS: [PONTIAC] Custom air conditioner ($421). Air injector exhaust control ($44). Console ($105). Cruise control ($63). Front disc brakes ($105). Rear window defogger ($21). Headrests ($42-$52). Capacitor ignition ($104-$115). Cornering lamps ($34). Low-fuel lamp ($6). Custom gauge panel cluster ($21-$36). Power antenna ($29). Power steering ($95-$105). AM/FM stereo ($239). Safeguard speedometer ($16). Reclining right-hand seat ($84). Super-Lift shock absorbers ($40). Front shoulder belts ($23-$26). Fender skirts ($26). Ride & handling package ($9). Strato Bucket seats on Bonneville coupe and convertible only ($114). Cordo top ($105-$132). Turbo-Hydra-Matic ($226). Four-speed manual transmission ($226). Three-speed manual transmission with floor shift ($42). Ventura Custom option with bench seats ($134). Ventura Custom convertible option with bucket seats ($206). Ventura Custom hardtop option with bucket seats ($248). Aluminum hubs and drums ($118-$135). Rally II wheels ($65-$73). 2 + 2 Sport Option ($389-$410). (Note: The 2 + 2 Sport Option included deluxe wheel discs and steering wheel, decor moldings, bucket seats, four-barrel 428-cid V-8, three-speed manual floor shift, dual exhausts and heavy-duty stabilizer bar. Lower 2 + 2 price applies to Catalina convertible; higher price to hardtop coupe.) The 265-hp base Catalina V-8 was a no-cost economy option in other full-sized lines. Base Bonneville V-8s were $35-$44 extra in Catalinas or

Executives with prices depending upon model and transmission. The 428-cid V-8 with 10.5:1 compression and four-barrel carburetor was optional in all full-sized Pontiacs at $79-$114 extra, with prices depending upon model, transmission, and use of air injector exhaust control. A 428-cid H.O. (high-output) V-8 was available in all full-sized Pontiacs for $119-$263 extra, with prices depending on model, transmission, and use of air injector exhaust control. **[TEMPEST/FIREBIRD]** Dual-stage air cleaner ($9). Custom air conditioner ($343). Carpeting ($19). GTO console ($68). Cruise control ($53). Remote control deck lid ($13). GTO tailpipe extensions ($21). Head rests ($42). Station wagon luggage carrier ($63). Remote control outside mirror ($7). Rally gauge cluster ($84). Power antenna ($29). AM/FM radio ($134). Reclining right-hand bucket seat ($84). Stereo tape player ($128). Tilt steering ($42). Three-speed manual transmission w/floor shift ($42). Three-speed manual transmission with full-synchromesh ($84). Four-speed manual transmission ($184). Automatic transmission with base OHC-6 ($226). Automatic transmission with 326-cid V-8 ($195). Turbo-Hydra-Matic in GTO only ($226). Wire wheel discs ($53-$70). Rally I wheels ($40-$57). Rally II wheels ($56-$72). Integral hubs and drums ($83-$100). Sprint package ($106-$127). (Sprint package includes heavy-duty stabilizer shaft, OHC six with four-barrel carburetor, three-speed manual transmission with floor shift, sport type shocks, front fender emblems, wheel opening moldings on Tempests and Tempest Customs, and Sprint side stripes on coupes and convertibles.) The 326-cid V-8 with 9.2:1 compression, two-barrel carburetion and 250 hp at 4600 rpm was $95 extra in Tempests. The Sprint OHC-6 with 10.5:1 compression, four-barrel carburetion and 207 hp at 5200 rpm was $58 extra in Tempests. The 326-cid V-8 with 10.5:1 compression, four-barrel carburetion and 285 hp at 5000 rpm was $159 extra in Tempests, except station wagons. (Note: Above options not available in GTOs.) **[GTO]** The 255-hp 400-cid V-8 with 8.6:1 compression and 255-hp at 4400 rpm was a no cost GTO economy option. A second option in this series was the RAM AIR 400-cid V-8 with the same specifications as base GTO engines. It also gave 360 hp, but at a higher peak of 5400 rpm.

FIREBIRD "MODEL-OPTION" PACKAGES

FIREBIRD SPRINT: Sprint models featured a 215-hp ohc six with four-barrel carburetion. A floor-mounted three speed manual gearbox and heavy-duty suspension was standard. Body still moldings with "3.8 Liter Overhead Cam" emblems were seen. Body side racing stripes were an option. The Firebird Sprint convertible was priced $3,019 and the Firebird Sprint coupe was $2,782. The additional weight over respective base models was 55 pounds.

FIREBIRD 326: Firebird 326s featured a 250-hp version of the base Tempest V-8 with two-barrel carburetion. The Firebird 326 convertible was priced $2,998 and weighed 3,415 pounds. The Firebird 326 coupe was priced $2,761 and weighed 3,123 pounds.

FIREBIRD 326-H.O.: Firebird 326-H.O.s used a 285-hp version of the base Tempest V-8 with 10.5:1 compression and four-barrel carburetion. Three-speed manual transmission with column shift, dual exhausts, H.O. side stripes, heavy-duty battery, and F70 x 14 wide oval tires were standard. The Firebird 326-H.O. convertible was priced $3,062 and the Firebird 326-H.O. coupe was priced $2,825.

FIREBIRD 400: Firebird 400s used a 325-hp version of the GTO V-8 with four-barrel carburetion. Standard equipment included dual scoop hood, chrome engine parts, three-speed heavy-duty floor shift, and sport-type suspension. The letters "400" appeared on the right-hand side of the deck lid. The Firebird 400 convertible was priced $3,177 and the Firebird 400 coupe was priced $2,777. Options included a Ram-Air induction setup that gave 325 hp at a higher rpm peak and cost over $600 extra.

1967 Pontiac Firebird coupe. OCW

HISTORICAL: Pontiacs were introduced in the fall of 1966 and the Firebird debuted Feb. 23, 1967. Calendar year production was 857,171 units. This was the only year that a Grand Prix convertible was ever offered. Interesting conversions of 1967 Pontiacs include the Dean Jeffries-built "Monkeemobile" GTO phaeton (made for the TV show) and the "Fitchbird," a performance-oriented package for Firebirds marketed by racing car builder/driver John Fitch. New features included 400-cid and 428-cid V-8s and the so-called "His-And-Her" transmission that allowed conventional shifting of the automatic gear selector. In magazine road tests, the 1967 Firebird Sprint hardtop with 215 hp did 0-to-60 mph in 10 seconds and the quarter-mile in 17.5 seconds. With the 325-hp Firebird 400 option, the numbers went down to 6.4 and 14.3, respectively. The Firebird 400 hardtop with the 325-hp motor was clocked by a second test driver at 14.7 seconds and 98 mph in the quarter-mile. A total of 7,724 Catalina 2 + 2s with the standard 428-cid/360-hp V-8 were built. Another 1,405 full-size Pontiacs had the 428 H.O./376-hp engine. The term Safari was used only for station wagons with wood-grained trim. The term Sports Coupe was used to describe Tempest and GTO two-door pillared coupes. The Bonneville Brougham package, available for four-door sedans and hardtops only, was $273 extra and included front foam seat cushions, power windows and Strato Bench seats.

1968 PONTIAC

1968 Pontiac Catalina four-door sedan. (JAG)

CATALINA — (V-8) — SERIES 252 — New styling features for full-sized 1968 Pontiacs included peripheral front bumpers, pointed noses, split grilles new interiors, revised instrument panels, and redesigned tail lamps. Standard equipment for Catalinas included General Motors safety features, cigar lighter, glove box and ashtray lamps, wood-grained dash trim, carpeting, concealed two-speed wipers, and a two-barrel V-8. Convertibles and station wagons had Morrokide seats and the nine-passenger wagon had a power tailgate window. Code 554 Ventura Custom trim option available on style numbers 25287 and 25267 with bucket seats ($178-$219) and all other Catalinas, except two-door sedans, with bench seats ($105). Ventura Custom option includes special interior trim and Ventura fender lettering. Catalina lettering appeared on the front fender tip, except cars with the Ventura package carried the Ventura name instead.

EXECUTIVE — (V-8) — SERIES 256 — Executives had all Catalina equipment, plus a deluxe steering wheel, decor moldings, deluxe

1968 Pontiac Catalina "Enforcer" police car. (JAG)

1968 Pontiac Executive four-door hardtop sedan. (JAG)

wheel discs and map, courtesy and trunk lamps. Executive lettering appeared behind the front wheel openings.

BONNEVILLE — (V-8) — SERIES 262 — Bonnevilles had all Executive features, plus fender skirts, carpeted lower door trim, elm burl vinyl dash trim, and a 340-hp V-8. Convertibles had leather and Morrokide interiors. Wagons had notch-back front seats with a folding armrest, a folding third seat, courtesy lamps, a power tailgate window, and a carpeted load area. The Bonneville name, in block letters, appeared behind the front wheel opening and on the deck lid latch panel. Bonneville taillights were of the same shape used a year earlier, but were now of a single design with the lenses being longer than those used on Catalinas and Executives. The code 511 Bonneville Brougham trim option was available on style numbers 26239 and 26287 ($273) and 26267 ($316). It included front foam cushions, spare tire cover, power windows, and Strato bench seat.

GRAND PRIX — (V-8) — SERIES 266 — Only the Grand Prix coupe was back for 1968. Standard were all General Motors safety features, plus deluxe wheel discs, fender skirts, dual exhausts, padded bucket seats with contoured backs and armrests, center console, and a 400-cid/350-hp four-barrel V-8 with three-speed manual attachment. New styling included a peripheral bumper, extra-long horizontal tail lamps integrated into bumper, down-swept rear deck, redesigned dash panel, and hidden headlights. A "GP" badge appeared on the left-hand grille and right-hand corner of the deck lid with engine displacement badges on rocker panel moldings.

TEMPEST — (6-CYL) — SERIES 233 — Tempests now had long hood/short deck styling. Two- and four-door models were built with different wheelbases. A peripheral bumper grille was used and taillights were placed in the bumper. Regular equipment on standard Tempests included GM safety features, heater and defroster, door armrests and an overhead valve six-cylinder engine.

TEMPEST CUSTOM — (6-CYL) — SERIES 235 — Tempest Customs had all features found on series 233 models, plus special interior and exterior trim, carpeting, Deluxe steering wheel, armrests with ashtrays, cigarette lighter, ignition buzzer alarm, front and rear body side marker lights, and dual horns. Station wagons and convertibles had all-Morrokide seats and carpeting, with panel courtesy lamps on convertibles. Tempest lettering along with custom badges appeared at tips of front fenders.

1968 Pontiac Grand Prix two-door hardtop coupe. (JAG)

1968 Pontiac Grand Prix two-door hardtop coupe. (JAG)

1968 Pontiac LeMans four-door hardtop. (JAG)

TEMPEST LEMANS — (6-CYL) — SERIES 237 AND SERIES 239 — Standard in LeMans were all GM safety features, plus disappearing wipers, dual horns, and Morrokide interior. Two-door models came with a choice of bucket or notch back armrest seats. The four-door hardtop had cloth and Morrokide upholstery and a choice of notch back or bench seats. A deluxe steering wheel, carpeting, cigar lighter, armrests and ashtrays, ignition alarm, panel courtesy lamps, ashtray, and glove box lamps were also featured. The LeMans convertible had a power top and special courtesy lights. The series 239 Safari was generally appointed in LeMans level trim with wood-grained interior and exterior paneling. The word LeMans was on the rear fender of each LeMans. The word Safari was on front of wood-trimmed station wagons.

GTO — (V-8) — SERIES 242 — Standard in GTOs were all GM safety features, dual exhausts, three-speed manual transmission with Hurst shifter, sports-type springs and shock absorbers, fast-back redline tires, bucket or notch back armrest seats, cigar lighter, carpeting, ignition alarm, disappearing wipers, panel courtesy, ashtray and glove box lamps, deluxe steering wheel, and 350-hp 400-cid four-barrel V-8 (or two-barrel 400-cid regular fuel V-8). GTOs had hidden headlights; a steel-reinforced "Endura" rubber front bumper; twin scoop hoods; GTO lettering on left-hand grille and right-hand deck lid; V-shaped badge behind front wheel opening; V-shaped nose emblems; and distinct tail lamps.

FIREBIRD — (6-CYL) — SERIES 223 — Base Firebird equipment included the standard GM safety features, front bucket seats, vinyl upholstery, simulated burl woodgrain dashboard, outside mirror, side marker lights, E70 x 14 black sidewall wide-oval tires with Space Saver spare, and 175-hp overhead cam six-cylinder engine. Styling was nearly identical to 1967-1/2 Firebirds except that vent

1968 Pontiac Firebird two-door hardtop. (JAG)

windows were replaced with one-piece side door glass. Technical changes included bias-mounted rear shock absorbers and multi-leaf rear springs.

I.D. DATA: VIN on left front door post. First symbol indicates GM division: 2=Pontiac. Second and third symbols indicate series: 23=Firebird; 33=Tempest; 35=Tempest Custom; 37=LeMans; 39=Tempest Safari; 42=GTO; 52=Catalina; 56=Star Chief; 62=Bonneville; 66=Grand Prix. Fourth and fifth symbols indicate body style and appear as last two symbols in body/style number column of charts below. Sixth symbol indicates model year: 8=1968. Seventh symbol tells assembly plant: L=Van Nuys, Calif.; 1=Oshawa, Ontario Canada; P=Pontiac, Mich.; C=South Gate, Calif.; E=Linden, N.J.; X=Kansas City, Kan.; R=Arlington, Texas; Z=Fremont, Calif.; B=Baltimore, Md.; K=Kansas City, Mo.; G=Framingham, Mass.; V=Lordstown, Ohio. Following symbols are sequential production number starting with 100001 at each assembly plant. Body/style number plate under hood tells manufacturer, Fisher style number, assembly plant, trim code, paint code, accessory codes. Style number consists of 68 (for 1968) prefix and four symbols that appear in second column of charts below. First two symbols indicate series; second two symbols indicate body type. VIN appears on front of engine at right-hand cylinder bank along with an alpha-numerical engine production code. Engine production codes included: [230-cid/175-hp OHC six] ZK/ZN. [230-cid/215-hp OHC six] ZD/ZE/ZO. [350-cid/265-hp V-8] WP/YN/WD/WC/YJ. [350-cid/320-hp V-8] WR/YM/YP/WK. [400-cid/265-hp V-8] XM/YA. [400-cid/290-hp] WA/WB/YC. [400-cid/330-hp V-8] WZ/YT. [400-cid/335-hp] WQ/WI/YW/XN. [400-cid/340-hp] WE/YE. [400-cid/350-hp] XZ/XH. [428-cid/375-hp V-8] WG/YH. [428-cid/390-hp V-8] WJ/YK. [400-cid/265-hp two-barrel GTO V-8; automatic only] XM. [400-cid/335-hp four-barrel special GTO V-8] WT/WW with synchromesh; YS with Turbo-Hydramatic. [400-cid/350-hp GTO special V-8] WT manual transmission only. [400-cid/360-hp special GTO V-8] WS/XS with synchromesh; YZ/XP Hydra-Matic.

1968 Pontiac Catalina two-door hardtop. (OCW)

1968 Pontiac LeMans four-door hardtop. (JAG)

1968 Pontiac GTO two-door convertible. (OCW)

1968 Pontiac Bonneville four-door sedan. (OCW)

1968 Pontiac Bonneville four-door hardtop. (OCW)

Model Number	Body Style Number	Body Type & Seating	Factory Price	Shipping Weight	Production Total
CATALINA (SERIES 252)					
252	25269	4d Hardtop-6P	3,004	3,888	94,441
252	25239	4d Hardtop-6P	3,158	4,012	41,727
252	25211	2d Sedan-6P	2,945	3,839	5,247
252	25287	2d Hardtop-6P	3,089	3,943	92,217
252	25267	2d Convertible-6P	3,391	3,980	7,339
252	25245	4d Sta Wagon-9P	3,537	4,408	13,363
252	25235	4d Sta Wagon-6P	3,390	4,327	21,848
EXECUTIVE (SERIES 256)					
256	25669	4d Sedan-6P	3,309	4,022	18,869
256	25639	4d Hardtop-6P	3,439	4,077	7,848
256	25687	2d Hardtop-6P	3,371	3,975	5,880
256	25645	4d Sta Wagon-9P	3,890	4,453	5,843
256	25635	4d Sta Wagon-6P	3,744	4,378	6,195
BONNEVILLE (SERIES 262)					
262	26239	4d Hardtop-6P	3,660	4,171	57,055
262	26287	2d Hardtop-6P	3,592	4,054	29,598
262	26267	2d Convertible-6P	3,800	4,090	7,358
262	26245	4d Sta Wagon-6P	3,987	4,485	6,926
262	26269	4d Sedan-6P	3,530	4,122	3,499
GRAND PRIX (SERIES 266)					
266	26657	2d Hardtop-6P	3,697	4,075	31,711
TEMPEST (SERIES 233)					
233	23369	4d Sedan-6P	2,509	3,307	11,590
233	23327	2d Coupe-6P	2,461	3,242	19,991
TEMPEST CUSTOM (SERIES 235)					
235	23569	4d Sedan-6P	2,602	3,297	17,304
235	23539	4d Hardtop-6P	2,728	3,382	6,147
235	23527	2d Coupe-6P	2,554	3,252	10,634
235	23537	2d Hardtop-6P	2,614	3,277	40,574
235	23567	2d Convertible-6P	2,839	3,337	3,518
235	23535	4d Sta Wagon-6P	2,906	3,667	8,253
TEMPEST LEMANS (SERIES 237)					
237	23739	4d Hardtop-6P	2,916	3,407	9,002
237	23727	2d Coupe-6P	2,724	3,287	8,439
237	23737	2d Hardtop-6P	2,786	3,302	110,036
237	23767	2d Convertible-6P	3,015	3,377	8,820
TEMPEST SAFARI (SERIES 239)					
239	23935	4d Sta Wagon-6P	3,017	3,677	4,414

1968 Pontiac Firebird two-door hardtop coupe. (OCW)

Model Number	Body Style Number	Body Type & Seating	Factory Price	Shipping Weight	Production Total
GTO (SERIES 242)					
242	24237	2d Hardtop-5P	3,101	3,506	77,704
242	24267	2d Convertible-5P	2,996	3,346	9,980
BASE FIREBIRD (SERIES 233)					
223	22337	2d Hardtop-5P	2,781	3,061	90,152
223	22367	2d Convertible-5P	2,996	3,346	16,960

NOTE 1: 240,971 Catalina passenger cars were built.

NOTE 2: 2,257 Catalina passenger cars had synchromesh and 238,714 had automatic.

NOTE 3: 35,211 Catalina station wagons were built.

NOTE 4: 289 Catalina station wagons had synchromesh and 34,922 had automatic.

NOTE 5: 32,597 Executive passenger cars were built.

NOTE 6: 47 Executive passenger cars had synchromesh and 32,550 had automatic.

NOTE 7: 12,038 Executive station wagons were built.

NOTE 8: 23 Executive station wagons had synchromesh and 12,015 had automatic.

NOTE 9: 98,005 Bonneville passenger cars were built.

NOTE 10: 208 Bonneville passenger cars had synchromesh and 97,797 had automatic.

1968 Pontiac Bonneville two-door convertible. (OCW)

1968 Pontiac Bonneville Safari four-door station wagon. (OCW)

1968 Pontiac Firebird two-door convertible. (OCW)

1968 Pontiac Firebird H.O. two-door convertible. (JAG)

NOTE 11: 6,926 Bonneville station wagons were built.

NOTE 12: Nine Bonneville station wagons had synchromesh and 6,917 had automatic.

NOTE 13: 495 Bonnevilles were provided for conversions.

NOTE 14: 31,711 Grand Prixs were built.

NOTE 15: 306 Grand Prixs had synchromesh and 31,405 had automatic.

NOTE 16: 31,581 standard Tempests were built.

NOTE 17: 5876 had synchromesh and 25,705 had automatic.

NOTE 18: 75,325 Custom Tempests were built.

NOTE 19: 8,302 had synchromesh and 67,023 had automatic.

NOTE 20: 136,297 LeMans cars were built.

NOTE 21: 12,233 LeMans cars had synchromesh and 124,074 had automatic.

NOTE 22: 122 LeMans Safaris had synchromesh and 4,292 had automatic.

NOTE 23: 87,684 GTOs were built.

NOTE 24: 36,299 had synchromesh and 51,385 had automatic.

FIREBIRD PRODUCTION NOTES

Model No.	Engine/Trim	Synchro.	Auto.	Total
Model 223	Standard OHC six	7,528	8,441	15,969
Model 224	Standard V-8	16,632	39,250	55,882
Model 225	Deluxe OHC six	1,216	1,309	2,525
Model 226	Deluxe V-8	7,534	25,202	32,736
Totals		32,910	74,202	107,112

PONTIAC ENGINES

ENGINE [Catalina with synchromesh]: V-8. Overhead valves. Cast-iron block. Displacement: 400 cid. Bore & stroke: 4.125 x 3.746 in. Compression ratio: 8.6:1. Brake horsepower: 265 at 4600 rpm. Five main bearings. Hydraulic valve lifters. Carburetor: Rochester two-barrel. (Optional Bonneville with Synchromesh)

ENGINE [Catalina/Executive with Hydra-Matic]: V-8. Overhead valves. Cast-iron block. Displacement: 400 cid. Bore & stroke: 4.125 x 3.746 in. Compression ratio: 10.5:1. Brake horsepower: 290 at 4600 rpm. Five main bearings. Hydraulic valve lifters. Carburetor: Rochester model 7028063 two-barrel.

ENGINE [Bonneville with Hydra-Matic]: V-8. Overhead valves. Cast-iron block. Displacement: 400 cid. Bore & stroke: 4.125 x 3.746 in. Compression ratio: 10.5:1. Brake horsepower: 340 at 4800 rpm. Five main bearings. Hydraulic valve lifters. Carburetor: Rochester model 7028263 four-barrel. [Optional in Executive with Hydra-Matic]

ENGINE [Grand Prix with Hydra-Matic]: V-8. Overhead valves. Cast-iron block. Displacement: 400 cid. Bore & stroke: 4.125 x 3.746 in. Compression ratio: 10.5:1. Brake horsepower: 350 at 5000 rpm. Five main bearings. Hydraulic valve lifters. High-lift camshaft. Carburetor: Carter AFB-4243S four-barrel.

ENGINE [Optional Bonneville/Grand Prix]: V-8. Overhead valves. Cast-iron block. Displacement: 428 cid. Bore & stroke: 4.125 x 4.00 in. Compression ratio: 10.5:1. Brake horsepower: 375 at 4800 rpm. Five main bearings. Hydraulic valve lifters. Carburetor: Rochester four-barrel.

ENGINE [Optional Bonneville/Grand Prix]: V-8. Overhead valves. Cast-iron block. Displacement: 428 cid. Bore & stroke: 4.125 x 4.00 in. Compression ratio: 10.75:1. Brake horsepower: 390 at 5200 rpm. Five main bearings. Hydraulic valve lifters. Carburetor: Rochester four-barrel.

TEMPEST ENGINES

ENGINE [Base Six]: Inline. Six-cylinder. Overhead valves. Cast-iron block. Displacement: 250 cid. Bore & stroke: 3.875 x 3.531 in. Compression ratio: 9.0:1. Brake horsepower: 175 at 4800 rpm. Hydraulic valve lifters. Carburetor: Rochester model 7028065 one-barrel.

ENGINE [Base Six]: Inline. Six-cylinder. Overhead valves. Cast-iron block. Displacement: 250 cid. Bore & stroke: 3.875 x 3.531 in. Compression ratio: 10.5:1. Brake horsepower: 215 at 4800 rpm. Hydraulic valve lifters. Carburetor: Rochester.

ENGINE [Base V-8]: Overhead valves. Cast-iron block. Displacement: 350 cid. Bore & stroke: 3.875 x 3.75 in. Compression ratio: 9.2:1. Brake horsepower: 265 at 4600 rpm. Hydraulic valve lifters. Carburetion: Rochester model 7028071 two-barrel.

ENGINE [Base V-8]: Overhead valves. Cast-iron block. Displacement: 350 cid. Bore & stroke: 3.875 x 3.75 in. Compression ratio: 10.5:1. Brake horsepower: 320 at 5100 rpm. Carburetion: Rochester.

LEMANS GTO ENGINES

ENGINE [Base V-8]: Overhead valves. Cast-iron block. Displacement: 400 cid. Bore & stroke: 4.125 x 3.746 in. Compression ratio: 8.6:1. Brake horsepower: 265 at 4600 rpm. Five main bearings. Hydraulic valve lifters. Carburetor: four-barrel.

ENGINE [Base V-8]: Overhead valves. Cast-iron block. Displacement: 400 cid. Bore & stroke: 4.125 x 3.746 in. Compression ratio: 10.75:1. Brake horsepower: 350 at 5000 rpm. Five main bearings. Hydraulic valve lifters. Carburetor: Rochester model 7028266 four-barrel.

ENGINE [Base V-8]: Overhead valves. Cast-iron block. Displacement: 400 cid. Bore & stroke: 4.125 x 3.746 in. Compression ratio: 10.5:1. Brake horsepower: 375 at 4800 rpm. Five main bearings. Hydraulic valve lifters. Carburetor: Rochester.

ENGINE [Base V-8]: Overhead valves. Cast-iron block. Displacement: 400 cid. Bore & stroke: 4.125 x 3.746 in. Compression ratio: 10.75:1. Brake horsepower: 375 at 4800 rpm. Five main bearings. Hydraulic valve lifters. Carburetor: Rochester.

1968 Pontiac GTO two-door hardtop. (OCW)

1968 Pontiac Tempest Safari four-door station wagon. (JAG)

FIREBIRD ENGINES

ENGINE [Base Six]: Inline. Six-cylinder. Overhead valves. Cast-iron block. Displacement: 250 cid. Bore & stroke: 3.875 x 3.531 in. Compression ratio: 9.0:1. Brake horsepower: 175 at 4800 rpm. Hydraulic valve lifters. Carburetor: Rochester model 7028065 one-barrel.

ENGINE [Base Six]: Inline. Six-cylinder. Overhead valves. Cast-iron block. Displacement: 250 cid. Bore & stroke: 3.875 x 3.531 in. Compression ratio: 10.5:1. Brake horsepower: 215 at 4800 rpm. Hydraulic valve lifters. Carburetor: Rochester.

ENGINE [Base V-8]: Overhead valves. Cast-iron block. Displacement: 350 cid. Bore & stroke: 3.875 x 3.75 in. Compression ratio: 9.2:1. Brake horsepower: 265 at 4600 rpm. Hydraulic valve lifters. Carburetion: Rochester model 7028071 two-barrel.

ENGINE [Base V-8]: Overhead valves. Cast-iron block. Displacement: 350 cid. Bore & stroke: 3.875 x 3.75 in. Compression ratio: 10.5:1. Brake horsepower: 320 at 5100 rpm. Hydraulic valve lifters. Carburetion: Rochester.

ENGINE [Base V-8]: Overhead valves. Cast-iron block. Displacement: 400 cid. Bore & stroke: 4.125 x 3.746 in. Compression ratio: 10.75:1. Brake horsepower: 330 at 4800 rpm. Five main bearings. Hydraulic valve lifters. Carburetor: Rochester four-barrel.

CHASSIS: Wheelbase: (Series 252, 266, and all Pontiac station wagons) 21 in.; (Series 256 and 262) 124 in.; (Tempest two-door) 112 in.; (Tempest four-door) 116 in.; (Firebird) 108 in. Overall Length: (All Pontiac station wagons) 217.8 in.; (Series 252 and 266) 216.5 in.; (Series 256 and 262) 223.5 in.; (Tempest station wagons) 211 in.; (Tempest two-door) 200.7 in.; (Tempest four-door) 204.7 in.; (Firebird) 188.8 in. Front tread: (Pontiac) 63 in.; (Tempest and Firebird) 60 in. Rear tread: (Pontiac) 64 in.; (Tempest and Firebird) 60 in.

OPTIONS: [PONTIAC] Custom air-conditioner ($421). Auxiliary gauge panel ($21-$37). Console ($105). Remote-control deck lid ($14). Rear window defogger ($21). Door guards ($6-$10). Electric clock ($16). Head restraints ($42-$53). Custom gear shift knob ($4). Underhood utility lamp ($7). Visor vanity mirror ($2-$4). Power brakes ($42). Power antenna ($30). Left power bucket seat ($69). Power steering ($105-$116). Power vent windows ($53). AM/FM Stereo ($239). Split back station wagon second seat ($37). Hood-mounted tachometer ($63). Strato bucket seats ($114). Wire wheel discs ($53-$74). Heavy-duty 15-inch wheels ($11). Aluminum hubs and drums ($126-$147). Rally II wheels ($63-$84). Transmission options included Turbo-Hydra-Matic ($237), Four-speed manual ($226), Close-ratio three-speed manual with floor shift ($42), and close-ratio four-speed manual ($226). The 265-hp two-barrel 400-cid V-8 was $9 extra on Catalinas and Executives with three-speed manual transmission. The 350-hp four-barrel 400-cid V-8 was $35-$44 extra on the same models. The 375-hp four-barrel 428-cid V-8 was $79-$114 extra on all Pontiacs with price depending on transmission. The 390-hp four-barrel 428-cid V-8 was $199-$263 extra on all Pontiacs with price depending on model and transmission. Dual exhausts were $31 extra. Safe-T-Track differential was $42 extra. A variety of axle ratios were available. [TEMPEST/GTO/FIREBIRD] Custom air conditioner ($360). Custom carpets ($19). Console ($51-$68). Cruise control ($53). Front disc brakes ($63). Auxiliary gauge cluster ($32). Rally gauge cluster ($51). Rally gauge cluster with tachometer ($84). Tinted windows ($35). Tinted windshield ($26). Right reclining bucket seat head restraint ($84). Dual horns ($4). Station wagon luggage carrier ($63). Four-way power seat ($70). Power brakes ($42). Power steering ($69). Left four-way power bucket seat ($70). AM/FM radio ($134). Rally stripes on GTO ($11). Rally stripes for Firebirds except 350 H.O. ($15). Safeguard speedometer ($16). Super-Lift shocks for Tempest/GTO ($42). Adjustable front and rear shocks for Firebird ($42). Hood-mounted tachometer ($63). Cordova top ($84-$95). Wire wheel discs ($53-$74). Rally I wheels ($40-$61). Rally II wheels. Transmission options included two-speed automatic ($195), four-speed manual ($184), and heavy-duty three-speed manual with floor shift ($84). The 265-hp two-barrel regular fuel 350-cid V-8 was $106 extra. The 320-hp four-barrel H.O. 350-cid V-8 was $170 extra. Dual exhausts were $31 extra. Safe-T-Track differential was $42 extra. GTO transmission options included Turbo-Hydramatic ($237) and close-ratio four-speed manual with floor shift ($184). The 366-hp four-barrel H.O. 400-cid V-8 was $631.12 extra. Dual exhausts were standard. Heavy-duty Safe-T-Track differential was $63 extra. Firebird transmission options

included all offered for Tempests and GTOs. Firebird engine options are listed in Firebird RPO packages section below.

FIREBIRD RPO PACKAGES

FIREBIRD 350 PACKAGE: Included three-speed manual transmission with column shift and F70 x 14 tires. Engine: 350-cid (3.88 x 3.75 Bore & stroke) V-8 with 9.2:1 compression, Rochester two-barrel carburetor and 265 hp at 4600 rpm. Price: $106 over base model cost.

FIREBIRD 350-H.O. PACKAGE: Included three-speed manual transmission with column shift, dual exhausts, H.O. side stripes, heavy-duty battery and four F70 x 14 tires. Engine: 350-cid V-8 with 10.5:1 compression, Rochester four-barrel carburetor and 320 hp at 5100 rpm. Price: $181 over base model cost.

FIREBIRD 400 PACKAGE: Included three-speed manual transmission with floor shift, chrome air cleaner, chrome rocker covers, chrome oil cap, sports type springs and shock absorbers, heavy-duty battery, dual exhausts, hood emblem and dual scoop hood, F70 x 14 red line or white sidewall tires, and "Power Flex" variable pitch cooling fan. Engine: 400-cid V-8 with 10.75:1 compression, Rochester four-barrel carburetor, and 330 hp at 4800 rpm. Price: $351-$435 depending on transmission. Lower price applies to cars with Turbo-Hydra-Matic four-speed manual transmissions.

FIREBIRD RAM AIR 400 PACKAGE: Same inclusions as above, except for addition of de-clutching fan and twin functional hood scoops. Engine: 400-cid V-8 with 10.75:1 compression, Rochester four-barrel carburetor, and 335 hp at 5000 rpm. Price: $616 over base model cost.

HISTORICAL: Production started Aug. 21, 1967. The model introductions were Sept. 21, 1967. Model year output was 910,977 cars. Calendar year output was 943,253 cars. The GTO Endura nose was a popular new option. This was the first year for two wheelbases in the Tempest series, with four-doors on the longer chassis. The 1968 Firebird 400 with the 335-hp option was capable of 0-to-60 mph in 7.6 seconds and the quarter-mile in 15.4 seconds. The 360-hp GTO hardtop did 0-to-60 mph in 6.6 seconds and the quarter-mile took 15.5 seconds. There were 6,252 standard 428 V-8 engines installed and 453 full-size 428 H.O. Pontiacs were built.

1969 PONTIAC

1969 Pontiac Catalina two-door hardtop. (OCW)

CATALINA — (V-8) — SERIES 252 — New styling features for full-sized 1969 Pontiacs included split bumpers, revised rooflines and vent-less windows. Wheelbases increased one inch. Catalinas had all GM safety features, carpeting, peripheral front bumpers with Endura rubber center inserts, "pulse" windshield wipers with concealed blades, front foam seat cushions, upper level ventilation systems and a choice of low-compression (regular fuel) two-barrel V-8s or a 290-hp 400-cid V-8. Station wagons had wood-grained dashboards and new two-way tailgates with power rear windows on nine-passenger styles. The Ventura trim package was offered for closed cars only.

EXECUTIVE — (V-8) — SERIES 256 — Standard equipment on Executive included everything found on Catalinas, plus deluxe wheel covers, three-spoke padded vinyl steering wheel, simulated elm burl dash trim, rear foam seat cushions, electric clock, and Morrokide upholstery. Executive Safaris also had wood-grained exterior paneling with simulated teakwood molding trim, vinyl floor mats, and a concealed cargo locker.

1969 Pontiac Executive Safari four-door station wagon. (OCW)

BONNEVILLE — (V-8) — SERIES 262 — Bonnevilles had all features found on Executives, plus a die-cast grille, choice of several Bonneville Custom interiors, extra-thick foam seat padding, front center fold-down armrest, fender skirts, carpeted lower door panels, and a 360-hp four-barrel V-8. The convertible had all-Morrokide upholstery with leather accents. Station wagons featured a notchback front seat with folding armrest, a folding third seat, and courtesy lamps. Bonneville lettering appeared on the left-hand grille, the rocker panel moldings, and the center edge of the deck lid. The Brougham option was again available, but for coupes and convertibles only.

GRAND PRIX — (V-8) — SERIES 276 — An all-new Grand Prix on an exclusive 118-in. platform was a popular offering this year. Styling highlights were a V-shaped grille, square headlamp surrounds, an aircraft inspired interior and, Pontiac claimed, the longest hood of any production car in history. Standard equipment included dual exhaust, Strato Bucket seats, padded integral console with floor shift, hidden radio antenna, carpeted lower door panels, upper level ventilation system, and "pulse" type recessed windshield wipers. An "SJ" option package was available. A 350-hp V-8 was standard.

TEMPEST — (6-CYL) — SERIES 233 — Tempests were mildly face-lifted with new grille and taillight treatments. Two-door hardtops and convertibles now had vent-less side window styling. Standard equipment on base models included all GM safety features, carpets, Morrokide accented upholstery trims, and an overhead valve six. A Tempest script was placed on the leading edge of front fenders.

TEMPEST CUSTOM — (6-CYL) — SERIES 235 — This was now called the Custom 'S' series and front fender scripts carried this designation. Standard equipment included all Tempest features, plus all-Morrokide upholstery, concealed windshield wipers, dual horns, ignition buzzer, and panel courtesy lamps on convertibles. Small hubcaps were a regular feature.

TEMPEST LEMANS — (6-CYL) — SERIES 237 AND 239 — LeMans models incorporated all Custom 'S' equipment, plus a 3.23:1 rear axle, deluxe three-spoke steering wheel, "pulse" wipers, lamp packages, and several seating arrangement choices. Two-door models were available with bucket or notchback seats; four-door hardtop buyers had a choice of bench or notchback seats with center armrests. LeMans convertibles had power tops and Safaris had wood-grained exterior paneling and concealed headlamps. The Sprint option was available for all six-cylinder Tempests, except station wagons. LeMans block lettering appeared on the front fender tips and there were bright metal window and wheel opening moldings.

1969 Pontiac Bonneville two-door convertible. (OCW)

1969 Pontiac Bonneville two-door convertible. (OCW)

Wood-trimmed station wagons had Safari fender scripts. The Safari was not a LeMans, but was close to it in overall level of trim.

GTO — (V-8) — SERIES 242 — GTOs were based on LeMans with additional standard equipment features including a 400-cid/350-hp V-8, dual exhausts, 3.55:1 rear axle ratio, heavy-duty clutch, three-speed gearbox with floor shifter, Power-Flex cooling fan, sports type springs and shock absorbers, red line wide-oval tires, carpeting, Deluxe steering wheel, and choice of bucket or notchback seats. A crosshatched grille insert with horizontal divider bars appeared and hidden headlights were standard. GTO lettering was seen on the left-hand grille, right-hand side of deck lid, and behind the front wheel openings. Tail lamps were no longer completely surrounded by bumpers and carried lenses with bright metal trim moldings. Side marker lights were of a distinctive rectangular shape, instead of the triangular type used on other Tempests. A special high-performance "The Judge" option was released Dec. 19, 1968. It included one of two available Ram Air V-8s as standard equipment as well as many other muscle car features. Though more expensive than base GTOs, a "The Judge" was the least expensive of several cars now on the market with comparable equipment.

FIREBIRD — (6-CYL) — SERIES 223 — Firebirds were restyled late in 1968 to incorporate revisions similar to those planned for the Chevrolet Camaro. Design changes included flatter wheel openings, front fender wind splits, new rooflines, and a creased lower beltline. The gas filler was moved behind the rear license plate and a boxier split bumper grille was used. Headlamps were set into square body-colored Endura bezels. The high-performance Trans Am was introduced March 8, 1969. This was the most highly refined "model-option" to come from Pontiac up to this point in time. Because of slow sales and late introductions of next-year models, 1969 Firebirds left in stock were carried over and sold through the following fall. Standard equipment for base Firebirds included vinyl bucket seats, grained dashboards, carpeting, outside mirrors, side marker lamps, and E70 x 14 tires. "Model-options" included Firebird Sprint, Firebird 350 and 350 HO, Firebird 400 and 400 HO, and Firebird RAM AIR 400, in addition to the midyear Trans Am.

1969 Pontiac Executive two-door hardtop. (OCW)

1969 Pontiac Grand Prix 'J' hardtop coupe. (OCW)

1969 Pontiac GTO two-door hardtop coupe. (OCW)

1969 Pontiac Firebird Trans Am two-door hardtop. (OCW)

1969 Pontiac Executive two-door sedan. (JAG)

1969 Pontiac Bonneville Brougham four-door hardtop. (OCW)

I.D. DATA: VIN on left top of instrument panel, visible through windshield. First symbol indicates GM division: 2=Pontiac. Second and third symbols indicate series: 23=Firebird; 33=Tempest; 35=Tempest Custom; 37=LeMans; 39=Tempest Safari; 42=GTO; 52=Catalina; 56=Star Chief; 62=Bonneville; 76=Grand Prix. Fourth and fifth symbols indicate body style and appear as last two symbols in body/style number column of charts below. Sixth symbol indicates model year: 9=1969. Seventh symbol tells assembly plant: A=Atlanta, Ga.; L=Van Nuys, Calif.; 1=Oshawa, Ontario Canada; P=Pontiac, Mich.; C=South Gate, Calif.; E=Linden, N.J.; X=Kansas City, Kan.; R=Arlington, Texas; Z=Fremont, Calif.; B=Baltimore, Md.; K=Kansas City, Mo.; G=Framingham, Mass.; V=Lordstown, Ohio. Following symbols are sequential production number starting with 100001 at each assembly plant. Body/style number plate under hood tells manufacturer, Fisher style number, assembly plant, trim code, paint code, accessory codes. Style number consists of 69 (for 1969) prefix and four symbols that appear in second column of charts below. First two symbols indicate series; second two symbols indicate body type. VIN appears on front of engine at right-hand cylinder bank along with an alpha-numerical engine production code. Engine production codes included: [250-cid/175-hp six] ZC/ZF/ZK/ZN. [250-cid/215-hp six] ZL/ZE. [250-cid/230-hp six] ZH/ZD. [350-cid/265-hp V-8] WU/YU/XS/XR/YN/WP/WM YE XB/WC XL YJ. [350 CID/325 HP V-8] WN/XG/[350-cid/330-hp V-8] WV/XU. [400-cid/265-hp V-8] XM/XX/YA/YB/YF. [400-cid/290-hp] WD/WE/YD/WA/WB. [400-cid/330-hp] WZ/YT. [400-cid/335-hp] WQ/ YW. [400-cid/345-hp] WH/XN. [400-cid/350-hp] WX/XH/Wt. [400-cid/350-hp] WT/YS. [400-cid/366-hp] WS/WW/YZ. [428-cid/340-hp] WG; [428-cid/360-hp] WG/YH/XJ/YL/XE. [428-cid/370-hp] XK/WF/XF. [428-cid/390-hp] WJ/YK/WL/XG.

Model Number	Body Style Number	Body Type & Seating	Factory Price	Shipping Weight	Production Total
CATALINA (SERIES 252)					
252	25269	4d Sedan-6P	3,090	3,945	48,590
252	25239	4d Hardtop-6P	3,244	4,005	38,819
252	25237	2d Hardtop-6P	3,174	2,935	84,006
252	25267	2d Convertible-6P	3,476	2,985	5,436
252	25246	4d Sta Wagon-9P	3,664	4,520	13,393
252	25236	4d Sta Wagon-6P	3,519	4,455	20,352
EXECUTIVE (SERIES 256)					
256	25669	4d Sedan-6P	3,394	4,045	14,831
256	25639	4d Hardtop-6P	3,525	4,065	6,522
256	25637	2d Hardtop-6P	3,456	2,970	4,492
256	25646	4d Sta Wagon-9P	4,017	4,545	6,805
256	25636	4d Sta Wagon-6P	3,872	4,475	6,411
BONNEVILLE (SERIES 262)					
262	26269	4d Sedan-6P	3,626	4,180	4,859
262	26239	4d Hardtop-6P	3,756	4,180	40,817
262	26237	2d Hardtop-6P	3,64,104	4,600	7,428
GRAND PRIX (SERIES 276)					
276	27657	2d Hardtop-5P	3,866	3,715	112,486
TEMPEST (SERIES 233)					
233	23369	4d Sedan-6P	2,557	3,250	9,741
233	23327	2d Coupe-6P	2,510	3,180	17,181
TEMPEST CUSTOM 'S' (SERIES 235)					
235	23569	4d Sedan-6P	2,651	3,235	16,532
235	23539	4d Hardtop-6P	2,777	3,315	3,918
235	23527	2d Coupe-6P	2,603	3,210	7,912
235	23537	2d Hardtop-6P	2,663	3,220	46,886
235	23567	2d Convertible-6P	2,888	3,265	2,379
235	23535	4d Sta Wagon-6P	2,956	5,696	6,963
TEMPEST LEMANS (SERIES 237)					
237	23769	4d Hardtop-6P	2,965	3,360	6,475
237	23727	2d Coupe-6P	2,773	3,225	5,033

1969 Pontiac GTO "The Judge" two-door hardtop. (OCW)

Model Number	Body Style Number	Body Type & Seating	Factory Price	Shipping Weight	Production Total
237	23737	2d Hardtop-6P	2,835	3,245	82,817
237	23767	2d Convertible-6P	3,064	3,290	5,676
TEMPEST SAFARI (SERIES 239)					
239	23936	4d Sta Wagon-6P	3,198	3,690	4,115
GTO (SERIES 242)					
242	24237	2d Hardtop-5P	2,831	3,080	58,126
242	24267	2d Convertible-5P	3,382	3,553	7,328
GTO "THE JUDGE" (SERIES 242)					
242	2437	2d Hardtop-5P	3,161	NA	6,725
242	24267	2d Convertible-5P	4,212	NA	108
FIREBIRD (SERIES 223)					
223	22337	2d Hardtop-5P	2,831	3,080	75,362
223	22367	2d Convertible-5P	3,045	3,330	11,649
FIREBIRD TRANS AM					
223	22337	2d Hardtop-5P	3,556	—	689
223	22367	2d Convertible-5P	3770	—	8

1969 Pontiac GTO two-door convertible. (OCW)

NOTE 1: 212,851 Catalina passenger cars were built.

NOTE 2: 837 Catalina passenger cars had synchromesh and 212,014 had automatic.

NOTE 3: 33,745 Catalina station wagons were built.

NOTE 4: 170 Catalina station wagons had synchromesh and 33,575 had automatic.

NOTE 5: 25,845 Executive passenger cars were built.

NOTE 6: 25 Executive passenger cars had synchromesh and 25,820 had automatic.

NOTE 7: 13,216 Executive station wagons were built.

NOTE 8: 14 Executive station wagons had synchromesh and 13,202 had automatic.

NOTE 9: 89,334 Bonneville passenger cars were built.

NOTE 10: 44 Bonneville passenger cars had synchromesh and 89,290 had automatic.

NOTE 11: 7,428 Bonneville station wagons were built.

NOTE 12: Seven Bonneville wagons had synchromesh and 7,421 had automatic.

NOTE 13: 447 Bonneville chassis were provided for conversions.

NOTE 14: 112,486 Grand Prix were built.

NOTE 15: 1,014 Grand Prix had synchromesh and 111,472 had automatic.

NOTE 16: Approximately 676 cars above had four-speed manual transmission.

NOTE 17: 26,922 standard Tempest were built.

NOTE 18: 4,450 had synchromesh and 22,472 had automatic.

NOTE 19: 84,590 Tempest Custom 'S' models were built.

NOTE 20: 4,045 Tempest 'S' had synchromesh and 80,545 had automatic.

NOTE 21: 100,001 LeMans passenger cars were built.

NOTE 22: 6,303 LeMans passenger cars had synchromesh and 93,698 had automatic.

NOTE 23: 86 Tempest Safaris had synchromesh and 4,029 had automatic.

NOTE 24: 72,287 GTOs and 'The Judge' optioned GTOs were built.

NOTE 25: 31,433 GTOs and Judges had synchromesh and 40,854 had automatic.

NOTE 26: 8,491 GTOs and Judges (including 362 convertibles) had RAM AIR III V-8s.

1969 Pontiac GTO "The Judge" two-door convertible. (OCW)

1969 Pontiac Firebird two-door hardtop coupe. (JAG)

NOTE 27: RAM AIR III engines were coded 'YZ' or 'WS'.

NOTE 28: 759 GTOs and Judges (including 59 convertibles) had RAM AIR IV V-8s.

NOTE 29: RAM AIR IV engines were coded 'XP' (automatic) or 'WW' (synchromesh).

NOTE 30: 87,709 Firebirds and Trans Ams were built.

NOTE 31: 20,840 Firebirds and Trans Ams had synchromesh; 66,868 had automatic.

NOTE 32: 114 Trans Ams had the L-74 RAM AIR III V-8 and Turbo-Hydra-Matic.

NOTE 33: 520 Trans Ams had the L-74 RAM AIR V-8 and synchromesh.

NOTE 34: All eight Trans Am convertibles were L-74s; four had manual gearboxes.

NOTE 35: Nine Trans Ams had the L-67 RAM AIR IV engine and Turbo-Hydra-Matic.

NOTE 36: 46 Trans Ams had the L-67 RAM AIR IV engine and synchromesh.

PONTIAC ENGINES

ENGINE [Catalina with synchromesh]: V-8. Overhead valves. Cast-iron block. Displacement: 400 cid. Bore & stroke: 4.125 x 3.746 in. Compression ratio: 8.6:1. Brake horsepower: 265 at 4600 rpm. Five main bearings. Hydraulic valve lifters. Carburetor: Rochester two-barrel. (No cost option for full-size Pontiacs with synchromesh.)

ENGINE [Catalina/Executive with Hydra-Matic]: V-8. Overhead valves. Cast-iron block. Displacement: 400 cid. Bore & stroke: 4.125 x 3.746 in. Compression ratio: 10.5:1. Brake horsepower: 290 at 4600 rpm. Five main bearings. Hydraulic valve lifters. Carburetor: Rochester model 7028066 two-barrel.

ENGINE [Bonneville with Hydra-Matic]: V-8. Overhead valves. Cast-iron block. Displacement: 428 cid. Bore & stroke: 4.125 x 4.00 in. Compression ratio: 10.5:1. Brake horsepower: 360 at 4600 rpm. Five main bearings. Hydraulic valve lifters. Carburetor: Rochester model 7029262 four-barrel. [Optional in Executive with Hydra-Matic.]

ENGINE [Grand Prix with Hydra-Matic]: V-8. Overhead valves. Cast-iron block. Displacement: 400 cid. Bore & stroke: 4.125 x 3.746 in. Compression ratio: 10.5:1. Brake horsepower: 350 at 5000 rpm. Five main bearings. Hydraulic valve lifters. High-lift camshaft. Carburetor: Rochester model 7029263 four-barrel.

ENGINE [Optional full-size Pontiacs]: V-8. Overhead valves. Cast-iron block. Displacement: 428 cid. Bore & stroke: 4.125 x 4.00 in. Compression ratio: 10.75:1. Brake horsepower: 390 at 5200 rpm. Five main bearings. Hydraulic valve lifters. Carburetor: Rochester four-barrel.

TEMPEST ENGINES

ENGINE [Base Six]: Inline. Six-cylinder. Overhead valves. Cast-iron block. Displacement: 250 cid. Bore & stroke: 3.875 x 3.531 in.

1969 Pontiac GTO two-door convertible. (OCW)

Compression ratio: 9.0:1. Brake horsepower: 175 at 4800 rpm. Hydraulic valve lifters. Carburetor: Rochester model 7028065 one-barrel.

ENGINE [Base Six]: Inline. Six-cylinder. Overhead valves. Cast-iron block. Displacement: 250 cid. Bore & stroke: 3.875 x 3.531 in. Compression ratio: 10.5:1. Brake horsepower: 215 at 4800 rpm. Hydraulic valve lifters. Carburetor: Rochester one-barrel.

ENGINE [Base V-8]: Overhead valves. Cast-iron block. Displacement: 350 cid. Bore & stroke: 3.875 x 3.75 in. Compression ratio: 9.2:1. Brake horsepower: 265 at 4600 rpm. Hydraulic valve lifters. Carburetion: Rochester two-barrel.

ENGINE [Base V-8]: Overhead valves. Cast-iron block. Displacement: 350 cid. Bore & stroke: 3.875 x 3.75 in. Compression ratio: 10.5:1. Brake horsepower: 330 at 5100 rpm. Hydraulic valve lifters. Carburetion: Four-barrel.

LEMANS GTO ENGINES

ENGINE [Base V-8]: Overhead valves. Cast-iron block. Displacement: 400 cid. Bore & stroke: 4.125 x 3.746 in. Compression ratio: 10.75:1. Brake horsepower: 350 at 5000 rpm. Five main bearings. Hydraulic valve lifters. Carburetor: Rochester model 7028266 four-barrel.

ENGINE [Base V-8]: Overhead valves. Cast-iron block. Displacement: 400 cid. Bore & stroke: 4.125 x 3.746 in. Compression ratio: 8.6:1. Brake horsepower: 265 at 4600 rpm. Five main bearings. Hydraulic valve lifters. Carburetor: Four-barrel.

ENGINE [Base V-8]: Overhead valves. Cast-iron block. Displacement: 400 cid. Bore & stroke: 4.125 x 3.746 in. Compression ratio: 10.5:1. Brake horsepower: 375 at 4800 rpm. Five main bearings. Hydraulic valve lifters. Carburetor: Rochester.

FIREBIRD ENGINES

ENGINE [Base Six]: Inline. Six-cylinder. Overhead valves. Cast-iron block. Displacement: 250 cid. Bore & stroke: 3.875 x 3.531 in. Compression ratio: 9.0:1. Brake horsepower: 175 at 4800 rpm. Hydraulic valve lifters. Carburetor: Rochester model 7028065 one-barrel.

ENGINE [Base Six]: Inline. Six-cylinder. Overhead valves. Cast-iron block. Displacement: 250 cid. Bore & stroke: 3.875 x 3.531 in. Compression ratio: 10.5:1. Brake horsepower: 215 at 4800 rpm. Hydraulic valve lifters. Carburetor: Rochester.

ENGINE [Base V-8]: Overhead valves. Cast-iron block. Displacement: 350 cid. Bore & stroke: 3.875 x 3.75 in. Compression ratio: 10.5:1. Brake horsepower: 320 at 5100 rpm. Hydraulic valve lifters. Carburetion: Rochester.

ENGINE [Base V-8]: Overhead valves. Cast-iron block. Displacement: 400 cid. Bore & stroke: 4.125 x 3.746 in. Compression ratio: 10.75:1. Brake horsepower: 330 at 4800 rpm. Five main bearings. Hydraulic valve lifters. Carburetor: Rochester four-barrel.

CHASSIS: Wheelbase: (Series 252 and all Pontiac station wagons) 122 in.; (Series 256 and 262) 125 in.; (Series 276) 118 in.; (Tempest two-door) 112 in.; (Tempest four-door) 116 in.; (Firebird) 108 in. Overall Length: (All Pontiac station wagons) 220.5 in.; (Series 252) 217.5 in.; (Series 256 and 262) 223.5 in.; (Series 276) 210.2 in.; (All Tempest station wagons) 211 in.; (Tempest two-door) 201.5 in.; (Tempest four-door) 205.5 in.; (Firebird) 191.1 in. Front

1969 Pontiac Firebird two-door convertible. (OCW)

1969 Pontiac Firebird Trans Am two-door convertible. (JAG)

tread: (Pontiac) 63 in.; (others) 60 in. Rear tread: (Pontiac) 64 in.; (others) 60 in.

OPTIONS [PONTIAC/TEMPEST] Heavy-duty aluminum front brake drums ($72). Load floor carpeting ($53). Console ($56). Cruise control ($58). GTO type exhaust extensions ($21). Instant air heater ($16). Luggage carrier for station wagons ($63-$84). Power rear antenna ($32). Power disc front brakes ($64-$74). Power door locks ($45-$68). Wonder Touch steering ($100-$105). GTO Rally Stripes ($14). GTO retractable headlight covers ($53). Custom Sport steering wheel ($34-$50). Tilt wheel with power steering ($45). Hood mounted tachometer ($63). Cordova top ($100-$142). Rally II wheels ($64-$84). Arctic wiper blades ($6). Station wagon rear window deflector ($26). Recessed wipers on base Tempest ($19). Leather GP trim ($199). Three-speed manual transmissions were provided at base prices, including a heavy-duty type in Grand Prix. Turbo-Hydra-Matic $227 extra. Grand Prix buyers had two other options, close or wide-ratio four-speed manual gearboxes, both at $185. The regular fuel V-8 was a no charge option in any line. The Bonneville four-barrel was $38 extra on lower lines. The 375-hp four-barrel 428-cid V-8 was $67-$105 extra on all Pontiacs (except Catalina and Executive station wagons) with price depending on series and transmission. The 390-hp four-barrel 428-cid HO V-8 was $150-$255 extra with the same qualifications. Dual exhaust and Safe-T-Track differential were priced as in 1968. (GTO) Transmission options included Turbo-Hydra-Matic/Turbo-Hydra-Matic/Hydra-Matic ($227) and wide or close-ratio four-speed manual ($185). The 366-hp and 370-hp RAM AIR V-8s were available with the price of RAM AIR IV set at $558. Dual exhausts were standard. Heavy-duty Safe-T-Track was again $63. **[FIREBIRD]** Custom air conditioner ($376). Heavy-duty battery ($4). Brake pedal trim package ($5). Electric clock ($16). Console ($54). Cruise control ($58). Remote control deck lid ($15). Rally gage cluster with tachometer ($84). Rally gauge cluster with clock ($47). Tinted windows ($33). Tinted windshield ($22). Custom stick-shift knob ($5). Leather and Morrokide trim ($199). Remote control outside mirror ($11). Power brakes ($42). Power steering ($105). Left power bucket seat ($74). Power convertible top ($53). Power windows ($105). Wire wheel discs ($53-$74). Rally II wheels ($63-$84). Turnpike cruise option package ($177). Transmission options included two-speed automatic ($174-$185); Turbo-Hydra-Matic ($195-$227); Three-speed manual with floor shift ($42); Heavy-duty three-speed manual with floor shift ($84) and wide or close-ratio four-speed manual ($185 each). The Sprint option package (Code 342) was $111-$132 and included the 215-hp OHC six, which was not offered separately. The

1969 Pontiac Firebird Trans Am two-door convertible. (JAG)

Standard Catalog of ® Pontiac, 2nd Edition

1969 Pontiac Firebird Trans Am two-door hardtop coupe. (JAG)

1969 Pontiac Executive four-door hardtop. (JAG)

265-hp two-barrel regular fuel 350-cid V-8 was $11 extra. The 330-hp four-barrel 350-cid HO V-8 was $175 extra. Dual exhausts and Safe-T-Track were priced as in 1968. Firebird Transmission options included all offered for Tempests and GTOs. Engine options are listed in Firebird RPO packages section below.

FIREBIRD RPO PACKAGES

FIREBIRD 350 PACKAGE: Option code 343. Engine code L-30. Included three-speed manual transmission with column shift and F70 x 14 tires. Engine: 350-cid V-8 with 9.2:1 compression, Rochester two-barrel carburetor and 265 hp at 4600 rpm. Price: $111 over base model cost.

FIREBIRD 350-HO PACKAGE: Option code 344. Engine code L-76. Included three-speed manual transmission with column shift, dual exhausts and heavy-duty battery. Engine: 350-cid V-8 with 10.5:1 compression, Rochester four-barrel carburetor and 325 hp at 5100 rpm. Price $186 over base model cost.

FIREBIRD 400 PACKAGE: Option code 345. Engine code W-S6. Included chrome engine parts, dual exhausts, heavy-duty battery, three-speed manual transmission with floor shift, F70 x 14 red stripe or white sidewall tires and variable pitch cooling fan. Engine: 400-cid V-8 with 10.75:1 compression, Rochester four-barrel carburetor and 330 hp at 4800 rpm. Special hood is used with non-functional scoops. Ride and handling package required. Price: $275-$358 over base model cost depending on transmission.

FIREBIRD RAM AIR 400 PACKAGE: Option code 348. Engine code L-74. Same inclusions as above except for addition of de-clutching fan and twin functional hood scoops with operating mechanism. Engine: Same as 1968. Price: $351-$435 over base model cost depending on transmission attachment.

FIREBIRD RAM AIR IV PACKAGE: Option code 347. Engine code L-67. Same equipment inclusions as above, plus special hood scoop emblems. Engine: 400-cid V-8 with special camshaft and valve train, 10.75:1 compression, Rochester four-barrel carburetor and 345 hp at 5400 rpm. Price: $832 over base model cost. Specific transmissions required.

TRANS AM PACKAGE: Code 322 UPC WS-4. Engine code L-74. Included heavy-duty three-speed manual gearbox with floor shifter; 3.55:1 axle; fiberglass-belted tires; heavy-duty shocks and springs; one-inch stabilizer bar; power front disc brakes; variable ratio power steering; engine air exhaust louvers; rear deck air foil; black textured grille; full-length body stripes; white and blue finish; leather covered steering wheel and special identification decals. Base engine specifications: See 1968 Firebird Ram Air 400 package listing optional engine package. Price for standard Trans Am: $725 over base model cost.

HISTORICAL: Production began Aug. 26, 1968. Introductions took place a month later, except for the Trans Am. It was introduced on March 8, 1969. Calendar year assemblies came to 772,104 cars for a 10.3 percent share of market. This was to be Pontiac's last year as America's third-ranking automaker. The 370-hp GTO Judge hardtop could do 0-to-60 mph in 6.2 seconds and the quarter-mile in 14.5 seconds. Bonneville Brougham trim group (Code 522) available for convertible ($316) and coupe ($273). Grand Prix "SJ" option ($316). Rally Group option ($153-$195). Turnpike Cruise package included tilt steering and four-way bench or bucket seat ($177-$208). Ventura package available on all Catalinas except convertible ($105). A short stroke 303-cid tunnel-port V-8 Trans Am engine was used in a small number of Firebirds used exclusively for SCCA Trans Am racing. There were 26,049 full-size Pontiacs with the standard 428-cid engine (360-hp). Also, there were 1,820 full-size Pontiacs with the 428 HO engine (390-hp).

1970 PONTIAC

1970 Pontiac Catalina four-door sedan. (OCW)

CATALINA — (V-8) — SERIES 252 — Radiator grilles inspired by Grand Prix, taillights set into bumpers, hoods with wider and flatter center bulges, hidden radio antennas, and wrapover front fender tips characterized 1970 Pontiacs. Catalinas had plain body sill moldings, Catalina or Ventura lettering behind front wheel openings, untrimmed taillights, the word "Pontiac" centered on edge of rear deck, horizontal blade grilles, and no fender skirts. Standard in Catalinas were carpeting, upper level ventilation, Endura side moldings, walnut-grained vinyl inserts, padded dashboards, and fiberglass black sidewall tires. Station wagons had Morrokide upholstery with power tailgate windows included on nine-passenger styles. The Ventura Custom option was available on all Catalinas except convertibles at $105 extra.

EXECUTIVE — (V-8) — SERIES 256 — Executives featured all Catalina equipment plus deluxe wheel covers, walnut-grained dash and door trim, Morrokide or cloth and Morrokide interiors, rear seat armrests, electric clock, and convenience lights. Executive lettering appeared behind the front wheel openings. Station wagons in this line included such extras as wood-grained exterior paneling and full carpeting. The balance of regular trim and equipment features were similar to that seen on Catalinas.

BONNEVILLE — (V-8) — SERIES 262 — Die-cast crosshatched grille inserts and horn ports, creased body still moldings with rear fender extensions, Bonneville front fender lettering, decorative taillight accents, and right-hand deck lid edge nameplates characterized Series 262 models outwardly. Standard equipment included all items found on Executives, plus extra-heavy padded bench seats, special interior trims, illuminated wiper and headlamp switches, fold-down front seat armrests, rear armrests with ashtrays, and larger tires. Bonneville station wagons did not have standard exterior paneling, but notch back front seats, folding third seats, courtesy lamps, and load area carpeting were included at base price. Brougham trim was optionally available on hardtops

1970 Pontiac Catalina two-door hardtop. (OCW)

and convertibles. The Bonneville Brougham package was available on style numbers 26237 and 26239 and included front foam cushions, power windows, visor vanity mirror, remote control mirror, electric clock, remote control deck lid, and heavy-duty air cleaner.

GRAND PRIX — (V-8) — SERIES 276 — A minimum of styling changes, such as tail lamp revisions and recessed door handles, appeared on 1970 Grand Prix. Series script replaced chrome slash moldings on the rear roof pillar. Standard equipment included dual exhaust, aircraft inspired interiors, front Strato Bucket seats, integral console with floor shift, carpeted lower door panels and trim panels, chrome body decor moldings, and special upholstery trims. The 'SJ' option was available again at $223-$244 extra and included 'SJ' badges, lamp group, larger tires and the 455-cid V-8.

TEMPEST — (6-CYL) — SERIES 233 — Tempests were given new Firebird-look bumper grilles, wraparound front parking and taillights, crease sculptured side styling and body color nose panels. Standard equipment included front door armrests; panel, ashtray and cigar lighter lamps; 37-amp Delcotrons; dome lamps; automatic interior lamp switches; in-the-windshield hidden antennas; wraparound side reflex markers; cloth and Morrokide interiors; fiberglass belted black sidewall tires; and side guard door beams. Tempest lettering was carried behind front wheel openings. In February 1970, the cut-price Tempest T-37 hardtop coupe was introduced. This move was followed by the appearance of a pair of economy type high-performance cars, the GT-37 coupe and GT-37 hardtop coupe.

LEMANS — (6-CYL) — SERIES 235 — LeMans nameplates were now attached to the mid-priced Tempests, which were formerly called Custom models. Added extras included loop pile carpets, Morrokide seats and sides, day/night rearview mirrors and rear armrests with ashtrays. Styling included body decor moldings, LeMans rear fender lettering, four short horizontal chrome slashes behind front wheel openings, and LeMans block letters on the right-hand edge of the deck lid.

LEMANS SPORT — (6-CYL) — SERIES 237 — The "high rung" Tempest line was now identified as the LeMans Sport series and had a "Sport" script below the rear fender model lettering. Standard equipment included all LeMans features plus glove compartment and ashtray lamps, front foam cushions, knit and expanded Morrokide trim, and padded wood-grained dashboards. Four-door hardtops had notch back seats; hardtop coupes and convertibles had bucket seats or notch back bench seats. The LeMans Sport Safari had exterior wood trim.

GTO — (V-8) — SERIES 242 — The GTOs utilized Tempest sheet metal combined with a standard Endura rubber nose. Twin oval cavities housed recessed grilles with GTO letters on the left-hand insert. There was also GTO lettering behind the front wheel openings and flared, crease-sculptured fenders. Standard equipment included bucket seats; vinyl trimmed padded dashboard; twin air scoops; heavy-duty clutch; sports type springs and shock absorbers; carpeting; glove box, ashtray and panel courtesy lamps; dual exhausts; Deluxe steering wheel; three-speed manual floor shift; and G78 x 14 black sidewall fiberglass tires. A Code 332-WT1 "The Judge" option

was again available at $337 over base model price. It included the 400-cid Ram Air V-8; Rally II wheels less trim rings; G70 x 14 fiberglass black sidewall tires; rear deck air foil; side stripes; Judge stripes and decals; black textured grilles; and T-handle shifters (on cars with manual gearboxes).

BASE FIREBIRD — (6-CYL) — SERIES 223 — Standard equipment on base Firebirds included a 250-cid 155-hp six, E78-14 black fiberglass tires, front and rear bucket type seats, vinyl upholstery, wood-grained dashboard, carpeting, outside rearview mirror, manual front disc brakes, six-inch wheel rims, and door storage pockets. Styling changes included Endura rubber front ends with dual recessed grilles; single headlights; split side marker lamps; enlarged wheel openings; flush door handles; and smooth, clean, curvy body panels. Firebird lettering and engine badges appeared behind front wheel cutouts.

FIREBIRD ESPRIT — (V-8) — SERIES 224 — The Esprit was outwardly identified by model script on the rear roof pillar, bright roof rail and wheel opening moldings, V-8 displacement badges under front fender Firebird lettering, and bird emblems above the grille. Standard equipment included all found on base models, plus knit vinyl upholstery, vinyl-covered Deluxe steering wheel, dual body-color outside sport mirrors, concealed windshield wipers and antenna, trunk floor mats, wheel trim rings, custom trim, decor moldings, and a 350-cid two-barrel V-8 with 8.8:1 compression and 255-hp at 4600 rpm. A three-speed manual gearbox with floor-mounted shift lever was regular equipment.

FIREBIRD FORMULA 400 — (V-8) — SERIES 226 — Standard equipment on Formula 400s included all GM safety features, 1-1/8-front and 5/8-in. rear stabilizer bars, high-rate springs, wind-up rear axle controls, F70 x 14 bias-belted black sidewall tires, seven-inch wheel rims, manual front disc brakes and rear drums, carpets, vinyl interiors, front and rear bucket type seats, dual outside sport mirrors, concealed wipers and antennas, and deluxe steering wheel. Power came from a 400-cid four-barrel V-8 with 10.25:1 compression and 265-hp at 4600 rpm, which was linked to a three-speed Hurst floor shift. External distinctions included extra-long twin hood scoops and Formula 400 nameplates.

TRANS AM — (V-8) — SERIES 228 — Trans Am had all GM safety features, plus front air dams; front and rear spoilers; shaker hood; side air extractors; rear end spoilers; aerodynamically styled outside mirrors with left-hand remote control type; front and rear stabilizers; heavy-duty shock absorbers and springs; engine-turned dash inserts; Rally gauge cluster; concealed wipers; bucket seats; carpets; vinyl upholstery; power brakes and steering; 11-in. wide 15-in. diameter Rally rims; and F60-15 white letter tires. Standard V-8 in the Trans Am was a 335-hp Ram Air engine. The factory called this the Ram Air HO. The 400-cid four-barrel V-8 was coded as the L74 engine. It had 10.5:1 compression heads and developed peak power at 5000 rpm. The base transmission was a wide-ratio four-speed manual gearbox with Hurst floor shift. Trans Ams had white or blue finish with contrasting racing stripes.

I.D. DATA: VIN on top of dash at left, viewable through windshield. First symbols tell GM division: 2=Pontiac. Second and third symbols tell series: 23=Firebird; 24=Esprit; 26=Formula 400; 28=Trans Am; 33=Tempest/T-37; 35=LeMans; 37=LeMans Sport; 42=GTO; 52=Catalina; 56=Executive; 62=Bonneville; 76=Grand Prix. Fourth and fifth symbols indicate body style and appear as last two digits of body/style number in charts below. Sixth symbol indicates model year: 0=1970. Seventh symbol indicates assembly plant: A=Atlanta, Ga.; B=Baltimore, Md.; C=South Gate, Calif.; E=Linden, N.J.; G=Framingham, Mass.; L=Van Nuys, Calif.; N=Norwood, Ohio; P=Pontiac, Mich.; R=Arlington, Texas; X=Kansas City, Kan.; Z=Fremont, Calif.; 1=Oshawa, Ontario Canada; 2=St. Therese, Quebec Canada. Remaining symbols are sequential unit production numbers at factory, starting with 100001. Fisher Body plate on cowl tells style number: (model year prefix 70, plus number in second column of charts below), body number, trim code, paint code and other data. Six-cylinder engine code stamped on distributor mounting on right side of block. V-8 engine code on front of block below right cylinder head. Engine production codes for 1970 were: [250-cid/155-hp six] CG/RF/ZB/ZG. [350-cid/255-hp V-8] WU/YU/W7/X7. [400-cid/265-hp V-8] XX/YB. [400-cid/290-hp V-8] WE/YD. [400-cid/330-hp V-8] WT/YS/XV/XZ. [400-cid/345-hp V-8] WS/YZ. [400-cid/350-hp V-8] WT/WX/YS/YH. [400-cid/366-hp V-8] WS/YZ. [400-cid/370-hp V-8] WW/WH/XP/XN. [455-cid/360-hp V-8] YH. [455-cid/370-hp V-8] WA/WG/YC/YA/XF.

1970 Pontiac Executive four-door sedan. (OCW)

Model Number	Body Style Number	Body Type & Seating	Factory Price	Shipping Weight	Production Total
CATALINA (SERIES 252)					
252	25269	4d Sedan-6P	3,164	3,997	84,795
252	25239	4d Hardtop-6P	3,319	4,042	35,155
252	25237	2d Hardtop-6P	3,249	3,952	70,350
252	25267	2d Convertible-6P	3,604	4,027	3,686
252	25246	4d Sta Wagon-9P	3,791	4,607	12,450
252	25236	4d Sta Wagon-6P	3,646	4,517	16,944
EXECUTIVE (SERIES 256)					
256	25669	4d Sedan-6	3,538	4,087	13,061
256	25639	4d Hardtop-6	3,669	4,132	5,376
256	25637	2d Hardtop-6	3,600	4,042	3,499
256	25646	4d Sta Wagon-9	4,160	4,632	5,629
256	25636	4d Sta Wagon-6	4,015	4,552	4,861
BONNEVILLE (SERIES 262)					
262	26269	4d Sedan-6P	3,770	4,181	3,802
262	26239	4d Hardtop-6P	3,900	4,226	44,241
262	26237	2d Hardtop-6P	3,832	4,111	23,418
262	26267	2d Convertible-6P	4,040	4,161	3,537
262	26246	4d Sta Wagon-9P	4,247	4,686	7,033
GRAND PRIX (SERIES 276)					
276	27657	2d Hardtop Cpe-5P	3,985	3,784	65,750
TEMPEST (SERIES 233)					
233	23369	4d Sedan-6P	2,670	3,295	9,187
233	23337	2d Hardtop-6P	2,750	3,360	Note 18
233	23327	2d Coupe-6P	2,623	3,225	11,977
TEMPEST (MIDYEAR ADDITIONS TO SERIES 233)					
T-37	23337	2d Hardtop Cpe-6P	2,683	3,250	20,883
GT-37	23337	2d Hardtop Cpe-6P	2,920	3,360	Note 18
GT-37	23327	2d Coupe-6P	2,907	3,300	Note 18
LEMANS (SERIES 235)					
235	23569	4d Sedan-6P	2,782	3,315	15,255
235	23539	4d Hardtop-6P	2,921	3,385	3,872
235	23527	2d Coupe-6P	2,735	3,240	5,656
235	23537	2d Hardtop-6P	2,795	3,265	52,304
235	23535	4d Sta Wagon-6P	3,092	3,585	7,165
LEMANS SPORT (SERIES 237)					
237	23739	4d Hardtop-6P	3,083	3,405	3,657
237	23727	2d Coupe-6P	2,891	3,265	1,673
237	23737	2d Hardtop-6P	2,953	3,290	58,356
237	23767	2d Convertible-6P	3,182	3,330	4,670
237	23736	4d Sta Wagon-6P	3,328	3,775	3,872
GTO (SERIES 242)					
242	24237	2d Hardtop-5P	3,267	3,641	32,737
242	24267	2d Convertible-5P	3,492	3,691	3,615
GTO (SERIES 242 with WT-1 "THE JUDGE" OPTION)					
242	24237	2d Hardtop-5P	3,604	—	3,629

1970 Pontiac Bonneville two-door convertible. (OCW)

1970 Pontiac Bonneville two-door convertible. (OCW)

1970 Pontiac Grand Prix SJ two-door hardtop coupe. (OCW)

1970 Pontiac Tempest GT-37 two-door sedan. (OCW)

1970 Pontiac Tempest GT-37 two-door sedan. (OCW)

1970 Pontiac GTO two-door hardtop coupe. (JAG)

1970 Pontiac Firebird Formula 400 two-door hardtop. (OCW)

Model Number	Body Style Number	Body Type & Seating	Factory Price	Shipping Weight	Production Total
242	24267	2d Convertible-5P	3,829	—	168
BASE FIREBIRD (SERIES 223)					
223	22387	2d Hardtop-4P	2,875	3,140	18,874
FIREBIRD ESPRIT (SERIES 224)					
224	22487	2d Hardtop-4P	3,241	3,435	18,961
FIREBIRD FORMULA 400 (SERIES 226)					
226	22687	2d Hardtop-4P	3,370	3,470	7,708
TRANS AM (SERIES 228)					
228	22887	2d Hardtop-5P	4,305	3,550	3,196

NOTE 1: 193,986 Catalina passenger cars were built.

NOTE 2: 579 Catalina passenger cars had synchromesh; 193,407 had automatic.

NOTE 3: 29,394 Catalina station wagons were built.

NOTE 4: 113 Catalina station wagons had synchromesh and 29,281 had automatic.

NOTE 5: 21,936 Executive passenger cars were built.

NOTE 6: Six Executive passenger cars had synchromesh and 21,930 had automatic.

NOTE 7: 10,490 Executive station wagons were built.

NOTE 8: Eight Executive wagons had synchromesh and 10,482 had automatic .

NOTE 9: 75,348 Bonneville passenger cars were built.

NOTE 10: 28 Bonneville passenger cars had synchromesh and 75,320 had automatic.

NOTE 11: 7,033 Bonneville station wagons were built.

NOTE 12: Six Bonneville wagons used synchromesh and 7,027 had automatic.

NOTE 13: A total of 65,750 Grand Prix were built.

NOTE 14: 500 Grand Prix had synchromesh and 65,250 had automatic.

NOTE 15: Of the cars with synchromesh, 329 had four-speed manual gearboxes.

NOTE 16: 42,047 Series 233 Tempests were built.

NOTE 17: 5,148 had synchromesh and 36,899 had automatic.

NOTE 18: Totals for all four-door sedans, two-door hardtops and two-door coupes are combined; no model breakouts.

NOTE 19: 1,419 GT-37 coupes and hardtops (combined) were built.

NOTE 20: 84,252 LeMans were made.

NOTE 21: 2,315 LeMans had synchromesh and 81,937 had automatic.

NOTE 22: 72,179 LeMans Sports were built.

NOTE 23: 3,413 LeMans Sports had synchromesh and 68,766 had automatic.

1970 Pontiac Firebird Formula 400 two-door hardtop. (OCW)

1970 Pontiac Executive Safari four-door station wagon. (OCW)

1970 Pontiac Tempest LeMans four-door hardtop. (OCW)

1970 Pontiac GTO two-door convertible. (OCW)

1970 Pontiac GTO "The Judge" two-door hardtop. (JAG)

1970 Pontiac Firebird Trans Am two-door Sport Coupe. (OCW)

1970 Pontiac Executive Safari four-door station wagon. (OCW)

NOTE 24: 40,149 GTOs and Judges were built in 1970.

NOTE 25: 16,033 GTOs and Judges had synchromesh and 24,116 had automatic.

NOTE 26: 366-hp Ram Air V-8s in 4,356 GTO/Judge hardtops and 288 convertibles.

NOTE 27: 370-hp Ram Air IV V-8s in 767 GTO/Judge hardtops and 37 convertibles.

NOTE 28: 18,874 base Firebirds were built.

NOTE 29: 2,899 base Firebirds had synchromesh and 15,975 had automatic.

NOTE 30: 3,134 Firebirds were built with six-cylinder power.

NOTE 31: 2,104 Firebird Esprits had synchromesh and 16,857 had automatic.

NOTE 32: 2,777 Firebird Formula 400s had synchromesh and 4,931 had automatic.

NOTE 33: 1,769 Trans Ams had synchromesh and 1,398 had automatic.

NOTE 34: 3,108 Trans Ams were L74s (1,339 with automatic; 1,769 with manual).

NOTE 35: 88 Trans Ams were LS1s (59 with automatic; 29 with manual).

BASE ENGINES

ENGINE [Catalina/Executive]: V-8. (Convertible and station wagon) 400-cid V-8 with two-barrel carburetor. Compression ratio: 10.0:1. Brake horsepower: 290 at 4600 rpm. (Other styles) 350-cid V-8 with two-barrel carburetor. Compression ratio: 8.8:1. Brake horsepower: 255 at 4600 rpm.

ENGINE [Bonneville Base V-8s]: This engine had overhead valves, cast-iron block, Bore & stroke: 4.15 x 4.21-in., five main bearings and hydraulic valve lifters. (Station wagon) V-8 with four-barrel carburetor. Displacement: 455-cid. Compression ratio: 10.75:1. Brake horsepower: 370 at 4600 rpm. (Other styles) V-8 with four-barrel carburetor. Displacement: 455-cid. Compression ratio: 10.0:1. Brake horsepower: 360 at 4300 rpm.

ENGINE [Grand Prix]: V-8 with four-barrel carburetor. Displacement: 400 cid. Compression ratio: 10.25:1. Brake horsepower: 350 at 5000 rpm. This engine was standard in Grand Prix.

ENGINE [Grand Prix with 'SJ' option]: V-8 with four-barrel carburetor. Displacement: 455-cid. Compression ratio 10.25:1. Brake horsepower: 370 at 4600 rpm.

ENGINE [Tempest/LeMans/Firebird]: Base six-cylinder: A Chevrolet manufactured Six with Bore & stroke: 3.88 x 3.53-in. Displacement:

1970 Pontiac Tempest LeMans four-door hardtop. (OCW)

1970 Pontiac GTO two-door convertible. (OCW)

250 cid. Compression ratio: 8.5:1 and Brake horsepower: 135 at 4600 rpm was standard in all Tempests, but not GTOs. This engine had overhead valves, cast-iron block, seven main bearings, hydraulic valve lifters, and a Rochester Model M or Model MV one-barrel carburetor.

ENGINE [GTO]: The standard engine in GTOs was the 400-cid four-barrel V-8 with Compression ratio: 10.25:1 and Brake horsepower: 350 at 5000 rpm.

Note: See options lists below for 1970 Pontiac engine options.

CHASSIS: Wheelbase: (series 252 and all Pontiac station wagons) 122 in.; (series 256 and 262) 125 in.; (series 276) 118 in.; (Tempest two-door) 112 in.; (Tempest four-door) 116 in.; (Firebird) 108 in. Overall Length: (all Pontiac station wagons) 220.9 in.; (series 252) 217.9 in.; (series 256 and 262) 223.9 in.; (series 276) 210.2 in.; (Tempest station wagons) 210.6 in.; (Tempest two-door) 202.5 in.; (Tempest four-door) 206.5 in.; (GTO) 202.9 in.; (Firebird) 191.6 in. Front tread: (Pontiac) 63 in. (others) 60 in. Rear tread: (Pontiac) 64 in.; (others) 60 in.

OPTIONS: [PONTIAC/GRAND PRIX/TEMPEST] Tempest air conditioning ($376). Pontiac air conditioning ($422). Automatic level control ($79). Auxiliary panel gauges ($21-$79). Cruise control ($63). Rear window defroster ($53). Driver-controlled GTO exhausts ($63). Tinted windshield ($22-$30). Tempest Instant Air ($16). Luggage carrier for station wagons ($63-$84). Left remote-control outside mirror ($11). Tempest wheelhouse moldings ($16). Power brakes ($42-$64). Remote-control deck lid ($15). Power front bucket seat for Tempest and Grand Prix ($73). AM/FM stereo ($239). Rally gauge cluster with tachometer for Tempest and Grand Prix ($84). Safeguard speedometer ($16). Catalina passenger car fender skirts ($37). Grand Prix leather trim ($199). Rally II wheel rims for passenger cars and Tempest station wagons ($63-$84). Base Tempest recessed wipers ($19). Bonneville Brougham trim ($378). Grand Prix 'SJ' group ($223-$244). GTO Judge package ($337). Turnpike Cruise package ($177-$208). Three-speed manual transmissions were provided at base prices, including a heavy-duty type in Grand Prix. Turbo-Hydra-Matic was $227 extra. Grand Prix had two other options, close- or wide-ratio four-speed manual gearboxes, both at $227 extra. The 400-cid two-barrel regular fuel V-8 (265-hp) was $53 extra in Catalinas with Turbo-Hydra-Matic. The four-barrel Bonneville V-8 was $47 more in Catalina station wagons, Catalina convertibles or Executives and $100 extra in other Catalinas. The two-barrel premium fuel 400-cid V-8 was $53 extra in Catalina coupes and hardtops. The 455-cid four-barrel V-8 with 10.0:1 compression

1970 Pontiac GTO "The Judge" two-door hardtop. (JAG)

1970 Pontiac Firebird Esprit two-door Sport Coupe. (OCW)

ratio and 360-hp at 4300 rpm was $150-$169 extra in Catalinas and Executives with price depending upon transmission. The 455-cid four-barrel high-performance V-8 with 10.25:1 compression and 370-hp at 4600 rpm was $200-$253 extra in Catalina and Executives, $95 extra in Bonnevilles and $58 extra in Grand Prix without decor packages. **[TEMPEST]** Transmission options included two-speed automatic on cars with six-cylinder power ($164-$174); Turbo-Hydra-Matic on V-8s ($227); three-speed manual with heavy-duty floor shift ($84) and wide-ratio four-speed manual ($185). The 255-hp regular fuel 350-cid V-8 with 8.8:1 compression was $111 extra. The 265-hp regular fuel two-barrel 400-cid V-8 with 8.8:1 compression ratio was $53-$163 extra in Tempests, with price depending upon model and transmission. The 400-cid four-barrel V-8 with 10.0:1 compression ratio and 330-hp at 4800 rpm was $210 extra. Dual exhausts were $31 extra and Safe-T-Track differential was $42-$63 extra. **(GTO)** Transmission options included Turbo-Hydra-Matic ($227) and wide- or close-ratio four-speed manual gearboxes ($185). The 366-hp HO V-8 was $169 extra on cars without "The Judge" options. The 370-hp Ram Air IV engine was $390 extra with "The Judge" and $558 extra on other GTOs. In midyear the 360-hp 455-cid V-8 was added as a third GTO power option. Dual exhausts were standard. Heavy-duty Safe-T-Track was again $63. **[FIREBIRD]** Air conditioning ($376). Electric clock ($16). Rally gauge cluster ($47). Rally gauge cluster with tachometer ($95). Cruise control ($58). Rear window defogger ($26). Electric rear window defroster ($53). Tinted glass, all windows ($33). Tinted windshield ($26). Dual horns ($4). Convenience lamps ($12). Dual outside mirrors in body color with left-hand remote-controlled ($26). Decor moldings ($47). Wonder Touch power brakes ($42). Power door locks ($45). Power door and seat back locks ($68). Variable ratio power steering ($105). Stereo tape player ($105). AM/FM push-button radio ($134). AM/FM stereo ($239). Cordova top ($74-$90). Deluxe steering wheel ($16). Formula steering wheel ($42-$58). Tilt steering wheel ($45). Wire wheel discs ($53-$74). Rally II rims ($63-$84). Transmission options included all offered for Tempests and GTOs. The 350-cid two-barrel V-8 was $111 extra in base Firebirds. The two-barrel regular fuel 400-cid V-8 was $53 extra in Esprits. The L74 Ram Air V-8 was $169 extra in Formula Firebirds. A mountain ratio performance axle was $17 extra. Safe-T-Track differential was $42 extra.

1970 Pontiac Firebird Trans Am two-door Sport coupe. (OCW)

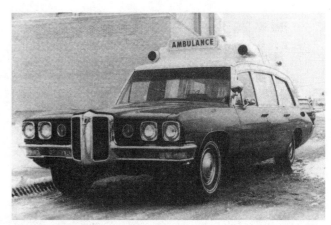

1970 Pontiac Superior ambulance. (JAG)

1970 Superior-Pontiac limousine and funeral car. (JAG)

HISTORICAL: Pontiacs were introduced Sept. 18, 1970, and the all-new second-generation Firebird bowed Feb. 26, 1971. Calendar year output was 422,212 units for sixth place in the sales rankings. The totals were pulled down by a painful UAW strike. The 1970 GTO with the 400-cid 366-hp V-8 was capable of 0-to-60 mph in six seconds flat. It did the quarter-mile in 14.6 seconds. The 455-cid 360-hp GTO hardtop registered 6.6 seconds 0-to-60 and a 14.8 second quarter-mile. The Firebird 400 with 330 hp did 0-to-60 mph in 6.4 seconds and covered the quarter-mile in 14.9 seconds. The W55 Turnpike Cruise option included cruise control, tilt steering wheel, and power seats. James McDonald became the new general manager of Pontiac Motor Division, replacing John Z. DeLorean, who moved to Chevrolet.

1971 PONTIAC

1971 Pontiac GTO convertible. (OCW)

CATALINA — (V-8) — SERIES 252 — Full-size Pontiacs had all-new styling with "fuselage" bodies, more massive V-shaped split radiator grilles and dual headlamps set high into the hood line with horizontal grilles below. Standard equipment on Catalinas included integral molded foam front seat cushion and solid foam back, loop-pile carpeting, cloth and Morrokide upholstery on hardtops and

1971 Pontiac Catalina two-door hardtop. (OCW)

sedans and all-Morrokide on convertibles, woodgrained dash accents, Deluxe steering wheel, center flow ventilation, glove box lamp, dual-action parallel sweep concealed wipers, bright rocker panel moldings, hood rear edge moldings, hub caps, roof drip moldings on hardtops, black sidewall tires, power front disc brakes and rear drums. Convertibles had rear quarter interior courtesy lamps. Catalina Safaris had all-Morrokide upholstery, ashtray lamps, vinyl cargo covering, right-hand outside mirror, power tailgate window, disappearing tailgate and L78-15 tires. Nine-passenger styles had forward facing third seats and split back second seats.

CATALINA BROUGHAM — (V-8) — SERIES 258 — Cars in this entirely new series had the same basic equipment as Catalinas, plus special luxury upholstery, electric clock, Castillian leather appearance instrument panel inserts, ashtray lamps, wheel opening moldings, Deluxe wheel covers, bright roof drip moldings, and rear foam-padded seats on four-door sedans. A Brougham script was placed on the rear roof pillar.

BONNEVILLE AND GRAND SAFARI — (V-8) — SERIES 262 — Bonnevilles were no longer top line Pontiacs, as a new Grand Ville series was placed even higher and had more standard features. Station wagons in Series 262 used a nameplate that was a mixture of both lines. They were called Grand Safaris. The wagons, however, used the Bonneville engines and series code. Identifying features of Bonnevilles include model nameplates on the left-hand grille and behind the front wheel wells, and slanting vertical slashes on the body sill moldings. Bonnevilles had the same basic equipment as Catalinas, plus ashtray; panel courtesy and trunk lamps; pedal trim plates; custom cushion steering wheel; electric clock; wheel well moldings; bright roof drip moldings; H78-15 tires; and power steering. The four-door sedan also had foam rear seat padding and side window reveal moldings. Grand Safaris had the same equipment as Catalina station wagons plus fold-down front seat center armrests; carpeted load area; dash panel courtesy lamps; pedal trim plates; electric clocks; custom cushion steering wheels; side window reveal moldings; wheel opening moldings; roof drip moldings; power steering; and Deluxe wheel covers. There were Grand Safari nameplates on the left-hand grille and behind the front wheel cutouts. Wood-grained exterior paneling was optional.

GRAND VILLE — (V-8) — SERIES 268 — Standard equipment on cars in Series 268 was the same as on Bonnevilles, plus Carpathian Elm burl vinyl instrument panel trim, rear door dome lamp switches, roof rail assist grips, formal roofline, belt reveal moldings and four-barrel V-8 power. The convertible and the hardtop coupe had notch-back bench seats and the former model also featured two rear quarter interior lamps. Several appearance distinctions such as crosshatched grille inserts and dual stacked horizontal taillights

1971 Pontiac Catalina two-door hardtop. (OCW)

1971 Pontiac Bonneville four-door hardtop. (OCW)

were shared with Bonnevilles. Grand Villes, however, did not have slash louvers on body sill moldings and used "Grand Ville" lettering on the left-hand grille and behind front fender cutouts.

GRAND PRIX — (V-8) — SERIES 276 — Grand Prix now had single headlamps (still in square housings), a bumper running across the grille and an attractive looking semi-boat tail rear end. Model script plates decorated the left-hand front panel, the roof pillars, and the right-hand edge of the deck lid. Buyers had a choice of notch back bench or bucket seats at the same price. Standard equipment included right-hand front door armrest ashtray; carpeted lower door panels; safety armrests with ashtrays; loop-pile carpets; foam seat padding; pedal trim plates; custom cushion steering wheel; Castillian leather appearance dash trim; upper level ventilation; courtesy and glove box lamps; concealed wipers; wheel opening, roof drip, belt reveal, and hood rear edge moldings; Deluxe wheel covers; power flex cooling fan; power steering; power brakes (with front discs); seven-inch wide safety wheel rims; G78-14 black sidewall tires and center console on cars with bucket seats. The 'SJ' option package was priced $195 extra. This option (code 324) included 455-cid four-barrel V-8, Rally gauge cluster, luggage lamp, body color outside mirrors (left-hand remote control), vinyl pin stripes, 'SJ' emblems and Delco X battery. A limited-edition Hurst SSJ Grand Prix was marketed.

LEMANS T-37 — (6 CYL) — SERIES 233 — Revisions to Pontiac intermediates included new model names, new series designations, redesigned grilles, and reworked GTO nose and hood. Pontiac T-37 lettering was seen behind the front wheel wells of the lowest priced models. Standard equipment included cloth and Morrokide bench seats, vinyl floor covering, Deluxe steering wheel, upper level ventilation in hardtops, black grained instrument panel, door operated dome lamp switches, conventional roof drip moldings, windshield and rear window reveal moldings, dual-action parallel sweep wipers, front disc brakes, and E78-14 black wall tires. Pillared coupes and sedans also had chrome edged ventipanes. The GT-37 was available again and was advertised as "The GTO For Kids Under 30." This option (code 334) was offered in just two hardtop versions. It included vinyl accent stripes, Rally II wheels (less trim rings), G70-14 tires (white-lettered), dual exhausts with chrome extensions, heavy-duty three-speed manual transmission with floor shift, body-colored outside mirrors (left-hand remote control), hood locking pins, and GT-37 nameplates. It was designed to provide buyers with a low-cost high-performance option.

1971 Pontiac Grand Safari four-door station wagon. (OCW)

1971 Pontiac Grand Ville four-door hardtop. (OCW)

LEMANS — (6-CYL) — SERIES 235 — LeMans models had the word "Pontiac" on the left-hand grille and carried vertical slash louvers behind the wheel wells and LeMans lettering under the rear fender crease lines. Extra features on LeMans included richer upholstery, loop-pile carpets, safety rear armrests with integral ashtrays, woodgrained dash, concealed wipers, rocker panel moldings, hood rear edge moldings, side window reveals on coupes, and vent windows on four-door styles. Station wagons had two-way tailgates and power front disc brakes.

LEMANS SPORT — (6-CYL) — SERIES 237 — Standard equipment in LeMans Sport models included all items found in LeMans models plus dual horns, pedal trim plates, ashtray and glove box lamps, courtesy lamps on convertibles, carpeted lower door panels, custom cushion steering wheel, and wheel well moldings. Buyers of two-door hardtops and convertibles had a choice of knit vinyl bucket seats or notch bench seats. The four-door hardtop used knit vinyl bench seats. LeMans Sport model nameplates were seen on the sides of rear fenders. GTO type Endura rubber noses were a $74 styling option for all LeMans Sport models including station wagons. This front end was also marketed as part of the code 602 LeMans Sport Endura styling option including GTO hood, GTO Endura bumper, and GTO headlamp assembly.

GTO — (V-8) — SERIES 242 — A new Endura nose piece identified the 1971 GTO. It had larger twin grille cavities, round parking lamps and integral body colored bumpers. Other characteristics included twin air slots at the front of the hood and GTO lettering on left-hand grille, front fender sides and right-hand edge of the deck lid. Standard equipment included all items found on LeMans models plus engine-turned aluminum dash inserts, dual exhausts with extensions through valance panel, power-flex cooling fan, heavy-duty stabilizer bars, shock absorbers and springs, and G70-14 black sidewall tires. For $395 extra "The Judge" option was available. This option (code 332) included 455-cid four-barrel HO V-8, Rally II wheels (less trim rings), hood air inlet system, T-handle gear shift control (with manual transmission), rear deck lid air foil, specific side stripes, "The Judge" decals, RAM AIR decals, and black-textured grille.

BASE FIREBIRD — (6-CYL) — SERIES 223 — Styling changes for 1971 Firebirds were of the minor variety. High-back seats were used, new wheel covers appeared, and all models, except the Trans Am, had simulated louvers behind the front wheel cutouts. Standard equipment on the basic Firebird included vinyl bucket seats, woodgrained dash, deluxe steering wheel, Endura front bumper, bright grille moldings, standard hubcaps, narrow rocker

1971 Pontiac GT-37 two-door hardtop. (OCW)

panel moldings, front disc brakes, and E78-14 tires. Base engine was the 145-hp 250-cid Six.

FIREBIRD ESPRIT — (V-8) — SERIES 224 — Esprits included custom trim features with knit vinyl upholstery, custom cushion steering wheel, trunk mat, bright roof drip moldings, wheel opening moldings, concealed wipers, twin body-colored outside mirrors, wheel trim rings, and dual horns as standard extras. Power was supplied by the two-barrel 350-cid V-8 with 8.0:1 compression ratio and 250 hp at 4400 rpm. A floor-mounted three-speed manual transmission was the standard gearbox.

FIREBIRD FORMULA — (V-8) — SERIES 226 — Standard equipment on Formula Firebirds included vinyl bucket seats, custom cushion steering wheel, flame chestnut wood-grain appearance dash panel, right and left body-colored outside mirrors, (left-hand remote-controlled), Endura rubber front bumper, fiberglass hood with simulated twin air scoops, black-textured grille insert, bright grille moldings, dual horns, front disc brakes, handling package, dual exhausts with chrome extensions, and the heavy-duty three-speed manual transmission. Also featured were standard hubcaps, F70-14 black sidewall tires, and Formula 350 or 400 or 455 identification numbering. Engine choices were the two-barrel 350-cid V-8, the four-barrel 400-cid V-8, or the four-barrel 455-cid V-8.

TRANS AM — (V-8) — SERIES 228 — Standard equipment on Trans Ams included vinyl bucket seats; Rally gauges (with clock and tachometer); Endura front bumper; Formula steering wheel; twin body-color outside mirrors (left-hand remote control); special honeycomb wheels; functional front fender air extractors; rear deck lid spoiler; black textured grille insert; bright grille moldings; front and rear wheel opening air spoilers; concealed wipers; Trans Am identification markings; performance dual exhausts with extensions; special air cleaner with rear-facing cold air intake on hood controlled by throttle; power flex cooling fan; power steering; Safe-T-Track differential; handling package; dual horns; power brakes with discs in front and drums at rear; and F60-15 white lettered tires. The RPO LS5 455 HO engine with four-barrel carburetion, 8.4:1 compression ratio, and 335 hp at 4800 rpm was standard in all Trans Ams, as was a heavy-duty three-speed manual gearbox with floor shifter.

VENTURA II — (6 CYL) — SERIES 213 — The Ventura II line was introduced on March 11, 1970, as an addition to the Pontiac family. It was based on the compact-sized Chevy II Nova with wider tail lamp lenses and split, twin-slot type grille. Standard equipment included all required safety features plus heater and defroster, outside rearview mirror, cloth and Morrokide upholstery, foam front seat padding, woodgrained dashboard accents, padded Morrokide door panels with woodgrained trim inserts, and E78 x 14 tires. The 250-cid six-cylinder 145-hp engine was base power plant. The Ventura Sprint

1971 Pontiac Grand Prix two-door hardtop. (OCW)

1971 Pontiac GT-37 two-door hardtop. (OCW)

Standard Catalog of ® Pontiac, 2nd Edition

1970 Pontiac GTO two-door convertible. (OCW)

option code 322 included three-speed manual transmission with floor shift, wheel trim rings, left-hand remote control color-keyed mirrors, custom carpets, custom sport steering wheel, blacked-out grille, side striping, 14 x 6-inch rims, and THR E78-14 white sidewall tires.

I.D. DATA: VIN on top of dash at left, viewable through windshield. First symbol tells GM division: 2=Pontiac. Second and third symbols tell series: 13=Ventura II; 23=Firebird; 24=Esprit; 26=Formula 400; 28=Trans Am; 33=Tempest/T-37; 35=LeMans; 37=LeMans Sport; 42=GTO; 52=Catalina; 58=Catalina Brougham; 62=Bonneville; 68=Grand Ville; 76=Grand Prix. Fourth and fifth symbols indicate body style and appear as last two digits of body/style number in charts below. Sixth symbol indicates model year: 1=1971. Seventh symbol indicates assembly plant: A=Atlanta, Ga.; B=Baltimore, Md.; C=South Gate, Calif.; D=Doraville, Ga.; E=Linden, N.J.; L=Van Nuys, Calif.; N=Norwood, Ohio; P=Pontiac, Mich.; R=Arlington, Texas; X=Kansas City, Kan.; Z=Fremont, Calif.; 1=Oshawa, Ontario, Canada; 2=St. Therese, Quebec, Canada. Remaining symbols are sequential unit production number at factory, starting with 100001. Fisher Body plate on cowl tells style number: (Model year prefix 71, plus number in second column of charts below), body number, trim code, paint code and other data. Six-cylinder engine code stamped on distributor mounting on right side of block. V-8 engine code on front of block below right cylinder head. Engine production codes for 1971 were: [250-cid/155-hp six] ZB/CAA/ZG/CAB. [307-cid/200-hp V-8] CCA/CCC. [350-cid/250-hp V-8] WR/WU/XU/XR/WN/WP/YN/YP. [400-cid/265-hp V-8] WS/WX/XX/YX. [400-cid/300-hp V-8] WT/WK/YS. [455-cid/280-hp V-8] WG/YG. [455-cid/325-hp V-8] WJ/YC/WL/WC/YE/YA.

Model Number	Body Style Number	Body Type & Seating	Factory Price	Shipping Weight	Production Total
CATALINA (SERIES 252)					
252	25269	4d Sedan-6P	3,421/3,770	4,033/4,077	59,355
252	25239	4d Hardtop-6P	3,590/3,939	4,063/4,170	22,333
252	25257	2d Hardtop-6P	3,521/3,870	3,998/4,042	46,257
252	25267	2d Convertible-6P	3,807/4,156	4,065/4,161	2,036
252	25235	4d Sta Wagon-6P	3,892/4,315	4,735/4,815	10,322
252	25245	4d Sta Wagon-9P	4,039/4,462	4,820/4,905	9,283
CATALINA BROUGHAM (SERIES 258)					
258	25869	4d Sedan-6P	3,629/4000	4,098/4149	6,069
258	25839	4d Hardtop-6P	3,783/4154	4,128/4179	9,001
258	25857	2d Hardtop-6P	3,713/4084	4,068/4119	8,823
BONNEVILLE AND GRAND SAFARI (SERIES 262)					
262	26269	4d Sedan-6P	3,968/4,210	4,188/4,213	6,513
262	26239	4d Hardtop-6P	4,098/4,340	4,248/4,273	16,393
262	26257	2d Hardtop-6P	4,030/4,272	4,163/4,188	8,778
262	26235	4d Sta Wagon-6P	4,401/4,643	4,843/4,855	3,613
262	26245	4d Sta Wagon-9P	4,548/4,790	4,913/4,970	5,972
GRAND VILLE (SERIES 268)					
268	26849	4d Hardtop-6P	4,324/4,566	4,278/4,303	30,524

1971 Pontiac GTO "The Judge" two-door hardtop. (OCW)

1971 Pontiac GTO "The Judge" two-door hardtop. (OCW)

Model Number	Body Style Number	Body Type & Seating	Factory Price	Shipping Weight	Production Total
268	26847	2d Hardtop-6P	4,255/4,497	4,198/4,223	14,017
268	26867	2d Convertible-6P	4,464/4,706	4,240/4,266	1,784
GRAND PRIX (SERIES 276)					
276	27657	2d Hardtop-5P	4,314/4,557	3,838/3,863	58,325
T-37 (SERIES 233)					
233	23327	2d Sedan-6P	2,747/2,868	3,189/3,445	7,184
233	23369	4d Sedan-6P	2,795/2,916	3,219/3,475	8,336
233	23337	2d Hardtop-6P	2,807/2,928	3,194/3,450	29,466
LEMANS (SERIES 235)					
235	23527	2d Sedan-6P	2,877/2,998	3,199/3,455	2,734
235	23569	4d Sedan-6P	2,025/3,046	3,229/3,485	11,979
235	23539	4d Hardtop-6P	3,064/3,185	3,314/3,570	3,186
235	23537	2d Hardtop-6P	2,938/3,059	3,199/3,455	40,966
235	23536	4d Sta Wagon-6P	3,353/3,474	3,765/3,995	6,311
235	23546	4d Sta Wagon-9P	3,465/3,586	3,825/4,045	4,363
LEMANS SPORT (SERIES 237)					
237	23739	4d Hardtop-6P	3,255/3,376	3,314/3,570	2,451
237	23737	2d Hardtop-6P	3,125/3,246	3,199/3,455	34,625
237	23767	2d Convertible-6P	3,359/3,480	3,289/3,545	3,865
GTO (SERIES 242)					
242	24237	2d Hardtop-5P	3,446	3,619	9,497
242	24267	2d Convertible-5P	3,676	3,664	661
GTO (WITH "THE JUDGE" OPTION)					
242	24237	2d Hardtop-5P	3,840	—	357
242	24267	2d Convertible-5P	4,070	—	17
BASE FIREBIRD (SERIES 223)					
223	22387	2d Hardtop-4P	3,047	3,164	23,021
FIREBIRD ESPRIT (SERIES 224)					
224	22487	2d Hardtop-4P	3,416	3,423	20,185
FIREBIRD FORMULA (SERIES 226)					
226	22687	2d Hardtop-4P	3,445	3,473	7,802
TRANS AM (SERIES 228)					
228	22887	2d Hardtop-4	4,594	3,578	2,116
VENTURA II (SERIES 213)					
213	21327	2d Coupe-5P	2,458	2,934	34,681
213	21369	4d Sedan-5P	2,488	2,983	13,803

NOTE 1: Automatic transmission standard after March 1971. Data above slash from fall 1970/below slash from March.

NOTE 2: 144 Catalina passenger cars had synchromesh and 129,893 had automatic.

NOTE 3: 30 Catalina station wagons had synchromesh and 19,586 had automatic.

NOTE 4: Automatic transmission standard after March 1971. Data above slash from fall 1970/below slash from March.

NOTE 5: Six Catalina Broughams had synchromesh and 23,886 had automatic.

NOTE 6: Automatic transmission standard after March 1971. Data above slash from fall 1970/below slash from March.

NOTE 7: Four Bonnevilles had synchromesh and 31,875 had automatic.

NOTE 8: All Grand Safaris had automatic.

NOTE 9: Automatic transmission standard after March 1971. Data above slash from fall 1970/below slash from March.

NOTE 10: Two Grand Villes had synchromesh and 46,328 had automatic.

NOTE 11: 194 Grand Ville chassis were supplied to professional car makers.

NOTE 12: Automatic transmission standard after March 1971. Data above slash from fall 1970/below slash from March.

NOTE 13: 116 Grand Prix had synchromesh and 58,208 had automatic.

NOTE 14: Data above slash for six/below slash for V-8.

1971 Pontiac Firebird Formula 400 two-door hardtop. (OCW)

NOTE 15: 5,525 T-37s had synchromesh and 39,461 had automatic.

NOTE 16: A combined total of 5,802 GT-37s were built as 1971 and 1971-1/2 models.

NOTE 17: Data above slash for six/below slash for V-8.

NOTE 18: 1,231 LeMans had synchromesh and 67,948 had automatic.

NOTE 19: Data above slash for six/below slash for V-8.

NOTE 20: 1,229 LeMans Sports had synchromesh and 39,712 had automatic.

NOTE 21: 2,287 GTOs had synchromesh and 7,945 had automatic.

NOTE 22: 2,778 base Firebirds had synchromesh and 20,244 had automatic.

NOTE 23: 2,975 base Firebirds were built with six-cylinder power plants.

NOTE 24: 947 Firebird Esprits had synchromesh and 19,238 had automatic.

NOTE 25: 1,860 Formula Firebirds had synchromesh and 5,942 had automatic.

NOTE 26: Data shown for Formula 350; Formula 400 was $100 extra; Formula 455 was $158 extra.

NOTE 27: 885 Trans Ams had synchromesh and 1,231 had automatic.

NOTE 28: 48,484 Ventura IIs were built.

NOTE 29: 8,542 Ventura IIs had synchromesh and 39,942 had automatic.

BASE ENGINES

ENGINE [Catalina]: Base two-barrel V-8 engine for all Catalinas. Displacement: 350 cid. Compression ratio: 8.0:1. Brake horse-power: 250 at 4400 rpm.

ENGINE [Catalina Safari/Catalina Brougham]: Base engine for all two-barrel V-8 Catalina Broughams. Displacement 400 cid. Compression ratio: 8.2:1. Brake horsepower: 265 at 4400 rpm.

ENGINE [Bonneville/Grand Safari]: Base V-8 for cars and station wagons in Series 262. Displacement: 455 cid. Compression ratio: 8.2:1. Brake horsepower: 280 at 4400 rpm.

ENGINE [Grand Ville]: Base four-barrel V-8 engine for Grand Villes. Displacement: 455 cid. Compression ratio: 8.2:1. Brake horsepower: 325 at 4400 rpm. This was the only Grand Ville engine.

ENGINE [Grand Prix]: Base four-barrel V-8 engine for Grand Prix. Displacement: 400 cid. Compression ratio: 8.2:1. Brake horse-power: 300 at 4800 rpm. The 455-cid V-8 used in Grand Villes was standard in the Grand Prix "SJ" and optional on base Grand Prix.

ENGINE [T-37/LeMans/LeMans Sport/Firebird/Ventura II Six]: Base engine for six-cylinder T-37s was the Chevrolet-built power-plant with a one-barrel carburetor. Displacement: 250 cid. Compression ratio: 8.5:1. Brake horsepower: 145 hp at 4200 rpm.

ENGINE [T-37/LeMans/LeMans Sport/Firebird V-8]: Base engines for eight-cylinder two-barrel carburetor T-37s. Displacement: 350 cid. Compression ratio: 8.0:1. Brake horsepower: 250 hp at 4400 rpm.

ENGINE [GTO]: Base four-barrel V-8. Displacement: 400 cid. Compression ratio: 8.2:1. Brake horsepower: 300 hp at 4800 rpm.

ENGINE [GTO "The Judge"]: The 335-hp four-barrel 455-cid HO V-8 was standard on cars with "The Judge" option.

OPTIONAL V-8 ENGINES

ENGINE [Optional V-8 (Standard in Firebird Esprit and Catalina; optional in LeMans)]: Displacement: 350 cid. Compression ratio: 8:1. Carburetion: two-barrel. Brake horsepower: 250 at 4400 rpm.

ENGINE [Optional V-8 (Standard in GTO)]: Displacement: 400 cid. Compression ratio: 8.2:1. Carburetion: four-barrel. Brake horse-power: 300 at 4800 rpm.

ENGINE [Optional V-8 (Standard in Grand Prix/Firebird Formula 400; optional in LeMans/Catalina)]: Displacement: 400 cid. Compression ratio: 8.2:1. Carburetion: four-barrel. Brake horsepower: 300 at 4800 rpm.

ENGINE [Optional V-8 (Standard in Bonneville; optional in Catalina)]: Displacement: 455 cid. Compression ratio: 8.2:1. Carburetion: two-barrel. Brake horsepower: 280 at 4400 rpm.

ENGINE [Optional V-8 (Standard in Grand Ville; optional in Firebird Formula 455/LeMans/GTO/Catalina/Bonneville)]: Displacement: 455 cid. Compression ratio: 8.2:1. Carburetion: four-barrel. Brake horsepower: 325 at 4400 rpm.

ENGINE [Optional V-8 (Standard on Trans Am; optional in GTO/LeMans)]: Displacement: 455 cid. Compression ratio: 8.4:1. Carburetion: four-barrel. Brake horsepower: 335 at 4800 rpm.

CHASSIS: Wheelbase: (All Pontiac station wagons) 127 in.; (Series 252 and 258) 123.5 in.; (Series 262 and 268) 126 in.; (Grand Prix) 118 in.; (Ventura) 111 in.; (Others) Same as 1970. Overall Length: (All Pontiac station wagons): 230.2 in.; (Series 252 and 258) 220.2 in.; (Series 262 and 268) 224.2 in.; (Grand Prix) 212.9 in.; (Tempest station wagons) 210.9 in.; (Tempest two-doors) 202.3 in.; (Tempest four-doors) 206.8 in.; (Firebird) 191.6 in.; (Ventura) 194.5 in.

OPTIONS: [PONTIAC/GRAND PRIX]: Automatic air conditioning ($521). Automatic level control ($79). Luggage carrier ($84). Electric clock ($18). Cruise control ($68). All tinted glass ($51). Tinted windshield ($36). Bumper guards ($16). Cornering lights ($37). Grand Prix power bucket seats ($79). 60/40 Bench seat with six-way power adjustments ($79). AM/FM stereo and tape system ($373). Grand Prix Rally gauge cluster with tachometer and clock ($84). Pontiac station wagon and GP cordova tops ($142). Cordova top on other Pontiacs ($119). Grand Prix wire wheel discs ($58). Rally II wheels ($63-$90). Custom Grand Ville trim group ($132-$237). Grand Prix "SJ" option ($195). **[TEMPEST/FIREBIRD]:** Manual air conditioning ($408). T-37 custom carpets ($21). Firebird rear console ($26). Firebird, GTO, and LeMans Sport front seat console ($60-$61). Cruise control ($63). All tinted glass ($38). Tinted windshield ($31). Bumper guards ($16). Formula and GTO air inlet hood ($84). Body-colored mirrors with left-hand remote control ($26). Firebird power brakes ($47). LeMans front disc brakes ($70). Wonder Touch brakes ($47). Tape player and stereo cassette ($134). Firebird Rally gauge cluster with tachometer and clock ($95). Firebird Formula rear deck spoiler ($33). Vinyl side stripes for two-door LeMans or GP ($31-$63). Tilt steering wheel with power steering required ($45). Formula steering wheel ($42). Hood-mounted tachometer on LeMans ($63). Firebird cordova top ($74-$90). LeMans cordova top ($100). Firebird and LeMans wire wheel discs ($84). Rally II wheels ($90). Honeycomb styled wheels on T-37 ($63); on other LeMans and Firebirds ($100-$126). LeMans Sport Endura styling option ($74). T-37 hardtop coupe "GT" option ($237). "The Judge" option ($395). Code 331 Firebird ride and handling package ($205) included honeycomb wheels, F60-15 white-lettered fiberglass tires, Trans Am front and rear stabilizer bars, and Trans Am rear springs. **[VENTURA II]** Manual air conditioner ($392). Custom carpets ($21). Front seat console ($59). Rear window defogger ($32). Left-hand remote control mirror ($26). Disc front brakes ($70). Wonder Touch brakes ($47). Power steering ($103). Custom cushion steering wheel ($16). Sun roof ($184). Rally II wheels ($63). Chrome wheel trim rings ($26). Custom bucket seat group ($242). Sprint option package ($233-$254).

[MIXED POWER TRAIN OPTIONS] The 350-cid two-barrel V-8 was $121 extra in base Firebirds, T-37s, and LeMans. The 400-cid two-barrel V-8 was $53 extra in Esprits and Catalinas and $174 extra in T-37 and LeMans. The 400-cid four-barrel V-8 was $100 extra in Formulas and Catalinas, $221 extra in all T-37s and LeMans

1971 Pontiac Firebird Trans Am two-door hardtop. (OCW)

1971 Pontiac Hurst SSJ Grand Prix two-door hardtop. (OCW)

(except standard in GTO), and $47 extra in Catalina Broughams. The 455-cid two-barrel V-8 was $58 extra in Catalina Broughams and $111 extra in Catalinas. The 455-cid four-barrel V-8 was $47 extra in Bonnevilles, $58 extra in GTO and Grand Prix, $105 extra in Catalina Broughams, and $158 extra in Catalinas. The 455-cid HO engine was standard in Trans Ams and "The Judge," $137 extra in other GTOs, $237 extra in Formula Firebirds, and $358 extra in T-37 and LeMans coupes and convertibles. In most cases, specific transmissions were required with the above power train options. Dual exhausts were $41 extra. Safe-T-Track differential was $46 extra. Heavy-duty Safe-T-Track differential was $67 extra. Special order, performance, and economy rear axles were each $11 extra. Heavy-duty batteries were $11 extra and Delco X maintenance free batteries were $26 extra. Optional in Ventura was a 307-cid Chevrolet V-8 with two-barrel carburetion, 8.5:1 compression ratio, and 200 hp at 4600 rpm.

HISTORICAL: Production of the 1971 models started Aug. 10, 1970, and the Ventura II was added to the line March 11, 1971. Model year production was 586,856 cars. Calendar year output was 728,615 cars for a 7.4 percent market share and number three ranking in the industry. A special Hurst SSJ Grand Prix was marketed this year. These cars were built in conjunction with Hurst Performance Products Co. Pontiac opened a 48,000 square foot emissions and testing laboratory and did a 100,000 square foot assembly plant expansion.

1972 PONTIAC

1972 Pontiac Catalina two-door hardtop. (OCW)

CATALINA — (V-8) — SERIES 2L — New energy-absorbing bumpers, redesigned radiator styled grilles, and revised tail light treatments characterized full-size Pontiacs for 1972. Catalinas featured front fender model lettering, horizontal blade grilles, and single deck tail lamps with chrome outlined quadrants. Standard equipment included solid foam front seat cushions with integral springs, solid foam front seat backs, nylon carpets, center-flow ventilation, front ashtrays, teakwood dash trim, ashtray and glove box lamps, trunk mat, and concealed wipers and windshield radio antennas. Other features included bright roof gutter moldings (on most models), hood

1972 Pontiac Bonneville two-door hardtop. (OCW)

rear edge moldings, power steering, power brakes with front discs, and G78-15 black sidewall tires. Closed body styles were upholstered in cloth and Morrokide. Convertibles featured all-Morrokide trims, twin rear quarter interior lamps and power tops with glass rear windows. Catalina Safaris also had all-Morrokide seats, deluxe steering wheel, vinyl load floor coverings, L78-15 tires, and power tailgate windows on nine-passenger jobs. All full-size Pontiacs had V-8 power and Turbo-Hydra-Matic transmission.

CATALINA BROUGHAM — (V-8) — SERIES 2M — Broughams had the same features as L Series Catalinas plus special interior trim, carpeted lower door panels, custom cushion steering wheel, electric clock, Deluxe wheel covers, and door handles with body-color inserts. Chrome signatures were seen on the roof pillar to identify Broughams externally. They used the same horizontal blade grille and single deck tail lamps as Catalinas.

BONNEVILLE — (V-8) — SERIES 2N — Bonnevilles had single deck taillights with chrome outline quadrants like Catalinas, but cross-hatched grille inserts like Grand Villes. Bonneville lettering appeared on the left-hand grille, behind the front wheel openings, and between the taillights. The standard equipment list was the same as the Catalina Brougham's, plus dash panel courtesy and trunk lamps, trunk compartment sidewall panels, formal roofline, bright metal window reveal moldings on four-door sedan, and H78-15 black sidewall tires. Bonneville Grand Safaris had the same equipment as Catalina station wagons, plus bench seats with center armrests, carpeted lower door panels and cargo area, custom cushion steering wheel, electric clock, dash panel courtesy lamps, and Deluxe wheel covers.

GRAND VILLE — (V-8) — SERIES 2P — Grand Villes featured Bonneville type crosshatched grilles and distinctive twin-deck slotted taillights. There was model identification lettering on the left-hand grille, behind the front wheel openings, and between the taillights. Standard equipment consisted of all items found on Bonnevilles, plus bench seats with folding center armrests (or notchback bench seats with center armrests), lighted front ashtrays, and, on convertibles, two rear quarter interior lamps and power operated tops with glass windows.

GRAND PRIX — (V-8) — SERIES 2K — Grand Prix featured high-intensity single headlamps, new cross-hatched grilles, model identification signature scripts, and semi-boattail rear deck styling with triple-lens horizontal taillights. Buyers had a choice of bucket or notch

1972 Pontiac Grand Ville four-door hardtop. (OCW)

1972 Pontiac Grand Prix two-door hardtop. (OCW)

back front bench seats. Standard equipment included carpeting; carpeted lower door panels; a console and floor shift (with bucket seats); custom cushion steering wheel; upper level ventilation; electric clock; front ashtrays; teakwood dash trim; ashtray, dash panel, and courtesy lamps; trunk compartment side panels; Deluxe wheel covers; concealed wipers; windshield antenna; and moldings for roof gutters, windshield, rear window, window sills, hood rear edge, wheel openings, and rocker panels. Other regular features included power steering, power brakes with front discs, power-flex cooling fan, dual exhausts, and G78-14 black sidewall tires. The "SJ" option package was again available and included a big V-8, body color outside mirrors, vinyl pinstripes, luggage and door courtesy lamps, and a Rally gauge cluster. All Grand Prix had automatic transmission. The code 332 Grand Prix "SJ" option included the 455-cid four-barrel V-8, body-color outside mirrors (left-hand remote control), vinyl accent stripes, luggage and door courtesy lamps, Delco X battery and Rally gauge cluster.

BASE LEMANS — (6-CYL) — SERIES 2D — Standard equipment included bench seats with cloth and Morrokide trim; front and rear foam seats; rear ashtrays in armrests (except coupe); loop-pile carpet (except coupe); Deluxe steering wheel; upper level ventilation (hardtop coupe); teakwood dash accents; windshield radio antenna; concealed wipers (except coupe); ventipanes (except hardtop coupe); chrome valance panel; and bright moldings on the roof gutters, windshield, rear window, and body sills of most styles. Station wagons had all-Morrokide seats, under-floor cargo compartments, vinyl cargo floor coverings, two-way tailgates with built-in steps, power brakes with front discs, and power tailgate windows on nine-passenger jobs. Standard tires were H78-14 size on Safaris and F78-14 size on other styles. The WW-4 option was available on LeMans style numbers 2027 and 2037 and included a 400-cid four-barrel V-8, four-speed manual transmission with floor shift, heavy-duty Safe-T-Track differential, front power disc brakes, custom carpet (coupe only) and the Ride and Handling package. The WW-5 option was available on LeMans style numbers 2027 and 2037 and included Turbo-Hydra-Matic or close-ratio four-speed manual transmission, 455-cid four-barrel H.O. V-8, heavy-duty Safe-T-Track differential, body-color outside mirrors (left-hand remote control), Formula steering wheel, roof drip moldings and carpet (coupe only), Rally gauge cluster with tachometer, Ride & Handling package, RAM AIR hood, and unitized ignition system.

LEMANS SPORT — (6-CYL) — SERIES D67 — The LeMans convertible was considered a separate sub-series called the LeMans

1972 Pontiac Luxury LeMans two-door hardtop. (OCW)

Sport line. This model carried special "Sport" signature scripts and had standard bucket seats. Many sources list this style with the LeMans series, but the factory broke it out separately in calculating production totals. The code 332 LeMans "GT" package was available on style numbers 2D37 and 2D67 and included three-speed heavy-duty manual transmission, G70 x 14 white-letter tires, body-color mirrors, Rally II wheels (less trim rings), vinyl tape stripes, dual exhausts with side splitters, and "GT" decals. The code 734 LeMans Sport option was available on style number 2D37 and included bucket seats, custom door and rear quarter trim, custom rear seat and special front fender nameplate.

LUXURY LEMANS — (V-8) — SERIES 2G — A distinctive grille treatment with twin cavities divided by bright horizontal blades was used on Luxury LeMans models. Twin-ribbed full-length body side moldings, fender skirts, and roof pillar letter badges were additional external distinctions. The standard equipment list was the same as for LeMans styles, plus all-Morrokide bucket seats in hardtop coupes or notchback bench seats in any body style. Interior trim features included all-Morrokide or cloth and Morrokide upholstery combinations, carpeted lower door panels with reflectors, custom cushion steering wheel, pedal trim plates, front door assist straps, bright armrest accents, ashtray lamp, and glove box lamp.

GTO — (V-8) — SERIES D OPTION — The GTO was no longer a separate series. There was a code 334 GTO option package available for the style number 2D37 LeMans hardtop coupe and the 2D27 LeMans two-door coupe. It included the Code T engine, three-speed heavy-duty manual floor shift transmission, G70-14 black sidewall tires, body-color mirrors, Endura styling option, special twin air slot hood, front fender air extractors, firm shock absorbers, front and rear stabilizer bars and GTO identification at a price of $344 over base model cost. The code X and code Y engines were optional. Only 5,807 GTOs left the factory and body style breakouts are not available. (Note: These cars are included in the LeMans production totals given above).

BASE FIREBIRD — (6-CYL) — SERIES 2S — The possibility of dropping the Firebird was raised this year and styling changes were minimal. There was a new honeycomb mesh grille insert, new interior trims, and redesigned hubcaps and wheel covers. Standard equipment in the basic model included front and rear bucket type seats with all-vinyl trim, solid foam seat cushions with integral springs, loop-pile carpet, Deluxe steering wheel, upper-level ventilation, woodgrained dash accents, ashtray light, Endura front bumper,

1972 Pontiac LeMans Sport two-door convertible. (OCW)

1972 Pontiac GTO "The Judge" two-door hardtop. (OCW)

1972 Pontiac Firebird Trans Am two-door hardtop. (JAG)

small full-width front air dam, hubcaps, windshield radio antenna, bright moldings on windshield, rear window and grille, thin body sill moldings, front disc brakes, three-speed manual column shift transmission, and E78-14 black sidewall tires.

FIREBIRD ESPRIT — (V-8) — SERIES 2T — The Esprit had model signature script moldings on the roof pillar. Standard equipment was the same as in basic Firebirds, plus custom cloth and Morrokide trim, distinctive door trim panels, perforated headliner, added sound insulation, custom cushion steering wheel, rear armrest ashtrays, trunk mat, dash assist grip, wheel trim rings, body-color mirrors (left-hand remote-control), body-color door handle inserts, concealed wipers, bright roof rail trim, window sill moldings, rear hood edge accents, wheel opening moldings, and wide rocker panel accent strips. Three-speed manual floor shift transmission was also included.

FIREBIRD FORMULA — (V-8) — SERIES 2U — Formula Firebirds had the same equipment features as Esprits, plus a fiberglass hood with forward-mounted twin air scoops, special Formula identification, 1-1/8-in. front stabilizer bars, firm control shock absorbers, dual exhausts with chrome extensions, and F70-14 tires.

FIREBIRD TRANS AM — (V-8) — SERIES 2V — Trans Ams had the same standard features as Firebirds, plus a Formula steering wheel; engine-turned dash trim; Rally gauge cluster with clock and tachometer; front air dam; front and rear wheel opening flares; full-width rear deck spoiler; engine air extractors; shaker hood; 15-in. Rally II rims with trim rings; black-textured grille inserts; fast-rate power steering; power brakes with front discs; 1-1/4-in. stabilizer bars; 7/8-in. rear stabilizer bars; special high-rate rear springs; Safe-T-Track differential; air cleaner with rear-facing cold air induction system; power-flex cooling fan; four-speed close-ratio manual transmission with floor shift (or Turbo-Hydra-Matic); and F60-15 white lettered tires.

VENTURA II — (6-CYL) — SERIES 2Y — There were virtually no changes in the 1972 Ventura II. Minor alterations included variations in fender lettering, interior trim modifications and a new steering wheel. Standard equipment included bench seats with cloth and Morrokide trim, front seat foam cushions, vinyl covered floor mats, rear ashtrays in armrests, deluxe steering wheel, woodgrained vinyl dash trim, hubcaps, front door vent windows, bright moldings on windshield and rear window, E78-14 black sidewall tires, and three-speed manual column shift transmission. Two specialty "model-options" were the Ventura "SD" and the Sprint. The code 332 Ventura (coupe) Sprint option included three-speed manual floor shift transmission, E78 x 14 whitewalls, body-colored mirrors (left-hand remote control), custom sport steering wheel, chrome wheel trim rings, custom carpets, blacked-out grille, side striping, 14 x 16-in. rims, and Sprint I decals. The Ventura "SD" (for "Sport Deluxe") was a limited-edition package offered only in cars built at Van Nuys, Calif. It was introduced in midyear and a production run of 500 units was predicted.

I.D. DATA: The serial numbering system was changed slightly this year. The first symbol was again the GM divisional code, using a '2' for Pontiacs. The second symbol was alphabetical, using letters to indicate series as follows: (Y) for Ventura; (S) for basic Firebird; (T) for Firebird Esprit; (U) for Formula Firebird; (V) for Trans Am; (D) for LeMans; (G) for Luxury LeMans; (L) for Catalina; (M) for Catalina Brougham; (N) for Bonneville; (P) for Grand Ville and (K) for Grand Prix. The third and fourth symbols indicated the body style. The fifth

symbol was a new numerical engine code as follows: VIN on top of dash at left, viewable through windshield. First symbol tells GM division: 2=Pontiac. Second symbol tells series: Y=Ventura II; S=Firebird; T=Esprit; U=Formula 400; V=Trans Am; D=LeMans; G=Luxury LeMans; K=Grand Prix; L=Catalina; M=Catalina Brougham; N=Bonneville; P=Grand Ville. Third and fourth symbols indicate body style and appear as last two letters of body/style number in charts below. Fifth symbol indicates engine (See chart at beginning of "Engines" section below). Sixth symbol indicates model year: 2=1972. Seventh symbol indicates assembly plant: A=Atlanta, Ga.; C=South Gate, Calif.; D=Doraville, Ga.; G=Framingham, Mass.; L=Van Nuys, Calif.; N=Norwood, Ohio; P=Pontiac, Mich.; W=Willow Run, Mich.; X=Kansas City, Kan.; Z=Fremont, Calif.; 2=St. Therese, Quebec Canada. Remaining symbols are sequential unit production number at factory, starting with 100001. Fisher Body plate on cowl tells style number: Model year prefix 72, plus (this year only) 1971 type body/style number codes, body number, trim code, paint code and other data. Six-cylinder engine code stamped on distributor mounting on right side of block. V-8 engine code on front of block below right cylinder head. Engine production codes for 1972 were: [250-cid/110-nhp six] W6/CBJ/Y6/CBG/CBA/CBC [307-cid/130-nhp V-8] CKG/CAY/CKH/CAZ/CTK/CMA. [350-cid/160-nhp V-8] WR/YU/YV/YR. [400-cid/180-nhp V-8] YX/ZX. [400-cid/200-nhp] WS/WK/YS/ZS. [400-cid/250-nhp] YY. [455-cid/190-nhp] YH/ZH. [455-cid/220-nhp] YC/YA. [455-cid/300-nhp] YB/YE. [455-cid/210-nhp] n.a. [455-cid/240-nhp] n.a. [455-cid/200-nhp] U. (Note: Horsepower ratings expressed in net horsepower or "nhp" terms).

Model Number	Body Style Number	Body Type & Seating	Factory Price	Shipping Weight	Production Total
CATALINA (2L SERIES)					
2L	2L69	4d Sedan-6P	3,713	4,154	83,004
2L	2L39	4d Hardtop-6P	3,874	4,179	28,010
2L	2L57	2d Hardtop-6P	3,808	4,129	60,233
2L	2L67	2d Convertible-6P	4,080	4,204	2,399
2L	2L35	4d Sta Wagon-6P	4,232	4,743	14,536
2L	2L45	4d Sta Wagon-9P	4,372	4,818	12,766
CATALINA BROUGHAM (2M SERIES)					
2M	2M69	4d Sedan-6P	3,916	4,188	8,007
2M	2M39	4d Hardtop-6P	4,062	4,238	8,762
2M	2M57	2d Hardtop Cpe-6P	3,996	4,158	10,545
BONNEVILLE (2N SERIES)					
2N	2N69	4d Sedan-6P	4,169	4,288	9,704
2N	2N39	4d Hardtop-6P	4,293	4,388	15,806
2N	2N57	2d Hardtop Cpe-6P	4,228	4,238	10,568
2N	2N35	4d Sta Wagon-6P	4,581	4,918	5,675
2N	2N45	4d Sta Wagon-9P	4,721	4,938	8,540
GRAND VILLE (2P SERIES)					
2P	2P49	4d Hardtop-6P	4,507	4,378	41,346
2P	2P47	2d Hardtop Cpe-6P	4,442	4,263	19,852
2P	2P67	2d Convertible-6P	4,640	4,333	2,213
GRAND PRIX (SERIES 2K)					
2K	2K57	2d Hardtop-5P	4,472	3,898	91,961
BASE LEMANS (20 SERIES)					
2D	2D27	2d Coupe-6P	2,722/2,840	3,294/3,510	6,855
2D	2D36	4d Sta Wagon-6P	3,271/3,389	3,799/4,015	8,332
2D	2D37	2d Hardtop-6P	2,851/2,969	3,234/3,450	80,383
2D	2D46	4d Sta Wagon-9P	3,378/3,496	3,839/4,055	5,266
2D	2D69	4d Sedan-6P	2,814/2,932	3,269/3,485	19,463
LEMANS SPORT (2D SUB-SERIES)					
2D	2D67	2d Convertible-5P	3,228/3,346	3,284/3,500	3,438

1972 Pontiac Firebird Trans Am two-door hardtop. (JAG)

1972 Pontiac Ventura II Sprint two-door sedan. (OCW)

Model Number	Body Style Number	Body Type & Seating	Factory Price	Shipping Weight	Production Total
LUXURY LEMANS (2G SERIES)					
2G	2G37	2d Hardtop-5P	3,196	3,488	8,641
2G	2639	4d Hardtop-6P	3,319	3,638	37,615
BASE FIREBIRD (2S SERIES)					
2S	2S87	2d Hardtop-4P	2,838/2,956	3,357/3,359	12,000
FIREBIRD ESPRIT (2T SERIES)					
2T	2T87	2d Hardtop-4P	3,194	3,359	11,415
FORMULA FIREBIRD (2U SERIES)					
2U	2U87	2d Hardtop-4P	3,221	3,424	5,250
FIREBIRD TRANS AM (2V SERIES)					
2V	2V87	2d Hardtop-4P	4,256	3,564	1,286
VENTURA II (SERIES 2Y)					
2Y	2Y69	4d Sedan-5P	2,454/2,544	2,979/3,129	21,584
2Y	2Y27	2d Coupe-5P	2,426/2,516	2,944/3,094	51,203

NOTE 1: Data above slash for six/below slash for V-8.

NOTE 2: 9,601 LeMans had synchromesh and 110,698 had automatic.

NOTE 3: 317 LeMans Sport "sport convertibles" made with synchromesh and 3,121 made with automatic.

NOTE 4: 269 Luxury LeMans had synchromesh and 45,987 had automatic.

NOTE 5: 1,263 Firebirds had synchromesh and 10,738 had automatic.

NOTE 6: 504 Firebird Esprits had synchromesh and 10,911 had automatic.

NOTE 7: 1,082 Formula Firebirds had synchromesh and 4,167 had automatic.

NOTE 8: 458 Trans Ams had synchromesh and 828 had automatic.

NOTE 9: 6,421 Ventura IIs had synchromesh and 26,644 had automatic.

ENGINES

Code*	Type	CID	Carb.	Comp. Ratio	Net HP at RPM
D	6-cyl	250	1-V	8.5:1	110 at 4200
F	V-8	307	2-V	8.5:1	140 at 4000
M	V-8	350	2-V	8.0:1	160 at 4400
N	V-8	350	2-V	8.0:1	175 at 4400**
R	V-8	400	2-V	8.2:1	175 at 4000
P	V-8	400	2-V	8.2:1	200 at 4000**
S	V-8	400	4-V	8.2:1	200 at 4000
T	V-8	400	4-V	8.2:1	250 at 4000**
V	V-8	455	2-V	8.2:1	185 at 4000
U	V-8	455	2-V	8.2:1	200 at 4000**
W	V-8	455	4-V	8.2:1	220 at 3600
Y	V-8	455	4-V	8.2:1	250 at 3600**
X	V-8	455	4-V	8.4:1	300 at 4000**

* VIN engine code; not engine production code.

** dual exhaust.

ENGINE [Catalina]: Base V-8 in Catalinas was the code N engine. The base V-8 in Catalina Safaris was the code R engine. Code S, V, Y, W, T, and U engines were optional.

ENGINE [Catalina Brougham]: Base V-8 in Catalina Broughams was the code R engine. Code S/V/Y/W/T/U engines were optional.

ENGINE [Bonneville]: Base V-8 in Bonnevilles was the code V engine. Code T/W/U engines were optional.

ENGINE [Grand Ville]: Base V-8 in Grand Ville was the code W engine. The only available option was the code Y engine.

ENGINE [Grand Prix]: Base V-8 in Grand Prix was the code S engine. Options were the code T/Y engines, with the latter included in the "SJ" option package as regular equipment.

ENGINE [LeMans]: Base six-cylinder power plant in LeMans was the code D engine. Base V-8 was the code M engine. Codes R/S/T/W/Y/X engines were other options.

ENGINE [Luxury LeMans]: Base V-8 in Luxury LeMans models was the code M engine. Code R/S/W/Y engines were additional options.

ENGINE [Base Firebird]: Base six-cylinder power plant in Firebirds was the code D engine. Base V-8 was the code M engine and the code N engine was optional.

ENGINE [Firebird Espirit]: Base V-8 in Firebirds Esprits was the code M engine. Options included code N and code R power plants.

ENGINE [Formula Firebird]: Base V-8 in Formula Firebirds was the code M engine. Options included the code N, T and X power plants. Depending on engines, cars were identified as Formula 350s, Formula 400s, or Formula 455s.

ENGINE [Trans Am]: The code X engine was the only Trans Am power plant this year.

ENGINE [Ventura II]: Base six-cylinder power plant in Ventura IIs was the code D engine. The code F engine was optional, except for cars registered in California, where the code M engine was used as the approved V-8.

CHASSIS: Wheelbase: Wheelbases for all lines were the same as 1971. Overall Length: For Venturas, Firebirds, and base LeMans overall lengths were the same as for comparable body styles in 1971. Luxury LeMans models were 202.8 in. long; all Pontiac Safaris were now 228 in. long; Catalinas were 222.4 in. long; Bonneville/Grand Villes were 226.2 in. long and Grand Prix were 213.6 in. long.

OPTIONS: Pontiac automatic air conditioning ($507). Firebird and LeMans air conditioning ($397). Formula or LeMans rear deck spoiler ($32-$46). Pontiac automatic level control ($77). Firebird rear seat console ($26). Ventura and Firebird front seat console ($57). LeMans two-door hardtop and Sport convertible console ($59). Cruise Control ($62-$67). Deck lid remote control ($14). Electric rear window defroster ($62). Base LeMans Endura styling option ($41). All-windows Soft-Ray glass ($39-$49). Soft-Ray windshield ($30-$35). Auxiliary gauge panel for Catalina ($38). Bumper guards ($5-$15). Warning lamps ($21). Auxiliary lamp group ($18). Convenience lamp group ($11). Safari luggage carrier ($62-$82). Front disc brakes ($46-$68). Wonder Touch brakes ($44-$46). Power bench seats ($67-$77-$103). Power left bucket seat ($77). Ventura power steering ($100). Variable ratio power steering for LeMans and Firebirds ($113). AM/FM Stereo and 8-Track ($363). Rally gauge cluster with clock and tachometer ($92). honeycomb wheels ($62-$123). Rally II wheel rims ($56-$87). Wood-grained Safari exterior paneling ($154). LeMans "GT" package ($23). Grand Ville Custom trim group ($231). Ventura sun roof ($179). LeMans Sport option ($164). Ventura Sprint option ($190). LeMans WW-4 performance option ($510-$796). LeMans WW5 RAM AIR option ($982-$995). Dual exhausts ($40). Performance or economy ratio rear axles ($10). Safe-T-Track differential was $45 extra and heavy-duty Safe-T-Track was $66 extra. Heavy-duty batteries were $10-$15 extra and a Delco X battery was $26 extra. Functional air inlet hoods for Formulas and specially-equipped LeMans models were $56 extra.

1972 Pontiac Bonneville Safari four-door station wagon. (OCW)

1972 Pontiac Firebird Formula 455 two-door hardtop. (OCW)

HISTORICAL: Production startup date was Aug. 12, 1971. Factory introductions were held Sept. 23, 1971. Model year output was 707,017 cars. Calendar year totals of 702,571 assemblies gave Pontiac Motor Div. fifth place. The 1972 GTO hardtop with 300 net hp was tested at 7.1 seconds 0-to-60 and 15.4 seconds in the quarter-mile. The 1972 Firebird Esprit did 0-to-60 mph in 9.9 seconds and the quarter-mile in 17.6 seconds. The GTO returned to option status this year and Pontiac made Turbo-Hydra-Matic and disc brakes standard on all models. On Oct. 1, 1972, Martin J. Caserio became Pontiac's general manager.

1973 PONTIAC

1973 Pontiac Catalina two-door hardtop. (OCW)

CATALINA — (V-8) — SERIES 2L — Catalina front-end styling was new and was characterized by full-width grilles having thin horizontal blades. Catalina lettering was seen behind the front wheel openings. Standard equipment was similar to the previous model year with small hubcaps, untrimmed wheel cutouts and thin body sill moldings. Tail lamp treatments were simpler than on other lines. The Catalina convertible and Catalina Brougham series were deleted. Base Catalinas came with a 350-cid two-barrel V-8, Turbo-Hydra-Matic and variable-ratio power steering.

1973 Pontiac Grand Ville two-door convertible. (OCW)

1973 Pontiac Grand Ville four-door hardtop. (OCW)

1973 Pontiac Grand Prix two-door hardtop. (OCW)

1973 Pontiac LeMans GTO two-door hardtop. (OCW)

1973 Pontiac Grand Am Colonnade two-door hardtop. (OCW)

1973 Pontiac Grand Am Colonnade two-door hardtop. (OCW)

1973 Pontiac Firebird Trans Am two-door hardtop. (OCW)

BONNEVILLE — (V-8) — SERIES 2N — Bonnevilles had a new "egg-crate" mesh grille running from side to side. Double twin-deck tail lamps were used along with wide body sill moldings having rear panel extensions. Bonneville lettering appeared on the left side of the grille, behind front wheel openings and between the tail lamps. Bonnevilles were now the same as Catalinas, but had higher levels of interior and exterior trim including Deluxe wheel covers, decor moldings and custom upholstery combinations. Fender skirts were no longer standard equipment, but other features were about the same as in 1972. A special RTS handling package was introduced for the hardtop. This Bonneville RTS coupe was priced $4,225 and included radial tires and heavy-duty underpinnings at this cost. Bonneville Safaris were moved to the Grand Ville series.

GRAND VILLE — (V-8) — SERIES 2P — Grand Ville passenger cars were now the same as other full-size Pontiacs. The new grille on this line was similar to the Bonneville type except that a signature script model badge was placed above the left-hand grille instead of on it. Stacked, horizontally-slit tail lamps were an exclusive feature. Full-wheel discs, wide body sill moldings, roof pillar nameplates (except convertible) and fender skirts were additional identification aids. Standard equipment was the same as in 1972. The Bonneville Safaris became Grand Ville Safaris. The big wagons were on a three-inch longer wheelbase than other Pontiacs. Safari features were about the same as those seen on 1972 Bonneville station wagons.

GRAND PRIX — (V-8) — SERIES 2K — The Grand Prix retained a link to previous styling themes, with several refinements. A new type of wide grille design was used and opera windows were an available styling option. The Grand Prix was on a shorter wheelbase and looked trimmer, even though overall size was increased. V-shaped hood styling was emphasized again. A new feature was African crossfire mahogany accents for the instrument panel. A custom cushion steering wheel and all-Morrokide trims were used. The general level of trim, appointments and standard equipment was the same as in 1972. The "SJ" option was offered again, with production counted separately for the first time. It included firm shock absorbers, thick front stabilizer bar, Rally RTS suspension and the 250-hp V-8.

LEMANS — (6-CYL) — SERIES 2D AND SERIES 2AF — Pontiac's A-body intermediate line had highly revised "Buck Rogers" styling this season. Design characteristics included V-shaped hoods, split rectangular grilles, single headlamps mounted in square housings, highly sculptured fenders and "Colonnade" style rooflines. The Colonnade styling provided heavier roof pillars to meet federal rollover standards with large window openings cut deep into the beltline in limousine style. LeMans lettering appeared behind the front wheel

1973 Pontiac Grand Am Colonnade four-door sedan. (OCW)

1973 Pontiac Luxury LeMans Colonnade two-door hardtop. (OCW)

opening and thin body sill moldings were used. The LeMans Sport convertible was discontinued and replaced by the Series 2AF LeMans Sport Coupe. This model constituted a separate sub-series and came standard with bucket seats and louvered rear quarter window styling. Station wagons were officially called Safaris again. Available options on the LeMans or LeMans Sport Coupes included the GT and GTO packages. Base models had a uniform vertical blade grille insert, with flat textured finish on the GTO. The GTO option also included the 400-cid four-barrel V-8, dual air scoop hood, wide oval tires, dual exhausts, floor mounted three-speed manual gearbox, rear sway bars, baby moon hubcaps, 15 x 7-in. wheel rims, specific body striping, and suitable model identification trim.

LUXURY LEMANS — (V-8) — SERIES 2AG — Luxury LeMans models also featured Colonnade styling, but with higher-level interior and exterior appointments, plus standard V-8 power. Styling features included wide beauty moldings running the full width of the body at about mid-wheel height; fender skirts with chrome edge moldings; rear deck beauty panels between the taillights; vertical blade grilles with vertical chrome division moldings; deluxe wheel covers; and "Luxury" signatures above the LeMans fender lettering. Luxury LeMans upholstery combinations were patterned after those seen in Grand Villes.

GRAND AM — (V-8) — SERIES 2AH — One of the most distinctive cars offered in the sales sweepstakes this model year was the Pontiac Grand Am. This A-body intermediate had an international flavor. Standard equipment included a sloping three-piece nose section of body-color injection-molded urethane plastic; twin sloping vertical-slot triple quadrant grilles; bucket seats with adjustable lumbar support; 14-in. custom cushion steering wheel; African crossfire mahogany dash trim; 10-in. diameter power front disc brakes; Grand Prix style dashboard; full-instrumentation with Rally gauge cluster; variable-ratio power steering; heavy-duty suspension; steel-belted wide-base G70-15 radial tires on 15 x 7-in. wheels; Pliacell shock absorbers; thick front and rear stabilizer bars; specific trim stripes; and special nameplates. Upholstery options included cloth with corduroy insert panels or perforated, leather-like Morrokide. A V-8 engine was also standard.

BASE FIREBIRD — (6-CYL) — SERIES 2F2 — Base Firebirds had a new "egg-crate" grille insert. Styling was not greatly changed from 1972, but the Endura nose had been substantially improved to meet U.S. government crash standards. Standard equipment was basically similar to that offered in 1972 models.

FIREBIRD ESPRIT — (V-8) — SERIES 2FT — The Firebird Esprit could be most easily identified by the model signature scripts on the

1973 Pontiac Luxury LeMans Colonnade two-door hardtop. (OCW)

1973 Pontiac Luxury LeMans Colonnade four-door hardtop. (OCW)

roof pillars. Also considered standard equipment were a custom interior, concealed windshield wipers, twin body-color mirrors (left-hand remote-control), and African crossfire mahogany dash and console accent panels.

FIREBIRD FORMULA — (V-8) — SERIES 2FU — Formula Firebirds could again be identified by the special twin-scoop hoods. Other features included a custom cushion steering wheel, heavy-duty suspension, black-textured grille, dual exhausts, and F70-14 tires, plus all items included on lower-priced lines.

FIREBIRD TRANS AM — (V-8) — SERIES 2FV — The most significant change to the Firebird Trans Am this season was the addition of the "chicken" graphics treatment for the hood. Stylist John Schinella created this modernized rendition of the legendary Indian symbol. Standard equipment included Formula steering wheel; Rally gauge cluster with clock and tachometer; full-width rear deck spoiler; power steering and front disc brakes; Safe-T-Track differential; wheel opening flares; front fender air extractors; dual exhausts with chrome extensions; heavy-duty underpinnings; Rally II wheels with trim rings; dual body-color mirrors (left-hand remote-controlled); F60-15 white-lettered tires; and a choice of Turbo-Hydra-Matic or four-speed manual transmission.

VENTURA — (6-CYL) — SERIES 2Y — The name Ventura II was shortened to Ventura and cars in the Y Series had several styling refinements. A "double-decker" twin slot grille was continued in use on cars with base level trim. Standard equipment included deluxe steering wheel, bench seats with cloth and Morrokide trim, front and rear armrests, high-low ventilation system, rubber floor mats, and hubcaps. A Sprint package including custom cushion steering wheel, custom carpeting, body-color outside mirrors, custom striping, model identification trim, and 14 x 6-in. wheel rims was available on two-door models. There was now a pair of two-door styles available, the notchback coupe and the hatchback coupe, along with a four-door notchback sedan. Cars with the Sprint package wore a Firebird-style twin rectangular grille.

VENTURA CUSTOM — (6-CYL) — SERIES 2Z — Ventura Customs included a choice of cloth or all-Morrokide upholstery, custom cushion steering wheel, bright metal front seat side panels, glove box lamp, nylon carpeting, deluxe wheel covers, pedal trim plates, body decor moldings and body sill beauty strips. The hatchback coupe included load area carpeting and a dome lamp, a fold-down rear seat and a Space Saver spare tire. As on base models Ventura block letters were seen behind the front wheel openings, but additional identification was provided by signature scripts reading "Custom" positioned on the rear roof pillars.

1973 Pontiac LeMans Safari four-door station wagon. (OCW)

1973 Pontiac Grand prix two-door hardtop. (OCW)

I.D. DATA: VIN on top of dash at left, viewable through windshield. First symbol tells GM division: 2=Pontiac. Second symbol tells series: Y=Ventura; Z=Ventura Custom; S=Firebird; T=Esprit; U=Formula 400; V=Trans Am; D=LeMans; F=LeMans Sport; G=Luxury LeMans; H=Grand Am; K=Grand Prix; L=Catalina; N=Bonneville; P=Grand Ville. Third and fourth symbols indicate body style and appear as last two digits of body/style number in charts below. Fifth symbol indicates engine. (See chart at beginning of "Engines" section below.) Sixth symbol indicates model year: 3=1973. Seventh symbol indicates assembly plant: A=Atlanta, Ga.; C=South Gate, Calif.; D=Doraville, Ga.; G=Framingham, Mass.; L=Van Nuys, Calif.; N=Norwood, Ohio; P=Pontiac, Mich.; Z=Fremont, Calif. Remaining symbols are sequential unit production number at factory, starting with 100001. Fisher Body plate on cowl tells style number: Model year prefix 73, plus new type body/style number codes (i.e., 2L69 for Catalina four-door sedan), body number, trim code, paint code and other data. Six-cylinder engine code stamped on distributor mounting on right side of block. V-8 engine code on front of block below right cylinder head. Engine production codes for 1972 were: [250 cid/100-nhp six] CCC-CCD-CCA-CCB-CDR-CDS-CAW. [350-cid/150-nhp V-8] YL-Y2-YR-Y7-YV-XR-XV-ZR-ZV-XC. [350-cid/175-nhp V-8] WV-ZB-ZD-WD-XC-X2-WF-WA-XF-WC-WL-WN-YW. [400-cid/170-nhp V-8] YP-Y4-YX-Y1-ZX-ZK-YZ. [400-cid/185-nhp V-8] P. [400-cid/200-nhp V-8] S. [400-cid/230-nhp V-8] WK-WS-WP-YS-Y3-YN-YT. [400-cid/250-nhp V-8] X4-X1-X3-XH-W5-Y6-YF-YG-XN-XX-X5-XZ-XK. [455-cid/215-nhp V-8] W. [455-cid/250-nhp V-8] WW-WT-YC-YA-ZC-ZZ-ZE-XE-XA-XJ-XL-XO-XT-X7-XY-XM. [455-cid/310-nhp Super-Duty V-8] ZJ-XD-W8-Y8.

Model Number	Body Style Number	Body Type & Seating	Factory Price	Shipping Weight	Production Total
CATALINA (2L SERIES)					
2L	L69	4d Sedan-6P	3,770	4,234	100,592
2L	L39	4d Hardtop-6P	3,938	4,270	31,663
2L	L57	2d Hardtop-6P	3,869	4,190	74,394
2L	L45	4d Sta Wagon-9P	4,457	4,873	14,654
2L	L35	4d Sta Wagon-6P	4,311	4,791	15,762
BONNEVILLE (2N SERIES)					
2N	N69	4d Sedan-6P	4,163	4,333	15,830
2N	N39	4d Hardtop-6P	4,292	4,369	17,202
2N	N57	2d Hardtop-6P	4,225	4,292	13,866
GRAND VILLE (2P SERIES)					
2P	P49	4d Hardtop-6P	4,592	4,376	44,09
2P	P47	2d Hardtop-6P	4,524	4,321	23,963
2P	P67	2d Convertible-6P	4,766	4,339	4,447
2P	P45	4d Sta Wagon-9P	4,821	4,925	10,776
2P	P35	4d Sta Wagon-6P	4,674	4,823	6,894
GRAND PRIX (2K SERIES)					
2K	K57	2d Hardtop-5P	4,583	4,025	133,150
2K	K57	'SJ' Hardtop-5P	4,962	4,400	20,749

1973 Pontiac Ventura two-door hatchback. (OCW)

1973 Pontiac Firebird Trans Am two-door hardtop. (OCW)

Model Number	Body Style Number	Body Type & Seating	Factory Price	Shipping Weight	Production Total
LEMANS (2AD SERIES)					
2AD	D29	4d Hardtop-6P	2,918/3,036	3,605/3,821	26,554
2AD	D37	2d Hardtop-6P	2,920/3,038	3,579/3,795	68,230
2AD	D45	4d Sta Wagon-9P	3,429/3,547	3,993/4,209	6,127
2AD	D35	4d Sta Wagon-6P	3,296/3,414	3,956/4,172	10,446
LEMANS SPORT (2AF SERIES)					
2AF	F37	2d Hardtop-5P	3,008/3,126	3,594/3,810	50,999
LUXURY LEMANS (2AG SERIES)					
2AG	G29	4d Hardtop-6P	3,344	3,867	9,377
2AG	G37	2d Hardtop-6P	3,274	3,799	33,916
GRAND AM (2AH SERIES)					
2AH	H29	4d Hardtop-6P	4,353	4,018	8,691
2AH	H37	2d Hardtop-6P	4,264	3,992	34,445
BASE FIREBIRD (SERIES 2FS)					
2FS	S87	2d Hardtop-4P	2,895/3,013	3,159/3,380	14,096
FIREBIRD ESPRIT (SERIES 2FT)					
2FT	T87	2d Hardtop-4P	3,249	3,309	17,249
FIREBIRD FORMULA (SERIES 2FU)					
2FU	U87	2d Hardtop-4P	3,276	3,318	10,166
FIREBIRD TRANS AM (SERIES 2FV)					
2FV	V87	2d Hardtop-4P	4,204	3,504	4,802
VENTURA (SERIES 2Y)					
2Y	Y69	4d Sedan-5P	2,481/2,599	3,124/3,336	21,012
2Y	Y27	2d Coupe-5P	2,452/2,570	3,064/3,276	49,153
2Y	Y17	2d Hatchback-5P	2,603/2,721	3,170/3,382	26,335
VENTURA CUSTOM (SERIES 2Z)					
2Z	Z69	4d Sedan-5P	2,638/2,756	3,157/3,369	(Note 8)
2Z	Z27	2d Coupe-5P	2,609/2,727	3,097/3,309	(Note 8)
2Z	Z17	2d Hatchback-5P	2,759/2,877	3,203/3,415	(Note 8)

NOTE 1: Data above slash for six/below slash for V-8.

NOTE 2: 4,806 LeMans/LeMans Sport two-door Colonnade hardtops had GTO option.

NOTE 3: 1,370 cars were built with six-cylinder power.

NOTE 4: Totals include base Venturas, Customs, and Sprints of same body style.

NOTE 5: Ventura Custom totals included in base Ventura chart above.

ENGINES

Code*	Type	CID	Carb.	Comp. Ratio	Net HP at RPM
D	6-cyl	250	1-V	8.25:1	100 at 3600
F	V-8	307	2-V	8.5:1	130 at 4000*
M	V-8	350	2-V	7.6:1	150 at 4000
N	V-8	350	2-V	7.6:1	175 at 4400**
R	V-8	400	2-V	8.0:1	170 at 3600
P	V-8	400	2-V	8.0:1	185 at 4000**
S	V-8	400	4-V	8.0:1	200 at 4000
T	V-8	400	4-V	8.0:1	250 at 4400**
W	V-8	455	4-V	8.0:1	215 at 3600
Y	V-8	455	4-V	8.0:1	250 at 4000**
X	V-8	455	4-V	8.4:1	310 at 4000**

* Canada only.

** Dual exhausts.

ENGINE [Catalina]: The base Catalina V-8 was the code M engine. Codes R-P-S-T-W-Y engines were optional. The code R engine was standard in Catalina Safaris.

ENGINE [Bonneville]: The base Bonneville V-8 was the code R engine. Code P-S-T-W-Y engines were optional.

ENGINE [Grand Ville]: The base Grand Ville V-8 was the code W engine. The code Y engine was optional.

ENGINE [Grand Prix]: The base Grand Prix V-8 was the code T engine. The code Y-X engines were optional.

ENGINE [LeMans-Ventura]: Base six-cylinder powerplant in LeMans models was the code D engine. Base V-8 in LeMans passenger cars was the code R engine. Code P-S-T-W-Y engines were optional in passenger cars. The code R engine was standard in Safari V-8s with code S-W engines as options. The code T engine was standard in cars with the GTO package.

ENGINE [Luxury LeMans]: Base V-8 powerplant in Luxury LeMans models was the code M engine. Code R-S-Y engines were optional.

ENGINE [Grand Am]: Base V-8 powerplant in Grand Ams was the code R engine. Code S-Y-X engines were optional.

ENGINE [Base Firebird]: Standard six-cylinder powerplant in basic Firebirds was the code D engine. Base V-8 was the code M engine. No other options were listed.

ENGINE [Firebird Espirit]: Base V-8 powerplant in Esprits was the code M engine. The only option was also a V-8, the code R engine.

ENGINE [Firebird Formula]: Base V-8 powerplant in the Formula Firebird series was the code M engine. Code R-Y-X engines were optional V-8s.

ENGINE [Firebird Trans Am]: Base V-8 powerplant in Trans Ams was the code Y engine. The code X engine was the only powertrain option.

OPTIONAL V-8 ENGINES

ENGINE [Optional V-8 (Standard in Catalina, Luxury LeMans, Firebird Esprit; Optional in Ventura/LeMans/Firebird)]: Displacement: 350 cid. Compression ratio: 7.6:1. Carburetion: two-barrel. Brake horsepower: 150 at 4000 rpm.

ENGINE [Optional V-8 (Optional in Ventura/LeMans/Catalina; Standard in Firebird Formula 350)]: Displacement: 350 cid. Compression ratio: 7.6:1. Carburetion: two-barrel. Brake horsepower: 175 at 4400 rpm.

ENGINE [Optional V-8 (Standard in Grand Am, Safari, Bonneville; Optional in LeMans/Catalina/Firebird Esprit)]: Displacement: 400 cid. Compression ratio: 8:1. Carburetion: two-barrel. Brake horsepower: 170 at 3600 rpm.

ENGINE [Optional V-8 (Optional in LeMans/Grand Am/Catalina)]: Displacement: 400 cid. Compression ratio: 8:1. Carburetion: two-barrel. Brake horsepower: 185 at 4000 rpm.

ENGINE [Optional V-8 (Standard in Grand Safari; Optional in Catalina/Bonneville)]: Displacement: 400 cid. Compression ratio: 8:1. Carburetion: four-barrel. Brake horsepower: 200 at 4000 rpm.

ENGINE [Optional V-8 (Standard in GTO, Grand Prix; Optional in LeMans/Grand Am/Formula 400/Catalina/Bonneville)]: Displacement: 400 cid. Compression ratio: 8:1. Carburetion: four-barrel. Brake horsepower: 230 at 4400 rpm.

ENGINE [Optional V-8 (Standard in Grand Ville; Optional in Catalina/Bonneville)]: Displacement: 455 cid. Compression ratio: 8:1. Carburetion: four-barrel. Brake horsepower: 215 at 3600 rpm.

ENGINE [Optional V-8 (Standard in Trans Am; Optional in Grand Prix/Grand Ville/Catalina/Bonneville/GTO/LeMans/Formula 455)]: Displacement: 455 cid. Compression ratio: 8:1. Carburetion: four-barrel. Brake horsepower: 250 at 4000 rpm.

ENGINE [Optional V-8 (optional in Trans Am/Formula 455)]: Displacement: 455 cid. Compression ratio: 8:1. Carburetion: four-barrel. Brake horsepower: 290 at 4000 rpm.

1973 Pontiac Ventura four-door sedan. (OCW)

1973 Pontiac Bonneville Superior laundaulet funeral car. (JAG)

CHASSIS: Wheelbase: (All Pontiac Safaris) 127 in.; (All Pontiac passenger cars) 124 in.; (A-body two-doors) 112 in.; (A-body four-doors) 116 in.; (Grand Prix) 116 in.; (Firebird) 108 in.; (Ventura) 111 in. Overall Length: (All Pontiac Safaris) 228.8 in.; (All Pontiac passenger cars) 224.8 in.; (Grand Am two-door) 208.6 in.; (Grand Am four-door) 212.6 in.; (Grand Prix) 216.6 in.; (Other A-body two-doors) 207.4 in.; (Other A-body four-doors) 211.4 in.; (A-body Safaris) 213.3 in. (Firebird) 192.1 in.; (Ventura) 197.5 in.

OPTIONS: Custom Safari option package ($317). GTO LeMans option package ($368). LeMans Ride & Handling package ($188). LeMans GT option ($237). Grand Prix "SJ" option ($379). Electric sunroof for A-body models ($325), Ventura sunroof ($179). Grand Prix electric sunroof ($325). Ventura vinyl top ($82) Firebird AM/FM stereo ($233); with tape deck ($363). Firebird power windows ($75). LeMans vinyl top ($97). LeMans AM/FM stereo ($233); with tape deck ($363). LeMans power windows ($103). LeMans Rally II wheels ($87). Pontiac six-way power seat ($103). Pontiac power windows ($129). Pontiac AM/FM stereo ($233); with tape deck ($363). Safari 60/40 bench seats ($77). Grand Prix vinyl roof ($116). Grand Prix power windows ($75).

HISTORICAL: Model year production was 919,872 units, the highest ever for Pontiac Motor Division. Calendar year output of 866,598 cars was also recorded for a 9.5 percent market share. On Nov. 27, 1972, a blue Catalina sedan became the 16th millionth Pontiac ever made. The SD-455 Trans Am was capable of 0-to-60 mph in 7.3 seconds and did the quarter-mile in 15 seconds. The 250-nhp Grand Am traveled from 0-to-60 mph in 7.9 seconds and made it down the drag strip in 15.7. Production of SD-455 Trans Ams totaled 252 cars, of which 180 had automatic transmission and 72 had manual transmission. Fifty Formula Firebirds also had the SD-455 muscle engine.

1974 PONTIAC

1974 Pontiac Grand Ville four-door hardtop. (OCW)

CATALINA — (V-8) — SERIES 2BL — The front and rear of 1974 Catalinas was restyled and some body styles also had new rooflines. A radiator grille was used again. It had a chrome shell with a broad vertical center bar forming two openings. Each was filled with a crosshatched grille accented by five bright horizontal division bars.

1974 Pontiac Catalina four-door sedan. (OCW)

Two-piece rectangular parking lamps were set into the front panel below the headlamps and above the bumper. Pontiac lettering appeared on the left front panel. Catalina lettering and engine displacement numbers were placed behind front wheel openings. Twin rectangular taillights were used at each side in the rear. Hardtop coupes featured Colonnade-type rooflines. All full-sized Pontiacs had the following as standard equipment: woodgrained dash trim; high/low ventilation; windshield radio antenna; front and rear energy-absorbing bumpers; ash trays; glove box lamp; inside hood release; nylon carpeting; safety belt warning system; windshield, roof drip, hood rear edge, and rear window moldings (except Grand Prix and Safaris); power steering; power brakes with front discs; Turbo-Hydra-Matic transmission; and V-8 engine. Catalinas also had a two-spoke steering wheel, cloth and Morrokide front bench seat, trunk mat, and G78-15 black sidewall tires. Catalina Safaris had all-Morrokide upholstery, storage compartments, Glide-Away tailgates, power tailgate windows, right-hand outside mirror, tailgate vertical rub stripes, rear quarter and tailgate window moldings, and L78-15 tires. The nine-passenger Safari came with a split-back second seat and rear-facing third seat.

BONNEVILLE — (V-8) — SERIES 28N — Bonnevilles featured "egg-crate" style grille inserts and one-piece horizontal parking lamps. Bonneville lettering was seen on the left-hand front body panel and behind the front wheel openings, as well as on the rear deck. Taillights were similar to the Catalina type, but accented with a deck latch panel beauty strip. Standard equipment included all items found on Catalinas, plus a choice of cloth and Morrokide or all-Morrokide upholstery; custom cushion steering wheel; electric clock; rear door light switches (on four-doors); dash courtesy lamps; pedal trim plates; trunk mat with side panels; deluxe wheel covers; decor moldings at wheel wells; wide body sill moldings with rear extensions; luggage lamp; rubber bumper strips; and H78-15 black sidewall tires.

GRAND VILLE — (V-8) — SERIES 2P — Grand Villes had the following features: Full-wheel discs, wide body sill moldings, roof pillar nameplates (except convertibles) and fender skirts. Standard equipment was about the same as in 1973. Station wagons were called Grand Safaris. The big wagons were on a three-inch longer wheelbase than other Pontiacs. Safari features were about the same as those seen on pre-1973 Bonneville Safari station wagons.

GRAND PRIX — (V-8) — SERIES 2GK — Grand Prix styling changes included a shorter grille that did not drop below the bumper line, thinner and more rectangular parking lamps, twin vertical taillights and a crease sculptured contour line behind the front wheel

1974 Pontiac Grand Ville two-door convertible. (OCW)

1974 Pontiac Grand Prix two-door hardtop coupe. (OCW)

opening. Standard equipment was the same as in Bonneville, plus carpeted lower door panels; black custom cushion steering wheel; cigar lighter and courtesy lamps; lateral restraint front bucket seats or notchback front bench seat; aircraft style wraparound instrument panel with integrated console (except with bench seats); rear quarter opera window styling; windowsill and wide body sill moldings; floor shift (bucket seats only); dual exhausts; and G78-15 tires. Approximately 92 percent of all Grand Prix had bucket seats and the 'SJ' option package, which collectors consider a separate model, was available again.

LEMANS AND LEMANS SPORT — (6-CYL) — SERIES 2AD/2AF — LeMans models had new front bumpers with rubber-faced protective guards, more angular front fender corner sections, twin rectangular grilles accented by bright horizontal division bars, and vertically curved taillights with new rear bumpers. Standard equipment in all A-body cars included woodgrained dash trim; deluxe two-spoke steering wheel; safety belt warning system; high/low ventilation, nylon carpeting; inside hood release; concealed wipers; windshield radio antenna; new energy-absorbing bumpers; hubcaps; manual front disc brakes; windshield, roof drip, body sill, rear and rear quarter window moldings; and F78-14 black sidewall tires. Base models had cloth-and-Morrokide front bench seats. The LeMans Sport coupe featured a notchback armrest front seat, woodgrained glove box trim, and louvered rear quarter window treatment.

LUXURY LEMANS — (V-8) — SERIES 2AG — Luxury LeMans models had special vertically segmented grille inserts; wide body sill moldings with front and rear extensions; distinctive curved vertical tail lamps accented with chrome moldings; a deck latch panel beauty strip; luxury scripts behind the front wheel openings and fender skirts. Standard equipment included deluxe wheel covers, custom cushion steering wheel, and V-8 power. The Luxury LeMans hardtop provided buyers with a choice of front bucket seats or a notchback type with armrest. This model also incorporated ashtrays and glove box lamps; cloth-and-Morrokide or all-Morrokide trims; door-pull straps; pedal trim plates; dual horns; decor moldings; and special taillight styling. The Luxury LeMans Safari came with woodgrained dash trim; all-Morrokide seats; under-floor storage compartment; liftgate; textured steel cargo floor; tailgate vertical rub strips; power front disc brakes; and all other base LeMans Safari station wagon features. The nine-passenger versions had a rear-facing third seat, electric tailgate release and swing-out rear quarter ventipanes.

GRAND AM — (V-8) — SERIES 2AH — Standard equipment for all Grand Ams was based on the Luxury LeMans list, with the following

1974 Pontiac LeMans GT Colonnade two-door hardtop. (OCW)

1974 Pontiac Luxury LeMans Colonnade two-door hardtop. (OCW)

variations: courtesy lamps; custom sport steering wheel; mahogany dash trim; electric clock; turn signal stalk headlight dimmer switch; integrated console with mahogany trim; floor-mounted gear shift lever; lateral-restraint bucket seats with adjustable lumbar support; custom finned wheel covers; Endura bumper protective strips; power brakes with front discs; Rally gauges with trip odometer; power steering; Turbo-Hydra-Matic transmission; and radial-tuned suspension with GR70-15 tires. Styling distinctions included a special vertically-segmented polyurethane nose panel, exclusive taillight design and specific striping and badge ornamentation.

BASE FIREBIRD — (6-CYL) — SERIES 2FS — New Firebird styling changes included a shovel-nosed Endura front end, a horizontal slotted taillight treatment, lowered rear fender line and twin horizontal rectangular grille inserts with vertical blades. All Firebird models had ashtrays lamps, nylon carpeting, high/low ventilation, Endura styling, and windshield radio antenna. The basic Firebird also featured a deluxe two-spoke steering wheel, single-buckle seat and shoulder belt arrangement, narrow rocker panel moldings and E78-14 tires.

FIREBIRD ESPRIT — (V-8) — SERIES 2FT — As usual, a model badge on the rear roof pillar was a trait of Esprit models. Standard extras on this line included custom cushion steering wheel, custom interior package, body-color door handle inserts, concealed wipers with articulated left arm, deluxe wheel covers, dual horns, dual outside mirrors (left-hand remote-controlled), roof drip and wheel opening moldings, wide body sill moldings, window sill and rear hood edge moldings, three-speed manual floor shift (with base engine only), safety belt warning system and E78-14 tires.

FORMULA FIREBIRD — (V-8) — SERIES 2FU — In addition to equipment standard in Esprits, Formula Firebirds featured hubcaps, dual-scoop fiberglass hoods, special heavy-duty suspension, black-textured grilles, dual exhausts, and F70-14 tires. Available model options included Formula 350, Formula 400, and Formula 455.

FIREBIRD TRANS AM — (V-8) — SERIES 2FV — Standard equipment on Trans Am included formula steering wheel, Rally gauges with clock and dash panel tachometer, swirl grain dash trim, full-width rear deck lid spoiler, power steering and front disc brakes, limited-slip differential, wheel opening air deflectors (flares), front fender air extractors, dual exhausts with chrome extensions, Rally II wheels with trim rings, special heavy-duty suspension, four-speed manual transmission (or M40 Turbo-Hydra-Matic), dual outside racing mirrors, and F60-15 white-lettered tires.

VENTURA — (6-CYL) — SERIES 2XY — The Firebird-style grille seen on 1973 Ventura Sprints was now used on all models in this

1974 Pontiac Luxury LeMans Colonnade two-door hardtop. (OCW)

Standard Catalog of ® Pontiac, 2nd Edition

1974 Pontiac Grand Am Colonnade two-door hardtop. (OCW)

line. There were minimal styling changes otherwise. Standard equipment included deluxe two-spoke steering wheel, bench front seat with cloth and Morrokide trim, woodgrained door inserts, front and rear armrests, high/low ventilation, rubber floor covering, hubcaps, vent windowless styling, and E78-14 tires. Cars with the Sprint option package (two-doors only) had black-textured grilles. The most interesting option was the GTO package, which was now available exclusively for Ventura coupes.

VENTURA CUSTOM — (6-CYL) — SERIES 2XZ — Ventura Customs had all features found on base models plus a choice of cloth or all-Morrokide trim, custom cushion steering wheel, bright-hand metal front seat side panels, glove box lamp, nylon carpeting, pedal trim plates, right-hand-hand door jamb switch, deluxe wheel covers and drip, scalp, and rocker panel moldings. Hatchback coupes also had load floor carpeting, fold-down seats, Space Saver spare tires, cargo area dome lights, and trimmed sidewalls.

I.D. DATA: VIN on top of dash at left, viewable through windshield. First symbol tells GM division: 2=Pontiac. Second symbol tells series: Y=Ventura; Z=Ventura Custom; S=Firebird; T=Esprit; U=Formula 400; V=Trans Am; D=LeMans; F=LeMans Sport; G=Luxury LeMans; H=Grand Am; K=Grand Prix; L=Catalina; N=Bonneville; P=Grand Ville. Third and fourth symbols indicate body style and appear as last two digits of body/style number in charts below. Fifth symbol indicates engine (See chart at beginning of "Engines" section below.) Sixth symbol indicates model year: 4=1974. Seventh symbol indicates assembly plant: A=Atlanta, Ga.; C=South Gate, Calif.; D=Doraville, Ga.; G=Framingham, Mass.; L=Van Nuys, Calif.; N=Norwood, Ohio; P=Pontiac, Mich.; W=Willow Run, Mich.; X=Kansas City, Kan.; Z=Fremont, Calif.; 1=Oshawa, Canada. Remaining symbols are sequential unit production number at factory, starting with 100001. Fisher Body plate on cowl tells style number (model year prefix 74, plus "2" for Pontiac and body/style number from charts below), plus body number, trim code, paint code and other data. Six-cylinder engine code stamped on distributor mounting on right-hand side of block. V-8 engine code on front of block below right-hand cylinder head. Engine production codes for 1972 were: [250-cid/100-nhp six] CCR-CCX-CCW. [350-cid/155-nhp V-8] WA-WB-YA-YB-YC-AA-ZA-ZB. [350-cid/170-nhp V-8] WN-WP-YN-YP-YS-ZP. [400-cid/175-nhp V-8] YH-YJ-AH-ZH-ZJ. [400-cid/200-nhp V-8] WT-YT-AT-ZT-YZ. [455-cid/215-nhp V-8] YY-YU-YX-AU-ZU-ZX-YW-ZW-YR. [455-cid/310-nhp Super-Duty V-8] W8-Y8.

Model Number	Body Style Number	Body Type & Seating	Factory Price	Shipping Weight	Production Total
CATALINA (SERIES 2BL)					
2BL	L69	4d Sedan-6P	4,190	4,294	46,025
2BL	L39	4d Hardtop-6P	4,347	4,352	11,769

1974 Pontiac Grand Am Colonnade four-door hardtop. (OCW)

1974 Pontiac Firebird Trans Am two-door hardtop. (OCW)

Model Number	Body Style Number	Body Type & Seating	Factory Price	Shipping Weight	Production Total
2BL	L57	2d Hardtop-6	4,278	4,279	40,657
2BL	L45	4d Sta Wagon-9P	4,834	5,037	6,486
2BL	L35	4d Sta Wagon-6P	4,692	4,973	5,662
BONNEVILLE (SERIES 2BN)					
2BN	N69	4d Sedan-6P	4,510	4,384	6,770
2BN	N39	4d Hardtop-6P	4,639	4,444	6,151
2BN	N57	2d Hardtop-6P	4,572	4,356	7,639
GRAND VILLE AND GRAND SAFARI — (V-8) — SERIES 2BP					
2BP	P49	4d Hardtop-6P	4,939	4,515	21,714
2BP	P47	2d Hardtop-6P	4,871	4,432	11,631
2BP	P67	2d Convertible-6P	5,113	4,476	3,000
2BP	P45	4d Sta Wagon-9P	5,256	5,112	5,255
2BP	P35	4d Sta Wagon-6P	5,109	5,011	2,894
GRAND PRIX (SERIES 2GK)					
GRAND PRIX J					
2GK	K57	2d Hardtop-6P	4,936	4,096	85,976
GRAND PRIX SJ					
2GK	K57	2d Hardtop-5P	5,321	4,300	13,84
LEMANS (SERIES 2AD)					
2AD	D29	4d Hardtop-6P	3,236/3,361	3,628/3,844	17,266
2AD	D37	2d Hardtop-6P	3,216/3,341	3,552/3,768	37,061
2AD	D45	4d Sta Wagon-9P	4,186	4,371	4,743
2AD	D35	4d Sta Wagon-6P	4,052	4,333	3,004
LEMANS SPORT (SERIES 2AF)					
2AF	F37	2d Hardtop-6P	3,300/3,425	3,580/3,796	37,955
LUXURY LEMANS (SERIES 2AG)					
2AG	G29	4d Hardtop-6P	3,759	3,904	4,513
2AG	G37	2d Hardtop-6P	3,703	3,808	25,882
2AG	G45	4d Sta Wagon-9P	4,459	4,401	1,178
2AG	G35	4d Sta Wagon-6P	4,326	4,363	952
GRAND AM (SERIES 2AH)					
2AH	H29	4d Hardtop-5P	4,623	4,073	3,122
2AH	H37	2d Hardtop-5P	4,534	3,992	13,961
FIREBIRD (SERIES 2FS)					
2FS	S87	2d Hardtop-4P	3,335/3,460	3,283/3,504	26,372
FIREBIRD ESPRIT (SERIES 2FT)					
2FT	T87	2d Hardtop-4	3,687	3,540	22,583
FORMULA FIREBIRD (SERIES 2FU)					
2FU	U87	2d Hardtop-4P	3,659		3,54814,51
FIREBIRD TRANS AM (SERIES 2FV)					
2FV	V87	2d Hardtop-4P	4,446	3,655	10,255
VENTURA (SERIES 2XY)					
2XY	Y69	4d Sedan-5P	2,921/3,046	3,169/3,398	21,012
2XY	Y27	2d Coupe-5P	2,892/3,017	3,184/3,376	49,153
2XY	Y17	2d Hatchback-5P	3,018/3,134	3,257/3,486	26,335
VENTURA WITH GTO OPTION					
2XY	Y27	2d Coupe-5P	3,212	3,400	(7,058)
VENTURA CUSTOM (SERIES 2XZ)					
2XZ	Z69	4d Sedan-5P	3,080/3,205	3,208/3,398	(Note 7)
2XZ	Z27	2d Coupe-5P	3,051/3,176	3,184/3,413	(Note 7)
2XZ	Z17	2d Hatchback-5P	3,176/3,301	2,362/3,491	(Note 7)
VENTURA CUSTOM W/GTO OPTION					
2XZ	Z27	2d Coupe-5P	3,371	3,437	(Note 8)

NOTE 1: Data above slash for six/below; no slash for V-8.

NOTE 2: 7,063 base Firebirds had six-cylinder engines.

NOTE 3: GTO option total (in parenthesis) included in Ventura coupe total.

NOTE 4: Ventura/Ventura Custom production combined by body style; see Ventura chart.

NOTE 5: Ventura/Ventura Custom GTO production combined; see Ventura chart.

ENGINES

Code*	Type	CID	Carb.	Comp. Ratio	Net HP at RPM
D	6-Cyl	250	1-V	8.2:1	100 at 3600

Code*	Type	CID	Carb.	Comp. Ratio	Net HP at RPM
M	V-8	350	2-V	7.6:1	155 at 4000
N	V-8	350	2-V	7.6:1	170 at 4000 **
J	V-8	350	4-V	7.6:1	185 at 4000
K	V-8	350	4-V	7.6:1	200 at 4000 **
R	V-8	400	2-V	7.6:1	175 at 3600
P	V-8	400	2-V	8.0:1	190 at 4000
S	V-8	400	4-V	8.0:1	200 at 4000
T	V-8	400	4-V	8.0:1	225 at 4000 **
W	V-8	455	4-V	8.0:1	215 at 3600
Y	V-8	455	4-V	8.0:1	250 at 4000 **
X	V-8	455	4-V	8.4:1	290 at 4000

NOTE: Dual exhausts are indicated by symbol (**)

ENGINE [Catalina]: Base V-8 in Catalina was the code R engine. Code P-S-T-W-Y engines were optional in federally certified cars. Code S and code T engines were not available for cars sold in California.

ENGINE [Bonneville]: Base V-8 in Bonnevilles was the code R engine. Code P-S-T-W-Y engines were optional in federally certified cars. Code S and T engines were not available for cars sold in California.

ENGINE [Grand Ville/Grand Safari]: Base V-8 in Grand Villes and Grand Safaris was the code W engine. The code Y engine was optional only in passenger cars.

ENGINE [Grand Prix]: Base V-8 in Grand Prix was the code T engine. The code Y powerplant was optional and was also part of the 'SJ' option package.

ENGINE [LeMans/LeMans Sport]: Base six-cylinder powerplant for passenger cars in both series was the code D engine. Base V-8 for Safaris and passenger cars was the code M engine. Code J-R-T-Y engines were optional in federally certified passenger cars. Code R-P-S-T-W engines were optional in federally certified Safaris. Code J and code S engines were not available in any cars sold in California. Code M and code T engines were not available in Safari station wagons sold in California.

ENGINE [Luxury LeMans]: Base V-8 in Luxury LeMans passenger cars was the code M engine. Code J-R-T-Y engines were optional in federally certified passenger cars. Base V-8 in Luxury LeMans Safaris [with federal certification] was the code M engine. Base V-8 in Luxury LeMans Safaris sold in California was the code R engine. Additional Safari options included code P-S-T-W engines. The code J engine was not available in passenger cars sold in California. The code S and code T engines were not available in Safaris sold in California.

ENGINE [Grand Am]: Base V-8 in Grand AM was the code P engine. Code T and code Y engines were optional. The code X Super-Duty 455-cid V-8, which had been listed as optional in 1973, but never issued, was no longer listed in 1974.

ENGINE [Base Firebird]: The standard six-cylinder powerplant in the basic Firebird was the code D engine. The base V-8 was the code M engine. There were no other options.

ENGINE [Firebird Espirit]: Base V-8 in Firebird Esprits was the code M engine. The code R engine was the only option in this line.

ENGINE [Formula Firebird]: Base V-8 in Formula Firebirds was the code M engine. Code R-T-Y-X engines were optional. All Firebirds built for sale in California were required to have automatic transmission.

1974 Pontiac Catalina Colonnade two-door hardtop. (OCW)

ENGINE [Firebird Trans Am]: Base V-8 in Trans Am was the code T engine. Code Y and code X engines were optional. The latter powerplant [SD-455] was officially called the LS2 option and was installed in 731 cars with Turbo-Hydra-Matic and 212 cars with synchromesh attachment.

ENGINE [Ventura]: The base six-cylinder powerplant for Venturas was the code D engine. The base V-8 for Venturas was the code M engine. The code J engine was included in the Ventura GTO option package and was a separate option in federally certified cars, but not in cars built for California sale.

ENGINE [Ventura Custom]: The base six-cylinder powerplant for Venturas was the code D engine. The base V-8 for Venturas was the code M engine. The code J engine was included in the Ventura GTO option package and was a separate option in federally certified cars, but not in cars built for California sale.

CHASSIS: Wheelbase: (B-body passenger cars) 124 in.; (B-body Safaris) 127 in.; (G-Body) 116 in.; (A-body two-doors) 112 in.; (A-body four-doors) 116 in.; (F-Body) 108 in.; (X-Body) 111 in. Overall Length: (B-body passenger cars) 226 in.; (B-body Safaris) 231.3 in.; (G-Body) 217.5 in.; (Grand Am two-door) 210.9 in.; (Grand Am four-door) 214.9 in.; (A-body two-door) 208.8 in.; (A-body Safaris) 216 in.; (A-body four-doors) 212.8 in.; (F-Body) 196 in.; (X-Body) 199.4 in. (Note: GM body nomenclature such as A-body now corresponds to first letter in body/style number).

OPTIONS: Pontiac and Grand Am air conditioning ($488-$522). Ventura air conditioning ($396). Firebird air conditioning ($412). Clock and Rally gauge cluster ($29-$49). Clock tachometer and Rally gauge cluster ($51-$100); with trip odometer on Grand Prix ($51-$90). Firebird rear seat console ($26). Ventura and Firebird front seat console ($58). Cruise control ($69-$70). Rear window defogger ($33-$38). LeMans air scoop hood ($87). LeMans D37 and Trans Am hood decals ($55). Formula Firebird RAM AIR hood ($56). Rear quarter windowless louver styling option on LeMans Sport ($35). Safari remote tailgate release ($14). Grand Prix reclining bucket seats ($112). Ventura bucket seats ($132). Grand Prix notchback seat ($50 credit since bucket seats were standard). Grand Am and Grand Prix accent stripes ($31). LeMans and Grand Prix electric sun roof ($325); manual sun roof ($275). Firebird radial tuned suspension with FR78-14 whitewall tires ($107-$145); same on Formula ($24-$36). Ventura radial tuned suspension ($113-$170); same with Sprint package ($91). Custom finned wheel covers on LeMans and Firebird ($24-$50). Honeycomb wheels on Grand Prix, Grand Am, and Firebird ($54-$123). Rally II rims ($37-$87). Transmission options included three-speed manual with column shift standard in Ventura and LeMans. Three-speed manual with floor shift in Venturas was $26 extra. Heavy-duty three-speed manual with floor shift was $82 extra in certain LeMans hardtops.

1974 Pontiac Ventura GTO two-door sedan. (OCW)

1974 Pontiac Bonneville Colonnade two-door hardtop. (OCW)

1975 Pontiac Catalina four-door hardtop. (OCW)

Four-speed manual was $197 extra in LeMans; $207 in Venturas and Firebirds and a $45 delete option in Grand Ams. M38 Turbo-Hydra-Matic was $221 extra in base Firebirds and certain LeMans; $206 extra in Venturas and $221 extra in Esprits, Formulas, and Luxury LeMans. M40 Turbo-Hydra-Matic was standard in Grand Am; a no-charge option in Trans Am; $21 extra in LeMans Safaris and $242 extra in LeMans, Esprit, and Formulas. Full-sized Pontiacs and Grand Prix had standard Turbo-Hydra-Matic .

OPTION PACKAGES: A code 308 custom trim package was available on style numbers FU87 and FV87 and included pedal trim, custom appointments, door handle decor inserts, Deluxe front bucket and custom rear seats and fitted trunk mat. A code 342 LeMans GT option package was available at $202-$246 and included Rally II wheels less trim rings, G70 x 14 tires, dual exhausts with chrome extensions, specific accent stripes, dual sport mirrors (left-hand remote control), wheel opening moldings and three-speed manual transmission with floor shift. The code 342 Grand Prix 'SJ' option sold for $354-$385 and included the 455-cid four-barrel V-8, body color mirrors (left-hand remote control), custom wheel covers, accent stripes, Delco X battery, Rally gauge cluster with trip odometer, GR70 x 15 steel-belted tires, special shock absorbers, and heavy-duty stabilizer bars. The code 341 Ventura Sprint option sold for $88-$168 and included specific front end styling, body-color sport mirrors, custom cushion steering wheel, custom carpets, cargo area carpeting, vinyl accent stripes, Rally II wheels less trim rings and a deck lid Sprint decal. The Ventura GTO option package sold for $195 and included a 350-cid four-barrel V-8, front and rear stabilizer bars, radial-tuned suspension, Pliacell shock absorbers, power steering, front and rear drum brakes, E78-14 tires, heavy-duty three-speed manual gearbox, dual exhausts with splitter extensions, 3.08:1 ratio axle; Rally II rims less trim rings, special grille driving lights, rear-facing "shaker" air scoop and computer selected high-rate rear springs. This was the 11th and last GTO.

HISTORICAL: The 1974 Pontiacs were introduced on Sept. 20, 1973. Model year production of 580,748 cars was registered and included LeMans models made in Canada. Calendar-year production was 502,083 units. A total of 212 Firebirds were built with LS2 SD-455 engines. This was the last year for a GTO (so far).

1975 PONTIAC

1975 Pontiac Catalina four-door sedan. (OCW)

CATALINA — (V-8) — SERIES 2BL — Full-sized Pontiacs were redesigned for 1975, with most models featuring new roofline treatments.

1975 Pontiac Grand Safari four-door station wagon. (OCW)

Catalinas had a distinctive radiator grille with a wide vertical center divider and chrome accent moldings forming three stacked rectangles on either side. Triple-stacked taillights were also used, which were shorter than those seen on other lines. The two-door notchback hardtop had an exclusive roofline featuring wide rear quarter windows, thin C-pillars, and a large backlight. Standard equipment was about the same as on 1974 Catalinas, except that a new efficiency system and radial-tuned suspension became regular features.

BONNEVILLE — (V-8) — SERIES 2BP — The N Series was dropped and Bonnevilles moved to the P Series (formerly Grand Ville) with Grand Safaris included. A radiator grille with crisscrossed dividers and "egg-crate" inserts was seen. Headlamps were mounted in rectangular housings with square parking lamps on the outside wrapping around the corners of the fenders. New rear quarter window treatments were employed. Taillights were wider than the Catalina type and wrapped around the corners of the rear fenders. Standard equipment was about the same as on 1975 Bonnevilles with the addition of the high-efficiency ignition system and radial-tuned suspension.

GRAND VILLE BROUGHAM — (V-8) — SERIES 2BR — Grand Ville Broughams were essentially Bonnevilles with a slightly higher level of interior and exterior appointments. Identifying features included wide body sill accent moldings with rear extensions, fender skirts and Grand Ville Brougham signature scripts behind the front wheel housings.

GRAND PRIX — (V-8) — SERIES 2GK — Styling refinements were seen in the grille, taillight design, and decorative trim of the 1975 Grand Prix. Both the grille and taillights were segmented to produce a more vertical look. The sports-oriented 'SJ' package returned and a new luxury-image 'U' option group was introduced. Modern collectors consider these to be separate models. So did Pontiac, and individual production totals are available for all three types of Grand Prix. Standard equipment was a near match for that featured the year before, except for ignition and suspension systems, which received the same improvements seen on full-size lines. The style number K57 coupe was available with the 'U' package including distinctive two-tone paint finish, deluxe wheel covers, outside mirrors, custom interior trim, and Cordova top. Every Grand Prix now had speedometers calibrated in kilometers and headlight dimmer switches built into the turn signal stalk.

LEMANS/LEMANS SPORT — (6-CYL) — SERIES 2AD/2AF — The 1975 base LeMans and LeMans Sport series were basically unchanged from the previous year except for a new "egg-crate" grille insert and some minor trim variations. An available styling option on two-door hardtop coupes was a louvered rear quarter window treatment, which was also standard on Series 2AF LeMans Sport sport coupes.

GRAND AM — (V-8) — SERIES 2AH — The Grand Am continued to feature a unique vertically segmented polyurethane nose and louvered

1975 Pontiac Bonneville four-door hardtop. (JAG)

1975 Pontiac Grand Ville two-door convertible. (JAG)

1975 Pontiac Grand Am four-door Colonnade hardtop. (OCW)

rear quarter windows on coupes. Little was changed except for some pin striping and grille insert details. The standard equipment list was about the same as in 1974 with the addition of the high-efficiency ignition system. At the end of the 1975 run this nameplate was temporarily dropped.

GRAND LEMANS — (V-8) — SERIES 2AG — The Luxury LeMans became the Grand LeMans this year. There was a distinctive grille design with six groupings of vertical blades arranged three on each side of the center divider. Stand-up hood ornaments appeared and fender skirts were used as standard equipment on all models, except Grand LeMans Safaris.

FIREBIRDS — (6-CYL) — SERIES 2FS (BASE)/2FT/(ESPRIT)/2FU/(FORMULA)/2FV/(TRANS AM) — Firebirds continued to look much the same as in 1974, except for a new roofline with a wrap-around backlight. High-Efficiency ignition and radial-tuned suspension systems were added to the equipment list. As usual, base models had conventional wipers and minimal trim. Esprits had concealed wipers, decor moldings, door handle inserts, and roof pillar signature scripts. Formulas featured heavy-duty chassis components and a distinctive twin scoop hood. The Trans Am had flares, spoilers, extractors, shaker hood scoop, and Firebird decals. There were some changes in a technical sense. The base powerplant in Esprit was now the Chevy-built Six. At the beginning of the year, the biggest engine for Trans Am was the 400-cid version. At midyear, the code Y engine (455-cid) was reinstated, but only with single exhausts and a catalytic converter. Due to the decrease in brute horsepower, the M38 Turbo Hydra-Matic was the only automatic transmission used. In addition, all Firebirds certified for sale in California were required to use this transmission.

VENTURA — (6-CYL) — SERIES 2XE (VENTURA S)/SERIES 2XY (VENTURA)/SERIES 2XZ (VENTURA CUSTOM)/SERIES 2XB (VENTURA SJ) — Venturas were completely restyled. The new 1975 frontal treatment featured distinctive grille ports with integral parking lights and an energy-absorbing front bumper. Rooflines were made somewhat slimmer with lower beltlines and more glass area than before. The Ventura was the basic model at the beginning of the year, with features about the same as 1974 base models. The GM efficiency system was made standard equipment, but on Venturas did not include radial tires. The next-step-up line was the Custom series with such things as custom interior trim, body decor moldings, and custom cushion steering wheel. Equipment variations over base models were again about the same as in 1974. A Ventura SJ series was new. Features included custom finned wheel covers; custom steering wheel; Grand Prix style instrument cluster; extra acoustical insulation; cigar lighter; rocker panel moldings; and decor trim for wheel openings, rear end, roof, and side windows. Interior

trims were similar to the Grand AM type and Ventura SJ lettering appeared behind the front wheel housings. In the middle of the model run a Ventura with less equipment than the base model was introduced as the Ventura S.

ASTRE — (4-CYL) — SERIES 2HC (ASTRE S)/SERIES 2HV (BASE ASTRE)/SERIES 2HX (ASTRE SJ) — Pontiac's entry in the 1975 sub-compact wars was the Astre. It was initially offered in hatchback coupe and Safari body styles, both of which came with base or SJ trim. The Astre S economy series was introduced at midyear and included the two original body styles, plus an exclusive notchback coupe. Standard equipment included all GM safety, anti-theft, convenience, and emissions control features, three-speed manual floor shift transmission, manual steering, manual brakes with front discs, heater and defroster, front bucket seats, carpeting, and A78-13 bias ply tires. The SJ models came standard with special upholstery, custom carpets, custom steering wheel, woodgrain dash inserts, Rally gauge cluster with tachometer and clock, Rally II wheels, and four-speed manual transmission. Also available was an Astre GT option package that added the two-jet induction system, front and rear stabilizer bars, Rally wheels, body-color sport mirrors, and radial-tuned suspension. A limited number of Astre-based panel delivery trucks were built in the U.S. for the Canadian market.

I.D. DATA: VIN on top of dash at left, viewable through windshield. First symbol tells GM division: 2=Pontiac. Second symbol tells series: X=Astre; B=Ventura SJ; S=Firebird; T=Esprit; U=Formula 400; V=Trans Am; D=LeMans; F=LeMans Sport; G=Luxury LeMans; H=Grand Am; K=Grand Prix; L=Catalina; P=Bonneville Grand Safari; R=Grand Ville Brougham. Third and fourth symbols indicate body style and appear as last two digits of body/style number in charts below. Fifth symbol indicates engine. (See chart at beginning of "Engines" section below.) Sixth symbol indicates model year: 5=1975. Seventh symbol indicates assembly plant: A=Atlanta, Ga.; C=South Gate, Calif.; G=Framingham, Mass.; L=Van Nuys, Calif.; N=Norwood, Ohio; P=Pontiac, Mich.; T=Tarrytown, N.Y.; U=Lordstown, Ohio; W=Willow Run, Mich.; X=Kansas City, Kan.; 1=Oshawa, Canada. Remaining symbols are sequential unit production numbers at factory, starting with 100001. Fisher Body plate on cowl tells style number: (model year prefix 75, plus division code and body/style number code (i.e. 2L69 for Catalina four-door sedan), body number, trim code, paint code and other data. Six-cylinder engine code stamped on distributor mounting on right side of block. V-8 engine code on front of block below right cylinder head. Engine production codes for 1975 were: [140-cid/78-nhp four-cylinder] BB-BC. [140-cid/87 hp four-cylinder] AM-AS-AR-AT-CAM-CAW-CBB-CBD-CAR-CAU. [140-cid/80-nhp four-cylinder] CAS-CAT. [250-cid/105-nhp six-cylinder] JU-JT-JL. [260-cid/110-nhp V-8]

1975 Pontiac Grand Prix two-door hardtop coupe. (OCW)

1975 Pontiac Grand Am two-door Colonnade hardtop. (OCW)

1975 Pontiac Grand LeMans two-door Colonnade hardtop. (OCW)

QA-QD-QE-QJ-TE-TJ. [350-cid/145 hp V-8] RI-RS. [350-cid/155 hp V-8] YA-YB. [350-cid/165-nhp V-8] RW-RX. [350-cid/175-nhp V-8] WN-YN-ZP-RN-RO. [400-cid/170-nhp V-8] YH. [400-cid/185-nhp V-8] YT-YM-YS-WT-ZT. [455-cid/200-nhp V-8] YW-YU-ZW-ZU-WX.

Model Number	Body Style Number	Body Type & Seating	Factory Price	Shipping Weight	Production Total
CATALINA (SERIES 2BL)					
2BL	L69	4d Sedan-6P	4,612	4,347	40,398
2BL	L57	2d Hardtop-6P	4,700	4,334	40,657
2BL	L45	4d Sta Wagon-9P	5,295	5,000	4,992
2BL	L35	4d Sta Wagon-6P	5,149	4,933	3,964
BONNEVILLE (SERIES 2BP)					
2BP	P49	4d Hardtop-6P	5,153	4,503	12,641
2BP	P47	2d Hardtop-6P	5,085	4,370	7,854
2BP	P45	4d Sta Wagon-9P	5,580	5,090	4,752
2BP	P35	4d Sta Wagon-6P	5,433	5,035	2,568
GRAND VILLE BROUGHAM (SERIES 2BR)					
2BR	R49	4d Hardtop-6P	5,896	4,558	15,686
2BR	R47	2d Hardtop-6P	5,729	4,404	7,447
2BR	R67	2d Conv-6P	5,858	5,035	4,519
GRAND PRIX (SERIES 2GK)					
GRAND PRIX J					
2GK	K57	2d Hardtop-5P	5,296	4,032	64,581
GRAND PRIX SJ					
2GK	K57	2d Hardtop-5P	5,573	—	7,146
GRAND PRIX LJ					
2GK	K57	2d Hardtop-5P	5,995	—	14,855
LEMANS (SERIES 2AD)					
2AD	D29	4d Hardtop-6P	3,612/3,742	3,729/3,948	15,065
2AD	D37	2d Hardtop-6P	3,590/3,720	3,656/3,875	20,636
2AD	D45	4d Sta Wagon-9P	4,688	4,500	2,393
2AD	D35	4d Sta Wagon-6P	4,555	4,401	3,898
LEMANS SPORT (SERIES 2AF)					
2AF	F37	2d Hardtop-5P	3,708/3,838	3,688/3,907	23,817
GRAND AM (SERIES 2AH)					
2AH	H29	4d Hardtop-5P	4,976	4,055	1,893
2AH	H37	2d Hardtop-5P	4,887	4,008	8,786
GRAND LEMANS (SERIES 2AG)					
2AG	G29	4d Hardtop-6P	4,157/4,287	3,786/3,905	4,906
2AG	G37	2d Hardtop-6P	4,101/4,231	3,723/3,942	19,310
2AG	G45	4d Sta Wagon-9P	4,882	4,500	1,501
2AG	G35	4d Sta Wagon-6P	4,749	4,462	1,393
FIREBIRDS (MODEL CODE INDICATES SERIES)					
FIREBIRD					
2FS	S87	2d Hardtop-4P	3,713/3,843	3,386/3,610	22,293
ESPRIT					
2FT	T87	2d Hardtop-4P	3,958/4,088	3,431/3,655	20,826
FORMULA					
2FU	U87	2d Hardtop-4P	4,349	3,631	13,67
TRANS AM					
2FV	V87	2d Hardtop-4P	4,740	3,716	27,274
VENTURA S (SERIES 2XE)					
2XE	E27	2d Coupe-5P	3,162/3,292	3,276/3,443	(Note 10)
VENTURA (SERIES 2XY)					
2XY	Y69	4d Sedan-5P	3,304/3,434	3,335/3,502	20,619
2XY	Y27	2d Coupe-5P	3,293/3,423	3,299/3,466	28,473

1975 Pontiac Formula Firebird two-door hardtop coupe. (OCW)

1975 Pontiac Firebird 350 two-door hardtop coupe. (OCW)

Model Number	Body Style Number	Body Type & Seating	Factory Price	Shipping Weight	Production Total
2XY	Y17	2d Hatchback-5P	3,432/3,562	3,383/3,550	8,841
VENTURA CUSTOM (SERIES 2XZ)					
2XZ	Z69	4d Sedan-5P	3,464/3,594	3,378/3,545	(Note 11)
2XZ	Z27	2d Coupe-5P	3,449/3,579	3,338/3,505	(Note 11)
2XZ	Z17	2d Hatchback-5P	3,593/3,565	3,398/3,565	(Note 11)
VENTURA SJ (SERIES 2XB)					
2XB	B69	4d Sedan-5P	3,846/3,976	3,370/3,537	1,449
2XB	B27	2d Coupe-5P	3,829/3,959	3,340/3,507	2,571
2XB	B17	2d Hatchback-5P	3,961/4,091	3,400/3,567	1,622
ASTRE S (SERIES 2HC)					
2HC	C11	2d Coupe-4P	2,841	2,416	8,339
2HC	C77	2d Hatchback-4P	2,954	2,487	40,809
2HC	C15	2d Sta Wagon-4P	3,071	2,539	15,322
BASE ASTRE (SERIES 2HV)					
2HV	V77	2d Hatchback-4P	3,079	2,499	(Note 13)
2HV	V15	2d Sta Wagon-4P	3,175	2,545	(Note 13)
2HV	N/A	2d Panel-2P	—	—	131
ASTRE SJ (SERIES 2HX)					
2HX	X77	2d Hatchback-4P	3,610	2,558	(Note 15)
2HX	X15	2d Sta Wagon-4P	3,686	2,602	(Note 15)

NOTE 1: Data above slash for six/below slash or no slash for V-8.

NOTE 2: 8,314 Firebirds were six-cylinders.

NOTE 3: 26,417 Trans Am had the 400-cid four-barrel (L78) engine.

NOTE 4: 20,277 L78 Trans Ams had Turbo-automatic and 6,140 had synchromesh.

NOTE 5: 857 Trans Ams were built with the 455-cid four-barrel (L75) engine.

NOTE 6: All L75 Trans Ams had synchromesh.

NOTE 7: Ventura S production included with base Ventura totals.

NOTE8: Ventura Custom production included with base Ventura/ Ventura S totals.

NOTE 9: Approximately 63 percent of all Venturas were built with V-8s.

NOTE 10: Astre output was broken out by body styles, but not by series.

NOTE 11: Base Astre production included with totals for same Astre S model.

NOTE 12: Astre SJ output included with totals for same Astre S model.

ENGINES

Code*	Type	CID	Carb.	Comp. Ratio	Net H.P. at RPM
A	4-cyl	140	1-V	8.0:1	78 at 4200(C)
B	4-cyl	140	2-V	8.0:1	87 at 4400(C)
D	6-cyl	250	1-V	8.25:1	105at3800(C)
E	V-8	350	2-V	8.0:1	145 at 3200(B)
H	V-8	350	4-V	8.0:1	165 at 3800(B)
F	V-8	260	2-V	8.0:1	110 at 3400(O)
M	V-8	350	2-V	7.6:1	155 at 4000
J	V-8	350	4-V	7.6:1	175 at 4400
R	V-8	400	2-V	7.6:1	170 at 4000
S	V-8	400	4-V	7.6:1	185 at 3600
Y	V-8	455	4-V	7.6:1	200 at 3500

NOTE: Letters after the horsepower rating for engines in the chart above indicate manufacture by Chevrolet (C), Buick (B), or Oldsmobile (O) divisions.

NOTE: Catalytic converters were required on all engines and dual exhausts were not available.

ENGINE [Catalina]: Base V-8 for federally certified Catalinas was the code R engine. Base V-8 for California Catalinas and federally certified Catalina Safaris was the code S engine. Base V-8 in California

147

1975 Pontiac Ventura three-door hatchback. (OCW)

1975 Pontiac Ventura two-door coupe. (OCW)

1975 Pontiac Astre GT three-door hatchback coupe. (OCW)

Safaris was the code Y engine, which was also optional in federally certified passenger cars.

ENGINE [Bonneville]: Bonneville engine offerings were the same used in Catalinas.

ENGINE [Grand Ville Brougham]: Base V-8 for Grand Ville Broughams was the code S engine. The code Y engine was optional. Both V-8s were available in cars certified for federal and California sale.

ENGINE [Grand Prix]: Base V-8 in Grand Prix was the code S engine. The code R engine was optional in federally certified cars only and the code Y engine was optional in all and was also part of the 'SJ' package.

ENGINE [LeMans/Grand LeMans/LeMans Sport]: Base six-cylinder powerplant for passenger cars in both series was the code D engine. The code M engine was the base V-8 for federally certified passenger cars. The code J engine was the base V-8 for California cars and the code S engine was optional in all passenger cars. The code R engine was base powerplant for federally certified Safaris. The code S engine was base V-8 for California Safaris and optional in others.

ENGINE [Grand Am]: Base V-8 in federally certified Grand Ams was the code R engine. The code S engine was base V-8 in cars built for California sale. The code Y engine was optional in all Grand Ams.

ENGINE [Firebird]: Base Firebirds and Esprits had the same engine offerings. For these models the code D six-cylinder powerplant was standard equipment. The code M engine was the base V-8 in cars certified for non-California sale. The code J engine was the base V-8 for California cars and optional in all others. This was also the base engine in Formulas. The code S engine was optional in Formulas and standard in Trans Ams. The code Y engine was released as a midyear option for Trans Ams.

ENGINE [Ventura]: Base six-cylinder powerplant for all Venturas was the code D engine. Base V-8 for all Venturas was the code F engine. The code H and J engines were optional in all Ventura series.

ENGINE [Astre]: Standard four-cylinder engine on coupes was the code A powerplant. The code B engine was standard in SJ and optional in other series.

CHASSIS: Wheelbase: (B-body Safari) 127 in.; (B-body passenger car) 123.4 in.; (Grand Prix) 116 in.; (A-body two-door) 112 in.; (A-body four-door) 116 in.; (Ventura) 111.1 in.; (Firebird) 108.1 in.; (Astre) 97 in. Overall Length: (B-body Safari) 231.3 in.; (B-body passenger car) 226 in.; (Grand Prix) 212.7 in.; (Grand AM four-door) 215 in.; (Grand Am two-door) 211 in.; (A-body Safaris) 215.4 in.; (LeMans four-door) 212 in.; (LeMans two-door) 208 in.; (Firebird) 196 in.; (Ventura) 199.6 in.; (Astre) 175.4 in.

OPTIONS: Astre vinyl roof ($79). Astre air conditioning ($398). Astre Safari luggage rack ($50). Astre AM/FM stereo ($213). Code B engine ($50). Ventura vinyl top ($87). Ventura tape deck ($215). Ventura, LeMans and Firebird AM/FM stereo ($233). LeMans and Firebird vinyl top ($99). LeMans Safari luggage rack ($68). LeMans and Grand Prix power seats ($70). LeMans and Pontiac AM/FM stereo with tape ($363). Firebird tape deck ($130). Pontiac six-way power seat ($117). Pontiac 60/40 seats ($81). Pontiac Safari luggage rack ($89). Grand Prix vinyl top ($119). Grand Prix power windows ($91). Grand Prix sun roof ($350). Grand Prix custom trim ($120). Ventura and LeMans power brakes ($47); with front discs ($70).

HISTORICAL: The 1974 Pontiacs appeared in showrooms on Sept. 27, 1974. Calendar-year output was 523,469 cars. A new sales promotion tool was a program of price rebates on compact models. Road testers found the 1975 Trans Am with the 185-nhp V-8 capable of 0-to-60 mph in 9.8 seconds and the quarter-mile in 16.8 seconds.

1976 PONTIAC

1976 Pontiac Astre two-door notchback coupe. (PGMC)

CATALINA — SERIES 2B — (V-8) — Pontiac's lowest-priced full-size model was similar in appearance to Bonneville (below), but had five thick horizontal bars across its grille. A Custom option, however, gave it the same new front-end look as Bonneville. Standard equipment included a 400-cid two-barrel V-8, Turbo-Hydra-Matic, power

1975 Pontiac Ventura three-door hatchback. (OCW)

1976 Pontiac Ventura SJ two-door Landau coupe. (PGMC)

1976 Pontiac Grand LeMans two-door hardtop. (PGMC)

brakes and steering, HR78 x 15 black sidewall SBR tires, radial-tuned suspension, and heater/defroster.

BONNEVILLE — SERIES 2B — (V-8) — Base and Brougham models were available in the top full-size line. Bonneville Brougham was the newest model, offered in two-door hardtop coupe or four-door hardtop sedan form. All models (including Grand Safari wagon) featured a new front-end look with quad rectangular headlamps. A new wrap-over "waterfall" grille looked like a set of many "fins" on each side of the divider bar, which held Pontiacs emblem. Headlamps were separated from the fender-tip wraparound park/signal lights. Wraparound tail lamps had upper and lower sections. Four-door wagons came with two seats, but a forward facing third seat was available. Standard equipment for the base Bonneville was similar to Catalina, but included a four-barrel 400-cid V-8, driver's remote mirror, accent paint stripes, power windows, and electric clock. Wagons came with a 455-cid V-8 engine and LR78 x 15 tires.

GRAND PRIX — SERIES 2G — (V-8) — Front-end appearance of Pontiac's personal-luxury coupe was the same as Bonneville (above), with the same sharp hood creases that came to a point at the front and the same new wrap-over-fin grille. New base engine was the 350-cid (5.7-liter) V-8. Grand Prix got a new full-width front seat with fold-down center armrest. Standard Grand Prix equipment included the 350-cid V-8 with two-barrel carburetor; Turbo-Hydra-Matic; power brakes and steering; GR78 x 15 black sidewall SBR tires; radial-tuned suspension; clock; heater/defroster; full-width seats with center armrest; window and hold moldings; rocker panel and wheel opening moldings; and roof drip moldings. Grand Prix SJ added the 400-cid four-barrel V-8, bucket seats (with console), special wheel covers and courtesy lights. A limited-edition Golden Anniversary model featured special paint and striping, removable roof panels, and a commemorative stand-up hood ornament. An LJ luxury appointments group included velour bucket seats, thick cut-pile carpeting, and two-tone body color.

LEMANS — SERIES 2A — (SIX/V-8) — Quad rectangular headlamps gave the LeMans a new front-end appearance. Base and the Grand LeMans came in two-door hardtop coupe and four-door hardtop sedan form, while the LeMans Sport Coupe was (obviously) a coupe only. Two-door models had a formal-look rear quarter window, while the Sport Coupes window was louvered. Park/signal lamps were at outer ends of a single bumper slot, next to the bumper guards. The LeMans grille consisted of thin vertical bars, arranged in sections per side of the peaked divider bar (which displayed a Pontiac emblem). Two four-door (two-seat) wagons were available: LeMans Safari and Grand LeMans Safari. Both could also have an optional rear-facing third seat. Grand LeMans had a wide variety of interior possibilities: standard notchback full-width seat (cloth and vinyl); optional 60/40 seating (cloth, vinyl, or velour); and bucket seats (perforated vinyl, corduroy, velour, or leather). LeMans standard equipment included the 250-cid six with three-speed manual shift, rocker panel moldings, FR78 x 15 SBR tires, radial-tuned suspension, and dual horns. Wagons had a 400-cid two-barrel V-8, Turbo-Hydra-Matic, power brakes and HR78 x 15 tires. Grand LeMans models had either a five-speed manual gearbox or Turbo-Hydra-Matic along with deluxe wheel covers and an electric clock. Both Grand LeMans and the Sport Coupe had wheel opening moldings and either full-width seating or bucket seats. A new five-speed manual transmission was available on the LeMans Sport Coupe.

FIREBIRD — SERIES 2F — (SIX/V-8) — Four models made up the famed Firebird lineup: base, Esprit, and performance-minded Formula and Trans Am. Each featured body-colored urethane bumpers at both ends this year. Base power plant was the 250-cid inline six, but Trans Am could go as high as a 455-cid V-8. New options this year included a canopy top, new appearance package (Formula only) and fuel economy indicator. Trans Am came in five body colors: Cameo White, Firethorn Red, Sterling Silver, Carousel Red and Goldenrod Yellow. Firebirds typical twin-section grille with mesh pattern sat in a sloping front panel. Single square headlamps were recessed. Park/signal lamps stood at the ends of a wide opening below the bumper strip. Standard Firebird/Esprit equipment included the 250-cid six with three-speed manual gearbox, dual horns, FR78 x 15 black sidewall SBR tires, power steering, and radial-tuned suspension. Esprit included sport mirrors (driver's side remote-controlled) and deluxe wheel covers. The Formula Firebird had a 350-cid two-barrel V-8, either a four-speed manual or Turbo-Hydra-Matic transmission, sport mirrors, and a full-length console. The Trans Am included an air dam, rear deck lid spoiler, shaker hood, Rally II wheels with trim rings, rally gauges, GR70 x 15 tires, and the 400-cid four-barrel V-8.

VENTURA — SERIES 2X — (SIX/V-8) — Compact in size, Ventura came in base and SJ trim, in three body styles: two-door coupe or hatchback and four-door sedan. Ventura rode a 111-in. wheelbase

1976 Pontiac Firebird Trans Am SE two-door hardtop. (PGMC)

1976 Pontiac Grand Prix LJ 50th Anniversary T-top coupe. (PGMC)

1976 Pontiac Bonneville Brougham four-door sedan. (PGMC)

and carried a standard 250-cid inline six-cylinder engine. Two V-8s were optional: 260- or 350-cid. A new five-speed manual gearbox became optional on models with the 260-cid V-8 engine. Options included cruise control and a landau coupe roof. An appearance group including special body striping and black window frames was offered on two-door models. Single round headlamps were mounted in squarish housings. On each side of a peaked divider bar were crosshatch grille inserts arranged in three rows (with two horizontal divider bars). Park/signal lamps stood behind bars at the outer ends of the grille. Venturas standard equipment included the 250-cid six with three-speed manual (floor lever) transmission, heater/defroster, E78 x 14 black sidewall tires, windshield and back window moldings, and carpeting. Hatchbacks and sedans also had roof drip moldings. Hatchbacks included a fold-down back seat. Ventura SJ added custom finned wheel covers, dual horns, courtesy lamps, rocker panel and wheel opening moldings, window moldings, and full-width front seats.

ASTRE — SERIES 2H — (FOUR) — Pontiacs subcompact came in two-door coupe or hatchback form or as a Safari two-door station wagon. Round headlamps sat in "squarish" recessed housings. A recessed two-section crosshatch (egg-crate) grille held rather large, inset parking/signal lights. On the body-color grille divider (a Pontiac "trademark") was the typical V-shaped emblem. Below the bumper was a wide air intake slot. Two new interior trim packages were available. The luxury version included doeskin seats, luxury door trim, upgraded sound insulation, and thick, cut-pile carpeting. Standard equipment included a 140-cid (2.3-liter) four-cylinder engine with one-barrel carburetor, three-speed manual gearbox (floor shift), front bucket seats, heater/defroster, A78 x 13 black sidewall tires, inside hood release, and window and roof drip moldings. A new five-speed manual gearbox (overdrive fifth gear) became optional. Astres GT option was offered on both hatchback and wagon, included a two-barrel version of the 140-cid four, four-speed gearbox, BR78 x 13 SBR tires, and rally gauge cluster.

SUNBIRD — SERIES 2H — (FOUR) — New for 1976, the sporty subcompact Sunbird rode a 97-in. wheelbase. Base engine was a 140-cid (2.3-liter) four, with new 231-cid (3.8-liter) V-6 from Buick optional. Sunbird's standard interior included bucket seats in cloth and Morrokide. Both rectangular quad headlamps and the twin crosshatch grille inserts were recessed between the customary Pontiac divider with V-shaped emblem. Standard equipment included a three-speed floor shift, a manual transmission, heater/defroster, front bucket seats, carpeting, custom wheel covers, window and roof drip moldings, wheel opening moldings, and A78 x 13 black sidewall tires. A luxury appointment group was optional. So was a new five-speed manual transmission.

I.D. DATA: The 13-symbol Vehicle Identification Number (VIN) was located on the upper left surface of the instrument panel, visible

1976 Pontiac Formula Firebird two-door hardtop. (PGMC)

through the windshield. The first digit is 2, indicating Pontiac division. The second symbol is a letter indicating series: C=Astre; M=Sunbird; Y=Ventura; Z=Ventura SJ; D=LeMans; F=LeMans Sport Coupe; G=Grand LeMans; S=Firebird; T=Firebird Esprit; U=Firebird Formula; W=Firebird Trans Am; L=Catalina; P=Bonneville; R=Bonneville Brougham; J=Grand Prix; K=Grand Prix SJ. Next come two digits that denote body type: 11=two-door pillar coupe; 17=two-door hatchback coupe; 27=two-door thin-pillar coupe; 37=two-door hardtop; 47=two-door hardtop; 57=two-door hardtop; 77=two-door hatchback coupe; 87=two-door hardtop; 29=four-door hardtop; 49=four-door hardtop; 69=four-door thin-pillar four-window sedan; 15=two-door station wagon; 35=four-door two-seat wagon; 45=four-door three-seat wagon. The fifth symbol is a letter indicating engine code: A=140-cid I4 one-barrel; B=140-cid I4 two-barrel; C=231-cid V-6 two-barrel; D=250-cid I6 one-barrel; F=260-cid V-8 two-barrel; H or M=350-cid V-8 two-barrel; E or J=350-cid V-8 four-barrel; R=400-cid V-8 two-barrel; S=400-cid V-8 four-barrel W=455-cid V-8 four-barrel. The sixth symbol denotes model year (6=1976). Next is a plant code: A=Lakewood, Ga.; C=South Gate, Calif.; G=Framingham, Mass.; L=Van Nuys, Calif.; N=Norwood, Ohio; P=Pontiac, Mich.; T=Tarrytown, N.Y.; U=Lordstown, Ohio; W=Willow Run, Mich.; X=Fairfax, Kan.; 1=Oshawa, Ontario; 2=Ste. Therese, Quebec. The final six digits are the sequential serial number, which began with 100,001.

Model Number	Body Style Number	Body Type & Seating	Factory Price	Shipping Weight	Production Total
CATALINA (V-8)					
2B	L57	2d Hardtop -6P	4,844	4,256	15,262
2B	L69	4d Sedan-6P	4,767	4,276	47,235
CATALINA SAFARI (V-8)					
2B	L35	4d Sta Wagon-6P	5,324	4,944	4,735
2B	L45	4d Sta Wagon-9P	5,473	5,000	5,513
BONNEVILLE (V-8)					
2B	P47	2d Hardtop -6P	5,246	4,308	9,189
2B	P49	4d Hardtop -6P	5,312	4,460	14,942
BONNEVILLE BROUGHAM (V-8)					
2B	R47	2d Hardtop -6P	5,734	4,341	10,466
2B	R49	4d Hardtop -6P	5,906	4,514	20,236
GRAND SAFARI (V-8)					
2B	P35	4d Sta Wagon-6P	5,746	5,035	3,462
2B	P45	4d Sta Wagon-9P	5,895	5,091	6,176
GRAND PRIX (V-8)					
2G	J57	2d Hardtop-5P	4,798	4,048	110,814
GRAND PRIX SJ (V-8)					
2G	K57	2d Hardtop-5P	5,223	4,052	88,232
GRAND PRIX LJ (V-8)					
2G	—	2d Hardtop -5P	—	—	29,045

1976 Pontiac Grand LeMans Safari four-door station wagon. (CP)

1976 Pontiac Astre three-door hatchback. (OCW)

1976 Pontiac Firebird Trans Am two-door hardtop. (JAG)

Model Number	Body Style Number	Body Type & Seating	Factory Price	Shipping Weight	Production Total
LEMANS (SIX/V-8)					
2A	D37	2d Hardtop-6P	3,768/3,908	3,651/3,826	21,130
2A	D29	4d Hardtop -6P	3,813/3,953	3,760/3,935	22,199
LEMANS SAFARI (V-8)					
2A	D35	4d Sta Wagon-6P	4,687	4,336	Note 2
2A	D45	4d Sta Wagon-9P	4,820	4,374	Note 2
LEMANS SPORT COUPE (SIX/V-8)					
2A	F37	2d Hardtop-6P	3,916/4,056	3,668/3,843	15,582
GRAND LEMANS (SIX/V-8)					
2A	G37	2d Hardtop -6P	4,330/4,470	3,747/3,922	14,757
2A	G29	4d Hardtop -6P	4,433/4,573	3,860/4,035	8,411
GRAND LEMANS SAFARI (V-8)					
2A	G35	4d Sta Wagon-6P	4,928	4,389	Note 2
2A	G45	4d Sta Wagon-9P	5,061	4,427	Note 2
FIREBIRD (SIX/V-8)					
2F	S87	2d Hardtop -4P	3,906/4,046	3,383/3,563	21,209
FIREBIRD ESPRIT (SIX/V-8)					
2F	T87	2d Hardtop -4P	4,162/4,302	3,431/3,611	22,252
FIREBIRD FORMULA (V-8)					
2F	U87	2d Hardtop -4P	4,566	3,625	20,613
FIREBIRD TRANS AM (V-8)					
F	W87	2d Hardtop -4P	4,987	3,640	46,701
VENTURA (SIX/V-8)					
2X	Y27	2d Coupe-5P	3,326/3,416	3,234/3,393	28,473
2X	Y17	2d Hatchback-5P	3,503/3,593	3,348/3,507	6,428
2X	Y69	4d Sedan-5P	3,361/3,451	3,271/3,430	27,773
VENTURA SJ (SIX/V-8)					
2X	Z27	2d Coupe-5P	3,612/3,702	3,290/3,449	4,815
2X	Z17	2d Hatchback-5P	3,775/3,865	3,380/3,539	1,823
2X	Z69	4d Sedan-5P	3,637/3,727	3,326/3,485	4,804
ASTRE (FOUR)					
2H	C11	2d Coupe-4P	3,064	2,439	18,143
2H	C77	2d Hatchback-4P	3,179	2,505	19,116
2H	C15	2d Safari Wag-4P	3,306	2,545	13,125
SUNBIRD (FOUR/V-6)					
2H	M27	2d Coupe-4P	3,431/3,607	2,653/ —	52,031

NOTE 1: LJ was actually a $625 option package for Grand Prix.

NOTE 2: A total of 8,249 two-seat (six-passenger) and 5,901 three-seat (nine-passenger) LeMans Safari wagons were produced (base and Grand).

NOTE 3: Data above slash for six/below slash or no slash for V-8.

ENGINE [Base Four Astre/Sunbird]: Inline. Overhead cam. Four-cylinder. Aluminum block and cast-iron head. Displacement: 140 cid. (2.3 liters). Bore & stroke: 3.50 x 3.63 in. Compression ratio: 7.9:1. Brake horsepower: 70 at 4400 rpm. Torque: 107 lbs.-ft. at 2400 rpm. Five main bearings. Hydraulic valve lifters. Carburetor: one-barrel Rochester. VIN Code: A.

1976 Pontiac Ventura SJ four-door sedan. (OCW)

1976 Pontiac Grand LeMans four-door sedan. (JAG)

ENGINE [Optional Four Astre/Sunbird]: Same as 140-cid four above, except Horsepower: 84 at 4400 rpm. Torque: 113 lbs.-ft. at 3200 rpm. Carburetor: two-barrel Holley 366829. VIN Code: B.

ENGINE [Optional V-6 Sunbird]: 90-degree, overhead-valve V-6. Cast-iron block and head. Displacement: 231 cid. (3.8 liters). Bore & stroke: 3.80 x 3.40 in. Compression ratio: 8.0:1. Brake horsepower: 105 at 3400 rpm. Torque: 185 lbs.-ft. at 2000 rpm. Four main bearings. Hydraulic valve lifters. Carburetor: two-barrel Rochester. VIN Code: C.

ENGINE [Base Six Ventura/Firebird/LeMans]: Inline. Overhead valve. Six-cylinder. Cast-iron block and head. Displacement: 250 cid. (4.1 liters). Bore & stroke: 3.87 x 3.53 in. Compression ratio: 8.3:1. Brake horsepower: 110 at 3600 rpm. Torque: 185 lbs.-ft. at 1200 rpm. Seven main bearings. Hydraulic valve lifters. Carburetor: one-barrel Rochester. VIN Code: D.

ENGINE [Optional V-8 (Ventura/LeMans)]: 90-degree, overhead valve V-8. Cast-iron block and head. Displacement: 260 cid. (4.3 liters). Bore & stroke: 3.50 x 3.39 in. Compression ratio: 7.5:1. Brake horsepower: 110 at 3400 rpm. Torque: 205 lbs.-ft. at 1600 rpm. Five main bearings. Hydraulic valve lifters. Carburetor: two-barrel Rochester. VIN Code: F.

ENGINE [Base V-8 (Grand Prix/ Firebird/ Formula); Optional (Firebird/LeMans)]: 90-degree, overhead valve V-8. Cast-iron block and head. Displacement: 350 cid. (5.7 liters). Bore & stroke: 3.88 x 3.75 in. Compression ratio: 7.6:1. Brake horsepower: 160 at 4000 rpm. Torque: 280 lbs.-ft. at 2000 rpm. Five main bearings. Hydraulic valve lifters. Carburetor: two-barrel Rochester. VIN Code: H or M.

ENGINE [Optional V-8 (Ventura)]: 90-degree, overhead valve V-8. Cast-iron block and head. Displacement: 350 cid. (5.7 liters). Bore & stroke: 3.80 x 3.85 in. Brake horsepower: 140 at 3200 rpm. Torque: 280 lbs.-ft. at 1600 rpm. Five main bearings. Hydraulic valve lifters. Carburetor: two-barrel Rochester.

ENGINE [Base V-8 (Catalina, Bonneville, LeMans Safari wagon); Optional V-8 (Ventura)]: Same as 350-cid V-8 above, with Rochester four-barrel carburetor. Horsepower: 155 at 3400 rpm. Torque: 280 lbs.-ft. at 1800 rpm.

ENGINE [Optional V-8 (LeMans/Grand Prix)]: 90-degree, overhead valve V-8. Cast-iron block and head. Displacement: 400 cid. (6.6 liters). Bore & stroke: 4.12 x 3.75 in. Compression ratio: 7.6:1. Brake horsepower: 170 at 4000 rpm. Torque: 310 lbs.-ft. at 1600 rpm. Five main bearings. Hydraulic valve lifters. Carburetor: two-barrel Rochester. VIN Code: R.

ENGINE [Base V-8 (Trans Am/Bonneville Brougham/Grand Prix SJ); Optional V-8 (LeMans/Firebird/Grand Prix/Catalina/ Bonneville)]: Same as 400-cid V-8 above, except Horsepower: 185 at 3600 rpm. Torque: 310 lbs.-ft. at 1600 rpm. Carburetor: four-barrel Rochester. VIN Code: S.

1976 Pontiac LeMans Sport Coupe two-door hardtop. (JAG)

1976 Pontiac Sunbird two-door coupe. (OCW)

1976 Pontiac Firebird Espirit two-door hardtop. (OCW)

ENGINE [Base V-8 (Catalina and Grand Safari wagons); Optional V-8 (LeMans/Firebird/Grand Prix/Catalina/Bonneville)]: 90-degree, overhead valve V-8. Cast-iron block and head. Displacement: 455 cid. (7.5 liters). Bore & stroke: 4.15 x 4.21 in. Compression ratio: 7.6:1. Brake horsepower: 200 at 3500 rpm. Torque: 330 lbs.-ft. at 2000 rpm. Five main bearings. Hydraulic valve lifters. Carburetor: four-barrel Rochester. VIN Code: W.

CHASSIS: Wheelbase: (Astre/Sunbird) 97.0 in.; (Ventura) 111.1 in.; (Firebird) 108.1 in.; (LeMans two-door) 112.0 in.; (LeMans four-door) 116.0 in.; (Grand Prix) 116.0 in.; (Catalina coupe/sedan) 123.4 in.; (Catalina station wagon) 127.0 in.; (Bonneville) 123.4 in. Overall Length: (Astre) 177.6 in.; (Sunbird) 177.8 in.; (Ventura) 199.6 in.; (Firebird) 196.8 in.; (LeMans two-door) 208.0 in.; (LeMans four-door) 212.0 in.; (LeMans station wagon) 215.4 in.; (G.P.) 212.7 in.; (Catalina coupe/sedan and Bonneville) 226.0 in.; (Catalina station wagon) 231.3 in. Height: (Astre hatchback) 50.0 in.; (Astre coupe/station wagon) 51.8 in.; (Sunbird) 49.8 in.; (Ventura two-door) 52.3 in.; (Ventura four-door) 53.2 in.; (Firebird) 49.1 in.; (LeMans two-door) 52.7 in.; (LeMans four-door) 53.5 in.; (LeMans station wagon) 55.3 in.; (Esprit/Formula) 49.4 in.; (Trans Am) 49.6 in.; (G.P.) 52.6 in.; (Catalina coupe) 53.5 in.; (Catalina sedan, Bonneville) 54.2 in.; (Catalina station wagon) 57.8 in. Width: (Astre/Sunbird) 65.4 in.; (Ventura) 72.4 in.; (Firebird) 73.0 in.; (LeMans) 77.4 in.; (G.P.) 77.8 in.; (Catalina coupe/sedan, Bonneville) 79.6 in.; (Catalina station wagon) 79.4 in. Front Tread: (Astre/Sunbird) 55.2 in.; (Ventura) 61.8 in.; (Firebird) 60.9 in.; (Firebird Formula) 61.3 in.; (Trans Am) 61.2 in.; (LeMans) 61.6 in.; (G.P.) 61.6 in.; (Catalina/Bonneville) 63.9 in. Rear Tread: (Astre/Sunbird) 54.1 in.; (Ventura) 59.6 in.; (Firebird) 60.0 in.; (Firebird Formula) 60.4 in.; (LeMans) 61.1 in.; (Trans Am) 60.3 in.; (G.P.) 61.1 in.; (Catalina/Bonneville) 64.0 in. Standard Tires: (Astre) A78 x 13; (Sunbird) A78 x 13 except V-6, B78 x 13; (Ventura) E78 x 14; (Firebird) FR78 x 15; (Firebird Formula) not available; (Trans Am) GR70 x 15; (LeMans) FR78 x 15 except station wagon, HR78 x 15; (G.P.) GR78 x 15; (Catalina) HR78 x 15 except station wagon, LR78 x 15; (Bonneville) HR78 x 15.

TECHNICAL: Transmission: Three-speed manual transmission standard on Astre, Sunbird, Ventura, LeMans and Firebird six (floor lever except Ventura/LeMans). Optional four-speed manual shift on

Astre/Sunbird four-cylinder. Optional four-speed on Astre/Sunbird six. Four-speed manual shift on Firebird V-8. Three-speed Turbo-Hydra-Matic standard on Grand Prix, Catalina and Bonneville; optional on others. Astre/Sunbird automatic available. Standard final drive ratio: (Astre) 2.92:1 with three-speed transmission, 2.93:1 with four-speed transmission, 2.92:1 with automatic transmission; (Sunbird) 2.92:1 with three-speed transmission, 2.93:1 with four-speed transmission, 2.92:1 with automatic transmission, 3.42:1 with 87 hp four, 2.56:1 with V-6; (Ventura six) 2.73:1 with three-speed transmission, 2.73:1 or 3.08:1 with automatic transmission; (Ventura V-8) 2.56:1; (Firebird six) 2.73:1; (Firebird V-8) 2.41:1; (LeMans) 2.73:1 with three-speed transmission, 2.73:1 or 3.08:1 with automatic transmission; (LeMans V-8-260) 3.08:1 with three-speed transmission, 2.73:1 with automatic transmission; (LeMans V-8-350/400) 2.41:1; (LeMans V-8-400 wagon) 2.56:1; (Trans Am) 3.08:1 with four-speed transmission, 3.23:1 with V-8-455; (Grand Prix) 2.41:1; (Catalina) 2.41:1 except wagon, 2.56:1; (Bonneville) 2.56:1. Steering: Recirculating ball. Front Suspension: (Astre) coil springs and control arms; (Firebird/LeMans) coil springs with lower trailing links and anti-sway bar; (others) coil springs and anti-sway bar. Rear Suspension: (Astre/Sunbird) rigid axle with coil springs, lower trailing radius arms and upper torque arms; (Ventura/Firebird) semi-elliptic leaf springs with anti-sway bar; (LeMans/Bonneville/Grand Prix) rigid axle with coil springs, lower trailing radius arms, upper torque arms and anti-sway bar; Brakes: Front disc, rear drum. Ignition: Electronic. Body construction: (Astre/Sunbird) unit; (Ventura) unit with front frame section; (Firebird) unit with separate partial frame; (others) separate body and frame. Fuel tank: (Astre) 16 gal.; (Sunbird) 18.5 gal.; (Ventura) 20.5 gal.; (Firebird) 20.2 gal.; (LeMans) 21.8 gal.; (Grand Prix) 25 gal.; (Catalina) 25.8 gal. except wagon, 22 gal.; (Bonneville) 25.8 gal.

DRIVETRAIN OPTIONS: Engines: 140-cid two-barrel four: Astre/Sunbird ($56). 231-cid V-6: Sunbird ($176). 260-cid two-barrel V-8: Ventura/LeMans ($90). 350-cid two-barrel V-8: Ventura/LeMans/Firebird ($140). 350-cid four-barrel V-8: Ventura/LeMans/Firebird ($195); Firebird Formula ($55); Grand Prix ($55). 400-cid two-barrel V-8: LeMans ($203); Grand Prix ($63). 400-cid four-barrel V-8: LeMans/Firebird ($258); LeMans wagon ($55); Firebird Formula ($118); Catalina/Bonneville ($73); Grand Prix ($118). 455-cid V-8: LeMans ($321); LeMans wagon ($118); Catalina/Bonneville ($137); Bonneville brougham ($64); Grand Prix ($181); Grand Prix SJ ($63). Performance package (455 V-8): Trans Am ($125). Transmission/Differential: Three-speed floor shift: Ventura ($29). Four-speed manual transmission: Astre/Sunbird ($60). Close-ratio four-speed: Firebird ($242). Five-speed manual transmission: Astre/Sunbird ($244); Ventura ($262); LeMans Sport Coupe ($262); Firebird ($262); Formula/

1976 Pontiac Firebird Espirit two-door hardtop. (OCW)

1976 Pontiac Grand Prix SJ two-door hardtop. (PGMC)

1976 Pontiac Bonneville Brougham two-door hardtop. (JAG)

Trans Am (NC). Turbo-Hydra-Matic: Astre ($244); Ventura/LeMans ($262); Grand LeMans (NC). M40 Turbo-Hydra-Matic: LeMans ($286); Grand LeMans ($24); LeMans wagon (NC). Safe-T-Track differential: Astre/Sunbird ($48); Ventura/LeMans/Firebird ($51); Catalina/Bonneville ($55); Grand Prix Suspension: Radial-tuned suspension: Astre ($130-$162). Rally RTS handling package: Astre ($12); Sunbird ($24); Ventura ($40); LeMans ($57-$101); Grand Prix ($66-$89). Firm ride package: Ventura/LeMans ($10); Catalina/Bonneville ($10). Super lift shock absorbers: LeMans ($46); Catalina/Bonneville ($47); Grand Prix ($46). Automatic level control: Catalina/Bonneville ($46-$93). Other: Heavy-duty radiator: Astre/Sunbird ($28); Ventura ($18). Super-cooling radiator: LeMans/Firebird/Grand Prix ($27-$49); Catalina/Bonneville ($27-$50). Heavy-duty battery ($15-$17). Heavy-duty alternator: LeMans/Firebird ($42); Catalina/Bonneville ($43); Grand Prix ($42). Engine block heater ($11-$12). Medium trailer group: LeMans ($97-$119); Catalina/Bonneville ($98-$121); Grand Prix ($97-$119). Heavy trailer group ($109-$165). California emissions ($50).

MAJOR CONVENIENCE/APPEARANCE OPTIONS: Air conditioning ($424-$512). Automatic air conditioning: LeMans ($513); Grand Prix ($542); Catalina/Bonneville ($549). Cruise control ($73); not available on Sunbird/Astre. Power seat: LeMans/Catalina/Bonneville/G.P. ($124-$126). Power windows ($99-$159); not available on Sunbird/Astre. Cornering lamps: Catalina/Bonneville/Grand Prix ($41). Power sun roof: LeMans/Grand Prix ($370). Removable sun roof: Sunbird ($149). Landau top: LeMans ($109-$119); Catalina/Bonneville ($125-$150). Rear-facing third seat: Safari ($149). Wood-grain siding: Safari wagons ($154-$156).

OPTION PACKAGES: Astre GT package: hatchback/Safari ($426-$465). Astre luxury appointment group: hatchback/Safari ($104). Astre custom exterior ($59-$88). Sunbird luxury appointment group ($139). Sunbird luxury trim group ($126). Ventura special appearance group: two-door ($70-$92). LeMans custom trim group: sedan ($88). Firebird custom trim group ($81). Firebird Formula appearance package ($100). Catalina custom group ($201-$228). Grand Prix LJ luxury appointments group ($336-$680). Grand Prix SJ golden anniversary package ($550).

HISTORICAL: Introduced: Sept. 25, 1975. Model year production: 748,842 units. Calendar year production (U.S.): 784,630 units. Calendar year sales by U.S. dealers: 753,093. Model year sales by U.S. dealers: 700,931. This was Pontiac's Golden Anniversary year, marking the 50th anniversary of the introduction of the Pontiac Series 6-27. Production rose for the model year and sales jumped even more. Only the sub-compact Astre found fewer customers in 1976 than the prior year.

1977 PONTIAC

CATALINA — SERIES 2B — (V-8) — Though reduced in outside dimensions and weighing considerably less than before, both Catalina and Bonneville offered more headroom and rear legroom. The new design featured less door glass curvature, as well as a higher roofline. Full-size models rode a 116-in. wheelbase. Front ends held quad rectangular headlamps. Mechanical features included a Freedom battery and engine/air conditioning electrical diagnostic connector. Catalinas had a new brushed-knit cloth interior. Catalina's horizontal-theme grille had a slightly V-shaped center vertical segment (with Pontiac v

1977 Pontiac Astre Safari three-door station wagon. (P)

emblem). It was part of a bold frame containing three horizontal bars (upper, lower and center), which stood ahead of a set of horizontal ribs, forming four sections in all (two on each side). Parking/signal lights were below the bumper rub strip, while two-section marker lenses wrapped around the front fender, following the line of the quad rectangular headlamps. Two horizontal slots were in the bumper, just inside the bumper guards. Base engine was a 231-cid (3.8-liter) V-6; 350-cid and 403-cid V-8s were optional. Safari and Grand Safari station wagons had a new three-way tailgate, two lockable storage areas, standard 350-cid V-8 and available rear-facing third seat. All full-size coupes and sedans had a CB radio option. Standard equipment included automatic transmission; power brakes and steering; FR78 x 15 black sidewall glass-belted radial tires; heater/defroster; and moldings at roof drip, window, wheel openings, and rocker panels.

BONNEVILLE — SERIES 2B — (V-8) — Offered in coupe and sedan form, the new Bonneville had a flush egg-crate-style grille pattern on each side of the central "V" segment (with Pontiac emblem). Left and right grille segments formed a 4 x 4 pattern, with each segment containing internal crosshatching to create a pattern within a pattern. The grille pattern was repeated in two bumper slots, just inside the bumper guards. Framing for the quad rectangular headlamps continued outward to enclose four-section marker lenses. Park/signal lights were in the bumper. Interior choices were Lombardy velour cloth or Morrokide. Base engine was the 350-cid (5.7-liter) four-barrel V-8 with a 6.6-liter V-8 available. The Bonneville Brougham included a luxury interior package and could be had with Valencia striped cloth trim. Standard Bonneville equipment was similar to the Catalina's, but included rear fender skirts, deluxe wheel covers, and a luxury steering wheel. The Bonneville Brougham added a Cordova top, driver's remote mirror, 60/40 seat with center armrest, power windows, and custom interior trim. Wagons had HR78 x 15 tires and a three-way tailgate with power back window.

GRAND PRIX — SERIES 2G — (V-8) — Three personal-luxury models of the Grand Prix were offered this year: base, sporty SJ, and luxury LJ. Base and LJ models had a standard 350-cid (5.7-liter) V-8, while the SJ came with a 6.6-liter V-8 (optional in the others). New Grand Prix options included CB radios and a digital AM/FM stereo information center and clock. This year's grille was

1977 Pontiac Formula Sunbird two-door coupe. (P)

1977 Pontiac Ventura SJ two-door coupe. (P)

1977 Pontiac LeMans Sport coupe two-door hardtop. (CP)

no longer a wrap-over style. It had only five vertical sections of bold elements on each side of the divider. The grille pattern repeated in two sections below the bumper. Quad rectangular headlamps were now separated by clear park/signal lights forming three separate units on each side. Narrow amber vertical marker lenses stood to the rear of the front fender tips. Both hood and deck lid showed sharp creases. Standard equipment included power brakes and steering, GR78 x 15 black sidewall steel-belted radial tires, three-speed automatic transmission, heater/defroster, wheel opening and rocker panel moldings, window and roof drip moldings, and a clock. The LJ added velour seat upholstery, a remote-controlled driver's mirror, and deluxe wheel covers. The SJ had a 6.6-liter V-8 engine, GR70 x 15 tires, Rally II wheels with trim rings, accent striping, bucket seats with console, Rally RTS handling package, and rally gauges.

LEMANS — SERIES 2A — (V-6/V-8) — The mid-size LeMans had a new front-end appearance and revised engine selections. Base engine was the 231-cid (3.8-liter) V-6, except for Safari wagons that had a standard 350-cid (5.7-liter) V-8. The 6.6-liter V-8 was available on all models. New LeMans options included 15-in. cast aluminum wheels, wire wheel covers and new-styled deluxe wheel covers. Grand LeMans could get a new AM/FM radio with digital clock. A LeMans GT option (for Sport coupe) included distinctive two-tone paint, bold striping, Rally RTS handling package and body-color Rally II wheels. Base LeMans models had quad rectangular headlamps alongside a grille made up only of heavy vertical bars, forming six sections on each side of a protruding center divider. That divider formed a point that carried forward from the prominent hood creases and contained the triangular Pontiac emblem at the tip. Headlamp frames continued outward to surround wraparound single-section marker lenses. Park/signal lights were at the outer ends of twin bumper slots. The Grand LeMans had a similar front-end look, but its grille sections included a horizontal divider forming a 5 x 2 pattern of square holes on each side. Each of those 20 holes contained a smaller square. One of the more notable Pontiacs of the decade was the Can Am—a performance version of the LeMans Sport coupe. Only 1,377 were produced. The Can Am included the performance T/A 400-cid (6.6-liter) V-8 (or a 403-cid V-8 in California) along with body-colored Rally II wheels, a blacked-out grille assembly, and GR70 x 15 SBR tires. The Can Am was promoted as a "fun car" along with Trans Am and was offered only in a

Cameo White body color. Standard equipment included Turbo-Hydra-Matic transmission, power brakes, variable-ratio power steering, front and rear stabilizer bars, body-color Rally II wheels, front/rear protective rubber bumper strips, and body-color dual sport mirrors (driver's side remote-controlled). A Grand Prix instrument panel assembly included a rally gauge cluster and clock. A Rally RTS handling package was standard. Appearance features included tri-tone colored accent tape striping on hood, front fenders, doors, and sport mirrors; black lower body side with accent stripe; black rocker panel moldings; full-width rear deck spoiler with tri-tone accent stripe (front and rear); tri-tone "Can Am" identification on front end, front fender, and rear deck; blacked-out windshield, backlight, door window, and belt moldings; and unique "Can Am" interior identification. The Trans Am-style "shaker" hood scoop had tri-tone "T/A 6.6" identification and accent stripes. Early Can Am models also included a selection of options: Saf-T-Track rear axle, white-letter GR70 x 15 tires, custom sport steering wheels, Soft Ray tinted glass, dual horns, front/rear floor mats, and custom color-keyed seatbelts. Other available options included an air-conditioning system, a radio and the choice of White, Black, or Firethorn interior trim color (or Firethorn-and-White) in notchback, full-width, or bucket seats.

FIREBIRD — SERIES 2F — (V-6/V-8) — New front-end styling for the Firebird coupe featured quad rectangular headlamps and an "aggressive" grille. Four models were offered: base, Esprit, and performance Formula and Trans Am. Formula's new hood held simulated air scoops and at its rear was a spoiler. The wheelbase was 108 in. and engine choices ranged from a 231-cid (3.8-liter) V-6 to the 403-cid (6.6-liter) V-8. Firebird's new grille was deeply recessed, directly in line with the quad rectangular headlamps. Its simple pattern consisted of a series of round-like (hexagonal) holes, resembling fencing more than a customary grille. A "Pontiac" nameplate went on the driver's side of the grille. Crossbar-trimmed amber park/signal lamps were also recessed, but into the outer ends of twin air intake slots below the bumper strip. The center front panel protruded forward to a slight point and contained the usual Pontiac emblem, but its sides were more sharply angled than the prior version. Esprit could have a new blue "Sky Bird" appearance package with blue velour seating, two-tone blue body and blue cast aluminum wheels. Firebird Formula came with a new 301-cid (5.0-liter) two-barrel V-8. Its body displayed blacked-out trim, dual hood scoops, and large "Formula" graphics on the lower door. The Trans Am had a new shaker hood and came with a standard 400- or 403-cid V-8. Also available was an optional "T/A 6.6" power plant.

1977 Pontiac Formula Firebird two-door hardtop. (P)

1977 Pontiac Grand LeMans two-door hardtop. (P)

1977 Pontiac Grand Prix SJ two-door hardtop. (P)

1977 Pontiac Grand Prix SJ two-door T-top hardtop. (P)

1977 Pontiac Catalina four-door sedan. (P)

1977 Pontiac Catalina four-door sedan. (P)

1977 Pontiac Bonneville two-door hardtop. (P)

VENTURA — SERIES 2X — (FOUR/V-6/V-8) — Ventura featured a new grille design, as well as a plusher interior with Grand Prix-style dash. Base and SJ models came in coupe, hatchback, and sedan models. Base engine was the 231-cid (3.8-liter) V-6, with a 301- or 350-cid V-8 available. Three-speed column shift was standard; four-speed manual optional with V-8 power; a five-speed with the available four-cylinder engine. Ventura's grille had a wide body-color center panel (with customary Pontiac emblem) to split the twin sections. Each section contained six rectangular holes (two rows), each of which had an internal vertical-theme pattern. Single round rectangular headlamps met two-section marker lenses on the fender sides. Front bumpers held two small slots. Parking/signal lamps were behind the outer grille section.

ASTRE — SERIES 2H — (FOUR) — Once again, the sub-compact Astre came in coupe, three-door hatchback, and two-door Safari Wagon forms. This year it had a fresh front-end look with a new grille, as well as revised interior trim. Astre's front end held single round headlamps in round recessed housings. On each side of the body-color V-shaped center panel (with Pontiac V-shaped emblem) were four holes in a single row that formed the grille. The outer "holes" were actually the park/signal lights, while the others contained a set of thin vertical strips. New Astre options included 13-in. cast aluminum wheels. A Luxury Trim group that included luxury seating, custom door trim with map pockets, rear ashtrays, and other extras was available in hatchback and Safari models. Base engine for the coupe was the 140-cid (2.3-liter) four, but hatchback and Safari models carried the new 151-cid (2.5-liter) "Iron Duke" four and standard four-speed manual transmission. A five-speed gearbox was optional, along with three-speed Turbo-Hydra-Matic.

SUNBIRD — SERIES 2H — (FOUR/V-6) — Like most other Pontiacs this year, Sunbird had a new grille and front-end appearance. Quad rectangular headlamps stood alongside a recessed grille that consisted of round elements, similar to the Firebird's. Base engine was the new 151-cid (2.5-liter) four, with 231-cid (3.8-liter) V-6 available. Also optional were cast-aluminum wheels. A new Sunbird Sport-Hatch (hatchback) version appeared with special paint and striping, joining the original two-door coupe.

PHOENIX — SERIES 2X — (FOUR/V-6/V-8) — Phoenix was a late arrival to the Pontiac lineup and replaced the Ventura late in 1977. Coupe, sedan, and hatchback models were offered. A wide center divider at the front held Pontiac lettering below a Pontiac emblem. Single rectangular headlamps and a grille with four vertical dividers characterized the front end. Base engine was the 231-cid (3.8-liter) V-6 with three-speed manual transmission. Standard equipment

1977 Pontiac Bonneville two-door hardtop. (P)

1977 Pontiac Bonneville Grand Safari four-door station wagon. (CP)

included E78 x 14 black sidewall tires, hubcaps, lighter, a heater and defroster, and a Grand Prix style instrument cluster.

I.D. DATA: Pontiac's 13-symbol Vehicle Identification Number (VIN) was located on the upper left surface of the instrument panel, visible through the windshield. The first digit is 2, indicating Pontiac division. The second symbol is a letter indicating series: C=Astre; M=Sunbird; X=Phoenix; Y=Ventura; Z=Ventura SJ; D=LeMans; F=LeMans Sport coupe; G=Grand LeMans; S=Firebird; T=Firebird Esprit; U=Firebird Formula; W=Firebird Trans Am; L=Catalina; N=Bonneville; Q=Bonneville Brougham; J=Grand Prix; K=Grand Prix LJ; H=Grand Prix SJ. Next come two digits that denote body type: 07=two-door hatchback coupe; 11=two-door pillared coupe; 17=two-door hatchback coupe; 27=two-door sport coupe; 37=two-door hardtop coupe; 57=two-door hardtop coupe; 77=two-door hatchback coupe; 87=two-door hardtop coupe; 29=four-door hardtop sedan; 69=four-door thin-pillar four-window sedan; 15=two-door station wagon; 35=four-door two-seat wagon. The fifth symbol is a letter indicating engine code: B=140-cid two-barrel I4; V=151-cid two-barrel I4; C=231-cid two-barrel V-6; Y=301-cid two-barrel V-8; U=305-cid four-barrel V-8; P=350-cid four-barrel V-8 (L76); R=350-cid four-barrel V-8 (L34); L=350-cid four-barrel V-8 (LM1); Z=400-cid four-barrel V-8; K=403-cid four-barrel V-8. The sixth symbol denotes model year (7=1977). Next is a plant code: A=Lakewood, Ga.; L=Van Nuys, Calif.; N=Norwood, Ohio; P=Pontiac, Mich.; T=Tarrytown, N.Y.; U=Lordstown, Ohio; W=Willow Run, Mich.; X=Fairfax, Kan.; 1=Oshawa, Ontario; 2=Ste. Therese, Quebec. The final six digits are the sequential serial number, starting with 100,001 (except Astre/Sunbird, 500,001).

Model Number	Body Style Number	Body Type & Seating	Factory Price	Shipping Weight	Production Total
CATALINA (V-6/V-8)					
2B	L37	2d Hardtop-6P	5,052/5,118	3,473/3,570	14,752
2B	L69	4d Sedan-6P	5,049/5,115	3,501/3,598	46,926
CATALINA SAFARI (V-8)					
2B	L35	4d Sta Wagon-6P	5,491	4,024	13,058
BONNEVILLE (V-8)					
2B	N37	2d Hardtop-6P	5,410	3,579	37,817
2B	N69	4d Sedan-6P	5,456	3,616	13,697
BONNEVILLE BROUGHAM (V-8)					
2B	Q37	2d Hardtop-6P	5,896	3,617	15,901
2B	Q69	4d Sedan-6P	5,991	3,680	47,465
GRAND SAFARI (V-8)					
2B	N35	4d Sta Wagon-6P	5,771	4,066	18,304
GRAND PRIX (V-8)					
2G	J57	2d Hardtop-6P	5,108	3,804	168,247
GRAND PRIX LJ (V-8)					
2G	K57	2d Hardtop-6P	5,471	3,815	66,741
GRAND PRIX SJ (V-8)					
2G	H57	2d Hardtop-6P	5,742	3,976	53,442
LEMANS (V-6/V-8)					
2A	D37	2d Hardtop-6P	4,045/4110	3550/3635	16,038

1977 Pontiac Astre two-door notchback coupe. (OCW)

1977 Pontiac Astre Formula two-door coupe. (OCW)

Model Number	Body Style Number	Body Type & Seating	Factory Price	Shipping Weight	Production Total
2A	D29	4d Hardtop-6P	4,093/4158	3638/3723	23,060
LEMANS SAFARI (V-8)					
2A	D35	4d Sta Wagon-6P	4,877	4135	10,081
LEMANS SPORT COUPE (V-6/V-8)					
2A	F37	2d Hardtop-6P	4,204/4269	3558/3643	12,277
LEMANS CAN AM (V-8)					
2A	not available	2d Hardtop-6P	—	—	1,377
GRAND LEMANS (V-6/V-8)					
2A	G37	2d Hardtop-6P	4,602/4,667	3,587/3,672	7,581
2A	G29	4d HT Sedan-6P	4,730/4,795	3,740/3,825	5,584
GRAND LEMANS SAFARI (V-8)					
2A	G35	4d Sta Wagon -6P	5,132	4,179	5,393
FIREBIRD (V-6/V-8)					
2F	S87	2d Hardtop-4P	4,269/4,334	3,264/3,349	30,642
FIREBIRD ESPRIT (V-6/V-8)					
2F	T87	2d Hardtop-4P	4,550/4,615	3,312/3,397	34,548
FIREBIRD FORMULA (V-8)					
2F	U87	2d Hardtop-4P	4,976	3,411	21,801
FIREBIRD TRANS AM (V-8)					
2F	W87	2d Hardtop-4P	5,456	3,526	68,745
VENTURA (V-6/V-8)					
2X	Y27	2d Coupe-5P	3,596/3,661	3,127/3,212	26,675
2X	Y17	2d Hatchback-5P	3,791/3,856	3,249/3,334	4,015
2X	Y69	4d Sedan-5P	3,650/3,715	3,167/3,252	27,089
VENTURA SJ (V-6/V-8)					
2X	Z27	2d Coupe-5P	3,945/4,010	3,206/3,291	3,418
2X	Z17	2d Hatchback-5P	4,124/4,189	3,293/3,378	1,100
2X	Z69	4d Sedan-5P	3,972/4,037	3,236/3,321	4,339
ASTRE (FOUR)					
2H	C11	2d Coupe-4P	3,304	2,480	10,327
2H	C77	2d Hatchback-4P	3,429	2,573	12,120
2H	C15	2d Safari Wag-4P	3,594	2,608	10,341
SUNBIRD (FOUR/V-6)					
2H	M27	2d Coupe-4P	3,659/3,779	2,662/ —	41,708
2H	M07	2d Hatchback-4P	3,784/3,904	2,693/ —	13,690
PHOENIX (V-6/V-8)					
2X	X27	2d Coupe	4,075/4,075	3,227/3,339	10,489
2X	X69	4d Sedan	4,122/4,122	3,275/3,387	13,639

NOTE 1: Prices and weights above slash for V-6/below slash for V-8.

NOTE 2: A third seat was available in all Catalina Safari wagons.

NOTE 3: A third seat was available in all Grand Safari wagons.

NOTE 4: A four-cylinder engine was available for $120 credit.

ENGINE [Base Four (Astre coupe); Optional (Sunbird)]: Inline. Overhead cam. Four-cylinder. Aluminum block. Displacement: 140 cid. (2.3 liters). Bore & stroke: 3.50 x 3.63 in. Compression ratio: 8.0:1. Brake horsepower: 84 at 4400 rpm. Torque: 117 lbs.-ft. at 2400 rpm. Five main bearings. Hydraulic valve lifters. Carburetor: two-barrel VIN Code: B.

ENGINE [Base Four (Astre hatchback/wagon and Sunbird); Optional (Astre coupe and Ventura)]: Inline. Overhead valve.

1977 Pontiac Sunbird two-door coupe. (OCW)

Standard Catalog of ® Pontiac, 2nd Edition

1977 Pontiac Ventura three-door hatchback. (OCW)

Four-cylinder. Cast-iron block and head. Displacement: 151 cid. (2.5 liters). Bore & stroke: 4.00 x 3.00 in. Compression ratio: 8.3:1. Brake horsepower: 90 at 4400 rpm. Torque: 128 lbs.-ft. at 2400 rpm. Five main bearings. Hydraulic valve lifters. Carburetor: two-barrel Holley 5210C. VIN Code: V.

ENGINE [Base V-6 (Ventura/Firebird/LeMans/Catalina); Optional (Sunbird)]: 90-degree, overhead-valve V-6. Cast-iron block and head. Displacement: 231 cid. (3.8 liters). Bore & stroke: 3.80 x 3.40 in. Compression ratio: 8.0:1. Brake horsepower: 105 at 3200 rpm. Torque: 185 lbs.-ft. at 2000 rpm. Four main bearings. Hydraulic valve lifters. Carburetor: two-barrel Rochester 2GC. VIN Code: C.

ENGINE [Base V-8 (Firebird Formula/Bonneville/Grand Prix); Optional (Ventura/Firebird/LeMans/Catalina)]: 90-degree, overhead valve V-8. Cast-iron block and head. Displacement: 301 cid. (5.0 liters). Bore & stroke: 4.00 x 3.00 in. Compression ratio: 8.2:1. Brake horsepower: 135 at 3800 rpm. Torque: 235-245 lbs.-ft. at 2000 rpm. (full-size, 250 at 1600). Five main bearings. Hydraulic valve lifters. Carburetor: two-barrel VIN Code: Y.

ENGINE [Optional V-8 (Ventura/Firebird)]: 90-degree, overhead valve V-8. Cast-iron block and head. Displacement: 305 cid. (5.0 liters). Bore & stroke: 3.74 x 3.48 in. Compression ratio: 8.5:1. Brake horsepower: 145 at 3800 rpm. Torque: 245 lbs.-ft. at 2400 rpm. Five main bearings. Hydraulic valve lifters. Carburetor: two-barrel Rochester 2GC. VIN Code: U.

ENGINE [Optional V-8 (Firebird/LeMans/Catalina/Bonneville/Grand Prix)]: 90-degree, overhead valve V-8. Cast-iron block and head. Displacement: 350 cid. (5.7 liters). Bore & stroke: 3.88 x 3.75 in. Compression ratio: 7.6:1. Brake horsepower: 170 at 4000 rpm. Torque: 280 lbs.-ft. at 1800 rpm. Five main bearings. Hydraulic valve lifters. Carburetor: four-barrel Rochester M4MC. VIN Code: P.

ENGINE [Alternate V-8 (Firebird/LeMans/Catalina/Bonneville/Grand Prix)]: 90-degree, overhead valve V-8. Cast-iron block and head. Displacement: 350 cid. (5.7 liters). Bore & stroke: 4.00 x 3.48 in. Compression ratio: 8.5:1. Brake horsepower: 170 at 3800 rpm. Torque: 270 lbs.-ft. at 2400 rpm. Five main bearings. Hydraulic valve lifters. Carburetor: four-barrel Rochester M4MC. Chevrolet-built. VIN Code: L.

ENGINE [Alternate V-8 (Firebird/LeMans/Catalina/Bonneville/Grand Prix)]: 90-degree, overhead valve V-8. Cast-iron block and head. Displacement: 350 cid. (5.7 liters). Bore & stroke: 4.06 x 3.38 in. Compression ratio: 8.0:1. Brake horsepower: 170 at 3800 rpm. Torque: 275 lbs.-ft. at 2000 rpm. Five main bearings. Hydraulic valve lifters. Carburetor: four-barrel Rochester M4MC. Oldsmobile-built. VIN Code: R.

ENGINE [Base V-8 (Grand Prix SJ); Optional (Firebird/LeMans/Catalina/Bonneville/Grand Prix)]: 90-degree, overhead valve V-8.

1977 Pontiac LeMans "Can Am" two-door hardtop. (OCW)

Cast-iron block and head. Displacement: 400 cid. (6.6 liters). Bore & stroke: 4.12 x 3.75 in. Compression ratio: 7.6:1. Brake horsepower: 180 at 3600 rpm. Torque: 325 lbs.-ft. at 1600 rpm. Five main bearings. Hydraulic valve lifters. Carburetor: four-barrel Rochester M4MC. VIN Code: Z.

ENGINE [Base V-8 Firebird Trans Am]: Same as 400-cid V-8 above, except Compression ratio: 8.0:1. Horsepower: 200 at 3600 rpm. Torque: 325 lbs.-ft. at 2400 rpm.

ENGINE [Alternate V-8 (Firebird/LeMans/Catalina/Bonneville/Grand Prix)]: 90-degree, overhead valve V-8. Cast-iron block and head. Displacement: 403 cid. (6.6 liters). Bore & stroke: 4.35 x 3.38 in. Compression ratio: 8.0:1. Brake horsepower: 185 at 3600 rpm. Torque: 320 lbs.-ft. at 2200 rpm. Five main bearings. Hydraulic valve lifters. Carburetor: four-barrel Rochester M4MC. VIN Code: K.

CHASSIS: Wheelbase: (Astre/Sunbird) 97.0 in.; (Ventura) 111.1 in.; (Firebird) 108.1 in.; (LeMans two-door) 112.0 in.; (LeMans four-door) 116.0 in.; (Grand Prix) 116.0 in.; (Catalina/Bonneville) 115.9 in. Overall Length: (Astre) 177.6 in.; (Sunbird) 177.8 in.; (Ventura) 199.6 in.; (Firebird) 196.8 in.; (LeMans two-door) 208.0 in.; (LeMans four-door) 212.0 in.; (LeMans Safari) 215.4 in.; (Grand Prix) 212.7 in.; (Catalina/Bonneville) 213.8 in.; (Catalina Safari) 214.7 in. Height: (Astre hatchback) 50.0 in.; (Astre coupe/Safari) 51.8 in.; (Sunbird) 49.8 in.; (Ventura two-door) 52.3 in.; (Ventura four-door) 53.2 in.; (Firebird) 49.1 in.; (Esprit/Formula) 49.4 in.; (Trans Am) 49.6 in.; (LeMans two-door Hardtop) 52.7 in.; (LeMans four-door sedan) 53.5 in.; (LeMans Safari) 55.3 in.; (Grand Prix) 52.6 in.; (Catalina/Bonneville) 53.9 in.; (Catalina/Bonneville sedan) 53.2 in.; (Catalina Safari) 57.3 in. Width: (Astre/Sunbird) 65.4 in.; (Ventura) 72.4 in.; (Firebird) 73.0 in.; (LeMans) 77.4 in.; (Grand Prix) 77.8 in.; (Catalina/Bonneville) 75.4 in. Front Tread: (Astre/Sunbird) 55.2 in.; (Ventura) 61.2 in.; (Ventura SJ) 61.8 in.; (Firebird) 60.9 in.; (Firebird Formula) 61.3 in.; (Trans Am) 61.2 in.; (LeMans) 61.6 in.; (Grand Prix) 61.6 in.; (Catalina/Bonneville) 61.7 in. Rear Tread: (Astre/Sunbird) 54.1 in.; (Ventura) 59.0 in.; (Firebird) 60.0 in.; (Firebird Formula) 60.4 in.; (Trans Am) 60.3 in.; (LeMans) 61.1 in.; (Grand Prix) 61.1 in.; (Catalina/Bonneville) 60.7 in. Standard Tires: (Astre) A78 x 13 except Safari BR78 x 13; (Sunbird) A78 x 13; (Ventura) E78 x 14; (Firebird) FR78 x 15; (Trans Am) GR70 x 15; (LeMans) FR78 x 15 except Safari HR78 x 15; (Grand Prix) not available; (Grand Prix SJ) GR70 x 15; (Catalina) FR78 x 15 except Safari HR78 x 15; (Bonneville) FR78 x 15.

TECHNICAL: Transmission: Three-speed manual transmission standard on Ventura, LeMans and Firebird. Four-speed manual

1977 Pontiac Firebird Trans Am two-door hardtop. (OCW)

1977 Pontiac LeMans GT two-door hardtop. (OCW)

1977 Pontiac Grand LeMans Safari station wagon. (OCW)

transmission standard on Astre/Sunbird and Firebird Formula; optional on Firebird and Ventura V-8. Five-speed manual transmission optional on Astre/Sunbird and Ventura four-cylinder. Three-speed Turbo-Hydra-Matic standard on other models, optional on all. Standard final drive ratio: (Astre coupe) 3.42:1; (Astre hatchback/Safari) 2.73:1; (Sunbird) 2.73:1 with four, 2.56:1 with V-6; (Ventura) 3.42:1 with four, 3.08:1 with V-6, 3.23:1 with V-8; (Firebird) 3.08:1 with four, 3.23:1 with V-8-301, 2.41:1 with V-8-350; (Trans Am) 3.23:1 or 3.42:1; (LeMans) 3.08:1 with V-6, 2.56:1 with V-8-301, 2.41:1 with V-8-350/400, 2.56:1 with V-8-403; (Grand Prix) 2.56:1 with V-8-301, 2.41:1 with V-8-350/400/403; (Catalina) 2.73:1 with V-6; (Bonneville) 2.41:1; (Safari) 2.56:1. Steering: Recirculating ball. Front Suspension: (Astre) coil springs and control arms; (Firebird/LeMans) coil springs with lower trailing links and anti-sway bar; (others) coil springs and anti-sway bar. Rear Suspension: (Astre/Sunbird) rigid axle with coil springs, lower trailing radius arms and upper torque arms; (Ventura/Firebird) semi-elliptic leaf springs with anti-sway bar; (LeMans/Bonneville/Grand Prix) rigid axle with coil springs, lower trailing radius arms, upper torque arms and anti-sway bar. Brakes: Front disc, rear drum. Ignition: Electronic. Body construction: (Astre/Sunbird) unit; (Ventura) unit with front frame section; (Firebird) unit with separate partial frame; (others) separate body and frame. Fuel Tank: (Astre) 16 gal.; (Sunbird) 18.5 gal.; (Ventura) 20.5 gal.; (Firebird) 20.2 gal.; (LeMans) 21.8 gal. except wagon, 22 gal.; (Grand Prix) 25 gal.; (Catalina/Bonneville) 20 gal. except Safari/Grand safari, 22.5 gal.

DRIVETRAIN OPTIONS: Engines: 140-cid two-barrel four: Astre ($20); Ventura coupe/sedan ($120 credit). 231-cid V-6: Sunbird ($120). 301-cid V-8: Ventura/Firebird/LeMans ($65); Catalina ($66). 305-cid two-barrel V-8: Ventura ($65). 350-cid four-barrel V-8: Ventura/LeMans/Firebird ($155); LeMans Safari ($90); Firebird Formula ($90); Grand Prix ($90). 400-cid four-barrel V-8: LeMans/Firebird ($220); LeMans wagon ($155); Firebird Formula ($155-$205); Trans Am ($50); Catalina ($223); Bonneville ($157); Grand Prix ($155). 403-cid four-barrel V-8: LeMans ($220); LeMans wagon ($155); Firebird Formula ($155); Catalina ($223); Bonneville ($157); Grand Prix ($155). Transmission/Differential: M15 three-speed manual transmission: LeMans ($282). Three-speed floor shift: Ventura ($31). Four-speed manual floor shift transmission: Ventura w/V-8-301 ($257). Four-speed manual transmission: Firebird ($257). Five-speed manual transmission: Astre/Sunbird ($248); Ventura four ($282). Turbo-Hydra-Matic: Astre/Sunbird/Ventura/Firebird ($248); LeMans (not available). Safe-T-Track differential: Astre/Sunbird ($50); Ventura/LeMans/Firebird ($54); Catalina/Bonneville/G.P. ($58). Brakes/Steering: Power brakes: Astre/Sunbird ($58); Ventura/LeMans/Firebird ($61). Power steering: Astre/Sunbird ($129); Ventura/LeMans ($146). Suspension: Rally RTS handling package: Astre ($55-$215); Sunbird ($44-$215); Ventura ($44); Firebird ($46-$116); LeMans ($36-$158); Catalina ($130-$156); Bonneville ($93-$111); Grand Prix ($34-$102). Firm

1977 Pontiac Ventura SJ four-door sedan. (OCW)

1977 Pontiac Bonneville Brougham two-door hardtop. (OCW)

ride package ($11) except Astre/Sunbird. Superlift shock absorbers: LeMans/Grand Prix ($49); Catalina/Bonneville ($50). Automatic level control: Catalina/Bonneville ($52-$102). Other: Heavy-duty radiator: Astre/Sunbird ($30); Ventura ($27-$55). Super-cooling radiator ($27-$55) except Astre/Sunbird. Heavy-duty battery ($16-$18). Maintenance-free battery ($31). Heavy-duty alternator: LeMans/Firebird ($45); Catalina/Bonneville ($46); Grand Prix ($45). Engine block heater ($12-$13). Class I trailer group: LeMans/ Grand Prix ($109-$133); Bonneville/Catalina ($110-$135). Medium trailer group: LeMans/ Grand Prix ($127-$151); Catalina/Bonneville ($128-$153). Heavy trailer group: Bonneville/Catalina ($139-$199). California emissions ($70). High-altitude option ($22).

OPTION PACKAGES: Astre Formula appearance group ($447-$558). Astre special appearance package: with Formula ($34). Astre luxury appointment group: hatchback/Safari ($147). Astre custom exterior ($63-$94). Astre custom interior ($141-$183). Sunbird Formula appearance group ($436-$543). Sunbird special appearance group ($82). Sunbird luxury appointment group ($147). Sunbird luxury trim group ($144). LeMans GT: Sport coupe ($446-$463). LeMans custom trim group: sedan/Safari ($92-$208). Firebird Skybird appearance package: Esprit ($325-$342). Trans Am special edition ($556-$1143). Firebird custom trim group ($27-$118). Firebird Formula appearance package ($127). Catalina special appearance group ($140). Bonneville special appearance group ($135). Safari custom trim group ($167-$286).

MAJOR CONVENIENCE/APPEARANCE OPTIONS: Air conditioning ($442-$540). Automatic air conditioning: LeMans/Grand Prix ($539-$552); Catalina/Bonneville ($579). Cruise control ($80-$84); not available on Sunbird/Astre. Power seat: LeMans/Catalina/Bonneville/Grand Prix ($137-$139). Power windows ($108-$151); not available on Sunbird/Astre. Cornering lamps: Catalina/Bonneville/Grand Prix ($44). Power glass sunroof: LeMans/Grand Prix ($625); Catalina/Bonneville ($898). Power steel sunroof: LeMans/Grand Prix ($394); Catalina/Bonneville ($735). Glass sunroof: Firebird ($587). Padded landau top: Grand Prix/LeMans ($180). Cordova vinyl top: Sunbird ($83-$144); Ventura ($93); LeMans ($111); Grand Prix ($121); Catalina/Bonneville ($135-$140). Canopy top: Firebird ($105). Landau vinyl top: Sunbird ($144); Ventura ($162); LeMans ($111); Grand Prix ($121). Canopy vinyl top: LeMans ($151); Catalina/Bonneville ($107-$112). Formal landau vinyl top: Catalina/Bonneville ($277-$282). Rear spoiler: Astre/Sunbird ($45); Firebird ($51).

HISTORICAL: Introduced: Sept. 30, 1976. Model year production: 911,050. Calendar year production (U.S.): 875,958. Calendar year sales by U.S. dealers: 808,467. Model year sales by U.S. dealers: 811,904. Sales rose considerably for the 1977 model year, paving the way for higher numbers the next time around. The downsized full-size models sold better than their bigger predecessors. Alex C. Mair was Pontiac's general manager at this time.

1978 PONTIAC

CATALINA — SERIES 2B — (V-6/V-8) — Styling of Catalina models was similar to 1977. A revised grille consisted of five horizontal strips over subdued vertical strips. Small clear park/signal lamps

1978 Pontiac Sunbird two-door coupe. (JAG)

were in the bumper. Alongside the quad rectangular headlamps were two-section amber wraparound marker lenses. The bright grille divider held no emblem. "Catalina" lettering went on the cowl. "Pontiac" lettering went over the driver's side headlamps. Wraparound tail lamps had three horizontal ribs, with back-up lights at the inner ends. The recessed license plate was on a level with the tail lamps. Catalina's base engine was the Buick-built 231-cid (3.8-liter) V-6, with 301-, 350- and 400- or 403-cid V-8 available. Equipment included automatic transmission, power brakes/steering, FR78 x 15 radial tires, front/rear bumper strips and heater/defroster.

BONNEVILLE — SERIES 2B — (V-8) — Like Catalina, the full-size Bonneville was similar to 1977, but had a revised grille. This one had four vertical divider bars on each side of the bright center divider (which had a Pontiac emblem), instead of the former egg-crate design. Wraparound marker lenses were in the same frames as headlamps, extending to four-section amber side marker lenses. "Pontiac" lettering went over the left headlamp again. The hood ornament was an octagon within an octagon. As before, small clear park/signal lamps were bumper mounted. The grille pattern repeated in twin narrow bumper slots. "Bonneville" lettering went on the lower cowl. Wraparound tail lamps were new. Standard equipment was similar to Catalina, but a two-barrel 301-cid V-8 was standard, along with fender skirts and wheel covers. The Bonneville Brougham added a 60/40 front seat, clock and power windows.

GRAND PRIX — SERIES 2G — (V-6/V-8) — Three Grand Prix models were offered again this year: base, sporty SJ and luxury LJ. All three now rode a 108-in. wheelbase, measuring 201.2 inches in length (nearly 17 inches shorter than their predecessors). Weights were cut by 600 to 750 pounds. The base Grand Prix had a notch-back front seat with either vinyl or cloth upholstery. Grand Prix LJ came with a loose-pillow style cloth notchback front seat. Optional on SJ and LJ: leather upholstery in Viscount design. Base engine was the 231-cid (3.8-liter) V-6, but LJ had a 301-cid (4.9-liter) two-barrel V-8 and LJ a four-barrel 301-cid V-8. Equipment also included a three-speed manual gearbox, wide rocker panel moldings, wheel opening moldings, clock, and P195/75R14 SBR black sidewall tires. SJ models added P205/70R14 tires, a 301-cid four-barrel V-8, power brakes and steering, automatic transmission, and vinyl front bucket seats. The Grand prix LJ had wide rocker panel moldings with extensions, a two-barrel 301-cid V-8, automatic transmission, power brakes, power steering, body-color mirrors, and deluxe wheel covers. The new-size Grand Prix displayed a rather tall grille in a bright, heavy frame with four vertical bars on each side of the bright center bar, which held no emblem. A tall hood ornament had 'GP' letters at the base. Clear park/signal lamps stood between each pair of quad headlamps, as in 1977. "Grand Prix" script went above the left headlamp. All told, the grille and the front end showed a more

1978 Pontiac Formula Sunbird Sport three-door hatchback. (OCW)

1978 Pontiac Formula Sunbird Sport three-door hatchback. (OCW)

upright, squared-off look than before. Hood creases were far less prominent, meeting the grille ends rather than coming to a point at the center. Large square-like tail lamps contained five horizontal divider ribs. The license plate was mounted in the deck lid.

LEMANS — SERIES 2A — (V-6/V-8) — The downsized mid-size Pontiacs were 8-17 inches shorter and 530 to 925 pounds lighter than before, boosting fuel economy without loss of interior space. LeMans and Grand LeMans came in two-door coupe and four-door sedan body styles, along with a four-door Safari wagon. Body features included soft, body-colored front/rear bumpers on coupes and sedans. Single rectangular headlamps were used. The headlamp dimmer was now column-mounted. An AM/FM stereo radio with cassette player was available. Options included power vent rear windows (for sedans). Base engine was the 231-cid (3.8-liter) V-6; optional, a 305-cid (5.0-liter) V-8. A wide body-color divider with emblem separated the grille into the customary twin sections. Each 3 x 3 crosshatch grille section stood over subdued vertical bars. Wraparound amber side marker lenses were split into three sections. Two small air slots were below the bumper strip. Wraparound tail lamps had two horizontal dividers and stretched full-width to the recessed license plate. Standard equipment included a three-speed manual floor shift, wheel opening moldings, P185/75R14 FBR black sidewall tires, hubcaps, and a heater/defroster. Grand LeMans added a hood ornament and moldings, lower body side moldings, and black rocker panel moldings.

GRAND AM — SERIES 2A — (V-8) — A single series with coupe and sedan models made up the Grand Am lineup, which featured a soft front-end panel and two-tone paint. Standard equipment included 205/70R14 steel-belted radial tires and Rally RTS suspension. Base engine was the 301-cid (4.9-liter) V-8; optional, a four-barrel version of the same power plant. Four body-color vertical strips separated each grille section in the sloping front panel into five segments. The protruding body-color center divider held a Pontiac emblem. Recessed single rectangular headlamps stood above clear park/signal lamps, with the same framework wrapping to clear/amber side marker lenses. "Grand Am" nameplates went on the forward end of front fenders. At the rear were horizontally ribbed wraparound tail lamps. Grand Am standard equipment was similar to that of the LeMans, but included an automatic transmission (four-speed manual transmission was optional), power brakes, power steering, two-tone paint, and P205/70R14 black sidewall SBR tires.

FIREBIRD — SERIES 2F — (V-6/V-8) — The appearance of the sporty Firebird was similar to 1977, with rectangular quad headlamps and a dark grille. Wide three-row tail lamps had back-up lights at the inner ends, close to the license plate. Tail lamp ribs filled most of the back panel. Base engine was the 231-cid (3.8-liter) V-6 with

1978 Pontiac Phoenix LJ two-door coupe. (CP)

1978 Pontiac Firebird Trans Am two-door coupe. (OCW)

1978 Pontiac LeMans Safari four-door Safari. (CP)

three-speed shift. Formula had a 305-cid (5.0-liter) V-8, while Trans Am carried a 400-cid four-barrel V-8. Equipment included Endura bumpers, hubcaps, dual horns, FR78 x 15 SBR tires, bucket seats, and a heater/defroster. Esprit added wheel covers, sport mirrors, bright hood and wheel opening moldings, and custom pedal trim. The Trans Am included a front air dam, black grille, rear spoiler, sport mirrors, rear wheel air deflectors, Rally II wheels, "shaker" hood and air cleaner, and rally instrument panel with tachometer. Formula and Trans Am models had power brakes. Automatic transmission was standard on the Formula and Trans Am, but Formula Firebird buyers could get a four-speed manual at no extra cost.

SUNBIRD — SERIES 2H — (FOUR/V-6) — The basic appearance of Pontiac's remaining subcompact was similar to 1977 with staggered, recessed quad rectangular headlamps at the ends of each front-end opening. This year's narrow grilles consisted of all vertical bars on each side of the tapered, body-color divider, which had a Pontiac emblem. 'Sunbird' script was on the cowl, below the body side molding. Bright tail lamp frames had two horizontal separator ribs. Back-up lights sat at the inner ends with amber lenses in the center of each unit. The base engine was the 151-cid (2.5-liter) four with four-speed manual transmission. Standard equipment included A78 x 13 tires (B78 x 13 on wagons), a heater/defroster, and bucket seats. Sport Coupe and hatchback models included bright grille and drip moldings and custom wheel covers.

PHOENIX — SERIES 2X — (FOUR/V-6/V-8) — Ventura was gone, but the compact Phoenix came in two-door coupe, four-door sedan and three-door hatchback forms. A wide center divider at the front held 'Pontiac' lettering below a Pontiac emblem. Grille framing extended to the single recessed rectangular headlamps and tall clear/marker side markers. The grille consisted of four vertical dividers, forming five sections on each side, with subdued vertical bars in each portion. A large Phoenix emblem was low on the cowl. Flush-mount tail lamps in bright frames had two divider ribs. Back-up lights were in the center of each lens set. Base engine was the 231-cid (3.8-liter) V-6 with three-speed manual transmission. Equipment included E78 x 14 black sidewall tires, hubcaps, lighter, heater/defroster and an instrument cluster similar to that used in the Grand Prix. The Phoenix LJ added a stand-up hood ornament, wheel opening and rocker panel moldings and deluxe wheel covers.

I.D. DATA: Pontiac's 13-symbol Vehicle Identification Number (VIN) was located on the upper left surface of the instrument panel, visible through the windshield. The first digit is 2, indicating Pontiac division. The second symbol is a letter indicating series:

E=Sunbird; M=Sunbird; Y=Phoenix; Z=Phoenix LJ; D=LeMans; F=Grand LeMans; G=Grand Am; S=Firebird; T=Firebird Esprit; U=Firebird Formula; W=Firebird Trans Am; L=Catalina; N=Bonneville; Q=Bonneville Brougham; J=Grand Prix; K=Grand Prix LJ; H=Grand Prix SJ. Next come two digits that denote body type: 07=two-door hatchback; 17=two-door hatchback; 27=two-door coupe; 37=two-door coupe; 87=two-door Hardtop; 19=four-door sedan (6-window); 69=four-door sedan (4-window); 15=two-door Safari; 35=four-door Safari. The fifth symbol is a letter indicating engine code: V=151-cid two-barrel I4; A=231-cid two-barrel V-6; Y=301-cid two-barrel V-8; W=301-cid four-barrel V-8; U=305-cid four-barrel V-8; X=350-cid four-barrel V-8; R=350-cid four-barrel V-8 (L34); L=350-cid four-barrel V-8 (LM1); Z=400-cid four-barrel V-8. The sixth symbol denotes model year (8=1978). Next is a plant code: A=Lakewood, Ga.; B=Baltimore; L=Van Nuys, Calif.; N=Norwood, Ohio; P=Pontiac, Mich.; T=Tarrytown, N.Y.; U=Lordstown, Ohio; W=Willow Run, Mich.; X=Fairfax, Kan.; 1=Oshawa, Ontario; 2=Ste. Therese, Quebec. The final six digits are the sequential serial number.

Model Number	Body Style Number	Body Type & Seating	Factory Price	Shipping Weight	Production Total
CATALINA (V-6/V-8)					
2B	L37	2d Coupe-6P	5,375/5,525	3,438/3,559	9,224
2B	L69	4d Sedan-6P	5,410/5,560	3,470/3,591	39,707
CATALINA SAFARI (V-8)					
2B	L35	4d Sta Wagon-6P	5,924	3,976	12,819
BONNEVILLE (V-8)					
2B	N37	2d Coupe-6P	5,831	3,581	22,510
2B	N69	4d Sedan-6P	5,931	3,637	48,647
BONNEVILLE BROUGHAM (V-8)					
2B	Q37	2d Coupe-6P	6,577	3,611	36,192
2B	Q69	4d Sedan-6P	6,677	3,667	17,948
GRAND SAFARI (V-8)					
2B	N35	4d Sta Wagon-6P	6,227	4,002	13,847
GRAND PRIX (V-6/V-8)					
2G	J37	2d Coupe-6P	4,800/5,030	3,101/3,224	127,253
GRAND PRIX LJ (V-8)					
2G	K37	2d Coupe-6P	5,815	3,216	65,122
GRAND PRIX SJ (V-8)					
2G	H37	2d Coupe-6P	6,088	3,229	36,069
LEMANS (V-6/V-8)					
2A	D27	2d Hardtop-6P	4,405/4,555	3,038/3,159	20,581
2A	D19	4d Hardtop-6P	4,480/4,630	3,047/3,168	22,728
LEMANS SAFARI (V-6/V-8)					
2A	D35	4d Sta Wagon-6P	4,937/5,086	3,225/3,372	15,714
GRAND LEMANS (V-6/V-8)					
2A	F27	2d Hardtop-6P	4,777/4,927	3,070/3,190	18,433
2A	F19	4d Hardtop-6P	4,881/5,031	3,098/3,218	21,252

1978 Pontiac Firebird Trans Am two-door SE coupe. (OCW)

1978 Pontiac Grand LeMans two-door coupe. (OCW)

1978 Pontiac Grand Prix SJ two-door coupe. (OCW)

1978 Pontiac Bonneville Brougham four-door sedan. (OCW)

1978 Pontiac Formula Sunbird Sport two-door hatchback. (JAG)

1978 Pontiac Phoenix LJ two-door coupe. (OCW)

1978 Pontiac Phoenix LJ four-door sedan. (OCW)

1978 Pontiac Firebird Espirit Red Bird two-door hardtop. (OCW)

Model Number	Body Style Number	Body Type & Seating	Factory Price	Shipping Weight	Production Total
GRAND LEMANS SAFARI (V-6/V-8)					
2A	F35	4d Sta Wagon-6P	5,265/5,415	3,242/3,389	11,125
GRAND AM (V-8)					
2A	G27	2d Coupe-6P	5,464	3,209	7,767
2A	G19	4d Sedan-6P	5,568	3,239	2,841
FIREBIRD (V-6/V-8)					
2F	S87	2d Hardtop-4P	4,545/4,695	3,254/3,377	32,672
FIREBIRD ESPRIT (V-6/V-8)					
2F	T87	2d Hardtop -4P	4,842/4,992	3,285/3,408	36,926
FIREBIRD FORMULA (V-8)					
2F	U87	2d Hardtop -4P	5,448	3,452	24,346
FIREBIRD TRANS AM (V-8)					
2F	W87	2d Hardtop -4P	5,799	3,511	93,341
SUNBIRD (FOUR/V-6)					
2H	E27	2d Coupe-4P	3,540/3,710	2,662/ —	20,413
2H	M07	2d Hatchback-4P	3,912/4,082	2,694/ —	25,380
2H	M27	2d Sport Coupe-4P	3,773/3,943	2,662/ —	32,572
2H	M15	2d Sta Wagon-4P	3,741/3,911	2,610/ —	8,424
PHOENIX (V-6/V-8)					
2X	Y27	2d Coupe-6P	3,872/4,022	3,119/3,215	26,143
2X	Y69	4d Sedan-6P	3,947/4,097	3,169/3,265	32,529
2X	Y17	2d Hatchback-6P	4,068/4,218	3,202/3,298	3,252
PHOENIX LJ (V-6/V-8)					
2X	Z27	2d Coupe-6P	4,357/4,507	3,228/3,324	6,210
2X	Z69	4d Sedan-6P	4,432/4,582	3,277/3,373	8,393

NOTE 1: Prices and weights above slash for V-6/below slash for V-8.

NOTE 2: A third seat was available in all Catalina Safari wagons.

NOTE 3: A four-cylinder engine for the Phoenix was available for $170 credit.

ENGINE [Base Four (Sunbird); Optional (Phoenix)]: Inline. Overhead valve. Four-cylinder. Cast-iron block and head. Displacement: 151 cid. (2.3 liters). Bore & stroke: 4.00 x 3.00 in. Compression ratio: 8.3:1. Brake horsepower: 85 at 4400 rpm. Torque: 123 lbs.-ft. at 2800 rpm. Five main bearings. Hydraulic valve lifters. Carburetor: two-barrel Holley 5210C. VIN Code: V.

ENGINE [Base V-6 (Phoenix/Firebird/LeMans/Catalina/Grand Prix); Optional (Sunbird)]: 90-degree, overhead-valve V-6. Cast-iron block and head. Displacement: 231 cid. (3.8 liters). Bore & stroke: 3.80 x 3.40 in. Compression ratio: 8.0:1. Brake horsepower: 105 at 3200-3400 rpm. Torque: 185 lbs.-ft. at 2000 rpm. Four main bearings. Hydraulic valve lifters. Carburetor: two-barrel Rochester 2GC. VIN Code: A.

ENGINE [Base V-8 (Grand Am/Bonneville/Grand Prix LJ); Optional (Grand Prix/Catalina)]: 90-degree, overhead valve V-8. Cast-iron block and head. Displacement: 301 cid. (5.0 liters). Bore & stroke: 4.00 x 3.00 in. Compression ratio: 8.2:1. Brake horsepower: 140 at 3600 rpm. Torque: 235 lbs.-ft. at 2000 rpm. Five main

1978 Pontiac Grand LeMans four-door sedan. (OCW)

1978 Pontiac Grand LeMans four-door Safari. (OCW)

1978 Pontiac Grand Am four-door sedan. (OCW)

bearings. Hydraulic valve lifters. Carburetor: two-barrel Rochester M2MC. VIN Code: Y.

ENGINE [Base V-8 (Grand Prix SJ); Optional (Grand Am/Grand Prix)]: Same as 301-cid V-8 above, with four-barrel carburetor [Rochester M4MC] Horsepower: 150 at 4000 rpm. Torque: 239 lbs.-ft. at 2000 rpm. VIN Code: W.

ENGINE [Base V-8 Firebird Formula; Optional Phoenix/Firebird/LeMans/Grand Prix SJ/LJ]: 90-degree, overhead valve V-8. Cast-iron block and head. Displacement: 305 cid. (5.0 liters). Bore & stroke: 3.74 x 3.48 in. Compression ratio: 8.4:1. Brake horsepower: 145 at 3800 rpm. Torque: 245 lbs.-ft. at 2400 rpm. Five main bearings. Hydraulic valve lifters. Carburetor: two-barrel Rochester 2GC. VIN Code: U.

ENGINE [Optional V-8 Firebird/Catalina/Bonneville]: 90-degree, overhead valve V-8. Cast-iron block and head. Displacement: 350 cid. (5.7 liters). Bore & stroke: 3.80 x 3.85 in. Compression ratio: 8.0:1. Brake horsepower: 155 at 3400 rpm. Torque: 280 lbs.-ft. at 1800 rpm. Five main bearings. Hydraulic valve lifters. Carburetor: four-barrel Rochester M4MC. Buick-built. VIN Code: X.

ENGINE [Alternate V-8 Firebird/Catalina/Bonneville]: 90-degree, overhead valve V-8. Cast-iron block and head. Displacement: 350 cid. (5.7 liters). Bore & stroke: 4.00 x 3.48 in. Compression ratio: 8.2:1. Brake horsepower: 170 at 3800 rpm. Torque: 270 lbs.-ft. at 2400 rpm. Five main bearings. Hydraulic valve lifters. Carburetor: four-barrel Rochester M4MC. Chevrolet-built. VIN Code: L.

ENGINE [Alternate V-8 Firebird/Catalina/Bonneville]: 90-degree, overhead valve V-8. Cast-iron block and head. Displacement: 350 cid. (5.7 liters). Bore & stroke: 4.06 x 3.38 in. Compression ratio: 7.9:1. Brake horsepower: 170 at 3800 rpm. Torque: 275 lbs.-ft. at 2000 rpm. Five main bearings. Hydraulic valve lifters. Carburetor: four-barrel Rochester M4MC. Oldsmobile-built. VIN Code: R.

ENGINE [Base V-8 (Trans Am); Optional (Firebird Formula/Catalina/Bonneville)]: 90-degree, overhead valve V-8. Cast-iron block and head. Displacement: 400 cid. (6.6 liters). Bore & stroke: 4.12 x 3.75 in. Compression ratio: 7.7:1. Brake horsepower: 180 at 3600 rpm. Torque: 325 lbs.-ft. at 1600 rpm. Five main bearings. Hydraulic valve lifters. Carburetor: four-barrel Rochester M4MC. VIN Code: Z.

ENGINE [Optional T/A V-8 Firebird Formula/Trans Am]: Same as 400-cid V-8 above, except Compression ratio: 8.1:1. Brake horsepower: 220 at 4000 rpm. Torque: 320 lbs.-ft. at 2800 rpm.

Note: A 403-cid V-8 was used in California models.

CHASSIS: Wheelbase: (Sunbird) 97.0 in.; (Phoenix) 111.1 in.; (Firebird) 108.1 in.; (LeMans) 108.1 in.; (Grand Prix) 108.1 in.; (Catalina/Bonneville) 115.9 in. Overall Length: (Sunbird) 177.8 in.; (Sunbird hatchback) 178.3 in.; (Sunbird Safari) 177.6 in.; (Phoenix) 203.4 in.; (Firebird) 196.8 in.; (LeMans coupe) 199.2 in.; (LeMans sedan) 198.5 in.; (LeMans Safari) 197.8 in.; (Grand Prix) 201.2 in.; (Catalina/

Bonneville) 214.3 in.; (Safari) 215.1 in. Height: (Sunbird) 49.6 in.; (Sunbird hatchback) 49.9 in.; (Sunbird Safari) 51.8 in.; (Phoenix) 52.3 in.; (Firebird) 49.3 in.; (Formula/Trans Am) 49.5 in.; (LeMans coupe) 53.5 in.; (LeMans sedan) 54.4 in.; (LeMans Safari) 54.8 in.; (Grand Prix) 53.3 in.; (Catalina/Bonneville coupe) 53.9 in.; (Catalina/Bonneville sedan) 54.5 in.; (Safari Wagon) 57.3 in. Width: (Sunbird) 65.4 in.; (Phoenix) 73.2 in.; (Firebird) 73.4 in.; (LeMans) 72.4 in.; (LeMans Safari) 72.6 in.; (Grand Prix) 72.8 in.; (Catalina/Bonneville) 78.0 in.; (Safari Wagon) 80.0 in. Front Tread: (Sunbird) 55.2 in. except hatchback, 54.7 in.; (Phoenix) 61.8 in.; (Firebird) 60.9 in.; (Firebird Formula) 61.3 in.; (Trans Am) 61.2 in.; (LeMans) 58.5 in.; (Grand Prix) 58.5 in.; (Catalina/Bonneville) 61.7 in.; (Safari) 62.1 in. Rear Tread: (Sunbird) 54.1 in. except hatchback, 53.6 in.; (Phoenix) 59.6 in.; (Firebird) 60.0 in.; (Firebird Formula) 60.4 in.; (Trans Am) 60.3 in.; (LeMans) 57.8 in.; (Grand Prix) 57.8 in.; (Catalina/Bonneville) 60.7 in.; (Safari) 64.1 in. Standard Tires: (Sunbird) A78 x 13 except wagon, B78 x 13; (Phoenix) E78 x 14; (Firebird) FR78 x 15; (Trans Am) GR70 x 15; (LeMans) P185/75R14; (Grand Am) P205/70R14; (Grand Prix) P195/75R14; (Catalina/Bonneville) FR78 x 15.

TECHNICAL: Transmission: Three-speed manual transmission standard on Phoenix, LeMans, Firebird and base Grand Prix (floor lever standard on Firebird and LeMans; optional on Phoenix). Four-speed manual transmission standard on Sunbird, optional on Firebird, Phoenix and Grand Am. Five-speed manual transmission optional on Sunbird. Three-speed Turbo Hydra-Matic transmission standard on other models; optional on all. Steering: Recirculating ball. Front Suspension: (Firebird/LeMans) coil springs with lower trailing links and anti-sway bar; (others) coil springs and anti-sway bar. Rear Suspension: (Sunbird) rigid axle with coil springs, lower trailing radius arms and upper torque arms; (Phoenix) semi-elliptic leaf springs; (Firebird) semi-elliptic leaf springs with anti-sway bar; (LeMans/Bonneville/Grand Prix) rigid axle with coil springs, lower trailing radius arms, upper torque arms and anti-sway bar. Brakes: Front disc, rear drum. Ignition: Electronic. Body construction: (Sunbird) unit; (Firebird) unit with separate partial frame; (others) separate body and frame. Fuel tank: (Sunbird) 18.5 gal. except wagon, 16 gal.; (Phoenix) 21 gal.; (Firebird) 21 gal.; (LeMans) 17.5 gal. except wagon, 18.3 gal.; (Grand Am) 15 gal.; (Grand Prix) 15 gal.; (Catalina/Bonneville) 21 gal. except wagon, 22 gal.

DRIVETRAIN OPTIONS: Engines: 140-cid two-barrel four in Phoenix ($170 credit). 231-cid V-6 in Sunbird ($170). 301-cid, two-barrel V-8 in Catalina/Grand Prix ($150). 301-cid, four-barrel V-8 in Grand Prix ($200); Grand Prix LJ ($50); Grand Am ($50). 305-cid, two-barrel V-8 in Phoenix/Firebird/LeMans/Grand Prix ($150). 350-cid, four-barrel V-8 in Phoenix/Firebird/Catalina ($265); LeMans Safari ($265); Firebird Formula ($115); Bonneville ($115). 400-cid, four-barrel V-8 in Firebird ($205). Catalina ($330); Bonneville ($180). T/A 400-cid, four-barrel V-8 in Formula ($280); Trans Am ($75). 403-cid,

1978 Pontiac Grand Am two-door hardtop. (OCW)

1978 Pontiac Grand Prix two-door hardtop. (OCW)

Standard Catalog of ® Pontiac, 2ⁿᵈ Edition

1978 Pontiac Catalina two-door coupe. (OCW)

four-barrel V-8 in Firebird Formula ($205); Catalina ($330); Bonneville ($180). Transmission/Differential: Three-speed floor shift in Phoenix ($33). Four-speed manual floor shift transmission in Phoenix w/V-8-305 ($125); Firebird/LeMans ($125); Formula ($182 credit). Five-speed manual transmission in Sunbird ($175). Turbo Hydra-Matic in Sunbird ($270); Phoenix/Firebird/LeMans/Grand Prix ($307); Formula/Trans Am (NC). Saf-T-Track differential in Sunbird ($56); LeMans/Firebird/Grand Prix ($60); Catalina/Bonneville ($64). Brakes/Steering: Power brakes in Sunbird (N/A); Phoenix/LeMans/Firebird/Grand Prix ($69). Power steering in Sunbird ($134); Phoenix/LeMans/Grand Prix ($152). Suspension: Rally RTS handling package in Sunbird ($230); Phoenix ($172-$217); LeMans ($42-$179); Catalina ($140-$169); Bonneville ($102-$120); Grand Prix ($67-$120). Firm ride package ($12) except Sunbird. Superlift shock absorbers in LeMans/Grand Prix ($52); Catalina/Bonneville ($53). Automatic level control in LeMans/Grand Prix/Catalina/Bonneville ($63-$116). Other: Heavy-duty radiator in Sunbird ($32); Phoenix ($31-$56). Super-cooling radiator ($31-$57) except Sunbird/Phoenix. Heavy-duty battery ($17-$20). Heavy-duty alternator in Sunbird/Phoenix/Firebird ($31); Catalina/Bonneville ($18-$49). Engine block heater ($13-$14). Class I trailer group for Bonneville/Catalina ($117-$143). Medium trailer group four LeMans/Grand Prix ($116-$141). Heavy trailer group four Bonneville/Catalina ($117-$178). California emissions ($75-$100). High-altitude option ($33).

OPTION PACKAGES: Sunbird Formula group ($448-$621). Sunbird appearance group in coupe ($87). Phoenix coupe/sedan appearance package ($73). Firebird "Skybird" appearance package for Esprit ($426-$461). Trans Am special edition ($1,259). Firebird custom trim group ($35-$154). Firebird Formula appearance package ($137). Firebird Trans Am special performance package ($249-$324). LeMans Safari security package ($35-$40). LeMans exterior paint appearance ($159). LeMans custom exterior (40-$75). LeMans custom trim group ($134-$247). Full-size exterior paint package ($159). Safari custom trim group ($205-$370). Grand Prix exterior appearance ($119-$165).

MAJOR CONVENIENCE/APPEARANCE OPTIONS: Air conditioning ($470-$581). Automatic air conditioning: LeMans/Grand Prix ($584); Catalina/Bonneville ($626). Cruise control ($90-$95); not available for Sunbird. Power seat: LeMans/Catalina/Bonneville/Grand Prix ($151). Power windows ($118-$190); not available for Sunbird. Cornering lamps: Catalina/Bonneville/Grand Prix ($47). Power glass sunroof for LeMans/Grand Prix ($699); Catalina/Bonneville ($895). Power steel sunroof for LeMans/Grand Prix ($499); Catalina/Bonneville ($695). Glass sunroof: Sunbird ($172). Hatch roof: Firebird/Grand Prix ($625). Full vinyl cordova top for Phoenix ($97); LeMans ($116); Grand Prix ($121); Catalina/Bonneville ($142). Padded landau top on Grand Prix/LeMans ($239); Catalina/Bonneville ($294). Landau cordova top on Sunbird ($153); Phoenix ($179). Canopy top on Firebird ($111). Rear-facing third seat: Safari ($175).

HISTORICAL: Introduced: Oct. 6, 1977. Model year production: 900,380 units. Calendar year production (U.S.): 867,008. Calendar year sales by U.S. dealers: 896,980. Model year sales by U.S. dealers: 871,391. Model year sales set a new record in 1978, beating the 1968 total. Contributing to the rise were strong sales of Trans Am and the shrunken mid-size models, but Sunbird also showed an increase.

1979 PONTIAC

CATALINA — SERIES 2B — (V-6/V-8) — Catalina coupe and sedan models were offered again, along with a Catalina Safari

1979 Pontiac Sunbird Astre Safari station wagon. (JAG)

wagon. Changes included a new grille, park/signal lamps, tail lamps, and side marker lamps. Wagons kept their former tail lamp design. Though similar to before, the new front end held a horizontal-themed grille made up of four rows (formerly six). Amber wrap-around front marker lenses were split into four sections instead of two. As before, small clear park/signal lamps were bumper-mounted. Rectangular quad headlamps continued. Base engine was the 231-cid (3.8-liter) V-6. A 350-cid four-barrel V-8 was available for high-altitude models. Safari wagons carried a 301-cid (4.9-liter) two-barrel V-8. A 350-cid four-barrel V-8 was used in California and a 403-cid V-8 was available in high-altitude regions. Both light- and heavy-duty trailering packages were optional. New "Cloud Dillon" cloth seat trim was used. Full-size options included wire wheel covers, power windows and door locks, power six-way 60/40 split front seats, air conditioning, AM/FM stereo, a padded landau Cordova top and a cushion-tilt steering wheel.

BONNEVILLE — SERIES 2B — (V-8) — Like Catalina models, the Bonneville and Bonneville Brougham received design changes including new grille, park/signal lamps, taillights, and side markers. All models had new deluxe wheel covers. For the first time, coupes could have optional cloth bucket seats with a console. Bonneville's base engine was a 301-cid (4.9-liter) two-barrel V-8 with a 350-cid four-barrel V-8 used in cars sold in California and high-altitude models. The Grand Safari became the Bonneville Safari. A third seat was available again. This year's seat trim was Chamonix cloth (Dante cloth in the Bonneville Brougham, which used a new pillow-style design). Bonneville's grille elements were whole vertical rectangles, not just single vertical bars as in 1978. Five of them appeared on each side of the center divider. Instead of four-section amber side marker lenses, this year's had two sections.

GRAND PRIX — SERIES 2G — (V-6/V-8) — Horizontal and vertical bars now made up the Grand Prix grille, forming a 3 x 7 pattern of wide holes on each side of a narrow center divider. Amber park/signal lenses went between each pair of rectangular quad headlamps.

LEMANS — SERIES 2A — (V-6/V-8) — Styling of the mid-size LeMans was similar to before, but the grille contained more holes that were now arranged in a 6 x 4 pattern. Amber side marker lenses now were split into four sections rather than three. Base engine was the 231-cid (3.8-liter) V-6 with three-speed manual transmission. Standard equipment included body-color bumpers

1979 Pontiac Formula Sunbird three-door hatchback. (OCW)

1979 Pontiac Formula Sunbird three-door hatchback. (OCW)

1979 Pontiac Phoenix LJ four-door sedan. (CP)

with rub strips, P185/75R14 glass-belted radial tires, hubcaps and wheel opening moldings. The Grand LeMans added a hood ornament and wind-split moldings, lower body side moldings, brushed aluminum center pillars, and door panel pull straps. Engine options included a 301-cid V-8 (with a two- or four-barrel carburetor) and a 305-cid four-barrel V-8. Safari wagons had a 5.0-liter V-8 as standard and could also have a 5.7-liter (350-cid) V-8.

GRAND AM — SERIES 2A — (V-8) — Except for amber park/signal and marker lenses, the appearance of the Grand Am changed little this year. Standard equipment was similar to that of the LeMans, but with power steering, two-tone body color, blackout tail lamps, P205/70R14 steel-belted radial tires, and a Rally RTS handling package.

FIREBIRD — SERIES 2F — (V-6/V-8) — Front ends of the new Firebirds were far different from predecessors. Quad rectangular headlamps now stood in separate recessed housings, in a sharply sloped center panel that had a peak and an emblem—but no grille. Instead, horizontally ribbed lower grilles went into twin slots below the bumper area, with clear park/signal lamps at outer ends. At the rear was a full-width horizontally ribbed panel. Base Firebird equipment included Buick's 231-cid (3.8-liter) V-6, three-speed manual shift, power steering, and FR78 x 15 steel-belted radials. Esprit added wheel covers, sport mirrors (driver's remote), and extra body moldings. Formula had a 301-cid V-8, automatic transmission, power brakes, black-accented grille, non-functional twin hood scoop, Rally II wheels with trim rings, console, and P225/70R15 black sidewall SBR tires. Trans Am had a 403-cid four-barrel V-8, four-speed manual transmission, power brakes, air dam, rear spoiler, "shaker" hood, and chrome side-splitter tailpipe extensions.

SUNBIRD — SERIES 2H — (FOUR/V-6) — The appearance of the sub-compact Sunbird was similar to 1978, but the small twin grilles now contained horizontal strips instead of vertical strips. Standard equipment was similar to 1978, with a standard 151-cid (2.5-liter) four and optional 231-cid V-6 or 305-cid V-8. A four-speed manual gearbox was standard. Tires were A78 x 13 except B78 x 13 with V-6 engines. Sport Coupe and Sport Hatch models added custom wheel covers, rocker panel and wheel opening moldings, and custom vinyl bucket seats.

PHOENIX — SERIES 2X — (V-6/V-8) — Each side of this year's Phoenix grille contained five side-by-side sections with subdued vertical bars in each one and clear park/signal lamps in outer ends. Otherwise, the appearance of the Phoenix was similar to 1978. The compact Pontiac came in three basic models: base coupe, two-door hatchback, and four-door sedan. The LJ series offered fancier versions of the coupe and sedan. New two-tone paint was offered in four different color combinations. The base Phoenix engine was the 231-cid (3.8-liter) V-6 and a 305-cid two-barrel V-8 was optional. A 350-cid V-8 was offered for cars sold in California and high-altitude

counties. The four-cylinder engine credit option was no longer available. Phoenix owners could get a light-duty trailer-towing package that handled trailers weighing up to one ton.

I.D. DATA: Pontiac's 13-symbol Vehicle Identification Number (VIN) was located on the upper left surface of the instrument panel, visible through the windshield. The first digit is 2 indicated Pontiac division. The second symbol is a letter indicating series: E=Sunbird; M=Sunbird Sport; Y=Phoenix; Z=Phoenix LJ; D=LeMans; F=Grand LeMans; G=Grand Am; S=Firebird; T=Firebird Esprit; U=Firebird Formula; W=Firebird Trans Am; L=Catalina; N=Bonneville; Q=Bonneville Brougham; J=Grand Prix; K=Grand Prix LJ; H=Grand Prix SJ. Next come two digits that denote body type: 07= two-door hatchback; 17=two-door hatchback; 27=two-door coupe; 37=two-door coupe; 87=four-door Hardtop; 19=four-door six-window sedan; 69=four-door four-window sedan; 15=two-door Safari; 35=four-door two-seat Safari. The fifth symbol is a letter indicating engine code: V=151-cid two-barrel I4; A=231-cid two-barrel V-6; Y=301-cid two-barrel V-8; W=301-cid four-barrel V-8; G=305-cid two-barrel V-8; H=305-cid four-barrel V-8; X=350-cid four-barrel V-8 (L37); R=350-cid four-barrel V-8 (L34); L=350-cid four-barrel V-8 (LM1); Z=400-cid four-barrel V-8; K=403-cid four-barrel V-8. The sixth symbol denotes model year (9=1979). Next is a plant code: A=Lakewood, Ga.; B=Baltimore, Md.; L=Van Nuys, Calif.; N=Norwood, Ohio; P=Pontiac, Mich.; T=Tarrytown, N.Y.; U=Lordstown, Ohio; W=Willow Run, Mich.; X=Fairfax, Kan.; 1=Oshawa, Ontario; 2=Ste. Therese, Quebec. The final six digits are the sequential serial number.

Model Number	Body Style Number	Body Type & Seating	Factory Price	Shipping Weight	Production Total
CATALINA (V-6/V-8)					
2B	L37	2d Coupe-6P	5,690/5,885	3,476/3,593	5,410
2B	L69	4d Sedan-6P	5,746/5,941	3,508/3,625	28,121
CATALINA SAFARI (V-8)					
2B	L35	4d Sta Wagon-6P	6,273	3,997	13,353
BONNEVILLE (V-8)					
2B	N37	2d Coupe-6P	6,205	3,616	34,127
2B	N69	4d Sedan-6P	6,330	3,672	71,906
BONNEVILLE BROUGHAM (V-8)					
2B	Q37	2d Coupe-6P	6,960	3,659	39,094
2B	Q69	4d Sedan-6P	7,149	3,726	17,364
BONNEVILLE SAFARI (V-8)					
2B	N35	4d Sta Wagon-6P	6,632	4,022	16,925
GRAND PRIX (V-6/V-8)					
2G	J37	2d Coupe-6P	5,113/5,308	3,126/3,205	124,815
GRAND PRIX LJ (V-8)					
2G	K37	2d Coupe-5P	6,192	3,285	61,175

1979 Pontiac Phoenix LJ two-door coupe. (CP)

1979 Pontiac Formula Firebird two-door hardtop. (JAG)

Standard Catalog of ® Pontiac, 2nd Edition

1979 Pontiac Formula Firebird two-door hardtop. (JAG)

Model Number	Body Style Number	Body Type & Seating	Factory Price	Shipping Weight	Production Total
GRAND PRIX SJ (V-8)					
2G	H37	2d Coupe-5P	6,438	3,349	24,060
LEMANS (V-6/V-8)					
2A	D27	2d Coupe-6P	4,608/4,803	3,036/3,115	14,197
2A	D19	4d Sedan-6P	4,708/4,903	3,042/3,121	26,958
LEMANS SAFARI (V-6/V-8)					
2A	D35	4d Sta Wagon-6P	5,216/5,411	3,200/3,328	27,517
GRAND LEMANS (V-6/V-8)					
2A	F27	2d Coupe-6P	4,868/5,063	3,058/3,137	13,020
2A	F19	4d Sedan-6P	4,993/5,188	3,087/3,166	28,577
GRAND LEMANS SAFARI (V-6/V-8)					
2A	F35	4d Sta Wagon-6P	5,560/5,755	3,234/3,362	20,783
GRAND AM (V-6/V-8)					
2A	G27	2d Coupe-6P	5,084/5,279	3,080/3,159	4,021
2A	G19	4d Sedan-6P	5,209/5,404	3,084/3,163	1,865
FIREBIRD (V-6/V-8)					
2F	S87	2d Hardtop-4P	4,825/5,020	3,257/3,330	38,642
FIREBIRD ESPRIT (V-6/V-8)					
2F	T87	2d Hardtop-4P	5,193/5,388	3,287/3,360	30,853
FIREBIRD FORMULA (V-8)					
2F	U87	2d Hardtop-4P	6,018	3,460	24,851
FIREBIRD TRANS AM (V-8)					
2F	W87	2d Hardtop-4P	6,299	3,551	117,108
FIREBIRD TRANS AM LIMITED EDITION (V-8)					
2F	X87	2d Hardtop-4P	10,620	3,551	—
SUNBIRD (FOUR/V-6)					
2H	E27	2d Coupe-4P	3,781/3,981	2,593/ —	40,560
2H	M07	2d Hatchback-4P	4,064/4,264	2,642/ —	24,221
2H	M27	2d Spt Coupe-4P	3,964/4,164	2,593/ —	30,087
2H	M15	2d Sta Wag-4P	4,138/4,338	2,651/ —	2,902
PHOENIX (V-6/V-8)					
2X	Y27	2d Coupe-6P	4,089/4,284	3,127/3,345	9,233
2X	Y69	4d Sedan-6P	4,189/4,384	3,177/3,395	10,565
2X	Y17	2d Hatchback-6P	4,239/4,434	3,210/3,428	923
PHOENIX LJ (V-6/V-8)					
2X	Z27	2d Coupe-6P	4,589/4,784	3,236/3,454	1,826
2X	Z69	4d Sedan-6P	4,689/4,884	3,285/3,503	2,353

NOTE 1: Prices and weights above slash for V-6/below slash for V-8.

NOTE 2: A third seat was available in all Safari wagons.

NOTE 3: Add $395 to I-4 prices for 305-cid V-8 in Sunbirds.

ENGINE [Base Four Sunbird]: Inline. Overhead valve. Four-cylinder. Cast-iron block and head. Displacement: 151 cid. (2.5 liters). Bore & stroke: 4.00 x 3.00 in. Compression ratio: 8.2:1. Brake horsepower: 85 at 4400 rpm. Torque: 123 lbs.-ft. at 2800 rpm. Five main bearings. Hydraulic valve lifters. Carburetor: two-barrel Rochester 2SE. VIN Code: V.

ENGINE [Base V-6 Phoenix/Firebird/LeMans/Catalina/Grand Prix]: Optional Sunbird] 90-degree, overhead-valve V-6. Cast-iron block and head. Displacement: 231 cid. (3.8 liters). Bore & stroke:

1979 Pontiac LeMans two-door coupe. (JAG)

1979 Pontiac Grand LeMans four-door sedan. (PGMC)

3.80 x 3.40 in. Compression ratio: 8.0:1. Brake horsepower: 105 at 3200-3400 rpm. Torque: 185 lbs.-ft. at 2000 rpm. Four main bearings. Hydraulic valve lifters. Carburetor: two-barrel Rochester M2ME. Buick-built. VIN Code: A.

ENGINE [Base V-8 (Bonneville/Grand Prix LJ/Safari); Optional (Firebird/LeMans/Grand Prix/Catalina)]: 90-degree, overhead valve V-8. Cast-iron block and head. Displacement: 301 cid. (5.0 liters). Bore & stroke: 4.06 x 3.04 in. Compression ratio: 8.1:1. Brake horsepower: 140 at 3600 rpm. Torque: 235 lbs.-ft. at 2000 rpm. Five main bearings. Hydraulic valve lifters. Carburetor: two-barrel Rochester M2MC. VIN Code: Y.

ENGINE [Base V-8 (Firebird Formula/Grand Prix SJ); Optional (Firebird/Trans Am/LeMans, Grand Am, Bonneville, Catalina, Grand Prix)]: Same as 301-cid V-8 above, with four-barrel Rochester M4MC carburetor. Horsepower: 150 at 4000 rpm. Torque: 240 lbs.-ft. at 2000 rpm. VIN Code: W.

ENGINE [Optional V-8 Sunbird/Phoenix]: 90-degree, overhead valve V-8. Cast-iron block and head. Displacement: 305 cid. (5.0 liters). Bore & stroke: 3.74 x 3.48 in. Compression ratio: 8.4:1. Brake horsepower: 145 at 3800 rpm. Torque: 245 lbs.-ft. at 2400 rpm. Five main bearings. Hydraulic valve lifters. Carburetor: two-barrel Rochester 2GC. VIN Code: U.

ENGINE [Alternate V-8 Sunbird/Phoenix/Firebird]: Same as 305-cid V-8 above, except Horsepower: 133 at 4000 rpm. Torque: 244

1979 Pontiac Firebird Trans Am two-door hardtop. (JAG)

1979 Pontiac Grand LeMans Safari four-door station wagon. (JAG)

1979 Pontiac Grand Am two-door coupe. (PGMC)

1979 Pontiac Grand Prix SJ two-door coupe. (JAG)

lbs.-ft. at 2000 rpm. [Optional V-8 LeMans] Same as 305-cid V-8 above, but with four-barrel carburetor. Horsepower: 150 at 4000 rpm. Torque: 225 lbs.-ft. at 2400 rpm. VIN Code: H.

ENGINE [Optional V-8 Phoenix/Firebird/Catalina/Bonneville/LeMans Safari]: 90-degree, overhead valve V-8. Cast-iron block and head. Displacement: 350 cid. (5.7 liters). Bore & stroke: 4.00 x 3.48 in. Compression ratio: 8.2:1. Brake horsepower: 160 at 3800 rpm. Torque: 260 lbs.-ft. at 2400 rpm. Five main bearings. Hydraulic valve lifters. Carburetor: four-barrel Rochester M4MC. Chevrolet-built. VIN Code: L.

ENGINE [Alternate V-8 Phoenix/Firebird/Catalina/Bonneville/LeMans Safari]: Same as 350-cid V-8 above, except Bore & stroke: 3.80 x 3.85 in. Compression ratio: 8.0:1. Brake horsepower: 155 at 3400 rpm. Torque: 280 lbs.-ft. at 1800 rpm. Buick-built. VIN Code: X.

ENGINE [Alternate V-8 Phoenix/Firebird/Catalina/Bonneville/LeMans Safari]: Same as 350-cid V-8 above, except Bore & stroke: 4.06 x 3.38 in. Compression ratio: 7.9:1. Brake horsepower: 160 at 3600 rpm. Torque: 270 lbs.-ft. at 2000 rpm. Oldsmobile-built. VIN Code: R.

ENGINE [Optional V-8 Firebird Formula/Trans Am]: 90-degree, overhead valve V-8. Cast-iron block and head. Displacement: 400 cid. (6.6 liters). Bore & stroke: 4.12 x 3.75 in. Compression ratio: 8.1:1. Brake horsepower: 220 at 4000 rpm. Torque: 320 lbs.-ft. at 2800 rpm. Five main bearings. Hydraulic valve lifters. Carburetor: four-barrel Rochester M4MC. VIN Code: Z.

ENGINE [Base V-8 (Trans Am); Optional (Firebird Formula)]: 90-degree, overhead valve V-8. Cast-iron block and head. Displacement: 403 cid. (6.6 liters). Bore & stroke: 4.35 x 3.38 in. Compression ratio: 7.9:1. Brake horsepower: 185 at 3600 rpm. Torque: 320 lbs.-ft. at 2000 rpm. Five main bearings. Hydraulic valve lifters. Carburetor: four-barrel Rochester M4MC. Oldsmobile-built. VIN Code: K.

CHASSIS: Wheelbase: (Sunbird) 97.0 in.; (Phoenix) 111.1 in.; (Firebird) 108.2 in.; (LeMans) 108.1 in.; (Grand Prix) 108.1 in.; (Catalina/Bonneville) 116.0 in. Overall Length: (Sunbird) 179.2 in.; (Sunbird Safari) 178.0 in.; (Phoenix) 203.4 in.; (Firebird) 196.8 in.; (LeMans) 198.5 in.; (LeMans Safari) 197.8 in.; (Grand Prix) 201.2 in.; (Catalina/Bonneville) 214.3 in.; (Safari) 215.1 in. Height: (Sunbird) 49.6 in.; (Sunbird Safari) 51.8 in.; (Phoenix coupe) 52.3 in.; (Phoenix sedan) 53.2 in.; (Firebird) 49.3 in.; (LeMans coupe) 53.5 in.; (LeMans sedan) 54.4 in.; (LeMans Safari) 54.8 in.; (Grand Prix) 53.3 in.; (Catalina/Bonneville coupe) 53.9 in.; (Catalina/Bonneville sedan) 54.5 in.; (Safari) 57.3 in. Width: (Sunbird) 65.4 in.; (Phoenix) 72.4 in.; (Firebird) 73.0 in.; (LeMans) 72.4 in.; (LeMans Safari) 72.6 in.; (Grand Prix) 72.7 in.; (Catalina/Bonneville) 76.4 in.; (Safari) 79.9

in. Front Tread: (Sunbird) 55.3 in.; (Phoenix) 61.9 in.; (Firebird) 61.3 in.; (LeMans) 58.5 in.; (Grand Prix) 58.5 in.; (Catalina/Bonneville) 61.7 in.; (Safari) 62.0 in. Rear Tread: (Sunbird) 54.1 in.; (Phoenix) 59.6 in.; (Firebird) 60.0 in.; (LeMans) 57.8 in.; (Grand Prix) 57.8 in.; (Catalina/Bonneville) 60.7 in.; (Safari) 64.1 in. Standard Tires: (Sunbird) A78 x 13; (Phoenix) E78 x 14; (Firebird) FR78 x 15; (Firebird Formula/Trans Am) P225/70R15; (LeMans) P185/75R14; (Grand Am) P205/70R14; (Grand Prix) P195/75R14; (Catalina/Bonneville) FR78 x 15.

TECHNICAL: Transmission: Three-speed manual transmission standard on Phoenix/LeMans/Firebird and base Grand Prix. Four-speed manual transmission standard for Sunbird, optional in Firebird, Phoenix and LeMans. Five-speed manual transmission optional in Sunbird. Three-speed Turbo-Hydra-Matic transmission standard in other models; optional on all. Standard final drive ratio: (Sunbird) 2.73:1 with four-cylinder engine and four-speed transmission; 2.93:1 with V-6 and four-speed transmission; (Phoenix) 3.08:1 with four-speed transmission; 2.56:1 with V-6 and automatic transmission; 2.41:1 with V-8 and automatic transmission; (Firebird V-6) 3.08:1 with three-speed transmission; (Firebird 302-cid V-8) 2.41:1, 3.08:1 or 2.73:1; (Firebird 350-cid V-8) 3.08:1; (Firebird 400-cid V-8) 3.23:1; (Firebird 403-cid V-8) 2.41:1; (LeMans V-6) 2.73:1 with three-speed transmission; 2.93:1 with four-speed transmission; 2.41:1 or 3.23:1 with automatic transmission; (LeMans V-8) 2.14:1, 2.29:1 or 2.73:1; (Grand Prix) 2.93:1 with V-6, 2.14:1 or 2.29:1 with V-8; (Catalina/Bonneville) 2.73:1 with V-6, 2.29:1 or 2.56:1 with V-8 301-cid; 2.41:1 with 350-cid V-8; (Safari) 2.56:1 or 2.73:1. Steering: Recirculating ball. Front Suspension: (Sunbird) coil springs and control arms; (Firebird/LeMans) coil springs with lower trailing links and anti-sway bar; (others) coil springs and anti-sway bar. Rear Suspension: (Sunbird) rigid axle with coil springs, lower trailing radius arms and upper torque arms; (Phoenix) rigid axle with semi-elliptic leaf springs; (Firebird) semi-elliptic leaf springs with anti-sway bar; (LeMans/Bonneville/Grand Prix) rigid axle with coil springs, lower trailing radius arms and upper torque arms. Brakes: Front disc, rear drum; four-wheel disc brakes available on Firebird Formula and Trans Am. Ignition: Electronic. Body construction: (Sunbird) unit; (Firebird) unit with separate partial frame; (others) separate body and frame. Fuel tank: (Sunbird) 18.5 gal. except wagon, 16 gal.; (Phoenix) 21 gal.; (Firebird) 21 gal.; (LeMans) 18.1 gal. except wagon, 18.2 gal.; (Grand Prix) 18.1 gal.; (Catalina/Bonneville) 21 gal.

DRIVETRAIN OPTIONS: Engines: 231-cid V-6: Sunbird ($200); Grand Prix LJ ($195 credit). 301-cid, two-barrel V-8: Firebird/LeMans/Catalina/Grand Prix ($195). 301-cid, four-barrel V-8: Firebird ($280); Firebird Formula ($85); Trans Am ($165 credit); LeMans/Grand Prix/Catalina

1979 Pontiac Grand Prix LJ two-door coupe. (PGMC)

1979 Pontiac Catalina two-door coupe. (PGMC)

1979 Pontiac Bonneville Brougham four-door sedan. (PGMC)

($255); Grand Prix LJ ($60); Bonneville ($60). 305-cid, two-barrel V-8: Sunbird ($395); Phoenix/Firebird ($195). 305-cid, four-barrel V-8: LeMans/Grand Prix ($255); Grand Prix LJ ($60). 350-cid, four-barrel V-8: Phoenix/Firebird/Catalina ($320); LeMans Safari ($320); Firebird Formula ($125); Bonneville ($125). Trans Am 400-cid, four-barrel V-8: Formula ($340); Trans Am ($90). 403-cid, four-barrel V-8: Firebird Formula ($250); Safari ($195). Transmission/Differential: Four-speed manual floor shift transmission: Phoenix with V-8-305 ($135); Firebird/LeMans/Grand Prix ($135); Grand Prix LJ/SJ ($200 credit). Five-speed manual transmission: Sunbird ($175). Turbo-Hydra-Matic: Sunbird ($295); Phoenix/Firebird/LeMans/Grand Prix ($335); Trans Am (NC). Limited-slip differential: Sunbird ($59); LeMans/Firebird/Grand Prix ($63); Catalina/Bonneville ($67). Brakes/Steering: Power brakes: Sunbird ($71); Phoenix/LeMans/Firebird/Grand Prix ($76). Power four-wheel disc brakes: Firebird Formula/Trans Am ($150). Power steering: Sunbird ($146); Phoenix/LeMans/Grand Prix ($163). Suspension: Rally RTS handling package: Sunbird ($38-$120); Phoenix ($182-$230); LeMans ($44-$189); Catalina ($150-$180); Bonneville ($109-$128); Grand Prix ($72-$128). Firm ride package ($13) except Sunbird. Superlift shock absorbers: LeMans/Grand Prix ($54); Catalina/Bonneville ($55). Automatic level control: LeMans/Grand Prix/Catalina/Bonneville ($66-$121). Other: Heavy-duty radiator: Sunbird ($33); Phoenix ($32-$59). Heavy-duty cooling: Sunbird ($26-$59). Super-cooling radiator ($32-$60) except Sunbird/Phoenix. Heavy-duty battery ($18-$21). Heavy-duty alternator: Sunbird/Phoenix/Firebird/LeMans/Grand Prix ($32); Catalina/Bonneville ($23-$55). Engine block heater ($14-$15). Light trailer group: Bonneville/Catalina ($122-$150). Medium trailer

1979 Pontiac Phoenix LJ four-door sedan. (OCW)

1979 Pontiac Firebird two-door hardtop. (OCW)

1979 Pontiac Firebird Trans Am two-door hardtop. (OCW)

group: LeMans/Grand Prix ($121-$148). Heavy trailer group: Bonneville/Catalina ($122-$187). California emissions ($83-$150). High-altitude option ($35).

OPTION PACKAGES: Sunbird Formula group ($415-$591). Sunbird sport hatchback graphics package ($73). Sunbird appearance group: cpe ($91). Phoenix custom exterior ($91-$97). Phoenix exterior appearance package ($166). Phoenix appearance package ($76). Firebird Red Bird appearance package: Esprit ($449-$491). Trans Am special edition ($674); with hatch roof ($1329). Firebird Formula appearance package ($92). Firebird Trans Am special performance package ($250-$434). LeMans Safari security package ($37-$42). LeMans luxury group ($148-$348). LeMans exterior paint appearance ($166). LeMans custom exterior ($46-$98). LeMans custom trim group ($145-$259). Full-size exterior paint package ($166). Grand Prix exterior appearance ($124-$172). Grand Prix appearance package ($197-$264).

MAJOR CONVENIENCE/APPEARANCE OPTIONS: Air conditioning ($496-$605). Automatic air conditioning: LeMans/Grand Prix ($653); Catalina/Bonneville ($688). Cruise control ($103-$108); not available for Sunbird. Power seat: LeMans/Catalina/Bonneville/Grand Prix ($163-$166). Power windows ($126-$205); not available for Sunbird. Cornering lamps: Catalina/Bonneville/Grand Prix ($49). Power glass sunroof: LeMans/Grand Prix ($729); Catalina/Bonneville ($925). Power steel sun roof: LeMans/Grand Prix ($529); Catalina/Bonneville ($725). Removable glass sunroof: Sunbird ($180). Hatch roof: Firebird/Grand Prix ($655). Full vinyl cordova top: Phoenix ($99); LeMans ($116); Catalina/Bonneville ($145). Padded landau top: Grand Prix/LeMans ($239); Catalina/Bonneville ($298). Landau top: Sunbird ($156); Phoenix ($190). Canopy top: Firebird ($116). Rear-facing third seat: Safari ($183). Wire wheels: Grand Prix ($425-$499).

HISTORICAL: Introduced: Sept. 28, 1978. Model year production: 907,412 units. Calendar year production (U.S.): 713,475. Calendar year sales by U.S. dealers: 781,042. Model year sales by U.S. dealers: 828,603 (including 42,852 early 1980 front-drive Phoenix models). Sales slipped a bit for the model year, with only the Sunbird and LeMans lines showing slight increases. Sunbird's "Iron Duke" four-cylinder engine switched to a cross-flow cylinder head and would soon be the standard power plant for many GM models, especially with transverse mounting in GM's new front-drive X-cars. An alternate version was supplied for rear-drive installations. At the end of 1979, Robert C. Stempel, who would later become head of General Motors, was named Pontiac's general manager.

1979 Pontiac Firebird Trans Am two-door hardtop. (OCW)

1980 Pontiac Sunbird Sport three-door hatchback. (AA)

CATALINA/BONNEVILLE — SERIES 2B — (V-6/V-8) — Full-size Pontiacs (Catalina, Bonneville, and Bonneville Brougham) all featured new front-end sheet metal as part of their first significant restyle since the 1977 debut in down-sized form. Weights were cut about 100 pounds, aerodynamics improved, and engine sizes reduced. The new design displayed a lower profile and more aerodynamic looking front, with new roof lines, sail panels, doors, and quarter panels. Lengthening both the front and rear overhang produced a longer overall look, even though dimensions did not change much. The hood was lowered and deck lid was raised. Air dams and baffles were added to the body. Coupes had a more formal roofline, while four-door sedans had a restyled upper window area. A compact spare added luggage space. Deck lids and tail lamp housings were new this year. The Catalina used narrow tail lamps, while the Bonneville's were of full-width wraparound design with two horizontal trim strips. For a change, Catalinas and Bonnevilles shared a similar front-end appearance. Both had a bold, all-bright vertical-themed grille (with the grille pattern extended below the bumper). It consisted of four vertical bars on each side of the bright divider, which held a Pontiac emblem. The flush bumper design included plastic inner fender skirts. Tungsten-halogen headlamps, which first appeared in midyear 1979, continued as an option. Headlamp bezels wrapped around the front fenders. Cornering lamps had body-colored bezels and were mounted higher on the fender this year, rather than in the lower body side molding. New park/signal lamps were set between the headlamps (similar to the 1979 Grand Prix arrangement). Front side markers had new amber lenses and two horizontal ribs. Coupes and sedans had new two-tone paint treatments and accent striping. Safari wagons again carried simulated woodgrain side paneling, but in a "planked" red elm design. Bonneville Safaris could have ordinary two-tone paint instead of the woodgrain. Bonnevilles had new full-length body side moldings as well as a new B-pillar appliqué. New landau padded roofs were also offered. Catalina upholstery was Dover II knit cloth, whereas Bonnevilles had new Patrician striped velour cloth. Brougham seating was Prima cloth knit, which had a longer nap than the former Dante

1980 Pontiac Phoenix SJ two-door coupe. (AA)

1980 Pontiac Firebird Esprit "Yellow Bird" two-door hardtop. (CP)

cloth. New Embassy leather was optional on Broughams. To improve ride and durability, the front suspension held new ball joints and a re-bushed front stabilizer bar. Wheel covers now had openings for improved brake and wheel bearing cooling. New tire sizes took higher inflation pressures. A new side frame jack was included. New options included electronic-tuned signal-seeking digital AM/FM stereo radios, extended-range speakers, and power outside mirrors. Base engine this year for both Catalina and Bonneville was the 231-cid (3.8-liter) V-6. Bonneville Brougham carried the new 265-cid (4.3-liter) V-8, which was optional on other models. Wagons had a 301-cid (4.9-liter) four-barrel V-8. The Oldsmobile-built diesel was available for Bonneville Brougham and Safari wagons only.

GRAND PRIX — SERIES 2G — (V-6/V-8) — Three Grand Prix models were offered again: base, luxury LJ, and sporty SJ. Standard engine was again the 231-cid (3.8-liter) V-6, except for in the SJ, which carried the new 301-cid (4.9-liter) E/C four-barrel V-8. Base and LJ models could have the new 265-cid (4.3-liter) V-8. California SJ models had a 305-cid V-8 with four-barrel carburetion, which was also optional on base and LJ models. Manual gearboxes were no longer available. Every Grand Prix had automatic transmission as well as power brakes and steering. Appearance changes included a new grille and grille bumper inserts, with a larger look than before. The all-bright grille contained vertical bars on each side of a fairly narrow bright divider. Between each pair of rectangular headlamps were clear park/signal lamps. Tail lamp housings, lenses, and bezels were new this year. 'GP' lettering was sonic-welded to the center of each lens. Grand Prix LJ and SJ had new tapered wheel opening moldings and revised multiple accent striping. The optional double two-tone paint treatment also was revised. Inside there were new cloth door-trim panels. Base models had a pull strap above dual bright and black moldings; SJ and LJ models offered a drop handle. New cloth seats went into base models, whereas LJ models had the same seating as base models with the luxury trim option. New options included electronic-tuned stereo radios and extended-range speakers. Halogen headlamps also were offered.

LEMANS — SERIES 2A — (V-6/V-8) — Design changes for the LeMans and Grand LeMans included new grilles, park/signal lamps, front side marker lamps and tail lamps (for coupes and sedans). Two new interior colors, blue and maroon, were available. LeMans door panels had new simulated welt-and-stitch lines centered between bright mylar moldings. Grand LeMans door panels had wide mylar moldings. All models had standard power brakes. Safari

1980 Pontiac Formula Firebird two-door hardtop. (CP)

1980 Pontiac Firebird Turbo Trans Am Indianapolis 500 Pace Car. (IMSC)

wagons could have a double two-tone paint treatment at no extra cost, instead of the standard simulated woodgraining. The woodgrain came in a new red elm pattern this year. New options included electronic-tuned stereo radios and extended-range speakers. Each grille section consisted of horizontal bars, with clear park/ signal lamps behind the outer ends. The wide center panel held a Pontiac emblem above "Pontiac" block lettering. Wraparound clear/ amber marker lenses had four horizontal trim ribs. Single rectangular headlamps were used. Base engine for coupes and sedans was Chevrolet's 229-cid (3.8-liter) V-6 with a three-speed manual gearbox. Other Pontiacs used Buick's 231-cid V-6. Options included the new 265-cid (4.3-liter) V-8 and Turbo-Hydra-Matic transmission, as well as a 301-cid (4.9-liter) four-barrel V-8. California models could have a 305-cid V-8.

GRAND AM — SERIES 2A — (V-8) — The Grand Am now came in coupe form only, carrying the 301-cid E/C engine (as in Trans Am) with automatic transmission. California Grand Ams had a 305-cid V-8 instead. In addition to a new soft-fascia front end, the Grand Am added ample standard equipment in an attempt to attain a performance image. The list included bucket seats (with console), sport mirrors, Rally IV wheels, and a custom sport steering wheel. A new silver upper body accent stripe was standard. The Rally RTS suspension had larger front and rear stabilizer bars. All Grand Am bodies had a new Ontario Gray lower accent color. Each of the twin grille sections was divided into three sections, with thin body-color separators between. Each section held horizontal strips. A wide, peaked center divider held a V-shaped Pontiac emblem that extended from the hood crease. The front bumper had two air slots. Single rectangular headlamps stood directly above clear park/signal lamps.

FIREBIRD — SERIES 2F — (V-6/V-8) — Appearance changes were minimal, but the Firebird got a sharply altered engine selection this year. Base engine for base and Esprit models remained the 231-cid (3.8-liter) V-6. A new 265-cid (4.3-liter) V-8 was optional along with a 301-cid (4.9-liter) four-barrel V-8. Trans Ams now carried the E/C 301-cid four-barrel V-8, which was optional on Formula models. Both the Trans Am and Formula could also get a new turbocharged 301-cid four-barrel. As in other models, California cars had a modified selection, including a 305-cid V-8 standard in the Trans Am and Formula. Base and Esprit Firebirds still had a three-speed

1980 Pontiac Grand LeMans four-door sedan. (PGMC)

1980 Pontiac Grand Am two-door coupe. (AA)

1980 Pontiac Grand Am two-door coupe. (AA)

1980 Pontiac Grand Prix SJ two-door coupe. (AA)

1980 Pontiac Grand Prix SJ two-door coupe. (AA)

1980 Pontiac Catalina two-door coupe. (AA)

1980 Pontiac Sunbird two-door coupe. (OCW)

manual transmission, while the Formula and Trans Am carried automatic transmissions. All California Firebirds were equipped with automatic transmission. Dual exhausts came in a lighter weight design this year. Turbocharged Firebirds included a unique hood with special bird decal. Turbo graphics went on the hood and deck lid spoiler. Another bird decal was available for non-turbo Trans Ams. A new "Yellow Bird" option package with gold accent striping replaced the former Redbird package. Trans Am buyers could again get a black-painted Special Edition package, either with or without a hatch roof. New Trans Am graphics colors included bronze-and-burgundy and a revised red-and-gold combination. New seating came in five colors. Dark blue was a new interior color. New optional electronic-tuned stereo radios came with a four-speaker system. Tungsten halogen headlamps remained available.

SUNBIRD — SERIES 2H — (FOUR/V-6) — Sunbird coupe, Sport Coupe and Sport Hatchback models were available, but the Sunbird Safari wagon was dropped. The Sunbird had a new egg-crate-pattern grille and new park/signal lamps. New seating came in five colors. Standard bucket seats now had smooth headrests. Luxury interior trim was now Ramrod striped velour. Options included new sport accent striping. Base engine was the cross-flow 151-cid (2.5-liter) four, with four-speed manual gearbox. Optional was a 231-cid (3.8-liter) V-6 and automatic transmission. The previously optional 305-cid V-8 had been dropped in mid-1979. The optional five-speed gearbox dropped out this year, too. An additional hatchback model (E07) was added later in the season.

PHOENIX — SERIES 2X — (FOUR/V-6) — The front-wheel-drive Phoenix compact debuted in April 1979 and entered its first full model year with minimal change. A two-door coupe and five-door (actually four-door) hatchback were offered. The base drive train was Pontiac's 151-cid (2.5-liter) four, mounted transversely, with a four-speed manual overdrive transaxle and floor-mounted gearshift lever. Chevrolet's 173-cid (2.8-liter) V-6 and automatic shift were optional. The front suspension used MacPherson struts; at the rear was a trailing axle with coil springs and track bar. Each of the twin grille sections consisted of large (3 x 3 pattern) holes over tight crosshatching. Clear vertical parking/signal lamps stood between the grille and the single rectangular headlamps. The horizontal tail lamps had two horizontal and two vertical trim strips, with back-up lights toward the center, next to the license plate. The body-colored bumpers had bright strips. Standard equipment included P185/80R13 glass-belted radial black sidewall tires, hubcaps with Pontiac

1980 Pontiac Phoenix five-door hatchback. (OCW)

crests and an AM radio. The Phoenix LJ added a stand-up hood ornament, bright wide rocker panel moldings, wheel covers, accent striping and sport mirrors. An SJ option package included black grilles and headlamp bezels, a Phoenix bird emblem on center pillar, vinyl bucket seats, P205 tires on Rally wheels, Rally RTS suspension and accent colors on the lower body and bumpers. New stripe colors were made available for the full year and base seating carried a different fabric. The sporty SJ option had new two-tone color combinations. A brushed aluminum B-pillar appliqué for the four-door hatchback was first available alone, then later only as part of a custom exterior group. Accent paint stripes were standard at first and then became optional.

I.D. DATA: Pontiac's 13-symbol Vehicle Identification Number (VIN) was located on the upper left surface of the instrument panel, visible through the windshield. The first digit is 2, indicating Pontiac division. The second symbol is a letter indicating series: E=Sunbird; M=Sunbird Sport; Y=Phoenix; Z=Phoenix LJ; D=LeMans; F=Grand LeMans; G=Grand Am; S=Firebird; T=Firebird Esprit; V=Firebird Formula; W=Firebird Trans Am; L=Catalina; N=Bonneville; R=Bonneville Brougham; J=Grand Prix; K=Grand Prix LJ; H=Grand Prix SJ. Next come two digits that denote body type: 07=two-door hatchback coupe; 27=two-door coupe; 37=two-door coupe; 87=two-door plain-back coupe; 19=four-door six-window sedan; 68=four-door six-window hatchback; 69=four-door four-window sedan; 35=four-door two-seat Safari. The fifth symbol is a symbol indicating engine code: V or 5=151-cid two-barrel I-4; 7=173-cid two-barrel V-6; A=231-cid two-barrel V-6; S=265-cid two-barrel V-8; W=301-cid four-barrel V-8; T=301-cid four-barrel Turbo V-8; H=305-cid four-barrel V-8; R=350-cid four-barrel V-8; N=350-cid diesel V-8. The sixth symbol denotes model year (A=1980). Next is a plant code: B=Baltimore; L=Van Nuys, Calif.; N=Norwood, Ohio; P=Pontiac, Mich.; T=Tarrytown, N.Y.; 7=Lordstown, Ohio; X=Fairfax, Kan.; 6=Oklahoma City; 1=Oshawa, Ontario Canada; 2=Ste. Therese, Quebec Canada. The final six digits are the sequential serial number.

Model Number	Body Style Number	Body Type & Seating	Factory Price	Shipping Weight	Production Total
CATALINA (V-6/V-8)					
2B	L37	2d Coupe-6P	6,341/6,521	3,394/3,503	3,319
2B	L69	4d Sedan-6P	6,397/6,577	3,419/3,528	10,408
CATALINA SAFARI (V-8)					
2B	L35	4d Sta Wag-6P	7,044	3,929	2,931
BONNEVILLE (V-6/V-8)					
2B	N37	2d Coupe-6P	6,667/6,847	3,431/3,540	16,771
2B	N69	4d Sedan-6P	6,792/6,972	3,478/3,587	26,112
BONNEVILLE BROUGHAM (V-8)					
2B	R37	2d Coupe-6P	7,696	3,571	12,374
2B	R69	4d Sedan-6P	7,885	3,639	21,249

1980 Pontiac Phoenix five-door hatchback. (OCW)

1980 Pontiac Phoenix SJ five-door hatchback. (OCW)

1980 Pontiac Phoenix SJ five-door hatchback. (OCW)

Model Number	Body Style Number	Body Type & Seating	Factory Price	Shipping Weight	Production Total
BONNEVILLE SAFARI (V-8)					
2B	N35	4d Sta Wag-6P	7,625	3,949	5,309
GRAND PRIX (V-6/V-8)					
2G	J37	2d Coupe-6P	6,219/6,399	3,139/3,263	72,659
GRAND PRIX LJ (V-6/V-8)					
2G	K37	2d Coupe-6P	6,598/6,778	3,279/3,406	34,968
GRAND PRIX SJ (V-8)					
2G	H37	2d Coupe-6P	7,296	3,291	7,087
LEMANS (V-6/V-8)					
2A	D27	2d Coupe-6P	5,274/5,454	3,024/3,104	9,110
2A	D19	4d Sedan-6P	5,377/5,557	3,040/3,120	20,485
LEMANS SAFARI (V-6/V-8)					
2A	D35	4d Sta Wagon-6P	5,861/6,041	3,232/3,359	12,912
GRAND AM (V-8)					
2A	G27	2d Coupe-6P	7,299	3,299	1,647
FIREBIRD (V-6/V-8)					
2F	S87	2d Hardtop-4P	5,604/5,784	3,269/3,342	29,811
FIREBIRD ESPRIT (V-6/V-8)					
2F	T87	2d Hardtop-4P	5,967/6,147	3,304/3,377	17,277
FIREBIRD FORMULA (V-8)					
2F	V87	2d Hardtop-4P	6,955	3,410	9,356
FIREBIRD TRANS AM (V-8)					
2F	W87	2d Hardtop-4P	7,179	3,429	50,896
SUNBIRD (FOUR/V-6)					
2H	E27	2d Coupe-4P	4,371/4,596	2,603/ —	105,847
2H	M07	2d Hatchback-4P	4,731/4,956	2,657/ —	52,952
2H	M27	2d Sport Cpe-4P	4,620/4,845	2,609/ —	29,180
2H	E07	2d Hatchback-4P	4,808/5,033	2,651/ —	Note 7
PHOENIX (FOUR/V-6)					
2X	Y37	2d Coupe-5P	5,067/5,292	2,496/2,535	49,485
2X	Y68	5d Hatchback-5P	5,251/5,476	2,539/2,578	72,875
PHOENIX LJ (FOUR/V-6)					
2X	Z37	2d Coupe-5P	5,520/5,745	2,531/2,570	23,674
2X	Z68	5d Hatchback-5P	5,704/5,929	2,591/2,630	32,257

NOTE 1: Prices and weights above slash for V-6/below slash for V-8.

NOTE 2: A third seat was available in all Safari wagons.

NOTE 3: Sunbird prices and weights above slash for I-4/below slash for V-6.

NOTE 4: Sunbird production included in hatchback figure above.

NOTE 5: Phoenix prices and weights above slash for I-4/below slash for V-6.

ENGINE [Base Four Sunbird/Phoenix]: Inline. Overhead valve. Four-cylinder. Cast-iron block and head. Displacement: 151 cid. (2.5 liters). Bore & stroke: 4.00 x 3.00 in. Compression ratio: 8.2:1. Brake horsepower: 86 at 4000 rpm (Phoenix 90 at 4000 rpm). Torque: 128 lbs.-ft. at 2400 rpm (Phoenix 134 lbs.-ft. at 2400). Five main bearings. Hydraulic valve lifters. Carburetor: two-barrel Rochester 2SE. VIN Code: V or 5.

ENGINE [Optional V-6 Phoenix]: 60-degree. Overhead valve six-cylinder. Cast-iron block and aluminum head. Displacement: 173 cid. (2.8 liters). Bore & stroke: 3.50 x 3.00 in. Compression ratio: 8.5:1. Brake horsepower: 115 at 4800 rpm. Torque: 150 lbs.-ft. at 2000 rpm. Four main bearings. Hydraulic valve lifters. Carburetor: two-barrel Rochester 2SE. VIN Code: 7.

ENGINE [Base V-6 LeMans]: 90-degree. Overhead-valve V-6. Cast-iron block and head. Displacement: 229 cid. (3.8 liters). Bore & stroke: 3.38 x 3.48 in. Compression ratio: 8.6:1. Brake horsepower: 115 at 4000 rpm. Torque: 175 lbs.-ft. at 2000 rpm. Four main bearings. Hydraulic valve lifters. Carburetor: two-barrel Rochester M2ME. Chevrolet-built. VIN Code: K.

ENGINE [Base V-6 Firebird/Grand Prix/Catalina/Bonneville; Optional Sunbird]: 90-degree. Overhead-valve V-6. Cast-iron block and head. Displacement: 231 cid. (3.8 liters). Bore & stroke: 3.80 x 3.40 in. Compression ratio: 8.0:1. Brake horsepower: 110 at 3800 rpm (Sunbird 115 at 3800). Torque: 190 lbs.-ft. at 1600 rpm (Sunbird 188 lb.ft. at 2000). Four main bearings. Hydraulic valve lifters. Carburetor: two-barrel Rochester M2ME. Buick-built. VIN Code: A.

ENGINE [Optional V-8 Firebird/LeMans/Grand Prix/Catalina/Bonneville]: 90-degree. Overhead valve V-8. Cast-iron block and head. Displacement: 265 cid. (4.3 liters). Bore & stroke: 3.75 x 3.00 in. Compression ratio: 8.3:1. Brake horsepower: 120 at 3600 rpm. Torque: 210 lbs.-ft. at 1600 rpm. Five main bearings. Hydraulic valve lifters. Carburetor: two-barrel. VIN Code: S.

ENGINE [Base V-8 Firebird Formula/Trans Am; Optional Firebird/LeMans/Grand Prix/Catalina/Bonneville]: 90-degree. Overhead valve V-8. Cast-iron block and head. Displacement: 301 cid. (5.0 liters). Bore & stroke: 4.06 x 3.04 in. Compression ratio: 8.1:1. Brake horsepower: 140 at 4000 rpm. Torque: 240 lbs.-ft. at 1800 rpm. Five main bearings. Hydraulic valve lifters. Carburetor: four-barrel Rochester. VIN Code: W.

ENGINE [Optional E/C V-8 Firebird Formula/Trans Am/Grand Am/Grand Prix SJ]: Same as 301-cid V-8 above, except Horsepower: 155 at 4400 rpm. Torque: 240 lbs.-ft. at 2200 rpm.

ENGINE [Turbocharged V-8 Firebird Formula/Trans Am]: Same as 301-cid V-8 above, with turbocharger. Compression ratio: 7.6:1. Horsepower: 210 at 4000 rpm. Torque: 345 lbs.-ft. at 2000 rpm. VIN Code: T.

ENGINE [Firebird/LeMans/Grand Am/Grand Prix sold in California]: Displacement: 305 cid. (5.0 liters). Bore & stroke: 3.74 x 3.48 in. Compression ratio: 8.4:1. Brake horsepower: 150 at 3800 rpm. Torque: 230 lbs.-ft. at 2400 rpm. Five main bearings. Hydraulic valve lifters. VIN Code: H.

ENGINE [Optional V-8 Safari and California full-size models]: 90-degree. Overhead valve V-8. Cast-iron block and head. Displacement: 350 cid. (5.7 liters). Bore & stroke: 4.06 x 3.39 in. Compression ratio: 8.0:1. Brake horsepower: 160 at 3600 rpm. Torque: 270 lbs.-ft. at 2000 rpm. Five main bearings. Hydraulic valve lifters. Carburetor: four-barrel Rochester E4MC. Oldsmobile-built. VIN Code: R.

1980 Pontiac Phoenix LJ coupe. (OCW)

1980 Pontiac Phoenix LJ coupe. (OCW)

1980 Pontiac Grand LeMans four-door Safari. (OCW)

1980 Pontiac Grand LeMans four-door Safari. (OCW)

ENGINE [Diesel V-8 Catalina/Bonneville/Safari]: 90-degree. Overhead valve V-8. Cast-iron block and head. Displacement: 350 cid. (5.7 liters). Bore & stroke: 4.06 x 3.39 in. Compression ratio: 22.5:1. Brake horsepower: 105 at 3200 rpm. Torque: 205 lbs.-ft. at 1600 rpm. Five main bearings. Hydraulic valve lifters. Fuel injection. Oldsmobile-built. VIN Code: N.

CHASSIS: Wheelbase: (Sunbird) 97.0 in.; (Phoenix) 104.9 in.; (Firebird) 108.2 in.; (LeMans) 108.1 in.; (Grand Prix) 108.1 in.; (Catalina/Bonneville) 116.0 in. Overall Length: (Sunbird) 179.2 in.; (Phoenix coupe) 182.1 in.; (Phoenix hatchback) 179.3 in.; (Firebird) 196.8 in.; (LeMans) 198.6 in.; (LeMans Safari) 197.8 in.; (Grand Prix) 201.4 in.; (Catalina/Bonneville) 214.0 in.; (Safari) 216.7 in. Height: (Sunbird) 49.6 in.; (Sunbird hatchback) 49.9 in.; (Phoenix coupe) 53.5 in.; (Phoenix sedan) 53.4 in.; (Firebird) 49.3 in.; (LeMans coupe) 53.5 in.; (LeMans sedan) 54.4 in.; (LeMans Safari) 54.8 in.; (Grand Prix) 53.3 in.; (Catalina/Bonneville coupe) 54.7 in.; (Catalina/Bonneville sedan) 55.2 in.; (Safari) 57.1 in. Width: (Sunbird) 65.4 in.; (Phoenix) 69.1 in.; (Firebird) 73.0 in.; (LeMans) 72.4 in.; (LeMans Safari) 72.6 in.; (Grand Prix) 72.7 in.; (Catalina/Bonneville) 76.4 in.; (Safari) 79.9 in. Front Tread: (Sunbird) 55.3 in.; (Phoenix) 58.7 in.; (Firebird) 61.3 in.; (LeMans) 58.5 in.; (Grand Prix) 58.5 in.; (Catalina/Bonneville) 61.7 in.; (Safari) 62.1 in. Rear Tread: (Sunbird) 54.1 in.; (Phoenix) 57.0 in.; (Firebird) 60.0 in.; (LeMans) 57.8 in. except Safarion, 58.0 in.; (Grand Prix) 57.8 in.; (Catalina/Bonneville) 60.7 in.; (Safari) 64.1 in. Standard Tires: (Sunbird) A78 x 13 except V-6, B78 x 13; (Phoenix) P185/80R13 GBR; (Firebird) P205/75R15 SBR; (Firebird Formula/Trans Am) P225/70R15 SBR; (LeMans) P185/75R14 GBR except Safari, P195/75R14 GBR; (Grand Am) P205/70R14 SBR; (Grand Prix) P195/75R14 SBR; (Catalina/Bonneville) P205/75R15 SBR; (Safari) P225/75R15.

TECHNICAL: Transmission: Three-speed manual transmission standard on base Firebird and LeMans. Four-speed manual transmission standard on Sunbird and Phoenix. Three-speed Turbo-Hydra-Matic transmission standard on other models, optional on all. Standard final drive ratio: (Sunbird) 2.73:1 or 2.93:1 with four, 2.93:1 with V-6 and four-speed, 2.56:1 with V-6 and automatic transmission; (Phoenix) 2.71:1 with four-speed transmission, 2.53:1 with four-cylinder engine and automatic transmission, 2.84:1 with V-6 and automatic transmission; (Firebird V-6) 3.08:1 with three-speed transmission, 2.56:1 with automatic transmission; (Firebird V-8) 2.41:1; (Firebird Trans Am/Formula) 2.41:1 except 3.08:1 with turbocharged engine or E/C V-8; (LeMans V-6) 2.73:1 with three-speed, 2.41:1 with automatic transmission; (LeMans V-8) 2.29:1 or 2.14:1; (LeMans Safari) 2.73:1 with V-6, 2.41:1 with 265-cid V-8, 2.29:1 with 301-cid V-8; (Grand Am) 2.93:1; (Grand Prix) 2.41:1 with V-6, 2.29:1 with 265-cid V-8, 2.14:1 with 301-cid V-8; (Grand Prix SJ) 2.93:1; (Catalina/Bonneville) 3.23:1 with V-6, 2.56:1 with 265-cid V-8, 2.41:1 with 301-cid V-8 or diesel; (Safari) 2.56:1 with 301-cid V-8, 2.73:1 with 350-cid V-8 or diesel. Steering: (Phoenix) rack and pinion; (others) recirculating ball. Front Suspension: (Sunbird) coil springs and control arms; (Phoenix) MacPherson struts with lower control arms and anti-sway bar; (Firebird/LeMans) coil springs with lower trailing links and anti-sway bar; (others) coil springs and anti-sway bar. Rear Suspension: (Sunbird) rigid axle with coil springs, lower trailing radius arms and upper torque arms; (Phoenix) single-beam trailing axle with track bar and coil springs; (Firebird) semi-elliptic leaf springs with anti-sway bar; (LeMans/Bonneville/Grand Prix) rigid axle with coil springs, lower trailing radius arms and upper torque arms. Brakes: Front disc, rear drum. Ignition: Electronic. Body construction: (Sunbird/Phoenix) unit; (Firebird) unit with separate partial frame; (others) separate body and frame. Fuel tank: (Sunbird) 18.5 gal.; (Phoenix) 14 gal.; (Firebird) 21 gal.; (LeMans) 18.1 gal. except wagon, 18.2 gal.; (Grand Prix) 18.1 gal.; (Catalina/Bonneville) 25 gal.; (Safari) 22 gal.

DRIVETRAIN OPTIONS: Engines: 173-cid V-6 in Phoenix ($225). 231-cid V-6 in Sunbird ($225). 265-cid two-barrel V-8 in Firebird ($150); in LeMans/Grand Prix/Catalina/Bonneville ($180). 301-cid four-barrel V-8 in Firebird ($325); in Trans Am ($180 credit); in LeMans/Grand Prix/Catalina/Bonneville ($295); in Bonneville Brougham ($115). E/C 301-cid, four-barrel V-8 in Firebird Formula ($150). Turbo 301-cid V-8 in Firebird Formula ($530); in Trans Am ($350). 305-cid four-barrel V-8 in LeMans/Grand Prix ($295); in Firebird ($295); in Grand Prix SJ ($150 credit); in Grand Am ($150 credit). 350-cid four-barrel V-8 in Catalina/Bonneville ($425); in Bonneville Brougham ($245); in Safari ($130). Diesel 350-cid V-8 in Bonneville Brougham ($915); in Safari ($860). Transmission/Differential: Turbo-Hydra-Matic in Sunbird ($320); in Phoenix ($337); in Firebird/LeMans ($358). Limited-slip differential: for Sunbird ($64); for LeMans/Firebird/Grand Prix ($68); for Catalina/Bonneville ($73). Brakes/Steering: Power brakes: for Sunbird/Phoenix ($76); for Firebird ($81). Power four-wheel disc brakes: for Firebird Formula/Trans Am ($162). Power steering: in Sunbird ($158); in Phoenix/Grand Prix ($164); in LeMans ($174). Suspension: Rally RTS handling package in Sunbird ($44-$227); in Phoenix ($52-$219); in LeMans ($142-$228); in Grand Am ($64); in Catalina/Bonneville ($45); in Grand Prix ($143-$157). Firm ride package ($14) except Sunbird. Superlift shock absorbers: for Phoenix ($55); for Catalina/Bonneville ($60). Automatic level control: Catalina/Bonneville ($72-$132). Other: Heavy-duty radiator: Sunbird ($36); Phoenix ($35-$60). H.D. cooling: Sunbird ($28-$64). Super-cooling radiator: Firebird ($35-$64); Catalina/Bonneville ($35-$65). Heavy-duty battery ($19-$23) except diesel ($46). Heavy-duty alternator: for Sunbird ($10-$34); for Phoenix ($10-$43); for Firebird ($15-$51); for LeMans/Grand Prix/Catalina/Bonneville ($15-$51). Engine block heater ($16). Light trailer group: Phoenix ($35-$74). Medium trailer group: for LeMans/Grand Prix ($132-$161); for Catalina/Bonneville ($133-$163). California emissions ($250) except diesel ($83).

OPTION PACKAGES: Sunbird Formula group ($496-$674). Sunbird Sport hatchback graphics package ($55). Phoenix custom exterior ($79-$123). Phoenix luxury trim package ($209-$324). Phoenix SJ option ($460-$502). Firebird "Yellow Bird" appearance package: Esprit ($505-$550). Trans Am Special Edition ($748); with hatch roof ($1,443). Firebird Formula appearance package ($100). Firebird Formula/Trans Am special performance package ($281-$481). LeMans Safari security package ($40-$45). LeMans luxury trim group ($161-$271). LeMans two-paint appearance ($180). LeMans custom exterior ($51-$107). LeMans custom trim group ($131-$305). Full-size exterior appearance package ($180). Grand Prix two-tone paint appearance ($134-$186); double two-tone ($213-$288). Full-size custom trim group. ($181-$435).

MAJOR CONVENIENCE/APPEARANCE OPTIONS: Air conditioning ($531-$647). Automatic air conditioning: LeMans/Grand Prix ($700); Catalina/Bonneville ($738). Cruise control ($105-$118); not available for Sunbird. Power seat ($165-$179); not available for Sunbird. Power windows ($132-$221); not available for Sunbird. Cornering lamps: Catalina/Bonneville/Grand Prix ($53). Power glass sunroof: LeMans/Grand Prix ($773); Catalina/Bonneville ($981). Power steel sunroof: LeMans/Grand Prix ($561); Catalina/Bonneville ($770). Removable glass sunroof: Sunbird ($193); Phoenix ($240). Hatch roof: Firebird/Grand Prix ($695). Full vinyl cordova top: LeMans ($124); Catalina/Bonneville ($155). Padded landau top:

1980 Pontiac Bonneville Brougham four-door sedan. (AA)

1980 Pontiac Bonneville Brougham four-door sedan (rear view). (OCW)

1980 Turbo Trans Am Indianapolis 500 Pace Car. (Indy Motor Speedway Corp.)

Phoenix ($179); Grand Prix/LeMans ($239); Catalina/Bonneville ($248). Landau top: Sunbird ($165). Rear-facing third seat: Safari ($199). Wire wheels: Grand Prix ($460-$540).

HISTORICAL: Introduced: Oct. 11, 1979, except Phoenix introduced April 19, 1979. Model year production: 770,821 units. Calendar year production (U.S.): 556,413. Calendar year sales by U.S. dealers: 614,897. Model year sales by U.S. dealers: 638,656 (not including 42,852 early 1980 front-wheel-drive Phoenix models counted in 1979 total). Production fell considerably for the 1980 model year. Unlike many models facing their final year in the lineup, Sunbird had a strong sales year. This was a bad time throughout the industry. Still, sagged sales caused Pontiac to slip back into fourth place among the GM divisions, after ranking No. 3 for three years. Even if Pontiac couldn't sell impressive numbers of cars, it supplied plenty of engines to the other GM divisions. A white limited edition Turbo Trans Am served as the Indianapolis 500 Pace Car. William E. Hoglund became general manager, after a brief turn by Robert Stempel.

1981 PONTIAC

1981 Pontiac T-1000 five-door hatchback sedan. (PGMC)

CATALINA/BONNEVILLE — SERIES 2B — (V-6/V-8) — Pontiac's full-size lineup again included Catalina, Bonneville, and Bonneville Brougham lines. The front-end appearance was similar to 1980, but the new grille had a tight crosshatch pattern repeated in twin bumper slots and park/signal lamps between the headlamps. The

1981 Pontiac T-1000 five-door hatchback sedan. (PGMC)

Bonneville also had new taillights and the Catalina sedan added new side window moldings. The base engine was the 231-cid (3.8-liter) V-6 hooked to an automatic transmission with a locking torque converter clutch. Models with the optional 307-cid (5.0-liter) V-8 required the new four-speed automatic transmission with overdrive top gear. Safari station wagons had the 307-cid V-8 and four-speed automatic transmission as standard. All full-size models could also have a 350-cid (5.7-liter) diesel V-8. Full-size standard equipment included power brakes and steering, P205/75R15 black sidewall tires, stand-up hood ornaments and wind-split moldings, bumper rub strips, rocker panel moldings and rear bumper guards. Catalina coupes and sedans had vinyl seat upholstery. The Bonneville added fender skirts, deluxe wheel covers, a notchback front seat, and hood edge moldings. The Bonneville Brougham included 60/40 notchback front seating, a remote driver's mirror, a clock, and power windows. Safari wagons had P225/75R15 tires, a three-way tailgate, a power tailgate window, driver's remote (passenger manual) outside mirrors, and simulated woodgrain paneling or (on Bonneville Safaris) optional two-tone paint.

GRAND PRIX — SERIES 2G — (V-6/V-8) — All-new sheet metal found its way onto Pontiac's Grand Prix personal-luxury coupe. The Grand Prix's new aerodynamic wedge profile featured a low front end and raised deck to improve the drag co-efficient by some 20 percent. Base and LJ models were offered, along with a new top-rung Grand Prix Brougham (which replaced the former SJ). Although similar in shape to the 1980 design, the new grille was wider, since parking and signal lamps were no longer between the rectangular headlamps. The horizontal-strip pattern of the grille extended below the bumper and appeared in two large slots. Small parking/signal lamps were mounted in the bumper strip. The base engine was the 231-cid (3.8-liter) V-6 with automatic transmission and lock-up torque converter clutch. A 265-cid (4.3-liter) V-8 or a 350-cid diesel were options. A new type of tire used higher pressure to cut rolling resistance. Standard equipment included power brakes and power steering, P195/75R14 black sidewall tires, bright-accented bumper strips, a stand-up hood ornament, hubcaps with crests, rocker panel and wheel opening moldings, and a notchback seat with center armrest. The Grand Prix LJ included wide rocker panel moldings (with extensions), dual body-color sport mirrors (driver's remote) and wide wheel opening moldings. The Grand Prix Brougham added a long list of equipment including opera lamps, a padded landau vinyl roof with formal back window, new finned wheel covers, power windows and a 60/40 front seat.

1981 Pontiac Phoenix SJ two-door coupe. (PGMC)

1981 Pontiac Formula Firebird two-door hardtop. (PGMC)

LEMANS — SERIES 2A — (V-6/V-8) — The LeMans had a lower, more horizontal front-end look that included a revised front fascia panel and grille. The twin egg-crate-style grilles had a 4 x 3 pattern on each side of a tapered center panel with the Pontiac emblem and contained new park/signal lamps at their outer ends. Rectangular quad headlamps were new and the wraparound marker lenses had two horizontal trim ribs. Wide wraparound taillights had one horizontal trim strip and a series of vertical strips that formed squares with back-up lenses at the center, adjoining the license plate. Sedans added a new formal roof. A fully-padded vinyl top was optional. Base engine was the 231-cid (3.8-liter) V-6 with three-speed manual shift (automatic in station wagons and in California). Automatic transmissions had a torque converter clutch. New standard equipment included power steering, a compact spare tire and a side-lift frame jack. Custom finned wheel covers were a new option. Standard equipment included P185/75R14 fiberglass-belted black sidewall tires, power brakes and steering, wheel opening moldings, body-color bumpers with bright rub strips and hubcaps with the Pontiac crest. Coupes had black/bright pillar moldings. Grand LeMans added a hood ornament and wind-split molding, window and lower body side moldings, black rocker panel moldings and a folding front center seat armrest.

FIREBIRD — SERIES 2F — (V-6/V-8) — The Firebird's appearance was the same as 1980, but engine selections were modified a bit this year. The Formula Firebird now carried a standard 265-cid (4.3-liter) V-8, which was optional on the base model and the Esprit. The Trans Am again had a 301-cid (4.9-liter) four-barrel V-8 with Electronic Spark Control. Both Trans Am and Formula models could have a turbocharged 301-cid V-8. The turbocharged V-8 was now available in California. As in 1980, a four-speed manual gearbox was available for Formula and Trans Am with the four-barrel 305-cid (5.0-liter) V-8. Standard power brakes now included a low-drag front caliper. A new two-color bird decal for the hood and reflective bird decal for Trans Am's gas filler door became available. Base Firebird standard equipment included the 231-cid (3.8-liter) V-6 and three-speed manual transmission (with floor shift lever and a console), power brakes, power steering, P205/75R15 SBR black sidewall

1981 Pontiac LeMans two-door coupe. (CP)

tires, a black-out grille with argent accents, hubcaps with Pontiac crests, and a rosewood woodgrain instrument panel appliqué. The Firebird Esprit added an automatic transmission, full wheel covers, wheel opening moldings, wide rocker panel moldings, and body-color sport mirrors (left remote-controlled). The Formula had a 265-cid (4.3-liter) two-barrel V-8 and automatic transmission, P225/70R15 tires, simulated twin hood air scoops, body-color mirrors, a rear deck spoiler, and Rally II wheels with trim rings. The Trans Am included the 301-cid V-8 and automatic, P225/70R15 tires, black-accent grille and headlamp bezels, wheel-opening air deflectors, side-split tailpipe extensions, engine-turned dash trim plate, rally gauges with tachometer, "shaker" hood, and Rally II wheels.

PHOENIX — SERIES 2X — (V-6/V-8) — Base and LJ models made up the Phoenix line again. They came in two-door Coupe or five-door Hatchback body styles. The base engine was the 151-cid (2.5-liter) four-cylinder with four-speed manual transaxle. An SJ option package included black body trim and solid color paint. SJ versions could also get an appearance package with two-tone paint, striping, and bold SJ Phoenix door graphics. New options for the SJ coupe included a deck lid spoiler and a front air dam. The year's new grille was dominated by vertical bars. A new multi-function turn signal lever controlled a pulse windshield wiper. New optional wide body side moldings came in all colors. Automatic transmissions could get a floor lever. Phoenix standard equipment included P185/80R13 fiberglass-belted tires, argent hubcaps with Pontiac crests, a compact spare tire, body-color bumpers with bright strips, a front bench seat, and an AM radio. Hatchbacks had bright rocker panel and wheel opening moldings. The LJ added a stand-up hood ornament and wind-split molding, bright wide rocker panel moldings, wheel covers, a notchback front seat with center armrest, dual horns, and bright window moldings.

T1000 — SERIES 2T — (FOUR) — Pontiac finally offered an equivalent to Chevrolet's subcompact rear-drive Chevette, with the same 1.6-liter four-cylinder engine. It debuted at the Chicago Auto Show in February 1981 as a midyear addition. See 1982 listing for more complete details.

1981 Pontiac "Bandit" Trans Am two-door hardtop. (CP)

1981 Pontiac Grand Prix Brougham two-door hardtop. (PGMC)

Standard Catalog of ® Pontiac, 2nd Edition

1981 Pontiac Catalina four-door sedan. (CP)

I.D. DATA: Pontiac had a new 17-symbol Vehicle Identification Number (VIN) this year, located on the upper left surface of the instrument panel, visible through the windshield. The first three symbols (1G2) indicate Pontiac division. Symbol four is restraint system (A=manual seatbelts). Symbol five is car line/series: M=T1000; Y=Phoenix; Z=Phoenix LJ; D=LeMans; F=Grand LeMans; S=Firebird; T=Firebird Esprit; V=Firebird Formula; W=Firebird Trans Am; X=Firebird Trans Am Turbo Special Edition; J=Grand Prix; K=Grand Prix LJ; P=Grand Prix Brougham; L=Catalina; N=Bonneville; R=Bonneville Brougham. In sixth and seventh position are two digits that denote body type: 07=two-door hatchback; 27=two-door coupe; 37=two-door hardtop; 87=two-door hardtop; 19=four-door six-window sedan; 68=five-door hatchback; 69=four-door four-window sedan; 35=four-door station wagon. Symbol eight is a letter indicating engine code: 5=151-cid two-barrel I-4; X=173-cid two-barrel V-6; A=231-cid two-barrel V-6; S=265-cid two-barrel V-8; W=301-cid four-barrel V-8; T=301-cid four-barrel Turbo V-8; H=305-cid four-barrel V-8; Y=307-cid four-barrel V-8; N=350-cid diesel V-8. Next is a check digit. The tenth symbol denotes model year (B=1981). Symbol eleven is a plant code: B=Baltimore; L=Van Nuys, Calif.; N=Norwood, Ohio; P=Pontiac, Mich.; T=Tarrytown, N.Y.; 7=Lordstown, Ohio; X=Fairfax, Kan.; 6=Oklahoma City; 1=Oshawa, Ontario Canada; 2=Ste. Therese, Quebec Canada. The final six digits are the sequential serial number.

Model Number	Body Style Number	Body Type & Seating	Factory Price	Shipping Weight	Production Total
CATALINA (V-6/V-8)					
2B	L37	2d Coupe-6P	7,367/7,417	3,421/3,540	1,074
2B	L69	4d Sedan-6P	7,471/7,521	3,429/3,548	6,456
CATALINA SAFARI (V-8)					
2B	L35	4d Sta Wagon-6P	8,666	3,924	2,912
BONNEVILLE (V-6/V-8)					
2B	N37	2d Coupe-6P	7,649/7,699	3,443/3,562	14,317
2B	N69	4d Sedan-6P	7,776/7,826	3,461/3,580	32,056
BONNEVILLE BROUGHAM (V-6/V-8)					
2B	R37	2d Coupe-6P	8,580/8,630	3,443/3,562	14,317
2B	R69	4d Sedan-6P	8,768/8,818	3,461/3,580	23,395
BONNEVILLE SAFARI (V-8)					
2B	N35	4d Sta Wagon-6P	9,205	3,949	6,855
GRAND PRIX (V-6/V-8)					
2G	J37	2d Hardtop-6P	7,424/7,474	3,166/3,287	74,786
GRAND PRIX LJ (V-6/V-8)					
2G	K37	2d Hardtop-6P	7,803/7,853	3,195/3,316	46,842
GRAND PRIX BROUGHAM (V-6/V-8)					
2G	P37	2d Hardtop-6P	8,936/8,986	3,231/3,342	26,083
LEMANS (V-6/V-8)					
2A	D27	2d Coupe-6P	6,689/6,739	3,035/3,151	2,578
2A	D69	4d Sedan-6P	6,797/6,847	3,052/3,168	22,186
LEMANS LJ (V-6/V-8)					
2A	D69/Y83	4d Sedan-6P	7,100/—	N/A	Note 3
LEMANS SAFARI (V-6/V-8)					
2A	D35	4d Sta Wagon-6P	7,316/7,366	3,240/3,386	13,358
GRAND LEMANS (V-6/V-8)					
2A	F27	2d Coupe-6P	6,976/7,026	3,063/3,179	1,819
2A	F69	4d Sedan-6P	7,153/7,203	3,108/3,224	25,241
GRAND LEMANS SAFARI (V-6/V-8)					
2A	F35	4d Sta Wagon-6P	7,726/7,776	3,279/3,425	16,683
FIREBIRD (V-6/V-8)					
2F	S87	2d Hardtop-4P	6,901/6,951	3,,275/3,350	20,541

Model Number	Body Style Number	Body Type & Seating	Factory Price	Shipping Weight	Production Total
FIREBIRD ESPRIT (V-6/V-8)					
2F	T87	2d Hardtop-4P	7,645/7,695	3,312/3,387	10,938
FIREBIRD FORMULA (V-6/V-8)					
2F	V87	2d Hardtop-4P	7,854/7,904	3,397/3,472	5,927
FIREBIRD TRANS AM (V-8)					
2F	W87	2d Hardtop-4P	8,322	3,419	33,493
2F	X87	2d Turbo SE-4P	12,257	—	Note 4
PHOENIX (FOUR/V-6)					
2X	Y37	2d Coupe-5P	6,307/6,432	2,450/2,555	31,829
2X	Y68	5d Hatch-5P	6,498/6,623	2,497/2,552	62,693
PHOENIX LJ (FOUR/V-6)					
2X	Z37	2d Coupe-5P	6,778/6,903	2,492/2,547	11,975
2X	Z68	5d Hatch-5P	6,969/7,094	2,552/2,607	21,372
T1000 (FOUR)					
2T	M08	3d Hatchback-4P	5,358	2,058	26,415
2T	M68	5d Hatchback-4P	5,504	2,122	43,779

NOTE 1: Prices and weights above slash for V-6/below slash for V-8.

NOTE 2: A third seat was available in all Safari wagons.

NOTE 3: LeMans production included in basic sedan total.

NOTE 4: Production included in basic Trans Am total.

NOTE 5: Phoenix prices and weights above slash for I-4/below slash for V-6.

ENGINE [Base Four T1000]: Inline. Overhead cam. Four-cylinder. Cast-iron block and head. Displacement: 97 cid. (1.6 liters). Bore & stroke: 3.23 x 2.98 in. Compression ratio: 8.6:1. Brake horsepower: 70 at 5200 rpm. Torque: 82 lbs.-ft. at 2400 rpm. Five main bearings. Hydraulic valve lifters. Carburetor: two-barrel Holley 5210C. VIN Code: 9.

ENGINE [Base Four Phoenix]: Inline. Overhead valve. Four-cylinder. Cast-iron block and head. Displacement: 151 cid. (2.5 liters). Bore & stroke: 4.00 x 3.00 in. Compression ratio: 8.2:1. Brake horsepower: 84 at 4000 rpm. Torque: 125 lbs.-ft. at 2400 rpm. Five main bearings. Hydraulic valve lifters. Carburetor: two-barrel Rochester 2SE. VIN Code: 5.

ENGINE [Optional V-6 Phoenix]: 60-degree. Overhead valve six-cylinder. Cast-iron block and aluminum head. Displacement: 173 cid. (2.8 liters). Bore & stroke: 3.50 x 3.00 in. Compression ratio: 8.5:1. Brake horsepower: 110 at 4800 rpm. Torque: 145 lbs.-ft. at 2400 rpm. Four main bearings. Hydraulic valve lifters. Carburetor: two-barrel Rochester. Chevrolet-built. VIN Code: X.

ENGINE [Base V-6 Firebird/LeMans/Grand Prix/Catalina/Bonneville]: 90-degree. Overhead-valve V-6. Cast-iron block and head. Displacement: 231 cid. (3.8 liters). Bore & stroke: 3.80 x 3.40 in. Compression ratio: 8.0:1. Brake horsepower: 110 at 3800 rpm. Torque: 190 lbs.-ft. at 1600 rpm. Four main bearings. Hydraulic valve lifters. Carburetor: two-barrel Rochester M2ME. Buick-built. VIN Code: A.

ENGINE [Base V-8 (Firebird Formula); Optional (Firebird/LeMans/Grand Prix/Catalina/Bonneville)]: 90-degree. Overhead valve V-8. Cast-iron block and head. Displacement: 265 cid. (4.3 liters). Bore & stroke: 3.75 x 3.00 in. Compression ratio: 8.3:1. Brake horsepower: 120 at 4000 rpm. Torque: 205 lbs.-ft. at 2000 rpm. Five main bearings. Hydraulic valve lifters. Carburetor: two-barrel Rochester E2ME. VIN Code: S.

ENGINE [Base V-8 (Safari); Optional (Firebird/Catalina/Bonneville/LeMans Safari)]: 90-degree. Overhead valve V-8. Cast-iron block and head. Displacement: 301 cid. (5.0 liters). Bore & stroke: 4.00 x 3.00 in. Compression ratio: 8.1:1. Brake horsepower: 135 at

1981 Pontiac Bonneville Brougham two-door coupe. (PGMC)

1981 Pontiac Bonneville Brougham ~~two-door coupe.~~ four sedan (OCW)

3600 rpm. Torque: 235 lbs.-ft. at 1600 rpm. Five main bearings. Hydraulic valve lifters. Carburetor: four-barrel Rochester E4ME. VIN Code: W.

ENGINE [Base V-8 (Firebird Trans Am); Optional (Firebird)]: Same as 301-cid V-8 above, except Brake horsepower: 150 at 4000 rpm. Torque: 245 lbs.-ft. at 2000 rpm.

ENGINE [Turbocharged V-8 Firebird Formula/Trans Am]: Same as 301-cid V-8 above, with turbocharger. Compression ratio: 7.5:1. Brake horsepower: 200 at 4000 rpm. Torque: 340 lbs.-ft. at 2000 rpm. VIN Code: T.

ENGINE [Optional V-8 Firebird Formula/Trans Am]: 90-degree. Overhead valve V-8. Cast-iron block and head. Displacement: 305 cid. (5.0 liters). Bore & stroke: 3.74 x 3.48 in. Compression ratio: 8.4:1. Brake horsepower: 145 at 3800 rpm. Torque: 240 lbs.-ft. at 2400 rpm. Five main bearings. Hydraulic valve lifters. Carburetor: four-barrel Rochester E4ME. Chevrolet-built. VIN Code: H.

ENGINE [Base V-8 (Safari); Optional (Catalina/Bonneville)]: 90-degree. Overhead valve V-8. Cast-iron block and head. Displacement: 307 cid. (5.0 liters). Bore & stroke: 3.80 x 3.38 in. Compression ratio: 8.0:1. Brake horsepower: 145 at 3800 rpm. Torque: 240 lbs.-ft. at 2400 rpm. Five main bearings. Hydraulic valve lifters. Carburetor: four-barrel Rochester E4ME. Oldsmobile-built. VIN Code: Y.

ENGINE [Diesel V-8 Grand Prix/Catalina/Bonneville/Full-size Safaris]: 90-degree. Overhead valve V-8. Cast-iron block and head. Displacement: 350 cid. (5.7 liters). Bore & stroke: 4.06 x 3.39 in. Compression ratio: 22.5:1. Brake horsepower: 105 at 3200 rpm. Torque: 205 lbs.-ft. at 1600 rpm. Five main bearings. Hydraulic valve lifters. Fuel injection. Oldsmobile-built. VIN Code: N.

CHASSIS: Wheelbase: (Phoenix) 104.9 in.; (Firebird) 108.2 in.; (LeMans) 108.1 in.; (Grand Prix) 108.1 in.; (Catalina/Bonneville) 116.0 in. Overall Length: (Phoenix Coupe) 182.1 in.; (Phoenix hatchback) 179.3 in.; (Firebird) 196.1 in.; (LeMans) 198.6 in.; (LeMans Wagon) 197.8 in.; (Grand Prix) 201.4 in.; (Catalina/Bonneville) 214.0 in.; (Safari Wagon) 216.7 in. Height: (Phoenix Coupe) 53.5 in.; (Phoenix Sedan) 53.4 in.; (Firebird) 49.3 in.; (LeMans) 53.5 in.; (LeMans Wagon) 54.4 in.; (Grand Prix) 54.7 in.; (Catalina/Bonneville Coupe) 56.0 in.; (Catalina/Bonneville Sedan) 56.7 in.; (Safari wag) 57.1 in. Width: (Phoenix) 69.1 in.; (Firebird) 73.0 in.; (LeMans) 72.4 in.; (LeMans Wagon) 71.9 in.; (Grand Prix) 72.7 in.; (Catalina/Bonneville) 75.4 in.; (Safari wagon) 75.8 in. Front Tread: (Phoenix) 58.7 in.; (Firebird) 61.3 in.; (LeMans) 58.5 in.; (Grand Prix) 58.5 in.; (Catalina/Bonneville) 61.7 in.; (Safari) 62.1 in. Rear Tread: (Phoenix) 57.0 in.; (Firebird) 60.0 in.; (LeMans) 57.8 in. except wagon, 58.0 in.; (Grand Prix) 57.8 in.; (Catalina/Bonneville) 60.7 in.; (Safari) 64.1 in. Standard Tires: (Phoenix) P185/80R13 GBR; (Firebird) P205/75R15 SBR; (Firebird Formula/Trans Am) P225/70R15 SBR; (LeMans) P185/75R14 GBR except wagon, P195/75R14 GBR; (Grand Prix) P195/75R14 SBR; (Catalina/Bonneville) P205/75R15 SBR; (Safari) P225/75R15 SBR.

TECHNICAL: Transmission: Three-speed manual transmission standard on base Firebird and LeMans. Four-speed manual standard on T1000 and Phoenix. Three-speed Turbo-Hydramatic standard on other models, optional on all. Four-speed overdrive automatic available on full-size models (standard on Safari). Standard final drive ratio: (Phoenix) 2.69:1 with four-speed transmission, 2.53:1 with four and automatic transmission, 2.84:1 with V-6 and automatic transmission, 2.96:1 or 3.33:1; with H.O. (high-output) V-6; (Firebird V-6) 3.08:1 with three-speed, 2.56:1 with automatic transmission; (Firebird V-8-265) 2.41:1; (Firebird V-8-301) 2.56:1; (Firebird Trans Am/Formula) 2.41:1 with V-8-265, 2.56:1 with V-8-301, 3.08:1 with turbo or 305 V-8; (LeMans V-6) 2.73:1 with three-speed,

2.41:1 with automatic transmission; (LeMans V-8) 2.29:1; (LeMans Safari) 2.73:1 with V-6, 2.41:1 with 265-cid V-8, 2.29:1 with 301-cid V-8; (Grand Prix) 2.41:1 with V-6, 2.29:1 with 265-cid V-8, 2.14:1 with 301-cid V-8; (Catalina/Bonneville) 2.73:1 with V-6, 2.41:1 with V-8 except 3.08:1 with 301-cid V-8 and four-speed automatic transmission; (Safari) 3.08:1 with 301-cid V-8, 2.73:1 with diesel. Steering: (Phoenix) rack and pinion; (others) recirculating ball. Front Suspension: (Phoenix) MacPherson struts with lower control arms and anti-sway bar; (Firebird/LeMans) coil springs with lower trailing links and anti-sway bar; (others) coil springs and anti-sway bar. Rear Suspension: (Phoenix) single-beam trailing axle with track bar and coil springs; (Firebird) semi-elliptic leaf springs with anti-sway bar; (LeMans/Grand Prix) rigid axle with coil springs, lower trailing radius arms and upper torque arms. Brakes: Front disc, rear drum. Ignition: Electronic. Body construction: (Phoenix) unit; (Firebird) unit with separate partial frame; (others) separate body and frame. Fuel Tank: (Phoenix) 14 gal.; (Firebird) 21 gal.; (LeMans) 18.1 gal. except wagon, 18.2 gal.; (Grand Prix) 18.1 gal.; (Catalina/Bonneville) 25 gal.; (Safari) 22 gal.

NOTE: Dimensions and technical details for T1000, added at mid-year, not available; see 1982 listing for data.

DRIVETRAIN OPTIONS: Engines: 173-cid V-6: Phoenix ($125). 265-cid two-barrel V-8: Firebird/LeMans/Grand Prix/Catalina/Bonneville ($50). 301-cid four-barrel V-8: Safari ($50). E/C 301-cid four-barrel V-8: Firebird ($215). Turbo 301-cid V-8: in Firebird Formula ($652); in Trans Am ($437). 305-cid, four-barrel V-8: in Firebird Formula ($75); in Trans Am ($140 credit). 307-cid, four-barrel V-8: in Catalina/Bonneville ($50). Diesel 350-cid V-8: in Grand Prix/Catalina/Bonneville Brougham ($695). Transmission/Differential: Turbo-Hydramatic in Phoenix/Firebird/LeMans ($349). Overdrive automatic transmission in Catalina/Bonneville Coupe/Sedan ($153). Limited-slip differential in Firebird/LeMans/Grand Prix/Catalina/Bonneville ($67). Brakes/Steering: Power brakes in Phoenix ($79). Power four-wheel disc brakes in Firebird ($158). Power steering in Phoenix ($168). Suspension: Rally RTS handling package: in Phoenix ($173-$245) except with SJ option ($173); in Catalina/Bonneville ($44). Rally handling suspension in LeMans ($202-$241). Superlift shock absorbers on Phoenix/Catalina/Bonneville ($57). Heavy-duty springs on Phoenix/LeMans/Grand Prix/Catalina/Bonneville ($14-$15). Automatic level control for Catalina/Bonneville ($85-$142). Others: Heavy-duty radiator for Phoenix ($38-$63). Heavy-duty cooling: for LeMans ($34); for Catalina/Bonneville ($34-$63). Super-cooling radiator: for Firebird ($34-$63); for Catalina/Bonneville ($34-$63). Heavy-duty battery ($22) except diesel ($44). Heavy-duty alternator: for Phoenix ($10-$43); for Firebird ($51); for LeMans/Grand Prix/Catalina/Bonneville ($15-$51). Engine block heater ($16). Light trailer group: for Phoenix ($120-$135); for LeMans/Catalina/Bonneville ($129-$158); for Grand Prix ($139-$158). Medium trailer group for Catalina/Bonneville ($129-$158). California emissions ($46) except diesel ($182).

OPTION PACKAGES: Phoenix custom exterior ($85-$130). Phoenix appearance package ($187). Phoenix SJ appearance package ($118). Phoenix luxury trim package ($223-$344). Phoenix SJ option ($404-$449). Trans Am Special Edition ($735); with hatch roof ($1,430). Firebird Formula appearance package ($200). Firebird Formula/Trans Am special performance package ($350-$546). Firebird custom trim ($45-$164). LeMans Safari security package ($40). LeMans luxury trim group ($160-$270). LeMans appearance

1981 Pontiac Grand LeMans four-door Safari station wagon. (OCW)

1981 Pontiac Grand LeMans four-door sedan. (OCW)

1981 Pontiac Grand Prix LJ coupe. (OCW)

package ($180). LeMans custom exterior ($44-$100). LeMans custom trim group ($130-$303). Grand Prix appearance ($184). Full-size appearance package ($177). Full-size custom trim group ($176-$398).

MAJOR CONVENIENCE/APPEARANCE OPTIONS: Air conditioning ($560-$625). Automatic air conditioning: for LeMans/Grand Prix ($677); for Catalina/Bonneville ($708); for Safari ($83). Cruise control ($132-$135). Power seat ($173). Power windows ($140-$211). Cornering lamps for Catalina/Bonneville/Grand Prix ($51-$52). Power glass sunroof: LeMans/Grand Prix ($773); Catalina/Bonneville ($981). Power steel sunroof: LeMans/Grand Prix ($561); Catalina/Bonneville ($704). Hatch roof for Firebird/Grand Prix ($663-$695). Full vinyl cordova top: on LeMans ($115); on Catalina/Bonneville ($142). Padded landau cordova top: on Phoenix ($178); on LeMans ($192); on Grand Prix/Bonneville ($222). Rear-facing third seat: Safari ($194).

HISTORICAL: Introduced: Sept. 25, 1980. Model year production: 600,543 units. Calendar year production (U.S.): 519,292. Calendar year sales by U.S. dealers: 552,384. Model year sales by U.S. dealers: 601,218 (including 34,424 early 1982 J2000 models). Production fell for the model year and for the second year in a row. Sales slipped too, but not by as much. Firebird sales dropped sharply, though part of the loss may have been due to expectations of a fully restyled version in 1982. Only Grand Prix showed a sales rise. Pontiac's CAFE figure for 1981 was just over 23 mpg (with 22 the required standard). In addition to sales of Pontiac's "Iron Duke" four-cylinder engine to other GM divisions, the four-cylinder Pontiac-built engine found its way under the hood of some American Motors'

1981 Pontiac Grand Prix LJ coupe (rear view). (OCW)

cars. Early in the year, Pontiac stopped making V-8 engines after building them in 1932 and from 1955-1981. William E. Hoglund was the division's new general manager.

1982 PONTIAC

1982 Pontiac T1000 three-door hatchback. (PGMC)

BONNEVILLE G — SERIES 2G — (V-6/V-8) — The old Catalina and Bonneville were gone, but a revised Bonneville G entered the lineup. This new Bonneville was a rear-drive car that was smaller and more fuel-efficient than its predecessor. It rode a 108.1-in. wheelbase. Base and Brougham trim levels were available on the formal-roof four-door sedan. A single station wagon model also was offered. Base engine was a 231-cid (3.8-liter) V-6 with three-speed automatic transmission. Options included either a 252-cid (4.1-liter) V-6 or a 350-cid V-8 diesel engine. A relatively narrow center divider (with emblem) separated the twin grilles, which were each made up of vertical bars. Quad rectangular headlamps stood directly above wide park/signal lamps. Two-row wraparound tail lamps had a checkerboard look. Standard Bonneville equipment included power brakes and steering, P195/75R14 black sidewall GBR tires, body-color bumpers, front bumper guards, wide rocker panels (with extensions), roof drip moldings, a stand-up hood ornament (with wind split), wheel opening moldings, wheel covers, and electric clock. Brougham added opera lamps, simulated teak instrument panel trim, and 60/40 front seat with fold-down armrest.

GRAND PRIX — SERIES 2G — (V-6) — The Grand Prix, which was restyled in 1981, continued its aero wedge shape with low front end and higher deck. Its appearance was similar to before, but with a tight pattern of vertical bars (formerly horizontal) in the twin grilles. The grille pattern was repeated in two tall bumper slots. Small park/signal lamps went into the bumper strip, which crossed the grille just below its up/down midpoint. "Grand Prix" script decorated the left grille. Base engine was the 231-cid (3.8-liter) V-6 from Buick with automatic transmission and a lock-up torque converter clutch. A 252-cid (4.1-liter) V-6 cost just $95 more. No gasoline V-8 was available, but a V-8 diesel cost $924. Four trim levels were available,

1982 Pontiac J2000 LE two-door coupe. (JG)

1982 Pontiac Phoenix four-door sedan. (PGMC)

including two new ones for the Brougham. The base Brougham was trimmed as in 1981, including a notchback loose-pillow 60/40 seat. A new Brougham Landau option included opera lamps, a formal back window, padded landau roof, power windows, and Tampico carpeting. Base, LJ, and Brougham models were offered.

FIREBIRD — SERIES 2F — (FOUR/V-6/V-8) — A new, aerodynamically restyled Firebird was 1982's foremost news from Pontiac. Instead of the previous four models, the revised Firebird came in three variations: base coupe, luxury SE coupe, and Trans Am coupe. Each one had its own suspension and tire setup. Base engine was now a fuel-injected 151-cid (2.5-liter) four hooked to four-speed manual gearbox. The SE carried a standard 173-cid (2.8-liter) two-barrel V-6, also with four-speed transmission. The Trans Am had a 305-cid (5.0-liter) four-barrel V-8 with a four-speed transmission. Trans Am buyers could also step up to a dual throttle-body (crossfire) fuel injection V-8 with fresh-air hood induction. A low nose now held electrically controlled hidden halogen headlamps. Park/signal lamps sat in squat slots inboard of the headlamps, barely visible with the headlamp doors shut. The twin air slots contained horizontal bars. At the rear was a large, contoured, frameless all-glass hatch. The tail lamps were housed in a full-width back panel. Reclining front bucket seats were standard. A new Formula steering wheel had an energy-absorbing hub. A WS6 suspension (optional on SE and Trans Am) included P215/65R15 steel-belted radial (SBR) tires on 7-in. aluminum wheels, larger stabilizer bars, four-wheel disc brakes, a posi-traction rear axle, and tuned springs, shocks, and bushings. Standard Firebird equipment included P195/75R14 glass-belted black sidewall tires, hubcaps, a black-finished grille, a front air dam, power brakes, power steering, a front stabilizer bar, side window defoggers, and a black-finished instrument panel. The Firebird SE added full-width black tail lamps, body-color body side moldings, lower accent paint (with striping), turbo cast aluminum wheels, P205/70R14 steel-belted black sidewall tires and rear stabilizer bar. The Trans Am included bird decals on hood and sail panel, front fender air extractors, front and rear wheel-opening flares, and an aero wing deck lid spoiler.

PHOENIX — SERIES 2X — (FOUR/V-6) — Fuel injection was added to the base Phoenix with the 151-cid (2.5-liter) four-cylinder engine this year. Standard equipment for the new Phoenix SJ coupe and hatchback included a high-output 173-cid (2.8-liter) V-6. A lower-powered version of the V-6 was optional in other Phoenix models, as was a three-speed automatic transmission to replace the standard four-speed manual shift. SJ included standard power steering and brakes, cast aluminum wheels, Rally RTS suspension,

1982 Pontiac Firebird SE two-door coupe. (PGMC)

a black grille, black moldings, and an SJ graphics package. The Phoenix steering gear was moved to the engine cradle this year, for better isolation. Styling was similar to 1981.

T1000 — SERIES 2T — (FOUR) — Differing little from Chevrolet's Chevette, the Pontiac T1000 contained the smallest four-cylinder engine ever used in a Pontiac. It had just 98 cid. or 1.6-liter displacement. A five-speed manual transmission was available this year on the T1000 three-door hatchback. A new dark argent grille with widely separated vertical bars and a wide center bar with emblem highlighted the front end. Single rectangular headlamps were set in black bezels. The T1000's small park/signal lamps were bumper-mounted and the bumpers held black rubber end caps. The tail lamps were of a wraparound style. The standard reclining bucket seats were upholstered in vinyl with Pompey cloth optional. Standard equipment included the 1.6-liter OHC four-cylinder engine, four-speed manual transmission, front and rear bumper guards with rub strips, an AM radio, P155/80R13 glass-belted black sidewall tires, wide black or bright body side moldings, argent styled steel wheels, wide vinyl-clad black rocker panel moldings, and black-finished window frames. Three-door hatchbacks had swing-out rear quarter windows.

J2000 — SERIES 2J — (FOUR) — Also new this year was the front-wheel-drive J2000 line. Introduced as an early 1982 model, the five-passenger subcompact's front-drive chassis rode on a 101.2-in. wheelbase. Two-door coupe, three-door hatchback, four-door sedan and four-door wagon bodies were available in base form. The sporty SE came only as a hatchback, while the luxury LE appeared as a coupe or sedan. Each model had standard reclining front bucket seats. Hatchbacks and wagons had full-folding back seats, while SE models had a split folding rear seat. An S model was added later. A sharply sloped front panel formed a tapered body-color center divider, with an emblem, between twin recessed grilles. Quad rectangular headlamps were used. The park/signal lamps were below the bumper strip. A full-width air slot between the parking lamps displayed an egg-crate pattern similar to that of the upper grilles. Wide wraparound tail lamps sat in a full-width panel with horizontal ribbing. There were back-up lenses in the center of each unit. Small rear license plate was bumper-mounted. Base J2000 engine was a transverse-mounted 112-cid (1.8-liter) four-cylinder with a two-barrel carburetor. It was hooked to a four-speed manual transaxle. The engine's fast-burn combustion chamber had a centrally positioned spark plug with high turbulence and 9.0:1 compression ratio. The electronic control module had built-in diagnostics. The front suspension used MacPherson struts. The rear suspension featured a double-crank

1982 Pontiac Phoenix SJ two-door coupe. (JG)

1982 Pontiac Firebird SE two-door coupe. (PGMC)

1982 Pontiac 6000 LE four-door sedan. (OCW)

trailing-twist rear axle. Variable-rate coil springs helped balance the front and rear suspensions. Standard equipment included power brakes, a locking fuel filler door, body-color bumpers with rub strips, swing-out rear quarter windows (except wagons), an AM radio with digital clock, Rally wheels, P175/80R13 fiberglass-belted tires, and reclining front bucket seats. Hatchbacks and LEs had wide body side moldings and rocker panel moldings. The SE added Viscount trim, a gauge set and a driver's side remote rearview mirror.

6000 — SERIES 2A — (FOUR/V-6) — Another new front-wheel-drive Pontiac was the 6000 model. Based on the Phoenix X-car design, the contemporary-styled 6000 carried five passengers and was designed with "internationally competitive" ride-and-handling characteristics. The Pontiac 6000 base and LE models came in two-door coupe or four-door sedan body styles. Standard power plant was a fuel-injected 151-cid (2.5-liter) four with three-speed automatic transmission. Vertical bars made up each side of the split grille. Recessed quad headlamps were used, with parking/signal lamps down in the bumper strip. The wraparound tail lamps had horizontal trim ribs. Back-up lights adjoined the license plate opening. Standard 6000 equipment included automatic transmission, power brakes, power steering, black rocker panel moldings, a front air dam, a black driver's mirror, wheel opening and roof drip moldings, P185/80R13 black sidewall GBR tires, hubcaps, an AM radio, side window defoggers, and a day/night mirror. The 6000 LE added deluxe wheel covers, lower door edge moldings, a locking gas filler door, overhead assist straps, and black-finished rocker panel areas.

I.D. DATA: Pontiac's 17-symbol Vehicle Identification Number (VIN) was on the upper left surface of the instrument panel, visible through the windshield. The first three symbols (1G2) indicate Pontiac division. Symbol four is restraint system (A=manual seatbelts). Symbol five is car line/series: L=T1000; B=J2000; E=J2000 S; C=J2000 LE; D=J2000 SE; Y=Phoenix; Z=Phoenix LJ; T=Phoenix SJ; F=6000; G=6000 LE; S=Firebird; X=Firebird SE; W=Firebird Trans Am; J=Grand Prix; K=Grand Prix LJ; P=Grand Prix Brougham; N=Bonneville G; R=Bonneville G Brougham. In sixth and seventh position are two digits that denote body type: 08=three-door hatchback coupe; 27=two-door coupe; 37=two-door coupe; 77=three-door hatchback; 87=two-door coupe; 19=four-door six-window sedan; 68=five-door hatchback sedan; 69=four-door four-window sedan; 35=four-door station wagon. Symbol eight is a letter indicating engine code: C=97-cid two-barrel I-4; O=109-cid two-barrel I-4; G=112-cid two-barrel I-4; R or 2=151-cid EFI I-4; X or 1=173-cid two-barrel V-6; Z=173-cid two-barrel H.O. V-6; A=231-cid two-barrel V-6; 4=252-cid four-barrel V-6; T=262-cid V-6 diesel; H=305-cid four-barrel V-8; 7=305-cid CFI V-8; N=350-cid V-8 diesel. Next is a check digit. The tenth symbol denotes model year (C=1982). Symbol eleven is a plant code: A=Lakewood, Ga.; G=Framingham, Mass.; K=Leeds,

1982 Pontiac Grand Prix coupe (Kyle Petty stock car). (PGMC)

Mo.; L=Van Nuys, Calif.; N=Norwood, Ohio; P=Pontiac, Mich.; T=Tarrytown, N.Y.; Y=Wilmington, Del.; 7=Lordstown, Ohio; 6=Oklahoma City; Okla. 1=Oshawa, Ontario Canada. The final six digits are the sequential serial number.

Model Number	Body Style Number	Body Type & Seating	Factory Price	Shipping Weight	Production Total
BONNEVILLE G (V-6)					
2G	N69	4d Sedan-6P	8,527	3,203	44,378
2G	N35	4d Sta Wagon-6P	8,414	3,380	16,100
BONNEVILLE G BROUGHAM (V-6)					
2G	R69	4d Sedan-6P	8,985	3,213	20,035
GRAND PRIX (V-6)					
2G	J37	2d Hardtop-6P	8,333	3,276	37,672
GRAND PRIX LJ (V-6)					
2G	K37	2d Hardtop -6P	8,788	3,276	29,726
GRAND PRIX BROUGHAM (V-6)					
2G	P37	2d Hardtop -6P	9,209	3,276	12,969
FIREBIRD (FOUR/V-6)					
2F	S87	2d Coupe-4P	7,996/8,121	—	41,683
FIREBIRD SE (V-6/V-8)					
2F	X87	2d Coupe-4P	9,624/9,819	—	21,719
FIREBIRD TRANS AM (V-8)					
2F	W87	2d Coupe-4P	9,658	—	52,960
PHOENIX (FOUR/V-6)					
2X	Y37	2d Coupe-5P	6,964/7,182	2,386/2,450	12,282
2X	Y68	5d Hatchback-5P	7,172/7,390	2,476/2,540	24,026
PHOENIX LJ (FOUR/V-6)					
2X	Z37	2d Coupe-5P	7,449/7,687	2,386/2,450	4,436
2X	Z68	5d Hatchback-5P	7,658/7,876	2,476/2,540	7,161
PHOENIX SJ (V-6)					
2X	T37	2d Coupe-5P	8,723	2,450	994
2X	T68	5d Hatchback-5P	8,884	2,540	268
T1000 (FOUR)					
2T	L08	3d Hatchback-4P	5,752	2,034	21,053
2T	L68	5d Hatchback-4P	5,945	2,098	23,416
J2000 (FOUR)					
2J	B27	2d Coupe-5P	6,999	2,295	15,865
2J	B77	3d Hatchback-5P	7,275	2,353	21,219
2J	B69	4d Sedan-5P	7,203	2,347	29,920
2J	B35	4d Sta Wagon-5P	7,448	2,418	16,014
J2000 S (FOUR)					
2J	E27	2d Coupe-5P	6,734	—	2,722
2J	E69	4d Sedan-5P	6,902	—	2,760
2J	E35	4d Sta Wagon-5P	7,208	—	1,245
J2000 LE (FOUR)					
2J	C27	2d Coupe-5P	7,372	2,300	6,313

1982 Pontiac 6000 LE two-door coupe. (OCW)

1982 Pontiac Bonneville G four-door station wagon. (JG)

1982 Pontiac Firebird two-door coupe. (OCW)

Model Number	Body Style Number	Body Type & Seating	Factory Price	Shipping Weight	Production Total
2J	C69	4d Sedan-5P	7,548	2,352	14,268
J2000 SE (FOUR)					
2J	D77	3d Hatchback-5P	7,654	2,358	8,533
6000 (FOUR/V-6)					
2A	F27	2d Coupe-5P	8,729/8,854 —		6,505
2A	F19	4d Sedan-5P	8,890/9,015 —		17,751
6000 LE (FOUR/V-6)					
2A	G27	2d Coupe-5P	9,097/9,222 —		7,025
2A	G19	4d Sedan-5P	9,258/9,383 —		26,253

Engine Note: A 305-cid V-8 cost $170 more than the V-6 on base Firebird.

NOTE 1: Firebird prices and weights above slash for four/below slash for V-6.

NOTE 2: Firebird SE prices and weights above slash for V-6/below slash for V-8.

Price Note: Phoenix V-6 price includes the required power brakes.

NOTE 3: Phoenix prices and weights above slash for I-4/below slash for V-6.

NOTE 4: J2000 prices rose $50-$93 shortly after introduction.

NOTE 5: 6000 prices and weights above slash for I-4/below slash for V-6.

ENGINE [Base Four T1000]: Inline. Overhead cam. Four-cylinder. Cast-iron block and head. Displacement: 97 cid. (1.6 liters). Bore & stroke: 3.23 x 2.98 in. Compression ratio: 9.2:1. Brake horsepower: 62 at 5200 rpm. Torque: 82 lbs.-ft. at 2400 rpm. Five main bearings. Hydraulic valve lifters. Carburetor: two-barrel Holley 6510C. VIN Code: C.

ENGINE [Base Four J2000]: Inline. Overhead valve. Four-cylinder. Cast-iron block and head. Displacement: 112 cid. (1.8 liters). Bore & stroke: 3.50 x 2.91 in. Compression ratio: 9.0:1. Brake horsepower: 88 at 5100 rpm. Torque: 100 lbs.-ft. at 2800 rpm. Five main bearings. Hydraulic valve lifters. Carburetor: two-barrel Rochester E2SE. VIN Code: G.

ENGINE [Optional Four J2000]: Inline. Overhead cam. Four-cylinder. Cast-iron block and aluminum head. Displacement: 109 cid. (1.8 liters). Bore & stroke: 3.34 x 3.13 in. Compression ratio: 9.0:1. Brake horsepower: 82 at 5200 rpm. Torque: 96 lbs.-ft. at 2800 rpm. Five main bearings. Hydraulic valve lifters. Carburetor: two-barrel Rochester. VIN Code: O.

ENGINE [Base Four Phoenix/Firebird/6000]: Inline. Overhead valve. Four-cylinder. Cast-iron block and head. Displacement: 151 cid. (2.5 liters). Bore & stroke: 4.00 x 3.00 in. Compression ratio: 8.2:1. Brake horsepower: 90 at 4000 rpm. Torque: 134 lbs.-ft. at 2400 rpm. Five main bearings. Hydraulic valve lifters. Throttle-body fuel injection. VIN Code: R or 2.

ENGINE [Optional V-6 Phoenix/Firebird/6000]: 60-degree. Overhead valve six-cylinder. Cast-iron block and aluminum head. Displacement: 173 cid. (2.8 liters). Bore & stroke: 3.50 x 3.00 in. Compression ratio: 8.5:1. Brake horsepower: 112 at 4800 rpm (Firebird, 105 at 4800). Torque: 145 lbs.-ft. at 2400 rpm (Firebird, 142 at 2400). Four main bearings. Hydraulic valve lifters. Carburetor: two-barrel Rochester E2SE. VIN Code: X or 1.

ENGINE [Optional V-6 Phoenix SJ]: High-output version of 173-cid V-6 above. Compression ratio: 8.9:1. Horsepower: 130 at 5400 rpm. Torque: 145 lbs.-ft. at 2400 rpm. VIN Code: Z.

ENGINE [Base V-6 Grand Prix/Bonneville]: 90-degree. Overhead-valve V-6. Cast-iron block and head. Displacement: 231 cid. (3.8 liters). Bore & stroke: 3.80 x 3.40 in. Compression ratio: 8.0:1. Brake horsepower: 110 at 3800 rpm. Torque: 190 lbs.-ft. at 1600 rpm. Four main bearings. Hydraulic valve lifters. Carburetor: two-barrel Rochester E2ME. Buick-built. VIN Code: A.

ENGINE [Optional V-6 Grand Prix]: 90-degree. Overhead-valve V-6. Cast-iron block and head. Displacement: 252 cid. (4.1 liters). Bore & stroke: 3.96 x 3.40 in. Compression ratio: 8.0:1. Brake horsepower: 125 at 4000 rpm. Torque: 205 lbs.-ft. at 2000 rpm. Four main bearings. Hydraulic valve lifters. Carburetor: two-barrel Buick-built. VIN Code: 4.

ENGINE [Diesel V-6 Pontiac 6000/Bonneville]: 90-degree. Overhead valve V-6. Cast-iron block and head. Displacement: 262 cid. (4.3 liters). Bore & stroke: 4.06 x 3.38 in. Compression ratio: 21.6:1. Brake horsepower: 85 at 3600 rpm. Torque: 165 lbs.-ft. at 1600 rpm. Four main bearings. Hydraulic valve lifters. Fuel injection. VIN Code: T.

ENGINE [Base V-8 (Firebird Trans Am); Optional (Firebird)]: 90-degree. Overhead valve V-8. Cast-iron block and head. Displacement: 305 cid. (5.0 liters). Bore & stroke: 3.74 x 3.48 in. Compression ratio: 8.6:1. Brake horsepower: 145 at 4000 rpm. Torque: 240 lbs.-ft. at 2000 rpm. Five main bearings. Hydraulic valve lifters. Carburetor: four-barrel Rochester E4ME. Chevrolet-built. VIN Code: H.

ENGINE [Optional V-8 Trans Am]: Same as 305-cid V-8 above, with throttle-body fuel injection. Compression ratio: 9.5:1. Horsepower: 165 at 4200 rpm. Torque: 240 lbs.-ft. at 2400 rpm. VIN Code: 7.

ENGINE [Diesel V-8 Grand Prix/Bonneville]: 90-degree. Overhead valve V-8. Cast-iron block and head. Displacement: 350 cid. (5.7 liters). Bore & stroke: 4.06 x 3.39 in. Compression ratio: 21.6:1. Brake horsepower: 105 at 3200 rpm. Torque: 205 lbs.-ft. at 1600 rpm. Five main bearings. Hydraulic valve lifters. Fuel injection. Oldsmobile-built. VIN Code: N.

CHASSIS: Wheelbase: (T1000 three-door hatchback) 94.3 in.; (T1000 five-door hatchback) 97.3 in.; (J2000) 101.2 in.; (Phoenix) 104.9 in.; (Firebird) 101.0 in.; (6000) 104.8 in.; (Grand Prix) 108.1 in.; (Bonneville) 108.1 in. Overall Length: (T1000 three-door hatchback) 161.9 in.; (T1000 five-door hatchback) 164.9 in.; (J2000 coupe) 169.4 in.; (J2000 sedan) 171.4 in.; (J2000 station wagon) 175.3 in.; (Phoenix coupe) 182.1 in.; (Phoenix hatchback) 179.3 in.; (Firebird) 189.8 in.; (6000) 188.7 in.; (Grand Prix) 201.9 in.; (Bonneville) 198.6 in.; (Bonneville station wagon) 197.8 in. Height: (T1000) 52.9 in.; (J2000 coupe) 51.3 in.; (J2000 sedan/station wagon) 53.3 in.; (Phoenix coupe) 53.5 in.; (Phoenix sedan) 53.4 in.; (Firebird) 49.8 in.; (6000) 53.3 in.; (Grand Prix) 54.7 in.; (Bonneville) 55.8 in.; (Bonneville station wagon) 56.1 in. Width: (T1000) 61.8 in.; (J2000) 64.9 in.; (Phoenix coupe) 69.1 in.; (Phoenix sedan) 69.6 in.; (Firebird) 72.0 in.; (6000) 67.7 in.; (Grand Prix) 72.1 in.; (Bonneville) 71.3 in.; (Bonneville station wagon) 72.6 in. Front Tread: (T1000) 51.2 in.; (J2000) 55.4 in.; (Phoenix) 58.7 in.; (Firebird) 60.7 in.; (6000) 58.7 in.; (Grand Prix) 58.5 in.; (Bonneville) 58.5 in. Rear Tread: (T1000) 51.2 in.; (J2000) 55.1 in.; (Phoenix) 57.0 in.; (Firebird) 60.6 in.; (6000) 56.9 in.; (Grand Prix) 57.8 in.; (Bonneville) 57.8 in.; (Bonneville station wagon) 58.0 in. Standard Tires: (T1000) P155/80R13 GBR BSW; (J2000) P175/80R13 GBR BSW; (Phoenix) P185/80R13 GBR BSW; (Firebird) P195/75R14 GBR BSW; (Firebird SE and Trans Am) P205/70R14 SBR BSW; (6000) P185/80R13 GBR BSW; (Grand Prix) P195/75R14 SBR BSW; (Bonneville) P195/75R14 GBR BSW.

TECHNICAL: Transmission: Four-speed manual standard on T1000/J2000/Phoenix and Firebird (base and SE). Three-speed Turbo-Hydra-Matic transmission standard on other models, optional on all. Standard final drive ratio: (T1000) 3.36:1; (J2000) 3.19:1 with 109 four, 3.32:1 with 112 four; (Phoenix) 3.32:1 except 3.65:1 with

1982 Pontiac Firebird Trans Am two-door coupe. (OCW)

Standard Catalog of ® Pontiac, 2nd Edition

H.O. V-6; (Firebird) 3.23:1 with V-6, 3.23:1 with V-8; (6000) 2.39:1 with four, 2.53:1 with V-6; (Grand Prix) 2.41:1 with V-6, 2.29:1 with V-8; (Bonneville) 2.73:1 with V-6, 2.41:1 with V-8. Steering: (T1000/J2000/Phoenix/6000) rack and pinion; (others) re-circulating ball. Front Suspension: (J2000/Phoenix) MacPherson struts with lower control arms and anti-sway bar; (Firebird) modified MacPherson struts with coil springs between lower control arm and X-member; (6000) MacPherson struts with coil springs; (others) coil springs and anti-sway bar. Rear Suspension: (T1000) rigid axle with longitudinal trailing radium arms, transverse bar, coil springs and anti-sway bar; (J2000) rigid axle with coil springs; (Phoenix) single-beam trailing axle with track bar and coil springs; (Firebird) torque arm/track bar with coil springs and anti-sway bar on SE and Trans Am; (6000) trailing arm and beam with coil springs and anti-sway bar; (Bonneville/Grand Prix) rigid axle with coil springs, lower trailing radius arms and upper torque arms. Brakes: Front disc, rear drum. Ignition: Electronic. Body construction: (T1000/J2000/Phoenix/Firebird/6000) unit; (others) separate body and frame. Fuel Tank: (T1000) 12.5 gal.; (J2000) 14 gal.; (Phoenix) 14 gal.; (Firebird) 16 gal.; (6000) 15.7 gal.; (Grand Prix) 18.2 gal.; (Bonneville) 20.6 gal.

DRIVETRAIN OPTIONS: Engines: 151-cid four in Firebird SE ($125 credit). 173-cid V-6 in Phoenix/Firebird/6000 ($125). 252-cid four-barrel V-6 in Grand Prix/Bonneville ($95). Diesel 262-cid V-6 in 6000 ($824). 305-cid four-barrel V-8: in Firebird ($295); in Firebird SE ($170-$195). Dual EFI engine package in Trans Am ($899). Diesel 350-cid V-8 in Grand Prix/Bonneville ($924). Transmission/Differential: Five-speed manual transmission in T1000 ($196). Turbo-Hydra-Matic: in T1000 ($380); in J2000 ($370); in Phoenix/Firebird ($396); in Trans Am ($72). Limited-slip differential in Firebird/Bonneville ($76). Brakes/Steering: Power brakes in T1000/Phoenix ($93). Power four-wheel disc brakes in Firebird ($255) but no charge with performance package. Power steering in T1000 ($190); in J2000 ($180); in Phoenix ($195). Suspension: Electronic suspension in 6000 ($165). Rally RTS handling package: in J2000 ($46); in Phoenix SJ ($88); in other V-6 Phoenix models ($317). Superlift shock absorbers in Phoenix/6000/Bonneville ($64). Heavy-duty springs in Phoenix/6000/Drand Prix/Bonneville ($16). Other: Heavy-duty radiator: in T1000 ($40-$70); in J2000 ($37-$67); in Phoenix ($72); in Firebird ($40). Heavy-duty cooling in 6000/Grand Prix/Bonneville ($40). Heavy-duty battery ($22-$25) except diesel ($50). Heavy-duty alternator: in J2000 ($25); in Phoenix ($16-$51); in Firebird ($15-$51); in Grand Prix/Bonneville ($51). Engine block heater ($17-$18). California emissions ($65) except diesel ($205).

OPTION PACKAGES: J2000 custom exterior group ($79). J2000 hatchback custom trim group ($195). Phoenix two-tone appearance package ($148-$176). Phoenix luxury trim package ($208-$356). Firebird Trans Am Recaro option ($2,486-$2,968). Firebird SE and Trans Am special performance package ($387-$417). Firebird custom exterior ($73-$134). Firebird luxury trim ($299-$844). Grand Prix Brougham Landau package ($810). Grand Prix appearance ($205). Bonneville two-tone paint appearance ($205). Bonneville wagon custom trim group ($211). Lamp groups: ($37-$45) except Bonneville ($21-$51).

MAJOR CONVENIENCE/APPEARANCE OPTIONS: Air conditioning ($595-$675). Cruise control ($145-$165); not available on 1000. Power seat ($183-$197); not available on 1000. Power windows ($152-$235); not available on 1000. Cornering lamps: Bonneville/Grand Prix ($58). Power glass sunroof: Grand Prix ($875). Removable glass sunroof: J2000/Phoenix/6000 ($261-$275). Hatchback roof: Firebird/Grand Prix ($790-$826). Full vinyl cordova top: Bonneville ($140). Padded landau cordova top: Phoenix ($195); Bonneville/ Grand Prix ($220). Wood-grain paneling: Bonneville wagon ($288).

HISTORICAL: Introduced: Sept. 24, 1981, except J2000, May 1981; T1000/Phoenix, Dec. 12, 1981 and Firebird/6000, Jan. 14, 1982. Model year production: 547,271 units. Calendar year production (U.S.): 411,324. Calendar year sales by U.S. dealers: 483,149. Model year sales by U.S. dealers: 461,845 (not including 34,424 early 1982 J2000 models counted in 1981 total). Production fell again for the model year. Sales slipped even further. Several Pontiacs (6000 and some Phoenix models) reached EPA estimates of 40 mpg (highway), while the T1000 managed 42 mpg and the new J2000 series 43 mpg on the highway. The new Firebird design received extensive wind tunnel testing.

1983 PONTIAC

1983 Pontiac 1000 three-door hatchback. (PGMC)

PARISIENNE — SERIES 2B — (V-6/V-8) — The full-size, rear-wheel-drive Parisienne had a conventional front-end appearance with quad rectangular headlamps and vertical-bar twin grilles. Two sedans and a station wagon were offered. Standard equipment included the 3.8-liter V-6 engine and three-speed automatic transmission, power brakes, power steering, P205/75R15 SBR black sidewall tires, narrow bright rocker panel and wheel opening moldings, color-keyed body side moldings, cloth 50/50 seating, bumper rub strips, and deluxe wheel covers. The Parisienne Brougham added luxury cloth 60/40 seating (with passenger recliner). Station wagons had P225/75R15 tires and a 5.0-liter V-8 engine with four-speed overdrive automatic.

BONNEVILLE — SERIES 2G — (V-6/V-8) — Mid-size Bonneville G sedans looked similar to 1982 models. Standard equipment included Buick's 231-cid (3.8-liter) V-6 with automatic transmission, power brakes, power steering, wide rocker panel moldings with extensions, wheel opening moldings/P195/75R14 tires, bumper guards and rub strips, an electric clock, and a day/night mirror. The Bonneville Brougham added cloth 60/40 notchback seating, opera lamps, and a bright pillar appliqué.

GRAND PRIX — SERIES 2G — (V-6/V-8) — Pontiac's personal-luxury coupes were said to get a more modern look this year, but little change was evident beyond a slightly revised grille pattern. The base engine was again the Buick-built 231-cid (3.8-liter) V-6 with three-speed automatic transmission. This year a V-8 option returned. It was a 5.0-liter engine with a four-barrel carburetor. The 350-cid diesel V-8 also was available. Standard equipment included power steering and brakes.

FIREBIRD — SERIES 2F — (FOUR/V-6/V-8) — Major changes to the Firebird were in the power train. Styling was similar to the 1982 redesign. Both four- and five-speed manual gearboxes were

1983 Pontiac J2000 four-door sedan. (PGMC)

1983 Pontiac J2000 LE four-door sedan. (OCW)

1983 Pontiac Phoenix SJ two-door coupe. (PGMC)

available this year, along with a four-speed automatic transmission. The Firebird SE got a high-output version of the 173-cid (2.8-liter) V-6, along with the five-speed transmission. Base models again carried a standard fuel-injected 151-cid (2.5-liter) four with four-speed manual shift. The Firebird SE had new cloth seats and a split-folding back seat (also available for other models in a custom trim package). New Lear Siegler articulated front bucket seats became optional. The Trans Am again carried a standard 5.0-liter V-8, but with the new five-speed transmission and a 3.73:1 axle ratio. Standard base Firebird equipment included power brakes, power steering, reclining front bucket seats and P195/75R14 glass-belted radial tires. The Firebird SE added P205/70R14 SBR tires on turbo cast aluminum wheels, a handling suspension, five-speed gearbox, sport mirrors, color-keyed body side moldings, and lower accent paint with striping. The Trans Am had a rear spoiler and wheel opening flares.

PHOENIX — SERIES 2X — (FOUR/V-6) — A restyling was intended to give Phoenix more of a "Pontiac" look. This year's grille consisted of all horizontal bars. Otherwise, its appearance was similar to 1982. A two-door coupe and five-door hatchback sedan came in base, LJ or sporty SJ trim. A fuel-injected 151-cid (2.5-liter) four with four-speed manual transaxle was standard and a 173-cid (2.8-liter) V-6 and automatic transmission were optional. The Phoenix SJ included a high-output 2.8-liter V-6 and a performance handling package with Goodyear Eagle GT SBR tires on six-inch cast aluminum turbo wheels. A different package with 13-in. wheels was available for other models. Standard equipment included an AM radio, a vinyl front bench seat, P185/80R13 glass-belted radials on Rally wheels, and color-keyed bumpers with black or bright rub strips. The LJ added a notchback front seat, narrow rocker panel moldings, black body side moldings, and charcoal wheel opening moldings. The SJ included power brakes, power steering, a tachometer, a handling suspension, wide black rocker panel moldings, front bucket seats, and P195/70R14 SBR tires on sport aluminum wheels.

1000 — SERIES 2T — (FOUR) — Body changes to the Pontiac 1000 (the "T1000" name was shortened) included more use of black

1983 Pontiac Phoenix LJ five-door hatchback. (PGMC)

1983 Pontiac Phoenix LJ five-door hatchback. (PGMC)

1983 Pontiac J2000 Sunbird two-door convertible. (PGMC)

1983 Pontiac Firebird Trans Am two-door coupe. (PGMC)

Standard Catalog of ® Pontiac, 2nd Edition

1983 Pontiac Firebird Trans Am two-door coupe. (PGMC)

accents to give a sporty, international feel to Pontiac's smallest model. The power train was again the overhead-cam 1.6-liter four with four-speed manual transmission. The standard AM radio could be deleted (for credit). Standard equipment also included reclining front bucket seats. Joining this year's option list were sport striping, a custom trim group, and black luggage rack. A diesel engine option was announced, but failed to materialize.

J2000 — SERIES 2J — (FOUR) — Base power train for the Pontiac J2000 series was now a fuel-injected, overhead-cam 1.8-liter four hooked to five-speed manual transaxle. Coupe, sedan, hatchback and Safari bodies were offered. Their appearance was similar to 1982, with the twin grilles now consisting of several horizontal bars. Recessed quad headlamps stood alongside the small grille inserts. At the center of the front-end panel was a wide, tapered divider with emblem. Small park/signal lamps were below the bumper strip. Standard equipment included power-operated brakes, bumper rub strips, a console, side window defoggers, fully reclining bucket seats, red instrument lighting, a woodgrained dash, wide body side moldings, and P175/80R13 glass-belted radial tires on Rally wheels. The J2000 LE's revised equipment list added an AM radio, bright rocker panel and wheel opening moldings, and a cushion steering wheel. The J2000 SE had P195/70R13 tires on finned turbo cast aluminum wheels and included a rear spoiler, power steering, two-tone paint, and a handling package. An all-new J2000 Sunbird convertible had power windows, fog lamps, and tinted glass. Lear Siegler adjustable front bucket seats were now available for the LE sedan or SE hatchback.

6000 — SERIES 2A — (FOUR/V-6) — The new Pontiac 6000 STE was created to appeal to buyers who craved European-style ride and handling. Offered in a choice of five subtle two-tone combinations, its distinctive body featured six front lights (including center fog lamps), wide body side moldings, and wraparound neutral-density dual-lens tail lamps. The inline lighting trio left little room for a grille on each side of the divider: just narrow black horizontal strips. Small park/signal lamps were in the bumper strip. A Driver Information Center displayed warnings and reminders for service. The orthopedic designed front bucket seats were fully adjustable. An

1983 Pontiac 6000 two-door coupe. (PGMC)

electronic-tuning seek/scan stereo radio with graphic equalizer and clock was standard. Also standard were automatic air conditioning, power mirrors, power windows, and power door locks. The power train consisted of a high-output 173-cid (2.8-liter) V-6 hooked to three-speed automatic transaxle. Hitting the ground were Goodyear Eagle GT steel-belted radial tires on 14-in. aluminum wheels. Electronic ride control, with an on-board air compressor adjusting pressure to the shock absorbers, was standard. The compressor could also be used to inflate a tire. Turning to the regular Pontiac 6000 series, a coupe and sedan were offered in base and LE trim, each with a standard fuel-injected 151-cid (2.5-liter) four and three-speed automatic transmission. Options included a 2.8-liter gas V-6 and 4.3-liter diesel V-6. Joining the option list was the Y99 high-performance rally suspension package. LE models had a 45/45 seat, with a recliner system optional. The twin grilles on the base and LE models again consisted of vertical bars. Standard Pontiac 6000 equipment included an AM radio, a rear stabilizer bar, power brakes, power steering, black mirrors, a black front air dam, black rocker panel moldings, vinyl notchback front seats, and P185/80R13 glass-belted tires on Rally wheels. The Pontiac 6000 LE added a black pillar appliqué, quartz digital clock, and map pockets. The Pontiac 6000 STE rode P195/70R14 tires and had power windows, speed control, tinted glass, air conditioning, an AM/FM stereo with cassette player and equalizer, two-tone paint, fog lamps, and much more on its basic equipment list.

I.D. DATA: Pontiac's 17-symbol Vehicle Identification Number (VIN) was on the upper left surface of the instrument panel, visible through the windshield. The first three symbols (1G2) indicate Pontiac division. Symbol four is restraint system (A=manual seatbelts). Symbol five is car line/series: L=Pontiac 1000; B=J2000; C=J2000 LE; D=J2000 SE; Y=Phoenix; Z=Phoenix LJ; T=Phoenix SJ; F=Pontiac 6000; G=Pontiac 6000 LE; H=Pontiac 6000 STE; S=Firebird; X=Firebird SE; W=Firebird Trans Am; J=Grand Prix; K=Grand Prix LJ; P=Grand Prix Brougham; N=Bonneville; R=Bonneville Brougham; L=Parisienne; T=Parisienne Brougham. In sixth and seventh position are two digits that denote body type: 08=three-door hatchback coupe; 27=two-door coupe; 37=two-door coupe;

1983 Pontiac Firebird two-door coupe. (PGMC)

1983 Pontiac 6000 two-door coupe. (PGMC)

1983 Pontiac 6000 STE four-door sedan. (PGMC)

1983 Pontiac Grand Prix Brougham two-door hardtop. (PGMC)

1983 Pontiac 6000 STE four-door sedan. (PGMC)

1983 Pontiac Bonneville Brougham four-door sedan. (PGMC)

1983 Pontiac 1000 five-door hatchback. (PGMC)

1983 Pontiac 1000 five-door hatchback. (PGMC)

77=three-door hatchback; 87=two-door coupe; 19=four-door six-window sedan; 68=five-door hatchback sedan; 69=four-door four-window sedan; 35=four-door station wagon. Symbol eight is a letter indicating engine code: C=98-cid two-barrel I-4; O=109-cid EFI I-4; P=122-cid EFI I-4; R or 2=151-cid EFI I-4; X or 1=173-cid two-barrel V-6; Z=173-cid two-barrel H.O. V-6; A=231-cid two-barrel V-6; T=262-cid diesel V-6; H=305-cid four-barrel V-8; 7=305-cid CFI V-8; N=350-cid diesel V-8. Next is a check digit. The tenth symbol denotes model year (D=1983). Symbol eleven is a plant code: A=Lakewood, Ga.; B=Baltimore, Md.; G=Framingham, Mass.; L=Van Nuys, Calif.; N=Norwood, Ohio; T=Tarrytown, N.Y.; Y=Wilmington, Del.; 7=Lordstown, Ohio; 1=Oshawa, Ontario Canada; 2=St. Therese, Quebec Canada. The final six digits are the sequential serial number.

Model Number	Body Style Number	Body Type & Seating	Factory Price	Shipping Weight	Production Total
PARISIENNE (V-6/V-8)					
2B	L69	4d Sedan-6P	9,609/9,889	—	9,279
2B	L35	4d Sta Wagon-6P	—/9,927	—	3,027
PARISIENNE BROUGHAM (V-6/V-8)					
2B	T69	4d Sedan-6P	9,879/10,159	—	5,139
BONNEVILLE (V-6/V-8)					
2G	N69	4d Sedan-6P	8,899/9,124	3,214/3,290	47,003
2G	N35	4d Sta Wagon-6P	9,112/9,337	3,275/3,351	17,551
BONNEVILLE BROUGHAM (V-6/V-8)					
2G	R69	4d Sedan-6P	9,399/9,624	3,210/3,286	19,335
GRAND PRIX (V-6/V-8)					
2G	J37	2d Hardtop-6P	8,698/8,923	—	41,511
GRAND PRIX LJ (V-6/V-8)					
2G	K37	2d Hardtop-6P	9,166/9,391	—	33,785
GRAND PRIX BROUGHAM (V-6/V-8)					
2G	P37	2d Hardtop-6P	9,781/10,006	—	10,502
FIREBIRD (FOUR/V-6)					
2F	S87	2d Cpe-4P	8,399/8,549	2,866/2,948	32,020
FIREBIRD SE (V-6/V-8)					
2F	X87	2d Cpe-4P	10,322/10,397	2,965/3,145	10,934
FIREBIRD TRANS AM (V-8)					
2F	W87	2d Cpe-4P	10,396	3,107	31,930
PHOENIX (FOUR/V-6)					
2X	Y37	2d Coupe-5P	6,942/7,192	2,485/2,549	7,205
2X	Y68	5d Hatchback-5P	7,087/7,337	2,542/2,606	13,377
PHOENIX LJ (FOUR/V-6)					
2X	Z37	2d Coupe-5P	7,489/7,739	2,526/2,590	2,251
2X	Z68	5d Hatchback-5P	7,698/7,948	2,574/2,638	3,635
PHOENIX SJ (V-6)					
2X	T37	2d Coupe-5P	8,861	2,581	853
2X	T68	5d Hatchback-5P	8,948	2,642	172
1000 (FOUR)					
2T	L08	3d Hatchback-4P	5,582	2,081	13,171
2T	L68	5d Hatchback-4P	5,785	2,130	12,806
J2000 (FOUR)					
2J	B27	2d Coupe-5P	6,499	2,353	22,063
2J	B77	3d Hatchback-5P	6,809	2,413	7,331

1983 Pontiac Firebird Trans Am two-door coupe. (OCW)

1983 Pontiac J2000 two-door coupe. (OCW)

Model Number	Body Style Number	Body Type & Seating	Factory Price	Shipping Weight	Production Total
2J	B69	4d Sedan-5P	6,621	2,412	24,833
2J	B35	4d Sta Wagon-5P	6,926	2,487	10,214
J2000 LE (FOUR)					
2J	C27	2d Coupe-5P	7,020	2,385	2,690
2J	C69	4d Sedan-5P	7,194	2,436	6,957
2J	C35	4d Sta Wagon-5P	7,497	2,517	1,780
2J	C67	2d Convertible-5P	—	—	626
J2000 SE (FOUR)					
2J	D77	3d Hatchback-5P	8,393	2,470	1,835
6000 (FOUR/V-6)					
2A	F27	2d Coupe-5P	8,399/8,549	2,693/2,741	3,524
2A	F19	4d Sedan-5P	8,569/8,719	2,736/2,779	20,267
6000 LE (FOUR/V-6)					
2A	G27	2d Coupe-5P	8,837/8,987	2,711/2,754	4,278
2A	G19	4d Sedan-5P	8,984/9,134	2,750/2,793	33,676
6000 STE (V-6)					
2A	H19	4d Sedan-5P	13,572	2,823	6,719

NOTE 1: Prices and weights above slash for V-6/ below slash for V-8.

NOTE 2: Firebird prices and weights above slash for four/below slash for V-6.

NOTE 3: A 305-cid V-8 cost $200-$225 more than the V-6 for the base Firebird.

NOTE 4: Firebird SE prices and weights above slash for V-6/below slash for V-8.

NOTE 5: Phoenix prices and weights above slash for four/below slash for V-6.

NOTE 6: 6000 prices and weights above slash for four/below slash for V-6.

ENGINE [Base Four Pontiac 1000]: Inline. Overhead cam. Four-cylinder. Cast-iron block and head. Displacement: 98 cid. (1.6 liters). Bore & stroke: 3.23 x 2.98 in. Compression ratio: 9.0:1. Brake horsepower: 65 at 5200 rpm. Torque: 80 lbs.-ft. at 3200 rpm. Five main bearings. Hydraulic valve lifters. Carburetor: two-barrel VIN Code: C.

ENGINE [Base Four J2000]: Inline. Overhead cam. Four-cylinder. Cast-iron block and aluminum head. Displacement: 109 cid. (1.8 liters). Bore & stroke: 3.34 x 3.13 in. Compression ratio: 9.0:1. Brake horsepower: 84 at 5200 rpm. Torque: 102 lbs.-ft. at 2800 rpm. Five main bearings. Hydraulic valve lifters. Electronic fuel injection. VIN Code: O.

ENGINE [Optional Four J2000]: Inline. Overhead valve. Four-cylinder. Cast-iron block and head. Displacement: 122 cid. (2.0 liters). Bore & stroke: 3.50 x 3.15 in. Compression ratio: 9.3:1. Brake

1983 Pontiac J2000 four-door station wagon. (OCW)

1983 Pontiac Phoenix SJ two-door coupe. (OCW)

horsepower: 88 at 4600 rpm. Torque: 110 lbs.-ft. at 2400 rpm. Five main bearings. Hydraulic valve lifters. Electronic fuel injection. VIN Code: P.

ENGINE [Base Four Phoenix/Firebird/Pontiac 6000]: Inline. Overhead valve. Four-cylinder. Cast-iron block and head. Displacement: 151 cid. (2.5 liters). Bore & stroke: 4.00 x 3.00 in. Compression ratio: 8.2:1. Brake horsepower: 90-94 at 4000 rpm. Torque: 132-135 lbs.-ft. at 2800 rpm. Five main bearings. Hydraulic valve lifters. Throttle-body fuel injection. VIN Code: R or 2.

ENGINE [Optional V-6 Phoenix/Firebird/Pontiac 6000]: 60-degree. Overhead valve six-cylinder. Cast-iron block and aluminum head. Displacement: 173 cid. (2.8 liters). Bore & stroke: 3.50 x 3.00 in. Compression ratio: 8.5:1. Brake horsepower: 112 at 4800 rpm (Firebird, 107 at 4800). Torque: 145 lbs.-ft. at 2400 rpm (Firebird, 145 at 2100). Four main bearings. Hydraulic valve lifters. Carburetor: two-barrel Rochester E2SE. VIN Code: X or 1.

ENGINE [Base V-6 Phoenix SJ/Firebird SE/Pontiac 6000 STE]: High-output version of 173-cid V-6 above. Compression ratio: 8.9:1. Horsepower: 130-135 at 5400 rpm. (Firebird, 125 hp) Torque: 145 lbs.-ft. at 2400 rpm. VIN Code: Z.

ENGINE [Base V-6 Grand Prix/Bonneville/Parisienne]: 90-degree. Overhead-valve V-6. Cast-iron block and head. Displacement: 231 cid. (3.8 liters). Bore & stroke: 3.80 x 3.40 in. Compression ratio: 8.0:1. Brake horsepower: 110 at 3800 rpm. Torque: 190 lbs.-ft. at 1600 rpm. Four main bearings. Hydraulic valve lifters. Carburetor: two-barrel Rochester E2ME. Buick-built. VIN Code: A.

ENGINE [Diesel V-6 Pontiac 6000]: 90-degree. Overhead valve V-6. Cast-iron block and head. Displacement: 260 cid. (4.3 liters). Bore & stroke: 4.06 x 3.38 in. Compression ratio: 21.6:1. Brake horsepower: 85 at 3600 rpm. Torque: 165 lbs.-ft. at 1600 rpm. Four main bearings. Hydraulic valve lifters. Fuel injection. VIN Code: T.

ENGINE [Base V-8 (Firebird Trans Am); Optional (Firebird/Grand Prix/Bonneville)]: 90-degree. Overhead valve V-8. Cast-iron block and head. Displacement: 305 cid. (5.0 liters). Bore & stroke: 3.74 x 3.48 in. Compression ratio: 8.6:1. Brake horsepower: 150 at 4000 rpm. Torque: 240 lbs.-ft. at 2400 rpm. Five main bearings. Hydraulic valve lifters. Carburetor: four-barrel Rochester E4ME. Chevrolet-built. VIN Code: H.

ENGINE [Optional V-8 Trans Am]: Same as 305-cid V-8 above, with crossfire fuel injection. Compression ratio: 9.5:1. Horsepower: 175 at 4200 rpm. Torque: 250 lbs.-ft. at 2800 rpm. VIN Code: 7.

ENGINE [Diesel V-8 Grand Prix/Bonneville/Parisienne]: 90-degree. Overhead valve V-8. Cast-iron block and head. Displacement: 350 cid.

1983 Pontiac Phoenix SJ two-door coupe. (PGMC)

185

1983 Pontiac Firebird Trans Am two-door coupe. (PGMC)

(5.7 liters). Bore & stroke: 4.06 x 3.39 in. Compression ratio: 21.6:1. Brake horsepower: 105 at 3200 rpm. Torque: 200 lbs.-ft. at 1600 rpm. Five main bearings. Hydraulic valve lifters. Fuel injection. Oldsmobile-built. VIN Code: N.

CHASSIS: Wheelbase: (Pontiac 1000 three-door hatchback) 94.3 in.; (Pontiac 1000 five-door hatchback) 97.3 in.; (J2000) 101.2 in.; (Phoenix) 104.9 in.; (Firebird) 101.0 in.; (Pontiac 6000) 104.8 in.; (Grand Prix) 108.1 in.; (Bonneville) 108.1 in. Overall Length: (Pontiac 1000 three-door hatchback) 161.9 in.; (Pontiac 1000 five-door hatchback) 164.9 in.; (J2000 coupe) 173.6 in.; (J2000 sedan/Safari) 175.9 in.; (Phoenix coupe) 182.1 in.; (Phoenix hatchback) 183.1 in.; (Firebird) 189.8 in.; (Pontiac 6000) 188.7 in.; (Grand Prix) 201.9 in.; (Bonneville) 198.6 in.; (Bonneville Safari) 197.8 in. Height: (Pontiac 1000) 52.9 in.; (J2000 coupe) 53.5 in.; (J2000 hatchback) 51.9 in.; (J2000 sedan/Safari) 54.8 in.; (Phoenix coupe) 53.5 in.; (Phoenix sedan) 53.4 in.; (Firebird) 49.8 in.; (Pontiac 6000) 54.8 in.; (Grand Prix) 54.7 in.; (Bonneville) 55.8 in.; (Bonneville Safari) 56.1 in. Width: (Pontiac 1000) 61.8 in.; (J2000) 68.6 in.; (Phoenix coupe) 69.1 in.; (Phoenix sedan) 69.6 in.; (Firebird) 72.0 in.; (Pontiac 6000) 68.2 in.; (Grand Prix) 72.1 in.; (Bonneville) 71.3 in.; (Bonneville wag) 72.6 in. Front Tread: (Pontiac 1000) 51.2 in.; (J2000) 55.5 in.; (Phoenix) 58.7 in.; (Firebird) 60.7 in.; (Pontiac 6000) 58.7 in.; (Grand Prix) 58.5 in.; (Bonneville) 58.5 in. Rear Tread: (Pontiac 1000) 51.2 in.; (J2000) 55.1 in.; (Phoenix) 57.0 in.; (Firebird) 61.6 in.; (Pontiac 6000) 57.0 in.; (Grand Prix) 57.8 in.; (Bonneville) 57.8 in. Standard Tires: (Pontiac 1000) P155/80R13 GBR BSW; (J2000) P175/80R13 GBR BSW; (J2000 SE) P195/70R13; (Phoenix) P185/80R13 GBR BSW; (Phoenix SJ) P195/70R14 SBR; (Firebird) P195/75R14 GBR BSW; (Firebird SE and Trans Am) P205/70R14 SBR BSW; (Pontiac 6000) P185/80R13 GBR BSW; (Pontiac 6000 STE) P195/70R14 SBR; (Grand Prix) P195/75R14 SBR BSW; (Bonneville) P195/75R14 GBR BSW.

TECHNICAL: Transmission: Four-speed manual standard on Pontiac 1000, Phoenix and base Firebird. Five-speed manual standard on J2000 and Firebird SE. Three-speed Turbo-Hydra-Matic standard on other models, Optional on all. Standard final drive ratio: (Pontiac 1000) 3.36:1 except 3.62:1 with five-speed transmission; (J2000) 3.83:1 with five-speed transmission, 3.91:1 with four-speed transmission, 3.18:1 with automatic transmission; (Phoenix) 3.32:1 except 3.06:1 with H.O. V-6; (Firebird) 3.42:1 with four-speed transmission, 3.73:1 with V-6 and five-speed transmission, 3.23:1 with V-8 and five-speed transmission, 3.08:1 with three-speed automatic transmission, 3.23:1 or 2.93:1 with four-speed automatic transmission; (Pontiac 6000) 2.39:1 except 3.33:1 with H.O. V-6; (Grand

Prix/Bonneville) 2.73:1 with V-6; 2.73:1 with V-8. Steering: (Pontiac 1000/J2000/Phoenix/Pontiac 6000) rack and pinion; (others) re-circulating ball. Front Suspension: (J2000/Phoenix/Pontiac 6000) MacPherson struts with lower control arms and anti-sway bar; (Firebird) modified MacPherson struts with coil springs between lower control arm and X-member; (others) coil springs and anti-sway bar. Rear Suspension: (Pontiac 1000) four-link rigid axle with torque tube and Panhard rod; (J2000) beam axle with coil springs and trailing arms; (Phoenix) single-beam trailing axle with track bar and coil springs; (Firebird) torque arm, track bar with coil springs and anti-sway bar; (Pontiac 6000) trailing arms and beam axle with coil springs and integral anti-sway bar; (Bonneville/Grand Prix) four-link rigid axle with coil springs, lower trailing radius arms and upper torque arms. Brakes: Front disc/rear drum. Ignition: Electronic. Body construction: (Pontiac 1000/J2000/Phoenix/Firebird/Pontiac 6000) unit; (others) separate body and frame. Fuel Tank: (Pontiac 1000) 12.5 gal.; (J2000) 14 gal.; (Phoenix) 14.6 gal.; (Firebird) 16 gal.; (Pontiac 6000) 15.7 gal.; (Grand Prix/Bonneville) 17.5 gal.

DRIVETRAIN OPTIONS: Engines: 2.0-liter four in J2000 ($50 credit). 151-cid four in Firebird SE ($300 credit). 173-cid V-6: in Phoenix/Firebird/Pontiac 6000 ($150). Diesel 262-cid V-6 in Pontiac 6000 ($599). 305-cid four-barrel V-8: in Firebird ($350-$375); in Firebird SE ($50-$75); in Grand Prix/Bonneville ($225). Crossfire EFI 305-cid V-8 in Trans Am ($858). Diesel 350-cid V-8 in Grand Prix/Bonneville ($799). Transmission/Differential: Four-speed manual transmission in J2000 ($75 credit). Five-speed manual transmission: in Pontiac 1000 ($75); in Firebird ($125). Three-speed automatic transmission: in Pontiac 1000 ($395); in J2000 ($320); in Phoenix/Firebird ($425); in Firebird SE ($195). Four-speed automatic transmission: in Firebird ($525); in Firebird SE and Trans Am ($295). Limited-slip differential in Firebird/Grand Prix/Bonneville ($95). Brakes/Steering: Power brakes: in Pontiac 1000 ($95); in Phoenix ($100). Power four-wheel disc brakes: Firebird ($274) but no charge (NC) with performance package Power steering: Pontiac 1000/J2000 ($199); Phoenix ($210). Suspension: Electronic suspension: Pontiac 6000 ($165). Rally handling package: in J2000 ($48); in Phoenix/Pontiac 6000/Firebird/Grand Prix ($50). Superlift shock absorbers: Pontiac 6000/Grand Prix/Bonneville ($64). Heavy-duty springs: Phoenix/Pontiac 6000/Grand Prix/Bonneville ($16). Other: Heavy-duty radiator: Pontiac 1000/J2000 ($40-$70). Heavy-duty cooling ($40-$70). Heavy-duty battery ($25) except diesel ($50). Heavy-duty alternator ($25-$51). Engine block heater ($18). California emissions ($75) except diesel ($215).

1983 Pontiac 6000 LE four-door sedan. (OCW)

1983 Pontiac Firebird Trans Am two-door coupe. (PGMC)

1983 Pontiac Firebird SE two-door coupe. (OCW)

OPTION PACKAGES: Pontiac 1000 custom trim ($151). J2000 custom exterior group ($56-$86). J2000 custom trim group ($249-$299). J2000 security package ($19). Phoenix upper exterior group ($98-$108); lower ($56). Firebird Trans Am Recaro option ($3,160-$3,610). Firebird SE and Trans Am special performance package ($408). Firebird custom exterior ($51-$112). Pontiac 6000 rally package ($618). Pontiac 6000 custom exterior ($56). Grand Prix Brougham Landau package ($549). Bonneville wagon custom trim group ($376). Lamp groups ($34-$46) except Bonneville ($22-$52) and Pontiac 6000 LE ($88).

MAJOR CONVENIENCE/APPEARANCE OPTIONS: Air conditioning ($625-$725). Cruise control ($170). Power seat ($210-$420); not available on Pontiac 1000. Power windows ($180-$255); not available on Pontiac 1000. Cornering lamps: Bonneville/Grand Prix ($68). Power glass sunroof: Grand Prix ($895). Removable glass sunroof: J2000/Phoenix/Pontiac 6000 ($295). Hatch roof: Firebird/Grand Prix ($825-$861). Full vinyl cordova top: Bonneville ($155). Padded top: on Phoenix ($215); on Bonneville/Grand Prix ($240). Louvered rear sunshields: on J2000 ($199); on Firebird ($210). Two-tone paint: on J2000 ($101); on Phoenix ($105-$135); on Grand Prix/Bonneville ($205). Lear Siegler bucket seats: on J2000 ($400); on Firebird ($400-$1,294). Wood-grain paneling: Bonneville station wagon ($283).

HISTORICAL: Introduced: Sept. 23, 1982, except Firebird, Nov. 18, 1982. Model year production: 462,279 units. Calendar year production (U.S.): 414,842. Calendar year sales by U.S. dealers: 553,135. Model year sales by U.S. dealers: 513,239. Production fell for the fourth year in a row. The Pontiac 6000 series posted a notable sales gain, partly due to the new Pontiac 6000 STE. Pontiac was trying to boost its performance image at this time, with the debut of a high-output V-8 for Trans Am as well as the Euro-styled Pontiac 6000 STE. Big (relatively) V-8s may have been popular with many buyers, but they didn't help Pontiac to meet CAFE fuel economy standards. Nevertheless, over one-fourth of 1983 engines were V-8s, as opposed to less than 16 percent a year earlier.

1984 PONTIAC

1984 Pontiac Fiero two-door coupe Indy Pace Car. (PGMC)

PARISIENNE — SERIES 2B — (V-6/V-8) — Pontiac's full-size rear-dive sedan held six passengers in the traditional style. Also available was a four-door station wagon and a Brougham four-door sedan. All Parisiennes rode on a 116-in. wheelbase. The overall appearance was similar to 1983. Each of the twin grilles contained six vertical bars with added vertical bars within each segment. Large parking-and-signal lamps were in the bumper, with quad rectangular headlamps above them. Wraparound amber side markers extended outward from the headlamp framework. Buick's 231-cid (3.8-liter) V-6 was the base power plant with three-speed automatic transmission. Wagons carried the 305-cid (5.0-liter) V-8 and four-speed overdrive automatic, a combination that optional on sedans. All models could also get an Oldsmobile-built 350-cid V-8 diesel engine. Standard equipment

1984 Pontiac Fiero two-door coupe. (PGMC)

included power brakes, power steering, cloth 50/50 seating, narrow bright rocker panel moldings, color-keyed body side moldings, two-tone paint, bumper rub strips, a quartz clock, P205/75R15 tires, and bright wheel opening moldings. The Parisienne Brougham had cloth 55/45 seating with a reclining passenger seat back.

BONNEVILLE — SERIES 2G — (V-6/V-8) — The station wagon was dropped from the Bonneville line this year, but an LE model joined the base and Brougham four-door sedans. The base engine was a 231-cid (3.8-liter) V-6 with three-speed automatic. A 305-cid (5.0-liter) gas V-8 or 350-cid diesel V-8 were optional with either three- or four-speed automatic transmissions. The Bonneville's appearance was similar to 1983. Standard equipment included the 231-cid V-6, three-speed automatic transmission, power brakes, power steering, wide rocker panel moldings with extensions, P195/75R14 tires, a clock, bumper guards, and rub strips and wheel opening moldings. The Bonneville Brougham added 55/45 cloth seating, opera lamps, and a padded vinyl Cordova top.

GRAND PRIX — SERIES 2G — (V-6/V-8) — The rear-dive, six-passenger personal-luxury Pontiac Grand Prix again came in three models: base, LE, and Brougham. The Grand Prix's appearance was similar to 1983, with many vertical bars in the side-by-side twin grilles. Standard equipment included the 231-cid (3.8-liter) V-6, three-speed automatic transmission, power brakes, power steering, P195/75R14 SBR tires, a cushioned steering wheel, formal rear quarter windows, narrow rocker panel moldings, wheel opening moldings, chrome lower bumpers, black bumper guards, a clock, and a woodgrained dash. The Grand prix LE added wide rocker panel moldings with extensions, a four-spoke sport steering wheel, color-keyed sport mirrors, and wide windowsill and hood edge moldings. The Grand Prix Brougham included power windows, 55/45 seating, and a teak-wood grain instrument panel.

FIREBIRD — SERIES 2F — (FOUR/V-6/V-8) — The Firebird's appearance was similar to 1983. The Firebird Trans Am got a performance boost with a high-output four-barrel version of the 305-cid (5.0-liter) V-8. That power plant—first offered as an option late in the 1983 model year 1984—replaced the former crossfire fuel-injected V-8. It was rated for 190 hp at 4800 rpm and produced 240 lbs.-ft. of torque. This year's Trans Am came with a standard five-speed manual gearbox and 3.73:1 axle ratio. It was capable of delivering 0-60 mph times

1984 Pontiac 1000 five-door hatchback. (PGMC)

1984 Pontiac 2000 Sunbird two-door convertible. (PGMC)

in the 7.2 second neighborhood and quarter miles in the low-15-seconds range. Four-cylinder engines in the base Firebird also got a boost with a swirl-port combustion chamber, a 9.0:1 compression ratio, and cooler spark plugs. The Firebird SE again came with a standard 173-cid (2.8-liter) high-output V-6. New SE features included a color-coordinated leather-wrapped steering wheel, shift lever, and parking brake handle. As before, Firebird could have the four-cylinder engine or 305 V-8 instead of its standard V-6. Trans Am buyers could get an optional aero package in 15 color combinations. It included new front and rear fascias, a bigger air dam, door and rocker panel extensions, and wide lower body graphics. Also available was a Recaro package with gold strobe graphics and gold deep-dish turbo wheels. Base Firebird equipment included a 151-cid (2.5-liter) four with four-speed manual shift, power brakes, power steering, P195/75R14 tires on Rally sport wheels, tinted liftback glass, and vinyl reclining front bucket seats. The Firebird SE included front and rear stabilizer bars, a high-output 2.8-liter V-6, a five-speed gearbox, a handling suspension, a tachometer, leather map pockets, cloth seat upholstery, lower accent paint (with striping), sport mirrors, color-keyed body side moldings, and P205/70R14 tires on turbo cast aluminum wheels. The Trans Am included the 305 V-8 with five-speed, black aerodynamic turbo cast aluminum wheels, rear wheel opening flares, a rear spoiler, and front fender air extractors.

PHOENIX — SERIES 2X — (FOUR/V-6) — For its final season, the X-bodied Phoenix compact came in the same body styles and trim levels with little change. The base engine was Pontiac's own 151-cid (2.5-liter) four-cylinder with fuel injection hooked to a four-speed manual transaxle. A high-output 173-cid (2.8-liter) V-6 was optional, along with the Y99 handling suspension. Standard equipment included an AM radio, vinyl bench seating, P185/80R13 tires, color-keyed bumpers, and halogen headlamps. The phoenix LE added cloth notchback seating, a three-spoke Formula steering wheel, custom wheel covers, narrow rocker panel moldings, wide black vinyl body side moldings, and charcoal wheel opening moldings. The phoenix SE included power brakes and steering, a leather-wrapped steering wheel, a tachometer, P195/70R14 tires on sport aluminum wheels, wide black rocker panel moldings, graphics, and cloth-upholstered reclining front bucket seats.

1984 Pontiac Phoenix five-door hatchback. (PGMC)

FIERO — SERIES 2P — (FOUR) — Displaying little trim apart from a tiny shield emblem ahead of its hood, the Fiero was described as a "revolutionary two-seat, mid-engine sports car." It was the first such model built in America. The sleek (if somewhat stubby) wedge-shaped Fiero had a compact front area with a drag coefficient of 0.377. Glass surfaces were nearly flush with the body and the headlamps were hidden. Flush-mounted at the rear were black, full-width, neutral-density reflex tail lamps. If trim was absent, black accents were not. The Fiero's "Enduraflex" body panel skins were corrosion-resistant. SMC plastic panels went on horizontal portions (hood, roof, deck lid, upper rear quarter panel). Reinforced reaction injection molded (RRIM) urethane panels with higher resistance to dents were used in vulnerable spots, including the front fenders and doors. The Fiero used a space frame of high-strength steel. It was described as being similar to a racing car's roll cage. The rear-wheel-drive Fiero rode a 93.4-in. wheelbase and carried a 92-hp, 151-cid (2.5-liter) four-cylinder engine. Three models were available. The first was a coupe with a four-speed transmission, 2.42:1 axle ratio and 13-in. tires. The second was the Sport Coupe with 4.10:1 axle ratio. The third was the SE with special WS6 performance handling package and standard rear deck luggage rack. Inside the cockpit was a free-standing instrument cluster with electric speedometer, a trip odometer, a gas gauge, a voltmeter, and a temperature gauge. Lights warned of the doors or engine compartment lid being ajar. There was an up-shift indicator light, a "seatbelts not affixed" light, an oil pressure warning light and a "check engine" light. A column-mounted lever controlled the turn signals, dimmed the headlights, operated the windshield wipers and washer, and activated the (optional) cruise control. Fiero standard equipment included a four-speed manual transmission, P185/80R13 black sidewall SBR tires, retractable halogen headlamps, a driver's remote mirror, body side moldings, rub strips, a full-length console, a tachometer, map pockets, reclining bucket seats, and a four-spoke steering wheel. The Fiero SE had P215/80R13 tires and a padded Formula steering wheel.

1000 — SERIES 2T — (FOUR) — As before, Pontiac's Chevette clone the Pontiac 1000 came in three- and five-door hatchback forms. A new sport package included a black spoiler, sport striping, black sport mirrors, special handling components, and a formula steering wheel. The base Pontiac 1000 engine was the 98-cid (1.6-liter) overhead-cam four with four-speed manual gearbox. Five-speed manual shifting was optional, as was a three-speed

1984 Pontiac 2000 Sunbird three-door hatchback. (PGMC)

1984 Pontiac Phoenix five-door hatchback. (PGMC)

1984 Pontiac Firebird Trans Am two-door coupe. (PGMC)

automatic transmission. Standard equipment included an AM radio, a front air dam, a clock, a mini console, a black or bright grille, argent styled steel Rally wheels, reclining front bucket seats, black rocker panel moldings, black bumper guards and rub strips, and a locking glove box.

2000 SUNBIRD — SERIES 2J — (FOUR) — The biggest news for Sunbird was a turbocharged 1.8-liter overhead-cam engine. It was standard on the SE model and optional in base and LE models except wagons. Pontiac claimed the turbo could hit 60 mph in nine seconds with standard four-speed manual transmission attachment. Along with the turbo four came a WS6 performance handling package, P205/60R14 Goodyear Eagle GT steel-belted radial tires on new turbo wheels, a tachometer, a turbo boost gauge, and power steering. Introduced in 1983, the Sunbird LE convertible included a power top, five-speed manual transmission, dual sport mirrors (driver's remote), power windows, special moldings, an AM radio, tinted glass, power brakes and steering, and rear-seat entrance lamps. Sunbird 2000 styling was similar to that of the 1983 Pontiac 2000, but the lower air slots were narrower and lacked the previous egg-crate pattern. Clear fog lamps replaced the usual small inset grilles on SE and LE models, giving them the look of the Pontiac 6000 STE. Standard equipment included a five-speed gearbox, Rally wheels, reclining front bucket seats, power brakes, P175/80R13 glass-belted tires, bumper rub strips, a digital clock, a console, and side window defoggers. The Sunbird 2000 LE added an AM radio, a Formula three-spoke steering wheel, cloth bucket seats, bright rocker panel moldings, and fog lamps. The Sunbird 2000 SE included a tachometer, power steering, a leather-wrapped steering wheel, turbo cast aluminum wheels, two-tone paint, black rocker panel moldings, P205/60R14 tires, and a handling package. Sunbird 2000 convertibles had power steering, a tachometer, power windows, a power top, tinted glass, bright rocker moldings, and sport mirrors (driver's side remote-controlled).

6000 — SERIES 2A — (FOUR/V-6) — Aero restyling highlighted this year's mid-size Pontiac 6000 series, which was headed by the performance-oriented Pontiac 6000 STE. This model featured an electronic instrument panel with digital speedometer and analog tachometer. A new bar-chart display showed fuel level, engine temperature, and voltage. The 6000 STE also included a programmable Driver's Information Center that monitored car systems. Electronics also controlled the ride and the stereo radio, which had a five-band graphic equalizer. No other Pontiac offered this radio. At the suspension, an air compressor automatically provided pressure to the shocks to maintain optimum height and increase the spring rate as

1984 Pontiac 6000 LE four-door station wagon. (PGMC)

the car's load changed. As before, the Pontiac 6000 STE had a minimal option list offering a choice of six two-tone colors, an extra-cost suede leather interior, and a removable sunroof. A high-output 173-cid (2.8-liter) V-6 rated at 130 hp provided the power to a three-speed automatic transaxle. Four-wheel disc brakes were new this year. A station wagon joined the basic Pontiac 6000 coupe and sedan. The base Pontiac 6000 engine was a 151-cid (2.5-liter) four with fuel injection. It came hooked to a three-speed automatic transaxle. Optional again was a 173-cid (2.8-liter) V-6 or a diesel V-6. Wider wraparound tail lamps now reached to the back-up lenses alongside the license plate. The front grille inserts now had a pattern made up of both vertical and horizontal bars. Standard Pontiac 6000 equipment included power brakes and steering, an AM radio, black rocker panel moldings, black bumper rub strips, mini bumper guards, vinyl notchback front seating, P185/75R14 tires on Rally wheels, body side moldings with black vinyl insert, and wheel opening moldings. The Pontiac 6000 LE added a black pillar appliqué, cloth upholstery, a locking fuel filler door, and map pockets. The Pontiac 6000 STE included the high-output V-6, power windows, an AM/FM stereo radio with cassette, black wide body side and rocker panel moldings, two-tone paint, air conditioning, four-wheel power disc brakes, tinted glass, electronic ride control, and reclining 45/45 front seats with cloth upholstery, dual six-way adjustment, and lumbar support. Standard Pontiac 6000 STE tires were P195/70R14 black sidewall models.

I.D. DATA: Pontiac's 17-symbol Vehicle Identification Number (VIN) was on the upper left surface of the instrument panel, visible through the windshield. The first three symbols (1G2) indicate Pontiac division. Symbol four is restraint system (A=manual seat belts). Symbol five is car line/series: E=Fiero; M=Fiero Sport; F=Fiero SE; L=T1000; B=2000 Sunbird; C=2000 Sunbird LE; D=2000 Sunbird SE; Y=Phoenix; Z=Phoenix LE; T=Phoenix SJ; F=Pontiac 6000; G=Pontiac 6000 LE; H=Pontiac 6000 STE; S=Firebird; X=Firebird SE; W=Firebird Trans Am; J=Grand Prix; K=Grand Prix LE; P=Grand Prix Brougham; N=Bonneville; R=Bonneville Brougham; S=Bonneville LE; L=Parisienne; T=Parisienne Brougham. In sixth and seventh position are two digits that denote body type: 08=three-door hatchback; 27=two-door coupe; 37=two-door coupe; 77=three-door hatchback; 87=two-door coupe; 19=four-door six-window sedan; 68=five-door hatchback; 69=four-door four-window sedan; 35=four-door station wagon. Symbol eight is an engine code: A=3.8-liter Buick-built two-barrel V-6; B=2.0-liter Chevrolet-built two-barrel I-4; C=1.6-liter Chevrolet-built two-barrel I-4; D=1.8-liter Isuzu-built diesel I-4; G=5.0-liter Chevrolet-built four-barrel V-8; H=5.0-liter Chevrolet/GM

1984 Pontiac Firebird Trans Am two-door coupe. (PGMC)

1984 Pontiac 6000 LE four-door station wagon. (PGMC)

1984 Pontiac Grand Prix two-door hardtop. (PGMC)

1984 Pontiac Bonneville LE four-door sedan. (PGMC)

Canada-built four-barrel V-8; J=1.8-liter Chevrolet-built MFI I-4; N=5.7-liter Oldsmobile-built diesel V-8; P=2.0-liter Chevrolet-built EFI I-4; R=2.5-liter Pontiac-built EFI I-4; T=4.3-liter Oldsmobile-built diesel V-6; X=2.8-liter Chevrolet/GM Canada-built two-barrel V-6; Z=5.0-liter Chevrolet-built four-barrel V-8; 0=1.8-liter GM do Brazil-built TBI I-4; 1=2.8-liter Chevrolet-built two-barrel V-6; 2=2.5-liter Pontiac-built EFI I-4. Next is a check digit. The tenth symbol denotes model year (E=1984). Symbol eleven is a plant code: B=Baltimore, Md.; L=Van Nuys, Calif.; N=Norwood, Ohio; P=Pontiac, Mich.; T=Tarrytown, N.Y.; X=Fairfax, Kan.; Y=Wilmington, Del.; 7=Lordstown, Ohio; 1=Oshawa, Ontario Canada; 2=St. Therese, Quebec Canada. The final six digits are the sequential serial number.

Model Number	Body Style Number	Body Type & Seating	Factory Price	Shipping Weight	Production Total
PARISIENNE (V-6/V-8)					
2B	L69	4d Sedan-6P	9,881/10,431	N/A	18,713
2B	L35	4d Sta Wagon-6P	—/10,394	3,948	16,599
PARISIENNE BROUGHAM (V-6/V-8)					
2B	T69	4d Sedan-6P	10,281/10,831	N/A	25,212
BONNEVILLE (V-6/V-8)					
2G	N69	4d Sedan-6P	9,131/9,506	3,214/3,290	40,908
BONNEVILLE LE (V-6/V-8)					
2G	S69	4d Sedan-6P	9,358/9,733	3,275/3,351	17,451
BONNEVILLE BROUGHAM (V-6/V-8)					
2G	R69	4d Sedan-6P	9,835/10,210	3,210/3,286	15,030
GRAND PRIX (V-6/V-8)					
2G	J37	2d Coupe-6P	9,145/9,520	—	36,893
GRAND PRIX LE (V-6/V-8)					
2G	K37	2d Coupe-6P	9,624/9,999	3,207	31,037
GRAND PRIX BROUGHAM (V-6/V-8)					
2G	P37	2d Coupe-6P	10,299/10,674	3,217	9,514
FIREBIRD (I-4/V-6)					
2F	X87	2d Coupe-4P	8,349/8,724	2,866/2,948	62.621
FIREBIRD SE (V-6/V-8)					
2F	X87	2d Coupe-4P	10,649/10,849	2,965/3,145	10,309
FIREBIRD TRANS AM (V-8)					
2F	W87	2d Coupe-4P	10,699	3,107	55,374
PHOENIX (FOUR/V-6)					
2X	Y37	2d Coupe-5P	7,090/7,440	2,485/2,549	7,461
2X	Y68	5d Hatchback-5P	7,165/7,515	2,542/2,606	11,545
PHOENIX LE (FOUR/V-6)					
2X	Z37	2d Coupe-5P	7,683/8,033	2,526/2,590	1,357
2X	Z68	5d Hatchback-5P	7,816/8,166	2,574/2,638	1,783
PHOENIX SJ (V-6)					
2X	T37	2d Coupe-5P	9,071	2,581	701
FIERO (FOUR)					
2P	E37	2d Coupe-2P	7,999	2,458	7,099
2P	M37	2d Sport Coupe-2P	8,999	2,458	62,070
2P	F37	2d SE Coupe-2P	9,599	2,458	67,671
1000 (FOUR)					
2T	L08	3d Hatchback-4P	5,621	2,081	19,628
2T	L68	5d Hatchback-4P	5,824	2,130	17,118

Model Number	Body Style Number	Body Type & Seating	Factory Price	Shipping Weight	Production Total
2000 SUNBIRD (FOUR)					
2J	B27	2d Coupe-5P	6,675	2,353	53,070
2J	B77	3d Hatchback-5P	6,995	2,413	12,245
2J	B69	4d Sedan-5P	6,799	2,412	59,312
2J	B35	4d Sta Wagon-5P	7,115	2,487	15,143
2000 SUNBIRD LE (FOUR)					
2J	C27	2d Coupe-5P	7,333	2,385	5,189
2J	C69	4d Sedan-5P	7,499	2,436	11,183
2J	C35	4d Sta Wagon-5P	7,819	2,517	2,011
2J	N/A	2d Convertible-4P	11,749	2,449	5,458
2000 SUNBIRD SE (FOUR)					
2J	D27	2d Coupe-5P	9,019	—	2,141
2J	D77	3d Hatchback-5P	9,489	—	2,165
2J	D69	4d Sedan-5P	9,185	—	1,373
6000 (FOUR/V-6)					
2A	F27	2d Coupe-5P	8,699/8,949	2,693/2,741	4,171
2A	F19	4d Sedan-5P	8,873/9,123	2,736/2,779	35,202
2A	F35	4d Sta Wagon-5P	9,221/9,471	2,911/—	8,423
6000 LE (FOUR/V-6)					
2A	G27	2d Coupe-5P	9,142/9,392	2,711/2,754	4,731
2A	G19	4d Sedan-5P	9,292/9,542	2,750/2,793	41,218
2A	G35	4d Sta Wagon-5P	9,612/9,862	2,919/—	9,211
6000 STE (V-6)					
2A	H19	4d Sedan-5P	14,437	2,823	19,236

NOTE 1: Prices and weights above slash for V-6/ below slash for V-8.

NOTE 2: A 305-cid V-8 cost $300 more than the V-6 on base Firebird.

NOTE 3: Phoenix prices and weights above slash for I-4/ below slash for V-6.

NOTE 4: Phoenix V-6 prices include $100 for the required power brakes.

NOTE 5: 6000 prices and weights above slash for I-4/ below slash for V-6.

ENGINE [Base Four Pontiac 1000]: Inline. Overhead cam. Four-cylinder. Cast-iron block and head. Displacement: 98 cid. (1.6 liters). Bore & stroke: 3.23 x 2.98 in. Compression ratio: 9.0:1. Brake horsepower: 65 at 5200 rpm. Torque: 80 lbs.-ft. at 3200 rpm. Five main bearings. Hydraulic valve lifters. Carburetor: two-barrel VIN Code: C.

ENGINE [Base Four Sunbird 2000]: Inline. Overhead cam. Four-cylinder. Cast-iron block and aluminum head. Displacement: 109 cid. (1.8 liters). Bore & stroke: 3.34 x 3.13 in. Compression ratio: 9.0:1. Brake horsepower: 84 at 5200 rpm. Torque: 102 lbs.-ft. at 2800 rpm. Five main bearings. Hydraulic valve lifters. Electronic fuel injection. VIN Code: 0.

ENGINE [Optional Turbo Four Sunbird 2000]: Same as 109-cid four above, with port fuel injection and turbocharger. Compression ratio: 8.0:1. Horsepower: 150 at 5600 rpm. Torque: 150 lbs.-ft. at 2800 rpm. VIN Code: J.

1984 Pontiac Bonneville LJ four-door sedan. (PGMC)

1984 Pontiac Parisienne four-door sedan. (PGMC)

1984 Pontiac Parisienne four-door sedan. (PGMC)

ENGINE [Optional Four Sunbird 2000]: Inline. Overhead valve. Four-cylinder. Cast-iron block and head. Displacement: 122 cid. (2.0 liters). Bore & stroke: 3.50 x 3.15 in. Compression ratio: 9.3:1. Brake horsepower: 88 at 4800 rpm. Torque: 110 lbs.-ft. at 2400 rpm. Five main bearings. Hydraulic valve lifters. Electronic fuel injection. VIN Code: P.

ENGINE [Base four Fiero/Phoenix/Firebird/Pontiac 6000]: Inline. Overhead valve. Four-cylinder. Cast-iron block and head. Displacement: 151 cid. (2.5 liters). Bore & stroke: 4.00 x 3.00 in. Compression ratio: 9.0:1. Brake horsepower: 92 at 4000-4400 rpm. Torque: 132-134 lbs.-ft. at 2800 rpm. Five main bearings. Hydraulic valve lifters. Throttle-body fuel injection. VIN Code: R or 2.

ENGINE [Optional V-6 Phoenix/Firebird/Pontiac 6000]: 60-degree. Overhead valve six-cylinder. Cast-iron block and aluminum head. Displacement: 173 cid. (2.8 liters). Bore & stroke: 3.50 x 3.00 in. Compression ratio: 8.5:1. Brake horsepower: 112 at 4800 rpm (Firebird, 107 at 4800). Torque: 145 lbs.-ft. at 2100 rpm. Four main bearings. Hydraulic valve lifters. Carburetor: two-barrel Rochester E2SE. VIN Code: X or 1.

ENGINE [Base V-6 Phoenix SJ/Firebird SE/Pontiac 6000 STE]: High-output version of 173-cid V-6 above. Compression ratio: 8.9:1. Horsepower: 130 at 5400 rpm (Firebird, 125 hp). Torque: 145 lbs.-ft. at 2400 rpm. VIN Code: Z.

ENGINE [Base V-6 Grand Prix/Bonneville/Parisienne]: 90-degree. Overhead-valve V-6. Cast-iron block and head. Displacement: 231 cid. (3.8 liters). Bore & stroke: 3.80 x 3.40 in. Compression ratio: 8.0:1. Brake horsepower: 110 at 3800 rpm. Torque: 190 lbs.-ft. at 1600 rpm. Four main bearings. Hydraulic valve lifters. Carburetor: two-barrel Rochester E2ME. Buick-built. VIN Code: A.

ENGINE [Diesel V-6 Pontiac 6000]: 90-degree. Overhead valve V-6. Cast-iron block and head. Displacement: 260 cid. (4.3 liters). Bore & stroke: 4.06 x 3.38 in. Compression ratio: 21.6:1. Brake horsepower: 85 at 3600 rpm. Torque: 165 lbs.-ft. at 1600 rpm. Four main bearings. Hydraulic valve lifters. Fuel injection. VIN Code: T.

ENGINE [Base V-8 (Firebird Trans Am); Optional (Firebird/ Grand Prix/Bonneville)]: 90-degree. Overhead valve V-8. Cast-iron block and head. Displacement: 305 cid. (5.0 liters). Bore & stroke: 3.74 x 3.48 in. Compression ratio: 8.6:1. Brake horsepower: 150 at 4000 rpm. Torque: 240 lbs.-ft. at 2400 rpm. Five main bearings. Hydraulic valve lifters. Carburetor: four-barrel Rochester E4ME. Chevrolet-built. VIN Code: H.

ENGINE [Optional V-8 Trans Am]: High-output version of 305-cid V-8. Compression ratio: 9.5:1. Brake horsepower: 190 at 4800 rpm. Torque: 240 lbs.-ft. at 3200 rpm.

ENGINE [Diesel V-8 Grand Prix/Bonneville/Parisienne]: 90-degree. Overhead valve V-8. Cast-iron block and head. Displacement: 350 cid. (5.7 liters). Bore & stroke: 4.06 x 3.39 in. Compression ratio: 22.5:1. Brake horsepower: 105 at 3200 rpm. Torque: 200 lbs.-ft. at 1600 rpm. Five main bearings. Hydraulic valve lifters. Fuel injection. Oldsmobile-built. VIN Code: N.

CHASSIS: Wheelbase: (Fiero) 93.4 in.; (Pontiac 1000 three-door Hatchback) 94.3 in.; (Pontiac 1000 five-door Hatchback) 97.3 in.; (Sunbird 2000) 101.2 in.; (Phoenix) 104.9 in.; (Firebird) 101.0 in.; (Pontiac 6000) 104.9 in.; (Grand Prix) 108.1 in.; (Bonneville) 108.1 in.; (Parisienne) 115.9 in. Overall Length: (Fiero) 160.7 in.; (Pontiac 1000 three-door Hatchback) 161.9 in.; (Pontiac 1000 five-door Hatchback) 164.7 in.; (Sunbird 2000) 173.7 in.; (Sunbird 2000

Safari) 175.8 in.; (Phoenix) 183.0 in.; (Firebird) 189.9 in.; (Pontiac 6000) 188.1 in.; (Pontiac 6000 Safari) 191.2 in.; (Grand Prix) 201.9 in.; (Bonneville) 198.5 in.; (Parisienne) 212.0 in.; (Parisienne Safari) 215.0 in. Height: (Fiero) 46.9 in.; (Pontiac 1000) 52.8 in.; (Sunbird 2000 coupe) 51.9 in.; (Sunbird 2000 Convertible) 52.7 in.; (Sunbird 2000 sedan) 53.8 in.; (Sunbird 2000 Safari) 54.1 in.; (Phoenix) 53.7 in.; (Firebird) 49.7 in.; (Pontiac 6000) 53.3-53.8 in.; (Grand Prix) 54.7 in.; (Bonneville) 55.8 in.; (Parisienne sedan) 56.4 in.; (Parisienne Safari) 58.1 in. Width: (Fiero) 68.9 in.; (Pontiac 1000) 61.8 in.; (Sunbird 2000 coupe/Convertible) 65.9 in.; (Sunbird 2000 Hatchback) 66.6 in.; (Sunbird 2000 sedan/Safari) 66.2 in.; (Phoenix coupe) 69.0-69.1 in.; (Firebird) 72.0 in.; (Pontiac 6000) 72.0 in.; (Grand Prix) 72.3 in.; (Bonneville) 71.6 in.; (Parisienne) 75.2 in. except Safari, 79.3 in. Front Tread: (Fiero) 57.8 in.; (Pontiac 1000) 51.2 in.; (Sunbird 2000) 55.4 in.; (Phoenix) 58.7 in.; (Firebird) 60.7 in.; (Pontiac 6000) 58.7 in.; (Grand Prix) 58.5 in.; (Bonneville) 58.5 in.; (Parisienne) 61.7 in.; (Parisienne Safari) 62.2 in. Rear Tread: (Fiero) 58.7 in.; (Pontiac 1000) 51.2 in.; (Sunbird 2000) 55.2 in.; (Phoenix) 57.0 in.; (Firebird) 61.6 in.; (Pontiac 6000) 57.0 in.; (Grand Prix) 57.8 in.; (Bonneville) 57.8 in.; (Parisienne) 60.7 in.; (Parisienne Safari) 64.1 in. Standard Tires: (Fiero) P185/80R13; (Pontiac 1000) P155/80R13; (Sunbird 2000) P175/80R13 GBR BSW; (Sunbird 2000 SE/Convertible) P195/70R13 SBR; (Phoenix) P185/80R13 GBR; (Phoenix SE) P195/70R14; (Firebird) P195/75R14; (Firebird Trans Am) P205/70R14 SBR BSW; (Pontiac 6000) P185/75R14 SBR; (Pontiac 6000 STE) P195/70R14 SBR; (Grand Prix) P195/75R14 SBR; (Bonneville) P195/75R14 SBR; (Parisienne sedan) P205/75R15 SBR; (Parisienne Safari) P225/75R15 SBR.

TECHNICAL: Transmission: Four-speed manual transmission standard in Fiero, Pontiac 1000, Phoenix and base Firebird. Five-speed manual transmission standard in Sunbird 2000 and Firebird SE; optional on Pontiac 1000. Three-speed Turbo-Hydra-Matic transmission standard in other models, optional on all. Four-speed overdrive automatic transmission available in Firebird, Pontiac 6000, Grand Prix, Bonneville, and Parisienne. Standard final drive ratio: (Fiero) 4.10:1 with four-speed, 3.18:1 with automatic transmission; (Pontiac 1000) 3.36:1; (Sunbird 2000) 2.55:1 with five-speed transmission, 2.96:1 or 3.32:1 with four-speed transmission, 3.33:1 or 3.43:1 with automatic transmission; (Phoenix four) 2.42:1 with four-speed transmission, 2.39:1 with automatic transmission; (Phoenix V-6) 2.69:1 with four-speed transmission, 2.84:1 with automatic transmission; (Phoenix H.O. V-6) 2.96:1 with four-speed transmission, 3.33:1 with automatic transmission; (Firebird) 3.42:1 with four-speed transmission, 3.73:1 with four- and five-speed transmissions or automatic transmission, 3.42:1 or 3.23:1 with V-6, 3.73:1 with H.O. V-6, 3.73:1 or 3.23:1 with V-8; (Firebird H.O. V-8) 3.23:1 with five-speed transmission, 3.42:1 with automatic transmission; (Pontiac 6000) 2.39:1 with four-cylinder engine, 2.84:1 or 3.06:1 with V-6, 3.33:1 with H.O. V-6; (Grand Prix/Bonneville) 2.41:1 with V-6, 2.29:1 or 2.73:1 with V-8; (Parisienne) 2.73:1. Steering: (Fiero/Pontiac 1000/Sunbird 2000/Phoenix/Pontiac 6000) rack-and-pinion; (others) recirculating ball. Front Suspension: (Sunbird 2000/Phoenix/Pontiac 6000) MacPherson struts with lower control arms and anti-sway bar; (Firebird) modified MacPherson struts with coil springs between lower control arm and X-member; (others) coil springs and anti-sway bar. Rear Suspension: (Fiero) MacPherson struts with lower control arms; (Pontiac 1000) four-link rigid axle with torque tube and Panhard rod; (Sunbird 2000) beam axle with coil springs and trailing arms; (Phoenix) single-beam trailing axle with track bar and coil

1984 Pontiac Fiero two-door coupe. (PGMC)

1984 Pontiac 6000 STE four-door sedan. (PGMC)

springs; (Firebird) torque arm/track bar with coil springs and anti-sway bar; (Pontiac 6000) trailing arms and beam axle with coil springs and integral anti-sway bar; (Bonneville/Grand Prix/Parisienne) four-link rigid axle with coil springs, lower trailing radius arms and upper torque arms. Brakes: Front disc, rear drum except Pontiac 6000 STE, four-wheel disc. Ignition: Electronic. Body construction: (Fiero/Pontiac 1000/Sunbird 2000/Phoenix/Firebird/Pontiac 6000) unit; (others) separate body and frame. Fuel Tank: (Fiero) 10.2 gal.; (Pontiac 1000) 12.5 gal.; (Sunbird 2000) 13.6 gal.; (Phoenix) 14.6 gal.; (Firebird) 15.9 gal.; (Pontiac 6000) 15.7 gal.; (Grand Prix/Bonneville) 18.1 gal.; (Parisienne sedan) 25 gal.; (Parisienne Safari) 22 gal.

DRIVETRAIN OPTIONS: Engines: Turbo 1.8-liter four in Sunbird 2000 ($1,309-$1,546). 2.0-liter four in Sunbird 2000 ($50 credit). 151-cid four in Firebird SE ($350 credit). 173-cid V-6 in Phoenix/Firebird/Pontiac 6000 ($250). H.O. 173-cid V-6 in Phoenix ($400). Diesel 262-cid V-6 in Pontiac 6000 ($575). 305-cid four-barrel V-8: in Firebird ($550); in Firebird SE ($220); in Grand Prix/Bonneville/Parisienne ($375). H.O. 305-cid V-8 in Trans Am ($530). Diesel 350-cid V-8 in Grand Prix/Bonneville/Parisienne ($801). Transmission/Differential: Four-speed manual transmission in Sunbird 2000 ($75 credit). Five-speed manual transmission: in Pontiac 1000 ($75); in Firebird ($125). Three-speed automatic transmission: in Pontiac 1000 ($395); in Sunbird 2000 ($320-$395); in Phoenix/Firebird ($425). Four-speed automatic transmission: in Firebird ($525); in Firebird SE and Trans Am ($295); in Pontiac 6000/Grand Prix/Bonneville/Parisienne ($175). Limited-slip differential: Firebird/Grand Prix/Bonneville/Parisienne ($95). Brakes/Steering: Power brakes: Pontiac 1000 ($95); Phoenix ($100). Power four-wheel disc brakes: Firebird ($179) but no charge (NC) with performance package Power steering: Pontiac 1000/Sunbird 2000 ($204); Phoenix ($215). Suspension: Electronic suspension: Pontiac 6000 ($165). Rally tuned suspension: Sunbird 2000 ($48); Phoenix/Pontiac 6000/Firebird/Grand Prix ($50); Parisienne ($49). Superlift shock absorbers: Pontiac 6000/Grand Prix/Bonneville/Parisienne ($64). Heavy-duty springs: Bonneville ($16). Other: Heavy-duty cooling ($40-$70). Heavy-duty battery ($25-$26) except diesel ($52). Heavy-duty alternator ($25-$51). Engine block heater ($18-$19). California emissions ($99).

OPTION PACKAGES: Fiero special performance package ($459). Pontiac 1000 sport/handling package ($464). Pontiac 1000 custom trim ($167). Sunbird 2000 custom exterior group ($86). Sunbird 2000 custom trim group ($308-$358). Sunbird 2000 security package ($19). Phoenix upper exterior group ($98-$108); lower ($56). Firebird Trans Am Recaro option ($3,061-$3,160). Firebird SE and Trans Am special performance package ($134-$408). Firebird aero exterior appearance package ($199). Firebird black appearance package ($123-$152). Firebird custom exterior ($51-$112). Pontiac 6000 rally package ($341-$449). Pontiac 6000 custom exterior ($56). Pontiac 6000 Station Wagon security package ($44). Grand Prix Brougham Landau package ($469). Lamp groups ($30-$47) except Pontiac 6000 LE ($79-$88).

MAJOR CONVENIENCE/APPEARANCE OPTIONS: Air conditioning ($630-$730). Cruise control ($175). Power seat ($210-$430); not available on Pontiac 1000/Fiero. Power windows ($185-$260); not available on Pontiac 1000. Cornering lamps: Bonneville/Grand Prix ($68); Parisienne ($55). Power glass sunroof: Sunbird 2000 ($300); Grand Prix ($895). Removable glass sunroof: Fiero/Sunbird 2000/Phoenix/Pontiac 6000 ($300). Hatch roof: Firebird/Grand Prix ($825-$861). Full vinyl cordova top: Bonneville ($160). Padded cordova landau top: Phoenix ($220); Grand Prix ($245). Sport landau

top: Pontiac 6000 ($735-$773). Padded top: Bonneville ($245); Parisienne ($185). Louvered rear sunshields: Sunbird 2000 ($199); Firebird ($210). Two-tone paint: Sunbird 2000 ($101-$151); Phoenix ($105-$135); Firebird ($205-$291); Grand Prix/Bonneville ($205). Lear Siegler bucket seats: Sunbird 2000 ($400); Firebird ($400-$759); leather ($945-$1304). Third seat: Pontiac 6000 Safari ($215). Wood-grain paneling: Pontiac 6000/LE Safari ($250-$325); Parisienne Safari ($387).

HISTORICAL: Introduced: Sept. 22, 1983. Model year production: 827,576 units. Calendar year production (U.S.): 491,370. Calendar year sales by U.S. dealers: 704,684. Model year sales by U.S. dealers: 707,007. After four bad years, Pontiac enjoyed a gigantic surge in production for model year 1984. Sales, too, rose markedly. Sunbird and Pontiac 6000 sales showed the greatest gains, along with the big Parisienne. The new Fiero delivered a claimed 12.5 second time to 60 mph with the standard four-speed manual gearbox, as well as EPA mileage estimates of 27 (city) and 47 (highway). With a 4.10:1 axle, acceleration time dropped by one second. Pontiac became part of the new GM C-P-C (Chevrolet-Pontiac-GM of Canada) group and J. Michael Losh took over as the division's general manager.

1985 PONTIAC

1985 Pontiac Fiero GT two-door coupe. (P)

PARISIENNE — SERIES 2B — (V-6/V-8) — Rear-drive was very much alive at Pontiac in the form of the last remaining full-size model—the Parisienne—that displayed a fresh look this year. Though similar overall to the 1984 edition, this year the sedan quarter panels, deck lid, and tail lamps came from the 1981 Bonneville, rather than Chevrolet Caprice (as had previously been the case). The new look included a revised bumper and rub strips and fender skirts with moldings. Extra-wide lower body side moldings and color-keyed body side moldings were also new. A new wind split hood molding became standard. Parisienne Broughams included opera lamps. The four-door sedan came in base and Brougham trim. The Safari wagon carried eight passengers. A new notchback seat with "loose pillow" style upholstery was standard and 45/55 seating was available. A fuel-injected 262-cid (4.3-liter) V-6 was now the base power plant with three-speed automatic transmission. Station wagons had a standard 5.0-liter V-8 (optional on sedan) and both could get the 350-cid diesel for the last time.

BONNEVILLE — SERIES 2G — (V-6/V-8) — Three trim levels made up the Bonneville line: Bonneville, Bonneville LE, and elegant Bonneville Brougham. All had a standard 231-cid (3.8-liter) V-6 with three-speed automatic transmission. All could be had with an optional 5.0-liter V-8 and three- or four-speed automatic transmission. A dozen body colors were available, including nine new ones. An electronic-tuning sound system was available for the first time. Standard equipment included power brakes and steering, bumper guards and rub strips, wide rocker panel moldings with extensions, wheel opening moldings, cloth notchback seating, a clock, and P195/75R14 steel-belted radial black sidewall tires. The Bonneville LE added belt reveal moldings, a pillar appliqué, and a sport steering

1932 Pontiac V-8 coupe with rumbleseat. (OCW)

1940 Pontiac Station Wagon. (OCW)
Owned by Pat and Ted Langmeyer of Sherborn, Massachusetts.

1948 Pontiac convertible coupe hydro 8-cylinder. (JAG)
Owned by Ted Cram.

1948 Pontiac Streamliner Eight four-door sedan. (JAG)

1953 Pontiac Chieftain. (JAG)

1953 Pontiac Chieftain Deluxe two-door sedan. (Photo by Tom Jevcak)

1954 Pontiac Star Chief Custom Catalina.
Photographed and owned by Dale Smith of North Branch, Minnesota.

1955 Pontiac Star Chief Custom Safari. (OCW)

1958 Pontiac Bonneville. (OCW)

1961 Pontiac Bonneville Catalina four-door sedan. (OCW)

1963 Pontiac Catalina Super Duty 421. (JAG) Owned by Dimitrio Toth.

1964 Pontiac Catalina 2 + 2 convertible. (JAG)

1975 Pontiac Grand Am. (OCW)

1982 Pontiac Trans Am. (OCW)

1984 Pontiac Fiero. (PMD)

1984 Pontiac Fiero. (PMD)

1986 Pontiac Grand Am SE Coupe. (PMD)

1988 Pontiac LeMans GSE. (PMD)

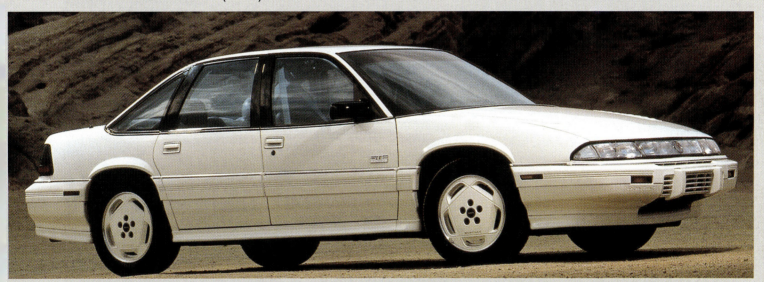

1990 Pontiac Grand Prix STE Turbo. (PMD)

1991 Pontiac Firebird GTA. (PMD)

1997 Pontiac Trans Am convertible with Ram Air. (PMD)

1999 Pontiac Grand Am SE Coupe. (PMD)

2001 Pontiac Aztek GT. (PMD)

Pontiacs at Car Shows

The old car hobby extends beyond having your dream car parked safely in your garage. Whether attending a local Friday night cruise-in that attracts thirty cars, or making vacation plans to attend a major national event that features thousands of cars, participating in car shows is the real joy of this hobby. Attending car shows as a participant or as a spectator allows us to meet old friends, make new ones, and share our common love for the automobiles of yesteryear. The following pages celebrate Pontiacs out of their garages and enjoyed by old car enthusiasts at car shows.

1927 Pontiac Landau four-door sedan. (JAG)
This was the most expensive of the 1927 offerings at a factory price of $975. Owned by Ron Brooks of Minnesota.

1934 Pontiac coupe. (JAG)
Features optional dual side-mounted tires with optional matching covers. This car was photographed at the annual car show in Appleton, Wisconsin.

1938 Pontiac 6 two-door Touring sedan. (JAG)
Shot at the POCI 2001 event in Red Wing, Minnesota, the "6" emblem is visible at the bottom center of the new-for-1938 grille design. Owned by John Hofmeyer of Fayette, Iowa.

1939 Pontiac convertible coupe. (JAG)
This photo, taken at the 2000 POCI convention in Grand Rapids, Michigan, provides a view of the optional fog lamps.

1940 Pontiac four-door sedan. (JAG)
A cigar lighter, automatic tuning six-tube radio, trunk light, and a rear view mirror were among the options available for this year.

1940 Pontiac Station Wagon. (JAG)
The Special Six station wagons for 1940 featured a single, side-mounted spare tire. This woody appeared at the 2000 Lake Geneva Classic Rally with optional whitewall tires and wheel trim rings. Owned by Larry Lange of Lake Geneva, Wisconsin.

1948 Pontiac Streamliner 8 four-door sedan. (JAG)
Pontiac produced 245,419 cars for model year 1948, of which 123,115 were Streamliner 8s.

1950 Pontiac Streamliner Deluxe Six four-door sedan. (JAG)
Deluxe appointments for 1950 included a chrome body strip, chrome wheel rings, chrome headlight rings, and stainless steel gravel guards. Pontiac Eights had an "8" between the words "Silver Streak" on the fenders, while Sixes did not. Owned by Carl Forsberg of Rosemont, Minnesota.

1951 Pontiac Chieftain Deluxe Eight four-door sedan. (JAG)
This car sports the optional windshield sun visor and appeared at the 2001 POCI event in Red Wing, Minnesota.

1953 Pontiac Chieftain Six four-door sedan. (JAG)
Pontiac produced 38,914 Chieftain Sixes for the year. Owned by Fred and Barb Dierks of Princeton, Minnesota.

1954 Pontiac Bonneville Special gull-wing coupe concept car. (JAG)

In addition to attending your local car shows this season, trips to car museums are an education in automobile history. A 1994 visit to the Gilmore Museum was rewarded with a view of Joe Bortz's Bonneville concept car.

1955 Pontiac Star Chief convertible. (JAG)

1955 was the last year for the optional illuminated Indian head hood ornament that was first available in 1949. Owned by Harold Cary of Mason City, Iowa.

1958 Barnette-Pontiac hearse-ambulance with Tri-Power. (JAG)

Tri-Power was a $93.50 option and its setup used three two-barrel Rochester carburetors, 10.5:1 cylinder heads, high-lift camshaft, and produced 300 hp at 4600 rpm.

1959 Pontiac Bonneville convertible. (JAG)

The V-8 standard in Bonnevilles this year was a 389 cid that produced 260 hp with synchromesh and 300 hp with Hydra-Matic transmissions.

1960 Pontiac Catalina Super Duty. (JAG)

This beauty features aluminum hubs and drums, better known as Pontiac 8-lug wheels. Owned by Larry Zidek of McHenry, Illinois.

1961 Pontiac Ventura. (JAG)

Distinguishing the Ventura from the Catalina this year were the chrome outline moldings for side spears, Ventura script inside the spear on the door, and bright metal roof drip moldings. Venturas also featured the aluminum hubs and drums (Pontiac 8-lug wheels) seen on this car. Owned by Steven Cayce.

1962 Pontiac Bonneville Safari four-door station wagon. (JAG)

The Custom Safari was the heaviest and most expensive Pontiac. It featured a two-toned, pleated Morrokide upholstery and a concealed luggage locker. Pontiac built 4,527 Safaris for the year.

1963 Pontiac LeMans convertible with 326. (JAG)

The 326-cid 260-hp V-8 engine was an option in Tempest models. Standard equipment included, dual sun visors, Deluxe steering wheel, custom interior, bucket seats, console, and power convertible top. Owned by Keith Baker of Pulaski, Wisconsin.

1963 Pontiac Catalina two-door hardtop. (JAG)

Pontiac produced 60,795 Catalinas in 1963. A three-speed manual transmission was standard, but $48 extra would get the Catalina owner a heavy-duty three-speed manual gearbox, and for $231 extra the four-speed manual or Super Hydra-matic transmission could be installed.

1964 Pontiac LeMans convertible. (JAG)

Pontiac produced 5,786 LeMans models with inline six-cylinder 215-cid 140-hp engines, and 11,773 models featuring optional V-8 powerplants.

1965 Pontiac Catalina two-door convertible. (JAG)

Available from the factory for $3,103, Pontiac produced 18,347 Catalina convertibles. Vehicles with the optional 2 + 2 package were trimmed with "421" engine badges on the front fenders, 2 + 2 numbering on the rear fenders and deck lid, and simulated louvers behind the front wheel cutouts.

1967 Pontiac Catalina two-door sedan. (JAG)

The two-door sedan is the rarest of the 1967 Catalinas as only 5,633 were built. Owned by Keith Anderson of Olympia, Washington.

1968 Pontiac Catalina convertible. (JAG)
The standard V-8 engine for Catalinas this year was the 400-cid 290-hp model that was accompanied by Turbo-Hydramatic transmission. Owned by Mac McConnell of Troy, Michigan.

1968 Pontiac Bonneville convertible. (JAG)
This beautiful convertible was shown at the POCI 2001 event in Red Wing, Minnesota. Standard equipment included all Executive features, fender skirts, carpeted lower door trim, elm burl vinyl dash trim, plus leather and Morrokide interiors. Owned by Earl Bert of Helena, Montana.

1968 Pontiac Firebird 400. (JAG)
The "400" package included chrome air cleaner, chrome rocker covers, chrome oil cap, dual exhausts, and a 400-cid 330-hp V-8 engine. Owned by Pat Redal of Sun Prairie, Wisconsin.

1969 Pontiac GTO. (JAG)
Making an appearance at the 2000 Lake Geneva Classic Car Rally was one of the 55,126 GTO hardtops produced by Pontiac in 1969. Hidden headlamps were standard. Here the doors are open exposing the dual headlamps.

1972 Pontiac LeMans Sport 350. (JAG)
The LeMans Sport option included bucket seats, custom door and rear quarter trim, custom rear seat and special front fender nameplate. Pontiac produced 3,438 LeMans Sports for the year. Owned by Dick Homblad of Shorewood, Wisconsin.

1973 Pontiac Grand Am Sport Coupe. (JAG)
According to Pontiac Historian John Sawruk, the automobile that became the Grand Am was originally intended to be the GTO. Owned by Chet Olszewski of Addison, Illinois.

1974 Pontiac Luxury LeMans. (JAG)
Pontiac built 25,882 Luxury LeMans models this year. Fender skirts were standard, as were the ashtray and glove box lamps. Owned by Bruce Rutherfurd of Monett, Missouri.

1977 Pontiac LeMans Can Am. (JAG)
Available only in Cameo White, the Can Am was promoted as a "fun car" along with the Trans Am. It included the Grand Prix instrument panel assembly, a Rally RTs handling package, and an interior trim color choice of White, Black, or Firethorn.

1985 Pontiac 1000 five-door hatchback. (P)

wheel. Bonneville Broughams included 55/45 notchback seats with cloth upholstery, lower door courtesy lights, and opera lamps.

GRAND PRIX — SERIES 2G — (V-6/V-8) — A new vertical-bar grille was evident at the Grand Prix's front end and new tail lamps were seen at the rear. Nine new paint colors were available, to make the total an even dozen. A Delco Sunbird AM radio was standard. The base engine remained the 231-cid (3.8-liter) V-6 with three-speed automatic transmission. The 5.0-liter V-8 with either three- or four-speed automatic transmission was optional. Standard equipment included formal rear quarter windows, power steering, power brakes, narrow rocker panel moldings, wheel opening moldings, chrome lower bumpers, mini black bumper guards, bright-accented bumper rub strips, a clock, and P195/75R14 steel-belted radials. The Grand Prix LE added wide rocker panel moldings with extensions, color-keyed sport mirrors, and wide windowsill and hood edge moldings. The Grand Prix Brougham added 55/45 notchback seating, power windows, and door courtesy lights.

FIREBIRD — SERIES 2F — (FOUR/V-6/V-8) — According to the Firebird's chief designer, John Schinella, the famed coupe became "more of a thoroughbred in 1985" with a "more aggressive" image and dramatic restyling. Also new was a V-8 power plant with tuned-port fuel injection that was intended to deliver a 0-60-mph time in the 8.1 second neighborhood. Optional in the Trans Am, this 205-hp V-8 produced 270 lbs.-ft. of torque. Engine choices also included the base 151-cid (2.5-liter) four, the fuel-injected 173-cid (2.8-liter) V-6, the standard 5.0-liter V-8 and a 190-hp high-output V-8. Firebird's standard ride/handling package now included all of the components of the former Y99 option except for special tires. An improved Y99 package included 15-in. wheels. The basic appearance was similar to 1984, but the Trans Am displayed new aero-tuned rocker and quarter panel extensions, a new hood with twin louvers near the front, and built-in fog lamps where the big air slots otherwise would be. Diamond spoke wheels were a new option this year.

FIERO — SERIES 2P — (FOUR) — A new Fiero GT model joined the original trio this year. It carried a 173-cid (2.8-liter) V-6 engine with multi-port fuel injection. The new V-6 was optional in Fiero Sport Coupes and Fiero SEs. The GT's appearance stemmed from the 1984 Fiero Indianapolis 500 Pace Car and included new "Enduraflex" front and rear fascias, rocker panel extensions, and an optional deck lid spoiler. A WS6 performance suspension and P215/60R14 Eagle GT tires on turbo-cast wheels were available. The standard 151-cid (2.5-liter) four came with a new Isuzu five-speed manual gearbox, while V-6 models had a four-speed manual transmission. Either model could be ordered with a three-speed automatic transmission. Other than the above, the Fiero's appearance was similar to 1984.

GRAND AM — SERIES 2N — (FOUR/V-6) — Ranked as a "sports specialty coupe," the Grand Am was targeted at youthful, upscale buyers who demanded good handling and performance and might otherwise turn to imports. The five-passenger coupe came in base and LE trim. The standard engine was a fuel-injected "Tech IV" 151-cid (2.5-liter) four-cylinder with five-speed manual gearbox. A 125-hp 181-cid (3.0-liter) V-6 with multi-port fuel injection and automatic transmission also was available, as was a Y99 rally suspension package that enhanced the basic model's handling characteristics. The Grand Am sported sculptured lines with smooth body curves

and had Pontiac's traditional (yet modern) split grille up front. A tapered hood sloped back to a flush-fitting, steeply-raked windshield. Inside the Grand Am were reclining front bucket seats, a console, instrument panel pods close to the steering wheel, an analog speedometer, and an analog gas gauge. Full analog gauges and electronic instruments were both optional. So was a six-function Driver Information Center. Optional hi-tech turbo-cast aluminum wheels and 215/60R14 Goodyear Eagle GT tires were said to give the car an "aggressive wide-track stance."

1000 — SERIES 2T — (FOUR) — At the entry-level end of the Pontiac scale, both three- and five-door Pontiac 1000 models could have the optional five-speed manual gearbox. The base engine remained the 1.6-liter overhead-cam four, with four-speed manual transmission. Seven new body colors were available and four new interior colors. The overall appearance was similar to 1984.

SUNBIRD — SERIES 2J — (FOUR) — A turbocharged power plant was available under the Sunbird's hood. It was based on a 150-hp version of the 1.8-liter OHC four-cylinder engine. The engine had multi-port fuel injection and delivered 150 lbs.-ft. of torque. The turbo option was available on both base Sunbird and Sunbird LE models, but not Sunbird wagons. It included P205/60R14 SBR tires on turbo-cast wheels, a WS6 suspension, a tachometer, a turbo boost gauge, power steering, new hood louvers, and special Turbo identification. Other models had a non-turbo edition of the 1.8-liter engine. Two-door notchback and hatchback coupes were offered, along with a four-door sedan, a four-door station wagon, and a convertible coupe. Appearance changed little from 1984. Standard equipment included a non-turbo 1.8-liter four-cylinder engine, a five-speed manual transmission, reclining front bucket seats, a remote hatch/trunk release, and a console. The Sunbird LE added an AM radio and wheel trim rings. Sunbird convertibles had power steering, power windows, and tinted glass. The Sunbird SE included the turbocharged engine and four-speed manual transaxle, as well as power steering and sport mirrors.

6000 — SERIES 2A — (FOUR/V-6) — A new 173-cid (2.8-liter) V-6 engine with multi-port fuel injection was available in the Pontiac 6000 series and standard in the performance-minded Pontiac 6000 STE. The base engine was a 151-cid (2.5-liter) "Tech IV" four. A carbureted 2.8 V-6 and a 4.3-liter diesel V-6 were optional. The STE got a front and rear restyling, as well as a few body changes that were evident from the side. A new front fascia included a wide bumper rub strip. At the rear were full-width, neutral-density tail lamps. Wider body side moldings were used. Standard again was an electronic instrument panel with Driver Information Center, but color was added to the cluster. In addition to two-door coupe and four-door sedan bodies, the Pontiac 6000 line again offered a station wagon with woodgrain side paneling and optional rear-facing third seat. The Pontiac 6000's grille shape was similar to 1984, but with a wider center divider bar and horizontal bars in each insert. The Pontiac 6000 STE again had a long standard equipment list, which included power four-wheel disc brakes, power windows, rally-tuned electronic ride control, an AM/FM stereo with cassette, 45/45 cloth upholstery with six-way adjustment and lumbar support, speed control, fog lamps, dual exhausts, electronic air conditioning, and two-tone paint.

I.D. DATA: Pontiac's 17-symbol Vehicle Identification Number (VIN) was on the upper left surface of the instrument panel, visible through the windshield. The first three symbols (1G2) indicate Pontiac division. Symbol four is restraint system (A=manual seat belts). Symbol five is car line/series: E=Fiero; M=Fiero Sport; F=Fiero SE; G=Fiero

1985 Pontiac Sunbird LE Turbo two-door convertible. (P)

1985 Pontiac Sunbird SE three-door hatchback. (P)

GT; L=T1000; B=Sunbird; C=Sunbird LE; D=Sunbird SE; E=Grand Am; V=Grand Am LE; F=Pontiac 6000; G=Pontiac 6000 LE; H=Pontiac 6000 STE; S=Firebird; X=Firebird SE; W=Firebird Trans Am; J=Grand Prix; K=Grand Prix LE; P=Grand Prix Brougham; N=Bonneville; R=Bonneville Brougham; S=Bonneville LE; L=Parisienne; T=Parisienne Brougham. In sixth and seventh position are two digits that denote body type: 08=three-door hatchback coupe; 27=two-door coupe; 37=two-door coupe; 77=three-door hatchback; 87=two-door coupe; 67=two-door convertible coupe; 19=four-door six-window sedan; 68=five-door hatchback sedan; 69=four-door four-window sedan; 35=four-door station wagon. Symbol eight is an engine code: A=3.8-liter Buick-built two-barrel V-6; B=2.0-liter Chevrolet-built two-barrel I-4; C=1.6-liter Chevrolet-built two-barrel I-4; D=1.8-liter Isuzu-built diesel I-4; G=5.0-liter Chevrolet-built four-barrel V-8; H=5.0-liter Chevrolet/GM Canada-built four-barrel V-8; J=1.8-liter Chevrolet-built MFI I-4; N=5.7-liter Oldsmobile-built diesel V-8; P=2.0-liter Chevrolet-built EFI I-4; R=2.5-liter Pontiac-built EFI I-4; T=4.3-liter Oldsmobile-built diesel V-6; X=2.8-liter Chevrolet/GM Canada-built two-barrel V-6; Z=5.0-liter Chevrolet-built four-barrel V-8; 0=1.8-liter GM do Brazil-built TBI I-4; 1=2.8-liter Chevrolet-built two-barrel V-6; 2=2.5-liter Pontiac-built EFI I-4. Next is a check digit. The tenth symbol denotes model year (F=1985). Symbol eleven is a plant code: A=Lakewood, Ga.; L=Van Nuys, Calif.; N=Norwood, Ohio; P=Pontiac, Mich.; T=Tarrytown, N.Y.; X=Fairfax, Kan.; M=Lansing, Mich.; 7=Lordstown, Ohio; 1=Oshawa, Ontario Casnada; 2=St. Therese, Quebec Canada. The final six digits are the sequential serial number.

Model Number	Body Style Number	Body Type & Seating	Factory Price	Shipping Weight	Production Total
PARISIENNE (V-6/V-8)					
2B	L69	4d Sedan-6P	10,395/10,635	3,350/ —	25,638
2B	L35	4d Sta Wagon-8P	— /10,495	3,944	17,638
PARISIENNE BROUGHAM (V-6/V-8)					
2B	T69	4d Sedan-6P	11,125/11,365	3,378/ —	38,831
BONNEVILLE (V-6/V-8)					
2G	N69	4d Sedan-6P	9,549/9,939	3,214/3,290	34,466
BONNEVILLE LE (V-6/V-8)					
2G	S69	4d Sedan-6P	9,789/10,179	3,275/3,351	10,503
BONNEVILLE BROUGHAM (V-6/V-8)					
2G	R69	4d Sedan-6P	10280/10669	3210/3286	8,425
GRAND PRIX (V-6/V-8)					
2G	J37	2d Coupe-6P	9,569/9,959	3,148/ —	30,365
GRAND PRIX LE (V-6/V-8)					
2G	K37	2d Coupe-6P	10,049/10,439	3,168/ —	21,195
GRAND PRIX BROUGHAM (V-6/V-8)					
2G	P37	2d Coupe-6P	10,749/11,139	3,186/ —	8,223

1985 Pontiac Grand Am LE two-door coupe. (P)

1985 Pontiac Grand Am LE two-door coupe. (P)

Model Number	Body Style Number	Body Type & Seating	Factory Price	Shipping Weight	Production Total
FIREBIRD (FOUR/V-6)					
2F	S87	2d Coupe-4P	8,763/9,013	2,866/2,948	46,644
FIREBIRD SE (V-6/V-8)					
2F	X87	2d Coupe-4P	11,063/11263	2,965/3,145	5,208
FIREBIRD TRANS AM (V-8)					
2F	W87	2d Coupe 4P	11,113	3,107	44,028
FIERO (FOUR)					
2P	E37	2d Coupe-2P	8,495	2,454	5,280
FIERO SPORT COUPE (V-6)					
2P	M37	2d Sport Coupe-2P	8,995	2,500	23,823
FIERO SE (V-6)					
2P	F37	2d Coupe-2P	9,995	2,525	24,734
FIERO GT (V-6)					
2P	G37	2d Coupe-2P	11,795	—	22,534
GRAND AM (FOUR/V-6)					
2N	E27	2d Coupe-5P	7,995/8,480	2,419/ —	40,273
GRAND AM LE (FOUR/V-6)					
2N	V27	2d Coupe-5P	8,485/8,970	2,447/ —	42,269
1000 (FOUR)					
2T	L08	3d Hatchback-4P	5,445	2,081	8,647
2T	L68	5d Hatchback-4P	5,695	2,130	8,216
SUNBIRD (FOUR)					
2J	B27	2d Coupe-5P	6,875	2,353	39,721
2J	B77	3d Hatchback-5P	7,215	2,413	5,235
2J	B69	4d Sedan-5P	6,995	2,412	44,553
2J	B35	4d Sta Wagon-5P	7,335	2,487	7,371
SUNBIRD LE (FOUR)					
2J	C27	2d Coupe-5P	7,555	2,385	3,424
2J	C69	4d Sedan-5P	7,725	2,436	6,287
2J	C35	4d Sta Wagon-5P	8,055	2,517	1,036
2J	C67	2d Convertible-4P	12,035	—	2,114
SUNBIRD SE (FOUR)					
2J	D27	2d Coupe-5P	9,295	2,360	965
2J	D77	3d Hatchback-5P	9,765	2,435	535
2J	D69	4d Sedan-5P	9,455	2,416	658
6000 (FOUR/V-6)					
2A	F27	2d Coupe-5P	8,899/9,159	2,698/2,741	4,493
2A	F19	4d Sedan-5P	9,079/9,339	2,736/2,779	54,424
2A	F35	4d Sta Wagon-5P	9,435/9,695	2,815/ —	8,491
6000 LE (FOUR/V-6)					
2A	G27	2d Coupe-5P	9,385/9,645	2,711/2,754	3,777
2A	G19	4d Sedan-5P	9,539/9,799	2,750/2,793	54,284
2A	G35	4d Wagon-5P	9,869/10,129	2,832/ —	8,025
6000 STE (V-6)					
2A	H19	4d Sedan-5P	14,829	2,823	22,728

NOTE 1: Prices and weights above slash for V-6/ below slash for V-8.

NOTE 2: Base Firebird prices and weights above slash for I-4/ below slash for V-6.

1985 Pontiac Firebird Trans Am two-door coupe. (P)

Standard Catalog of ® Pontiac, 2ⁿᵈ Edition

1985 Pontiac 6000 STE four-door sedan. (AA)

NOTE 3: A 305-cid V-8 cost $300 more than the V-6 on base Firebird.

NOTE 4: Firebird SE prices and weights above slash for V-6/ below slash for V-8.

NOTE 5: Grand Am prices and weights above slash for I-4/ below slash for V-6.

ENGINE [Base Four Pontiac 1000]: Inline. Overhead cam. Four-cylinder. Cast-iron block and head. Displacement: 98 cid. (1.6 liters). Bore & stroke: 3.23 x 2.98 in. Compression ratio: 9.0:1. Brake horsepower: 65 at 5200 rpm. Torque: 80 lbs.-ft. at 3200 rpm. Five main bearings. Hydraulic valve lifters. Carburetor: two-barrel. VIN Code: C.

ENGINE [Base Four Sunbird]: Inline. Overhead cam. Four-cylinder. Cast-iron block and aluminum head. Displacement: 109 cid. (1.8 liters). Bore & stroke: 3.34 x 3.13 in. Compression ratio: 9.0:1. Brake horsepower: 82 at 5200 rpm. Torque: 102 lbs.-ft. at 2800 rpm. Five main bearings. Hydraulic valve lifters. Electronic fuel injection. VIN Code: 0.

ENGINE [Optional turbocharged Four Sunbird]: Same as 109-cid four above, with port fuel injection and turbocharger. Compression ratio: 8.0:1. Brake horsepower: 150 at 5600 rpm. Torque: 150 lbs.-ft. at 2800 rpm. VIN Code: J.

ENGINE [Optional Four Sunbird]: Inline. Overhead valve. Four-cylinder. Cast-iron block and head. Displacement: 122 cid. (2.0 liters). Bore & stroke: 3.50 x 3.15 in. Compression ratio: 9.3:1. Brake horsepower: 88 at 4800 rpm. Torque: 110 lbs.-ft. at 2400 rpm. Five main bearings. Hydraulic valve lifters. Electronic fuel injection. VIN Code: P.

ENGINE [Base Four Fiero/Grand Am/Firebird/Pontiac 6000]: Inline. Overhead valve. Four-cylinder. Cast-iron block and head. Displacement: 151 cid. (2.5 liters). Bore & stroke: 4.00 x 3.00 in. Compression ratio: 9.0:1. Brake horsepower: 92 at 4400 rpm (Firebird/88 at 4400). Torque: 132-134 lbs.-ft. at 2800 rpm. Five main bearings. Hydraulic valve lifters. Throttle-body fuel injection. VIN Code: U or 2.

ENGINE [Optional V-6 Pontiac 6000]: 60-degree. Overhead valve six-cylinder. Cast-iron block and aluminum head. Displacement: 173 cid. (2.8 liters). Bore & stroke: 3.50 x 3.00 in. Compression ratio: 8.5:1. Brake horsepower: 112 at 4800 rpm. Torque: 145 lbs.-ft. at 2100 rpm. Four main bearings. Hydraulic valve lifters. Carburetor: two-barrel. VIN Code: X.

ENGINE [Base V-6 (Firebird SE/Pontiac 6000 STE); Optional (Fiero/Firebird)]: Fuel-injected version of 173-cid V-6 above. Compression ratio: 8.9:1. Brake horsepower: 130 at 4800 rpm (Firebird, 135 at 5100). Torque: 160-165 lbs.-ft. at 3600 rpm. VIN Code: 5, 9 or W.

1985 Pontiac 6000 STE four-door sedan. (AA)

1985 Pontiac Grand Prix Brougham two-door coupe. (OCW)

ENGINE [Optional V-6 Grand Am]: 90-degree. Overhead-valve V-6. Cast-iron block and head. Displacement: 181 cid. (3.0 liters). Bore & stroke: 3.80 x 2.70 in. Compression ratio: 9.0:1. Brake horsepower: 125 at 4900 rpm. Torque: 154 lbs.-ft. at 2400 rpm. Four main bearings. Hydraulic valve lifters. Fuel injection. VIN Code: L.

ENGINE [Base V-6 Grand Prix/Bonneville]: 90-degree. Overhead-valve V-6. Cast-iron block and head. Displacement: 231 cid. (3.8 liters). Bore & stroke: 3.80 x 3.40 in. Compression ratio: 8.0:1. Brake horsepower: 110 at 3800 rpm. Torque: 190 lbs.-ft. at 1600 rpm. Four main bearings. Hydraulic valve lifters. Carburetor: two-barrel Rochester E2ME. Buick-built. VIN Code: A.

ENGINE [Base V-6 Parisienne]: 90-degree. Overhead-valve V-6. Cast-iron block and head. Displacement: 262 cid. (4.3 liters). Bore & stroke: 4.00 x 3.48 in. Compression ratio: not available. Brake horsepower: 130 at 3600 rpm. Torque: 210 lbs.-ft. at Sunbird rpm. Four main bearings. Throttle-body fuel injection. VIN Code: 7.

ENGINE [Diesel V-6 Pontiac 6000]: 90-degree. Overhead valve V-6. Cast-iron block and head. Displacement: 260 cid. (4.3 liters). Bore & stroke: 4.06 x 3.38 in. Compression ratio: 21.6:1. Brake horsepower: 85 at 3600 rpm. Torque: 165 lbs.-ft. at 1600 rpm. Four main bearings. Hydraulic valve lifters. Fuel injection. VIN Code: T.

ENGINE [Base V-8 (Firebird Trans Am); Optional (Firebird/ Grand Prix/Bonneville/Parisienne)]: 90-degree. Overhead valve V-8. Cast-iron block and head. Displacement: 305 cid. (5.0 liters). Bore & stroke: 3.74 x 3.48 in. Compression ratio: 9.5:1. Brake horsepower: 165 at 4200 rpm. Torque: 250 lbs.-ft. at 2400 rpm. Five main bearings. Hydraulic valve lifters. Carburetor: four-barrel. Chevrolet-built. VIN Code: H.

ENGINE [Optional V-8 Trans Am]: High-output version of 305-cid V-8. Compression ratio: 9.5:1. Brake horsepower: 190 at 4800 rpm. Torque: 240 lbs.-ft. at 3200 rpm. VIN Code: G. Optional V-8 [Trans Am] Fuel-injected version of 305-cid V-8. Horsepower: 205 at 4400 rpm. Torque: 275 lbs.-ft. at 3200 rpm. VIN Code: F.

ENGINE [Diesel V-8 Parisienne]: 90-degree. Overhead valve V-8. Cast-iron block and head. Displacement: 350 cid. (5.7 liters). Bore & stroke: 4.06 x 3.39 in. Compression ratio: 22.5:1. Brake horsepower: 105 at 3200 rpm. Torque: 200 lbs.-ft. at 1600 rpm. Five main bearings. Hydraulic valve lifters. Fuel injection. Oldsmobile-built. VIN Code: N.

CHASSIS: Wheelbase: (Fiero) 93.4 in.; (Pontiac 1000 three-door hatchback) 94.3 in.; (Pontiac 1000 five-door hatchback) 97.3 in.; (Sunbird) 101.2 in.; (Grand Am) 103.4 in.; (Firebird) 101.0 in.; (Pontiac 6000) 104.8 in.; (Grand Prix) 108.1 in.; (Bonneville) 108.1 in.;

1985 Pontiac Grand Prix Brougham two-door coupe. (OCW)

1985 Pontiac Bonneville Brougham four-door sedan. (P)

(Parisienne) 116.0 in. Overall Length: (Fiero) 160.7 in.; (Pontiac 1000 three-door hatchback) 161.9 in.; (Pontiac 1000 five-door hatchback) 164.9 in.; (Sunbird) 175.4 in.; (Sunbird Safari) 176.5 in.; (Grand Am) 177.5 in.; (Firebird) 189.9 in.; (Pontiac 6000) 188.8 in.; (Pontiac 6000 Safari) 191.2 in.; (Grand Prix) 201.9 in.; (Bonneville) 200.2 in.; (Parisienne) 212.4 in.; (Parisienne Safari) 215.1 in. Height: (Fiero) 46.9 in.; (Pontiac 1000) 52.8-52.9 in.; (Sunbird coupe) 51.9 in.; (Sunbird convertible) 52.7 in.; (Sunbird sedan) 53.8 in.; (Sunbird Safari) 54.1 in.; (Grand Am) 52.5 in.; (Firebird) 49.7 in.; (Pontiac 6000) 53.3-53.8 in.; (Grand Prix) 54.7 in.; (Bonneville) 55.8 in.; (Parisienne sedan) 56.4 in.; (Parisienne Safari) 58.1 in. Width: (Fiero) 68.9 in.; (Pontiac 1000) 61.8 in.; (Sunbird coupe/convertible) 65.9 in.; (Sunbird hatch) 66.6 in.; (Sunbird sedan/Safari) 66.2 in.; (Grand Am) 67.3 in.; (Firebird) 72.4 in.; (Pontiac 6000) 67.7-67.8 in.; (Grand Prix) 72.3 in.; (Bonneville) 71.6 in.; (Parisienne) 76.4 in. except Safari, 79.3 in. Front Tread: (Fiero) 57.8 in.; (Pontiac 1000) 51.2 in.; (Sunbird) 55.4 in.; (Grand Am) 55.6 in.; (Firebird) 60.7 in.; (Pontiac 6000) 58.7 in.; (Grand Prix) 58.5 in.; (Bonneville) 58.5 in.; (Parisienne) 61.8 in.; (Parisienne Safari) 62.2 in. Rear Tread: (Fiero) 58.7 in.; (Pontiac 1000) 51.2 in.; (Sunbird) 55.2 in.; (Grand Am) 55.1 in.; (Firebird) 61.6 in.; (Pontiac 6000) 56.9 in.; (Grand Prix) 57.8 in.; (Bonneville) 57.8 in.; (Parisienne) 60.8 in.; (Parisienne Safari) 64.1 in. Standard Tires: (Fiero) P185/80R13; (Pontiac 1000) P155/80R13 GBR BSW; (Sunbird) P175/80R13 SBR BSW; (Grand Am) P185/80R13 SBR BSW; (Firebird) P195/75R14 SBR BSW; (Firebird SE) P205/70R14 SBR BSW; (Pontiac 6000) P185/75R14 SBR; (Pontiac 6000 STE) P195/70R14 SBR; (Grand Prix) P195/75R14 SBR; (Bonneville) P195/75R14 SBR; (Parisienne sedan) P205/75R15 SBR; (Parisienne Safari) P225/75R15 SBR.

TECHNICAL: Transmission: Four-speed manual transmission standard on Fiero, Pontiac 1000 and base Firebird. Five-speed manual transmission standard on Sunbird, Firebird and Grand Am, optional on Pontiac 1000. Three-speed Turbo-Hydra-Matic transmission standard on other models. Four-speed overdrive automatic transmission available on Firebird, Pontiac 6000, Grand Prix, Bonneville, and Parisienne. Standard final drive ratio: (Fiero) not available; (Pontiac 1000) 3.36:1; (Sunbird) 2.55:1 with five-speed transmission, 2.96:1 or 3.32:1 with four-speed transmission, 3.33:1 or 3.43:1 with automatic transmission; (Grand Am) 2.48:1 with five-speed, 2.84:1 with automatic transmission; (Firebird) 3.42:1 with four-speed, 3.73:1 with four- and five-speed transmission or automatic transmission, 3.42:1 with V-6, 3.27:1 with V-8; (Trans Am) 3.27:1 except 3.70:1 with H.O. V-8 and 3.27:1 with FI V-8; (Pontiac 6000) 2.39:1 with four, 2.84:1 or 3.06:1 with V-6; (Pontiac 6000 STE) 3.18:1; (Grand Prix/Bonneville) 2.41:1; (Parisienne) 2.56:1; (Parisienne Safari) 2.73:1. Steering: (Fiero/Pontiac 1000/Sunbird/Phoenix/

1985 Pontiac Parisienne Brougham four-door sedan. (JG)

Pontiac 6000) rack and pinion; (others) recirculating ball. Front Suspension: (Sunbird/Phoenix/Pontiac 6000) MacPherson struts with lower control arms and anti-sway bar; (Grand Am) MacPherson struts and anti-sway bar; (Firebird) modified MacPherson struts with coil springs between lower control arm and X-member; (others) coil springs and anti-sway bar. Rear Suspension: (Fiero) MacPherson struts with lower control arms; (Pontiac 1000) four-link rigid axle with torque tube and Panhard rod; (Sunbird) beam axle with coil springs and trailing arms; (Grand Am) semi-independent beam axle with trailing arms and coil springs; (Firebird) torque arm/track bar with coil springs and anti-sway bar; (Pontiac 6000) trailing arms and beam axle with coil springs and integral anti-sway bar; (Bonneville/Grand Prix/Parisienne) four-link rigid axle with coil springs, lower trailing radius arms and upper torque arms. Brakes: Front disc, rear drum except Pontiac 6000 STE, four-wheel disc. Ignition: Electronic. Body construction: (Fiero/Pontiac 1000/Sunbird/Phoenix/Firebird/Pontiac 6000) unit; (others) separate body and frame. Fuel Tank: (Fiero) 10.2 gal.; (Pontiac 1000) 12.2 gal.; (Sunbird) 13.6 gal.; (Grand Am) 13.6 gal.; (Firebird) 15.9 gal.; (Pontiac 6000) 15.7 gal.; (Grand Prix/Bonneville) 18.1 gal.; (Parisienne sedan) 25 gal.; (Parisienne Safari) 22 gal.

DRIVETRAIN OPTIONS: Engines: Turbo 1.8-liter four in Sunbird ($1,248-$1,486); standard on SE. 173-cid, two-barrel V-6 in Pontiac 6000 ($260). 173-cid FI V-6: in Fiero ($595); in Firebird ($350); in Pontiac 6000 ($435). 181-cid V-6 in Grand Am ($560). Diesel 262-cid V-6 in Pontiac 6000 ($335). 305-cid four-barrel V-8: in Firebird ($650); in Firebird SE ($300); in Grand Prix/Bonneville ($390); in Parisienne ($240). H.O. 305-cid V-8 four-barrel or FI in Trans Am ($695). Diesel 350-cid V-8: in Parisienne sedan ($341); in Parisienne Safari ($101). Transmission/Differential: Four-speed manual transmission: in Fiero SE ($50 credit); in Sunbird ($75 credit). Five-speed manual transmission in Pontiac 1000 ($75). Three-speed automatic transmission: in Fiero ($425-$475); in Fiero GT ($750); in Pontiac 1000 ($395); in Sunbird ($350-$425); in Grand Am ($425). Four-speed automatic transmission: in Firebird ($325); in Pontiac 6000/Grand Prix/Bonneville/Parisienne ($175). Limited-slip differential: in Firebird/Grand Prix/Bonneville/Parisienne ($95-$100). Brakes/Steering: Power brakes for Pontiac 1000 ($94). Power four-wheel disc brakes for Firebird ($179) but no charge (NC) with performance package. Power steering: in Pontiac 1000 ($204); in Sunbird ($215). Suspension: Electronic suspension: Pontiac 6000 ($165). Rally tuned suspension: for Firebird ($30); for Sunbird/Grand Am/Pontiac 6000/Firebird/Grand Prix ($50); for Parisienne ($49). Superlift shock absorbers for Pontiac 6000/Grand Prix/Bonneville/Parisienne ($64). Heavy-duty springs: Parisienne ($16).

1985 Pontiac Parisienne four-door sedan. (JG)

1985 Pontiac Parisienne Brougham four-door sedan. (JG)

Standard Catalog of ® Pontiac, 2ⁿᵈ Edition

Other: Heavy-duty cooling ($40-$70). Heavy-duty battery ($25-$26) except diesel ($52). Heavy-duty alternator ($25-$51). Engine block heater ($18-$19). California emissions ($99).

OPTION PACKAGES: Fiero special performance package ($174-$491). Pontiac 1000 sport/handling package ($464). Pontiac 1000 custom trim ($167). Sunbird custom exterior group ($86). Sunbird custom trim group ($308-$358). Sunbird security package ($19). Firebird Trans Am special performance package ($664). Firebird black appearance package ($123-$152). Firebird custom exterior ($51-$112). Firebird luxury interior trim ($349-$359). Pontiac 6000 Sport Landau Coupe ($665-$703). Pontiac 6000 rally package ($441-$479). Pontiac 6000 custom exterior ($56). Pontiac 6000 Safari security package ($44). Grand Prix Brougham Landau package ($469). Lamp groups ($21-$47) except Pontiac 6000 LE ($79-$88).

MAJOR CONVENIENCE/APPEARANCE OPTIONS: Air conditioning ($630-$730). Cruise control ($175). Power seat ($215-$488); not available on Pontiac 1000/Fiero. Power windows ($185-$260); not available on Pontiac 1000. Cornering lamps: Bonneville/Grand Prix ($68); Parisienne ($55). Power glass sunroof: Parisienne ($1,195). Removable glass sunroof: Fiero/Sunbird/Grand Am/Pontiac 6000 ($300-$310). Hatch roof: Firebird/Grand Prix ($825-$875). Full vinyl roof: Bonneville ($160). Padded cordova landau roof: Grand Prix ($245). Aero wing spoiler: Trans Am ($199). Padded full vinyl roof: Bonneville ($245); Parisienne ($185). Louvered rear sunshields: Sunbird ($199); Firebird ($210). Two-tone paint: Sunbird ($101-$151); Firebird/Pontiac 6000 ($205); Grand Prix/Bonneville ($205-$291); Parisienne sedan ($205). Lear Siegler bucket seats: Sunbird ($400); Firebird ($400-$759); leather ($945-$1,304). Recaro bucket seats: Firebird ($636-$995). Wood-grain paneling on Parisienne Safari ($345).

HISTORICAL: Introduced: Oct. 2, 1984, except Sunbird/Firebird, Nov. 8, 1984; Pontiac 1000, Nov. 11, 1984; and Fiero, Jan. 10, 1985. Model year production: 735,161 units. Calendar year production (U.S.): 684,901. Calendar year sales by U.S. dealers: 796,795. Model year sales by U.S. dealers: 785,643. First built only in Canada, the Pontiac 6000 series expanded production to the Tarrytown, New York, plant for 1985. Sales rose moderately for the model year, with Pontiac 6000 and Parisienne posting impressive increases. Small cars weren't doing as well. Fiero sales continued relatively strong, if beneath expectations. The Pontiac 6000 was Pontiac's best selling car. Well over half of Pontiacs now carried fuel-injected engines.

1986 PONTIAC

1986 Pontiac Fiero GT two-door coupe. (PGMC)

PARISIENNE — SERIES 2B — (V-6/V-8) — Once again, the full-size rear-wheel-drive Pontiacs came in Parisienne or Parisienne Brougham trim as a four-door sedan or as an eight-passenger station wagon. New fine-textured velour cloth trim went into Brougham sedans. Turbo-finned cast aluminum wheels were optional on sedans. Optional instruments now included a voltmeter instead of a fuel economy gauge. Base engine was a 4.3-liter fuel-injected V-6, with three-speed automatic transmission. Station wagons carried a 5.0-liter V-8 and four-speed automatic transmission.

1986 Pontiac Fiero GT two-door coupe. (PGMC)

BONNEVILLE — SERIES 2G — (V-6/V-8) — Appearance of the Bonneville was similar to 1985. The six-passenger mid-size sedan came in base, LE, and Brougham trim, in a dozen body colors. Base engine was the 231-cid (3.8-liter) V-6 with three-speed automatic. Optional: a 5.0-liter V-8 with four-speed overdrive automatic transmission. Standard equipment included power brakes and steering, an AM radio, a notchback front seat with fold-down center armrest, and custom wheel covers. The Bonneville LE added a four-spoke sport steering wheel, pillar appliqué, and belt reveal moldings. The Bonneville Brougham added a 55/45 front seat, a cushion steering wheel and door courtesy lamps.

GRAND PRIX — SERIES 2G — (V-6/V-8) — As before, three Grand Prix series were available on the rear-drive personal-luxury coupe: base, LE, and Brougham. Standard engine was Buick's 231-cid (3.8-liter) V-6 with three-speed automatic transmission. A 5.0-liter V-8 with four-speed overdrive automatic was optional. The taillights and bezels were slightly revised. Three-section tail lamps had a 'GP' octagon in the center lens. Though similar to 1985, this year's grille had fewer vertical bars. Interiors had a notchback seat with center armrest. A new optional visor vanity mirror came with dual-intensity lamps. Only 200 examples of the Grand Prix 2+2 coupe were built and all of them sold by dealers in southeastern United States. The Grand Prix 2+2 was a street version of a NASCAR racecar that was driven by Richard Petty in the 1986-1987 season. Under the hood of the Grand Prix 2+2 was a 165-hp version of the 305-cid V-8 that produced 245 lbs.-ft. of torque. Selling price of the Grand Prix 2+2 was $18,214, but dealers quickly marked up the few units available to around $22,000. Pontiac claimed a quarter-mile time of 17.6 seconds for this model with a trap speed of 80 mph. The Grand Prix 2+2 had a gray body with twin-shade red striping on the lower panels. A 'Pontiac 2+2' nameplate in red/gray on black went on the left of the black honeycomb grille. 'Pontiac 2+2' lettering also went on the door and 'Pontiac Grand Prix' identification was seen on the deck. The 2+2 option was RPO code Y97.

FIREBIRD — SERIES 2F — (FOUR/V-6/V-8) — New tail lamps and center filler panel gave the base 1986 Firebird a modified look that was different from that of the upscale Firebirds. New lower body accent paint with sports striping became standard. Also standard were dual sport mirrors and a rear spoiler. The optional hood bird graphic decal also changed in appearance. All models had a power pull-down hatch with electric remote release optional. All

1986 Pontiac 1000 five-door hatchback. (PGMC)

1986 Pontiac Sunbird Turbo GT three-door hatchback. (PGMC)

models carried 15-in. tires. New options included a programmable, electrically-controlled day/night mirror. All base and SE Firebirds with V-6 or V-8 now had the optional Rally Tuned suspension with P215/65R15 tires on seven-inch Rally II wheels. New lightweight pistons went into the base "Tech IV" 151-cid (2.5-liter) four, which was connected to a standard five-speed manual gearbox. The Firebird SE carried a standard 173-cid (2.8-liter) V-6 with multi-port fuel injection. Both base and SE Firebirds could have a 5.0-liter four-barrel V-8 with either a five-speed manual or automatic transmission. The Trans Am had a standard 155-hp version of the 5.0-liter V-8 and a tuned-port fuel injection option that delivered 190 hp. A five-speed manual shifter was standard and a four-speed overdrive automatic was required with the tuned-port-injection (TPI) engine. The standard Y99 Rally Tuned suspension came with P215/60R15 tires on seven-inch cast aluminum wheels. The Trans Am's WS6 suspension package included four-wheel disc brakes, a limited-slip differential, larger front and rear stabilizer bars, and P245/50VR16 Gatorback tires. A new back-lit instrument cluster included an electric speedometer, which read up to 140 mph when equipped with the TPI V-8.

FIERO — SERIES 2P — (FOUR/V-6) — Four coupes made up the two-seat Fiero line: base, Sport and SE. A black-accented aero package gave the Fiero SE its own styling cues. Its standard 151-cid (2.5-liter) fuel-injected "Tech IV" four featured dual-trumpet exhausts and a five-speed manual transaxle (from Isuzu). Optional again was a 173-cid (2.8-liter) V-6 with multi-port fuel injection. The Fiero SE came with a standard Rally Tuned suspension, including 14-in. cast aluminum wheels. Four-cylinder Fiero SE models had P195/70R14 tires. Those with a V-6 used P215/60R14 tires. The Fiero's standard reclining bucket seats wore Pallex cloth trim. Optional leather, suede and cloth trim replaced the former fleece and suede option. Standard tires for base and Sport Coupe Fieros were size P185/75R14 models with new tri-tech wheel covers. Aluminum wheels were optional. New sail-panel stereo speakers replaced the former headrest units. Body colors included Black, Silver, Red, White, and Gold. The Fiero's overall appearance was similar to 1985, but the smooth-surfaced front end now held a single center air slot with separate openings for the park/signal lamps. A fastback GT model was announced for late arrival.

1986 Pontiac Sunbird GT three-door hatchback. (PGMC)

1986 Pontiac Grand Am SE two-door coupe. (PGMC)

GRAND AM — SERIES 2N — (FOUR/V-6) — A sporty four-door sedan joined the original Grand Am coupe, along with a "sophisticated" SE series aimed at enthusiasts. The SE, said its design studio head, offered a "boldly aggressive appearance." The approach was similar to that used for the 6000 STE. This edition had an aero ground-effects package that included a low front bumper air dam, side skirts, and deep rear extension, as well as flush composite headlamps and built-in fog lamps. The Grand Am SE also had a unique monochrome paint treatment with the grille, emblems, and cast aluminum wheels color-coordinated to the body. At the rear were neutral-density tail lamps. The standard engine was a 181-cid (3.0-liter) V-6 with multi-port fuel injection hooked to a three-speed automatic. The Y99 Rally Tuned suspension included thick front and rear stabilizer bars and P215/60R14 Eagle GT tires. Grand Am SE interiors contained tone-on-tone Pallex seat trim, color-coordinated with the body color. Standard equipment included a four-way (manual-control) driver's bucket seat; a leather-wrapped steering wheel, parking brake handle and gearshift knob; a header-mounted reading lamp; a rear roof courtesy lamp; a visor vanity mirror and a seek/scan AM/FM stereo. Options included a six-speaker sound system, tilt steering, and cruise control. The appearances of the "ordinary" base and LE Grand Ams changed little this year, except for new high-gloss black moldings on LE models. The base engine was the "Tech IV" 151-cid (2.5-liter) four-cylinder with fuel injection and a five-speed manual transaxle. A new Flame Red shade was one of the dozen available body colors. Turbo-cast aluminum wheels were optional again. Base and LE Grand Ams could also get the 3.0-liter V-6 with three-speed automatic transmission.

1000 — SERIES 2T — (FOUR) — For its final year, the sub-compact 1000 again came in two body styles: three- and five-door hatchbacks. The standard engine was a 1.6-liter OHC four with four-speed manual transmission. A five-speed manual transmission and automatic transmission were optional. An optional sport handling package included a heavier front stabilizer bar and a rear stabilizer bar, as well as cast aluminum wheels, dual mirrors, and sport body striping. Also optional was a new four-spoke steering wheel. Standard equipment included a Delco AM radio, a front mini-console, reclining front seats, and a folding full-width back seat.

SUNBIRD — SERIES 2J — (FOUR) — The most notable of the Sunbird's changes was the new GT offered as a coupe, hatchback, convertible, and sedan. The station wagon remained available in the base line. The SE line included a convertible. Aimed at enthusiasts, the Sunbird GT included a sloped front fascia with partly hidden

1986 Pontiac Grand Am SE two-door coupe. (PGMC)

1986 Pontiac Grand Am SE four-door sedan. (PGMC)

1986 Pontiac Trans Am two-door coupe. (PGMC)

quad halogen headlamps and a rear spoiler. GT equipment included narrow black body side moldings and dual sport mirrors. Two-door GT models also had wheel flares, turbo aluminum wheels, and P215/60R14 Eagle GT tires. A turbocharged version of the 1.8-liter engine, rated at 150 hp, delivered a claimed 8.5-second 0-to-60 mph time. The Sunbird GT also included a performance handling package and power steering. Inside was a back-lit, round-dial instrument cluster that included a turbo boost gauge, a tachometer, and an electric speedometer. A rally console extension included a thumbwheel mileage/event reminder. The four-spoke rally urethane steering wheel had horn bars on each side of the hub and leather wrapping was optional. Genor cloth upholstery was standard. Base and SE models were still around, but the Sunbird LE became an option package for base sedans and wagons, rather than a model on its own. Sedans and wagons got a black-out tail lamp treatment to replace the former bright framing. Sunbird SE models had a revised tail lamp design, wide body side moldings, fog lamps (making six front lights in all) and black-out trim on the belt moldings, drip rails and door handles. All models had a back-lit instrument cluster with standard temperature gauge. The base four-cylinder, 1.8-liter engine developed 84 hp, but the former 2.0-liter option was no longer available.

6000 — SERIES 2A — (FOUR/V-6) — Most notable of the improvements in the 1986 Pontiac 6000 line was standard anti-lock braking which was introduced during the model year on the 6000 STE (as part of its standard four-wheel power disc brake system). Radio controls were moved to the steering wheel this year and duplicated on the dashboard. The 6000 STE had a revised grille (lacking the traditional Pontiac split design), along with aerodynamic flush halogen headlamps and fog lamps. The standard STE engine was a 173-cid (2.8-liter) V-6 with multi-port fuel injection delivering 130 hp. The standard three-speed automatic transmission was now connected to a 3.18:1 rear axle. An electronic instrument cluster remained standard and had a new vacuum fluorescent unit. A pod held the controls for power windows, power door locks, and power mirrors. As before, the Pontiac 6000 STE had an almost non-existent options list that listed only six-way power driver and passenger seats with recliners, a sunroof, and suede interior trim. Pontiac 6000 base and LE models had a standard 151-cid (2.5-liter) four with a three-speed automatic transmission. Options included both carbureted and fuel-injected versions of the 2.8-liter V-6. A four-speed overdrive automatic transmission was available for V-6 models.

I.D. DATA: Pontiac's 17-symbol Vehicle Identification Number (VIN) was on the upper left surface of the instrument panel, visible through the windshield. The first three symbols (1G2) indicate Pontiac division. Symbol four is restraint system (A=manual seatbelts). Symbol five is car line/series: E=Fiero; M=Fiero Sport; F=Fiero SE; G=Fiero GT; L=T1000; B=Sunbird; U=Sunbird GT; D=Sunbird SE; E=Grand Am; V=Grand Am LE; W=Grand Am SE; F=6000; G=6000 LE; E=6000 SE; H=6000 STE; S=Firebird; X=Firebird SE; W=Firebird Trans Am; J=Grand Prix; K=Grand Prix LE; P=Grand Prix Brougham; N=Bonneville; R=Bonneville Brougham; S=Bonneville LE; L=Parisienne; T=Parisienne Brougham. In sixth and seventh position are two digits that denote body type: 08=three-door hatchback coupe; 27=two-door coupe; 37=two-door coupe; 77=three-door hatchback; 87=two-door coupe; 97=two-door coupe; 67=two-door convertible; 19=four-door six-window sedan; 68=five-door hatchback; 69=four-door four-window sedan; 35=four-door station wagon. Symbol eight is an engine code: A=3.8-liter U.S.-built two-barrel V-6; C=1.6-liter U.S.-built two-barrel I-4; D=1.8-liter Japan-built diesel I-4; F=5.0-liter U.S./Canada-built 5.0-liter FI V-8; G=5.0-liter U.S./Canada-built four-barrel V-8; H=5.0-liter U.S./Canada-built four-barrel V-8; J=1.8-liter Brazil-built FI I-4; L=3.0-liter U.S.-built FI V-6; P=2.0-liter U.S.-built EFI I-4; R=2.5-liter U.S.-built EFI I-4; R=2.5-liter U.S.-built FI I-4; S=2.8-liter U.S.-built FI V-6; U=2.5-liter U.S.-built I-4; W=2.8-liter U.S./Canada/Mexico-built FI I-4; X=2.8-liter U.S./Canada/Mexico-built two-barrel V-6; Y=5.0-liter U.S.-built four-barrel V-8; Z=4.3-liter U.S.-built FI V-6; 0=1.8-liter Brazil-built FI I-4; 2=2.5-liter U.S./Canada-built FI I-4; 9=2.8-liter U.S./Canada/Mexico-built FI V-6. Next is a check digit. The tenth symbol denotes model year (G=1986). Symbol eleven is a plant code: A=Lakewood, Ga.; L=Van Nuys, Calif.; N=Norwood, Ohio; P=Pontiac, Mich.; T=Tarrytown, N.Y.; X=Fairfax, Kan.; M=Lansing, Mich.; 7=Lordstown, Ohio; 1=Oshawa, Ontario; 2=St. Therese, Quebec. The final six digits are the sequential serial number.

Model Number	Body Style Number	Body Type & Seating	Factory Price	Shipping Weight	Production Total
PARISIENNE (V-6/V-8)					
2B	L69	4d Sedan-6P	11,169/11,734	3,427/—	27,078
2B	L35	4d Sta Wagon-8P	—/11,779	—/3,985	14,464
PARISIENNE BROUGHAM (V-6/V-8)					
2B	T69	4d Sedan-6P	11,949/12,514	3,456/—	43,540
BONNEVILLE (V-6/V-8)					
2G	N69	4d Sedan-6P	10,249/10,964	3,143/—	27,801
BONNEVILLE LE (V-6/V-8)					
2G	S69	4d Sedan-6P	10,529/11,244	3,152/—	7,179
BONNEVILLE BROUGHAM (V-6/V-8)					
2G	R69	4d Sedan-6P	11,079/11,794	3,172/—	5,941
GRAND PRIX (V-6/V-8)					
2G	J37	2d Coupe-6P	10,259/10,974	3,161/—	21,668

1986 Pontiac Firebird two-door coupe. (PGMC)

1986 Pontiac 6000 STE four-door wagon. (PGMC)

1986 Pontiac Bonneville Brougham four-door sedan. (PGMC)

Model Number	Body Style Number	Body Type & Seating	Factory Price	Shipping Weight	Production Total
GRAND PRIX 2+2 (V-6/V-8)					
2G	N/A	2d Coupe-5P	—/18,214	—	200
GRAND PRIX LE (V-6/V-8)					
2G	K37	2d Coupe-6P	10,795/11,510	3,178/—	13,918
GRAND PRIX BROUGHAM (V-6/V-8)					
2G	P37	2d Coupe-6P	11,579/12,294	3,201/—	4,798
FIREBIRD (FOUR/V-6)					
2F	S87	2d Coupe-4P	9,279/9,629	2,789/—	59,334
FIREBIRD SE (V-6/V-8)					
2F	X87	2d Coupe-4P	11,995/12,395	2,909/—	2,259
FIREBIRD TRANS AM (V-8)					
2F	W87	2d Coupe-4P	12,395	3,132	48,870
FIERO (FOUR/V-6)					
2P	E37	2d Coupe-2P	8,949/—	2,480	9,143
FIERO SPORT COUPE (FOUR/V-6)					
2P	M37	2d Sport Coupe-2P	9,449/—	2,493	24,866
FIERO SE (FOUR/V-6)					
2P	F37	2d Coupe-2P	10,595/11,240	7,499	32,305
FIERO GT (V-6)					
2P	G97	2d Coupe-2P	—/12,875	—	17,660
GRAND AM (FOUR/V-6)					
2N	E27	2d Coupe-5P	8,549/9,624	2,423/—	69,545
2N	E69	4d Sedan-5P	8,749/9,824	2,496/—	49,166
GRAND AM LE (FOUR/V-6)					
2N	V27	2d Coupe-5P	9,079/10,154	2,458/—	48,530
2N	V69	4d Sedan-5P	9,279/10,354	2,521/—	31,790
GRAND AM SE (V-6)					
2N	W27	2d Coupe-5P	11,499	2,605	15,506
2N	W69	4d Sedan-5P	11,749	2,683	8,957
1000 (FOUR)					
2T	L08	3d Hatchback-4P	5,749	2,059	12,266
2T	L68	5d Hatchback-4P	5,969	2,118	9,423
SUNBIRD (FOUR)					
2J	B69	4d Sedan-5P	7,495	2,336	60,080
2J	B35	4d Sta Wagon-5P	7,879	2,397	7,445
SUNBIRD SE (FOUR)					
2J	D27	2d Coupe-5P	7,469	2,285	37,526
2J	D77	3d Hatchback-5P	7,829	2,330	3,822
2J	D67	2d Convertible-4P	12,779	2,464	1,598
SUNBIRD GT (FOUR)					
2J	U27	2d Coupe-5P	9,459	2,396	18,118
2J	U77	3d Hatchback-5P	9,819	2,419	2,442
2J	U69	4d Sedan-5P	9,499	2,398	2,802
2J	U67	2d Convertible-4P	14,399	2,573	1,268
6000 (FOUR/V-6)					
2A	F27	2d Coupe-6P	9,549/10,159	2,668/—	4,739
2A	F19	4d Sedan-6P	9,729/10,339	2,713/—	81,531
2A	F35	4d Sta Wagon-6P	10,095/10,705	2,849/—	10,094

1986 Pontiac Grand Prix 2+2 Aerodynamic coupe. (PGMC)

216

1986 Pontiac Grand Prix 2+2 Aerodynamic coupe. (PGMC)

Model Number	Body Style Number	Body Type & Seating	Factory Price	Shipping Weight	Production Total
6000 LE (FOUR/V-6)					
2A	G27	2d Coupe-6P	10,049/10,659	2,687/—	4,803
2A	G19	4d Sedan-6P	10,195/10,805	2,731/—	67,697
2A	G35	4d Wagon-6P	10,579/11189	2,867/—	7,556
6000 SE (V-6)					
2A	E19	4d Sedan-6P	—/11,179	—	7,348
2A	E35	4d Wagon-6P	—/11,825	—	1,308
6000 STE (V-6)					
2A	H19	4d Sedan-5P	15,949	3,039	26,299

NOTE 1: Parisienne, Bonneville, and Grand Prix prices and weights above slash for V-6/belowslash for V-8.

NOTE 2: Base Firebird prices and weights above slash for I-4/ below slash for V-6.

NOTE 3: A 305-cid V-8 cost $400 more than the V-6 on base Firebird.

NOTE 4: Firebird SE prices and weights above slash for V-6/below-slash for V-8.

NOTE 5: Fiero prices and weights above slash for I-4/ below slash for V-6.

NOTE 6: Grand Am prices and weights above slash for I-4/ below slash for V-6.

NOTE 7: Grand Am SE is a V-6 only model.

NOTE 8: 6000 prices and weights above slash for I-4/ below slash for V-6.

ENGINE [Base Four 1000]: Inline. Overhead cam. Four-cylinder. Cast-iron block and head. Displacement: 98 cid. (1.6 liters). Bore & stroke: 3.23 x 2.98 in. Compression ratio: 9.0:1. Brake horsepower: 65 at 5200 rpm. Torque: 80 lbs.-ft. at 3200 rpm. Five main bearings. Hydraulic valve lifters. Carburetor: two-barrel. VIN Code: C.

ENGINE [Base Four Sunbird]: Inline. Overhead cam. Four-cylinder. Cast-iron block and aluminum head. Displacement: 109 cid. (1.8 liters). Bore & stroke: 3.34 x 3.13 in. Compression ratio: 8.8:1. Brake horsepower: 84 at 5200 rpm. Torque: 98 lbs.-ft. at 2800 rpm. Five main bearings. Hydraulic valve lifters. Electronic fuel injection. VIN Code: 0.

ENGINE [Optional Turbo Four Sunbird]: Same as 109-cid four above, with multi-port fuel injection and turbocharger. Compression ratio: 8.0:1. Brake horsepower: 150 at 5600 rpm. Torque: 150 lbs.-ft. at 2800 rpm. VIN Code: J.

ENGINE [Base Four Fiero/Grand Am/Firebird/6000]: Inline. Overhead valve. Four-cylinder. Cast-iron block and head. Displacement: 151 cid. (2.5 liters). Bore & stroke: 4.00 x 3.00 in. Compression ratio: 9.0:1. Brake horsepower: 92 at 4400 rpm. (Firebird: 88 at 4400). Torque: 132-134 lbs.-ft. at 2800 rpm. Five main bearings. Hydraulic valve lifters. Throttle-body fuel injection. VIN Code: R or U.

ENGINE [Optional V-6 6000]: 60-degree. Overhead valve six-cylinder. Cast-iron block and aluminum head. Displacement: 173 cid.

1986 Pontiac Bonneville Brougham four-door sedan. (PGMC)

1986 Pontiac Parisienne Brougham four-door sedan. (PGMC)

(2.8 liters). Bore & stroke: 3.50 x 3.00 in. Compression ratio: 8.5:1. Brake horsepower: 112 at 4800 rpm. Torque: 145 lbs.-ft. at 2100 rpm. Four main bearings. Hydraulic valve lifters. Carburetor: two-barrel. VIN Code: X.

ENGINE [Base V-6 (Firebird SE/6000 STE); Optional (Fiero/Firebird)]: Fuel-injected version of 173-cid V-6 above. Compression ratio: 8.9:1. Brake horsepower: 125 at 4800 rpm. (Fiero: 140 at 5200; Firebird, 135 at 5100). Torque: 155-175 lbs.-ft. at 3600 rpm. VIN Code: S, W, or 9.

ENGINE [Base V-6 (Grand Am SE); Optional (Grand Am)]: 90-degree. Overhead-valve V-6. Cast-iron block and head. Displacement: 181 cid. (3.0 liters). Bore & stroke: 3.80 x 2.70 in. Compression ratio: 9.0:1. Brake horsepower: 125 at 4900 rpm. Torque: 150 lbs.-ft. at 2400 rpm. Four main bearings. Hydraulic valve lifters. Multi-port fuel injection. VIN Code: L.

ENGINE [Base V-6 Grand Prix/Bonneville]: 90-degree. Overhead-valve V-6. Cast-iron block and head. Displacement: 231 cid. (3.8 liters). Bore & stroke: 3.80 x 3.40 in. Compression ratio: 8.0:1. Brake horsepower: 110 at 3800 rpm. Torque: 190 lbs.-ft. at 1600 rpm. Four main bearings. Hydraulic valve lifters. Carburetor: two-barrel Buick-built. VIN Code: A.

ENGINE [Base V-6 Parisienne]: 90-degree. Overhead-valve V-6. Cast-iron block and head. Displacement: 262 cid. (4.3 liters). Bore & stroke: 4.00 x 3.48 in. Compression ratio: N/A. Brake horsepower: 130 at 3600 rpm. Torque: 210 lbs.-ft. at 2000 rpm. Four main bearings. Hydraulic valve lifters. Throttle-body fuel injection. VIN Code: Z.

ENGINE [Base V-8 (Firebird Trans Am/Parisienne wagon); Optional (Firebird/Grand Prix/Bonneville/Parisienne)]: 90-degree. Overhead valve V-8. Cast-iron block and head. Displacement: 305 cid. (5.0 liters). Bore & stroke: 3.74 x 3.48 in. Compression ratio: 9.5:1. Brake horsepower: 150 at 4200 rpm. (Trans Am: 155 at 4000; Parisienne: 165 at 4200). Torque: 235-245 lbs.-ft. at 2000-2400 rpm. Five main bearings. Hydraulic valve lifters. Carburetor: four-barrel Chevrolet-built. VIN Code: H.

ENGINE [Optional V-8 Trans Am]: High-output version of 305-cid V-8. Compression ratio: 9.5:1. Brake horsepower: 190 at 4800 rpm. Torque: 240 lbs.-ft. at 3200 rpm. VIN Code: G.

ENGINE [Optional V-8 Trans Am]: Fuel-injected version of 305-cid V-8. Brake horsepower: 205 at 4000 rpm. Torque: 270 lbs.-ft. at 3200 rpm. VIN Code: F.

CHASSIS: Wheelbase: (Fiero) 93.4 in.; (Pontiac 1000 three-door hatchback) 94.3 in.; (Pontiac 1000 five-door hatchback) 97.3 in.; (Sunbird) 101.2 in.; (Grand Am) 103.4 in.; (Firebird) 101.0 in.; (Pontiac 6000) 104.9 in.; (Grand Prix) 108.1 in.; (Bonneville) 108.1 in.; (Parisienne) 116 in. Overall Length: (Fiero) 160.7 in.; (Pontiac 1000 three-door hatchback) 161.9 in.; (Pontiac 1000 five-door hatchback) 164.9 in.; (Sunbird) 175.4 in.; (Sunbird Safari) 176.5 in.; (Grand Am) 177.5 in.; (Firebird) 188.1 in.; (Pontiac 6000) 188.8 in.; (Pontiac 6000 Safari) 193.2 in.; (Grand Prix) 201.9 in.; (Bonneville) 200.2 in.; (Parisienne) 212.3 in.; (Parisienne Safari) 215.1 in. Height: (Fiero) 46.9 in.; (Pontiac 1000) 52.8-52.9 in.; (Sunbird coupe) 51.9 in.; (Sunbird convertible) 52.7 in.; (Sunbird sedan) 53.8 in.; (Sunbird Safari) 54.1 in.; (Grand Am) 52.5 in.; (Firebird) 50 in.; (Pontiac 6000 coupe) 53.3 in.; (Pontiac 6000 coupe) 53.7 in.; (Pontiac 6000 Safari) 54.1 in. (Grand Prix) 54.7 in.; (Bonneville) 55.8 in.; (Parisienne sedan) 56.6 in.; (Parisienne Safari) 57.4 in. Width: (Fiero) 68.9 in.; (Pontiac 1000) 61.8 in.; (Sunbird coupe/convertible) 65.9 in.; (Sunbird hatch) 66.6 in.; (Sunbird sedan/Safari) 66.2 in.; (Grand Am) 66.5 in.; (Firebird) 72.4 in.; (Pontiac 6000) 72 in.; (Grand Prix) 72.3 in.; (Bonneville) 71.6 in.; (Parisienne) 75.3 in.

except Safari, 79.3 in. Front Tread: (Fiero) 57.8 in.; (Pontiac 1000) 51.2 in.; (Sunbird) 55.4 in.; (Grand Am) 55.5 in.; (Firebird) 60.7 in.; (Pontiac 6000) 58.7 in.; (Grand Prix) 58.5 in.; (Bonneville) 58.5 in.; (Parisienne) 61.8 in.; (Parisienne Safari) 62.2 in. Rear Tread: (Fiero) 58.7 in.; (Pontiac 1000) 51.2 in.; (Sunbird) 55.2 in.; (Grand Am) 55.1 in.; (Firebird) 61.6 in.; (Pontiac 6000) 56.9 in.; (Grand Prix) 57.8 in.; (Bonneville) 57.8 in.; (Parisienne) 60.8 in.; (Parisienne Safari) 64.1 in. Standard Tires: (Fiero) P185/75R14 SBR BSW; (Fiero SE) P195/70R14; (1000) P155/80R13 GBR BSW; (Sunbird) P175/80R13 SBR BSW; (Grand Am) P185/80R13 SBR BSW; (Firebird) P215/65R15 SBR BSW; (6000) P185/75R14 SBR; (6000 STE) P195/70R14 SBR; (Grand Prix) P195/75R14 SBR; (Bonneville) P195/75R14 SBR; (Parisienne sedan) P205/75R15 SBR; (Parisienne Safari) P225/75R15 SBR.

TECHNICAL: Transmission: Four-speed manual transmission standard on Fiero V-6 and 1000. Five-speed manual transmission standard on Fiero four, Sunbird, Firebird and Grand Am; optional on 1000. Three-speed Turbo-Hydra-Matic transmission standard on other models. Four-speed overdrive automatic transmission available on Firebird, 6000, Grand Prix, and Bonneville; standard on Parisienne. Standard final drive ratio: (Fiero) 2.48:1 with five-speed transmission, 3.18:1 with automatic transmission; (Fiero V-6) 2.96:1 with four-speed transmission, 3.06:1 with automatic transmission; (1000) 3.36:1; (Sunbird) 2.55:1 with five-speed transmission, 3.43:1 with automatic transmission; (Sunbird turbo) 2.96:1 with four-speed transmission, 3.33:1 with automatic transmission; (Grand Am) 2.48:1 with five-speed transmission, 2.84:1 with automatic transmission; (Firebird) 3.73:1 or 3.70:1 with four, 3.42:1 with V-6, 2.77:1 with V-8; (Trans Am) 3.27:1 except 3.70:1 with H.O. V-8; (6000) 2.39:1 with four, 2.84:1 or 3.06:1 with V-6; (6000 STE) 3.18:1; (Grand Prix/Bonneville) 2.41:1; (Parisienne) 2.56:1; (Parisienne wagon) 2.73:1. Steering/Suspension/Brakes/Body: same as 1985, except anti-lock braking on 6000 STE. Fuel Tank: (Fiero) 10.2 gal.; (1000) 12.2 gal.; (Sunbird) 13.6 gal.; (Grand Am) 13.6 gal.; (Firebird) 15.5 gal.; (6000) 15.7 gal.; (Grand Prix/Bonneville) 18.1 gal.; (Parisienne sedan) 25 gal.; (Parisienne wagon) 22 gal.

DRIVETRAIN OPTIONS: Engines: Turbo 1.8-liter four: in Sunbird ($1,511); in Sunbird SE convertible ($1,296); standard in GT. 173-cid two-barrel V-6 in Pontiac 6000 ($435). 173-cid FI V-6: in Fiero ($645); in Firebird ($350); in Pontiac 6000 ($560). 181-cid V-6 in Grand Am ($610). 262-cid V-6 in Grand Prix ($150). 305-cid four-barrel V-8: in Firebird ($750); in Firebird SE ($400); in Grand Prix/Bonneville ($540); in Parisienne ($390). H.O. 305-cid V-8 four-barrel or FI in Trans Am ($695). Transmission/Differential: Four-speed manual transmission: in Fiero SE ($50 credit); in Sunbird ($75 credit). Five-speed manual transmission: in 1000 ($75); in Sunbird GT ($75). Three-speed automatic transmission: in Fiero ($465); in Fiero GT ($515); in Sunbird ($390- $465); in Grand Am ($465). Four-speed automatic transmission: in Firebird ($465); in 6000/Grand Prix/Bonneville/Parisienne ($175). Limited-slip differential in Firebird/Grand Prix/Bonneville/Parisienne ($100). Brakes/Steering: Power brakes in T1000 ($100). Power four-wheel disc brakes in Firebird ($179) but no charge (NC) with performance package. Power steering in T1000/Sunbird ($215). Suspension: Rally tuned suspension: in Fiero/Sunbird/Grand Am/6000/Grand Prix/Parisienne ($50). Superlift shock absorbers in 6000/GRAND PRIX/Bonneville/Parisienne ($64). Heavy-duty springs in Parisienne

1986 Pontiac 6000 STE four-door sedan. (PGMC)

1986 Pontiac Grand Am four-door sedan. (PGMC)

($16). Other: Heavy-duty cooling ($40-$70). Heavy-duty battery ($26). Heavy-duty alternator ($25-$51). Engine block heater ($18-$19). California emissions ($99).

OPTION PACKAGES: 1000 sport/handling package ($358). 1000 custom trim ($151). Sunbird custom exterior group ($86). Sunbird custom trim group ($244-$493). Sunbird security package ($19). Firebird Trans Am special performance package ($664). Firebird luxury interior trim ($349-$359). 6000 custom exterior ($56). Grand Prix Brougham Landau package ($469). Lamp groups ($21-$47).

MAJOR CONVENIENCE/APPEARANCE OPTIONS: Air conditioning ($645-$750). Cruise control ($175); Not available on 1000. Power seat ($215-$225); Not available on 1000/Fiero. Dual eight-way power seats: 6000 STE ($508). Power windows ($195-$285); Not available on 1000. Cornering lamps: Bonneville/Grand Prix ($68); Parisienne ($55). Power glass sunroof: Parisienne ($1230). Removable glass sunroof: Fiero/Sunbird/Grand Am/6000 ($310). Hatch roof: Firebird/Grand Prix ($850-$886). Full vinyl roof: Bonneville ($160). Padded landau roof: Grand Prix ($245-$322). Padded full vinyl roof: Bonneville ($245); Parisienne ($185). Rear spoiler: Fiero ($269); Firebird SE ($70). Louvered rear sunshields: Sunbird ($199); Firebird ($210); Trans Am ($95). Two-tone paint: Sunbird ($101-$151); Grand Am ($101); Firebird/6000 ($205); Grand Prix/Bonneville ($205); Parisienne sedan ($205). Recaro bucket seats: Firebird ($636-$995).

HISTORICAL: Introduced: Oct. 3, 1985, except Grand Am, Aug. 28, 1985 and Fiero, Jan. 3, 1986. Model year production: 952,943 units. Calendar year production (U.S.): 775,247. Calendar year sales by U.S. dealers: 841,441. Model year sales by U.S. dealers: 840,137. Pontiac's anti-lock braking (ABS), like that of other GM divisions, came from the Teves organization in West Germany. The division's market share rose by one percent in model year 1986, as a result of moderately increased sales. Even with V-6 power available, Fiero sales continued below the anticipated level and fell this year (though over 71,000 did find customers). Grand Am, on the other hand, wasn't so far from doubling its 1985 sales total. Pontiac's version of the N-body design attracted considerably more buyers than the equivalents from Buick and Oldsmobile. Firebird sales slipped a bit, but the Trans Am remained popular. Grand Prix and Bonneville declined rather sharply. Poor sales of the subcompact 1000 prompted its discontinuance for 1987, when a new front-drive Bonneville appeared. Pontiac was also planning to introduce a Korean import under the LeMans name for 1987.

1987 PONTIAC

1987 Pontiac Fiero GT two-door coupe. (PGMC)

SAFARI — SERIES 2L — (V-8) — Although the Safari name was used on 1987 Sunbird and 6000 wagons, the separate Safari series still offered Pontiac's massive (for 1987) full-sized station wagon. It used the traditional front engine, rear-wheel-drive layout that dated back many years. This model was the only remaining "Parisienne" model, but that model name was no longer used. Standard Safari features included tinted glass, air conditioning, AM/FM stereo radio, dual sport mirrors, whitewall tires, and a 5.0-liter V-8 coupled to a four-speed automatic transmission. For towing purposes, the Safari was available with a seven-wire trailer light cable, plus an optional heavy-duty cooling system. Additional standard fare included soft ray tinted glass, Power Master front disc/rear drum power brakes, white-accented bumper rub strips front and rear, carpeting on the floor and load floor, carpeted lower door panels, a center high-mounted stop light, extensive anti-corrosion protection, the GM Computer Command Control system, an inside hood release, a remote-control driver's mirror, power steering, a notchback front seat with center armrest, a rear-facing third seat with Hartford vinyl trim, load-carrying rear springs, a front stabilizer bar, a three-spoke steering wheel, a tailgate window control, and custom wheel covers.

BONNEVILLE — SERIES 2H — (V-6) — The Bonneville badge went on an all-new front-wheel-drive sedan in 1987. Pontiac described it as a "state-of-the-art" Sports Sedan. It was in the full-size car class and was constructed with a great deal of attention paid to detail to give it a high-quality image. Aggressive, aerodynamic looks characterized this contemporary new entry. All models were powered by a transversely-mounted V-6 with a sequential fuel injection (SFI) system. This engine was teamed with a four-speed automatic transaxle. Power rack-and-pinion steering, power disc brakes, and a fully-independent MacPherson strut suspension system provided precise road feel. Styling cues started with a fluid shape featuring a bold and aggressively tapered nose that swept to reveal a narrow horizontal grille opening proudly showcasing the Pontiac crest. The roofline was designed to give generous head room, while a gently curved rear window swept into the carefully sculptured rear deck. The rear view of the Bonneville was dominated by a boldly ribbed taillight design, with lamps that wrapped neatly around each body corner for maximum visibility. The cumulative design effect was one of smoothness combined with an aggressive road stance. "We wanted to create a more youthful, sophisticated sedan," said John Schinella, chief designer of Pontiac Design Studio 2. "Smooth, graceful surfaces, rounded front and rear curves and more contemporary proportions have helped to achieve a more integral design for the all-new Bonneville." The interior featured round gauges, back-lit dials and pointers, an electric speedometer, fuel and engine temperature gauges, and a function monitoring system with graphic tell-tales. A rich wood-look treatment on the instrument panel blended with the four-spoke steering wheel for total driver appeal. Seating was carefully tailored and sculpted to provide excellent support and long distance comfort. Door map pockets were a standard feature, along with tinted glass and air conditioning. There were two models (base Bonneville and Bonneville LE), plus an RPOY80 Bonneville SE option package. Standard on the base model was acoustical insulation, Aero Torque wheel covers, a front center armrest seat, automatic front safety belts (effective November 1986), carpets, a center high-mounted stop light, cluster warning lights, a compact spare tire, complete instrumentation, a Delco Freedom II battery, dual horns, extensive corrosion protection, flow-through ventilation, the GM Computer Command Control system, an inside hood release, a dome lamp, a glove box lamp, a trunk lamp, lower door panel carpeting, a multi-function control lever, power rack-and-pinion steering, a UL6 Delco AM radio with clock, and fluidic windshield wipers. LE models added a rear seat with pull-down center armrest, deluxe carpets, deluxe trunk trim, dual side view sport mirrors, power windows with door pod switches, right- and left-hand manual front seat recliners, a 45/55 split bench front seat with armrest, and wide body side moldings. The Bonneville SE also featured complete rally instrumentation with a tachometer, controlled-cycle windshield wipers, a driver information center, gas pressure struts, special springs, a leather-wrapped steering wheel, a rally-tuned suspension, a tilt steering wheel, 15 x 6-in. Tri-Port cast aluminum wheels, and Eagle GT steel-belted radial tires.

GRAND PRIX — SERIES 2G — (V-6/V-8) — Pontiac's rear-dive intermediate luxury coupe was fading in popularity by 1987. It offered comfortable, reliable motoring combined with mediocre fuel economy. Three trim levels were offered: Grand Prix, Grand Prix LE and Grand Prix Brougham. Returning again was the limited-edition 2+2 model with a fastback rear window treatment designed to enhance aerodynamics and homologate the special "big window" body for NASCAR Grand National stock car racing. Every Grand Prix featured mini bumper guards front and rear; carpeted lower door areas; a center high-mounted stop light; front and rear lower chrome bumpers; a compact spare tire; custom wheel covers; a Delco Freedom II battery; a dome light; dual horns; dual rectangular headlights; an electronic clock; an engine coolant recovery system; extensive anti-corrosion protection; a formal roofline with formal rear quarter windows; a front stabilizer bar; a glove compartment with lock and key; the GM Computer Command Control system; an inside hood release; a multi-function control lever; power steering; and a wind-split hood ornament. Grand Prix LEs also featured color-keyed safety belts, dual sport side view mirrors, a 55/45 notchback front seat in Pallex cloth with fold-down center armrest, a four-spoke sport steering wheel, and wide rocker panel moldings. The Grand Prix Brougham added door courtesy lamps, power windows, Majestic cloth seat trim (instead of Pallex cloth) and a luxury cushion steering wheel. The 2+2 was designed for fans of luxury sport driving. It included performance-oriented power and handling features. Styling changes began up front with a rounded front fascia incorporating a four-sectioned honeycomb grille-work. The upper sections blended smoothly into the molded fascia panel, while the lower sections were mounted in the body-colored bumper. A deep front air dam added to the sporty character. Like the front fascia, it was made of reaction injection molded (RIM) urethane. Further back, the aerodynamic flavor of the fastback model continued with a sweeping, permanently fixed rear window. A fiberglass panel covered the area between the rear seat and the aft portion of the window. This panel was finished in matte black to reduce glare on the window. Access to the luggage compartment was possible through an abbreviated fiberglass rear deck lid. A four-inch high spoiler, molded into the deck lid, enhanced the smooth airflow over the vehicle and also served as a housing for the center high-mounted stoplight. The 2+2 came with a high-performance drive train. Its specifically-tuned suspension featured four gas-filled shocks, 77 N-mm front and 24 N-mm rear coil springs, 29mm front and 16mm rear stabilizer bars, 15x7-in. Rally II wheels and Goodyear Eagle GT tires. Complimenting the performance suspension of the 2+2 was a firm 12.7:1 steering ratio. Interior features included a leather-wrapped three-spoke tilt steering wheel, cloth-covered front bucket seats, a center console, rally cluster instrumentation (with tachometer and digital clock), and an AM/FM stereo with seek-and-scan and a cassette deck. Air conditioning, cruise control, full tinted glass, dual sport mirrors, power windows, and power locks were also standard in 2+2s. They were finished in a Silver primary exterior color with Gray interior.

FIREBIRD — SERIES 2F — (V-6/V-8) — The sporty F-body Firebird had few changes for 1987. The dropping of the SE coupe was the big one. A new Formula option was offered. A body-color aero spoiler with a high-mounted stoplight embedded in it was one change. Base Firebirds also had a new seat with adjustable headrest and Ripple cloth upholstery. New options included body-color body side moldings, molded door panel trim (except GTA), and availability of the Y99 performance suspension on base models. A 5.7-liter multi-port fuel injected V-8 performance engine was optional in cars with the Formula package and standard in the GTA, which was itself a new Trans Am option. A four-way manual adjustable seat was now standard in Trans Ams. Base Firebirds featured a full-length console with instrument panel, side window defoggers, a front air dam, the GM Computer Command Control system, a hatchback "pull-down" feature, rectangular-shaped concealed quartz halogen headlights, a U63 Delco AM radio, cloth reclining front bucket seats, a folding rear seat, a three-spoke Formula steering wheel, a lockable storage compartment, and "wet-arm" (fluidic) windshield wipers. Formulas added a body-color aero rear deck lid spoiler, analog instrumentation, a domed hood, 16 x 8-in. Hi-Tech aluminum wheels and a special performance suspension. The Trans Am added an aero body skirting package, hood and front fender air extractors, hood air louvers, fog lamps, soft ray tinted glass, and a rally-tuned suspension. GTAs added articulating front bucket seats, a limited-slip rear axle, a special aero package, a special performance suspension, a leather-wrapped steering wheel, and lightweight 16 x 8-in. diamond-spoke gold-colored wheels.

1987 Pontiac Sunbird SE two-door coupe. (PGMC)

FIERO — SERIES 2P — (FOUR/V-6) — The Fiero was Pontiac's distinctive P-body two-passenger, mid-engined sports car. A lineup of sporty Fieros drove into 1987 with a full range of fun-to-drive model offerings: Coupe, Sport Coupe, SE coupe, and GT coupe. Each had distinctive styling and performance features that appealed to every taste and budget. New for the base coupe and Sport Coupe were exciting new front and rear fascias that gave each model a cleaner, more aerodynamic look. All except the GT also had a new front license plate carrier. New SE colors were offered, too. The standard 2.5-liter EFI four had increased air flow and power for 1987 due to enlargements of both the throttle-body-injection (TBI) system and the intake manifold. It featured an updated Direct Ignition System. This system replaced the ignition distributor with a solid state, multiple-coiled, computer-controlled spark plug firing system for improved efficiency and reduced engine maintenance. The Fiero coupe and Sport Coupe came equipped with 14-in. Tri-Tech wheel covers. The 14-in. Hi-Tech Turbo wheels were optional on the Sport Coupe. The interiors of the base coupe and Sport Coupe carried a four-spoke steering wheel, a full-length console, cloth-appointed bucket seats and trim, and clean instrumentation. The Fiero SE was aimed at driving enthusiasts. It had unique styling with an optional rear deck lid spoiler. Inside were complete instrumentation in backlit gauges, a full-length console, a four-spoke sport steering wheel, and Pallex cloth trim on Euro-style bucket seats. GT colors available at the start of the year were again Black and Silver, plus a new Medium Red Metallic. Other colors were added later. The Fiero GT, which was introduced in mid-1986, returned in 1987. It included the Gertag/GM gearbox and a 2.8-liter 135-hp V-6 good for 8-second 0-to-60-mph times. With optional automatic transmission the same acceleration took 9 seconds. The GT had fastback styling, exclusive use of the WS6 performance suspension, and 15-in. diamond-spoke aluminum wheels with different size tires front and rear. It also had dual twin-trumpet exhausts and an optional wing spoiler. Inside was a back-lit instrument cluster with tachometer, trip odometer, temperature and fuel gauges, a leather-wrapped three-spoke steering wheel, and Euro-style bucket seats.

GRAND AM — SERIES 2N — Pontiac's Grand Am was an upscale N-body front-wheel-drive compact. New features for 1987 included a backlit analog gauge cluster, passive seat belts, redesigned manual shifter knob, raised rear speakers, and nine new paint colors: Light Sapphire Metallic, Medium Sapphire Metallic, Medium Garnet Metallic, Light Rosewood Metallic, Medium Rosewood Metallic, Light Copper Metallic, Medium Copper Metallic, Beige, and Black Metallic. New 14-in. wheels with Tri-Port wheel covers and 195/70R14 tires were a new option for base and LE models. A split-folding rear seat was new for LEs and SEs and was standard in SEs. Other new options included an Ultima cloth articulating seat and new leather trim for LE and SE and a 2.0-liter Turbo engine at mid-year. Composite lamps were now standard on LEs. A new console with integral armrest was optional in base models and standard in others. The 2.5-liter engine utilized a new tuned intake manifold with high-flow cylinder head. Last, but not least came new four-spoke urethane- and leather-clad steering wheels. Standard equipment included an acoustic insulation package; automatic front safety belts (after January 1987); front and rear soft fascia bumpers; a center high-mounted stop light; a compact spare tire; a Delco Freedom II battery; dual front radio speakers; dual horns; anti-corrosion protection; fluidic windshield washers; a flush windshield and backlight; a glove compartment; the GM Computer Command Control system; a headlights-on warning; a heater vent system with ducted rear-seat heat; an inside hood release; a low-noise engine cooling fan; a multi-function control lever; a U63 Delco AM radio; rear seat integral headrests; reclining front bucket seats; soft ray tinted glass; and wide body side moldings. LEs also had a deluxe cloth interior; deluxe color-keyed safety belts; deluxe exterior ornamentation; deluxe Thaxton carpeting; dual sport side-view mirrors and two-tone paint. The SE also included composite headlights; cruise control; deluxe integral fog lamps; a remote fuel filler; power door locks; a UM7 Delco AM/FM stereo; rally gauges with a tachometer; a rear seat center armrest; specific monotone paint treatment with color-keyed grille emblems and aluminum wheels; a Rally Tuned suspension; tilt steering; and a visor vanity mirror.

1000 — SERIES 2T — (FOUR) — The 1000 was Pontiac's version of Chevy's Chevette. Both were derived from the four-cylinder Opel T-body sub-compact (Opel was a GM-owned German automaker). A split grille with vertical segmentation characterized the Pontiac edition. It bowed in mid-1981 as the T1000 and had not been expected back in 1987. However, it did return for one last year. This sub-compact was an economical entry-level model good for little more than around-town use. It came in three-door and five-door body styles, both with simple and boxy styling. In its 1987 *Product Highlights and Changes* folder issued Feb. 19, 1987, Pontiac Motor Div. listed no revisions for 1000s. The Pontiac 1000 did not even get new paint colors. Standard equipment included front and rear bumper guards, front and rear bumper rub strips, chrome-plated steel bumpers, all-vinyl seats, a cigar lighter, cut-pile carpets, an AM radio with clock, a front mini console, an inside hood release, reclining front bucket seats, a sport steering wheel, a Delco Freedom II battery, anti-corrosion treatment, and a fluidic windshield washer/wiper system. The standard interior featured a folding full-width rear seat.

SUNBIRD — SERIES 2J — (FOUR) — The J-body Sunbirds were much-improved spin-offs of the Chevrolet Vega/Pontiac Astre sub-compact cars. Base Sunbird models were carried over from 1986 without changes, except for a new manual transmission shift knob and several new interior trims and exterior finishes. New body colors for 1987 Sunbirds included Light Sapphire Metallic; Dark Sapphire Metallic; Medium Rosewood Metallic; and Dark Rosewood Metallic. Standard equipment included a front air dam, dual rectangular headlights, front and rear bumpers, a cigar lighter, cut-pile carpeting, a front floor console, an inside hood release, reclining bucket seats, side window defoggers, a Delco Freedom II battery, extensive anti-corrosion protection, and a fluidic windshield washer system. When cloth trim was ordered, a new low-back front bucket seat with separate headrest was included for added comfort. The level 1 cloth trim option was of a luxurious new "Ripple cloth" design. An LE (Luxury Edition) option was available for the two-door sedan and Safari wagon. It included the GT-style six-lamp front fascia, custom trim, high-tech taillights, a deluxe console, and LE identification. Specific new front and rear fascias were added to the SE (Sport Edition) model, which also carried black exterior moldings. The SE front included new semi-hidden headlights. The Sunbird GT had a standard turbocharged engine, new color-keyed fender flares (except sedan), a color-keyed spoiler, and mirrors with monochromatic finish. The Gertag/GM five-speed, revised axle half shafts and WS6 performance suspension were standard on GTs. The latter included 28-mm front/21-mm rear stabilizer bars, high-rate springs and rear bushings, 14.0:1 ratio power steering, and P215/60R14 tires. New body side striping could be ordered for solid color GTs, while those with optional two-tone paint treatments included specific body striping as standard equipment. New to the options list was an Easy-Entry passenger seat, an Ultima cloth articulating seat, and new 13-in. aluminum Sport Tech wheels

1987 Pontiac 6000 STE four-door sedan. (PGMC)

(replacing Turbo Torque wheels). The old Safari name was added to wagons.

6000 — SERIES 2A — (I-4/V-6) — There were no styling changes for the 1987 Pontiac 6000. New for the base model was a tethered gas cap, a lightweight scissors jack, composite headlights, a revised instrument panel appliqué, 14-in. cast aluminum wheels, restyled taillight lenses and bezels, a bright grille, and an improved Delco maintenance-free battery. Also the 6000 Station Wagon used the Safari name, as did other Pontiac wagons. The LE was dropped as a model and became an interior trim option for the base 6000. It included wide body side moldings, two-tone lower paint accents, new door map pockets, and London/Empress cloth interior trim. The LE model's B-pillar appliqués became a delete-option. New for 6000 SEs was a standard aero package and rear deck lid spoiler, door map pockets, new taillight lenses with black bezels, a new black grille, and newly optional leather seat inserts. Changes in STE models included a new body-color lower air dam, new body-color taillight bezels, a "wet-arm" wiper system, new door map pockets, and button type front floor mat retainers. The black rocker panel moldings used previously were deleted. Standard equipment on base 6000s included acoustical insulation; black door window frames; carpeted lower door panels; a center high-mounted stop light; a compact spare tire; composite headlights; cut-pile carpeting; a Delco Freedom II battery; extensive anti-corrosion protection; a fluidic windshield wiper/washer system; a black front air dam; front and rear door lamp switches; a glove compartment with lock; the GM Computer Command Control system; an inside hood release; warm red instrument panel lighting; a multi-function control lever; a Delco U63 AM radio; radio noise suppression equipment; side window defoggers and soft fascia front; and rear bumpers. Cars with the LE option also had color-keyed safety belts; door map pockets, dual horns, a locking fuel filler door, lower two-tone paint accents, map pockets on front seat backs, and a four-spoke sport steering wheel. Added on SE models were front bucket seats and a console; a dual outlet sport exhaust system; rally gauges with a tachometer; and a leather-wrapped SE steering wheel. The top-of-the-line 6000 STE also had an accessory kit with flares; a raincoat and first aid supplies; controlled-cycle wipers; deluxe carpeted floor mats; a driver information center; electronically operated side view mirrors; electronic ride control system; the GM Computer Control system; a locking fuel filler door; power door locks; a Delco "touch control" AM/FM stereo with cassette; a rear seat with fold-down center armrest; a specific STE leather-wrapped steering wheel with integral radio controls; a tilt steering wheel; a visor vanity mirror; and a windshield sun shade with pockets.

I.D. DATA: Pontiac's 17-symbol Vehicle Identification Number (VIN) was on the upper left surface of the instrument panel, visible through the windshield. The first symbol indicates country of origin: 1=U.S.; 2= Canada; J=Japan. The second symbol indicates manufacturer: G=General Motors; G=Suzuki; 8=Isuzu; Y=NUMMI. The third symbol G indicates make: 2=Pontiac division. The fourth and fifth symbols indicate body type and series: A/E=6000 SE; A/F=6000; A/G=6000 LE; A/H=6000 STE; B/L=Safari; F/S=Firebird; F/W=Firebird Trans Am; G/J=Grand Prix; G/K=Grand Prix LE; G/P=Grand Prix Brougham; H/X=Bonneville; H/Z=Bonneville LE; J/B=Sunbird; J/D=Sunbird SE; J/U=Sunbird GT; M/R=Firefly (U.S. Customs Territories); N/E=Grand Am; N/V=Grand Am LE; N/W=Grand Am SE; P/E=Fiero coupe; P/F=Fiero SE coupe; P/G=Fiero GT coupe; P/M=Fiero Sport Coupe; T/L=Pontiac 1000. The sixth seventh symbol denotes body type: 1=two-door coupe/sedan styles 11, 27, 37, 47, 57, 97; 2=two-door hatchback styles 07, 08, 77 and 87; 3=two-door convertible style 67; 5=four-door sedan styles 19, 23, 33 and 69; 6=four-door hatchback style 68; 8=four-door station wagon style 35. Symbol seven indicates restraint code: 1=manual belts; 4=automatic belts. Symbol eight is an engine code: A=3.8-liter U.S.-built two-barrel V-6; C=1.6-liter U.S.-built two-barrel I-4; F=5.0-liter U.S./Canada-built 5.0-liter FI V-8; H=5.0-liter U.S./Canada-built four-barrel V-8; K=2.0-liter U.S.-built FI I-4; L=3.0-liter U.S.-built FI V-6; P=2.0-liter U.S.-built EFI I-4; M=2.0-liter U.S.-built FI I-4; R=2.5-liter U.S.-built EFI I-4; S=2.8-liter Mexico-built FI V-6; U=2.5-liter U.S.-built FI I-4; W=2.8-liter U.S./Canada/Mexico-built FI I-4; Y=5.0-liter U.S.-built four-barrel V-8; Z=4.3-liter U.S.-built FI V-6; 3=3.8-liter U.S.-built FI V-6; 8=5.7-liter U.S./Canada-built V-8; 9=2.8-liter Mexico-built FI V-6. Next is a check digit. The tenth symbol denotes model year (H=1987). Symbol eleven is a plant code: A=Lakewood, Ga.; L=Van Nuys, Calif.; N=Norwood, Ohio; P=Pontiac, Mich.;

1987 Pontiac Grand Prix 2+2 Aerodynamic coupe. (PGMC)

T=Tarrytown, N.Y.; X=Fairfax, Kan.; M=Lansing, Mich.; 7=Lordstown, Ohio; 1=Oshawa, Ontario; 2=St. Therese, Quebec. The final six digits are the sequential serial number.

Model Number	Body Style Number	Body Type & Seating	Factory Price	Shipping Weight	Production Total
SAFARI SERIES 2L (V-8)					
2L	BL8	4d Sta Wagon-8P	13,959	4,109	11,935
BONNEVILLE SERIES H/X (V-6)					
2H	HX5	4d Sport Sedan-5P	13,399	3,316	Note 1
BONNEVILLE LE SERIES H/Z (V-6)					
2H	HZ5	4d Sport Sedan-5P	14,866	3,316	Note 1
BONNEVILLE SE SERIES H/Z5 (V-6)					
2H	HZ5/Y80	4d Sport Sedan-5P	15,806	3,324	Note 1
GRAND PRIX SERIES 2G (V-6/V-8)					
2G	J37	2d Coupe-5P	11,069	3,231	Note 2
GRAND PRIX LE SERIES 2G (V-6/V-8)					
2G	K37	2d Coupe-5P	11,799	3,263	Note 2
GRAND PRIX BROUGHAM SERIES 2G (V-6/V-8)					
2G	P37	2d Coupe-5P	12,519	3,265	Note 2
GRAND PRIX 2+2 SERIES 2G (V-6/V-8)					
2G	RPOY97	2d Aero Coupe-5P	17,800	3,530	Note 2/3
FIREBIRD SERIES 2F (V-6)					
2F	S87	2d Coupe-5P	10,359	3,105	Note 4
FIREBIRD SERIES 2F (V-8)					
2F	S87	2d Coupe-5P	13,259	3,274	Note 4
FIERO SERIES P/E (I-4/V-6)					
2P	E37	2d Coupe-2P	8,299	2,546	Note 5
FIERO SERIES P/M (I-4/V-6)					
2P	M37	2d Sport Coupe-2P	9,989	2,546	Note 5
FIERO SERIES P/F (I-4/V-6)					
2P	F37	2d Coupe-2P	11,239	2,567	Note 5
FIERO SERIES P/G (I-4/V-6)					
2P	G37	2d Coupe-2P	13,489	2,708	Note 5
GRAND AM SERIES 2N (I-4/V-6)					
2N	E27	2d Coupe-5P	9,299	2,492	Note 6
2N	E69	4d Sedan-5P	9,499	2,565	Note 6
GRAND AM LE SERIES 2N (I-4/V-6)					
2N	V27	2d Coupe-5P	9,999	2,528	Note 6
2N	V69	4d Sedan-5P	10,199	2,590	Note 6
GRAND AM SE SERIES 2N (I-4/V-6)					
2N	W27	2d Coupe-5P	12,659	2,608	Note 6
2N	W69	4d Sedan-5P	12,899	2,686	Note 6
1000 SERIES 2T (I-4)					
2T	L08	3d Hatchback-4P	5,959	2,114	Note 7
2T	L68	5d Hatchback 4P	6,099	2,173	Note 7
SUNBIRD SERIES 2J (I-4)					
2J	B69	4d Sedan-5P	7,999	2,404	Note 8
2J	B35	4d Safari-5P	8,529	2,466	Note 8
SUNBIRD SE SERIES 2J (I-4/I-4 Turbo)					
2J	D27	2d Coupe-5P	7,979	2,353	Note 8
2J	D77	3d Hatchback-5P	8,499	2,466	Note 8
2J	D87	2d Convertible-5P	13,799	2,532	Note 8
SUNBIRD GT SERIES 2J (I-4/I-4 Turbo)					
2J	U27	2d Coupe-5P	10,299	2,353	Note 8
2J	U69	4d Sedan-5P	10,349	2,404	Note 8
2J	U77	3d Hatchback-5P	10,699	2,399	Note 8
2J	U67	2d Convertible-5P	15,569	2,532	Note 8
6000 SERIES 2A (I-4/V-6)					
2A	F27	2d Coupe-5P	10,499	2,792	Note 9
2A	F19	4d Sedan-5P	10,499	2,755	Note 9
2A	F35	4d Safari-5P	10,899	2,925	Note 9
6000 LE SERIES 2A (I-4/V-6)					
2A	G19	4d Sedan-5P	11,099	2,824	Note 9
2A	G35	4d Safari-5P	11,499	2,977	Note 9
6000 SE SERIES 2A (I-4/V-6)					
2A	E19	4d Sedan-5P	12,389	2,986	Note 9
2A	E35	4d Safari-5P	13,049	3,162	Note 9
6000 STE SERIES 2A (I-4/V-6)					
2A	H19	4d Sedan-5P	18,099	3,101	Note 9

NOTE 1: Bonneville series production totaled 111,419 cars.

NOTE 2: Grand Prix series production totaled 16,542 cars.

NOTE 3: Only 200 Grand Prix 2+2s are believed to have been built.

NOTE 4: Firebird series production totaled 80,439 cars.

NOTE 5: Fiero series production totaled 44,432 cars.

NOTE 6: Grand Am series production totaled 226,507 cars.

NOTE 7: 1000 series production totaled 5,628 cars.

NOTE 8: Sunbird series production totaled 87,286 cars.

NOTE 9: 6000 series production totaled 138,518 cars.

SAFARI ENGINE

ENGINE [Standard V-8]: V-block. Overhead valves. Eight-cylinder. Cast-iron block. Displacement: 307 cid. (5.0L). Bore & stroke: 3.80 x 3.85 in. Brake horsepower: 140 at 3200 rpm. Fuel system: four-barrel carburetor. RPO Code: LV2. Produced in U.S. and Canada. Standard V-8 in all Safaris. [VIN code Y].

BONNEVILLE ENGINE

ENGINE [Base Six]: V-block. Overhead valves. Six-cylinder. Cast-iron block. Displacement: 231 cid. (3.8L). Bore & stroke: 3.80 x 3.40 in. Brake horsepower: 150 at 4400 rpm. Fuel system: EFI/SFI. RPO Code: LG3. Standard V-6 in all Bonneville models. [VIN code 3].

GRAND PRIX ENGINES

ENGINE [Base Six]: V-block. Overhead valves. Six-cylinder. Cast-iron block. Displacement: 231 cid. (3.8L). Bore & stroke: 3.80 x 3.40 in. Brake horsepower: 110 at 3800 rpm. Fuel system: two-barrel carburetor. RPO Code: LD5. Standard V-6 (with three-speed automatic) in all Grand Prix models except 2+2. [VIN code A].

ENGINE [Optional Six]: V-block. Overhead valves. Six-cylinder. Cast-iron block. Displacement: 263 cid. (4.3L). Bore & stroke: 4.00 x 3.48 in. Brake horsepower: 140 at 4200. Fuel system: EFI/TBI. RPO Code: LB4. Optional V-6 with three-speed automatic in all Grand Prix models except 2+2. Also available in same models with optional four-speed automatic. [VIN code Z].

ENGINE [Base V-8]: V-block. Overhead valves. Eight-cylinder. Cast-iron block. Displacement: 305 cid. (5.0L). Bore & stroke: 3.74 x 3.48 in. Brake horsepower: 150 at 4000 rpm. Fuel system: four-barrel carburetor. RPO Code: LG4. Produced in U.S. and Canada. Standard V-8 in all Grand Prix including 2+2. [VIN code H].

FIREBIRD ENGINES

ENGINE [Base V-6]: V-block. Overhead valves. Six-cylinder. Cast-iron block and aluminum head. Displacement: 173 cid. (2.8L). Bore & stroke: 3.50 x 2.99 in. 135 at 5100 rpm. Fuel system: EFI/MFI. RPO Code: LB8. Standard with five-speed manual in base Firebird. Available with four-speed automatic in base Firebird. [VIN code W].

ENGINE [Base V-8]: V-block. Overhead valves. Eight-cylinder. Cast-iron block and head. Displacement: 305 cid. (5.0L). Bore & stroke: 3.74 x 3.48 in. Brake horsepower: 155 at 4200 rpm. Fuel system: four-barrel carburetor. RPO Code: LG4. Produced in U.S. or Canada. Standard with five-speed manual in base Firebird V-8, Formula, and Trans Am. Available with four-speed automatic in same models. [VIN code E].

ENGINE [Optional V-8]: V-block. Overhead valves. Eight-cylinder. Cast-iron block and head. Displacement: 305 cid. (5.0L). Bore & stroke: 3.74 x 3.48 in. Brake horsepower: 165 at 4400 rpm. Fuel system: four-barrel carburetor. RPO Code: LB9. Produced in U.S. or Canada. Available with five-speed manual in Formula and Trans Am (delete-option in GTA). Available with four-speed automatic in same applications. [VIN code F].

ENGINE [GTA V-8]: V-block. Overhead valves. Eight-cylinder. Cast-iron block and head. Displacement: 350 cid. (5.7L). Bore & stroke: 3.74 x 3.48 in. Brake horsepower: 210 at 4000 rpm. Torque: 315 lbs.-ft. at 3200 rpm. Fuel system: four-barrel carburetor. RPO Code: B2L. Standard with four-speed automatic in GTA (optional in Formula and Trans Am). Includes low-profile air induction system with aluminum plenum and individual aluminum tuned runners, an extruded dual fuel rail assembly with computer controlled fuel injectors, and a special low-restriction exhaust system. [VIN code 8].

FIERO ENGINES

ENGINE [Base Four]: Inline. Overhead valves. Four-cylinder. Cast-iron block and head. Displacement: 151 cid. (2.5L Tech IV). Bore & stroke: 4.00 x 3.00 in. Compression ratio: 9.0:1. Brake horsepower:

98 at 4800 rpm. Torque: 132-134 lbs.-ft. at 2800 rpm. Five main bearings. Hydraulic valve lifters. Fuel system: EFI/TBI. RPO Code: LR8. Standard with five-speed manual in base, Sport Coupe and SE. Available with three-speed automatic in same models. [VIN code U].

ENGINE [Optional Six]: V-block. Overhead valves. Six-cylinder. Cast-iron block and aluminum head. Displacement: 173 cid. (2.8L). Bore & stroke: 3.50 x 2.99 in. Compression ratio: 8.9:1. Brake horsepower: 135 at 4500 rpm. Torque: 160-165 lbs.-ft. at 3600 rpm. Fuel system: EFI/MFI. RPO Code: L44. Standard with five-speed manual in GT (optional in SE). Available with three-speed automatic in SE and GT. [VIN code W].

GRAND AM ENGINES

ENGINE [Base Four]: Inline. Overhead valves. Four-cylinder. Cast-iron block and head. Displacement: 151 cid. (2.5L Tech IV). Bore & stroke: 4.00 x 3.00 in. Compression ratio: 9.0:1. Brake horsepower: 98 at 4800 rpm. Torque: 132-134 lbs.-ft. at 2800 rpm. Five main bearings. Hydraulic valve lifters. Fuel system: EFI/TBI. RPO Code: L68. Standard with five-speed manual in base and LE (credit option in SE). Available with three-speed automatic, except in SE. [VIN code R].

ENGINE [Optional Six]: V-block. Overhead valves. Six-cylinder. Cast-iron block and aluminum head. Displacement: 181 cid. (3.0L). Bore & stroke: 3.80 x 2.70 in. Brake horsepower: 125 at 4900 rpm. Fuel system: EFI/MFI. RPO Code: LN7. Standard with three-speed automatic in SE (optional in base and LE). [VIN code L].

PONTIAC 1000 ENGINE

ENGINE [Base Four]: Inline. OHC. Four-cylinder. Cast-iron block and head. Displacement: 98 cid. (1.6L). Bore & stroke: 3.23 x 2.98 in. Compression ratio: 9.0:1. Brake horsepower: 65 at 5200 rpm. Torque: 80 lbs.-ft. at 3200 rpm. Five main bearings. Hydraulic valve lifters. Fuel system: 2V carburetor. RPO Code: L17. Standard with four-speed manual. Optional with five-speed manual or three-speed automatic. [VIN code C].

SUNBIRD ENGINES

ENGINE [Base Four]: Inline. OHC. Four-cylinder. Cast-iron block and aluminum head. Displacement: 121 cid. (2.0L). Bore & stroke: 3.39 x 3.39 in. Brake horsepower: 96 at 4800 rpm. Fuel system: EFI/TBI. RPO Code: LT2. Standard with five-speed manual in base, Safari, and SE (optional in GT). Available with three-speed automatic in all. [VIN code K].

ENGINE [Optional Four]: Inline. OHC. Four-cylinder. Turbocharged. Cast-iron block and aluminum head. Displacement: 121 cid. (2.0L). Bore & stroke: 3.39 x 3.39 in. Brake horsepower: 165 at 5600 rpm. Fuel system: EFI/MFI. RPO Code: LT3. Standard with five-speed manual in GT (optional in SE). Available with three-speed automatic in SE and GT. [VIN code M].

6000 ENGINES

ENGINE [Base Four]: Inline. Overhead valves. Four-cylinder. Cast-iron block and head. Displacement: 151 cid. (2.5L Tech IV). Bore & stroke: 4.00 x 3.00 in. Compression ratio: 9.0:1. Brake horsepower: 98 at 4800 rpm. Torque: 132-134 lbs.-ft. at 2800 rpm. Five main bearings. Hydraulic valve lifters. Fuel system: EFI/TBI. RPO Code: LR8. Standard with three-speed automatic in base 6000, base Safari, 6000 LE and Safari LE. [VIN code U].

ENGINE [Standard V-6]: V-block. Overhead valves. Six-cylinder. Cast-iron block and aluminum head. Displacement: 173 cid. (2.8L). Bore & stroke: 3.50 x 2.99 in. Brake horsepower: 125 at 4800 rpm. Fuel system: EFI/MFI. RPO Code: LB6. Standard V-6 (with three-speed automatic) in all 6000 models except STE. Standard in STE with four-speed automatic (and optional in all other models). Also available as a delete-option, with five-speed manual transmission, in SE and STE models. [VIN code 9].

CHASSIS

SAFARI CHASSIS: Wheelbase: 116.0 in. (all). Overall length: 215.1 in. (all). Width: 79.3 in. (all). Height: 57.4 in. (all). Front tread: 62.1 in. Rear tread: 64.1 in. Tires: P225/75R15 WSW steel-belted radials.

BONNEVILLE CHASSIS: Wheelbase: 110.8 in. (all). Overall length: 198.7 in. (all). Width: 72.1 in. (all). Height: 55.5 in. (all). Front tread: 58.7 in. Rear tread: 57.0 in. Standard tires: 205/75R14 BSW (All except SE). Standard tires: 215/65R15 Goodyear Eagle GT (SE).

GRAND PRIX CHASSIS: Wheelbase: 108.1 in. (all). Overall length: 201.9 in. (all). Width: 72.3 in. (all). Height: 54.7 in. (all). Front tread:

55.4 in. Rear tread: 55.1 in. Standard tires: 195/75R14 (All except 2+2). Standard tires: 215/65R15 Goodyear Eagle GT (2+2).

FIREBIRD CHASSIS: Wheelbase: 101.0 in. (All). Overall length: 188.0 (Base/Formula); 191.6 in. (Trans Am/GTA). Width: 72.0 in. (all). Height: 49.7 in. (all). Front tread: 60.7 in. Rear tread: 61.6 in. Standard tires: P215/65R15 BSW (Base/Formula/GTA). Standard tires: P215/65R15 RWL (Trans Am).

FIERO CHASSIS: Wheelbase: 93.4 in. (all). Overall length: 162.7 in. (coupe/Sport Coupe); 165.1 in. (SE/GT). Width: 69 in. (all) Height: 46.9 in. (all). Front tread: 57.8 in. Rear tread: 57.8 in. Standard tires: P185/75R15 BSW (coupe, Sport Coupe); P195/70R14 BSW (SE); P205/60R14 front and P215/60R14 rear (GT).

GRAND AM CHASSIS: Wheelbase: 103.4 in. (coupe/sedan). Overall length: 177.5 (all). Width: 66.9 in. (coupe); 67.5 in. (sedan). Height: 52.5 (coupe/sedan). Front tread: 55.6 in. Rear tread: 55.1 in. Standard tires: P185/80R13 BSW (Base/LE). Standard tires: P215/60R14 (SE).

PONTIAC 1000 CHASSIS: Wheelbase: 94.3 in. (all). Overall length: 161.9 in. (three-door); 164.9 in. (five-door). Width: 61.8 in. (all) Height: 52.8 in. (all). Front tread: 51.2 in. Rear tread: 51.2 in. Standard tires: P155/80R13 BSW (all).

SUNBIRD CHASSIS: Wheelbase: 101.2 in. (all). Overall length: 173.7 in. (coupe/hatchback/convertible); 175.7 (sedan); 175.9 (Wagon). Width: 66.0 in. (coupe/convertible); 66.3 in. (Others) Height: 51.9 in. (coupe/hatchback/convertible); 53.8 in. (sedan); 54.1 in. (Safari Wagon). Front tread: 54.4 in. Rear tread: 54.1 in. Standard tires: P175/80R13 BSW (all except Turbo). Standard tires: P215/60R14 (Turbo).

6000 CHASSIS: Wheelbase: 104.9 in. (all). Overall length: 188.8 in. (coupe/sedan); 193.2 in. (Safari). Width: 72 in. (all). Height: 53.3 in. (coupe); 53.7 in. (sedan); 54.1 in. (Safari). Front tread: 58.7 in. Rear tread: 57.0 in. Standard tires: 185/75R14 (All except STE). Standard tires: 195/70R14 (STE).

TECHNICAL

SAFARI TECHNICAL: Chassis: Front engine/rear drive. Base transmission: Four-speed automatic. Axle ratio: 2.73:1 (standard). Axle ratio: 3.08:1 (optional). Front suspension: Control arms with coil springs. Rear suspension: Live axle, links and coil springs. Front brakes: Power-assisted vented discs. Rear brakes: Power-assisted drums. Fuel tank: 22.0 gal.

BONNEVILLE TECHNICAL: Chassis: Front engine/front drive. Base transmission: Four-speed automatic. Axle ratio: 2.73:1 (standard with 3.8L V-6 in Base Bonneville and Bonneville SE). Axle ratio: 2.97:1 (standard with 3.8L V-6 in Bonneville SE). Front suspension: MacPherson struts with coil springs. Rear suspension: MacPherson struts with coil springs. Front brakes: Power-assisted vented discs. Rear brakes: Power-assisted drums. Fuel tank: 18.0 gal.

GRAND PRIX TECHNICAL: Chassis: Front engine/rear drive. Base transmission (except 2+2): Three-speed automatic with overdrive. Base transmission (2+2): Turbo-Hydra-Matic THM 200-4R four-speed overdrive automatic. Optional transmission (except 2+2): Four-speed automatic. Axle ratio: 2.41:1 (standard with 3.8L V-6 and three-speed automatic; with 4.3L V-6 and four-speed automatic; and with 5.0L V-8 and four-speed automatic, except in 2+2). Axle ratio: 2.29:1 (standard with 4.3L V-6 and three-speed automatic). Axle ratio: 3.08:1 (standard in Grand Prix 2+2 with 5.0L V-8; optional in other models with 3.8L V-6 and three-speed automatic; optional in

1987 Pontiac Bonneville LE four-door sedan. (PGMC)

other models with 4.3L V-6 and four-speed automatic; and optional in other models with 5.0L V-8 and four-speed automatic). Axle ratio: 2.73:1 (optional with 4.3L V-6 and three-speed manual). Front suspension: MacPherson struts with coil springs. Rear suspension: Beam axle with coil springs. Front brakes: Power-assisted vented discs. Rear brakes: Power-assisted drums. Fuel tank: 13.6 gal.

FIREBIRD TECHNICAL: Chassis: Front engine/rear drive. Base transmission: Five-speed manual with overdrive. Optional transmission: Four-speed automatic. Axle ratio: 3.42:1 (with V-6). Axle ratio: 3.23:1 (with 5.0-liter 4V V-8 and five-speed manual). Axle ratio: 2.73:1 (with 5.0-liter 4V V-8 and four-speed automatic). Axle ratio: 3.08:1 (with 5.0-liter TPI V-8 and five-speed manual). Axle ratio: 2.77:1 (with 5.7-liter V-8). Axle ratio: 3.45:1 (with 5.0-liter TPI V-8 and five-speed manual). Front suspension: MacPherson struts with coil springs. Rear suspension: Live axle with coil springs. Front brakes: Power-assisted vented discs. Rear brakes: Power-assisted drums (rear disc brakes standard on GTA). Fuel tank: 15.5 (V-6/TPI V-8s). Fuel tank: 16.2 gal. (four-barrel V-8).

FIERO TECHNICAL: Chassis: Mid-engine/rear drive. Base transmission: Three-speed automatic. Optional transmission (with V-6): Gertag-designed GM-developed five-speed manual. Axle ratio: 3.18:1 (manual) or 2.84 (automatic). Steering: Rack-and-pinion. Front suspension: Independent control arms with coil springs. Rear suspension: Independent control arms with coil springs. Front brakes: Disc. Rear brakes: disc. Fuel tank: 12 gal.

GRAND AM TECHNICAL: Chassis: Front engine/front drive. Base transmission: Five-speed manual with overdrive. Optional transmission: Three-speed automatic. Axle ratio: 3.35:1 (with 2.5-liter engine and manual). Axle ratio: 3.61:1 (with Turbo engine and manual). Axle ratio: 2.84:1 (with 3.0-liter engine or 2.5L engine with automatic). Axle ratio: 3.18:1 (with Turbo engine and automatic). Front suspension: MacPherson struts with coil springs. Rear suspension: Beam axle with coil springs. Front brakes: Power-assisted vented discs. Rear brakes: Power-assisted drums. Fuel tank: 13.6 gal.

PONTIAC 1000 TECHNICAL: Chassis: Front engine/front drive. Base transmission: Four-speed manual. Optional transmission: Three-speed automatic or five-speed manual. Front suspension: Independent control arms with coil springs. Rear suspension: Live axle with links and coil springs. Front brakes: Vented disc. Rear brakes: drum. Fuel tank: 12.2 gal.

SUNBIRD TECHNICAL: Chassis: Front engine/front drive. Base transmission: Five-speed manual with overdrive. Optional transmission: Three-speed automatic. Front suspension: MacPherson struts with coil springs. Rear suspension: Beam axle with coil springs. Front brakes: Power-assisted vented discs. Rear brakes: Power-assisted drums. Fuel tank: 13.6 gal.

6000 TECHNICAL: Chassis: Front engine/front drive. Base transmission: Three-speed automatic with overdrive. Optional transmissions: Four-speed automatic and five-speed manual. Axle ratio: 2.39:1 (with 2.5-liter). Axle ratio: 3.33:1 (with 2.8-liter V-6 and four-speed automatic). Axle ratio: 3.18:1 (performance ratio with 2.8-liter V-6 and three-speed automatic). Axle ratio: 3.61:1 (with 2.8L V-6 and five-speed manual). Front suspension: MacPherson struts with coil springs. Rear suspension: Beam axle with coil springs. Front brakes: Power-assisted vented discs. Rear brakes: Power-assisted drums (ABS vented discs on STE). Fuel tank: 15.7 gal.

OPTIONS

SAFARI OPTIONS: W61 option group #1 ($882). W63 option group #2 ($1,309). G80 limited-slip axle ($100). Y08 cooling system ($40-$66). C49 electric rear window defogger ($145). NB2 California emissions system ($99). K05 engine block heater ($44). U14 rally gauges ($71). V55 roof rack with rear air deflector ($155). B34 carpeted front and rear floor mats ($35). UM6 ETR AM/FM stereo with cassette, etc. ($122). UX1 AM/FM ETR stereo with cassette, graphic equalizer, clock, etc. ($272). UL5 AM/FM stereo delete ($273 credit). U75 power antenna ($70). A65 notch back seat with Hartford or Pallex cloth trim (no charge). AM6 55/45 split notchback seat with Hartford or Pallex cloth trim ($133). AT6 reclining passenger seat with 55/45 seats only ($70). G66 Superlift shock absorbers ($64). U94 trailer wiring package ($30). YD1 trailering package with or without engine block heater ($40-$66). N91 wire wheel covers with locking package ($214). BX3 simulated woodgrain siding with door edge moldings and wood-tone body side molding ($345).

1987 Pontiac Bonneville SE four-door sedan. (PGMC)

BONNEVILLE OPTIONS: W61 Bonneville sedan option group #1 ($457). W63 Bonneville sedan option group #2 ($837). W67 Bonneville sedan option group #3 ($1,369). W61 Bonneville LE option group #1 ($790). W63 Bonneville LE option group #2 ($1,066). W67 Bonneville LE sedan option group #3 ($1,593). W61 Bonneville SE option group #1 ($580). W63 Bonneville SE option group #2 ($856). W67 Bonneville SE sedan option group #3 ($1,333). WS1 Bonneville performance value package #1 ($215). WS3 Bonneville LE performance value package #2 ($356). Y80 Bonneville SE option group, includes QYZ tires, PG5 aluminum wheels, CD4 pulse wipers, NP5 leather-wrapped steering wheel, C75 lamp package with fog lamps, UW1 driver information center, AS7 split seat, D55 console, Y99 suspension, sporty exhausts, black door lock cylinders, and gray window sill moldings on Bonneville LE ($940). V08 heavy-duty cooling system ($66). C49 electric rear window defogger ($145). UW1 driver information center in LE, requires U21 rally gauges ($125). G67 electronic ride control, except on SE or teamed with Y99 rally suspension ($170). NB2 California emissions ($99). K05 engine block heater ($44). B34 carpeted front and rear floor mats ($35). B53 carpeted front and rear floor mats ($35). U21 gauges in Bonneville and Bonneville SE ($100). Y56 luggage carrier ($115). DD8 automatic tilt rearview mirror ($80). D64 two-tone paint ($105). UM7 ETR AM/FM stereo ($178). UM6 AM/FM stereo with cassette and clock ($300). UX1 AM/FM ETR stereo with cassette and more ($450). UT4 AM/FM ETR stereo with "everything" ($775 in Base and LE; $685 in SE). UTO Bose sound system ($1,248 in SE; $1,298 in Base and LE). UL5 AM radio delete ($56 credit). US7 power radio antenna ($70). AT6 reclining passenger seat in base Bonneville, requires 45/55 seat ($70). A78 reclining seats, requires 45/55 seat, in base Bonneville ($140). A80 reclining power seats ($150). AM6 55/45 notchback seat with center armrest in base Bonneville with cloth trim ($133). AM6 55/45 notchback seat with center armrest in Bonneville LE with Majestic cloth and leather trim ($379). AS7 45/55 seat with console and cloth trim in Bonneville LE ($110). AS7 45/55 seat with console and Majestic cloth and leather trim in Bonneville LE ($489); in Bonneville SE ($379). CF5 power glass sunroof including courtesy and dual reading lamps ($1,254-$1,284). Y99 Rally Tuned suspension ($50). Tire options ($76-$206). N91 wire wheel covers with locking package ($199). PD6 14-in diamond-spoke aluminum wheels with locking package ($215). PG5 15-in. Tri-Port aluminum wheels with locking package ($246). U89 trailering wiring harness ($30).

GRAND PRIX OPTIONS: W61 Grand Prix coupe option group #1 ($1,313). W63 Grand Prix coupe option group #2 ($1,867). W61 Grand Prix LE option group #1 ($1,844). W63 Grand Prix LE option group #2 ($2,117). W61 Grand Prix Brougham option group #1 ($1,874). W63 Grand Prix Brougham option group #2 ($2,078). WS1 Grand Prix performance value package #1 ($703). WS3 Grand Prix LE performance value package #2 ($500). LB4 4.3L V-6 ($200). LG4 5.0L four-barrel V-8 ($590). MX0 four-speed automatic transmission ($175). C60 air conditioning ($775). G80 limited-slip axle ($100). V10 Cold weather group ($18-$44). V08 heavy-duty cooling system ($66-$96). C49 electric rear window defogger ($145). NB2 California emissions ($99). U14 rally cluster with trip odometer ($71). U21 rally gauge cluster with tachometer ($153). AO1 tinted glass ($120). CC1 hatch roof with removable glass panels and rear courtesy lamps, not available with sunroof ($906). B34 carpeted front and rear floor mats ($35). B53 carpeted front and rear floor mats ($35). BX2 wide rocker panel molding for base Grand Prix without two-tone paint ($86). B84 two-tone paint with custom upper accent stripes on base or LE Grand Prix ($205). W71 sport two-tone paint treatment on base Grand Prix ($291); on Grand Prix LE ($205). UK4 AM/FM stereo ($178). UK5 AM/FM stereo with cassette ($300). UX1 AM/FM ETR stereo with cassette and more ($450). UL5 AM radio delete ($56 credit). U75 rear mounted power radio antenna ($70). AM6 55/45 notchback seat with center armrest in base Grand Prix with Ripple cloth trim ($133). AR9 bucket seats with recliners and console with Ripple cloth trim in base Grand Prix ($292). AR9 bucket seats with recliners and console with Pallex cloth trim in Grand Prix LE ($89). AR9 bucket seats with recliners and console with Pallex cloth and leather trim in Grand Prix LE ($389). AT6 reclining passenger seat in Grand Prix without bucket seats ($60). D90 painted upper body accent stripes ($65). CF5 power glass sunroof including manual sliding sun shade ($925). Y99 rally-tuned suspension ($50). Tire options ($68-$156). AB6 padded formal landau roof including rear window insert and exterior opera lamps ($337). C04 padded landau roof, not available with two-tone paint W70 ($260). PB7 14-in. Argent Silver Rally II wheels with trim rings ($125). PD8 14-in. turbo-finned aluminum wheels with locking package ($246). N91 wire wheel covers with locking package ($214).

FIREBIRD OPTIONS: W61 Firebird coupe option group #1 ($1,273). W63 Firebird coupe option group #2 ($1,792). W61 Firebird Formula option group #1 ($1,273). W63 Firebird Formula option group #2 ($1,842). W61 Firebird Trans Am coupe option group #1 ($1,697). W63 Firebird Trans Am coupe option group #2 ($1,949). W61 Firebird GTA coupe option group #1 ($1,701). W63 Firebird GTA coupe option group #2 ($1,958). WS1 base Firebird performance value package #1 ($265). WS3 base Firebird performance value package #2 ($709). WS1 Trans Am performance value package #1 ($839). W66 Formula option for base Firebird, includes LG4 5.0L V-8, QDZ tires, N96 Hi-Tech Turbo wheels, WS6 performance package, U21 gauge cluster, rear aero wing spoiler and Formula exterior ornamentation ($1,070). Y84 GTA option for Trans Am consists of B2L 5.7L V-8, QDZ tires, PW7 gold diamond spoke wheels, WS6 performance package, KC4 oil cooler, J65 four-wheel disc brakes, G80 limited-slip axle, articulating seats with custom trim, DD9 power paddle type mirrors, NP5 leather appointment group, B34 front and rear mats, and GTA exterior ornamentation ($2,700). G4 5.0L V-8 ($400). LB9 5.0L TPI V-8, except in GTA ($745). LB9 5.0L TPI V-8 in GTA ($300 credit). B2L 5.7L V-8 in Formula or Trans Am, requires MX0 automatic transmission, KC4 oil cooler, WS6 performance package, J65 four-wheel disc brakes, and G80 limited-slip axle ($1,045). MX0 four-speed automatic transmission ($490). MM5 five-speed manual transmission in GTA ($490 credit). C60 air conditioning ($825). G80 limited-slip axle ($100). UA1 heavy-duty battery ($26). DX Trans Am hood decal ($95). C49 electric rear window defogger ($145). NB2 California emissions ($99). KC4 engine oil cooler ($110). U21 rally gauge cluster with tachometer, trip odometer in base Firebird ($150). U52 electronic instrument cluster ($275). CC1 locking hatch roof ($920). B34 front and rear floor mats ($35). Dual remote-control power sport mirrors ($91). WX1 two-tone lower accent paint delete base Firebird and Formula ($150 credit). J65 four-wheel power disc brakes ($179). UM7 seek-and-scan stereo radio equipment ($217). UM6 seek-and-scan stereo radio equipment with cassette ($339). UX1 seek-and-scan ETR radio with

1987 Pontiac Bonneville SE four-door sedan. (PGMC)

graphic equalizer and cassette ($489). UT4 seek-and-scan stereo radio equipment with cassette, graphic equalizer, "touch control" and more ($529). UQ7 subwoofer speaker system ($150). UL5 AM radio delete ($56 credit). U75 power antenna ($70). D42 cargo security screen ($69). AH3 four-way manual seat adjuster ($35). B20 custom interior with reclining bucket seats and Pallex cloth trim ($319-$349). B20 custom interior with reclining bucket seats and Pallex cloth and leather trim ($619-$649). B20 custom interior with articulating bucket seats and Pallex cloth trim ($619-$649). Y99 rally-tuned suspension ($59). WS6 special performance package including QDZ tires and performance suspension components on Trans Am ($385). Optional tires ($68-$318) depending upon model. [NOTE: QDZ tires are P245/50VR16.] N24 15-in. Hi-Tech color-coordinated turbo wheels with locks ($215). N90 15-in. diamond-spoke color-coordinated wheels with lock ($215).

FIERO OPTIONS: W61 Fiero coupe option group #1 ($1,317). W61 Fiero Sport Coupe option group #1 ($1,217). W61 Fiero SE coupe option group #1 ($1,127). W61 Fiero GT coupe option group #1 ($1,181). W63 Fiero Sport Coupe option group #2 ($1,581). W63 Fiero SE coupe option group #2 ($1,613). WS1 Performance value package ($259). MM5 five-speed manual transmission (no charge). MX1 three-speed automatic transmission ($490). C60 air conditioning ($775). UA1 heavy-duty battery ($26). V08 heavy-duty cooling system, except with coupe or GT or L44 engine ($40 with A/C or $70 w/o A/C). C49 electric rear window defogger ($145). NB2 California emissions ($99). Engine block heater, except base coupe ($18). A01 tinted glass with A/C in coupe or Sport Coupe ($120); in SE or GT (no charge). V56 luggage rack, except with base coupe or optional deck lid spoiler ($115). B34 carpeted front floor mats ($24). U63 AM radio equipment in coupe ($122). UM7 seek-and-scan stereo radio equipment ($217-$317). UM8 seek-and-scan stereo radio equipment with cassette ($339-$439). UX1 seek-and-scan stereo radio equipment with cassette, graphic equalizer and more ($160-$489). UT4 seek-and-scan stereo radio equipment with cassette, graphic equalizer, touch control and more ($200-$529). UQ6 speaker system ($150). UL5 AM radio delete ($58 credit). UL5 AM/FM radio delete ($373 credit). AR9 suede leather and Pallex cloth trim for SE and GT ($375). D80 rear deck lid spoiler ($269). AD3 glass sunroof ($375). N78 14-in. High Tech turbo aluminum wheels with locks for Sport Coupe or SE only ($241). Plus, various tire and wheel options.

GRAND AM OPTIONS: W61 Grand Am coupe option group #1 ($1,128). W63 Grand Am coupe option group #2 ($1,304). W67 Grand Am coupe option group #3 ($1,609). W61 Grand Am sedan option group #1 ($1,128). W63 Grand Am sedan option group #2 ($1,304). W67 Grand Am sedan option group #3 ($1,734). W61 Grand Am LE coupe option group #1 ($1,575). W63 Grand Am LE coupe option group #2 ($1,853). W61 Grand Am LE sedan option group #1 ($1,211). W63 Grand Am LE sedan option group #2 ($1,978). W61 Grand Am SE coupe option group #1 ($906). W63 Grand Am SE coupe option group #2 ($1,210). W61 Grand Am SE sedan option group #1 ($981). W63 Grand Am SE sedan option group #2 ($1,210). WS1 base/LE performance value package #1 ($319). WS3 base/LE performance value package #2 ($728). L68 engine in SE with MM5 transmission ($660 credit). LN7 engine in base/LE models, requires MX1 transmission ($660). MM5 five-speed manual transmission in SE ($490 credit). MX1 three-speed automatic transmission in Grand Am/Grand Am LE ($490). C60 air conditioning ($675). C49 electric rear window defogger ($145). Y80 driver enthusiast package ($799). NB2 California emissions ($99). K05 engine block heater ($18). U14 rally gauge cluster with tachometer and trip odometer ($127). V56 rear deck luggage carrier ($115). B34 carpeted front floor mats, base model ($33). B53 carpeted front floor mats, LE/SE models ($33). UM7 seek-and-scan stereo radio equipment ($217). UM8 seek-and-scan stereo radio equipment with cassette ($132-$339). UX1 seek-and-scan ETR radio with graphic equalizer and cassette ($282-$489). UT4 seek-and-scan stereo radio equipment with cassette, graphic equalizer, "touch control" and more ($322-$529). UL5 AM radio delete ($56 credit). AR9 custom seats with Pallex cloth and leather trim in LE/SE ($150). AQ9 articulating seat, except base model ($450). AD3 removable sunroof ($350). Y99 rally-tuned suspension ($59). Optional tires ($68-$318) depending upon model. N78 14-in. Hi-Tech Turbo wheels.

PONTIAC 1000 OPTIONS: W61 option group #1 ($835). W63 option group #2 ($988). MM5 five-speed manual transmission ($75). MX1 three-speed automatic transmission ($450). C60 air

1987 Pontiac Grand Am LE two-door coupe. (PGMC)

conditioning ($675). V10 cold climate group ($44). C49 electric rear window defogger ($145). NB2 California emissions ($99). A01 tinted glass ($105). B37 Carpeted front and rear floor mats ($33). N41 power steering, with automatic transmission required ($225). U69 AM/FM radio ($92). U58 AM/FM radio with three speakers ($119). UL5 AM radio delete ($56 credit). AR9 Oxen vinyl trim bucket seats (standard) or Genor cloth trim bucket seats ($30). D88 mid-body accent stripes ($60). AD3 removable glass sunroof ($350). White sidewall tires ($61 extra). P06 wheel trim rings ($39).

SUNBIRD OPTIONS: W61 Sunbird sedan & Safari Wagon option group #1 ($433). W63 Sunbird sedan and Safari Wagon option group #2 ($1,531). W67 Sunbird sedan and Safari option group #3 ($1,895-$1,945). W61 Sunbird SE, except convertible, option group #1 ($383). W63 Sunbird SE, except convertible, option group #2 ($1,481). W67 Sunbird SE, except convertible, option group #3 ($1,644). W61 Sunbird SE convertible, option group #1 ($972). W63 Sunbird SE convertible, option group #2 ($1,135). Turbo engine as SE option ($1,312-$1,527). WS1 Performance value package for SE convertible ($278). MX1 three-speed automatic transmission ($415). C60 air conditioning ($675). D06 armrest front seat ($58). D06 custom console ($45). D07 custom trim ($45 charge to $45 credit, depending on model). DM1 Turbo decal (no charge). C49 electric rear window defogger ($145). NB2 California emissions ($99). K05 engine block heater ($18). U14 rally gauge cluster ($49). U21 rally gauge cluster with tachometer ($127). A01 tinted glass with A/C in coupe or Sport Coupe ($105). V56 rear deck luggage carrier ($115). Roof luggage carrier for Safari ($115). B34 carpeted front floor mats ($24). Two-tone paint ($101-$151). U63 AM radio equipment ($122). UM7 seek-and-scan stereo radio equipment ($217-$317). UM8 seek-and-scan stereo radio equipment with cassette ($339-$439). UT4 seek-and-scan stereo radio equipment with cassette, graphic equalizer, "touch control" and more ($529-$629). UL5 AM radio delete ($58 credit). D42 cargo area security screen for hatchback only ($69). AR9 Ripple cloth bucket seats for Sunbird/Sunbird SE ($75). AH13 manual seat adjuster ($35). D80 deck lid spoiler ($70). D98 accent striping ($61). D88 sport stripes for Sunbird GT ($55). AD3 removable glass sunroof, except convertible. Rally tuned suspension ($50). Optional tires ($64-$388) depending upon model. B20 custom trim groups ($168-$643). Y91 LE Custom group ($443-$493). PX1 13-in. Sport Tech aluminum wheels and locks ($215). N78 14-in. Hi-Tech Turbo wheels.

6000 OPTIONS: [Except STE] W61 6000 coupe option group #1 ($1,274). W63 6000 coupe option group #2 ($1,700). W67 6000 coupe option group #3 ($1,907). W61 6000 sedan option group #1 ($1,274). W63 6000 sedan option group #2 ($1,750). W67 6000 sedan option group #3 ($2,032). W61 6000 Safari option group #1 ($1,274). W63 6000 Safari option group #2 ($1,781). W67 6000 Safari option group #3 ($2,013). W61 6000 LE sedan option group #1 ($1,522). W63 6000 LE sedan option group #2 ($1,999). W67 6000 LE sedan option group #3 ($2,032). W61 6000 LE Safari option group #1 ($1,513). W63 6000 LE Safari option group #2 ($1,980). W67 6000 LE Safari option group #3 ($2,294). W61 6000 SE sedan option group #1 ($1,461). W63 6000 SE sedan option group #2 ($1,949). W67 6000 SE sedan option group #3 ($2,137). W61 6000 SE Safari option group #1 ($1,452). W63 6000 SE Safari option group #2 ($1,930). W67 6000 SE Safari option group #3 ($2,118). WS1 performance value package #1 ($260). WS3 performance value package #2 ($549). LB6 2.8L V-6 in 6000/6000LE ($610). MX0 four-speed automatic transmission ($175). MM5 five-speed manual transmission, 6000STE only ($440 credit). C60 air conditioning ($775). BC5 carpeted sidewalls and tailgate in Safari.

V10 cold weather group ($18-$44). CS1 Safari rear window deflector ($40). C49 electric rear window defogger ($145). NB2 California emissions ($99). U21 rally gauge cluster with tachometer ($100). U52 electronic instrument cluster with tachometer ($150-$250). AQ1 tinted glass ($120). V56 deck lid luggage carrier ($115). V55 roof top luggage carrier ($115). B34 carpeted front and rear floor mats ($35). UM7 seek-and-scan stereo radio equipment ($217). UM8 seek-and-scan stereo radio equipment with cassette ($339). UX1 AM/FM ETR stereo with cassette and more ($489). UL5 AM radio delete ($56 credit). U75 rear-mounted power radio antenna ($70). WV4 bicycle roof carrier ($70). WV3 roof carrier ski racks on Safari SE ($70). AQ4 Safari third seat with swing-out windows ($215). AT6 reclining passenger seat ($45). A76 reclining driver and passenger seats ($90). B20 custom trim ($125). A65 notchback center arm rear seat with Ripple cloth trim ($30). AM6 45/55 split bench seat with center armrest and Ripple cloth or Sierra vinyl trim in 6000 or Empress/London cloth trim in LE ($133). AS7 45/55 split bench seat ($83). AR9 bucket seats with leather trim ($320). D90 upper painted accent stripes ($40). AD3 glass sunroof ($350-$365). CF5 power glass sunroof ($918). Y99 rally tuned suspension on 6000 and 6000 LE ($50). Various tire options ($68-$130). WW9 Sport Landau top, 6000 coupe, includes Landau top, D55 sport mirrors, vinyl accent stripes, and N91 wire wheel covers. N78 aluminum sport wheels with locks ($215). N91 simulated wire wheel covers ($214). C25 rear window wiper/washer ($125). Simulated woodgrain side trim.

6000 STE OPTIONS: AG9 power seat locks delete option ($538 credit). AG3 memory control seat ($150). NB2 California emissions ($99). AS7 45/55 split bench seat with suede, Pallex cloth and leather trim ($545). CF5 power glass sunroof ($895).

NOTE: Full option package contents, descriptions, and applications information can often be determined by consulting factory literature. The data above is edited for size and clarity. This information provided only as a guide to help collectors appraise the relative value of cars with numerous options. Option prices originally charged by individual dealers may have varied.

HISTORICAL: Pontiac sales and market share dropped in the model-year. The model-year sales totals were 715,536 units. This total included the following sub-totals by car-line: [6000] 7,582; [1988 LeMans imported] 26,948; [Sunbird] 81,930; [Fiero] 47,156; [Firebird] 77,635; [Grand Am] 216,065; [6000] 133,881; [Bonneville] 95,324; [Grand Prix] 17,088 and [Parisienne Safari] 11,927. This gave Pontiac 6.8 percent of the U.S. car market, down from 7.5 percent a year earlier. Production of Firebirds was cut back to one factory this year. The F-cars were made only in the Van Nuys, Calif., assembly plant. The Norwood, Ohio, factory was permanently closed in August 1987. Dow Chemical Co. teamed with Pontiac to build a special Grand Am "idea" car featuring Dow advanced materials. Under its hood was a 3-liter turbocharged four with Dow magnesium engine block that produced 313 hp at 5500 rpm and 326 lbs.-ft. of torque at 4500 rpm. It also had Dow brake fluid and coolant, plus special Dow plastics and foam materials incorporated in its interior and exterior design. Pontiac participated in motor sports with the Entech Camel Lights Fiero racing car. It featured a carbon fiber/aluminum body on a chassis with honeycomb, bonded monocoque construction. The suspension was of double wishbone pushrod design in front and lower wishbone/top rockers design at the rear. Under the engine cover was a 182-cid Super-Duty four-cylinder Pontiac engine. A company named Corporate Concepts Limited, from Capac, Mich., marketed a 1987 MERA Fiero Conversion that gave the Fiero the look of a Lamborghini or Ferrari. It came with a 135-hp version of the Fiero's V-6. More excitement was generated

1987 Pontiac Trans Am GTA two-door coupe. (PGMC)

by a futuristic-looking concept vehicle called the Trans Sport, which was the prototype for what would become a production APV minivan. In January 1987, *Car and Driver* named the Bonneville SE one of the 10 best cars of the year. On the vehicle service front, Pontiac dealers introduced new GM-CAMS technology to enhance service department diagnostics. On Aug. 18, 1987, a plane crash in Detroit took the lives of 14 General Motors employees bound for the GM Desert Proving Ground at Mesa, Ariz. They included four members of the Chevrolet-Pontiac-Canada (CPC) Engineering Dept., Lewis E. Dresch, 45, Patrick A. Gleason, 49, John Matthews, 38 and Jay T. Strausbaugh, 29. J. Michael Losh was general manager of Pontiac Motor Div. in 1987. E.M. Schlesinger was general sales and service manager. William J. O'Neil was director of public relations.

1988 PONTIAC

1988 Pontiac LeMans two-door Aerocoupe. (PGMC)

SAFARI — SERIES 2L — (V-8) — Pontiac's 1988 Safari was a traditional full-size station wagon offering luxury, passenger roominess, comfort, generous cargo capacity, and power to handle large loads. Safari's superior eight-passenger carrying capacity was enhanced with a comprehensive list of standard equipment including a rear-facing third seat, air conditioning, a stereo radio, dual sport mirrors, tinted glass, and whitewall radial tires. The standard power train was unchanged, but new axle ratios were specified for better performance. An electronic spark control system was added for better fuel economy. It was EPA-rated for 17 mpg city/24 mpg highway. The interior of the Safari received some improvements such as new sun visors with a center support, new accelerator and brake pedals, and new power seat controls mounted on door pods. Also new were five exterior colors (Light Blue Metallic, Dark Blue Metallic, Camel Metallic, Dark Brown Metallic, and Medium Red Metallic) and a pair of new interior trim colors (Dark Blue and Camel). Standard on all big Safaris was a 5.0-liter four-barrel V-8; air conditioning with Soft-Ray tinted glass; Powermaster front disc/rear drum brakes; white-accented front/rear bumper rub strips; carpeting throughout; a center high-mounted stop lamp; the GM Computer Command Control system; an inside hood release; dual sport mirrors (left-hand remote-controlled); power steering; a UM7 Delco ETR AM/FM stereo; a notchback front seat with center armrest; a rear-facing third seat with Hartford vinyl trim; load-carrying springs; a front stabilizer bar; a three-spoke steering wheel; a full-coil suspension; a tailgate window control; P225/75R15 steel-belted radial whitewall tires; a four-speed automatic transmission; and custom wheel covers.

BONNEVILLE — SERIES 2H — (V-6) — The aerodynamic Bonneville front-wheel-drive Sports Sedan returned in 1988. The LE became the base model. The SE was now the middle model. On top was a new SSE. All Bonnevilles had new dual sport mirrors (left-hand remote-controlled), woodgrained interior trim plates, a standard AM/FM stereo and two new exterior colors called Caramel Metallic and Medium Brown Metallic. New Bonneville LE features included new wheels, color-accented exterior trim and a passenger visor mirror. SEs now had variable-ratio power steering, a new

1988 Pontiac Sunbird GT two-door convertible. (PGMC)

"3800" V-6, a new seat and some new standard "options." The SSE was a Euro-style luxury touring car with a high price sticker and a page and a quarter-long list of added standard equipment from tuned dual exhaust outlets to automatic headlight sentinel control. Standard on the LE model was a 3.8-liter V-6 engine with sequential fuel-injection (SFI); acoustical insulation; air conditioning; a front seat with center armrest; body-frame integral construction; carpets; a center high-mounted stop lamp; cluster warning lights; a compact spare tire; complete instrumentation; a Delco Freedom II battery; dual horns; extensive corrosion protection; flow-through ventilation; the GM Computer Command Control system; independent front/rear suspension; an inside hood release; a dome lamp; a glove box lamp; a trunk lamp; lower door map pockets (except with the UW4 speaker system); lower door panel carpeting; dual sport side view mirrors; power rack-and-pinion steering; a UM7 Delco ETR AM/FM radio; automatic front safety belts; rear seat safety shoulder belts; a systems monitor feature; a four-speed automatic transmission; a passenger visor-vanity mirror; Aero Torque wheel covers; wide body side moldings; and dual fluidic concealed windshield wipers. SE models added or substituted a 3.3-liter SFI 3800 V-6 engine; a rear seat pull-down armrest; complete rally instrumentation with a tachometer; controlled-cycle wipers; cruise control; a driver information center; gas pressurized struts; front/rear door interior courtesy lamps; power windows with door pod switches; right- and left-hand manual front seat recliners; a 45/55 split bench front seat; special springs; a leather-wrapped steering wheel; a Rally Tuned suspension; tilt steering; P215/65R15 Eagle GT steel-belted radial tires; and 15 x 6-in. Tri-Port cast-aluminum wheels. The Bonneville SSE also added or substituted aero extentions on doors and rocker panels; automatic air conditioning; front disc/rear drum anti-lock brakes; a console with power seat controls; duplicate steering wheel radio controls; an electronic compass; electronic ride control; a flash-to-pass headlight control; the GM protection plan; headlight washers; key-activated power door locks; heated blue-tint power mirrors; a UT4 Delco ETR "touch control" AM/FM stereo with cassette and Delco-Loc; a rear seat armrest with storage compartment; 45/55 10-way power adjustable front seats; a six-speaker sound system; a special purpose suspension; P215/60R16 BSW Goodyear Eagle GT+4 tires; and Aero-Cast 16 x 7-in. aluminum wheels.

GRAND PRIX — SERIES 2G — (V-6/V-8) — A totally new aerodynamically styled, front-wheel-drive Grand Prix bowed in 1988. It came in three trim levels: Grand Prix, Grand Prix LE, and Grand Prix SE. The exterior of this new Grand Prix featured a Pontiac-style split grille, wraparound taillights, soft fascia bumpers, and an aggressive-looking stance. The sleek body had a drag coefficient of .299 and was one of the world's most wind-cheating production cars of the year. It had an aggressively tapered nose and a low hood line

1988 Pontiac Grand Am SE two-door coupe. (PGMC)

promoting smooth airflow towards the flush-mounted 62-degree windshield. The Grand Prix's side windows were also flush and the door handles were recessed into the body "B" pillars. The Grand Prix also had flush-fitting composite halogen headlights and hidden windshield wipers. It featured a MacPherson strut front suspension with tapered-top coil springs that permitted the lowering of the hood line. A totally new tri-link rear suspension was employed. Suspension components were "lubed-for-life" and all strut cartridges were designed for easier servicing. Excellent braking performance was provided by a four-wheel-disc brake system using composite material rotors. The front rotors were of vented design with twin-piston calipers. Solid rotors and single-bore calipers were found at the rear. Select Grand Prix models were available in five exterior colors: Metallic Silver, Metallic Camel, Metallic Medium Gray, Metallic Medium Red, and White. The Grand Prix and Grand Prix LE were also offered in Metallic Black, Light Metallic Blue, and Medium Metallic Blue, as well as a non-metallic Red. Interiors came in Blue, Camel, and Medium Gray on all models. Standard equipment included a 2.8-liter MFI V-6; acoustical insulation; four-wheel power disc brakes; composite halogen headlights; dual horns; dual sport mirrors (left-hand remote); a glove box with combination lock; an ashtray light; a glove box light; a dome light; rack-and-pinion steering; a UM7 Delco ETR AM/FM stereo; a remote fuel filler door release; a notchback front bench seat with armrest and Ripple cloth trim; side window defoggers; four-wheel independent suspension; P195/75R14 steel-belted radial tires; a four-speed automatic transmission; wet-arm windshield wipers; and custom wheel covers. The Grand Prix LE added or substituted analog instrumentation with a tachometer; coolant temperature; oil pressure and voltmeter gauges; door map pockets; a luggage compartment light; an underhood light; an instrument panel courtesy light; power windows with illuminated switches; a rear folding armrest seat with a pass-through to the luggage compartment; and 60/40 split reclining front seats in Pallex cloth trim. The Grand Prix SE added or substituted cruise control; dual exhausts; fog lamps; an overhead console with storage and lights; articulating power bucket seats and rear-passenger bucket seat; a Rally Tuned suspension; a tilt steering wheel; P215/65R15 Goodyear Eagle GT+4 tires; a five-speed manual transmission; and color-keyed 15-in. aluminum sport wheels.

FIREBIRD — SERIES 2F — (V-6/V-8) — The sporty F-body Firebird had 17 major changes and engineering highlights for 1988. Base models shared an improved Tuned Port Induction (TPI) system on V-8 engines, which also had new serpentine accessory belt drives. Base models now came with standard 15 x 7 in. deep-dish Hi-Tech Turbo or diamond spoke aluminum wheels, a redesigned four-spoke steering wheel, an AM/FM stereo with seek-and-scan and clock, Pallex cloth interior trim, a new Camel colored interior, monotone paint treatments, and a choice of two new exterior colors (Silver Blue Metallic or Orange Metallic). Formulas had new 16 x 8 in. Hi-Tech Turbo cast-aluminum wheels and a new 5.0-liter throttle-body-injection (TBI) V-8 engine that was also standard in the Trans Am. All TPI 5.0-liter and 5.7-liter engines now came with full-gauge analog clusters and a 140-mph speedometer. New features for GTA models included a remote deck lid release; a power antenna; a right-hand visor-vanity mirror; power windows; power door locks; body side moldings; air conditioning; tinted glass; a lamp group; the Pass Key theft deterrent system; controlled-cycle wipers; a rear window defogger; cruise control; tilt steering; an AM/FM stereo with cassette and graphic equalizer; steering wheel-mounted radio controls; integral

1988 Pontiac Firebird Trans Am GTA two-door coupe. (PGMC)

1988 Pontiac 6000 STE four-door sedan. (PGMC)

rear seat headrests; and Metrix cloth interior trim (optional for the Trans Am). In addition, leather-trimmed articulating front bucket seats were a new GTA model option. Base Firebirds featured a 2.8-liter MFI V-6; a center high-mounted stop lamp; complete analog instrumentation; a full-length console with instrument panel; side window defoggers; a front air dam; the GM Computer Command Control system; a hatch "pull-down" feature; rectangular-shaped concealed quartz halogen headlights; monochromatic paint; a UM7 Delco ETR AM/FM stereo; cloth reclining front bucket seats; a folding rear seat; a four-spoke steering wheel; a lockable storage compartment; P215/65R15 BSW tires; a five-speed manual transmission; "wet-arm" windshield wipers; and 15 x 7-in. Hi-Tech Turbo or diamond-spoke cast-aluminum wheels. Formulas added or substituted a 5.0-liter EFI V-8, a body-color aero rear deck lid spoiler, a domed hood, Formula graphics, 16 x 8-in. Hi-Tech aluminum wheels, the WS6 special performance suspension, and two-tone paint and striping. Trans Ams added or substituted a body aero package, hood and front fender air extractors, hood air louvers, fog lamps, soft ray tinted glass, and the Y99 Rally Tuned suspension. GTAs added the 5.7-liter TPI V-8; four-wheel disc brakes; air conditioning; cruise control; dual power mirrors; power articulating front bucket seats; power deck lid release; power door locks; power windows; a Delco UT4 ETR "touch control" AM/FM stereo with cassette and anti-theft feature; a special performance suspension; a leather-wrapped steering wheel; steering wheel radio controls; P245/50VR16 Goodyear Eagle tires; a four-speed automatic transmission; and 16 x 8-in. gold-colored lightweight diamond-spoke aluminum wheels.

FIERO — SERIES 2P — (FOUR/V-6) — Pontiac's distinctive P-body two-passenger, mid-engined sports car remained in the lineup with coupe and GT models for 1988. Each had distinctive styling and performance features. In addition, a new Formula option package was released for the coupe. The Formula group included the spirited 2.8-liter MFI V-6 engine, a GM Muncie/Gertag five-speed transaxle, the WS6 suspension with special front and rear shocks, special springs, 15-in. black diamond-spoke wheels and Goodyear Eagle GT+4 tires (P205/60R15 front/P215/60R15 rear), a 28mm front stabilizer bar, special bushings, and special front/rear control arms. A rear spoiler and Formula graphics completed the package. Standard in base coupes, the famous Tech IV engine had a new secondary force balancer system to smooth and quiet engine operation, plus a redesigned crankshaft with a gear drive for the balancers located in the pan. The in-the-pan oil pump and filter were also redesigned. Also new were completely redesigned independent front and rear suspension systems, a revised four-wheel disc brake system, standard High-Tech Turbo cast wheels, radial spare tires, a standard AM/FM stereo sound system, an interior upgrade to Pallex cloth trim, a new Camel interior color, and a new midyear Bright Yellow exterior color. New standard features for GTs included Eagle GT+4 tires, Metrix cloth trim, and monochromatic exterior colors. New GT model options were black or gold diamond-spoke cast-aluminum wheels, an inflatable lumbar support seat and "soft" leather seat trim. Every Fiero coupe featured black-finished air deflectors; body side moldings; door handles and lock cylinders; reclining bucket seats; a center high-mounted stop lamp; clearcoat paint; color-keyed safety belts; a compact spare radial tire; a Delco Freedom II battery; a dome lamp; dual map lights; Enduraflex body panels; extensive anti-corrosion protection; a full-length console; the GM Computer Command Control system; halogen headlights with a retracting feature; hobnail carpeting; a locking fuel filler door; a map

1988 Pontiac Grand Prix SE two-door coupe. (PGMC)

pocket on instrument panel; front/rear side marker lights; "mill and drill" construction; a left-hand remote-controlled sport mirror; a right-hand manual sport mirror; a multi-function control lever; a UM7 Delco AM/FM ETR radio; a radio noise suppression kit; side window defoggers; soft fascia system in front and rear; space-frame body construction; a four-spoke rally steering wheel; sun visors; independent front and rear suspension; a five-speed manual transmission; Hi-Tech turbo aluminum wheels; and the 2.8-liter Tech IV engine with EFI. The Formula added or substituted the 2.8-liter V-6 engine with EFI; a rear deck spoiler; special front and rear shock absorbers; special springs; a 23mm rear stabilizer bar; the WS6 performance suspension; P205/60R15 (front) and P215/60R15 (rear) Goodyear Eagle GT+4 tires; a tuned dual-port exhaust system; and 15-in. diamond-spoke black-finished aluminum wheels. The GT added or substituted an aero package with special aerodynamic front and rear fascias; body side skirts; controlled-cycle windshield wipers; an instrumentation package with console-mounted lamp group; deluxe luggage compartment trim; sun visor map pockets; a monochromatic exterior color scheme; power windows; a UM6 Delco AM/FM ETR radio; a remote deck lid release; Soft-Ray tinted glass; a deluxe three-spoke leather-wrapped tilt steering wheel; and the choice of gold-finished diamond-spoke aluminum wheels in addition to black-finished diamond-spoke aluminum wheels.

GRAND AM — SERIES 2N — This upscale N-body front-drive compact was one of Pontiac's best selling cars and a top performing vehicle. Introduced for 1988 was a 2.3-liter DOHC 16-valve four-cylinder engine that was available in all models. Standard equipment for base and LE editions was an improved 2.5-liter balance shaft four-cylinder engine with an automatic transaxle. A 2.0-liter MFI Turbo four-cylinder engine was standard in SE models. Also new-for-1988 were body-color grilles for all models; a standard split-back folding seat on SEs; a new glove box lock; cup holders; improved lighting for the heat/vent/air conditioning (HVAC) control panel; a revised trim plate design for the instrument panel cluster and console; Pallex cloth interior trim for base models (Metrix cloth became standard in LE and SE models); a standard AM/FM stereo system in all models; dual outside sport mirrors on all models; a new Camel interior trim color; and two new exterior colors (Camel Metallic and Maroon Metallic). Standard equipment included: 2.5-liter Tech IV engine with EFI; an acoustic insulation package; black-finish door handles and lock cylinders; power front disc/rear drum brakes; reclining front bucket seats; front/rear soft bumper fascias; automatic front safety belts; a center high-mounted stop lamp; a compact spare tire; complete analog instrumentation; a floor-mounted console; a Delco Freedom II battery; dual front radio speakers; dual horn; anti-corrosion protection; front-wheel-drive; a glove compartment; the GM Computer Command Control system; a "headlights-on" warning signal; a heater vent system with ducted rear-seat heat; an inside hood release; a low-noise engine cooling fan; dual sport side view mirrors; a multi-function control lever; Pallex cloth upholstery; power rack-and-pinion steering; a UM7 Delco AM/FM ETR stereo radio; rear-seat integral headrests; side window defogger; soft ray tinted glass; MacPherson strut front suspension; five-speed manual transmission; custom wheel covers; and wide body side moldings. Grand Am LEs added or substituted composite headlights; deluxe color-keyed safety belts; deluxe exterior ornamentation; front console with armrest; Metrix cloth upholstery; two-tone

paint; and custom color-keyed wheel covers. The Grand Am SE added or substituted a 2.0-liter four-cylinder Turbo engine with MFI; cruise control; deluxe Thaxton carpets; deluxe integral fog lamps; a remote fuel filler; a leather appointment group with four-spoke rally steering wheel, shift knob, and brake release handle; power door locks; rally gauges and a tachometer; a rear seat center armrest; a specific monotone paint treatment with color-keyed grille; emblems and aluminum wheels; a Rally Tuned suspension with 28mm front/21mm rear stabilizer bars; a tilt steering wheel; P215/60R14 Eagle GT+4 tires; and specific SE cast-aluminum wheels.

LEMANS — SERIES 2T — (FOUR) — A Korean-built car made by Daewoo Motor Co. Ltd. revived a classic Pontiac nameplate. The all-new LeMans replaced the Pontiac 1000 as the company's entry-level offering. Four versions were offered: Aerocoupe Value Leader, LE Aerocoupe, GSE sedan, and SE sedan. Standard equipment for the Value Leader model started with a 1.6-liter EFI four; power front disc/rear drum brakes; an electric rear window defogger; extensive anti-corrosion protection; a folding rear seat; a full-size spare tire; adjustable headrests; mounting provisions for an integral roof luggage rack; a rear compartment light; an ashtray light; a glove box light; a two-tone lower body side paint accent; a luggage compartment security cover; a left-hand remote-control mirror; a one-key locking system; rack-and-pinion steering; reclining front bucket seats; a side window defogger; a soft headliner; a MacPherson front strut suspension with stabilizer bar; a semi-independent trailing arm/torsion bar rear suspension with coil springs; P175/70R13 steel-belted radial tires; a four-speed manual transmission; a trip odometer; twill cloth upholstery; two-tone paint; custom wheel covers; and wide body side moldings. Every Aerocoupe LE and GSE sedan added or substituted front and rear assist handles; full analog instrumentation; dual remote-control sport mirrors; a UM7 Delco AM/FM ETR stereo; Soft-Ray tinted glass; swing-out rear windows (Aerocoupe only); a tachometer; a five-speed manual transmission and a visor-vanity mirror. The GSE sedan added or substituted fog lamps; Mosaik/Turin cloth upholstery; specific SE up-level bucket seats; special seat height adjusters; a split-folding rear seat; and a tilt steering wheel.

SUNBIRD — SERIES 2J — (FOUR) — The 1988 J-body Sunbirds were even more improved spin-offs of the Chevrolet Vega/Pontiac Astre. There were six models (including a new coupe) in three series: Base, SE and GT Turbo. Both base Sunbirds and SEs came with a 2.0-liter EFI engine and standard five-speed manual gearbox. Interiors were upgraded with monotone Pallex cloth upholstery and a Delco ETR AM/FM stereo as standard features. Two new colors Medium Red Metallic and Camel Metallic were introduced. Also new were Goodyear P185/80R13 standard tires on base and SE models and Goodyear P215/60R14 Eagle GT+4s on the wagon with Rally Tuned suspension. Other 1988 changes included wide body side moldings as standard equipment on base models and color-keyed seat belts as standard equipment on GTs. Standard base-model equipment included the new OHC four-cylinder motor; black-finished door window frames; wipers and wide body side moldings; power front disc/rear drum brakes; reclining front bucket seats; a center high-mounted stop light; clearcoat paint; a compact spare;

1988 Pontiac Grand Prix SE two-door coupe. (PGMC)

cut-pile carpeting; a Delco Freedom II battery; front door lamp switches; dual rectangular headlights; extensive anti-corrosion protection; fluidic wipers; a front air dam; a front floor console; front-wheel-drive; the GM Computer Command Control system; an inside hood release; a day/night rearview mirror; rack-and-pinion steering; a UM7 Delco ETR AM/FM stereo; side window defoggers; MacPherson strut front suspension; a five-speed manual transmission; warm red instrument panel lighting; and five-port wheel covers. The Sunbird SE added or substituted new coupe styling with wraparound front parking lights and partially hidden halogen headlights. The Sunbird GT added or substituted a turbocharged four-cylinder engine; a special hood with simulated air louvers; higher-rate springs and bushings; sport side view mirrors; power steering; special instrumentation with a turbo boost gauge; a special performance suspension with 28mm front and 21mm rear stabilizer bars; a tachometer and trip odometer; P215/60R14 steel-belted BSW tires; 14-in. Turbo cast Hi-Tech aluminum wheels; and wheel flares.

6000 — SERIES 2A — (I-4/V-6) — The 6000 and 6000 LE were aimed at the family car marketplace. They combined a smooth, comfortable ride with pleasant looks, lots of space and economy of operation. Both trim levels were available in four-door sedans or Safari station wagons. Standard power train for both was a 2.5-liter four-cylinder EFI engine with three-speed automatic transaxle. A 2.8-liter MFI V-6 was optional. Interiors of the entry-level 6000 sedan and Safari received a new standard Pallex seat fabric for up-level comfort. The 6000 LE received redesigned contour seats covered with London/Empress fabric. Standard on both levels and models was an AM/FM stereo sound system, tinted glass, color-keyed wheel covers (available in four colors) and P185/75R14 tires. Six new metallic colors were offered: Light Blue, Dark Blue, Camel, Dark Brown, Medium Maroon, and Medium Rosewood. The 6000 SE sedan and Safari were aimed at driving enthusiasts who wanted better road handling in a 6000-type car. They both had unique aero styling, a 2.8-liter V-6, a five-speed manual transaxle and road-hugging P195/70R14 Goodyear Eagle GT+4 all-season tires mounted on color-keyed Turbo Torque cast-aluminum wheels. A four-speed automatic transmission was optional. The SE interior featured Metrix cloth over reclining seats, a leather-wrapped steering wheel, a center shift console and a fully backlit instrument cluster. The 6000 STE featured a 2.8-liter aluminum head V-6 with direct-fire ignition, serpentine drive belts and standard four-speed automatic transaxle (five-speed manual optional). Also included were two-tone paint treatments, body-colored lower front air dam, composite headlights, integral fog lights, and specific taillight bezels. Anti-lock brakes were included on the STE, plus new 15-in. aluminum wheels and P195/70R15 Goodyear Eagle GT+4 tires. The suspension was completely re-tuned, as well. At midyear, the STE interior added contoured front seats with power-adjustable lumbar and headrest operation, a redesigned rear seat with integral cup holders and larger headrests. A Delco-Loc radio anti-theft system was integrated into the steering wheel hub-mounted radio controls. A warning sticker aimed at deterring theft of the system was included in the car owner's manual and could be affixed to its windows. Also, a new Metrix cloth seat trim with color-keyed seat belts was standard in STEs and an upgraded Ventura cloth and leather interior was made available during the year. A new plateau in the 6000 model offering was the 6000 STE-AWD. This was an STE model with full-time all-wheel-drive system

1988 Pontiac Grand Prix LE two-door coupe. (PGMC)

1988 Pontiac Bonneville SE four-door sedan. (PGMC)

that improved directional control, traction, and handling under most driving conditions. It was introduced late in the model-year. Exclusive to Pontiac, it was the first application of all-wheel-drive to a General Motors passenger car. It also marked the first mass-production usage of a high-torque, transverse-mounted 3.1-liter V-6 engine and automatic transmission combination in a full-time all-wheel-drive vehicle. Standard equipment on base 6000s included a 2.5-liter Tech IV engine; acoustical insulation; black door window frames; carpeted lower door panels; a center high-mounted stop lamp; a compact spare tire; composite headlights; cut-pile carpeting; a Delco Freedom II battery; extensive anti-corrosion protection; fluidic windshield wiper/washer system with dual nozzles; a black front air dam; front-wheel-drive; a glove compartment with lock; the GM Computer Command Control system; an inside hood release; warm red instrument panel lighting; MacPherson strut front suspension; a multi-function control lever; a Delco UM7 AM/FM stereo; radio noise suppression equipment; side window defoggers; soft fascia front and rear bumpers; a trailing-arm-and-beam rear suspension with integral stabilizer bar; a three-speed automatic transmission; and Tri-Port wheel covers. Cars with the LE option also had right- and left-hand door map pockets, dual horns, locking fuel filler door, lower two-tone paint accents, map pockets on front seat backs, and a four-spoke Sport steering wheel. Added or substituted on SE models were a 2.8-liter V-6; front bucket seats and a console; a dual outlet sport exhaust system; electronic ride control (Safari SE only); dual sport side view mirrors; rally gauges with tachometer; specific springs and bushings; 28mm front/22mm rear stabilizer bars; a leather-wrapped SE steering wheel; a Rally Tuned suspension; Goodyear Eagle GT+4 P195/70R14 tires; and Sport aluminum wheels with locks. The top-of-the-line 6000 STE added or substituted: a road kit with flares; a raincoat and first aid supplies; four-wheel anti-lock disc brakes; controlled-cycle wipers; deluxe carpeted floor mats; a driver information center; electrically operated side view mirrors; an electronic ride control system; the GM protection plan; a lighted visor-vanity mirror; a locking fuel filler door; lower accent two-toning; map pockets on seat backs; power door locks; a Delco UT4 "touch control" AM/FM stereo with cassette; a rear seat with fold down center armrest; a specific STE leather-wrapped steering wheel with integral radio controls; a tilt steering wheel; a four-speed automatic transmission; specific STE wheels; and a windshield sun shade with pockets.

I.D. DATA: Pontiac's 17-symbol Vehicle Identification Number (VIN) was on the upper left surface of the instrument panel, visible through the windshield. The first symbol indicates country of origin: 1=U.S.; 2= Canada; J=Japan;K=Korea; 3=Mexico. The second symbol indicates manufacturer: G=General Motors; G=Suzuki; 8=Isuzu; Y=NUMMI; L=Daewoo. The third symbol G indicates make: 2=Pontiac division. The fourth and fifth symbols indicate body type and series: A/E=6000 SE; A/F=6000; A/G=6000 LE; A/H=6000 STE; B/L=Safari; F/S=Firebird; F/W=Firebird Trans Am; W/J=Grand Prix; W/K=Grand Prix LE; W/P=Grand Prix Brougham; H/X=Bonneville LE; H/Y=Bonneville SSE; H/Z=Bonneville SE; J/B=Sunbird; J/D=Sunbird SE; J/U=Sunbird GT; M/R=Firefly (U.S. Customs Territories); N/E=Grand Am; N/V=Grand Am LE; N/W=Grand Am SE; P/E=Fiero coupe; P/F=Fiero SE coupe; P/G=Fiero GT coupe; P/M=Fiero Sport Coupe; T/N=LeMans; T/R=LeMans SE; T/S=LeMans GSE; T/X=LeMans coupe. The sixth symbol denotes body type: 1=two-door coupe/sedan styles 11, 27, 37, 47, 57, 97; 2=two-door hatchback styles 07, 08, 77 and 87; 3=two-door convertible style 67; 5=four-door sedan styles 19 and 69; 6=four-door hatchback style 68;

229

1988 Pontiac LeMans GSE three-door hatchback. (PGMC)

8=four-door station wagon style 35. Symbol seven indicates restraint code: 1=manual belts; 3=manual belts with driver's airbag; 4=automatic belts. Symbol eight is an engine code: C=3.8-liter U.S.-built FI V-6; D=2.3-liter U.S.-built FI I-4; E=5.0-liter U.S.-built FI V-8; F=5.0-liter U.S.-built 5.0-liter FI V-8; K=2.0-liter U.S.-built FI I-4; M=2.0-liter U.S.-built FI I-4; R=2.5-liter U.S.-built EFI I-4; S=2.8-liter Mexico-built FI V-6; T=3.1-liter Mexico-built FI V-6; U=2.5-liter U.S.-built FI I-4; W=2.8-liter U.S./Canada/Mexico-built FI I-4; Y=5.0-liter U.S.-built four-barrel V-8; 3=3.8-liter U.S.-built FI V-6; 6=1.6-liter Korean-built FI I-4; 8=5.7-liter U.S.-built FI V-8; 9=2.8-liter Mexico-built FI V-6. Next is a check digit. The tenth symbol denotes model year (J=1988). The 11th symbol indicates the GM assembly plant (B=Baltimore, Md. T&B; B=Lansing, Mich.; B=Pupyong, Korea; C=Lansing, Mich.; D=Doraville, Ga.; E=Pontiac East, Mich. T&B; F=Fairfax II, Kan.; F=Flint T&B; G=Framingham, Mass.; H=Flint, Mich.; J=Janesville, Wis.; K=Leeds, Mo.; K=Kosai, Japan; L=Van Nuys, Calif.; M=Lansing, Mich; N=Norwood, Ohio; P=Pontiac, Mich.; R=Arlington, Texas; S=St. Louis, Mo.; S=Ramos Arizpe, Mexico; T=Tarrytown, N.Y.; U=Hamtramck, Mich; V=Pontiac, Mich. (T&B); X=Fairfax I, Kansas; Y=Wilmington, Del.; Z=Fremont, Calif.; Z=Ft. Wayne, Ind. T&B; 0= Pontiac, Mich. (T&B); 1=Oshawa Canada #2; 1=Wentzville, Mo. T&B; 2=Morraine, OH T&B; 2=Ste. Therese Canada; 3=Detroit, Mich. T&B; 3=St. Eustache, PQ; 3=Kawasaki, Japan; 4=Orion, Mich.; 4=Scarborough, Ontario Canada; 5=Bowling Green, Ken.; 5=London, Ontario, Canada; 6=Oklahoma City, Okla.; 7=Lordstown, Ohio; 7=Flusawa, Japan; 8=Shreveport, La. T&B; 9=Detroit, Mich. (CAD); 9=Oshawa, Ontario, Canada #1. Pontiacs are not produced at all of these GM plants. The last six symbols are the consecutive unit number at the factory.

Model Number	Body Style Number	Body Type & Seating	Factory Price	Shipping Weight	Production Total
SAFARI SERIES B/L (V-8)					
2L	BL8	4d Sta Wagon-8P	14,519	4,109	Note 1
BONNEVILLE LE SERIES H/X (V-6)					
2H	HX5	4d Sport Sedan-5P	14,099	3,275	Note 2
BONNEVILLE SE SERIES H/Z (V-6)					
2H	HZ5	4d Sport Sedan-5P	16,299	3,341	Note 2
BONNEVILLE SSE SERIES H/Z5 (V-6)					
2H	HZ5/Y80	4d Sport Sedan-5P	21,879	3,481	Note 2
GRAND PRIX SERIES W/J (V-6/V-8)					
2G	WJ1	2d Coupe-5P	12,539	3,038	Note 3
GRAND PRIX LE SERIES W/K (V-6/V-8)					
2G	WK1	2d Coupe-5P	13,239	3,056	Note 3
GRAND PRIX SE SERIES W/P (V-6/V-8)					
2G	WP1	2d Coupe-5P	15,249	3,113	Note 3
FIREBIRD – SERIES F/S (V-6)					
2F	FS2	2d Coupe-5P	10,999	3,102	Note 4
FIREBIRD SERIES F/S (V-8)					
2F	FS2	2d Coupe-5P	11,399	—	Note 4
FIREBIRD FORMULA SERIES F/S (V-8)					
2F	FS2	2d Coupe-5P	11,999	3,296	Note 4
FIREBIRD TRANS AM SERIES F/W (V-8)					
2F	FW2	2d Coupe-5P	13,999	3,355	Note 4
FIREBIRD TRANS AM GTA SERIES F/W (V-8)					
2F	FW2	2d Coupe-5P	19,299	3,406	Note 4
FIERO SERIES 2P (I-4/V-6)					
2P	PE1	2d Coupe-2P	8,999	2,597	Note 5
FIERO FORMULA SERIES 2P (I-4/V-6)					
2P	PE1	2d Coupe -2P	10,999	2,602	Note 5
FIERO GT SERIES 2P (I-4/V-6)					
2P	PG7	2d Coupe -2P	13,999	2,790	Note 5
GRAND AM SERIES 2N (I-4/V-6)					
2N	NE1	2d Coupe-5P	9,869	2,493	Note 6
2N	NE5	4d Sedan-5P	10,069	2,565	Note 6

Model Number	Body Style Number	Body Type & Seating	Factory Price	Shipping Weight	Production Total
GRAND AM LE SERIES 2N (I-4/V-6)					
2N	NV1	2d Coupe-5P	10,569	2,519	Note 6
2N	NV5	4d Sedan-5P	10,769	2,591	Note 6
GRAND AM SE SERIES 2N (I-4/V-6)					
2N	NW1	2d Coupe-5P	12,869	2,713	Note 6
2N	NW5	4d Sedan-5P	13,099	2,781	Note 6
LEMANS AEROCOUPE VALUE LEADER SERIES T/X (I-4)					
2T	TX2	3d Coupe-4P	5,995	2,019	Note 7
LEMANS AEROCOUPE LE SERIES T/N (I-4)					
2T	TN2	3d Coupe-4P	7,325	2,058	Note 7
LEMANS SE SERIES T/S (I-4)					
2T	TR5	4d Sedan-4P	7,925	2,121	Note 7
LEMANS GSE SERIES T/R (I-4)					
2T	TS5	4d Sedan-4P	8,399	2,150	Note 7
SUNBIRD SERIES J/B (I-4)					
2J	JB5	4d Sedan-5P	8,499	2,367	Note 8
SUNBIRD SE SERIES J/D (I-4/I-4)					
2J	JD5	4d Sedan-5P	8,799	2,427	Note 8
2J	JD1	2d Coupe-5P	8,599	2,394	Note 8
2J	JD8	4d Sta Wagon-5P	9,399	2,427	Note 8
SUNBIRD GT TURBO SERIES J/U (I-4/I-4 Turbo)					
2J	JU1	2d Coupe-5P	10,899	2,412	Note 8
2J	JU3	2d Convertible-5P	16,199	2,577	Note 8
6000 SERIES 2A (I-4/V-6)					
2A	AF5	4d Sedan-5P	11,199	2,755	Note 9
2A	AF8	4d Safari-5P	11,639	2,925	Note 9
6000 LE SERIES 2A (I-4/V-6)					
2A	AG5	4d Sedan-5P	11,839	2,824	Note 9
2A	AG8	4d Safari-5P	12,299	2,977	Note 9
6000 SE SERIES 2A (I-4/V-6)					
2A	AE5	4d Sedan-5P	12,739	2,986	Note 9
2A	AE8	4d Safari-5P	13,699	3,162	Note 9
6000 STE SERIES 2A (I-4/V-6)					
2A	AH5	4d Sedan-5P	18,699	3,101	Note 9

NOTE 1: Safari series production totaled 6,397 cars.

NOTE 2: Bonneville series production totaled 108,563 cars.

NOTE 3: Grand Prix series production totaled 86,357 cars.

NOTE 4: Firebird series production totaled 62,455 cars.

NOTE 5: Fiero series production totaled 26,401 cars.

NOTE 6: Grand Am series production totaled 235,371 cars.

NOTE 7: LeMans series production totaled 64,037 cars.

NOTE 8: Sunbird series production totaled 93,689 cars.

NOTE 9: 6000 series production totaled 90,934 cars.

SAFARI ENGINE

ENGINE [Standard V-8]: V-block. OHV. Eight-cylinder. Cast-iron block. Displacement: 307 cid. (5.0L). Bore & stroke: 3.80 x 3.39 in. Compression ratio: 8.0.1. Brake horsepower: 140 at 3200 rpm. Torque: 255 lbs.-ft. at 2000 rpm. Fuel system: Four-barrel carburetor. RPO Code: LV2. Standard V-8 in all Safaris. [VIN code Y].

BONNEVILLE ENGINE

ENGINE [Standard LE]: V-block. OHV. Six-cylinder. Cast-iron block and head. Aluminum intake manifold. Displacement: 231 cid. (3.8L). Bore & stroke: 3.80 x 3.40 in. Compression ratio: 8.5:1. Brake horsepower: 150 at 4400 rpm. Torque: 200 lbs.-ft. at 2000 rpm. Fuel system: SFI. RPO Code: LG3. Standard in Bonneville LE model. [VIN code W, S, or 9].

ENGINE [Standard SE/SSE]: V-block. OHV. "3800" six-cylinder. Cast-iron block and head. Aluminum intake manifold. Displacement:

1988 Pontiac LeMans GSE three-door hatchback. (PGMC)

231 cid. (3.8L). Bore & stroke: 3.80 x 3.40 in. Compression ratio: 8.5:1. Brake horsepower: 165 at 5200 rpm. Torque: 210 lbs.-ft. at 2000 rpm. Fuel system: SFI. RPO Code: LN3. Standard in Bonneville SE/SSE model. [VIN code W, S or 9].

GRAND PRIX ENGINES

ENGINE [Standard]: V-block. OHV. Six-cylinder. Cast-iron block and aluminum head. Displacement: 173 cid. (2.8L). Bore & stroke: 3.50 x 2.99 in. Compression ratio: 8.8:1. Brake horsepower: 130 at 4800 rpm. Torque: 160 lbs.-ft. at 3600 rpm. Fuel system: MPFI. RPO Code: LB6. Standard in Grand Prix. Produced in U.S., Canada, or Mexico. [VIN code W, S or 9].

FIREBIRD ENGINES

ENGINE [Base V-6]: V-block. OHV. Six-cylinder. Cast-iron block and head. Aluminum intake manifold. Displacement: 173 cid. (2.8L). Bore & stroke: 3.50 x 2.99 in. Compression ratio: 8.5:1. Brake horsepower: 135 at 4900 rpm. Torque: 160 lbs.-ft. at 3900 rpm. Fuel system: EFI/TBI. RPO Code: LB8. Standard in base Firebird. Produced in U.S., Canada, or Mexico. [VIN code W, S, or 9].

ENGINE [Base V-8]: V-block. OHV. Eight-cylinder. Cast-iron block and head. Aluminum intake manifold. Displacement: 305 cid. (5.0L). Bore & stroke: 3.74 x 3.48 in. Brake horsepower: 170 at 4000 rpm. Torque: 255 lbs.-ft. at 2400 rpm. Compression ratio: 9.3:1. Fuel system: EFI/TBI. RPO Code: L03. Produced in U.S. or Canada. Standard Formula and Trans Am. Available in base Firebird. [VIN code E or F].

ENGINE [Optional V-8]: V-block. OHV. Eight-cylinder. Cast-iron block and head. Aluminum intake manifold. Displacement: 305 cid. (5.0L). Bore & stroke: 3.74 x 3.48 in. Brake horsepower: 190 at 4000 rpm (automatic) or 215 at 4400 rpm (manual). Torque: 295 lbs.-ft. at 2800 rpm (automatic) or 285 lbs.-ft. at 3200 rpm (manual). Compression ratio: 9.3:1. Fuel system: TPI. RPO Code: LB9. Available with five-speed manual in Formula and Trans Am (delete option in GTA). Available with four-speed automatic in same applications. [VIN code E or F].

ENGINE [GTA V-8]: V-block. OHV. Eight-cylinder. Cast-iron block and head. Aluminum intake manifold. Displacement: 350 cid. (5.7L). Bore & stroke: 4.00 x 3.48 in. Brake horsepower: 225 at 4400 rpm. Torque: 330 lbs.-ft. at 3200 rpm. Compression ratio: 9.3:1. Fuel system: EFI/TPI. RPO Code: B2L. Standard with four-speed automatic in GTA (optional in Formula and Trans Am). Includes low-profile air induction system with aluminum plenum and individual aluminum tuned runners, an extruded dual fuel rail assembly with computer controlled fuel injectors and a special low-restriction single exhaust system. [VIN code 8].

FIERO ENGINES

ENGINE [Base Four]: Inline. OHV. Four-cylinder. Cast-iron block and head. Aluminum intake manifold. Displacement: 151 cid. (2.5L Tech IV). Bore & stroke: 4.00 x 3.00 in. Compression ratio: 9.0:1. Brake horsepower: 98 at 4800 rpm. Torque: 135 lbs.-ft. at 3200 rpm. Five main bearings. Hydraulic valve lifters. Fuel system: EFI/TBI. RPO Code: LR8. Standard with five-speed manual in base Fiero. Produced in U.S., Canada, or Mexico. [VIN code U].

ENGINE [Optional Six]: V-block. OHV. Six-cylinder. Cast-iron block and head. Aluminum intake manifold. Displacement: 173 cid. (2.8L).

1988 Pontiac Grand Am LE four-door sedan. (PGMC)

Bore & stroke: 3.50 x 2.99 in. Compression ratio: 8.5:1. Brake horsepower: 135 at 4500 rpm. Torque: 165 lbs.-ft. at 3600 rpm. Fuel system: MPFI. RPO Code: L44. Standard in Formula Fiero and Fiero GT. [VIN code W, S, or 9].

GRAND AM ENGINES

ENGINE [Standard Grand Am/Grand Am LE]: Inline. OHV. Cast-iron block and head. Aluminum intake manifold. Displacement: 151 cid. (2.5L Tech IV). Bore & stroke: 4.00 x 3.00 in. Compression ratio: 9.0:1. Brake horsepower: 98 at 4800 rpm. Torque: 135 lbs.-ft. at 3200 rpm. Five main bearings. Hydraulic valve lifters. Fuel system: EFI/TBI. RPO Code: L68. Standard in base Grand Am and Grand AM LE. [VIN code U].

ENGINE [Standard Grand Am SE]: Inline. OHC. Turbocharged (Garret T2.5 turbocharger). Cast-iron block. Aluminum head and intake manifold. Displacement: 2.0-liter Turbo. Bore & stroke: 3.39 x 3.39 in. Compression ratio: 8.0:1. Brake horsepower: 165 at 5600 rpm. Torque: 175 lbs.-ft. at 4000 rpm. Fuel system: MPFI. RPO Code: LT3. Standard in Grand Am SE, optional in Grand Am LE. Produced in Brazil or Australia.

ENGINE [Optional Four]: Inline. DOHC. 16-Valve. Four-cylinder. Cast-iron block. Aluminum head and intake manifold. Displacement: 140 cid. (2.3L). Quad 4 16-valve. Bore & stroke: 3.62 x 3.35 in. Compression ratio: 9.5:1. Brake horsepower: 150 at 5200 rpm. Torque: 160 lbs.-ft. at 4400 rpm. Fuel system: MPFI. RPO Code: LD2. Optional in Grand Am, Grand Am LE and Grand Am SE. [VIN code D].

LEMANS ENGINE

ENGINE [Base Four]: Inline. OHV. Four-cylinder. Cast-iron block. Aluminum head and intake manifold. Displacement: 98 cid. (1.6L). Bore & stroke: 3.11 x 3.21 in. Compression ratio: 8.6:1. Brake horsepower: 74 at 5600 rpm. Torque: 90 lbs.-ft. at 2800 rpm. Fuel system: EFI/TBI. RPO Code: L73. Standard with four-speed manual. Produced in the Republic of South Korea. [VIN code 6].

SUNBIRD ENGINES

ENGINE [Base]: Inline. OHC. Four-cylinder. Cast-iron block. Aluminum head and intake manifold. Displacement: 121 cid. (2.0L). Bore & stroke: 3.39 x 3.39 in. Compression ratio: 8.8:1. Brake horsepower: 96 at 4800 rpm. Torque: 118 lbs.-ft. at 3600 rpm. Fuel system: EFI/TBI. RPO Code: LT2. Standard in Sunbird sedan, Sunbird SE Safari, Sunbird SE coupe, and Sunbird SE sedan. Produced in Brazil or Australia. [VIN code K].

ENGINE [Optional Four]: Inline. OHC. Four-cylinder. Turbocharged (Garrett T2.5 turbocharger). Cast-iron block. Aluminum head and intake manifold. Displacement: 121 cid. (2.0L). Bore & stroke: 3.39 x 3.39 in. Compression ratio: 8.0:1. Brake horsepower: 165 at 5600 rpm. Torque: 175 lbs.-ft. at 4000 rpm. Fuel system: MPFI with Turbo. RPO Code: LT3. Standard in Sunbird Turbo GT (optional in Sunbird SE coupe and Sunbird SE sedan). [VIN code M].

6000 ENGINES

ENGINE [Base Four]: Inline. OHV. Four-cylinder. Cast-iron block and head. Aluminum intake manifold. Displacement: 151 cid. (2.5L Tech IV). Bore & stroke: 4.00 x 3.00 in. Compression ratio: 9.0:1. Brake horsepower: 98 at 4800 rpm. Torque: 135 lbs.-ft. at 3200 rpm. Five main bearings. Hydraulic valve lifters. Fuel system: EFI/TBI. RPO Code: LR8. Standard in 6000 and 6000 LE. [VIN code U].

ENGINE [Optional Six]: V-block. OHV. Six-cylinder. Cast-iron block. Aluminum head and intake manifold. Displacement: 173 cid. (2.8L). Bore & stroke: 3.50 x 2.99 in. Compression ratio: 8.8:1. Brake horsepower: 125 at 4500 rpm. Torque: 160 lbs.-ft. at 3600 rpm. Fuel system: MPFI. RPO Code: LB6. Standard in 6000 SE /STE sedan and Safari; optional in base 6000 and 6000 LE sedan and Safari. Produced in U.S., Canada, or Mexico. [VIN code W, S, or 9].

ENGINE [Standard STE All-Wheel-Drive]: V-block. OHV. Six-cylinder. Cast-iron block. Aluminum head and intake manifold. Displacement: 189 cid. (3.1L). Bore & stroke: 3.50 x 3.30 in. Compression ratio: 8.8:1. Brake horsepower: 135 at 4800 rpm. Torque: 180 lbs.-ft. at 3600 rpm. Fuel system: MPFI. RPO Code: LHO. Standard in 6000 STE All-Wheel-Drive model. [VIN code T].

CHASSIS

SAFARI CHASSIS: Wheelbase: 116.0 in. (all). Overall length: 215.1 in. (all). Width: 79.3 in. (all). Height: 57.4 in. (all). Front tread: 60.3 in. Rear tread: 59.8 in. Tires: P225/75R15.

BONNEVILLE CHASSIS: Wheelbase: 110.8 in. (all). Overall length: 198.7 in. (all). Width: 72.1 in. (all). Height: 55.5 in. (all). Front tread: 58.7 in. Rear tread: 57.0 in. Standard tires: 205/75R14 BSW (LE). Standard tires: 215/65R15 Goodyear Eagle GT (SE). Standard tires: P215/60R16 BSW (SSE).

GRAND PRIX CHASSIS: Wheelbase: 107.6 in. (all). Overall length: 194.1 in. (all). Width: 71.0 in. (all). Height: 53.3 in. (all). Front tread: 59.5 in. Rear tread: 58.0 in. Standard tires: 195/75R14 (base and LE). Standard tires: 215/65R15 Goodyear Eagle GT (SE).

GRAND AM CHASSIS: Wheelbase: 103.4 in. (coupe/sedan). Overall length: 177.5 in. (coupe/sedan). Width: 66.5 in. (coupe/sedan). Height: 52.5 in. (coupe/sedan). Front tread: 55.6 in. Rear tread: 55.1 in. Standard tires: P185/80R13 BSW (Base/LE). Standard tires: P215/60R14 (SE).

FIREBIRD CHASSIS: Wheelbase: 101.0 in. (all). Overall length: 188.1 in. (Base/Formula); 191.6 in. (Trans Am/GTA). Width: 72.4 in. (coupe). Height: 50.0 in. (coupe). Front tread: 60.7 in. Rear tread: 61.6 in. Standard tires: P215/65R15 BSW (Base). Standard tires (Formula/Trans Am/GTA): P245/50VR16 RWL.

FIERO CHASSIS: Wheelbase: 93.4 in. (all). Overall length: 162.7 in. (coupe, Sport Coupe); 165.1 in. (SE, GT). Width: 69 in. (all) Height: 46.9 in. (all). Front tread: 57.8 in. Rear tread: 57.8 in. Standard tires: P185/75R15 BSW (coupe); P205/60R14 front and P215/60R14 rear (Formula/GT).

PONTIAC LEMANS CHASSIS: Wheelbase: 99.21 in. (all). Overall length: 163.70 in. (three-door); 171.89 in. (four-door). Height: 54.72 in. (all). Standard tires: P175/70R13 BSW (all).

SUNBIRD CHASSIS: Wheelbase: 101.2 in. (all). Overall length: 178.2 in. (coupe and convertible); 181.7 (sedan); 175.9 (Safari). Width: 65.0 in. (coupe/sedan/convertible); 66.3 in. (Safari) Height: 50.4 in. (coupe); 53.8 in. (sedan); 52.6 in. (convertible); 54.1 in. (Safari Wagon). Front tread: 55.6 in. (coupe and sedan); 55.4 in. (Safari and convertible). Rear tread: 55.2 in. (all). Standard tires: P185/80R13 BSW (except convertible and GTs). Standard tires: P215/60R14 (convertible). Standard tires: P215/60R14 (GT). Optional tires with Y99 Rally Tuned suspension on Sunbird SE wagon only: P215/60R14 Goodyear Eagle GT+4. Optional tires with WS6 special performance suspension: P215/60R14 Goodyear Eagle GT+4.

6000 CHASSIS: Wheelbase: 104.9 in. (all). Overall length: 188.8 in. (sedan); 193.2 in. (Safari). Width: 72 in. (all). Height: 53.7 in. (sedan); 54.1 in. (Safari). Front tread: 58.7 in. Rear tread: 57.0 in. Standard tires: 185/75R14 (All except STE). Standard tires: 195/70R14 (STE).

TECHNICAL

SAFARI TECHNICAL: Front engine/rear drive. Base transmission: Four-speed automatic. Axle ratio: 2.93:1 (standard). Axle ratio: 3.23:1 (optional). Front suspension: Control arms with coil springs. Rear suspension: Live axle, links and coil springs. Front brakes: Power-assisted vented discs. Rear brakes: Power-assisted drums. Fuel tank: 22.0 gal.

BONNEVILLE TECHNICAL: Front engine/front drive. Base transmission: Four-speed automatic. Axle ratio: 2.73:1 (standard with 3.8L V-6 in Base Bonneville and Bonneville SE). Axle ratio: 2.97:1 (standard with 3.8L V-6 in Bonneville SE/SSE). Front suspension: MacPherson struts with coil springs. Rear suspension: MacPherson struts with coil springs. Front brakes: Power-assisted vented Anti-lock brake system standard with SSE. Fuel tank: 18.0 gal.

GRAND PRIX TECHNICAL: Chassis: Front engine/front drive. Standard drive train: 2.8L V-6 with five-speed manual transaxle. Optional drive train: 2.8L V-6 with four-speed automatic transaxle. Axle ratio: 3.61:1 (manual); 3.33:1 (automatic). Front suspension: MacPherson struts with tapered top coil springs. Rear suspension: Tri-link independent suspension. Four-wheel power disc brakes. Fuel tank: 16.0 gal.

FIREBIRD TECHNICAL: Chassis: Front engine/rear drive. Base transmission: Five-speed manual with overdrive. Optional transmission: Four-speed automatic. Axle ratio: 3.08:1 (with 5.0L TBI and manual). Axle ratio: 2.73:1 (with 5.0L TBI and four-speed automatic). Axle ratio: 3.45:1 (with 5.0L TPI and five-speed manual). Axle ratio: 3.23:1 (with 5.0L TPI and four-speed automatic). Axle ratio: 3.27:1 (with 5.7L and four-speed automatic and with 5.0L TPI and four-speed automatic in GTA/Trans Am only). Front suspension:

1988 Pontiac Fiero Formula two-door coupe. (PGMC)

MacPherson struts with coil springs. Rear suspension: Live axle with coil springs. Front brakes: Power-assisted vented discs. Rear brakes: Power-assisted drums (rear disc brakes standard on GTA). Fuel tank: 15.5.

FIERO TECHNICAL: Chassis: Mid-engine/rear drive. Base transmission: Three-speed automatic. Optional transmission (with V-6): Gertag-designed GM-developed five-speed manual. Axle ratio: 3.35:1 (2.5L with manual). Axle ratio: 2.84:1 (2.5L with automatic). Axle ratio: 3.61:1 (2.8L with manual). Axle ratio: 3.33:1 (2.8L with automatic). Steering: Rack-and-pinion. Front suspension: Independent control arms with coil springs. Rear suspension: Independent control arms with coil springs. Front brakes: Disc. Rear brakes: disc. Fuel tank: 12 gal. discs. Rear brakes: Power-assisted drums.

GRAND AM TECHNICAL: Chassis: Front engine/front drive. Base transmission: Five-speed manual with overdrive. Optional transmission: Three-speed automatic. Axle ratio: 3.35:1 (with 2.5L engine and manual). Axle ratio: 3.61:1 (with 2.0L engine and manual or 2.3L engine and manual). Axle ratio: 2.84:1 (with 2.3L and automatic or 2.5L and automatic). Axle ratio: 3.18:1 with 2.0L and automatic). Front suspension: MacPherson struts with coil springs. Rear suspension: Beam axle with coil springs. Front brakes: Power-assisted vented discs. Rear brakes: Power-assisted drums. Fuel tank: 13.6 gal.

LEMANS TECHNICAL: Chassis: Front engine/front drive. Base transmission: Four-speed manual. Optional transmission: Three-speed automatic or five-speed manual. Axle ratio: 3.43:1 with automatic. Axle ratio: 3.74:1 with manual. Front suspension: Hydraulic cartridge shocks. Rear suspension: Coil springs. Front brakes: Vented disc. Rear brakes: drum.

SUNBIRD TECHNICAL: Chassis: Front engine/front drive. Base transmission: Five-speed manual with overdrive. Optional transmission: Three-speed automatic. Axle ratio: 3.45:1 (with 2.0L engine and manual). Axle ratio: 3.18:1 (with 2.0L engine and automatic). Axle ratio: 3.61:1 with Turbo engine and manual). Axle ratio: 3.18:1 with Turbo engine and automatic). Front suspension: MacPherson struts with coil springs. Rear suspension: Beam axle with coil springs. Front brakes: Power-assisted vented discs. Rear brakes: Power-assisted drums. Fuel tank: 13.6 gal.

6000 TECHNICAL: Chassis: Front engine/front drive. Base transmission: Three-speed automatic with overdrive. Optional transmissions: Four-speed automatic and five-speed manual. Axle ratio: 2.84:1 (with three-speed automatic). Axle ratio: 3.33:1 (with four-speed automatic). Axle ratio: 3.61:1 (with five-speed manual). Front suspension: MacPherson struts with coil springs. Rear suspension: Beam axle with coil springs. Front brakes: Power-assisted vented discs. Rear brakes: Power-assisted drums (ABS vented discs on STE). Fuel tank: 15.7 gal.

OPTIONS

SAFARI OPTIONS: Power antenna. Heavy-duty cooling. Electric rear window defogger. Front and rear floor mats. Gauge package including coolant temperature and voltmeter gauges. Luggage carrier including rear air deflector. Power door locks, including power tailgate lock. Power windows. UM6 Delco radio equipment. UX1 Delco radio equipment. 55/45 split front seat with passenger recliner. Superlift shock absorbers. Simulated woodgrain exterior body siding. Trailer wiring harness. Simulated wire wheel covers with locking package. Safari full-size station wagon option group #1, includes tilt steering, lamp group, cruise control, and controlled-cycle windshield wipers. Safari full-size station wagon option group #2, includes tilt steering, lamp group, cruise control, controlled-cycle windshield wipers, power door locks, power windows, power driver's seat with 55/45 split seat only, carpeted sidewalls and tailgate, cornering lamps, dual remote-control OSRV mirrors, front and rear bumper guards, illuminated passenger visor-vanity mirror, and halogen headlights.

BONNEVILLE OPTIONS: Power antenna. Electric rear window defogger. Gauge package including driver information center (included with 45/45 seat option). Leather seat trim. Two-tone paint. Power door locks, Power windows. UM6 Delco radio equipment. UT4 Delco radio equipment. 45/55 split front seat. 45/45 split front seat. Power sunroof. Theft-deterrent system. 14-in. diamond-spoke aluminum wheels with locking package. Bonneville LE option group #1 includes controlled-cycle windshield wipers, tilt steering, and lamp group. Bonneville LE option group #2 includes controlled-cycle windshield wipers, tilt steering, cruise control, and lamp group. Bonneville LE option group #3 includes controlled-cycle windshield wipers, tilt steering, cruise control, lamp group, power door locks, power windows, power driver's seat, deck lid release, and illuminated passenger visor-vanity mirror. Bonneville LE option group #4 includes controlled-cycle windshield wipers, tilt steering, cruise control, lamp group, power door locks, power windows, power driver's seat, deck lid release, illuminated passenger visor-vanity mirror, leather-wrapped steering wheel, lighted entry system, electric fuel door lock, power sport mirrors, and power passenger seat. Bonneville SE option group #1 includes lamp group and power door locks, plus all standard SE extras. Bonneville SE option group #2 includes lamp group and power door locks, power driver's seat, deck lid release, illuminated passenger visor-vanity mirror and fog lamps, plus all standard SE extras. Bonneville SE option group #3 includes lamp group and power door locks, power driver's seat, deck lid release, illuminated passenger visor-vanity mirror, fog lamps, lighted entry system, electric fuel door lock, power sport mirrors, power passenger seat and twilight sentinel, plus all standard SE extras.

GRAND PRIX OPTIONS: Electronic control air conditioning. Electric rear window defogger. Front and rear carpeted floor mats. Mechanical analog gauges with tachometer and trip odometer. Lower accent two-tone paint. UM6 Delco ETR AM/FM stereo. UX1 Delco ETR AM/FM stereo. High-performance sound system with six speakers and power amplifier. Power antenna. Power door locks. Power windows. 40/60 split seat with folding armrest. Reclining bucket seats with console. P195/70R15 Goodyear Eagle GT+4 BSW radial tires, requires 15-in. wheels. P215/65R15 Goodyear Eagle GT+4 BSW tires teamed with Y99 Rally Tuned suspension. Four-speed automatic transaxle. Five-speed manual transaxle. 15-in. styled sport wheels. 15-in. aluminum wheels (color-keyed on SE) with locking packages. Base Grand Prix option group #1 includes air conditioning with electronic control, tilt steering, lamp group and right-hand vanity mirror. Base Grand Prix option group #2 includes air conditioning with electronic control, tilt steering, lamp group, right-hand vanity mirror, cruise control, and controlled-cycle wipers. Base Grand Prix option group #3 includes air conditioning with electronic control, tilt steering, lamp group, right-hand vanity mirror, cruise control, controlled-cycle wipers, power windows with illuminated switches, power door locks with illuminated switches, and remote

deck lid release. Grand Prix LE option group #1 includes air conditioning with electronic control, tilt steering, right-hand vanity mirror, cruise control, controlled-cycle wipers, and power door locks with illuminated switches, plus standard LE extras. Grand Prix LE option group #2 includes air conditioning with electronic control, tilt steering, cruise control, controlled-cycle wipers, power door locks with illuminated switches, deck lid release, power driver's seat, and illuminated passenger visor-vanity mirror, plus standard LE extras. Grand Prix LE option group #3 includes air conditioning with electronic control, tilt steering, cruise control, controlled-cycle wipers, power door locks with illuminated switches, deck lid release, power driver's seat, illuminated passenger visor-vanity mirror, rearview mirror with dual reading lamps, leather appointment group, security lighting including illuminated entry, and time-delay headlight shut-off and power mirrors, plus standard LE extras. Grand Prix SE option group #1 includes right-hand visor-vanity mirror, power door locks with illuminated switches, deck lid release and power driver's seat, plus standard SE extras. Grand Prix SE option group #2 includes power door locks with illuminated switches, deck lid release, power driver's seat, illuminated passenger visor-vanity mirror, power mirrors, and console extension with electronic compass, trip computer, and service reminder, plus standard SE extras.

FIREBIRD OPTIONS: Air conditioning with Soft-Ray tinted glass. Limited-slip axle. Four-wheel disc brakes. Electric rear window defogger. 5.0-liter EFI V-8. 5.0-liter TPI high-output V-8. 5.7-liter TPI high-output V-8. Gauge package, requires electronic air conditioning controls. Hatch roof with removable glass panels. Luxury trim group. Power antenna. Power door locks. Power windows. UM6 Delco ETR AM/FM stereo. UX1 Delco ETR AM/FM stereo. Subwoofer six-speaker system. Articulating bucket seats with inflatable lumbar and backwing bolsters. Leather seat trim. Four-speed automatic transmission. Deep-dish Hi-Tech 15-in. Turbo cast-aluminum wheels with locking package (no-charge option). 15-in. diamond-spoke cast-aluminum wheels. 16-in. diamond-spoke cast-aluminum wheels. 16-in Hi-Tech Turbo cast-aluminum wheels, available with WS6 suspension only. Base Firebird option group #1 includes air conditioning with Soft-Ray tinted glass, tilt steering, custom-colored safety belts, body side moldings, controlled-cycle windshield wipers, and passenger visor-vanity mirror. Base Firebird option group #2 includes air conditioning with Soft-Ray tinted glass, tilt steering, custom-colored safety belts, body side moldings, controlled-cycle windshield wipers, passenger visor-vanity mirror, lamp group, cruise control, remote deck lid release, and four-way manual driver's seat adjuster. Base Firebird option group #3 includes air conditioning with Soft-Ray tinted glass, tilt steering, custom-colored safety belts, body side moldings, controlled-cycle windshield wipers, passenger visor-vanity mirror, lamp group, cruise control, remote deck lid release, four-way manual driver's seat adjuster, power windows, and power door locks. Firebird Formula option group #1 includes air conditioning with Soft-Ray tinted glass, tilt steering, custom-colored safety belts, body side moldings, controlled-cycle windshield wipers, and passenger visor-vanity mirror. Firebird Formula option group #2 includes air conditioning with Soft-Ray tinted glass, tilt steering, custom-colored safety belts, body side moldings, controlled-cycle windshield wipers, passenger visor-vanity mirror, lamp group, cruise control, remote deck lid release, and four-way manual driver's seat adjuster. Firebird Formula option group #3 includes air conditioning with Soft-Ray tinted glass, tilt steering, custom-colored safety belts, body side moldings, controlled-cycle windshield wipers, passenger visor-vanity mirror, lamp group, cruise control, remote deck lid release, four-way manual driver's seat adjuster, power windows, and power door locks. Firebird Trans Am option group #1 includes air conditioning with Soft-Ray tinted glass, tilt steering, custom-colored safety belts, body side moldings, controlled-cycle windshield wipers, passenger visor-vanity mirror, lamp group, cruise control, remote deck lid release, and standard Trans Am extras. Firebird Trans Am option group #3 includes air conditioning with Soft-Ray tinted glass, tilt steering, custom-colored safety belts, body side moldings, controlled-cycle windshield wipers, passenger visor-vanity mirror, lamp group, cruise control, remote deck lid release, power windows, power door locks, leather appointments group, and power sport mirrors, plus standard Trans Am extras.

FIERO OPTIONS: Air conditioning with Soft-Ray tinted glass. Electric rear window defogger. Deck lid luggage carrier. Front floor carpets. Power door locks. Power windows. UM6 Delco ETR AM/FM

1988 Pontiac Firebird Formula two-door coupe. (PGMC)

1988 Pontiac Bonneville SSE four-door sedan. (PGMC)

stereo. UX1 Delco ETR AM/FM stereo. Inflatable driver's side lumbar-support bucket seat. Reclining bucket seat with Ventura cloth and leather trim. Rear deck lid spoiler (not available with deck lid luggage carrier). Subwoofer speaker system, requires stereo and air conditioning. Removable sunroof. P195/70R14 Eagle GT+4 steel-belted radial tires. Three-speed automatic transmission. Gold- or black-finished diamond-spoke aluminum wheels (gold on GT only). Base coupe and Formula option group #1 with tilt steering, comfort-cycle wipers, and tinted glass. Base coupe and Formula option group #2 with air conditioning, tinted glass, tilt steering, controlled-cycle wipers, lamp group, passenger visor-vanity mirror, and cruise control. Base coupe and Formula option group #3 with air conditioning, tinted glass, tilt steering, controlled-cycle wipers, lamp group, passenger visor-vanity mirror, cruise control, power door locks, and power windows. GT coupe option group #1 adds tinted glass, passenger visor-vanity mirror, cruise control, power door locks, and power sport windows to regular standard features for GT model.

GRAND AM OPTIONS: Air conditioning. Electric rear window defogger. 2.0-liter four-cylinder turbo engine with MFI. 2.3-liter Quad 4 engine. Gauge package. Deck lid luggage carrier. Pontiac performance sound system, requires power windows. UM6 Delco ETR AM/FM stereo. UX1 Delco ETR AM/FM stereo. Articulating bucket seats with inflatable lumbar and backwing bolsters. Removable sunroof with air deflector. Three-speed automatic transmission. Tri-Port wheels, requires P195/70R14 tires. Hi-Tech Turbo aluminum wheels with locking package. Base Grand Am option group #1 includes air conditioning, tilt steering, and custom console. Base Grand Am option group #2 includes air conditioning, tilt steering, custom console, lamp group, controlled-cycle wipers, and cruise control. Base Grand Am option group #3 includes air conditioning, tilt steering, custom console, lamp group, controlled-cycle wipers, cruise control, power windows, and power door locks. Grand Am LE option group #1 includes air conditioning, tilt steering, lamp group, controlled-cycle wipers, and cruise control, plus standard LE extras. Grand Am LE option group #2 includes air conditioning, tilt steering, lamp group, controlled-cycle wipers, cruise control, remote gas filler, visor-vanity mirror, remote deck lid release, and split-folding rear seat, plus standard LE extras. Grand Am LE option group #3 includes air conditioning, tilt steering, lamp group, controlled-cycle wipers, cruise control, remote gas filler, visor-vanity mirror, remote deck lid release, split-folding rear seat, power windows, power door locks, fog lamps including header and front courtesy lamps, and power driver's seat, plus standard LE extras. Grand AM SE option package #1 includes tilt steering, lamp group, and power windows, plus standard SE extras. Grand AM SE option package #2 includes tilt steering, lamp group, power windows, power driver's seat, lighted visor-vanity mirror, and power sport mirrors, plus standard SE extras.

LEMANS OPTIONS: Air conditioning, requires power steering. Front and rear carpeted floor mats. Power steering. UM6 Delco DIN-size AM/FM stereo cassette. UM7 Delco ETR DIN-size AM/FM stereo. Black-finished roof luggage rack. Sunroof. Three-speed automatic transmission.

SUNBIRD OPTIONS: Air conditioning with Soft-Ray tinted glass. Custom interior trim. Electric rear window defogger. Rally gauge cluster with trip odometer. Deck lid luggage carrier. Roof luggage carrier. Front /rear carpeted floor mats. Power door locks. Power

windows, requires power door locks. UM6 Delco ETR AM/FM stereo. UX1 Delco ETR AM/FM stereo radio. Articulating bucket seats with lumbar and backwing bolsters, requires custom trim. Sunroof with removable glass. Three-speed automatic transmission. 14-in. Hi-Tech Turbo cast-aluminum wheels with locking package. 13-in. Sport Tech cast-aluminum wheels, except GT. Base and SE option group #1 with tinted glass, power steering and sport mirrors. Base and SE option package #2 with tinted glass, power steering, sport mirrors, color-keyed seat belts, tilt steering, controlled-cycle wipers, and four-spoke steering wheel. Base and SE option package #3 with tinted glass, power steering, sport mirrors, color-keyed seat belts, air conditioning, tilt steering, controlled-cycle wipers, four-spoke steering wheel, lamp group, cruise control, and front seat armrest. Sunbird GT coupe option group #1 including tinted glass, air conditioning, tilt steering, and controlled cycle wipers, plus GT standard extras. Sunbird GT convertible option group #1 including air conditioning, tilt steering, and controlled cycle wipers, plus GT convertible standard extras. Sunbird GT coupe option group #2 including tinted glass, air conditioning, tilt steering, controlled cycle wipers, lamp group, cruise control, front seat armrest, remote deck lid release, and visor-vanity mirror, plus GT coupe standard extras. Sunbird GT coupe option group #3 including tinted glass, air conditioning, tilt steering, controlled cycle wipers, lamp group, cruise control, front seat armrest, remote deck lid release, visor-vanity mirror, power windows, power door locks, and leather-wrapped steering wheel, plus GT coupe standard extras. Sunbird GT convertible option group #3 including air conditioning, tilt steering, controlled cycle wipers, lamp group, cruise control, front seat armrest, remote deck lid release, and leather-wrapped steering wheel, plus GT convertible standard extras.

6000 OPTIONS: Air conditioning with Soft-Ray tinted glass. Sport mirrors. 2.8-liter V-6 with MFI. Analog instrument cluster with tachometer. Electronic instrument cluster with tachometer. UM6 Delco ETR AM/FM stereo. UX1 Delco ETR AM/FM stereo. Simulated woodgrain Safari paneling. Paint stripes. Power glass sunroof, includes reading lamps, not available on Safari. Four-speed automatic transmission with overdrive. Five-speed manual transmission. Aluminum sport wheels with locking package. Simulated wire wheel covers with locking package. Base 6000 option group #1 includes air conditioning with Soft-Ray tinted glass, sport mirrors, and tilt steering. Base 6000 option group #2 includes air conditioning with Soft-Ray tinted glass, sport mirrors, tilt steering, custom-exterior group, sport steering wheel, cruise control, lamp group, and concealed-cycle wipers. Base 6000 option group #3 includes air conditioning with Soft-Ray tinted glass, sport mirrors, tilt steering, custom exterior group, sport steering wheel, cruise control, lamp group, concealed-cycle wipers, power door locks, deck lid release, visor-vanity mirror, and power windows. 6000 LE option group #1 includes air conditioning with Soft-Ray tinted glass, sport mirrors, tilt steering, cruise control, lamp group, and concealed-cycle wipers, plus standard LE extras. 6000 LE option group #2 includes air conditioning with Soft-Ray tinted glass, sport mirrors, tilt steering, cruise control, lamp group, concealed-cycle wipers, power door locks, deck lid release, visor-vanity mirror, and power windows, plus standard LE extras. 6000 LE option group #3 includes air conditioning with Soft-Ray tinted glass, sport mirrors, tilt steering, cruise control, lamp group, concealed-cycle wipers, power door locks, deck lid release, power windows, illuminated visor-vanity mirror, and mirror with dual reading lamps, plus standard LE extras. 6000 SE option group #1 includes air conditioning with Soft-Ray tinted glass, tilt steering, cruise control, lamp group, and controlled-cycle wipers, plus standard SE extras. 6000 SE option group #2 includes air conditioning with Soft-Ray tinted glass, tilt steering, cruise control, lamp group and controlled-cycle wipers, power door locks, deck lid release, visor-vanity mirror, and power windows, plus standard SE extras. 6000 SE option group #3 includes air conditioning with Soft-Ray tinted glass, tilt steering, cruise control, lamp group and controlled-cycle wipers, power door locks, deck lid release, visor-vanity mirror, power windows, power driver's seat, and mirror with reading lamp, plus standard SE extras.

HISTORICAL: The new 6000 STE (GM's first all-wheel-drive car) was predicted to be the hot "image" product of the year. It reflected an effort to make Pontiac A-body cars distinctive from those of other GM divisions. Unfortunately, its introduction was delayed, making it impossible to hit even its low-volume production target of approximately 3,000 units. It was, however, the new LeMans (sourced from Daewoo of Korea) that increased the company's model-year unit sales volume. The total was 740,928 cars sold, an increase of more than 25,000. This broke down as follows: [1000] 366; [Daewoo LeMans] 54,671; [Sunbird] 77,864; [Fiero] 27,304; [Firebird] 59,459; [Grand Am] 221,438; [6000] 103,003; [Bonneville] 109,862; [RWD Grand Prix] 2,850; [FWD Grand Prix] 76,723; [Full-size Safari] 7,388. Pontiac regained the number three slot in the U.S. auto sales charts, a position it had last held 15 years earlier in 1973. The front-wheel-drive Bonneville—which had been somewhat of a sales disappointment in 1987—had a more respectable showing this season, although it was the new front-wheel-drive Grand Prix—introduced at midyear—that became a first-year success story. The top-selling Grand Am also gained from 1987. All 1988 Firebirds were built in Van Nuys, California. All 1988 Parisienne-style Safaris were built in Lakewood, Georgia. All front-wheel-drive Grand Prixs were built at the Fairfax plant near Kansas City. All Grand Ams were made in Lansing, Mich. All Bonnevilles were built at Willow Run, Mich. Pontiac 6000s were built at Tarrytown, N.Y. and Oklahoma City, Okla. Sunbirds were manufactured at Lordstown, Ohio. Additional U.S. market cars were sourced from Canadian factories. Michael J. Losh continued as Pontiac Motor Div.'s general manager in 1988, with E.M. Schlesinger heading up sales and service responsibilities. Bill O'Neill once again handled public relations. John Sawruk was official Pontiac Historian.

1989 PONTIAC

1989 Pontiac LeMans GSE three-door hatchback. (PGMC)

SAFARI — SERIES 2L — (V-8) — Pontiac's 1989 Safari remained a traditional full-size station wagon based on what had once been the Parisienne. Standard on all big Safaris was a 5.0-liter four-barrel V-8; air conditioning with Soft-Ray tinted glass; Powermaster front disc/rear drum brakes; white-accented front/rear bumper rub strips; carpeting throughout; a center high-mounted stop lamp; The GM Computer Command Control system; an inside hood release; dual sport mirrors (left-hand remote-controlled); power steering; a UM7 Delco ETR AM/FM stereo; a notchback front seat with center armrest; a rear-facing third seat with Hartford vinyl trim; load-carrying springs; front stabilizer bar; a three-spoke steering wheel; full-coil suspension; a tailgate window control; P225/75R15 steel-belted radial whitewall tires; a four-speed automatic transmission; and custom wheel covers.

BONNEVILLE — SERIES 2H — (V-6) — The Pontiac Bonneville offered performance in a full-size touring sedan. There were three models with the luxurious Bonneville LE at the bottom and the sporty Bonneville SE above it. The top-of-the-line Bonneville SSE was a European-inspired high-performance "luxo" sedan. Bonneville for 1989 featured evolutionary, rather than revolutionary changes. All Bonnevilles were again powered by the 3.8-liter "3800" V-6

engine. This was a 90-degree V-6 with multi-port sequential fuel injection. It developed 165 hp and 210 lbs.-ft. of torque. The 3800, equipped with a balance shaft to eliminate the primary engine shaking force normally found on 90-degree V-6s, was teamed with a four-speed (three plus overdrive) automatic transaxle. Antilock brakes (ABS) were available on all Bonnevilles and continued as standard equipment on the SSE. The ABS contributed greatly to vehicle maneuverability, enabling the car to stop in a controlled straight line under all surface conditions. Additional detail improvements throughout the line served to enhance driving comfort and utility. A new Grand Prix-style steering wheel with hub-mounted radio and climate controls, in conjunction with automatic air conditioning, was available on LE and SE models and standard on SSE models. The lineup included three sound systems, a base UM7 four-speaker system, an optional six-speaker system, and a Delco "Enhanced Audio" system with eight speakers, which was standard on SSEs. Storage space throughout the car was increased and the trunk utility was improved by raising the rear speakers. A cargo security net was standard in the trunks of SE/SSE models and optional in LEs. Glove box capacity was increased 50 percent. An additional front seat storage armrest was added for the Level II 55/45 seats. Also, map pockets in the doors were redesigned to improve overall customer convenience. The Bonneville LE emphasized aerodynamic styling, plus good ride and handling. Its changes for 1989 included a new 2.84:1 final drive ratio for improved part throttle response and grade load driveability. The LE came with standard P205/75R14 tires on 14 x 6-in. wheels. A urethane Grand Prix style steering wheel was standard, along with redesigned instruments, a new 115-mph speedometer and front and rear floor mats. The Bonneville SE added or substituted a Y99 suspension with P215/65R15 Eagle GT+4 tires and 15 x 6-in. Tri-Port cast aluminum wheels as standard content. The SE also had a leather-wrapped steering wheel, standard 45/55 seats with storage provisions and full analog instrumentation with a tachometer and 115 mph speedometer. A prestigious full-size touring sedan with European flair and style, the Bonneville SSE boasted head-turning aerodynamic styling. It also combined outstanding handling with excellent ride quality and comfort. Pontiac said that it rivaled some of the world's finest touring sedans in features and quality. The SSE was equipped with its own unique suspension that included ABS brakes, variable-ratio power steering, firmer springs, larger 32mm front anti-roll bar, electronic load leveling and Goodyear P215/60R16 Eagle GT+4 all-season tires. Its standard wheels were 16 x 7-in. body-colored alloys. At mid-year, 16 x 7-in. gold cross-lace wheels were made optional. Inside, the SSE created the finest ergonomic environment possible in an American production car. The deeply-hooded SSE-specific instrument panel featured large, legible full-analog gauges including an electronic compass and driver information center. Standard interior features included redundant radio and heat/vent/AC (HVAC) controls in the steering wheel hub. The new center console between the 45/45 bucket seats contained a storage bin, two accessory power plugs for operating multiple appliances and power seat control switches. The improved Bonneville SSE sound system utilized a subwoofer, two 6 x 6-in. dual voice coil speakers, and two titanium tweeters in the package shelf, plus two 6 x 9-in. speakers with dual titanium tweeters in the front doors.

GRAND PRIX — SERIES 2G — (V-6/V-8) — Entering its first full year of production, the highly-touted Pontiac Grand Prix sported a combination of eye-catching good looks, driver-oriented interior features, and multi-level performance that begged to be taken on the road. The standard engine was a 130-hp V-6. Late in the year, a larger 3.1-liter engine was released. Standard equipment included three-point rear seat belts, air conditioning, and a radio with seek up/seek down function. The base model was the Grand Prix. Electronic air conditioning and front and rear floor mats were added to its standard equipment list, along with a number of new options. The Grand Prix LE offered a higher level of standard equipment and interior trim. Standard equipment included electronic-controlled air conditioning, SE instrumentation, and power windows with an express-down feature. There was also a 60/40 front seat with a folding center armrest. Standard tires were size P195/75R14 all-season radials. The Grand Prix SE was a quick, stylish, driver-friendly coupe that came standard with the Y99 rally-tuned suspension and a choice of a 2.8-liter four-/five-speed manual or 3.1-liter V-6 four-speed automatic drivetrain. Both engines featured SE-specific dual

1989 Pontiac Sunbird LE two-door coupe. (PGMC)

exhausts. On the exterior, the SE had the belt moldings and hood rear edge molding changed from chrome to black. There was a distinctive front fascia with integral fog lights, an exclusive taillight treatment, body side moldings, and aero body extensions. The SE interior had articulated power bucket seats with adjustable thigh support and electrically adjusted head restraints. In the rear, bucket seats were divided by a large pass-through to the carpeted trunk. Electronic air conditioning, power windows (with driver's express-down feature), power mirrors, and cruise control were installed on all Grand Prix SEs, along with a leather-wrapped tilting sport steering wheel, an LCD speedometer and fuel gauge and analog gauges including a tachometer. In the spring of 1989, Pontiac announced an exciting limited-edition run of 2000 Turbo Grand Prixs. These cars were powered by a McLaren-developed 3.1-liter turbocharged V-6 producing over 200 hp. A special Garrett turbocharger added the real muscle and was designed to effectively eliminate turbo lag while maximizing torque. A specific four-speed automatic transmission backed up the powerhouse engine. Specific struts, springs and standard antilock brakes were also featured on the turbocharged Grand Prix. "Rounding" out the contents were P245/50ZR16 Goodyear Eagle GT+4 tires and 16 x 8-in. gold cross-lace alloy wheels. All SE options were standard on the Turbo, except a power sunroof and leather interior. Also included was a camel-colored interior, heads-up display (HUD) instrumentation, specific front and rear fascias, deep aerodynamic body side skirting, functional hood louvers, special "fat tire" fenders, new Bright Red or Metallic Black finish and specific gold-colored cloisonné emblems. One 1989 Turbo Grand Prix was selected as the Official Pace Car for the Daytona 500 stock car race on February 19, 1989.

FIREBIRD — SERIES 2F — (V-6/V-8) — For 1989 Pontiac's premium performer, the Firebird, continued its more-than-two-decades heritage of high-powered excitement. From performance machine enthusiasts to sporty car buyers looking for trademark styling, the Firebird offered a complete range of power and price. Again there were four regular models: Firebird, Formula, Trans Am and Trans Am GTA. There was also a special limited-edition 25th Anniversary "Indy Pace Car" version of the GTA with a high-output V-6 pirated from the Buick GNX. All Firebirds came with V-8s and the base model also came with a V-6 for entry-level sports car buyers. Multec fuel injectors were added to 1989 engines for more reliability and less susceptibility to fuel fouling. The self-adjusting rear disc brakes were completely revised with a new caliper and rotor design. Pass Key anti-theft protection, previously standard only on the GTA, became standard on all Firebirds. An electronically coded resistor embedded in the ignition key activated a control module in the ignition lock, which determined when the anti-theft vehicle start-up system should be activated. GM noted that the system had been successful in reducing Corvette thefts by 40 percent and said that it should be helpful in holding down Firebird owners' insurance premiums. Door glass seals were improved for better sealing and less wind noise. The entire Firebird line also got clearcoat paint over the base color for a long-lasting high gloss finish. New in the color lineup was Bright Blue Metallic. Standard equipment across the entire 1989 Firebird lineup included three-point lap and shoulder belts for rear seat occupants. Available

options now offered across the F-car line included removable T-tops, a variety of radios, and an all-new compact digital disc player with the Delco II theft deterrent system that rendered the unit inoperative if power was interrupted. The lowest-priced Firebird was the base model with a standard 2.8-liter V-6 and five-speed manual transmission. For 1989, V-6s received the FE1 suspension package with 30mm front and 18mm rear anti-roll bars. Added standard equipment for V-8 models included a Trans Am-style F41 suspension and air conditioning. The base Firebird carried the same exterior striping package as the Formula. The Formula Firebird was aimed at buyers interested in high-performance "street machines" and was designed to provide maximum "oomph" for a minimum price. This package provided the Trans Am engine, which had a 10-hp boost in power due to the use of a new dual catalytic converter low-back-pressure exhaust system. Pontiac claimed this equated to a two- to three-second cut in 0-to-60 mph acceleration times. Also standard on Formulas was the WS6 suspension and tire package, air conditioning, and a revised exterior graphics package with narrower body side stripes. The Trans Am had a standard 5.0-liter TBI 170-hp V-8 engine, five-speed manual transmission, and limited-slip differential. Also included were F41 underpinnings with 34mm front and 23mm rear anti-roll bars and recalibrated springs and shocks, Firestone Firehawk GTX tires, 15 x 7-in. cast aluminum wheels and air conditioning. Described as the "ultimate Firebird" (even though it wasn't in 1989) was the Trans Am GTA. It had a 5.7-liter 235-hp TPI V-8 borrowed from the Corvette; plus five-speed manual transmission; a limited-slip differential; the WS6 performance suspension with 36mm front and 24mm rear anti-roll bars; deflected-disc gas-filled shocks and struts; 16-in. lightweight cross-laced aluminum wheels; Z-rated Goodyear tires; cloth articulating bucket seats; air conditioning; cruise control; power windows; power door locks; a power antenna; a AM/FM cassette radio with graphic equalizer; and redundant radio controls on the steering wheel hub. Also included on the GTA notchback were 45/55 split folding rear seats with integral headrests. Leather bucket seats with increased thigh support and inflatable lumbar and side bolsters were optional. To commemorate the 20th anniversary of the first Firebird Trans Am, a special series of 1,500 20th Anniversary Trans Ams was produced. These cars were above the level of the GTA model and were really the "ultimate" Trans Ams of this year. Power was provided by a 3.8-liter turbocharged V-6 that developed 250 hp. It was coupled to a four-speed automatic transmission and limited-slip rear axle. All 20th Anniversary Trans Ams were painted White and had Camel colored interiors. Externally, the GTA emblem on the nose was changed to a special "20th Anniversary" insignia. A similar cloisonné emblem could be found on the sail panels. "Turbo Trans Am" emblems on the front fenders replaced the standard GTA script in the same location. Also included with this model was a larger, baffled, competition-type 18-gal. fuel tank, four-wheel power disc brakes, 16-in. gold-finished lightweight diamond-spoke aluminum wheels, stainless steel exhaust splitters, analog gauges with turbo boost gauge, unique contoured rear seats, and packaged-in-the-car Official Pace Car decals that could be installed by Pontiac dealers at the request of the buyer.

1989 Pontiac Grand Am SE two-door coupe. (PGMC)

1989 Pontiac Formula Firebird two-door coupe. (PGMC)

GRAND AM — SERIES 2N — The fifth N-body Grand Am front-drive compact was the best-selling Pontiac. It had new looks to complement its already popular performance and roadability. Models offered were the LE coupe, LE sedan, SE coupe, and SE sedan. A new front treatment featured a new hood, fenders, grille, and fascia cover that gave a more swept-back, aerodynamic profile. At the rear, both trim levels had new fascias, end panels, bumpers, and taillights. The license plate opening was relocated to the rear fascia. Side marker lights and parking lights were modified for 1989 and a new one-piece side molding was seen. Paint work featured a two-layer basecoat/clearcoat system. Ride and comfort in all models was improved by new deflected-disc valving in the MacPherson strut front suspension. To ensure long life even beyond GM's six-year/100,000-mile warranty against rust-through, the Grand Am hood and fenders were made of steel galvanized on both sides. Inside the 1989 Grand Am were a sporty, redesigned steering wheel and revised instrument panel graphics, including a new higher-reading speedometer. On coupes, the passenger seat slid forward to allow easier rear entrance and a mechanical "memory" returned the seat to its original position. All Grand Ams were equipped with new three-point rear seat belts and a shoulder harness. An all-new compact digital disc player and a choice of radios were available for all models, along with an optional performance sound system. The Grand Am LE offered distinctive exterior styling at an affordable price. Its new rear end treatment featured amber turn signals and back-up lights between the taillights. The SE models were easy to spot with their monochromatic exteriors. Standard features included composite headlights; integrated front fog lights; a rally tuned suspension (RTS) with 28mm front and 21mm rear anti-roll bars; P215.60R14 tires on newly designed body-color aluminum wheels; revised "clean-look" neutral density taillights incorporating back-up lights; wheel opening flares; new and larger body aero skirting; leather-covered sport steering wheel; shift lever and parking brake; rally instrumentation (including tachometer); cruise control; and split rear seat backs. As a prelude to 1990, Pontiac announced plans to build just 200 special Grand Am SEs equipped with a 2.3-liter Twin Cam 16-valve High Output four-cylinder engine linked to a manual transaxle. Pontiac suggested that these cars, scheduled to be built late in the model-year, would enable the division to gain experience with the car in the marketplace prior to its scheduled production in 1990.

LEMANS — SERIES 2T — (FOUR) — For 1989, the LeMans continued the sporty, fun-to-dive character of Pontiac's smallest performer initially introduced in June of 1987. Featuring distinctive European styling and engineering by GM's Adam Opel subsidiary in West Germany and assembly by Daewoo Motor Co. in South Korea, all LeMans models offered high quality in an affordably priced compact that returned the best fuel economy figures in the Pontiac lineup. All five LeMans models featured fuel-injected engines, front-wheel-drive, power-assisted front disc brakes, rack-and-pinion steering, and a clean, wind-cheating aero design. Front suspension was by MacPherson struts with anti-roll bar. Rear suspension was by semi-independent torsion beam and coil springs, with trailing arms and an anti-roll bar. The LeMans Value Leader

Aerocoupe featured a 1.6-liter 74-hp EFI engine, four-speed manual transaxle, fully reclining seats, and a fold-down rear seat back. The next-step-up LeMans SE was offered in Aerocoupe and sedan models. Both had the base engine, but with a five-speed manual transaxle. The brakes were 8.9-in. solid discs up front. The suspension used 20mm front and 18mm rear anti-roll bars. Also standard was tinted glass and a Delco AM/FM radio with clock. Swing-out rear windows were featured on the Aerocoupe, while the sedan had roll-down rear door glass. The Aerocoupe also came with interior door map pockets and a tachometer. A three-speed automatic transmission, power steering, and air conditioning were available. The LeMans SE offered a 2.0-liter OHC engine, a five-speed manual transaxle, larger tires and wheels, tilt steering, a tachometer, a black air dam, and integral fog lamps. It had larger 10-in. vented disc brakes. The front seats had height adjusters, while the 60/40 split rear seat had fold-down seat backs. On the top of the LeMans lineup was the GSE. It added or substituted body-color cast alloy wheels, semi-metallic brake pads, even larger 10.1-in. front disc brakes, a sport suspension, and 18.3:1 power steering. The GSE also had an exterior aero fascia, rocker extensions, a body-color rear deck lid spoiler, and integrated fog lights. Found at the rear were unique GSE turn signal lenses. A three-spoke steering wheel and full instrumentation (with tachometer) were also included.

SUNBIRD — SERIES 2J — (FOUR) — The 1989 Pontiac Sunbird was an aggressively styled, sporty, affordable American car designed to compete head-on with small domestic and imported sedans and sport coupes. Five models were offered and new features across the line included deflected-disc front struts for improved handling, a redesigned instrument panel, a Grand Prix type steering wheel, a Delco Advanced Radio Concept (ARC) sound system, a redesigned console and parking brake lever, and three-point rear seat and shoulder belts. A compact digital disc player was a new option. All models also featured plastisol protection against nicks for lower body paint and clearcoat finishes. The most affordable Sunbird models were the LE Sport Coupe and LE Sport Sedan. Both had a completely restyled front end including new lower hood and fender profiles, fascia, grille, front and side marker lamps, and composite headlights for a sleeker, sportier look and better aerodynamics. A large protective side molding wrapped around the LE Sport Coupe. Sunbird LE models used 22mm front stabilizer bars and the suspension was refined for improved handling without ride degradation. The middle line was the Sunbird SE. It included only a sport coupe. Its standard features included a front with partially hidden headlights and rally instrumentation. The top-of-the-line Sunbird GT coupe and convertible featured a turbocharged four-cylinder engine, a special performance suspension (with 28mm front and 19mm rear stabilizer bars), higher-rate springs, fatter tires, and a quicker 14:1 steering ratio. Sunbird GT styling emphasized sportiness with wheel flares, aero-style covers over the partly hidden headlights and standard fog lamps. Two-tone paint with a unique body stripe was available in Black over Silver, Black over Red, and Black over Bright Blue. Also included was rally instrumentation.

6000 — SERIES 2A — (I-4/V-6) — The Pontiac 6000 line for 1989 provided a complete selection of mid-size cars that catered to a variety of driving needs from the fully-equipped STE all-wheel-drive (AWD) model to solid transportation in the 6000 sedan and Safari

1989 Pontiac 600 STE four-door AWD sedan. (PGMC)

wagon. Five models were offered in all. The 6000 sedans had a new appearance with the roofline, upper rear quarter, and trunk lid all restyled. There was a revised taillight treatment and a new rounded backlight (rear window). All 6000 LE and SE models had a six-light front appearance including integrated fog lamps. All 6000s had a two-stage basecoat/clearcoat paint system. Three-point rear seat and shoulder belts were standard on all models. Base models were the LE sedan and Safari. The 2.5-liter engine was now standard equipment, along with a three-speed automatic transaxle (four-speed automatic transaxle in Safaris), a suspension with 22mm front and 20mm rear anti-roll bars, and P185/75R14 tires. The 6000 SE also came as a four-door sedan or Safari. Both had a standard 2.8-liter V-6, a four-speed automatic transaxle, a radial tuned suspension, larger tires, aluminum sport wheels, and front disc/rear drum brakes. Electronic ride control was included for SE Safari wagons. The SE exteriors were enhanced by body-color front grilles and body side moldings. Also standard was cruise control, controlled cycle wipers, power windows, power door locks, an AM/FM stereo cassette radio, and a leather-wrapped four-spoke tilt steering wheel. The 6000 STE was replaced by the 6000 STE AWD model, which came only as a four-door sedan. It was GM's first all-wheel-drive production car. The AWD system provided improved driving safety and security, increased mobility in low-traction conditions, and improved overall handling and performance. The difference could be seen in the AWD's improved acceleration, traction, and high-speed stability. No driver action was required to activate the automatic all-wheel-drive system. An electro-mechanical center differential locking system was provided for extreme conditions and could be activated by a console-mounted switch. Activating the switch ensured drive power to at least one wheel on the front and rear of the vehicle. A planetary center differential provided a 60 percent front/40 percent rear drive torque split. The STE AWD was the first mass-produced car to be powered by a high-torque, transverse V-6 and automatic transaxle. It had fully independent front and rear suspensions with electronic ride control. At the front, new outer steering links were used, along with a new (27mm) anti-roll bar. At the rear a thick (22mm) anti-roll bar was used in combination with a composite transverse leaf spring. Four-wheel-disc anti-lock brakes were standard, as was quicker-ratio steering. The P195/70R15 Goodyear Eagle GT+4 tires were mounted on specific cast aluminum wheels with gold ports. The STE AWD was available only in two monochromatic paint schemes: Medium Red Metallic and Dark Blue Metallic. The model also had body-color bumpers, aero moldings, a new deck lid spoiler, body color mirrors, and new fog lamps. Inside the standard radio/cassette with graphic equalizer featured controls in the center of the new four-spoke leather-wrapped tilt steering wheel. A power driver's seat with lumbar support, power windows, power door locks, and cruise control were standard. An on-board inflator system was mounted in the trunk.

I.D. DATA: Pontiac's 17-symbol Vehicle Identification Number (VIN) was on the upper left surface of the instrument panel, visible through the windshield. The first symbol indicates country of origin: 1=U.S.; 2= Canada; J=Japan; K=Korea; 3=Mexico. The second symbol indicates manufacturer: G=General Motors; G=Suzuki; 8=Isuzu;

1989 Pontiac Grand Prix SE two-door coupe. (PGMC)

1989 Pontiac Grand Prix two-door coupe. (PGMC)

Y=NUMMI and L=Daewoo. The third symbol G indicates make: 2=Pontiac division. The fourth and fifth symbols indicate body type and series: A/E=6000 SE; A/F=6000; A/G=6000 LE; A/H=6000 STE; B/L=Safari; F/S=Firebird; F/W=Firebird Trans Am; H/X=Bonneville LE; HY=Bonneville SSE; H/Z=Bonneville SE; J/B=Sunbird; J/D=Sunbird SE; J/U=Sunbird GT; M/R=Firefly (U.S. Customs Territories); N/E=Grand Am; N/W=Grand Am SE; T/N=LeMans; T/R=LeMans SE; T/S=LeMans GSE; T/X=LeMans Aero Coupe; W/J=Grand Prix; W/K=Grand Prix LE; W/P=Grand Prix SE. The sixth symbol denotes body type: 1=two-door coupe/sedan styles 11, 27, 37, 47, 57, 97; 2=two-door hatchback styles 07, 08, 77 and 87; 3=two-door convertible style 67; 5=four-door sedan styles 19 and 69; 6=four-door hatchback style 68; 8=four-door station wagon style 35. the seventh symbol indicates restraint system: 1=manual belts; 3=manual belts with driver's airbag; 4=automatic belts. Symbol eight is an engine code: A=2.3-liter U.S.-built fuel-inject I-4; C=3.8-liter U.S.-built fuel-injected V-6; D=2.3-liter U.S.-built fuel-injected I-4; E=5.0-liter U.S./Canada-built fuel-injected V-8; F=5.0-liter U.S.-built fuel-injected V-8; K=2.0-liter U.S.-built fuel-injected I-4; M=2.0-liter U.S.-built fuel-injected I-4; R=2.5-liter U.S.-built fuel-injected I-4; S=2.8-liter Mexico-built fuel-injected V-6; T=3.1-liter Mexico-built fuel-injected V-6; U=2.5-liter U.S.-built fuel-injected I-4; V=3.1-liter U.S.-built FI V-6; W=2.8-liter U.S./Canada/Mexico-built fuel-injected V-6; Y=5.0-liter U.S.-built four-barrel V-8; 6=1.6-liter Korean-built fuel-injected I-4; 7=3.8-liter U.S.-built fuel-injected V-6; 8=5.7-liter U.S.-built fuel-injected V-8. Next is a check digit. The tenth symbol denotes model year (K=1989). The 11th symbol indicates the GM assembly plant (B=Baltimore, Md. T&B; B=Lansing, Mich.; B=Pupyong, Korea; C=Lansing, Mich.; D=Doraville, Ga.; E=Linden, N.J.; E=Pontiac East, Mich. T&B; F=Fairfax II, Kan.; F=Flint T&B; G=Framingham, Mass.; H=Flint, Mich.; J=Janesville, Wis.; K=Leeds, Mo.; K=Kosai, Japan; L=Van Nuys, Calif.; M=Lansing, Mich; P=Pontiac, Mich.; R=Arlington, Texas; S=Ramos Arizpe, Mexico; T=Tarrytown, N.Y.; U=Hamtramck, Mich; V=Pontiac, Mich. (T&B); W=Willow Run, Mich.; W=Iwata, Japan; X=Fairfax I, Kansas; Y=Wilmington, Del.; Z=Fremont, Calif.; Z=Ft. Wayne, Ind. T&B; 0= Pontiac, Mich. (T&B); 1=Oshawa, Canada #2; 1=Wentzville, Mo. T&B; 2=Morraine, OH T&B; 2=Ste. Therese, Canada; 3=Detroit, Mich. T&B; 3=Kawasaki, Japan; 4=Orion, Mich.; 4=Scarborough, Ontario, Canada; 5=Bowling Green, Ken.; 5=London, Ontario, Canada; 6=Oklahoma City, Okla.; 7=Lordstown, Ohio; 7=Flusawa, Japan; 8=Shreveport, La. T&B; 9=Oshawa, Ontario, Canada #1. Pontiacs are not produced at all of these GM plants. The last six symbols are the consecutive unit number at the factory.

Model Number	Body Style Number	Body Type & Seating	Factory Price	Shipping Weight	Production Total
SAFARI SERIES 2L (V-8)					
2L	BL8	4d Sta Wagon-8P	15,659	4,109	Note 1
BONNEVILLE LE SERIES H/X (V-6)					
2H	HX5	4d Sport Sedan-5P	14,829	3,275	Note 2
BONNEVILLE SE SERIES H/Z (V-6)					
2H	HZ5	4d Sport Sedan-5P	17,199	3,327	Note 2
BONNEVILLE SSE SERIES H/Y5 (V-6)					
2H	HZ5/Y80	4d Sport Sedan-5P	22,899	3,481	Note 2
GRAND PRIX SERIES 2W (V-6/V-8)					
2G	WJ1	2d Coupe-5P	13,899	3,167	Note 3
GRAND PRIX LE SERIES 2W (V-6/V-8)					
2G	WK1	2d Coupe-5P	14,949	3,188	Note 3
GRAND PRIX SE SERIES 2W (V-6/V-8)					
2G	WP1	2d Coupe-5P	15,999	3,217	Note 3

1989 Pontiac Bonneville SSE four-door sedan. (PGMC)

Model Number	Body Style Number	Body Type & Seating	Factory Price	Shipping Weight	Production Total
FIREBIRD SERIES F/S (V-6)					
2F	FS2	2d Coupe-5P	11,999	3,083	Note 4
FIREBIRD SERIES F/S (V-8)					
2F	FS2	2d Coupe-5P	12,399	3,300	Note 4
FIREBIRD FORMULA SERIES F/S (V-8)					
2F	FS2	2d Coupe-5P	13,949	3,318	Note 4
FIREBIRD TRANS AM SERIES F/W (V-8)					
2F	FW2	2d Coupe-5P	15,999	3,337	Note 4
FIREBIRD TRANS AM GTA SERIES F/W (V-8)					
2F	FW2	2d Coupe-5P	20,399	3,486	Note 4
GRAND AM LE SERIES 2N (I-4/V-6)					
2N	NE1	2d Coupe-5P	10,469	2,508	Note 5
2N	NE5	4d Sedan-5P	10,669	2,592	Note 5
GRAND AM SE-- SERIES 2N (I-4/V-6)					
2N	NW1	2d Coupe-5P	13,599	2,739	Note 5
2N	NW5	4d Sedan-5P	13,799	2,826	Note 5
LEMANS SERIES 2T (I-4)					
LEMANS AEROCOUPE SERIES T/X (I-4)					
2T	TX2	3d Coupe-4P	6,399	2,136	Note 6
LEMANS LE SERIES T/N (I-4)					
2T	TN2	3d Coupe-4P	7,699	2,180	Note 6
2T	TN5	4d Sedan-4P	7,999	2,235	Note 6
LEMANS GSE SERIES T/S (I-4)					
2T	TS2	3d Coupe-4P	9,149	2,302	Note 6
LEMANS SE SERIES T/R (I-4)					
2T	TR5	4d Sedan-4P	9,429	2,357	Note 6
SUNBIRD LE SERIES 2J (I-4)					
2J	JB5	4d Sedan-5P	8,949	2,433	Note 7
2J	JB1	2d Coupe-5P	8,849	2,418	Note 7
SUNBIRD SE SERIES 2J (I-4/I-4 Turbo)					
2J	JD1	2d Coupe-5P	9,099	2,376	Note 7
SUNBIRD GT TURBO SERIES 2J (I-4/I-4 Turbo)					
2J	JU1	2d Coupe-5P	11,399	2,422	Note 7
2J	JU3	2d Convertible-5P	16,899	2,577	Note 7
6000 LE SERIES A/F (I-4)					
2A	AF5	4d Sedan-5P	11,969	2,676	Note 8
6000 LE SERIES A/G (I-4/V-6)					
2A	AG5	4d Sedan-5P	12,579	2,760	Note 8
2A	AG8	4d Safari-5P	13,769	2,897	Note 8
6000 SE SERIES A/E (I-4/V-6)					
2A	AE5	4d Sedan-5P	15,399	2,762	Note 8
2A	AE8	4d Safari-5P	16,699	2,899	Note 8
6000 STE SERIES A/H (I-4/V-6)					
2A	AH5	4d Sedan-5P	22,599	3,381	Note 8

NOTE 1: Safari series production totaled 5,146 cars.

NOTE 2: Bonneville series production totaled 108,653 cars.

NOTE 3: Grand Prix series production totaled 136,747 cars.

NOTE 4: Firebird series production totaled 64,406 cars.

NOTE 5: Grand Am series production totaled 246,418 cars.

NOTE 6: LeMans series production totaled 44,641 cars.

NOTE 7: Sunbird series production totaled 139,644 cars.

NOTE 8: Pontiac 6000 series production totaled 100,586 cars.

SAFARI ENGINE

ENGINE [Base V-8]: V-block. OHV. Eight-cylinder. Cast-iron block. Displacement: 307 cid. (5.0L). Bore & stroke: 3.80 x 3.39 in. Compression ratio: 8.0:1. Brake horsepower: 140 at 3200 rpm. Torque: 255 lbs.-ft. at 2000 rpm. Fuel system: Four-barrel carburetor. RPO Code: LV2. Standard V-8 in all Safaris. [VIN code Y].

BONNEVILLE ENGINE

ENGINE [Base Six (LE/SE/SSE)]: V-block. OHV. "3800" six-cylinder. Cast-iron block and head. Aluminum intake manifold. Displacement:

231 cid. (3.8L). Bore & stroke: 3.80 x 3.40 in. Compression ratio: 8.5:1. Brake horsepower: 165 at 5200 rpm. Torque: 210 lbs.-ft. at 2000 rpm. Fuel system: SFI. RPO Code: LN3. Standard in Bonneville LE/SE/SSE model. [VIN code W, S, or 9].

GRAND PRIX ENGINES

ENGINE [Base Six]: V-block. OHV. Six-cylinder. Cast-iron block and aluminum head. Displacement: 173 cid. (2.8L). Bore & stroke: 3.50 x 2.99 in. Compression ratio: 8.9:1. Brake horsepower: 130 at 4500 rpm. Torque: 170 lbs.-ft. at 3600 rpm. Fuel system: EFI/MPI. RPO Code: LB6. Standard in Grand Prix. Produced in U.S., Canada, or Mexico. [VIN code W, S, or 9].

ENGINE [Optional Six]: V-block. OHV. Six-cylinder. Cast-iron block and aluminum head. Displacement: 191 cid. (3.1L). Bore & stroke: 3.50 x 3.31 in. Compression ratio: 8.8:1. Brake horsepower: 140 at 4500 rpm. Torque: 185 lbs.-ft. at 3600 rpm. Fuel system: EFI/MPI. RPO Code: LHO. Standard in Grand Prix with four-speed automatic transaxles after midyear. Not available with three-speed automatic. [VIN code T].

ENGINE [Optional Six]: V-block. OHV. Six-cylinder. Turbo. Cast-iron block and aluminum head. Displacement: 191 cid. (3.1L). Bore & stroke: 3.50 x 3.31 in. Compression ratio: 8.65:1. Brake horsepower: 205 at 4800 rpm. Torque: 220 lbs.-ft. at 3200 rpm. Fuel system: EFI/MPI. RPO Code: LHO with LG5 American Sun Roof Corp. (ASC)/McLaren Turbo conversion. [VIN code T].

FIREBIRD ENGINES

ENGINE [Base V-6]: V-block. OHV. Six-cylinder. Cast-iron block and head. Aluminum intake manifold. Displacement: 173 cid. (2.8L). Bore & stroke: 3.50 x 2.99 in. Compression ratio: 8.5:1. Brake horsepower: 135 at 4900 rpm. Torque: 160 lbs.-ft. at 3900 rpm. Fuel system: EFI/TBI. RPO Code: LB8. Standard in base Firebird. Produced in U.S., Canada, or Mexico. [VIN code W, S, or 9].

ENGINE [Base V-8]: V-block. OHV. Eight-cylinder. Cast-iron block and head. Aluminum intake manifold. Displacement: 305 cid. (5.0L). Bore & stroke: 3.74 x 3.48 in. Brake horsepower: 170 at 4000 rpm. Torque: 255 lbs.-ft. at 2400 rpm. Compression ratio: 9.3:1. Fuel system: EFI/TBI. RPO Code: L03. Produced in U.S. or Canada. Standard Formula and Trans Am. Available in base Firebird. [VIN code E or F].

ENGINE [Optional V-8]: V-block. OHV. Eight-cylinder. Cast-iron block and head. Aluminum intake manifold. Displacement: 305 cid. (5.0L). Bore & stroke: 3.74 x 3.48 in. Brake horsepower: 190 at 4000 rpm (automatic) or 225 at 4400 rpm (manual/dual exhausts). Torque: 295 lbs.-ft. at 2800 rpm (automatic) or 285 lbs.-ft. at 3200 rpm (manual). Compression ratio: 9.3:1. Fuel system: TPI. RPO Code: LB9. Available with five-speed manual in Formula and Trans Am (delete option in GTA). Available with four-speed automatic in same applications. [VIN code E or F].

ENGINE [GTA V-8]: V-block. OHV. Eight-cylinder. Cast-iron block and head. Aluminum intake manifold. Displacement: 350 cid. (5.7L). Bore & stroke: 4.00 x 3.48 in. Brake horsepower: 235 at 4400 rpm. Torque: 330 lbs.-ft. at 3200 rpm. Compression ratio: 9.3:1. Fuel system: EFI/TPI. RPO Code: B2L. Standard with four-speed automatic in GTA (optional in Formula and Trans Am). Includes low-profile air induction system with aluminum plenum and individual aluminum tuned runners, an extruded dual fuel rail assembly with computer controlled fuel injectors and a special low-restriction single exhaust system. [VIN code 8].

1989 Pontiac Firebird two-door coupe. (PGMC)

ENGINE [Standard Indy Pace Car Turbo V-6]: V-block. Garrett T3 turbocharger. OHV. Six-cylinder. Cast-iron block and head. Aluminum intake manifold. Displacement: 231 cid. (3.8L). Bore & stroke: 3.80 x 3.40 in. Brake horsepower: 250 at 4400 rpm. Torque: 340 lbs.-ft. at 2800 rpm. Compression ratio: 8.0:1. Fuel system: EFI/SFI. RPO Code: LG3. Standard in 20th Anniversary Trans Am Indy Pace Car. [VIN code W, S, or 9].

GRAND AM ENGINES

ENGINE [Standard LE]: Inline. OHV. Cast-iron block and head. Aluminum intake manifold. Displacement: 151 cid. (2.5L Tech IV). Bore & stroke: 4.00 x 3.00 in. Compression ratio: 9.0:1. Brake horsepower: 110 at 5200 rpm. Torque: 135 lbs.-ft. at 3200 rpm. Five main bearings. Hydraulic valve lifters. Fuel system: EFI. RPO Code: L68. Standard in Grand Am LE. [VIN code U/R].

ENGINE [Standard SE]: Inline. OHC. Turbocharged (Garret T2.5 turbocharger). Cast-iron block. Aluminum head and intake manifold. Displacement: 2.0-liter Turbo. Bore & stroke: 3.39 x 3.39 in. Compression ratio: 8.0:1. Brake horsepower: 165 at 5600 rpm. Torque: 175 lbs.-ft. at 4000 rpm. Fuel system: MPFI. RPO Code: LT3. Standard in Grand Am SE, not available in Grand Am LE. [VIN code M].

ENGINE [Optional LE/SE]: Inline. DOHC. 16-Valve. Four-cylinder. Cast-iron block. Aluminum head and intake manifold. Displacement: 140 cid. (2.3L MFI). Quad 4 16-valve. Bore & stroke: 3.62 x 3.35 in. Compression ratio: 9.5:1. Brake horsepower: 150 at 5200 rpm. Torque: 160 lbs.-ft. at 4400 rpm. Fuel system: MPFI. RPO Code: LD2. Optional in Grand Am LE and delete-option in Grand Am SE. [VIN code D].

ENGINE [Optional SE]: Inline. DOHC. Quad IV HO. 16-Valve. Four-cylinder. Cast-iron block. Aluminum head and intake manifold. Displacement: 140 cid. (2.3L MFI High Output). Quad 4 16-valve. Bore & stroke: 3.62 x 3.35 in. Compression ratio: 10.0:1. Brake horsepower: 180 at 6200 rpm. Torque: 155 lbs.-ft. at 5200 rpm. Fuel system: MPFI. RPO Code: LD2. Optional in SE. [VIN code A].

LEMANS ENGINES

ENGINE [Base Four (VL/LE)]: Inline. OHV. Four-cylinder. Cast-iron block. Aluminum head and intake manifold. Displacement: 97.5 cid. (1.6L). Bore & stroke: 3.11 x 3.21 in. Compression ratio: 8.6:1. Brake horsepower: 74 at 5600 rpm. Torque: 90 lbs.-ft. at 2800 rpm. Fuel system: EFI/TBI. RPO Code: L73. Standard with four-speed manual Value Leader and LeMans LE. [VIN code 6].

ENGINE [Base Four (SE/GSE)]: Inline. OHC. Four-cylinder. Cast-iron block. Aluminum head and intake manifold. Displacement: 121 cid. (2.0L). Bore & stroke: 3.39 x 3.39 in. Compression ratio: 8.8:1. Brake horsepower: 95 at 4800 rpm. Torque: 118 lbs.-ft. at 3600 rpm. Fuel system: EFI/TBI. RPO Code: LT2. Standard with five-speed manual LeMans SE and GSE models. [VIN code K].

SUNBIRD ENGINES

ENGINE [Base Four (LE/SE)]: Inline. OHC. Four-cylinder. Cast-iron block. Aluminum head and intake manifold. Displacement: 121 cid. (2.0L). Bore & stroke: 3.39 x 3.39 in. Compression ratio: 8.8:1. Brake horsepower: 96 at 4800 rpm. Torque: 118 lbs.-ft. at 3600 rpm. Fuel system: EFI/TBI. RPO Code: LT2. Standard in Sunbird LE and Sunbird SE models. [VIN code K].

ENGINE [Base Four (GT)]: Inline. OHC. Four-cylinder. Turbocharged (Garrett T2.5 turbocharger). Cast-iron block. Aluminum head and intake manifold. Displacement: 121 cid. (2.0L). Bore & stroke: 3.39 x 3.39 in. Compression ratio: 8.0:1. Brake horsepower: 165 at 5600 rpm. Torque: 175 lbs.-ft. at 4000 rpm. Fuel system: MPFI with Turbo. RPO Code: LT3. Standard in Sunbird Turbo GT (optional in Sunbird SE Sport Coupe and Sunbird SE Sport Sedan). [VIN code M].

6000 ENGINES

ENGINE [Base Four]: Inline. OHV. Four-cylinder. Cast-iron block and head. Aluminum intake manifold. Displacement: 151 cid. (2.5L Tech IV). Bore & stroke: 4.00 x 3.00 in. Compression ratio: 9.0:1. Brake horsepower: 98 at 4800 rpm. Torque: 135 lbs.-ft. at 3200 rpm. Five main bearings. Hydraulic valve lifters. Fuel system: EFI/TBI. RPO Code: LR8. Standard in 6000 LE. [VIN code U].

ENGINE [Optional Six]: V-block. OHV. Six-cylinder. Cast-iron block. Aluminum head and intake manifold. Displacement: 173 cid. (2.8L). Bore & stroke: 3.50 x 2.99 in. Compression ratio: 8.91. Brake horsepower: 130 at 4500 rpm. Torque: 17 lbs.-ft. at 3600 rpm. Fuel system: EFI. RPO Code: LB6. Standard in 6000 SE. [VIN code W, S, or 9].

1989 Pontiac Sunbird GT two-door convertible. (PGMC)

ENGINE [Base Six (STE-AWD)]: V-block. OHV. Six-cylinder. Cast-iron block. Aluminum head and intake manifold. Displacement: 191 cid. (3.1L). Bore & stroke: 3.50 x 3.31in. Brake horsepower: 135 at 4800 rpm. Torque: 180 lbs.-ft. at 3600 rpm. Fuel system: EFI. RPO Code: LHO. Standard in 6000 STE AWD. [VIN code T].

CHASSIS

SAFARI CHASSIS: Wheelbase: 116.0 in. (all). Overall length: 215.1 in. (all). Width: 79.3 in. (all). Height: 57.4 in. (all). Front tread: 60.3 in. Rear tread: 59.8 in. Tires: P225/75R15.

BONNEVILLE CHASSIS: Wheelbase: 110.8 in. (all). Overall length: 198.7 in. (all). Width: 72.1 in. (all). Height: 55.5 in. (all). Front tread: 60.3 in. Rear tread: 59.8 in. Standard tires: 205/75R14 BSW (LE). Standard tires: 215/65R15 Goodyear Eagle GT+4 (SE). Standard tires: P215/60R16 BSW (SSE).

GRAND PRIX CHASSIS: Wheelbase: 107.5 in. (all). Overall length: 193.9 in. (all). Width: 70.9 in. (all). Height: 53.3 in. (all). Front tread: 59.5 in. Rear tread: 58.0 in. Standard tires: 195/75R14 (base and LE). Standard tires: 215/60R15 Goodyear Eagle GT (SE). Standard tires: P245/50ZR16 (ASC/McLaren Turbo).

FIREBIRD CHASSIS: Wheelbase: 101.0 in. (all). Overall length: 188.1 in. (Base/Formula); 191.6 in. (Trans Am/GTA). Width: 72.4 in. (all). Height: 50.0 in. (all). Front tread: 60.7 in. Rear tread: 61.6 in. Tires: P215/65R15 Firestone Firehawk FX (Level I). Standard tires: P215/65R15 Firestone Firehawk GTX (Level II). Tire: P245/50ZR16 Goodyear Eagle ZR50 "Gatorback."

GRAND AM CHASSIS: Wheelbase: 103.4 in. (Coupe/sedan). Overall length: 180.1 in. (all). Width: 66.5 in. (all). Height: 52.5 in. (all). Front tread: 55.6 in. Rear tread: 55.2 in. Standard tires: P185/80R13 BSW (LE). Standard tires: P215/60R14 (SE).

LEMANS CHASSIS: Wheelbase: 99.2 in. (all). Overall length: 163.70 in. (three-door); 172.4 in. (four-door). Height: 53.5 in. (Aero-coupe); 53.7 in. (sedan). Standard tires: P175/70R13 BSW (all).

SUNBIRD CHASSIS: Wheelbase: 101.2 in. (all). Overall length: 178.2 in. (Coupe and convertible); 181.7 in. (sedan). Width: 65.0 in. (sedan/convertible); 66.0 in. (Coupe/convertible). Height: 50.4.in. (Coupe); 53.8 in. (sedan); 51.9 in. (convertible). Front tread: 55.6 in. (all). Rear tread: 55.2 in. (all). Standard tires: P185/80R13 BSW (LE). Standard tires: P195/70R14 (SE). Standard tires: P215/60R14 Eagle GT+4 (GT). Optional tires with WS6 special performance suspension: P215/60R14 Goodyear Eagle GT+4.

6000 CHASSIS: Wheelbase: 104.9 in. (all). Overall length: 188.8 in. (sedan); 193.2 in. (Safari). Width: 72.0 in. (all). Height: 53.7 in. (sedan); 54.1 in. (Safari). Front tread: 58.7 in. Rear tread: 57.0 in. Standard Tires: 185/75R14 (LE). Standard tires: 195/70R14 Goodyear Eagle GT+4 (SE and STE FWD).

TECHNICAL

SAFARI TECHNICAL: Chassis: Front engine/rear drive. Base transmission: Four-speed automatic. Axle ratio: 3.31:1 (SSE interim). Axle ratio: 2.97:1 (SE). Axle ratio: 2.84:1 (LE). Front suspension: Control arms with coil springs. Rear suspension: Live axle, links and coil springs. Front brakes: Power-assisted vented discs. Rear brakes: Power-assisted drums. Fuel tank: 22.0 gal.

BONNEVILLE TECHNICAL: Chassis: Front engine/front drive. Base transmission: Four-speed automatic. Axle ratio: 2.73:1 (standard with 3.8L V-6 in Base Bonneville and Bonneville SE). Axle ratio: 2.97:1 (standard with 3.8L V-6 in Bonneville SE/SSE). Front suspension: MacPherson struts with 20N-mm coil springs and 30mm anti-roll bar (LE). Front suspension: MacPherson struts with 28N-mm coil springs and 32mm anti-roll bar (SE). Front suspension: MacPherson struts with 24N-mm coil springs and 32mm anti-roll bar (SSE). Rear suspension: MacPherson struts with variable rate (48-65 N-mm) coil springs and 14mm anti-roll bar (LE). Rear suspension: MacPherson struts with variable rate (55-75 N-mm) coil springs and 18mm anti-roll bar (SE). Rear suspension: MacPherson struts with 47 N-mm coil springs and 18mm anti-roll bar (SSE). Steering: Power-assisted rack-and-pinion with 18.0:1 constant ratio, 2.97 turns lock-to-lock and 12.1-ft. left/11.9-ft. right turning circle (LE/SE). Steering: Power-assisted rack-and-pinion with 15.3-19.0:1 variable ratio, 2.79 turns lock-to-lock and 11.7-ft. left/12.4-ft. right turning circle (SSE). Front brakes: Power-assisted 10.1-in. vented discs. Rear brakes: Power-assisted 8.9-in. drums. Anti-lock brake system standard with SSE. Fuel tank: 18.0 gal.

GRAND PRIX TECHNICAL: Chassis: Front engine/front drive. Standard drivetrain: 2.8L V-6 with five-speed manual transaxle or (midyear) 3.1L V-6 with four-speed automatic transaxle. Optional drivetrain: 3.1L ASC/McLaren Turbo V-6 with four-speed automatic transaxle. Axle ratio: 3.41:1 (2.8L with manual); 3.33:1 (2.3L, 3.1L with automatic and 3.1L ASC/McLaren Turbo). Front suspension: MacPherson struts with tapered top coil springs, lower A arm and 28mm anti-roll bar (30mm anti-roll bar with Y99 suspension). Rear suspension: Tri-link independent suspension with 12mm anti-roll bar (transverse fiberglass leaf spring and 12mm anti-roll bar with Y99 option). Steering: Power-assisted rack-and-pinion with 14.0:1 ratio, 2.25 turns lock-to-lock and 39.7-ft. turning circle (interim) or 15.7:1 ratio, 2.89 turns lock-to-lock, and 37.4-ft. turning circle. Four-wheel power disc brakes. Front brakes: 10.5-in. composite vented discs. Rear brakes: 10.1-in. composite solid discs. Fuel tank: 16.0 gal.

FIREBIRD TECHNICAL: Chassis: Front engine/rear drive. Base transmission: Five-speed manual. Optional transmission: Four-speed automatic. Front suspension: Fully independent with modified MacPherson strut and low-friction ball bearing upper strut mount and 30mm (Level I) or 34mm (Level II), or 36mm (Level III) anti-roll bar. Rear suspension: Live axle with coil springs, longitudinal lower control arm and torque arm, transverse track bar and 18mm (Level I) or 23mm (Level II) or 24mm (Level III) anti-roll bar. Steering: Power re-circulating ball; 14.1:1 ratio (Level I), or 12.7:1 quick ratio with sport effort valving (Levels II and III). Turns lock-to-lock: 2.72 (Level I), 2.47 (Level II), or 2.26 (Level III). Turning circle: 39.1 ft. (Level I) or 32.6 ft. (Levels II and III). Brakes: Power vented 10.5-in. front disc/9.5-in. rear drum on Coupes and Formula with 5,0L EFI; power four-wheel vented disc 10.5-in. front/11.7-in. rear with 5.7L or 5.0L with TPI and five-speed on GTA or Formula-assisted vented discs. Rear brakes: Power-assisted 7.87-in. drums. Fuel tank: 13.6 gal.

GRAND AM TECHNICAL: Chassis: Front engine/front drive. Base transmission: Five-speed manual with overdrive. Optional transmission: Three-speed automatic. Axle ratio: 3.35:1 (with 2.5L engine and manual). Axle ratio: 3.61:1 (with 2.0L engine and manual or 2.3L engine and manual). Axle ratio: 2.84:1 (with 2.3L and automatic or 2.5L and automatic). Axle ratio: 3.18:1 (with 2.0L and automatic. Stall torque ratio: 2.48:1 (with automatic). Front suspension: MacPherson struts with coil springs and 24mm anti-roll bar (28mm anti-roll bar with WS6 suspension). Rear suspension: Trailing crank arm with twist arm, coil springs and 21mm anti-roll bar. Steering: Power-assisted rack-and-pinion, 16.1:1 ratio, 2.88 turns lock-to-lock and 35.4-ft. (left); 37.8-ft. (right) turning circle. Front brakes:

Power-assisted 9.72-in. vented discs. Rear brakes: Power-assisted 7.87-in. drums. Fuel tank: 13.6 gal.

LEMANS TECHNICAL: Chassis: Front engine/front drive. Base transmission: Four-speed manual. Optional transmission: Three-speed automatic or five-speed manual. Axle ratio: 3.43:1 with 1.6L and automatic. Axle ratio: 3.18:1 with 2.0L and three-speed automatic. Axle ratio: 3.72:1 with 1.6L and four-speed manual; or either engine and five-speed manual. Front suspension: deflected disc, MacPherson struts, and (20mm with 1.6L/22mm with 2.0L) stabilizer bars. Rear suspension: Coil springs, semi-independent torsion beam, trailing arms, and 18mm anti-roll bar. Steering: Rack-and-pinion 24.5:1 ratio (18.3:1 power-assisted on GTE). Turns lock-to-lock: 3.5 (power); 4.57 (manual). Turning circle: 32.8 ft. Front brakes: 9.25-in. solid discs (1.6L) or 10.1-in. vented disc (2.0L) power-assisted. Rear brakes: 7.9 x 1.8 -in. drum (both engines) power-assisted.

SUNBIRD TECHNICAL: Chassis: Front engine/front drive. Base transmission: Five-speed manual. Optional transmission: Three-speed automatic. Axle ratio: 3.45:1 with base engine and five-speed manual. Axle ratio: 3.18:1 with 2.0L TBI engine and three-speed automatic. Axle ratio: 3.61:1 with 1.6L with 2.0L Turbo and five-speed manual. Front suspension: deflected disc, MacPherson struts and (22mm with 2.0L TBI/28mm with 2.0L Turbo) stabilizer bars. Rear suspension: Coil springs, semi-independent torsion beam, trailing arms (and 18mm anti-roll bar with 2.0L Turbo). Steering: Rack-and-pinion 16.0:1 ratio. Turns lock-to-lock: 2.88. Turning circle: 34.3 ft. Front brakes: 9.72-in. vented disc power-assisted. Rear brakes: 7.87 x 1.77-in. drum power-assisted.

6000 TECHNICAL: Chassis: Front engine/front drive. Base transmission: Three-speed automatic with overdrive. Optional transmissions: Four-speed automatic. Axle ratio: 2.84:1 (with three-speed automatic and 2.5L or 2.8L engines). Axle ratio: 3.33:1 (with four-speed automatic with 2.8L engine). Axle ratio: 3.42:1 (with four-speed automatic and 3.1L engine). Front suspension: MacPherson struts with 22mm (LE), 28mm (SE), or 27mm (STE AWD). Rear suspension: Independent, transverse composite leaf spring and 22mm anti-roll bar (STE AWD); or trailing arms and track bar, Panhard rod, coil springs and 22mm anti-roll bar (SE), 20mm anti-roll bar standard. Steering: Power-assisted rack-and-pinion with 17.5:1 ratio, 3.05 turns lock-to-lock and 36.96-ft. turning circle. Front brakes: Power assisted vented discs 9.72-in. (standard); 10.24-in. (medium-/heavy-duty), 10.2-in. (STE). Rear brakes: Power assisted 8.86-in. drum (standard); 8.86-in. drum (medium-/heavy-duty), 10.3-in solid discs (STE). Fuel tank: 15.7-gal.

OPTIONS

SAFARI OPTIONS: 1SA option package #1 ($412). 1SB option package #2 ($1,474). V08 heavy-duty cooling system ($40). C49 electric rear window defogger ($150). NB2 California emissions system ($100). U39 instrument cluster with gauges and trip odometer ($71). V55 roof top luggage carrier with rear air deflector ($155). AU3 power door locks, includes tailgate lock ($255). A31 power windows ($295) UM7 AM/FM ETR stereo system ($122). UX1 Delco sound system ($272). U75 power antenna ($70). AM6 55/45 split bench seat with Pallex cloth trim ($133). AT6 reclining passenger seat with AM6 only ($45). G66 Superlift shock absorbers ($64). N94 simulated wire wheel covers with locking package ($230). BX3 simulated exterior woodgrain siding, includes door edge moldings and wood-toned body side moldings ($345).

BONNEVILLE OPTIONS: 1SA Bonneville LE option package #1 ($259). 1SB Bonneville LE option package #2 ($444). 1SC Bonneville LE option package #3 ($1,365). 1SA Bonneville SE option package #1 ($284). 1SB Bonneville SE option package #2 ($695). 1SC Bonneville SE option package #3 ($1,183). R6A Bonneville LE value option package ($474). R6A Bonneville SE value option package. ($327). C49 electric rear window defogger ($150). NB2 California emissions system ($100). UB3 gauge cluster ($100). V56 deck lid luggage carrier ($115). D84 two-tone paint ($105). JM4 power anti-lock brakes ($925). AU3 power door locks ($205). A31 power windows ($365). UM6 Delco radio equipment ($122). UT4 radio equipment package ($550-$722). U1A compact disc player ($754-$876). UW6 six-speaker performance sound system ($100). US7 power antenna ($70). A78 custom interior in LE ($70). A65 notchback seat with custom trim in LE ($133). AS7 custom interior trim with split bench seat and console ($235). B20 custom interior with 45/55 split seat in Empress/London cloth trim ($120-$618) depending on value

1989 Pontiac Grand Am LE four-door sedan. (PGMC)

1989 Pontiac Firebird Trans Am Indy 500 pace car. (PGMC)

package options or individual option). CF5 power glass sunroof ($1,284). Various tire options ($48-$164). QNS Y99 rally tuned suspension package ($116-$164). PF7 15-in. diamond-spoke wheels with locking package on LE ($296). AL7 45/55 articulating split bench seat with Ventura leather trim on SSE ($679). UA6 anti-theft deterrent system ($15).

GRAND PRIX OPTIONS: 1SA Grand Prix option package #1 ($183). 1SB Grand Prix option package #2 ($423). 1SC Grand Prix option package #3 ($858). 1SA Grand Prix LE option package #1 ($520). 1SB Grand Prix LE option package #2 ($863). 1SC Grand Prix LE option package #3 ($1,139). 1SA Grand Prix SE option package #1 ($455). 1SB Grand Prix SE option package #2 ($898). R6A Grand Prix value option package ($408). R6A Grand Prix LE value option package. ($425). LG5 ASC/McLaren Turbo conversion ($4,888). MX0 four-speed automatic in Grand Prix SE ($640). MM5 five-speed manual transmission in Grand Prix and LE ($615 credit). JL9 anti-lock power brakes ($925). C49 electric rear window defogger ($150). DK4 electronic information center ($4,275). NB2 California emissions system ($100). UB3 gauge cluster ($85). V56 deck lid luggage carrier ($115). D84 two-tone paint ($105). AU3 power door locks ($155). CF5 power sunroof ($650-$675). A31 power windows ($230). UM6 Delco radio equipment ($132). UX1 Delco radio equipment ($325-$447). UW4 speakers ($125). U75 power antenna ($70). AM6 40/60 split bench seat with Ripple cloth trim in base Grand Prix ($133). AR9 bucket seats with front console and Ripple cloth trim in base Grand Prix with/without value option package ($60-$193). AR9 bucket seats with front console and Pallex cloth trim in Grand Prix LE ($110). AC9 bucket seats with front console and Ventura leather trim in Grand Prix LE ($450). Various tire options ($48-$72). QGW rally tuned suspension package ($184-$232). PF1 15-in. styled steel wheels, except SE ($145). PH3 15-in. aluminum sport wheels with locking package ($120-$265). NWO 16-in. aluminum sport wheels, with/without value option package ($155-$300). 13P 16-in. bright-faced aluminum sport wheels with locking package for Grand Prix SE (no charge).

FIREBIRD OPTIONS: 1SA Firebird option group #1 ($311). 1SB Firebird option group #2 ($187). 1SA Formula option group #1 ($701). 1SB Formula option group #2 ($517). 1SA Trans Am option group #1 ($701). 1SB Trans Am option group #2 ($552). R6A Trans Am value package ($1,089). R6A Trans Am GTA value package ($1,020). LO3 5.0-liter TBI V-8 engine in base Firebird ($400). LB9 5.0L MPI V-8 in Formula and Trans Am ($745). LB9 5.0L MPI V-8 in Trans Am GTA ($300 credit). B2L 5.7L MPI V-8 in Formula and Trans Am ($1,045). MM5 five-speed manual transmission in Trans Am GTA with LB9 ($490 credit). MX0 four-speed automatic transmission, except in GTA ($515). C60 air conditioning ($795). G80 limited-slip axle ($100). C49 electric rear window defogger ($150). N10 dual converter exhaust ($155). KC4 engine oil cooler ($110). NB2 California emissions ($100). CC1 Hatch roof ($920). TR9 lamp group ($34). D66 deluxe two-tone paint ($150). WX1 lower accent two-tone paint delete on Formulas ($150 credit). J65 power brakes ($179). AU3 power door locks ($155). DG7 power remote sport mirrors ($91). A31 power windows ($250). UM6 Delco radio equipment ($132). UX1 Delco radio equipment ($282). UT4 Delco radio equipment ($315-$447). UA1 Delco radio equipment ($79 in GTA) ($526). U75 power antenna ($70). D42 cargo area security screen ($69). AR9 custom reclining bucket seats with Pallex cloth trim (no

charge). B20 luxury interior with Metrix cloth trim in Trans Am ($293). AQ9 articulating bucket seats with Ventura leather trim in GTA ($450). QLC high-performance WS6 performance suspension ($385). N24 15-in. charcoal deep-dish Hi-Tech Turbo aluminum wheels with locking package on Formula or GTA (no charge). PEO 16-in. deep-dish Hi-Tech Turbo aluminum wheels with locking package on Formula (no charge). PW7 16-in. color-coordinated diamond-spoke aluminum wheels in silver or gold with locking package on Trans Am or GTA only (no charge).

GRAND AM OPTIONS: 1SA Grand Am option group #1 ($876-$1,011 based on trim level and body style). 1SB Grand Am option group ($1,139-$1,350 based on trim level and body style). 1SC Grand Am option group #3 ($1,350 all). 1SD Grand Am option group #4 ($2,072-$2,197 based on trim level and body style). R6A value package ($416). R6B value package ($216). LD 2.3-liter MPI engine ($600 in LE; $108 delete-option in SE). MX1 three-speed automatic transmission ($515). C60 air conditioning ($695). C49 electric rear window defogger ($150). T96 fog lamps for LE only ($97). NB2 California emissions package ($100). UB3 rally cluster gauges and trip odometer in LE ($127). V56 deck lid luggage carrier ($115). D84 custom two-tone paint for LE ($101). D84 custom two-tone paint ($101). AU3 power door locks ($155 Coupe/$205 sedan). A31 power windows, requires custom console in LE ($220 Coupe/$295 sedan). UM6 Delco radio equipment ($122). UX1 Delco radio equipment ($150-$272). U1D Delco radio equipment ($423-$545). UW4 performance sound system ($125). AR9 custom reclining bucket seats with Pallex cloth trim (no charge). A09 articulating bucket seats ($245-$450). B20 custom interior with Metrix cloth in LE only ($119-$269 depending on value option package). AD3 removable glass sunroof ($350). Various tire options ($68-$278 extra). N78 14-in. Hi-Tech Turbo aluminum wheels with locking package ($265).

LEMANS OPTIONS: C60 air conditioning requires power steering and not available in Value Leader Aerocoupe ($660). N40 power steering, requires air conditioning in Aerocoupe or SE sedan ($214). UM7 Delco ETR stereo in Value Leader Aerocoupe ($307). UM6 Delco ETR AM/FM with cassette and more in Value Leader Aerocoupe ($429). UM6 Delco ETR AM/FM with cassette and more in LE/SE/GSE ($122). V54 painted roof luggage rack ($95). AD3 removable sunroof ($350). MX1 three-speed automatic transmission ($420).

SUNBIRD OPTIONS: 1SA Sunbird option group #1 ($383-$1,013 based on trim level and body style). 1SB Sunbird option group ($680-$1,286 based on trim level and body style). 1SC Sunbird option group #3 ($1,624-$1,711 based on trim level and body style). R6A value package ($442-$445 based on trim level). R6B value package ($366 all). LT2 2.0-liter TBI engine as delete-option in GT ($768 credit). LT3 Turbo engine, mandatory extras and specific options, except in GT ($1,169-$1,434). MX1 three-speed automatic transmission ($440). C60 air conditioning ($695). C49 electric rear window defogger ($150). NB2 California emissions package ($100). U39 really cluster gauges and trip odometer in LE ($49). TR9 lamp group ($44 in sedan/$38 in Coupe). V56 deck lid luggage carrier ($115). D84 custom two-tone paint for LE ($101). D86 deluxe two-tone paint for GT ($101). AU3 power door locks ($155 Coupe/$205 sedan). A31 power windows, requires power door locks ($220 Coupe/$295 sedan/no charge convertible). UM7 Delco radio equipment (standard/no charge). UM6 Delco radio equipment ($152 additional). U1C Delco radio equipment ($244-$396). AK1 color-keyed seat belts for LE/SE only ($26). B20 custom interior with Metrix cloth in GT Coupe only ($335). B20 custom interior with Metrix cloth in GT convertible only ($142). N36 rally steering wheel in LE/SE only ($26). AD3 removable glass sunroof ($350). Various tire options ($68-$276 extra). PX1 13-in. Sport Tech aluminum wheels with locking package ($265). N78 14-in Hi-Tech Turbo aluminum wheels with locking package ($265).

6000 OPTIONS: 1SA option package #1 for 6000 LE sedan ($975). 1SB option package #2 for 6000 LE sedan ($1,160). 1SC option package #3 for 6000 LE sedan ($2,076). 1SA option package #1 for 6000 LE Safari ($975). 1SB option package #2 for 6000 LE Safari ($1,715) 1SC option package #3 for 6000 LE Safari ($2,066). 1SA option package #1 for 6000 SE sedan ($1,118). 1SA option package #2 for 6000 SE Safari ($1,068). R6A value option package for 6000 LE sedan ($395). R6B value option package for 6000 LE sedan ($180). R6B value option package for 6000 LE sedan ($385). LB6

1989 Pontiac Firebird Trans Am Indy 500 pace car. (PGMC)

2.8-liter MFI V-6 in LE sedan ($610). MX0 four-speed automatic transmission ($200). C60 air conditioning ($795). C49 electric rear window defogger ($150). D86 two-tone paint ($115). AU3 power door locks ($205). A31 power windows ($310). UM6 Delco ETR AM/FM stereo ($122). U1A Delco ETR AM stereo/FM stereo ($519-$554). AM6 45/55 split bench seat ($133). B20 custom interior with 45/55 split seat in Empress/London cloth ($360-$493). Various tire options (no charge to $68). N78 Sport aluminum wheels with locking package ($265). BX3 woodgrain exterior siding for Safari ($295).

NOTE: Full option package contents, descriptions, and applications information can often be determined by consulting factory literature. The data above is edited for size and clarity. This information provided only as a guide to help collectors appraise the relative value of cars with numerous options. Prices for items included as part of a value option package are usually much less than individual prices. Option prices charged by individual dealers may also vary.

HISTORICAL: Pontiac's new HUD instrumentation was available only as standard equipment on Turbo Grand Prix. This HUD optically projected key instrument displays to a focal point near the front of the vehicle. It could be viewed through the lower windshield, allowing the driver to view the data while keeping his or her eyes on the road. Vehicle speed, turn signal indicators, the high beam indicator, low fuel warning, and "check gauges" warning that monitors low oil pressure and high coolant temperatures are the features of the HUD system displays. Pontiac Motor Div. had an active motor sports program in 1989. After finishing third in the Winston Cup manufacturers championship in 1988 (only five points behind the winner), Pontiac was looking forward to the 1989 NASCAR/Winston Cup season with great anticipation. Those returning to drive Pontiac Grand Prix included Rusty Wallace (No. 27 Kodiak/Mobil One/AC Delco Pontiac), Richard Petty (No. 43 STP/Prestone/Goody's Pontiac), Michael Waltrip (No. 30 Country Time/All-Pro/Post Pontiac) and Morgan Shepherd (No. 75 Valvoline Pontiac). In addition, Kyle Petty (No. 42 Peak/Uniden Pontiac), Greg Sacks (No. 88 Crisco/AC Spark Plug Pontiac), Hut Stricklin (No. 57 Heinz Pontiac) and Dale Jarrett (No. 29 Hardee's/Coke Pontiac) were among other "Poncho" pilots. Other Pontiac drivers were Ernie Irvan (No. 2), Ken Bouchard (No. 10), Jim Sauter (No. 31), Joe Ruttman (No. 45), Mickey Gibbs (No. 48), Jimmy Means (No. 52), Derrike Cope (No. 68), J.D. McDuffie (No. 70) and Jimmy Horton (No. 80). In all, 17 teams were using Pontiacs in 1989 NASCAR competition.

1989 Pontiac Turbo Grand Prix coupe. (PGMC)

1990 PONTIAC

1990 Pontiac LeMans GSE three-door hatchback. (PGMC)

Note: 1990 and newer Pontiac models arranged from low to high series.

LEMANS — SERIES 2T — (FOUR) — The 1990 LeMans was Pontiac's lowest-priced car, but had no shortage of Pontiac style or performance relative to other cars in the entry-level subcompact class. It again combined European styling, German engineering, and Asian craftsmanship in a highly affordable, economical, and fun package. The LeMans featured the highest fuel economy of the entire Pontiac line (31 mpg city/40 mpg highway) and the long list of standard features made every LeMans model competitive with other imports. There were four 1990 models: Aerocoupe "Value Leader," LE Aerocoupe, LE sedan, and GSE Aerocoupe. There were several product changes for 1990. The first was a ride and handling improvement package with new spring and shock insulators and a re-tuned suspension for with larger stabilizer bar for 1.6-liter models. It gave improved performance and a quieter cabin. The second change was a brake feel improvement package on all 1.6-liter cars. It included a larger master cylinder and recalibrated front suspension struts. Third came quicker steering on the GSE model. A two-point motorized passive restraint system was added to all LeMans for added front seat comfort, convenience, and safety. All models also had revised door panels. A redesigned standard stereo radio and optional cassette with knob controls were featured on all models except the Value Leader Aerocoupe. Every LeMans was equipped with roof rail moldings that accepted an optional luggage rack kit for greater cargo carrying capability. Also continued from 1990-1/2 was a new cam belt tensioner for 1.6-liter engines. Standard equipment in the Value Leader Aerocoupe included a 1.6-liter TBI engine, four-speed manual transmission, P175/70R13 tires, and 9.5-in. solid front disc brakes. The LeMans LE sedan and Aerocoupe added or substituted a five-speed manual gearbox and AM/FM stereo with clock. Externally, the LE sedan had black side mirrors and wide black moldings with bright accents. Light Flame Red Metallic finish was no longer available on the LE sedan. On the Aerocoupe, lower accent two-tone paint in a new Silver color was standard. In addition, a new-for-1990 color was Medium Smoke Gray Metallic. It was available only on Aerocoupes. Externally, the LE Aerocoupe had swing-out rear quarter windows. Internally, the LE sedan had reclining front and folding rear seats, roll-down rear windows, tinted glass, and child safety rear door lock. The LeMans GSE Aerocoupe added or substituted a 2.0-liter throttle-body-injected (TBI) engine, P185/60R14 tires, 10.1-in. vented front disc brakes, rack-and-pinion steering, a Sport suspension featuring 22mm front and 18mm rear stabilizer bars, slot alloy wheels, and power steering. Externally, it had aero fascias and rocker extensions, body-color outside rearview mirrors, a deck lid spoiler, narrower body side moldings, and fog lamps. Interior appointments included rally instrumentation, tinted glass, swing-out rear quarter windows, height-adjustable reclining sport seats, specific GSE interior trim, 60/40 split fold down rear seats, a luggage compartment security cover, and an AM/FM stereo. The LeMans was designed after the Opel Kadett. Both the car and the standard engine were built in Korea by Daewoo Motor Co., as part of a joint venture between GM and the Daewoo group.

1990 Pontiac Firebird Trans Am GTA two-door coupe. (PGMC)

SUNBIRD — SERIES 2J — (FOUR) — The 1990 Pontiac Sunbird offered buyers sporty, expressive styling and performance in an affordably priced, American-built car. Sunbird models appealed to a wide range of car enthusiasts from buyers of economy Sports Sedans to convertible lovers, to those seeking all-out performance. All Sunbirds were equipped with new low-tension passive restraint systems, with color-keyed seat belts in all models. Improved acoustics helped make the interior more pleasant. The drive axle splines were now free-floating and had a smoother finish, which allowed them to slide smoothly in their housings. This minimized shudder upon acceleration. The interior lighting system gained a new 45-second delay-off feature for added convenience. A new color option was Bright Torch Red. All Sunbirds had clearcoat finish. Three additional changes highlighted the year: An LE convertible replaced the GT convertible; dramatic new styling updates characterized the SE and GT models and Pontiac offered Sunbird buyers new tire choices and wheel designs. The LE convertible replaced the Sunbird GT convertible, making ownership of a Pontiac ragtop more affordable. The LE convertible featured hydraulic top action and a snap-on boot to cover the top when lowered. The was a Convertible Sport package that included a turbo engine, fatter tires, Hi-tech Turbo wheels, the WS6 suspension, GT-type steering, rally instrumentation, and an engine block heater. The LE convertible also came with power windows, power door locks, tinted glass, power steering, and black sport mirrors as standard equipment. The SE offered buyers the aggressive look of the GT at a lower cost. It had a GT-style front-end treatment, larger 14-in. road wheels and P185/75R14 tires, plus standard gauges (trip, fuel, voltage, oil pressure and temperature), and the same normally aspirated four-cylinder engine used in the LE. The top Sunbird model was the GT. It had an all-new front hood, fenders, fascia, and semi-hidden headlights. Also new was an aero package, replacing 1989's wheel flares with new fenders, a new front fascia with air dam, a new rear fascia, and side rocker extensions. The side aero panels included an integral body side molding for protection against parking lot dents. In the exterior lighting department, fog lights were standard on the GT. The 14-in. cast aluminum wheels were also of a new design. The WS6 suspension was standard. Power came from a turbocharged four-cylinder engine coupled to a GM Muncie/Gertag five-speed manual transmission. Rally instrumentation was standard equipment, along with tinted glass, power steering, black dual sport mirrors, an AM/FM stereo cassette, and full instrumentation (including a tachometer) as standard equipment. During the model-year, a new "Value Leader" version of the Sunbird was introduced. It offered the coupe and the sedan with less standard equipment.

GRAND AM — SERIES 2N —- The 1990 Grand Am delivered Pontiac performance in an agile, front-wheel-drive compact package with a contemporary design. Thanks to its universal appeal to a broad range of buyers, the Grand Am was Pontiac's top-selling line. General Motors produced the one millionth Grand Am in June 1989. The Grand Am lineup consisted of a coupe and a sedan and both came in LE and SE trim levels. Changes for 1990 included a new standard 2.3-liter H.O. engine with double overhead cams (DOHC) with more power on SE models, reduced noise levels (with all engines), a new drive axle design, bigger wheels and tires, new optional "express-down" power windows, and delayed interior

lighting on all cars. Vanity mirrors on both sides were standard on all models. Slate Gray replaced Gray as an interior option. Standard in both LE models was a 2.5-liter Tech IV engine, five-speed manual transmission, an AM/FM radio, a new up-level console, Tri-Lace wheel covers, an interior lighting package, and P185/75R14 tires. The LE coupe also added bucket seats. A new Sport Option package was available for LEs. It featured a monotone paint theme in White, Slate Gray, or Bright Red. Fog lamps and P195/70R14 tires on Hi-tech Turbo aluminum wheels were also included in the Sport Option package. Beechwood was available as an interior color only with the LE Sport Option. Expressive styling and high-performance were offered in the Grand Am SE. A 2.3-liter High Output version of the Quad-4 16-valve DOHC engine was standard. It was teamed with a five-speed Gertag manual transmission. An engine-oil cooler was standard in this high-compression (10.1:1) power plant. Other standard equipment included a WS6 suspension; monotone paint treatment; aerodynamic front; side and rear body skirting; black-finished window frames and mirrors; neutral density taillights; an AM/FM stereo cassette radio; air conditioning; controlled cycle wipers; fog lamps; cruise control; a remote deck lid release; power door locks; power windows with express-down; split folding rear seats; a four-spoke rally steering wheel; a leather shift knob; leather parking brake handle; a rally instrument panel; deluxe cloth upholstery; and P205/55R16 Eagle GT+4 tires on color-coordinated 16 x 6-in. aluminum wheels (or machine-faced aluminum wheels).

FIREBIRD — SERIES 2F — (V-6/V-8) — For 1990, Firebirds had a larger and more powerful base V-6. All TPI V-8s (standard in Trans Ams) had a speed density metering system. All Firebirds also had an inflatable airbag restraint system, a new self-adjusting parking brake, dual body-color sport mirrors and new instrument panel switches for the rear defogger, rear hatch release, and fog lamps. Brilliant Red Metallic was a new color replacing Flame Red. Base Firebirds had new seat and armrest trim, plus a different rear spoiler design. Standard features included a five-speed manual gearbox, an FE1 suspension, P215/65R15 tires, front disc/rear drum brakes and an AM/FM stereo with clock. Hi-tech aluminum wheels (15 x 7 in.) were standard. The Formula model had more of a performance image. Its equipment list added an aero-style rear deck lid spoiler, air conditioning, tinted glass, the WS6 sport suspension, P245/50ZR16 tires, and a TBI V-8 engine. The Formula's 6-in. deep-dish Hi-tech wheels had machined-finished faces and silver metallic ports. The Trans Am had a more powerful V-8, an F41 handling suspension, a limited-slip differential, P215/65R15 Firehawk GTX tires, and 15-in. deep-dish Hi-tech turbo aluminum wheels with machined faces and charcoal metallic ports, plus a leather appointment group. The luxury version of the Trans Am was the GTA. Its standard features included a 5.7-liter TPI V-8, a dual catalytic converter exhaust system, a four-speed automatic transmission, four-wheel disc brakes, P245/50ZR-16 Goodyear performance tires, and 16 x 8 in. gold crosslace aluminum wheels. Also standard were a leather-wrapped steering wheel, articulating custom bucket seats with inflatable lumbar and lateral supports, a rear defogger, a cargo screen, a full-featured Delco ETR AM/FM stereo cassette with equalizer, a power antenna, power side view mirrors, power windows, and power door locks.

6000 — SERIES 2A — (I-4/V-6) — New features for 1990 Pontiac 6000s included passive restraint belts in all models, use of the 3.1-liter V-6 and an all-wheel-drive option for the SE (replacing the previous 6000 STE all-wheel-drive model). All models had composite headlights and fog lamps, a front air dam, dual outside rearview mirrors, black door, roof and reveal moldings, and tinted glass. Standard equipment on the lowest-priced 6000 LE sedan also included a 2.5-liter EFI four-cylinder engine, three-speed automatic transmission, front-wheel-drive, P185/75R14 tires, and an AM/FM stereo with clock. Highly contoured front seats with Pallex cloth trim were standard. A newly available color was Maple Red. Air conditioning and a rear defogger were standard on the LE Safari wagon, which also had swing-out rear quarter windows and a rear-facing third seat. The 3.1-liter engine was standard in Safari wagons with a four-speed automatic transmission. The 6000 SE sedan and Safari wagon also had the 3.1-liter V-6, plus electronic ride control, P195/70R15 Goodyear Eagle GT+4 tires, power windows, cruise control, power door locks, and an AM/FM cassette stereo with seek-and-scan feature and a clock. The SE model also included 15-in. cast aluminum wheels, trailing arm and beam rear suspension, a dual outlet exhaust system, a Level II suspension system, body color aero moldings, a remote deck lid release, a six-way power driver's seat, a power rearview mirror, and reading lamps. The SE Safari wagon also had a roof top luggage rack, a power tailgate release, a split folding second seat, and a rear window wiper. The 6000 SE AWD option on the SE sedan had a full-time all-wheel-drive system that required no special driver actions to take advantage of its outstanding grip under all conditions. The all-wheel-drive feature included ABS anti-lock disc brakes at all four wheels, the 3.1-liter V-6 with three-speed automatic transmission, a fully independent rear suspension, specific aluminum wheels with locks, quicker-ratio power steering, and dual outlet exhausts. This model-option came only in Medium Red Metallic or Dark Blue Metallic, both with gold accents and emblems, special badges, a unique rear spoiler, and specific fog lights. Also included were power windows, power door locks, cruise control, controlled-cycle wipers, air conditioning, an AM/FM stereo cassette radio, and front seat back map pockets.

GRAND PRIX — SERIES 2G — (V-6/V-8) — The Grand Prix was again Pontiac's personal sports machine. It came in five models from the responsive Grand Prix LE all the way up to a powerful Turbo Grand Prix coupe. General features included eye-catching styling, a driver-oriented cockpit, and a complete performance spectrum. Changes in the 1990 Grand Prix lineup included the addition of a four-door sedan, a redesigned analog gauge cluster with new pod switches, a 2.3-liter 16-valve engine option (the 2.8-liter V-6 was dropped), and new Pallex/Metrix cloth upholstery replacing the previous Ripple/Pallex cloth interior choices. New paint colors included Bright Red and Slate Gray Metallic throughout the line, plus Black Metallic, Medium Blue Metallic, and Bright Red for the SE. Camel Metallic, Medium Gray Metallic, and Red finishes were dropped. On interiors, Slate Gray replaced Medium Gray. Standard equipment on the LE coupe and sedan included a 2.3-liter 16-valve DOHC "Quad Four" engine, a three-speed automatic transmission, P195/75R14 (sedan) or P205/65R15 (coupe) tires, air conditioning, 60/40 reclining front seats, and an AM/FM stereo with clock. A five-speed manual gearbox was offered only for coupes with the optional 3.1-liter MFI V-6. Both models with this engine could also be optioned with a four-speed automatic transmission. Other standard features included styled wheel covers on sedans and styled steel wheels on coupes and standard Pallex cloth seat trim in both body types. The Grand Prix SE coupe added or substituted the following standard features: The 3.1-liter V-6, five-speed manual transmission, P215/60R16 tires, power windows, power reclining front seats with articulated thigh, lumbar, lateral and head support, cruise control, an AM/FM stereo with graphic equalizer, clock and steering wheel controls, and a six-speaker sound system with amplifier. Also included on the SE were a Y99 rally-tuned suspension, split dual exhausts, 16 x 6 cast aluminum wheels with white, bright red or medium blue machined faces, exterior aero body skirting, fog lamps, specific front and rear fascias, and a monochromatic color scheme. The SE was also appointed in richer Metrix cloth upholstery. The Grand Prix Special Touring Edition (STE) sedan added even more standard equipment including power reclining bucket front seats with lumbar and articulated thigh supports, a keyless entry system and a Hi-performance eight-speaker sound system. The STE also had an analog instrument cluster, Metrix cloth trim, a specific con-

toured three-passenger rear seat with luggage pass-through, a leather-wrapped steering wheel, tilt steering, controlled-cycle wipers, a rear window defogger, and an overhead mini-console. Its P215/60R16 Goodyear Eagle GT+4 tires were mounted on specific STE alloy wheel rims. The STE had a distinctive front end with a unique fascia and integral grille. A light bar containing integral fog lights extended across the entire width of the car. At the rear, the STE had another specific fascia and full-width taillights. A monochromatic paint scheme was standard, with optional lower accent paint treatments available at extra-cost. The top-of-the-line Turbo Grand Prix coupe added a 3.1-liter turbocharged V-6, a standard four-speed automatic transmission, ABS brakes, and 245/50ZR16 tires. Also included were gold cross-lace wheels, a monochromatic paint scheme, a unique ground effects package, functional hood louvers, a heads-up instrument panel display, and rear bucket seats with integral headrests.

BONNEVILLE — SERIES 2H — (V-6) — The 1990 Pontiac Bonneville continued to blend style and performance. Models offered were the capable and well-equipped LE, the sportier SE, and the Euro-style look of the Bonneville SSE. Six changes were highlighted: A redesigned front body/frame structure; new wheels and tire combinations; a new grille and taillights; deck lid lock cover for LE/SE models; a new grille for the SSE; seat-mounted safety belts; new express-down power windows; and new remote keyless entry system. All Bonnevilles were powered by a 3.8-liter SFI V-6 coupled with a four-speed automatic transmission. Features of the Bonneville LE included an F41 suspension; P205/75R14 tires; 14-in. wheel covers; a 2.84:1 rear axle; manual air conditioning; an AM/FM stereo with clock; and 45/55 reclining split seat with armrest. The Bonneville SE added or substituted P215/60R Eagle GT+4 tires; 16-in. six-spoke wheels; a 2.97:1 final drive ratio; a cassette stereo; a 45/55 reclining split seat with storage armrest; a rear window defogger; power windows with express-down feature; and power door locks. Also included on the SE was a rear deck lid spoiler, Metrix cloth upholstery, a re-tuned suspension, and variable-ratio power steering. The formerly optional fog lamps, interior lamp group, and rear deck lid release were standard for 1990. The Bonneville SSE added or substituted the following over SE features: ABS brakes; an FE2 suspension with electronic-level control and variable-ratio steering; 16-in. Aerolite wheels; a 3.33:1 final drive ratio; automatic air conditioning with temperature indicator light; steering wheel controls for radio/heat/vent and A/C functions; an AM/FM stereo with cassette and graphic equalizer; 45/55 bucket seats with console; a remote keyless entry system; and a theft deterrent system. The SSE had a European-like monochromatic color scheme with wide body-color moldings with gold protective inserts. The door frame, B-pillar, wheel opening, windshield, and side window moldings had high-gloss black finish to distinguish them from the SE (gray moldings) and LE (bright moldings). A standard rear deck lid spoiler emphasized the sporty nature of this "touring sedan." The door handles were a unique combination of body color and black. A new outside rearview mirror and a new grille enhanced the exterior. The wheels were done in body color, too. Headlight washers and fog lights were included. The interior featured specific gauges, a driver information center, a leather-wrapped steering wheel, and eight radio speakers. Also included on the SSE were an electric fuel filler door release, an electric deck lid release, heated and blue-tinted OSRV mirrors, a rear window defogger, and deluxe trunk trim with a deck lid inner liner. The trunk was fitted with a security net, a rear cargo compartment closeout, a trunk-mounted tire inflator, and a roadside emergency kit.

TRANS SPORT — SERIES 2U — (V-6) — The Pontiac Trans Sport was introduced in 1990. This MPV (Multi-Purpose-Vehicle) was a van in body style, but had a car-like front-wheel-drive chassis and drive train. It was based on an exciting "concept vehicle" that Pontiac built and exhibited in 1986. The Trans Sport featured a space frame substructure attached to a sturdy ladder frame. Body panels were made of reinforced composite materials. There were two models called the (entry-level) Transport and Trans Sport SE. Both were powered by an electronically fuel-injected 3.1-liter V-6 developing 120 hp and coupled to a three-speed automatic transmission. The entry-level Transport was equipped with 2+3 seating with front buckets and a mid-mounted bench. The interior was trimmed in Pallex cloth. The less expensive model had its own lower body treatment. The fascias and aero moldings were done in a contrasting color, which was either Silver Metallic or Medium Gray Metallic, depending

1990 Pontiac 6000 SE AWD four-door sedan. (PGMC)

on body color. The rear portion of the roof could be ordered in gloss black (standard) or body color (a delete-option). Also standard were an AM/FM radio with clock and P205/70R-14 tires on 14-in. wheels. The Trans Sport SE featured 2+2+2 modular seating with Metrix cloth trim and specific SE seats. A monocromatic exterior was standard and the roof had the gloss black treatment that accentuated its deep-tinted glass areas. Front air conditioning, a rear air flow distribution system, an AM/FM cassette radio with seek-and-scan and digital clock, a leather-clad steering wheel, 15-in. cast aluminum road wheels, and P195/70R-15 Goodyear Eagle GT+4 tires were also standard, along with automatic load leveling, a built-in tire inflator, lamp group, tilt steering, and cruise control.

I.D. DATA: Pontiac's 17-symbol Vehicle Identification Number (VIN) for passenger cars was on the upper left surface of the instrument panel, visible through the windshield. The first symbol indicates country of origin: 1=U.S.; 2= Canada; 3=Mexico; J=Japan; K=Korea. The second symbol indicates manufacturer: G=General Motors; G=Suzuki; 8=Isuzu; Y=NUMMI; L=Daewoo; C=CAMI. The third symbol G indicates make: 2=Pontiac division; 5=Pontiac incomplete; 7=GM of Canada; N=Pontiac Multi-Purpose Vehicle; Y=Pontiac Truck. The fourth and fifth symbols for passenger cars indicated body type and series: A/ J=6000 SE; A/F=6000 LE; F/S=Firebird; F/W=Firebird Trans Am; H/ X=Bonneville LE; HY=Bonneville SSE; H/Z=Bonneville SE; J/B=Sunbird LE; J/D=Sunbird SE; J/U=Sunbird GT; M/R=Firefly LE/Firefly Turbo; M/T=Firefly (U.S. Customs Territories); N/E=Grand Am LE; N/ W=Grand Am SE; T/N=LeMans; T/S=LeMans GSE; T/X=LeMans Aerocoupe; W/J=Grand Prix LE; W/T=Grand Prix STE; W/P=Grand Prix SE. On Trans Sports the fourth symbol indicated the GVWR/brake system and the fifth symbol indicating line and chassis type was a "U" for All-Purpose Vehicle 4x2. The sixth symbol on passenger cars denoted body type: 1=two-door coupe/sedan styles 11, 27, 37, 47, 57, 97; 2=two-door hatchback styles 07, 08, 77 and 87; 3=two-door convertible style 67; 4=two-door station wagon style 15; 5=four-door sedan styles 19 and 69; 6=four-door hatchback/liftback style 68; 7=four-door liftback style 68; 8=four-door station wagon style 35. The sixth symbol on Trans Sports indicated series: 1=1/2-ton. The seventh symbol on passenger cars indicated the type of restraint system: 1=manual belts; 3=manual belts with driver airbag; 4=automatic belts. The seventh symbol on Trans Sports indicated body type: 6=All-Purpose Vehicle. Symbol eight for passenger cars was an engine code: A=2.3-liter fuel-inject I-4; C=3.8-liter fuel-injected V-6; D=2.3-liter fuel-injected I-4; E=5.0-liter fuel-injected V-8; F=5.0-liter fuel-injected V-8; K=2.0-liter fuel-injected I-4; M=2.0-liter fuel-injected I-4; R=2.5-liter fuel-injected I-4; T=3.1-liter fuel-injected V-6; U=2.5-liter fuel-injected I-4; V=3.1-liter fuel-injected V-6; 6=1.6-liter fuel-injected I-4; 8=5.7-liter fuel-injected V-8. The seventh symbol for Trans sports was also an engine code: D=3.1-liter fuel-injected V-6. The ninth symbol for cars and trucks is a check digit. The tenth symbol for cars and trucks denotes model year (L=1990). The 11th symbol for cars and trucks indicates the GM assembly plant (A=Lakewood, CA; B=Baltimore, Md. T&B; B=Lansing, Mich.; B=Pupyong, Korea; C=Lansing, Mich.; D=Doraville, Ga.; E=Linden, N.J.; E=Pontiac East, Mich. T&B; F=Fairfax II, Kan.; F=Flint T&B; H=Flint, Mich.; J=Janesville, Wis.; J=Janesville, Wis. T&B; K=Kosai, Japan; L=Van Nuys, Calif.; M=Lansing, Mich; R=Arlington, Texas; S=Ramos Arizpe, Mexico; T=Tarrytown, N.Y.; U=Hamtramck, Mich; V=Pontiac, Mich. (T&B); W=Willow Run, Mich.; W=Iwata, Japan; Y=Wilmington, Del.; Z=Fremont, Calif.; Z=Ft. Wayne, Ind. T&B; 0= Pontiac, Mich. (T&B); 1=Oshawa, Canada #2; 1=Wentzville, Mo. T&B; 2=Morraine, OH T&B; 2=Ste. Therese, Canada; 3=Detroit, Mich. T&B; 3=Kawasaki, Japan; 4=Orion, Mich.; 4=Scarborough, Ontario, Canada; 5=Bowling Green, Ken.; 6=Ingersoll, Ontario, Canada; 6=Oklahoma City, Okla.; 7=Lordstown, Ohio; 7=Flusawa, Japan; 8=Shreveport, La. T&B; 9=Oshawa, Ontario, Canada #1. Pontiacs are not produced at all of these GM plants. The last six symbols are the consecutive unit number at the factory.

Model Number	Body Style Number	Body Type & Seating	Factory Price	Shipping Weight	Production Total
LEMANS AEROCOUPE SERIES T/X (I-4)					
2T	TX2	3d V/L Coupe-4P	7,254	2,136	Note 1
LEMANS SERIES T/N (I-4)					
2T	TN2	3d Coupe-4P	8,554	2,180	Note 1
2T	TN5	4d Sedan-4P	8,904	2,235	Note 1
LEMANS GSE SERIES T/S (I-4)					
2T	TS2	3d Coupe-4P	10,764	2,302	Note 1
SUNBIRD VALUE LEADER SERIES J/B (I-4)					
2J	JB5	4d Sedan-5P	7,958	2,398	Note 2

1990 Pontiac Bonneville SSE four-door sedan. (PGMC)

Model Number	Body Style Number	Body Type & Seating	Factory Price	Shipping Weight	Production Total
2J	JB1	2d Coupe-5P	7,858	2,376	Note 2
SUNBIRD LE SERIES J/B (I-4)					
2J	JB5	4d Sedan-5P	8,899	2,500	Note 2
2J	JB1	2d Coupe-5P	8,799	2,478	Note 2
2J	JB3	2d Convertible-5P	13924	2,431	Note 2
SUNBIRD SE SERIES J/D (I-4/I-4 Turbo)					
2J	JD1	2d Coupe-5P	9,204	2,568	Note 2
SUNBIRD GT TURBO SERIES J/U (I-4/I-4 Turbo)					
2J	JU1	2d Coupe-5P	11,724	2,674	Note 2
GRAND AM LE SERIES N/E (I-4/V-6)					
2N	NE1	2d Coupe-5P	10,544	2,566	Note 3
2N	NE5	4d Sedan-5P	10,744	2,623	Note 3
GRAND AM SE SERIES N/W (I-4/V-6)					
2N	NW1	2d Coupe-5P	14,894	2,767	Note 3
2N	NW5	4d Sedan-5P	15,194	2,842	Note 3
FIREBIRD SERIES F/S (V-6)					
2F	FS2	2d Coupe-5P	11,320	3,106	Note 4
FIREBIRD SERIES F/S (V-8)					
2F	FS2	2d Coupe-5P	11,670	3,266	Note 4
FIREBIRD FORMULA SERIES F/S (V-8)					
2F	FS2	2d Coupe-5P	14,610	3,338	Note 4
FIREBIRD TRANS AM SERIES F/W (V-8)					
2F	FW2	2d Coupe-5P	16,510	3,338	Note 4
FIREBIRD TRANS AM GTA SERIES F/W (V-8)					
2F	FW2	2d Coupe-5P	23,320	3,554	Note 4
6000 LE SERIES A/F (I-4)					
2A	AF5	4d Sedan-5P	12,149	2,837	Note 5
6000 LE SERIES A/F (V-6)					
2A	AF5	4d Sedan-5P	12,809	2,886	Note 5
2A	AF8	4d Safari-5P	15,309	3,156	Note 5
6000 SE SERIES A/J (I-4/V-6)					
2A	AJ5	4d Sedan-5P	16,909	3,015	Note 5
2A	AJ8	4d Safari-5P	18,509	3,201	Note 5
GRAND PRIX LE SERIES W/J (I-4/V-6)					
2G	WJ5	4d Sedan-5P	14,564	3,280	Note 6
2G	WJ1	2d Coupe-5P	14,564	3,189	Note 6
GRAND PRIX SE SERIES W/P (V-6)					
2G	WPJ1	2d Coupe-5P	17,684	3,284	Note 6
GRAND PRIX SE TURBO SERIES W/L (V-6)					
2G	WJ1/LG5	2d Coupe-5P	23,775	3,500	Note 6
GRAND PRIX STE SERIES W/T (V-6/V-8)					
2G	WT5	4d Sedan-5P	18,539	3,385	Note 6
BONNEVILLE LE SERIES H/X (V-6)					
2H	HX5	4d Sport Sedan-5P	15,774	3,309	Note 7
BONNEVILLE SE SERIES H/Z (V-6)					
2H	HZ5	4d Sport Sedan-5P	19,144	3,392	Note 7
BONNEVILLE SSE SERIES H/Y (V-6)					
2H	HZ5/Y80	4d Sport Sedan-5P	23,994	3,567	Note 7
TRANS SPORT SERIES M/U (V-6)					
2U	U06	Minivan	15,495	3,500	Note 8
2U	U06	Minivan	18,625	3,500	Note 8

NOTE 1: LeMans series production totaled 39,081 cars.

NOTE 2: Sunbird series production totaled 143,932 cars.

NOTE 3: Grand Am series production totaled 197,020 cars.

NOTE 4: Firebird series production totaled 46,760 (includes 1991 model vehicles introduced early in the 1990 model year).

NOTE 5: 6000 series production totaled 66,398 cars.

NOTE 6: Grand Prix series production totaled 128,067 cars.

NOTE 7: Bonneville series production totaled 85,844 cars.

NOTE 8: Trans Sport series production totaled 40,750 units.

LEMANS ENGINES

ENGINE [Base Four (VL/LE)]: Inline. OHV. Four-cylinder. Cast-iron block. Aluminum head and intake manifold. Displacement: 97.5 cid.

(1.6L). Bore & stroke: 3.11 x 3.21 in. Compression ratio: 8.6:1. Brake horsepower: 74 at 5600 rpm. Torque: 90 lbs.-ft. at 2800 rpm. Fuel system: EFI/TBI. RPO Code: L73. Standard with four-speed manual Value Leader and LeMans LE. [VIN code 6].

ENGINE [Base Four (GSE)]: Inline. OHC. Four-cylinder. Cast-iron block. Aluminum head and intake manifold. Displacement: 121 cid. (2.0L). Bore & stroke: 3.39 x 3.39 in. Compression ratio: 8.8:1. Brake horsepower: 96 at 4800 rpm. Torque: 118 lbs.-ft. at 3600 rpm. Fuel system: EFI/TBI. RPO Code: LT2. Standard with five-speed manual LeMans GSE models. [VIN code K].

SUNBIRD ENGINES

ENGINE [Base Four (LE/SE)]: Inline. OHC. Four-cylinder. Cast-iron block. Aluminum head and intake manifold. Displacement: 121 cid. (2.0L). Bore & stroke: 3.39 x 3.39 in. Compression ratio: 8.8:1. Brake horsepower: 96 at 4800 rpm. Torque: 118 lbs.-ft. at 3600 rpm. Fuel system: EFI/TBI. RPO Code: LT2. Standard in Sunbird LE and Sunbird SE models. [VIN code K].

ENGINE [Base Four (GT)]: Inline. OHC. Four-cylinder. Turbocharged (Garrett T2.5 turbocharger). Cast-iron block. Aluminum head and intake manifold. Displacement: 121 cid. (2.0L). Bore & stroke: 3.39 x 3.39 in. Compression ratio: 8.0:1. Brake horsepower: 165 at 5600 rpm. Torque: 175 lbs.-ft. at 4000 rpm. Fuel system: MPFI with Turbo. RPO Code: LT3. Standard in Sunbird Turbo GT (optional in Sunbird LE convertible). [VIN code M].

GRAND AM ENGINES

ENGINE [Standard LE]: Inline. OHV. Cast-iron block and head. Aluminum intake manifold. Displacement: 151 cid. (2.5L Tech IV). Bore & stroke: 4.00 x 3.00 in. Compression ratio: 9.0:1. Brake horsepower: 110 at 5200 rpm. Torque: 135 lbs.-ft. at 3200 rpm. Five main bearings. Hydraulic valve lifters. Fuel system: EFI/TBI. RPO Code: L68. Standard in Grand AM LE. [VIN code U/R].

ENGINE [Standard SE with manual transmission]: Inline. DOHC. 16-valve. Quad-4 High-Output. Cast-iron block. Aluminum head and intake manifold. Displacement: 138 cid. (2.3-liter). Bore & stroke: 3.62 x 3.35 in. Compression ratio: 10.0:1. Brake horsepower: 180 at 6200 rpm. Torque: 160 lbs.-ft. at 5200 rpm. Fuel system: MPFI. RPO Code: LGO. Standard and exclusive in Grand Am SE with five-speed Manual transmission. [VIN code A].

ENGINE [Standard SE with automatic transmission]: Inline. DOHC. 16-valve. Quad-4. Cast-iron block. Aluminum head and intake manifold. Displacement: 138 cid. (2.3-liter). Bore & stroke: 3.62 x 3.35 in. Compression ratio: 9.5:1. Brake horsepower: 160 at 6200 rpm. Torque: 155 lbs.-ft. at 5200 rpm. Fuel system: MPFI. RPO Code: LD2. Standard in SE with automatic; optional in LE with automatic. [VIN code D].

FIREBIRD ENGINES

ENGINE [Base V-6]: V-block. OHV. Six-cylinder. Cast-iron block and head. Aluminum intake manifold. Displacement: 191 cid. (3.1L). Bore & stroke: 3.50 x 3.31 in. Compression ratio: 8.75:1. Brake horsepower: 135 at 4400 rpm. Torque: 180 lbs.-ft. at 3600 rpm. Fuel system: EFI/MFI. RPO Code: L (H.O.) Standard in base Firebird. Produced in U.S., Canada, or Mexico. [VIN code T].

ENGINE [Base V-8]: V-block. OHV. Eight-cylinder. Cast-iron block and head. Aluminum intake manifold. Displacement: 305 cid. (5.0L). Bore & stroke: 3.74 x 3.48 in. Brake horsepower: 170 at 4400 rpm. Torque: 255 lbs.-ft. at 2400 rpm. Compression ratio: 9.3:1. Fuel system: EFI/TBI. RPO Code: L03. Produced in U.S. or Canada. Standard Formula. Available in base Firebird. [VIN code E or F].

ENGINE [Optional V-8]: V-block. OHV. Eight-cylinder. Cast-iron block and head. Aluminum intake manifold. Displacement: 305 cid. (5.0L). Bore & stroke: 3.74 x 3.48 in. Brake horsepower: 200 at 4400 rpm (Formula with automatic and Trans Am with five-speed manual) or 225 at 4600 rpm (GTA and Formula with five-speed manual). Torque: 300 lbs.-ft. at 3200 rpm (Formula with automatic and Trans Am with five-speed manual) or 290 lbs.-ft. at 3200 rpm (GTA and Formula with five-speed manual). Compression ratio: 9.3:1. Fuel system: EFI/TPI. RPO Code: LB9. Available with five-speed manual in Formula and Trans Am (delete option in GTA). [VIN code E or F].

ENGINE [GTA V-8]: V-block. OHV. Eight-cylinder. Cast-iron block and head. Aluminum intake manifold. Displacement: 350 cid. (5.7L). Bore & stroke: 4.00 x 3.48 in. Brake horsepower: 235 at 4400 rpm. Torque: 340 lbs.-ft. at 3200 rpm. Compression ratio: 9.3:1. Fuel system: EFI/TPI. RPO Code: B2L. Standard with four-speed automatic

in GTA (optional in Formula and Trans Am). Includes low-profile air induction system with aluminum plenum and individual aluminum tuned runners, an extruded dual fuel rail assembly with computer controlled fuel injectors, and a special low-restriction single exhaust system. [VIN code 8].

6000 ENGINES

ENGINE [Base Four]: Inline. OHV. Four-cylinder. Cast-iron block and head. Aluminum intake manifold. Displacement: 151 cid. (2.5L Tech IV). Bore & stroke: 4.00 x 3.00 in. Compression ratio: 9.0:1. Brake horsepower: 112 at 5200 rpm. Torque: 135 lbs.-ft. at 3200 rpm. Five main bearings. Hydraulic valve lifters. Fuel system: EFI/TBI. RPO Code: LR8. Standard in 6000 LE. [VIN code U].

ENGINE [Base Six (LE Safari; SE sedan and Safari)]: V-block. OHV. Six-cylinder. Cast-iron block. Aluminum head and intake manifold. Displacement: 191 cid. (3.1L). Bore & stroke: 3.50 x 3.31 in. Brake horsepower: 135 at 4400 rpm. Torque: 180 lbs.-ft. at 3600 rpm. Fuel system: EFI/MFI Code: L (H.O.) Standard in 6000 SE sedan and Safari and LE Safari. [VIN code T].

GRAND PRIX ENGINES

ENGINE [Base Four]: Inline. DOHC. 16-valve. Quad-4. Cast-iron block. Aluminum head and intake manifold. Displacement: 138 cid. (2.3L). Bore & stroke: 3.62 x 3.35 in. Compression ratio: 9.5:1. Brake horsepower: 160 at 6200 rpm. Torque: 155 lbs.-ft. at 5200 rpm. Fuel system: MPFI. RPO Code: LD2. Standard in SE with automatic; optional in LE with automatic. [VIN code D].

ENGINE [Base Six (SE and STE); Optional (LE)]: V-block. OHV. Six-cylinder. Cast-iron block and aluminum head. 191 cid. (3.1L). Bore & stroke: 3.50 x 3.31 in. Compression ratio: 8.75:1. Brake horsepower: 135 at 4400 rpm. Torque: 180 lbs.-ft. at 3600 rpm. Fuel system: EFI/MPI. RPO Code: L (H.O.) [VIN code T].

ENGINE [Optional Six]: V-block. OHV. Six-cylinder. Turbo. Cast-iron block and aluminum head. 191 cid. (3.1L). Bore & stroke: 3.50 x 3.31 in. Compression ratio: 8.75:1. Brake horsepower: 205 at 4800 rpm. Torque: 220 lbs.-ft. at 3200 rpm. Fuel system: EFI/MPI. RPO Code: L (H.O.) with LG5 American Sun Roof Corp. (ASC)/McLaren Turbo conversion. [VIN code T].

BONNEVILLE ENGINE

ENGINE [Base Six (LE/SE/SSE)]: V-block. OHV. "3800" six-cylinder. Cast-iron block and head. Aluminum intake manifold. Displacement: 231 cid. (3.8L). Bore & stroke: 3.80 x 3.40 in. Compression ratio: 8.5:1. Brake horsepower: 165 at 5200 rpm. Torque: 210 lbs.-ft. at 2000 rpm. Fuel system: SFI. RPO Code: LN3. Standard in Bonneville LE/SE/SSE model. [VIN code W, S, or 9].

TRANS SPORT ENGINE

ENGINE [Base Six]: V-block. OHV. Six-cylinder. Cast-iron block and head. Aluminum intake manifold. Displacement: 191 cid. (3.1L). Bore & stroke: 3.50 x 3.31 in. Compression ratio: 8.5:1. Brake horsepower: 120 at 4200 rpm. Torque: 175 lbs.-ft. at 2200 rpm. Fuel system: EFI/TBI. RPO Code: LG6. Standard in base Firebird. Produced in U.S., Canada, or Mexico. [VIN code T].

CHASSIS

LEMANS CHASSIS: Wheelbase: 99.2 in. (all). Overall length: 163.7 in. (three-door); 172.4 in. (four-door). Height: 53.5 in. (Aerocoupe); 53.7 in. (sedan). Standard tires: P175/70R13 BSW (all).

1990 Pontiac Sunbird LE two-door convertible. (PGMC)

1990 Pontiac Grand Am SE two-door coupe. (PGMC)

SUNBIRD CHASSIS: Wheelbase: 101.2 in. (all). Overall length: 182 in. (coupe and convertible). Width: 67.0 in. coupe/convertible). Height: 50.4.in. (coupe); 51.9 in. (convertible). Front tread: 55.6 in. (all). Rear tread: 55.2 in. (all). Standard tires: P185/75R14 BSW (LE). Standard tires: P185/75R14 (SE). Standard tires: P215/60R14 Eagle GT+4 (GT).

GRAND AM CHASSIS: Wheelbase: 103.4 in. (coupe/sedan). Overall length: 180.1 in. (all). Width: 66.5 in. (all). Height: 52.5 in. (all). Front tread: 55.6 in. Rear tread: 55.2 in. Standard tires: P185/80R13 BSW (LE). Standard tires: P215/60R14 (SE).

FIREBIRD CHASSIS: Wheelbase: 101.0 in. (All). Overall length: 188.1 in. (Base/Formula); 191.6 in. (Trans Am/GTA). Width: 72.4 in. (all). Height: 50.0 in. (all). Front tread: 60.7 in. Rear tread: 61.6 in. Standard tires: P215/65R15 (Base Firebird and Trans Am). Tire: P245/50ZR16 Goodyear Eagle ZR50 "Gatorback" (Formula and GTA).

6000 CHASSIS: Wheelbase: 104.9 in. (all). Overall length: 188.8 in. (sedan); 193.2 in. (Safari). Width: 72.0 in. (all). Height: 53.7 in. (sedan); 54.1 in. (Safari). Front tread: 58.7 in. Rear tread: 57.0 in. Standard Tires: 185/75R14 (LE). Standard tires: 195/70R14 Goodyear Eagle GT+4 (SE).

GRAND PRIX CHASSIS: Wheelbase: 107.5 in. (all). Overall length: 193.9 in. (coupe). Overall length: 195.0 in. (sedan). Width: 72 in. (all). Height: 53.3 in. (all). Front tread: 59.5 in. Rear tread: 58.0 in. Standard tires: 195/75R14 (base and LE). Standard tires: 215/60R15 Goodyear Eagle GT (SE/STE). Standard tires: P245/50ZR16 (ASC/McLaren Turbo).

BONNEVILLE CHASSIS: Wheelbase: 110.8 in. (all). Overall length: 198.7 in. (all). Width: 72.1 in. (all). Height: 55.5 in. (all). Front tread: 60.3 in. Rear tread: 59.8 in. Standard tires: 205/75R14 BSW (LE). Standard tires: 215/65R15 Goodyear Eagle GT+4 (SE). Standard tires: P215/60R16 BSW (SSE).

TRANS SPORT CHASSIS: Wheelbase: 109.9 in. (all). Overall length: 194.5 in. (all). Width: 74.2 in. (all). Height: 65.5 in. (all). Standard tires: 205/70R14 BSW (Base). Standard tires: 195/70R15 Goodyear Eagle GT+4 (SE).

TECHNICAL

LEMANS TECHNICAL: Chassis: Front engine/front drive. Base transmission: Four-speed manual. Optional transmission: Three-speed automatic or five-speed manual. Axle ratio: 3.43:1 with 1.6L and automatic. Axle ratio: 3.18:1 with 2.0L and three-speed automatic. Axle ratio: 3.72:1 with 1.6L and four-speed manual or either engine and five-speed manual. Front suspension: deflected disc, MacPherson struts and 22mm stabilizer bar. Rear suspension: Coil springs, semi-independent torsion beam, trailing arms and 18mm anti-roll bar. Steering: Rack-and-pinion 24.5:1 ratio (18.3:1 power-assisted on GSE). Turns lock-to-lock: 3.1:1 (GSE); 3.5 (power); 4.57 (manual). Turning circle: 32.8 ft. Front brakes: 9.25-in. solid discs (1.6L) or 10.1-in. vented disc (2.0L) power-assisted. Rear brakes: 7.9 x 1.8 -in. drum (both engines) power-assisted.

SUNBIRD TECHNICAL: Chassis: Front engine/front drive. Base transmission: Five-speed manual. Optional transmission: Three-speed automatic. Axle ratio: 3.45:1 with base engine and five-speed manual. Axle ratio: 3.18:1 with 2.0L TBI engine and three-speed automatic. Axle ratio: 3.61:1 with 2.0L Turbo and five-speed manual. Axle ratio: 3.18:1 with three-speed automatic (2.08:1 optional). Front suspension: deflected disc, MacPherson struts and (22mm with 2.0L TBI/28mm with 2.0L Turbo) stabilizer bars. Rear suspension: Coil springs, semi-independent torsion beam, trailing arms (and

21mm anti-roll bar with 2.0L Turbo). Steering: Rack-and-pinion 16.0:1 ratio (14.0:1 on GT). Turns lock-to-lock: 3.0 (2.5 on GT). Turning circle: 34.3 ft. (all). Front brakes: 9.72-in. vented disc power-assisted. Rear brakes: 7.87 x 1.77-in. drum power-assisted.

GRAND AM TECHNICAL: Chassis: Front engine/front drive. Base transmission: Five-speed manual with overdrive. Optional transmission: Three-speed automatic. Axle ratio: 3.18:1 (with 2.5L engine and automatic SE). Axle ratio: 2.84:1 (with 2.5L engine and automatic LE). Axle ratio: 3.18:1 (with 2.3L engine and automatic SE). Axle ratio: 2.48:1 (with 2.3L engine and manual). Axle ratio: 3.61 (with 2.3L H.O. and manual). Stall torque ratio: 2.48:1 (with automatic). Front suspension: MacPherson struts with coil springs and 24mm anti-roll bar (28mm anti-roll bar with standard WS6 suspension on SE). Rear suspension: Trailing crank arm with twist arm, coil springs, (and 21mm anti-roll bar on SE). Steering (LE): Power-assisted rack-and-pinion, 16.0:1 ratio, 3.0 turns lock-to-lock, and 35.4-ft. (left); 37.8-ft. (right) turning circle. Steering (SE): Power-assisted rack-and-pinion, 14.0:1 ratio, 2.5 turns lock-to-lock and 35.4-ft. (left); 37.8-ft. (right) turning circle. Front brakes: Power-assisted 9.7-in. vented discs. Rear brakes: Power-assisted 7.87-in. drums. Fuel tank: 13.6 gal.

FIREBIRD TECHNICAL: Chassis: Front engine/rear drive. Base transmission: Five-speed manual. Optional transmission: Four-speed automatic. Front suspension: Fully independent with modified MacPherson strut and low-friction ball bearing upper strut mount and 30mm (Level I) or 34mm (Level II), or 36mm (Level III) anti-roll bar. Rear suspension: Live axle with coil springs, longitudinal lower control arm and torque arm, transverse track bar and 18mm (Level I) or 23mm (Level II) or 24mm (Level III) anti-roll bar. Steering: Power re-circulating ball; 14.1:1 ratio (Level I), or 12.7:1 quick ratio with sport effort valving (Levels II and III). Turns lock-to-lock: 2.72 (Level I), 2.47 (Level II), or 2.26 (Level III). Turning circle: 39.1 ft. (Level I) or 32.6 ft. (Levels II and III). Brakes: Power vented 10.5-in. front disc/9.5-in. rear drum on coupes and Formula with 5.0L EFI; power four-wheel vented disc 10.5-in. front and 11.7-in. rear with 5.7L or 5.0L with TPI and five-speed on GTA or Formula-assisted vented discs. Rear brakes: Power-assisted 7.87-in. drums. Fuel tank: 13.6 gal.

6000 TECHNICAL: Chassis: Front engine/front drive. Base transmission: Three-speed automatic with overdrive. Optional transmissions: Four-speed automatic. Axle ratio: 2.84:1 (with three-speed automatic and 2.5L or 3.1L engines). Axle ratio: 3.33:1 (with four-speed automatic and 3.1L engine). Axle ratio: 3.18:1 (with three-speed automatic and 3.1L engine in SE AWD). Front suspension: MacPherson struts with 22mm (LE), 28mm (SE), or 27mm (STE AWD). Rear suspension: Independent, transverse composite leaf spring and 22mm anti-roll bar (STE AWD); or trailing arms and track bar, Panhard rod, coil springs and 22mm anti-roll bar (SE), 20mm anti-roll bar standard. Steering: Power-assisted rack-and-pinion with 17.5:1 ratio (16.0:1 in SE AWD), 3.05 turns lock to lock and 36.96-ft. (38.5 with STE AWD) turning circle. Front brakes: Power assisted vented discs 9.72-in. (standard); 10.24-in. (medium-/heavy-duty), 10.2-in (STE). Rear brakes: Power assisted 8.86-in. drum (standard); 8.86-in. drum (medium-/heavy-duty), 10.3-in solid discs (STE). Fuel tank: 15.7-gal.

GRAND PRIX TECHNICAL: Chassis: Front engine/front drive. Standard drive train: 2.3L Quad-4 with three-speed automatic transaxle. Optional drive train: 3.1L MFI V-6 with five-speed manual transaxle. Optional drive train: 3.1L ASC/McLaren Turbo V-6 with four-speed automatic transaxle. Axle ratio: 3.18 (2.3L with three-speed automatic). Axle ratio: 3.33 (3.1L MFI V-6 with four-speed automatic). Axle ratio: 3.61 (3.1L Turbo with five-speed manual). Front suspension: MacPherson struts with tapered top coil springs, lower A arm and 28mm anti-roll bar (30mm anti-roll bar with Y99 suspension). Rear suspension: Tri-link independent suspension with 12mm anti-roll bar (transverse fiberglass leaf spring and 12mm anti-roll bar with Y99 option). Steering: Power-assisted rack-and-pinion with 15.5:1 ratio, 2.89 turns lock-to-lock and 37.4-ft. turning circle (standard). Steering: Power-assisted rack-and-pinion with 14.0:1 ratio, 2.25 turns lock-to-lock and 39.7-ft. turning circle (Y99). Steering: Power-assisted rack-and-pinion with 15.7:1 ratio, 2.25 turns lock-to-lock and 39.7-ft. turning circle (STE with Y99). Four-wheel power disc brakes. Front brakes: 10.5-in. composite vented discs. Rear brakes: 10.1-in. composite solid discs. Fuel tank: 16.0 gal.

BONNEVILLE TECHNICAL: Chassis: Front engine/front drive. Base transmission: Four-speed automatic. Axle ratio: 2.84:1 (standard with 3.8L V-6 in Bonneville LE). Axle ratio: 2.97:1 (standard with 3.8L V-6 in Bonneville SE.) Axle ratio: 3.33:1 (standard with 3.8L V-6 in Bonneville SSE). Front suspension: MacPherson struts with 24N-mm coil springs and 30mm anti-roll bar (LE). Front suspension: MacPherson struts with 248N-mm coil springs and 32mm anti-roll bar (SE). Front suspension: MacPherson struts with 24N-mm coil springs and 32mm anti-roll bar (SSE). Rear suspension: MacPherson struts with variable rate (48-65 N-mm) coil springs and 14mm anti-roll bar (LE). Rear suspension: MacPherson struts with constant-rate (47 N-mm) coil springs and 14mm anti-roll bar (LE/SE). Rear suspension: MacPherson struts with 47 N-mm coil springs and 18mm anti-roll bar (SSE). Steering: Power-assisted rack-and-pinion with 18.1:1 constant ratio, 2.97 turns lock-to-lock and 39.7-ft. left/39.0-ft. right turning circle (LE/SE). Steering: Power-assisted rack-and-pinion with 15.3:1 to 18.0:1 variable ratio, 2.79 turns lock-to-lock and 38.4-ft. left/40.7-ft. right turning circle (SSE). Front brakes: Power-assisted 10.1-in. vented discs. Rear brakes: Power-assisted 8.9-in. drums. Anti-lock brake system standard with SSE. Fuel tank: 18.0 gal.

TRANS SPORT TECHNICAL: Chassis: Front engine/front drive. Transmission: Three-speed automatic. Axle ratio: 3.18:1 (all). Front suspension: MacPherson struts with 24N-mm coil springs and 30mm anti-roll bar (LE). Front suspension: MacPherson strut, stamped lower control arms, 28mm stabilizer bar. Rear suspension: Open-section transverse beam on stamped steel trailing arms, tube shocks, coil springs, and 25.4mm stabilizer bar. Steering: Power-assisted rack-and-pinion with 15.7:1 ratio and 42.5-ft. turning circle. Front brakes: Power-assisted 10.2-in. vented rotors, 182 sq. in. swept area. Rear brakes: Power-assisted 8.86 x 1.77-in. finned composite cast-iron drums with 98.5 sq. in. swept area. Fuel tank: 20.0 gal.

OPTIONS

LEMANS OPTIONS: MX1 three-speed automatic transmission ($445). C60 air conditioning requires power steering and not available in Value Leader Aerocoupe ($680). B37 front and rear floor mats ($33). N40 power steering, requires air conditioning in Aerocoupe or SE sedan ($214). UM7 Delco ETR stereo in Value Leader Aerocoupe ($307). UM6 Delco ETR AM/FM with cassette and more in Value Leader Aerocoupe ($429). UM6 Delco ETR AM/FM with cassette and more in LE/SE/GSE ($122). V54 painted roof luggage rack ($95). AD3 removable sunroof ($350). WDV warranty enhancements for New York ($65).

SUNBIRD OPTIONS: 1SB Sunbird LE coupe option group #1 ($416). 1SC Sunbird LE coupe option group #2 ($1,462). 1SD Sunbird LE coupe option group #3 ($1,657). 1SB Sunbird LE sedan option group #1 ($416). 1SC Sunbird LE sedan option group #2 ($1,468). 1SD Sunbird LE sedan option group #3 ($1,863). 1SB Sunbird LE convertible option group #1 ($1,046). 1SC Sunbird LE convertible option group #2 ($1,368). 1SB Sunbird SE coupe option group #1 ($416). 1SC Sunbird SE coupe option group #2 ($1,413). 1SD Sunbird SE coupe option group #3 ($1,886). 1SB Sunbird GT coupe option group #1 ($1,122). 1SC Sunbird SE coupe option group #2 ($1,367). R6A Sunbird LE value package ($374). R6A Sunbird SE coupe value package ($469). LT2 2.0-liter engine in GT

1990 Pontiac Trans Sport SE Minivan. (PGMC)

($768 credit). LT3 Turbo engine, mandatory extras and specific options, optional only in LE convertible ($1,023-$1,402). MX1 three-speed automatic transmission ($465). C60 air conditioning ($720). K34 cruise control ($195). C49 electric rear window defogger ($160). NB2 California emissions package ($100). D84 custom two-tone paint for LE ($101). AU3 power door locks ($175 coupe/$215 sedan). A31 power windows, requires power door locks ($230 coupe/$295 sedan/no charge convertible). UM7 Delco radio equipment (standard/no charge). UM6 Delco radio equipment ($1,702 additional). U1C Delco radio equipment ($226-$396). AR9 reclining bucket seats with Pallex cloth trim (no charge). T43 rear deck lid with spoiler for LE convertible ($70). AD3 removable glass sunroof ($350). QME tire option ($114). PX1 13-in. N78 14-in Hi-tech Turbo aluminum wheels with locking package ($265-$335).

GRAND AM OPTIONS: 1SB Grand Am LE coupe option group #1 ($910). 1SC Grand Am LE coupe option group #2 ($1,105). 1SD Grand Am LE coupe option group #3 ($1,817). 1SB Grand Am LE sedan option group #1 ($910). 1SC Grand Am LE sedan option group #2 ($1,105). 1SD Grand Am LE sedan option group #3 ($1,922). 1SB Grand Am SE coupe and sedan option group #1 ($321). R6A Grand Am LE coupe value package ($394). R6B Grand Am LE coupe value package without 1SD package ($455). R6B Grand Am LE coupe value package with 1SD package ($40). R6B Grand Am LE sedan value package ($520). Advertising ($200). LD2 Quad-4 2.3-liter MPI engine ($660 in LE; $108 delete-option in SE). LGO Quad-4 High-Output engine (standard on SE/Manual). MX1 three-speed automatic transmission ($540). C60 air conditioning ($720). C49 electric rear window defogger ($160). NB2 California emission requirements ($100). UB3 rally cluster gauges and trip odometer in LE ($127). V56 deck lid luggage carrier ($115). D84 custom two-tone paint for LE ($101). AU3 power door locks ($175 coupe/$215 sedan). A31 power windows, requires custom console in LE ($240 coupe/$305 sedan). W30 Sport Option package includes SE-style front and rear fascias, SE tail lamps, SE Aero package less wheel flares, Quad-4 H.O. engine, dual exhausts, five-speed manual transmission, P195/70R14 black sidewall tires; Hi-tech Turbo wheels, specific FE2 suspension, rally gauges with tachometer and interior courtesy lamps for LE coupe/sedan ($1,164-$1,718 depending on specific package). UM6 Delco radio equipment ($140). U1D Delco radio equipment ($405-$545). AR9 custom reclining bucket seats with Pallex cloth trim (no charge). AD3 removable glass sunroof ($350). QMB tire option ($78 extra). N78 14-in Hi-tech Turbo aluminum wheels with locking package ($265).

FIREBIRD OPTIONS: 1SB Firebird option group #1 ($865). 1SB Firebird option group #2 ($1,603).1SB Formula/Trans Am option group #1 ($495). 1SC Firebird and Formula option group #2 ($889). 1SC Firebird and Formula option group #2 ($854). R6A Firebird and Formula value package ($820). R6A Trans Am value package ($889). R6A Trans Am value package ($1,020). Advertising ($200). LO3 5.0-liter TBI V-8 engine in base Firebird ($350). LB9 5.0L MPI V-8 in Formula and Trans Am ($745). LB9 5.0L MPI V-8 in Trans Am GTA ($300 credit). B2L 5.7L MPI V-8 in Trans Am ($300). B2L 5.7L MPI V-8 in Formula ($1,020). MM5 five-speed manual transmission in Trans Am GTA with LB9 ($515 credit). MX0 four-speed automatic transmission, except in GTA ($515). C60 air conditioning ($805). G80 limited-slip axle ($100). C49 electric rear window defogger ($160). N10 dual converter exhaust ($155). KC4 engine oil cooler ($110). NB2 California emissions ($100). CC1 Hatch roof ($920). D66 deluxe two-tone paint ($150). WX1 lower accent two-tone paint delete on Formulas ($150 credit). J65 four-wheel disc power brakes ($179). AU3 power door locks ($175). A31 power windows ($260). UM6 Delco radio equipment ($150). UX1 Delco radio equipment ($300). U1A Delco radio equipment ($226-$526). U75 power antenna ($75). D42 cargo area security screen ($69). AQ9 articulating bucket seats with Ventura leather trim in GTA ($450). QLC high-performance WS6 performance suspension ($385).

6000 OPTIONS: 1SB option package #1 for 6000 LE sedan ($995). 1SC option package #2 for 6000 LE sedan ($1,190). 1SD option package #3 for 6000 LE sedan ($2,058). 1SB option package #1 for 6000 LE Safari ($190). 1SC option package #2 for 6000 LE Safari ($385). 1SD option package #3 for 6000 LE Safari ($1,243). 1SB option package #1 for 6000 SE sedan ($343). 1SB option package #1 for 6000 SE Safari ($293). R6A value option package for 6000 LE sedan ($413). R6B value option package for 6000 LE sedan

1990 Pontiac Turbo Grand Prix STE four-door sedan. (PGMC)

1990 Pontiac Grand Prix STE four-door sedan. (PGMC)

($413). R6B value option package for 6000 LE sedan ($413). LB6 2.8-liter MFI V-6 in LE sedan ($660). MX0 four-speed automatic transmission ($200). C60 air conditioning ($805). C49 electric rear window defogger ($160). D86 two-tone paint ($115). AU3 power door locks ($205). A31 power windows ($310). UM6 Delco ETR AM/FM stereo ($122). U1A Delco ETR AM stereo/FM stereo ($501-$536). AM6 45/55 split bench seat ($133). B20 custom interior with 45/55 split seat in Empress/London cloth ($350-$483). Various tire options (no charge to $68). N78 Sport aluminum wheels with locking package ($265). BX3 woodgrain exterior siding for Safari ($295).

GRAND PRIX OPTIONS: 1SB Grand Prix LE coupe option package #1 ($190). 1SC Grand Prix LE coupe option package #2 ($470). 1SD Grand Prix LE coupe option package #3 ($1,603). 1SE Grand Prix LE coupe option package #4 ($2,162). 1SB Grand Prix LE sedan option package #1 ($190). 1SC Grand Prix LE sedan option package #2 ($385). 1SD Grand Prix LE sedan option package #3 ($1,808). 1SE Grand Prix LE sedan option package #4 ($2,487). 1SB Grand Prix SE coupe option package #1 ($561). LG5 Turbo coupe Option Package ($888 credit). R6A Grand Prix LE coupe value option package ($865). R6A Grand Prix LE sedan value option package ($409). R6B Grand Prix LE sedan value option package ($464). R6A Grand Prix SE coupe value option package ($975). R6A Grand Prix STE sedan value option package. ($975). LG5 ASC/McLaren Turbo conversion ($5,236). MX0 four-speed automatic in Grand Prix SE ($200). MX0 four-speed automatic in Grand Prix SE ($640). MM5 five-speed manual transmission in Grand Prix LE ($440 credit). JL9 anti-lock power brakes ($925). C49 electric rear window defogger ($160). NB2 California emissions system ($100). D84 two-tone paint ($105). AU3 power door locks ($175-$215). CF5 power sunroof ($650 or $450 with Turbo conversion). A31 power windows ($240-$301). UM6 Delco radio equipment ($140). UX1 Delco radio equipment ($400). U1A stereo sound system ($226-$666 depending on model). AM9 bucket seat with Pallex cloth trim in Grand Prix LE ($110). AN3 Custom Cloth bucket seat in Grand Prix LE ($140). AQ9 articulating Sport bucket seats with front console and Ventura leather trim ($450-$650). AC3 power seat ($270). BYP Sport Appearance package including SE styling elements for LE coupe ($160-$285).

BYP Sport Appearance package including SE styling elements for LE sedan ($480). Various tire options ($54-$72). PF1 15-in. styled steel wheels, except SE ($145). PH3 15-in. aluminum sport wheels with locking package ($125-$265).

BONNEVILLE OPTIONS: 1SB Bonneville LE option package #1 ($269). 1SC Bonneville LE option package #2 ($464). 1SD Bonneville LE option package #3 ($1,716). 1SE Bonneville LE option package #3 ($2,414). 1SB Bonneville SE option package #1 ($330). 1SC Bonneville SE option package #2 ($810). R6A Bonneville LE value option package ($940). R6A Bonneville SE value option package. ($465). R6A Bonneville SE value option package ($610). R6A Bonneville SE value option package. ($535). Advertising ($200). C49 electric rear window defogger ($160). NB2 California emissions system ($100). D84 two-tone paint ($105). JM4 power anti-lock brakes ($925). AU3 power door locks ($215). A31 power windows ($375). UM6 Delco radio equipment ($140). UT4 radio equipment package ($580-$655). U1A compact disc player ($666-$1,031). US7 power antenna ($75). AS7 custom interior trim with split bench seat and console ($235). B20 custom interior with 45/55 split seat in Metrix cloth trim ($230-$705 depending on value package options or individual option). AG1 six-way power seat in LE ($270). CF5 power glass sunroof ($1,230). Various tire options ($70-$164). PF7 15-in. diamond-spoke wheels with locking package on LE ($296). Bonneville SSE R6A value option package ($1,080). UA1 AM/FM stereo in Bonneville SSE ($186). CF5 power glass sunroof in SSE ($1,230). UA6 theft deterrent system in SSE ($150). WDV warranty enhancements for New York ($65).

TRANS SPORT OPTIONS: 1SB Trans Sport option package #1 ($1,195). 1SC Trans Sport option package #2 ($1,960). 1SB Trans Sport SE option package #1 ($765). Advertising ($200). C67 air conditioning in Trans Sport ($805). NB2 California emissions system ($100). B2Q black roof delete (no charge). C49 electric rear window defogger ($160). AJ1 glass package in Trans Sport ($245). AB5 power door locks ($255). A31 power windows ($240). UM6 Delco radio equipment ($140). U1A compact disc player ($376-$516). AB3 six-passenger seating package ($525). ZP7 seven-passenger seating package ($675). N78 14-in. aluminum wheels ($265).

NOTE: Full option package contents, descriptions, and applications information can often be determined by consulting factory literature. The data above is edited for size and clarity. This information provided only as a guide to help collectors appraise the relative value of cars with numerous options. Prices for items included as part of a value option package are usually much less than individual prices. Option prices charged by individual dealers may also vary.

HISTORICAL: Pontiac's model-year production included 143,932 Sunbirds, 197,020 Grand Ams, 46,760 Firebirds, 66,398 Pontiac 6000s, 85,844 Bonnevilles and 128,067 Grand Prixs. In addition, 34,226 LeMans models were built in Canada and 40,771 Trans Ports left the factory counted as "trucks." Model-year sales (not counting LeMans and Trans Sport units) were 596,414 for an 8.8 percent market share. Ed Lechtzin became PMD's director of public relations. One of the cars that seemed to promote itself was the hot-selling Grand Am. In the Summer 1990 issue of PMD's *Action Track*, it was reported that 3,500 people working at the 572-acre Fairfax, Kansas factory were building 650 Grand Prix in two shifts a day, except on Wednesdays, when each shift built only 300 cars because team meetings to improve quality and productivity were held.

1990 Pontiac Turbo Grand Prix STE four-door sedan. (PGMC)

1991 PONTIAC

1991 Pontiac Sunbird GT two-door coupe. (PGMC)

LEMANS — SERIES 2T — (FOUR) — The Pontiac LeMans was based on the German Opel Kadett and built in Korea. The 1991 LeMans line consisted of the Aerocoupe and the LE coupe and the LE sedan. The GSE was discontinued. All models featured motorized passive seat belts, fully reclining bucket seats, an electric rear window defogger, vented front disk brakes, an electronically fuel-injected engine and front-wheel-drive. The Aerocoupe also had a four-speed manual transmission, P175R/70R13 tires, steel wheels with full wheel covers and a two-spoke steering wheel. The LE models added or substituted a five-speed manual transmission, gray lower accent paint, and an AM/FM stereo with clock. New for 1991 were body-color and gray accent moldings (replacing black body side moldings), new Chester and Sarah cloth interior trims (replacing Twill cloth), a new manual transmission shift boot (replacing the molded rubber type), a new cam belt tensioner (1.6-liter engine) and a 10-minute rear defroster time-out (replacing five-minute time-out).

SUNBIRD — SERIES 2J — (FOUR) — The 1991 Sunbird was a sporty and expressive front-wheel-drive sub-compact. Four coupes, one convertible coupe and two sedans were offered in base, LE, SE, and GT car-lines. New features for 1991 included a 3.1-liter V-6 engine; a stainless steel exhaust system; dual exhausts on GT models; new 15-in. specific GT wheels; a quarter-wave tuner for the two-liter engine; a new Medium Camel interior (replacing Beechwood); added acoustical ride insulation; colored visor vanity mirrors; a self-aligning steering wheel; and a new Bright Red exterior color. Standard equipment on the Sunbird coupe and sedan included a 2.0-liter MFI engine, a five-speed manual transmission, P185/75R14 tires, steel wheels with tri-lace wheel covers, power rack and pinion steering, and an AM/FM stereo with clock. The Sunbird LE coupe and sedan had the same basic equipment, but a few upgraded interior/exterior trim items. The Sunbird LE convertible added or substituted P185/75R14 tires, power door locks, power windows, dual sport mirrors, and tinted glass. As compared to LE models, the Sunbird SE coupe added or substituted P195/70R14 tires, Hi-Tech Turbo wheels, a rear deck lid spoiler, dual sport mirrors, and tinted glass. The top-of-the-line Sunbird GT coupe featured a 3.1-liter EFI V-6, a five-speed manual transmission, P205/55R15 Eagle GT+4 tires, a Sport suspension, GT specific 15-in. alloy wheels, a rear deck lid spoiler, dual Sport mirrors, tinted glass, power rack and pinion steering, and an AM/FM cassette stereo with clock.

GRAND AM — SERIES 2N — (FOUR/V-6) — Since its re-introduction as a 1985 model, the Grand Am had become Pontiac's most popular nameplate. Its sales topped the one million mark and nearly a quarter-million Grand Ams were sold in 1989 alone. The 1991 Grand Am line continued to offer the same type of appeal with many features and attractive pricing aimed at a broad range of buyers. The line included two body styles that came in six models. The Grand Am, the Grand Am LE and the Grand Am SE were all offered as a coupe or as a sedan. New features for 1991 included larger front brakes and redesigned cables, a shorter manual shift lever, a new Black color (replacing Black Metallic) and redesigned seat recliner

handles. LE models also had a new Sport Performance package and monotone exterior treatment. SEs also came with ABS VI anti-lock brakes. A 3.77:1 first gear ratio was new for Grand Ams with the 2.3-liter H.O. engine and a five-speed manual transmission. Standard equipment on the Grand Am coupe and sedan included the 2.5-liter EFI engine, the five-speed manual transmission, P185/75R14 tires, 14-in steel wheels with tri-lace wheel covers, easy-entry bucket seats (coupes only) and an AM/FM stereo with clock. The Grand Am LE had the same basic equipment features with slightly upgraded interior and exterior trim. The SE models added or substituted a 2.3-liter H.O. MFI "Quad Four" engine, ABS IV anti-lock brakes, 16-in. color-keyed aluminum wheels, an instrumentation package, air conditioning, split folding rear seats, cruise control, a tilt steering wheel, power windows (with driver-window "express-down" feature), power door locks and an AM/FM cassette stereo with clock.

FIREBIRD — SERIES 2F — (V-6/V-8) — The new 1991 Firebirds were actually introduced in the spring of 1990. Their most visible change was a new exterior appearance. All models benefited from restyled front and rear fascias. The front fascias, made of body color resilient "Endura" thermoplastic, incorporated low-profile turn signals and integral air dams. At the rear, the GTA, Trans Am, and Formula were fitted with a redesigned rear deck lid spoiler. New fascias on GTA and Trans Am models incorporated restyled taillights. The Sport Appearance package on the base Firebird included fog lights in the fascia and carried the aero look to the sides with distinctive lateral skirting. The headlights were more compact, without sacrificing light output. Available in 1991 for all 5.0- and 5.7-liter TPI V-8s was a new "Street Legal Performance" (SLP) package of GM high-performance hardware. The SLP kit, available from GM dealers, boosted engine performance without modifications to the power plants. The kit could be dealer-installed or owner-installed. All 1991 Firebirds were protected by a Pass-Key theft deterrent system. All Firebirds had a driver's side airbag. The standard radio was upgraded to an AM/FM cassette stereo and the GTA included a cassette with five-band graphic equalizer. Acoustics were improved in all models. New colors included Dark Green Metallic and a Bright White. Standard Firebird equipment included a 3.1-liter MFI V-6, a four-speed automatic transmission, the FE1 suspension, P215/65R15 tires, 15 x 7-in. Hi-Tech aluminum wheels, disc/drum brakes, new front/rear fascias, and an AM/FM stereo with cassette and clock. The Formula added or substituted a 5.0-liter TBI V-8, a five-speed manual gearbox, the WS6 Sport Suspension, P245/50ZR16 tires, 16 x 8 -in. Hi-Tech Turbo aluminum wheels, a limited-slip differential, and air conditioning. The Trans Am added or substituted a 5.0-liter TPI V-8, the F41 Rally Tuned suspension, 16 x 8-in. diamond spoke wheels, an aero package with special side treatment, a leather appointment group (including leather-wrapped steering wheel), and a four-way manual driver's seat adjuster. Standard equipment for the Trans Am GTA included the 5.7-liter TPI V-8, a four-speed automatic transmission, the WS6 Sport suspension, P245/50ZR16 tires, 16 x 8-in. diamond spoke wheels, a limited-slip differential, disc/drum brakes, a Performance Enhancement group (with engine oil cooler, dual converters and performance axle), new front/rear fascias, an aero package with side treatment, air conditioning, an upgraded sound system, a power antenna, the leather appointment group, a four-way manual driver's seat, power windows and power door locks, cruise control, a remote deck lid release, and power outside mirrors.

1991 Pontiac Firebird Formula two-door coupe. (PGMC)

6000 — SERIES 2A — (I-4/V-6) — New features for 1991 Pontiac 6000s were few. They consisted primarily of a new Light Camel Metallic exterior color, a new Tan interior color, and the dropping of two models, the 600 SE Safari wagon and the 6000 SE All-Wheel-Drive sedan. That left the LE sedan, LE Safari wagon, and SE sedan in the lineup. All 6000s came with composite headlights, fog lamps, a front air dam, dual sport outside mirrors, and black door and window moldings. The 6000 SE carried the full card of standard features, while the LE sedan allowed buyers to equip their cars to fit their needs. The 6000 LE Safari wagon provided all the size benefits of a traditional station wagon. Standard features of the LE sedan included a 2.5-liter EFI four-cylinder engine, a three-speed automatic transmission, P185/75R14 tires, 14-in. rims with tri-lace wheel covers, and an AM/FM stereo radio with clock. The 6000 LE Safari wagon added or substituted a 3.1-liter base V-6 with EFI, a four-speed automatic transmission, and air conditioning. In addition to the Safari wagon's equipment, the 6000 SE had P195/70R15 Eagle GT+4 tires, 15-in. aluminum sport wheels, power windows, cruise control, power door locks, a custom trim package with bucket seats and gauges, and an AM/FM cassette stereo with clock.

GRAND PRIX — SERIES 2G — (V-6/V-8) — The Grand Prix had some of the most exciting changes in the 1991 Pontiac lineup. There was a revised model range, with the Grand Prix GTP replacing the Grand Prix Turbo coupe. This car looked like the turbocharged model, but had an all-new 210-hp Twin Dual Cam V-6. A new four-speed electronic automatic transmission could be had only with the new engine. Coupes had a new exterior appearance. There was also a new SE coupe sport appearance package, plus a new Aero Performance package. New-for-1991 colors included Bright Blue Metallic, Bright White, Black, and Turquoise. Also new was a Generation II head-up display option. Models available included the LE sedan, SE coupe, SE sedan, GT coupe, and STE sedan. The GTP was considered a model-option. Standard equipment for LEs included the 2.3-liter Quad 4 engine, a three-speed automatic transmission, 15-in. sport wheel covers, P205/70R15 touring tires, air conditioning, 45/55 split reclining front seats, and an AM/FM stereo with clock. The SE coupe and sedan added or substituted upscale interior and exterior trims. The GT coupe added or substituted a 3.1-liter MFI V-6; the Y99 Rally Tuned suspension; 16-in. cast aluminum wheels; P21560R/16 Eagle GT+4 tire; power windows; power door locks; front bucket seats with power articulated supports; a power driver's seat; cruise control; an AM/FM cassette stereo with equalizer, clock, and steering wheel controls; and a six-speaker sound system. The Grand Prix STE sedan had most of the GT features, but its 16-in. cast aluminum wheels were different. Also found on the Grand Prix STE were an electronic information center, a remote keyless entry system, an eight-speaker sound system, and power reclining front articulated bucket seats. Standard features of the GTP-optioned coupe included the 3.4-liter Twin Dual Cam V-6, a five-speed manual transmission, the Y99 Rally Tuned suspension, an Aero Performance package, P225/60R16 Eagle GT+4 tires on 16 x 8-in. aluminum wheels, air conditioning, power windows, power door locks, front articulated bucket seats, a power driver's seat, cruise control, an AM/FM cassette with equalizer, clock and steering wheel controls, and a six-speaker sound system.

BONNEVILLE — SERIES 2H — (V-6) — The Bonneville remained Pontiac's full-size Touring Sedan in 1991. Innovations for the year included a new brake-transmission interlock; London/Empress cloth trims for SE models (optional on LE); 15-in. bolt-on wheel covers for LE models; and P215/65R-15 tires for LE models. The LE was the low model, the SE was the middle model and the SSE was the top-of-the-line. The LE gave buyers a choice of 45/55 bucket seats with a center console or a 45/55 split bench seat with center armrest. Standard equipment included a four-spoke steering wheel, an AM/FM stereo radio with clock, manual air conditioning, the F41 suspension, and a 2.84:1 final drive ratio. The SE model added or substituted power express windows, P21560R-16 tires, 16-in. six-spoke wheels, a 2.97:1 final drive ratio, an AM/FM stereo cassette, a 45/55 reclining split front seat with armrest, a rear window defogger, and power door locks. A full rally instrumentation package including tachometer, voltmeter, engine and oil temperature gauges, and trip odometer was also included at no extra cost. The Bonneville SSE added or substituted the following over SE features: ABS brakes, the FE2 suspension with electronic-level control and variable-ratio steering, 16-in. Aerolite wheels (gold cross-lace wheels were a no-

1991 Pontiac Grand Prix GTP two-door coupe. (PGMC)

cost option), a 3.33:1 final drive ratio, automatic air conditioning with temperature indicator light, steering wheel controls for radio/heat/vent and A/C functions, an AM/FM stereo with cassette and graphic equalizer, an eight-speaker sound system, 45/55 12-way articulating bucket seats with console, a specific instrument package with full gauges, compass and Driver Information Center, a remote keyless entry system, a theft-deterrent system, a rear window defogger, a power antenna, a remote deck lid release, and express-down power windows. The SSE again sported a distinctive monochromatic paint treatment. The trunk was fitted with a security net, a rear cargo compartment close-out, a trunk-mounted tire inflator, and a roadside emergency kit.

TRANS SPORT — SERIES 2U — (V-6) — The 1991 Trans Sport came in Trans Sport (base) and Trans Sport SE models. Standard features of the base model included 2+3 seating with a bench-type second seat, an AM/FM radio with clock, and P205/70R-14 tires. The Trans Port SE added or substituted 2+2+2 seating, a leather steering wheel, tilt steering, cruise control, deep-tinted glass, power outside rearview mirrors, electronic control front air conditioning, an AM/FM cassette stereo, Electronic Ride Control, P205/65R-15 tires, 15-in. wheels (with Medium Red, White, or machine-faced finish), and a package including a lamp group. New features for 1991 included a stainless steel exhaust system, a roof luggage carrier, larger outside rearview mirrors, and a self-aligning steering wheel. The standard tires used on each model were upgraded and the SE's new standard power mirrors could also be added to the base model at extra cost. The SE also offered a new 2+3+2 seating option. New colors of Bright Red and Medium Blue Metallic were also offered for the monochromatic-finished SE. Base Trans Sport seats were trimmed with Pallex cloth. Uplevel Metrix fabric was found inside the higher-priced SE.

I.D. DATA: Pontiac's 17-symbol Vehicle Identification Number (VIN) for passenger cars was on the upper left surface of the instrument panel, visible through the windshield. The first symbol indicates country of origin: 1=U.S.; 2= Canada; 3=Mexico; J=Japan; K=Korea. The second symbol indicates manufacturer: G=General Motors; G=Suzuki; 8=Isuzu; Y=NUMMI; L=Daewoo; C=CAMI. The third symbol G indicates make: 2=Pontiac division; 5=Pontiac incomplete; 7=GM of Canada; M=Pontiac Multi-Purpose Vehicle; Y=Pontiac Truck. The fourth and fifth symbols for passenger cars indicated body type and series: A/J=6000 SE; A/F=6000 LE; F/S=Firebird; F/W=Firebird Trans Am; H/X=Bonneville LE; HY=Bonneville SSE; H/Z=Bonneville SE; J/C=Sunbird; J/B=Sunbird LE; J/D=Sunbird SE; J/U=Sunbird GT; M/R=Firefly (U.S. Customs Territories); N/G=Grand Am; N/E=Grand Am LE; N/W=Grand Am SE; T/N=LeMans; T/S=LeMans GSE; T/X=LeMans Aerocoupe; W/J=Grand Prix LE; W/T=Grand Prix STE; W/P=Grand Prix SE. On Trans Sports the fourth symbol indicated the GVWR/brake system and the fifth symbol indicating line and chassis type was a "U" for All-Purpose Vehicle 4x2. The sixth symbol on passenger cars denoted body type: 1=two-door coupe/sedan styles 11, 27, 37, 47, 57, 97; 2=two-door hatchback styles 07, 08, 77 and 87; 3=two-door convertible style 67; 4=two-door station wagon style 15; 5=four-door sedan styles 19 and 69; 6=four-door hatchback/liftback style 68; 8=four-door station wagon style 35. The sixth symbol on Trans Sports indicated series: 6=All-Purpose Vehicle. The seventh symbol on passenger cars indicated the type of restraint system: 1=manual belts; 3=manual belts with driver airbag; 4=passive automatic belts. The seventh symbol on Trans Sports indicated body type: 6=All-Purpose Vehicle. Symbol eight for passenger cars was an engine code: A=RPO LG0 2.3-liter fuel-inject I-4; C=RPO LN3 3.8-liter fuel-injected V-6; D=RPO LD2 2.3-liter fuel-injected I-4; E=RPO L03 5.0-liter fuel-injected V-8; F=RPO LB9 5.0-liter fuel-injected V-8; K=RPO LT2 2.0-liter fuel-injected I-4; R=RPO LR8 2.5-liter fuel-injected I-4; T=RPO LH0 3.1-liter fuel-injected V-6; U=RPO L68 2.5-liter fuel-injected I-4; X=RPO LQ1 3.4-liter fuel-injected V-6; 6=RPO L73 1.6-liter fuel-injected I-4; 8=RPO L98 5.7-liter fuel-injected V-8. The seventh symbol for Trans sports was also an engine code: D=3.1-liter fuel-injected V-6. The ninth symbol for cars and trucks is a check digit. The tenth symbol for cars and trucks denotes model year (M=1991). The 11th symbol for cars and trucks indicates the GM assembly plant (A=Lakewood, CA; B=Baltimore, Md. T&B; B=Lansing, Mich.; B=Pupyong, Korea; C=Lansing, Mich.; D=Doraville, Ga.; E=Linden, N.J.; E=Pontiac East, Mich. T&B; F=Fairfax II, Kan.; F=Flint T&B; H=Flint, Mich.; J=Janesville, Wis.; J=Janesville, Wis. T&B; K=Kosai, Japan; L=Van Nuys, Calif.; M=Lansing, Mich; R=Arlington, Texas; S=Ramos Arizpe, Mexico; T=Tarrytown, N.Y.; U=Hamtramck, Mich; V=Pontiac, Mich. (T&B); W=Willow Run, Mich.; W=Iwata, Japan; Y=Wilmington, Del.; Z=Fremont, Calif.; Z=Ft. Wayne, Ind. T&B; 0= Pontiac, Mich. (T&B); 1=Oshawa, Canada #2; 1=Wentzville, Mo. T&B; 2=Morraine, OH T&B; 2=Ste. Therese, Canada; 3=Detroit, Mich. T&B; 3=Kawasaki, Japan; 4=Orion, Mich.; 4=Scarborough, Ontario, Canada; 5=Bowling Green, Ken.; 6=Ingersoll, Ontario, Canada; 6=Oklahoma City, Okla.; 7=Lordstown, Ohio; 7=Flusawa, Japan; 8=Shreveport, La. T&B; 9=Oshawa, Ontario, Canada #1. Pontiacs are not produced at all of these GM plants. The last six symbols are the consecutive unit number at the factory.

Model Number	Body Style Number	Body Type & Seating	Factory Price	Shipping Weight	Production Total
LEMANS AEROCOUPE SERIES T/X (I-4)					
2T	TX2	3d Coupe-4P	7,574	2,169	—
LEMANS LE SERIES T/N (I-4)					
2T	TN2	3d Coupe-4P	8,304	2,191	—
2T	N5	4d Sedan-4P	8,754	2,246	—
BASE SUNBIRD SERIES J/C (I-4)					
2J	JC5	4d Sedan-5P	8,784	2,592	Note 1
2J	JC1	2d Coupe-5P	7,858	2,376	Note 1
SUNBIRD LE SERIES J/B (I-4)					
2J	JB5	4d Sedan-5P	9,544	2,608	Note 1
2J	JB1	2d Coupe-5P	9,444	2,590	Note 1
2J	JB3	2d Convertible-5P	14,414	2,775	Note 1
SUNBIRD SE SERIES J/D (I-4/I-4 TURBO)					
2J	JD1	2d Coupe-5P	10,694	2,617	Note 1
SUNBIRD GT TURBO SERIES J/U (I-4/I-4 Turbo)					
2J	JU1	2d Coupe-5P	12,444	2,793	Note 1
GRAND AM LE SERIES N/G (I-4/V-6)					
2N	NG1	2d Coupe-5P	10,174	2,566	Note 2
2N	NG5	4d Sedan-5P	10,374	2,566	Note 2
GRAND AM LE SERIES N/E (I-4/V-6)					
2N	NE1	2d Coupe-5P	11,124	2,508	Note 2
2N	NE5	4d Sedan-5P	11,324	2,592	Note 2
GRAND AM SE SERIES N/W (I-4)					
2N	NW1	2d Coupe-5P	16,344	2,739	Note 2
2N	NW5	4d Sedan-5P	16,544	2,826	Note 2
FIREBIRD SERIES F/S (V-6)					
2F	FS2	2d Coupe-5P	12,690	3,121	Note 3
2F	FS3	2d Convertible-5P	19,159	—	Note 3
FIREBIRD SERIES F/S (V-8)					
2F	FS2	2d Coupe-5P	13,040	3,287	Note 3
2F	FS3	2d Convertible-5P	19,509	—	Note 3
FIREBIRD FORMULA SERIES F/S (V-8)					
2F	FS2	2d Coupe-5P	15,530	3,370	Note 3

Model Number	Body Style Number	Body Type & Seating	Factory Price	Shipping Weight	Production Total
FIREBIRD TRANS AM SERIES F/W (V-8)					
2F	FW2	2d Coupe-5P	17,530	3,343	Note 3
2F	FW3	2d Convertible-5P	22,980	—	Note 3
FIREBIRD TRANS AM GTA SERIES F/W (V-8)					
2F	FW2	2d Coupe-5P	24,530	3,456	Note 3
6000 LE SERIES A/F (I-4)					
2A	AF5	4d Sedan-5P	12,999	2,843	Note 4
6000 LE SERIES A/F (V-6)					
2A	AF5	4d Sedan-5P	13,659	2,970	Note 4
2A	AF8	4d Safari-5P	16,699	3,162	Note 4
6000 SE SERIES A/J (I-4/V-6)					
2A	AJ5	4d Sedan-5P	18,399	3,370	Note 4
GRAND PRIX LE SERIES 2W (I-4)					
2G	WH5	4d Sedan-5P	14,294	3,248	Note 5
GRAND PRIX LE SERIES 2W (V-6)					
2G	WH5	4d Sedan-5P	14,294	3,274	Note 5
GRAND PRIX SE SERIES 2W (I-4)					
2G	WJ5	4d Sedan-5P	15,284	3,252	Note 5
2G	WJ1	2d Coupe-5P	14,894	3,188	Note 5
GRAND PRIX SE SERIES 2W (V-6)					
2G	WJ5	4d Sedan-5P	15,284	3,278	Note 5
2G	WJ1	2d Coupe-5P	14,294	3,274	Note 5
GRAND PRIX GT- SERIES 2W (V-6)					
2G	WP1	2d Coupe-5P	19,154	3,323	Note 5
GRAND PRIX STE SERIES 2W (V-6/V-8)					
2G	WT5	4d Sedan-5P	19,994	3,400	Note 5
BONNEVILLE LE SERIES H/X (V-6)					
2H	HX5	4d Sport Sedan-5P	16,834	3,323	Note 6
BONNEVILLE SE SERIES H/Z (V-6)					
2H	HZ5	4d Sport Sedan-5P	20,464	3,376	Note 6
BONNEVILLE SSE SERIES H/Y (V-6)					
2H	HY5	4d Sport Sedan-5P	25,264	3,551	Note 6
TRANS SPORT SERIES U (V-6)					
2U	U06	Minivan	15,619	3,514	Note 7
TRANS SPORT SE SERIES U (V-6)					
2U	U06	Minivan	18,889	3,626	Note 7

NOTE 1: Sunbird series production totaled 118,615 cars.

NOTE 2: Grand Am series production totaled 147,467 cars.

NOTE 3: Firebird series production totaled 20,332 cars.

NOTE 4: 6000 series production totaled 19,603 cars.

NOTE 5: Grand Prix series production totaled 114,718 cars.

NOTE 6: Bonneville series production totaled 88,355 cars.

NOTE 7: Trans Sport series production totaled 27,181 cars.

LE MANS ENGINE

ENGINE [Base Four VL/LE]: Inline. OHV. Four-cylinder. Cast-iron block. Aluminum head and intake manifold. Displacement: 97.5 cid. (1.6L). Bore & stroke: 3.11 x 3.21 in. Compression ratio: 8.6:1. Brake horsepower: 74 at 5600 rpm. Torque: 90 lbs.-ft. at 2800 rpm. Fuel system: EFI/TBI. RPO Code: L73. Standard with four-speed manual Value Leader and LeMans LE. [VIN code 6].

SUNBIRD ENGINES

ENGINE [Base Four LE/SE]: Inline. OHC. Four-cylinder. Cast-iron block. Aluminum head and intake manifold. Displacement: 121 cid. (2.0L). Bore & stroke: 3.39 x 3.39 in. Compression ratio: 8.8:1. Brake horsepower: 96 at 4800 rpm. Torque: 118 lbs.-ft. at 3600 rpm. Fuel system: EFI/TBI. RPO Code: LT2. Standard in Sunbird LE and Sunbird SE models. [VIN code K].

ENGINE [Base Six GT]: V-block. OHV. Six-cylinder. Cast-iron block and aluminum head. Displacement 191 cid. (3.1L). Bore & stroke: 3.50 x 3.31 in. Compression ratio: 8.9:1. Brake horsepower: 140 at 4500 rpm. Torque: 180 lbs.-ft. at 3600 rpm. Fuel system: EFI/MPI. RPO Code: [VIN code T].

GRAND AM ENGINES

ENGINE [Standard base/LE]: Inline. OHV. Cast-iron block and head. Aluminum intake manifold. Displacement: 151 cid. (2.5L Tech IV). Bore & stroke: 4.00 x 3.00 in. Compression ratio: 9.0:1. Brake horsepower: 110 at 5200 rpm. Torque: 135 lbs.-ft. at 3200 rpm. Five main bearings. Hydraulic valve lifters. Fuel system: EFI. RPO Code: L68. Standard in Grand AM/LE. [VIN code U/R].

ENGINE [Standard SE with automatic transmission]: Inline. DOHC. 16-valve. Quad-4. Cast-iron block. Aluminum head and intake manifold. Displacement: 138 cid. (2.3L). Bore & stroke: 3.62 x 3.35 in. Compression ratio: 9.5:1. Brake horsepower: 160 at 6200 rpm. Torque: 155 lbs.-ft. at 5200 rpm. Fuel system: MPFI. RPO Code: LD2. Standard in SE with automatic; optional in LE with automatic. [VIN code D].

1991 Pontiac Grand Prix STE four-door sedan. (PGMC)

1991 Pontiac Bonneville SSE four-door sedan. (PGMC)

ENGINE [Standard SE with manual transmission]: Inline. DOHC. 16-valve. Quad-4 High-Output. Cast-iron block. Aluminum head and intake manifold. Displacement: 138 cid. (2.3L). Bore & stroke: 3.62 x 3.35 in. Compression ratio: 10.0:1. Brake horsepower: 180 at 6200 rpm. Torque: 160 lbs.-ft. at 5200 rpm. Fuel system: MPFI. RPO Code: LG0. Standard and exclusive in Grand Am SE with five-speed manual transmission. [VIN code A].

FIREBIRD ENGINES

ENGINE [Base V-6]: V-block. OHV. Six-cylinder. Cast-iron block and head. Aluminum intake manifold. Displacement: 191 cid. (3.1L). Bore & stroke: 3.50 x 3.31 in. Compression ratio: 8.5:1. Brake horsepower: 140 at 4400 rpm. Torque: 180 lbs.-ft. at 3600 rpm. Fuel system: EFI/MFI. RPO Code: L H.O. Standard in base Firebird. [VIN code T].

ENGINE [Base V-8]: V-block. OHV. Eight-cylinder. Cast-iron block and head. Aluminum intake manifold. Displacement: 305 cid. (5.0L). Bore & stroke: 3.74 x 3.48 in. Brake horsepower: 170 at 4400 rpm. Torque: 255 lbs.-ft. at 2400 rpm. Compression ratio: 9.3:1. Fuel system: EFI/TBI. RPO Code: L03. Standard Formula. Available in base Firebird. [VIN code E or F].

ENGINE [Optional V-8]: V-block. OHV. Eight-cylinder. Cast-iron block and head. Aluminum intake manifold. Displacement: 305 cid. (5.0L). Bore & stroke: 3.74 x 3.48 in. Brake horsepower: 205 at 4200 rpm (Formula, Trans Am and GTA with automatic); 230 hp at 4400 rpm (all others). Torque: 300 lbs.-ft. at 3200 rpm (GTA/Formula with manual; optional Trans Am); Torque: 285 lbs.-ft. at 3200 rpm (GTA, Trans Am and Formula with five-speed manual). Compression ratio: 9.3:1. Fuel system: EFI/TPI. RPO Code: LB9. Available with five-speed manual in Formula and Trans Am (delete option in GTA). [VIN code E or F].

ENGINE [GTA V-8]: V-block. OHV. Eight-cylinder. Cast-iron block and head. Aluminum intake manifold. Displacement: 350 cid. (5.7L). Bore & stroke: 4.00 x 3.48 in. Brake horsepower: 240 at 4400 rpm. Torque: 340 lbs.-ft. at 3200 rpm. Compression ratio: 9.3:1. Fuel system: EFI/TPI. RPO Code: B2L. Standard with four-speed automatic in GTA (optional in Formula and Trans Am). Includes Performance Enhancement group with dual catalytic converter exhausts, engine oil cooler and performance axle ratio. [VIN code 8].

PONTIAC 6000 ENGINES

ENGINE [Base Four]: Inline. OHV. Four-cylinder. Cast-iron block and head. Aluminum intake manifold. Displacement: 151 cid. (2.5L Tech IV). Bore & stroke: 4.00 x 3.00 in. Compression ratio: 9.0:1. Brake horsepower: 110 at 5200 rpm. Torque: 135 lbs.-ft. at 3200 rpm. Five main bearings. Hydraulic valve lifters. Fuel system: EFI. RPO Code: LR8. Standard in 6000 LE sedan. [VIN code U].

ENGINE [Standard LE Safari; SE sedan]: V-block. OHV. Six-cylinder. Cast-iron block. Aluminum head and intake manifold. Displacement: 191 cid. (3.1L). Bore & stroke: 3.50 x 3.31 in. Brake horsepower: 140 at 4400 rpm. Torque: 185 lbs.-ft. at 3200 rpm. Fuel system: EFI/MFI Code: L H.O. Standard in 6000 SE sedan and LE wagon. [VIN code T].

GRAND PRIX ENGINES

ENGINE [Base Four]: Inline. DOHC. 16-valve. Quad-4. Cast-iron block. Aluminum head and intake manifold. Displacement: 138 cid. (2.3L). Bore & stroke: 3.63 x 3.35 in. Compression ratio: 9.5:1. Brake horsepower: 160 at 6200 rpm. Torque: 155 lbs.-ft. at 5200 rpm. Fuel system: MPFI. RPO Code: LD2. Standard in LE/SE. [VIN code D].

ENGINE [Base Six (STE and GT); Optional (LE/SE)]: V-block. OHV. Six-cylinder. Cast-iron block and aluminum head. Displacement: 191 cid. (3.1L). Bore & stroke: 3.50 x 3.31 in. Compression ratio: 8.8:1. Brake horsepower: 140 at 4400 rpm. Torque: 185 lbs.-ft. at 3200 rpm. Fuel system: EFI/MPI. RPO Code: L H.O. [VIN code T].

ENGINE [Base Six (GTP); Optional (others except LE)]: V-block. OHV. Six-cylinder. Cast-iron block and aluminum head. Displacement: 207 cid. (3.4L). Bore & stroke: 3.62 x 3.31 in. Compression ratio: 9.25:1. Brake horsepower: 210 at 5200 rpm. Torque: 215 lbs.-ft. at 4000 rpm. Fuel system: EFI/MPI. [VIN code X].

BONNEVILLE ENGINE

ENGINE [Base Six LE/SE/SSE]: V-block. OHV. "3800" six-cylinder. Cast-iron block and head. Aluminum intake manifold. Displacement: 231 cid. (3.8L). Bore & stroke: 3.80 x 3.40 in. Compression ratio: 8.5:1. Brake horsepower: 165 at 4800 rpm. Torque: 210 lbs.-ft. at 2000 rpm. Fuel system: SFI. RPO Code: LN3. Standard in Bonneville LE/SE/SSE model. [VIN code W, S, or 9].

TRANS SPORT ENGINE

ENGINE [Base Six]: V-block. OHV. Six-cylinder. Cast-iron block and head. Aluminum intake manifold. Displacement: 191 cid. (3.1L). Bore & stroke: 3.50 x 3.31 in. Compression ratio: 8.5:1. Brake horsepower: 120 at 4200 rpm. Torque: 175 lbs.-ft. at 2200 rpm. Fuel system: EFI/TBI. RPO Code: LG6. Standard in base Firebird. [VIN code T].

CHASSIS

LEMANS CHASSIS: Wheelbase: 99.2 in. (all). Overall length: 163.70 in. (three-door); 172.4 in. (four-door). Height: 53.5 in. (Aerocoupe); 53.7 in. (sedan). Width: 65.5 in. (three-door); 65.7 in. (four-door). Front tread: 55.1 in. (all) Rear tread: 55.4 in. (all). Standard tires: P175/70R13 BSW (all). Fuel tank: 13.2 gal.

SUNBIRD CHASSIS: Wheelbase: 101.2 in. (all). Overall length: 181.3 in. (all). Overall width: 66.3 in. (all). Height: 52.0.in. (coupe); 53.6 in. sedan; 52.1 in. (convertible). Front tread: 55.6 in. (all). Rear tread: 55.2 in. (all). Standard tires: P185/75R14 BSW (all except SE and GT coupes). Standard tires: P195/70R14 (SE coupe). Standard tires: P205/55R15 Eagle GT+4 (GT).

GRAND AM CHASSIS: Wheelbase: 103.4 in. (all). Overall length: 180.1 in. (all). Width: 66.5 in. (all). Height: 52.5 in. (all). Front tread: 55.6 in. Rear tread: 55.2 in. Standard tires: P185/75R15 BSW (base/LE). Standard tires: P205/55R15 (SE).

FIREBIRD CHASSIS: Wheelbase: 101.0 in. (all). Overall length: 195.1 in. (base/Formula); 195.2 in. (Trans Am/GTA). Width: 72.4 in. (all). Height: 49.7 in. (all). Front tread: 60.7 in. Rear tread: 61.6 in. Standard tires: P215/65R15 (base Firebird). Standard tires: P215/60R16 (Trans Am). Standard tires: P245/50ZR16 Goodyear Eagle ZR50 "Gatorback" (Formula/GTA).

6000 CHASSIS: Wheelbase: 104.9 in. (all). Overall length: 185.8 in. (sedan); 193.2 in. (wagon). Width: 72.0 in. (all). Height: 53.7 in. (sedan); 54.1 in. (wagon). Front tread: 58.7 in. (sedan); 56.7 in. (wagon). Rear tread: 57.0 in. (all). Standard Tires: 185/75R14 (LE). Standard tires: 195/70R15 Goodyear Eagle GT+4 (SE).

GRAND PRIX CHASSIS: Wheelbase: 107.5 in. (all). Overall length: 193.9 in. (coupe); 194.8 in. (sedan). Width: 70.9 in. (all). Height: 52.8 in. (all). Front tread: 59.5 in. Rear tread: 58.0 in. Standard tires: 205/70R15 (LE/SE). Standard tires: 215/60R15 Goodyear Eagle GT+4 (STE/GT). Standard tires: P225/60R16 Eagle GT+4 (GTP).

BONNEVILLE CHASSIS: Wheelbase: 110.8 in. (all). Overall length: 198.7 in. (all). Width: 72.1 in. (all). Height: 54.1 in. (all). Front tread: 60.3 in. Rear tread: 59.8 in. Standard tires: 205/75R14 BSW (LE). Standard tires: 215/65R15 Goodyear Eagle GT+4 (SE). Standard tires: P215/60R16 BSW (SSE).

TRANS SPORT CHASSIS: Wheelbase: 109.8 in. (all). Overall length: 194.5 in. (all). Width: 74.6 in. (all). Height: 65.2 in. (all). Standard tires: 205/70R14 BSW (base). Standard tires: P205/65R15 (SE).

TECHNICAL

LEMANS TECHNICAL: Chassis: Front engine/front drive. Standard transmission: Four-speed manual (Aerocoupe only). Standard transmission: Five-speed manual (LE only). Optional transmission: Three-speed automatic (LE only). Axle ratio: 3.43:1 with 1.6L and automatic. Axle ratio: 3.72:1 (both manual). Front suspension: deflected disc, MacPherson struts and 22mm stabilizer bar. Rear suspension: Coil springs, semi-independent torsion beam, trailing arms, and 18mm anti-roll bar. Steering: Rack-and-pinion 24.5:1 ratio (18.3:1 power-assisted optional LEs). Turns lock-to-lock: 3.5

(power); 4.57 (manual). Turning circle: 32.8 ft. Front brakes: 9.25-in. vented discs. Rear brakes: 7.9 x 1.8-in. drums (power-assisted}.

SUNBIRD TECHNICAL: Chassis: Front engine/front drive. Base transmission: Five-speed manual. Optional transmission: Three-speed automatic. Axle ratio: 3.45:1 with 2.0-liter engine and five-speed manual. Axle ratio: 3.18:1 with 2.0L TBI engine and three-speed automatic. Axle ratio: 3.45:1 with 3.1-liter V-6 and five-speed manual. Axle ratio: 2.08:1 with 3.1-liter V-6 and three-speed automatic in base Sunbird. Axle ratio: 2.53:1 with 3.1-liter V-6 and three-speed automatic in SE and base Sunbird. Axle ratio: 2.84:1 with 3.1-liter V-6 and three-speed automatic in LE convertible and SE. Front suspension: deflected disc, MacPherson struts and (22mm with 2.0L TBI/28mm with 3.1L MFI) stabilizer bars. Rear suspension: Coil springs, semi-independent torsion beam, trailing arms (and 21mm anti-roll bar with 3.1L MFI). Steering: Rack-and-pinion 16.0:1 ratio (14.0:1 on GT). Turns lock-to-lock: 3.0 (2.5 on GT). Turning circle: 34.3 ft. (all). Front brakes: 9.72-in. vented disc power-assisted. Rear brakes: 7.87 x 1.77-in. drum power-assisted.

GRAND AM TECHNICAL: Chassis: Front engine/front drive. Base transmission: Five-speed manual with overdrive. Optional transmission: Three-speed automatic. Axle ratio: 3.18:1 (with 2.3L and 2.5L engines and automatic SE). Axle ratio: 2.84:1 (with 2.3L and 2.5L engines and automatic LE). Axle ratio: 3.35:1 (with 2.5L engine and manual). Axle ratio: 3.61:1 (with 2.3L H.O. engine and manual). Stall torque ratio: 2.48:1 (2.3L with automatic). Stall torque ratio: 2.35:1 (2.5L with automatic). Front suspension: MacPherson struts with coil springs and 24mm anti-roll bar (28mm anti-roll bar with Sport Performance and WS6 suspensions). Rear suspension: Trailing crank arm with twist arm, coil springs, (and 21mm anti-roll bar with Sport Performance and WS6 suspensions). Steering (Standard): Power-assisted rack-and-pinion, 16.0:1 ratio, 2.88 turns lock-to-lock and 35.4-ft. (left); 37.8-ft. (right) turning circle. Steering (Sport Performance and WS6): Power-assisted rack-and-pinion, 14.0:1 ratio, 2.5 turns lock-to-lock and 35.4-ft. (left); 37.8-ft. (right) turning circle. Front brakes: Power-assisted 10.24-in. vented discs. Rear brakes: Power-assisted 7.87-in. drums. (ABS standard on SE). Fuel tank: 13.6 gal.

FIREBIRD TECHNICAL: Chassis: Front engine/rear drive. Base transmission: Four-speed automatic (Firebird/GTA). Optional transmission: Five-speed manual. (Formula/Trans Am). Front suspension: Modified MacPherson strut with 30mm (FE1), 34mm (F41), or 36mm (WS6) anti-roll bar. Rear suspension: Live axle with coil springs, control arms, torque arm, track bar and 18mm (FE1) or 23mm (F41 and WS6) anti-roll bar. Steering: Power re-circulating ball; 14.0:1 ratio (FE1), or 12.7:1 quick ratio with sport effort valving (F41 and WS6). Turns lock-to-lock: 2.57 (FE1), or 2.14 (F41 and WS6). Turning circle: 38.5 ft. (FE1) or 38.5 ft. (F41 and WS6). Brakes: Power vented 10.5-in. front disc/9.5 x 2.0-in. rear drum. Fuel tank: 15.5 gal.

6000 TECHNICAL: Chassis: Front engine/front drive. Base transmission: Three-speed automatic with overdrive. Optional transmission: Four-speed automatic. Axle ratio: 2.84:1 (with three-speed automatic and 2.5L or 3.1L engines). Axle ratio: 3.33:1 (with four-speed automatic and 3.1L engine). Front suspension: MacPherson struts with 14.5 N-mm coil springs on LE (16 N-mm on SE; and 23.5 N-mm Fleet models) and 22mm (27mm on SE and 24mm all wagons) anti-roll bars. Rear suspension: Trailing arm and open channel, Panhard rod track bar and 26.9 N-mm coil springs on LE sedan (32 N-mm on LE wagon and SE sedan (*) and 22mm anti-roll bar on SE, 20mm anti-roll bar standard. Steering: Power-assisted rack-and-pinion with 17.5:1 ratio, 3.05 turns lock-to-lock and 36.96-ft. turning circle. Front brakes: Power assisted vented discs 9.72-in. (standard); 10.24-in. (medium-/heavy-duty). Rear brakes: Power assisted 8.86-in. drum (all). Fuel tank: 15.7-gal.

(*) Fleet model rear suspension has 40.5 N-mm coil springs for sedan and 48.3 N-mm for wagon.

GRAND PRIX TECHNICAL: Chassis: Front engine/front drive. Standard drive train: 2.3L Quad-4 with three-speed automatic transaxle. Optional drive train: 3.1L MFI V-6 with five-speed manual transaxle. Optional drive train: 3.4L Twin Dual Cam V-6 with five-speed manual transaxle. Axle ratio: 3.18 (2.3L with three-speed automatic). Axle ratio: 3.33 (3.1L MFI V-6 with four-speed automatic). Axle ratio: 3.67 (3.4L with five-speed manual). Axle ratio: 3.43 (3.4L with four-speed manual). Front suspension: MacPherson struts with tapered top coil springs, lower A arm and 28mm anti-roll bar (34mm anti-roll bar with Y99 suspension). Rear suspension: Tri-link independent suspension with 12mm anti-roll bar (transverse fiberglass leaf spring and 12mm anti-roll bar with 3.1L; 14mm anti-roll bar with 3.4-liter engine.). Steering: Power-assisted rack- and-pinion with 15.7:1 ratio (14.0:1 with Y99 3.4-liter; 15.7:1 with 3.1-liter engine); 2.6 turns lock-to-lock and 36.77-ft. turning circle (standard). Steering: Power-assisted rack-and-pinion with 15.7:1 ratio, 2.25 turns lock-to-lock and 39.7-ft. turning circle (STE with Y99). Four-wheel power disc brakes. Front brakes: 10.5-in. x 1.04-in. composite vented discs. Rear brakes: 10.1-in. x 0.5-in. composite solid discs. Fuel tank: 15.5 gal.

BONNEVILLE TECHNICAL: Chassis: Front engine/front drive. Base transmission: Four-speed automatic. Axle ratio: 2.84:1 (standard with 3.8L V-6 in Bonneville LE). Axle ratio: 2.97:1 (standard with 3.8L V-6 in Bonneville SE.) Axle ratio: 3.33:1 (standard with 3.8L V-6 in Bonneville SSE). Front suspension: MacPherson struts with 20 N-mm coil springs and 28mm anti-roll bar (LE). Front suspension: MacPherson struts with 24.2 N-mm coil springs and 32mm anti-roll bar (SE). Front suspension: MacPherson struts with 24 N-mm coil springs and 32mm anti-roll bar (SSE). Rear suspension: MacPherson struts with variable rate (48-65 N-mm) coil springs and 14mm anti-roll bar (LE). Rear suspension: MacPherson struts with variable-rate (55-65 N-mm) coil springs and 18mm anti-roll bar (SE). Rear suspension: MacPherson struts with 47 N-mm coil springs and 18mm anti-roll bar (SSE). Steering: Power-assisted rack- and-pinion with 18.1:1 constant ratio, 2.97 turns lock-to-lock and 39.7-ft. left/39.0-ft. right turning circle (LE/SE). Steering: Power-assisted rack- and-pinion with 15.3:1 to 18.0:1 variable ratio, 2.79 turns lock-to-lock and 38.4-ft. left/40.7-ft. right turning circle (SSE). Front brakes: Power-assisted 10.1-in. vented discs. Rear brakes: Power-assisted 8.9-in. drums. Anti-lock brake system standard with SSE. Fuel tank: 18.0 gal.

TRANS SPORT TECHNICAL: Chassis: Front engine/front drive. Transmission: Three-speed automatic. Axle ratio: 3.18:1 (all). Front suspension: MacPherson struts with 24 N-mm coil springs and 30mm anti-roll bar (LE). Front suspension: MacPherson strut, stamped lower control arms, 28mm stabilizer bar. Rear suspension: Open-section transverse beam on stamped steel trailing arms, tube shocks, coil springs and 25.4mm stabilizer bar. Steering: Power-assisted rack-and-pinion with 15.7:1 ratio and 38-ft. turning circle. Front brakes: Power-assisted 10.2-in. vented rotors, 182 sq. in. swept area. Rear brakes: Power-assisted 8.86 x 1.58-in. finned composite cast-iron drums with 98.5 sq. in. swept area. Fuel tank: 20.0 gal.

OPTIONS

LEMANS OPTIONS: R6A value package for Value Leader model ($662). R6A Value package for SE model ($355). MX1 three-speed automatic transmission ($475). C60 air conditioning, requires power steering and not available in Value Leader Aerocoupe ($705). B37 front and rear floor mats ($33). N40 power steering, requires air conditioning in Aerocoupe or SE sedan ($225). UM7 Delco ETR stereo in Value Leader Aerocoupe ($307). UM6 Delco ETR AM/FM with cassette and more in Value Leader Aerocoupe ($429). UM6 Delco ETR AM/FM with cassette and more in LE/SE/GSE ($122). AD3 removable sunroof ($350). WDV warranty enhancements for New York ($65).

SUNBIRD OPTIONS: 1SB Sunbird LE coupe and sedan option group #1 ($158). 1SC Sunbird LE coupe and sedan ($914). 1SD Sunbird LE coupe and sedan ($1,114). 1SB Sunbird LE convertible

1991 Pontiac Grand Am LE four-door sedan. (PGMC)

($910). 1SC Sunbird LE convertible ($804). 1SB Sunbird SE coupe and sedan ($910). 1SC option for SE coupe and sedan ($1,470). 1SB Sunbird GT coupe ($862-$910). L H.O. engine, except no cost in GT ($660). MX1 three-speed automatic transmission ($495). C60 air conditioning ($745). DO6 front seat armrest in GT and SE ($58). NB2 California emissions ($100). K34 cruise control ($225). A90 remote deck lid release ($60). AO1 tinted glass ($105). TR9 lamp group ($29). AU3 power door locks ($210-$250). A31 power windows, requires power door locks ($265 SE/GT coupe/$330 sedan/no charge convertible). UM6 Delco radio equipment ($170 additional). U1C Delco radio equipment ($396). U39 rally gauges ($127). AM9 split folding rear seat ($150). T43 rear deck lid spoiler on LE convertible ($70). N33 tilt steering wheel ($135). AD3 removable glass sunroof ($350). CD4 controlled cycle wipers on LE ($65). B20 white vinyl trim on LE convertible ($75). D84 Custom two-tone paint on LE ($101). WDV New York warranty enhancements ($65). QME touring tires ($114). N78 14-in. Hi-Tech Turbo aluminum wheels ($275).

GRAND AM OPTIONS: 1SB package on LE coupe ($810). 1SC package on LE coupe ($1,265). 1SB package on LE sedan ($850). 1SC package on LE sedan ($1,370). R6A Value option package on SE coupe and sedan ($394). LD2 Quad-4 2.3-liter MPI engine in SE models ($660). LD2 Quad-4 2.3-liter MPI engine in GT models ($140 credit). LGO Quad-4 H.O. engine (standard on SE and LE with manual shift and W32 performance package). MX1 three-speed automatic transmission ($555). W32 Sport Performance package including monotone paint treatment, Hi-Tech Turbo aluminum wheels, fog lamps, aero body skirting, rally cluster and more ($1,271-$1,650 depending upon option pairings). UB3 rally gauge cluster ($127). C60 air conditioning ($745). NB2 California emissions ($100). K34 cruise control ($225). A90 remote deck lid release ($60). C49 electric rear window defogger ($170). V56 luggage carrier ($115). AU3 power door locks ($210-$250). AC3 power driver seat in SE ($305). A31 express down power windows in SE and GT coupe ($275). A31 express down power window in SE or GT sedan ($340). AM9 split folding rear seat ($150). N33 tilt steering ($145). AD3 removable glass sunroof ($350). CD4 controlled cycle wipers ($65). AR9 Custom cloth reclining seats with Pallex cloth in base and LE and Metrix cloth in SE (no charge). WDV warranty enhancements ($65). UM6 Delco sound system ($140). U1D Delco sound system ($405-$545). QME touring tires with Ride & Handling suspension ($114). N78 14-in. Hi-Tech Turbo aluminum wheels ($275).

FIREBIRD OPTIONS: 1SB Firebird V-6 option group ($888). 1SB Firebird V-8 option group ($33). 1SB Formula/Trans Am option group ($223). 1SB Firebird V-8 convertible ($225). 1SB Trans Am convertible option group ($183). 1SC Firebird V-6 option group ($979). 1SC Firebird V-8 option group ($419). 1SC Formula option group ($419). 1SC Trans Am option group ($384). R6A Firebird and Formula value package ($820). R6B Value Option package Firebird and Formula ($814). R6A Trans Am value package ($889). R6A Trans AM GTA Value Option package ($1,020). LO3 5.0-liter TBI V-8 engine in base Firebird ($350). LB9 5.0L MPI V-8 in Formula and Trans Am ($745). B2L 5.7L MPI V-8 in Trans Am ($300). B2L 5.7L MPI V-8 in Formula ($1,045). MM5 five-speed manual transmission in Trans Am GTA with LB9 ($515 credit). MX0 four-speed automatic transmission, except in GTA ($530). C60 air conditioning ($830). G80 limited-slip axle ($100). K34 cruise control, except GTA ($225). A90 rear deck lid release in Trans Am ($60). C49 rear window defogger, except GTA ($170). NB2 California emissions ($100). CC1 Hatch roof ($920). DG7 dual Sport mirror, left-h and remote-control, except GTA ($91). R6P Performance Enhancement group with dual converter exhaust, four-wheel disc brake, engine oil cooler and more ($265). AU3 power door locks ($210). A31 power windows ($280). U75 power antenna ($85). UX1 Delco sound system ($150). U1A Delco radio equipment ($226-$376). D42 cargo area security screen ($69). AH3 four-way adjustable power driver seat, except GTA ($35). AR9 Custom Pallex cloth reclining bucket seat, no cost option, but not available on GTA. AQ9 articulating bucket seats with Ventura leather trim in GTA ($450). W68 Sport Appearance package with front and rear Trans Am fascias, fog lamps, and Trans Am aero side moldings for Firebird only ($450). QLC high-performance WS6 performance suspension ($313). WDV New York warranty enhancements ($25).

6000 OPTIONS: 1SB option package #1 for 6000 LE sedan ($1,009). 1SC option package #2 for 6000 LE sedan ($1,024). 1SD

1991 Pontiac Grand Am LE four-door sedan. (PGMC)

option package #3 for 6000 LE sedan ($1,399). 1SB option package #1 for 6000 LE wagon ($190). 1SC option package #2 for 6000 LE wagon ($400). 1SD option package #3 for 6000 LE wagon ($570). 1SB option package #1 for 6000 SE sedan ($73). R6A value option package for 6000 LE sedan ($463). R6B value option package for 6000 LE sedan ($478). R6B value option package for 6000 LE sedan ($248). R6B Value Option package for LE wagon ($518). L H.O. 3.1-liter MFI V-6 in LE sedan ($660). MX0 four-speed automatic transmission ($200). C60 air conditioning ($830). K34 cruise control ($225). A90 rear deck lid release ($60). C49 electric rear window defogger ($170). D86 two-tone paint ($115). AU3 power door locks ($250-$290). A31 power windows ($345). B34 front and rear carpet mats ($45). AG1 power seat ($305). UM6 Delco ETR AM/FM stereo ($140). UX1 Delco ETR AM stereo/FM stereo ($310). UA1 Delco sound system ($536). A65 three-passenger seating in base LE ($183). B20 custom interior with 45/55 split seat in Metrix cloth ($350-$533). Various tire options (no charge to $68). N78 Sport aluminum wheels with locking package ($275). BX3 woodgrain exterior siding for wagon ($295).

GRAND PRIX OPTIONS: 1SB Grand Prix LE ($190). 1SC Grand Prix LE ($400). 1SB Grand Prix SE sedan ($415). 1SC Grand Prix SE sedan ($533). 1SD Grand Prix SE sedan ($869). 1SB Grand Prix SE coupe ($190). 1SC Grand Prix SE coupe ($415). 1SD Grand Prix SE coupe ($428). 1SE Grand Prix SE coupe ($764). 1SB Grand Prix GT coupe ($411). 1SB Grand Prix STE sedan ($500). R6A Value Option for Grand Prix SE coupe ($703). R6B Value Option package for Grand Prix SE coupe ($733). R6A Value Option Package for Grand Prix SE sedan ($699). R6B Value Option package for Grand Prix SE sedan ($399). R6A Value Option package for Grand Prix GT coupe ($825). R6B Value Option package for Grand Prix GT coupe ($801). R6A Value Option package for Grand Prix STE sedan ($801). MX0 four-speed automatic in Grand Prix SE ($200). A90 remote deck lid release ($60). C49 electric rear window defogger ($170). NB2 California emissions system ($100). D84 two-tone paint ($105). JL9 power antilock brakes ($925). CF5 power glass sunroof ($670-$695). AUO Remote Keyless Entry system ($135). UB3 rally gauge cluster with tach ($85). UV6 heads-up display, requires Graphite, Gray, or Beige interior trim and bucket seats ($250). V56 rear deck lid luggage carrier ($115). B37 front and rear carpet mats ($45). DG7 dual Sport mirrors ($78). DH6 dual illuminated visor vanity mirrors ($86). A31 power windows on coupe ($275). A31 power windows on sedan ($340). AU3 power door locks on coupe ($210). AU3 power door locks on sedan ($250). B20 Custom interior trim ($324-$328). BYP Sport Appearance package with lower aero ground effects ($595-$680 depending on model and other options). B4U Aero Appearance package ($2,795). Y99 rally handling suspension ($50). UM6 Delco radio equipment ($140). UX1 Delco radio equipment ($540-$590). U1A stereo sound system ($226-$816 depending on model). AR9 bucket seat with Pallex cloth trim in Grand Prix LE ($110). AN3 Custom Cloth bucket seat in Grand Prix LE ($140). AC3 power seat ($305). B20 Custom interior trim ($328). PH3 15-in. aluminum sport wheels with locking package ($275). WDV warranty enhancements for New York ($65).

BONNEVILLE OPTIONS: 1SB Bonneville LE option package ($269). 1SC Bonneville LE option package ($629). 1SD Bonneville

1991 Pontiac Firebird Trans Am GTA two-door coupe. (PGMC)

1991 Pontiac Trans Port SE All-Purpose-Vehicle (minivan). (PGMC)

1992 Pontiac Grand Am SE four-door sedan. (PGMC)

LEMANS — SERIES 2T — (FOUR) — The Pontiac LeMans was based on the German Opel Kadett and built in Korea. The 1992 LeMans line consisted of the SE "Value Leader" Aerocoupe, the SE Aerocoupe and the SE Sedan. New for 1992 was a sport-tuned exhaust system, amber section taillights, revised engine calibration, new Bright Yellow (Aerocoupe) paint, and the SE badge replacing the LE badge. Standard equipment on the LeMans SE "Value Leader" included a 1.6-liter TBI engine, four-speed manual transmission, P175/70R13 black sidewall tires, 9.25-in. vented front disc brakes, steel wheels, Custom wheel covers, wide body side moldings, and a Custom two-spoke sport steering wheel. The LeMans SE Aerocoupe added or substituted a five-speed manual transmission, styled steel wheels, a three-spoke steering wheel, and a Delco AM/FM stereo with clock. The LeMans SE Sedan had all the same equipment as the SE "Value Leader" Aerocoupe, plus a five-speed manual transmission and a Delco AM/FM stereo with clock.

SUNBIRD — SERIES 2J — (FOUR) — Over half the buyers of Sunbirds were under 35 years old. This was the affordable Pontiac model's 10th anniversary. There were three series: LE, SE, and GT. A convertible came in the SE line. New functional features included the addition of multi-point fuel injection (and 17 hp) to the 2.0-liter engine, standard antilock brakes on all models, the addition of a brake/transmission shift interlock, and a 1.6-gal. larger fuel tank. There were also four exterior updates: new optional 14- and 15-in. SE wheel covers, a monotone appearance for the GT, monotone LE and SE appearances with red stripes, and four new exterior colors. On the interior, the 1992 models had standard automatic door locks, new interior door trim on coupes and convertibles, new front seats and seat fabrics on all models, and a new Graphite interior color. Standard equipment on the Sunbird LE coupe and sedan included the 2.0-liter MPFI V-6 engine, a five-speed manual transmission, antilock brakes, P185/75R14 tires, power rack and pinion steering, a Delco ETR AM/FM stereo with seek-and-scan and clock, a stainless steel exhaust system, an illuminated entry system, and automatic door locks. The Sunbird SE coupe and sedan had the same basics, while the Sunbird SE convertible added a fully automatic electro-hydraulic top, reclining front bucket seats with grid cloth trim, power door locks, power windows, dual sport mirrors, and tinted glass. A new convertible option was the "Special Appearance Package" which included white accents, white body striping, 15-in. aluminum wheels, and nameplate decals with any one of five exterior colors. A white vinyl trim interior was also available for ragtops. The Sunbird GT added or substituted a 3.1-liter MPFI V-6, P195/65R15 Goodrich T/A touring tires, a dual exhaust system, 15-in. machine-faced aluminum wheels, tinted glass, and a rear deck lid spoiler.

GRAND AM — SERIES 2N — Pontiac's most popular car-line was dramatically redesigned for 1992. Available were SE and GT coupes and sedans. The dramatic exterior styling stressed aerodynamic enhancements. Each body style had its own distinctive roof design and flush-mounted window glass. The door frames wrapped into the roof for easier entry and exit. The rear doors of sedans were larger and opened 80 degrees from closed position. Grand Am sedans also came with fully retracting rear windows. Though on the

LE option package ($1,039). 1SB Bonneville SE option package ($265). 1SC Bonneville SE option package ($315). 1SB Bonneville SSE option package ($1,259). R6A Bonneville LE value option package ($408). R6A Bonneville SSE value option package ($1,080). C49 electric rear window defogger ($170). NB2 California emissions system ($100). D84 Custom two-tone paint ($105). JM4 power front disc/rear drum ABS brakes ($925). AU3 power door locks ($250). A31 power windows ($410). AUO remote keyless entry system ($136). Z05 Convenience package ($315). US7 power antenna ($85). UM6 Delco radio equipment ($140). UX1 Delco sound system ($615-$805). U1A compact disc player ($226-$1,031). AS7 45/45 split front seat with console and London/Empress cloth trims for LE and SE models ($235). B320 Custom interior trim ($130-$620). AG1 power seat ($305). CF5 power glass sunroof ($1,230). PXO 16-in. spoke cast aluminum wheels ($340). PF7 15-in. six-spoke cast aluminum wheels ($306). QPJ touring tires ($76). QGW touring tires ($88). WDV warranty enhancements ($65).

TRANS SPORT OPTIONS: 1SB Trans Sport option package #1 ($1,210). 1SC Trans Sport option package #2 ($935). 1SB Trans Sport SE option package #1 ($275). R6A Value Option package for Trans Sport ($348). C67 air conditioning in Trans Sport ($830). V54 luggage rack ($145). NB2 California emissions system ($100). DG7 dual outside mirrors ($48). C49 electric rear window defogger ($170). AJ1 glass package in Trans Sport ($245). AB5 power door locks ($290-$300). A31 power windows ($275). UM6 Delco radio equipment ($140). U1A compact disc player ($376-$516). AB3 six-passenger seating package ($525). ZP7 seven-passenger seating package ($675). Rear air distribution system ($110). N78 14-in. aluminum wheels ($275).

NOTE: Full option package contents, descriptions, and applications information can often be determined by consulting factory literature. The data above is edited for size and clarity. This information provided only as a guide to help collectors appraise the relative value of cars with numerous options. Prices for items included as part of a value option package are usually much less than individual prices. Option prices charged by individual dealers may also vary.

HISTORICAL: In its third incarnation, the Grand Am became Pontiac's most popular nameplate, as well as one of the best-selling American-made cars. Its sales topped the one million mark in 1989. Production was 246,000 that year, 197,020 in 1990 and 170,622 in 1991. Lordstown, Ohio autoworkers also stayed busy building Pontiac's second best-selling model, the Sunbird. With model-year production of 91,465, the Grand Prix was the third best selling Pontiac. The 6000 was built in Oklahoma City and losing popularity. Only 34,721 were made. The Wentzville, Mo., GM assembly plant turned out 42,797 Bonnevilles this model year. PMD also made 18,319 Trans Sports in a factory in Tarrytown, N.Y.

same wheelbase as 1991, the Grand Ams were longer and had more interior room. All models now featured two-side galvanized steel body panels and stainless steel exhaust systems. Exterior lighting was enhanced with new high-strength headlamp composite material (polycarbonate). Functional changes included new 2.3-liter Quad 4 and 3.3-liter V-6 engines, ABS on all models, a larger fuel tank, electronic variable orifice (EVO) steering, torque-axis engine mountings, new brake/transmission shift interlock, a more rounded aerodynamic body appearance, split grilles, ribbed body side moldings, and engine tuning and cam chain enhancements. Exterior updates included wrap-in lamps all around, standard fog lamps, flush body-color door handles, a rear deck-mounted radio antenna, low lift-over trunks, high-mounted backlights, and all double-galvanized sheet metal. Interior upgrades included a more comfortable rear seating package, new instrument panel, a new console, new door panels, twin instrument panel glove boxes, cup storage provisions, an easy-access fuse panel, a headliner storage console, a new instrument cluster, column-mounted lights/wiper controls, new seat fabrics, revised radio appearances, and standard automatic door locks. Standard equipment on SE models included fog lamps, monotone paint treatments with wide body side moldings, P185/75R14 tires, bolt-on 14-in. wheel covers, a Delco ETR AM/FM stereo with auto-reversing cassette, a 2.3-liter Quad Four OHC engine, a five-speed manual transmission, ABS brakes, and power rack-and-pinion steering. The GT added or substituted aero body moldings, dual/dual chrome-tipped exhaust outlets, neutral-density taillights, P205/55R16 tires, specific 16-in cast aluminum wheels, rally gauges with a tachometer, and a 2.3-liter H.O. DOHC 16-valve four-cylinder engine.

FIREBIRD — SERIES 2F — (V-6/V-8) — Pontiac announced the first Firebird convertible in 21 years in 1991 and only 2,000 were built. The open model was continued in 1992. The full line consisted of Firebird, Firebird Formula, Trans Am, and Trans Am GTA models. The convertible was available as a base Firebird or as a Trans Am. Other changes for 1992 included structural enhancements and non-asbestos brake pads. New Yellow, Dark Jade Gray Metallic, and Dark Aqua Metallic exterior paint colors were also added. The interiors had revised AM/FM cassette radio graphics and new knobs and rings, plus a revised Beige interior. Standard features of the base Firebird included a 3.1-liter MPFI V-6, a five-speed manual transmission, the FE1 suspension, P215/65R15 tires, 15x7-in. Hi-Tech aluminum wheels, disc/drum brakes, and a Delco ETR AM/FM stereo with auto-reverse, cassette and clock. The Firebird Formula added or substituted a 5.0-liter EFI V-8, the WS6 Sport suspension, P245/50ZR16 tires, 15x7-in. deep-dish High-Tech aluminum wheels, air conditioning, and a leather appointment group with leather-wrapped steering wheel. The Trans Am added or substituted the following over base Firebird features: the 5.0-liter TPI V-8, the F41 Rally-Tuned suspension, P215/60R16 tires, 16x8-in. diamond-spoke wheels, a limited-slip differential, an aero package with special side treatment, and air conditioning. The Trans AM GTA added or substituted the following over the Trans Am: the 5.7-liter TPI V-8, a four-speed automatic transmission, the WS6 Sport suspension, P245/50ZR16 tires, dual catalytic converters, a performance axle, a Delco ETR AM/FM stereo with CD and five-band equalizer, a power antenna, the leather appointment group, a four-way manual driver's seat adjuster, power windows and door locks, cruise control, a remote deck lid release, a rear window defogger and power outside mirrors. Both convertibles came with a choice of Black or Beige cloth tops that stowed away neatly, under a tonneau cover. Both ragtops carried the aero package as standard equipment (including fog lights, brake cooling ducts in the front fascias, and a distinctive body side treatment). The Trans Am convertible also had functional hood louvers, air extractors, and the available leather-clad articulated bucket seats.

GRAND PRIX — SERIES 2G — (V-6/V-8) — Pontiac's sporty mid-size car line had enhanced styling and performance for 1992. The focus for the year was on strengthening the Grand Prix sedan lineup and increasing the status of the LE sedan. Functional improvements for 1992 included standard antilock brakes on the GT, GTP, and STE models, a standard 3.1-liter V-6 for LEs and SEs (replacing a 2.3-liter engine), a second gear start switch available with a 3.4-liter automatic drive train, a new 3.4-liter DOHC V-6 available for LE sedans, new P215/60R16 touring tires standard on the SE sedan, and P225/60R15 Eagle GT+4 tires standard on the

STE. Exterior changes included a new LE sedan with an STE-inspired appearance, grid-pattern GT taillights for the LE and SE models, new 16-in. five-blade aluminum wheels for the SE sedan and GT coupe (and required on the LE sedan with 3.4-liter V-6), red molding insert stripes for SE sedans, an optional Sport Appearance package for SE sedans, and four new body colors (Bright Aqua, Light Gray, Light Beige, and Jade Gray). In addition, three new interior colors (Graphite, Gray, and Beige) were offered. The SE coupe featured the 3.1-liter MFI V-6; a three-speed automatic transmission; 15-in. bolt-on wheel covers; P20570R15 touring tires; air conditioning; 45/55 split reclining front seats (or articulated power bucket seats with thigh; lumbar and lateral support). and a Delco ETR AM/FM stereo with clock. The GT coupe featured a 3.1-liter MFI V-6; a four-speed automatic transmission; the Y99 Rally tuned suspension; ABS brakes; 16-in. cast aluminum wheels; P225/60R16 Eagle GT+4 tires; air conditioning; power windows; power door locks; power bucket seats with thigh; lumbar and lateral support; cruise control; and a Delco ETR AM/FM stereo cassette with equalizer and steering wheel controls and six-speaker sound system. The GTP coupe featured a 3.4-liter Twin Dual Cam V-6; a five-speed manual transmission; the Y99 Rally Tuned suspension; ABS brakes; an aero performance package; P245/50ZR16 tires; air conditioning; power windows; power door locks; a power driver's seat; cruise control; a Delco ETR AM/FM stereo cassette with equalizer and steering wheel controls; and a six-speaker sound system. The LE sedan included the 3.1-liter MFI V-6, a three-speed automatic transmission, 15-in. bolt-on wheel covers, P205/70R15 touring tires, air conditioning, 45/55 split reclining front seats and a Delco ETR AM/FM stereo with clock. The SE sedan featured a 3.1-liter MFI V-6; a three-speed automatic transmission; 15-in. bolt-on wheel covers or 16-in. cast aluminum wheels; P215/60R16 touring tires; air conditioning; 45/55 split reclining front seats (or articulated power bucket seats with thigh; lumbar and lateral support); and a Delco ETR AM/FM stereo with clock. The STE sedan included the 3.1-liter MFI V-6; a four-speed automatic transmission; the Y99 Rally Tuned suspension; P225/60R16 Eagle GT+4 tires; an electronic information center; air conditioning; power windows; power door locks; a power driver's seat; cruise control; a remote keyless entry system; a Delco ETR AM/FM cassette stereo with equalizer and steering wheel controls; and an eight-speaker sound system with subwoofer amplifier.

BONNEVILLE — SERIES 2H — (V-6) — The Bonneville's 35th year was celebrated with some progress in styling and more standard features than ever before. Major changes to the exterior and interior and a new Sport package were the focus of the program for the SE, SSE, and SSEi models. An enhanced 3800 V-6 was standard (this engine was supercharged in SSEi), along with new torque-axis engine mounts; an electronic four-speed automatic transmission; dual airbags; an anti theft deterrent system; ABS brakes; larger diameter front brakes; retained accessory power; a heated windshield on SSEi models; traction control on SSEi models; a heads-up instrument display on SSEi models; driver-selected transmission controls with the supercharged V-6; and a Two-Flow Electronic variable-ratio steering (standard on SE with Sport Appearance package). New exterior features included all-new sheet metal; flush glass; two levels of new body fascias; new headlights; two levels of new taillights; standard round fog lights; three levels of new body

1992 Pontiac Firebird Trans Am two-door convertible. (PGMC)

side moldings; a low lift-over deck lid design; three types of new aluminum wheels; and two new tire types (depending on the model). Interior changes for 1992 included a new instrument panel; a new floor console; a new storage console and assist handles in upper-level headliners; three new seating levels; new fabrics on Level 1 trims; new front and rear door trim designs; new rear seat armrests with pass-through to trunk; new steering wheels with redundant radio controls; three levels of new dash clusters; and an eight-speaker sound system standard on SSEi. Major standard equipment varied by model. On SEs, the list included a driver's side airbag; rack-and-pinion power steering; a 3.8-liter 3800 series TPI V-6; a four-speed electronic automatic transmission; P215/65R15 black sidewall touring tires; 15-in. bolt-on wheel covers; manual air conditioning; a Delco ETR AM/FM stereo with seek-and-scan and clock; a 45/55 reclining split seat with armrest; an armrest rear seat with dual cup holders and a pass-through to the trunk; express-down power windows; power door locks; black wide body moldings; and a Pass-Key II theft deterrent system. On SSEs, the standard features list included ABS brakes; a driver's side airbag; rack-and-pinion variable-ratio power steering; a 3.8-liter 3800 series TPI V-6; a four-speed electronic automatic transmission; an electric leveling system; P215/65R15 black sidewall touring tires; 16-in. Aerolite color-keyed (or silver) aluminum wheels; manual air conditioning; a Delco ETR AM/FM cassette stereo with equalizer; six speakers and steering wheel controls; 45/45 bucket seats with a console; an armrest rear seat with dual cup holders and pass-through to trunk; a driver information center; a rear window defogger; express-down power windows; power door locks; a Pass Key II theft deterrent system; a ribbed monotone moldings appliqué; and monotone ground effects. On SSEis, the standard features list included ABS brakes; dual front airbags; rack-and-pinion variable-ratio power steering; a 3.8-liter 3800 series supercharged TPI V-6; a four-speed electronic automatic transmission with selectable controls; an electric leveling system; a traction-control system; P225/60R16 Eagle GT+4 black sidewall touring tires or P225/60ZR16 speed-rated GT+4 performance tires; 16-in. Aerolite color-keyed (or silver) aluminum wheels; automatic air conditioning; a Delco ETR AM/FM cassette stereo with equalizer; six speakers and steering wheel controls; 45/45 12-way articulating bucket seats with console and recliner controls; an armrest rear seat with dual cup holders and pass-through to trunk; a driver information center; a rear window defogger; a Remote Keyless entry system; an illuminated entry system with retained accessory power; a full-feature anti-theft system; express-down power windows; power door locks; a Pass Key II theft deterrent system; a ribbed monotone moldings appliqué; and monotone ground effects.

TRANS SPORT — SERIES 2U — (V-6) — The 1992 Trans Sport again came in two models. They were renamed SE and GT. Functional changes for 1992 included an antilock braking system, a new optional trailer towing package, a standard 3800 series V-6 engine for the GT (optional on SE), a new rear air conditioning system, an integrated power roof antenna, and an optional Remote Keyless entry system. New for the exterior were steel wheels with 15-in. bolt-on wheel covers, new tire sizes and styles, and four new body colors. Interior updates included a four-way manual seat adjuster, an optional sunroof, rear "saddlebag" storage provisions, and a rear convenience net. Standard equipment on the SE included a 3.1-liter EFI V-6, three-speed automatic transmission, ABS brakes, P205/70R15 tires on 15-in. wheels, 15-in. bolt-on wheel covers, 2+3 seating with a bench seat in the second position, Delco ETR AM/FM radio with clock, and integrated roof antenna. The GT model's features list included the 3.8-liter EFI V-6, four-speed automatic transmission, ABS brakes, electronic ride control, P205/70R15 touring tires, Sport cast aluminum wheels, 2+2+2 seating, a leather steering wheel, tilt steering, cruise control, deep tinted glass, power outside rearview mirrors, electronic control front air conditioning, Delco ETR AM/FM stereo cassette radio, and integrated roof antenna.

I.D. DATA: Pontiac's 17-symbol Vehicle Identification Number (VIN) for passenger cars was on the upper left surface of the instrument panel, visible through the windshield. The first symbol indicates country of origin: 1=U.S.; 2= Canada; 3=Mexico; J=Japan; K=Korea. The second symbol indicates manufacturer: G=General Motors; G=Suzuki; 8=Isuzu; Y=NUMMI; L=Daewoo; C=CAMI. The third symbol G indicates make: 2=Pontiac division; 7=GM of Canada; M=Pontiac Multi-Purpose Vehicle. The fourth and fifth symbols for passenger cars indicated body type and series: F/S=Firebird; F/W=Firebird Trans Am; H/

1992 Pontiac Bonneville SSEi four-door sedan. (PGMC)

X=Bonneville SE; HY=Bonneville SSEi; H/Z=Bonneville SSE; J/B=Sunbird SE and convertible; J/C=Sunbird LE; J/D=Sunbird GT; M/R=Firefly (U.S. Customs Territories); N/E=Grand Am SE; N/W=Grand Am GT; T/N=LeMans SE Aerocoupe and sedan; T/X=LeMans; W/H=Grand Prix LE; W/J=Grand Prix SE; W/T=Grand Prix STE; W/P=Grand Prix GT/GTP. On Trans Sports the fourth symbol indicated the GVWR/brake system and the fifth symbol indicating line and chassis type was a "U" for All-Purpose Vehicle 4x2. The sixth symbol on passenger cars denoted body type: 1=two-door coupe/sedan styles 11, 27, 37, 47, 57, 97; 2=two-door hatchback styles 07, 08, 77 and 87; 3=two-door convertible style 67; 4=two-door Safari style 15; 5=four-door sedan styles 19 and 69; 6=four-door hatchback/liftback style 68; 8=four-door Safari style 35. The sixth symbol on Trans Sports indicated series: 0=All-Purpose Vehicle. The seventh symbol on passenger cars indicated the type of restraint system: 1=manual belts; 2=active manual belts with dual airbags; 3=active manual belts with driver airbag; 4=passive automatic belts; 5=passive automatic belts with driver airbag. The seventh symbol on Trans Sports indicated body type: 6=All-Purpose Vehicle. Symbol eight for passenger cars was an engine code: A=RPO LG0 2.3-liter fuel-injected (MFI) I-4; D=RPO LD2 2.3-liter fuel-injected (MFI) I-4; E=RPO L03 5.0-liter fuel-injected (TBI) V-8; F=RPO LB9 5.0-liter fuel-injected (MFI) V-8; H=RPOI LE4 2.0-liter fuel-injected (MFI) I-4; L=RPO L27 3.8-liter fuel-injected (MFI) V-6; N=RPO LG7 3.3-liter fuel-injected (MFI) V-6; R=RPO LR8 2.5-liter fuel-injected (TBI) I-4; T=RPO LH0 3.1-liter fuel-injected (MFI) V-6; X=RPO LQ1 3.4-liter fuel-injected (MFI) V-6; 1=RPO L67 3.8-liter fuel-injected (MFI) V-6; 3=RPO L40 2.3-liter fuel-injected (MFI) I-4; 6=RPO L73 1.6-liter fuel-injected (TBI) I-4; 8=RPO L98 5.7-liter fuel-injected (MFI) V-8. The seventh symbol for Trans sports was also an engine code: D=RPO LG6 3.1-liter fuel-injected (TBI) V-6; L=RPO L27 3.8-liter fuel-injected (MFI) V-6. The ninth symbol for cars and trucks is a check digit. The tenth symbol for cars and trucks denotes model year (N=1992). The 11th symbol for cars and trucks indicates the GM assembly plant (A=Lakewood, GA; B=Baltimore, Md. T&B; B=Pupyong, Korea; C=Lansing, Mich.; D=Doraville, Ga.; E=Linden, N.J.; E=Pontiac East, Mich. T&B; F=Fairfax II, Kan.; F=Flint T&B; H=Flint, Mich.; J=Janesville, Wis. T&B; K=Kosai, Japan; L=Van Nuys, Calif.; M=Lansing, Mich; R=Arlington, Texas; S=Ramos Arizpe, Mexico; T=Tarrytown, N.Y.; U=Hamtramck, Mich; W=Willow Run, Mich.; W=Iwata, Japan; Y=Wilmington, Del.; Z=Fremont, Calif.; Z=Ft. Wayne, Ind.; Z=Spring Hill, Tenn.; 0= Pontiac, Mich. (T&B); 1=Oshawa, Canada #2; 1=Wentzville, Mo. T&B; 2=Morraine, OH T&B; 2=Ste. Therese, Canada; 3=Detroit, Mich. T&B; 3=Kawasaki, Japan; 4=Orion, Mich.; 4=Scarborough, Ontario, Canada; 5=Bowling Green, Ken.; 6=Ingersoll, Ontario, Canada; 6=Oklahoma City, Okla.; 7=Lordstown, Ohio; 7=Lordstown, Ohio T&B; 7=Flusawa, Japan; 8=Shreveport, La. T&B; 9=Oshawa, Ontario, Canada #1. Pontiacs are not produced at all of these GM plants. The last six symbols are the consecutive unit number at the factory.

Model Number	Body Style Number	Body Type & Seating	Factory Price	Shipping Weight	Production Total
LEMANS VALUE LEADER SERIES T/X (I-4)					
2T	TX2	3d Coupe-4P	8,050	2,164	Note 1
LEMANS SE AEROCOUPE AND SEDAN SERIES T/N (I-4)					
2T	TN2	3d Coupe-4P	8,750	2,186	Note 1
2T	TN5	4d Sedan-4P	9,465	2,241	Note 1
SUNBIRD LE SERIES 2J (I-4)					
2J	JC5	4d Sedan-5P	9,720	2,502	Note 2
2J	JC1	2d Coupe-5P	9,620	2,484	Note 2

Model Number	Body Style Number	Body Type & Seating	Factory Price	Shipping Weight	Production Total
SUNBIRD SE SERIES 2J (I-4)					
2J	JB5	4d Sedan-5P	10,480	2,502	Note 2
2J	JB1	2d Coupe-5P	10,380	2,484	Note 2
2J	JB3	2d Convertible-5P	15,345	2,694	Note 2
SUNBIRD GT SERIES 2J (V-6)					
2J	JD1	2d Coupe-5P	12,820	2,682	Note 2
GRAND AM SE SERIES N/E (Quad Four)					
2N	NE1	2d Coupe-5P	11,899	2,728	Note 3
2N	NE5	4d Sedan-5P	11,999	2,777	Note 3
GRAND AM SE SERIES N/E (V-6)					
2N	NE1	2d Coupe-5P	12,359	—	Note 3
2N	NE5	4d Sedan-5P	12,459	—	Note 3
GRAND AM GT SERIES N/W (Quad Four)					
2N	NW1	2d Coupe-5P	13,699	2,804	Note 3
2N	NW5	4d Sedan-5P	13,799	2,846	Note 3
FIREBIRD SERIES F/S (V-6)					
2F	FS2	2d Coupe-5P	12,505	3,121	Note 4
2F	FS3	2d Convertible-5P	19,375	3,280	Note 4
FIREBIRD SERIES F/S (V-8)					
2F	FS2	2d Coupe-5P	12,874	3,281	Note 4
2F	FS3	2d Convertible-5P	19,744	3,440	Note 4
FIREBIRD FORMULA SERIES F/S (V-8)					
2F	FS2	2d Coupe-5P	16,205	3,370	Note 4
FIREBIRD TRANS AM SERIES F/W (V-8)					
2F	FW2	2d Coupe-5P	18,105	3,343	Note 4
2F	FW3	2d Convertible-5P	23,875	3,441	Note 4
FIREBIRD TRANS AM GTA SERIES F/W (V-8)					
2F	FW2	2d Coupe-5P	25,880	3,456	Note 4
GRAND PRIX LE SERIES W/H (V-6)					
2G	WH5	4d Sedan-5P	14,890	3,243	Note 5
GRAND PRIX SE SERIES W/J (V-6)					
2G	WJ5	4d Sedan-5P	16,190	3,282	Note 5
2G	WJ1	2d Coupe-5P	15,390	3,214	Note 5
GRAND PRIX STE SERIES W/T (V-6)					
2G	WT5	4d Sedan-5P	21,635	3,434	Note 5
GRAND PRIX GT/GTP SERIES W/P (V-6)					
2G	WP1	2d Coupe-5P	20,340	3,357	Note 5
BONNEVILLE SE SERIES H/X (V-6)					
2H	HX5	4d Sport Sedan-5P	18,5999	3,362	Note 6
BONNEVILLE SSE SERIES H/Z (V-6)					
2H	HZ5	4d Sport Sedan-5P	23,999	3,507	Note 6
BONNEVILLE SSEi SERIES H/Y (V-6)					
2H	HY5	4d Sport Sedan-5P	28,045	3,607	Note 6
TRANS SPORT SE SERIES U (V-6)					
2U	U06	Minivan	16,225	3,599	Note 7
TRANS SPORT GT SERIES U (V-6)					
2U	U06	Minivan	20,935	3,678	Note 7

NOTE 1: LeMans series production totaled 19,499 cars.

NOTE 2: Sunbird series production totaled 73,979 cars.

NOTE 3: Grand Am series production totaled 190,025 cars.

NOTE 4: Firebird series production totaled 25,180 cars.

NOTE 5: Grand Prix series production totaled 106,583 cars.

NOTE 6: Bonneville series production totaled 116,002 cars.

NOTE 7: Trans Sport series production totaled 30,900 cars.

LEMANS ENGINE

ENGINE [Standard ALL]: Inline. OHV. Four-cylinder. Cast-iron block. Aluminum head and intake manifold. Displacement: 97.5 cid.

1992 Pontiac Trans Sport GT minivan. (PGMC)

(1.6L). Bore & stroke: 3.11 x 3.21 in. Compression ratio: 8.6:1. Brake horsepower: 74 at 5600 rpm. Torque: 90 lbs.-ft. at 2800 rpm. Fuel system: EFI/TBI. RPO Code: L73. Standard with four-speed manual LeMans SE "Value Leader" Aerocoupe; standard with five-speed manual transmission in other models. [VIN code 6].

SUNBIRD ENGINES

ENGINE [Base Four LE/SE]: Inline. OHC. Four-cylinder. Cast-iron block. Aluminum head and intake manifold. Displacement: 121 cid. (2.0L). Bore & stroke: 3.38 x 3.38 in. Compression ratio: 9.2:1. Brake horsepower: 111 at 5200 rpm. Torque: 125 lbs.-ft. at 3600 rpm. Fuel system: EFI/MPFI. Code: LT2. Standard in Sunbird LE and Sunbird SE models. [VIN code K].

ENGINE [Base Six GT]: V-block. OHV. Six-cylinder. Cast-iron block and aluminum head. Displacement: 191 cid. (3.1L). Bore & stroke: 3.50 x 3.31 in. Compression ratio: 8.8:1. Brake horsepower: 140 at 4200 rpm. Torque: 185 lbs.-ft. at 3600 rpm. Fuel system: EFI/MPFI. [VIN code T].

GRAND AM ENGINES

ENGINE [Base Four SE]: Inline. Quad-4 OHC. Cast-iron block. Aluminum head and intake manifold. Displacement: 138 cid. (2.3L). Bore & stroke: 3.63 x 3.35 in. Compression ratio: 9.5:1. Brake horsepower: 120 at 5200 rpm. Torque: 140 lbs.-ft. at 3200 rpm. Fuel system: MPFI. RPO Code: L4O. Standard in SE. [VIN code A].

ENGINE [Optional Four SE]: Inline. Quad-4 DOHC. 16-valve. Cast-iron block. Aluminum head and intake manifold. Displacement: 138 cid. (2.3L). Bore & stroke: 3.63 x 3.35 in. Compression ratio: 9.5:1. Brake horsepower: 160 at 6200 rpm. Torque: 155 lbs.-ft. at 5200 rpm. Fuel system: MPFI. RPO Code: LD2. Optional in SE. [VIN code D].

ENGINE [Base Four GT]: Inline. Quad-4 H.O. DOHC. 16-valve. Quad-4 High-Output. Cast-iron block. Aluminum head and intake manifold. Displacement: 138 cid. (2.3L). Bore & stroke: 3.63 x 3.35 in. Compression ratio: 10.0:1. Brake horsepower: 180 at 6200 rpm. Torque: 160 lbs.-ft. at 5200 rpm. Fuel system: MPFI. RPO Code: LG0. Standard and exclusive in Grand Am SE with five-speed Manual transmission. [VIN code A].

ENGINE [Optional Six SE/GT]: V-block. OHV. Six-cylinder. Cast-iron block and aluminum head. Displacement: 204 cid. (3.3L). Bore & stroke: 3.70 x 3.16 in. Compression ratio: 9.0:1. Brake horsepower: 160 at 5200 rpm. Torque: 185 lbs.-ft. at 2000 rpm. Fuel system: MFI. RPO Code LG7. Optional in Grand Am SE and GT. [VIN code N].

FIREBIRD ENGINES

ENGINE [Base V-6]: V-block. OHV. Six-cylinder. Cast-iron block and head. Aluminum intake manifold. Displacement: 191 cid. (3.1L). Bore & stroke: 3.50 x 3.31 in. Compression ratio: 8.8:1. Brake horsepower: 140 at 4400 rpm. Torque: 185 lbs.-ft. at 3200 rpm. Fuel system: EFI/MFI. RPO Code: L H.O. Standard in base Firebird. [VIN code T].

ENGINE [Base V-8]: V-block. OHV. Eight-cylinder. Cast-iron block and head. Aluminum intake manifold. Displacement: 305 cid. (5.0L). Bore & stroke: 3.74 x 3.48 in. Brake horsepower: 170 at 4000 rpm. Torque: 255 lbs.-ft. at 2400 rpm. Compression ratio: 9.3:1. Fuel system: EFI/TBI. RPO Code: LO3. Standard Formula. Available in base Firebird. [VIN code E or F].

ENGINE [Optional V-8]: V-block. OHV. Eight-cylinder. Cast-iron block and head. Aluminum intake manifold. Displacement: 305 cid. (5.0L). Bore & stroke: 3.74 x 3.48 in. Brake horsepower: 205 at 4200 rpm. Torque: 285 lbs.-ft. at 3200 rpm. Compression ratio: 9.3:1. Fuel system: EFI/TPI. RPO Code: LB9. Available with five-speed manual in Formula and Trans Am (delete option in GTA). [VIN code E or F].

ENGINE [GTA V-8]: V-block. OHV. Eight-cylinder. Cast-iron block and head. Aluminum intake manifold. Displacement: 350 cid. (5.7L). Bore & stroke: 4.00 x 3.48 in. Brake horsepower: 240 at 4400 rpm. Torque: 340 lbs.-ft. at 3200 rpm. Compression ratio: 9.3:1. Fuel system: EFI/TPI. RPO Code: B2L. Standard with four-speed automatic in GTA (optional in Formula and Trans Am). Includes Performance Enhancement group with dual catalytic converter exhausts, engine oil cooler, and performance axle ratio. [VIN code 8].

GRAND PRIX ENGINES

ENGINE [Base Six (STE and GT); Optional (LE/SE)]: V-block. OHV. Six-cylinder. Cast-iron block and aluminum head. Displacement: 191 cid. (3.1L). Bore & stroke: 3.50 x 3.31 in. Compression ratio: 8.8:1. Brake horsepower: 140 at 4400 rpm. Torque: 185 lbs.-ft. at 3200 rpm. Fuel system: EFI/MPI. RPO Code: L H.O. [VIN code T].

1992 Pontiac Grand Am GT two-door coupe. (PGMC)

ENGINE [Base Six (GTP); Optional (all except LE)]: V-block. OHV. Six-cylinder. Cast-iron block and aluminum head. Displacement: 207 cid. (3.4L). Bore & stroke: 3.62 x 3.31 in. Compression ratio: 9.25:1. Brake horsepower: 210 at 5200 rpm. Torque: 215 lbs.-ft. at 4000 rpm. Fuel system: EFI/MPI. [VIN code X].

BONNEVILLE ENGINES

ENGINE [Base Six SE/SSE]: V-block. OHV. "3800" six-cylinder. Cast-iron block and head. Aluminum intake manifold. Displacement: 231 cid. (3.8L). Bore & stroke: 3.80 x 3.40 in. Compression ratio: 8.5:1. Brake horsepower: 170 at 4800 rpm. Torque: 220 lbs.-ft. at 3200 rpm. Fuel system: SFI. RPO Code: L27. Standard in Bonneville SE/SSE models. [VIN code C].

ENGINE [Base Six SSEi]: V-block. OHV. "3800" supercharged six-cylinder. Cast-iron block and head. Aluminum intake manifold. Displacement: 231 cid. (3.8L). Bore & stroke: 3.80 x 3.40 in. Compression ratio: 8.5:1. Brake horsepower: 205 at 4400 rpm. Torque: 260 lbs.-ft. at 2800 rpm. Fuel system: SFI and supercharged. RPO Code: L67. Standard and exclusive in Bonneville SSEi model. [VIN code 1].

TRANS SPORT ENGINES

ENGINE [Base Six SE]: V-block. OHV. Six-cylinder. Cast-iron block and head. Aluminum intake manifold. Displacement: 191 cid. (3.1L). Bore & stroke: 3.50 x 3.31 in. Compression ratio: 8.5:1. Brake horsepower: 120 at 4400 rpm. Torque: 175 lbs.-ft. at 2200 rpm. Fuel system: EFI/TBI. RPO Code: LG6. Standard in base Firebird. [VIN code T].

ENGINE [Base Six GT]: V-block. OHV. "3800" six-cylinder. Cast-iron block and head. Aluminum intake manifold. Displacement: 231 cid. (3.8L). Bore & stroke: 3.80 x 3.40 in. Compression ratio: 8.5:1. Brake horsepower: 165 at 4300 rpm. Torque: 220 lbs.-ft. at 3200 rpm. Fuel system: SFI. RPO Code: L27. Standard in Transport GT. [VIN code C].

CHASSIS

PONTIAC LEMANS CHASSIS: Wheelbase: 99.2 in. (all). Overall length: 163.70 in. (three-door); 172.4 in. (four-door). Height: 53.5 in. (Aerocoupe); 53.7 in. (sedan). Width: 65.5 in. (three-door); 65.7 in. (four-door). Front track: 55.1 in. (all) Rear track: 55.4 in. (all). Standard tires: P175/70R13 BSW (all). Fuel tank: 13.2 gal.

SUNBIRD CHASSIS: Wheelbase: 101.3 in. (all). Overall length: 180.7 in. (all). Overall width: 66.3 in. (all). Height: 52.0.in. (coupe). Front tread: 55.6 in. (all). Rear tread: 55.2 in. (all). Standard tires: P185/75R14 BSW (all except SE and GT coupes). Standard tires: P195/65R15 Goodrich T/A touring tires. (GT coupe).

GRAND AM CHASSIS: Wheelbase: 103.4 in. (all). Overall length: 186.9 in. (all). Width: 68.6 in. (all). Height: 53.1 in. (all). Standard tires: P185/75R14 BSW (SE). Standard tires: P205/55R16 (GT).

FIREBIRD CHASSIS: Wheelbase: 101.0 in. (all). Overall length: 195.1 in. (Base/Formula); 195.2 in. (Trans Am/GTA). Width: 72.4 in. (all). Height: 49.7 in. (all). Front tread: 60.7 in. Rear tread: 61.6 in. Standard tires: P215/65R15 (Base Firebird). Standard tires: P215/60R16 (Trans Am). Standard tires: P245/50ZR16 Goodyear Eagle ZR50 "Gatorback" (Formula and GTA).

GRAND PRIX CHASSIS: Wheelbase: 107.5 in. (all). Overall length: 194.8 in. (coupe). Overall length: 194.8 in. (sedan). Width: 71.9 in. (all). Height: 53.3 in. (all). Standard tires: See model description.

BONNEVILLE CHASSIS: Wheelbase: 110.8 in. (all). Overall length: 200.6 in. (all). Width: 73.6 in. (all). Height: 55.5 in. (all). Standard tires: See model descriptions.

TRANS SPORT CHASSIS: Wheelbase: 109.8 in. (all). Overall length: 194.5 in. (all). Width: 74.6 in. (all). Height: 65.7 in. (all). Standard tires: 205/70R15 BSW (SE). Standard tires: P205/70R15 touring tires (GT).

TECHNICAL

LEMANS TECHNICAL: Chassis: Front engine/front drive. Standard transmission: Four-speed manual (SE Aerocoupe "Value Leader" only). Standard transmission: Five-speed manual (Other Models). Optional (except "Value Leader") three-speed automatic transmission. Axle ratio: 3.43:1 with 1.6L and automatic. Axle ratio: 3.72:1 (both manual). Front suspension: deflected disc, MacPherson struts and 22mm stabilizer bar. Rear suspension: Coil springs, semi-independent torsion beam, trailing arms and 18mm anti-roll bar. Steering: Rack-and-pinion 24.5:1 ratio (18.3:1 power-assisted optional, except "Value Leader"). Turns lock-to-lock: 3.5 (power); 4.57 (manual). Turning circle: 32.8 ft. Front brakes: 9.25-in. vented discs. Rear brakes: 7.9 x 1.8-in. drums (power-assisted).

SUNBIRD TECHNICAL: Chassis: Front engine/front drive. Base transmission: Five-speed manual. Optional transmission: Three-speed automatic. Axle ratio: 3.45:1 with five-speed manual. Axle ratio: 3.18:1 with three-speed automatic. Front suspension [Level I]: Deflected disc, MacPherson struts and (22mm with 2.0L TBI/28mm with 3.1L MFI) stabilizer bars. Front suspension [Level II]: Deflected disc, MacPherson struts and 28mm stabilizer bars. Rear suspension: Coil springs, semi-independent torsion beam, trailing arms and 21mm anti-roll bar. Steering: Rack-and-pinion 16.0:1 ratio (14.0:1 on cars with base 14-in. tires). Turns lock-to-lock: 3.0 (2.5 on GT). Turning circle: 34.3 ft. (all). Front brakes: 10.5-in. vented disc power-assisted. Rear brakes: 7.87 x 1.77-in. drum power-assisted.

GRAND AM TECHNICAL: Chassis: Front engine/front drive. Base transmission: Five-speed manual with overdrive (M32 or MV5). Optional transmission: Three-speed automatic (MD9). Axle ratio: 3.58:1 (with M32 five-speed). Axle ratio: 2.84:1 (with MD9 automatic). Axle ratio: 3.94:1 (with MV5 five-speed manual). Level I suspension: [Front] Deflected disc; MacPherson struts with coil springs and 26mm anti-roll bar; [Rear] Coil springs; semi-independent torsion beam, trailing arms. Level II suspension: [Front] Deflected disc; MacPherson struts with coil springs and 28mm anti-roll bar; [Rear] Coil springs; semi-independent torsion beam, trailing arms. Level III suspension: [Front] Deflected disc; MacPherson struts, 18mm. direct-acting anti-roll bar. [Rear] Coil springs; semi-independent torsion beam, trailing arms and defected disc, gas-charged shocks. Steering (Level I): Power-assisted rack-and-pinion, 16.0:1 ratio, 2.98 turns lock-to-lock and 34.1-ft. turning circle. Steering (Level II): Power-assisted rack-and-pinion, 14.0:1 ratio, 2.5 turns lock-to-lock and 36.4-ft. turning circle. Front brakes: 259.5mm diameter vented discs. Rear brakes: 2.00mm diameter drums. Fuel tank: 15.2 gal.

FIREBIRD TECHNICAL: Chassis: Front engine/rear drive. Base transmission: Four-speed automatic (Firebird/GTA). Optional transmission: Five-speed manual. (Formula/Trans Am). Front suspension: Modified MacPherson strut with 30mm (FE1), 34mm (F41), or 36mm (WS6) anti-roll bar. Rear suspension: Live axle with coil springs, control arms, torque arm, track bar, coil springs and 18mm (FE1), 23mm (F41) or 33mm (WS6) anti-roll bar. Steering: Power re-circulating ball; 14.1:1 ratio (FE1), or 12.7:1 quick ratio with sport effort valving (F41 and WS6). Turns lock-to-lock: 2.57 (FE1), or 2.14 (F41 and WS6). Turning circle: 38.5 ft. (all). Brakes: Power vented 10.5-in. front disc/9.5 x 2.0-in. rear drum (10.5-in. rear vented discs on GTA and optional others). Fuel tank: 15.5 gal.

GRAND PRIX TECHNICAL: Chassis: Front engine/front drive. Standard drive train SE and LE sedan: 3.1L MFI V-6 with three-speed automatic. Standard drive train GT coupe and STE sedan: 3.1L MFI V-6 with five-speed manual transaxle. Optional drive train GTP coupe: 3.4L Twin Dual Cam V-6 with five-speed manual transaxle. Final Drive Ratios: [five-speed manual] 2.84:1; [M13 four-speed manual] 2.40:1; [ME9 four-speed manual] 2.33:1; [three-speed manual] 2.84:1. Front suspension: MacPherson struts with tapered top coil springs, lower A arm and 28mm anti-roll bar (34mm anti-roll bar with Y99 suspension). Rear suspension: Tri-link independent suspension, transverse fiberglass leaf spring and 10mm anti-roll bar (12mm anti-roll bar with Y99). Steering: Power-assisted rack-and-pinion with 15.7:1 ratio (14.0:1 with 3.4-liter V-6). 2.6 turns lock-to-lock (2.26 with GT/STE) and 36.7-ft. (39-ft. GT/STE) turning circle. Front brakes: 10.51-in. vented discs, power-assisted. Rear brakes: 10.1-in. solid discs, power-assisted. Fuel tank: 16.5 gal.

BONNEVILLE TECHNICAL: Chassis: Front engine/front drive. Base transmission: Four-speed automatic. Axle ratio: 2.84:1 (standard all). Front suspension: Deflected-disc, MacPherson struts with 32mm stabilizer bar (F41/FE2 and FE1). Rear suspension: Coil springs, semi-independent torsion beam, trailing arms and 21mm stabilizer bar (F41/FE2) or 17mm stabilizer bar (FE1). Steering (SE): Power-assisted rack-and-pinion with 16.54:1 ratio, 2.79 turns lock-to-lock and 39.4-ft. (left)/40-ft. (right) turning circle. Steering (W21/SSE/SSEi): Power-assisted rack-and-pinion with 14.93:1 to 18.91:1 variable ratio, 2.86 turns lock-to-lock and 38.7-ft. (left)/40.3-ft. (right) turning circle. Front brakes: Power-assisted 10.9-in. vented discs. Rear brakes: Power-assisted 8.85-in. drums. (Antilock brake system standard with SSE). Fuel tank: 18.0 gal.

TRANS SPORT TECHNICAL: Chassis: Front engine/front drive. Transmission: Three-speed automatic. Axle ratio: 3.18:1 (3.1L V-6). Axle ratio: 3.06:1 (3.4L V-6). Front suspension: MacPherson struts with 24 N-mm coil springs and 30mm anti-roll bar (LE). Front suspension: MacPherson strut, stamped lower control arms, 28mm stabilizer bar. Rear suspension: Open-section transverse beam on stamped steel trailing arms, tube shocks, coil springs and 25.4mm stabilizer bar. Steering: Power-assisted rack-and-pinion with 15.7:1 ratio and 38-ft. turning circle. Front brakes: Power-assisted 10.2-in. vented rotors, 182 sq. in. swept area. Rear brakes: Power-assisted 8.86 x 1.58-in. finned composite cast-iron drums with 98.5 sq. in. swept area. Fuel tank: 20.0 gal.

OPTIONS

LEMANS OPTIONS: R6A value package for Value Leader model ($662). R6A Value package for SE model ($355). MX1 three-speed automatic transmission ($475). C60 air conditioning, requires power steering and not available in Value Leader Aerocoupe ($705). B37 front and rear floor mats ($33). N40 power steering, requires air conditioning in Aerocoupe or SE sedan ($225). UM7 Delco ETR stereo in Value Leader Aerocoupe ($307). UM6 Delco ETR AM/FM with cassette and more in Value Leader Aerocoupe ($429). UM6 Delco ETR AM/FM with cassette and more in LE/SE/GSE ($122). AD3 removable sunroof ($350). WDV warranty enhancements for New York ($25).

SUNBIRD OPTIONS: 1SB Sunbird LE coupe and sedan option group #1 ($903). 1SB Sunbird SE coupe and sedan option group #1 ($158). 1SC option for SE coupe and sedan ($671). TR9 option group for SE coupe and sedan ($1,135). 1SB Sunbird SE convertible option group #1 ($955). 1SC option for SE convertible ($827). 1SB option group for GT coupe ($955). R6A option group for LE coupe and sedan ($258). R6A option group for SE coupe and convertible ($258). R6B option group for SE coupe and convertible ($790). R6A option group for SE sedan ($258). R6B option group for SE sedan ($720). L H.O. engine, except no cost in GT ($585). MX1 three-speed automatic transmission ($495). W25 Special Appearance package ($316-$599 depending on value option packages it's teamed with). C60 air conditioning ($745). DO6 front seat armrest in GT and SE ($58). NB2 California emissions ($100). K34 cruise control ($225). C49 electric rear window defogger ($170). AO1 tinted glass ($105). TR9 lamp group ($29). D35 Sport mirrors ($53). A31 power windows, requires power door locks ($265 SE/GT coupe/$230 sedan/no charge convertible). UM6 Delco radio equipment ($170 additional). U1C Delco radio equipment ($396).

GRAND AM OPTIONS: 1SB package on GT coupe ($1,327). 1SC package on GT coupe ($1,838). 1SB package on GT sedan ($1,327). 1SC package on GT sedan ($1,903). 1SB package on SE coupe ($565). 1SC package on SE coupe ($976). 1SB package on SE sedan ($565). 1SC package on SE sedan ($1,041). R6A Value option package on SE coupe and sedan ($253). R6B Value option package on SE coupe and sedan ($431). LD2 Quad-4 2.3-liter MPI engine in SE models ($410). LD2 Quad-4 2.3-liter MPI engine in GT models ($140 credit). LGO Quad-4 High-Output engine (standard on SE/Manual). LG7 3.3-liter V-6 in SE ($460). MX1 three-speed automatic transmission ($555). C60 air conditioning ($830). C49 electric rear window defogger ($170). K34 cruise control ($225). UB3 rally gauges ($111). NB2 California emission requirements ($100). K34 cruise control ($225). C49 electric rear window defogger ($170). UB3 rally gauges for SE ($111). DG7 dual sport mirrors ($86). AC3 power seat with Sport interior group ($305). AC3 power seat without Sport interior group ($340). NV7 variable effort power steering ($62). A31 express down power windows in SE and GT

coupe ($275). A31 express down power window in SE or GT sedan ($340). AM9 split folding rear seat ($150). CD4 controlled cycle wipers ($65). B20 Sport interior group, SE and GT ($265). WDV warranty enhancements ($25). UM6 Delco sound system ($140). UW6 full-range speakers ($85). U1A Delco sound system ($460-$600). QMW touring tires with Ride & Handling suspension ($141). QPD touring tires with Ride & Handling suspension ($158). PC1 custom wheel covers ($275). V2C 16-in. custom wheels on GT ($396). PG1 crosslace wheel covers on SE without value package ($55). UB3 rally gauges with tach ($78-$127). AM9 split folding rear seat ($150). T43 rear deck lid spoiler SE convertible without value package or W25 Special Appearance package ($70). N33 tilt steering wheel ($145). AD3 glass sunroof SE coupe and GT ($350). CD4 controlled cycle windshield wipers ($65). B20/11N9 white vinyl trim for LE coupe, SE coupe, SE convertible and GT ($75). D84 two-tone paint on SE ($101). WDV warranty enhancement for New York ($25). QME tires without value option package ($141). QPD touring tires with Ride & Handling package ($158). N78 14-in. Hi-Tech Turbo aluminum wheels ($220-$275). PG1 15-in. crosslace wheel covers ($55). PF7 cast aluminum wheels with locking package ($220-$275).

FIREBIRD OPTIONS: 1SB Firebird V-6 option group ($413). 1SB Firebird V-8 option group ($223). 1SB Formula/Trans Am option group ($223). 1SB Firebird V-6 convertible ($390). 1SB Firebird V-8 convertible ($225). 1SB Trans Am convertible option group ($225). 1SC Firebird V-6 option group ($804). 1SC Firebird V-8 option group ($484). 1SC Formula/Trans Am option group ($484). 1SC Firebird V-6 convertible ($721). 1SC Firebird V-8 convertible ($401). 1SC Trans Am convertible option group ($366). R6A Firebird and Formula value package ($814). R6A Trans Am convertible value package ($680). L H.O. 3.1-liter MPFI V-6 engine in base Firebird coupe and convertible ($369). LB9 5.0L MPI V-8 in Formula and Trans Am ($745). LB9 5.0L MPI V-8 in Trans Am GTA ($300 credit). B2L 5.7L MPI V-8 in Trans Am ($300). B2L 5.7L MPI V-8 in Formula ($1,045). MM5 five-speed manual transmission in Trans Am GTA with LB9 ($530 credit). MX0 four-speed automatic transmission, except in GTA ($530). C60 air conditioning ($830). G80 limited-slip axle ($100). K34 cruise control, except GTA ($225). A90 rear deck lid release in Trans Am ($60). C49 rear window defogger, except GTA ($170). NB2 California emissions ($100). CC1 Hatch roof ($914). DG7 dual Sport mirror, left-hand remote-control, except GTA ($91). R6P Performance Enhancement group with dual converter exhaust, four-wheel disc brake, engine oil cooler and more ($444). AU3 power door locks ($210). A31 power windows ($280). U75 power antenna ($75). UM6 Delco radio equipment ($150). U1A Delco radio equipment ($226-$376). D42 cargo area security screen ($69). AH3 four-way adjustable power driver seat, except GTA ($35). AR9 Custom Pallex cloth reclining bucket seat, no cost option, but not available on GTA. AQ9 articulating bucket seats with Ventura leather trim in GTA ($475). AQ9 articulating bucket seats with Ventura leather trim in Trans Am convertible ($780). QLC high-performance WS6 performance suspension ($313).

6000 OPTIONS: 1SB option package #1 for 6000 LE sedan ($995). 1SC option package #2 for 6000 LE sedan ($1,190). 1SD option package #3 for 6000 LE sedan ($2,058). 1SB option package #1 for 6000 LE Safari ($190). 1SC option package #2 for 6000 LE Safari ($385). 1SD option package #3 for 6000 LE Safari ($1,243). 1SB option package #1 for 6000 SE sedan ($343). 1SB option package

1992 Pontiac Bonneville SE four-door sedan. (PGMC)

Standard Catalog of ® Pontiac, 2nd Edition

#1 for 6000 SE Safari ($293). R6A value option package for 6000 LE sedan ($413). R6B value option package for 6000 LE sedan ($413). R6B value option package for 6000 LE sedan ($413). LB6 2.8-liter MFI V-6 in LE sedan ($660). MX0 four-speed automatic transmission ($200). C60 air conditioning ($805). C49 electric rear window defogger ($160). D86 two-tone paint ($115). AU3 power door locks ($205). A31 power windows ($310). UM6 Delco ETR AM/FM stereo ($122). U1A Delco ETR AM stereo/FM stereo ($501-$564). AM6 45/55 split bench seat ($133). B20 custom interior with 45/55 split seat in Empress/London cloth ($350-$483). Various tire options (no charge to $68). N78 Sport aluminum wheels with locking package ($265). BX3 woodgrain exterior siding for Safari ($295).

GRAND PRIX OPTIONS: 1SB Grand Prix LE ($175). 1SC Grand Prix LE ($540). 1SB Grand Prix SE sedan ($450). 1SC Grand Prix SE sedan ($1,023). 1SD Grand Prix SE sedan ($1,389). 1SB Grand Prix SE coupe ($450). 1SC Grand Prix SE coupe ($718). 1SD Grand Prix SE coupe ($1,084). 1SB Grand Prix GT coupe ($841). 1SB Grand Prix STE sedan ($1,145). R6A Value Option for Grand Prix LE sedan ($543). R6B Value Option package for Grand Prix LE sedan ($488), R6A Value Option Package for Grand Prix SE coupe ($818). R6B Value Option package for Grand Prix SE coupe ($753). R6C Value Option package for Grand Prix SE coupe ($2,228). R6A Value Option package for Grand Prix SE sedan ($584). R6B Value Option package for Grand Prix SE sedan ($774). R6C Value Option package for Grand Prix SE sedan ($1,457). LQ1 3.4L DOHC 24-valve Twin Dual Cam V-6 ($995). MX0 four-speed automatic in Grand Prix SE ($200). MM5 five-speed manual transmission in Grand Prix LE ($200 credit). A90 remote deck lid release ($60). C49 electric rear window defogger ($170). NB2 California emissions system ($100). D84 two-tone paint ($105). JL9 power antilock brakes ($450). AUO Remote Keyless Entry system ($135). CF5 power sunroof ($670-$695). UB3 rally gauge cluster with tachometer ($85). U68 electric compass with trip computer and service reminder ($285). UV6 heads-up display, requires Graphite, Gray, or Beige interior trim and bucket seats ($250). V56 rear deck lid luggage carrier ($115). B20 Custom interior trim ($45). DG7 dual Sport mirrors ($78). DH6 dual illuminated visor vanity mirrors ($86). KD1 transmission oil cooler ($75). N33 tilt steering wheel ($450). A31 power windows on coupe ($275). A31 power windows on sedan ($340). AU3 power door locks on coupe ($210). AU3 power door locks on sedan ($250). BYP Sport Appearance package with lower aero ground effects ($385-$690 depending on model and other options). B4U Aero Appearance package ($2,080-$2,595). Y99 rally handling suspension ($50). NC5 dual split exhausts ($90). WDV warranty enhancements ($25). UM6 Delco radio equipment ($140). UX1 Delco radio equipment ($540-$590). U1A stereo sound system ($766-$816 depending on model). US7 power antenna ($85). AR9 bucket seat with Pallex cloth trim in Grand Prix LE ($110). AN3 Custom Cloth bucket seat in Grand Prix LE ($140). AQ9 articulating Sport bucket seats with front console and Ventura leather trim ($475). AC3 power seat ($305). B20 Custom interior trim ($324-$383). QPE touring tires ($112). QXJ P22560R-16 tires ($150). QLC P245/50ZR16 tires with GTP coupe ($209). PH3 15-in. aluminum sport wheels with locking package ($275). NWO 16-in. aluminum Sport wheels ($275).

BONNEVILLE OPTIONS: 1SB Bonneville SE option package ($383). 1SC Bonneville SE option package ($901). 1SD Bonneville SE option package ($1,242). 1SB Bonneville SSE option package ($845). R6A Bonneville SE value option package ($845). R6B Bonneville SE value option package. ($424). R6C Bonneville SE value option package ($200). R6A Bonneville SSE value option package. ($1,835). R6A Bonneville SSEi value option package. ($1,195). AS7 45/45 bucket seats and console ($220-$315). AL7 leather trim package ($779-$1,419 depending on other options). B20 Custom interior trim ($130). AG1 six-way power seat ($305). AUO Remote Keyless Entry system ($135). B57 monotone appearance package ($180). C97 illuminated entry system ($75). CF5 power glass sunroof ($1,216-$1,326). C49 electric rear window defogger ($170). C50 heated windshield ($250) JM4 power front disc/rear drum antilock braking system ($450). K05 engine block heater ($18). NB2 California emissions system ($100). NW9 Traction Control system ($175). PF5 16-in. five-blade cast aluminum wheels ($340). PF7 15-in. six-spoke cast aluminum wheels ($306). QPJ touring tires ($76). QNX touring tires ($74). R7E premium equipment package ($1,345). T2U convenience group ($213). T2Z enhancement group ($206). T43

rear deck lid spoiler ($95). UA6 Theft Deterrent system ($190). UM6 Delco radio equipment ($140). UX1 Delco sound system ($460-$650). U1A compact disc player ($226-$876). US7 power antenna ($85). V92 trailer provisions ($150-$614 depending on other options and Value Packages). WDV warranty enhancements ($25). W21 SE Sport package ($591-$1,185 depending on model, options and Value Packages).

TRANS SPORT OPTIONS: 1SB Trans Sport option package #1 ($1,195). 1SC Trans Sport option package #2 ($1,960). 1SB Trans Sport SE option package #1 ($765). Advertising ($200). C67 air conditioning in Trans Sport ($805). NB2 California emissions system ($100). B2Q black roof delete (no charge). C49 electric rear window defogger ($160). AJ1 glass package in Trans Sport ($245). AB5 power door locks ($255). A31 power windows ($240). UM6 Delco radio equipment ($140). U1A compact disc player ($376-$516). AB3 six-passenger seating package ($525). ZP7 seven-passenger seating package ($675). N78 14-in. aluminum wheels ($265).

NOTE: Full option package contents, descriptions and applications information can often be determined by consulting factory literature. The data above is edited for size and clarity. This information provided only as a guide to help collectors appraise the relative value of cars with numerous options. Prices for items included as part of a value option package are usually much less than individual prices. Option prices charged by individual dealers may also vary.

HISTORICAL: Total production in U.S. and Canada included 27,567 Firebirds; 119,319 Grand Prixs; 208,568 Grand Ams; 1,208 Tempests; 124,511 Bonnevilles; 106,752 Sunbirds and 41,529 Trans Sports for a total of 629,454 units. John Middlebrook was Pontiac Motor Division's general manager in 1992. E.M. Schlesinger was in charge of general sales and service. E.S. Lechtzin was the company's director of public relations. Lynn Myers was the director of marketing and production planning. B. L. Warner was chief engineer.

1993 PONTIAC

1993 Pontiac Sunbird SE two-door coupe. (PGMC)

LEMANS — SERIES 2T — (FOUR) — The Pontiac LeMans was based on the German Opel Kadett and built in Korea. The 1993 LeMans line consisted of the "Value Leader" Aerocoupe, the SE Aerocoupe, and the SE sedan. New for 1993 was a revised, less angular front and rear appearance due to new bumpers and fascias, new side marker lamps, parking lamps and turn signals, black body side moldings, and revised HVAC controls. There were two new colors: Bright Turquoise (Aerocoupe "Value Leader") and Light Aqua Metallic. More contemporary 13-in. custom wheel covers were finished in argent silver on the Aerocoupe "Value Leader" and SE sedan. Standard equipment on the LeMans "Value Leader" included a 1.6-liter TBI engine, a four-speed manual transmission, P175/70R13 black side wall tires, 9.25-in. vented front disc brakes, steel wheels, an electric rear window defogger, halogen headlamps, and remote sport mirrors. The LeMans SE Aerocoupe added or substituted a five-speed manual transmission, styled steel wheels, a three-spoke steering wheel, and a Delco AM/FM stereo with clock.

The LeMans SE sedan had all the same equipment as the SE "Value Leader" Aerocoupe, plus a five-speed manual transmission and a Delco AM/FM stereo with clock.

SUNBIRD — SERIES 2J — (FOUR) — An acoustics package was added across the line in 1993, making Sunbirds quieter. There were again three series comprising the Sunbird lineup: LE, SE, and GT. New features included a Sport Appearance Package for the SE coupe, a glass convertible rear window with available defogger for the SE convertible, a low-oil-level sensor on the 2.0L engine, three new exterior colors (Bright White, Light Gray Metallic, and Light Teal Metallic), three new interior colors (Beige, Gray, and Arctic White) and a trunk cargo net. Standard equipment on the Sunbird included the MPFI 2.0-liter four-cylinder engine (LE and SE coupes), a five-speed manual transmission, reclining front bucket seats, antilock brakes, P185/75R14 tires, power rack and pinion steering, a Delco ETR AM/FM stereo with seek-and-scan and a clock, a stainless steel exhaust system, and automatic door locks. The Sunbird SE convertible offered Soft-Ray tinted glass, rear quarter courtesy lights and a front seat armrest and storage bin. The Sunbird GT added or substituted a 3.1-liter MPFI V-6 mated to a Getrag five-speed manual transmission featuring a new concentric slave cylinder clutch design, P195/65R15 tires, and a dual exhaust system.

GRAND AM — SERIES 2N — Pontiac's best seller, the Grand Am, was again available as SE and GT coupes and sedans. The Grand Am's Quad Four engine received improvements to enhance noise reduction. Functional changes included one new exterior color (Gray Purple Metallic), two new interior colors (Beige and New Gray), battery rundown protection, axle ratio changes, revised HVAC controls and graphics and a revised base instrument panel appliqué. Standard equipment included fog lamps, P185/75R14 tires, bolt-on 14-in. wheel covers, a Delco ETR AM/FM stereo with seek-and-scan and clock, a 2.3-liter Quad OHC four-cylinder engine, a five-speed manual transmission, stainless steel exhaust, ABS brakes, and power rack-and-pinion steering. The GT added or substituted dual chrome-tipped exhaust outlets, neutral-density taillights, P205/55R16 tires, specific 16-in. cast aluminum wheels, rally gauges with a tachometer, and a 2.3-liter H.O. DOHC 16-valve Quad four-cylinder engine.

FIREBIRD — SERIES 2F — (V-6/V-8) — Pontiac's fourth-generation Firebird arrived in 1993 with 90 percent new content. This radical revision found most every component of the Firebird completely new or extensively updated. The full line consisted of Firebird, Firebird Formula, and Trans Am. Included among the many changes for 1993 were a 68-degree windshield angle, new aluminum wheels and tires, composite body panels that were resistant to minor impacts and rust, new instrumentation, a locking glove box, and new front and rear suspensions. A new 3.4-liter V-6 was standard on the Firebird and an LT1 5.7-liter V-8 was standard on Formula and Trans Am models. A six-speed manual transmission was also standard on Formulas and Trans Ams. Other new features included advanced four-wheel antilock brakes (standard on Firebirds with four-wheel disc brakes including all Formulas and Trans Ams) and dual front airbags. A keyless entry system was now available on all Firebirds and standard on Trans Ams. Colors offered in 1993 were: Dark Green Metallic, Yellow, Bright Red, Medium Red Metallic, Bright Blue Metallic, Gray Purple Metallic, Bright White, and Black. Standard features on all Firebird models included front air dam, tinted glass, sport mirrors, an aerodynamic rear-deck spoiler, side-window defogers, a four-spoke steering wheel with adjustable steering column, P215/60R16 steel-belted touring tires, rear-wheel drive, rack-and-pinion steering, and a five-speed manual transmission.

GRAND PRIX — SERIES 2W — (V-6/V-8) — Pontiac touted the 1993 Grand Prix lineup as offering sport styling, performance, and safety "for buyers seeking affordable, controlled performance and distinctive styling in a mid-sized automobile." New features included an optional "second-gear start" transmission with the 3.1-liter V-6 (for enhanced starting on slippery roads); a new Ruby Red interior color; a Sport Appearance Package for the LE sedan; an available four-speed electronic automatic transmission (for cars with the 3.1-liter engine); standard automatic door locks; and provisions for installation of a cellular car phone. Standard on all Grand Prix models were air conditioning; power door locks; a 3.1-liter MFI V-6; fog lamps; rear-seat headrests; rack-and-pinion steering; four-wheel power disc brakes; and a stainless steel exhaust system. The SE

1993 Pontiac Grand Am GT two-door coupe. (PGMC)

coupe also included a 3.1-liter MFI V-6; a three-speed automatic transmission; 15-in. bolt-on wheel covers; P20570R15 touring tires; 45/55 split reclining front seats; and a Delco ETR AM/FM stereo with clock. The GT coupe included a 3.1-liter MFI V-6; a four-speed automatic transmission; the Y99 rally suspension; 16-in. cast aluminum wheels; P225/60R16 Eagle GT+4 tires; rally gauges with tachometer; power windows; power bucket seats with thigh; lumbar and lateral support; cruise control; and a Delco ETR AM/FM stereo cassette with equalizer and steering wheel controls. The GTP coupe added a 3.4-liter Twin Dual Cam V-6; a five-speed manual transmission; the Y99 Rally Tuned suspension; an "aero" performance package; P245/50ZR16 tires; power windows; a power driver's seat; cruise control; a Delco ETR AM/FM stereo cassette with equalizer and steering wheel controls; and a six-speaker sound system. The Grand Prix LE sedan included a 3.1-liter MFI V-6; a three-speed automatic transmission; 15-in. bolt-on wheel covers; P205/70R15 touring tires; 45/55 split reclining front seats; and a Delco ETR AM/FM stereo with clock. The Grand Prix SE sedan included a 3.1-liter MFI V-6; a three-speed automatic transmission; 16-in. cast aluminum wheels; P215/60R16 touring tires; 45/55 split reclining front seats and a Delco ETR AM/FM stereo with clock. Finally; the Grand Prix STE sedan also featured a 3.1-liter MFI V-6; a four-speed automatic transmission; the Y99 Rally Tuned suspension; P225/60R16 Eagle GT+4 tires; rally gauges with a tachometer; power windows; power driver's seat; cruise control; a remote keyless entry system; a Delco ETR AM/FM cassette stereo with equalizer; and steering-wheel-mounted redundant radio controls.

BONNEVILLE — SERIES 2H — (V-6) — Pontiac's luxury import sedan fighter, the Bonneville, received additional firepower in the SLE package for 1993. The SLE makeover of the standard Bonneville SE joined the Pontiac flagship SSE and SSEi models in attracting import-oriented buyers. Pontiac promoted buying American and said, "The Bonneville SLE is a driver-oriented, sophisticated sports sedan, designed and engineered to perform and handle like import luxury sedans that cost thousands of dollars more." In addition to the SLE package, other new features offered on Bonneville models included three new exterior colors (Gray Purple Metallic, Light Gray Metallic, and Bright White), standard monotone appearance on the base model, ABS graphics added to 16-in. five-blade cast-aluminum wheels, revised turn signal, wiper and cruise stalk controls, antilock brakes on all models. Two new interior colors (Ruby Red and Medium Gray) were offered. Also standard was a soft-touch graphite instrument panel trim plate on all Bonnevilles with bucket seats. A supercharged 3800 Series V-6 engine was available in the Bonneville SSE along with traction control, 16-in. tires and wheels and an RPO Y52 Performance and Handling Package to replace the former W21 Sport Appearance Package. Major standard equipment varied by model. On SEs, the list included a driver's side airbag; rack-and-pinion power steering; the 3.8-liter 3800 series TPI V-6; a four-speed electronic automatic transmission; P215/65R15 black sidewall touring tires; 15-in. bolt-on wheel covers; manual air conditioning; a Pass-Key II theft deterrent system; tinted windows; and a stainless steel single exhaust system. On Bonneville SSEs the standard features list included a driver's side airbag; rack-and-pinion variable-ratio power steering; a 3.8-liter 3800 series TPI V-6; a four-speed electronic automatic transmission; an electronic load leveling system; P215/60R16 black sidewall Eagle GA touring tires; 16-in. Aerolite color-keyed (or silver) aluminum wheels; a manual air-conditioning system; a driver information center; the Pass Key II theft deterrent system; cruise control; a stainless steel split-dual-exhaust system; a monotone ground effects package; a leather-wrapped steering wheel with radio controls; and a convenience net in trunk. For the Bonneville SSEi the standard features list included dual front airbags; rack-and-pinion variable-ratio power steering; a 3.8-liter 3800 series supercharged TPI V-6; a four-speed electronic automatic transmission; an electronic load-leveling system; a traction-control system; P225/60ZR16 Eagle GT+4 black sidewall tires; 16-in. Aerolite color-keyed (or silver) aluminum wheels; automatic air conditioning; a leather-wrapped steering wheel with radio controls; a driver information center; the Pass-Key II theft-deterrent system; a monotone ground effects package; stainless steel split dual exhaust; tinted glass; and a remote keyless entry system.

TRANS SPORT — SERIES 2U — (V-6) — With the discontinuation of the GT version of the Trans Sport, the 1993 Pontiac minivan lineup consisted only of the Trans Sport SE. A new, standard "Quiet Package" was the big news on the improvement front. It greatly reduced outside noise levels. Trans Sport SE purchasers could still add on all the up-level features found on the previous year's GT version at extra cost. New features for the SE included a pop-up sunroof (at mid-year); one new interior color Ruby Red; a lockable under-dash storage area; larger HVAC (heating; ventilation; and air conditioning) controls; redundant radio controls; an AM/FM Stereo cassette with graphic equalizer; cargo lamps; a leather seating area option; and increased wheel caster. Standard equipment included a 3.1 liter V-6 with electronic fuel injection; a three-speed automatic transmission; an antilock braking system; a stainless steel exhaust system; an integrated roof antenna; tinted glass; P205/70R15 black sidewall all-season tires; 15-in. styled bolt-on wheel covers; analog instrumentation with tachometer; and intermittent wipers.

I.D. DATA: Pontiac's 17-symbol Vehicle Identification Number (VIN) for passenger cars was on the upper left surface of the instrument panel, visible through the windshield. The first symbol indicates country of origin: 1 or 4=U.S.; 2=Canada; 3=Mexico; J=Japan; K=Korea. The second symbol indicates manufacturer: G=General Motors; G=Suzuki; 8=Isuzu; Y=NUMMI; L=Daewoo; C=CAMI. The third symbol G indicates make: 2=Pontiac division; 5=Pontiac incomplete; 7=GM of Canada; M=Pontiac Multi-Purpose Vehicle. The fourth and fifth symbols for passenger cars indicated body type and series: F/S=Firebird; F/V=Firebird Formula or Trans Am; H/X=Bonneville SE; HY=Bonneville SSEi; H/Z=Bonneville SSE; J/B=Sunbird SE and convertible; J/C=Sunbird LE; J/D=Sunbird GT (two-door); L/T=Tempest (Export only); N/E=Grand Am SE; N/W=Grand Am GT; T/N=LeMans SE Aerocoupe and sedan; T/X=LeMans; W/H=Grand Prix LE; W/J=Grand Prix SE; W/T=Grand Prix STE; W/P=Grand Prix GT/GTP. On Trans Sports the fourth symbol indicated the GVWR/brake system and the fifth symbol indicating line and chassis type was a "U" for All-Purpose Vehicle 4x2. The sixth symbol on passenger cars denoted body type: 1=two-door coupe/sedan styles 27, 37, 47, 57, 97; 2=two-door hatchback/liftback styles 07, 08, 77 and 87; 3=two-door convertible style 67; 4=two-door Safari style 15; 5=four-door sedan styles 19 and 69; 6=four-door hatchback/liftback styles 29, 68; 8=four-door Safari style 35. The sixth symbol on Trans Sports indicated series: 0=All-Purpose Vehicle. The seventh symbol on passenger cars indicated the type of restraint system: 1=manual belts; 2=active manual belts

1993 Pontiac Formula Firebird two-door coupe. (PGMC)

1993 Pontiac Firebird two-door coupe. (PGMC)

with dual airbags; 3=active manual belts with driver airbag; 4=passive automatic belts; 5=passive automatic belts with driver airbag. The seventh symbol on Trans Sports indicated body type: 6=All-Purpose Vehicle. Symbol eight for passenger cars was an engine code: A=RPO LG0 2.3-liter fuel-injected (MFI) I-4; D=RPO LD2 2.3-liter fuel-injected (MFI) I-4; H=RPO LE4 2.0-liter fuel-injected (MFI) I-4; L=RPO L27 3.8-liter fuel-injected (MFI) V-6; N=RPO LG7 3.3-liter fuel-injected (MFI) V-6; P=RPO LT1 5.7-liter fuel-injected (MFI) V-8; S=RPO L32 3.4-liter fuel-injected (MFI) V-6; T=RPO LH0 3.1-liter fuel-injected (MFI) V-6; X=RPO LQ1 3.4-liter fuel-injected (MFI) V-6; 1=RPO L67 3.8-liter fuel-injected (MFI) V-6; 3=RPO L40 2.3-liter fuel-injected (MFI) I-4; 6=RPO L73 1.6-liter fuel-injected (TBI) I-4. The seventh symbol for Trans sports was also an engine code: D=RPO LG6 3.1-liter fuel-injected (TBI) V-6; L=RPO L27 3.8-liter fuel-injected (MFI) V-6. The ninth symbol for cars and trucks is a check digit. The tenth symbol for cars and trucks denotes model year (P=1993). The 11th symbol for cars and trucks indicates the GM assembly plant (A=Lakewood, Ga.; B=Baltimore, Md. T&B; B=Pupyong, Korea; C=Lansing, Mich.; D=Doraville, Ga.; E=Linden, N.J.; E=Pontiac East, Mich. T&B; F=Fairfax II, Kan.; F=Flint, Mich. T&B; H=Flint, Mich.; J=Janesville, Wis. T&B; K=Kosai, Japan; K=Linden, N.J. T&B; L=Van Nuys, Calif.; M=Lansing, Mich.; M=Mexico City, Mexico; R=Arlington, Texas; S=Ramos Arizpe, Mexico; T=Tarrytown, N.Y.; U=Hamtramck, Mich.; W=Willow Run, Mich.; W=Iwata, Japan; Y=Wilmington, Del.; Z=Fremont, Calif.; Z=Ft. Wayne, Ind.; Z=Spring Hill, Tenn.; 0=Pontiac, Mich. (T&B); 1=Oshawa, Canada #2; 1=Oshawa, Canada T&B; 1=Wentzville, Mo. T&B; 2=Morraine, Ohio T&B; 2=Ste. Therese, Canada; 3=Detroit, Mich. T&B; 3=Kawasaki, Japan; 4=Orion, Mich.; 4=Scarborough, Ontario, Canada; 5=Bowling Green, Ky.; 6=Ingersoll, Ontario, Canada; 6=Oklahoma City, Okla.; 7=Lordstown, Ohio; 7=Flusawa, Japan; 8=Shreveport, La. T&B; 8=Tillonburg, Ontario, Canada (CANEXPO); 9=Oshawa, Ontario, Canada #1. Pontiacs are not produced at all of these GM plants. The last six symbols are the consecutive unit number at the factory.

Model Number	Body Style Number	Body Type & Seating	Factory Price	Shipping Weight	Production Total
LEMANS (VALUE LEADER) SERIES T/X (I-4)					
2T	TX2	3d Coupe-4P	8,154	2,137	Note 1
LEMANS SE SERIES T/N (I-4)					
2T	TN2	3d Aerocoupe-4P	9,054	2,175	Note 1
2T	TN5	4d Sedan-4P	9,854	2,203	Note 1
SUNBIRD LE SERIES J/C (I-4)					
2J	JC5	4d Sedan-5P	9,382	2,502	Note 2
2J	JC1	2d Coupe-5P	9,382	2,484	Note 2
SUNBIRD SE SERIES J/B (I-4)					
2J	JB5	4d Sedan-5P	10,380	2,502	Note 2
2J	JB1	2d Coupe-5P	10,380	2,484	Note 2
2J	JB3	2d Convertible-5P	15,403	2,694	Note 2
SUNBIRD GT SERIES J/D (V-6)					
2J	JD1	2d Coupe-5P	12,820	2,682	Note 2
GRAND AM SE SERIES 2N (Quad 4)					
2N	NE1	2d Coupe-5P	12,624	2,728	Note 3
2N	NE5	4d Sedan-5P	12,524	2,777	Note 3
GRAND AM SE SERIES N/E (V-6)					
2N	NE1	2d Coupe-5P	12,984	—	Note 3
2N	NE5	4d Sedan-5P	13,084	—	Note 3
GRAND AM GT SERIES N/W (Quad 4)					
2N	NW1	2d Coupe-5P	13,924	2,804	Note 3
2N	NW5	4d Sedan-5P	14,024	2,846	Note 3
FIREBIRD SERIES F/S (V-6)					
2F	FS2	2d Coupe-5P	13,995	3,241	Note 4

Model Number	Body Style Number	Body Type & Seating	Factory Price	Shipping Weight	Production Total
FIREBIRD FORMULA SERIES F/V (V-8)					
2F	FV2	2d Coupe-5P	17,995	3,381	Note 4
FIREBIRD TRANS AM SERIES F/V (V-8)					
2F	FV2	2d Coupe-5P	21,395	3,452	Note 4
GRAND PRIX LE SERIES W/H (V-6)					
2G	WH5	4d Sedan-5P			14,890
3,333	Note 5				
GRAND PRIX SE SERIES W/J (V-6)					
2G	WJ5	4d Sedan-5P	16,190	3,369	Note 5
2G	WJ1	2d Coupe-5P	15,390	3,231	Note 5
GRAND PRIX STE SERIES W/T (V-6)					
2G	WT5	4d Sedan-5P	21,635	3,506	Note 5
GRAND PRIX GT- SERIES W/P (V-6)					
2G	WP1	2d Coupe-5P	20,340	3,326	Note 5
BONNEVILLE SE SERIES H/X (V-6)					
2H	HX5	4d Sport Sedan-5P	19,444	3,444	Note 6
BONNEVILLE SSE SERIES H/Z (V-6)					
2H	HZ5	4d Sport Sedan-5P	24,844	3,587	Note 6
BONNEVILLE SSEi SERIES H/Y (V-6)					
2H	HY5	4d Sport Sedan-5P	29,444	3,690	Note 6
TRANS SPORT SE SERIES U (V-6)					
2U	U06	Minivan	16,689	3,598	26,385

NOTE 1: LeMans series production totaled 7,550 cars.

NOTE 2: Sunbird series production totaled 82,902 cars.

NOTE 3: Grand Am series production totaled 224,255 cars.

NOTE 4: Firebird series production totaled 14,112 cars.

NOTE 5: Grand Prix series production totaled 106,083 cars.

NOTE 6: Bonneville series production totaled 98,724 cars.

LEMANS ENGINE

ENGINE [Standard all]: Inline. OHV. Four-cylinder. Cast-iron block. Aluminum head and intake manifold. Displacement: 97.5 cid (1.6L). Bore & stroke: 3.11 x 3.21 in. Compression ratio: 8.6:1. Brake horsepower: 74 at 5600 rpm. Torque: 90 lbs.-ft. at 2800 rpm. Fuel system: EFI/TBI. RPO Code: L73. Standard with four-speed manual LeMans "Value Leader" Aerocoupe; standard with five-speed manual transmission in other models. [VIN code 6].

SUNBIRD ENGINES

ENGINE [Base Four LE/SE]: Inline. OHC. Four-cylinder. Cast-iron block. Aluminum head and intake manifold. Displacement: 121 cid (2.0L). Bore & stroke: 3.38 x 3.38 in. Compression ratio: 9.2:1. Brake horsepower: 110 at 5200 rpm. Torque: 124 lbs.-ft. at 3600 rpm. Fuel system: MPFI. Code: LE4. Standard in Sunbird LE and Sunbird SE models.

ENGINE [Base Six GT]: V-block. OHV. Six-cylinder. VIN code K Cast-iron block and aluminum head. Displacement: 191 cid (3.1L). Bore & stroke: 3.50 x 3.31 in. Compression ratio: 8.9:1. Brake horsepower: 140 at 4200 rpm. Torque: 185 lbs.-ft. at 3200 rpm. Fuel system: MPFI. [VIN code T].

GRAND AM ENGINES

ENGINE [Standard Four SE]: Inline. Quad-4 OHC. Cast-iron block. Aluminum head and intake manifold. Displacement: 138 cid (2.3L). Bore & stroke: 3.63 x 3.35 in. Compression ratio: 9.5:1. Brake horsepower: 115 at 5200 rpm. Torque: 140 lbs.-ft. at 3200 rpm. Fuel system: MPFI. RPO Code: L40. Standard in SE. [VIN code A].

ENGINE [Optional Four SE]: Inline. Quad-4 DOHC. 16-valve. Cast-iron block. Aluminum head and intake manifold. Displacement: 138 cid (2.3L). Bore & stroke: 3.63 x 3.35 in. Compression ratio: 9.5:1. Brake horsepower: 155 at 6000 rpm. Torque: 150 lbs.-ft. at 4800 rpm. Fuel system: MPFI. RPO Code: LD2. Optional in SE. [VIN code D].

ENGINE [Base Four GT]: Inline. Quad-4 H.O. DOHC. 16-valve. Quad-4 High-Output. Cast-iron block. Aluminum head and intake manifold. Displacement: 138 cid (2.3L). Bore & stroke: 3.63 x 3.35 in. Compression ratio: 10.0:1. Brake horsepower: 175 at 6200 rpm. Torque: 155 lbs.-ft. at 5200 rpm. Fuel system: MPFI. RPO Code: LG0. Standard in Grand Am GT with five-speed manual transmission. [VIN code A].

ENGINE [Optional Six SE/GT]: V-block. OHV. Six-cylinder. Cast-iron block and aluminum head. Displacement: 204 cid (3.3L). Bore & stroke: 3.70 x 3.16 in. Compression ratio: 9.0:1. Brake horsepower: 160 at 5200 rpm. Torque: 185 lbs.-ft. at 2000 rpm. Fuel system: MFI. RPO Code LG7. Optional in Grand Am SE and GT. [VIN code N].

FIREBIRD ENGINES

ENGINE [Base V-6]: V-block. OHV. Six-cylinder. Cast-iron block and head. Aluminum intake manifold. Displacement: 207 cid (3.4L). Bore & stroke: 3.62 x 3.31 in. Compression ratio: 9.0:1. Brake horsepower: 160 at 4600 rpm. Torque: 200 lbs.-ft. at 3200 rpm. Fuel system: EFI. RPO Code: L32. Standard in Firebird. Not available in Formula and Trans Am. [VIN code S].

ENGINE [Base V-8]: V-block. OHV. Eight-cylinder. Cast-iron block and head. Aluminum intake manifold. Displacement: 350 cid (5.7L). Bore & stroke: 4.00 x 3.48 in. Compression ratio: 10.5:1. Brake horsepower: 270 at 4800 rpm. Torque: 325 lbs.-ft. at 2400 rpm. Fuel system: PFI. RPO Code: LT1. Standard in Formula and Trans Am. Not available in Firebird. [VIN code P].

GRAND PRIX ENGINES

ENGINE [Base Six LE/SE, STE, and GT]: V-block. OHV. Six-cylinder. Cast-iron block and aluminum head. Displacement: 191 cid (3.1L). Bore & stroke: 3.50 x 3.31 in. Compression ratio: 8.9:1. Brake horsepower: 140 at 4200 rpm. Torque: 185 lbs.-ft. at 3200 rpm. Fuel system: MPFI. RPO Code: L H.O. [VIN code T or M].

ENGINE [Base Six (GTP); Optional (all others)]: V-block. OHV. Six-cylinder. Cast-iron block and aluminum head. Displacement: 207 cid (3.4L). Bore & stroke: 3.62 x 3.30 in. Compression ratio: 9.25:1. Brake horsepower: 210 at 5200 rpm. Torque: 215 lbs.-ft. at 4000 rpm. Fuel system: MPFI. RPO Code: LQ1. [VIN code X or S].

BONNEVILLE ENGINES

ENGINE [Standard SE/SSE]: V-block. OHV. "3800" six-cylinder. Cast-iron block and head. Aluminum intake manifold. Displacement: 231 cid (3.8L). Bore & stroke: 3.80 x 3.40 in. Compression ratio: 9.0:1. Brake horsepower: 170 at 4800 rpm. Torque: 225 lbs.-ft. at 3200 rpm. Fuel system: SPFI. RPO Code: L27. Standard in Bonneville SE/SSE models. [VIN code C].

ENGINE [Standard SSEi]: V-block. OHV. "3800" supercharged six-cylinder. Cast-iron block and head. Aluminum intake manifold. Displacement: 231 cid (3.8L). Bore & stroke: 3.80 x 3.40 in. Compression ratio: 9.0:1. Brake horsepower: 205 at 4400 rpm. Torque: 260 lbs.-ft. at 2600 rpm. Fuel system: SPFI and supercharged. RPO Code: L67. Standard and exclusive in Bonneville SSEi model. [VIN code 1].

TRANS SPORT ENGINES

ENGINE [Standard SE]: V-block. OHV. Six-cylinder. Cast-iron block and head. Aluminum intake manifold. Displacement: 191 cid (3.1L). Bore & stroke: 3.50 x 3.31 in. Compression ratio: 8.5:1. Brake horsepower: 120 at 4400 rpm. Torque: 175 lbs.-ft. at 2200 rpm. Fuel system: EFI/TBFI. RPO Code: LG6. Standard in SE. [VIN code T].

ENGINE [Optional SE]: V-block. OHV. "3800" six-cylinder. Cast-iron block and head. Aluminum intake manifold. Displacement: 231 cid (3.8L). Bore & stroke: 3.80 x 3.40 in. Compression ratio: 9.0:1. Brake horsepower: 170 at 4800 rpm. Torque: 225 lbs.-ft. at 3200 rpm. Fuel system: SPFI. RPO Code: L27. [VIN code 3 or C].

CHASSIS

LEMANS CHASSIS: Wheelbase: 99.2 in. (all). Overall length: 167.90 in. (three-door); 176.9 in. (four-door). Height: 53.5 in. (Aerocoupe); 53.7 in. (sedan). Width: 65.5 in. (three-door); 65.7 in. (four-door). Front tread: 55.1 in. (all). Rear tread: 55.4 in. (all). Standard tires: P175/70R13 BSW (all). Fuel tank: 13.2 gal.

SUNBIRD CHASSIS: Wheelbase: 101.3 in. (all). Overall length: 180.7 in. (all). Overall width: 66.3 in. (all). Height: 52.0 in. (coupe and convertible), 53.6 in. (sedan). Front tread: 55.6 in. (all). Rear tread: 55.4 in. (all). Standard tires: P185/75R14 BSW (all except SE and GT coupes). Standard tires: P195/65R15. (GT coupe).

1993 Pontiac Bonneville SE four-door sedan. (PGMC)

GRAND AM CHASSIS: Wheelbase: 103.4 in. (all). Overall length: 186.9 in. (all). Width: 68.6 in. (all). Height: 53.2 in. (all). Front tread: 55.9 in. (all). Rear tread: 55.4 in. (all). Standard tires: P185/75R14 BSW (SE). Standard tires: P205/55R16 (GT).

FIREBIRD CHASSIS: Wheelbase: 101.1 in. (all). Overall length: 195.6 in. (Firebird/Formula); 197.0 in. (Trans Am). Width: 74.5 in. (all). Height: 52.0 in. (Firebird/Formula); 51.7 in. (Trans Am). Front tread: 60.7 in. (all). Rear tread: 60.6 in. (all). Standard tires: P215/60R16 (Firebird); P235/55R16 (Formula); P245/50ZR16 (Trans Am).

GRAND PRIX CHASSIS: Wheelbase: 107.5 in. (all). Overall length: 194.8 in. (coupe); 194.9 in. (sedan). Width: 71.9 in. (all). Height: 53.3 in. (coupe); 54.8 in. (sedan). Standard tires: See model description.

BONNEVILLE CHASSIS: Wheelbase: 110.8 in. (all). Overall length: 199.5 in. (SE); 201.2 in. (SSE/SSEi). Width: 73.6 in. (all). Height: 55.5 in. (all). Standard tires: See model descriptions.

TRANS SPORT CHASSIS: Wheelbase: 109.8 in. Overall length: 194.5 in. Width: 74.6 in. Height: 65.7 in. Standard tires: P205/70R15 BSW.

TECHNICAL

LEMANS TECHNICAL: Chassis: Front engine/front drive. Standard transmission: Four-speed manual (Aerocoupe "Value Leader" only). Standard transmission: Five-speed manual (other models). Optional (except "Value Leader") three-speed automatic transmission. Axle ratio: 3.43:1 with 1.6L and automatic. Axle ratio: 3.72:1 (both manual). Front suspension: deflected disc, MacPherson struts and 22mm stabilizer bar. Rear suspension: Coil springs, semi-independent torsion beam, trailing arms and 18mm anti-roll bar. Steering: Rack-and-pinion 24.5:1 ratio (18.3:1 power-assisted optional, except "Value Leader"). Turns lock-to-lock: 3.5 (power); 4.57 (manual). Turning circle: 32.8 ft. Front brakes: 9.25-in. vented discs. Rear brakes: 7.9 x 1.8-in. drums (power-assisted).

SUNBIRD TECHNICAL: Chassis: Front engine/front drive. Base transmission: Five-speed manual. Optional transmission: Three-speed automatic. Axle ratio: 3.45:1 with five-speed manual. Axle ratio: 3.18:1 with three-speed automatic. Front suspension [Level I]: Deflected disc, MacPherson struts and (22mm with 2.0L TBI/28mm with 3.1L MFI) stabilizer bars. Front suspension [Level II]: Deflected disc, MacPherson struts and 28mm stabilizer bars. Rear suspension: Coil springs, semi-independent torsion beam, trailing arms and 21mm anti-roll bar. Steering: Rack-and-pinion 16.0:1 ratio (14.0:1 on cars with base 14-in. tires). Turns lock-to-lock: 3.0 (2.5 on base tire). Turning circle: 34.3 ft. (all). Front brakes: 10.25-in. vented disc power-assisted. Rear brakes: 7.87 x 1.77-in. drum power-assisted.

GRAND AM TECHNICAL: Chassis: Front engine/front drive. Base transmission: Five-speed manual with overdrive (M32 or MV5). Optional transmission: Three-speed automatic (MD9). Axle ratio: 3.58:1 (with M32 five-speed manual). Axle ratio: 3:18:1 (with MD9 automatic). Axle ratio: 3.94:1 (with MV5 five-speed manual). Level I suspension: [Front] Deflected disc; MacPherson struts and 26mm anti-roll bar; [Rear] Coil springs; semi-independent torsion beam, trailing arms. Level II suspension: [Front] Deflected disc; MacPherson struts and 28mm anti-roll bar; [Rear] Coil springs; semi-independent torsion beam, trailing arms. Level III suspension: [Front] Deflected disc; MacPherson struts, 18mm direct-acting anti-roll bar. [Rear] Coil springs; semi-independent torsion beam, trailing arms and defected disc, gas-charged shocks. Steering (Level I): Power-assisted rack-and-pinion, 16.0:1 ratio, 2.98 turns lock-to-lock and 34.1-ft. turning circle. Steering (Level II & III): Power-assisted rack-and-pinion, 14.0:1 ratio, 2.5 turns lock-to-lock and 36.4-ft. turning circle. Front brakes: 259.5mm diameter vented discs. Rear brakes: 200.0mm diameter drums. Fuel tank: 15.2 gal.

FIREBIRD TECHNICAL: Chassis: Front engine/rear drive. Base transmission: Five-speed manual (Firebird); six-speed manual (Formula/Trans Am). Optional transmission: Four-speed automatic (all). Front suspension: Short/long arm (SLA) design with gas-filled monotube shocks including front stabilizer bar. Rear suspension: Live axle with revised spring mass and rates with gas-filled monotube shocks. Steering: Power assist rack-and-pinion. Turning circle: 37.8 ft. (Formula). Brakes: Advanced Delco-Moraine ABS VI four-wheel antilock brakes (all); front disc/rear drum (Firebird); four-wheel disc (Formula and Trans Am). Fuel tank: 15.5 gal.

GRAND PRIX TECHNICAL: Chassis: Front engine/front drive. Standard drive train all except GTP coupe: 3.1L MPFI V-6 with

1993 Pontiac Grand Prix LE four-door sedan. (PGMC)

three-speed automatic. Standard drive train GT coupe and optional all others: 3.4L Twin Dual Cam MPFI V-6 with five-speed manual transaxle. Final Drive Ratios: [M27 five-speed manual] 3.67:1; [M13 four-speed electronic automatic--optional on all] 3.43:1; [MD9 three-speed automatic] 2.84:1; [M13 four-speed electronic automatic--standard GT and STE/optional LE and SE] 3.33:1. Front suspension: MacPherson struts with tapered coil springs, lower A arm and 28mm anti-roll bar with Y99 rally suspension). Rear suspension: Tri-link independent suspension, transverse fiberglass leaf spring and 12mm anti-roll bar (12mm anti-roll bar with Y99 and 3.1-liter V-6/14mm with Y99 and 3.4-liter V-6). Steering: Power-assisted rack-and-pinion with 15.7:1 ratio (14.0:1 with 3.4-liter V-6); 2.6 turns lock-to-lock (2.26 with GT/STE) and 36.7-ft. (39-ft. GT/STE) turning circle. Front brakes: 10.51-in. vented discs, power-assisted. Rear brakes: 10.1-in. solid discs, power-assisted. Fuel tank: 16.5 gal.

BONNEVILLE TECHNICAL: Chassis: Front engine/front drive. Base transmission: Four-speed electronic automatic. Axle ratio: 2.84:1 (3800 V-6); 3.06:1 (supercharged 3800 V-6). Front suspension: Deflected-disc, MacPherson struts with 32mm stabilizer bar (F41/FE2 and FE1). Rear suspension: Coil springs, semi-independent torsion beam, trailing arms, and 21mm stabilizer bar (F41/FE2) or 17mm stabilizer bar (FE1). Steering (SE): Power-assisted rack-and-pinion with 16.54:1 ratio, 2.79 turns lock-to-lock and 39.4-ft. (left)/40.0-ft. (right) turning circle. Steering (Y52/SSE/SSEi): Power-assisted rack-and-pinion with 14.93:1 to 18.91:1 variable ratio, 2.86 turns lock-to-lock and 38.7-ft. (left)/40.3-ft. (right) turning circle. Front brakes: Power-assisted 10.9-in. vented discs. Rear brakes: Power-assisted 8.85-in. drums. Fuel tank: 18.0 gal.

TRANS SPORT TECHNICAL: Chassis: Front engine/front drive. Transmission: (MD9) Three-speed automatic; optional (M13) four-speed automatic. Axle ratio: 3.18:1 (3.1L V-6). Axle ratio: 3.06:1 (3.4L V-6). Front suspension: MacPherson struts, stamped lower control arms, 28mm stabilizer bar. Rear suspension: Open-section transverse beam on stamped steel trailing arms, tube shocks, coil springs and 25.4mm stabilizer bar. Steering: Power-assisted rack-and-pinion with 15.7:1 ratio and 38-ft. turning circle. Front brakes: 10.2-in. vented rotors, 182 sq. in. swept area. Rear brakes: 8.86 x 1.58-in. finned composite cast-iron drums with 98.5 sq. in. swept area. Fuel tank: 20.0 gal.

OPTIONS

LEMANS OPTIONS: MX1 three-speed automatic transmission for SE ($475). C60 air conditioning, requires power steering and not available in Value Leader Aerocoupe ($705). B37 front and rear floor mats ($33). N40 power steering, requires air conditioning in Aerocoupe or SE sedan ($225). UM7 Delco ETR stereo in Value Leader Aerocoupe ($307). UM6 Delco ETR AM/FM with cassette and more in Value Leader Aerocoupe ($429). UM6 Delco ETR AM/FM with cassette and more in SE ($122). AD3 removable sunroof ($350). WDV warranty enhancements for New York ($25).

SUNBIRD OPTIONS: 1SB Sunbird LE and SE option group ($903). 1SC Sunbird LE and SE option group ($1,352). 1SD Sunbird LE and SE option group ($2,238). 1SB Sunbird SE convertible option group ($1,136). 1SC Sunbird SE convertible option group ($2,020). 1SB option group for GT coupe ($1,136). B4U Sport Appearance Package for SE coupe, requires V-6 ($612). L H.O. 3.1-liter MPFI V-6, standard in GT coupe ($585). W25 Special Appearance package ($524-$599 depending on value option packages it's teamed with). C60 air conditioning ($745). DO6 front seat armrest in GT and SE ($58). NB2 California emissions ($100). K34 cruise control ($225). C49 electric rear window defogger ($170). AO1 tinted glass ($105). TR9 lamp group ($29). D35 Sport mirrors ($53). A31 power windows, requires power door locks ($265 SE/GT coupe/$330 sedan/no charge convertible). UN6 Delco radio equipment ($170). U1C Delco radio equipment ($396).

GRAND AM OPTIONS: 1SB package on GT coupe/sedan ($1,467). 1SC package on GT coupe ($1,892). 1SC package on GT sedan ($1,957). 1SD package on GT coupe ($2,310). 1SD package on GT sedan ($2,375). 1SB package on SE coupe/sedan ($975). 1SC package on SE coupe/sedan ($1,405). 1SD package on SE coupe ($1,892). 1SD package on SE sedan ($1,957). LD2 Quad-4 2.3-liter MPI engine in SE models ($410). LD2 Quad-4 2.3-liter MPI engine in GT models ($140 credit). LGO Quad-4 High-Output engine, standard on GT (no charge). LG7 3.3-liter V-6 in SE ($460/$90 credit in GT). MX1 three-speed automatic transmission ($555). C60 air conditioning ($830). C49 electric rear window defogger ($170). K34 cruise control ($225). UB3 rally gauges ($111). NB2 California emission requirements ($100). DG7 dual sport mirrors ($86). AC3 power seat with Sport interior group ($340). NV7 variable effort power steering ($62). A31 express down power windows in SE and GT coupe ($275). A31 express down power window in SE or GT sedan ($340). AM9 split folding rear seat ($150). CD4 controlled cycle wipers ($65). WDV warranty enhancements ($25). UM6 Delco sound system ($140). U1A Delco sound system ($460-$600). PG1 crosslace wheel covers on SE without value package ($55).

FIREBIRD OPTIONS: C60 air conditioning included in option groups 1SA, 1SB, 1SC, and 1SD. B35 rear floor mats included in all except optional in Formula 1SA group. B84 body side moldings included in all except optional in Formula 1SA group. A31 power windows included in all except Firebird 1SB group and Formula 1SA group. AU3 power door locks included in all except optional in Firebird 1SB group and Formula 1SA group. AH3 driver's side four-way manual seat adjuster included in select models except optional in Formula 1SA group (not available in Formula 1SB or 1SC groups). K34 cruise control included in all except optional in Firebird 1SB group and Formula 1SA group. DG7 dual Sport mirrors included in all except optional in Firebird 1SB group and Formula 1SA group. AU0 remote keyless entry included in Firebird 1SD, Formula 1SC and Trans Am 1SA groups, optional in all others. UX1 cassette with equalizer, steering wheel controls and 10-speaker sound system included in Firebird 1SD, Formula 1SC and Trans Am 1SA groups, optional in all others.

GRAND PRIX OPTIONS: 1SB Grand Prix LE ($370). 1SC Grand Prix LE ($929). 1SB Grand Prix SE sedan ($996). 1SC Grand Prix

1993 Pontiac Firebird Trans Am two-door coupe. (PGMC)

SE sedan ($1,379). 1SD Grand Prix SE sedan ($1,975). 1SB Grand Prix SE coupe ($931). 1SC Grand Prix SE coupe ($1,314). 1SD Grand Prix SE coupe ($1,910). 1SB Grand Prix GT coupe ($306). LQ1 3.4L 24-valve Twin Dual Cam V-6 ($995). MX0 four-speed automatic ($200). MM5 five-speed manual transmission in Grand Prix GT coupe ($200 credit)/STE sedan ($225 credit). A90 remote deck lid release ($60). C49 electric rear window defogger ($170). NB2 California emissions system ($100). AUO remote keyless entry system ($135). CF5 power sunroof ($695). UB3 rally gauge cluster ($250). U68 electric compass with trip computer and service reminder ($285). UV6 head-up display, requires bucket seats ($250). V56 rear deck lid luggage carrier ($115). B20 Custom interior trim ($355). DG7 dual Sport mirrors ($78). N33 tilt steering wheel ($145). A31 power windows ($275). BYP Sport Appearance package with lower aero ground effects ($366-$783 depending on model and other options). B4U Aero Appearance package ($2,565-$2,595). WDV warranty enhancements ($25). UM6 Delco radio equipment ($140). UX1 Delco radio equipment ($590). U1A stereo sound system ($226-$816 depending on model). US7 power antenna ($85). AN3 bucket seats ($140). B20 Custom interior trim ($110-$416). QPE touring tires ($112). QXJ P225/60R16 tires ($150). QLC P245/50ZR16 tires with GTP coupe ($209). PH3 15-in. aluminum sport wheels ($275). NWO 16-in. aluminum Sport wheels ($275).

BONNEVILLE OPTIONS: 1SB Bonneville SE option package ($383). 1SC Bonneville SE option package ($1,041). 1SD Bonneville SE option package ($1,467). 1SB Bonneville SSE option package ($1,270). B20 Custom interior trim ($265). AUO remote keyless entry system ($135). CF5 power glass sunroof ($1,216-$1,230). C49 electric rear window defogger ($170). K05 engine block heater ($18). NB2 California emissions system ($100). NW9 Traction Control system ($175). PF5 16-in. five-blade cast aluminum wheels ($340). QNX touring tires ($74). QVF tires ($90). T43 rear deck lid spoiler ($95). UA6 Theft Deterrent system ($190). UM6 Delco radio equipment ($140). UX1 Delco sound system ($375-$650). U1A compact disc player ($226-$876). US7 power antenna ($85). V92 trailer provisions ($150-$689 depending on other options and Value Packages). WDV warranty enhancements ($25). Y52 Performance & Handling package ($739).

TRANS SPORT OPTIONS: 1SB Trans Sport SE option package ($1,035). 1SC Trans Sport SE option package ($1,883). 1SD Trans Sport SE option package ($2,428). C67 air conditioning ($830). NB2 California emissions system ($100). B2Q black roof delete (no charge). C49 electric rear window defogger ($170). AJ1 glass package ($245). AB5 power door locks ($300). D84 custom two-tone paint ($60). NK4 leather-wrapped steering wheel ($60). V54 roof luggage carrier ($145). KO5 engine block heater ($18). UM6 Delco radio equipment ($140). U1A compact disc player ($226-$701). AG9 six-way power driver's seat ($270). ZP7 seven-passenger seating package ($870). PH3 aluminum wheels with locks ($275).

NOTE: Full option package contents, descriptions, and applications information can often be determined by consulting factory literature. The data above is edited for size and clarity. This information provided only as a guide to help collectors appraise the relative value of cars with numerous options. Prices for items included as part of a value option package are usually much less than individual prices. Option prices charged by individual dealers may also vary.

HISTORICAL: With John Middlebrook continuing on as general manager, Pontiac Motor Div. produced over 567,000 units in the

1993 Pontiac Trans Sport SE minivan. (PGMC)

1993 Pontiac Bonneville SSEi four-door sedan. (PGMC)

1993 model year. Official production totals for U.S. and Canada cars included 15,475 Firebirds; 116,008 Grand Prixs; 247,498 Grand Ams; 877 Tempests (export only); 104,806 Bonnevilles; 116,408 Sunbirds; 10,874 LeMans and 34,797 Trans Sports for a grand total of 646,743 units. Sales for the calendar year were 544,302 cars and 28,324 "trucks." That added up to 6.39 percent of the total U.S. car market and 18.71 percent of all GM sales.

1994 PONTIAC

1994 Pontiac Grand Am GT two-door coupe. (PGMC)

SUNBIRD — SERIES 2J — (FOUR) — Pontiac's sub-compact Sunbird offered a streamlined lineup. From the previous year's six Sunbird models, four model offerings were left. Gone were the GT coupe and SE sedan, while the SE convertible became the LE convertible. New features included the Sport Appearance Package—now standard on the SE coupe—plus two new exterior colors (Brilliant Blue and Dark Purple); dual outside rearview mirrors; and tinted glass standard on all models. Also on the standard equipment list were a rear deck lid spoiler; controlled-cycle windshield wipers; 15-in. wheels and tires (now standard on the LE convertible); automatic door unlock/relock; lamp group now standard on all models; and power train noise and vibration reductions. Standard features across-the-lineup included a four-wheel antilock braking system; a stainless steel exhaust system; an oil level indicator; side window defoggers; a grid cloth fabric interior; an illuminated entry system; rear quarter courtesy lights; a Delco ETR AM/FM stereo with seek-and-scan and a clock; reclining front bucket seats; a black fixed-mast antenna; an air dam; bumpers and fascias with integral rub strips; Sport mirrors; fluidic windshield wipers; and a front floor console. The standard features of the LE coupe and sedan included a 2.0-liter OHC four-cylinder MPFI engine with a five-speed manual transmission; P185/75R14 black sidewall all-season tires; and custom 14-in. bolt-on wheel covers. The LE convertible featured the 2.0-liter OHC four-cylinder MPFI engine with a five-speed manual transmission; a convertible top with electro-hydraulic operation and a glass back window; a two-passenger rear seat; P195/65R15 black sidewall touring tires; 15-in. crosslace wheel covers; and power windows with driver's side "express-down" feature. The SE coupe came with a 3.1-liter V-6 MPFI engine with a five-speed manual transmission; aero body extensions; specific front and rear fascia with semi-hidden headlamps; fog lamps; P195/65R15 black sidewall touring tires; 15-in. crosslace wheel covers; an odometer; and carpeted front and rear floor mats.

GRAND AM — SERIES 2N — Pontiac's Grand Am was again the automaker's sales leader and was again available as SE and GT coupes and sedans for 1994. Functional changes included four new exterior colors: Dark Green Metallic; Light Gray Metallic; Brilliant Blue Metallic; and Medium Blue Metallic; 16-in. Sport aluminum wheels; a rear deck lid spoiler (standard on GT; optional on SE); a power sunroof; a driver's side airbag; an automatic door lock/unlock/re-lock feature; a leather interior option (Gray or Beige); theater dimming interior lights; exit lighting; the 3.1-liter 3100 SFI V-6 engine option; a four-speed automatic transmission; a remote keyless entry system; and an air-conditioning system with R134A refrigerant replacing R12 refrigerant. Grand Am standard equipment included a four-wheel antilock braking system; the GM Computer Command Control system; a fixed mast antenna; bumpers and soft fascias with integral rub strips; tinted glass; fog lamps; Sport mirrors; "wet-arm" windshield wipers; a driver's side airbag; power automatic door locks; an illuminated entry system (new for 1994); a Delco ETR AM/FM stereo with seek up/down and a clock; a Grid Cloth fabric interior; 45/45 reclining front bucket seats; a three-passenger rear seat with integrated headrests; a four-spoke Sport steering wheel; and an overhead compartment. Standard equipment on the SE coupe and sedan included a 2.3-liter OHC Quad four-cylinder engine with a five-speed manual transmission; P185/75R14 black sidewall tires and 14-in. custom bolt-on wheel covers. The GT coupe and sedan came with a 2.3-liter Quad 4 DOHC H.O. 16-valve four-cylinder engine with a five-speed manual transmission; aero body extensions including front; rear and side skirts; neutral density wrap-around taillights; P205/55R16 black sidewall Eagle GT+4 tires; 16-in. bright-faced aluminum or white wheels; air conditioning; controlled-cycle windshield wipers; analog instrumentation including a tachometer and trip odometer; a tilt-wheel adjustable steering column; and a stainless steel exhaust system with dual-dual chrome-tipped outlets.

FIREBIRD — SERIES 2F — (V-6/V-8) — Pontiac's theme for its Firebird 1994 lineup could have been the "return of the ragtop." Each of its series—Firebird, Formula and Trans Am—had its 1993 coupe-only offering bolstered with the addition of a convertible. The Trans Am convertible was part of its GT series, while the coupe version was offered both as a Trans Am and a GT. New features for the overall Firebird line included a new Dark Aqua Metallic exterior color; flood-lit interior door switches; visor straps; a Delco 2001 Series radio; a compact disc player (without graphic equalizer); a 5.7-liter SFI V-8; a Mass Air Flow Control System; a four-speed electronically-controlled automatic transmission; driver-selectable automatic transmission controls; a six-speed manual transmission with a 1-4 gear skip shift feature; a 3.42:1 axle ratio; a traction-control system (V-8 automatic only) and two-component clearcoat paint. Standard equipment for all Firebirds included: four-wheel antilock brakes; a stainless steel exhaust system; GM's Computer Command Control system; a low-oil-level monitor and warning; a front air dam; a black fixed-mast antenna; one-piece resilient body color bumpers and fascias; tinted glass; a rear deck lid spoiler; controlled-cycle windshield wipers; dual front airbags; side window defoggers; a Metrix Cloth fabric interior; a locking glove box; reclining front bucket seats and folding rear seats; a tilt-wheel adjustable steering column; and GM's Pass-Key II theft deterrent system. SLP Engineering, Inc., of Toms River, N.J., created 250 Firebird-based performance cars called Firehawks. They were built from 1994 Pontiac Formula coupes. The Firehawks were sold through Pontiac dealers with GMAC financing offered to buyers of the road racers. The Firehawk was offered with a six-speed manual transmission or a four-speed automatic transmission in hardtop or T-top versions. Beyond the distinctive Firehawk graphics on the car, the other giveaway feature was twin hood scoops that the SLP engineers called "functional cold-air induction." The air channeled into the engine bay fed a 5.7-liter, 300-hp V-8 with a compression ratio of 10.25:1. This combination produced 0-to-60 mph in 4.9 seconds. The Firehawk rode on a 17-in. tire-and-wheel combination and the manufacturer's suggested retail price (MSRP) was $24,244.

GRAND PRIX — SERIES 2W — (V-6/V-8) — The Grand Prix lineup for 1994 was reduced from five models the previous year to two models called the SE coupe and sedan. The revamped lineup received an increased level of standard equipment as well as many new features. Among the changes were dual front airbags (standard on SE coupe and sedan), a "Special Edition coupe" package; new Brilliant Blue, Dark Teal, and Medium Teal exterior colors; a new Teal interior color; a GTP Performance Package for the SE coupe; a GT Performance Package for the SE sedan; 15-in. Sport wheel covers; 16-in. five-spoke aluminum wheels; a new instrument panel; a low-oil-level sensor for the 3.1-liter engine; rotary HVAC and headlamp controls; stalk-mounted windshield wiper and cruise controls; electronic actuated cruise control; a Delco 2001 Series radio; automatic door locks with the unlock and re-lock feature; a trip computer with outside temperature display; a single-stroke parking brake; the 3.1-liter 3100 SFI V-6 engine (or optional 210-hp 3.4-liter SFI DOHC V-6); R134A air conditioning refrigerant; and the Pass-Key II theft deterrent system. Standard equipment found on both the SE coupe and sedan included a black fixed-mast radio antenna; soft fascia type bumpers with integral rub strips; tinted and safety laminated glass; fog lamps; lower aero ground effects; "wet-arm" controlled-cycle windshield wipers; electronic air conditioning; mechanical analog instrumentation; a three-passenger rear seat with integrated headrests; a tilt-wheel adjustable steering column; power windows with the "express-down" feature; four-wheel disc brakes; a stainless steel exhaust system; the GM Computer Command Control engine-management system; the 3.1-liter 3100 SFI V-6; and an electronically-controlled four-speed automatic transmission with second-gear-start feature.

BONNEVILLE — SERIES 2H — (V-6) — Pontiac dropped the SSEi model for 1994 and offered a new Bonneville SSEi Supercharger Package (WA6) as an option on the SSE sedan only. The revised two-model lineup offered many new features for 1994 including electronic brake and engine-traction control; a rear deck lid spoiler (available with all exterior colors); standard 15-in. bolt-on wheel covers for Bonneville SE models; standard 16-in. torque-star cast-aluminum wheels for Bonneville SSE models; gray ports on optional 16-in. five-blade wheels for Bonneville SE models; black windshield wipers; and front license plate bracket on the Bonneville SSE. The Bonneville SLE grille was now standard on SE models. There was monotone paint treatment on the SSE grille, a new RPO B57 Monotone Appearance Package, high gloss black body side appliqués, fascia inserts on Monotone Appearance Package (and the SLE Package on Bonneville SE models), and black windshield and header moldings with the SLE Package on the SE model. Dual airbags were now standard on SE and SSE. Also new for the year was an electronic auto-calibrating compass, an available six-way power adjustable passenger seat, a Delco 2001 Series radio family, a new Medium Blue interior color, Computer Command Ride suspension, and a remote trunk release that activated with the ignition off. Standard equipment found on Bonneville SE and SSE sedans included composite polymer bumpers and fascias; fog lamps; tinted glass; manual air conditioning; power door locks; a "warning lights" cluster that included security system lighting; a rear-seat pass-through; a tilt-wheel adjustable steering column; the Pass-Key II theft deterrent system; power windows with the "express down" feature; four-wheel antilock brakes; a brake/transmission shift interlock safety feature; and the 3800 Series SFI V-6 engine with electronically-controlled four-speed automatic transmission.

TRANS SPORT — SERIES 2U — (V-6) — The Trans Sport SE again comprised Pontiac's minivan lineup. Changes for 1994 were many and included updated exterior styling; fog lamps; a "hidden" lift-gate handle; a molded-in rear step pad; a center high-mounted stop lamp; a monotone paint treatment; new Light Blue Metallic; Medium Blue Metallic; and Bright Aqua Metallic exterior colors; a new Blue interior color; optional solar privacy glass; a standard driver's side airbag; integral child seat(s); a redesigned forward instrument panel; five- and seven-passenger seating; fold-and-stow modular seats; Milli-weave cloth fabric upholstery; thinner/lighter (32 lbs.) modular seats; automatic power door locks; vinyl door and sidewall trim; traction control; a power sliding door; and a coin holder in the under-dash storage

1994 Pontiac Firebird two-door convertible. (PGMC)

compartment. Standard equipment included the 3.1-liter V-6 engine; a three-speed automatic transmission; four-wheel antilock braking system; a stainless steel exhaust system; GM's Computer Command Control system; a four-way manual driver's side seat adjuster; face-level HVAC vents; a front side window defogger; a "wet-arm" controlled-cycle windshield wiper system; an integrated roof antenna; composite polymer bumpers with integral rub strips; tinted glass; P205/70R15 black sidewall all-season tires; 15-in. bolt-on styled wheel covers; and a lower aero molding.

I.D. DATA: Pontiac's 17-symbol Vehicle Identification Number (VIN) for passenger cars was on the upper left surface of the instrument panel, visible through the windshield. The first symbol indicates country of origin: 1 or 4=U.S.; 2=Canada; 3=Mexico; J=Japan. The second symbol indicates manufacturer: G=General Motors; G=Suzuki; 8=Isuzu; Y=NUMMI; C=CAMI. The third symbol G indicates make: 2=Pontiac division; 5=Pontiac incomplete (1G5); 7=GM of Canada; M=Pontiac Multi-Purpose Vehicle. The fourth and fifth symbols for passenger cars indicated body type and series: F/S=Firebird; F/V=Firebird Formula or Trans Am; H/X=Bonneville SE; H/Z=Bonneville SSE; J/B=Sunbird LE and convertible; J/L=Sunbird SE; N/E=Grand Am SE; N/W=Grand Am GT; W/J=Grand Prix SE. On Trans Sports the fourth symbol indicated the GVWR/brake system and the fifth symbol indicating line and chassis type was a "U" for All-Purpose Vehicle 4x2. The sixth symbol on passenger cars denoted body type: 1=two-door coupe/sedan styles 27, 37, 47, 57, 97; 2=two-door hatchback/liftback styles 07, 08, 77 and 87; 3=two-door convertible style 67; 4=two-door Safari style 15; 5=four-door sedan styles 19 and 69; 6=four-door hatchback/liftback styles 29, 68; 8=four-door Safari style 35. The sixth symbol on Trans Sports indicated series: 0=All-Purpose Vehicle. The seventh symbol on passenger cars indicated the type of restraint system: 1=manual belts; 2=active manual belts with dual airbags; 3=active manual belts with driver airbag; 4=passive automatic belts; 5=passive automatic belts with driver airbag; 6=passive automatic belts with dual airbags. The seventh symbol on Trans Sports indicated body type: 6=All-Purpose Vehicle. Symbol eight for passenger cars was an engine code: A=RPO LG0 2.3-liter fuel-injected (MFI) I-4; D=RPO LD2 2.3-liter fuel-injected (MFI) I-4; H=RPO LE4 2.0-liter fuel-injected (MFI) I-4; L=RPO L27 3.8-liter fuel-injected (MFI) V-6; M=RPO L82 3.1-liter fuel-injected (MFI) V-6; P=RPO LT1 5.7-liter fuel-injected (MFI) V-8; S=RPO L32 3.4-liter fuel-injected (MFI) V-6; T=RPO LH0 3.1-liter fuel-injected (MFI) V-6; X=RPO LQ1 3.4-liter fuel-injected (MFI) V-6; 1=RPO L67 3.8-liter fuel-injected (MFI) V-6; 3=RPO L40 2.3-liter fuel-injected (MFI) I-4; 4=RPO LN2 2.2-liter fuel-injected (MFI) I-4. The seventh symbol for Trans Sports was also an engine code: D=RPO LG6 3.1-liter fuel-injected (TBI) V-6; G=RPO LD2 2.3-liter fuel-injected (MFI) I-4; L=RPO L27 3.8-liter fuel-injected (MFI) V-6. The ninth symbol for cars and trucks is a check digit. The tenth symbol for cars and trucks denotes model year (R=1994). The 11th symbol for cars and trucks indicates the GM assembly plant (B=Baltimore, Md. T&B; C=Lansing, Mich.; D=Doraville, Ga.; E=Pontiac East, Mich.; T&B; F=Fairfax II, Kan.; F=Flint T&B; H=Flint, Mich.; J=Janesville, Wis. T&B; K=Kosai, Japan; K=Linden, N.J. T&B; M=Lansing, Mich,; (A); M=Mexico City, Mexico; R=Arlington, Texas; S=Ramos Arizpe, Mexico; T=Tarrytown, N.Y.; U=Hamtramck, Mich.; W=Iwata, Japan; Y=Wilmington, Del.; Z=Fremont, Calif.; Z=Ft. Wayne, Ind.; Z=Spring Hill, Tenn.; 0=Pontiac West, Mich. (T&B); 1=Oshawa, Canada #2; 1=Oshawa, Canada T&B; 1=Wentzville, Mo. T&B; 2=Morraine, Ohio T&B;

2=Ste. Therese Canada; 3=Detroit, Mich. T&B; 3=Kawasaki, Japan; 4=Orion, Mich.; 5=Bowling Green, Ken.; 6=Ingersoll, Ontario Canada; 6=Oklahoma City, Okla.; 7=Lordstown, Ohio; 7=Flusawa, Japan; 8=Shreveport, La. T&B; 8=Tillonburg, Ontario Canada (CANEXPO); 9=Oshawa, Ontario Canada #1. Pontiacs are not produced at all of these GM plants. The last six symbols are the consecutive unit number at the factory.

Model Number	Body Style Number	Body Type & Seating	Factory Price	Shipping Weight	Production Total
SUNBIRD LE SERIES J/B (I-4)					
2J	JB5	4d Sedan-5P	9,382	2,502	Note 1
2J	JB1	2d Coupe-5P	9,382	2,484	Note 1
2J	JB3	2d Convertible-5P	15,524	2,661	Note 1
SUNBIRD SE SERIES J/L (I-4)					
2J	JL1	2d Coupe-5P	12,424	2,682	Note 1
GRAND AM SE SERIES N/E (Quad 4)					
2N	NE1	2d Coupe-5P	12,514	2,736	Note 2
2N	NE5	4d Sedan-5P	12,614	2,793	Note 2
GRAND AM GT SERIES N/W (Quad 4)					
2N	NW1	2d Coupe-5P	15,014	2,822	Note 2
2N	NW5	4d Sedan-5P	15,114	2,882	Note 2
FIREBIRD SERIES F/S OR CONVERTIBLE F/V (V-6)					
2F	FS2	2d Coupe-5P	13,995	3,232	Note 3
2F	FV3	2d Convertible-5P	21,179	3,346	Note 3
FIREBIRD FORMULA SERIES F/V (V-8)					
2F	FV2	2d Coupe-5P	17,995	3,369	Note 3
2F	FV3	2d Convertible-5P	24,279	3,485	Note 3
FIREBIRD TRANS AM SERIES F/V (V-8)					
2F	FV2	2d Coupe-5P	19,895	3,461	Note 3
FIREBIRD TRANS AM GT SERIES F/V (V-8)					
2F	FV2	2d Coupe-5P	21,395	3,478	Note 3
2F	FV3	2d Convertible-5P	26,479	—	Note 3
GRAND PRIX SE SERIES W/J (V-6)					
2W	WJ5	4d Sedan-5P	16,174	3,370	Note 4
2W	WJ1	2d Coupe-5P	16,770	3,275	Note 4
BONNEVILLE SE SERIES H/X (V-6)					
2H	HX5	4d Sport Sedan-5P	20,424	3,446	Note 5
BONNEVILLE SSE SERIES H/Z (V-6)					
2H	HZ5	4d Sport Sedan-5P	25,884	3,587	Note 5
TRANS SPORT SE SERIES U (V-6)					
2U	U06	Minivan	17,369	3,576	43,694

NOTE 1: Sunbird series production totaled 103,738 cars.

NOTE 2: Grand Am series production totaled 254,919 cars.

NOTE 3: Firebird series production totaled 51,523 cars.

NOTE 4: Grand Prix series production totaled 148,405 cars.

NOTE 5: Bonneville series production totaled 87,926 cars.

SUNBIRD ENGINES

ENGINE [Base Four LE]: Inline. OHC. Four-cylinder. Cast-iron block. Aluminum head and intake manifold. Displacement: 121 cid. (2.0L). Bore & stroke: 3.38 x 3.38 in. Compression ratio: 9.2:1. Brake horsepower: 110 at 5200 rpm. Torque: 124 lbs.-ft. at 3600 rpm. Fuel system: MPFI. Code: LE4. Standard in Sunbird LE Series models. [VIN code H].

ENGINE [Base Six SE]: V-block. OHV. Six-cylinder. Cast-iron block and aluminum head. Displacement: 191 cid. (3.1L). Bore & stroke: 3.51 x 3.31 in. Compression ratio: 8.9:1. Brake horsepower: 140 at 4200 rpm. Torque: 185 lbs.-ft. at 3600 rpm. Fuel system: MPFI. Standard in Sunbird SE coupe, optional in LE Series models. [VIN code T or M].

1994 Pontiac Firebird Trans Am 25th Anniversary two-door coupe. (PGMC)

GRAND AM ENGINES

ENGINE [Standard SE]: Inline. Quad-4 OHC. Cast-iron block. Aluminum head and intake manifold. Displacement: 138 cid. (2.3L). Bore & stroke: 3.63 x 3.35 in. Compression ratio: 9.5:1. Brake horsepower: 115 at 5200 rpm. Torque: 140 lbs.-ft. at 3200 rpm. Fuel system: MPFI. RPO Code: L40. Standard in SE coupe/sedan. [VIN code A].

ENGINE [Optional GT]: Inline. Quad-4 DOHC. 16-valve. Cast-iron block. Aluminum head and intake manifold. Displacement: 138 cid. (2.3L). Bore & stroke: 3.63 x 3.35 in. Compression ratio: 9.5:1. Brake horsepower: 155 at 6000 rpm. Torque: 150 lbs.-ft. at 4800 rpm. Fuel system: MPFI. RPO Code: LD2. Optional in GT coupe/sedan. [VIN code D].

ENGINE [Standard GT]: Inline. Quad-4 H.O. DOHC. 16-valve. Cast-iron block. Aluminum head and intake manifold. Displacement: 138 cid. (2.3L). Bore & stroke: 3.63 x 3.35 in. Compression ratio: 10.0:1. Brake horsepower: 175 at 6200 rpm. Torque: 150 lbs.-ft. at 5200 rpm. Fuel system: MPFI. RPO Code: LG0. Standard in Grand Am GT coupe/sedan with MV5 five-speed manual transmission. [VIN code A].

ENGINE [Optional Six SE/GT]: V-block. OHV. Six-cylinder. Cast-iron block and aluminum heads. Displacement: 191 cid. (3.1L). Bore & stroke: 3.51 x 3.31 in. Compression ratio: 9.5:1. Brake horsepower: 155 at 5200 rpm. Torque: 185 lbs.-ft. at 4000 rpm. Fuel system: SPFI. RPO Code L82. Optional in Grand Am SE and GT coupe/sedan. [VIN code M or T].

FIREBIRD ENGINES

ENGINE [Base V-6]: V-block. OHV. Six-cylinder. Cast-iron block and heads. Aluminum intake manifold. Displacement: 207 cid. (3.4L). Bore & stroke: 3.62 x 3.31 in. Compression ratio: 9.0:1. Brake horsepower: 160 at 4600 rpm. Torque: 200 lbs.-ft. at 3600 rpm. Fuel system: SPFI. RPO Code: L32. Standard in Firebird. Not available in Formula and Trans Am. [VIN code S or X].

ENGINE [Base V-8 Formula/Trans Am]: V-block. OHV. Eight-cylinder. Cast-iron block and heads. Aluminum intake manifold. Displacement: 350 cid. (5.7L). Bore & stroke: 4.00 x 3.48 in. Compression ratio: 10.5:1. Brake horsepower: 275 at 5000 rpm. Torque: 325 lbs.-ft. at 2400 rpm. Fuel system: SPFI. RPO Code: LT1. Standard in Formula and Trans Am. Not available in Firebird. [VIN code P].

GRAND PRIX ENGINES

ENGINE [Base Six SE]: V-block. OHV. Six-cylinder. Cast-iron block and cast aluminum heads. Displacement: 191 cid. (3.1L). Bore & stroke: 3.51 x 3.31 in. Compression ratio: 9.5:1. Brake horsepower: 160 at 5200 rpm. Torque: 185 lbs.-ft. at 4000 rpm. Fuel system: SPFI. RPO Code: L82. [VIN code T or M].

ENGINE [Optional Six SE]: V-block. DOHC. Six-cylinder. Cast-iron block and cast aluminum heads. Displacement: 207 cid. (3.4L). Bore & stroke: 3.62 x 3.30 in. Compression ratio: 9.25:1. Brake horsepower: 210 at 5000 rpm. Torque: 215 lbs.-ft. at 4000 rpm. Fuel system: SPFI. RPO Code: LQ1. [VIN code X or S].

BONNEVILLE ENGINES

ENGINE [Base Six SE/SSE]: V-block. OHV. "3800" six-cylinder. Cast-iron block and heads. Aluminum intake manifold. Displacement: 231 cid. (3.8L). Bore & stroke: 3.80 x 3.40 in. Compression ratio: 9.0:1. Brake horsepower: 170 at 4800 rpm. Torque: 225 lbs.-ft. at 3200 rpm. Fuel system: SPFI. RPO Code: L27. Standard in Bonneville SE/SSE. [VIN code C].

ENGINE [Optional Six SSE]: V-block. OHV. "3800" supercharged six-cylinder. Cast-iron block and heads. Aluminum intake manifold. Displacement: 231 cid. (3.8L). Bore & stroke: 3.80 x 3.40 in. Compression ratio: 9.0:1. Brake horsepower: 225 at 5000 rpm. Torque: 275 lbs.-ft. at 3200 rpm. Fuel system: SPFI and supercharged. RPO Code: L67. Optional in Bonneville SSE. [VIN code 1].

TRANS SPORT ENGINES

ENGINE [Optional Four]: Inline. Quad-4 DOHC. 16-valve. Cast-iron block. Aluminum head and intake manifold. Displacement: 138 cid. (2.3L). Bore & stroke: 3.63 x 3.35 in. Compression ratio: 9.5:1. Brake horsepower: 155 at 6000 rpm. Torque: 150 lbs.-ft. at 4800 rpm. Fuel system: MPFI. RPO Code: LD2. [VIN code G].

ENGINE [Base Six SE]: V-block. OHV. Six-cylinder. Cast-iron block and heads. Aluminum intake manifold. Displacement: 191 cid. (3.1L). Bore & stroke: 3.50 x 3.31 in. Compression ratio: 8.5:1.

Brake horsepower: 120 at 4400 rpm. Torque: 175 lbs.-ft. at 2200 rpm. Fuel system: EFI/TBFI. RPO Code: LG6. Standard in SE. [VIN code T or M].

ENGINE [Optional Six SE]: V-block. OHV. "3800" six-cylinder. Cast-iron block and heads. Aluminum intake manifold. Displacement: 231 cid. (3.8L). Bore & stroke: 3.80 x 3.40 in. Compression ratio: 9.0:1. Brake horsepower: 170 at 4800 rpm. Torque: 225 lbs.-ft. at 3200 rpm. Fuel system: SPFI. RPO Code: L27. [VIN code 3 or C].

CHASSIS

SUNBIRD CHASSIS: Wheelbase: 101.3 in. (all). Overall length: 180.7 in. (all). Overall width: 66.2 in. (all). Height: 52.2.in. (LE/SE coupe); 52.4 in. (LE convertible), 53.9 in. (LE sedan). Front tread: 55.6 in. (all). Rear tread: 55.4 in. (all). Standard tires: See model descriptions.

GRAND AM CHASSIS: Wheelbase: 103.4 in. (all). Overall length: 186.9 in. (all). Width: 67.5 in. (all). Height: 53.2 in. (all). Front tread: 55.9 in. (all). Rear tread: 55.4 in. (all). Standard tires: See model descriptions.

FIREBIRD CHASSIS: Wheelbase: 101.1 in. (all). Overall length: 195.6 in. (Firebird/Formula); 197.0 in. (Trans Am). Width: 74.5 in. (all). Height: 52.0 in. (Firebird/Formula); 51.7 in. (Trans Am). Front tread: 60.7 in. (all). Rear tread: 60.6 in. (all). Standard tires: P215/60R16 (Firebird); P235/55R16 (Formula/Trans Am); P245/50ZR16 (Trans Am GT).

GRAND PRIX CHASSIS: Wheelbase: 107.5 in. (all). Overall length: 194.8 in. (coupe); 194.9 in. (sedan). Width: 71.9 in. (all). Height: 52.8 in. (coupe); 54.8 in. (sedan). Front tread: 59.5 in. (all). Rear tread: 58.0 in. (all). Standard tires: P215/60/R16 (coupe). P205/70R15 (sedan).

BONNEVILLE CHASSIS: Wheelbase: 110.8 in. (all). Overall length: 199.5 in. (SE); 201.2 in. (SSE). Width: 74.5 in. (all). Height: 55.7 in. (all). Front tread: 60.4 in. (SE); 60.8 in. (SSE). Rear tread: 60.3 in. (SE); 60.6 in. (SSE). Standard tires: P215/65R15 (SE); P225/60R16 (SSE).

TRANS SPORT CHASSIS: Wheelbase: 109.8 in. Overall length: 192.2 in. Width: 74.6 in. Height: 65.7 in. Front tread: 59.2 in. Rear tread: 61.4 in. Standard tires: See model descriptions.

TECHNICAL

SUNBIRD TECHNICAL: Chassis: Front engine/front drive. Base transmission: (MK7) five-speed manual (2.0-liter L4)/(MG2) five-speed manual (3.1-liter V-6). Optional transmission: (MD9) three-speed automatic. Axle ratio: 3.45:1 with 2.0-liter L4 and five-speed manual/3.61:1 with 3.1-liter V-6 and five-speed manual. Axle ratio: 3.18:1 with 2.0-liter L4 and three-speed automatic/2.53:1 with 3.1-liter V-6 and three-speed automatic (2.84:1 on LE convertible). Front suspension [Level I]: Deflected disc, MacPherson struts and (22mm with 14-in. tires & wheels/28mm with optional tires/wheels) stabilizer bars. Rear suspension [Level I]: Coil springs, semi-independent torsion beam, trailing arms, 19mm anti-roll bar with optional tires/wheels. Front suspension [Level II]: Deflected disc, MacPherson struts and 28mm stabilizer bars. Rear suspension: Coil springs, semi-independent torsion beam, trailing arms and 19mm anti-roll bar. Steering: Rack-and-pinion 16.0:1 ratio (14.0:1 on cars with optional tires/wheels). Turns lock-to-lock: 3.0 (2.5 on optional tires/wheels). Turning circle: 35.3 ft. (all). Front brakes: 10.2-in. vented discs. Rear brakes: 7.87 x 1.77-in. drums, power-assisted.

GRAND AM TECHNICAL: Chassis: Front engine/front drive. Base transmission: Five-speed manual with overdrive (M32 or MV5). Optional transmissions: four-speed automatic (M13)/three-speed automatic (MD9). Axle ratio: 3.58:1 (with M32 five-speed manual); 3.94:1 (with MV5 five-speed manual); 3.43:1 (with M13 four-speed automatic and L40 Quad OHC four-cylinder engine); 3.73:1 (with M13 four-speed automatic and LD2 Quad 4 engine); 2:53:1 (with MD9 three-speed automatic). Front suspension (Standard SE): Deflected disc; MacPherson struts, 27 N-mm spring and 22mm stabilizer bar. Rear Suspension (Standard SE): 23/39 N-mm dual rate springs, semi-independent trailing arms linked with torsion beam, 19.5mm stabilizer bar. Front suspension (Standard GT): Deflected disc; MacPherson struts, 27 N-mm spring and 24mm stabilizer bar (automatic)/30mm (manual). Rear suspension (Standard GT): 28/47 N-mm dual rate springs, semi-independent trailing arms linked with torsion beam, 19.5mm stabilizer bar. Steering: Power-assisted rack-and-pinion, 14.0:1 ratio. Turns lock-to-lock: 2.5. Turning circle: 36.4 ft. Front brakes: 259.5mm diameter vented discs. Rear brakes: 200.0mm diameter drums. Fuel tank: 15.2 gal.

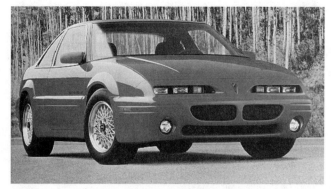

1994 Pontiac Grand Prix SE two-door coupe. (PGMC)

FIREBIRD TECHNICAL: Chassis: Front engine/rear drive. Base transmission: (M49) Five-speed manual (Firebird); (MM6) six-speed manual (Formula/Trans Am). Optional transmission: (MD8) four-speed automatic (all). Front suspension: (F41 Firebird) short/long arm (SLA)/coil over monotube gas-charged shocks, tubular stabilizer bar with links, 30mm stabilizer bar. (FE2 Formula/Trans Am) SLA/coil over monotube gas-charged shocks, tubular stabilizer bar with links, 30mm stabilizer bar. Rear suspension: (F41 Firebird) Salisbury axle with torque arm, trailing arm, track bar, coil springs, 17mm stabilizer bar. (FE2 Formula/Trans Am) Salisbury axle with torque arm, trailing arm, track bar, coil springs, 19mm stabilizer bar. Steering: Power, rack-and-pinion with 16.9:1 ratio (Firebird)/14.4:1 (Formula/Trans Am). Turns lock-to-lock: 2.67 (Firebird)/2.28 (Formula/Trans Am). Turning circle: (Firebird) 37.9 ft. (left) 40.6 ft. (right)/(Formula/Trans Am) 37.7 ft. (left) 40.1 ft. (right). Front brakes: (Firebird/Formula/Trans Am) 10.7 in. vented disc. Rear brakes: (Firebird) 9.5 in. power assisted Duo-Servo drum. (Formula/Trans Am) 11.4 in. power assisted vented disc. Fuel tank: 15.5 gal.

GRAND PRIX TECHNICAL: Chassis: Front engine/front drive. Standard drive train: (L82) 3.1L SPFI V-6 engine with (M13) four-speed electronic automatic transmission. Final drive ratios: 3.43:1 with (M13) four-speed electronic automatic, optional on all. 3.33:1 (M13) four-speed electronic automatic, standard on SE coupe/sedan. Front suspension: MacPherson struts with tapered coil springs, lower "A" arm and 28mm anti-roll bar (34mm anti-roll bar with Y99 rally suspension). Rear suspension: Tri-link independent suspension, transverse fiberglass leaf spring and 12mm anti-roll bar (12mm anti-roll bar with Y99 and 3.1-liter V-6/14mm with Y99 and 3.4-liter V-6). Steering: Power-assisted rack- and-pinion with 15.7:1 ratio (14.0:1 with 3.4-liter V-6). Turns lock-to-lock: 2.6 (2.26 with Y99 and 3.4-liter V-6). Turning circle: 36.7-ft. (39-ft. with Y99 and 3.4-liter V-6). Front brakes: 10.51-in. vented discs, power-assisted. Rear brakes: 10.1-in. solid discs, power-assisted. Fuel tank: 16.5 gal.

BONNEVILLE TECHNICAL: Chassis: Front engine/front drive. Base transmission: (M13) four-speed electronic automatic. Axle ratio: 2.84:1 (3800 V-6); 2.97:1 (supercharged 3800 V-6). Front suspension: (SE) Standard FE1: deflected-disc, MacPherson struts, coil spring over strut (22 N-mm), 30mm stabilizer bar. (SSE) Standard FE2: deflected-disc, MacPherson struts, coil spring over strut (26 N-mm), 32mm stabilizer bar. Rear suspension: (SE) Standard FE1: coil springs (variable rate 48-65 N-mm), independent lower A-arm, 17mm stabilizer bar. (SSE) Standard FE2: automatic level control coil springs (47 N-mm), Chapman struts, independent lower A-arm, 22mm stabilizer bar. Optional front suspension: (SE) F41: Performance and Handling, deflected-disc, MacPherson struts, coil spring over strut (26 N-mm), 32mm stabilizer bar; (SSE) FW1: Computer Command Ride, deflected-disc, MacPherson struts, coil spring over strut (26 N-mm), 32mm stabilizer bar. Optional rear suspension: (SE) F41: coil springs (variable rate 55-75 N-mm), Chapman struts, independent lower A-arm, 17mm stabilizer bar. (SSE) FW1: automatic level control coil springs (47 N-mm), Chapman struts, independent lower A-arm, 22mm stabilizer bar. Steering (Standard SE): Power-assisted rack-and-pinion with 16.54:1 ratio, 2.79 turns lock-to-lock and 39.4-ft. turning circle. (SSE/optional SE): Variable-effort rack-and-pinion with 14.93:1 to 18.91:1 ratio, 2.86 turns lock-to-lock and 40.5-ft. turning circle. Front brakes: 10.9-in. vented discs (all). Rear brakes: Power-assisted 8.85-in. drums (all). Fuel tank: 18.0 gal.

TRANS SPORT TECHNICAL: Chassis: Front engine/front drive. Transmission: (MD9) three-speed automatic; optional (M13) four-speed automatic. Axle ratio: 3.06:1 (3.1L V-6); 3.06:1 (3.8L V-6). Front suspension: MacPherson struts with coil springs (27 N-mm), stamped lower control arms and modular iron steering knuckles, 27mm stabilizer bar. Rear suspension: Open-section transverse beam on stamped steel trailing arms, tube shocks, 48-56 N-mm variable rate coil springs (base suspension)/48.3 N-mm coil springs (up-level suspension, electronic leveling) 25.4mm stabilizer bar. Steering: Rack-and-pinion with integral power unit with 15.7:1 ratio. Turns lock-to-lock: 3.05. Turning circle: 43.1 ft. Front brakes: 10.9 x 1.3-in. single caliper disc. Rear brakes: 8.86 x 1.77-in. leading trailing drum. Fuel tank: 20.0 gal.

OPTIONS

SUNBIRD OPTIONS: 1SB Sunbird LE coupe/sedan option group ($1,234). 1SC Sunbird LE coupe/sedan option group ($1,974). 1SD Sunbird LE coupe/sedan option group ($1,969). 1SB Sunbird LE convertible option group ($1,366). 1SB Sunbird SE coupe option group ($1,234). 1SC Sunbird SE coupe option group ($1,904). L H.O. 3.1-liter MPFI V-6, standard in SE coupe ($712). W25 Special Appearance package ($316-$330 depending on value option packages). C60 air conditioning ($785). YF5 California emissions ($100). N33 tilt steering wheel ($145). K34 cruise control ($225). C49 electric rear window defogger ($170). A31 power windows ($265 LE/SE coupe/$330 LE sedan/no charge convertible). UN6 Delco radio equipment ($170). U1C Delco radio equipment ($396).

GRAND AM OPTIONS: 1SB package on GT coupe/sedan ($535). 1SC package on GT coupe ($1,046). 1SC package on GT sedan ($1,111). 1SB package on SE coupe/sedan ($1,575). 1SC package on SE coupe ($2,086). 1SD package on SE sedan ($2,151). LD2 Quad-4 2.3-liter MPI engine in SE models ($410). LD2 Quad-4 2.3-liter MPI engine in GT models ($140 credit). LGO Quad-4 High-Output engine, standard on GT (no charge). L82 3.1-liter V-6 in SE ($410/$140 credit in GT). MX1 three-speed automatic transmission ($555). MX0 four-speed automatic transmission ($755). C60 air conditioning ($830). C49 electric rear window defogger ($170). K34 cruise control ($225). UB3 rally gauges ($111). YF5 California emission requirements ($100). DG7 dual sport mirrors ($86). AC3 power seat with Sport interior group ($340). CF5 power sunroof ($595). A31 express down power windows ($275-$340 depending on value option packages). AM9 split folding rear seat ($150). WDV warranty enhancements ($25). UM6 Delco sound system ($140). UX1 Delco sound system ($375).

FIREBIRD OPTIONS: 1SB Firebird coupe option package ($1,005). 1SC Firebird coupe option package ($2,421). 1SB Formula coupe option package ($906). 1SC Formula coupe option package ($1,491). 1SB Firebird convertible option package ($485). 1SB Formula convertible option package ($485). C60 air conditioning ($895 on Firebird, standard on Formula/Trans Am). AU0 remote keyless entry ($135). MX0 four-speed automatic transmission ($775). B84 body color side moldings ($60). CC1 hatch roof ($895). U1C Delco sound system with CD player ($226). UP3 Delco sound system with CD player and graphic equalizer ($676). K34 cruise control, standard on Trans Am/Trans Am GT ($225). YF5 California emission requirements ($100). AR9 articulating bucket seats with leather ($780). C49 rear window defogger ($170).

GRAND PRIX OPTIONS: 1SB Grand Prix SE sedan ($717). 1SC Grand Prix SE sedan ($1,912). LQ1 3.4L DOHC V-6 ($1,125). A90

remote deck lid release ($60). C49 electric rear window defogger ($170). AU0 remote keyless entry system ($135). CF5 power sunroof ($695). UV8 cellular phone provisions ($35). UV6 head-up display ($250). B20 Custom interior trim ($391-$1,103 depending on value option packages). B4S GTP Performance package for Grand Prix SE coupe ($1,605). B4Q GT Performance package for Grand Prix SE sedan ($2,103-$2,198 depending on value option packages). JL9 antilock brakes ($450). UN6 Delco radio equipment ($170). UT6 Delco radio equipment ($225-$400 depending on value option packages). U1C Delco radio equipment ($226-$396 depending on value option package). AC3 six-way power driver's seat ($305). QPE touring tires for Grand Prix SE sedan ($112). QXJ P225/60R16 tires ($150). PH3 15-in. aluminum Sport wheels for Grand Prix SE sedan ($275). NWO 16-in. aluminum Sport wheels for Grand Prix SE sedan ($275).

BONNEVILLE OPTIONS: 1SB Bonneville SE option package ($628). 1SC Bonneville SE option package ($1,281). 1SD Bonneville SE option package ($1,942). 1SB Bonneville SSE option package ($1,440). WA6 SSEi supercharger package, requires P225/60ZR16 tires ($1,167). AU0 remote keyless entry system ($135). CF5 power glass sunroof ($981-$995). C49 electric rear window defogger ($170). KO5 engine block heater ($18). NW9 traction control system ($175). PF5 16-in. five-blade cast-aluminum wheels ($340). QNX touring tires ($84). T43 rear deck lid spoiler ($110). UN6 Delco radio equipment ($170). U1C Delco sound system ($396). UP3 Delco sound system with compact disc player ($686). US7 power antenna ($85). Y52 Performance & Handling package ($649).

TRANS SPORT OPTIONS: 1SB Trans Sport SE option package ($1,388). 1SC Trans Sport SE option package ($2,383). 1SD Trans Sport SE option package ($2,933). B2Q black roof delete (no charge). C49 electric rear window defogger ($170). AJ1 glass package ($245). AB5 power door locks ($300). V54 roof luggage carrier ($175). KO5 engine block heater ($18). UM6 Delco radio equipment ($140). U1A Delco sound system with compact disc player ($206-$541). ZP7 seven-passenger seating package ($870). PH3 aluminum wheels with locks ($275). L27 3.8L V-6 with four-speed auto transmission ($819). E58 power sliding door ($295). C54 pop-up sunroof ($300). NW9 traction control ($350).

NOTE: Full option package contents, descriptions, and applications information can often be determined by consulting factory literature. The data above is edited for size and clarity. This information provided only as a guide to help collectors appraise the relative value of cars with numerous options. Prices for items included as part of a value option package are usually much less than individual prices. Option prices charged by individual dealers may also vary.

HISTORICAL: Despite bitterly cold weather across the country and earthquakes in California, PMD rode a hot, steady track to sales success in 1994. General manager John Middlebrook spoke of the ways in which value, performance and safety translated into solid sales at Pontiac dealerships. Sales of new Pontiacs for the calendar year rose nearly eight percent to 586,343 units. The Trans Sport added 34,841 additional purchases to the PMD total. PMD's overall domestic model-year production climbed almost five percent o 594,988 units. Model year production for the U.S. and Canada included 515,523 Firebirds; 148,405 Grand Prixs; 254,921 Grand Ams; 5,592 Fireflys (export); 87,926 Bonnevilles; 131,233 Sunbirds and 43,694 Trans Sports for a grand total of 723,294 units. Calendar-year sales were over 600,000 units (586,343 cars and 34,841 Trans Sport "trucks"). In the GM stable, 19.2 percent of new-vehicle sales were earned by PMD and Pontiac held a 6.5 percent share of the total U.S. market.

1994 Pontiac Trans Sport minivan APV. (PGMC)

1995 PONTIAC

SUNFIRE — SERIES 2J — (FOUR) — Previously known as the Sunbird, Pontiac's 1995 sub-compact model had a new Sunfire name and new styling, engineering and technology. It was essentially an all-new car. Standard features of the Sunfire included a 2.2-liter OHV four-cylinder engine for the SE (the GT was powered by a 2.3-liter DOHC 16-valve Quad 4); an aluminized stainless steel

1995 Pontiac Sunfire four-door sedan. (PGMC)

exhaust system; dual airbags; tinted glass; anti-lock braking system; a coil-over-shock rear suspension; rear HVAC vents; a tilt-wheel adjustable steering column; a tachometer; a 4.9-liter glove box; and lamps in the trunk and glove box. Other amenities included a folding rear seat for extra cargo room (also found in SE convertibles) and optional traction control on GT coupes.

GRAND AM — SERIES 2N — The 2.3-liter DOHC Quad 4 engine became standard equipment in Pontiac's best-selling car—the Grand Am. Other new features included an improved rear suspension with spring-on-center design; a balance shaft system added to the Quad 4 engine; variable effort steering (available on the GT); direct drive power steering; a "stepper motor" cruise control system; black body side inserts (available on the GT); a new Medium Dark Purple Metallic exterior color; and a choice of 15-in. Star-cast aluminum wheels; 15-in. five-blade wheel covers or 14-in. Custom wheel covers. The Grand Am SE came with P195/70R14 tires and the Grand Am GT came with P205/55R16 Goodyear Eagle RSA tires. Other standard equipment on both the SE and GT lines included a fixed-mast antenna; tinted glass; fog lamps; Sport mirrors; "wet-arm" windshield wipers; bumpers and soft fascias with integral rub strips; a driver's side airbag; power automatic door locks with unlock and re-lock; a Delco ETR AM/FM stereo with seek up/down and a clock; a Grid Cloth fabric interior; 45/45 reclining front bucket seats; a three-passenger rear seat with integrated headrests; a four-spoke Sport steering wheel; a four-wheel anti-lock braking system; GM's Computer Command Control; and a stainless steel exhaust system.

FIREBIRD — SERIES 2F — (V-6/V-8) — Pontiac's lone rear-wheel drive vehicle was offered in 1995 in coupe and convertible versions in three series: Firebird, Formula, and Trans Am. The Canadian-produced muscle machines had several changes. First, a traction-control system was available for V-8-powered cars with either manual or automatic transmission. Blue Green Chameleon, Medium Dark Purple Metallic, and Bright Silver Metallic were new exterior colors. New Bright Red (all) and Bright White (convertible only) leather interiors were seen. Also new were 16-in. five-spoke aluminum wheels on V-8-powered Firebirds; all-weather speed-rated P245/50Z16 tires; a power antenna; a four-spoke Sport steering wheel; and a remote compact disc changer (as a dealer-installed option). Across-the-line standard features included soft fascia-type bumpers; a fixed-mast black rear radio antenna; tinted glass; Sport mirrors; controlled-cycle windshield wipers; dual front airbags; a Metrix cloth fabric interior; a locking glove box; analog instrumentation; a Delco ETR AM/FM stereo radio with auto-reverse cassette; a clock and a Delco theft lock; reclining front bucket seats; folding rear seats; a tilt-wheel adjustable steering column; the Pass-Key II theft deterrent system; a four-wheel anti-lock braking system; a brake/transmission shift interlock (with automatic transmission); a low-oil-level monitor and warning; GM's Computer Command Control system; and a stainless steel exhaust system. Features that were standard equipment exclusively to the Firebird, Formula, and Trans Am convertibles included cruise control; an electric rear window defogger; power automatic door locks; a remote keyless entry system; a four-way manual front driver seat; a two-way manual front passenger seat; and power windows with an "express-down" feature.

GRAND PRIX — SERIES 2W — (V-6) — The Grand Prix was offered in 1995 as either an SE coupe or sedan. There was a new GTP Performance Package for the coupe and a GT Performance

Package for the sedan, as well as a White Appearance Package for the Grand Prix SE coupe. Such options added depth to the Grand Prix lineup. Changes were minimal this year. They included a new Red Orange Metallic exterior color, new up-level 16-in. H-rated Goodyear P225/60R16 RSA tires, an engine oil-level monitor for cars with the 3.4-liter DOHC V-6, and a brake/transmission shift interlock system. Five-spoke aluminum wheels were available on the Grand Prix SE coupe. EVO variable-effort power steering was offered as part of the Grand Prix GT and GTP packages. Other new features included a floor console with improved and repositioned dual cup holders and an ashtray, a new storage armrest with flip-out cup holder, and a removable coin holder in models with split bench seats. The glove box latch and right-hand HVAC vent were now color-keyed to match the interior. Standard equipment on both the SE coupe and sedan included a black fixed-mast radio antenna; tinted and safety laminated glass; soft fascia-type bumpers with integral rub strips; fog lamps; "wet-arm" controlled-cycle windshield wipers; dual front airbags; electronic push-button air conditioning; power automatic door locks with unlock and re-lock features; mechanical analog instrumentation including a tachometer; a Cordae Cloth fabric interior; a three-passenger rear seat with integrated headrests; a tilt-wheel adjustable steering column; power windows with the "express down" feature; four-wheel disc brakes; a Pass-Key II theft-deterrent system; GM's Computer Command Control; and a stainless steel exhaust system.

BONNEVILLE — SERIES 2H — (V-6) — For 1995, the SE and SSE sedan versions again comprised the Bonneville lineup. The Sports Luxury Edition (SLE) package was available to upgrade the SE sedan. An additional option to enhance the SLE package was the supercharged 3800 V-6 engine. For the SSE sedan, buyers could opt for the SSEi Supercharger Package as an upgrade option. New features for the Bonneville in 1995 included a 205-hp 3800 Series II V-6 as standard power plant on SE and SSE models; the availability of Computer Command Ride on SEs; standard cruise control and rally gauges with the tachometer and lamp group; a new Graphite color interior trim in cloth or leather; new tachometer red line for 3800 Series II engine (6000 rpm); a Cobra-head shifter (with bucket seats); a Graphite colored "soft-touch" instrument panel trim plate; color-coordinated interior components; a Graphite steering wheel and column (available with all interior trim colors); a rear seat child shoulder harness comfort guide; an improved automatic HVAC system (automatic air conditioning was now available in the SE); and 16-in. machine-faced crosslace cast wheels. Standard features found on both the SE and SSE sedans included: soft fascia-type bumpers with integral rub strips; fog lamps; tinted glass; dual front airbags; front three-point active height-adjustable safety belts; manual air conditioning; power door locks; back-lit analog instrumentation including a tachometer; power windows with the "express down" feature; a tilt-wheel adjustable steering column; a Pass-Key II theft deterrent system; a four-wheel anti-lock braking system; and a brake/transmission shift interlock.

TRANS SPORT — SERIES 2U — (V-6) — Changes on Pontiac's 1995 minivan offering, the Trans Sport SE, were minimal. New features included Traction Control (carried over from a mid-1994 introduction), a brake/transmission shift interlock, a new Dark Teal Metallic exterior color, three-spoke 15-in. aluminum wheels, a four-spoke steering wheel (available with duplicate radio controls), a Doral Cloth fabric interior, and an available overhead console.

I.D. DATA: Pontiac's 17-symbol Vehicle Identification Number (VIN) for passenger cars was on the upper left surface of the instrument panel; visible through the windshield. The first symbol indicates country of origin: 1 or 4=U.S.; 2=Canada; 3=Mexico. The second symbol indicates manufacturer: G=General Motors; Y=NUMMI; C=CAMI. The third symbol G indicates make: 2=Pontiac division; 5=Pontiac incomplete (1G5); 7=GM of Canada; M=Pontiac Multi-Purpose Vehicle. The fourth and fifth symbols for passenger cars indicated body type and series: F/S=Firebird and convertible; F/V=Firebird Formula or Trans Am and convertible; H/X=Bonneville SE; H/Z=Bonneville SSE; J/B=Sunfire LE and convertible; J/D=Sunfire GT; N/E=Grand Am SE; N/W=Grand Am GT; W/J=Grand Prix SE. On Trans Sports the fourth symbol indicated the GVWR/brake system and the fifth symbol indicating line and chassis type was a "U" for All-Purpose Vehicle 4x2. The sixth symbol on passenger cars denoted body type: 1=two-door coupe/sedan styles 27, 37, 47, 57, 97; 2=two-door hatchback/liftback styles 07, 08, 77 and 87; 3=two-door convertible style 67; 4=two-door Safari style 15; 5=four-door sedan styles 19 and 69; 6=four-door hatchback/liftback styles 29, 68; 8=four-door Safari style 35. The sixth symbol on Trans Sports indicated series: 0=All-Purpose Vehicle. The seventh symbol on passenger cars indicated the type of restraint system: 1=manual belts; 2=active manual belts with dual airbags; 3=active manual belts with driver airbag; 4=passive automatic belts; 5=passive automatic belts with driver airbag; 6=passive automatic belts with dual airbags. The seventh symbol on Trans Sports indicated body type: 6=All-Purpose Vehicle. Symbol eight for passenger cars was an engine code: D=RPO LD2 2.3-liter fuel-injected (MFI) I-4; K=RPO L36 3.8-liter fuel-injected (MFI) V-6; M=RPO L82 3.1-liter fuel-injected (MFI) V-6; P=RPO LT1 5.7-liter fuel-injected (MFI) V-8; S=RPO L32 3.4-liter fuel-injected (MFI) V-6; X=RPO LQ1 3.4-liter fuel-injected (MFI) V-6; 1=RPO L67 3.8-liter fuel-injected (MFI) V-6; 4=RPO LN2 2.2-liter fuel-injected (MFI) I-4. The seventh symbol for Trans Sports was also an engine code: D=RPO LG6 3.1-liter fuel-injected (TBI) V-6; L=RPO L27 3.8-liter fuel-injected (MFI) V-6. The ninth symbol for cars and trucks is a check digit. The tenth symbol for cars and trucks denotes model year (S=1995). The 11th symbol for cars and trucks indicates the GM assembly plant (B=Baltimore, Md. T&B; B=Lansing (GENASYS); C=Lansing, Mich.; D=Doraville, Ga.; E=Pontiac East, Mich. T&B; F=Fairfax II, Kan.; F=Flint, Mich. T&B; H=Flint, Mich., J=Janesville, Wis. T&B, K=Linden, N.J. T&B, M=Lansing, Mich. (A), M=Mexico City, Mexico, R=Arlington, Texas, S=Ramos Arizpe, Mexico, T=Tarrytown, N.Y., U=Hamtramck, Mich., W=Iwata Japan; Y=Wilmington, Del.; Z=Fremont, Calif.; Z=Ft. Wayne, Ind.; Z=Spring Hill, Tenn.; 1=Oshawa Canada #2; 1=Oshawa Canada T&B; 2=Morraine, Ohio T&B; 2=Ste. Therese Canada; 3=Detroit, Mich. T&B; 3=Kawasaki Japan; 4=Orion, Mich.; 5=Bowling Green, Ken.; 6=Ingersoll, Ontario Canada; 6=Oklahoma City, Okla.; 7=Lordstown, Ohio; 7=Flusawa Japan; 8=Shreveport, La. T&B; 8=Tillonburg Ontario Canada (CAN-EXPO); 9=Oshawa Ontario Canada #1. Pontiacs are not produced at all of these GM plants. The last six symbols are the consecutive unit number at the factory.

Model Number	Body Style Number	Body Type & Seating	Factory Price	Shipping Weight	Production Total
SUNFIRE SE SERIES J/B (I-4)					
2J	B69S	4d Sedan-5P	11,709	2,723	Note 1
2J	B37S	2d Coupe-5P	11,559	2,679	Note 1
2J	B69S	2d Convertible-5P	—	2,835	Note 1
SUNFIRE GT SERIES J/D (I-4)					
2J	D37S	2d Coupe-5P	—	2,829	Note 1
GRAND AM SE SERIES N/E (Quad 4)					
2N	E37S	2d Coupe-5P	13,399	2,749	Note 2
2N	E69S	4d Sedan-5P	13,499	2,806	Note 2
GRAND AM GT SERIES N/W (Quad 4)					
2N	W37S	2d Coupe-5P	15,349	2,888	Note 2
2N	W69S	4d Sedan-5P	15,449	2,941	Note 2
FIREBIRD SERIES F/S (V-6)					
2F	S87S	2d Coupe-5P	15,359	3,230	Note 3
2F	S67S	2d Convertible-5P	22,439	3,346	Note 3
FIREBIRD FORMULA SERIES F/V (V-8)					
2F	V87S	2d Coupe-5P	19,599	3,373	Note 3
2F	V67S	2d Convertible-5P	25,629	3,489	Note 3
FIREBIRD TRANS AM SERIES F/V (V-8)					
2F	V87S	2d Coupe-5P	21,569	3,445	Note 3
2F	V67S	2d Convertible-5P	27,639	3,610	Note 3
GRAND PRIX SE SERIES W/J (V-6)					
2W	J37S	4d Sedan-5P	17,169	3,370	Note 4
2W	J19S	2d Coupe-5P	17,919	3,275	Note 4
BONNEVILLE SE SERIES H/X (V-6)					
2H	X69S	4d Sport Sedan-5P	21,389	3,446	Note 5
BONNEVILLE SSE SERIES H/Z (V-6)					
2H	Z69S	4d Sport Sedan-5P	26,389	3,587	Note 5
TRANS SPORT SERIES U (V-6)					
2U	M06S	Minivan	18,429	3,540	55,813

NOTE 1: According to official Pontiac Motor Div. production totals for U.S. and Canada 81,097 "Sunbirds" were built. According to *Ward's 2000 Automotive Yearbook*, 81,355 Sunfires were made for the U.S. market.

NOTE 2: According to official Pontiac Motor Div. production totals for U.S. and Canada 291,144 Grand Ams were built.

NOTE 3: According to official Pontiac Motor Div. production totals for U.S. and Canada 56,723 Firebirds were built.

NOTE 4: According to official Pontiac Motor Div. production totals for U.S. and Canada 143,729 Grand Prixs were built.

NOTE 5: According to official Pontiac Motor Div. production totals for U.S. and Canada 96,761 Bonnevilles were built.

SUNFIRE ENGINES

ENGINE [Base Four SE]: Inline. OHV. Four-cylinder. Cast-iron block. Cast aluminum head. Displacement: 133 cid. (2.2L). Bore & stroke: 3.50 x 3.46 in. Compression ratio: 9.0:1. Brake horsepower: 120 at 5200 rpm. Torque: 130 lbs.-ft. at 4000 rpm. Fuel system: MPFI. RPO Code: LN2. Standard in Sunfire SE coupe, convertible, and sedan.

ENGINE [Base Four GT]: Inline. DOHC Quad 4. Four-cylinder. Cast-iron block. Cast aluminum head. Displacement: 138 cid. (2.3L). Bore & stroke: 3.63 x 3.35 in. Compression ratio: 9.5:1. Brake horsepower: 150 at 6000 rpm. Torque: 145 lbs.-ft. at 4800 rpm. Fuel system: MPFI. RPO Code: LD2. Standard in Sunfire GT coupe.

GRAND AM ENGINES

ENGINE [Standard SE/GT]: Inline. Quad-4 DOHC. Cast-iron block. Cast aluminum head. Displacement: 138 cid. (2.3L). Bore & stroke: 3.63 x 3.35 in. Compression ratio: 9.5:1. Brake horsepower: 150 at 6000 rpm. Torque: 145 lbs.-ft. at 4800 rpm. Fuel system: MPFI. RPO Code: LD2. Standard in SE/GT coupes and sedans.

ENGINE [Optional SE/GT]: V-block. OHV. Cast-iron block. Cast aluminum head. Displacement: 191 cid. (3.1L). Bore & stroke: 3.51 x 3.31 in. Compression ratio: 9.5:1. Brake horsepower: 155 at 5200 rpm. Torque: 185 lbs.-ft. at 4000 rpm. Fuel system: SPFI. RPO Code: L82. Optional in SE/GT coupes and sedans.

FIREBIRD ENGINES

ENGINE [Base V-6]: V-block. OHV. Six-cylinder. Cast-iron block and heads. Aluminum intake manifold. Displacement: 207 cid. (3.4L). Bore & stroke: 3.62 x 3.31 in. Compression ratio: 9.0:1. Brake horsepower: 160 at 4600 rpm. Torque: 200 lbs.-ft. at 3600 rpm. Fuel system: SPFI. RPO Code: L32. Standard in Firebird. Not available in Formula and Trans Am.

ENGINE [Base V-8 Formula/Trans Am]: V-block. OHV. Eight-cylinder. Cast-iron block and aluminum heads. Aluminum intake manifold. Displacement: 350 cid. (5.7L). Bore & stroke: 4.00 x 3.48 in. Compression ratio: 10.5:1. Brake horsepower: 275 at 5000 rpm. Torque: 325 lbs.-ft. at 2400 rpm. Fuel system: SPFI. RPO Code: LT1. Standard in Formula and Trans Am. Not available in Firebird.

GRAND PRIX ENGINES

ENGINE [Standard SE]: V-block. OHV. Six-cylinder. Cast-iron block and cast aluminum heads. Displacement: 191 cid. (3.1L). Bore & stroke: 3.51 x 3.31 in. Compression ratio: 9.5:1. Brake horsepower: 160 at 5200 rpm. Torque: 185 lbs.-ft. at 4000 rpm. Fuel system: SPFI. RPO Code: L82.

ENGINE [Optional SE]: V-block. DOHC. Six-cylinder. Cast-iron block and cast aluminum heads. Displacement: 207 cid. (3.4L). Bore & stroke: 3.62 x 3.30 in. Compression ratio: 9.25:1. Brake horsepower: 210 at 5000 rpm. Torque: 215 lbs.-ft. at 4000 rpm. Fuel system: SPFI. RPO Code: LQ1.

BONNEVILLE ENGINES

ENGINE [Base Six SE/SSE]: V-block. OHV. "3800" six-cylinder. Cast-iron block and heads. Aluminum intake manifold. Displacement: 231 cid. (3.8L). Bore & stroke: 3.80 x 3.40 in. Compression ratio: 9.4:1. Brake horsepower: 205 at 5200 rpm. Torque: 230 lbs.-ft.

1995 Pontiac Grand Am GT two-door coupe. (PGMC)

1995 Pontiac Firebird two-door coupe. (PGMC)

at 4000 rpm. Fuel system: SPFI. RPO Code: L36. Standard in Bonneville SE/SSE.

ENGINE [Optional Six SE/SSE]: V-block. OHV. "3800" supercharged six-cylinder. Cast-iron block and heads. Aluminum intake manifold. Displacement: 231 cid. (3.8L). Bore & stroke: 3.80 x 3.40 in. Compression ratio: 9.0:1. Brake horsepower: 225 at 5000 rpm. Torque: 275 lbs.-ft. at 3200 rpm. Fuel system: SPFI and supercharged. RPO Code: L67. Optional in Bonneville SSE, available in SE only through SLE option package.

TRANS SPORT ENGINES

ENGINE [Base Six SE]: V-block. OHV. Six-cylinder. Cast-iron block and heads. Aluminum intake manifold. Displacement: 191 cid. (3.1L). Bore & stroke: 3.50 x 3.31 in. Compression ratio: 8.5:1. Brake horsepower: 120 at 4400 rpm. Torque: 175 lbs.-ft. at 2200 rpm. Fuel system: TBFI. RPO Code: LG6. Standard in SE.

ENGINE [Optional Six SE]: V-block. OHV. "3800" six-cylinder. Cast-iron block and heads. Aluminum intake manifold. Displacement: 231 cid. (3.8L). Bore & stroke: 3.80 x 3.40 in. Compression ratio: 9.0:1. Brake horsepower: 170 at 4800 rpm. Torque: 225 lbs.-ft. at 3200 rpm. Fuel system: SPFI. RPO Code: L27.

CHASSIS

SUNFIRE CHASSIS: Wheelbase: 104.1 in. (all). Overall length: 181.9 in. (SE/GT coupes); 181.7 in. (SE sedan); 182.4 in. (SE convertible). Overall width: 67.4 in. (SE/GT coupes); 67.3 in. (SE sedan); 68.4 in. (SE convertible). Height: 53.2 in. (SE/GT coupes); 54.8 in. (SE sedan); 53.9 in. (SE convertible). Front tread: 57.6 in. (all). Rear tread: 56.8 in. (SE/GT coupes and SE sedan); 56.7 in. (SE convertible). Standard tires: P195/70R14 (SE coupe/sedan); P195/65R15 (SE convertible); P205/55R16 (GT coupe).

GRAND AM CHASSIS: Wheelbase: 103.4 in. (all). Overall length: 186.9 in. (all). Width: 67.5 in. (all). Height: 53.2 in. (all). Front tread: 55.9 in. (all). Rear tread: 55.4 in. (all). Standard tires: See model descriptions.

FIREBIRD CHASSIS: Wheelbase: 101.1 in. (all). Overall length: 195.6 in. (Firebird/Formula); 197.0 in. (Trans Am). Width: 74.5 in. (all). Height: 52.0 in. (Firebird/Formula/Trans Am coupes); 52.7 in. (Firebird/Formula/Trans Am convertibles). Front tread: 60.7 in. (all). Rear tread: 60.6 in. (all). Standard tires: P215/60R16 (Firebird); P235/55R16 (Formula); P245/50ZR16 (Trans Am).

GRAND PRIX CHASSIS: Wheelbase: 107.5 in. (all). Overall length: 194.8 in. (coupe); 194.9 in. (sedan). Width: 71.9 in. (all). Height: 52.8 in. (coupe); 54.8 in. (sedan). Front tread: 59.5 in. (all). Rear tread: 58.0 in. (all). Standard tires: P215/60/R16 (coupe); P205/70R15 (sedan).

BONNEVILLE CHASSIS: Wheelbase: 110.8 in. (all). Overall length: 199.5 in. (SE); 201.1 in. (SSE). Width: 74.5 in. (all). Height: 55.7 in. (all). Front tread: 60.4 in. (SE); 60.8 in. (SSE). Rear tread: 60.3 in. (SE); 60.6 in. (SSE). Standard tires: P215/65R15 (SE); P225/60R16 (SSE).

TRANS SPORT CHASSIS: Wheelbase: 109.8 in. Overall length: 192.2 in. Width: 74.6 in. Height: 65.7 in. Front tread: 59.2 in. Rear tread: 61.4 in. Standard tires: P205/70R15.

TECHNICAL

SUNFIRE TECHNICAL: Chassis: Front engine/front drive. Base transmission: five-speed manual (MK7). Optional transmissions: five-speed manual (MD9, optional on SE coupe/convertible, standard on

GT coupe); four-speed automatic (MN4, all). Axle ratio: 3.58:1 with 2.2-liter L4 and five-speed manual/3.94:1 with 2.3-liter Quad 4 and five-speed manual/3.91:1 with 2.3-liter Quad 4 and four-speed automatic. Front suspension: Dual path deflected disc front struts, 19mm anti-roll bar (20mm on GT coupe with 16-in. wheels), cross-axis front ball joints. Rear suspension: Tubular rear axle with coil over shock design. Steering: Rack-and-pinion mounted on cradle (SE and GT), 15.7:1 ratio (13.96:1 on GT). Turns lock-to-lock: 2.88 (2.33 on GT). Turning circle: 37.2 ft. (all). Front brakes: 10.2-in. vented discs. Rear brakes: 7.87 x 1.77-in. drums, power assisted. Fuel tank: 15.2 gal.

GRAND AM TECHNICAL: Chassis: Front engine/front drive. Base transmission: Five-speed manual (M32). Optional transmissions: four-speed automatic (M13, optional on SE and GT)/three-speed automatic (MD9, optional on SE only). Axle ratio: 3.94:1 (with M32 five-speed manual); 2.84:1 (with MD9 three-speed automatic and LD2 Quad 4 engine); 3.69:1 (with M13 four-speed automatic and LD2 Quad 4 engine); 2:93:1 (with M13 four-speed automatic and L82 V-6). Front suspension (Standard SE): Deflected disc; MacPherson struts, 27 N-mm spring and 22mm stabilizer bar. Rear Suspension (Standard SE): 21 N-mm springs, semi-independent trailing arms, spring-on-center linked with torsion beam, 18mm stabilizer bar. Front suspension (Standard GT): Deflected disc; MacPherson struts, 27 N-mm spring and 24mm stabilizer bar (automatic)/30mm (manual). Rear suspension (Standard GT): 25 N-mm springs, semi-independent trailing arms, spring-on-center linked with torsion beam, 22mm stabilizer bar. Steering: Power-assisted rack-and-pinion, 13.96:1 ratio. Turns lock-to-lock: 2.5. Turning circle: 35.3 ft. Front brakes: 259.5mm diameter vented discs. Rear brakes: 200.0mm diameter drums. Fuel tank: 15.2 gal.

FIREBIRD TECHNICAL: Chassis: Front engine/rear drive. Base transmission: (M49) Five-speed manual (Firebird); (MM6) six-speed manual (Formula/Trans Am). Optional transmission: (MD8) Four-speed automatic (all). Axle ratio: 3.23:1 (with M49 five-speed manual); 3.42:1 (with MM6 six-speed manual); 3.23:1 (with MD8 four-speed automatic and 3.4-liter V-6); 2.73:1 (with MD8 four-speed automatic and 5.7-liter V-8. Front suspension: (F41 Firebird) Short/long arm (SLA)/coil over mono-tube gas-charged shocks, tubular stabilizer bar with links, 30mm stabilizer bar. (FE2 Formula/Trans Am) SLA/coil over mono-tube gas-charged shocks, tubular stabilizer bar with links, 30mm stabilizer bar. Rear suspension: (F41 Firebird) Salisbury axle with torque arm, trailing arm, track bar, coil springs, 17mm stabilizer bar. (FE2 Formula/Trans Am) Salisbury axle with torque arm, trailing arm, track bar, coil springs, 19mm stabilizer bar. Steering: Power, rack-and-pinion with 16.9:1 ratio (Firebird)/14.4:1 (Formula/Trans Am). Turns lock-to-lock: 2.67 (Firebird)/2.28 (Formula/Trans Am). Turning circle: (Firebird) 37.9 ft. (left) 40.6 ft. (right)/(Formula/Trans Am) 37.7 ft. (left) 40.1 ft. (right). Front brakes: (Firebird/Formula/Trans Am) 10.7 in. vented disc. Rear brakes: (Firebird) 9.5 in. power assisted Duo-Servo drum. (Formula/Trans Am) 11.4 in. power assisted vented disc. Fuel tank: 15.5 gal.

GRAND PRIX TECHNICAL: Chassis: Front engine/front drive. Base transmission: (M13) four-speed electronic automatic transmission. Final Drive Ratios: 3.33:1 with (M13) four-speed electronic automatic and 3.1-liter V-6; 3.43:1 with (M13) four-speed electronic automatic and 3.4-liter V-6. Front suspension: MacPherson struts with tapered coil springs, lower "A" arm and 28mm anti-roll bar

1995 Pontiac Trans Sport minivan APV. (PGMC)

(34mm anti-roll bar with Y99 rally suspension). Rear suspension: Tri-link independent suspension, transverse fiberglass leaf spring and 12mm anti-roll bar (12mm anti-roll bar with Y99 and 3.1-liter V-6/14mm with Y99 and 3.4-liter V-6). Steering: Power-assisted rack-and-pinion with 15.7:1 ratio (14.0:1 with 3.4-liter V-6). Turns lock-to-lock: 2.6 (2.26 with Y99 and 3.4-liter V-6). Turning circle: 36.7 ft. (39 ft. with Y99 and 3.4-liter V-6). Front brakes: 10.51-in. vented discs, power-assisted. Rear brakes: 10.1-in. solid discs, power-assisted. Fuel tank: 17.1 gal.

BONNEVILLE TECHNICAL: Chassis: Front engine/front drive. Base transmission: (M13) four-speed electronic automatic. Axle ratio: 2.84:1 (3800 V-6); 2.97:1 (supercharged 3800 V-6). Front suspension: (SE) Standard FE1: deflected-disc, MacPherson struts, coil spring over strut (22 N-mm), 30mm stabilizer bar. (SSE) Standard FE2: deflected-disc, MacPherson struts, coil spring over strut (26 N-mm), 32mm stabilizer bar. Rear suspension: (SE) Standard FE1: coil springs (variable rate 48-65 N-mm), independent lower "A" arm, 17mm stabilizer bar. (SSE) Standard FE2: automatic level control coil springs (47 N-mm), Chapman struts, independent lower "A" arm, 22mm stabilizer bar. Optional front suspension: (SE) Y52: Computer Command Ride, deflected-disc, MacPherson struts, coil spring over strut (26 N-mm), 32mm stabilizer bar. (SSE) FW1: Computer Command Ride, deflected-disc, MacPherson struts, coil spring over strut (26 N-mm), 32mm stabilizer bar. Optional rear suspension: (SE) Y52: automatic level control coil springs (47 N-mm), Chapman struts, independent lower "A" arm, 22mm stabilizer bar. (SSE) FW1: automatic level control coil springs (47 N-mm), Chapman struts, independent lower "A" arm, 22mm stabilizer bar. Steering (Standard SE): Power-assisted rack-and-pinion with 16.54:1 ratio, 2.79 turns lock-to-lock and 39-ft. turning circle. (SSE/optional SE): Variable-effort rack-and-pinion with 14.93:1 to 18.91:1 ratio, 2.86 turns lock-to-lock and 40.5-ft. turning circle. Front brakes: 10.9-in. vented discs (all). Rear brakes: Power-assisted 8.85-in. drums (all). Fuel tank: 18.0 gal.

TRANS SPORT TECHNICAL: Chassis: Front engine/front drive. Transmission: (MD9) Three-speed automatic; optional (M13) four-speed automatic. Axle ratio: 3.06:1 (with either three-speed automatic and 3.1L V-6 or four-speed automatic and 3.8L V-6). Front suspension: MacPherson strut with coil springs (27 N-mm), stamped lower control arms and nodular iron steering knuckles, 27mm stabilizer bar. Rear suspension: Open-section transverse beam on stamped steel trailing arms, tube shocks, 48-56 N-mm variable rate coil springs (base suspension)/48.3 N-mm coil springs (uplevel suspension), electronic leveling, 25.4mm stabilizer bar. Steering: Rack-and-pinion with integral power unit with 15.7:1 ratio. Turns lock-to-lock: 3.05. Turning circle: 43.1 ft. Front brakes: 10.9 x 1.3-in. single caliper disc. Rear brakes: 8.86 x 1.77-in. leading trailing drum. Fuel tank: 20.0 gal.

OPTIONS

SUNFIRE OPTIONS: 1SB Sunfire SE Series option group ($1,295). 1SC Sunfire SE Series option group ($1,665). 1SD Sunfire SE Series option group ($2,226 coupe/$2,331 sedan). C60 air conditioning ($785). YF5 California emissions ($100). N33 tilt steering wheel ($145). K34 cruise control ($225). C49 electric rear window defogger ($170). A31 power windows ($265 SE coupe/$330 SE

sedan/no charge convertible). UN6 Delco stereo equipment ($195). UT6 Delco stereo equipment ($230). T43 rear deck lid spoiler ($70). MX1 three-speed automatic transmission ($495). CF5 power sunroof ($556). R6A Convenience Package ($80).

GRAND AM OPTIONS: 1SB package on SE coupe/sedan ($1,575). 1SC package on SE coupe ($2,021). 1SC package on SE sedan ($2,286). 1SB package on GT coupe/sedan ($597). 1SC package on GT coupe ($1,243). 1SC package on GT sedan ($1,308). L82 3.1-liter V-6 ($350). MX1 three-speed automatic transmission ($555, not available on GT). MX0 four-speed automatic transmission ($755). C60 air conditioning ($830). C49 electric rear window defogger ($170). K34 cruise control ($225). UB3 rally gauges ($111). YF5 California emission requirements ($100). CF5 power sunroof ($595). A31 express down power windows ($275-$340 depending on value option packages). AM9 split folding rear seat ($150). AX3 remote keyless entry ($135). UM6 Delco sound system ($140). UX1 Delco sound system ($375).

FIREBIRD OPTIONS: 1SB Firebird coupe option package ($1,005). 1SC Firebird coupe option package ($2,614). 1SB Formula coupe option package ($1,076). 1SC Formula coupe option package ($1,684). 1SB Firebird convertible option package ($508). 1SB Formula convertible option package ($508). C60 air conditioning ($895 on Firebird, standard on Formula/Trans Am). AU0 remote keyless entry ($135). MX0 four-speed automatic transmission ($775). B84 body color side moldings ($60). CC1 hatch roof ($995). U1C Delco sound system with CD player ($100). UP3 Delco sound system with CD player and graphic equalizer ($100-$573, depending on value option packages). K34 cruise control, ($225, standard on Trans Am). YF5 California emission requirements ($100). AR9 articulating bucket seats with leather ($780). GU5 rear performance axle ($175, not available on Firebird).

GRAND PRIX OPTIONS: 1SB Grand Prix SE sedan ($742). 1SC Grand Prix SE sedan ($1,937). A90 remote deck lid release ($60). C49 electric rear window defogger ($170). AUO Remote keyless entry system ($135). CF5 power sunroof ($646). UV8 cellular phone provisions ($35). UV6 head-up display ($250). B20 Custom interior trim ($393-$1,063 depending on value option packages). B4S GTP Performance Package for Grand Prix SE coupe ($2,256). B4Q GT Performance package for Grand Prix SE sedan ($1,825-$2,275 depending on value option packages). JL9 anti-lock brakes ($450). UN6 Delco stereo equipment ($195). UT6 Delco stereo equipment ($150-$325 depending on value option packages). U1C Delco stereo equipment ($125-$295 depending on value option package). AG1 six-way power driver's seat ($305). QPE touring tires for Grand Prix SE sedan ($112). PH3 15-in. aluminum Sport wheels for Grand Prix SE sedan ($259). NWO aluminum Sport wheels for Grand Prix SE sedan ($259).

BONNEVILLE OPTIONS: 1SB Bonneville SE option package ($270). 1SC Bonneville SE option package ($923). 1SD Bonneville SE option package ($1,584). 1SB Bonneville SSE option package ($1,440). WA6 SSEi supercharger package ($1,167, SSE). FW1 Computer Command Ride ($380, SSE). L67 Supercharged 3.8L 3800 V-6 ($1,187, SE). AUO Remote keyless entry system ($135). CF5 power glass sunroof ($981-$995). C49 electric rear window defogger ($170). K05 engine block heater ($18). NW9 Traction Control system ($175). PF5 16-in. five-blade cast aluminum wheels ($340). T2Z enhancement group ($206, SE). T43 rear deck lid spoiler ($110). UN6 Delco stereo equipment ($170). U1C Delco sound system ($295). UP3 Delco sound system with compact disc player ($485). US7 power antenna ($85). Y52 Performance & Handling package ($1,199, SE).

TRANS SPORT OPTIONS: 1SB Trans Sport SE option package ($1,418). 1SC Trans Sport SE option package ($2,513). 1SD Trans Sport SE option package ($3,093). 1SE Trans Sport SE option package ($4,197). L27 3.8L V-6 with four-speed automatic ($819). ZP7 seven-passenger seating ($705-$870 depending on value option packages). B2Q black roof delete (no charge). C49 electric rear window defogger ($170). AJ1 glass package ($245). AB5 power door locks ($300). V54 roof luggage carrier ($175). KO5 engine block heater ($18). UM6 Delco stereo equipment ($140). U1A Delco sound system with compact disc player ($206-$541). PH6 15-in. aluminum wheels ($259). E58 power sliding door ($350). C54 pop-up sunroof ($300). NW9 traction control ($350). AG9 six-way power driver's seat ($270). G67 Auto Level Control ($200).

NOTE: Full option package contents, descriptions, and applications information can often be determined by consulting factory literature.

1995 Pontiac Bonneville SSEi four-door sedan. (PGMC)

1995 Pontiac Sunfire two-door convertible. (PGMC)

1996 Pontiac Sunfire SE two-door convertible. (PGMC)

1995 Pontiac Bonneville SE four-door sedan. (PGMC)

The data above is edited for size and clarity. This information provided only as a guide to help collectors appraise the relative value of cars with numerous options. Prices for items included as part of a value option package are usually much less than individual prices. Option prices charged by individual dealers may also vary.

HISTORICAL: PMD's overall domestic model-year production was 78,795 units. Calendar-year sales were 566,826 cars, plus 32,297 Trans Sports. In the General Motors stable, 19.3 percent of new-vehicle sales were being earned by PMD and Pontiac products held a 6.6 percent share of the total U.S. market.

1996 PONTIAC

1996 Pontiac Sunfire SE four-door sedan. (PGMC)

SUNFIRE — CARLINE J — (FOUR) — The 1996 Pontiac Sunfire was considered a small car. It carried forward the Sunfire's 1995 introduction and again used a standard 2.2-liter four-cylinder engine. A 2.4-liter Twin Cam four-cylinder engine was a new option in 1996. **SE coupe:** Standard equipment included a rear-mounted fixed-mast antenna; soft fascia type bumpers; Soft-Ray tinted glass; composite halogen headlamps; breakaway sport mirrors (left-hand remote-controlled); body side moldings; P195/70R14 all-season black sidewall tires; compact spare; a low-liftover trunk; PC1 14-in.

custom bolt-on wheel covers; wet-arm pulse windshield wipers; extensive acoustic insulation; dual airbags; a front seat console armrest with storage bin; Milliweave cloth interior trim; instrumentation with analog speedometer/odometer; tachometer; cooling temperature gauge; oil pressure indicator and trip odometer; headlamp-on warning signal; carpeted luggage compartment; front and rear carpeted floor mats; day/night rearview mirror; twin visor vanity mirrors with covers; UM7 Delco ETR AM/FM stereo with seek up/down and clock; 45/45 reclining front bucket seats; full-folding rear three-passenger seat with integrated headrests; four-spoke steering wheel; front center armrest with cassette and CD storage; front door map pockets; glove compartment with lock; Delco Freedom battery; antilock braking with power front discs and rear drums; Brake/transmission shift interlock feature (with automatic transmission); five-speed manual transmission; stainless steel exhaust system; extensive anti-corrosion protection; GM Computer Command Control system; PASSLock theft system; power rack-and-pinion steering; and MacPherson front suspension. **SE sedan:** In addition or in place of SE coupe standard equipment, the SE sedan featured child-restraint rear door locks, but did not have the Easy-Entry front passenger seat. **SE convertible:** In addition to or in place of the SE sedan standard equipment, the SE convertible featured a rear deck lid spoiler; P195/65R15 black sidewall steel-belted radial touring tires; 15-in. bolt-on wheel covers; R134A air conditioning; a convenience package with deck-lid release; trunk net; reading lamps; and overhead console storage; dual reading lights mounted in the rearview mirror; tilt steering; and three-speed automatic transmission. **GT coupe:** In addition or in place of SE coupe standard equipment, the Sunfire GT featured aero extensions, a rear deck lid spoiler, P205/55R16 steel-belted radial black sidewall tires, PGO 16-in. GT-specific cast aluminum wheels, tilt steering, the 2.4-liter Twin Cam four-cylinder engine, and five-speed manual transmission, but body side moldings, a console armrest and power rack-and-pinion steering were deleted from the ragtop's standard equipment list.

GRAND AM — CARLINE N — (FOUR) — The 1996 Pontiac Grand Am was considered a medium-priced car. This line offered a coupe and sedan in SE and GT trim levels. Changed little since its 1987 redesign, the Grand Am shared components with other GM models, but was aimed at younger buyers preferring a sportier car. The base engine was the 2.4-liter, 150-hp Twin Cam four. A 3.1-liter V-6 was optional. **SE coupe/sedan:** Standard equipment on SE models included a fixed-mast antenna; a soft fascia and bumper with integral rub strips; Soft-Ray tinted glass; composite wraparound headlamps; daytime running lamps; fog lamps; sport mirrors (left-hand mirror

1996 Pontiac Sunfire SE four-door sedan. (PGMC)

remote-controlled); wide body-color body side moldings; P195/70R14 steel-belted radial tires; compact spare; a low-liftover trunk with trim protector; 14-in. custom bolt-on wheel covers; wet-arm windshield wipers; acoustical insulation; dual airbags; a front console; cup holders with "Aladdin" feature; a deck lid release; automatic power door locks with unlock/relock; rear child restraint (sedan); fuel filler door release; instrumentation; analog gauges with trip odometer; tachometer; fuel; temperature gauge and trip odometer; headlamp-on warning; interior lamp group with illuminated entry lamp; carpeted luggage compartment; day/night rearview mirror; twin visor vanity mirrors; Delco ETR stereo with seek up/down and clock; safety belts; Cordae cloth 45/45 reclining front bucket seats; rear three-passenger seat with integrated headrests; four-spoke steering wheel; front center armrest with cup holders and "Aladdin" feature; front door map pockets; glove compartment; litter bag hook; anti-corrosion protection; Delco Freedom battery; antilock braking with power front discs and rear drums; Brake/transmission shift interlock feature (with automatic transmission); stainless steel exhaust system; polished oval exhaust outlets; GM Computer Command Control system; 2.4-liter twin-cam four-cylinder engine; five-speed manual transmission; power rack-and-pinion steering; and MacPherson front suspension. **GT coupe:** In addition or in place of SE equipment, the Grand Am GT included aerodynamic body extensions; a rear deck lid spoiler; Goodyear RSA Eagle P205/55R16 steel-belted radial tires; specific GT 16-in. three-spoke cast aluminum wheels; controlled-cycle windshield wipers; air conditioning; a leather-wrapped four-spoke steering wheel; tilt steering; and a cast aluminum and stainless steel dual exhaust system.

FIREBIRD — CARLINE F — (V-6/V-8) — The 1996 Firebirds were members of a dwindling breed: the rear-wheel-drive American muscle car. **Firebird:** Standard equipment included a black fixed-mast antenna; soft fascia type bumpers; composite doors; fenders; fascias and roof (except convertible); a rear deck spoiler; Solar-Ray tinted glass; concealed quartz-halogen headlights; front license plate bracket; lighted rear license plate bracket; dual sport mirrors (left-hand mirror remote controlled) or left- and right-hand power remote mirrors with blue glass on all convertibles and Trans Am coupe; two-coat-component waterborne basecoat/clearcoat paint; rear deck lid spoiler with integrated center high-mounted stop lamp; one-piece multi-color tail lamp lenses; P215/60R16 steel-belted radial black sidewall touring tires; high-pressure T125/70D15 compact spare tire on 15 x 4-in. steel wheel; bright silver 16 x 8-in. sport cast aluminum wheels; controlled-cycle windshield wipers; extensive acoustical insulation; driver and passenger airbags; air conditioning (convertible only); full-length console with cup holder and storage box adjoining to instrument panel; cruise control (convertible only); electric rear window defogger (convertible only); power side windows; automatic power door locks (convertible only); Metrix cloth seat fabric; locking glove box; hatch release or rear deck lid release on convertibles; instrumentation including analog speedometer; tachometer; coolant temperature gauge; oil pressure gauge; voltmeter and trip odometer; ashtray lamp; dome lamp (except convertible); glove box lamp; rear seat courtesy lamp (convertible only); trunk lamp (convertible only); carpeted front floor mats; day/night rearview mirror with reading lamps; left- and right-hand covered visor vanity mirrors; Delco 2001 series electronically-tuned AM/FM stereo radio with cassette and seven-band equalizer; clock; touch control; seek up/down; search and replay and Delco theft lock; remote compact disc player pre-wiring and four-speaker coaxial sound system (convertible and Trans am coupe only); rear deck lid

1996 Pontiac Grand Am SE two-door coupe. (PGMC)

1996 Pontiac Grand Am GT four-door sedan. (PGMC)

release; safety belts; two-way manual reclining front bucket seats; folding rear seat; four-spoke steering wheel; adjustable tilt steering column; power window controls with driver side "express-down" feature for convertible only (requires power mirrors and power door locks); 105-ampere alternator; extensive anti-corrosion protection; Delco Freedom II battery; four-wheel antilock-braking system with front discs and rear drums; brake/transmission interlock with automatic transmission; stainless steel exhaust system (federal); General Motors Computer Command Control system; low-oil-level monitor and warning; driver-selectable transmission controls (automatic transmission only); V-6 normal second gear start (coupe only); power rack-and-pinion steering; short and long arm suspension with front and rear stabilizer bars and F41 Ride & Handling package; PASS-Key II theft-deterrent system; 3.8-liter V-6; and five-speed manual transmission. **FORMULA:** Formula models also include (in addition or in place of the above) neutral-density tail lamps with smooth-contour lenses; P235/55R16 steel-belted radial touring tires; air conditioning; 125-ampere alternator; four-wheel power disc brakes; electric rear window defogger (convertible only); power door locks (convertible only); rear seat courtesy lamps (convertible only); trunk lamp (convertible only); driver-selectable transmission control (with automatic transmission only); V-6 normal second gear start (convertible only); 5.7-liter V-8; and six-speed manual transmission. **TRANS AM:** Trans Am models also include (in addition to or in place of Formula features) a power antenna (convertible only); fog lamps; body-color body side moldings; P245/50ZR16 speed-rated tires (all-weather tires type on convertible only); cruise control; electric rear window defogger; automatic power door locks; rear floor mats (convertible only); Delco 2001 series electronically-tuned AM/FM stereo with auto reverse cassette and seven-band graphic equalizer (convertible only); four-way manual driver's seat and two-way manual front passenger seat; leather-wrapped steering wheel including leather-wrapped shift knob and parking brake handle (coupe only); leather-wrapped steering wheel with radio controls; including leather-wrapped shift knob and parking brake (convertible only); and power window controls with driver side "express-down" feature (requires power mirrors and power door locks).

GRAND PRIX — CARLINE W — (V-6/V-8) — The 1996 Pontiac Grand Prix was considered a medium-sized moderate-priced car. This line offered a coupe in SE and GTP trim levels and a sedan in SE and GT trim levels. The Grand Prix shared components with the Buick Regal and Oldsmobile Cutlass Supreme, but had more performance-oriented handling characteristics. The base engine was the 3.1-liter V-6. A 3.4-liter V-6 was optional, but delivered only slightly more performance and consumed more fuel. **SE coupe:** Standard equipment included (B4U) package with specific front and rear fascias with round fog lamps; lower-body aerodynamic skirting; wheel flares; 16 x 8-in. aluminum wheels; P225/60R16 performance tires; dual; split exhausts; sport suspension; fixed-mast antenna; a soft fascia type bumpers with integral rub strips; flush-fitting glass; completely Soft-Ray tinted and safety laminated; mini quad halogen headlamps; fog lamps; body-color remote-control sport mirrors. (coupe only); split dual exhausts (coupe only); steel-belted-radial black sidewall P215/60R16 touring tires or P225/60R16 black sidewall Eagle GT+4 tires (with 3.4-liter DOHC V-6 and B4U package); compact spare; 16 x 7-in. five-spoke cast-aluminum wheels (coupe only); wet-arm windshield wipers; extensive acoustic insulation package; dual airbags; electric push-button air conditioning; front floor console with storage (included on sedan with bucket seats);

cruise control (coupe only); deck lid release (coupe only); electric rear window defogger (coupe only); flush door handles; power door locks with unlock/relock feature; Cordae cloth interior; instrumentation including a mechanical analog speedometer; tachometer; coolant temperature gauge; fuel gauge and trip odometer; entry lighting; fully-carpeted luggage compartment trim; day/night rearview mirror; left- and right-hand covered visor vanity mirrors (coupe only); Delco 2001 Series ETR AM/FM stereo with seek up/down; auto reverse; cassette and clock; leather-wrapped steering wheel including steering-wheel radio controls (available in coupes with cassette and CD player only); seat and shoulder belts for driver and all passengers; front sport bucket seats with reclining backs; three-passenger rear seat with integrated headrests; four-spoke urethane steering wheel with airbag (coupe only; not available with base radio); locking instrument panel storage compartment; front door map pockets; pocketed visors (coupe only); turn-signal reminder; power windows with lighted switch and "express-down" feature; Delco Freedom II battery; four-wheel disc brakes; brake/transmission shift interlock; stainless steel dual exhaust system (included on GT sedan); extensive anti-corrosion protection; front-wheel drive; GM Computer Command Control; PASS-Key II theft-deterrent system; 3.1-liter 3100 sequential fuel-injection V-6 engine; and ECT four-speed automatic transmission. **SE sedan:** In addition to or in place of SE coupe equipment the Grand Prix SE sedan included: composite halogen headlamps; left-hand remote and right-hand manual rearview mirrors; P205/70R15 black sidewall touring tires; 15-in. wheel with bolt-on sport wheel covers; 45/55 split front seat with folding armrest; reclining left- and right-hand seat backs; and front center armrest with storage compartment (with 45/55 split bench seat).

BONNEVILLE — CARLINE H — (V-6) — The Bonneville was Pontiac's large car and, when properly equipped, represented one of the best large cars in the General Motors lineup. It was related to the Buick LeSabre and Olds Eighty-Eight, but had a firmer suspension and faster-acting steering. It was a true five-passenger sedan with room for three adults in the rear compartment. The standard engine was a V-6, with a supercharged V-6 optional. **SE sedan:** Standard Bonneville SE equipment included: a four-speaker sound system (not available with UT6/UT3 radios); 15-in. bolt-on wheel covers; four-wheel ABS brake system; extensive acoustical interior insulation; two-side galvanized steel doors; quarter panels; hood; deck lid; rocker panels and fenders; Delco Freedom II battery; brake/transmission interlock safety feature; power front disc/rear drum brakes; soft fascia type bumpers with integral rub strips; cruise control; daytime running lamps with Twilight Sentinel; electric rear window defogger; power door locks; 3800 Series II V-6 engine with sequential fuel-injection; stainless steel single exhaust system; flash-to-pass feature; fog lamps; front center armrest with storage compartment and cup holders; Soft-Ray tinted glass; composite halogen headlamps; instrument panel including cluster warning lamps for oil pressure; check engine; brakes; security system and airbag; backlit instruments including analog speedometer; fuel gauge; coolant temperature gauge; oil pressure gauge; voltage gauge and tachometer; lamp group including front overhead console lamp; ashtray lamp; glove box lamp and headlamps-on warning lamp; rear assist handles; rear rail courtesy lamps and trunk lamp; front and rear floor mats; left- and right-hand covered front visor vanity mirrors; sport-type outside rearview mirrors (left-hand remote-controlled); wide ribbed monotone body moldings; rear-seat pass through; three-point active safety belts; 45/55 split-bench front seat with manual recliners

and storage armrests with dual cup holders; Doral cloth upholstery; Delco ETR AM/FM stereo with four-speaker sound system; adjustable four-spoke tilting urethane steering wheel; power rack-and-pinion steering; systems monitoring functions with coolant temperature light; oil pressure indicator; battery voltage light and parking brake light; PASS-key II theft-deterrent system; P215/65R15 steel-belted radial black sidewall touring tires; ECT four-speed automatic transmission; and power windows with driver's side "express down." **SSE/SSEi sedan:** In addition to or in place of the above, the Bonneville SSE/SSEi models included: six-speaker sound system (not available with the UM7 radio); accessory emergency road kit; air conditioning with an automatic outside air temperature indicator; power antenna; a front floor storage console with storage compartment and heating; ventilation and air-conditioning vents; a deck lid release with valet lock-out; a six-way power driver's bucket seat; an electric compass and a Driver Information Center (with a boost gauge in supercharged models); a stainless steel dual rectangular split exhaust system (with supercharged engine); a entry illumination system; a keyless entry system; electric load leveling; a luggage compartment cargo net; heated and blue-tinted mirrors; a monotone ground effects package with aggressive-looking ribbed moldings and appliqué; a 45/45 bucket seat center console with storage compartment; Doral cloth seat trim; a Delco 2001 Series ETR AM/FM stereo system with auto-reverse cassette and seven-band equalizer; a rear center storage-type armrest with dual cup holders (standard with leather seating areas only); a four-spoke leather-wrapped steering wheel with radio controls (UT6 and UP3 radios); variable-effort power steering (standard Y52 CCR handling package on SE); P225/60R16 Goodyear Eagle GA black sidewall steel-belted radial touring tires; left- and right-hand covered visor vanity mirrors; and silver, three-blade-design, cast-aluminum 16-in. wheel covers.

TRANS SPORT — CARLINE U — (V-6) — The Trans Sport was Pontiac's plastic-bodied, front-wheel-drive minivan. Consumer magazines criticized its blind spots, wimpy suspension, poor fuel economy and "ponderous" handling. Reliability was another often-mentioned problem. Standard Trans Sport SE equipment included: an integrated roof antenna; soft fascia bumpers with integral rub strips; a center high-mounted stop lamp; dent-and-rust-resistant composite body panels; integral round fog lamps; heat-repelling pinkish solar-tinted glass with four flip-out rear side glass windows; composite halogen headlamps; left-hand remote-control sport mirror and right-hand manual sport mirror with fold-and-stow feature; black front roof treatment; lower aerodynamic moldings; wide body side moldings; monotone paint theme; 18-in. step-in height rear liftgate with hidden handle; two-speed wiper/washer and integral cargo lamps; P205/70R15 all-season black sidewall tires; a compact spare tire with hoist cable; 15-in. bolt-on styled wheel covers; controlled-cycle wet-arm windshield wipers; "Quiet Package" acoustical insulation; a driver's-side airbag; front air conditioning; side window defoggers; Doral cloth fabric; instrumentation including an analog speedometer; odometer; tachometer; low-coolant sensor; low-oil sensor; voltmeter and trip odometer; doorway; glove compartment; liftgate; security; headlamp-on and warning (with tones) lamps; a lap group with overhead consolette; map lights; rear dome reading lamps; a lamp group without overhead consolette; map lights; rear dome reading lamps; cargo area lamps and underhood lamp; front and rear floor mats; day/night rearview mirror; left- and right-hand covered visor vanity mirrors; power windows with driver "express-down" feature; Delco ETR AM/FM stereo

1996 Pontiac Grand Am SE four-door sedan. (PGMC)

1996 Pontiac Firebird two-door coupe. (PGMC)

1996 Pontiac Ram Air Formula Firebird WS6 two-door coupe. (PGMC)

with clock; safety belts; reclining front bucket seats with four-way adjustable headrests and armrest; five-passenger second-row bench seat; four-way manually-adjustable front driver's seat; four-spoke sport steering wheel with airbag; lower console with center instrument panel cup-and-mug-holder tray; front and side door map pockets; lockable under-dash storage; a covered upper instrument panel; a lower instrument panel glove box with lockable coin holder; a front seat back mesh net; a lower left rear quarter closed storage compartment; lower right rear quarter jack storage; upper rear quarter open storage with cup holder; a Delco Freedom II battery; power front disc/rear drum antilock brakes; four-wheel brake/trans-mission interlock system; long-life engine coolant; stainless steel exhaust system; 20-gallon fuel tank; GM Computer Command Control; power rack-and-pinion steering; 3.4-liter V-6 engine; and four-speed automatic transmission.

I.D. DATA: The vehicle identification number (VIN) is located on the top left-hand surface of the instrument panel and is visible through the windshield. The VIN has 17 symbols. The first symbol indicates the country of manufacture (1 or 4=United States; 2=Canada). The second symbol indicates the manufacturer (G=General Motors). The third symbol indicates the make/division (2=Pontiac; 5=Pontiac incomplete; M=Pontiac MPV and 7=GM of Canada). The fourth, fifth symbols indicate the car line and series (F/S=Firebird and convertible; F/V=Formula-Trans Am and convertible; H/X=Bonneville SE; H/Z=Bonneville SSE/SSEi; J/B=Sunfire SE and convertible; J/D=Sunfire GT; N/E=Grand Am SE; N/W= Grand Am GT; W/J=Grand Prix SE; W/M=Grand Prix; U=All-Purpose Vehicle 4x2). The sixth symbol indicates body style (1=two-door coupe models 27, 37, 47 and 57; 2=two-door models 07, 08, 77, 87; 3=two-door convertible model 67; 5=four-door sedan models 19 and 69; 6=four-door models 29 and 68; 0=All-Purpose Vehicle). The seventh symbol indicates the restraint system: 1=Active manual belts; 2=Active manual belts with driver and passenger inflatable restraints; 3=Active manual belts with driver inflatable restraint; 4=Passive (automatic) belts; 5=Passive (automatic) belts with driver inflatable restraint; 6=Passive (automatic) belts with driver and passenger inflatable restraints; 7=Active (manual) belt driver and passive (automatic) belt passenger with driver inflatable restraint. The eighth symbol indicates the engine type: K=RPO L36 3.8-liter V-6; M=RPO L82 3.1-liter V-6; P=RPO LT1 5.7-liter V-8; T=RPO LD9 2.4-liter L4; X=RPO LQ1 3.4-liter V-6; 1=RPO L67 3.8-liter V-8; 4=RPO LN2 2.2-liter L4 and E=RPO LA1 3.4-liter V-6. (Note: All Pontiac engines made in U.S. except "M" also made in Canada and "X" made in Canada only; all are MFI multi-point fuel-injected engines). The ninth symbol is a check digit. The 10th symbol indicates model year (T=1996). The 11th symbol indicates the GM assembly plant (B=Baltimore, Md., T&B; B=Lansing, Mich., GENASYS; C=Lansing, Mich.; C=Charlotte, Mich. T&B; D=Doraville, Ga.; E=Pontiac, Mich., East T&B; F=Fairfax II, Kan.; F=Flint T&B; G=Silao, Mexico; H=Flint, Mich.; J=Janesville, Wis.; K=Linden, N.J., T&B; M=Lansing, Mich.; M=Toluco Mexico; R=Arlington, Texas; S=Ramos Arizpe Mexico; T=Tarrytown, N.Y.; U=Hamtramck, Mich.; Y=Wilmington, Del.; Z=Fremont, Calif.; Z=Spring Hill, Tenn.; Z=Ft. Wayne, Ind. T&B; 1=Oshawa Canada #2; 1=Wentzville, Mo., T&B; 2=Morraine, Ohio, T&B; 2=Ste. Therese Canada; 3=Detroit, Mich., T&B; 3=Kawasaki Japan; 4=Orion, Mich.; 5=Bowling Green, Ky.; 6=Ingersoll, Ontario Canada; 6=Oklahoma City, Okla.; 7=Lordstown, Ohio; 7=Flusawa Japan; 8=Shreveport, La. T&B; 8= Tillisonburg, Ohio, CANEXPO; 9=Oshawa, Ontario Canada,

#1). Pontiacs are not produced at all of these plants. The last six symbols are the consecutive unit number at the factory.

Model Number	Body Style Number	Body Type & Seating	Factory Price	Shipping Weight	Production Total
SUNFIRE SE SERIES B (I-4)					
J/B	B37T	2d Coupe-4	11,504	2,679	Note 1
J/B	B69T	4d Sedan-4P	11,674	2,723	Note 1
J/B	B67T	2d Convertible-4P	17,734	2,835	Note 1
SUNFIRE GT SERIES D (I-4)					
J/D	D37T	2d Coupe-4P	13,214	2,829	Note 1
GRAND AM SE SERIES E (I-4)					
N/E	E37T	2d Coupe-4	13,499	2,881	Note 2
N/E	E69T	4d Sedan-4P	13,499	2,954	Note 2
GRAND AM GT SERIES W (I-4)					
N/W	W67T	2d Coupe-4P	15,499	2,932	Note 2
N/W	W69T	2d Sedan-4P	15,499	3,011	Note 2
FIREBIRD SERIES S (V-6)					
F/S	S87T	2d Coupe-4P	15,614	3,131	Note 3
F/S	S67T	2d Convertible-4P	22,444	3,346	Note 3
FORMULA SERIES V (V-8)					
F/V	V87T	2d Coupe-4P	19,464	3,373	Note 3
F/V	V67T	2d Convertible-4P	25,284	3,489	Note 3
TRANS AM SERIES V (V-8)					
F/V	V87T	2d Coupe-4P	21,414	3,345	Note 3
F/V	V67T	2d Convertible-4P	27,364	3610	Note 3
GRAND PRIX SE SERIES J (V-6)					
W/J	J37T	2d Coupe-4	18,359	3,243	Note 4
W/J	J19T	4d Sedan-4P	17,089	3,318	Note 4
BONNEVILLE SE SERIES X (V-6)					
X	X69T	4d Sedan-6P	21,589	3,446	Note 5
BONNEVILLE SLE/SSEi SERIES X (V-6)					
Z	Z69T	4d Sedan-6P	26,559	3,587	Note 5
TRANS SPORT SE SERIES U (I-4)					
U	M06T	Minivan-6p	19,394	3,593	Note 6

NOTE 1: Model-year production total was 131,759 Sunfires of all types.

NOTE 2: Model-year production total was 229,117 Grand Ams of all types.

NOTE 3: Model-year production total was 32,799 Firebirds of all types.

NOTE 4: Model-year production total was 83,587 Grand Prixs of all types.

NOTE 5: Model-year production total was 74,191 Bonnevilles of all types.

NOTE 6: Model-year production total was 25,142 Trans Sports of all types.

SUNFIRE ENGINES

ENGINE [Base Four SE]: Inline. OHV. Four-cylinder. Cast-iron block. Aluminum head and intake manifold. Two valves per cylinder. Displacement: 133 cid. (2.2L). Bore & stroke: 3.50 x 3.46 in. Compression ratio: 9.0:1. Net horsepower: 120 at 5200 rpm. Torque: 130 lbs.-ft. at 4000 rpm. Fuel system: SFI. VIN Code: 4. RPO Code: LN2.

ENGINE [Base Four (GT); Optional (SE)]: Inline. DOHC. Four-cylinder. Cast-iron block. Aluminum head and intake manifold. Four valves per cylinder. Displacement: 138 cid. (2.4L). Bore & stroke: 3.54 x 3.79 in. Compression ratio: 9.5:1. Net horsepower: 150 at 6000 rpm. Torque: 155 lbs.-ft. at 4400 rpm. Fuel system: SFI. VIN Code: T. RPO Code: LD9.

GRAND AM ENGINES

ENGINE [Base Four SE/GT]: Inline. DOHC. Four-cylinder. Cast-iron block. Aluminum head and intake manifold. Four valves per cylinder. Displacement: 138 cid. (2.4L). Bore & stroke: 3.54 x 3.79 in. Compression ratio: 9.5:1. Net horsepower: 150 at 6000 rpm.

1996 Pontiac Ram Air Firebird Trans Am two-door coupe. (PGMC)

1996 Pontiac Firebird two-door T-Top coupe. (PGMC)

Torque: 155 lbs.-ft. at 4400 rpm. Fuel system: SFI. VIN Code: T. RPO Code: LD9.

ENGINE [Optional Six]: V-block. OHV. Six-cylinder. Cast-iron block and head. Aluminum intake manifold. Displacement: 191 cid. (3.1L). Bore & stroke: 3.50 x 3.31 in. Compression ratio: 9.5:1. Brake horsepower: 155 at 5200 rpm. Torque: 185 lbs.-ft. at 4000 rpm. Fuel system: SFI. VIN Code: M. RPO Code: L82.

FIREBIRD ENGINES

ENGINE [Base Six V-6]: V-block. OHV. Six-cylinder. Cast-iron block and head. Aluminum intake manifold. Displacement: 231 cid. (3.8L). Bore & stroke: 3.80 x 3.40 in. Compression ratio: 9.0:1. Brake horsepower: 200 at 5200 rpm. Torque: 225 lbs.-ft. at 4000 rpm. Fuel system: SFI. VIN Code: K. RPO Code: L36.

ENGINE [Base V-8]: V-block. OHV. Eight-cylinder. Cast-iron block and head. Aluminum intake manifold. Displacement: 350 cid. (5.7L). Bore & stroke: 4.00 x 3.48 in. Brake horsepower: 285 at 5000 rpm. Torque: 325 lbs.-ft. at 2400 rpm. Compression ratio: 10.5:1. Fuel system: SFI. VIN Code: 5. RPO Code: LT1.

GRAND PRIX ENGINES

ENGINE [Base V-6]: V-block. OHV. Six-cylinder. Cast-iron block and head. Aluminum intake manifold. Displacement: 191 cid. (3.1L). Bore & stroke: 3.50 x 3.31 in. Compression ratio: 9.5:1. Brake horsepower: 160 at 5200 rpm. Torque: 185 lbs.-ft. at 4000 rpm. Fuel system: SFI. VIN Code: M. RPO Code: L82.

ENGINE [Optional V-6]: V-block. DOHC. Six-cylinder. Cast-iron block and head. Aluminum intake manifold. Displacement: 206 cid. (3.4L). Bore & stroke: 3.62 x 3.31 in. Compression ratio: 9.7:1. Brake horsepower: 215 at 5200 rpm. Torque: 215 lbs.-ft. at 4,000 rpm. Fuel system: SFI. VIN Code: X. RPO Code: LQ1.

BONNEVILLE ENGINE

ENGINE [Base Six SE/SSE]: "3800" SFI Series II V-6. V-block. OHV. Six-cylinder. Cast-iron block and head. Aluminum intake manifold. Displacement: 231 cid. (3.8L). Bore & stroke: 3.80 x 3.40 in. Compression ratio: 9.0:1. Brake horsepower: 205 at 5200 rpm. Torque: 230 lbs.-ft. at 4000 rpm. Fuel system: SFI. VIN Code: K RPO Code: L36

ENGINE [Supercharged Six SSEi]: "3800" Supercharged Series II V-6. V-block. OHV. Six-cylinder. Cast-iron block and head. Aluminum intake manifold. Displacement: 231 cid. (3.8L). Bore & stroke: 3.80 x 3.40 in. Compression ratio: 8.5:1. Brake horsepower: 240 at 5200 rpm. Torque: 280 lbs.-ft. at 3200 rpm. Fuel system: SFI. VIN Code: 1 RPO Code: L67

TRANS SPORT ENGINE

ENGINE [Base V-6]: V-block. DOHC. Six-cylinder. Cast-iron block and head. Aluminum intake manifold. Displacement: 207 cid. (3.4L). Bore & stroke: 3.62 x 3.31. Compression ratio: 9.5:1. Brake horsepower: 180 at 5200 rpm. Torque: 205 lbs.-ft. at 4,000 rpm. Fuel system: SFI. VIN Code: E. RPO Code: LA1.

CHASSIS

SUNFIRE CHASSIS: Wheelbase: (All) 104.1 in. Overall length: (coupe) 182 in.; (sedan) 181.7 in.; (convertible) 182.4 in. Overall width: (coupe) 67.4 in.; (sedan) 67.3; (convertible) 68.4. Height: (coupe) 53.2 in.; (sedan) 54.8 in.; (convertible) 51.9 in. Standard tires: (SE coupe and sedan) steel-belted radial P195/70R14 black sidewall all-season; (SE convertible) steel-belted radial P195/65R15

black sidewall touring; (GT) steel-belted radial P205/55R16 black sidewall Performance.

GRAND AM CHASSIS: Wheelbase: (All) 103.4 in. Overall length: (coupe) 187.3 in.; (sedan) 186.9 in. Width: (All) 68.7 in. Height: (All) 53.5 in. Front tread: 55.6 in. Rear tread: 55.2 in. Standard tires: (SE) steel-belted radial P195/70R14 black sidewall; (GT) steel-belted radial P205/55R16 black sidewall Eagle RSA.

FIREBIRD CHASSIS: Wheelbase: (All) 101.0 in. Overall length: (Firebird/Formula) 195.6 in.; (Trans Am) 197 in. Width: (All) 74.5 in. Height: (Firebird/Formula coupe) 52.0 in.; (Firebird/Formula convertible) 52.7 in.; (Trans Am coupe) 51.7 in.; (Trans Am convertible) 52.4 in. Front tread: 60.7 in. Rear tread: 61.6 in. Standard tires: (Firebird) steel-belted radial P215/60R15 black sidewall touring; (Formula) steel-belted radial P235/55R16 touring; (Trans Am) P245/50ZR16 speed-rated, all-weather.

GRAND PRIX CHASSIS: Wheelbase: (All) 107.5 in. Overall length: (coupe) 194.8 in.; (sedan) 194.9 in. Width: (All) 71.9 in. Height: (coupe) 52.9 in.; (sedan) 52.8 in. Front tread: 59.5 in. Rear tread: 58.0 in. Standard tires: (SE coupe w/B4U) 225/60R16 Performance; (SE coupe) steel-belted radial 215/60R16 black sidewall touring; (SE coupe with DOHC V-6) P225/60R16 black sidewall Eagle GT+4; (SE sedan) P205/70R15 black sidewall touring.

BONNEVILLE CHASSIS: Wheelbase: (All) 110.8 in. Overall length: (All) 201.2 in. Width: (All) 74.5 in. Height: (All) 55.7 in. Front tread: 60.3 in. Rear tread: 59.8 in. Standard tires: (SE) steel-belted radial 215/65R15 black sidewall touring; (SSE) steel-belted radial P225/60R16 black sidewall Eagle GA touring.

TRANS SPORT CHASSIS: Wheelbase: 109.8 in. Overall length: 192.2 in. Width: 74.6 in. Height: 65.7 in. Standard tires: 205/70R-15 black sidewall all-season.

TECHNICAL

SUNFIRE TECHNICAL: Chassis: Front engine/front drive. Base transmission: Five-speed manual. Optional transmission: Three-speed automatic. Front suspension: MacPherson struts. Rear suspension: Coil springs, semi-independent torsion beam, trailing arms. Steering: Rack-and-pinion. Front brakes: vented disc power-assisted. Rear brakes: drum power-assisted.

GRAND AM TECHNICAL: Chassis: Front engine/front drive. Base transmission: Five-speed manual with overdrive. Optional transmission: Three-speed automatic. Axle ratio: 3.18:1 (with 2.3L and 2.5L engines and automatic SE). Axle ratio: 2.84:1 (with 2.3L and 2.5L engines and automatic LE). Axle ratio: 3.35:1 (with 2.5L engine and manual). Axle ratio: 3.61:1 (with 2.3L H.O. engine and manual). Stall torque ratio: 2.48:1 (2.3L with automatic). Stall torque ratio: 2.35:1 (2.5L with automatic). Front suspension: MacPherson struts with coil springs and 24mm anti-roll bar (28mm anti-roll bar with Sport Performance and WS6 suspensions). Rear suspension: Trailing crank arm with twist arm, coil springs, (and 21mm anti-roll bar with Sport Performance and WS6 suspensions). Steering (Standard): Power-assisted rack-and-pinion, 16.0:1 ratio, 2.88 turns lock-to-lock, and 35.4-ft. (left); 37.8-ft. (right) turning circle. Steering (Sport Performance and WS6): Power-assisted rack-and-pinion, 14.0:1 ratio, 2.5 turns lock-to-lock, and 35.4-ft. (left); 37.8-ft. (right) turning circle. Front brakes: Power-assisted 10.24-in. vented discs. Rear brakes: Power-assisted 7.87-in. drums. (ABS standard on SE). Fuel tank: 13.6 gal.

FIREBIRD TECHNICAL: Chassis: Front engine/rear drive. Base transmission: Four-speed automatic (Firebird/GTA). Optional transmission: Five-speed manual. (Formula/Trans Am). Front

1996 Pontiac Firebird two-door convertible. (PGMC)

Standard Catalog of ® Pontiac, 2nd Edition

1996 Pontiac Grand Prix SE four-door sedan. (PGMC)

suspension: Modified MacPherson strut with 30mm (FE1), 34mm (F41), or 36mm (WS6) anti-roll bar. Rear suspension: Live axle with coil springs, control arms, torque arm, track bar, and 18mm (FE1) or 23mm (F41 and WS6) anti-roll bar. Steering: Power re-circulating ball; 14.0:1 ratio (FE1), or 12.7:1 quick ratio with sport effort valving (F41 and WS6). Turns lock-to-lock: 2.57 (FE1), or 2.14 (F41 and WS6). Turning circle: 38.5 ft. (FE1) or 38.5 ft. (F41 and WS6). Brakes: Power vented 10.5-in. front disc/9.5 x 2.0-in. rear drum. Fuel tank: 15.5 gal.

GRAND PRIX TECHNICAL: Chassis: Front engine/front drive. Standard drive train: 2.3L Quad-4 with three-speed automatic transaxle. Optional drive train: 3.1L MFI V-6 with five-speed manual transaxle. Optional drive train: 3.4L Twin Dual Cam V-6 with five-speed manual transaxle. Axle ratio: 3.18 (2.3L with three-speed automatic). Axle ratio: 3.33 (3.1L MFI V-6 with four-speed automatic). Axle ratio: 3.67 (3.4L with five-speed manual). Axle ratio: 3.43 (3.4L with four-speed manual). Front suspension: MacPherson struts with tapered top coil springs, lower A arm and 28mm anti-roll bar (34mm anti-roll bar with Y99 suspension). Rear suspension: Tri-link independent suspension with 12mm anti-roll bar (transverse fiberglass leaf spring and 12mm anti-roll bar with 3.1L; 14mm anti-roll bar with 3.4-liter engine.). Steering: Power-assisted rack-and-pinion with 15.7:1 ratio (14.0:1 with Y99 3.4-liter; 15.7:1 with 3.1-liter engine); 2.6 turns lock-to-lock, and 36.77-ft. turning circle (standard). Steering: Power-assisted rack-and-pinion with 15.7:1 ratio, 2.25 turns lock-to-lock, and 39.7-ft. turning circle (STE with Y99). Four-wheel power disc brakes. Front brakes: 10.5-in. x 1.04-in. composite vented discs. Rear brakes: 10.1-in. x 0.5-in. composite solid discs. Fuel tank: 15.5 gal.

BONNEVILLE TECHNICAL: Chassis: Front engine/front drive. Base transmission: Four-speed automatic. Axle ratio: 2.84:1 (standard with 3.8L V-6 in Bonneville LE). Axle ratio: 2.97:1 (standard with 3.8L V-6 in Bonneville SE.) Axle ratio: 3.33:1 (standard with 3.8L V-6 in Bonneville SSE). Front suspension: MacPherson struts with 20 N-mm coil springs and 28mm anti-roll bar (LE). Front suspension: MacPherson struts with 24.2 N-mm coil springs and 32mm anti-roll bar (SE). Front suspension: MacPherson struts with 24 N-mm coil springs and 32mm anti-roll bar (SSE). Rear suspension: MacPherson struts with variable rate (48-65 N-mm) coil springs and 14mm anti-roll bar (LE). Rear suspension: MacPherson struts with variable-rate (55-65 N-mm) coil springs and 18mm anti-roll bar (SE). Rear suspension: MacPherson struts with 47 N-mm coil springs and 18mm anti-roll bar (SSE). Steering: Power-assisted rack-and-pinion with 18.1:1 constant ratio, 2.97 turns lock-to-lock, and 39.7-ft. left/39.0-ft. right turning circle (LE/SE). Steering: Power-assisted rack-and-pinion with 15.3:1 to 18.0:1 variable ratio, 2.79 turns lock-to-lock, and 38.4-ft. left/40.7-ft. right turning circle (SSE). Front brakes: Power-assisted 10.1-in. vented discs. Rear brakes: Power-assisted 8.9-in. drums. Antilock brake system standard with SSE. Fuel tank: 18.0 gal.

TRANS SPORT TECHNICAL: Chassis: Front engine/front drive. Transmission: Three-speed automatic. Axle ratio: 3.18:1 (all). Front suspension: MacPherson struts with 24 N-mm coil springs and 30mm anti-roll bar (LE). Front suspension: MacPherson strut, stamped lower control arms, 28mm stabilizer bar. Rear suspension: Open-section transverse beam on stamped steel trailing arms, tube shocks, coil springs and 25.4mm stabilizer bar. Steering: Power-assisted rack-and-pinion with 15.7:1 ratio, and 38-ft. turning circle. Front brakes: Power-assisted 10.2-in. vented rotors, 182 sq. in. swept area. Rear brakes: Power-assisted 8.86 x 1.58-in. finned composite cast-iron drums with 98.5 sq. in. swept area. Fuel tank: 20.0 gal.

OPTIONS

SUNFIRE OPTIONS: LD9 2.4-liter Twin Cam 16-valve four-cylinder engine, standard GT; not available with MX1 transmission; requires tire upgrade on SE coupe and sedan ($3,950). FE9 Federal emissions with LD9 and MX0 (no cost); FE9 50-state emissions with LD9 and MM5 (no cost). FE9 50-state emissions with LD9 and MM5 with L82 (no cost). YF5 California emissions with LD9 and MX0 ($100). YF5 50-state emissions with LD9 and MM5 and L82 (no cost). NG1 N.Y./Mass. Emissions with LD9 and MX0 ($100). NG1 50-state emissions with LD9 and MM5 and L82 (no cost). QPD P195/65R15 black sidewall steel-belted radial touring tires, standard SE convertible; not available with GT coupe; requires PG1 or PF7 wheels ($131). Milliweave cloth front bucket seat trim standard without Sport interior; with Sport interior ($95). 10N5 front bucket seats with white vinyl trim and sport interior ($145). 1SA Sunfire SE coupe and sedan option package including vehicle with standard equipment (no cost). 1SB Sunfire SE coupe and sedan option group ($1,305). 1SC Sunfire SE coupe and sedan ($1,675). 1SD Sunfire SE coupe ($2,531) or SE sedan ($2,636). 1SA Sunfire SE convertible option package including vehicle with standard equipment (no cost). 1SB Sunfire SE convertible group ($741). 1SC Sunfire SE convertible ($1,511). 1SA Sunfire GT coupe option package including vehicle with standard equipment (no cost). 1SB Sunfire GT coupe ($1,616). 1SC Sunfire GT coupe ($2,386). C60 air conditioning ($795). C41 non-air-conditioning (no cost). R6A convenience package ($41-80). K34 cruise control ($225). C49 electric window defogger ($170). K05 engine block heater ($18). VK3 front license plate bracket (no cost). AU3 power door locks ($210-$250). DG7 dual power sport mirrors ($86). A31 power windows, requires power door locks (SE/GT coupe $265; sedan $330; convertible, no cost). UK3 steering wheel radio controls ($125). UN6 Delco radio equipment ($125). UT6 ETR AM/FM stereo with cassette and equalizer (with 1SA $230; with 1SB or 1SC $35). UP3 ETR AM/FM stereo with CD and equalizer (with 1SA $330; with 1SB or 1SC $135; with 1SD $100). AUO remote keyless entry ($135). N33 tilt steering wheel ($145). T43 rear deck lid spoiler ($95). CF5 power sunroof ($556-595). MM5 five-speed transmission ($550 credit in SE convertible w/LD9). MX1 three-speed automatic transmission ($550). MX0 four-speed automatic transmission ($795 except SE convertible $245). PG1 15-in. bolt-on wheel covers; requires QPD tires (no cost). PF7 15-in. aluminum wheels; not available on GT, requires QPD tires ($275).

GRAND AM OPTIONS: L82 3.1-liter 3100 SFI V-6 ($395). FE9 Federal emissions with LD9 and MX0 (NC); FE9 50-state emissions with LD9 and MM5 (no cost). FE9 50-state emissions with LD9 and MM5 with L82 (no cost). YF5 California emissions with LD9 and MX0 ($100) YF5 50-state emissions with LD9 and MM5 and L82 (no cost) NG1 N.Y./Mass. Emissions with LD9 and MX0 ($100). NG1 50-state emissions with LD9 and MM5 and L82 (no cost). QPD P195/65R15 touring tires, not available GT ($131). QMS P205/55R16 touring tires, not available GT ($223). QLG P205/55R16 STL performance tires (standard equipment, GT only). SE bucket seats with cloth seating and Sports Interior group ($220). GT interior trim ($170). 225 bucket seats with leather seating area ($645-$845). Sport interior group (package). 1SA SE option package (no cost). 1SB SE option package includes air conditioning; tilt steering; cycle wipers; cruise control; rear defogger, and radio with cassette ($1,630). 1SC SE coupe option package includes 1SB plus variable-effort power steering; split folding rear seat; power windows; power mirrors; remote

1996 Pontiac Grand Prix SE two-door coupe. (PGMC)

1996 Pontiac Bonneville SE four-door Sport Sedan. (PGMC)

1996 Pontiac Bonneville SLE four-door Sport Sedan. (PGMC)

keyless entry ($2,353). 1SC SE sedan option package includes 1SB plus variable-effort power steering; split folding rear seat; power windows; power mirrors; remote keyless entry ($2,418). 1SA GT option package (no cost). 1SB GT option package includes cruise control; rear defogger and radio with cassette; and variable-effort power steering ($652). 1SC GT coupe option package includes 1SB plus split folding rear seat; power windows; power mirrors; remote keyless entry ($1,313). 1SC GT sedan option package includes 1SB plus split folding rear seat; power windows; power mirrors; remote keyless entry ($1,378). C60 air conditioning ($830). C41 no air conditioning, not available GT (NC). K34 cruise control with resume-speed function ($225). C49 electric rear window defogger ($170). K05 engine block heater ($18). VK3 front license plate bracket (no cost). AUO remote keyless entry ($135). AG1 six-way driver's power seat ($340). A31 power windows with express down ($290 coupe; $355 sedan). UK3 steering wheel radio controls ($125). UN6 ETR AM/FM stereo with cassette ($195). UT6 ETR AM/FM stereo with CD, equalizers, six speakers (without 1SB or 1SC $305; with 1SB or 1SC $110). UP3 ETR AM/FM stereo with CD, equalizers, six speakers (without 1SB or 1SC $405; with 1SB or 1SC $210). UN1 ETR AM/FM stereo with CD, cassette, equalizers, six speakers (without 1SB or 1SC $600; with 1SB or 1SC $405). AM9 spilt folding rear seat ($150). T43 rear deck spoiler (standard GT; $150 SE). D58 delete rear deck spoiler on GT ($150 credit). N33 tilt steering (standard GT; $145 SE). CF5 power glass sunroof ($595). MM5 five-speed manual transmission (standard). MX0 four-speed automatic transmission ($795). PG1 15-in. bolt-on wheel covers for SE (no cost). PF7 15-in. crosslaced aluminum wheels for SE ($275). PG0 16-in. SE sport aluminum wheels ($300). V2C aluminum silver wheels (no cost). CD4 controlled cycle wipers for SE ($65).

FIREBIRD OPTIONS: FE9 Federal emissions (no cost). YF5 50 California emissions (no cost). NG1 N.Y./Mass. Emissions (no cost). NB8 Calif./NY/Mass. Emissions override, requires FE9 (no cost). NC7 Federal emissions override, requires YF5 or NG1 (no cost). QCB P235/55R16 black sidewall touring tires for Firebird, standard Formula and Trans Am; not available Trans Am convertible ($132). QFZ P245/50ZR16 black sidewall steel-belted radial all-weather performance tires for Formula and Trans Am coupe ($225). QLC P245/50ZR16 black sidewall steel-belted radial performance tires for Formula and Trans Am ($225). QFK P275/40ZR17 speed-rated tires for Formula and Trans Am coupe with WS6 only (no cost). AR9 articulating bucket seats (Firebird and Formula coupe $804; convertible $829). AQ9 articulating bucket seats including articulating headrests (Trans Am with Metrix cloth trim $320; Trans Am with Prado leather trim $829). 1SA Firebird coupe option package, includes vehicle with standard equipment (no cost). 1SB Firebird option group ($1,078). 1SC Firebird option group ($2,499). 1SA Formula coupe option package, includes vehicle with standard equipment (no cost). 1SB Formula coupe option group ($1,184). 1SC Formula coupe option group ($1,604). 1SA Firebird and Formula convertible option package, includes vehicle with standard equipment (no cost). 1SB Firebird and Formula convertible group ($580). 1SA Trans Am coupe/convertible option package, includes vehicle with standard equipment (no cost). R6A Firebird and Formula value package ($820). R6B value package Firebird and Formula ($814). Y82 Trans Am coupe option (standard). Y84 Trans Am convertible option (standard). Y87 3800 performance package ($535). WS6

Ram Air performance and handling package, includes Ram Air induction system; functional air scoops; 17-in. five-spoke aluminum wheels; P275/40ZR17 speed-rated tires and dual oval exhaust outlets ($2,995). B84 body color side moldings ($60). UA6 content theft alarm ($90). K34 cruise control ($225). C49 electric rear window defogger ($170). CC1 hatch roof ($970). DE4 hatch roof sunshades ($25). VK3 front license plate bracket (no cost). B35 rear carpet floor mats, standard Trans Ams ($15). DG7 dual sport mirrors ($96). U75 power antenna, requires radio upgrade, standard on Trans Am convertible ($85). AU3 power door locks ($220). A31 power windows ($290). W52 ETR AM/FM stereo with auto-reverse, graphic equalizer, clock, seek up/down, remote CD pre-wire, and four coaxial speakers ($73). W53 ETR AM/FM stereo with CD player, graphic equalizer, clock, seek up/down, and four coaxial speakers ($173). W54 ETR AM/FM stereo with auto-reverse, graphic equalizer, clock, seek up/down, remote CD pre-wiring, and 10-speaker sound system ($115). W55 ETR AM/FM stereo with CD player, graphic equalizer, clock, seek up/down. and 10-speaker sound system ($115). W58 ETR AM/FM stereo with CD player, graphic equalizer, clock, seek up/down. and four-speaker sound system ($100). W59 ETR AM/FM stereo with auto-reverse cassette, graphic equalizer, clock, seek up/down, remote CD pre-wiring, and six-speaker sound system ($50). W73 ETR AM/FM stereo with CD player, graphic equalizer, clock, seek up/down, and six-speaker sound system ($150). U1S trunk mounted remote 12-disc CD changer ($595). GU5 performance axle ($175). AUO remote keyless entry ($135). AH3 manual four-way-adjustable driver's seat ($35). AG1 six-way power driver's seat ($270-$305). UK3 steering wheel radio controls (Firebird/Formula $200; Trans Am $125). NW9 traction control ($450). MX0 four-speed automatic transmission ($790). T43 up-level rear deck lid spoiler, Trans Am only ($395). PO5 chrome aluminum wheels, not available with 1SA Firebird coupe ($500).

GRAND PRIX OPTIONS: L82 3.1-liter 3100 SFI V-6 (standard). LQ1 3.4-liter DOHC V-6 with split dual exhaust and sport suspension, with B4S only (no cost). FE9 50-state emissions (no cost). YF5 50-state emissions (no cost). NG1 50-state emissions (no cost). QVG P225/60R16 black sidewall STL performance tires for coupe (standard). QIN P205/70R15 black sidewall STL touring tires for sedan (standard). QPE P215/60R16 black sidewall STL touring tires for sedan ($112). QVG P225/60R16 black sidewall STL performance tires, available for sedan with B4Q only (no cost). B9/AR9 SE coupe bucket seat interior with Cordae cloth trim (standard). B20 SE coupe custom interior group (C3/B20 sport buckets with Doral cloth $391; 23/B20 sport buckets with Prado leather trim $866). B6 SE sedan 45/55 split bench seat with Cordea cloth trim (standard). B9/AR9 SE sedan bucket seats ($70). (A variety of specific B20 custom interior group options were available at prices from $393 to $1,063). 1SA option package for SE coupe, includes vehicle and standard equipment (standard). 1SB option package for SE sedan ($742). 1SC option package for SE sedan ($1,937). B4S performance package ($1,635). B4M white Special Edition package ($295). B5Z high-polished five-spoke wheels ($495). B4Q GT performance package (sedan with 1SB $2,275; sedan with 1SC $1,825). K34 cruise control ($225). A90 remote deck lid release ($60). C49 electric rear window defogger ($170). B37 front and rear floor carpet mats ($45 or standard with B20). K05 engine block heater ($18). NC5 split dual exhausts, sedan ($90 or no cost with B4Q). UV6 heads-up display ($250). U40 trip computer ($199). VK3 front license plate bracket (no cost). DD2 dual covered visor vanity mirrors ($14 or no cost with B20 or sedan with 1SB/1SC). US7 power antenna ($85). JL9 power antilock brakes for coupe without B4S or sedan without B4Q or 1SC ($450). U1C AM/FM stereo with CD player (coupe $125; sedan without 1SB/1SC $295; sedan with 1SB/1SC $150). UT6 ETR AM/FM stereo with auto-reverse, seven-band equalizer, and eight-speaker sound system ($150 to $375 depending on model and other options on car). UP3 ETR AM/FM stereo with CD and equalizer ($250 to $425 depending on model and other options on car). UN6 AM/FM stereo with auto-reverse (sedan with 1SB/1SC no cost; without 1SB/1SC $195). UK3 steering wheel radio controls (from no cost with specific other options to $175). AUO remote keyless entry ($135). D81 rear deck lid spoiler for coupe without B4M/B5Z ($175). CF5 power glass sunroof ($646). R6S 16-in. crosslaced silver aluminum wheels, coupe with B4S only (no cost). R6G 16-in. crosslaced gold aluminum wheels, coupe with B4S only (no cost). PF9 16-in. five-spoke aluminum wheels, coupe with B4S only (no cost). NOW 16-in. five-blade aluminum wheels (for sedan with B4Q no cost; for sedan without B4Q $259).

BONNEVILLE OPTIONS: L36 3.8-liter 3800 Series II SFI V-6 for SE/SEE models (standard). L67 3.8-liter 3800 SFI supercharged V-6 (SSE no cost; SE $1,362). FE9 50-state emissions (no cost). YF5 50-state emissions (no cost). NG1 50-state emissions (no cost). QPH P215/65R15 black sidewall steel-belted radial touring Tires on SE (no cost). QNX P225/60R16 black sidewall steel-belted radial touring tires (SSE standard; SE with 1SD or Y52 no cost; other SE's $84). QVG P225/60HR16 black sidewall steel-belted radial performance tires (SSE requires WA6 or included with supercharged SSE). AM6 45/55 split bench seat interior (standard). AS7 bucket seats ($314 with 1SB; $218 with 1SC; no cost with 1SD). AS7/1SD leather trim bucket seats ($1,213 with 1SB; $1,067 with 1SC; no cost with 1SD). SSE bucket seats with cloth trim (standard). AS7 bucket seats with leather trim ($779). AL7 articulating bucket seats with leather trim, not available on 1SA ($1,024). SE sedan 1SB option package ($836). SE sedan 1SC option package ($1,287). SE sedan 1SD option package ($3,057). SSE sedan. 1SA option package, includes vehicle and standard equipment (standard). SSE sedan 1SB option package ($1,250). Y52 Computer Command ride and handling package (with 1SC $1,183; with 1SD without L67 $775; with L67 $600). WA6 SSEi supercharger package, includes 3.8-liter 3800 V-6 supercharged engine with driver-selectable shift four-speed transmission; cluster with turbo boost gauge; P225/60H16 performance tires; traction control; SSEi floor mats; and SSEi nameplates (with 1SA $1,342; SSE with 1SB $1,167). UA6 anti-theft alarm system ($190). FW1 Computer Command Ride, SSE ($380). KO5 engine block heater ($18). VK3 front license plate bracket (no cost). C68 automatic electric air conditioning; AG1 power driver's seat (with 1SA $305; with 1SB/1SC/1SD no cost). AG2 power passenger's seat (with 1SA $305; with 1SB/1SC/1SD no cost). US7 power antenna without 1SD, UT6 or UP3 ($85). UK3 leather-wrapped steering wheel (with UP3 or UT6 no cost; others $125-$175). UN6 ETR AM/FM stereo with cassette without 1SB/1SC/1SD ($195). U1C ETR AM/FM stereo with CD with 1SB/1SC/1SD $100; without 1SB/1SC/1SD $295. UW6 six

1996 Pontiac Bonneville SSEi four-door Sport Sedan. (PGMC)

speaker performance sound system ($100), UN6 ETR AM/FM stereo with CD, equalizers, six speakers (SE sedan without 1SD or leather $385; with leather without 1SD $335; with 1SD $150). UP3 ETR AM/FM stereo with CD, equalizers, seven speakers (without 1SD or leather $485; without 1SD with leather $435; with 1SD $250; SSE $100). AUO remote keyless entry without 1SD or 1SC ($135). D58 rear deck lid spoiler delete ($110 credit). T43 rear deck lid spoiler, SE sedan without 1SD ($110). CF5 power glass sunroof ($995). NW9 traction control ($175). N73 16-in. gold aluminum crosslace wheels without 1SD or Y52 ($324). PA2 16-in. aluminum machine face crosslace wheels without 1SD or Y52 ($324). PF5 16-in. five-blade aluminum wheels, SE sedan without 1SD ($324).

TRANS SPORT OPTIONS: FE9 50-state emissions (no cost). YF5 50-state emissions (no cost). NG1 50-state emissions (no cost). XIN P205/70R15 black sidewall all-season touring tires (with P42 or 1SE no cost; without P42 or 1SE $35). ZP7/C7 seven-passenger Doral cloth seating (with 1SB/1SC/1SD no cost; others $705). ZP7/27 seven-passenger Prado leather seating (with 1SD/1SE $870). 1SA Trans Sport option package, includes vehicle with standard equipment (no cost). 1SB Trans Sport option package (no cost). 1SC Trans Sport option package ($1,883). 1SD Trans Sport option package ($2,263). 1SE Trans Sport option package ($3,367). C34 front-and-rear air conditioning in Trans Sport ($450). G67 Auto Level Control ($170-$200). C49 electric rear window defogger ($170). KO5 engine block heater ($18). VK3 front license plate bracket (no cost). AJ1 deep-tinted glass ($245) AD8 one integral child seat ($125). AD9 two integral child seats ($225). V54 luggage rack, includes saddlebag storage ($175). DK6 overhead console ($175). D84 two-tone paint, requires PH6 wheels and XIN tires ($125). AB5 power door locks ($300). AG9 driver six-way power seat ($270). E58 power sliding door; A31 power windows ($275). UM6 Delco radio equipment ($140). UX1 ETR AM/FM with cassette and 5-band equalizer (with 1SD $315; with 1SE no cost). U1A ETR AM/FM CD and five-band equalizer (with 1SD $541; with 1SE $226). AUO remote keyless entry ($135). C54 pop-up sunroof ($300). V92 trailer provisions ($150). P42 15-in. self-sealing touring tires ($185). PH6 15-in. aluminum wheels ($259). 15P 15-in. aluminum wheels ($259).

NOTE: Full option package contents, descriptions, and applications information can often be determined by consulting factory literature. The data above is edited for size and clarity. This information provided only as a guide to help collectors appraise the relative value of cars with numerous options. Prices for items included as part of a value option package are usually much less than individual prices. Option prices charged by individual dealers may also vary.

1996 Pontiac Bonneville SSEi four-door Sport Sedan. (PGMC)

1996 Pontiac Bonneville SSEi four-door Sport Sedan. (PGMC)

HISTORICAL: Pontiac's total 1996 model-year production was 579,360 vehicles including 2,345 Firefly models and 420 Sunrunner models. This includes units manufactured in Canada and other countries that were intended for distribution in the United States. Calendar-year sales were 529,710 cars and 21,397 Trans Sport MPVs, for a grand total of 551,107 vehicles. General Motors merged its Pontiac and GMC divisions in 1996 to create the Pontiac-GMC Division with 3,736 franchised dealers. Roy S. Roberts was appointed general manager of the new division.

1997 PONTIAC

1997 Pontiac Sunfire GT two-door coupe. (PGMC)

1997 Pontiac Sunfire SE four-door sedan. (PGMC)

SUNFIRE — CARLINE J — (FOUR) — Pontiac added Mexican production in 1997, building Sunfire coupes at an assembly plant in Ramos Arizpe, Mexico, as well as at Lordstown, Ohio. The Sunfire convertibles were built in Lansing, Mich. There was more standard equipment on this year's SE convertible, including a four-speed automatic transmission, delay wipers, a rear window defogger, and cruise control. All Sunfires were modified to comply with new dynamic side-impact government crash standards. **SE coupe and sedan:** Dual front airbags; power front disc/rear drum four-wheel antilock brakes; child-resistant rear door lock system in sedan; RPO LN2 2.2-liter overhead valve four-cylinder 120-hp engine; Soft-Ray tinted glass; analog instrumentation with tachometer; dual break-away exterior mirrors (left-hand mirror remote controlled); PASS-Lock theft deterrent system; AM/FM stereo radio with seek up/down; clock and fixed mast antenna; five-passenger seating with Milli-weave cloth trim (front reclining bucket seats and three-passenger full-folding rear seat); P195/70R14 all-season black sidewall tires with compact spare tire; RPO MM5 five-speed manual transmission; wet-arm windshield wipers with fixed-delay pulse; 14-in. custom bolt-on wheel covers. **SE convertible:** In addition to or in place of the SE coupe and sedan standard equipment, the SE convertible featured P195/65R15 black sidewall steel-belted radial touring tires; 15-in. custom bolt-on wheel covers; R134A air conditioning; cruise control; electric rear window defogger; tilt steering; controlled-cycle windshield wipers; and RPO MX0 four-speed automatic transmission. **GT coupe:** In addition or in place of SE coupe standard equipment, the Sunfire GT featured P205/55R16 steel-belted radial black sidewall tires, PGO 16-in. GT-specific cast aluminum wheels, and 2.4-liter Twin Cam four-cylinder engine.

GRAND AM — CARLINE N — (FOUR) — Grand Am's SE and GT trim levels returned, each offering a coupe and sedan. Drive train availability mirrored what was offered the previous year. Changes were minimal with one exception being the addition of previously optional air conditioning as standard equipment on all 1997 Grand Ams. Calendar-year sales of 204,078 units put the Grand Am in 10th spot among U.S. car sales with a 2.5 percent market share. **SE coupe/sedan:** Four-gauge cluster with tachometer and trip odometer; dual front airbags; air conditioning; power front disc/rear drum four-wheel antilock brakes; automatic power door locks; child-resistant rear sedan door locks; RPO LD9 2.4-liter Twin Cam 150-hp four-cylinder engine; Soft-Ray tinted glass; dual exterior sport mirrors (left-hand remote controlled; right-hand manual); PASSLock theft-deterrent system; AM/FM stereo radio with seek up/down; clock and fixed mast antenna; front reclining bucket seats with cloth trim; three-passenger rear bench seat with headrests; P195/70R14

black sidewall tires; compact spare tire; RPO MM5 five-speed manual transmission; wet-arm windshield wipers; and 14-in. custom bolt-on wheel covers. **GT coupe:** In addition or in place of SE equipment, the Grand Am GT included an adjustable tilt steering wheel, P205/55R16 black sidewall Eagle RSA performance tires, a larger compact spare tire, controlled-cycle windshield wipers, and 16-in. cast aluminum GT wheels.

FIREBIRD — CARLINE F — (V-6/V-8) — "Either you get it or you don't!" That's what a talented and perceptive copywriter said about '97 Firebirds. "The first rule of success is to equip yourself with the proper tools. This axiom not only applies to business, but to automobiles as well. Firebird provides drivers with what's needed for command of the road." Models and engines carried over from 1996, but new performance and appearance options were added. A Ram Air Performance and Handling Package was offered for convertibles. Ram Air ragtops featured a 5.7-liter V-8, twin scoops with Ram Air logos on each "nostril," high-polished dual exhaust tips, and 17-in. aluminum rims. A new package, introduced in mid-1996, was a Sport and Appearance Package for V-6 Firebirds with ground effects, fog lamps, and dual exhausts with cast aluminum extensions. New Firebird interior features included a console with an auxiliary power outlet for electronic devices, a pull-out cup holder, and revised storage. Air conditioning became standard and all-leather power seats were now available. A four-way seat adjuster and daytime running lamps were added standard equipment. New options included a 500-watt Monsoon sound system. **Firebird coupe:** Standard equipment included dual front airbags; air conditioning; power front disc/rear drum four-wheel antilock brakes; side window defoggers; RPO L36 3800 Series II 200-hp SFI V-6 engine; Solar-Ray tinted glass; full instrumentation with tachometer and trip odometer; sport exterior mirrors; left-hand remote controlled; PASS-Key II theft-deterrent system; AM/FM stereo ETR radio and cassette with seven-band graphic equalizer; touch control; search-and-replay; Delco theft lock; clock; seek up/down; remote CD prewiring; four-speaker coaxial sound system and fixed mast antenna; reclining front bucket seats with cloth trim; four-way dual; manual front seat adjusters; rear two-passenger folding seat; tilt steering column; P215/60R16 touring tires with high-pressure compact spare; RPO MM5 five-speed manual transmission; controlled-cycle windshield wipers; and 16-in. cast aluminum wheels. **Formula coupe:** Formula models also include (in addition or in place of the above) brake/transmission shift interlock; four-wheel power disc brakes with antilock; RPO LT1 5.7-liter 285-hp SFI V-8 engine; P235/55R16 touring tires with high-pressure compact spare; and RPO MX0 four-speed automatic transmission. **Trans Am coupe:** Trans Am models

1997 Pontiac Grand Am GT four-door sedan. (PGMC)

286

1997 Pontiac Grand Am GT four-door sedan. (PGMC)

also include (in addition to or in place of Formula features) cruise control; electric rear window defogger; power door locks; leather appointment group with leather-wrapped steering wheel; shift knob and parking brake handle; and dual power mirrors with blue-tinted glass. **Firebird/Formula convertibles:** convertibles also include (in addition to or in place of respective coupe features) audible content theft-deterrent system; cruise control; rear window defogger; power door locks; remote keyless entry; dual blue-tinted power mirrors; six-speaker sound system; and power windows. **Trans Am convertible:** Trans Am convertibles also include (in addition to or in place of Firebird/Formula convertible features) remote keyless entry and P245/50ZR16 all-season speed-rated tires.

GRAND PRIX — CARLINE W — (V-6/V-8) — The 1997 Grand Prix series had an all-new Wide Track stance and revised model lineup. There was an SE sedan and GT coupe and sedan. Produced at the Fairfax assembly plant in Kansas City, Kansas, the Grand Prix featured a two-inch wider front track and a three-inch longer wheelbase. It had a low-profile roof, new front and rear fascias, aerodynamic headlamps with reflector optics, standard integrated fog lamps, new sculpted tail lamps that integrated lighting functions, and twin post body-colored power mirrors. Inside was an all-new "cockpit" interior. The SE sedan used the 3.1-liter V-6 with an electronically-controlled four-speed automatic transmission. GT models used the 3800 Series II 3.8-liter V-6. A GT option was a GTP Performance package with a supercharged 240-hp 3800 Series II engine and driver-selectable shift. **Grand Prix SE:** Standard equipment included dual front airbags; air conditioning; brake/transmission shift interlock; four-wheel power disc brakes with antilock; automatic programmable door locks with delayed locking and lockout protection (rear child security locks in SE sedan); RPO L82 3.1-liter 3100 160-hp SFI V-6; Soft-Ray tinted glass; analog instrumentation including tachometer and trip odometer; dual body-color exterior power mirrors; AM/FM ETR stereo radio with seek-scan feature and four speakers; six-way manually adjustable driver's bucket seat with two-way manual lumbar support; three-passenger rear bench seat with integrated headrests; tilt steering wheel; P205/70R15 black sidewall touring tires; RPO MX0 four-speed automatic transmission; wet-arm controlled-cycle windshield wipers; and power windows with driver's side "express down" feature. **Grand Prix GT:** In addition to or in place of SE equipment, standard GT features included cruise control (sedan only), RPO L36 3800 Series II 195-hp V-6, dual outlet exhausts with bright tips, AM/FM stereo radio with cassette (sedan only), P225/60R16 touring tires, and 16-in. cast aluminum wheels.

BONNEVILLE — CARLINE H — (V-6) — Pontiac said that the 1997 Bonneville was built "for the American Autobahn." New for the year was an ETC four-speed automatic transmission with the supercharged engine, an adjustable "heads-up" display, a Delco/Bose premium sound system, Magnasteer variable effort power steering, remote keyless entry, and electronic load leveling. The last three features were standard on SSEs and optional on SEs. Model-year sales held steady at 77,105 units. **SE sedan:** Standard Bonneville SE equipment included dual front airbags; manual air conditioning; analog instrument cluster with tachometer; brake/transmission shift interlock; power front disc/rear drum brakes with four-wheel antilock; cruise control with resume; electric rear window defogger; automatic power door locks with lockout protection and delayed locking feature; RPO L36 3.8-liter 3800 Series II 205-hp SFI V-6; Soft-Ray tinted glass; dual sport outside mirrors (left-hand remote control;

right-hand manual); PASS-Key II theft-deterrent system; AM/FM stereo radio with clock; four speakers and fixed mast antenna; six-passenger seating with 45/55 split front bench seat with manual recliners; tilt steering wheel; storage armrest with dual cup holders; rear split bench seat with trunk pass through; P215/65R15 black sidewall touring tires with compact spare; RPO MX0 four-speed automatic transmission; 15-in. bolt-on wheel covers; and power windows with driver's side "express down" feature. **SSE/SSEi sedan:** In addition to or in place of the above, the Bonneville SSE/SSEi models included automatic air conditioning with outside temperature indicator; driver information center with electric compass; door ajar light; hood ajar light and service reminders; stainless steel dual exhaust system; remote keyless entry; dual heated power exterior mirrors with blue tint; AM/FM stereo radio with auto-reverse cassette; seven-band equalizer; clock; touch control; seek up/down; search-and-replay feature; leather-wrapped steering wheel with radio controls; power antenna; six-speaker sound system and Delco theft lock; five-passenger seating with 45/45 six-way power front bucket seats; P225/60R16 black sidewall touring tires with compact spare; and 16-in. cast aluminum wheels. **Special Edition 40th Anniversary Bonneville:** This special production model was available in both SE and SSE models and could be ordered in either of two special anniversary colors: Dark Cherry Metallic or Silver Mist Metallic (available in spring). The Special Edition 40th Anniversary Bonneville offered exclusive content, including factory-installed 40th anniversary badging on left and right front panels, special 40th anniversary floor mats, rear spoiler, 16-in. aluminum wheels, leather seating areas, and 1SB option package. With the Bonneville SE the 1SB package included variable-effort power steering, six-way power driver's seat, power outside sport mirrors, illuminated entry system, remote deck lid release, AM/FM stereo with cassette, and trunk storage net. With the Bonneville SSE model the 1SB package included traction control, theft-deterrent alarm system, six-way power front passenger seat, Bose eight-speaker sound system, Eye-Cue™ head-up display, and electrochromic inside rearview mirror.

TRANS SPORT — CARLINE U — (V-6) — An all-new steel-bodied eight-passenger Trans Sport MPV made in Doraville, Ga., replaced the plastic-bodied 1996 model. It was offered with a choice of two wheelbases and a driver's side rear door was optional on long-wheelbase versions. A revamp of the rear suspension made the longer model capable of carrying a 4 x 8-foot sheet of plywood with the tailgate closed. Trans Sport exclusives included modular seating and a Montana package with SUV styling cues, extra-traction tires, and a traction-control system. **Trans Sport SE Standard Wheelbase:** Standard equipment included a driver and front passenger airbag; integrated roof antenna; brake/transmission shift interlock safety feature; power front disc/rear drum four-wheel antilock brakes; soft fascia with integral rub strips; child security door lock; front side window defoggers; power door locks with signal-key automatic locking doors; 3.4-liter 3400 SFI V-6 engine; stainless steel exhaust system; solar-coated heat-repelling glass windshield; four flip-out rear side glass windows (Soft-Ray tinted); GM Computer Command Control; instrumentation including analog speedometer; odometer; tachometer; coolant temperature gauge; low oil indicator; low coolant indicator; voltmeter; trip odometer and door ajar signal; blue-tinted power left- and right-hand sport mirrors with fold-and-stow feature; Delco ETR AM/FM stereo radio with clock; rear window wipers; front reclining bucket seats with rotating headrest; manual lumbar adjustment and inboard armrest; seven-passenger split

1997 Pontiac Grand Am SE two-door coupe. (PGMC)

1997 Pontiac Grand Am SE four-door sedan. (PGMC)

folding modular 2-2-3 bench seat with integrated headrests (standard/extended wheelbase models); four-way manual adjusting driver's seat; four-spoke adjustable; tilting sport steering wheel with airbag; fully-independent MacPherson strut front suspension; rear coil spring suspension; P205/70R15 all-season steel-belted radial tires; four-speed automatic ETC transmission; Doral cloth upholstery; wet-arm controlled-cycle windshield wipers; and 15-in. styled wheels with bolt-on covers. **Trans Sport SE Extended Wheelbase**: Standard equipment included a driver and front passenger airbag; integrated roof antenna; brake/transmission shift interlock safety feature; power front disc/rear drum four-wheel antilock brakes; soft fascia with integral rub strips; child security door lock; front side window defoggers; power door locks with signal-key automatic locking doors; 3.4-liter 3400 SFI V-6 engine; stainless steel exhaust system; solar-coated heat-repelling glass windshield; four flip-out rear side glass windows (Soft-Ray tinted); GM Computer Command Control; instrumentation including analog speedometer; odometer; tachometer; coolant temperature gauge; low oil indicator; low coolant indicator; voltmeter; trip odometer and door ajar signal; blue-tinted power left- and right-hand sport mirrors with fold-and-stow feature; Delco ETR AM/FM stereo radio with clock; rear window wipers; front reclining bucket seats with rotating headrest; manual lumbar adjustment and inboard armrest; seven-passenger split folding modular 2-2-3 bench seat with integrated headrests (standard/extended wheelbase models); four-way manual adjusting driver's seat; four-spoke adjustable; tilting sport steering wheel with airbag; fully-independent MacPherson strut front suspension; rear coil spring suspension; P215/70R15 all-season tires; four-speed automatic ETC transmission; Doral cloth upholstery; wet-arm controlled-cycle windshield wipers; and 15-in. styled wheels with bolt-on covers.

I.D. DATA: The vehicle identification number (VIN) is located on the top left-hand surface of the instrument panel and is visible through the windshield. The VIN has 17 symbols. The first symbol indicates the country of manufacture (1 or 4=United States; 2=Canada; 3=Mexico). The second symbol indicates the manufacturer (G=General Motors). The third symbol indicates the make/division (2=Pontiac; M=MPV and 7=GM of Canada). The fourth, fifth symbols indicate the car line and series (F/S=Firebird and convertible; F/V=Formula-Trans Am and convertible; H/X=Bonneville SE; H/Z=Bonneville SSE/SSEi; J/B=Sunfire SE and convertible; J/D=Sunfire GT; N/E=Grand Am SE; N/W= Grand Am GT; W/J=Grand Prix SE; W/P=Grand Prix GT; U=All-Purpose Vehicle 4x2; X=All-Purpose Vehicle Extended 4x2). The sixth symbol indicates body style (1=two-door coupe models 27, 37, 47 and 57; 2=two-door models 07, 08, 77, 87; 3=two-door convertible model 67; 5=four-door sedan models 19 and 69; 6=four-door models 29 and 68; 6=All-Purpose Vehicle). The seventh symbol indicates the restraint system: 2=Active manual belts with driver and passenger inflatable restraints; 4=Active manual belts front and side. The eighth symbol indicates the engine type: K=RPO L36 3.8-liter V-6; M=RPO L82 3.1-liter V-6; P=RPO LT1 5.7-liter V-8; T=RPO LD9 2.4-liter L4; 1=RPO L67 3.8-liter V-8; 4=RPO LN2 2.2-liter L4 and E=RPO LA1 3.4-liter V-6. (Note: All Pontiac engines made in U.S. except "M" also made in Canada; all are MFI multi-point fuel-injected engines). The ninth symbol is a check digit. The 10th symbol indicates model year (V=1997). The 11th symbol indicates the GM assembly plant (B=Baltimore, Md., T&B; B=Lansing, Mich., GENASYS; C=Lansing, Mich.; C=Charlotte, Mich., T&B; D=Doraville, Ga.; E=Pontiac, Mich.,

East T&B; F=Fairfax II, Kan.; F=Flint, Mich., T&B; G=Silao Mexico; H=Flint, Mich.; J=Janesville, Wis.; K=Linden, N.J., T&B; M=Lansing, Mich.; M=Toluca Mexico; R=Arlington, Texas; R=Russelsheim Germany; S=Ramos Arizpe Mexico; T=Shreveport, La.; U=Hamtramck, Mich.; Y=Wilmington, Del.; Z=Fremont, Calif.; Z=Spring Hill, Tenn.; Z=Ft. Wayne, Ind. T&B; 1=Oshawa Canada, T&B; 1=Oshawa Canada, #2; 1=Wentzville, Mo., T&B; 2=Morraine, Ohio, T&B; 2=Ste. Therese Canada; 3=Detroit, Mich., T&B; 3=Kawasaki Japan; 4=Orion, Mich.; 5=Bowling Green, Ken.; 6=Ingersoll, Ontario Canada; 6=Oklahoma City, Okla.; 7=Lordstown, Ohio; 7=Flusawa Japan; 8=Shreveport, La., T&B; 8=Tillisonburg, Ohio, CANEXPO; 9=Oshawa, Ontario Canada, #1). Pontiacs are not produced at all of these plants. The last six symbols are the consecutive unit number at the factory.

Model Number	Body Style Number	Body Type & Seating	Factory Price	Shipping Weight	Production Total
SUNFIRE SE SERIES B (I-4)					
J/B	B37V	2d Coupe-4P	12,599	2,679	Note 1
J/B	B69V	4d Sedan-4P	12,699	2,723	Note 1
J/B	B67V	2d Convertible-4P	19,399	2,835	Note 1
SUNFIRE GT SERIES D (I-4)					
J/D	D37V	2d Coupe-4P	14,219	2,829	Note 1
GRAND AM SE SERIES E (I-4)					
N/E	E37V	2d Coupe-4	15,159	2,881	Note 2
N/E	E69V	4d Sedan-4P	15,159	2,954	Note 2
GRAND AM GT SERIES W (I-4)					
N/W	W37V	2d Coupe-4P	16,399	2,932	Note 2
N/W	W69V	4d Sedan-4P	16,399	3,011	Note 2
FIREBIRD SERIES S (V-6)					
F/S	S87V	2d Coupe-4P	17,649	3,131	Note 3
F/S	S67V	2d Convertible-4P	23,559	3,346	Note 3
FORMULA SERIES V (V-8)					
F/V	V87V	2d Coupe-4P	21,179	3,373	Note 3
F/V	V67V	2d Convertible-4P	26,949	3,489	Note 3
TRANS AM SERIES V (V-8)					
F/V	V87V	2d Coupe-4P	23,339	3,345	Note 3
F/V	V87V	2d Convertible-4P	28,899	3610	Note 3
GRAND PRIX SE SERIES J (V-6)					
W/J	J69V	4d Sedan-4P			18,579
3,381	Note 4				
GRAND PRIX GT SERIES P (V-6)					
W/J	P37V	2d Coupe-4	19,359	3,396	Note 4
W/J	P69V	4d Sedan-4P	20,359	3,414	Note 4
BONNEVILLE SE SERIES X (V-6)					
X	X69V	4d Sedan-6P	22,719	3,446	Note 5
BONNEVILLE SSE SERIES Z (V-6)					
Z	Z69V	4d Sedan-6P	27,769	3,587	Note 5
BONNEVILLE SSEi SERIES Z (Supercharged V-6)					
Z	Z69V	4d Sedan-6P	29,111	3,691	Note 5
TRANS SPORT SE REGULAR WHEELBASE SERIES U (I-4)					
U	N06V	3d Minivan	21,049	3,702	Note 6
TRANS SPORT SE EXTENDED WHEELBASE SERIES U (I-4)					
U	M06V	3d Minivan	22,009	3,825	Note 6
U	M16V	4d Minivan	23,939	3,920	Note 6

NOTE 1: Model-year production total was 157,590 Sunfires of all types.

NOTE 2: Model-year production total was 235,738 Grand Ams of all types.

NOTE 3: Model-year production total was 32,692 Firebirds of all types.

NOTE 4: Model-year production total was 159,140 Grand Prixs of all types.

NOTE 5: Model-year production total was 79,392 Bonnevilles of all types.

1997 Pontiac Firebird two-door coupe. (PGMC)

NOTE 6: Model-year production total was 63,820 Trans Sports of all types.

SUNFIRE ENGINES

ENGINE [Base Four SE]: Inline. OHV. Four-cylinder. Cast-iron block. Aluminum head and intake manifold. Two valves per cylinder. Displacement: 133 cid. (2.2L). Bore & stroke: 3.50 x 3.46 in. Compression ratio: 9.0:1. Net horsepower: 120 at 5200 rpm. Torque: 130 lbs.-ft. at 4000 rpm. Fuel system: SFI. VIN Code: 4. RPO Code: LN2.

ENGINE [Base Four (GT); Optional (SE)]: Inline. DOHC. Four-cylinder. Cast-iron block. Aluminum head and intake manifold. Four valves per cylinder. Displacement: 146 cid. (2.4L). Bore & stroke: 3.54 x 3.79 in. Compression ratio: 9.5:1. Net horsepower: 150 at 6000 rpm. Torque: 155 lbs.-ft. at 4400 rpm. Fuel system: SFI. VIN Code: T. RPO Code: LD9.

GRAND AM ENGINES

ENGINE [Base Four SE/GT]: Inline. DOHC. Four-cylinder. Cast-iron block. Aluminum head and intake manifold. Four valves per cylinder. Displacement: 146 cid. (2.4L). Bore & stroke: 3.54 x 3.79 in. Compression ratio: 9.5:1. Net horsepower: 150 at 6000 rpm. Torque: 155 lbs.-ft. at 4400 rpm. Fuel system: SFI. VIN Code: T. RPO Code: LD9.

ENGINE [Optional Six]: V-block. OHV. Six-cylinder. Cast-iron block and head. Aluminum intake manifold. Displacement: 191 cid. (3.1L). Bore & stroke: 3.50 x 3.31 in. Compression ratio: 9.5:1. Brake horsepower: 155 at 5200 rpm. Torque: 185 lbs.-ft. at 4000 rpm. Fuel system: SFI. VIN Code: M. RPO Code: L82.

FIREBIRD ENGINES

ENGINE [Base V-6]: V-block. OHV. Six-cylinder. Cast-iron block and head. Aluminum intake manifold. Displacement: 231 cid. (3.8L). Bore & stroke: 3.80 x 3.40 in. Compression ratio: 9.4:1. Brake horsepower: 200 at 5200 rpm. Torque: 225 lbs.-ft. at 4000 rpm. Fuel system: SFI. VIN Code: K. RPO Code: L36.

ENGINE [Base V-8]: V-block. OHV. Eight-cylinder. Cast-iron block and head. Aluminum intake manifold. Displacement: 350 cid. (5.7L). Bore & stroke: 4.00 x 3.48 in. Brake horsepower: 285 at 5000 rpm. Torque: 325 lbs.-ft. at 2400 rpm. Compression ratio: 10.5:1. Fuel system: SFI. VIN Code: 5. RPO Code: LT1.

GRAND PRIX ENGINES

ENGINE [Base V-6]: V-block. OHV. Six-cylinder. Cast-iron block and head. Aluminum intake manifold. Displacement: 191 cid. (3.1L). Bore & stroke: 3.50 x 3.31 in. Compression ratio: 9.5:1. Brake horsepower: 160 at 5200 rpm. Torque: 185 lbs.-ft. at 4000 rpm. Fuel system: SFI. VIN Code: M. RPO Code: L82.

ENGINE [Optional V-6]: V-block. Six-cylinder. Cast-iron block and head. Aluminum intake manifold. Displacement: 231 cid. (3.4L). Bore & stroke: 3.80 x 3.40 in. Compression ratio: 9.0:1. Brake horsepower: 195 at 5200 rpm. Torque: 220 lbs.-ft. at 4,000 rpm. Fuel system: SFI. VIN Code: X. RPO Code: L36.

BONNEVILLE ENGINES

ENGINE [Base Six SE/SSE]: "3800" SFI Series II V-6. V-block. OHV. Six-cylinder. Cast-iron block and head. Aluminum intake manifold. Displacement: 231 cid. (3.8L). Bore & stroke: 3.80 x 3.40 in. Compression ratio: 9.0:1. Brake horsepower: 205 at 5200 rpm. Torque: 230 lbs.-ft. at 4000 rpm. Fuel system: SFI. VIN Code: K RPO Code: L36

1997 Pontiac Firebird Trans Am two-door convertible. (PGMC)

1997 Pontiac Formula Firebird two-door coupe. (PGMC)

ENGINE [Supercharged Six SSEi]: "3800" Supercharged Series II V-6. V-block. OHV. Six-cylinder. Cast-iron block and head. Aluminum intake manifold. Displacement: 231 cid. (3.8L). Bore & stroke: 3.80 x 3.40 in. Compression ratio: 8.5:1. Brake horsepower: 240 at 5200 rpm. Torque: 280 lbs.-ft. at 3200 rpm. Fuel system: SFI. VIN Code: 1 RPO Code: L67

TRANS SPORT ENGINE

ENGINE [Base V-6]: V-block. DOHC. Six-cylinder. Cast-iron block and head. Aluminum intake manifold. Displacement: 207 cid. (3.4L). Bore & stroke: 3.62 x 3.31 in. Compression ratio: 9.5:1. Brake horsepower: 180 at 5200 rpm. Torque: 205 lbs.-ft. at 4,000 rpm. Fuel system: SFI. VIN Code: E. RPO Code: LA1.

CHASSIS

SUNFIRE CHASSIS: Wheelbase: (All) 104.1 in. Overall length: (coupe) 182 in.; (sedan) 181.7 in.; (convertible) 182.4 in. Overall width: (coupe) 67.4 in.; (sedan) 67.3; (convertible) 68.4. Height: (coupe) 53.2 in.; (sedan) 54.8 in.; (convertible) 51.9 in. Standard tires: (SE coupe and sedan) steel-belted radial P195/70R14 black sidewall all-season; (SE convertible) steel-belted radial P195/65R15 black sidewall touring; (GT) steel-belted radial P205/55R16 black sidewall performance type.

GRAND AM CHASSIS: Wheelbase: (All) 103.4 in. Overall length: (SE coupe and SE sedan) 186.9 in.; (GT coupe and sedan) 187.3 in. Width: (All) 68.7 in. Height: (All) 53.5 in. Front tread: 55.6 in. Rear tread: 55.2 in. Standard tires: (SE) steel-belted radial P195/70R14 black sidewall; (GT) steel-belted radial P205/55R16 black sidewall Eagle RSA.

FIREBIRD CHASSIS: Wheelbase: (All) 101.0 in. Overall length: (Firebird/Formula) 195.6 in.; (Trans Am) 197 in. Width: (All) 74.5 in. Height: (Firebird/Formula coupe) 52.0 in.; (Firebird/Formula convertible) 52.7 in.; (Trans Am coupe) 51.7 in.; (Trans Am convertible) 52.4 in. Front tread: 60.7 in. Rear tread: 61.6 in. Standard tires: (Firebird) steel-belted radial P215/60R15 black sidewall touring; (Formula) steel-belted radial P235/55R16 touring; (Trans Am convertible) P245/50ZR16 speed-rated, all-weather.

GRAND PRIX CHASSIS: Wheelbase: (All) 110.5 in. Overall length: (All) 196.5. Width: (All) 72.7 in. Height: (All) 54.7 in. Standard tires: (SE sedan) 205/70R15 black sidewall touring; (GT coupe and sedan) P225/60R16 black sidewall touring.

BONNEVILLE CHASSIS: Wheelbase: (All) 110.8 in. Overall length: (SE sedan) 200.5 in.; (SSE/SSEi sedan) 201.1 in. Width: (All) 74.5 in. Height: (All) 55.7 in. Front tread: 60.3 in. Rear tread: 59.8 in. Standard tires: (SE) steel-belted radial 215/65R15 black sidewall touring. (SSE) steel-belted radial P225/60R16 black sidewall touring.

TRANS SPORT CHASSIS: Wheelbase: (Standard three-door) 112 in.; (Extended three-door) 120 in.; (Extended four-door) 120 in. Overall length: (Standard three-door) 187.4 in.; (Extended three-door) 201.4 in.; (Extended four-door) 201.4 in. Width: (All) 72.2 in. Height: (Standard three-door) 67.4 in.; (Extended three-door) 68.1 in.; (Extended four-door) 68.1 in. Standard tires: (Standard wheelbase) 205/70R-15 black sidewall all-season; (Extended wheelbase) P215/70R15 black sidewall all-season.

TECHNICAL

SUNFIRE TECHNICAL: Chassis: Front engine/front drive. Base transmission: Five-speed manual. Optional transmission: Three-speed automatic. Front suspension: MacPherson struts. Rear

1997 Pontiac Ram Air Firebird Trans Am two-door coupe. (PGMC)

suspension: Coil springs, semi-independent torsion beam, trailing arms. Steering: Rack-and-pinion. Front brakes: vented disc power-assisted. Rear brakes: drum power-assisted.

GRAND AM TECHNICAL: Chassis: Front engine/front drive. Base transmission: Five-speed manual with overdrive. Optional transmission: Three-speed automatic. Front suspension: MacPherson struts. Rear suspension: Trailing crank arm with twist arm, coil springs. Steering (Standard): Power-assisted rack-and-pinion. Steering (Sport Performance and WS6): Power-assisted rack-and-pinion, 14.0:1 ratio. Front brakes: Power-assisted vented discs. Rear brakes: Power-assisted drums. Fuel tank: 13.6 gal.

FIREBIRD TECHNICAL: Chassis: Front engine/rear drive. Base transmission: Five-speed manual. Front suspension: Modified MacPherson strut with anti-roll bar. Rear suspension: Live axle with coil springs, control arms, torque arm, track bar and anti-roll bar. Steering: Power re-circulating ball. Brakes: Power four-wheel discs with ABS.

GRAND PRIX TECHNICAL: Chassis: Front engine/front drive. Front suspension: MacPherson struts. Rear suspension: Tri-link independent suspension with anti-roll bar. Steering: Power-assisted rack-and-pinion. Four-wheel power disc brakes.

BONNEVILLE TECHNICAL: Chassis: Front engine/front drive. Base transmission: Four-speed automatic. Front suspension: MacPherson struts with anti-roll bar. Front suspension: (SE) MacPherson struts with anti-roll bar; (SSE) MacPherson struts with anti-roll bar. Rear suspension: MacPherson. Steering: Power-assisted rack-and-pinion. Brakes: Power front disc/rear drum with four-wheel ABS.

TRANS SPORT TECHNICAL: Chassis: Front engine/front drive. Transmission: Three-speed automatic. Front suspension: MacPherson strut, stamped lower control arms, stabilizer bar. Rear suspension: Open-section transverse beam on stamped steel trailing arms, tube shocks, coil springs and stabilizer bar. Steering: Power-assisted rack-and-pinion. Front brakes: Power-assisted vented rotors. Rear brakes: Power-assisted finned composite cast-iron drums.

OPTIONS

SUNFIRE OPTIONS: 1SA Sunfire SE coupe and sedan option package including vehicle with standard equipment (no cost). 1SB Sunfire SE coupe and sedan option group ($1,355). 1SC Sunfire SE coupe and sedan ($1,735). 1SD Sunfire SE coupe ($2,745) or SE sedan ($2,850). 1SA Sunfire SE convertible option package including vehicle with standard equipment (no cost). 1SB Sunfire SE convertible group ($765). 1SC Sunfire SE convertible ($1,205). 1SA Sunfire GT coupe option package including vehicle with standard equipment (no cost). 1SB Sunfire GT coupe ($1,845). 1SC Sunfire GT coupe ($2,570). FE9 Federal emissions with LD9 and MX0 (no cost). YF5 California emissions ($170). NG1 NY/Mass. Emissions ($170). LD9 2.4-liter Twin Cam four-cylinder engine for SE coupe or sedan ($450). QPF P195/65R15 black sidewall STL touring tires for SE coupe and sedan ($131). AS5 sport interior package with front bucket seats in Patina/Redondo cloth trim ($180). AS5 sport interior package with front bucket seats in Santos vinyl trim ($180). C60 custom air conditioning ($830). C41 non-air-conditioning (no cost). R6A convenience package ($41-80). K34 cruise control ($235). C49 electric window defogger ($180). K05 engine block heater ($20). VK3 front license plate bracket (no cost). AU3 power door locks

($220-$280). DG7 dual power sport mirrors ($90). A31 power windows, requires power door locks (SE/GT coupe $290; sedan $355). UK3 steering wheel radio controls ($125). UN6 Delco radio equipment ($195). UT6 ETR AM/FM stereo with cassette and equalizer (with 1SA $230; with 1SB or 1SC $35; with 1SD $100 credit). UP3 ETR AM/FM stereo with CD and equalizer (with 1SA $330; with 1SB or 1SC $135). AUO remote keyless entry ($150). DT4 smoker's package ($15). N33 tilt steering wheel ($150). T43 rear deck lid spoiler ($125). CF5 power sunroof ($556-595). MM5 five-speed transmission ($810 credit in SE convertible). MX1 three-speed automatic transmission ($550). MX0 four-speed automatic transmission ($810). PG1 15-in. bolt-on wheel covers (no cost). PF7 15-in. aluminum wheels; not available on GT ($280).

GRAND AM OPTIONS: 1SA SE option package (no cost). 1SB SE option package includes tilt steering; cycle wipers; cruise control; rear defogger; and radio with cassette ($825). 1SC SE coupe option package includes 1SB plus variable-effort power steering; split folding rear seat; power windows; power mirrors; remote keyless entry ($1,582). 1SC SE sedan option package includes 1SB plus variable-effort power steering; split folding rear seat; power windows; power mirrors; remote keyless entry ($1,647). 1SA GT option package (no cost). 1SB GT option package includes cruise control; rear defogger and radio with cassette; and variable-effort power steering ($672). 1SC GT coupe option package includes 1SB plus split folding rear seat; power windows; power mirrors; remote keyless entry ($1,367). 1SC GT sedan option package includes 1SB plus split folding rear seat; power windows; power mirrors; remote keyless entry ($1,432). R5B includes UP3 sound system and CF5 power glass sunroof ($405-$600). FE9 Federal emissions (no cost). YF5 California emissions ($170). NG1 N.Y./Mass. Emissions ($170). L82 3.1-liter 3100 SFI V-6 ($405). QPD P195/65R15 touring tires, not available GT ($131). QMS P205/55R16 touring tires, not available GT ($223). B20 SE bucket seats with Cordae or Impulse cloth trim and Sports Interior group ($220). B20 bucket seats with Prado leather seating areas ($645-$860). K34 cruise control with resume-speed function ($235). C49 electric rear window defogger ($180). K05 engine block heater ($20). VK3 front license plate bracket (no cost). A31 power windows with express down ($290 coupe; $355 sedan). UK3 steering wheel radio controls ($125). UN6 ETR AM/FM stereo with cassette ($195). UT6 ETR AM/FM stereo with CD, equalizers, six speakers (without 1SB or 1SC $305; with 1SB or 1SC $110). UP3 ETR AM/FM stereo with CD, equalizers, six speakers (without 1SB or 1SC $405; with 1SB or 1SC $210). UN1 ETR AM/FM stereo with CD, cassette, equalizers, six speakers (without 1SB or 1SC $600; with 1SB or 1SC $405; with R6B $195). AUO remote keyless entry ($150). AG1 six-way power driver's seat ($340). AM9 split folding rear seat ($165). DT4 smoker's package ($15). T43 rear deck spoiler (standard GT; $170 SE). D58 delete rear deck spoiler on GT ($170 credit). N33 tilt steering (standard GT; $150 SE). CF5 power glass sunroof ($595). MM5 five-speed manual transmission (standard). MX0 four-speed automatic transmission ($810). PG1 15-in. bolt-on wheel covers for GT (no cost). PF7 15-in. cross-laced aluminum wheels for SE ($300). PG0 16-in. SE sport aluminum wheels ($325). 16P Bright White wheels for GT only (no cost). CD4 controlled cycle wipers for SE ($65).

FIREBIRD OPTIONS: 1SA Firebird coupe option package, includes vehicle with standard equipment (no cost). 1SB Firebird option group ($1,936). 1SA Formula coupe option package, includes vehicle with standard equipment (no cost). 1SB Formula coupe option group ($1,121). 1SA Trans Am coupe option package, includes vehicle with standard equipment (no cost). 1SA Firebird and Formula convertible option package, includes vehicle with standard equipment (no cost).

1997 Pontiac Grand Prix SE four-door sedan. (PGMC)

1997 Pontiac Grand Prix GT four-door sedan. (PGMC)

1SB Firebird and Formula convertible group ($435). 1SA Trans Am convertible option package, includes vehicle with standard equipment (no cost). R6A Firebird and Formula value package ($820). FE9 Federal emissions (no cost). YF5 50 California emissions (Firebird no cost; Formula/Trans Am $170). NG1 NY/Mass. Emissions (Firebird no cost; Formula/Trans Am $170). NB8 Calif./NY/Mass. Emissions override, requires FE9 (no cost). NC7 Federal emissions override, requires YF5 or NG1 (no cost). QCB P235/55R16 black sidewall touring tires for Firebird, standard Formula and Trans Am; not available Trans Am convertible ($132). QFZ P245/50ZR16 black sidewall steel-belted radial all-weather performance tires for Formula and Trans Am coupe ($245). QLC P245/50ZR16 black sidewall steel-belted radial performance tires for Formula and Trans Am ($245). QFK P275/40ZR17 speed-rated tires for Formula and Trans Am coupe with WS6 only (no cost). 23/AN3 articulating bucket seats with Prado leather (Firebird and Formula $804). 28/AQ9 articulating bucket seats with Prado leather (Trans Am coupe $829; Trans Am convertible $804). Y82 Trans Am coupe option (standard). Y84 Trans Am convertible option (standard). W68 Sport Appearance package includes aero components, fog lamps, dual outlet exhausts for base models, requires QCB tires and automatic transmission ($1,449). Y87 3800 performance package includes limited-slip differential, four-wheel disc brakes, up-level steering, dual outlet exhausts, QCB tires, and 3.42:1 axle if ordered with MX0 transmission, base models only ($550). 1LE Performance Package includes special handling suspension, larger stabilizer bars, stiffer springs, Koni shocks ($1,175). WS6 Ram Air performance and handling package, includes Ram Air induction system; functional air scoops; 17-in. five-spoke aluminum wheels; P275/40ZR17 speed-rated tires; and dual oval exhaust outlets ($3,345). UA6 content theft alarm ($90). K34 cruise control ($235). C49 electric rear window defogger ($180). CC1 hatch roof ($995). VK3 front license plate bracket (no cost). DG7 dual sport mirrors ($96). U75 power antenna, requires radio upgrade, standard on Trans Am convertible ($85). AU3 power door locks ($220). AG1 six-way power driver's seat ($270). A31 power windows ($290). W53 ETR AM/FM stereo with CD player, graphic equalizer, clock, seek up/down, and four coaxial speakers ($100). W54 ETR AM/FM stereo with auto-reverse, graphic equalizer, clock, seek up/down, remote

1997 Pontiac Grand Prix GT four-door sedan and Trans Sport Montana. (PGMC)

1997 Pontiac Grand Prix GTP four-door sedan. (PGMC)

CD pre-wiring, and 10-speaker sound system (coupes with 1SA $230; coupes with 1SB $130). W55 ETR AM/FM stereo with CD player, graphic equalizer, clock, seek up/down and 10-speaker sound system (coupes with 1SA $330; coupes with 1SB $230). W73 ETR AM/FM stereo with CD player, graphic equalizer, clock, seek up/down, and six-speaker sound system ($100). U1S trunk mounted remote 12-disc CD changer ($595). GU5 performance axle ($225). AUO remote keyless entry ($150). UK3 steering wheel radio controls (Firebird/Formula $200; Trans am $125). MN6 six-speed manual transmission in Formula/Trans Am (no cost). NW9 traction control ($450). MX0 four-speed automatic transmission ($815). PO5 chrome aluminum wheels, not available with 1SA Firebird coupe ($595).

GRAND PRIX OPTIONS: RPO L82 3.1-liter 3100 SFI V-6 (standard). RPO L36 3.8-liter 3800 Series II SFI V-6 in SE models ($415). L67 3.8-liter 3800 Series II supercharged SFI V-6, in GT models with BS4 GTP performance package (no cost). FE9 Federal emissions (no cost). YF5 California emissions ($170). NG1 NY/Mass. emissions ($170). QIN P205/70R15 black sidewall STL touring tires for sedan (standard). QNX P225/60R16 black sidewall STL touring tires for SE sedan ($160). QVG P225/60R16 black sidewall STL performance tires, available for sedan with B4S GTP performance package only (no cost). B6/AM6 45-55 split bench seat with Doral cloth in SE (no cost). B9/AR9 SE coupe bucket seat interior with leather trim ($475-$575 depending on model and option packages). B9/AR9 bucket seats with leather seating ($475-$575 depending on model and option packages). B19 SE custom interior group ($80-$210 depending on model and option packages). 1SA option package for SE sedan, includes vehicle and standard equipment (standard). 1SB option package for SE sedan ($670). 1SC option package for SE sedan ($1,305). 1SA option package for GT coupe, includes vehicle and standard equipment (standard). 1SB option package for GT coupe ($670). 1SC option package for GT coupe ($1,305). 1SD option package for GT coupe ($2,099). 1SA option package for GT sedan, includes vehicle and standard equipment (standard). 1SB option package for GT sedan ($765). 1SC option package for GT sedan ($1,589). B4S GTP performance package includes GTP nameplates, 3800 supercharged engine, four-speed automatic transmission with driver select shift, D81 rear deck lid spoiler, U40 trip computer, QVG tires, NV7 Magnasteer and QD1 wheels ($1,326-$1,526 depending upon model and option packages). CJ2 air conditioning with automatic temperature control and dual comfort zone ($195). U77 rear window antenna ($40). AN2 child seat ($125). C49 electric rear window defogger ($180). DD8 electrochromic inside rear view mirror ($60). K05 engine block heater ($20). Eye-Cue™ heads-up display ($250). KA1 heated driver's bucket seat with dual setting ($50). U40 trip computer ($200). VK3 front

1997 Pontiac Grand Prix GTP four-door sedan. (PGMC)

1997 Pontiac Bonneville SSE four-door Sport Sedan. (PGMC)

license plate bracket (no cost). AG1 six-way power driver's seat ($270). AG6 four-way power lumbar driver's seat ($100). TR9 premium lighting package (GT coupe $184; other models $214). UN6 AM/FM stereo with auto-reverse cassette and four speakers (GT coupe $195). U1C AM/FM stereo, seek-scan, CD player and four speakers ($100). UT6 ETR AM/FM stereo with graphic equalizer, steering wheel radio controls and eight-speaker premium sound system ($275 to $325 depending on model and other options on car). UP3 ETR AM/FM stereo with CD, graphic equalizer, steering wheel radio controls and eight-speaker premium sound system ($250 to $595 depending on model and other options on car). U1S multi-disc CD changer ($595). UQ3 premium sound system ($125). UK3 steering wheel radio controls ($125-$175 depending upon model and option packages). R7K rear seat pass through ($50). AUO remote keyless entry ($150). D81 rear deck lid spoiler ($175). CF5 power glass sunroof ($646). UA6 theft deterrent system ($60). NV7 variable-effort Magnasteer system ($93). NWO 16-in. aluminum machine-faced wheels for SE ($259). R6G 16-in. crosslace silver aluminum wheels (GT no cost; SE $259). RBG 16-in. crosslace Champagne-colored wheels (GT no cost; SE $259). 16P Bright White wheels for Bright White GTs only (no cost).

BONNEVILLE OPTIONS: SE sedan 1SA option package, includes vehicle and standard equipment (standard). SE sedan 1SB option package ($848). SE sedan 1SC option package ($1,144). SE sedan 1SD option package ($3,084). SSE sedan 1SA option package, includes vehicle and standard equipment (standard). SSE sedan 1SB option package ($1,455). FE9 Federal emissions (no cost). YF5 California emissions ($170). NG1 NY/Mass. emissions ($170). L67 3.8-liter 3800 SFI supercharged V-6 (SSE no cost; SE $1,362). QNX P225/60R16 black sidewall steel-belted radial touring tires (SSE standard; SE with 1SD or Y52 no cost; other SE's $84). QVG P225/60HR16 black sidewall steel-belted radial performance tires (SSE requires WA6 or included with supercharged SSEi). AM6 45/55 split bench seat interior (standard). AS7 bucket seats ($314 with 1SB; $218 with 1SC; no cost with 1SD). AS7/1SD leather trim bucket seats ($1,213 with 1SB; $1,067 with 1SC; no cost with 1SD). AS7 bucket seats with leather trim ($779). AL7 articulating bucket seats with leather trim, not available on 1SA ($1,024). Y52 Computer Command ride and handling package (with 1SC $1,183; with 1SD without L67 $775; with L67 $600). WA6 SSEi supercharger package, includes 3.8-liter 3800 V-6 supercharged engine with driver-selectable shift four-speed transmission; cluster with turbo boost gauge; P225/60H16 performance tires; traction control; SSEi

floor mats and SSEi nameplates (with 1SA $1,342; SSE with 1SB $1,167). UA6 anti-theft alarm system ($190). FW1 Computer Command Ride, SSE ($380). KO5 engine block heater ($20). VK3 front license plate bracket (no cost). AG1 power driver's seat (with 1SA $305; with 1SB/1SC/1SD no cost). AG2 power passenger's seat (with 1SA $305; with 1SB/1SC/1SD no cost). AUO remote keyless entry without 1SD, UT6 or UP3 ($85). UK3 leather-wrapped steering wheel (with UP3 or UT6 no cost; others $125-$175). UN6 ETR AM/FM stereo with cassette without 1SB/1SC/1SD ($195). U1C ETR AM/FM stereo with CD with 1SB/1SC/1SD ($100); without 1SB/1SC/1SD ($295). UW6 six-speaker performance sound system ($100). UT6 ETR AM/FM stereo with CD, equalizers, six speakers (SE sedan without 1SD or leather $385; with leather without 1SD $335; with 1SD $150). UP3 ETR AM/FM stereo with CD, equalizers, seven speakers (without 1SD or leather $485; without 1SD with leather $435; with 1SD $250; SSE $100). AUO remote keyless entry without 1SD or 1SC ($135). D58 rear deck lid spoiler delete ($110 credit). T43 rear deck lid spoiler, SE sedan without 1SD ($110). CF5 power glass sunroof ($995). NW9 traction control ($175). N73 16-in. gold aluminum crosslace wheels without 1SD or Y52 ($324). PA2 16-in. aluminum machine face crosslace wheels without 1SD or Y52 ($324). PF5 16-in. five-blade aluminum wheels, SE sedan without 1SD ($324). PO5 18-in. aluminum chrome Torque Star wheels (SE sedan without 1SD or Y52 $919; SE sedan with 1SD or Y52 $595; SSE $595).

TRANS SPORT OPTIONS: 1SA Trans Sport SE option package, includes vehicle with standard equipment (no cost). 1SB Trans Sport SE option package ($460). 1SC Trans Sport SE option package ($1,410). 1SD Trans Sport option package ($2,451). FE9 Federal emissions (no cost). YF5 California emissions ($170). NG1 NY/Mass. emissions ($170). ABA seven-passenger split bench Doral cloth seating, regular wheelbase ($335). ABB seven-passenger modular bucket seats with Multra/Diva cloth trim, regular wheelbase (without 1SD or WX4 $450; with 1SD or WX4 $115; extended wheelbase $115). ABD captain's chairs with Multra/Diva cloth (without 1SD or WX4 $600; with 1SD or WX4 $265; extended wheelbase $265). ZP8 eight-passenger seating with Multra/Diva cloth (without 1SD or WX4 $600; with 1SD or WX4 $265; extended wheelbase $265). WJ6 leather seating areas, includes UK3 leather steering wheel with radio controls ($1,055). C34 front-and-rear air conditioning in Trans Sport ($460). C49 electric rear window defogger ($180). KO5 engine block heater ($20). AJ1 deep-tinted glass ($245). C36 rear heater for extended-wheelbase model (with C34 or WX4 $167; without C34 or WX4 $177). AN2 one integral child seat ($125). AN5 two integral child seats ($225). V54 luggage rack, includes saddlebag storage ($175). WX4 Montana package (regular-wheelbase

1997 Pontiac Bonneville SE four-door Sport Sedan. (PGMC)

1997 Pontiac Bonneville SSEi four-door Sport Sedan. (PGMC)

1997 Pontiac Extended Wheelbase Trans Sport Minivan. (PGMC)

1997 Pontiac Extended Wheelbase Trans Sport Montana Minivan. (PGMC)

1998 Pontiac Sunfire SE four-door sedan. (PGMC)

without 1SD ($1,537); regular wheelbase with 1SD ($1,027); extended-wheelbase without 1SD ($1,164); extended-wheelbase with 1SD ($989). D84 two-tone paint ($125). AG1 six-way power driver's seat ($270). AG9 six-way power passenger seat ($305). E58 power sliding door ($350-$400). A31 power windows ($275). AU0 remote keyless entry ($150). UN6 Delco radio equipment ($195). UT6 AM/FM cassette with equalizer and rear seat audio ($150 with leather seat group or $335). U1C AM/FM CD player ($100). UP3 AM/FM CD player with equalizer and rear audio ($250 with leather seat group or $435). UM1 AM/FM cassette with equalizer, dual playback CD player, and rear seat audio ($350 with leather seat group or $535). UZ5 extended-range co-axial speakers ($50). G67 Auto Level Control ($180). R6A safety and security package (with P42 or WX4 $60; others $210). XPU P215/70R15 touring tires (regular wheelbase $73; extended wheelbase $35). P42 self-sealing touring tires ($150). V92 trailering provisions ($150). PH3 15-in. aluminum wheels ($259). CF5 sunroof, extended-wheelbase three-door model ($520 with 1SD or $695 without 1SD).

NOTE: Full option package contents, descriptions, and applications information can often be determined by consulting factory literature. The data above is edited for size and clarity. This information provided only as a guide to help collectors appraise the relative value of cars with numerous options. Prices for items included as part of a value option package are usually much less than individual prices. Option prices charged by individual dealers may also vary.

HISTORICAL: Pontiac-GMC's U.S. car model-year production rose to 730,988 units in 1997. That included 2,200 Firefly models and 416 Sunrunner models. During the calendar year, it sold 556,662 cars and 51,961 light trucks. This gave the division a 7.5 percent share of the total market and a 23.4 percent share of GM's combined passenger car and light truck sales. Roy S. Roberts continued as general manager of Pontiac-GMC Div. Starting late in 1997, the division began preparations to move its offices into GM's new World Headquarters building in Detroit's Renaissance Center.

1998 PONTIAC

1998 Pontiac Sunfire GT two-door coupe. (PGMC)

SUNFIRE — CARLINE J — (FOUR) — For 1998, the Pontiac Sunfire's 2.2-liter engine was enhanced with roller rocker arms, a new intake manifold, combustion chamber improvements, and a new cylinder head design. Reduced-power airbags were standard. Model-year U.S. sales were 86,794 units. **SE coupe and sedan:** Standard equipment included dual front airbags; a rear fixed-mass antenna; power front disc/rear drum four-wheel antilock brakes; a transmission shift interlock safety feature with automatic transmission; a child-resistant rear door lock system in sedana; the RPO LN2 2.2-liter overhead valve four-cylinder engine; a stainless steel exhaust system; Soft-Ray tinted glass; analog instrumentation (with a speedometer; odometer; tachometer; coolant temperature gauge; oil pressure indicator and trip odometer); dual breakaway exterior sport mirrors (left-hand remote controlled; right-hand manual); a day/night inside rearview mirror; right- and left-hand visor vanity mirrors with covers; a Delco ETR AM/FM stereo radio with seek up/down and clock; UM7 seating with front 45/45 reclining bucket seats (easy-entry front passenger seat in coupe only) and fully-folding three-passenger rear bench seat with integrated headrests; a four-spoke sport steering wheel; power rack-and-pinion steering; the PASS-Lock™ theft deterrent system; P195/70R14 all-season black sidewall tires with a compact spare tire; the RPO MM5 five-speed manual transmission; wet-arm windshield wipers with fixed-delay pulse; wet-arm windshield wipers with fixed delay pulse feature; and 14-in. custom bolt-on wheel covers. **SE convertible:** In addition to or in place of the SE coupe and sedan standard equipment, the SE convertible featured R134A air conditioning; cruise control; an electric rear window defogger; the 2.2-liter overhead valve four-cylinder engine; a UP3 ETR AM/FM radio with seek up/down, CD, graphic equalizer, digital clock, and premium speaker sound system; a tilt steering wheel with adjustable column; P195/65R15 black sidewall steel-belted radial touring tires; a four-speed automatic transmission with traction control; wet-arm controlled-cycle windshield wipers; and 15-in. custom bolt-on wheel covers. **GT coupe:** In addition or in place of SE coupe standard equipment, the Sunfire GT coupe featured the 2.4-liter Twin Cam four-cylinder engine; an easy-entry front passenger bucket seat; P205/55R16 steel-belted radial black sidewall performance tires; a five-speed manual transmission; wet-arm pulse windshield wipers with fixed-delay feature; and GT-specific 16-in. cast aluminum wheels. Cruise control was deleted from the GT coupe's standard equipment list.

GRAND AM — CARLINE N — (FOUR) — Aside from having less powerful dual airbags and modified inboard seat belt buckles in coupes, the 1998 Grand Am models were unchanged from the previous year. New 1999 Grand Ams began entering Pontiac showrooms in the spring of 1998. Model-year sales hit 174,812 units. **SE coupe/sedan:** Extensive acoustical insulation; dual airbags; a fixed

1998 Pontiac Sunfire SE two-door convertible. (PGMC)

mast antenna; a brake/transmission shift interlock safety feature with automatic transmission; power front disc/rear drum four-wheel antilock brakes; automatic power door locks with unlock/re-lock feature; child-resistant rear sedan door locks; the RPO LD9 2.4-liter Twin Cam 150-hp four-cylinder engine; a stainless steel exhaust system; polished oval exhaust outlets; Soft-Ray tinted glass; GM Computer Command Control; analog gauges (with a speedometer; odometer; tachometer; fuel gauge; temperature gauge and trip odometer); dual exterior sport mirrors (left-hand remote controlled; right-hand manual); a day/night inside rearview mirror; a right-hand visor vanity mirror; a Delco ETR AM/FM stereo radio with seek up/down and clock; Cordea cloth 45/45 front reclining bucket seats with easy-entry passenger seat; a three-passenger rear bench seat with integrated headrests; a four-spoke sport steering wheel; power rack and pinion steering; P195/70R14 black sidewall tires; a five-speed manual transmission; wet-arm windshield wipers; and 14-in. custom bolt-on wheel covers. **GT coupe:** In addition or in place of SE equipment, the Grand Am GT coupe included air conditioning; a stainless steel dual exhaust system; cast aluminum dual extensions; a leather appointment group (including leather-wrapped steering wheel; cobra head shifter and parking brake handle); a four-spoke sport tilt steering wheel with adjustable column; P205/55R16 black sidewall Eagle RSA performance tires; a larger compact spare tire; controlled-cycle windshield wipers; and specific three-spoke 16-in. cast aluminum GT wheels.

FIREBIRD — CARLINE F — (V-6/V-8) — "The automotive family tree includes the branch that bore muscle cars—those revered, big-engined road rockets of yore," said PMD's 1998 sales catalog. "As often happens when a species evolves, the strong get stronger." The hot, rear-dive 2+2 Firebird offered just five model choices in 1998, after dropping the Formula convertible. Previously base, Formula, and Trans Am convertibles were offered, but ragtop production failed to top 3,000 units in 1996-1997. Production numbers for 1998 were close to 2,100 ragtops. Coupes were again featured in base, Formula, and Trans Am trim levels. Formulas and Trans Ams got a new, all-aluminum 5.7-liter 305-hp V-8 with a six-speed manual transmission. A Ram Air package provided 320 hp. Styling was freshened with a front fascia that incorporated a new headlamp design. There were updated taillights, too. Suspension tuning was revised and base models received a one-piece driveshaft. Firebird V-8s with four-speed automatic transmissions had a larger torque converter. All Firebirds got standard four-wheel disc brakes. A mid-year Formula option was an AutoCross package with a beefed-up suspension. A $1,125-delete option that turned the Formula into a stripped-down street performance car was also new. **Firebird coupe:** Standard equipment on the base Firebird coupe included extensive acoustical insulation; dual front airbags; air conditioning; a black fixed mast antenna at right rear; a brake/transmission shift interlock safety feature with automatic transmission; power four-wheel disc brakes with four-wheel ABS; the RPO L36 3800 Series II 200-hp SFI V-6 engine; cruise control; electric rear and side window defoggers; Solar-Ray tinted glass; instrumentation (including an electric analog speedometer; a tachometer; odometer; coolant temperature indicator; oil pressure gauge; voltmeter and LED trip odometer); sport exterior mirrors (left-hand remote controlled); a day/night inside rearview mirror with reading lamps; left- and right-hand covered visor vanity mirrors; a Delco AM/FM stereo ETR radio and cassette (with seven-band graphic equalizer, touch control, search-and-

1998 Pontiac Grand Am SE four-door sedan. (PGMC)

replay, Delco theft lock, clock, seek up/down, remote CD prewiring, and four-speaker coaxial sound system); reclining front bucket seats; four-way driver and passenger front seat manual adjusters; a rear two-passenger folding seat; a four-spoke sport tilt steering wheel with adjustable column; the PASS-Key II theft-deterrent system; P215/60R16 touring tires with a high-pressure compact spare; the RPO MM5 five-speed manual transmission; controlled-cycle windshield wipers; and bright silver 16-in. five-spoke cast aluminum wheels. **Formula coupe:** Formula models also included (in addition or in place of the above) a power antenna; power door locks; power automatic sport mirrors with blue glass; a Delco 500-watt peak power Monsoon AM/FM stereo (with CD, seven-band graphic equalizer, clock, Touch Control, seek up/down, search, and replay; Delco anti-theft lock; high-performance 10-speaker sound system in coupe or six-speaker sound system in convertible; HSS speakers and tweeters in doors; 6.5-in. subwoofers in sail panels; subwoofer amp and four speakers; and tweeters in rear quarter panels); a leather-wrapped steering wheel with radio controls (including leather-wrapped steering wheel; shift knob and parking brake handle); P245/50ZR16 speed-rated all-weather tires; and power window controls with driver's "express down" feature (power mirrors and door locks required). **Trans Am:** Trans Am models also included (in addition to or in place of Formula features) an audible content theft-deterrent system, remote keyless entry, and a six-way power front driver's seat.

GRAND PRIX — CARLINE W — (V-6/V-8) — The all-new-for-'97 "Wide-Track" Grand Prix was slightly refined for 1998. De-powered airbags were standard equipment. Full-function traction control was used on models with the supercharged 3.8-liter V-6 and a new 4T65-E automatic transmission was standard on models with a normally-aspirated V-6. Model-year sales were 119,512 units. **Grand Prix SE:** Standard equipment included extensive acoustical insulation; dual front airbags; air conditioning; a fixed mast antenna; a brake/transmission shift interlock safety feature; four-wheel power disc brakes with antilock; automatic programmable door locks with delayed locking and lockout protection (rear child security locks in SE sedan); the RPO L82 3.1-liter 3100 160-hp SFI V-6; a stainless steel exhaust system; completely flush fitting Soft-Ray safety-laminated tinted glass; GM Computer Command Control; mechanical analog instrumentation (including tachometer; fuel gauge; coolant temperature indicator and trip odometer); body-colored and power-operated remote-control left- and right-hand sport-style outside rearview mirrors; a Delco ETR AM/FM stereo radio with seek/scan feature and clock; front sport bucket seats with Doral cloth interior fabric; a three-passenger rear bench seat with integrated head rests; a six-way manually adjustable driver's bucket seat with two-way manual lumbar support; front seat back storage pockets; a four-spoke sport tilt steering wheel with adjustable column; P205/70R15 black sidewall steel-belted radial touring tires; a four-speed ETC automatic transmission; 15-in. sport wheel covers; wet-arm controlled-cycle windshield wipers; and power windows with driver's side "express down" feature. **Grand Prix GT:** In addition to or in place of SE equipment, standard GT features included cruise control; the RPO L36 3800 Series II 195-hp V-6; a stainless steel exhaust system with dual bright outlet exhausts; a Delco 2001 series ETR AM/FM stereo radio with cassette, clock seek up/down, and auto reverse; a leather-wrapped sport steering wheel; P225/

1998 Pontiac Grand Am SE two-door coupe. (PGMC)

Standard Catalog of ® Pontiac, 2nd Edition

1998 Pontiac Formula Firebird two-door coupe. (PGMC)

60R16 black sidewall tires; and five-spoke 16 x 6.5-in. cast aluminum wheels.

BONNEVILLE — CARLINE H — (V-6) — Assembled in Orion Township and Flint, Mich., the Bonneville SE and SSE sedans mirrored the previous models, except that the optional supercharged 3.8-liter V-6 was no longer available on SE sedans. The SE sedan's optional Computer Command Ride (Y52) package was also discontinued. Now standard was a "next-generation" airbag system. Newly optional was an OnStar navigation system. SE models could also be ordered with the optional Special Edition Package featuring SLE exterior badges, plus SSE body side cladding, fascias, fog lamps, and grille. Model-year sales were 61,516 cars. Total '98 model output was 65,465 Bonnevilles. **SE sedan:** Standard Bonneville SE equipment included extensive acoustical insulation; dual front airbags; manual air conditioning; a brake/transmission shift interlock safety feature; power front disc/rear drum brakes with four-wheel antilock; cruise control with resume; an electric rear window defogger; automatic power door locks with lockout protection and delayed locking feature; the RPO L36 3.8-liter 3800 Series II SFI V-6; a stainless steel exhaust system; Soft-Ray tinted glass; backlit instrumentation (including analog speedometer; fuel and coolant temperature gauge; oil pressure gauge; voltmeter and tachometer); dual sport outside mirrors (left-hand remote control; right-hand manual); dual covered visor vanity mirrors; the PASS-Key II theft-deterrent system; a Delco ETR AM/FM stereo radio with clock, four speakers, and fixed mast antenna; six-passenger seating with a 45/55 split front bench seat with manual recliners; a four-spoke sport tilt steering wheel with adjustable column; a storage armrest with dual cup holders; Cartagena cloth upholstery; P215/65R15 black sidewall touring tires; a four-speed automatic transmission; 15-in. bolt-on wheel covers; and power windows with driver's side "express down" feature. **SSE/SSEi sedan:** In addition to or in place of the above, the Bonneville SSE/SSEi models included automatic air conditioning with an outside temperature indicator; a driver information center with electric compass; a door ajar light; hood ajar light and service reminders; an illuminated entry system; stainless steel dual exhaust system; remote keyless entry; dual heated power exterior mirrors with blue tint; a Delco 2001 series ETR AM/FM stereo radio with CD player, clock, theft lock, and Bose eight-speaker sound system; five-passenger seating with 45/45 six-way non-articulated power front bucket seats and leather seating areas; a leather-wrapped steering wheel with radio controls; Magnasteer variable-ratio power steering; a full-feature theft-deterrent system; P225/60R16 black sidewall Eagle LS touring tires; and three-blade silver 16-in. cast aluminum wheels.

TRANS SPORT — CARLINE U — (V-6) — The 1998 Trans Sport MPV got side-impact airbags for front passengers as standard equipment. Of course, they were of the new, lower-power type used in all Pontiacs this year. Dual sliding doors were now available on the short-wheelbase model and a power passenger-side sliding door was optional. The second- and third-row modular bench/bucket seats were also redesigned. **Trans Sport SE Regular Wheelbase:** Standard equipment on the regular wheelbase model included driver and front passenger airbags; an integrated roof antenna; a brake/transmission shift interlock safety feature; power front disc/rear drum four-wheel antilock brakes; a soft fascia with integral rub strips; child security door locks; front side window defoggers; power door locks with signal-key automatic locking doors; the 3.4-liter 3400 SFI V-6 engine; a stainless steel exhaust system; a solar-coated

heat-repelling glass windshield; four flip-out rear side glass windows (Soft-Ray tinted); GM Computer Command Control; instrumentation (including analog speedometer; odometer; tachometer; coolant temperature gauge; low oil indicator; low coolant indicator; voltmeter; trip odometer and door ajar signal); blue-tinted power left- and right-hand sport mirrors with fold-and-stow feature; a Delco ETR AM/FM stereo radio with clock; rear window wipers; front reclining bucket seats with rotating headrests; manual lumbar adjustment and inboard armrests; seven-passenger split folding modular 2-2-3 bench seating with integrated headrests (optional on regular wheelbase model); a four-way manual adjusting driver's seat; a four-spoke adjustable tilting sport steering wheel with airbag; a fully-independent MacPherson strut front suspension; a rear coil spring suspension; P205/70R15 all-season steel-belted radial tires; a four-speed automatic ETC transmission; Doral cloth upholstery; wet-arm controlled-cycle windshield wipers; and 15-in. styled wheels with bolt-on covers. **Trans Sport SE Extended Wheelbase:** Standard equipment on extended wheelbase models included: driver and front passenger airbags; an integrated roof antenna; a brake/transmission shift interlock safety feature; power front disc/rear drum four-wheel antilock brakes; a soft fascia with integral rub strips; child security door locks; front side window defoggers; power door locks with signal-key automatic locking doors; the 3.4-liter 3400 SFI V-6 engine; a stainless steel exhaust system; a solar-coated heat-repelling glass windshield; four flip-out rear side glass windows (Soft-Ray tinted); GM Computer Command Control; instrumentation (including analog speedometer; odometer; tachometer; coolant temperature gauge; low oil indicator; low coolant indicator; voltmeter; trip odometer and door ajar signal); blue-tinted power left- and right-hand sport mirrors with fold-and-stow feature; a Delco ETR AM/FM stereo radio with clock; rear window wipers; front reclining bucket seats with rotating headrests; manual lumbar adjustment and inboard armrests; seven-passenger split folding modular 2-2-3 bench seating with integrated headrests (standard/extended wheelbase models); a four-way manual adjusting driver's seat; a four-spoke adjustable; tilting sport steering wheel with airbag; a fully-independent MacPherson strut front suspension; a rear coil spring suspension; P215/70R15 all-season tires; a four-speed automatic ETC transmission; Doral cloth upholstery; wet-arm controlled-cycle windshield wipers; and 15-in. styled wheels with bolt-on covers.

I.D. DATA: The vehicle identification number (VIN) is located on the top left-hand surface of the instrument panel and is visible through the windshield. The VIN has 17 symbols. The first symbol indicates the country of manufacture (1 or 4=United States; 2=Canada; 3=Mexico). The second symbol indicates the manufacturer (G=General Motors). The third symbol indicates the make/division (2=Pontiac; M=Pontiac MPV and 7=GM of Canada). The fourth, fifth symbols indicate the car line and series (F/S=Firebird and convertible; F/V=Formula-Trans Am and convertible; H/X=Bonneville SE; H/Z=Bonneville SSE/SSEi; J/B=Sunfire SE and convertible; J/D=Sunfire GT; N/E=Grand Am SE; N/W=Grand Am GT; W/J=Grand Prix SE; W/P=Grand Prix GT; U=All-Purpose Vehicle 4 x 2; X=All-Purpose Vehicle Extended 4 x 2). The sixth symbol indicates body style (1=two-door coupe models 27, 37, 47 and 57; 2=two-door models 07, 08, 77, 87; 3=two-door convertible model 67; 5=four-door sedan models 19 and 69; 6=four-door sedan models 29 and 68; 8=four-door Station Wagon model 35; 0=All-Purpose Vehicle). The seventh symbol indicates the restraint system: 2=Active manual belts with driver and passenger inflatable restraints; 4=Active manual belts front and side. The eighth symbol indicates the engine type: G=LS1 5.7-liter V-8; K=RPO L36 3.8-liter V-6; M=RPO L82 3.1-liter V-6; T=RPO LD9 2.4-liter L4; 1=RPO L67 3.8-liter V-8; 4=RPO LN2 2.2-liter L4 and E=RPO LA1 3.4-liter V-6. (Note: All Pontiac engines made in U.S. except "M" also made in Canada; all are MFI multi-point fuel-injected engines). The ninth symbol is a check digit. The 10th symbol indicates model year (W=1998). The 11th symbol indicates the GM assembly plant (B=Baltimore, Md..,T&B; B=Lansing, Mich., GENA-SYS; C=Lansing, Mich.; C=Charlotte, Mich.,T&B; D=Doraville, Ga.; E=Pontiac, Mich., East, T&B; F=Fairfax II, Kan.; F=Flint, Mich., T&B; G=Silao Mexico; H=Flint, Mich.; J=Janesville, Wis.; K=Linden, N.J., T&B; M=Lansing, Mich.; M=Toluca Mexico; R=Arlington, Texas; S=Russelsheim Germany; S=Ramos Arizpe Mexico; T=Shreveport, La.; U=Hamtramck, Mich.; Y=Wilmington, Del.; Z=Fremont, Calif.; Z=Spring Hill, Tenn.; Z=Ft. Wayne, Ind.,

T&B; 0=Lansing, Mich.; 1=Oshawa Canada, T&B; 1=Oshawa Canada, #2; 1=Wentzville, Mo., T&B; 2=Morraine, Ohio, T&B; 2=Ste. Therese Canada; 3=Detroit, Mich., T&B; 3=Kawasaki Japan; 4=Orion, Mich.; 5=Bowling Green, Ken.; 6=Ingersoll, Ontario Canada; 6=Oklahoma City, Okla.; 7=Lordstown, Ohio; 7=Flusawa Japan; 8=Shreveport, La., T&B; 8= Tillisonburg, Ohio, CANEXPO; 9=Oshawa, Ontario Canada, #1). Pontiacs are not produced at all of these plants. The last six symbols are the consecutive unit number at the factory.

Model Number	Body Style Number	Body Type & Seating	Factory Price	Shipping Weight	Production Total
SUNFIRE SE SERIES B (I-4)					
J/B	B37V	2d Coupe-4	12,995	2,637	Note 1
J/B	B69V	4d Sedan-4P	12,995	2,674	Note 1
J/B	B67V	2d Convertible-4P	19,995	2,870	Note 1
SUNFIRE GT SERIES D (I-4)					
J/D	D37V	2d Coupe-4P	15,995	2,822	Note 1
GRAND AM SE SERIES E (I-4)					
N/E	E37V	2d Coupe-4P	15,399	2,835	Note 2
N/E	E69V	4d Sedan-4P	15,549	2,877	Note 2
GRAND AM GT SERIES W (I-4)					
N/W	W37V	2d Coupe-4P	16,849	2,945	Note 2
N/W	W69V	2d Sedan-4P	16,999	2,987	Note 2
FIREBIRD SERIES S (V-6)					
F/S	S87V	2d Coupe -4P	18,540	3,340	Note 3
F/S	S67V	2d Conv-4P	24,830	3,492	Note 3
FORMULA SERIES V (V-8)					
F/V	V87V	2d Coupe -4P	23,390	3,455	Note 3
TRANS AM SERIES V (V-8)					
F/V	V87V	2d Coupe -4P	26,500	3,477	Note 3
F/V	V67V	2d Convertble-4P	30,240	3,605	Note 3
GRAND PRIX SE SERIES J (V-6)					
W/J	J69V	4d Sedan-4P	19,345	3,381	Note 4
GRAND PRIX GT SERIES (V-6)					
W/J	P37V	2d Coupe-4P	22,125	3,396	Note 4
W/J	P69V	4d Sedan-4P	24,825	3,414	Note 4
BONNEVILLE SE SERIES X (V-6)					
X	X69V	4d Sedan-6P	22,995	3,446	Note 5
BONNEVILLE SSE SERIES Z (V-6)					
Z	Z69V	4d Sedan-6P	29,995	3,587	Note 5
BONNEVILLE SSEi SERIES Z (Supercharged V-6)					
Z	Z69V	4d Sedan-6P	31,165	3,691	Note 5
TRANS SPORT SE REGULAR WHEELBASE SERIES U (V-6)					
U	N06V	3d Minivan	21,410	3,730	Note 6
U	M06V	4d Minivan	22,950	3,780	Note 6
TRANS SPORT SE EXTENDED WHEELBASE SERIES X (V-6)					
U	M16V	4d Minivan	23,660	3,942	Note 6

NOTE 1: Model-year production total was 139,174 Sunfires of all types.

NOTE 2: Model-year production total was 111,610 Grand Ams of all types.

NOTE 3: Model-year production total was 33,299 Firebirds of all types.

NOTE 4: Model-year production total was 142,346 Grand Prixs of all types.

NOTE 5: Model-year production total was 68,329 Bonnevilles of all types.

NOTE 6: Model-year production total was 79,267 Trans Sports of all types.

SUNFIRE ENGINES

ENGINE [Base Four SE]: Inline. OHV. Four-cylinder. Two valves per cylinder. Displacement: 133 cid. (2.2L). Bore & stroke: 3.50 x 3.46 in. Compression ratio: 9.0:1. Net horsepower: 115 at 5000 rpm. Torque: 135 lbs.-ft. at 3600 rpm. Fuel system: SFI. VIN Code: 4. RPO Code: LN2.

1998 Pontiac Firebird Trans Am two-door convertible. (PGMC)

1998 Pontiac Grand Prix GTP two-door coupe. (PGMC)

ENGINE [Base Four (GT/SE Convertible); Optional (SE)]: Inline. DOHC. Four-cylinder. Four valves per cylinder. Displacement: 146 cid. (2.4L). Bore & stroke: 3.54 x 3.79 in. Compression ratio: 9.5:1. Net horsepower: 150 at 5600 rpm. Torque: 155 lbs.-ft. at 4400 rpm. Fuel system: SFI. VIN Code: T. RPO Code: LD9.

GRAND AM ENGINES

ENGINE [Base Four SE/GT]: Inline. DOHC. Four-cylinder. Four valves per cylinder. Displacement: 146 cid. (2.4L). Bore & stroke: 3.54 x 3.79 in. Compression ratio: 9.5:1. Net horsepower: 150 at 600 rpm. Torque: 155 lbs.-ft. at 4400 rpm. Fuel system: SFI. VIN Code: T. RPO Code: LD9.

ENGINE [Optional Six]: V-block. OHV. Six-cylinder. Cast-iron block and head. Aluminum intake manifold. Displacement: 191 cid. (3.1L). Bore & stroke: 3.50 x 3.31 in. Compression ratio: 9.5:1. Brake horsepower: 155 at 5200 rpm. Torque: 185 lbs.-ft. at 4000 rpm. Fuel system: SFI. VIN Code: M. RPO Code: L82.

FIREBIRD ENGINES

ENGINE [Base V-6]: V-block. OHV. Six-cylinder. Displacement: 231 cid. (3.8L). Bore & stroke: 3.80 x 3.40 in. Compression ratio: 9.4:1. Brake horsepower: 200 at 5200 rpm. Torque: 225 lbs.-ft. at 4000 rpm. Fuel system: SFI. VIN Code: K. RPO Code: L36.

ENGINE [Base V-8]: V-block. OHV. Eight-cylinder. Aluminum block and head. Aluminum intake manifold. Displacement: 350 cid. (5.7L). Bore & stroke: 4.00 x 3.48 in. Brake horsepower: 305 at 5200 rpm. Torque: 335 lbs.-ft. at 4000 rpm. Compression ratio: 10.5:1. Fuel system: SFI. VIN Code: G. RPO Code: LT1.

ENGINE [Optional V-8]: V-block. OHV. Ram Air. Eight-cylinder. Cast-iron block and head. Aluminum intake manifold. Displacement: 350 cid. (5.7L). Bore & stroke: 4.00 x 3.48 in. Brake horsepower: 320 at 5200 rpm. Torque: 345 lbs.-ft. at 4400 rpm. Compression ratio: 10.5:1. Fuel system: SFI. RPO Code: LT1.

GRAND PRIX ENGINES

ENGINE [Base V-6]: V-block. OHV. Six-cylinder. Displacement: 191 cid. (3.1L). Bore & stroke: 3.50 x 3.31 in. Compression ratio: 9.5:1. Brake horsepower: 160 at 5200 rpm. Torque: 185 lbs.-ft. at 4000 rpm. Fuel system: SFI. VIN Code: M. RPO Code: L82.

ENGINE [Optional V-6]: V-block. Six-cylinder. Displacement: 231 cid. (3.4L). Bore & stroke: 3.80 x 3.40 in. Compression ratio: 9.0:1. Brake horsepower: 195 at 5200 rpm. Torque: 220 lbs.-ft. at 4000 rpm. Fuel system: SFI. VIN Code: X. RPO Code: L36.

BONNEVILLE ENGINES

ENGINE [Base Six SE/SSE]: "3800" SFI Series II V-6. V-block. OHV. Six-cylinder. Displacement: 231 cid. (3.8L). Bore & stroke: 3.80 x 3.40 in. Compression ratio: 9.0:1. Brake horsepower: 205 at 5200 rpm. Torque: 230 lbs.-ft. at 4000 rpm. Fuel system: SFI. VIN Code: K RPO Code: L36

ENGINE [Optional Supercharged SSEi]: "3800" Supercharged Series II V-6. V-block. OHV. Six-cylinder. Displacement: 231 cid. (3.8L). Bore & stroke: 3.80 x 3.40 in. Compression ratio: 8.5:1. Brake horsepower: 240 at 5200 rpm. Torque: 280 lbs.-ft. at 3200 rpm. Fuel system: SFI. VIN Code: 1 RPO Code: L67

TRANS SPORT ENGINE

ENGINE [Base V-6]: V-block. DOHC. Six-cylinder. Displacement: 207 cid. (3.4L). Bore & stroke: 3.62 x 3.31 in. Compression ratio:

9.5:1. Brake horsepower: 180 at 5200 rpm. Torque: 205 lbs.-ft. at 4000 rpm. Fuel system: SFI. VIN Code: E. RPO Code: LA1.

CHASSIS

SUNFIRE CHASSIS: Wheelbase: (All) 104.1 in. Overall length: (All) 181.9 in. Overall width: (coupe/convertible) 67.4 in.; (sedan) 67.3. Height: (coupe) 53.0 in.; (sedan) 54.7 in.; (convertible) 53.7 in. Standard tires: (SE coupe and sedan) steel-belted radial P195/70R14 black sidewall all-season; (SE convertible) steel-belted radial P195/65R15 black sidewall touring; (GT) steel-belted radial P205/55R16 black sidewall performance.

GRAND AM CHASSIS: Wheelbase: (All) 103.4 in. Overall length: (SE coupe and SE sedan) 186.9 in.; (GT coupe and sedan) 187.3 in. Width: (All) 68.7 in. Height: (All) 53.5 in. Standard tires: (SE) steel-belted radial P195/70R14 black sidewall; (GT) steel-belted radial P205/55R16 black sidewall Eagle RSA.

FIREBIRD CHASSIS: Wheelbase: (All) 101.0 in. Overall length: (Firebird/Formula) 193.4 in.; (Trans Am) 193.8 in. Width: (All) 74.5 in. Height: (Firebird/Formula coupe) 52.0 in.; (Firebird convertible) 52.7 in.; (Trans Am coupe) 51.7 in.; (Trans Am convertible) 52.4 in. Standard tires: (Firebird) steel-belted radial P215/60R16 black sidewall touring; (Formula/Trans Am) P245/50ZR16 speed-rated, all-weather.

GRAND PRIX CHASSIS: Wheelbase: (All) 110.5 in. Overall length: (All) 196.5. Width: (All) 72.7 in. Height: (All) 54.7 in. Standard tires: (SE sedan) 205/70R15 black sidewall touring; (GT coupe and sedan) P225/60R16 black sidewall touring.

BONNEVILLE CHASSIS: Wheelbase: (All) 110.8 in. Overall length: (SE sedan) 200.5 in.; (SSE/SSEi sedan) 201.1 in. Width: (All) 74.5 in. Height: (All) 55.7 in. Front tread: 60.3 in. Rear tread: 59.8 in. Standard tires: (SE) steel-belted radial 215/65R15 black sidewall touring. (SSE) steel-belted radial P225/60R16 black sidewall touring.

TRANS SPORT CHASSIS: Wheelbase: (Standard three-door) 112 in.; (Four-door) 112 in.; (Extended four-door) 120 in. Overall length: (Standard three- and four-doors) 187.3 in.; (Extended four-door) 201.3 in. Width: (All) 72.7 in. Height: (Standard three- and four-doors) 67.4 in.; (Extended four-door) 68.1 in. Standard tires: (Standard wheelbase) 205/70R-15 black sidewall all-season; (Extended wheelbase) P215/70R15 black sidewall all-season.

TECHNICAL

SUNFIRE TECHNICAL: Chassis: Front engine/front drive. Base transmission: Five-speed manual. Optional transmission: Three-speed automatic. Front suspension: MacPherson struts. Rear suspension: Coil springs, semi-independent torsion beam, trailing arms. Steering: Rack-and-pinion. Front brakes: Vented disc power-assisted. Rear brakes: Drum power-assisted.

GRAND AM TECHNICAL: Chassis: Front engine/front drive. Base transmission: Five-speed manual with overdrive. Optional transmission: Three-speed automatic. Front suspension: MacPherson struts. Rear suspension: Trailing crank arm with twist arm, coil springs. Steering (Standard): Power-assisted rack-and-pinion. Steering (Sport Performance and WS6): Power-assisted rack-and-pinion, 14.0:1 ratio. Front brakes: Power-assisted vented discs. Rear brakes: Power-assisted drums. Fuel tank: 13.6 gal.

FIREBIRD TECHNICAL: Chassis: Front engine/rear drive. Base transmission: Five-speed manual. Front suspension: Modified MacPherson strut with anti-roll bar. Rear suspension: Live axle with coil springs, control arms, torque arm, track bar and anti-roll bar. Steering: Power recirculating ball. Brakes: Power four-wheel discs with ABS.

GRAND PRIX TECHNICAL: Chassis: Front engine/front drive. Front suspension: MacPherson struts. Rear suspension: Tri-link independent suspension with anti-roll bar. Steering: Power-assisted rack-and-pinion. Four-wheel power disc brakes.

BONNEVILLE TECHNICAL: Chassis: Front engine/front drive. Base transmission: Four-speed automatic. Front suspension: MacPherson struts with anti-roll bar. Front suspension: (SE) MacPherson struts with anti-roll bar; (SSE) MacPherson struts with anti-roll bar. Rear suspension: MacPherson. Steering: Power-assisted rack-and-pinion. Brakes: Power front disc/rear drum with four-wheel ABS.

TRANS SPORT TECHNICAL: Chassis: Front engine/front drive. Transmission: Three-speed automatic. Front suspension: MacPherson strut, stamped lower control arms, stabilizer bar. Rear suspension: Open-section transverse beam on stamped steel trailing arms, tube shocks, coil springs and stabilizer bar. Steering: Power-assisted rack-and-pinion. Front brakes: Power-assisted vented rotors. Rear brakes: Power-assisted finned composite cast-iron drums.

OPTIONS

SUNFIRE OPTIONS: 1SA Sunfire SE coupe and sedan option package including vehicle with standard equipment (no cost). 1SB Sunfire SE coupe and sedan option group ($2,130). 1SC Sunfire SE coupe ($3,015) and sedan ($3,051). 1SD Sunfire SE coupe ($3,700) or SE sedan ($3,740). 1SE Sunfire SE coupe ($4,655) or SE sedan ($4,760). 1SA Sunfire SE convertible option package including vehicle with standard equipment (no cost). 1SB Sunfire SE convertible group ($1,800). 1SA Sunfire GT coupe option package including vehicle with standard equipment (no cost). 1SB Sunfire GT coupe ($1,740). 1SC Sunfire GT coupe ($2,245). C41 non-air-conditioning not desired (no cost). C60 custom air conditioning ($830). C49 electric window defogger ($180). FE9 Federal emissions with LD9 and MX0 (no cost). YF5 California emissions ($170). NG1 NY/Mass. Emissions ($170). K05 engine block heater ($20). VK3 front license plate bracket (no cost). R9P power package, coupe and convertible ($380) or sedan ($445). UN6 Delco radio equipment ($195). UT6 ETR AM/FM stereo with cassette and equalizer ($100 credit). UP3 ETR AM/FM stereo with CD and equalizer (no charge). DT4 smoker's package ($15). T43 rear deck lid spoiler ($150). R6B Sun & Sound package ($170). CF5 power sunroof ($556-595). QPD P195/65R15 black sidewall tires, except GT ($135). MM5 five-speed transmission ($600 credit in SE coupe or sedan with 1SB and $810 credit in others). MX0 four-speed automatic transmission SE coupe/sedan without 1SB and 1SC ($210); GT coupe ($810). MX1 three-speed automatic transmission, SE coupe/sedan only ($600). PF7 15-in. aluminum wheels; not available on GT ($295).

GRAND AM OPTIONS: 1SA SE option package (no cost). 1SB SE option package includes tilt steering; cycle wipers; cruise control; rear defogger and radio with cassette ($545). 1SC SE option package ($995). 1SD SE option package coupe ($1,870); sedan ($1,935). 1SE option package coupe ($2,575); sedan ($2,640). 1SA GT option package (no cost). 1SB GT option package ($375). 1SC GT sedan ($1,480); coupe ($1,415). 1SD GT sedan ($2,535); coupe ($2,470). C49 electric rear window defogger ($180). FE9 Federal emissions (no cost). YF5 California emissions ($170). NG1 N.Y./Mass. emissions ($170). L82 3.1-liter 3100 SFI V-6 ($450). K05 engine block heater ($20). B20 bucket seats with Prado leather seating areas ($475-$810). VK3 front license plate bracket (no cost). UN1 ETR AM/FM stereo with CD, cassette, equalizers, six speakers (with 1SB or 1SC $405; with R6B $195). UN6 ETR AM/FM

1998 Pontiac Grand Prix GT two-door coupe. (PGMC)

1998 Pontiac Tran Sport Extended wheelbase Minivan. (PGMC)

1998 Pontiac Bonneville SSEi four-door Sport sedan. (PGMC)

stereo with cassette ($210). UP3 ETR AM/FM stereo with CD, equalizers, six speakers ($210). UT6 ETR AM/FM stereo with CD, equalizers, six speakers ($110). AG1 six-way power driver's seat ($340). DT4 smoker's package ($15). CF5 power glass sunroof ($595). QFB P195/70R 14 black sidewall steel-belted radial tires (no charge). QPD P195/65R15 touring tires, not available GT ($135). QMS P205/55R16 touring tires, not available on GT ($225). MX0 four-speed automatic transmission ($810). 16P Bright White wheels for GT only (no charge). PF7 15-in. cross-laced aluminum wheels for SE ($300). PG0 16-in. SE sport aluminum wheels ($325). PG1 15-in. bolt-on wheel covers for GT (no cost).

FIREBIRD OPTIONS: 1SA Firebird coupe option package, includes vehicle with standard equipment (no cost). 1SA Plus Firebird coupe option package, includes vehicle with standard equipment plus power door locks, power windows, power sport mirrors with blue tint, power antenna, automatic transmission and power seat ($1,510). 1SB Firebird option group ($1,505). 1SC Firebird option group ($2,450). 1SA convertible option package, includes vehicle with standard equipment (no cost). 1SB Firebird and Formula convertible group ($435). 1SA Trans Am convertible option package, includes vehicle with standard equipment (no cost). VK3 front license plate bracket (no cost). FE9 Federal emissions (no cost). YF5 50 California emissions ($170). NG1 N.Y./Mass. Emissions ($170). 1LE Autocross Package for Formula, includes special handling suspension, larger stabilizer bars, stiffer springs, Koni shocks ($1,175). GU5 performance axle ($225). NW9 traction control ($450). R7Q 1LE standard equipment delete (credit of $1,125). WS6 Ram Air performance and handling package ($3,100). Y87 3800 performance package ($440). U1S trunk mounted remote 12-disc CD changer ($595). W54 ETR AM/FM Monsoon stereo with auto-reverse, graphic equalizer, clock, seek up/down, remote CD pre-wiring and 10-speaker sound system ($330). W55 ETR AM/FM Monsoon stereo with CD player, graphic equalizer, clock, seek up/down and 10-speaker sound system ($430). W59 Delco 500-watt peak power Monsoon AM/FM stereo (with CD, graphic equalizer, clock, seek up/down, search and replay, and high-performance 10-speaker sound system ($430). CC1 hatch roof ($995). R7X security package ($240). AQ9 articulating bucket seats with lumbar supports ($650). AG1 six-way power driver's seat ($270). W68 Sport Appearance package includes aero components, fog lamps, dual outlet exhausts for base models, requires QCB tires and automatic transmission ($990). QCB P235/55R16 black sidewall touring tires for Firebird, standard Formula and Trans Am; not available Trans Am convertible ($135). MM5 five-speed manual transmission ($815 credit). MN6 six-speed manual transmission (no cost). MX0 four-speed automatic transmission ($815). PO5 chrome aluminum 16-in. wheels ($595).

GRAND PRIX OPTIONS: 1SA option package for SE, includes vehicle and standard equipment (standard). 1SB option package for SE ($540). 1SC option package for SE ($1,665). 1SD option package for SE ($2,905). 1SB option package for GT coupe ($670). 1SC option package for GT coupe ($1,305). 1SD option package for GT coupe ($2,099). 1SA option package for GT, includes vehicle and standard equipment (standard). 1SB option package for GT ($755). 1SC option package for GT sedan ($2,115); for GT coupe ($2,085). CJ2 air conditioning with automatic temperature control and dual comfort zone ($195). U77 rear window antenna (no charge with UP3, UT6 or U1C). TR9 premium lighting package ($185-$215). FE9 Federal emissions (no cost). YF5 California emissions ($170). NG1 NY/Mass. emissions ($170). K05 engine block heater ($20). RPO L82 3.1-liter 3100 SFI V-6 (standard). RPO L36 3.8-liter 3800

1998 Pontiac Firebird Trans Am. (PGMC)

Series II SFI V-6 in SE models ($415). L67 3.8-liter 3800 Series II supercharged SFI V-6, in GT models with BS4 GTP performance package (no cost). B4S GTP performance package includes GTP nameplates, 3800 supercharged engine, four-speed automatic transmission with driver select shift, D81 rear deck lid spoiler, U40 trip computer, QVG tires, NV7 Magnasteer, and QD1 wheels ($1,410-$1,610 depending upon model and option packages). U1C AM/FM stereo, seek-scan, CD player and four speakers ($140). U1S multi-disc CD changer ($595). UP3 ETR AM/FM stereo with CD, graphic equalizer, steering wheel radio controls and eight-speaker premium sound system ($125 to $290 depending on model and other options on car). UT6 ETR AM/FM stereo with graphic equalizer, steering wheel radio controls and eight-speaker premium sound system ($190). AM6 45-55 split bench seat with Doral cloth in SE (no cost). B9/AR9 SE coupe bucket seat interior with leather trim (no charge). AR9 bucket seats with leather seating ($475). AG1 six-way power driver's seat ($270). AG6 four-way power lumbar driver's seat ($100). AN2 child seat ($75-$125). KA1 heated driver's bucket seat with dual setting ($50). D81 rear deck lid spoiler ($175). CF5 power glass sunroof ($650). UA6 theft deterrent system ($60). QIN P205/70R15 black sidewall STL touring tires for sedan (standard). QNX P225/60R16 black sidewall STL touring tires for SE sedan ($160). QVG P225/60R16 black sidewall STL performance tires, available for sedan with B4S GTP performance package only (no cost). MWO 16-in. aluminum machine-faced wheels for SE ($260). R6G 16-in. crosslaced Champagne-colored aluminum wheels (GT no cost; SE $260). R6S 16-in. crosslaced silver-colored wheels (GT no cost; SE $260). 16P Bright White wheels for Bright White GTs only (no cost). V2C high-polished 16-in. five-spoke aluminum wheels ($325).

BONNEVILLE OPTIONS: SE sedan 1SA option package, includes vehicle and standard equipment (standard). SE sedan 1SB option package ($1,125). SE sedan 1SC option package ($2,030). SE sedan 1SD option package ($3,135). SSE sedan 1SA option package, includes vehicle and standard equipment (standard). US7 power antenna without 1SD, UT6 or UP3 ($85). FW1 Computer Command

1998 Pontiac Firebird Trans Am. (PGMC)

Ride, SSE ($380). FE9 Federal emissions (no cost). YF5 California emissions ($170). NG1 NY/Mass. emissions ($170). NB8 emissions override (no cost). L67 3.8-liter 3800 SFI supercharged V-6, available only with SSEi supercharger package (no cost). KO5 engine block heater ($20). H4U Special edition package, includes specific SLE exterior badging and specific SSE body side cladding, front and rear fascias, fog lamps, and grille ($600). WA6 SSEi supercharger package, includes 3.8-liter 3800 V-6 supercharged engine with driver-selectable shift four-speed transmission; cluster with turbo boost gauge; P225/60H16 performance tires; traction control; SSEi floor mats; and SSEi nameplates, SSE only ($1,170). RD9 radio equipment enhancement package ($275). UP3 ETR AM/FM stereo with CD, equalizers, seven speakers ($100-$320). UT6 ETR AM/FM stereo with CD, equalizers, six speakers ($220). UN6 ETR AM/FM stereo with cassette ($100 credit). AM645/55 split bench seat in SE (no cost). AS7 bucket seats with 1SB ($220). AS7 leather trim bucket seats with 1SB ($1,345); with 1SC ($850). AL7 articulating 45/45 bucket seats with leather trim in SSE ($245). AG2 power passenger's seat ($305). D58 rear deck lid spoiler delete ($110 credit). CF5 power glass sunroof ($980-$995). UA6 anti-theft alarm system ($190). QNX P225/60R16 black sidewall steel-belted radial touring tires, SE without 1SD ($85). NW9 traction control ($175). N73 16-in. gold aluminum crosslace wheels without 1SD or Y52 ($325). PO5 18-in. aluminum chrome Torque Star wheels (SE sedan without 1SD or Y52 $920; SE sedan with 1SD or Y52 $595; SSE $595). QNX tires on SE without 1SC or 1SD ($325).

TRANS SPORT OPTIONS: 1SA Trans Sport SE option package, includes vehicle with standard equipment (no cost). 1SB Trans Sport SE option package ($460). 1SC Trans Sport option package ($1,410). 1SD Trans Sport option package ($2,451). FE9 Federal emissions (no cost). YF5 California emissions ($170). NG1 NY/Mass. emissions ($170). ABA seven-passenger split bench Doral cloth seating, regular wheelbase ($335). ABB seven-passenger modular bucket seats with Multra/Diva cloth trim, regular wheelbase (without 1SD or WX4 $450; with 1SD or WX4 $115; extended wheelbase $115). ABD captain's chairs with Multra/Diva cloth (without 1SD or WX4 $600; with 1SD or WX4 $265; extended wheelbase $265). ZP8 eight-passenger seating with Multra/Diva cloth (without 1SD or WX4 $600; with 1SD or WX4 $265; extended $265). WJ6 leather seating areas, includes UK3 leather steering wheel with radio controls ($1,055). C34 front-and-rear air conditioning in Trans Sport ($460). C49 electric rear window defogger ($180). KO5 engine block heater ($20). AJ1 deep-tinted glass ($245). C36 rear heater for extended-wheelbase model (with C34 or WX4 $167; without C34 or WX4 $177). AN2 one integral child seat ($125). AN5 two integral child seats ($225). V54 luggage rack, includes saddlebag storage ($175). WX4 Montana package (regular-wheelbase without 1Sd $1,537; regular wheelbase with 1SD $1,027; extended-wheelbase without 1SD $1,164; extended-wheelbase with 1SD $989). D84 two-tone paint ($125). AG1 six-way power driver's seat ($270). AG9 six-way power passenger seat ($305). E58 power sliding door ($350-$400). A31 power windows ($275). AU0 remote keyless entry ($150). UN6 Delco radio equipment ($195). UT6 AM/FM cassette with equalizer and rear seat audio ($150 with leather seat group or $335). U1C AM/FM CD player ($100) UP3 AM/FM CD player with equalizer and rear audio ($250 with leather seat group or $435). UM1 AM/FM cassette with equalizer, dual playback CD player and rear seat audio ($350 with leather seat group or $535). UZ5 extended-range co-axial speakers ($50). G67 Auto Level Control ($180). R6A safety and security package (with P42 or WX4 $60; others $210). XPU P215/70R15 touring tires (regular wheelbase $73; extended wheelbase $35). P42 self-sealing touring tires ($150). V92 trailering provisions ($150). PH3 15-in. aluminum wheels ($259). CF5 sunroof, extended-wheelbase three-door model ($520 with 1SD or $695 without 1SD).

NOTE: Full option package contents, descriptions, and applications information can often be determined by consulting factory literature. The data above is edited for size and clarity. This information provided only as a guide to help collectors appraise the relative value of cars with numerous options. Prices for items included as part of a value option package are usually much less than individual prices. Option prices charged by individual dealers may also vary.

HISTORICAL: Pontiac-GMC's U.S. car model-year production dropped to 575,582 units in 1998. That included 1,557 Firefly. In late 1997 and early 1998, the division moved its offices into GM's new World Headquarters building in Detroit's Renaissance Center. Roy S. Roberts continued as general manager of Pontiac-GMC Div.

1999 PONTIAC

1999 Pontiac Sunfire SE two-door coupe. (PGMC)

SUNFIRE — CARLINE J — (FOUR) — For 1999, a convertible was added to the Pontiac Sunfire line. There were also some technical changes to the 2.4-liter four-cylinder engine including revisions to its fuel injectors, fuel rails, exhaust manifolds, and catalytic converter. Standard equipment on the **Sunfire SE** coupe and sedan included extensive acoustical insulation; dual airbags; a rear-mounted fixed-mast antenna; front disc/rear drum brakes with four-wheel ABS; rear-compartment child-resistant door locks in the SE sedan; a 2.2-liter overhead valve four-cylinder engine with stainless steel exhaust system; Soft-Ray tinted glass; GM Computer Command Control; analog instrumentation (including speedometer; odometer; tachometer; coolant temperature gauge; oil pressure indicator and trip odometer); sport-style breakaway exterior mirrors (left-hand remote-controlled); a RPO UM7 Delco ETR stereo radio with seek up/down and a clock; front 45/45 reclining bucket seats; an easy-entry front passenger seat in coupe only; a three-passenger folding rear seat with integral headrests; a four-spoke Sport steering wheel; power rack-and-pinion steering; a PASSLock™ theft-deterrent system; P195/70R14 black sidewall steel-belted radial tires; a five-speed manual transmission; "wet-arm" fixed-delay "pulse" windshield wipers; and 14-in. bolt-on custom wheel covers. **GT convertible:** The GT convertible had the following equipment in addition to or in place of SE sedan equipment, an air-conditioning system using R134A refrigerant; cruise control; an electric rear window defogger; a 2.4-liter Twin Cam four-cylinder engine; a UP3 Delco ETR stereo radio (with seek up/down; graphic equalizer; digital clock and premium sound system); an adjustable tilt steering wheel; P195/65R15 steel-belted radial black sidewall touring tires; a four-speed automatic transmission with traction control; controlled-cycle "wet-arm" windshield wipers; and 15-in. bolt-on custom wheel covers. **GT coupe:** The GT coupe had the following equipment in addition to or in place of GT convertible equipment, P205/55R16 steel-belted radial black sidewall performance tires, a five-speed manual transmission, "wet-arm" windshield wipers with a fixed-delay pulse feature, and 16-in. GT-specific cast aluminum wheels (cruise control deleted).

1999 Pontiac Sunfire GT two-door coupe. (PGMC)

GRAND AM — CARLINE N — (FOUR) — The new 1999 Grand Am coupe and sedan were introduced in the spring of 1998. Changes made after the 1999 model-year changeover included the addition of a GT coupe and sedan with a 175-hp version of the 3.4-liter V-6 engine. The GT models also had unique front and rear fascias, plus a specially-tuned suspension, and performance type tires. **SE coupe/sedan:** Standard equipment included Gen II dual airbags; air conditioning; a brake/transmission shift interlock safety feature (with automatic transmission); power front disc/rear drum four-wheel antilock brakes; automatic power door locks with unlock/relock feature; child-resistant rear sedan door locks; the RPO LD9 2.4-liter 16-valve Twin Cam four-cylinder engine; an illuminated entry system with automatic lighting control; tinted glass; dual black exterior sport mirrors (left-hand remote controlled; right-hand manual); a day/night inside rearview mirror; a right-hand visor vanity mirror; a Delco ETR AM/FM stereo radio; front bucket seats; power steering; a tilt steering wheel; a tachometer; a PASSLock II theft-deterrent system; P215/60R15 black sidewall touring tires; a four-speed ECT automatic transmission; auto trip; Cartegena cloth upholstery; intermittent windshield wipers; and bolt-on wheel covers. **SE1:** The SE1 trim level included, in addition to in-place of SE equipment, cruise control; dual black power mirrors; an AM/FM ETR stereo radio with cassette; front bucket seats with manual four-way driver seat adjustment and power forward-back adjustment; a split-back fold-down rear seat; five-spoke aluminum wheels; and power windows with driver's side "express down" feature. **SE2:** The SE2 trim level included, in addition to or in place of SE1, the 3.4-liter EFI V-6 engine; remote keyless entry; an AM/FM ETR stereo (with CD, seven-band graphic equalizer, and high-performance speaker system); up-level front sport bucket seats (with manual four-way driver's seat and power front-back and height adjustment and manual lumbar support); a leather-wrapped steering wheel with redundant radio controls; speed-sensitive power steering; P225/50R16 touring tires; Redondo/Patina cloth upholstery; and multi-spoke aluminum wheels. The **GT coupe** included, in addition to or in place of SE equipment, four-wheel disc brakes; the 3.4-liter 3400 SFI V-6 with Ram Air induction; dual power exterior mirrors; an AM/FM radio with auto reverse cassette; four speakers and a clock; a four-way driver power seat; a split folding rear seat; the sport interior group; uplevel design seats; a leather-wrapped steering wheel; shift knob and brake handle; variable-effort power steering; P205/55R16 performance tires; power windows; and 16-in. machine-faced wheels. **GT1:** In addition to GT goodies, the GT1 package included remote keyless entry, a radio upgrade, a power driver's seat, and a power sunroof.

FIREBIRD — CARLINE F — (V-6/V-8) — The availability of GM's traction control system was extended to V-6-powered Firebirds this year. All Firebirds with a V-8 and some with a V-6 had a Torsen II slip-reduction rear axle. An Electronic Brakeforce Distribution (EBD) system replaced the old hydraulic proportioning valve for improved brake performance. Also new was a solenoid-based Bosch antilock braking system. An enhanced sensing and a diagnostic module or SDM recorded vehicle speed, engine rpm, throttle position, and brake use in the last five seconds prior to airbag deployment. **Firebird coupe:** Standard equipment for the Firebird coupe included extensive acoustical insulation; dual front airbags; air conditioning; a black fixed-mast antenna at right rear; a brake/transmission shift interlock safety feature (with automatic transmission); power four-

1999 Pontiac Sunfire GT two-door convertible. (PGMC)

1999 Pontiac Grand Am SE two-door coupe. (PGMC)

wheel disc brakes with four-wheel ABS; the RPO L36 3800 Series II 200-hp SFI V-6 engine; cruise control; electric rear and side window defoggers; Solar-Ray tinted glass; instrumentation (including electric analog speedometer; tachometer; odometer; coolant temperature indicator; oil pressure gauge; voltmeter and LED trip odometer); sport exterior mirrors (left-hand remote controlled; right-hand manual); a day/night inside rearview mirror with reading lamps; left- and right-hand covered visor vanity mirrors; a Delco AM/FM stereo ETR radio and cassette (with seven-band graphic equalizer, touch control, search-and-replay, Delco theft lock, clock, seek up/down, remote CD prewiring, and four-speaker coaxial sound system); reclining front bucket seats; four-way driver and passenger front seat manual adjusters; a rear two-passenger folding seat; a four-spoke sport tilt steering wheel with adjustable column; the PASS-Key II theft-deterrent system; P215/60R16 touring tires with a high-pressure compact spare; the RPO MM5 five-speed manual transmission; controlled-cycle windshield wipers; and bright silver 16-in. five-spoke cast aluminum wheels. **Formula Coupe:** Formula models also included (in addition to or in place of the above) a power antenna; power door locks; power automatic sport mirrors with blue glass; a Delco 500-watt peak power Monsoon AM/FM stereo (with CD, seven-band graphic equalizer, clock, touch control, seek up/down, search and replay, Delco anti-theft lock, high-performance 10-speaker sound system in coupe or six-speaker sound system in convertible, HSS speakers and tweeters in doors, 6.5-in. subwoofers in sail panels, subwoofer amp and four speakers and tweeters in rear quarter panels); a leather-wrapped steering wheel with radio controls (including leather-wrapped shift knob and parking brake handle); P245/50ZR16 speed-rated all-weather tires; and power window controls with driver's "express down" feature (requires power mirrors and door locks). **Trans Am:** Trans Am models also included (in addition to or in place of Formula features) an audible content theft-deterrent system, remote keyless entry, and a six-way power front driver's seat.

GRAND PRIX — CARLINE W — (V-6/V-8) — Changes for the 1999 version of the "Wide-Track" Grand Prix included an Enhanced Traction System (throttle-intervention traction control) for SE and GT models. The non-turbo 3.8-liter V-6 jumped up to 200 hp. The theft-deterrent system was now included with remote keyless entry. The standard sound system was also upgraded and the GTP version of the Grand Prix—which was previously an option—was now a separate series with a coupe and a sedan. **Grand Prix SE:** Standard equipment for the Grand Prix SE included extensive acoustical insulation; dual front airbags; air conditioning; a fixed mast antenna; a brake/transmission shift interlock safety feature; four-wheel power disc brakes with antilock; automatic programmable door locks with delayed locking and lockout protection (rear child security locks in SE sedan); the RPO L82 3.1-liter 3100 160-hp SFI V-6; a stainless steel exhaust system; completely flush fitting Soft-Ray safety-laminated tinted glass; GM Computer Command Control; mechanical analog instrumentation (including tachometer; fuel gauge; coolant temperature indicator and trip odometer); a Driver Information Center (including trunk ajar; ETS on/off; low washer fluid; check tire pressure; check oil soon and ETS low-traction indicators); body-colored and power-operated remote-control left- and right-hand sport rearview mirrors; left- and right-hand covered visor

1999 Pontiac Grand Am SE four-door sedan. (PGMC)

1999 Pontiac Grand Am SC/T four-door sedan. (PGMC)

vanity mirrors; a Delco ETR AM/FM stereo radio with seek/scan feature and clock; front sport bucket seats with Doral cloth interior fabric; a three-passenger rear bench seat with integrated headrests; a two-way manually adjustable driver's bucket seat with two-way manual lumbar support; front seat back storage pockets; a four-spoke sport tilt urethane steering wheel with adjustable column and airbag; P205/70R15 black sidewall steel-belted radial touring tires; a four-speed ETC automatic transmission; 15-in. sport-style bolt-on wheel covers; wet-arm controlled-cycle windshield wipers and power windows with lighted switches; and the driver's side "express down" feature. **Grand Prix GT Coupe:** In addition to or in place of SE equipment; standard GT coupe features included cruise control; the RPO L36 3800 Series II 200-hp V-6; a stainless steel exhaust system with dual bright outlet exhausts; a Delco 2001 series ETR AM/FM stereo radio (with cassette, clock, seek up/down, and auto reverse), a leather-wrapped sport steering wheel; P225/60R16 black sidewall tires; and five-spoke 16 x 6.5-in. cast-aluminum wheels. **Grand Prix GT Sedan:** In addition to or in place of SE equipment, standard Grand Prix GT sedan features included a Delco 2001 series ETR AM/FM stereo radio with cassette, a clock, seek up/down, and auto reverse.

BONNEVILLE — CARLINE H — (V-6) — There were no major changes in the 1999 Pontiac Bonneville because it was scheduled for a complete change for model-year 2000. **SE Sedan:** Standard Bonneville SE equipment included extensive acoustical insulation; dual front airbags; manual air conditioning; a brake/transmission shift interlock safety feature; power front disc/rear drum brakes with four-wheel antilock; cruise control; an electric rear window defogger; automatic power door locks with lockout protection and delayed locking feature; the RPO L36 3.8-liter 3800 Series II SFI V-6; a stainless steel exhaust system; Soft-Ray tinted glass; backlit instrumentation (including an analog speedometer); a Systems Monitor (including fuel and coolant temperature gauges; an oil pressure gauge; a voltmeter and a tachometer); sport outside mirrors (left-hand remote control; right-hand manual); dual covered visor vanity mirrors; the PASS-Key II theft-deterrent system; a Delco ETR AM/FM stereo radio (with clock; four speakers and fixed mast antenna); six-passenger seating with a 45/55 split front bench seat with manual recliners; a four-spoke sport tilt urethane steering wheel with

adjustable column; a storage armrest with dual cup holders; Cartagena cloth upholstery; a rear seat pass through; P215/65R15 black sidewall touring tires; a four-speed automatic transmission; 15-in. bolt-on wheel covers; and power windows with driver's side "express down" feature. **SSE/SSEi Sedan:** In addition to or in place of the above, the Bonneville SSE/SSEi models included: automatic air conditioning with an outside temperature indicator; a power mast antenna; instrumentation with a heads-up display; a Driver Information Center (with electric compass, door ajar light, hood ajar light, and service reminders); an illuminated entry system; a stainless steel dual exhaust system; remote keyless entry; dual heated power exterior mirrors with blue tint; a Delco 2001 series ETR AM/FM stereo radio (with CD player, clock, theft lock, and Bose eight-speaker sound system); five-passenger seating with 45/45 six-way non-articulated power front bucket seats and leather seating areas; a leather-wrapped steering wheel with radio controls; Magnasteer variable-ratio power steering; a full-feature theft-deterrent system; P225/60R16 black sidewall Eagle LS touring tires (Eagle RSA standard on SSEi); and three-blade silver 16-in. cast aluminum wheels.

MONTANA — CARLINE U — (V-6) — In 1999, the name of the Trans Sport All-Purpose Vehicle (a.k.a. Multi-Purpose Vehicle) was changed to Montana. This reflected the popularity of the previous Montana option group. Puncture-sealing tires were now standard equipment. The 3.4-liter V-6 engine was upgraded and now had 185 hp and 210 lbs.-ft. of torque. New options included a Sport Performance option group and a Vision package with a drop-down LCD color monitor for rear seat passengers. A video cassette player and a CD player were added to the options list. **Montana Sport Regular Wheelbase:** Standard equipment on the regular wheelbase model included driver and front passenger airbags; and integral roof antenna; a brake/transmission shift interlock safety feature; power front disc/rear drum four-wheel antilock brakes; a soft fascia with integral rub strips; child security door locks; front-compartment side window defoggers; power door locks with signal-key automatic locking doors; a 3.4-liter 3400 SFI V-6 engine; a stainless steel exhaust system; a solar-coated heat-repelling glass windshield; four flip-out rear side glass windows (Soft-Ray tinted); GM Computer Command Control; instrumentation (including an analog speedometer, odometer, tachometer, coolant temperature gauge, low oil indicator, low

1999 Pontiac Grand Am GT two-door coupe. (PGMC)

1999 Pontiac Firebird two-door coupe. (PGMC)

1999 Pontiac Formula Firebird WS6 two-door coupe. (PGMC)

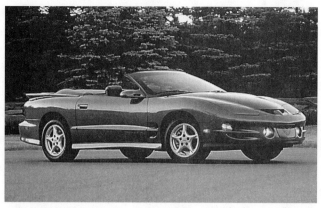

1999 Pontiac Firebird Trans Am two-door convertible. (PGMC)

coolant indicator, voltmeter, trip odometer, and door ajar signal); blue-tinted power left- and right-hand sport mirrors with a fold-and-stow feature; a Delco ETR AM/FM stereo radio with clock; rear window wipers; front reclining bucket seats (with rotating headrests, manual lumbar adjustment, and inboard armrest); seven-passenger split folding modular 2-2-3 bench seating with integral headrests (optional in regular wheelbase models); a four-way manual adjusting driver's seat; a four-spoke adjustable tilting sport steering wheel with airbag; a fully-independent MacPherson strut front suspension; a rear coil spring suspension; P205/70R15 all-season steel-belted radial tires; a four-speed automatic ETC transmission; Doral cloth upholstery; wet-arm controlled-cycle windshield wipers; and 15-in. styled wheels with bolt-on covers. **Montana Sport Extended Wheelbase**: Standard equipment on the extended wheelbase models included driver and front passenger airbags; an integral roof antenna; a brake/transmission shift interlock safety feature; power front disc/rear drum four-wheel antilock brakes; a soft fascia with integral rub strips; child security door locks; front-compartment side window defoggers; power door locks with signal-key automatic locking doors; the 3.4-liter 3400 SFI V-6 engine; a stainless steel exhaust system; a solar-coated heat-repelling glass windshield; four flip-out rear side glass windows (Soft-Ray tinted); GM Computer Command Control; instrumentation (including analog speedometer, odometer, tachometer, coolant temperature gauge, low oil indicator, low coolant indicator, voltmeter, trip odometer, and door ajar signal); blue-tinted power left- and right-hand sport mirrors with the fold-and-stow feature; a Delco ETR AM/FM stereo radio with clock; rear window wipers; front reclining bucket seats (with rotating headrests, manual lumbar adjustment, and inboard armrests); seven-passenger split folding modular 2-2-3 bench seating with integral headrests; a four-way manual adjusting driver's seat; a four-spoke adjustable tilting sport steering wheel with airbag; a fully-independent MacPherson strut front suspension; a rear coil spring suspension; P215/70R15 all-season tires; a four-speed automatic ETC transmission; Doral cloth upholstery; wet-arm controlled-cycle windshield wipers; and 15-in. styled wheels with bolt-on covers.

I.D. DATA: The vehicle identification number (VIN) is located on the top left-hand surface of the instrument panel and is visible through the windshield. The VIN has 17 symbols. The first symbol indicates the country of manufacture (1 or 4=United States; 2=Canada; 3=Mexico). The second symbol indicates the manufacturer (G=General Motors). The third symbol indicates the make/division (2=Pontiac; M=Pontiac MPV and 7=GM of Canada). The fourth and fifth symbols indicate the car line and series: F/S=Firebird and convertible; F/V=Formula and convertible; H/X=Bonneville SE; H/Z=Bonneville SSE/SSEi; J/B=Sunfire SE and convertible; J/D=Sunfire; N/E=Grand Am SE; N/W= Grand Am GT; W/J=Grand Prix SE; W/P=Grand Prix GT; WR=Grand Prix GTP; U=All-Purpose Vehicle 4 x 2; X=All-Purpose Vehicle Extended 4 x 2. The sixth symbol indicates body style (1=two-door coupe models 27, 37, 47 and 57; 2=two-door coupe models 07, 08, 77, 87; 3=two-door convertible model 67; 5=four-door sedan models 19 and 69; 6=four-door sedan models 29 and 68; 8=four-door station wagon model 35; 0=All-Purpose Vehicle). The seventh symbol indicates the restraint system: 2=Active manual belts with driver and passenger inflatable restraints; 4=Active manual belts front and side. The eighth symbol indicates the engine type: G=LS1 5.7-liter V-8; K=RPO L36 3.8-liter V-6; M=RPO L82 3.1-liter V-6; T=RPO LD9 2.4-liter L4; 1=RPO L67 3.8-liter V-8; 4=RPO LN2 2.2-liter L4 and E=RPO LA1 3.4-liter V-6. (Note: All Pontiac engines made in U.S. except "M" also made in Canada; all are MFI multi-point fuel-injected engines.) The ninth symbol is a check digit. The 10th symbol indicates model year (X=1999). The 11th symbol indicates the GM assembly plant (B=Baltimore, Md., T&B; B=Lansing, Mich., GENASYS; C=Lansing, Mich.; C=Charlotte, Mich., T&B; D=Doraville, Ga.; E=Pontiac East, Mich., T&B; F=Fairfax II, Kan.; F=Flint, Mich., T&B; G=Silao Mexico; H=Flint, Mich.; J=Janesville, Wis.; K=Linden, N.J., T&B; M=Lansing, Mich.; M=Toluca Mexico; R=Arlington, Texas; R=Russelsheim Germany; S=Ramos Arizpe Mexico; T=Shreveport, La.; U=Hamtramck, Mich.; Y=Wilmington, Del.; Z=Fremont, Calif.; Z=Spring Hill, Tenn.; Z=Ft. Wayne, Ind., T&B; 0=Lansing, Mich.; 1=Oshawa Canada, T&B; 1=Oshawa Canada, #2; 1=Wentzville, Mo., T&B; 2=Morraine, Ohio, T&B; 2=Ste. Therese Canada; 3=Detroit, Mich., T&B; 3=Kawasaki Japan; 4=Orion, Mich.; 5=Bowling Green, Ky.; 6=Ingersoll, Ontario Canada; 6=Oklahoma City, Okla.; 7=Lordstown, Ohio; 7=Flusawa Japan; 8=Shreveport, La., T&B; 8=Tillisonburg, Ohio, CANEXPO; 9=Oshawa, Ontario Canada, #1). Pontiacs are not produced at all of

1999 Pontiac Firebird Trans Am two-door coupe. (PGMC)

1999 Pontiac Firebird Trans Am 30th Anniversary two-door coupe. (PGMC)

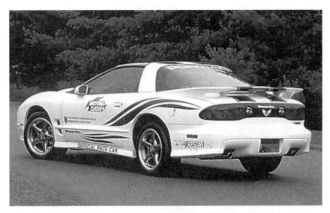

1999 Pontiac Firebird Trans Am 30th Anniversary two-door coupe Daytona 500 Pace Car edition. (PGMC)

1999 Pontiac Firebird Trans Am 30th Anniversary two-door convertible. (PGMC)

these plants. The last six symbols are the consecutive unit number at the factory.

Model Number	Body Style Number	Body Type & Seating	Factory Price	Shipping Weight	Production Total
SUNFIRE SE SERIES B (I-4)					
J/B	B37V	2d Coupe-4P	13,225	2,630	Note 1
J/B	B69V	4d Sedan-4P	13,225	2,670	Note 1
J/B	B67V	2d Convertible-4P	21,655	2,998	Note 1
SUNFIRE GT SERIES D (I-4)					
J/D	D37V	2d Coupe-4P	16,225	2,822	Note 1
GRAND AM SE SERIES E (I-4)					
N/E	E37V	2d Coupe-4P	16,395	3,050	Note 2
N/E	E69V	4d Sedan-4P	16,595	3,116	Note 2
GRAND AM GT SERIES W (V-6)					
N/W	W37V	2d Coupe-4P	21,095	3,050	Note 2
N/W	W69V	2d Sedan-4P	21,495	3,116	Note 2
FIREBIRD SERIES S (V-6)					
F/S	S87V	2d Coupe-4P	18,700	3,402	Note 3
F/S	S67V	2d Convertible-4P	25,320	3,492	Note 3
FORMULA SERIES V (V-8)					
F/V	V87V	2d Coupe-4P	23,600	3,514	Note 3
TRANS AM SERIES V (V-8)					
F/V	V87V	2d Coupe-4P	26,710	3,536	Note 3
F/V	V67V	2d Convertible-4P	30,780	3,605	Note 3
GRAND PRIX SE SERIES J (V-6)					
W/J	J69V	4d Sedan-4P	19,975	3,381	Note 4
GRAND PRIX GT SERIES P (V-6)					
W/J	P37V	2d Coupe-4P	21,555	3,396	Note 4
W/J	P69V	4d Sedan-4P	24,825	3,414	Note 4
GRAND PRIX GTP SERIES R (V-6)					
W/J	P37V	2d Coupe-4P	23,735	—	Note 4
W/J	P69V	4d Sedan-4P	26,435	—	Note 4
BONNEVILLE SE SERIES X (V-6)					
X	X69V	4d Sedan-6P	23,495	3,446	Note 5
BONNEVILLE SSE SERIES Z (V-6)					
Z	Z69V	4d Sedan-6P	30,495	3,587	Note 5
BONNEVILLE SSEi SERIES Z (Supercharged V-6)					
Z	Z69V	4d Sedan-6P	31,665	3,691	Note 5
MONTANA REGULAR WHEELBASE SERIES N (V-6)					
U	N06V	3d Minivan	21,655	3,730	Note 6
MONTANA EXTENDED WHEELBASE SERIES M (V-6)					
U	M06V	4d Minivan	23,445	3,803	Note 6
U	M16V	4d Minivan	24,455	3,942	Note 6

Model Number	Body Style Number	Body Type & Seating	Factory Price	Shipping Weight	Production Total
MONTANA SPORT EXTENDED WHEELBASE SERIES M (V-6)					
U	M06V	4d Minivan	25,335	3,828	Note 6
U	M16V	4d Minivan	26,335	3,967	Note 6

NOTE 1: Model-year production total was 121,825 Sunfires of all types.

NOTE 2: Model-year production total was 331,196 Grand Ams of all types.

NOTE 3: Model-year production total was 36,219 Firebirds of all types.

NOTE 4: Model-year production total was 155,317 Grand Prixs of all types.

NOTE 5: Model-year production total was 54,384 Bonnevilles of all types.

NOTE 6: Model-year production total was 81,718 Montanas of all types.

SUNFIRE ENGINES

ENGINE [Base Four SE]: Inline. OHV. Four-cylinder. Two valves per cylinder. Displacement: 133 cid. (2.2L). Bore & stroke: 3.50 x 3.46 in. Compression ratio: 9.0:1. Net horsepower: 115 at 5000 rpm. Torque: 135 lbs.-ft. at 3600 rpm. Fuel system: SFI. VIN Code: 4. RPO Code: LN2.

ENGINE [Base Four (GT/SE Convertible); Optional (SE)]: Inline. DOHC. Four-cylinder. Four valves per cylinder. Displacement: 146 cid. (2.4L). Bore & stroke: 3.54 x 3.79 in. Compression ratio: 9.5:1. Net horsepower: 150 at 5600 rpm. Torque: 155 lbs.-ft. at 4400 rpm. Fuel system: SFI. VIN Code: T. RPO Code: LD9.

GRAND AM ENGINES

ENGINE [Base Four SE/GT]: Inline. DOHC. Four-cylinder. Four valves per cylinder. Displacement: 146 cid. (2.4L). Bore & stroke: 3.54 x 3.79 in. Compression ratio: 9.5:1. Net horsepower: 150 at 5600 rpm. Torque: 155 lbs.-ft. at 4400 rpm. Fuel system: SFI. VIN Code: T. RPO Code: LD9.

ENGINE [Optional Six]: V-block. OHV. Six-cylinder. Cast iron block and head. Aluminum intake manifold. Displacement: 207 cid. (3.4L). Bore & stroke: 3.62 x 3.31 in. Compression ratio: 9.5:1. Brake horsepower: 170 at 4800 rpm. Torque: 195 lbs.-ft. at 4000 rpm. Fuel system: SFI. VIN Code: M. RPO Code: L82.

1999 Pontiac Firebird Trans Am 30th Anniversary two-door convertible. (PGMC)

1999 Pontiac Grand Prix GT two-door coupe. (PGMC)

1999 Pontiac Grand Prix GT four-door sedan. (PGMC)

FIREBIRD ENGINES

ENGINE [Base V-6]: V-block. OHV. Six-cylinder. Displacement: 231 cid. (3.8L). Bore & stroke: 3.80 x 3.40 in. Compression ratio: 9.4:1. Brake horsepower: 200 at 5200 rpm. Torque: 225 lbs.-ft. at 4000 rpm. Fuel system: SFI. VIN Code: K. RPO Code: L36.

ENGINE [Base V-8]: V-block. OHV. Eight-cylinder. Aluminum block and head. Aluminum intake manifold. Displacement: 350 cid. (5.7L). Bore & stroke: 3.90 x 3.62 in. Brake horsepower: 305 at 5200 rpm. Torque: 335 lbs.-ft. at 4000 rpm. Compression ratio: 10.5:1. Fuel system: SFI. VIN Code: G. RPO Code: LT1.

GRAND PRIX ENGINES

ENGINE [Base V-6]: V-block. OHV. Six-cylinder. Displacement: 191 cid. (3.1L). Bore & stroke: 3.50 x 3.31 in. Compression ratio: 9.5:1. Brake horsepower: 160 at 5200 rpm. Torque: 185 lbs.-ft. at 4000 rpm. Fuel system: SFI. VIN Code: M. RPO Code: L82.

ENGINE [Optional V-6]: V-block. Six-cylinder. Displacement: 231 cid. (3.8L). Bore & stroke: 3.80 x 3.40 in. Compression ratio: 9.4:1. Brake horsepower: 200 at 5200 rpm. Torque: 225 lbs.-ft. at 4,000 rpm. Fuel system: SFI. VIN Code: X. RPO Code: L36.

ENGINE [Optional V-6; GTP only]: V-block. Six-cylinder. Displacement: 231 cid. (3.8L). Bore & stroke: 3.80 x 3.40 in. Compression ratio: 8.5:1. Brake horsepower: 240 at 5200 rpm. Torque: 280 lbs.-ft. at 3200 rpm. Fuel system: SFI. VIN Code: X. RPO Code: L36.

BONNEVILLE ENGINES

ENGINE [Base V-6 SE/SSE]: "3800" SFI Series II V-6. V-block. OHV. Six-cylinder. Displacement: 231 cid. (3.8L). Bore & stroke: 3.80 x 3.40 in. Compression ratio: 9.0:1. Brake horsepower: 205 at 5200 rpm. Torque: 230 lbs.-ft. at 4000 rpm. Fuel system: SFI. VIN Code: K RPO Code: L36.

ENGINE [Optional Supercharged Six SSEi]: "3800" Supercharged Series II V-6. V-block. OHV. Six-cylinder. Displacement: 231 cid. (3.8L). Bore & stroke: 3.80 x 3.40 in. Compression ratio: 8.5:1. Brake horsepower: 240 at 5200 rpm. Torque: 280 lbs.-ft. at 3200 rpm. Fuel system: SFI. VIN Code: 1 RPO Code: L67.

MONTANA ENGINE

ENGINE [Base V-6]: V-block. DOHC. Six-cylinder. Displacement: 207 cid. (3.4L). Bore & stroke: 3.62 x 3.31 in. Compression ratio: 9.5:1. Brake horsepower: 185 at 5200 rpm. Torque: 210 lbs.-ft. at 4,000 rpm. Fuel system: SFI. VIN Code: E. RPO Code: LA1.

CHASSIS

SUNFIRE CHASSIS: Wheelbase: (all) 104.1 in. Overall length: (All except SE sedan) 181.9 in.; (SE sedan) 181.7 in. Overall width: (All except SE sedan) 68.4 in.; (SE sedan) 67.9 in. Height: (Coupe) 53.0 in.; (Sedan) 54.7 in. (Convertible) 54.1 in.

GRAND AM CHASSIS: Wheelbase: (all) 106.7 in. Overall length: 186.3 in. Width: (all) 70.4 in. Height: (all) 55.1 in.

FIREBIRD CHASSIS: Wheelbase: (all) 101.0 in. Overall length: (Firebird/Formula) 193.3 in.; (Trans Am) 193.7 in. Width: (all) 74.4 in. Height: (Firebird/Formula) 51.2 in.; (Trans Am) 51.8 in.

GRAND PRIX CHASSIS: Wheelbase: (all) 110.5 in. Overall length: (all) 196.5. Width: (all) 72.7 in. Height: (all) 54.7 in.

BONNEVILLE CHASSIS: Wheelbase: (all) 110.8 in. Overall length: (SE Sedan) 200.5 in.; (SSE/SSEi Sedan) 202.1 in. Width: (all) 74.5 in. Height: (all) 55.7 in. Front tread: 60.3 in. Rear tread: 59.8 in.

MONTANA CHASSIS: Wheelbase: (Standard three-door) 112 in.; (Four-door) 112 in.; (Extended four-door) 120 in. Overall length: (Standard three- and four-doors) 187.3 in.; (Extended four-door) 201.3 in. Width: (all) 72.7 in. Height: (Standard three- and four-doors) 67.4 in.; (Extended four-door) 68.1 in.

Note: See standard equipment lists for tire sizes.

TECHNICAL

SUNFIRE TECHNICAL: Front engine/front drive. Base transmission: Five-speed manual. Optional transmission: Three-speed automatic. Front suspension: MacPherson struts. Rear suspension: Coil springs, semi-independent torsion beam, trailing arms. Steering: Rack-and-pinion. Front brakes: vented disc power-assisted. Rear brakes: drum power-assisted.

GRAND AM TECHNICAL: Front engine/front drive. Base transmission: Five-speed manual with overdrive. Optional transmission: Three-speed automatic. Front suspension: MacPherson struts. Rear suspension: Trailing crank arm with twist arm, coil springs. Steering (Standard): Power-assisted rack-and-pinion. Steering (Sport Performance and WS6): Power-assisted rack-and-pinion, 14.0:1 ratio. Front brakes: Power-assisted vented discs. Rear brakes: Power-assisted drums. Fuel tank: 13.6 gal.

FIREBIRD TECHNICAL: Front engine/rear drive. Base transmission: Five-speed manual. Front suspension: Modified MacPherson strut with anti-roll bar. Rear suspension: Live axle with coil springs, control arms, torque arm, track bar and anti-roll bar. Steering: Power recirculating ball. Brakes: Power four-wheel discs with ABS.

GRAND PRIX TECHNICAL: Front engine/front drive. Front suspension: MacPherson struts. Rear suspension: Tri-link independent suspension with anti-roll bar. Steering: Power-assisted rack-and-pinion. Brakes; Four-wheel power disc brakes.

BONNEVILLE TECHNICAL: Front engine/front drive. Base transmission: Four-speed automatic. Front suspension: MacPherson struts with anti-roll bar. Front suspension: (SE) MacPherson struts with anti-roll bar; (SSE) MacPherson struts with anti-roll bar. Rear suspension: MacPherson. Steering: Power-assisted rack-and-pinion. Brakes: Power front disc/rear drum with four-wheel ABS.

TRANS SPORT TECHNICAL: Front engine/front drive. Transmission: Three-speed automatic. Front suspension: MacPherson strut, stamped lower control arms, stabilizer bar. Rear suspension: Open-section transverse beam on stamped steel trailing arms, tube shocks, coil springs and stabilizer bar. Steering: Power-assisted rack-and-pinion. Front brakes: Power-assisted vented rotors. Rear brakes: Power-assisted finned composite cast iron drums.

OPTIONS

SUNFIRE OPTIONS: 1SA Sunfire SE Coupe and Sedan option package including vehicle with standard equipment (no cost). 1SB Sunfire SE Coupe ($2,130) and Sedan ($2,280) option group. 1SC Sunfire SE Coupe ($3,225) and Sedan ($3,415). SE Convertible option package including vehicle with standard equipment (no cost). 1SA Sunfire GT Coupe option package including vehicle with standard equipment (no cost). 1SB Sunfire GT Coupe ($2,245). C41 air-conditioning not desired. C60 custom air conditioning ($830). K34 cruise control ($235). C49 electric window defogger ($180). FE9 Federal emissions with LD9 and MX0 (no cost). YF5 California emissions (no cost). NG1 NY/Mass. Emissions (no cost). RPO LD (engine ($450). K05 engine block heater ($20). VK3 front license plate bracket (no cost). R9P power package, Coupe and Convertible ($380) or Sedan ($445). UN6 Delco radio equipment ($195). UT6 ETR AM/FM stereo with cassette and equalizer ($270 credit). UP3 ETR AM/FM stereo with CD and equalizer ($370). R7X Security package ($370-$410). DT4 smoker's package ($15). T43 rear deck lid spoiler ($150). AS5 Sport Interior package ($180). CF5 power sunroof ($556-$595). QPD P195/65R15 black sidewall tires,

1999 Pontiac Bonneville SE four-door Sport Sedan. (PGMC)

Standard Catalog of ® Pontiac, 2nd Edition

1999 Pontiac Bonneville SLE four-door Sport Sedan. (PGMC)

except GT ($135). MM5 five-speed transmission ($600 credit in SE Coupe or Sedan with 1SB and $810 credit in others). MX0 four-speed automatic transmission SE Coupe/Sedan without 1SB and 1SC ($210); GT Coupe ($810). MX1 three-speed automatic transmission, SE Coupe/Sedan only ($600). PG1 15-in. wheel covers, requires QPD tires (no charge). PF7 15-in. aluminum wheels; not available on GT ($295).

GRAND AM OPTIONS: K34 cruise control: ($235). FE9 Federal emissions (no cost). YF5 California emissions ($170). NG1 N.Y./Mass. Emissions ($170). LA1 3.4-liter 3400 SFI V-6 ($595). LD9 2.4-liter Twin Cam 16-valve four-cylinder engine ($595 credit as part of SE package delete). K05 engine block heater ($20). DT4 smoker's package ($15). VK3 front license plate bracket (no cost). UN1 ETR AM/FM stereo with CD, cassette, equalizer, six speakers ($195-$665 depending on model). UN6 ETR AM/FM stereo with cassette ($195). UP3 ETR AM/FM stereo with CD, equalizer, six speakers ($210-$470 depending on model and equipment). AUO remote keyless entry ($150). AG1 6-way power seat ($265). B20 Prado leather bucket seats ($475). T43 rear deck lid spoiler ($195 or standard with GT). CF5 power glass sunroof ($595).

FIREBIRD OPTIONS: 1SA Firebird Coupe option package, includes vehicle with standard equipment (no cost). 1SB Plus Firebird Coupe option package, includes vehicle with standard equipment plus power door locks, power windows, power sport mirrors with blue tint, power antenna, automatic transmission, and power seat ($1,510). 1SC Firebird option group ($2,450). 1SA Convertible option package, includes vehicle with standard equipment (no cost). GU5 3.23:1 performance axle ($300). FE9 Federal emissions (no cost). YF5 50 California emissions (no cost). NG1 N.Y./Mass. Emissions (no cost). CC1 hatch roof ($995). Y87 3800 performance package ($490). 1LE Autocross Package for Formula, includes special handling suspension, larger stabilizer bars, stiffer springs, Koni shocks ($1,175). WS6 Ram Air performance and handling package ($3,150). R7Q 1LE standard equipment delete (credit of $1,125). U1S trunk-mounted, remote 12-disc CD changer ($595). W54 ETR AM/FM Monsoon stereo with auto-reverse, graphic equalizer, clock, seek up/down, remote CD pre-wiring and 10-speaker sound system ($330). W55 ETR AM/FM Monsoon stereo with CD player, graphic equalizer, clock, seek up/down and 10-speaker sound system ($430). AQ9 articulating bucket seats with lumbar supports ($155). AG1 six-way power driver's seat ($270). W68 Sport Appearance package includes aero components, fog lamps, dual outlet exhausts for base models, requires QCB tires and automatic transmission ($1,040). QCB P235/55R16 black sidewall touring tires for Firebird, standard Formula and Trans Am; not available Trans Am Convertible ($135). MW9 traction control system ($250-$450). MM5 five-speed manual transmission (no charge). MN6 six-speed manual transmission (no cost). MX0 four-speed automatic transmission ($815). PO5 chrome aluminum 16-in. wheels ($595).

GRAND PRIX OPTIONS: 1SA option package for SE, includes vehicle and standard equipment (standard). 1SB option package for SE ($345). 1SC option package for SE ($1,285). 1SA option package for GT, includes vehicle and standard equipment (standard). 1SB option package for GT ($815). 1SC option package for GT Sedan ($1,360-$1,390). 1SD package for GT ($2,830-$2,860). 1SA package for GTP (standard). 1SB package for GTP ($525-$555). 1SC package for GTP ($1,620-$1,650). K34 cruise control ($235). FE9 Federal emissions (no cost). YF5 California emissions (no

cost). NG1 NY/Mass. emissions (no cost). KO5 engine block heater ($20). RPO L82 3.1-liter 3100 SFI V-6 (standard). RPO L36 3.8-liter 3800 Series II SFI V-6 in SE models ($415). L36 3.8-liter 3800 Series II supercharged SFI V-6 ($415 but standard in GTP). UV6 heads-up display ($275). VK3 license plate bracket (no cost). U1C AM/FM stereo, seek-scan, CD player and four speakers ($140). U1S multi-disc CD changer ($460). UP3 ETR AM/FM stereo with CD, graphic equalizer, steering wheel radio controls and eight-speaker premium sound system ($165). UN6 ETR AM/FM stereo with auto reverse, six-speaker sound system, and fixed mast antenna (standard). U85 premium sound system ($395-$495). KA1 heated driver's bucket seat with dual setting ($50). AG6 four-way power lumbar driver's seat ($100). AG1 six-way power driver's seat ($270). AM6 45/55 split bench seat with Doral cloth in SE (no cost). D81 rear deck lid spoiler ($175). CF5 power glass sunroof ($570). QNX P225/60R16 black sidewall STL touring tires for SE Sedan ($160). NWO 16-in. aluminum machine-faced wheels for SE ($295). V2C high-polished 16-in. five-spoke aluminum wheels ($325).

BONNEVILLE OPTIONS: SE Sedan 1SA option package, includes vehicle and standard equipment (standard). SE Sedan 1SB option package ($1,125). SE Sedan 1SC option package ($2,030). SE Sedan 1SD option package ($3,135). SSE Sedan 1SA option package, includes vehicle and standard equipment (standard). US7 power antenna without 1SD, UT6 or UP3 ($85). FW1 Computer Command Ride, SSE ($380). FE9 Federal emissions (no cost). YF5 California emissions ($170). NG1 NY/Mass. emissions ($170). NB8 emissions override (no cost). L67 3.8-liter 3800 SFI supercharged V-6, available only with SSEi supercharger package (no cost). KO5 engine block heater ($20). H4U Special edition package, includes specific SLE exterior badging and specific SSE body side cladding, front and rear fascias, fog lamps and grille ($600). WA6 SSEi supercharger package, includes 3.8-liter 3800 V-6 supercharged engine with driver-selectable shift four-speed transmission; cluster with turbo boost gauge; P225/60H16 performance tires; traction control; SSEi floor mats; and SSEi nameplates, SSE only ($1,170). RD9 radio equipment enhancement package ($275). UP3 ETR AM/FM stereo with CD, equalizer, seven speakers ($100-$320). UT6 ETR AM/FM stereo with CD, equalizer, six speakers ($220). UN6 ETR AM/FM stereo with cassette ($100 credit). AM6 45/55 split bench seat in SE (no cost). AS7 bucket seats with 1SB ($220). AS7 leather trim bucket seats with 1SB ($1,345); with 1SC ($850). AL7 articulating 45/45 bucket seats with leather trim in SSE ($245). AG2 power passenger's seat ($305). D58 rear deck lid spoiler delete ($110 credit). CF5 power glass sunroof ($980-$995). UA6 anti-theft alarm system ($190). QNX P225/60R16 black sidewall steel-belted radial touring tires, SE without 1SD ($85). NW9 traction control ($175). N73 16-in. gold aluminum crosslace wheels without 1SD or Y52 ($325). PO5 18-in. aluminum chrome Torque Star wheels (SE Sedan without 1SD or Y52 $920; SE Sedan with 1SD or Y52 $595; SSE $595). QNX tires on SE without 1SC or 1SD ($325).

MONTANA OPTIONS: 1SA Montana SE option package, includes vehicle with standard equipment (no cost). 1SB Montana SE option package ($460). 1SC Montana option package ($1,410). 1SD Montana option package ($2,451). FE9 Federal emissions (no cost). YF5 California emissions ($170). NG1 NY/Mass. emissions ($170). ABA seven-passenger split bench Doral cloth seating, regular wheelbase ($335). ABB seven-passenger modular bucket seats with Multra/Diva cloth trim, regular wheelbase (without 1SD or WX4

1999 Pontiac Extended Wheelbase Montana Minivan. (PGMC)

$450; with 1SD or WX4 $115; extended wheelbase $115). ABD captain's chairs with Multra/Diva cloth (without 1SD or WX4 $600; with 1SD or WX4 $265; extended wheelbase $265). ZP8 eight-passenger seating with Multra/Diva cloth (without 1SD or WX4 $600; with 1SD or WX4 $265; extended wheelbase $265). WJ6 leather seating areas, includes UK3 leather steering wheel with radio controls ($1,055). C34 front-and-rear air conditioning in Montana ($460). C49 electric rear window defogger ($180). KO5 engine block heater ($20). AJ1 deep-tinted glass ($245). C36 rear heater for extended-wheelbase model (with C34 or WX4 $167; without C34 or WX4 $177). AN2 one integral child seat ($125). AN5 two integral child seats ($225). V54 luggage rack, includes saddlebag storage ($175). WX4 Montana package (regular-wheelbase without 1SD $1,537; regular wheelbase with 1SD $1,027; extended-wheelbase without 1SD $1,164; extended-wheelbase with 1SD ($989). D84 two-tone paint ($125). AG1 six-way power driver's seat ($270). AG9 six-way power passenger seat ($305). E58 power sliding door ($350-$400). A31 power windows ($275). AU0 remote keyless entry ($150). UN6 Delco radio equipment ($195). UT6 AM/FM cassette with equalizer and rear seat audio ($150 with leather seat group or $335). U1C AM/FM CD player ($100). UP3 AM/FM CD player with equalizer and rear audio ($250 with leather seat group or $435). UM1 AM/FM cassette with equalizer, dual playback CD player and rear seat audio ($350 with leather seat group or $535). UZ5 extended-range co-axial speakers ($50). G67 Auto Level Control ($180). R6A safety and security package (with P42 or WX4 $60; others $210). XPU P215/70R15 touring tires (regular wheelbase $73; extended wheelbase $35). P42 self-sealing touring tires ($150). V92 trailering provisions ($150). PH3 15-in. aluminum wheels ($259). CF5 sunroof, extended-wheelbase three-door model ($520 with 1SD or $695 without 1SD).

NOTE: Full option package contents, descriptions and applications information can often be determined by consulting factory literature. The data above is edited for size and clarity. This information provided only as a guide to help collectors appraise the relative value of cars with numerous options. Prices for items included as part of a value option package are usually much less than individual prices. Option prices charged by individual dealers may also vary.

HISTORICAL: Pontiac's total output of 1999 model U.S. passenger cars was 629,938 units including 113,421 Sunfires, 265,590 Grand Ams, 41,226 Firebirds, 155,317 Grand Prixs, and 54,384 Bonnevilles. Model-year sales of U.S. cars were 553,390 for a 6.4 percent market share. That was up from 476,212 cars and a 5.9 percent share of market in 1998. These figures do not include Montanas or Canadian units.

2000 PONTIAC

2000 Pontiac Bonneville SLE four-door sedan. (PGMC)

Note: PASS-Key II but PASSKey III is the correct way to write each.
SUNFIRE — CARLINE J — (FOUR) — For the year 2000, Pontiac Sunfire models featured redesigned front and rear fascias. A Gertag five-speed manual transmission was now standard on the coupe and the sedan, but optional on the convertible. The instrument panel and center console featured updated appearances. Another new

addition for the year was restyled 15- and 16-in. aluminum wheels. New brake system components improved the Sunfire's stopping ability. **SE coupe and sedan:** Standard equipment on the Sunfire SE coupe and sedan included extensive acoustical insulation; dual airbags; a rear-mounted fixed-mast antenna; front disc/rear drum brakes with four-wheel ABS; rear-compartment child-resistant door locks in the SE sedan; a 2.2-liter overhead valve four-cylinder engine with stainless steel exhaust system; Soft-Ray tinted glass; GM Computer Command Control; analog instrumentation (including speedometer; odometer; tachometer; coolant temperature gauge; oil pressure indicator and trip odometer); sport-style breakaway exterior mirrors (left-hand remote-controlled); a RPO UM7 Delco ETR stereo radio with seek up/down and a clock; front 45/45 reclining bucket seats; an easy-entry front passenger seat in coupe only; a three-passenger folding rear seat with integral headrests; a four-spoke Sport steering wheel; power rack-and-pinion steering; a PASSLock™ theft-deterrent system; P195/70R14 black sidewall steel-belted-radial tires; a five-speed manual transmission; "wet-arm" fixed-delay "pulse" windshield wipers; and 14-in. bolt-on custom wheel covers. **GT convertible:** The Sunfire GT convertible had the following equipment in addition to or in place of SE sedan equipment: an air-conditioning system using R134A refrigerant; cruise control; an electric rear window defogger; a 2.4-liter Twin Cam four-cylinder engine; a UP3 Delco ETR stereo radio (with seek up/down; a graphic equalizer; a digital clock and a premium sound system); an adjustable tilt steering wheel; P195/65R15 steel-belted radial black sidewall touring tires; a four-speed automatic transmission with traction control; controlled-cycle "wet-arm" windshield wipers; and 15-in. bolt-on custom wheel covers. **GT coupe:** The GT coupe had the following equipment in addition to or in place of GT convertible equipment; P205/55R16 steel-belted radial black sidewall performance tires; a five-speed manual transmission; "wet-arm" windshield wipers with a fixed-delay pulse feature; and 16-in. GT-specific cast aluminum wheels (cruise control deleted).

GRAND AM — CARLINE N — (FOUR) — Changes in the Grand Am for 2000 included the inclusion of a five-speed manual transmission as standard equipment on SE models in combination with the 2.4-liter DOHC four-cylinder engine. Both the 2.4-liter four and the 3.4-liter V-6 now met LEV emissions standards. A composite intake manifold was introduced to save weight and "tumble" incoming air for improved combustion. Also added to the Grand Am's standard equipment list were tether anchors for a rear child seat. **SE coupe and sedan:** Standard equipment for the SE models included Gen II dual airbags; air conditioning; a brake/transmission shift interlock safety feature (with automatic transmission); power front disc/rear drum four-wheel antilock brakes; automatic power door locks with unlock/relock feature; child-resistant rear sedan door locks; the RPO LD9 2.4-liter 16-valve Twin Cam 155-hp four-cylinder engine; an illuminated entry system with automatic lighting control; tinted glass; dual black exterior sport mirrors (left-hand remote controlled; right-hand manual); a day/night inside rearview mirror; a right-hand visor vanity mirror; a Delco ETR AM/FM stereo radio; front bucket seats; power steering; a tilt steering wheel; a tachometer; the PASS-Lock II theft-deterrent system; P215/60R15 black sidewall touring tires; a four-speed ECT automatic transmission; auto trip; Cartegena cloth upholstery; intermittent windshield wipers; and bolt-on wheel covers. **SE1:** The SE1 level also included, in addition to or in place of SE features; cruise control; dual black power mirrors; an

2000 Pontiac Bonneville SLE four-door sedan. (PGMC)

AM/FM ETR stereo radio with cassette; front bucket seats (with manual four-way driver seat adjustment and power forward-back adjustment); a split-back fold-down rear seat; five-spoke aluminum wheels; and power windows with the driver's side "express down" feature. **SE2:** The SE2 level included, in addition to or in place of SE1, the 3.4-liter 170-hp SFI V-6 engine; remote keyless entry; an AM/FM ETR stereo (with CD seven-band graphic equalizer and high-performance speaker system); uplevel front sport bucket seats (with manual four-way driver's seat and power forward-back and height adjustments and manual lumbar support); a leather-wrapped steering wheel with redundant radio controls; speed-sensitive power steering; P225/50R16 touring tires; Redondo/Patina cloth upholstery; and multi-spoke aluminum wheels. **GT coupe:** The GT coupe included, in addition to or in place of SE equipment, four-wheel disc brakes; a 3.4-liter 175-hp 3400 SFI V-6 with Ram Air induction; dual power exterior mirrors; an AM/FM radio (with auto reverse cassette; four speakers and clock); a four-way power driver's seat; a split folding rear seat; the sport interior group; uplevel design seats; a leather-wrapped steering wheel; shift knob and brake handle; variable-effort power steering; P205/55R16 performance tires; power windows and 16-in. machine-faced wheels. In addition to GT; a GT1 package included reote keyless entry; a radio upgrade; a power driver's seat; and a power sunroof.

FIREBIRD — CARLINE F — (V-6/V-8) — Starting in 2000, all Firebirds complied with California's new LEV (low-emissions-vehicles) rules. Two rear child seat tether anchors were added on all models. The throttle linkage on all V-8-powered Firebirds was revised. Both Formula and Trans Am models equipped with the WS6 Ram Air package sported new 17-in. alloy wheel rims. **Firebird coupe:** Standard Firebird coupe equipment included extensive acoustical insulation; dual front airbags; air conditioning; a black fixed-mast antenna at right rear; the brake/transmission shift interlock safety feature (with automatic transmission); power four-wheel disc brakes with four-wheel ABS; the RPO L36 3800 Series II 200-hp SFI V-6 engine; cruise control; electric rear and side window defoggers; Solar-Ray tinted glass; instrumentation (including electric anaolog speedometer; tachometer; odometer; coolant temperature indicator; oil pressure gauge; voltmeter and LED trip odometer); sport exterior mirrors (left-hand remote controlled); a day/night inside rearview mirror with reading lamps; left- and right-hand covered visor vanity mirrors; a Delco AM/FM stereo ETR radio and cassette (with seven-band graphic equalizer, touch control, search-and-replay, Delco theft lock, clock, seek up/down, remote CD prewiring, and four-speaker coaxial sound system); reclining front bucket seats; four-way driver and passenger front seat manual adjusters; a rear two-passenger folding seat; a four-spoke sport tilt steering wheel with adjustable column; the PASS-Key II theft-deterrent system; tilt steering column; P215/60R16 touring tires with a high-pressure compact spare; the RPO MM5 five-speed manual transmission; controlled-cycle windshield wipers; and bright silver 16-in. five-spoke cast aluminum wheels. **Formula coupe:** Formula models also included, in addition to or in place of the above, a power antenna; power door locks; power automatic sport mirrors with blue glass; a Delco 500-watt peak power Monsoon AM/FM stereo (with CD, seven-band graphic equalizer, clock, touch control, seek up/down, search and replay, Delco antitheft lock, high-performance 10-

2000 Pontiac Sunfire SE four-door sedan. (PGMC)

speaker sound system in coupe or six-speaker sound system in convertible, HSS speakers and tweeters in doors, 6.5-in. subwoofers in sail panels, subwoofer amp, and four speakers and tweeters in rear quarter panels); a leather-wrapped steering wheel with radio controls (including leather-wrapped shift knob and parking brake handle); P245/50ZR16 speed-rated all-weather tires; and power window controls with driver's "express down" feature (requires power mirrors and door locks). **Trans Am:** Trans Am models also included, in addition to or in place of Formula features, an audible content theft-deterrent system, remote keyless entry, and a six-way power front driver's seat.

GRAND PRIX — CARLINE W — (V-6/V-8) — A Grand Prix Daytona Pace Car replica was introduced in 2000. Horsepower was increased on the 3.1-liter V-6 and all engines complied with LEV regulations. Revisions to the Grand Prix's front airflow deflector reduced air drag and enhanced fuel economy. The GM PassKey III theft-deterrent system was standard on all models and all had the new child seat tether anchors. **Grand Prix SE:** Standard Grand Prix SE equipment included extensive acoustical insulation; dual front airbags; air conditioning; a fixed mast antenna; the brake/transmission shift interlock safety feature; four-wheel power disc brakes with antilock; automatic programmable door locks with delayed locking and lockout protection (rear child security locks in SE sedan); the RPO L82 3.1-liter 3100 SFI V-6; a stainless steel exhaust system; completely flush fitting Soft-Ray safety-laminated tinted glass; GM Computer Command Control; mechanical analog instrumentation (including tachometer, fuel gauge, coolant temperature indicator, and trip odometer); a Driver Information Center (including trunk ajar, ETS on/off, low washer fluid, check tire pressure, check oil soon, and ETS low-traction indicators); body-colored; power-operated remote-control left- and right-hand sport-style outside rearview mirrors; left- and right-hand covered visor vanity mirrors; a Delco ETR AM/FM stereo radio with seek/scan feature and clock; front sport bucket seats with Doral cloth interior fabric; a three-passenger rear bench seat with integrated head rests; a two-way manually-adjustable driver's bucket seat with two-way manual lumbar support; front seat back storage pockets; a four-spoke sport tilt urethane steering wheel with adjustable column and airbag; P205/70R15 black sidewall steel-belted radial touring tires; a four-speed ETC automatic transmission; 15-in. sport-style bolt-on wheel covers; wet-arm controlled-cycle windshield wipers; and power windows with lighted switches and the driver's side "express down" feature. **Grand Prix**

2000 Pontiac Grand Am SE two-door coupe. (PGMC)

2000 Pontiac Grand Prix GTP four-door sedan. (PGMC)

2000 Pontiac Firebird Trans Am two-door convertible. (PGMC)

GT coupe: In addition to or in place of SE equipment, standard GT coupe features included cruise control; the RPO L36 3800 Series II V-6; a stainless steel exhaust system with dual bright outlet exhausts; a Delco 2001 series ETR AM/FM stereo radio (with cassette, clock, seek up/down, and auto reverse); a leather-wrapped sport steering wheel; P225/60R16 black sidewall tires; and five-spoke 16 x 6.5-in. cast aluminum wheels. **Grand Prix GT sedan:** In addition to or in place of SE equipment, standard GT sedan features included a Delco 2001 series ETR AM/FM stereo radio with cassette, clock, seek up/down, and auto reverse.

BONNEVILLE — CARLINE H — (V-6) — An all-new 2000 Bonneville cost less than a similarly-equipped 1999 version. The new car came in SE, SLE, and SSEi levels. Standard in all were seat-mounted safety belts, dual front and side airbags, four-wheel antilock disc brakes, and the PassKey III theft-deterrent system. The SLE and SSEi also featured dual-climate-control and a driver-information center with programmable functionality. The SSEi came with a supercharged 3.8-liter V-6 with dual exhausts. A StabiliTrak stability system, a heads-up display, a memory driver's seat, heated outside mirrors, and the OnStar system were all standard in the SSEi. **SE sedan:** Standard Bonneville SE equipment included the RPO L36 3.8-liter 3800 Series II V-6; a four-speed automatic transmission; a Spacesaver spare tire; a front stabilizer bar; a self-leveling suspension; front disc/rear drum ABS brakes; front side-mounted airbags; rear door child safety locks; child seat anchors; rear center lap belt; headrests; an antitheft system; daytime running lights; dusk-sensing headlamps; front fog lights; a rear window defogger; bucket front seats; cloth upholstery; a six-way power driver's seat with adjustable lumbar support; a rear bench seat with pass-through center armrest; power door locks; power windows; power mirrors; a Delco AM/FM cassette stereo; a six-speaker sound system; cruise control; power steering; a tilt adjustable steering wheel; remote-control left- and right-hand outside mirrors; front and rear cup holders; a remote trunk release; front door map pockets; a cargo net; a front center console with storage space; air conditioning; front and rear reading lights; left- and right-hand illuminated visor/vanity mirrors; front and rear floor mats; a tachometer; a clock; and a rear deck lid spoiler. **SLE sedan:** In addition to or in place of the above, the Bonneville SLE model included 17-in. wheel rims; P235/55R17 tires; front and rear stabilizer bars; traction control; heated mirrors; audio and cruise controls on the steering wheel; a dual-zone climate control system; a leather-wrapped steering wheel; an external temperature display; a compass; and the OnStar telecommunications system. **SSEi sedan:** In addition to or in place of the above, the Bonneville SSEi sedan had a supercharged 240-hp V-6; a stability-control system; leather upholstery; a 12-way power driver's seat and a 12-way passenger seat; a reverse-tilt passenger-side mirror; an AM/FM cassette stereo with CD; Bose speakers; speed-proportional power steering; a universal remote; an auto-dimming inside rearview mirror; a memory seat-and-mirrors system; and a heads-up display.

MONTANA — CARLINE U — (V-6) — The 2000 Montana featured an upgraded electrical system that used fewer wires and electrical connections to carry digitally-coded information and provide oil-life monitoring. An upgraded instrument cluster featured a new message center and additional reading lamps. An improved antilock braking system shortened stopping distances by up to 10 percent. Like all Pontiacs, the Montana now had a LEV-compliant engine. **Montana Sport Standard Wheelbase:** Standard Montana Sport Standard

Wheelbase equipment included driver and front passenger airbags; an integrated roof antenna; the brake/transmission shift interlock safety feature; power front disc/rear drum four-wheel antilock brakes; a soft fascia with integral rub strips; child security door locks; front side window defoggers; power door locks with signal-key automatic locking doors; the 3.4-liter 3400 SFI V-6 engine; a stainless steel exhaust system; a solar-coated heat-repelling glass windshield; four flip-out rear side glass windows (Soft-Ray tinted); GM Computer Command Control; instrumentation (including analog speedometer, odometer, tachometer, coolant temperature gauge, low oil indicator, low coolant indicator, voltmeter, trip odometer, and door ajar signal); blue-tinted power left- and right-hand sport mirrors with the fold-and-stow feature; a Delco ETR AM/FM stereo radio with clock; rear window wipers; front reclining bucket seats (with rotating headrests, manual lumbar adjustment, and inboard armrests); seven-passenger split folding modular 2-2-3 bench seating with integrated headrests (optional regular wheelbase models); a four-way manual adjusting driver's seat; a four-spoke adjustable tilting sport steering wheel (with airbag); a fully-independent MacPherson strut front suspension; a rear coil spring suspension; P205/70R15 all-season steel-belted radial tires; a four-speed automatic ETC transmission; Doral cloth upholstery; wet-arm controlled-cycle windshield wipers; and 15-in. styled wheels with bolt-on covers. **Montana Sport Extended Wheelbase**: Standard equipment for the extended wheelbase Montana Sport model included driver and front passenger airbags; an integrated roof antenna; the brake/transmission shift interlock safety feature; power front disc/rear drum four-wheel antilock brakes; a soft fascia with integral rub strips; child security door locks; front side window defoggers; power door locks with signal-key automatic locking doors; the 3.4-liter 3400 SFI V-6 engine; a stainless steel exhaust system; a solar-coated heat-repelling glass windshield; four flip-out rear side glass windows (Soft-Ray tinted); GM Computer Command Control; instrumentation (including analog speedometer, odometer, tachometer, coolant temperature gauge, low oil indicator, low coolant indicator, voltmeter, trip odometer, and door ajar signal); blue-tinted power left- and right-hand sport mirrors with the fold-and-stow feature; a Delco ETR AM/FM stereo radio with clock; rear window wipers; front reclining bucket seats (with rotating headrests, manual lumbar adjustment, and inboard armrests); seven-passenger split folding modular 2-2-3 bench seat with integrated headrests; a four-way manual adjusting driver's seat; a four-spoke adjustable tilting sport steering wheel (with airbag); a fully-independent McPherson strut front suspension; a rear coil spring suspension; P215/70R15 all-season tires; a four-speed automatic ETC transmission; Doral cloth upholstery; wet-arm controlled-cycle windshield wipers; and 15-in. styled wheels with bolt-on covers.

I.D. DATA: The vehicle identification number (VIN) is located on the top left-hand surface of the instrument panel and is visible through the windshield. The VIN has 17 symbols. The first symbol indicates the country of manufacture (1 or 4=United States; 2=Canada; 3=Mexico; W=Germany). The second symbol indicates the manufacturer (G=General Motors, GENASYS L.C.; Y=NUMMI; C=CAMMI; O=Opel). The third symbol indicates the make/division (2=Pontiac; M=Pontiac MPV and 7=GM of Canada). The fourth symbol (trucks) indicates the GVWR range and brake system. The fourth and fifth symbols (passenger cars) indicate the car line and series F/S=Firebird and convertible; F/V=Formula and convertible; H/X=Bonneville SE; H/Y=Bonneville SLE; H/Z=Bonneville SSEi; J/B=Sunfire and convertible; J/D=Sunfire; N/E=Grand Am SE; N/F=Grand Am SE1; N/G=Grand Am SE2; N/V=Grand Am GT1; N/W= Grand Am GT; W/J=Grand Prix SE; W/P=Grand Prix GT; W/

2000 Pontiac Firebird two-door coupe. (PGMC)

2000 Pontiac Bonneville SSE four-door sedan. (PGMC)

2000 Pontiac Bonneville SLE four-door sedan. (PGMC)

R=Grand Prix GTP. The fifth and sixth symbols (trucks) indicate car line and series: U/0=Montana All-Purpose Vehicle 4x2; U/1=Montana All-Purpose Vehicle 4 x 2 luxury; U/2=Montana All-Purpose Vehicle 4 x 2 economy; X/0=Montana All-Purpose Vehicle Extended-Wheelbase 4 x 2; X/1=Montana All-Purpose Vehicle luxury Extended-Wheelbase 4 x 2; X/2= Montana All-Purpose Vehicle economy Extended-Wheelbase 4 x 2. The sixth symbol (passenger cars only) indicates body style: (1=two-door coupe models 27, 37, 47 and 57; 2=two-door models 07, 08, 77, 87; 3=two-door convertible model 67; 5=four-door sedan models 19 and 69; 6=four-door sedan models 29 and 68; 8=four-door station wagon model 35. The seventh symbol (passenger cars) indicates the restraint system: 2=Active manual belts with driver and passenger inflatable restraints; 4=Active manual belts front and side; 6=Active manual belts with dual airbags and automatic passenger side sensor; 7=Active manual belts with dual front-and-side airbags in front and rear. The seventh symbol (trucks) indicates body style: 3=All-Purpose Vehicle (Montana). The eighth symbol indicates the engine type: E=RPO LA1 3.4-liter fuel-injected (MFI) V-6; G=RPO LS1 5.7-liter fuel-injected (MFI) V-8; J=RPO LG8 3.1-liter fuel-injected (SFI) V-6; K=RPO L36 3.8-liter fuel-injected (MFI) V-6; T=RPO LD9 2.4-liter fuel-injected (MFI) I-4; 1=RPO L67 3.8-liter fuel-injected (MFI) V-6; 4=RPO LN2 2.2-liter fuel-injected (MFI) I-4; E=RPO LA1 3.4-liter fuel-injected (MFI) V-6. (Note: All Pontiac engines made in U.S.). The ninth symbol is a check digit. The 10th symbol indicates model year (Y=2000). The 11th symbol indicates the GM assembly plant (B=Baltimore, Md., T&B; B=Lansing, Mich., GENASYS; C=Lansing, Mich.; D=Doraville, Ga.; E=Pontiac East, Mich., T&B; F=Fairfax II, Kan.; F=Flint, Mich., T&B; G=Silao Mexico; H=Flint, Mich.; J=Janesville, Wis., T&B; K=Linden, N.J., T&B; M=Lansing, Mich; M=Toluca Mexico; R=Arlington, Texas; R=Russelsheim Germany; S=Ramos Arizpe Mexico; T=Shreveport, La.; U=Hamtramck, Mich.; Y=Wilmington, Del.; Z=Fremont, Calif.; Z=Spring Hill, Tenn.; Z=Ft. Wayne, Ind. T&B; 0=Lansing, Mich.; 1=Oshawa Canada, #1; 1=Oshawa Canada, #2; 1=Wentzville, Mo., T&B; 2=Morraine, Ohio, T&B; 2=Ste. Therese, Canada; 3=Kawasaki Japan; 4=Orion, Mich.; 5=Bowling Green, Ky.; 6=Ingersoll, Ontario Canada; 6=Oklahoma City, Okla.; 7=Lordstown, Ohio; 7=Flusawa Japan; 8=Shreveport, La., T&B; 8=Tillisonburg, Ohio, CANEXPO; 9=Oshawa, Ontario Canada, #1). Pontiacs are not produced at all of these plants. The last six symbols are the consecutive unit number at the factory.

Model Number	Body Style Number	Body Type & Seating	Factory Price	Shipping Weight	Production Total
SUNFIRE SE SERIES B (I-4)					
J/B	B37V	2d Coupe-4P	14,515	2,630	Note 1
J/B	B69V	4d Sedan-4P	14,615	2,670	Note 1
SUNFIRE GT SERIES D (I-4)					
J/B	D67V	2d Convertible-4P	22,255	2,892	Note 1
J/D	D37V	2d Coupe -4P	16,805	2,822	Note 1
GRAND AM SE SERIES E (I-4)					
N/E	E37V	2d Coupe-4P	16,590	3,066	Note 2
N/E	E69V	4d Sedan-4P	16,890	3,116	Note 2
GRAND AM SE1 SERIES F (I-4)					
N/F	E37V	2d Coupe-4P	20,130	3,091	Note 2
N/F	E69V	4d Sedan-4P	20,430	3,168	Note 2
GRAND AM GT SERIES W (V-6)					
N/W	W37V	2d Coupe-4P	21,720	3,091	Note 2
N/W	W69V	2d Sedan-4P	22,020	3,168	Note 2

Model Number	Body Style Number	Body Type & Seating	Factory Price	Shipping Weight	Production Total
FIREBIRD SERIES S (V-6)					
F/S	S87V	2d Coupe-4P	18,700	3,402	Note 3
F/S	S67V	2d Convertible-4P	25,320	3,492	Note 3
FORMULA SERIES V (V-8)					
F/V	V87V	2d Coupe-4P	23,600	3, 514	Note 3
TRANS AM SERIES V (V-8)					
F/V	V87V	2d Coupe-4P	26,710	3,536	Note 3
F/V	V67V	2d Convertible-4P	30,780	3,605	Note 3
GRAND PRIX SE SERIES J (V-6)					
W/J	J69V	4d Sedan-4P	20,495	3,373	Note 4
GRAND PRIX GT SERIES P (V-6)					
W/P	P37V	2d Coupe-4	22,075	3,396	Note 4
W/P	P69V	4d Sedan-4P	22,225	3,414	Note 4
GRAND PRIX GTP SERIES R (V-6)					
W/R	R37V	2d Coupe-4	24,480	3,505	Note 4
W/R	R69V	4d Sedan-4P	24,990	3,523	Note 4
BONNEVILLE SE SERIES X (V-6)					
X	X69V	4d Sport Sedan-6P	23,495	3,446	Note 5
BONNEVILLE SLE SERIES Y (V-6)					
Y	Z69V	4d Sport Sedan-6P	30,495	3,587	Note 5
BONNEVILLE SSEi SERIES Z (Supercharged V-6)					
Z	Z69V	4d Sport Sedan-6P	31,665	3,691	Note 5
MONTANA REGULAR WHEELBASE SERIES N (V-6)					
U	N06V	3d Minivan	21,655	3,730	Note 6
MONTANA EXTENDED WHEELBASE SERIES M (V-6)					
U	M06V	4d Minivan	23,445	3,803	Note 6
U	M16V	4d Minivan	24,455	3,942	Note 6
MONTANA SPORT EXTENDED WHEELBASE SERIES M (V-6)					
U	M06V	4d Minivan	25,335	3,828	Note 6
U	M16V	4d Minivan	26,335	3,967	Note 6

NOTE 1: Production of 2000 Sunfires was 140,265 units in the U.S. and Canada.

NOTE 2: Production of 2000 Grand Ams was 255,855 units in the U.S. and Canada.

NOTE 3: Production of 2000 Firebirds was 31,826 units in the U.S. and Canada.

NOTE 4: Production of 2000 Grand Prixs was 172,811 units in the U.S. and Canada.

NOTE 5: Production of 2000 Bonnevilles was 62,463 units in the U.S. and Canada.

NOTE 6: Model-year production total was 81,718 Montanas of all types.

SUNFIRE ENGINES

ENGINE [Base Four SE]: Inline. OHV. Four-cylinder. Two valves per cylinder. Displacement: 133 cid. (2.2L). Bore & stroke: 3.50 x 3.46 in. Compression ratio: 9.0:1. Net horsepower: 115 at 5000 rpm. Torque: 135 lbs.-ft. at 3600 rpm. Fuel system: SFI. VIN Code: 4. RPO Code: LN2.

ENGINE [Base Four (GT/SE Convertible); Optional (SE)]: Inline. DOHC. Four-cylinder. Four valves per cylinder. Displacement: 146 cid. (2.4L). Bore & stroke: 3.54 x 3.79 in. Compression ratio: 9.5:1. Net horsepower: 150 at 5600 rpm. Torque: 155 lbs.-ft. at 4400 rpm. Fuel system: SFI. VIN Code: T. RPO Code: LD9.

GRAND AM ENGINES

ENGINE [Base Four SE/GT]: Inline. DOHC. Four-cylinder. Four valves per cylinder. Displacement: 146 cid. (2.4L). Bore & stroke: 3.54 x 3.79 in. Compression ratio: 9.5:1. Net horsepower: 150 at 5600 rpm. Torque: 155 lbs.-ft. at 4400 rpm. Fuel system: SFI. VIN Code: T. RPO Code: LD9.

ENGINE [Optional Six]: V-block. OHV. Six-cylinder. Cast-iron block and head. Aluminum intake manifold. Displacement: 207 cid. (3.4L). Bore & stroke: 3.62 x 3.31 in. Compression ratio: 9.5:1. Brake horsepower: 170 at 4800 rpm. Torque: 195 lbs.-ft. at 4000 rpm. Fuel system: SFI. VIN Code: M. RPO Code: L82.

FIREBIRD ENGINES

ENGINE [Base V-6]: V-block. OHV. Six-cylinder. Displacement: 231 cid. (3.8L). Bore & stroke: 3.80 x 3.40 in. Compression ratio: 9.4:1. Brake horsepower: 200 at 5200 rpm. Torque: 225 lbs.-ft. at 4000 rpm. Fuel system: SFI. VIN Code: K. RPO Code: L36.

ENGINE [Base V-8]: V-block. OHV. Eight-cylinder. Aluminum block and head. Aluminum intake manifold. Displacement: 350 cid. (5.7L). Bore & stroke: 3.90 x 3.62 in. Brake horsepower: 305 at 5200 rpm. Torque: 335 lbs.-ft. at 4000 rpm. Compression ratio: 10.5:1. Fuel system: SFI. VIN Code: G. RPO Code: LT1.

GRAND PRIX ENGINES

ENGINE [Base V-6]: V-block. OHV. Six-cylinder. Displacement: 191 cid. (3.1L). Bore & stroke: 3.50 x 3.31 in. Compression ratio: 9.5:1. Brake horsepower: 160 at 5200 rpm. Torque: 185 lbs.-ft. at 4000 rpm. Fuel system: SFI. VIN Code: M. RPO Code: L82.

ENGINE [Optional V-6]: V-block. Six-cylinder. Displacement: 231 cid. (3.8L). Bore & stroke: 3.80 x 3.40 in. Compression ratio: 9.4:1. Brake horsepower: 200 at 5200 rpm. Torque: 225 lbs.-ft. at 4,000 rpm. Fuel system: SFI. VIN Code: X. RPO Code: L36.

ENGINE [Optional V-6; GTP only]: V-block. Six-cylinder. Displacement: 231 cid. (3.8L). Bore & stroke: 3.80 x 3.40 in. Compression ratio: 8.5:1. Brake horsepower: 240 at 5200 rpm. Torque: 280 lbs.-ft. at 3200 rpm. Fuel system: SFI. VIN Code: X. RPO Code: L36.

BONNEVILLE ENGINES

ENGINE [Base V-6 SE/SSE]: "3800" SFI Series II V-6. V-block. OHV. Six-cylinder. Displacement: 231 cid. (3.8L). Bore & stroke: 3.80 x 3.40 in. Compression ratio: 9.0:1. Brake horsepower: 205 at 5200 rpm. Torque: 230 lbs.-ft. at 4000 rpm. Fuel system: SFI. VIN Code: K RPO Code: L36.

ENGINE [Optional Supercharged V-6 SSEi]: "3800" Supercharged Series II V-6. V-block. OHV. Six-cylinder. Displacement: 231 cid. (3.8L). Bore & stroke: 3.80 x 3.40 in. Compression ratio: 8.5:1. Brake horsepower: 240 at 5200 rpm. Torque: 280 lbs.-ft. at 3200 rpm. Fuel system: SFI. VIN Code: 1 RPO Code: L67.

MONTANA ENGINE

ENGINE [Base V-6]: V-block. DOHC. Six-cylinder. Displacement: 207 cid. (3.4L). Bore & stroke: 3.62 x 3.31 in. Compression ratio: 9.5:1. Brake horsepower: 185 at 5200 rpm. Torque: 210 lbs.-ft. at 4,000 rpm. Fuel system: SFI. VIN Code: E. RPO Code: LA1.

CHASSIS

SUNFIRE CHASSIS: Wheelbase: (all) 104.1 in. Overall length: (All except SE sedan) 181.9 in.; (SE sedan) 181.7 in. Overall width: (All except SE sedan) 68.4 in.; (SE sedan) 67.9 in. Height: (coupe) 53.0 in.; (sedan) 54.7 in.; (convertible) 54.1 in.

GRAND AM CHASSIS: Wheelbase: (all) 106.7 in. Overall length: 186.3 in. Width: (all) 70.4 in. Height: (all) 55.1 in.

FIREBIRD CHASSIS: Wheelbase: (all) 101.0 in. Overall length: (Firebird/Formula) 193.3 in.; (Trans Am) 193.7 in. Width: (all) 74.4 in. Height: (Firebird/Formula) 51.2 in.; (Trans Am) 51.8 in.

GRAND PRIX CHASSIS: Wheelbase: (all) 110.5 in. Overall length: (all) 196.5. Width: (all) 72.7 in. Height: (all) 54.7 in.

BONNEVILLE CHASSIS: Wheelbase: (all) 112.2 in. Overall length: (all) 202.6 in. Width: (all) 74.2 in. Height: (all) 56.6 in.

MONTANA CHASSIS: Wheelbase: (Standard three-door) 112 in.; (Four-door) 112 in.; (Extended four-door) 120 in. Overall length: (Standard three- and four-doors) 187.3 in.; (Extended four-door) 201.3 in. Width: (all) 72.7 in. Height: (Standard three- and four-doors) 67.4 in.; (Extended four-door) 68.1 in.

Note: See standard equipment lists for tire sizes.

TECHNICAL

SUNFIRE TECHNICAL: Chassis: Front engine/front drive. Base transmission: Five-speed manual. Optional transmission: Three-speed automatic. Front suspension: MacPherson struts. Rear suspension: Coil springs, semi-independent torsion beam, trailing arms. Steering: Rack-and-pinion. Front brakes: vented disc power-assisted. Rear brakes: drum power-assisted.

GRAND AM TECHNICAL: Chassis: Front engine/front drive. Base transmission: Five-speed manual with overdrive. Optional transmission: Three-speed automatic. Front suspension: MacPherson struts. Rear suspension: Trailing crank arm with twist arm, coil springs. Steering (Standard): Power-assisted rack-and-pinion. Steering (Sport Performance and WS6): Power-assisted rack-and-pinion, 14.0:1 ratio. Front brakes: Power-assisted vented discs. Rear brakes: Power-assisted drums. Fuel tank: 13.6 gal.

FIREBIRD TECHNICAL: Chassis: Front engine/rear drive. Base transmission: Five-speed manual. Front suspension: Modified MacPherson strut with anti-roll bar. Rear suspension: Live axle with coil springs, control arms, torque arm, track bar and anti-roll bar. Steering: Power recirculating ball. Brakes: Power four-wheel discs with ABS.

GRAND PRIX TECHNICAL: Chassis: Front engine/front drive. Front suspension: MacPherson struts. Rear suspension: Tri-link independent suspension with anti-roll bar. Steering: Power-assisted rack-and-pinion. Four-wheel power disc brakes.

BONNEVILLE TECHNICAL: Chassis: Front engine/front drive. Base transmission: Four-speed automatic. Front suspension: MacPherson struts with anti-roll bar. Front suspension: (SE) MacPherson struts with anti-roll bar; (SSE) MacPherson struts with anti-roll bar. Rear suspension: MacPherson. Steering: Power-assisted rack-and-pinion. Brakes: Power front disc/rear drum with four-wheel ABS.

TRANS SPORT TECHNICAL: Chassis: Front engine/front drive. Transmission: Three-speed automatic. Front suspension: MacPherson strut, stamped lower control arms, stabilizer bar. Rear suspension: Open-section transverse beam on stamped steel trailing arms, tube shocks, coil springs and stabilizer bar. Steering: Power-assisted rack-and-pinion. Front brakes: Power-assisted vented rotors. Rear brakes: Power-assisted finned composite cast-iron drums.

OPTIONS

SUNFIRE OPTIONS: 1SA Sunfire SE coupe and sedan option package including vehicle with standard equipment (no cost). 1SB Sunfire SE coupe ($2,130) and sedan ($2,280) option group. 1SC Sunfire SE coupe ($3,225) and sedan ($3,415). SE convertible option package including vehicle with standard equipment (no cost). 1SA Sunfire GT coupe option package including vehicle with standard equipment (no cost). 1SB Sunfire GT coupe ($2,245). C41 non-air-conditioning not desired (no cost). C60 custom air conditioning ($830). K34 cruise

2000 Pontiac Bonneville SSEi four-door sedan. (PGMC)

2000 Pontiac Montana minivand APV. (PGMC)

2000 Pontiac Sunfire GT two-door coupe. (PGMC)

2000 Pontiac Sunfire GT two-door convertible. (PGMC)

control ($235). C49 electric window defogger ($180). FE9 Federal emissions with LD9 and MX0 (no cost). YF5 California emissions (no cost). NG1 NY/Mass. Emissions (no cost). RPO LD (engine ($450). K05 engine block heater ($20). VK3 front license plate bracket (no cost). R9P power package, coupe and convertible ($380) or sedan ($445). UN6 Delco radio equipment ($195). UT6 ETR AM/FM stereo with cassette and equalizer ($270 credit). UP3 ETR AM/FM stereo with CD and equalizer ($370). R7X Security package: ($370-$410). DT4 smoker's package ($15). T43 rear deck lid spoiler ($150). AS5 Sport Interior package: ($180). CF5 power sunroof ($556-$595). QPD P195/65R15 black sidewall tires, except GT ($135). MM5 five-speed transmission ($600 credit in SE coupe or sedan with 1SB and $810 credit in others). MX0 four-speed automatic transmission SE coupe/sedan without 1SB and 1SC ($210); GT coupe ($810). MX1 three-speed automatic transmission, SE coupe/sedan only ($600). PG1 15-in. wheel covers requires QPD tires (no charge). PF7 15-in. aluminum wheels; not available on GT ($295).

GRAND AM OPTIONS: K34 cruise control: ($235). FE9 Federal emissions (no cost). YF5 California emissions ($170). NG1 N.Y./Mass. Emissions ($170). LA1 3.4-liter 3400 SFI V-6 ($595). LD9 2.4-liter Twin Cam 16-valve four-cylinder engine ($595 credit as part of SE package delete). K05 engine block heater ($20). DT4 smoker's package; ($15). VK3 front license plate bracket (no cost). UN1 ETR AM/FM stereo with CD, cassette, equalizers, six speakers ($195-$665 depending on model). UN6 ETR AM/FM stereo with cassette ($195). UP3 ETR AM/FM stereo with CD, equalizers, six speakers ($210-$470 depending on model and equipment). AUO remote keyless entry ($150). AG1 6-way power seat ($265). B20 Prado leather bucket seats ($475). T43 rear deck lid spoiler ($195 or standard with GT). CF5 power glass sunroof ($595).

FIREBIRD OPTIONS: 1SA Firebird coupe option package, includes vehicle with standard equipment (no cost). 1SB Plus Firebird coupe option package, includes vehicle with standard equipment plus power door locks, power windows, power sport mirrors with blue tint, power antenna, automatic transmission, and power seat ($1,510). 1SC Firebird option group ($2,450). 1SA convertible option package, includes vehicle with standard equipment (no cost). GU5 3.23:1 performance axle ($300). FE9 Federal emissions (no cost). YF5 50 California emissions (no cost). NG1 N.Y./Mass. Emissions (no cost). CC1 hatch roof ($995). Y87 3800 performance package ($490). 1LE Autocross Package for Formula, includes special handling suspension, larger stabilizer bars, stiffer springs, Koni shocks ($1,175). WS6 Ram Air performance and handling package ($3,150). R7Q 1LE standard equipment delete (credit of $1,125). U1S trunk mounted remote 12-disc CD changer ($595). W54 ETR AM/FM Monsoon stereo with auto-reverse, graphic equalizer, clock, seek up/down, remote CD pre-wiring and 10-speaker sound system ($330). W55 ETR AM/FM Monsoon stereo with CD player, graphic equalizer, clock, seek up/down and 10-speaker sound system ($430). AQ9 articulating bucket seats with lumbar supports ($155). AG1 six-way power driver's seat ($270). W68 Sport Appearance package includes aero components, fog lamps, dual outlet exhausts for base models, requires QCB tires and automatic transmission ($1,040). QCB P235/55R16 black sidewall touring tires for Firebird, standard Formula and Trans Am; not available Trans Am convertible

($135). MW9 traction control system ($250-$450). MM5 five-speed manual transmission (no charge). MN6 six-speed manual transmission (no cost). MX0 four-speed automatic transmission ($815). PO5 chrome aluminum 16-in. wheels ($595).

GRAND PRIX OPTIONS: 1SA option package for SE, includes vehicle and standard equipment (standard). 1SB option package for SE ($345). 1SC option package for SE ($1,285). 1SA option package for GT, includes vehicle and standard equipment (standard). 1SB option package for GT ($815). 1SC option package for GT sedan ($1,360-$1,390). 1SD package for GT ($2,830-$2,860). 1SA package for GTP (standard). 1SB package for GTP ($525-$555). 1SC package for GTP ($1,620-$1,650). K34 cruise control ($235). FE9 Federal emissions (no cost). YF5 California emissions (no cost). NG1 NY/Mass. emissions (no cost). K05 engine block heater ($20). RPO L82 3.1-liter 3100 SFI V-6 (standard). RPO L36 3.8-liter 3800 Series II SFI V-6 in SE models ($415). L36 3.8-liter 3800 Series II supercharged SFI V-6 ($415 but standard in GTP). UV6 heads-up display ($275) VK3 license plate bracket (no cost). U1C AM/FM stereo, seek-scan, CD player, and four speakers ($140). U1S multi-disc CD changer ($460). UP3 ETR AM/FM stereo with CD, graphic equalizer, steering wheel radio controls and eight-speaker premium sound system ($165). UN6 ETR AM/FM stereo with auto reverse, 6-speaker sound system and fixed mast antenna (standard). U85 premium sound system ($395-$495). KA1 heated driver's bucket seat with dual setting ($50). AG6 four-way power lumbar driver's seat ($100). AG1 six-way power driver's seat ($270). AM6 45-55 split bench seat with Doral cloth in SE (no cost). D81 rear deck lid spoiler ($175). CF5 power glass sunroof ($570). QNX P225/60R16 black sidewall STL touring tires for SE sedan ($160). NWO 16-in. aluminum machine-faced wheels for SE ($295). V2C high-polished 16-in. five-spoke aluminum wheels ($325).

BONNEVILLE OPTIONS: 1SC option group ($1,840). A51 leather bucket seats package in SLE ($850). AG2 6-way power passenger seat ($330-$530). AM6 split bench seat ($150). CF5 power glass sunroof ($1,080). K05 engine block heater ($35). KA1 heated front seats ($295). N94 17-in. wheels on SLE/SSEi, includes bright chrome high-polished multi-spoke cast aluminum wheels. NP5 leather-wrapped steering wheel with radio controls in SE ($175). NW9 traction control in SE ($175). U1P Delco AM/FM stereo with CD player ($100), U1Q Delco AM/FM stereo with CD and cassette in SE and SLE ($200). U1S trunk-mounted 12-disc CD changer, in SE requires 1SC ($595).

2000 Pontiac Bonneville SSEi four-door sedan. (PGMC)

MONTANA OPTIONS: 1SA Montana SE option package, includes vehicle with standard equipment (no cost). 1SB Montana SE option package ($460). 1SC Montana option package ($1,410). 1SD Montana option package ($2,451). FE9 Federal emissions (no cost). YF5 California emissions ($170). NG1 NY/Mass. emissions ($170). ABA seven-passenger split bench Doral cloth seating, regular wheelbase ($335). ABB seven-passenger modular bucket seats with Multra/Diva cloth trim, regular wheelbase (without 1SD or WX4 $450; with 1SD or WX4 $115; extended wheelbase $115). ABD captain's chairs with Multra/Diva cloth (without 1SD or WX4 $600; with 1SD or WX4 $265; extended wheelbase $265). ZP8 eight-passenger seating with Multra/Diva cloth (without 1SD or WX4 $600; with 1SD or WX4 $265; extended wheelbase $265). WJ6 leather seating areas, includes UK3 leather steering wheel with radio controls ($1,055). C34 front-and-rear air conditioning in Montana ($460). C49 electric rear window defogger ($180). KO5 engine block heater ($20). AJ1 deep-tinted glass ($245). C36 rear heater for extended-wheelbase model (with C34 or WX4 $167; without C34 or WX4 $177). AN2 one integral child seat ($125). AN5 two integral child seats ($225). V54 luggage rack, includes saddlebag storage ($175). WX4 Montana package (regular-wheelbase without 1SD $1,537; regular wheelbase with 1SD $1,027; extended-wheelbase without 1SD $1,164; extended-wheelbase with 1SD ($989). D84 two-tone paint ($125). AG1 six-way power driver's seat ($270). AG9 six-way power passenger seat ($305). E58 power sliding door ($350-$400). A31 power windows ($275). AU0 remote keyless entry ($150). UN6 Delco radio equipment ($195). UT6 AM/FM cassette with equalizer and rear seat audio ($150 with leather seat group or $335). U1C AM/FM CD player ($100). UP3 AM/FM CD player with equalizer and rear audio ($250 with leather seat group or $435). UM1 AM/FM cassette with equalizer, dual playback CD player and rear seat audio ($350 with leather seat group or $535). UZ5 extended-range co-axial speakers ($50). G67 Auto Level Control ($180). R6A safety and security package (with P42 or WX4 $60; others $210). XPU P215/70R15 touring tires (regular wheelbase $73; extended wheelbase $35). P42 self-sealing touring tires ($150). V92 trailering provisions ($150). PH3 15-in. aluminum wheels ($259). CF5 sunroof, extended-wheelbase three-door model ($520 with 1SD or $695 without 1SD).

NOTE: Full option package contents, descriptions, and applications information can often be determined by consulting factory literature. The data above is edited for size and clarity. This information provided only as a guide to help collectors appraise the relative value of cars with numerous options. Prices for items included as part of a value option package are usually much less than individual prices. Option prices charged by individual dealers may also vary.

HISTORICAL: Pontiac's total output of 1999 model U.S. passenger cars was 629,938 units including 113,421 Sunfires, 265,590 Grand Ams, 41,226 Firebirds, 155,317 Grand Prixs and 54,384 Bonnevilles. Model-year sales of U.S. cars were 553,390 for a 6.4 percent market share. That was up from 476,212 cars and a 5.9 percent share of market in 1998. These figures do not include Montanas or Canadian units.

2001 PONTIAC

2001 Pontiac Sunfire SE two-door coupe. (PGMC)

SUNFIRE — CARLINE J — (FOUR) — The 2001 Pontiac Sunfire delivered at a budget price. Its spirited performance, dynamic styling,

2001 Pontiac Sunfire SE Sun & Sound two-door coupe. (PGMC)

and numerous comfort and convenience features combined to create a sporty, affordable combination for the budget-minded driver. Changes for 2001 included making an AM/FM stereo with cassette standard on SE models and making a rear spoiler standard on all models. The convertible and the White vinyl interior choice were discontinued. The 2001 model lineup gave buyers a choice of three well-equipped versions: the SE sedan, the SE coupe and the GT coupe. The Sunfire SE coupe and sedan used a standard 2.2-liter overhead-valve engine that produces 115 hp. The GT coupe upped the ante with 150 hp from a 2.4-liter Twin Cam engine. Both engines were attached to a five-speed manual transmission built by the German transmission manufacturer Getrag. It featured excellent shift feel, as well as a synchronized reverse gear for easy engagement and a reverse lockout feature for enhanced safety. The 2.2-liter engine was also available with a three- or four-speed automatic transmission. In addition to the rear spoiler on all models, the Sunfire's sporty design featured side ribs and rocker panel moldings on the SE coupe and sedan. Sunfire front fascias included rounded turn signal lamps on the SE and integral fog lamps on the GT coupe. Both SE versions got 14-in. steel wheels with bolt-on wheel covers that contributed to a sporty look. Fifteen-inch aluminum wheels were also available on the SE coupe and sedan. Sixteen-inch aluminum wheels with P205/55R16 tires were standard on the GT coupe, increasing its handling and road-holding ability. Sunfire's front reclining bucket seats and full fold-down rear seat were trimmed in Fanfare cloth on Sunfire SEs and Patina/Redondo cloth on GTs. The GT model's shift knob, parking brake handle and steering wheel were wrapped in leather. The user-friendly instrument panel cluster included an analog speedometer, digital LCD odometer and trip odometer, a tachometer, a coolant temperature gauge, and a fuel gauge. A lighted P-R-N-D-L indicator on the console provided excellent readability at night. The Sunfire's front floor console featured an integral armrest that combined sportiness with practicality. It included two forward-mounted cup holders, a concealed coin holder, and ample storage space for tapes, CDs, and other items. A padded armrest was provided. The Sunfire featured a standard AM/FM radio and cassette player with one AM and two FM bands (six presets per band), seek/scan and preset scan functions, and a theft-deterrent system helped keep the radio where it belonged. A retained accessory feature allowed the radio to remain powered for 10 minutes after power was switched off or until the driver's door opened. Standard features like four-wheel anti-lock brakes, driver and front passenger airbags, side door beams, and daytime running lamps worked together to help protect the safety of the driver and occupants. A standard PASSLock II™ theft-deterrent system immobilized the vehicle if an attempt to start it without the proper key was made. Content theft protection—included with the remote keyless entry and power door lock security package—flashed the daytime running lamps and dome lamp and sounded the horn during an unauthorized attempt to open the doors. Additional standard equipment on SE coupes included a Space Saver spare tire, front and rear ABS disc brakes, child seat anchors, an emergency release in the trunk, daytime running lights, intermittent windshield wipers, a rear defogger, bucket front seats, a folding rear seat, power steering, front cup holders, front door pockets, a 12-volt power outlet, a front console with storage space, air conditioning, dual vanity mirrors, and front and rear floor mats. The SE sedan had standard rear door child safety locks. The GT coupe also had front and rear stabilizer bars, front fog lights,

2001 Pontiac Grand AM SE2 two-door coupe. (PGC)

a six-speaker sound system, a tilt-adjustable steering wheel, front seat back storage space, and a clock.

GRAND AM — CARLINE N — (FOUR) — For years the Grand Am had consistently ranked as one of the top 10 selling U.S. automobiles. The Grand Am exterior was replete with Pontiac design cues like cat's-eye headlamps, a twin-port grille, round driving lamps, and ribbed lower body contours. At the rear, bold exhaust outlets, integrated tail lamp housings, and matching round lamps carried on the Pontiac legacy. GT models sported distinctive front and rear fascias, color-keyed body side cladding, twin-post body color sport mirrors, wheel treatments, and a standard rear deck spoiler. The base 2.4-liter Twin Cam 16-valve engine delivered impressive performance. The electrical terminals on the Twin Cam's throttle body were even gold plated for enhanced reliability. The optional 3400 V-6 delivered 170 hp. Grand Am GTs featured a standard Ram Air version of the same engine with cold-air induction and low-restriction exhaust system that boosted output to 175 hp. Grand Am's 4T45-E automatic transaxle, standard with the 3400 V-6, was engineered for operation with an Enhanced Traction System that automatically limits front wheel spin in slippery conditions. Manufactured by Getrag, the five-speed transmission standard on SE models was loaded with special features. A composite shifter base helped isolate power train noise and vibration from the Grand Am's interior. All gears were ground and honed for smooth, quiet operation. Closely-spaced ratios help the engine to provide brisk, quick acceleration. An overdrive fifth gear delivered quiet and efficient highway cruising. The Grand Am's world-class body structure optimized stiffness while minimizing weight. The 25 Hz body rigidity set a standard for compact cars. A four-wheel independent suspension used aluminum suspension knuckles to reduce unsprung weight for responsive ride and handling. A torque-axis power train mounting system used two mounts to support the mass of the engine and transaxle, with two others specifically tuned to resist torque and damp idle vibrations. Mounting Grand Am's power rack-and-pinion steering system directly to the hydro-formed chassis cradle provided precise "on-center" feel with excellent isolation of road disturbances. Grand Am's interior focused on the driver features like large, circular instruments backlit with warm, red illumination. The instrument panel had a seamless design with low gloss and soft touch. Large, round knobs made operating the climate controls a breeze. The ample center console accommodated large beverage cups while providing storage, a coin holder, and an armrest. A steel cage with reinforced pillars, side-guard door beams and a full-frame front chassis cradle provided outstanding occupant protection along with high-performance handling and a superior ride. Grand Ams had manual lap/shoulder safety belts for all outboard positions and lap belts for the center seating positions. The frontal-impact airbags worked in conjunction with safety belts to help protect the driver and right front passenger. The rear shoulder belts included child comfort guides and anchors in all three rear-seating positions now attached to both the upper and lower tether straps provided on child safety seats. Changes for 2001 Grand Ams included newly upgraded Delco sound systems for all models (a Monsoon ® premium audio system was standard on GT models and available on SE models). Lower child safety-seat anchors were added to rear seat and a new Wave/Form cloth interior trim was

introduced, along with new 15-in. aluminum, twin five-spoke wheels. Galaxy Silver Metallic, Champagne Beige Metallic, and Dark Bronzemist Metallic were new exterior colors. The Grand Am SE2 equipment level was discontinued. An AM/FM stereo with a seek feature and auto-reverse cassette was standard on the Grand Am SE. The standard system on SE1 and GT models replaced the cassette with a CD player and added a seven-band equalizer and digital clock. Standard on GT1s was an AM/FM stereo with cassette and a CD player, a graphic equalizer, a clock, and a Monsoon ® premium audio system. Standard on GT and GT1 were Monsoon's ® eight optimally placed speakers. The standard SE coupe and sedan feature the Twin Cam engine, a five-speed transmission, air-conditioning, 15-in. wheels and tires, and the Delco AM/FM sound system with auto-reverse cassette. The Grand Am SE1 added cruise control, power windows, power sport mirrors, a power height-adjustment system for the driver's seat, a split-folding rear seat, and five-spoke cast-aluminum wheels. GT models took everything standard on the SE1 and wrapped it in distinctive exterior accents with unique front and rear fascias, color-keyed side cladding, twin-post mirrors, a rear deck lid spoiler, and special GT tail lamps. Goodyear RSA P225/50R16 tires were mounted on 16-in, five-spoke cast aluminum GT-specific wheels. Other standard performance features included four-wheel-disc brakes with ABS, variable-effort power steering and an upgraded suspension system consisting of firmer bushings, solid front and rear anti-roll bars and specific spring rates. Leather seating surfaces were available in all GT editions. The Grand Am GT1 added automatic transmission, an enhanced traction system, remote keyless entry, 16-in. aluminum wheels and redundant steering-wheel controls. The GT1 also featured a six-way power driver's seat and a power sunroof. Grand Am standard equipment included five-mph bumpers, ABS, air-conditioning, a tilt steering wheel, programmable door locks with lockout protection, battery rundown protection, an electric remote trunk release, an oil life sensor, the PASSLock II ™ theft-deterrent system, a sealed-for-life transmission, and illuminated entry with theater dimming. For SE1 models, the "Solid Value" Package contained 16-in. aluminum wheels and tires, a Monsoon ® eight-speaker sound system with AM/FM stereo, cassette player, and CD, and a power sunroof. The GT models' "Solid Value" Package was similar, upgrading the aluminum wheels to 16-in. ChromeTech wheels. Customers opting for the GT1 "Solid Value" Package received leather seating surfaces and 16-in. ChromeTech wheels.

FIREBIRD — CARLINE F — (V-6/V-8) — "Firebird: The muscle car lives," said Pontiac in its Advanced Media Information book for the 2001 Firebird. The F-car remained true to its heritage while taking performance to new levels, although enthusiasts of the nameplate would be shocked by the announcement, in the fall of 2001, that General Motors would soon be stopping Firebird (and Camaro) production. For over three decades, the Pontiac Firebird had defined high-powered driving excitement. The 2001 lineup started with Firebird coupe and convertible. Firebird hood and rear quarter panels were made of two-sided galvanized steel, while the doors, hatch, roof, fenders, and fascias were formed from composite materials that were lightweight and impervious to rust or corrosion. Base Firebird features included a hidden headlamp design, integrated fog lamps, fender-mounted air extractors, and a sleek, aerodynamically

2001 Pontiac Grand Am GT two-door coupe. (PGMC)

shaped body. Standard equipment included air conditioning, four-wheel disc brakes with ABS, cruise control, a fold-down rear seat, and a center console with an auxiliary power outlet and dual cup holders. The Firebird convertible added a standard up-level Monsoon ® sound system with CD player and eight speakers, a six-way power driver's seat, a leather-wrapped steering wheel with redundant radio controls, remote keyless entry, an alarm, power door locks, power windows, power outside mirrors, and a power radio antenna. Firebird Formula coupe appointments included low-profile Z-speed-rated tires, Silver 16-in. five-spoke sport wheels, and a performance-oriented suspension. It also included a 10-speaker version of the Monsoon ® CD audio system. The ultimate expression of Firebird muscle, the Trans Am, was offered in both coupe and convertible editions. Standard equipment included removable coupe roof panels, leather seat surfaces, and an up-level rear spoiler for the Trans Am coupe. Bright Silver Metallic paint was replaced with Sunset Orange Metallic. A new Camel Accent interior color was also added. To make the ride even better for those on the inside, the shock absorbers were improved for better ride isolation and shake elimination on all models. A 5.7-liter Gen III LS1 V-8 was standard on the Formula and Trans Am. It had a new camshaft and a new intake manifold and the external EGR valve was eliminated for a gain of five horsepower (to 310 hp). Trans Am drivers who opted for Ram Air enjoyed 15 additional horsepower. Standard for the base Firebird coupe and convertible was a 3800 V-6 that delivered 200 hp. It came hooked to a five-speed manual or available four-speed automatic transmission. A slick-shifting six-speed manual transmission was also available at no extra charge. An optional Hurst shifter was available on models equipped with the six-speed transmission. The 3800 V-6 Performance package combined wider P235/55R16 touring tires with a Torsen II limited-slip differential, uplevel steering, dual exhaust outlets, and a 3.42:1 axle ratio (available only with the automatic transmission). Trans Ams equipped with Pontiac's exclusive WS6 Ram Air Performance and Handling package benefited from functional air scoops, Ram Air induction, a dual-outlet exhaust system, a power-steering cooler, and a suspension tuned for maximum handling performance. The package included P275/40ZR17 performance radial tires on 9 x 17-in. highly-polished alloy wheels featuring a five-spoke spoke design. A Sports Appearance package offered for Firebird and Firebird convertible included dual exhaust outlets, a distinctive chin spoiler, rocker panel extensions, and a deeper rear valance. The Firebird's high-performance attitude was not limited to its engine compartment—it was also found in the wide selection of audio systems available. Base equipment for the Firebird coupe was a Delco 2001 Series electronically tuned radio with AM/FM stereo, a CD player, a seven-band graphic equalizer, four speakers, a clock, and touch controls for seek, search, and replay. All convertibles featured a standard Monsoon ® radio and eight speakers. A similar system with 10 speakers was standard in Formula and Trans Am coupes and optional in the Firebird coupe. Firebirds featured safety-cage construction with side-door beams, manual lap/shoulder safety belts, driver and passenger frontal impact airbags, and two rear compartment child safety seat top tether anchors. Crash-avoidance features included standard four-wheel disc brakes with electronic brake force distribution and ABS, a brake/transmission shift interlock system, automatic daytime running lamps, fog lamps, and tires with built-in wear indicators and available traction control. A PASSKey II theft-deterrent system was also standard.

2001 Pontiac Firebird two-door convertible. (PGMC)

GRAND PRIX — CARLINE W — (V-6/V-8) — Introduced in the middle of the 2000 model year, Pontiac's latest Wide Track Grand Prix provided smooth cornering, excellent handling and a firm grip on the road in a hot-looking package. The Grand Prix's muscular front-end design flaunted aggressive grille openings between the headlamps combined with a graphite-colored lower valance. Body-color fascias that integrated reflector-optic headlamps, directional signals, side marker lamps, and round fog lamps added to the low, sporty look. Inside, everything was geared toward keeping the driver in command. Large, analog instrumentation with red backlighting was easy to read with controls canted toward the driver and a floor console within convenient reach. A standard Driver Information Center (DIC) in the instrument cluster kept the driver updated on various operating conditions such as traction system activation, the need for an oil change, or a door ajar. An available trip computer added "driving range," "oil life used," "average fuel economy" and "fuel used since last reset" information. The most obvious change in the 2001 Grand Prix SE was its new front end. It looked sleeker with its twin GT-like raised grille ports, fog lamps, and body-colored lower valance panel. The Grand Prix Wide Track family consisted of three trim levels, the SE sedan, the GT coupe, and sedan and the GTP coupe and sedan. Standard equipment in all models included a spoiler; air conditioning; an automatic transmission; four-wheel disc brakes with ABS; a tilting and adjustable steering column; power windows; power mirrors; owner-programmable power door locks; and a rear window defogger. Standard dual airbags worked in conjunction with safety belts to help keep front seat occupants safer. The SE's new athletic appearance was also backed up by a high-powered 3.1L 175-hp V-6 paired with a four-speed automatic transmission. A sport-tuned suspension and traction control were other features. New to the Grand Prix SE sedan was the optional Wide Track Smart package with exterior features including a standard rear deck lid spoiler, 16-in. five-spoke silver-painted aluminum wheels, and P225/60R16 steel-belted-radial black sidewall touring tires. Inside were Graphite or Dark Taupe Cyclone Cloth bucket seats with six-way power driver's seat controls, an AM/FM stereo with cassette player, a six-speaker sound system, and cruise control. A remote deck lid release, a rear seat pass-through, and a trunk net added extra convenience and cargo carrying capacity. The Wide Track Smart package was available in Grand Prix SE's most popular exterior colors: Arctic White, Silvermist Metallic, Dark Forest Green Metallic, Black, Redfire Metallic, and Dark Bronzemist Metallic. A 200-hp 3800 V-6 was standard in Grand Prix GTs. Top-of-the-line GTPs were powered by a supercharged 3800 V-6 that pumped out a whopping 240 hp. The Grand Prix GT and GTP lines offered Special Edition coupe and sedan models. These carried over the aggressive deck lid spoiler and had heat extractors on their hoods, roof fences, and bright dual/dual exhaust tips pirated from last-year's limited-edition Grand Prix Daytona Pace Car replica. Inside, there were unique two-tone leather seats (Graphite with Medium Gray inserts), painted trim plates and a machined door emblem. A Special Edition decal on the rear deck lid and unique chrome multi-spoke wheels further set these cars apart from anything else on the road. The Special Edition GT and GTP were available in four exterior colors: Galaxy Silver, Black, Bright Red, and White. A factory-installed OnStar ® system was optional on GTs and standard on GTPs. A standard manual, dual-zone HVAC system replaced the automatic type, giving occupants more hands-on temperature control. A new steering wheel provided improved controls for the driver's ease of operation. A

2001 Pontiac Firebird two-door coupe. (PGMC)

2001 Pontiac Firebird WS6 Trans Am Ram two-door coupe. (PGMC)

compass and outside air temperature display were now included in the available electrochromatic mirror. GT and GTP models also got a new Medium Gray leather interior option. Outside, a new 16-in. three-spoke aluminum wheel for GT and GTP models was available in painted and polished aluminum. A spoiler, a license plate cover, and a backlight antenna were standard equipment. A new Galaxy Silver Metallic color was added. GT and GTP models also benefited from standard Magnasteer variable-effort power rack-and-pinion steering. The supercharged GTP's Driver Information Center added an engine boost-pressure display. Crash-avoidance features on Grand Prixs included the four-wheel antilock brakes, an Enhanced Traction System, automatic daytime running lamps with automatic exterior lamp control, and tires with built-in tread wear indicators. The PASSKey III theft-deterrent system included a transponder circuit in the ignition key to communicate with circuits onboard the car to authorize start-up and drive-away.

BONNEVILLE — CARLINE H — (V-6) — Following its complete redesign for the 2000 model year, the 2001 Bonneville focused on improvements that increased luxury, convenience, and safety for driver and passengers. The Bonneville was available in three models—SE, SLE, and SSEi—each with a high level of standard equipment. The 2001 Bonneville featured the widest overall track in its class. Four-wheel antilock disc brakes were standard on all Bonnevilles, with a Delco-Bosch 5.3 system providing electronic proportioning. An available traction-control system used brake application and engine torque modulation to increase driver control in slippery conditions. The Bonneville's Pontiac heritage showed through in its robust silhouette, its cat's eye headlamps, its integrated wide body side sculpting, the wide dihedral V-shapes in the hood and deck lid, and the car's muscular haunches. A new color was Ivory White. The Bonneville SE was a true sport sedan that seated five or six comfortably in its roomy interior. Standard features on the SE included independent front and rear touring suspension with electronic level control, a tire pressure monitor, daytime running lamps with twilight sentinel, a PASSKey III security system, power windows with express-down feature on driver and passenger sides, power outside rearview mirrors, and a trunk pass-through. The Bonneville SE also featured standard 16-in. wheels with bolt-on wheel covers along with steel-belted radial, black sidewall P225/60R16 touring tires. Five-spoke 16-in. cast aluminum wheels were available. Bonneville SE and SLE models were powered by a 205-hp 3800 Series II V-6 mated to a 4T65-E four-speed electronic automatic transmission. The Bonneville SLE placed an even stronger emphasis on style, performance, and convenience. Among its standard features were a six-way power driver's seat, a remote keyless entry system, an antitheft alarm system, a dual-zone climate control system, independent front and rear performance suspension with electronic level control, a 3.05:1 performance axle ratio, a rear deck spoiler, and a Driver Information Center. Heated, tinted power outside rearview mirrors were standard on both SLE and SSEi models. The Bonneville SSEi took content to the highest level with the StabiliTrak system, a Head-Up display, variable-effort steering, 12-way articulating driver and passenger leather bucket seats with memory, a trunk accessory kit, and more. The SSEi's standard engine added a supercharger and heavy-duty transaxle with a lower axle ratio for higher output of 240 hp. A 17-in. multi-lace cast aluminum wheel was standard on SLE and SSEi models, with a chrome high-polished multi-spoked 17-in. wheel

available. Steel belted P235/55R17 black sidewall speed-rated tires were standard on SLE and SSEi models. Parallel parking was easier in the SSEi, which had passenger-side mirrors that dipped automatically to give the driver a better view of the curb. Inside, the Bonneville's programmable features included an available dual-climate control system with separate temperature and fan controls for the driver and front seat passengers, heated seats with position memory, specialized seek/scan and memory functions on the premium Bose ® sound system, automatic power door locks, outside rearview mirror position-and-perimeter lighting, and 45/45 bucket seats in Geneva Cloth or available leather. A 55/45 bench seat with center storage armrest was available on the SE, in cloth only, for six-passenger seating. Driver and passenger six-way power adjusters were offered in the SE and SLE. SSEi buyers enjoyed standard 12-way articulating power driver and passenger bucket leather seats with driver-position memory. Bonnevilles featured Delco Electronics 100 series radios with TheftLock™ and Radio Data Systems (RDS) technology. SE and SLE models included an AM/FM stereo auto-reverse cassette system with automatic tone control and remote CD changer capability. The top-of-the-line Delco radio with a seven-band equalizer was standard on the Bonneville SSEi.

MONTANA — CARLINE U — (V-6) — The Pontiac Montana was engineered to be a functional minivan. It came in two different sizes: a 112-in. wheelbase and a long 120-in. wheelbase, both with two sliding doors. All Montanas offered optional power-operated passenger-side sliding doors and a variety of seating configurations. For 2001, a next-generation OnStar system was standard on all models. A HomeLink universal garage door opener was available as a new option. MontanaVision—available on the 121-in. wheelbase model—was a fully integrated, factory-installed rear-seat entertainment system with LCD video screen, a hi-fi videocassette player, tape storage, a full-function remote control with onscreen display, wireless headsets, enhanced sound quality, six headphone jacks with dedicated volume controls, a video game input for connecting a camcorder or computer game, and rear-seat audio controls. A rear-parking-aid option was available on the extended model. The 2001 Montana's all-new look came from a redesigned front grille and fascia combined with a new rear fascia. A factory-installed luggage rack was now standard. A new Black color was added to Montana's paint offerings. The Montana got a new third row stowable seat with convenience center enabling customers to have "space on demand" to accommodate their changing needs. The Montana could seat seven with four captain's chairs and a split-folding bench in the rear seating row. The flip-and-fold second- and third-row seats were readily removable without tools. Other available seating variations included a new stowable third row seat, eight-passenger seating with modular buckets in the middle row and a split bench seat in the rear row. Six-passenger seating with modular buckets in the middle and rear rows was also available on the regular wheelbase version. Air conditioning was standard and an optional package provided heating and air conditioning ducts for rear-seat passengers. Auxiliary power outlets were provided in both the front passenger compartment and the rear cargo area. A wealth of onboard storage was found in places like seatback map pockets, a lockable glove box, rear cargo sidewalls, and a double-bin center console. A small overhead console contained a storage bin, dual map lights, and an interior lamp override switch. The standard radio provided electronic tuning for the AM/FM stereo, a CD player, an electronic equalizer, and extended-range coaxial speakers. Occupant protection features included safety cage construction, sliding side doors with high-strength guard beams, and

2001 Pontiac Firebird WS6 Trans Am Ram Air two-door convertible. (PGMC)

child safety locks. Next generation airbags and safety belts with pre-tensioner systems and height adjustment were standard for front-seat passengers. Seat-mounted side airbags are also included as standard equipment. Second row seats now had lower anchors and tethers in two positions. Heated outside mirrors, standard air conditioning, and a rear window defogger helped maintain visibility during inclement weather. Puncture-sealant tires added extra safety. A 3.4-liter V-6 powered the Montana. A special Sport Performance and Handling package contained a sport suspension, 15-in. cast aluminum wheels, touring performance tires, all-weather traction control, automatic load leveling and special saddlebag storage pockets. The blending of new enhancements with proven family-pleasing features made the 2001 Montana a good choice for young families looking for practicality, rugged sportiness, and driving fun.

AZTEK — CARLINE A/B — (V-6) — The Pontiac Aztek originated as a sport recreation vehicle (SRV) concept unveiled at the 2000 North American International Auto Show in Detroit, Mich. It advanced to full production status for the 2001 model year. The Aztek drew design cues from the Grand Prix Sport Sedan, including its wide-track stance, roomy interior, low entry height, and advanced technology. It was available with all-wheel drive. Features included a flat load floor and lightweight flip-fold-or-remove modular seating. A portable console/cooler was standard on Aztek GTs. The Aztek GT also featured removable utility packs nested in its front door trim for handy portable storage of cameras, CD players, cell phones, and other gear. Aztek's rugged center console also included dual cup-holders and power outlets, along with a mat that featured a molded-in coin holder. With the back seats removed the Aztek offered 93.5 cu. ft. of cargo space. The fold-down tailgate had two molded-in seating surfaces and cup holders. Two optional cargo storage systems offered Aztek owners additional versatility. An innovative sliding rear cargo tray system could support up to 400 lbs. of sports gear or home improvement materials. A second option was a re-configurable rear cargo net system. Pontiac's design trademarks included cats-eye headlamps, oversize fog lamps, a twin-port grille with ram-air slots in the hood, and protective side cladding. Aztek's cockpit had a functional look. An innovative VERSATRAK AWD system was engineered specifically for the Aztek. With absolutely no pulling of levers, punching of buttons or other driver action, VERSA-TRAK AWD directed torque to those wheels with the best traction on demand when you need it. After wheel slippage ceased, the clutches disengaged and the Aztek reverted back to front-wheel drive. The Aztek GT included a standard two-line dot-matrix Driver Information Center (DIC) located below its speedometer. The Aztek GT was the first GM product to showcase the latest new-generation heads-up display (HUD) in which small pixels created virtual images of data presented in the driver's line of vision. The Aztek offered four different audio entertainment systems.

I.D. DATA: The Vehicle Identification Number (VIN) is located on the top left-hand surface of the instrument panel and is visible through the windshield. The VIN has 17 symbols. The first symbol indicates the country of manufacture (1 or 4=United States; 2=Canada; 3=Mexico; W=Germany). The second symbol indicates the manufacturer (G=General Motors). The third symbol indicates the make/division (2=Pontiac; M=Pontiac MPV and 7=GM of Canada). The fourth symbol (trucks) indicates the GVWR range and brake system. The fourth and fifth symbols (passenger cars) indicate the car line and series F/S=Firebird and Convertible; F/V=Formula and Convertible; H/X=Bonneville SE; H/Y=Bonneville SLE;

2001 Pontiac Grand Prix SE four-door sedan. (PGMC)

2001 Pontiac Grand Prix Special Edition four-door sedan. (PGMC)

H/Z=Bonneville SSEi; J/B=Sunfire; J/D=Sunfire; N/E=Grand Am SE; N/F=Grand Am SE1; N/G=Grand Am SE2; N/V=Grand Am GT1; N/W= Grand Am GT; W/J=Grand Prix SE; W/K=Grand Prix SE1; W/P=Grand Prix GT; W/R=Grand Prix GTP. The fifth and sixth symbols (trucks) indicate car line and series: A/O=Aztek SRV 4 x 2; B/O=Aztek SRV 4 x 4; U/O=Montana All-Purpose Vehicle 4 x 2; U/1=Montana All-Purpose Vehicle 4 x 2 luxury; U/2=Montana All-Purpose Vehicle 4 x 2 economy; X/O=Montana All-Purpose Vehicle Extended-Wheelbase 4 x 2; X/1=Montana All-Purpose Vehicle luxury Extended-Wheelbase 4 x 2; X/2=Montana All-Purpose Vehicle economy Extended-Wheelbase 4 x 2. The sixth symbol (passenger cars only) indicates body style (1=two-door coupe models 27, 37, 47 and 57; 2=two-door models 07, 08, 77, 87; 3=two-door convertible model 67; 5=four-door sedan models 19 and 69; 6=four-door sedan models 29 and 68; 8=four-door station wagon model 35. The seventh symbol (passenger cars) indicates the restraint system: 1=Active manual belts; 2=Active manual belts with driver and passenger inflatable restraints; 4=Active manual belts front and side; 5=Active manual belts with driver and passenger front and side airbags; 6=Active manual belts with driver and passenger front and side airbags and passenger sensor; 7=Active manual belts with driver and passenger front and side airbags and rear passenger compartment side airbags. The seventh symbol (trucks) indicates body style: 3=All-Purpose Vehicle (Montana and Aztek). The eighth symbol indicates the engine type: E=RPO LA1 3.4-liter fuel-injected (MFI) V-6; G=RPO LS1 5.7-liter fuel-injected (MFI) V-8; K=RPO L36 3.8-liter fuel-injected (MFI) V-6; T=RPO LD9 2.4-liter fuel-injected (MFI) I-4; 1=RPO L67 3.8-liter fuel-injected (MFI) V-6; 4=RPO LN2 2.2-liter fuel-injected (MFI) I-4; E=RPO LA1 3.4-liter fuel-injected (MFI) V-6 in Montana and Aztek. (Note: All Pontiac engines made in U.S.). The ninth symbol is a check digit. The 10th symbol indicates model year (1=2001). The 11th symbol indicates the GM assembly plant (B=Baltimore, Md., T&B; B=Lansing, Mich., GENASYS; C=Lansing, Mich.; D=Doraville, Ga.; E=Pontiac East, Mich., T&B; F=Fairfax II, Kan.; F=Flint, Mich., T&B; G=Silao Mexico; H=Flint, Mich.; J=Janesville, Wis., (T&B); K=Linden, N.J., T&B; M=Lansing, Mich; M=Toluca Mexico; R=Arlington, Texas; R=Russelsheim Germany; S=Ramos Arizpe Mexico; T=Shreveport, La.; U=Hamtramck, Mich; Y=Wilmington, Del.; Z=Fremont, Calif.; Z=Spring Hill, Tenn.; Z=Ft. Wayne, Ind. T&B; 0=Lansing, Mich.; 1=Oshawa Canada, T&B; 1=Oshawa Canada, #2; 1=Wentzville, Mo., T&B; 2=Morraine, Ohio, T&B; 2=Ste. Therese Canada; 3=Kawasaki Japan; 4=Orion, Mich.; 5=Bowling Green, Ken.; 6=Ingersoll, Ontario Canada; 6=Oklahoma City, Okla.; 7=Lordstown, Ohio; 7=Flusawa Japan; 8=Shreveport, La., T&B; 8=Tillisonburg, Ohio, CANEXPO; 9=Oshawa, Ontario Canada #1). Pontiacs are not produced at all of these plants. The last six symbols are the consecutive unit number at the factory.

Model Number	Body Style Number	Body Type & Seating	Factory Price	Shipping Weight	Production Total
SUNFIRE SE SERIES B (I-4)					
J/B	B37V	2d Coupe-4P	14,250	2,606	Note 1
J/B	B69V	4d Sedan-4P	13,459	2,644	Note 1
SUNFIRE GT SERIES D (I-4)					
J/D	D37V	2d Coupe -4P	15,286	2,771	Note 1
GRAND AM SE SERIES E (I-4)					
N/E	E37V	2d Coupe-4P	16,205	3,066	Note 3
N/E	E69V	4d Sedan-4P	16,505	3,116	Note 3

Standard Catalog of ® Pontiac, 2nd Edition

2001 Pontiac Bonneville SE four-door Sport Sedan. (PGMC)

Model Number	Body Style Number	Body Type & Seating	Factory Price	Shipping Weight	Production Total
GRAND AM GT SERIES W (I-4)					
N/W	W67V	2d Coupe-4P	20,385	3,099	Note 3
N/W	W69V	2d Sedan-4P	20,685	3,118	Note 3
FIREBIRD SERIES S (V-6)					
F/S	S87V	2d Coupe-4P	18,855	3,323	Note 5
F/S	S67V	2d Convertible-4P	25,475	3,402	Note 5
FORMULA SERIES V (V-8)					
F/V	V87V	2d Coupe-4P	24,035	3,341	Note 5
TRANS AM SERIES V (V-8)					
F/V	V87V	2d Coupe-4P	27,145	3,397	Note 5
F/V	V-67V	2d Convertible-4P	31,215	3,514	Note 5
GRAND PRIX SE SERIES J (V-6)					
W/J	J69V	4d Sedan-4P	20,455	3,384	Note 7
GRAND PRIX GT SERIES (V-6)					
W/J	P37V	2d Coupe-4P	21,960	3,429	Note 7
W/J	P69V	4d Sedan-4P	22,110	3,496	Note 7
GRAND PRIX GTP SERIES (V-6)					
W/J	R37V	2d Coupe-4P	25,450	3,495	Note 7
W/J	R69V	4d Sedan-4P	25,630	3,559	Note 7
BONNEVILLE SE SERIES X (V-6)					
X	X69V	4d SE Sed-6P	25,220	3,590	Note 9
BONNEVILLE SLE SERIES X (V-6)					
Z	Z69V	4d SSE Sed-6P	28,190	3,650	Note 9
BONNEVILLE SSEi SERIES X (Supercharged V-6)					
Z	Z69V	4d SSEi Sed-6P	32,560	3,790	Note 9
MONTANA REGULAR WHEELBASE SERIES U (V-6)					
U	U	Minivan 6-seat	25,040	3,803	Note 11
U	U	Minivan 7-seat	25,040	3,803	Note 11
MONTANA SPORT REGULAR WHEELBASE SERIES U (V-6)					
U	U	Minivan 7-seat	28,555	3,803	Note 11
MONTANA VISION REGULAR WHEELBASE SERIES U (V-6)					
U	U	Minivan 8-seat	32,135	3,803	Note 11
MONTANA EXTENDED WHEELBASE SERIES X (V-6)					
U	X	Minivan 7-seat	27,380	3,942	Note 11
U	X	Minivan 7-seat	28,505	3,942	Note 11
MONTANA EXTENDED WHEELBASE/CONVENIENCE SERIES X (V-6)					
U	X	Minivan 7-seat	29,935	3,942	Note 11
MONTANA SPORT EXTENDED WHEELBASE SERIES X (V-6)					
U	X	Minivan 7-seat	30,440	3,942	Note 11
U	X	Minivan 7-seat	30,290	3,942	Note 11
MONTANA VISION EXTENDED WHEELBASE SERIES X (V-6)					
U	X	Minivan 7-seat	32,735	3,942	Note 11
U	X	Minivan 8-seat	32,135	3,942	Note 11
AZTEK (FWD) SERIES AO3 (I-4)					
A	AO3	4d Sport Utility	21,995	3,779	Note 13
AZTEK (AWD) SERIES AO3 (I-4)					
A	AO3	4d Sport Utility	24,660	3,779	Note 13
AZTEK GT (FWD) SERIES BO3 (I-4)					
A	BO3	4d Sport Utility	24,995	4,043	Note 13
AZTEK GT (AWD) SERIES BO3 (I-4)					
A	BO3	4d Sport Utility	27,465	4,043	Note 1

Note 1: Calendar-year production through Sept. 29, 2001 was 88,755 including 2,340 built in Mexico.

Note 2: A $655 dealer destination charge applied to Sunfire models.

Note 3: Calendar-year production through Sept. 29, 2001 was 154,335.

Note 4: A $655 dealer destination charge applied to Grand Am models.

Note 5: Calendar-year production through Sept. 29, 2001 was 14,204 (all built in Canada).

Note 6: A $655 dealer destination charge applied to Firebird models.

Note 7: Calendar-year production through Sept. 29, 2001 was 98,131.

Note 8: A $655 dealer destination charge applied to Grand Prix models.

Note 9: Calendar-year production through Sept. 29, 2001 was 17,507.

Note 10: A $655 dealer destination charge applied to Bonneville models.

Note 11: Calendar-year production through Sept. 29, 2001 was 59,066.

Note 12: Montana prices include a $640 dealer destination charge.

Note 13: Not available at publication date.

Note 14: Aztek prices include a $550 dealer destination charge.

SUNFIRE ENGINES

ENGINE [Base Four SE]: Inline. OHV. Four-cylinder. Cast-iron block and cast aluminum cylinder head. Aluminum intake manifold. Two valves per cylinder. Displacement: 134 cid. (2.2L). Bore & stroke: 3.50 x 3.46 in. Compression ratio: 9.0:1. Net horsepower: 115 at 5000 rpm. Torque: 135 lbs.-ft. at 3600 rpm. Fuel system: SFI. VIN Code: 4. RPO Code: LN2.

ENGINE [Base Four (GT/SE Convertible); Optional (SE)]: Inline. DOHC. Four-cylinder. Four valves per cylinder. Cast-iron block and cast aluminum head. Aluminum intake manifold. Displacement: 146 cid. (2.4L). Bore & stroke: 3.54 x 3.70 in. Compression ratio: 9.5:1. Net horsepower: 150 at 5600 rpm. Torque: 155 lbs.-ft. at 4400 rpm. Fuel system: SFI. VIN Code: T. RPO Code: LD9.

GRAND AM ENGINES

ENGINE [Base Four SE/GT]: Inline. DOHC. Four-cylinder. Four valves per cylinder. Cast-iron block and cast aluminum cylinder head. Aluminum intake manifold. Displacement: 146 cid. (2.4L). Bore & stroke: 3.54 x 3.70 in. Compression ratio: 9.5:1. Net horsepower: 150 at 5600 rpm. Torque: 155 lbs.-ft. at 4400 rpm. Fuel system: SFI. VIN Code: T. RPO Code: LD9.

ENGINE [Optional Six]: V-block. OHV. Six-cylinder. Cast-iron block and aluminum cylinder head. Aluminum intake manifold. Displacement: 207 cid. (3.4L). Bore & stroke: 3.62 x 3.31 in. Compression ratio: 9.5:1. Brake horsepower: 170 at 4800 rpm. Torque: 195 lbs.-ft. at 4000 rpm. Fuel system: SFI. VIN Code: M. RPO Code: LA1.

FIREBIRD ENGINES

ENGINE [Base V-6]: V-block. OHV. Six-cylinder. Cast-iron block. Cast-iron cylinder head. Displacement: 231 cid. (3.8L). Bore & stroke: 3.80 x 3.40 in. Compression ratio: 9.4:1. Brake horsepower: 200 at 5200 rpm. Torque: 225 lbs.-ft. at 4000 rpm. Fuel system: SFI. VIN Code: K. RPO Code: L36.

ENGINE [Base V-8]: V-block. OHV. Eight-cylinder. Aluminum block and cylinder head. Aluminum intake manifold. Displacement: 350 cid. (5.7L). Bore & stroke: 3.90 x 3.62 in. Brake horsepower: 310 at 5200 rpm. Torque: 340 lbs.-ft. at 4000 rpm. Compression ratio: 10.5:1. Fuel system: SFI. VIN Code: G. RPO Code: LS1.

ENGINE [WS6 RAM AIR V-8]: V-block. OHV. Eight-cylinder. Aluminum block and cylinder head. Aluminum intake manifold. Ram-air induction. Displacement: 350 cid. (5.7L). Bore & stroke: 3.90 x 3.62 in. Brake horsepower: 325 at 5200 rpm. Torque: 350 lbs.-ft. at 4000 rpm. Compression ratio: 10.5:1. Fuel system: SFI. VIN Code: G. RPO Code: LS1.

GRAND PRIX ENGINES

ENGINE [Base V-6]: V-block. Six-cylinder. Cast-iron block. Cast-iron cylinder head. Displacement: 231 cid. (3.8L). Bore & stroke:

2001 Pontiac Bonneville SLE four-door Sport Sedan. (PGMC)

3.80 x 3.40 in. Compression ratio: 9.4:1. Brake horsepower: 200 at 5200 rpm. Torque: 225 lbs.-ft. at 4,000 rpm. Fuel system: SFI. VIN Code: K. RPO Code: L36.

ENGINE [Optional V-6]: V-block. Six-cylinder. Supercharged. Cast-iron block. Cast-iron cylinder head. Displacement: 231 cid. (3.8L). Bore & stroke: 3.80 x 3.40 in. Compression ratio: 8.5:1. Brake horsepower: 240 at 5200 rpm. Torque: 280 lbs.-ft. at 3,200 rpm. Fuel system: SFI. VIN Code: 1. RPO Code: L67.

BONNEVILLE ENGINES

ENGINE [Base V-6 SE/SSE]: "3800" SFI Series II V-6. V-block. OHV. Six-cylinder. Displacement: 231 cid. (3.8L). Bore & stroke: 3.80 x 3.40 in. Compression ratio: 9.4:1. Brake horsepower: 205 at 5200 rpm. Torque: 230 lbs.-ft. at 4000 rpm. Fuel system: SFI. VIN Code: K. RPO Code: L36.

ENGINE [Optional Supercharged V-6 SSEi]: "3800" Supercharged Series II V-6. V-block. OHV. Six-cylinder. Displacement: 231 cid. (3.8L). Bore & stroke: 3.80 x 3.40 in. Compression ratio: 8.5:1. Brake horsepower: 240 at 5200 rpm. Torque: 280 lbs.-ft. at 3200 rpm. Fuel system: SFI. VIN Code: 1. RPO Code: L67.

MONTANA ENGINE

ENGINE [Base V-6]: V-block. DOHC. Six-cylinder. Cast-iron block. Aluminum cylinder head. Displacement: 207 cid. (3.4L). Bore & stroke: 3.62 x 3.31 in. Compression ratio: 9.5:1. Brake horsepower: 185 at 5200 rpm. Torque: 210 lbs.-ft. at 4,000 rpm. Fuel system: SFI. VIN Code: E. RPO Code: LA1.

AZTEK ENGINE

ENGINE [Base V-6]: V-block. DOHC. Six-cylinder. Cast-iron block. Aluminum cylinder head. Displacement: 207 cid. (3.4L). Bore & stroke: 3.62 x 3.31 in. Compression ratio: 9.5:1. Brake horsepower: 185 at 5200 rpm. Torque: 210 lbs.-ft. at 4,000 rpm. Fuel system: SFI. VIN Code: E. RPO Code: LA1.

CHASSIS

SUNFIRE CHASSIS: Wheelbase: (all) 104.1 in. Overall length: (coupe) 182 in.; (sedan) 181.8 in. Overall width: (coupe) 68.4 in.; (sedan) 67.9 in. Height: (coupe) 53.0 in.; (sedan) 54.7 in. Front tread: (all) 57.6 in. Rear tread: (coupe) 56.4 in.; (sedan) 56.6 in.

GRAND AM CHASSIS: Wheelbase: (all) 107 in. Overall length: 186.3 in. Width: (all) 70.4 in. Height: (all) 55.1 in. Front tread: (all) 59 in. Rear tread: (all) 59.1 in.

FIREBIRD CHASSIS: Wheelbase: (all) 101.1 in. Overall length: (Firebird/Formula) 193.3 in.; (Trans Am) 193.7 in. Width: (all) 74.4 in. Height: (Firebird/Formula coupe) 51.2 in.; (Trans Am coupe) 51.2 in.; (All Convertibles) 51.8 in. Front Tread: (all) 60.7 in. Rear tread: (all) 60.6 in.

GRAND PRIX CHASSIS: Wheelbase: (all) 110.5 in. Overall length: (all) 197.5 in. Width: (all) 72.7 in. Height: (all) 54.7 in. Front Tread: (all) 61.76 in. Rear tread: (all) 61.1 in.

BONNEVILLE CHASSIS: Wheelbase: (all) 112.2 in. Overall length: (SE sedan) 202.6 in.; (SSE/SSEi sedan) 202.6 in. Width: (all) 74.2 in. Height: (all) 56.6 in. Front tread: 62.6 in. Rear tread: 62.1 in.

MONTANA CHASSIS: Wheelbase: (Standard three-door) 112 in.; (Four-door) 112 in.; (Extended four-door) 121 in. Overall length: (Standard three- and four-doors) 187.3 in.; (Extended four-door) 200.9 in. Width: (all) 72 in. Height: (Standard three- and four-doors)

2001 Pontiac Bonneville SSEi four-door Sport Sedan. (PGMC)

2001 Pontiac Montana EWB minivan. (PGMC)

67.4 in.; (Extended four-door) 68.2 in. Front tread: (Regular) 61.5 in.; (Extended) 61.8 in. Rear tread: (Both) 63.3 in.

AZTEK CHASSIS: Wheelbase: (all) 108.3 in. Overall length: (all) 182.1 in. Width: (all) 73.7 in. Height: (all) 66.7 in. without roof rack. Front tread: (all) 62.7 in. Rear tread: (all) 63.8 in.

TECHNICAL

SUNFIRE TECHNICAL: Chassis: Front engine/front drive. Base transmission: Five-speed manual. Optional transmission: Three-speed automatic. Front suspension: Deflected-disc MacPherson struts. Rear suspension: Trailing tubular control arms with twist beam, coil springs and 18-mm stablizer bar on GT coupe. Steering: Rack-and-pinion. Front brakes: vented disc power-assisted. Rear brakes: drum power-assisted. Standard tires: (SE) P195/70R14 all-season black sidewall; (GT) P205/55R16 black sidewall performance-type. Fuel tank: 15 gal.

GRAND AM TECHNICAL: Chassis: Front engine/front drive. Base transmission: Five-speed manual with overdrive. Optional transmission: Three-speed automatic. Front suspension: MacPherson struts with lower control arms, 29 Nm spring and 24-mm hollow stabilizer bar. Rear suspension: Tri-link independent with 17.5 Hm spring and 15.3-mm solid stabilizer bar. Steering (Four-cylinder): Power-assisted rack-and-pinion. Steering (Six-cylinder) C-spring EVO variable effort. Power-assisted rack-and-pinion, 14.7:1 ratio. Front brakes: Power-assisted vented discs. Rear brakes: Power-assisted drums. Standard tires: (SE/SE1) P215/60R15 black sidewall touring; (GT/GT1) P225/50R16 black sidewall touring. Fuel tank: 14.3 gal.

FIREBIRD TECHNICAL: Chassis: Front engine/rear drive. Base transmission: Five-speed manual. Front suspension: (Firebird F41) SLA/coil over monotube gas-charged shocks, tubular stabilizer bars with links and 28-mm stabilizer bar; (Formula Trans Am FE2) SLA/coil over monotube gas-charged shocks, tubular stabilizer bar with links and 30-mm stablizer bar. Rear suspension: (Firebird F41) Salisbury axle with torque arm, trailing arm, track bar, coil springs and 15mm stabilizer bar; (Formula Trans Am FE2) Salisbury axle with torque arm, trailing arm, track bar, coil springs and 19mm stabilizer bar. Steering: (Firebird) Power rack and pinion, 16.9:1 ratio, 2.67 turns lock-to-lock, 37.9-ft. turn circle; (Formula/Trans Am) Power rack and pinion, 14.4:1 ratio, 2.28 turns lock-to-lock, 37.75-ft. turn circle. Front brakes: (All) 11.9-in. vented disc/302.3 mm. Rear brakes: (All) 12-in. vented disc, power-assisted, 304.8 mm. Standard tires: (Firebird) P215/60R16 steel-belted radial black sidewall touring; (Formula) P245/50ZR16 speed-rated, all-weather; (Trans Am) P245/50ZR16 speed-rated, all-weather. Fuel tank: 16.8 gal.

GRAND PRIX TECHNICAL: Chassis: Front engine/front drive. Front suspension: MacPherson struts with coil springs, lower A-arm and 30mm hollow anti-roll bar. Rear suspension: Independent, tri-link, coil-over-strut, 18mm anti-roll bar. Steering: Low-friction power-assisted rack-and-pinion, 17.6:1 ratio, 2.26 turns lock-to-lock and 35.6 ft. Turn circle. (MagnaSteer™ variable-effort power steering optional). Front brakes: 10.9-in. vented discs, power assisted. Rear brakes: 10.9-in. solid discs, power assisted, standard ABS. Standard tires: (SE) P205/70R15 black sidewall touring; (GT) P225/60R16 black sidewall; (GTP) P225/60R16 black sidewall performance-type. Fuel tank: 17.5 gal.

BONNEVILLE TECHNICAL: Chassis: Front engine/front drive. Base transmission: Four-speed automatic. Standard FE1 front

2001 Pontiac Aztek FWD Sport Recreational Vehicle. (PGMC)

suspension: Deflected-disc MacPherson struts with 27 Nm coil spring over strut and 29mm stabilizer bar. Optional FE2 front suspension: Deflected-disc MacPherson struts with 27 Nm coil spring over strut and 30mm stabilizer bar. Standard FE1 rear suspension: Automatic level control (variable rate 48-65 Nm), 36mm coil springs, Cadiz shocks and independent lower control arm. Optional FE2 rear suspension: Automatic level control (variable rate 48-65 Nm), 36mm coil springs, Cadiz shocks and independent lower control arm and 20mm stabilizer bar. Steering: (Standard) Power-assisted variable-ratio rack-and-pinion, 15.3:1 to 20.3:1 ratio, 3.2 turns lock-to-lock and 40.5-ft. turn circle; (Optional SSEi only) Mag-E variable-ratio rack-and-pinion, 15.3:1 to 20.3:1 ratio, 3.2 turns lock-to-lock and 40.5-ft. turn circle Front brakes: (Grand Prix SE) 10.9-in vented discs; (Grand Prix SLE and SSEi only) 11.9-in. vented discs. Rear brakes: (All) 11.1-in. discs, power assisted, antilock. Tires: (SE) P225/60R16 Firestone Affinity; (SLE/SSEi) P235/55R17 Goodyear Eagle RSA. Fuel tank: 18.5 gal.

MONTANA TECHNICAL: Chassis: Front engine/front drive. Transmission: Three-speed automatic. Front suspension: MacPherson strut with 27 Nm coil springs, stamped lower control arms and 34mm stabilizer bar. Rear suspension: Open-section twist axle with integral stabilizer bar, 30mm base gas shocks, 32mm self-leveling air shocks (sport suspension); 27 Nm base coil springs and 36mm stabilizer bar. Rack-and-pinion steering, 17.5:1 ratio, 3.05 turns lock-to-lock and 37.4-ft. turn circle. Front brakes: Power-assisted vented rotors. Rear brakes: Power-assisted finned composite cast-iron drums. Front tread: 61.8 in. Rear tread: 63.3 in. Standard tires: P215/70R15 all-season touring tires with sealant and raised white outline letters. Fuel tank: 25 gal.

AZTEK TECHNICAL: Chassis: Transversely-mounted front engine/front transaxle (AWD optional). Transmission: Four-speed automatic. Front suspension: Independent strut type with coil springs and anti-roll bar. Rear suspension: (FWD) trailing twist beam axle with integral anti-roll bar and coil springs; (AWD) short and long control arms with one toe-control link per side, coil springs and anti-roll bar. Power-assisted rack-and-pinion steering. Brakes: (FWD) Vented disc/drum with power assist and ABS; (AWD) Vented disc/disc with power assist and ABS. Front tread: 62.7 in. Rear tread: 63.8 in. Standard tires: P215/70R15 all-season black sidewall. Fuel tank: 18 gal.

OPTIONS

SUNFIRE OPTIONS: RPO 1SB option group on GT coupe ($1,480); on SE coupe ($1,115); on SE sedan ($1,115). RPO 1SC option group on GT coupe ($2,135); on SE coupe ($1,865); on SE sedan ($1,905). RPO 1SX 75th anniversary package includes four-sped automatic transmission with traction control, AM/FM stereo CD player with programmed equalizer and Monsoon 8-speaker sound system with 8-channel amplifier, cruise control, remote keyless entry, theft-deterrent system, power door locks, adjustable-tilt wheel, controlled-cycle windshield wipers, trunk net, reading lamps, overhead storage and assist handles ($2,465). CD4 controlled-cycle wet arm windshield wipers (no charge). CF5 glass power sunroof ($595). K05 engine block heater ($35). K34 cruise control ($235). LD9 Twin Cam 16-valve SFI I-4 engine ($450). MM5 five-speed manual transmission, requires 1SB or 1SC and not available with LD9 engine ($810 credit). M33 four-speed automatic transmission

($810). N33 tilt-steering column SE, included in 1SB, 1SC and 1SX, not available with 1SA (no charge). PB1 15-in. custom bolt-on wheel covers ($295). PF7 15-in. rally cast-aluminum wheels ($295). QPD P195/65R15 SBR touring tires ($135). R6B Sun and Sound package ($1,844-$2,555). R6B Sun and Storm package ($2,270-$2,690). R6S Special Edition package ($2,105-$2,485). R7X SE coupe/sedan security package ($370). R9P GT power package ($380-$445). U1P Delco 100 series ETR AM/FM stereo with CD player ($155). U1Q Delco 100 series ETR AM/FM stereo with cassette ($100). U85 Monsoon premium sound system ($195). VK4 front license plate bracket. (no charge).

GRAND AM OPTIONS: AS5 leather bucket seats in GT/GT1 ($475). CF5 power glass sunroof ($695). K05 engine block heater ($35). K34 cruise control in SE ($235). LA1 3.4-liter SFI V-6 in SE1 ($655). MX0 Four-speed electronically-controlled automatic transmission in SE/SE1 ($825). NW0 16-in. cast-aluminum GT-specific wheels on GT/GT1 (no charge). PY0 16-in. multi-spoke cast-aluminum wheels on SE1 ($490). PY1 16-in. ChromeTech cast-aluminum wheels on GT/GT1 ($645). R6B Solid Value appearance package for GT ($1,535). R6B Solid Value appearance package for SE1 ($1,525). R6S Solid value appearance package for GT ($1,120). T43 rear deck lid spoiler ($195). U1P Delco ETR AM/FM stereo with CD player in SE ($175). U1Q Delco ETR AM/FM stereo with CD and cassette in GT ($195). U1Q Delco ETR AM/FM stereo with CD and cassette in SE1 ($340). U85 Monsoon eight-speaker premium sound system in SE1 (no charge). YF5 California emissions requirements (no charge). Z03 Grand Am GT1 75th anniversary package includes 16-in. Chrome-Tech cast-aluminum wheels, up-level seat trim and 75th anniversary exterior badges and fender emblems ($1,270)

FIREBIRD OPTIONS: 1SA Firebird coupe option package, includes vehicle with standard equipment (no cost). 1SB Plus Firebird coupe option package, includes vehicle with standard equipment plus power door locks, power windows, power sport mirrors with blue tint, power antenna, automatic transmission, and power seat ($1,505-$1,510). 1SC Firebird option group ($2,450). 1SH NHRA Special four-speed automatic edition Formula package, includes P245/50ZR16 high-performance tires, 3.23:1 rear axle, power steering cooler, four-speed automatic transmission, and chrome wheels. ($1,170). 1SH NHRA Special six-speed manual edition Formula package, includes P245/50ZR16 high-performance tires, 3.23:1 rear axle, power steering cooler, Hurst shifter, six-speed manual transmission and chrome wheels. ($1,170). 1SX base Firebird 75th anniversary package, includes remote keyless entry, theft-deterrent system, six-way power driver's seat, 16 x 8-in. chrome five-spoke cast aluminum wheels, 3.8-liter V-6, power antenna, power windows, power door locks, and power mirrors ($4,530). 1SX Firebird Formula 75th anniversary (automatic) package, includes remote keyless entry, theft-deterrent system, six-way power driver's seat, 16 x 8-in. chrome five-spoke cast aluminum wheels, P245/50ZR16 performance tires, performance rear axle, and four-speed automatic transmission. ($2,850). 1SX Firebird Formula 75th anniversary (manual) package, includes hatch roof, remote keyless entry, theft-deterrent system, six-way power driver's seat, traction control, 16 x 8-in. chrome five-spoke cast aluminum wheels, six-speed manual transmission, and Hurst shifter ($2,875). AG1 six-way power driver's seat ($270). AQ9 Custom Prado leather bucket seats with adjustable lumbar support

2001 Pontiac Aztek AWD Sport Recreational Vehicle. (PGMC)

($185). AR9 Front bucket seats with Prado leather seating surfaces in convertible ($575). AR9 Front bucket seats with Prado leather seating surfaces in Formula, requires 1SB ($575). AR9 Front bucket seats with Prado leather seating surfaces in Hatchback, requires 1SC ($575). BBS Hurst Performance shift linkage in Formula or Trans Am ($325). CC1 removable hatch roof ($995). GU5 rear performance axle in Trans Am ($300). GU5 rear performance axle in Formula ($300). MM5 five-speed manual transmission in hatchback with 1SA, 1SB or 1SX required ($815 credit). MN6 six-speed manual transmission in Trans Am or Formula, includes "skip shift" feature (no charge). MX0 four-speed automatic transmission with overdrive in Firebird ($815). NW9 traction control in Formula or Trans Am ($450); in hatchback or convertible ($850). PQ5 16 x 8-in. chrome five-spoke cast aluminum wheels on Formula ($595). QCB P235/55R16 touring tires on hatchback or convertible ($135). R6M New Jersey cost surcharge, required in N.J. (no charge to customer). R7X protection group on Formula ($240). R9P power package for hatchback (no charge). UTS 12-disc CD player, trunk mounted ($595). V12 power steering cooler ($100). W53 Delco 2001 series ETR AM/FM stereo with CD player in hatchback with 1SA or 1SB (no charge). W54 Monsoon series ETR AM/FM stereo with auto-reverse cassette ($330-$430). W55 Monsoon series ETR AM/FM stereo with CD player ($430). W68 Sport Appearance package for convertible or hatchback ($1,040). WS6 Performance & Handling package for Trans Am ($3,390). X10 Monsoon series ETR AM/FM stereo with auto-reverse cassette in convertible ($100 credit). Y3C GT package for hatchback (no charge). Y87 3800 V-6 performance package for convertible ($490). YF5 California emissions requirements (no charge).

GRAND PRIX OPTIONS: 1SA option package for SE, includes vehicle and standard equipment (standard). 1SB option package for GT ($765-$1,415). 1SB Wide Track Smart package ($1,050). 1SC option package for GT coupe ($1,572). 1SC option package for GT sedan ($1,602). 1SD package for GT coupe ($3,362). 1SC package for GT sedan ($3,392). Ag1 six-way power driver's seat, GT ($270). AL9 four-way power driver's seat, GT ($130). AP9 trunk cargo net ($30). AR9 leather accent bucket seats, GT ($520). AR9 leather accent bucket seats, GTP ($520). B4U Special Edition package, GT ($2,515). CF5 glass power sunroof with express open, GT ($795). CF5 glass power sunroof with express open, GTP ($795). K05 engine block heater ($35). K34 cruise control ($235). KA1 heated driver's seat ($100). R6M New Jersey cost surcharge (no charge). R7K rear seat pass through, SE sedan ($60). R7X SE security package ($210). TR9 premium lighting package, GT coupe ($607). TR9 premium lighting package, GT sedan ($637). U1C AM/FM stereo, seek-scan, CD player, and four speakers ($110). UB5 Bose high-performance stereo, GT ($395) or GTP ($390). UP3 Delco 2001 series ETR AM/FM stereo with CD player ($150). UV6 Eye-Cue heads-up display, GT ($325). V2C 16 x 6.5-in. high-polished cast-aluminum wheels on GT/GTP ($325).

BONNEVILLE OPTIONS: SE sedan 1SC option package ($1,840). A51 bucket seats with leather seating surfaces in SLE ($850) AG2 six-way power passenger's seat in SE/SLE ($530). AM6 split bench seat in SE ($150). CF5 power glass sunroof ($1,080). K05 engine block heater ($35). KA1 heated front seats ($295). N94 17-in. wheels on SLE/SSEi ($595). NP5 leather-wrapped steering wheel with radio controls in SE ($175). NW9 traction control in SE ($175).

2001 Pontiac Aztek AWD Sport Recreational Vehicle. (PGMC)

R7W 75th anniversary package includes AM/FM stereo, CD player, cassette player with auto reverse, equalizer, power glass sunroof with express open, and six-way power front passenger's seat ($1,210). U1P Delco AM/FM stereo with CD player in SE and SLE ($100). U1Q Delco AM/FM stereo with CD and cassette in SE or SLE ($200). U1S 12-disc trunk-mounted CD changer ($595).

MONTANA OPTIONS: 1SA Montana SE option package, includes vehicle with standard equipment (no cost). 1SB Montana SE option package ($460). 1SC Montana option package ($1,410). 1SD Montana option package ($2,451). FE9 Federal emissions (no cost). YF5 California emissions ($170). NG1 NY/Mass. emissions ($170). ABA seven-passenger split bench Doral cloth seating, regular wheelbase ($335). ABB seven-passenger modular bucket seats with Multra/Diva cloth trim, regular wheelbase (without 1SD or WX4 $450; with 1SD or WX4 $115; extended wheelbase $115). ABD captain's chairs with Multra/Diva cloth (without 1SD or WX4 $600; with 1SD or WX4 $265; extended wheelbase $265). ZP8 eight-passenger seating with Multra/Diva cloth (without 1SD or WX4 $600; with 1SD or WX4 $265; extended wheelbase $265). WJ6 leather seating areas, includes UK3 leather steering wheel with radio controls ($1,055). C34 front-and-rear air conditioning in Montana ($460). C49 electric rear window defogger ($180). KO5 engine block heater ($20). AJ1 deep-tinted glass ($245). C36 rear heater for extended-wheelbase model (with C34 or WX4 $167; without C34 or WX4 $177). AN2 one integral child seat ($125). AN5 two integral child seats ($225). V54 luggage rack, includes saddlebag storage ($175). WX4 Montana package (regular-wheelbase without 1SD $1,537; regular wheelbase with 1SD $1,027; extended-wheelbase without 1SD $1,164; extended-wheelbase with 1SD $989. D84 two-tone paint ($125). AG1 six-way power driver's seat ($270). AG9 six-way power passenger seat ($305). E58 power sliding door ($350-$400). A31 power windows ($275). AU0 remote keyless entry ($150). UN6 Delco radio equipment ($195). UT6 AM/FM cassette with equalizer and rear seat audio ($150 with leather seat group or $335). U1C AM/FM CD player ($100) UP3 AM/FM CD player with equalizer and rear audio ($250 with leather seat group or $435). UM1 AM/FM cassette with equalizer, dual playback CD player and rear seat audio ($350 with leather seat group or $535). UZ5 extended-range co-axial speakers ($50). G67 Auto Level Control ($180). R6A safety and security package (with P42 or WX4 $60; others $210). XPU P215/70R15 touring tires (regular wheelbase $73; extended wheelbase $35). P42 self-sealing touring tires ($150). V92 trailering provisions ($150). PH3 15-in. aluminum wheels ($259). CF5 sunroof, extended-wheelbase three-door model ($520 with 1SD or $695 without 1SD).

AZTEK OPTIONS: Roof rack system with side rails and cross bars for base Aztek. P215/70R16 touring tires with raised white lettering and puncture sealant feature for Aztek GT. Trailer provisions for both trim levels. 16-in. 3-on-3 spoke cast-aluminum wheels for AWD models only, both trim levels. Reconfigurable cargo net system for base Aztek. Cruise control for base Aztek. Leather seating surfaces for Aztek GT. OnStar Communication and assistance Service for Aztek GT. Pontiac 100 series AM/FM stereo with CD, graphic equalizer, RDS, clock, TheftLock, and six-speaker sound system for base Aztek. Pontiac 100 series AM/FM stereo with compact disc player, auto-reverse cassette, graphic equalizer, RDS, clock, touch control, seek up/down, search and replay, TheftLock, rear cargo audio controls, and Pioneer premium 10-speaker sound system for both models. In-dash CDX receiver with AM/FM and multi CD storage capability (6) with RDS, random disc function, speed-compensated volume control, graphic equalizer, clock, TheftLock, rear cargo audio controls, and Pioneer 10-speaker premium sound system for both models. Rear audio controls for Aztek GT without sunroof. Adjustable six-way power driver's seat for base Aztek. Power passenger seat for Aztek GT, requires optional leather. Four-passenger seating with removable captain's chairs with recliners, fold-down seat backs, halo headrests and armrests for Aztek GT. Smoker's package for both models. Sliding rear cargo tray for both models. Power sunroof with express open for both models. Vehicle theft deterrent alarm system for Aztek GT. Four-wheel disc brakes with AWD models, both trim levels. Engine block heater, both models. State emission equipment, both models. AWD with independent short and long arm control and coil springs, for both models. Automatic level control system including auxiliary air inflator and hose, for both models.

NOTE: Full option package contents, descriptions, and applications information can often be determined by consulting factory literature. The data above is edited for size and clarity. This information provided only as a guide to help collectors appraise the relative value of cars with numerous options. Prices for items included as part of a value option package are usually much less than individual prices. Option prices charged by individual dealers may also vary.

HISTORICAL: Pontiac Motor Div. proudly celebrated its 75th anniversary in 2001. The company marked the milestone year by commissioning Krause Publications to produce a hardcover book called *75 Years of Pontiac: The Official History*. Pontiac Motor Div. also transported a collection of historic vehicles and concept cars to events such as the Detroit Auto Show, the Chicago Auto Show, the New York Auto Show, the Iola Old Car Show, the Pontiac Oakland Club International Convention, and the Woodward Dream Cruise. At the latter event, held in the Detroit, Mich. area in August, a "once-in-75-years" collection of 35 rare and unique Pontiacs was seen. The exhibit also featured a production of classic Pontiac commercials highlighting advertising campaigns from its past to present. On Sept. 25, 2001, General Motors Corp. announced plans to drop the Pontiac Firebird and Chevrolet Camaro after 2002 and close the Canadian plant where they were made. GM termed the halt in production a "hiatus," rather than a final termination and said that the decision to drop the two cars was due to a drop in demand in the sporty car segment, which experienced a 53 percent decline in sales in the past decade.

2002 PONTIAC

2002 Pontiac Sunfire SE two-door coupe. (PGMC)

SUNFIRE — CARLINE J — (FOUR) — The 2002 Pontiac Sunfire picked up right where the 2001 left off, offering spirited performance at just the right price. New was a top-line 2.2-liter dual overhead cam four-cylinder engine, more standard equipment on all models, and new colors. The model lineup gave buyers a choice of the SE sedan, SE coupe, and GT coupe. The base Sunbird engine was a 2.2-liter 2200 inline four. An "Ecotec" version of the 2.2-liter four was due later in 2001, but was not available at the start of production. This 140-hp engine featured twin overhead camshafts with four valves per cylinder. Its quiet operation was aided by twin balance shafts located in the cylinder block that canceled the shaking forces inherent in an inline four-cylinder engine. The new engine could run

2002 Pontiac Sunfire SE two door coupe. (PGMC)

smoothly from idle to maximum engine speed. It was also the lightest engine GM produced in its displacement class and one of the most compact four-cylinders in the world. According to published output figures and EPA mileage ratings, with a five-speed manual transmission, it got 33 mpg. The GT coupe upped performance with 150 hp from a 2.4-liter Twin Cam engine. A tilt steering wheel became standard on all Sunfires. An auxiliary power outlet was made standard on all models, although not at the start of production. An electronic trunk release also became standard. Polo Green Metallic, Spring Green, and Mayan Gold were new colors. A new Driver Convenience package included cruise control, intermittent wipers, a trunk cargo net, assist handles, overhead storage provisions, and reading lamps. Both Sunfire SEs got 14-in. steel wheels with bolt-on wheel covers. Sixteen-inch cast-aluminum wheels with P205/55R16 performance tires were standard on the GT. Other standard features included four-wheel antilock brakes, driver and front passenger airbags, side door beams, and daytime running lamps. Safety equipment included three-point passive safety belts and top tether rear seat anchorages to ensure proper installation of child restraint seats. The Sunfire's standard PASSLock II theft-deterrent system immobilized the vehicle if an attempt to start it without the proper key was made. Content theft protection, included with the remote keyless entry and power door lock security package that flashed daytime running lamps and dome lamp and sounded the horn during an unauthorized attempt to open the doors. Sunfire audio packages included a Radio Data System (RDS) that let listeners seek and scan stations. The premium audio system for SE coupe and GT coupe models was Monsoon's ® 200-watt, eight-speaker world-shaker. Sunfires featured a user-friendly instrument panel cluster including an analog speedometer, a digital LCD odometer and trip odometer, a tachometer, a coolant temperature gauge, and a fuel gauge. The front floor console with integral armrest combined sportiness with practicality. It included two forward-mounted cupholders, a concealed coin holder and ample storage space for tapes, CDs, and other items. For 2002, customers who wanted to add personal touches to their Sunfire had many options and accessories available. American Racing custom chrome-plated wheels were available in either 15- or 16-in. sizes. An aerodynamic ground effects package featured urethane body side moldings and front and rear fascia extensions for a "look fast" appearance. Body side graphics were available to complement the vehicle's exterior color and a ram air hood could be ordered to project a performance look. Customers could also add carbon fiber outside mirrors for a street rod look or a rear wing spoiler for a track-ready look. An interior trim kit featured laser-cut carbon fiber or brushed aluminum panels for the dash, doors, and console. Also available was a Speed Glo Gauge kit that created a soft green or cool blue glow at night with the flip of a switch. Dealer-installed accessories included a sunroof with electronic "open," "vent," and "close" functions, as well as an "auto-close" feature that shut it when the vehicle was turned off.

GRAND AM — CARLINE N — (FOUR) — In the compact coupe and sedan segment, the Grand Am had long enjoyed a solid reputation for performance and reliability. Its athletic design, responsive handling, fully-independent suspension, and driver-focused interior set it apart. For 2002, the Grand Am featured the new EcoTec 2.2L inline four as its base engine. A new console with integrated cupholder was standard on all Grand Ams. The GT also got standard 16-in. five-spoke aluminum torqued wheels (16-in. five-spoke Chrome-Tech torqued wheels were optional on GTs). Dark Tropic Teal was a new fall color. The 3400 V-6 that was optional in 2002 SE editions

2002 Pontiac Grand AM SE two-door coupe. (PGC)

2002 Pontiac ~~Grand Am GT~~ *Trans Am WS6 Ram Air* two-door coupe. (PGMC)

delivered 170 hp. Grand Am GTs upped the ante with a Ram Air version with cold-air induction and low-restriction exhausts that boosted output to 175 hp. The Grand Am SE and SE1 models included a list of standard features not often found in the compact class and GTs took everything that's standard on SE1s and wrapped it in distinctive exterior accents like unique front and rear fascias, color-keyed side cladding, twin-post mirrors, a deck lid spoiler, and special tail lamps. Other standard performance features included four-wheel-disc brakes with ABS, variable-effort power steering, and an upgraded suspension system consisting of firmer bushings, solid front and rear anti-roll bars, and specific spring rates. On all Grand Ams, buyers got 5-mph bumpers, ABS, air-conditioning, a tilt steering wheel, programmable door locks with lock-out protection, battery rundown protection, an electric remote trunk release, an oil life sensor, the PASSLock II theft-deterrent system, a sealed-for-life transmission, and an illuminated entry system with theater dimming. A four-wheel independent suspension with aluminum suspension knuckles reduced unsprung weight for a responsive ride and better handling.

FIREBIRD — CARLINE F — (V-6/V-8) — On Sept. 25, 2001 General Motors announced that the 2002 Firebird would be the last of the breed. However, the automaker left the gate open to use the Firebird name on a new type of car in the future. Whether that will happen, only time will tell, but changes in the 2002 models were quite naturally modest. A power antenna was made standard on all models, along with power remote mirrors, power automatic door locks, and power windows with "express-down" driver's side window controls. A power steering cooler also became standard equipment on all cars with V-8 engines. Formula Firebird coupes got four new standard features such as a removable hatch roof with sunshades, remote keyless entry, a six-way power driver's seat, and an audible theft deterrent system. A 3.8-liter V-6 and five-speed manual transmission were standard on the Firebird coupe. The Firebird convertible combined the same engine with a 4L60-E four-speed automatic transmission. The Formula coupe and both Trans Am models used the same standard drive train as the Formula coupe. The base Firebirds featured hidden headlamps, integrated fog lamps, fender-mounted air extractors, and a sleek, aerodynamic body. Standard equipment included air conditioning, four-wheel disc brakes with ABS, cruise control, a fold-down rear seat, and a center console with an auxiliary power outlet and dual cupholders. The convertible added a standard up-level Monsoon ® sound system with CD player and eight speakers, plus a six-way power driver's seat, a leather-wrapped steering wheel with redundant radio controls, remote keyless entry, alarm and power door locks, "express down" windows, outside mirrors, and an outside radio antenna. Formula coupe appointments included low profile Z-speed-rated tires, silver 16-in. five-spoke sport wheels, a performance-oriented suspension and a 10-speaker version of the Monsoon ® CD audio system. The Trans Am came in both coupe and convertible editions with standard removable roof panels with sunshades, leather seating surfaces, and an uplevel rear spoiler for the coupe. Both Firebird engines were significantly improved for the 2001 model year. Both had Delco-Remy's latest-generation starter, which produced more torque per amp and drew less current for extended starter and battery life. The 5.7L LS1 V-8 introduced leading-edge technologies to the grand tradition of the GM small-block V-8, including all-aluminum construction and a thermoplastic intake manifold. Measured by mass, package size, performance, or cost to the customer, the 5.7L LS1 matched the world's best overhead cam V-8s. This new small-block V-8 proved

that cam-in-block engines could meet the demands of a new decade and stringent emissions standards. Formula and Trans Am drivers got 310 hp and Trans Am drivers opting for Ram Air got 325 hp. Available transmissions for the LS1 included a six-speed manual. The 3800 V-6 Performance Package featured a Torsen II limited-slip differential, up-level steering, dual outlet exhaust, and a 3.42:1 axle ratio (with automatic transmission only). Trans Am coupe and convertible models with the WS6 Ram Air Performance and Handling package benefited from functional air scoops, Ram Air induction, low-restriction dual-outlet exhaust, and a suspension specifically tuned for maximum handling performance. The WS6 package also sported P275/40ZR17 performance radial tires mounted on 9 x 17-in. highly polished alloy wheels featuring a five-spoke spoke design.

GRAND PRIX — CARLINE W — (V-6/V-8) — There were 11 major changes in the 2002 Grand Prix. The Grand Prix GT and GTP coupe and sedan models were available with special 40th Anniversary package to celebrate the "GP's" four decades of production. Five new items became standard equipment on GTs: a six-way power driver's seat, a trunk cargo net, a security package with theft deterrent and power door locks, a steering wheel with radio controls, and an AM/FM stereo with compact disc player. The SE sedan got two new standard features: cruise control and a remote trunk release. Ivory White, Dark Tropic Teal Metallic, and Dark Cherry Metallic were new exterior colors. The Grand Prix SE models came standard with a 3.1-liter V-6 and 4T65E four-speed automatic transmission. The Grand Prix GT added a 3.8-liter V-6 hooked to the same transmission. The GTP added the 3.8-liter supercharged V-6, again with the same transmission. The 40th Anniversary option package included special appointments like a unique rear spoiler, exclusive hood heat extractors, a dual-dual exhaust system, roof "fences" that mirrored the production car's NASCAR cousin, special wheels, and Dark Cherry paint. Inside, the milestone year was commemorated with interior seat emblems, as well as two-tone leather seats, door trim and steering wheel done in Ruby Red and Graphite, as well as a Ruby Red leather shift knob and Ruby Red soft touch paint cluster and console trim plates. A sport-tuned suspension with front and rear stabilizer bars was found on all Grand Prix models. Standard four-wheel antilock brakes and traction control helped keep a driver in command under less-than-perfect driving conditions. Inside the large analog instrumentation with red backlighting was easy to read. The controls were canted toward the driver and a floor console was within convenient reach. A standard Driver Information Center (DIC) in the instrument cluster kept drivers updated on various operating conditions such as traction system activation, the need for an oil change, or a door ajar. The supercharged GTP added an engine boost pressure display. The Grand Prix included contoured front bucket seats, manual lap/shoulder safety belts for all outboard positions, manual lap safety belts for center seating positions, and driver and passenger front-impact airbags. Also standard were four-wheel antilock brakes, an Enhanced Traction System, daytime running lamps with automatic exterior lamp control, and tires with built-in tread wear indicators.

BONNEVILLE — CARLINE H — (V-6) — The 2002 Pontiac Bonneville had 13 notable changes. There were new front and rear fascias for Bonneville SE models, while new badging dressed up the Bonneville SLE and Bonneville SSEi models. New dual oval exhaust tips were seen on SLE and SSEi models, which also got new 17-in. optional

2002 Pontiac Firebird two-door coupe. (PGMC)

chrome wheels. New 17-in. aluminum wheels were standard on Bonnevilles. Also new was a redesigned center console with cup holders. A Monsoon audio system was now standard on SSEi models. All Bonnevilles now had LATCH child safety seat anchors, an interior trunk release handle, and new Peak Expression cloth-and-fabric interior trims. Dark Blue Metallic and Granite Metallic were new exterior colors and the Polo Green introduced in April 2001 was continued. The Bonneville SE employed the 3.8-liter V-6 and 4T65-E four-speed automatic transmission, as did the Bonneville SLE. The SSEi combined the same transmission with the supercharged 3.8-liter V-6. The Bonneville SE remained a true Sport Sedan that seated five or six comfortably. Standard features on the SE now included a CD player, 16-in. aluminum wheels, a six-way power driver's seat, remote keyless entry and an anti-theft alarm system, as well as independent front and rear touring suspensions with electronic level control, a tire pressure monitor, daytime running lamps with twilight sentinel, the PASSKey III security system, power windows with express-down driver and passenger, power outside rearview mirrors, a rear-deck spoiler, and a trunk pass-through. The Bonneville added standard 17-in. inch five-spoke aluminum wheels, a dual-play audio system, a dual-zone climate control system, independent front and rear performance suspensions with electronic level control, a 3.05:1 performance axle ratio, a rear deck spoiler, and a Driver Information Center. The Bonneville SSEi took the content to its highest level with the StabiliTrak system, heads-up display, magnetic variable-effort steering, 12-way articulating driver, and passenger leather bucket seats with memory and a trunk accessory kit. Four-wheel ABS was standard on all Bonnevilles, with a Delco-Bosch 5.3 system providing electronic proportioning. The available traction control system used brake application and engine torque modulation to increase driver control in slippery conditions. Inside the Bonneville was an array of programmable personalization usually found in more expensive luxury vehicles. The 45/45 bucket seats in Peak Expression cloth were standard with Connolly leather trim available. A 55/45 bench seat with center storage armrest was available on the SE, in cloth only, for six-passenger seating. Bonneville interior components were engineered to help minimize trauma to occupants in the event of a collision. An integral quarter panel with one-piece side frame inner and outer stampings, a stiff overall body, strong seat and safety belt anchors, and excellent cross-car integrity worked together to help the Bonneville offer buyers extreme crashworthiness.

MONTANA — CARLINE U — (V-6) — VERSATRAK AWD was a new standard feature of the 2002 Montana. Also new was an optional DVD entertainment system and extra-cost Thunder Sport appearance package. Pontiac again offered the minivan in regular wheelbase and extended wheelbase models all using the same 3.4-liter V-6 and four-speed automatic transmission. The addition of GM's VERSATRAK AWD system to the Montana created a minivan with all-wheel drive that still allowed for a flat load floor in the rear, without removing the third-row seat. The new Thunder Sport appearance package was available on all extended wheelbase models. It consisted of 16-in. chrome wheels, fully independent front and rear suspensions, a unique two-tone leather interior, a rear spoiler and special "Thunder" badging. The new Gen III entertainment system featured a DVD player with wireless remote and a seven-inch video screen with on-screen programming, auxiliary stereo RCA jacks for video game systems and camcorders, and wireless headphones with separate volume controls. A variety of seating configurations inside the Montana accommodated the active demands of any family. Montana's "space on demand" capabilities included an available third-row stowable seat with convenience center. It was available with an eight-passenger seating configuration

2002 Pontiac Firebird two-door convertible. (PGMC)

2002 Pontiac Grand Prix GTP four-door sedan. (PGMC)

on Extended Wheelbase models. In all, the Montana seated seven with four captain's chairs and a split-folding bench in the rear seating row. Flip and fold second- and third-row seats were readily removable without tools. Buyers could also opt for eight-passenger seating with modular buckets in the middle row and a bench seat in the rear. Six-passenger seating with captain's chairs in the middle row and buckets in the rear row was available on the regular-wheelbase version. While air conditioning was standard, an optional Montana package provided heating and air conditioning ducts for rear-seat passengers, along with auxiliary controls for selecting temperature and fan speed on extended-wheelbase models. Auxiliary power outlets were provided in both the front passenger compartment and the rear cargo area. A special Sport Performance and Handling package contained a sport suspension, 15-in. cast-aluminum wheels, touring performance tires, all-weather traction control, and automatic load leveling.

AZTEK — CARLINE A/B — (V-6) — After a rough first year due to its controversial appearance, the Aztek entered the 2002 model year with a revised two-model lineup that included the Aztek front-wheel-drive model and the Aztek VERSATRAK AWD model. The Aztek GT was eliminated. The exterior appearance was freshened with a monotone exterior treatment with a rear spoiler. Revised Aztek option packaging produced four choices: 1SA Aztek; 1SB Aztek Basic Plus; 1SC Aztek Comfort & Security; and 1SD Aztek Deluxe. Champagne Beige was a new exterior color. New standard equipment included a console/cooler, an AM/FM stereo radio with CD, and three-spoke 16-in. cast-aluminum wheels. Heated seats were now standard on Azteks with optional leather seating. A leather-wrapped steering wheel with radio controls was now standard on Azteks with the dual-play radio and in-dash six-disc CDX receiver. A new interior option was Hanglide premium cloth trim in Red Accent on five-passenger seats. Pontiac also promised Aztek buyers expanded availability of the OnStar system (which was not available with a sunroof), the theft deterrent alarm system, the 16-in. Three-on-Three cast-aluminum wheels, and the 16-in. puncture sealant tires. Another new option package for all-wheel-drive Azteks included 17-in. cast-aluminum wheels and tires. All Azteks used the 3.8-liter V-6 and four-speed automatic transmission. Aztek buyers again got bucket seats in front with a choice of a three-passenger flip/fold 50/50-split seat or dual captain chairs in back. Aztek retained its wide, low and flat load floor. Removing the back seats opened up 93.5 cu. ft. of cargo space. A dozen securely attached cargo anchors, a rear convenience net and storage areas built into the side trim and tailgate sill helped keep track of loose ends. Two optional cargo storage systems offered Aztek owners versatility. The sliding rear cargo tray system supported up to 400 pounds of cargo. The second option was the reconfigurable rear cargo net system. The MacPherson strut front suspension was fitted with four-stage shock absorbers valving for optimum ride and handling. The short-and-long-arm independent (SLA) rear suspension, designed specifically for VERSATRAK AWD models, gave the Aztek suspension a significant handling edge over live-axle systems, particularly on irregular pavement. An optional automatic level-control system added a bladder around each rear shock absorber. Air pressure inside the bladder was supplied by an on-board compressor and maintained a flat vehicle attitude when heavy loads were carried or when a trailer was attached. Included with the auto-level system was an auxiliary accessory outlet located behind the rear interior trim, an air hose, and a pressure gauge.

2002 Pontiac Grand Prix GT four-door sedan. (PGMC)

I.D. DATA: The vehicle identification number (VIN) is located on the top left-hand surface of the instrument panel and is visible through the windshield. The VIN has 17 symbols. The first symbol indicates the country of manufacture (1 or 4=United States; 2=Canada; 3=Mexico; W=Germany). The second symbol indicates the manufacturer (G=General Motors). The third symbol indicates the make/division (2=Pontiac; M=Pontiac MPV and 7=GM of Canada). The fourth symbol (trucks) indicates the GVWR range and brake system. The fourth and fifth symbols (passenger cars) indicate the car line and series F/S=Firebird and Convertible; F/V=Formula and Convertible; H/X=Bonneville SE; H/Y=Bonneville SLE; H/Z=Bonneville SSEi; J/B=Sunfire; J/D=Sunfire; N/E=Grand Am SE; N/F=Grand Am SE1; N/G=Grand Am SE2; N/V=Grand Am GT1; N/W= Grand Am GT; W/J=Grand Prix SE; W/K=Grand Prix SE1; W/P=Grand Prix GT; W/R=Grand prix GTP. The fifth and sixth symbols (trucks) indicate car line and series: A/O=Aztek SRV 4 x 2; B/O=Aztek SRV 4 x 4; U/O=Montana All-Purpose Vehicle 4 x 2; U/1=Montana All-Purpose Vehicle 4 x 2 luxury; U/2=Montana All-Purpose Vehicle 4 x 2 economy; X/O=Montana All-Purpose Vehicle Extended-Wheelbase 4 x 2; X/1=Montana All-Purpose Vehicle luxury Extended-Wheelbase 4 x 2; X/2=Montana All-Purpose Vehicle economy Extended-Wheelbase 4 x 2. The sixth symbol (passenger cars only) indicates body style (1=two-door coupe models 27, 37, 47 and 57; 2=two-door models 07, 08, 77, 87; 3=two-door Convertible model 67; 5=four-door sedan models 19 and 69; 6=four-door sedan models 29 and 68; 8=four-door station wagon model 35. The seventh symbol (passenger cars) indicates the restraint system: 1=Active manual belts; 2=Active manual belts with driver and passenger inflatable restraints; 4=Active manual belts front and side; 5=Active manual belts with driver and passenger front and side airbags; 6=Active manual belts with driver and passenger front and side airbags and passenger sensor; 7=Active manual belts with driver and passenger front and side airbags and rear passenger compartment side airbags. The seventh symbol (trucks) indicates body style: 3=All-Purpose Vehicle (Montana and Aztek). The eighth symbol indicates the engine type. The ninth symbol is a check digit. The 10th symbol indicates model year (2=2002). The 11th symbol indicates the GM assembly plant (B=Baltimore, Md., T&B; B=Lansing, Mich., GENASYS; C=Lansing, Mich.; D=Doraville, Ga.; E=Pontiac East, Mich., T&B; F=Fairfax II, Kan.; F=Flint, Mich., T&B; G=Silao Mexico; H=Flint, Mich.; J=Janesville, Wis., T&B; K=Linden, N.J., T&B; M=Lansing, Mich.; M=Toluca Mexico; R=Arlington, Texas; R=Russelsheim Germany; S=Ramos Arizpe Mexico; T=Shreveport, La.; U=Hamtramck, Mich.; Y=Wilmington, Del.; Z=Fremont, Calif.; Z=Spring Hill, Tenn.; Z=Ft. Wayne, Ind., T&B; 0=Lansing, Mich.; 1=Oshawa Canada, T&B; 1=Oshawa Canada, #2; 1=Wentzville, Mo., T&B; 2=Morraine, Ohio, T&B; 2=Ste. Therese Canada; 3=Kawasaki Japan; 4=Orion, Mich.; 5=Bowling Green, Ken.; 6=Ingersoll, Ontario Canada; 6=Oklahoma City, Okla.; 7=Lordstown, Ohio; 7=Flusawa Japan; 8=Shreveport, La., T&B; 8=Tillisonburg, Ohio, CANEXPO; 9=Oshawa, Ontario Canada, #1). Pontiacs are not produced at all of these plants. The last six symbols are the consecutive unit number at the factory.

Model Number	Body Style Number	Body Type & Seating	Factory Price	Shipping Weight	Production Total
SUNFIRE SE SERIES B (I-4)					
J/B	B37V	2d Coupe-4P	15,080	2,606	Note 1
J/B	B69V	4d Sedan-4P	15,580	2,644	Note 1
SUNFIRE GT SERIES D (I-4)					
J/D	D37V	2d Coupe-4P	17,395	2,771	Note 1

Model Number	Body Style Number	Body Type & Seating	Factory Price	Shipping Weight	Production Total
GRAND AM SE SERIES E (I-4)					
N/E	E37V	2d Coupe-4P	17,255	3,066	Note 1
N/E	E69V	4d Sedan-4P	17,405	3,116	Note 1
GRAND AM SE1 SERIES E (I-4)					
N/E	E37V	2d Coupe-4P	18,695	3,166	Note 1
N/E	E69V	4d Sedan-4P	18,845	3,216	Note 1
GRAND AM GT SERIES W (I-4)					
N/W	W37V	2d Coupe-4P	21,145	3,099	Note 1
N/W	W69V	2d Sedan-4P	21,295	3,118	Note 1
GRAND AM GT1 SERIES W (I-4)					
N/W	W37V	2d Coupe-4P	22,415	3,199	Note 1
N/W	W69V	2d Sedan-4P	22,565	3,218	Note 1
FIREBIRD SERIES S (V-6)					
F/S	S87V	2d Coupe-4P	20,090	3,323	Note 1
F/S	S67V	2d Convertible-4P	27,005	3,402	Note 1
FORMULA SERIES V (V-8)					
F/V	V87V	2d Coupe-4P	26,035	3, 341	Note 1
TRANS AM SERIES V (V-8)					
F/V	V87V	2d Coupe-4P	28,065	3,397	Note 1
F/V	V67V	2d Convertible-4P	32,135	3,514	Note 1
GRAND PRIX SE SERIES J (V-6)					
W/J	J69V	4d Sedan-4P	21,575	3,384	Note 1
GRAND PRIX GT SERIES (V-6)					
W/J	P37V	2d Coupe-4P	23,545	3,429	Note 1
W/J	P69V	4d Sedan-4P	23,695	3,496	Note 1
GRAND PRIX GTP SERIES (V-6)					
W/J	R37V	2d Coupe-4P	26,235	3,495	Note 1
W/J	R69V	4d Sedan-4P	26,415	3,559	Note 1
BONNEVILLE SE SERIES X (V-6)					
X	X69V	4d Sport Sedan-6P	26,185	3,590	
BONNEVILLE SLE SERIES Z (V-6)					
Z	Z69V	4d Sport Sedan-6P	29,375	3,650	Note 1
BONNEVILLE SSEi SERIES Z (Supercharged V-6)					
Z	Z69V	4d Sport Sedan-6P	33,625	3,790	Note 1
MONTANA REGULAR WHEELBASE FRONT-WHEEL DRIVE SERIES U (V-6)					
U	U	Minivan 6-seat	24,990	3,803	Note 1
U	U	Minivan 7-seat	27,390	3,850	Note 1
MONTANA EXTENDED WHEELBASE FRONT-WHEEL DRIVE SERIES X (V-6)					
U	X	Minivan 7-seat	25,900	3,942	Note 1
MONTANA EXTENDED WHEELBASE ALL-WHEEL DRIVE SERIES X (V-6)					
U	X	Minivan 7-seat	30,860	4,142	Note 1
MONTANA VISION EXTENDED WHEELBASE FRONT-WHEEL DRIVE SERIES X (V-6)					
U	X	Minivan 7-seat	30,975	3,942	Note 1
MONTANA VISION EXTENDED WHEELBASE ALL-WHEEL DRIVE SERIES X (V-6)					
U	X	Minivan 8-seat	34,465	4,142	Note 1
AZTEK (FWD) SERIES AO3 (I-4)					
A	AO3	4d Sport Utility	20,545	3,779	Note 1
AZTEK (AWD) SERIES AO3 (I-4)					
A	AO3	4d Sport Utility	23,545	4,043	Note 1

NOTE 1: Not available at time of publication.

SUNFIRE ENGINES

ENGINE [Base Four SE]: Inline. OHV. Four-cylinder. Cast-iron block and cast-aluminum cylinder head. Aluminum intake manifold. Two valves per cylinder. Displacement: 134 cid. (2.2L). Bore x stroke: 3.50 x 3.46 in. Compression ratio: 9.0:1. Net horsepower: 115 at 5000 rpm. Torque: 135 lbs.-ft. at 3600 rpm. Fuel system: SFI. VIN Code: 4. RPO Code: LN2.

ENGINE [Base Four (GT early production); Optional (SE)]: Inline. DOHC. Four-cylinder. Four valves per cylinder. Cast-iron block and cast-aluminum head. Aluminum intake manifold. Displacement: 146 cid. (2.4L). Bore x stroke: 3.54 x 3.70 in. Compression ratio: 9.5:1. Net horsepower: 150 at 5600 rpm. Torque: 155 lbs.-ft. at 4400 rpm. Fuel system: SFI. VIN Code: T. RPO Code: LD9.

ENGINE [Base Four (GT late production); Optional (SE)]: Inline. OHV. ECOTEC FOUR Four-cylinder. Cast-aluminum block and cast-

2002 Pontiac Bonneville SE four-door Sport Sedan. (PGMC)

Standard Catalog of ® Pontiac, 2nd Edition

aluminum cylinder head. Aluminum intake manifold. Two valves per cylinder. Displacement: 134 cid. (2.2L). Bore x stroke: 3.39 x 3.72 in. Compression ratio: 10.0:1. Net horsepower: 140 at 5600 rpm. Torque: 150 lbs.-ft. at 4000 rpm. Fuel system: SFI. VIN Code: 4. RPO Code: L61.

GRAND AM ENGINES

ENGINE [Base Four SE/SE1]: Inline. OHV. ECOTECH Four-cylinder. Cast-aluminum block and cast-aluminum cylinder head. Aluminum intake manifold. Two valves per cylinder. Displacement: 134 cid. (2.2L). Bore & stroke: 3.39 x 3.72 in. Compression ratio: 10.0:1. Net horsepower: 140 at 5600 rpm. Torque: 150 lbs.-ft. at 4000 rpm. Fuel system: SFI. VIN Code: 4. RPO Code: L61.

ENGINE [Base V-6 SE1]: V-block. OHV. Six-cylinder. Cast-iron block and aluminum cylinder head. Aluminum intake manifold. Displacement: 207 cid. (3.4L). Bore & stroke: 3.62 x 3.31 in. Compression ratio: 9.5:1. Brake horsepower: 170 at 4800 rpm. Torque: 195 lbs.-ft. at 4000 rpm. Fuel system: SFI. VIN Code: M. RPO Code: LA1.

ENGINE [Base V-6 GT]: V-block. OHV. Six-cylinder. RAM AIR. Cast-iron block and aluminum cylinder head. Aluminum intake manifold. Displacement: 207 cid. (3.4L). Bore & stroke: 3.62 x 3.31 in. Compression ratio: 9.5:1. Brake horsepower: 175 at 5200 rpm. Torque: 205 lbs.-ft. at 4000 rpm. Fuel system: SFI. VIN Code: M. RPO Code: LA1.

FIREBIRD ENGINES

ENGINE [Base V-6 Firebird coupe and convertible]: V-block. OHV. Six-cylinder. Cast-iron block. Cast-iron cylinder head. Displacement: 231 cid. (3.8L). Bore & stroke: 3.80 x 3.40 in. Compression ratio: 9.4:1. Brake horsepower: 200 at 5200 rpm. Torque: 225 lbs.-ft. at 4000 rpm. Fuel system: SFI. VIN Code: K. RPO Code: L36.

ENGINE [Base V-8 Formula and Trans Am]: V-block. OHV. Eight-cylinder. Aluminum block and cylinder head. Aluminum intake manifold. Displacement: 350 cid. (5.7L). Bore & stroke: 3.90 x 3.62 in. Brake horsepower: 310 at 5200 rpm. Torque: 340 lbs.-ft. at 4000 rpm. Compression ratio: 10.5:1. Fuel system: SFI. VIN Code: G. RPO Code: LS1.

ENGINE [Optional V-8 Formula and Trans Am WS6 RAM AIR]: V-block. OHV. Eight-cylinder. Aluminum block and cylinder head. Aluminum intake manifold. Ram-air induction. Displacement: 350 cid. (5.7L). Bore & stroke: 3.90 x 3.62 in. Brake horsepower: 325 at 5200 rpm. Torque: 350 lbs.-ft. at 4000 rpm. Compression ratio: 10.5:1. Fuel system: SFI. VIN Code: G. RPO Code: LS1.

GRAND PRIX ENGINES

ENGINE [Base V-6 SE]: V-block. Six-cylinder. Cast-iron block. Cast-aluminum cylinder head. Displacement: 191 cid. (3.1L). Bore & stroke: 3.51 x 3.31 in. Compression ratio: 9.6:1. Brake horsepower: 175 at 5200 rpm. Torque: 195 lbs.-ft. at 4000 rpm. Fuel system: SFI. RPO Code: LG8.

ENGINE [Base V-6 GT]: V-block. Six-cylinder. Cast-iron block and cylinder head. Displacement: 231 cid. (3.8L). Bore & stroke: 3.80 x 3.40 in. Compression ratio: 9.4:1. Brake horsepower: 200 at 5200 rpm. Torque: 225 lbs.-ft. at 4000 rpm. Fuel system: SFI. VIN Code: K. RPO Code: L36.

ENGINE [Optional V-6 GTP]: V-block. Six-cylinder. Supercharged. Cast-iron block and cylinder head. Displacement: 231 cid. (3.8L). Bore & stroke: 3.80 x 3.40 in. Compression ratio: 8.5:1. Brake horsepower: 240 at 5200 rpm. Torque: 280 lbs.-ft. at 3200 rpm. Fuel system: SFI. VIN Code: 1. RPO Code: L67.

2002 Pontiac Bonneville SLE four-door Sport Sedan. (PGMC)

2002 Pontiac Bonneville SSEi four-door Sport Sedan. (PGMC)

BONNEVILLE ENGINES

ENGINE [Base V-6 SE/SLE]: "3800" SFI Series II V-6. V-block. OHV. Six-cylinder. Displacement: 231 cid. (3.8L). Bore & stroke: 3.80 x 3.40 in. Compression ratio: 9.4:1. Brake horsepower: 205 at 5200 rpm. Torque: 230 lbs.-ft. at 4000 rpm. Fuel system: SFI. VIN Code: K RPO Code: L36.

ENGINE [Optional Supercharged V-6 SSEi]: "3800" Supercharged Series II V-6. V-block. OHV. Six-cylinder. Displacement: 231 cid. (3.8L). Bore & stroke: 3.80 x 3.40 in. Compression ratio: 8.5:1. Brake horsepower: 240 at 5200 rpm. Torque: 280 lbs.-ft. at 3200 rpm. Fuel system: SFI. VIN Code: 1 RPO Code: L67.

MONTANA ENGINE

ENGINE [Base V-6]: V-block. DOHC. Six-cylinder. Cast-iron block. Aluminum cylinder head. Displacement: 207 cid. (3.4L). Bore & stroke: 3.62 x 3.31 in. Compression ratio: 9.5:1. Brake horsepower: 185 at 5200 rpm. Torque: 210 lbs.-ft. at 4000 rpm. Fuel system: SFI. VIN Code: E. RPO Code: LA1.

AZTEK ENGINE

ENGINE [Base V-6]: V-block. DOHC. Six-cylinder. Cast-iron block. Aluminum cylinder head. Displacement: 207 cid. (3.4L). Bore & stroke: 3.62 x 3.31 in. Compression ratio: 9.5:1. Brake horsepower: 185 at 5200 rpm. Torque: 210 lbs.-ft. at 4000 rpm. Fuel system: SFI. VIN Code: E. RPO Code: LA1.

CHASSIS

SUNFIRE CHASSIS: Wheelbase: (all) 104.1 in. Overall length: (coupe) 182 in.; (sedan) 181.8 in. Overall width: (coupe) 68.4 in.; (sedan) 67.9 in. Height: (coupe) 53.0 in.; (sedan) 54.7 in. Front tread: (all) 57.6 in. Rear tread: (coupe) 56.4 in.; (sedan) 56.6 in.

GRAND AM CHASSIS: Wheelbase: (all) 107 in. Overall length: 186.3 in. Width: (all) 70.4 in. Height: (all) 55.1 in. Front tread: (all) 59 in. Rear tread: (all) 59.1 in.

FIREBIRD CHASSIS: Wheelbase: (all) 101.1 in. Overall length: (Firebird/Formula) 193.3 in.; (Trans Am) 193.7 in. Width: (all) 74.4 in. Height: (Firebird/Formula coupe) 51.2 in.; (Trans Am coupe) 51.2 in.; (All Convertibles) 51.8 in. Front Tread: (all) 60.7 in. Rear tread: (all) 60.6 in.

GRAND PRIX CHASSIS: Wheelbase: (all) 110.5 in. Overall length: (all) 197.5 in. Width: (all) 72.7 in. Height: (all) 54.7 in. Front Tread: (all) 61.76 in. Rear tread: (all) 61.1 in.

BONNEVILLE CHASSIS: Wheelbase: (all) 112.2 in. Overall length: (all) 202.6 in. Width: (all) 74.2 in. Height: (all) 56.6 in. Front tread: 62.6 in. Rear tread: 62.1 in.

MONTANA CHASSIS: Wheelbase: (Regular Wheelbase) 112 in.; (Extended Wheelbase) 121 in. Overall length: (Regular Wheelbase) 187.3 in.; (Extended Wheelbase) 200.9 in. Width: (all) 72 in. Height: (Regular Wheelbase) 67.4 in.; (Extended Wheelbase) 68.2 in. Front tread: (Regular Wheelbase) 61.5 in.; (Extended Wheelbase) 61.8 in. Rear tread: (Both) 63.3 in.

AZTEK CHASSIS: Wheelbase: (all) 108.3 in. Overall length: (all) 182.1 in. Width: (all) 73.7 in. Height: (all) 66.7 in. without roof rack. Front tread: (all) 62.7 in. Rear tread: (all) 63.8 in.

TECHNICAL

SUNFIRE TECHNICAL: Chassis: Front engine/front drive. Base transmission: Five-speed manual. Optional transmission: Three-speed automatic. Front suspension: (SE) Deflected disc MacPherson

2002 Pontiac Montana RWB minivan. (PGMC)

struts with lower control arms, spring and 18-mm anti-roll bar; (GT) Deflected disc MacPherson struts with lower control arms, spring and 22-mm anti-roll bar. Rear suspension: Trailing tubular control arms with twist beam; coil springs; 18-mm anti-roll bar on GT coupe. Steering: Rack-and-pinion. Front brakes: vented disc power-assisted. Rear brakes: drum power-assisted. Standard tires: (SE) P195/70R14 all-season black sidewall; (GT) P205/55R16 black sidewall performance-type. Fuel tank: 15 gal.

GRAND AM TECHNICAL: Chassis: Front engine/front drive. Base transmission: Five-speed manual with overdrive. Optional transmission: Three-speed automatic. Front suspension: MacPherson struts with lower control arms, 29 Nm spring and 24-mm hollow stabilizer bar. Rear suspension: Tri-link independent with 17.5 Nm spring and 15.3-mm solid stabilizer bar. Steering (Four-cylinder): Power-assisted rack-and-pinion. Steering (Six-cylinder) C-spring EVO variable effort. Power-assisted rack-and-pinion, 14.7:1 ratio. Front brakes: Power-assisted vented discs. Rear brakes: Power-assisted drums. Standard tires: (SE/SE1) P215/60R15 black sidewall touring; (GT/GT1) P225/50R16 black sidewall touring. Fuel tank: 14.3 gal.

FIREBIRD TECHNICAL: Chassis: Front engine/rear drive. Base transmission: Five-speed manual. Front suspension: (Firebird F41) SLA/coil over monotube gas-charged shocks, tubular stabilizer bars with links and 28-mm stabilizer bar; (Formula Trans Am FE2) SLA/coil over monotube gas-charged shocks, tubular stabilizer bar with links and 30-mm stabilizer bar. Rear suspension: (Firebird F41) Salisbury axle with torque arm, trailing arm, track bar, coil springs and 15mm stabilizer bar; (Formula Trans Am FE2) Salisbury axle with torque arm, trailing arm, track bar, coil springs and 19mm stabilizer bar. Steering: (Firebird) Power rack and pinion, 16.9:1 ratio, 2.67 turns lock-to-lock, 37.9-ft. turn circle; (Formula/Trans Am) Power rack and pinion, 14.4:1 ratio, 2.28 turns lock-to-lock, 37.75-ft. turn circle. Front brakes: (All) 11.9-in. vented disc/302.3 mm. Rear brakes: (All) 12-in. vented disc, power-assisted, 304.8 mm. Standard tires: (Firebird) P215/60R16 steel-belted radial black sidewall touring; (Formula) P245/50ZR16 speed-rated, all-weather; (Trans Am) P245/50ZR16 speed-rated, all-weather. Fuel tank: 16.8 gal.

GRAND PRIX TECHNICAL: Chassis: Front engine/front drive. Front suspension: MacPherson struts with coil springs, lower A-arm and 30mm hollow anti-roll bar. Rear suspension: Independent, tri-link, coil-over-strut, 18mm anti-roll bar. Steering: Low-friction power-assisted rack-and-pinion, 17.6:1 ratio, 2.26 turns lock-to-lock and 35.6 ft. Turn circle. (MagnaSteer™ variable-effort power steering optional). Front brakes: 10.9-in. vented discs, power assisted. Rear brakes: 10.9-in. solid discs, power assisted, standard ABS. Standard tires: (SE) P205/70R15 black sidewall touring; (GT) P225/60R16 black sidewall; (GTP) P225/60R16 black sidewall performance-type. Fuel tank: 17.5 gal.

BONNEVILLE TECHNICAL: Chassis: Front engine/front drive. Base transmission: Four-speed automatic. Standard FE1 front suspension: Deflected-disc MacPherson struts with 27 Nm coil spring over strut and 29mm stabilizer bar. Optional FE2 front suspension: Deflected-disc MacPherson struts with 27 Nm coil spring over strut and 30mm stabilizer bar. Standard FE1 rear suspension: Automatic level control (variable rate 48-65 Nm), 36mm coil springs, Cadiz shocks and independent lower control arm. Optional FE2 rear suspension: Automatic level control (variable rate 48-65 Nm), 36mm coil springs, Cadiz shocks and independent lower control arm and 20mm stabilizer bar. Steering: (Standard) Power-assisted variable-ratio rack-and-pinion,

15.3:1 to 20.3:1 ratio, 3.2 turns lock-to-lock and 40.5-ft. turn circle; (Optional SSEi only) Mag-E variable-ratio rack-and-pinion, 15.3:1 to 20.3:1 ratio, 3.2 turns lock-to-lock and 40.5-ft. turn circle Front brakes: (Grand Prix SE) 10.9-in vented discs; (Grand Prix SLE and SSEi only) 11.9-in. vented discs. Rear brakes: (All) 11.1-in. discs, power assisted, antilock. Tires: (SE) P225/60R16 Firestone Affinity; (SLE/SSEi) P235/55R17 Goodyear Eagle RSA. Fuel tank: 18.5 gal.

MONTANA TECHNICAL: Chassis: Front engine/front drive. Transmission: Three-speed automatic. Front suspension: MacPherson strut with 27 Nm coil springs, stamped lower control arms and 34mm stabilizer bar. Rear suspension: Open-section twist axle with integral stabilizer bar, 30mm base gas shocks, 32mm self-leveling air shocks (sport suspension); 27 Nm base coil springs and 36mm stabilizer bar. Rack-and-pinion steering, 17.5:1 ratio, 3.05 turns lock-to-lock and 37.4-ft. turn circle. Front brakes: Power-assisted vented rotors. Rear brakes: Power-assisted finned composite Cast-iron drums. Front tread: 61.8 in. Rear tread: 63.3 in. Standard tires: P215/70R15 all-season touring tires with sealant and raised white outline letters. Fuel tank: 25 gal.

AZTEK TECHNICAL: Chassis: Transversely-mounted front engine/front transaxle (AWD optional). Transmission: Four-speed automatic. Front suspension: Independent strut type with coil springs and anti-roll bar. Rear suspension: (FWD) trailing twist beam axle with integral anti-roll bar and coil springs; (AWD) short and long control arms with one tow-control link per side, coil springs and anti-roll bar. Power-assisted rack-and-pinion steering. Brakes: (FWD) Vented disc/drum with power assist and ABS; (AWD) Vented disc/disc with power assist and ABS. Front tread: 62.7 in. Rear tread: 63.8 in. Standard tires: P215/70R15 all-season black sidewall. Fuel tank: 18 gal.

OPTIONS

SUNFIRE OPTIONS: [SE coupe] PB1 15-in. custom bolt-on wheel covers ($55). LD9 2.4-liter Twin cam engine ($450). MM5 five-speed manual transmission ($810 credit). CD4 controlled cycle windshield wipers ($65). K34 cruise control ($235). U1P Delco 100 series ETR AM/FM stereo with CD player ($155). K05 engine block heater ($35). U85 Monsoon premium sound system ($195). R6M New Jersey cost surcharge (no cost). 1SA option group 1 (no cost). 1SB option group 2 ($965). QPD P195/65R15 SBR touring tires ($135). CF5 power glass sunroof ($595). PDC security package ($370). PCR Sun and Storm package ($1,770). [SE sedan] PB1 15-in. custom bolt-on wheel covers ($55). LD9 2.4-liter Twin cam engine ($450). MM5 five-speed manual transmission ($810 credit). CD4 controlled cycle windshield wipers ($65). K34 cruise control ($235). K05 engine block heater ($35). R6M New Jersey cost surcharge (no cost). 1SA option group 1 (no cost). 1SB option group 2 ($1,115). QPD P195/65R15 SBR touring tires ($135). PDN power package ($445). PDC security package ($410). PCN Special Edition package ($1,375). [GT coupe] PB1 15-in. custom bolt-on wheel covers ($55). MX0 four-speed automatic transmission ($810). MM5 five-speed manual transmission ($810 credit). U1P Delco 100 series ETR AM/FM stereo with CD player ($155). K05engine block heater ($35). VK4 front license plate bracket ($100). U85 Monsoon premium sound system ($195). 1SA option group 1 (no cost). R6M New Jersey cost surcharge (no cost). 1SB

2002 Pontiac Montana EWB minivan. (PGMC)

Standard Catalog of ® Pontiac, 2nd Edition

option group 2 ($1,480). 1SC option group 3 ($1,989). CF5 power glass sunroof ($555). PDN power package ($380). PCR Sun and Storm package ($2,190). PCR Sun and Storm package ($1,770).

GRAND AM OPTIONS: [SE coupe/sedan] MX0 four-speed automatic transmission ($825). YF5 California emissions requirements (no cost). K34 cruise control ($235). K05 engine block heater ($35). NC7 Federal emissions override (no cost). FE9 Federal emissions requirements (no cost). R6M New Jersey cost surcharge (no cost). NB8 Northeast states emissions override (no cost). NG1 Northeast states emissions requirements (no cost). [SE1 coupe/sedan] PY1 16-in. ChromeTech cast-aluminum wheels ($595). LA1 3.4-liter SFI V-6 ($715). MX0 four-speed automatic transmission ($825). YF5 California emissions requirements (no cost). U1Q Delco ETR AM/FM stereo with CD and cassette ($340). K05 engine block heater ($35). NC7 Federal emissions override (no cost). FE9 Federal emissions requirements (no cost). R6M New Jersey cost surcharge (no cost). NB8 Northeast states emissions override (no cost). NG1 Northeast states emissions requirements (no cost). CF5 power glass sunroof ($695). PCH Solid Value option package ($1,005). [GT coupe/sedan] PY2 16-in. ChromeTech cast-aluminum wheels ($645). YF5 California emissions requirements (no cost). U1Q Delco ETR AM/FM stereo with CD and cassette ($195). K05 engine block heater ($35). NC7 Federal emissions override (no cost). FE9 Federal emissions requirements (no cost). R6M New Jersey cost surcharge (no cost). NB8 Northeast states emissions override (no cost). NG1 Northeast states emissions requirements (no cost). CF5 power glass sunroof ($695). PCH Solid Value option package ($910). AS5 Sport Interior group ($575). [GT1 coupe] PY2 16-in. ChromeTech cast-aluminum wheels ($645). YF5 California emissions requirements (no cost). K05 engine block heater ($35). NC7 Federal emissions override (no cost). FE9 Federal emissions requirements (no cost). R6M New Jersey cost surcharge (no cost). NB8 Northeast states emissions override (no cost). NG1 Northeast states emissions requirements (no cost). PCR Solid Value option package ($900). AS5 Sport Interior group ($575).

FIREBIRD OPTIONS: [Firebird coupe] U1S trunk-mounted 12-disc CD changer ($595). P05 16 x 8-in. chrome five-spoke cast-aluminum wheels ($595). Y87 3.8-liter V-6 Performance package ($430). Y87 3.8-liter V-6 Performance package ($430). MX0 four-speed overdrive automatic transmission ($815). MM5 five-speed manual transmission ($815 credit). AG1 six-way power driver's seat ($270). 1SA base equipment group (no cost). NC7 Federal emissions override (no cost). FE9 Federal emissions requirements (no cost). AR9 front bucket seats with Prado leather seating surfaces ($575). W55 Monsoon series ETR AM/FM stereo with CD player ($430). R6M New Jersey cost surcharge (no cost). NB8 Northeast states emissions override (no cost). NG1 Northeast states emissions requirements (no cost). 1SB Option Group 2 ($1,755). CC1 removable hatch roof ($995). PDC security package ($240). W68 Sport Appearance package ($1,040). NW9 traction control ($250). [Firebird convertible] U1S trunk-mounted 12-disc CD changer ($595). P05 16 x 8-in. chrome five-spoke cast-aluminum wheels ($595). Y87 3.8-liter V-6 Performance package ($430). Y87 3.8-liter V-6 Performance package ($430). MM5 five-speed manual transmission (no cost). 1SA base equipment group (no cost). NC7 Federal emissions override (no cost). AR9 front bucket seats with Prado leather seating surfaces ($575). R6M New Jersey cost surcharge (no cost). NB8 Northeast states emissions override (no cost). NG1 Northeast states emissions requirements (no cost). W68 Sport Appearance package ($1,040). [Firebird Formula coupe] U1S trunk-mounted 12-

2002 Pontiac Aztek FWD Sport Recreational Vehicle. (PGMC)

2002 Pontiac Aztek AWD Sport Recreational Vehicle. (PGMC)

disc CD changer ($595). P05 16 x 8-in. chrome five-spoke cast-aluminum wheels ($595). MN6 six-speed manual transmission (no cost). AG1 six-way power driver's seat ($270). 1SA base equipment group (no cost). NC7 Federal emissions override (no cost). FE9 Federal emissions requirements (no cost). AR9 front bucket seats with Prado leather seating surfaces ($575). BBS Hurst performance shift linkage ($325). 1SH NHRA Special four-speed automatic edition package ($1,070). 1SH NHRA special six-speed manual edition package ($1,095). R6M New Jersey cost surcharge (no cost). NB8 Northeast states emissions override (no cost). NG1 Northeast states emissions requirements (no cost). GU5 performance rear axle ($300). CC1 removable hatch roof ($995). NW9 traction control ($450). [Firebird Trans Am coupe/convertible] U1S trunk-mounted 12-disc CD changer ($595). P05 16 x 8-in. chrome five-spoke cast-aluminum wheels ($595). Z15 35th Anniversary Coolector Edition ($3,000). MN6 six-speed manual transmission (no cost). 1SA base equipment group (no cost). 54U Collector Edition Yellow paint (no cost). NC7 Federal emissions override (no cost). FE9 Federal emissions requirements (no cost). BBS Hurst performance shift linkage ($325). 1SH NHRA Special four-speed automatic edition package ($1,070). 1SH NHRA special six-speed manual edition package ($1,095). R6M New Jersey cost surcharge (no cost). NB8 Northeast states emissions override (no cost). NG1 Northeast states emissions requirements (no cost). WS6 Performance and Handling package ($3,290). GU5 performance rear axle ($300). NW9 traction control ($450).

GRAND PRIX OPTIONS: [GT coupe] V2C 16 x 6.5-in. high-polished cast-aluminum wheels ($325). AL9 four-way power lumbar driver's seat ($130). U85 Bose premium sound system ($395). UP3 Delco 2001 series ETR AM/FM stereo with CD player ($50). K05 engine block heater ($35). UV6 Eye-Cue Heads-Up display ($325). KA1 heated driver's seat ($100). R6M New Jersey cost surcharge (no cost). 1SA option group 1 (no cost). 1SB option group 2 ($810). 1SC option group 3 ($2,680). CF5 power glass sunroof with express-open ($795). TR9 premium lighting package and OnStar ($610). [GT sedan] V2C 16 x 6.5-in. high-polished cast-aluminum wheels ($325). AL9 four-way power lumbar driver's seat ($130). U85 Bose premium sound system ($395). UP3 Delco 2001 series ETR AM/FM stereo with CD player ($50). K05 engine block heater ($35). UV6 Eye-Cue Heads-Up display ($325). KA1 heated driver's seat ($100). R6M New Jersey cost surcharge (no cost). 1SA option group 1 (no cost). 1SB option group 2 ($840). 1SC option group 3 ($2,710). CF5 power glass sunroof with express-open ($795). TR9 premium lighting package and OnStar ($640). [GTP coupe/sedan] V2C 16 x 6.5-in. high-polished cast-aluminum wheels ($325). AL9 four-way power lumbar driver's seat ($130). U85 Bose premium sound system ($325). K05 engine block heater ($35). KA1 heated driver's seat ($100). AR9 leather accent bucket seats ($520). 1SA option group 1 (no cost). CF5 power glass sunroof with express-open ($795).

BONNEVILLE OPTIONS: [SE sedan] U1S trunk-mounted 12-disc CD changer ($595). AG2 six-way power passenger seat ($530). YF5 California emission requirements (no cost). U1Q Delco AM/FM stereo with CD and cassette ($100). K05 engine block heater ($35). NC7 Federal emissions override (no cost). 1SZ heat and seat discount ($200 credit). NP5 leather-wrapped steering wheel with radio controls ($175). NG1 Northeast states emissions requirements (no cost). 1SB option group 2 (no cost). 1SC option group 3 ($2,130). CF5 power glass sunroof ($1,080). AM6 split bench seat ($150).

2002 Pontiac Aztek AWD Sport Recreational Vehicle. (PGMC)

NW9 traction control ($175). [SLE sedan] U1S trunk-mounted 12-disc CD changer ($595). N89 17-in. wheels ($595). AG2 six-way power passenger seat ($530). A51L bucket seats with leather seating surfaces ($850). YF5 California emission requirements (no cost). K05 engine block heater ($35). NC7 Federal emissions override (no cost). 1SZ heat and seat discount ($200 credit). NG1 Northeast states emissions requirements (no cost). 1SA option group 1 (no cost). CF5 power glass sunroof ($1,080). [SSEi sedan] U1S trunk-mounted 12-disc CD changer ($595). N89 17-in. wheels ($595). YF5 California emission requirements (no cost). K05 engine block heater ($35). NC7 Federal emissions override (no cost). FE9 Federal emissions requirements (no cost). KA1 heated front seats ($295). NG1 Northeast states emissions requirements (no cost). 1SB option group 2 (no cost). CF5 power glass sunroof ($1,080).

MONTANA OPTIONS: [FWD four-door 6-seat] PH13 15-in. silver-painted cast-aluminum sport wheels ($325). R6M New Jersey cost surcharge (no cost). 1SV option package (no cost). [FWD four-door] PH3 15-in. silver-painted cast-aluminum sport wheels ($325). ABE eight-passenger seating (no cost). U1Q AM/FM stereo with CD and cassette ($100). U1Q AM/FM stereo with CD and cassette ($440). G67 automatic level control ($200). PDD convenience package no. 1 ($610). PDD convenience package no. 1 (no cost). PDY convenience package no. 2 ($540). U68 Driver information Center ($185). K05 engine block heater ($35). KA1 heated driver and passenger seats ($195). R6M New Jersey cost surcharge (no cost). 1SA option package (no cost). PCV premium seating package ($1,885). PDC safety and security package ($500). B4U sport performance and handling package ($720). NW9 traction control ($195). D84 two-tone paint ($150). [FWD four-door extended wheelbase] PH3 15-in. silver-painted cast-aluminum sport wheels ($325). UC6 six-disc CD changer in-dash sound system ($395). UC6 six-disc CD changer in-dash sound system ($735). ABF eight-passenger seating with stowable third row seat ($235). U1Q AM/FM stereo with CD and cassette ($100). U1Q AM/FM stereo with CD and cassette ($440). G67 automatic level control ($200). PDD convenience package no. 1 (no cost). PDD convenience package no. 1 ($1,060). PDY convenience package no. 2 ($1,795). U68 Driver information Center ($185). K05 engine block heater ($35). KA1 heated driver and passenger seats ($195). R6M New Jersey cost surcharge (no cost). 1SA option package (no cost). E59 power sliding driver's side door ($350). PCV premium seating package ($1,275). PCV premium seating package ($2,335). PDC safety and security package ($500). B4U sport performance and handling package ($720). H4T Thunder Sport package ($1,200). NW9 traction control ($195). V92 trailer provisions ($165). D84 two-tone paint ($150). [AWD four-door extended wheelbase] PH3 15-in. silver-painted cast-aluminum sport wheels ($325). UC6 six-disc CD changer in-dash sound system ($395). UC6 six-disc CD changer in-dash sound system ($735). ABF eight-passenger seating with stowable third row seat ($235). U1Q AM/FM stereo with CD and cassette ($100). U1Q AM/FM stereo with CD and cassette ($440). PDD convenience package no. 1 ($1,060). PDY convenience package no. 2 ($1,795). K05 engine block heater ($35). KA1 heated driver and passenger seats ($195). R6M New Jersey cost surcharge (no cost). 1SX option package (no cost). E59 power sliding driver's side door ($350). PCV premium seating package ($1,275). PCV premium seating package ($2,335). H4T Thunder Sport package ($1,200).

D84 two-tone paint ($150). [Montana Vision FWD four-door extended wheelbase] PH3 15-in. silver-painted cast-aluminum sport wheels ($325). UC6 six-disc CD changer in-dash sound system ($295). ABF eight-passenger seating with stowable third row seat ($235). U1Q AM/FM stereo with CD and cassette ($100). G67 automatic level control ($200). U68 Driver Information Center ($185). K05 engine block heater ($35). 1SE extended-wheelbase equipment group (no cost). KA1 heated driver and passenger seats ($195). R6M New Jersey cost surcharge (no cost). E59 power sliding driver's side door ($350). PCV premium seating package ($1,175). B4U sport performance and handling package ($395). H4T Thunder Sport package ($1,200). NW9 traction control ($195). V92 trailer provisions ($165). D84 two-tone paint ($150). [Montana Vision AWD four-door extended wheelbase] PH3 15-in. silver-painted cast-aluminum sport wheels ($325). UC6 six-disc CD changer in-dash sound system ($295). ABF eight-passenger seating with stowable third row seat ($235). U1Q AM/FM stereo with CD and cassette ($100). K05 engine block heater ($35). KA1 heated driver and passenger seats ($195). R6M New Jersey cost surcharge (no cost). E59 power sliding driver's side door ($350). PCV premium seating package ($1,175). H4T Thunder Sport package ($1,200). D84 two-tone paint ($150).

AZTEK OPTIONS: [FWD] AG1 six-way power driver's seat and sliding rear cargo tray ($500). UC6 AM/FM radio with six-disc in-dash CD changer and rear audio ($295). UC6 AM/FM radio with six-disc in-dash CD changer and rear audio ($720). U1Q AM/FM radio with CD cassette and rear audio ($425). U1Q AM/FM radio with CD cassette and rear audio ($510). 1SA basic package (no cost). 1SB basic plus package ($985). 1SC comfort and security package ($3,150). 1SD deluxe package ($5,125). K05 engine block heater ($35). R6M New Jersey cost surcharge (no cost). QGO P215/70R16 all-season tires with puncture sealant ($150). CF5 power glass sunroof ($140). CF5 power glass sunroof ($650). CF5 power glass sunroof ($140). CF5 power glass sunroof ($240). 14D red accent "Hanglide" upholstery ($100). V92 trailer tow package ($365). [AWD] N85 17-in. five-spoke cast-aluminum wheels with P235/55R17 all-season tires ($200). AG1 six-way power driver's seat and sliding rear cargo tray ($500). UC6 AM/FM radio with six-disc in-dash CD changer and rear audio ($295). UC6 AM/FM radio with six-disc in-dash CD changer and rear audio ($720). UC6 AM/FM radio with six-disc in-dash CD changer and rear audio ($805). U1Q AM/FM radio with CD cassette and rear audio ($425). U1Q AM/FM radio with CD cassette and rear audio ($510). 1SA basic package (no cost). 1SB basic plus package ($985). 1SC comfort and security package ($3,080). 1SD deluxe package ($5,055). K05 engine block heater ($35). R6M New Jersey cost surcharge (no cost). QGO P215/70R16 all-season tires with puncture sealant ($150). CF5 power glass sunroof ($140). CF5 power glass sunroof ($650). CF5 power glass sunroof ($140). CF5 power glass sunroof ($240). 14D red accent "Hanglide" upholstery ($100). V92 trailer tow package ($365).

NOTE: Full option package contents, descriptions, and applications information can often be determined by consulting factory literature. The data above is edited for size and clarity. This information provided only as a guide to help collectors appraise the relative value of cars with numerous options. Prices for items included as part of a value option package are usually much less than individual prices. Option prices charged by individual dealers may also vary.

HISTORICAL: Pontiac Motor Div. marked the 40th anniversary of the Grand Prix nameplate in 2002. Pontiac continued its evolution into the 21st Century with an updated model lineup and with the all-new Pontiac Vibe waiting in the wings. The company's future looked just as bright as its storied past. "Pontiac has delivered robust driving excitement for 75 years," said Pontiac-GMC general manager Lynn Myers. "And as Pontiac enters its 76th year, we continue to define what 21st century driving excitement is all about. From the serious performance of the Bonneville SSEi and "Wide Track" Grand Prix to the brawny muscle of the Firebird line, from the versatility of the Aztek to the rugged Montana, from the fun and excitement of Grand Am and Sunfire to the all-new trend-setting Vibe, we truly have something for everyone who is youthful in age or attitude."

STYLE NUMBER DESIGNATIONS

The cars of Oakland (1907 to 1931) and Pontiac (1926 to 1995) are listed by the model year and the official factory style number. The style number is located on the firewall identification plate inside the engine compartment. (Cars manufactured prior to 1933 utilize the term job number synonymously with the term style number.)

OAKLAND

1907-25

Standard Sedan ....SED
Special Sedan.....................................SPESED
Landaulet Sedan....................................LETSED
Brougham Sedan.....................................BRSED
Custom Sedan ....CUSSED
Landau Sedan ....LANSED
Sport Sedan ....SSED
Two-door Sedan ....COACH
Standard Coupe ....COUPE
Landau Coupe ....LCoupe
Sport Coupe..SCoupe
Convertible Coupe ....CCoupe
Business Coupe...................................BCoupe
Roadster ....ROAD
Sport Roadster....................................SROAD
Phaeton ....PHAE
Sport Phaeton ....SPHAE
Runabout .... RUN
Speedster ....SPDTR

1926

Standard 6330
Landau Sedan 6360
Two-door Sedan 6340
Landau Coupe 6350
Sport Roadster....................................SROAD
Sport Phaeton ....SPHAE

1927

Standard Sedan 7060
Landau Sedan 7080
Two-door Sedan 7070
Landau Coupe 7090
Sport Roadster....................................SROAD
Sport Phaeton ....SPHAE

1928

Standard Sedan 7500
Landau Sedan 7520
Two-door Sedan 7510
Landau Coupe 7530
Sport Coupe 7540
Sport Roadster....................................SROAD
Sport Phaeton ....SPHAE

1929

Standard Sedan 8770
Special Sedan................................. 8775
Landaulet Sedan 8780
Brougham Sedan............................. 8820
Two-door Sedan 8790
Standard Coupe 8800
Convertible Coupe 8810
Sport Roadster....................................SROAD
Sport Phaeton ....SPHAE

1930

Standard Sedan 30359
Custom Sedan 30360
Two-door Sedan 30351
Standard Coupe.............................. 30357
Sport Coupe 30358
Sport Roadster....................................SROAD
Sport Phaeton ....SPHAE

1931

Standard Sedan 31359
Custom Sedan 31369
Two-door Sedan 31351
Standard Coupe 31357
Sport Coupe 31358
Convertible....................................... 31368
Sport Roadster....................................SROAD
Sport Phaeton ....SPHAE

PONTIAC

1926 Six

Standard Coupe.................................. 6640

Deluxe Coupe 6640D
Two-door Sedan 6650
Landau Sedan 7160
Deluxe Landau Sedan................... 7160D

1926 Stewart bodies

Roadster .... ROAD
Sport Roadster .... SROAD
Phaeton ....TOUR

1927 Six

Standard Coupe 7430
Two-door Sedan 7440
Landau Sedan 7450
Deluxe Landau Sedan................... 7450D
Sport Coupe 7460

1927 Stewart bodies

Roadster... ROAD
Sport Roadster .... SROAD
Phaeton ....TOUR

1928 Six

Standard Sedan 8220
Landaulet 8230
Two-door Sedan 8240
Standard Coupe 8250
Landau Coupe 8260

1928 Stewart bodies

Roadster... ROAD
Sport Roadster .... SROAD
Phaeton ....TOUR

1929 Six

Standard Sedan 8920
Landaulet Sedan 8930
Two-door Sedan 8940
Standard Coupe 8950
Convertible Coupe (rumble seat) 8960

1929 Stewart bodies

Roadster... ROAD
Sport Roadster .... SROAD
Phaeton ....TOUR

1930 Six

Two-door Sedan 30301
Standard Sedan 30302
Standard Coupe 30307
Sport Coupe (rumble seat) 30306
Custom Sedan 30309

1930 Stewart bodies

Roadster... ROAD
Sport Roadster .... SROAD
Phaeton ....TOUR

1931 Six

Two-door Sedan 31301
Standard Coupe 31307
Sport Coupe (rumble seat).....................31308
Standard Sedan 31309
Convertible Coupe (rumble seat) 31318
Custom Sedan 31319

1931 Stewart bodies

Roadster... ROAD
Sport Roadster .... SROAD
Phaeton ....TOUR

1932 Six

Two-door Sedan 32301
Sport Coupe 32308
Four-door Sedan 32309
Business Coupe...............................32317
Convertible Coupe 32318
Custom Sedan 32319

1932 V-8

Two-door Sedan 32351
Sport Coupe 32358
Four-door Sedan 32359

Business Coupe....................................32367
Convertible Coupe 32368
Custom Sedan 32369

1933 Eight

Two-door Sedan 33301
Four-door Sedan 33309
Standard Coupe.............................. 33317
Convertible Coupe 33318
Sport Coupe 33328
Touring Sedan................................. 33331
Roadster .... ROAD

1934 Eight

Two-door Standard Sedan 34301
Four-door Standard Sedan 34309
Standard Coupe.............................. 34317
Convertible Coupe 34318
Four-door Touring Sedan 34319
Sport Coupe 34328
Two-door Touring Sedan................. 34331

1935 Master Six

Business Coupe................................2107A
Two-door Sedan 2101A
Two-door Touring Sedan.................2111A
Four-door Sedan..............................2109A
Four-door Touring Sedan.................2119A

1935 Deluxe Six

Business Coupe................................ 2107
Sport Coupe 2157
Convertible Coupe 2167
Two-door Sedan 2101
Two-door Touring Sedan................. 2111
Four-door Sedan.............................. 2109
Four-door Touring Sedan.................2119

1935 Deluxe Eight

Business Coupe................................ 2007
Opera Coupe 2077
Sport Coupe 2057
Convertible Coupe 2067
Two-door Sedan 2001
Two-door Touring Sedan.................2011
Four-door Sedan.............................. 2009
Four-door Touring Sedan.................2019

1936 Master Six

Business Coupe................................2607A
Sport Coupe 2657A
Convertible Coupe 2667A
Two-door Sedan 2601A
Two-door Sedan 2601AB
Two-door Touring Sedan................. 2611A
Two-door Touring Sedan.................2611AB
Four-door Sedan..............................2609A
Four-door Touring Sedan.................2619A

1936 Deluxe Six

Business Coupe................................ 2607
Sport Coupe 2657
Convertible Coupe 2667
Two-door Sedan 2601
Two-door Touring Sedan.................2611
Four-door Sedan.............................. 2609
Four-door Touring Sedan................. 2619

1936 Deluxe Eight

Business Coupe................................ 2807
Sport Coupe 2857
Convertible Coupe 2867
Two-door Sedan 2801
Two-door Touring Sedan.................2811
Four-door Sedan.............................. 2809
Four-door Touring Sedan................. 2819

1937 Six

Business Coupe................................2627B
Sport Coupe 2627
Convertible Coupe 2667
Two-door Sedan 2601
Two-door Touring Sedan.................2611

Four-door Sedan................................ 2609
Four-door Touring Sedan........................ 2619
Four-door Convertible Sedan 2649
Station Wagon .... STAWAG

1937 Eight
Business Coupe..........................2827B
Sport Coupe................................ 2827
Convertible Coupe 2867
Two-door Sedan 2801
Two-door Touring Sedan 2811
Four-door Sedan............................. 2809
Four-door Touring Sedan 2819
Four-door Convertible Sedan 2849

1938 Six
Business Coupe..........................2627B
Sport Coupe................................ 2627
Convertible Coupe 2667
Two-door Sedan ....: 2601
Two-door Touring Sedan 2611
Four-door Sedan............................. 2609
Four-door Touring Sedan 2619
Four-door Convertible Sedan 2649
Station Wagon .... STAWAG

1938 Eight
Business Coupe..........................2827B
Sport Coupe................................ 2827
Convertible Coupe 2867
Two-door Sedan 2801
Two-door Touring Sedan 2811
Four-door Sedan............................. 2809
Four-door Touring Sedan 2819
Four-door Convertible Sedan 2849

1939 Quality Six
Business Coupe..........................2527B
Sport Coupe................................ 2527
Two-door Touring Sedan 2511
Four-door Touring Sedan 2519
Station Wagon .... STAWAG

1939 Deluxe Six
Business Coupe..........................2627B
Sport Coupe................................ 2627
Convertible Coupe 2667
Two-door Touring Sedan 2611
Four-door Touring Sedan 2619

1939 Deluxe Eight
Business Coupe..........................2827B
Sport Coupe................................ 2827
Convertible Coupe 2867
Two-door Touring Sedan 2811
Two-door Sunroof Sedan 2811A
Four-door Touring Sedan 2819
Four-door Sunroof Sedan 2819A

1940 Special Six
Business Coupe..........................2527B
Sport Coupe................................ 2527
Two-door Touring Sedan 2511
Four-door Touring Sedan 2519
Station Wagon .... STAWAG

1940 Deluxe Six
Business Coupe..........................2627B
Sport Coupe................................ 2627
Convertible Coupe 2667
Two-door Touring Sedan 2611
Four-door Touring Sedan 2619

1940 Deluxe Eight
Business Coupe..........................2827B
Sport Coupe................................ 2827
Convertible Coupe 2867
Two-door Touring Sedan 2811
Four-door Touring Sedan 2819

1940 Torpedo Eight
Sport Coupe................................2927C
Four-door Touring Sedan 2919

1941 Deluxe Torpedo Six
Business Coupe..........................2527B
Sport Coupe................................ 2527
Convertible Coupe 2567
Two-door Sedan 2511
Four-door four-window Sedan 2569
Four-door six-window Sedan 2519
Station Wagon .... STAWAG

1941 Streamliner Six
Coupe.....................................2627D

Four-door Sedan 2609D

1941 Custom Six
Coupe.......................................2427
Four-door six-window Sedan...................2419

1941 Deluxe Torpedo Eight
Business Coupe 2727B
Sport Coupe................................2727
Convertible Coupe 2767
Two-door Sedan 2711
Four-door four-window Sedan..................2769
Four-door six-window Sedan..................2719
Station Wagon .... STAWAG

1941 Streamliner Eight
Coupe.......................................2827
Four-door Sedan...........................2809

1941 Super Streamliner Eight
Coupe.....................................2827D
Four-door Sedan 2809D

1941 Custom Eight
Coupe.......................................2927
Four-door six-window Sedan..................2919

1942 Torpedo Six
Business Coupe 2527B
Sport Coupe 2527
Sedan Coupe 2507
Convertible Coupe 2567
Two-door Sedan 2511
Four-door four-window Sedan..................2569
Four-door six-window Sedan..................2519

1942 Streamliner Six
Coupe.......................................2607
Four-door six-window Sedan..................2609
Station Wagon ....STAWAG

1942 Streamliner Chieftain Six
Coupe......................................2607D
Four-door six-window Sedan..................2609D
Station Wagon ....STAWAG

1942 Torpedo Eight
Business Coupe 2727B
Sport Coupe 2727
Sedan Coupe 2707
Convertible Coupe 2767
Two-door Sedan 2711
Four-door four-window Sedan..................2769
Four-door six-window Sedan..................2719

1942 Streamliner Eight
Coupe.......................................2807
Four-door six-window Sedan..................2809
Station Wagon ....STAWAG

1942 Streamliner Chieftain Eight
Coupe......................................2807D
Four-door six-window Sedan..................2809D
Station Wagon ....STAWAG

1946 Torpedo Six
Business Coupe 2527B
Sport Coupe 2527
Sedan Coupe 2507
Convertible Coupe 2567
Two-door Sedan 2511
Four-door Sedan 2519

1946 Streamliner Six
Sedan Coupe 2607
Four-door Sedan 2609
Station Wagon Sedan ....STAWAG

1946 Torpedo Eight
Business Coupe 2727B
Sport Coupe 2727
Sedan Coupe 2707
Convertible Coupe 2767
Two-door Sedan 2711
Four-door Sedan 2719

1946 Streamliner Eight
Sedan Coupe 2807
Four-door Sedan 2809
Station Wagon Standard ....STAWAG

1947 Torpedo Six
Business Coupe 2527B
Sport Coupe 2527
Sedan Coupe 2507

Convertible Coupe 2567
Two-door Sedan 2511
Four-door Sedan............................ 2519

1947 Streamliner Six
Sedan Coupe 2607
Four-door Sedan 2609
Station Wagon Standard................... STAWAG

1947 Torpedo Eight
Business Coupe..........................2727B
Sport Coupe................................ 2727
Sedan Coupe 2707
Convertible Coupe 2767
Two-door Sedan 2711
Four-door Sedan............................ 2719

1947 Streamliner Eight
Coupe 2807
Four-door Sedan............................ 2809
Station Wagon Standard................... STAWAG

1948 Torpedo Six
Business Coupe..........................2527B
Sport Coupe................................ 2527
Sedan Coupe 2507
Sedan Coupe 2507D
Convertible Coupe 2567
Two-door Sedan 2511
Four-door Sedan............................ 2519
Four-door Sedan...........................2519D

1948 Streamliner Six
Coupe 2607
Coupe 2607D
Four-door Sedan 2609
Four-door Sedan...........................2609D
Station Wagon Standard................... STAWAG
Station Wagon Deluxe .... STAWAG

1948 Torpedo Eight
Business Coupe..........................2727B
Sport Coupe................................ 2727
Sedan Coupe 2707
Sedan Coupe 2707D
Convertible................................ 2767
Two-door Sedan 2711
Four-door Sedan 2719
Four-door Sedan...........................2719D

1948 Streamliner Eight
Coupe 2807
Coupe 2807D
Four-door Sedan............................ 2809
Four-door Sedan...........................2809D
Station Wagon Standard................... STAWAG
Station Wagon Deluxe .... STAWAG

1949 Chieftain Six and Eight
Business Coupe..........................2527B
Sedan Coupe 2527
Sedan Coupe Deluxe..........................2727D
Convertible Coupe Deluxe................... 2567DX
Two-door Sedan 2511
Two-door Sedan Deluxe 2511D
Four-door Sedan............................ 2569
Four-door Sedan Deluxe 2569D

1949 Streamliner Six and Eight
Sedan Coupe............................... 2507
Sedan Coupe Deluxe..........................2507D
Four-door Sedan............................ 2508
Four-door Sedan Deluxe 2508D
Wood Station Wagon 2561
Deluxe Wood Station Wagon..................2561D
Metal Station Wagon 2562
Deluxe Metal Station Wagon 2562
Sedan Delivery 2571

1950 Chieftain Six and Eight
Business Coupe..........................2527B
Sedan Coupe 2527
Sedan Coupe Deluxe..........................2527D
Convertible Coupe Deluxe................. 2567DTX
Catalina Coupe Deluxe..........................2537D
Catalina Super Deluxe.......................2537SD
Two-door Sedan 2511
Two-door Sedan Deluxe 2511D
Four-door Sedan............................ 2569
Four-door Sedan Deluxe 2569D

1950 Streamliner Six and Eight
Sedan Coupe................................ 2507

Sedan Coupe Deluxe.............................2507D
Four-door Sedan.................................. 2508
Four-door Sedan Deluxe 2508D
Station Wagon 2562
Station Wagon Deluxe 2562D
Sedan Delivery 2571

1951 Chieftain Six and Eight
Business Coupe.................................2527B
Sedan Coupe 2527
Sedan Coupe Deluxe.........................2527D
Convertible Coupe Deluxe................ 2567DTX
Catalina Coupe Deluxe 2537D
Catalina Super Deluxe 2537SD
Two-door Sedan 2511
Two-door Sedan Deluxe 2511D
Four-door Sedan 2569
Four-door Sedan Deluxe 2569D

1951 Streamliner Six and Eight
Sedan Coupe 2507
Sedan Coupe Deluxe.........................2507D
Station Wagon 2562
Station Wagon Deluxe 2562D
Sedan Delivery 2571

1952 Chieftain Six and Eight
Convertible Coupe Deluxe................ 2567DTX
Catalina Coupe Deluxe 2537D
Catalina Super Deluxe 2537SD
Two-door Sedan 2511
Two-door Sedan Deluxe 2511D
Four-door Sedan 2569
Four-door Sedan Deluxe 2569D
Station Wagon 2562
Station Wagon Deluxe 2562
Sedan Delivery 2571

1953 Chieftain Six and Eight
Convertible Coupe Deluxe................ 2567DTX
Catalina Coupe Deluxe 2537D
Catalina Custom 2537SD
Two-door Sedan 2511W
Two-door Sedan Deluxe 2511WD
Four-door Sedan................................ 2569W
Four-door Sedan Deluxe 2569WD
Station Wagon 2-seat 2562F
Station Wagon 3-seat 2562
Station Wagon Deluxe 2562DF
Sedan Delivery 2571

1954 Chieftain Six and Eight
Catalina Coupe Deluxe 2537D
Catalina Coupe Super Deluxe 2537SD
Two-door Sedan 2511W
Two-door Sedan Deluxe 2511WD
Four-door Sedan................................ 2569W
Four-door Sedan Deluxe 2569WD
Station Wagon 3-seat 2562
Station Wagon 2-seat 2562F
Station Wagon Deluxe 2562DF

1954 Star Chief Eight
Convertible Coupe 2867DTX
Catalina Coupe Custom......................2837SD
Four-door Sedan Deluxe 2869WD
Four-door Sedan Custom 2869WSD

1955 Chieftain 25
Catalina Coupe 870 ....2537D
Two-door Sedan 860 2511
Two-door Sedan 870 ....2511D
Four-door Sedan 860.......................... 2519
Four-door Sedan 870..........................2719D
Four-door Station Wagon 860............. 2562
Four-door Station Wagon 870.............. 2562DF
Two-door Station Wagon 860 .... 2563F

1955 Star Chief 25
Custom. Station Wagon 2564DF

1955 Star Chief 28
Convertible Coupe 2867DTX
Catalina Custom Coupe 2837SD
Four-door Sedan................................2819D
Four-door Custom Sedan 2819SD

1956 Chieftain 27
Catalina Coupe 860 2737
Catalina Coupe 870 ....2737D
Catalina Sedan 860 2739
Catalina Sedan 870 ....2739D
Two-door Sedan 860 2711

Four-door Sedan 860 2719
Four-door Sedan 870..........................2719D
Four-door Station Wagon 860 ....2762FC
Four-door Station Wagon 870 ....2762DF
Two-door Station Wagon 860.................2768

1956 Star Chief 27
Custom Station Wagon 2764DF

1956 Star Chief 28
Convertible Coupe 2867DTX
Catalina Coupe Custom 2837SD
Catalina SD Custom 2839SD
Four-door Sedan 2819D

1957 Chieftain 27
Catalina Coupe 2737
Catalina Sedan.................................. 2739
Two-door Sedan 2711
Four-door Sedan 2719
Four-door Station Wagon 2762FC
Two-door Station Wagon......................2763F

1957 Super Chief 27
Catalina Coupe 2737D
Catalina Sedan.................................. 2739D
Four-door Sedan 2719D
Four-door Safari 2762DF

1957 Star Chief 27
Four-door Safari Custom....................2762SDF
Two-door Safari Custom......................2764DF

1957 Star Chief 28
Convertible Coupe 2867DTX
Convertible Custom (Bonneville)........ 2867SDX
Catalina Coupe Custom 2837SD
Catalina Sedan Custom 2839SD
Four-door Sedan 2819D
Four-door Sedan 2819SD

1958 Bonneville 25
Sport Coupe 2547SD
Convertible Coupe 2567SD

1958 Chieftain 25
Convertible Coupe 2567

1958 Chieftain 27
Catalina Coupe 2731
Catalina Sedan..................................2739
Two-door Sedan 2741
Four-door Sedan 2749
Four-door Safari 2794

1958 Star Chief 27
Four-door Safari 2793D
Four-door Safari 2793SD

1958 Super Chief 28
Catalina Coupe 2831D
Catalina Sedan..................................2839D
Four-door Sedan 2849D

1958 Star Chief 26
Catalina Coupe 2831SD
Catalina Sedan..................................2839SD
Four-door Sedan 2849SD

1959 Catalina 21
Two-door Sport Sedan 2111
Four-door Sedan 2119
Four-door Safari 2135
Two-door Sport Coupe 2137
Four-door Vista 2139
Four-door Safari 2145
Two-door Convertible Coupe...............2167

1959 Star Chief 24
Two-door Sport Sedan 2411
Four-door Sedan 2419
Four-door Vista 2439

1959 Bonneville 27
Four-door Safari 2735

1959 Bonneville 28
Two-door Sport Coupe 2837
Four-door Vista..................................2839
Two-door Convertible Coupe...............2867

1960 Catalina 21
Two-door Sport Sedan 2111
Four-door Sedan 2119
Four-door Safari 2135
Two-door Sport Coupe 2137

Four-door Vista 2139
Four-door Safari 2145
Two-door Convertible Coupe 2167

1960 Ventura 23
Two-door Sport Coupe 2337
Four-door Vista 2339

1960 Star Chief 24
Two-door Sport Sedan........................2411
Four-door Sedan 2419
Four-door Vista 2439

1960 Bonneville 27
Four-door Safari.................................2735

1960 Bonneville 28
Two-door Sport Coupe 2837
Four-door Vista 2839
Two-door Convertible Coupe 2867

1961 Tempest 21
Four-door Sedan................................2119
Two-door Custom Coupe 2117
Two-door Standard Coupe 2127
Four-door Safari 2135

1961 Catalina 23
Two-door Sport Sedan........................2311
Four-door Safari 6-Passenger 2335
Two-door Sport Coupe 2337
Four-door Vista 2339
Four-door Safari 9-Passenger 2345
Two-door Convertible Coupe 2367
Four-door Sedan 2369

1961 Ventura 25
Two-door Sport Coupe 2537
Four-door Vista 2539

1961 Star Chief 26
Four-door Vista 2639
Four-door Sedan 2669

1961 Bonneville 27
Four-door Safari 6-Passenger 2735

1961 Bonneville 28
Two-door Sport Coupe 2837
Four-door Vista 2839
Two-door Convertible Coupe 2867

1962 Tempest 21
Two-door Sport Coupe........................2117
Four-door Sedan................................2119
Two-door Standard Coupe 2127
Four-door Safari 2135
Two-door Convertible Coupe 2167

1962 Catalina 23
Two-door Sport Coupe........................2311
Four-door Safari 5-Passenger 2335
Four-door Vista 2339
Four-door Safari 9-Passenger 2345
Two-door Sport Coupe 2347
Two-door Convertible Coupe 2367
Four-door Sedan 2369

1962 Star Chief 26
Four-door Vista 2639
Four-door Sedan 2669

1962 Bonneville 27
Four-door Safari 6-Passenger 2735

1962 Bonneville 28
Four-door Vista 2839
Two-door Sport Coupe 2847
Two-door Convertible Coupe 2867

1962 Grand Prix 29
Two-door Sport Coupe........................2947

1963 Tempest Standard
Two-door Coupe (with post)................2127
Four-door Station Wagon 2135
Four-door Sedan (with post)...............2119

1963 Tempest Custom
Two-door Coupe (with post)................2117
Convertible Coupe 2167

1963 LeMans
Two-door Coupe (with post)................2217
Two-door Convertible Coupe 2267

1963 Catalina
Two-door Sport Sedan (with post) 2311

2-seat Station Wagon 2335
Two-door Sport Coupe............................ 2347
Four-door Hardtop 2339
3-seat Station Wagon 2345
Two-door Convertible Coupe 2367
Four-door Sedan (with post) 2369

1963 Star Chief
Four-door Hardtop 2639
Four-door Sedan (with post) 2669

1963 Bonneville
Four-door Station Wagon........................ 2835
Two-door Sport Coupe............................ 2847
Four-door Hardtop 2839
Two-door Convertible Coupe 2867

1963 Grand Prix
Two-door Sport Coupe............................ 2957

1964 Tempest Standard
Two-door Coupe (with post)...................... 2027
Four-door Station Wagon........................ 2035
Four-door Sedan (with post) 2069

1964 Tempest Custom
Two-door Coupe (with post) 2127
Four-door Station Wagon........................ 2135
Four-door Sedan (with post) 2169
Two-door Convertible Coupe 2167

1964 LeMans
Two-door Coupe (with post)...................... 2227
Two-door Hardtop Coupe 2237
Two-door Convertible Coupe 2267

1964 Catalina
Two-door Sport Sedan (with post) 2311
2-seat Station Wagon 2335
Two-door Sport Coupe............................ 2347
Four-door Hardtop 2339
3-seat Station Wagon 2345
Two-door Convertible Coupe 2367
Four-door Sedan (with post) 2369

1964 Star Chief
Four-door Hardtop 2639
Four-door Sedan (with post) 2669

1964 Bonneville
Four-door Station Wagon........................ 2835
Two-door Sport Coupe............................ 2847
Four-door Hardtop 2839
Two-door Convertible Coupe 2867

1964 Grand Prix
Two-door Sport Coupe............................ 2957

1965 Tempest
Two-door Coupe 23327
Four-door Station Wagon 2-seat.............. 23335
Four-door Sedan 23369

1965 Tempest Custom
Two-door Coupe 23527
Two-door Station Wagon 2-seat 23535
Two-door Hardtop 23537
Two-door Convertible............................. 23567
Four-door Sedan................................. 23569

1965 LeMans
Two-door Coupe 23727
Two-door Hardtop 23737
Two-door Convertible............................. 23767
Four-door Sedan................................. 23769

1965 Catalina
Two-door Sedan 25211
Four-door Station Wagon 2-seat............. 25235
Two-door Hardtop 25237
Four-door Hardtop 25239
Four-door Station Wagon 3-seat............. 25245
Two-door Convertible............................. 25267
Four-door Sedan................................. 25269

1965 Star Chief
Four-door Hardtop 25639
Four-door Sedan 25669

1965 Bonneville
Four-door Station Wagon 2-seat............. 26235
Two-door Hardtop 26237
Four-door Hardtop 26239
Two-door Convertible............................. 26267

1965 Grand Prix
Two-door Hardtop 26657

1966 Tempest
Two-door Sport Coupe.......................... 23307
Four-door Sedan................................. 23369
Four-door Station Wagon 2-seat.............. 23335

1966 Tempest Custom
Two-door Sport Coupe.......................... 23507
Four-door Sedan 23569
Two-door Hardtop 23517
Four-door Hardtop 23539
Four-door Station Wagon 2-seat............. 23535

1966 LeMans
Two-door Sport Coupe 23707
Two-door Hardtop 23717
Four-door Hardtop 23739
Two-door Convertible............................. 23767

1966 GTO
Two-door Coupe................................. 24207
Two-door Hardtop 24217
Two-door Convertible............................ 24267

1966 Catalina
Two-door Sedan................................. 25211
Four-door Station Wagon 2-seat............. 25235
Four-door Station Wagon 3-seat............. 25245
Four-door Hardtop 25239
Two-door Convertible............................ 25267
Four-door Sedan 25269
Two-door Hardtop 25237

1966 Catalina 2+2
Two-door Sport Coupe.......................... 25437
Two-door Convertible............................ 25467

1966 Star Chief Executive
Two-door Hardtop 25637
Four-door Hardtop.............................. 25639
Four-door Sedan 25669

1966 Bonneville
Two-door Hardtop 26237
Four-door Hardtop 26239
Two-door Convertible............................ 26267
Four-door Station Wagon 3-seat............. 26245

1966 Grand Prix
Two-door Hardtop 26657

1967 Firebird
Two-door Hardtop 22337
Two-door Convertible............................ 22367

1967 Tempest
Two-door Sport Coupe 23307
Four-door Sedan 23369
Four-door Station Wagon 2-seat............. 23335

1967 Tempest Custom
Two-door Coupe................................. 23507
Four-door Sedan 23569
Two-door Hardtop 23517
Four-door Hardtop 23539
Two-door Convertible............................ 23567
Two-door Station Wagon 2-seat.............. 23535

1967 LeMans
Two-door Sport Coupe 23707
Two-door Hardtop 23717
Four-door Hardtop 23739
Two-door Convertible............................ 23767

1967 Tempest Safari
Four-door Station Wagon 2-seat.............. 23935

1967 GTO
Two-door Sport Coupe 24207
Two-door Hardtop 24217
Two-door Convertible............................ 24267

1967 Catalina
Two-door Sedan................................. 25211
Four-door Sedan 25269
Two-door Hardtop 25287
Four-door Hardtop.............................. 25239
Two-door Convertible............................ 25267
Four-door Station Wagon 2-seat............. 25235
Four-door Station Wagon 3-seat............. 25245

1967 Executive
Two-door Hardtop.............................. 25687
Four-door Hardtop............................... 25639
Four-door Sedan 25669
Four-door Station Wagon 2-seat.............. 25635

Four-door Station Wagon 3-seat 25645

1967 Bonneville
Two-door Hardtop 26287
Four-door Hardtop 26239
Two-door Convertible............................ 26267
Four-door Station Wagon 3-seat 26245

1967 Grand Prix
Two-door Hardtop 26657
Two-door Convertible............................ 26667

1968 Firebird
Two-door Hardtop 22337
Two-door Convertible............................ 22367

1968 Tempest
Two-door Coupe 23327
Four-door Sedan................................. 23369

1968 Tempest Custom
Two-door Coupe 23257
Two-door Station Wagon 2-seat 23535
Two-door Hardtop 23537
Four-door Hardtop 23539
Two-door Convertible............................ 23567
Four-door Sedan................................. 23569

1968 LeMans
Two-door Coupe 23727
Two-door Hardtop 23737
Four-door Hardtop 23739
Two-door Convertible............................ 23767

1968 Tempest Safari
Four-door Station Wagon 2-seat 23935

1968 GTO
Two-door Hardtop 24237
Two-door Convertible............................ 24267

1968 Catalina
Two-door Sedan 25211
Four-door Sedan................................. 25269
Two-door Hardtop 25287
Four-door Hardtop 25239
Two-door Convertible............................ 25267
Four-door Station Wagon 2-seat 25235
Four-door Station Wagon 3-seat 25245

1968 Executive
Four-door Station Wagon 2-seat 25635
Four-door Hardtop 25639
Four-door Station Wagon 3-seat 25645
Four-door Sedan................................. 25669
Two-door Hardtop 25687

1968 Bonneville
Four-door Hardtop 26239
Four-door Station Wagon 3-seat 26245
Two-door Convertible............................ 26267
Four-door Sedan................................. 26269
Two-door Hardtop 26287

1968 Grand Prix
Two-door Hardtop 26657

1969 Firebird
Two-door Hardtop 22337
Two-door Convertible............................ 22367

1969 Tempest
Two-door Sport Coupe........................... 23327
Four-door Sedan................................. 23369

1969 Custom "S"
Two-door Sport Coupe........................... 23527
Four-door Sedan................................. 23569
Two-door Hardtop 23537
Four-door Hardtop 23539
Two-door Convertible............................ 23567
Four-door Station Wagon 2-seat 23535
Four-door Station Wagon 3-seat 23536

1969 LeMans Sport
Two-door Sport Coupe 23727
Two-door Hardtop 23737
Four-door Hardtop 23739
Two-door Convertible............................ 23767

1969 LeMans Safari
Four-door Station Wagon 2-seat 23936

1969 GTO
Two-door Hardtop 24237
Two-door Convertible............................ 24267

1969 Catalina
Four-door Sedan................................. 25269

Two-door Hardtop 25237
Four-door Hardtop 25239
Two-door Convertible 25267
Four-door Station Wagon 2-seat............ 25236
Four-door Station Wagon 3-seat............ 25246

1969 Executive
Four-door Sedan 25669
Two-door Hardtop 25637
Four-door Hardtop 25639
Four-door Station Wagon 2-seat............ 25636
Four-door Station Wagon 3-seat............ 25646

1969 Bonneville
Four-door Sedan 26269
Two-door Hardtop 26237
Four-door Hardtop 26239
Two-door Convertible 26267
Four-door Station Wagon 3-seat............ 26246

1969 Grand Prix
Two-door Hardtop J 27647
Two-door Hardtop SJ 27657

1970 Firebird
Two-door Hardtop 22387
Two-door Esprit Hardtop 22487
Two-door Formula Hardtop.................... 22687
Two-door Trans Am Hardtop.................. 22887

1970 Tempest
Two-door Coupe 23327
Two-door Hardtop 23337
Four-door Sedan................................. 23369

1970 LeMans
Two-door Coupe 23527
Four-door Station Wagon 2-seat............ 23535
Two-door Hardtop 23537
Four-door Hardtop 23539
Four-door Sedan................................. 23569

1970 LeMans Sport
Two-door Coupe 23727
Two-door Hardtop 23737
Four-door Hardtop 23739
Two-door Convertible 23767
Four-door Station Wagon 2-seat............ 23736

1970 GTO
Two-door Hardtop 24237
Two-door Convertible........................... 24267

1970 Catalina
Four-door Station Wagon 2-seat............ 25236
Two-door Hardtop 25237
Four-door Hardtop 25239
Four-door Station Wagon 3-seat............ 25246
Two-door Convertible........................... 25267
Four-door Sedan................................. 25269

1970 Executive
Four-door Station Wagon 2-seat............ 25636
Two-door Hardtop 25637
Four-door Hardtop 25639
Four-door Station Wagon 3-seat............ 25646
Four-door Sedan................................. 25669

1970 Bonneville
Two-door Hardtop 26237
Four-door Hardtop 26239
Four-door Station Wagon 3-seat............ 26245
Two-door Convertible........................... 26267
Four-door Sedan................................. 26269

1970 Grand Prix
Two-door Hardtop J 27647
Two-door Hardtop SJ........................... 27657

1971 Ventura II
Two-door Coupe 21327
Four-door Sedan................................. 21369
Two-door Coupe 21427
Four-door Sedan................................. 21469

1971 Firebird
Two-door Hardtop 22387
Two-door Esprit Hardtop 22487
Two-door Formula Hardtop.................... 22687
Two-door Trans Am Hardtop.................. 22887

1971 T37
Two-door Coupe 23327
Two-door Hardtop 23337
Four-door Sedan................................. 23369

1971 LeMans
Two-door Coupe 23327

Four-door Station Wagon 2-seat............. 23536
Two-door Hardtop 23537
Four-door Hardtop 23539
Four-door Station Wagon 3-seat............. 23546
Four-door Sedan 23569

1971 LeMans Sport
Two-door Hardtop 23737
Four-door Hardtop 23739
Two-door Convertible 23767

1971 GTO
Two-door Hardtop 24237
Two-door Convertible 24267

1971 Catalina
Four-door Station Wagon 2-seat............. 25235
Four-door Hardtop 25239
Four-door Station Wagon 3-seat............. 25245
Two-door Hardtop 25257
Two-door Convertible 25267
Four-door Sedan 25269

1971 Catalina Brougham
Four-door Hardtop 25839
Two-door Hardtop 25857
Four-door Sedan 25869

1971 Bonneville
Four-door Station Wagon 2-seat............. 26235
Four-door Hardtop 26239
Four-door Station Wagon 3-seat............. 26245
Two-door Hardtop 26257
Four-door Sedan 26269

1971 Grand Ville
Two-door Hardtop 26847
Four-door Hardtop 26849
Two-door Convertible 26867

1971 Grand Prix
Two-door Hardtop J............................... 27647
Two-door Hardtop SJ 27657

1972 Ventura II
Two-door Sedan 21327
Four-door Sedan 21369
Two-door Sedan 21427
Four-door Sedan 21469

1972 Firebird
Two-door Hardtop 22387
Two-door Esprit Hardtop 22487
Two-door Formula Hardtop..................... 22687
Two-door Trans Am Hardtop 22887

1972 LeMans
Two-door Sedan 23527
Two-door Hardtop 23537
Four-door Sedan 23569
Four-door Station Wagon 2-seat............. 23536
Four-door Station Wagon 3-seat............. 23546

1972 LeMans Sport
Two-door Convertible 23867
LeMans Luxury Two-door HT 24437
Four-door Hardtop 24439

1972 Catalina
Two-door Hardtop 25257
Four-door Hardtop 25239
Four-door Sedan 25269
Two-door Convertible 25267
Four-door Station Wagon 2-seat............. 25235
Four-door Station Wagon 3-seat............. 25245

1972 Catalina Brougham
Two-door Hardtop 25857
Four-door Hardtop 25839
Four-door Sedan 25869

1972 Bonneville
Two-door Hardtop 26257
Four-door Hardtop 26239
Four-door Sedan 26269
Four-door Station Wagon 2-seat............. 26235
Four-door Station Wagon 3-seat............. 26245

1972 Grand Ville
Two-door Hardtop 26847
Four-door Hardtop 26849
Two-door Convertible 26867

1972 Grand Prix
Two-door Hardtop J............................... 27647
Two-door Hardtop SJ 27657

1973 Ventura
Two-door Hatchback.............................2XY17
Two-door Notchback Sedan 2XY27
Four-door Notchback Sedan..................2XY69
Two-door Hatchback.............................2XZ17
Two-door Notchback Sedan 2XZ27
Four-door Notchback Sedan..................2XZ69

1973 Firebird
Two-door Hardtop 2FS87
Two-door Esprit Hardtop 2FT87
Two-door Formula Hardtop.....................2FU87
Two-door Trans Am Hardtop 2FV87

1973 LeMans
Four-door Hardtop 6-Window 2AD29
Four-door Station Wagon 2-seat 2AD35
Two-door Hardtop 2AD37
Four-door Station Wagon 3-seat 2AD45

1973 LeMans Sport
Two-door Hardtop 2AF37
LeMans Luxury Four-door HT 2AG29
Two-door Notchback Hardtop 2AH37

1973 Grand Am
Four-door 6W Hardtop..........................2AH29
Two-door Hardtop 2AH37

1973 Grand Prix
Two-door Notchback Hardtop J2GK57
Two-door Notchback Hardtop SJ2GK57

1973 Catalina
Four-door Station Wagon 2-seat 2BL35
Four-door Hardtop 4-Window 2BL39
Four-door Station Wagon 3-seat 2BL45
Two-door Notchback Hardtop 2BL57
Four-door Sedan 4-Window 2BL69

1973 Bonneville
Four-door Hardtop 4-Window 2BN39
Two-door Hardtop 2BN57
Four-door Sedan 4-Window.....................2BN69

1973 Grand Ville
Four-door Station Wagon 2-seat 2BP35
Four-door Station Wagon 3-seat 2BP45
Two-door Notchback Hardtop 2BP47
Four-door Hardtop 4-Window 2BP49
Two-door Convertible.............................2BP67

1974 Ventura
Two-door Hatchback..............................2XY17
Two-door Notchback Sedan 2XY27
Four-door Notchback Sedan...................2XY69

1974 Ventura Custom
Two-door Hatchback..............................2XZ17
Two-door Notchback Sedan 2XZ27
Four-door Notchback Sedan...................2XZ69

1974 Firebird
Two-door Hardtop 2FS87
Two-Door Esprit Hardtop 2FT87
Two-door Formula Hardtop.....................2FU87
Two-door Trans Am Hardtop 2FV87

1974 LeMans
Four-door Notchback Hardtop 2AD29
Four-door Station Wagon 2-seat 2AD35
Two-door Notchback Hardtop 2AD37
Four-door Station Wagon 3-seat 2AD45

1974 LeMans Sport
Two-door Notchback Hardtop 2AF37
LeMans Luxury 4-door Hardtop 2AG29
Four-door Station Wagon 2-seat 2AG35
Two-door Notchback Hardtop 2AG37
Four-door Station Wagon 3-seat 2AG45

1974 Grand Am
Four-door Notchback Hardtop 2AH29
Two-door Notchback Hardtop 2AH37

1974 Grand Prix
Two-door Notchback Hardtop 2GK57
Two-door Notchback Hardtop S...........J2GK57

1974 Catalina
Four-door Station Wagon 2-seat 2BL35
Four-door Notchback Hardtop 2BL39
Four-door Station Wagon 3-seat 2BL45
Two-door Notchback Hardtop 2BL57
Four-door Notchback Sedan....................2BL69

1974 Bonneville
Four-door Notchback Hardtop 2BN39

Two-door Notchback Hardtop 2BN57
Four-door Notchback Sedan.................. 2BN69

1974 Grand Ville
Four-door Station Wagon 2-seat........... 2BP35
Four-door Station Wagon 3-seat........... 2BP45
Two-door Notchback Hardtop 2BP47
Four-door Notchback Hardtop 2BP49
Two-door Convertible........................... 2BP67

1975 Astre
Two-door Station Wagon 2HV15
Two-door Hatchback............................. 2HV77

1975 Astre SJ
Two-door Station Wagon 2HX15
Two-door Hatchback............................. 2HX77

1975 Ventura
Two-door Hatchback 2XY17
Two-door Notchback Sedan 2XY27
Four-door Notchback Sedan................. 2XY69

1975 Ventura SJ
Two-door Hatchback 2XB17
Two-door Notchback Sedan 2XB27
Four-door Notchback Sedan.................. 2XB69

1975 Firebird
Two-door Hardtop 2FS87
Two-door Esprit Hardtop 2FT87
Two-door Formula Hardtop 2FU87
Two-door Trans Am Hardtop................. 2FW87

1975 LeMans
Four-door Notchback Hardtop 2AD29
Four-door Station Wagon 2-seat........... 2AD35
Two-door Notchback Hardtop 2AD37
Four-door Station Wagon 3-seat........... 2AD45

1975 LeMans Sport
Two-door Notchback Hardtop 2AF37

1975 Grand LeMans
Four-door Notchback Hardtop 2AG29
Four-door Station Wagon 2-seat........... 2AG35
Two-door Notchback Hardtop 3AG37
Four-door Station Wagon 3-seat........... 2AG45

1975 Grand Am
Four-door Notchback Hardtop 2AH29
Two-door Notchback Hardtop 2AH37

1975 Grand Prix
Two-door Notchback Hardtop 2GK57
Two-door Notchback Hardtop SJ........... 2GK57

1975 Catalina
Four-door Station Wagon 2-seat............ 2BL35
Four-door Station Wagon 3-seat............ 2BL45
Two-door Notchback Hardtop 2BL57
Four-door Notchback Sedan.................. 2BL69

1975 Bonneville
Four-door Station Wagon 2-seat........... 2BP35
Four-door Station Wagon 3-seat........... 2BP45
Two-door Notchback Hardtop 2BP47
Four-door Notchback Hardtop 2BP49

1975 Grand Ville
Two-door Notchback Hardtop 2BR47
Four-door Notchback Hardtop 2BR49
Two-door Convertible........................... 2BR67

1975 Grand Ville
Four-door Station Wagon 2-seat........... 2BP35
Four-door Station Wagon 2-seat........... 2BP45
Two-door Notchback Hardtop 2BP47
Four-door Notchback Hardtop 2BP49
Two-door Convertible........................... 2BP67

1976 Astre
Coupe C11
Safari C15
Hatchback... C77

1976 LeMans
Sedan D29
Safari D35
Coupe D37
Sport Coupe.. F37

1976 Grand LeMans
Sedan G29
Safari G35
Coupe G37

1976 Grand Prix
Coupe J57
Coupe SJ (LJ optional)............................... K57

1976 Catalina
Safari L35
Coupe L57
Sedan L69

1976 Sunbird
Coupe..M27

1976 Grand Safari
Grand Safari.. P35

1976 Bonneville
Coupe P47
Sedan P49

1976 Bonneville Brougham
Coupe R47
Sedan R49

1976 Firebird
Firebird S87
Esprit T87
Formula U87
Trans Am W87

1976 Ventura
Hatchback Y17
Coupe Y27
Sedan Y69

1976 Ventura SJ
Hatchback Z17
Coupe Z27
Sedan Z69

1977 Astre
Coupe.. C11
Safari C15
Hatchback C77

1977 LeMans
Sedan D29
Safari D35
Coupe D37
Sport Coupe F37

1977 Grand LeMans
Sedan G29
Safari G35
Coupe G37

1977 Grand Prix
Coupe SJ H57
Coupe J H37
Sedan K57

1977 Catalina
Safari L35
Coupe L37
Sedan.. L69

1977 Sunbird
Coupe..M27
Sport Hatch..M07
Grand Safari N35

1977 Bonneville
Coupe N37
Sedan N69

1977 Bonneville Brougham
Coupe Q37
Sedan Q69

1977 Firebird
Firebird S87
Esprit T87
Formula U87
Trans Am... W87

1977 Ventura
Hatchback Y17
Coupe Y27
Sedan Y69

1977 Ventura SJ
Hatchback Z17
Coupe Z27
Sedan Z69

1977 Phoenix
Coupe X27

Sedan X69

1978 LeMans
Coupe D27
Sedan D19
Wagon D35

1978 Grand LeMans
Coupe F27
Sedan F19
Wagon F35

1978 Grand Am
Coupe..G27
Sedan..G19

1978 Grand Prix
Coupe JK37
Coupe LJ K37
Coupe SJ K37

1978 Catalina
Coupe L37
Sedan L69
Wagon L35

1978 Bonneville
Coupe N37
Sedan N69

1978 Grand Safari
Grand Safari N35

1978 Bonneville Brougham
Coupe Q37
Sedan Q69

1978 Sunbird
Coupe E27
Sport Coupe M27
Sport Hatch M07
Sport Safari M15

1978 Phoenix
Hatchback.. Y17
Coupe Y27
Sedan Y69

1978 Phoenix LJ
Coupe Z27
Sedan Z69

1978 Firebird
Firebird...S87
Esprit.. T87
Formula...U87
Trans Am W87
10th Anniversary..................................... X87

1979 LeMans
Coupe D27
Sedan D19
Wagon D35

1979 Grand LeMans
Coupe F27
Sedan F19
Wagon F35

1979 Grand Am
Coupe..G27
Sedan..G19

1979 Grand Prix
Coupe..J37
Coupe LJK37
Coupe S JH37

1979 Catalina
Coupe L37
Sedan L69
Wagon L35

1979 Bonneville
Coupe N37
Sedan N69

1979 Grand Safari
Grand Safari N35

1979 Bonneville Brougham
Coupe Q37
Sedan Q69

1979 Sunbird
Coupe E27
Sport Coupe...M27

Sport Hatch M07
Sport Safari M15

1979 Phoenix
Hatchback Y17
Coupe Y27
Sedan Y69

1979 Phoenix LJ
Coupe Z27
Sedan Z69

1979 Firebird
Firebird S87
Esprit T87
Formula U87
Trans Am W87
Anniversary X87

1980 Sunbird
Coupe E27
Sport Coupe M27
Sport Hatch M07

1980 Grand Prix
Grand Prix J K37
Grand Prix LJ K37
Grand Prix SJ H37

1980 Catalina
Coupe L37
Sedan L69

1980 Bonneville
Coupe N37
Sedan N69
Safari N35

1980 Bonneville Brougham
Coupe R37
Sedan R69

1980 Phoenix
Coupe Z37
Five-Door Hatchback Z68

1980 Firebird
Firebird S87
Esprit T87
Formula V87
Trans Am Z87
Pace Car X87

1980 LeMans
Coupe D27
Sedan D19
Safari D35

1980 Grand LeMans
Coupe F27
Sedan F19
Safari F35

1980 Grand Am
Coupe G27

1981 Sunbird
Coupe E27
Sport Coupe M27
Sport Hatch M07
Hatch E07

1981 Grand Prix
Grand Prix J37
Grand Prix LJ K37
Grand Prix Brougham P37

1981 Catalina
Coupe L37
Sedan L69
Safari L35

1981 Bonneville
Coupe N37
Sedan N69
Safari N35

1981 Bonneville Brougham
Coupe R37
Sedan R69

1981 Phoenix
Coupe Y37
Five-door Hatch Y68

1981 Phoenix LJ
Coupe Z37

Five-door Hatch Z68

1981 Firebird
Firebird S87
Esprit T87
Formula V87
Trans Am W87

1981 LeMans
Coupe D27
Sedan D69
Safari D35

1981 Grand LeMans
Coupe F27
Sedan F69
Safari F35

1982 Firebird
Firebird S87
Trans Am W87
Firebird SE X87

1982 6000
Coupe F27
Sedan F19

1982 6000 LE
Coupe G27
Sedan G19

1982 Grand Prix
Grand Prix J37
Grand Prix LJ K37
Grand Prix Brougham P37

1982 Bonneville Model G
Sedan N69
Wagon N35

1982 Model G Brougham
Sedan R69

1982 T1000
3-door Hatchback Coupe L08
Five-door Hatch Sedan L68

1982 J2000
Coupe B27
Sedan B69
Three-door Hatchback B77
Wagon B35

1982 J2000 LE
Coupe C27
Sedan C69

1982 J2000 SE
Three-door Hatchback D77

1982 Phoenix
Coupe Y37
Five-door Hatchback Y68

1982 Phoenix LJ
Coupe Z37
Five-door Hatchback Z68

1982 Phoenix SJ
Coupe T37
Five-door Hatchback T68

1983 Firebird
Firebird S87
Trans Am W87
Firebird SE X87

1983 6000
Coupe F27
Sedan F19

1983 6000 LE
Coupe G27
Sedan G19

1983 6000 STE
Sedan H19

1983 Grand Prix
Grand Prix J37
Grand Prix LJ K37
Grand Prix Brougham P37

1983 Bonneville Model G
Sedan N69
Wagon N35

1983 Model G Brougham
Sedan R69

1983 1000
Three-door Hatchback Coupe L08
Five-door Hatch Sedan L68

1983 2000
Coupe B27
Sedan B69
Three-door Hatchback B77
Wagon B57

1983 2000 LE
Coupe C27
Sedan C69
Wagon C35

1983 2000 SE
Three-door Hatchback D77

1983 Phoenix
Coupe Y37
Five-door Hatchback Y68

1983 Phoenix LJ
Coupe Z37
Five-door Hatchback Z68

1983 Phoenix SJ
Coupe T37
Five-door Hatchback T68

1984 Firebird
Firebird S87
Trans Am W87
Firebird SE X87

1984 6000
Coupe F27
Sedan F19
Wagon F35

1984 6000 LE
Coupe G27
Sedan G19
Wagon G35

1984 6000 STE
Sedan H19

1984 Grand Prix
Grand Prix J37
Grand Prix LE K37
Grand Prix Brougham P37

1984 Bonneville
Bonneville N69
Bonneville LE S69
Bonneville Brougham R69

1984 Parisienne
Sedan L69
Wagon L35

1984 Parisienne Brougham
Sedan T69

1984 Phoenix
Coupe Y37
Four-door Hatchback Y68

1984 Phoenix LE
Coupe Z37
Five-door Hatchback Z68

1984 Phoenix SE
Coupe T37

1984 1000
Three-door Hatchback L08
Five-door Hatchback L68

1984 Fiero
Coupe E37
Sport Coupe M37
SE Coupe F37

1984 2000 Sunbird
Coupe B27
Sedan B69
Three-door Hatchback B77
Wagon B35

1984 2000 Sunbird LE
Coupe D27
Sedan D69
Three-door Hatchback D77

1984 2000 Sunbird LE Two-door Convertible
Two-door Convertible C67

1985 Firebird
Firebird....S87
Trans Am....W87
Firebird SE....X87

1985 6000
Coupe....F27
Sedan....F19
Wagon....F35

1985 6000 LE
Coupe....G27
Sedan....G19
Wagon....G35

1985 6000 STE
Sedan....H19

1985 Grand Am
Grand Am....E27
Grand LE....V27

1985 Grand Prix
Grand Prix....J37
Grand Prix LE....K37
Grand Prix Brougham....P37

1985 Bonneville
Bonneville....N69
Bonneville LE....S69
Bonneville Brougham....R69

1985 Parisienne
Sedan....L69

1985 Parisienne Brougham
Sedan....T69

1985 Phoenix
Coupe....Y37
Four-door Hatchback....Y68

1985 Phoenix LE
Coupe....Z37
Five-door Hatchback....Z68

1985 Phoenix SE
Coupe....T37

1985 1000
Three-door Hatchback....L08
Five-door Hatchback....L68

1985 Fiero
Coupe....E37
Sport Coupe....M37
SE Coupe....F37

1985 Sunbird
Coupe....B27
Sedan....B69
Three-door Hatchback....B77
Wagon....B35

1985 Sunbird LE
Coupe....C37
Sedan....C69
Wagon....C35

1985 Sunbird SE
Coupe....D27
Sedan....D69
Three-door Hatchback....D77

1985 Sunbird LE Two-door Convertible
Two-door Convertible....C67

1986 Firebird
Firebird....S87
Trans Am....W87
Firebird SE....X87

1986 6000
Coupe....F27
Sedan....F19
Wagon....F35

1986 6000 LE
Coupe....G27
Sedan....G19
Wagon....G35

1986 6000 STE
Sedan....H19
SE Sedan....E19
SE Wagon....E35

1986 Grand Am
Grand Am....E27
Sedan....E69
Grand Am LE Coupe....V27
Sedan....V69
SE Coupe....W27
SE Sedan....W69

1986 Grand Prix
Grand Prix....J37
Grand Prix LE....K37
Grand Prix Brougham....P37

1986 Bonneville
Bonneville....N69
Bonneville LE....S69
Bonneville Brougham....R69

1986 Parisienne
Sedan....L69
Wagon....L35

1986 Parisienne Brougham
Sedan....T69

1986 1000
Three-door Hatchback....L08
Five-door Hatchback....L68

1986 Fiero
Coupe....E37
Sport Coupe....M37
SE Coupe....F37
GT Coupe....G97

1986 Sunbird
Sedan....B69
Wagon....B35

1986 Sunbird SE
Coupe....D27
Two-door Convertible....D67
Three-door Hatchback....D77

1986 Sunbird GT
Coupe....U27
Sedan....U69
Three-door Hatchback....U77
Two-door Convertible....U67

1987 Firebird
Firebird....S87
Trans Am....W87
Trans Am GTA (Option Package)....W87

1987 6000
Coupe....F27
Sedan....F19
Wagon....F35

1987 6000 LE
Sedan....G19
Wagon....G35

1987 6000 STE
Sedan....H19
SE Sedan....E19
SE Wagon....E35

1987 Grand Am
Grand Am Coupe....E27
Sedan....E69
Grand Am LE Coupe....V27
Sedan....V69
SE Coupe....W27
SE Sedan....W69

1987 Grand Prix
Grand Prix....J37
Grand Prix LE....K37
Grand Prix Brougham....P37

1987 Bonneville
Bonneville....X69
Bonneville LE....Z69

1987 Safari
Wagon....L35

1987 1000
Three-door Hatchback....L08
Five-door Hatchback....L68

1987 Fiero
Base Coupe....E37
Sport Coupe....M37
SE Coupe....F37
GT coupe....G97

1987 Sunbird
Sedan....B69
Wagon....B35

1987 Sunbird SE
Coupe....D27
Two-door Convertible....D67
Three-door Hatchback....D77

1987 Sunbird GT
Coupe....U27
Sedan....U69
Three-door Hatchback....U77
Two-door Convertible (GT)....U67

1988 Firebird
Firebird....S87
Formula (Option Package)....W66
Trans Am....W87
Trans Am GTA (Option Package)....Y84

1988 6000
Sedan....F19
Wagon....F35

1988 6000 LE
Sedan....G19
Wagon....G35

1988 6000 STE
Sedan....H19
SE Sedan....E19
SE Wagon....E35

1988 Grand Am
Grand Am Coupe....E27
Sedan....E69
Grand Am LE Coupe....V27
Sedan....V69
SE Coupe....W27
SE Sedan....W69

1988 Grand Prix
Grand Prix....J37
Grand Prix LE....K37
Grand Prix SE....P37

1988 Bonneville
Bonneville LE....X69
Bonneville SE....Z69
Bonneville SSE....Y69

1988 Safari
Wagon....L35

1988 Fiero
Coupe Base....E37
Formula Package....W66
GT....G97

1988 Sunbird
Sedan....B69
Wagon....D35

1988 Sunbird SE
Coupe....D27
SE Wagon....D35

1988 Sunbird GT
Coupe....U37
Two-door Convertible (GT)....U67

1988 LeMans
Value Leader....X08
Aerocoupe....N08
Sedan....W19
SE Sedan....R19

1989 Firebird
Firebird....S87
Formula (Option Package)....W66
Trans Am....W87
Trans Am GTA (Option Package)....Y84

1989 6000 LE
Sedan....F69
Wagon....F35

1989 6000 STE
Sedan....H69
SE Sedan....J69
SE Wagon....J35

1989 Grand Am
LE Coupe....E27
Sedan LE....E69

SE Coupe W27
SE Sedan..W69

1989 Grand Prix
Coupe J37
LE Coupe K37
SE Coupe P37

1989 Bonneville
LE Sedan..X69
SE Sedan..Z69
SSE Sedan..Y69

1989 Safari
Wagon..L35

1989 Sunbird
LE Coupe B37
LE Sedan...B69
SE Coupe D37
GT Coupe U37
GT Two-door Convertible....................U67

1989 LeMans
3-DR Aerocoupe X08
(Value Leader)
LE Aerocoupe 08
LE Sedan...N19
SE Sedan...R19
GSE Aerocoupe..................................S08

1990 Firebird
Firebird...S87
Formula (Option Package)..................W66
Trans Am W87
Trans Am GTA (Option Package) Y84

1990 6000 LE
Sedan F69
Wagon...F35

1990 6000 STE
SE Sedan J69
SE Sedan AWD J69
SE Wagon.. J35

1990 Grand Am
LE Coupe E27
Sedan LE E69
SE Coupe W27
SE Sedan...W69

1990 Grand Prix
Coupe J37
SE Coupe P37
Four-door Sedan J19
Four-door STE Sedan.........................T19

1990 Bonneville
LE Sedan...X69
SE Sedan...Z69
SSE Sedan...Y69

1990 Sunbird
LE Coupe B37
LE Sedan...B69
SE Coupe D37
GT Coupe U37
LE Two-door Convertible B67

1990 LeMans
Three-door Aerocoupe.......................X08
(Value Leader)
LE Aerocoupe N08
LE Sedan...N19
GSE Aerocoupe..................................S08

1990 Trans Sport
FWD Minivan M06

1991 Firebird
Hatchback Coupe S87
Trans Am Hatchback Coupe.................W87

1991 6000
LE Sedan F69
LE Wagon F35
SE Sedan... J69

1991 Grand Am
Coupe G27
Sedan G69
LE Coupe E27
LE Sedan...E69
SE Coupe W27
SE Sedan...W69

1991 Grand Prix
LE Sedan H19
SE Sedan J19
SE Coupe J37
GT Coupe P37
STE Sedan T19

1991 Bonneville
LE Sedan...X69
SE Sedan...Z69
SSE Sedan...Y69

1991 Sunbird
Coupe C37
Sedan C69
LE Coupe B37
LE Sedan...B69
LE Two-door Convertible.....................B67
SE Coupe D37
GT Coupe U37

1991 LeMans
Three-door Aerocoupe X08
(Value Leader)
LE three-door Aerocoupe N08
LE Sedan...N19

1991 Trans Sport
Minivan...M06

1992 Firebird
Firebird Two-door Convertible S67
Firebird S87
Formula (W66)................................... S87
Trans Am Two-door Convertible.......... W67
Trans Am W87
Trans Am GTA Y84/W87

1992 Grand Am
SE Coupe E37
SE Sedan...E69
GT Coupe W37
GT Sedan...W69

1992 Grand Prix
LE Sedan H19
SE Sedan J19
SE Coupe J37
GT Coupe P37
STE Sedan T19

1992 Bonneville
SE Sedan X69
SSE Sedan...Z69
SSEI Sedan..Y69

1992 Sunbird
LE Coupe C37
LE Sedan C69
SE Coupe B37
SE Sedan...B69
SE Two-door Convertible B67
GT Coupe D37

1992 LeMans
Aerocoupe (Value Leader) X08
SE Aerocoupe N08
SE Sedan...N19

1992 Trans Sport
Trans Sport SE M06
Trans Sport GT Y92/M06

1993 Firebird
Firebird Two-door Coupe.....................S87P
Formula Two-door Coupe.....................V87P
Trans Am Two-door Coupe V87P/Y83

1993 Grand Am
SE Two-door Coupe E37P
SE Four-door Sedan E69P

1993 Grand Prix
LE Four-door Sedan............................H19P
SE Two-door Coupe J37N
SE Four-door Sedan J19P
GT Two-door Coupe P37N
STE Four-door Sedan T19P

1993 Bonneville
SE Four-door Sedan X69P
SSE Four-door Sedan Z69P
SSEI Four-door Sedan.........................Y69P

1993 Sunbird
LE Two-door Coupe C37P

LE Four-door Sedan C69P
SE Two-door Coupe B37P
SE Four-door Sedan B69P
SE Two-door Convertible......................B67P

1993 LeMans
Value Leader 3-DR Aerocoupe..............X08P
SE 3-DR Aerocoupe N08P
SE Four-door Sedan N19P

1993 Trans Sport
SE Minivan...M06P

1994 Firebird
Firebird Two-door Coupe S87R
Formula Two-door Coupe V87R
Trans Am Two-door Coupe.............V87R/Y82

1994 Grand Am
SE Two-door Coupe E37R
SE Four-door Sedan E69R

1994 Grand Prix
SE Four-door Sedan J19R
SE Two-door Coupe J37R

1994 Bonneville
SE Four-door Sedan X69R
SSE Four-door Sedan Z69R

1994 Sunbird
LE Two-door Coupe............................ B37R
LE Four-door Sedan B69R
SE Two-door Coupe L37R
LE Two-door Convertible B67R

1994 Trans Sport
SE Minivan...MO6R

1995 Firebird
Two-door Coupe S87S
Two-door Convertible..........................S67S

1995 Formula Firebird
Two-door Coupe V87S
Two-door Convertible..........................V67S

1995 Firebird Trans Am
Two-door Coupe V87S
Two-door Convertible V67S

1995 Grand Am
SE Two-door Coupe E37S
SE Four-door Sedan E69S
GT Two-door Coupe W37S
GT Four-door Sedan...........................W69S

1995 Grand Prix
SE Two-door Coupe J37S
SE Four-door Sedan............................J19S

1995 Bonneville
SE Four-door Sedan X69S
SSE Four-door Sedan Z69S

1995 Sunfire
SE Two-door Coupe B37S
SE Four-door Sedan...........................B69S
SE Two-door Convertible......................B67S
GT Two-door Coupe D37S

1995 Trans Sport
SE Minivan...MO6S

1996 Firebird
Two-door Coupe S87T
Two-door Convertible..........................S67T

1996 Formula Firebird
Two-door Coupe V87T
Two-door Convertible V67T

1996 Firebird Trans Am
Two-door Coupe V87T
Two-door Convertible..........................V67T

1996 Grand Am
SE Two-door Coupe E37T
SE Four-door Sedan E69T
GT Two-door Coupe W37T
GT Four-door Sedan...........................W69T

1996 Grand Prix
SE Two-door Coupe J37T
SE Four-door Sedan............................J19T

1996 Bonneville
SE Four-door Sedan X69T

SSE Four-door Sedan Z69T

1996 Sunfire
SE Two-door Coupe B37T
SE Four-door Sedan B69T
SE Two-door Convertible B67T
GT Two-door Coupe D37T

1996 Trans Sport
SE Minivan..MO6T

1997 Firebird
Two-door Coupe S87V
Two-door Convertible................................S67V

1997 Formula Firebird
Two-door Coupe V87V
Two-door Convertible................................V67V

1997 Firebird Trans Am
Two-door Coupe V87V
Two-door Convertible................................V67V

1997 Grand Am
SE Two-door Coupe E37V
SE Four-door Sedan E69V
GT Two-door Coupe W37V
GT Four-door Sedan W69V

1997 Grand Prix
SE Four-door Sedan J69V
GT Two-door Coupe P37V
GT Four-door Sedan J69V

1997 Bonneville
SE Four-door Sedan X69V
SSE Four-door Sedan Z69V
SSEi Four-door Sedan Z69V

1997 Sunfire
SE Two-door Coupe B37V
SE Four-door Sedan B69V
SE Two-door Convertible B67V
GT Two-door Coupe D37V

1997 Trans Sport
SE Three-door Minivan NO6V
SE Three-door Extended Minivan............MO6V
SE Four-door Extended Minivan..............M16V

1998 Firebird
Two-door Coupe S87V
Two-door Convertible................................S67V

1998 Formula Firebird
Two-door Coupe V87V

1998 Firebird Trans Am
Two-door Coupe V87V
Two-door Convertible................................V67V

1998 Grand Am
SE Two-door Coupe E37V
SE Four-door Sedan E69V
GT Two-door Coupe W37V
GT Four-door Sedan..................................W69V

1998 Grand Prix
SE Four-door Sedan J69V
GT Two-door Coupe P37V
GT Four-door Sedan..................................P69V

1998 Bonneville
SE Four-door Sedan X69V
SSE Four-door Sedan Z69V
SSEi Four-door Sedan................................Z69V

1998 Sunfire
SE Two-door Coupe B37V
SE Four-door Sedan B69V
SE Two-door Convertible B67V
GT Two-door Coupe D37V

1998 Trans Sport
SE Three-door Minivan NO6V
SE Three-door Extended Minivan............MO6V
SE Four-door Extended Minivan..............M16V

1999 Firebird
Two-door Coupe S87V
Two-door Convertible................................ S67V

1999 Formula Firebird
Two-door Coupe......................................V87V

1999 Firebird Trans Am
Two-door Coupe......................................V87V
Two-door Convertible V67V

1999 Grand Am
SE Two-door Coupe..................................E37V
SE Four-door Sedan E69V
GT Two-door Coupe..................................W37V
GT Four-door Sedan W69V

1999 Grand Prix
SE Four-door Sedan J69V
GT Two-door Coupe..................................P37V
GT Four-door Sedan P69V
GTP Two-door Coupe R37V
GTP Four-door Sedan................................R69V

1999 Bonneville
SE Four-door Sedan X69V
SSE Four-door Sedan Z69V
SSEi Four-door Sedan Z69V

1999 Sunfire
SE Two-door Coupe..................................B37V
SE Four-door Sedan B69V
SE Two-door Convertible B67V
GT Two-door Coupe..................................D37V

1999 Montana
SE Three-door Minivan NO6V
SE Three-door Extended Minivan MO6V
SE Four-door Extended Minivan M16V

1999 Montana Sport
SE Three-door Extended Minivan............MO6V
SE Four-door Extended Minivan M16V

2000 Firebird
Two-door Coupe......................................S87V
Two-door Convertible S67V

2000 Formula Firebird
Two-door Coupe......................................V87V

2000 Firebird Trans Am
Two-door Coupe......................................V87V
Two-door Convertible V67V

2000 Grand Am
SE Two-door Coupe..................................E37V
SE Four-door Sedan E69V
SE1 Two-door Coupe E37V
SE1 Four-door Sedan E69V
GT Two-door Coupe..................................W37V
GT Four-door Sedan W69V

2000 Grand Prix
SE Four-door Sedan J69V
GT Two-door Coupe..................................P37V
GT Four-door Sedan P69V
GTP Two-door Coupe R37V
GTP Four-door Sedan R69V

2000 Bonneville
SE Four-door Sedan X69V
SLE Four-door Sedan Z69V
SSEi Four-door Sedan Z69V

2000 Sunfire
SE Two-door Coupe..................................B37V
SE Four-door Sedan B69V
SE Two-door Convertible D67V
GT Two-door Coupe..................................D37V

2000 Montana
SE Three-door Minivan NO6V
SE Three-door Extended Minivan M06V
SE Four-door Extended Minivan M16V

2000 Montana Sport
SE Three-door Extended Minivan M06V
SE Four-door Extended Minivan M16V

2001 Firebird
Two-door Coupe.......................................S87V
Two-door Convertible S67V

2001 Formula Firebird
Two-door Coupe V87V

2001 Firebird Trans Am
Two-door Coupe V87V
Two-door Convertible................................V67V

2001 Grand Am
SE Two-door Coupe E37V
SE Four-door Sedan E69V
GT Two-door Coupe W37V
GT Four-door Sedan W69V

2001 Grand Prix
SE Four-door Sedan J69V
GT Two-door Coupe P37V
GT Four-door Sedan P69V
GTP Two-door Coupe.................................R37V
GTP Four-door Sedan R69V

2001 Bonneville
SE Four-door Sedan X69V
SLE Four-door Sedan Z69V
SSEi Four-door Sedan Z69V

2001 Sunfire
SE Two-door Coupe B37V
SE Four-door Sedan B69V
GT Two-door Coupe D37V

2001 Montana
SE Three-door Minivan............................ N06V
SE Three-door Extended Minivan.............M06V
SE Four-door Extended Minivan...............M16V

2001 Montana Sport
SE Three-door Extended Minivan.............M06V
SE Four-door Extended Minivan...............M16V

2002 Firebird
Two-door Coupe..S87V
Two-door Convertible................................S67V

2002 Formula Firebird
Two-door Coupe..V87V

2002 Firebird Trans Am
Two-door Coupe..V87V
Two-door Convertible................................V67V

2002 Grand Am
SE Two-door Coupe E37V
SE Four-door Sedan...................................E69V
SE1 Two-door Coupe E37V
SE1 Four-door Sedan E69V
GT Two-door Coupe W37V
GT Four-door Sedan W69V
GT1 Two-door Coupe W37V
GT1 Four-door Sedan.................................W69V

2002 Grand Prix
SE Four-door Sedan...................................J69V
GT Two-door Coupe P37V
GT Four-door Sedan...................................P69V
GTP Two-door Coupe.................................R37V
GTP Four-door Sedan R69V

2002 Bonneville
SE Four-door Sedan...................................X69V
SLE Four-door Sedan Z69V
SSEi Four-door Sedan................................Z69V

2002 Sunfire
SE Two-door Coupe B37V
SE Four-door Sedan...................................B69V
GT Two-door Coupe D37V

2002 Montana
SE Three-door Minivan...............................N06V
SE Three-door Extended Minivan.............M06V
SE Four-door Extended Minivan...............M16V

2002 Montana Sport
SE Three-door Extended Minivan.............M06V
SE Four-door Extended Minivan...............M16V

INTERESTING PONTIAC FACTS

By John Sawruk

• Pontiac's first postwar V-8 design was a flathead.

• Pontiac built an experimental car in 1954 with an L-head six-cylinder in the rear mounted transversely.

• The 1955 GMC L'Universelle Show Van had a front-wheel drive Pontiac V-8 powertrain.

• The 1956 Pontiac Club de Mer show car had a brushed metal skin. Guess who the head of Pontiac Advance Design was at that point?

• The 1957 and 1958 Pontiac fuel injection systems used different intake manifolds; 1957 was tubular and 1958 was cast.

• Pontiac used Cadillac bodies during development of the transaxle, which led to the 1961 Tempest.

• The first 1961 Tempest four-cylinder engines were made by putting bob weights in place of piston and rod assemblies in 1958 V-8 engines in Chieftains.

• 1958 big Pontiacs were used to develop the XB-60 "rope-drive" transaxle for the 1961 Tempest.

• Around 1959 Pontiac made 389 cid aluminum cylinder blocks in conjunction with Reynolds Aluminum. They had no liners. In the same period, aluminum heads without seat inserts were made; valve seat wear was a serious problem.

• Drawings of never made Pontiacs originally planned include:

— The elusive 1954 Sedan Delivery, marked "Canceled 9/14/53".

— A 1954 Business Coupe and Sedan Coupe, marked "Canceled 8/17/53".

— A 1954 short wheelbase convertible.

— A 1956 proposal with the transmission mounted under the seat. It had a flat floor and two driveshafts.

• Various 1959 studies with different side trim or models versus what was released for production. These included a Star Chief Safari station wagon and a "Ventura," which was the beginning of the Grand Prix concept.

— A 1961 Star Chief two-door sedan.

— A 1962 Ventura series (not just a Catalina with the Ventura option).

— 1963 Tempests with different front end styling versus what was finally used in production.

— A 1966 Ventura Safari station wagon with woodgrain.

• The name "Ventura" was often used on concept sketches for proposed Pontiacs and Tempests.

• There are reports of a factory prototype 1964 Tempest with a turbine engine.

• There are reports of a factory prototype 1964 Tempest with front-wheel drive.

• Pontiac partially developed a Rochester six-barrel carburetor. It had a 3-2 barrels on a common base.

• The 1966 Tri-Power and 1967 four-barrel intake manifold/carburetor/air cleaner systems had equivalent power. The restrictive Tri-Power intake manifold was replaced by a 1967 four-barrel design that was related to the early 1960's NASCAR manifold. In addition, the small Tri-Power air cleaners were quite restrictive also versus the large element used with the four-barrel.

• One Pontiac OHC V-8 is currently running in a private owner's car.

• Several different Pontiac OHC V-8s were built.

• There was a plan for cast iron eight-lug wheels for the 1966 Tempest. Brake drum distortion and high unsprung weight killed the program.

• Pontiac built a 1967 Firebird with a ground effects machine in the trunk to increase traction.

• Many Canadian Pontiacs, including the Canadian specific muscle cars, used Chevrolet engines.

• A 1968 GTO Hatchback prototype was built. It was white with blue stripes (ala the 1969 Trans Am).

• The prototype 1969 Trans Am was silver. It has a fiberglass hood with push down and rotate style hood locks.

• Some 1970 GTOs were equipped with an optional vacuum controlled exhaust system called "The Tiger Button". A knob, similar to that used for RAM AIR, changed the exhaust sound. Few were sold before the option was canceled.

• A drawing has been found that indicates the original plan for the 1971 GT-37 was to have it use the 1970 GT-37 stripe, which is the same as the 1969 Judge.

• The major change in 1971 vs. 1970 horsepower ratings didn't come from the change in compression ratio. Instead, it comes from the use of more realistic net hp ratings in 1971 (which included a fan, an air cleaner, exhaust system, etc.) versus the gross hp used in 1970.

• The 1972 "A" duck tail spoiler was never installed in production. Factory pictures exist showing it installed on a LeMans GT and a GTO. Some parts appear to have been sold through GM Parts Division and installed.

• The 1972 GTO was originally going to have a 350 cid four-barrel engine as standard.

• What became the 1973 Grand Am was originally intended to be the GTO.

• One 1973 "A" SD 455 was built. It was in a Grand Am and was an engineering prototype. There were no production 1973 "A" SD 455s.

• No 1973 production "A" cars were produced with functional NASA scoops. However, one prototype, now in private hands, does exist. In addition, some other units may have been sold through GM Parts Division and installed.

• What became the 1973 "A" was intended to be released as a 1972, but was delayed by the long GM strike.

• SD455 Formula Firebirds came from the factory with Trans Am hoods and shakers.

• There was a 1959 proposal for a Pontiac version of the El Camino. One prototype still exists in a private owner's hands. This proposal resurfaced in 1978. A prototype vehicle, using the Grand Am appearance, was built. This vehicle, now updated to 1980 appearance, is in the Pontiac Historical Vehicle Collection. A similar proposal, using LeMans sheet metal, was proposed to be sold by GM Truck and Coach.

• The 1979 Firebird Type K came close to going into production. The build process required that a Firebird be partially built in the plant, transferred to an outside body facility, and then returned to the plant for completion. As a result, the total number of Firebirds able to be built was reduced due to the assembly line interruptions. A financial analysis of the situation showed Pontiac would lose profit from this situation and the project was canceled.

• One of the 1980 Phoenix optional trims combined a basically black interior with saddle colored seat inserts. The trim brochure shows saddle inserts on the door trim panels also, but due to a factory error, some cars were built with all black door panels.

• Many factory photos and Product Description Manuals (an assembly guide) are incorrect versus how the cars were actually made.

• The 1953 and 1954 Pontiacs had provisions to accommodate the V-8 finally introduced in 1955. Some people have reported seeing possible 1953-'54 prototype V-8 cars in Pontiac/Detroit area junkyards.

• The first stamped steel rocker arm (to be used in the 1955 Pontiac and Chevy engines, ultimately) was made at home by a Pontiac Engineer.

- Notes from Pete Estes indicate the 1959 "Wide-Track was primarily viewed as a styling feature, with the handling advantage seen as secondary."

- Pontiac built experimental 1961 Tempests with 316, 347, and 389 cid engines.

- A 1961 Tempest was built with a side-mounted radiator and an engine compartment with seals.

- A 1961 Catalina was built with a 336 cid V-8 for performance and economy testing.

- Automatic overdrive transmissions were tried in large Pontiacs in 1961 and 1969, at least.

- While "Ventura" was used as a generic code name for many Pontiac styling proposals, a document has been found that indicates it was the intended name for what became the 1962 Grand Prix. It also says the car was to use special springs for a one inch lower ride height.

- Vinyl tops for large Pontiac coupe models were announced as being available as of 1-30-62. "Cobra" grain vinyl was used.

- A 35,000 mile chassis lube was intended for the 1962 Tempest.

- The 1963 Tempest 326 cid V-8 was really a 336. In 1964 it became a 326.

- A 421 cid SOHC V-8 "Sports Engine" was seriously developed by Pontiac. A 395 cid was also proposed. 1963 test data on the 421 SOHC showed the four-barrel version produced more power than the Tri-power one.

- An Engineering report dated 5-29-63 is titled "Preliminary Performance and Fuel Economy Comparison - G.T.O. (with periods!) versus 326 HO engine and 326 low compression ratio engine".

- Data was found that indicates an informational description of what became the 1964 GTO was published inside Pontiac on 7-3-63, revised 8-13-63, 8-19-63, and 10-18-63. The 8-13-63 list indicates the GTO crest was to be red, white, and blue. It also shows that the GTO was intended to have a 116 inch wheelbase (with a modified suspension) versus the Tempest 115 inches.

- Pontiac designed and built a front-wheel drive 1964 Tempest with a 326 cid V-8. It used unequal length driveshafts. The engine was mounted longitudinally.

- There was a plan for a six bolt rocker cover for the 1964 Pontiac V-8.

- There was a Hilborn-like fuel injection system designed by Pontiac Engineering for the GTO.

- Pontiac tested a water heated 2-4 barrel ram intake manifold for the 1965 GTO engine.

- A RPD speed-density fuel injection system was tested on a 1965 GTO engine with a modified 3-2 manifold, a ram manifold, and a cross-ram manifold.

- A 265 cid OHC6 was built for possible use in the Catalina and Tempest. It apparently had a longer stroke. One-barrel and four-barrel versions were built.

- 1966 Engineering Bulletin #66-22, dated 10-14-65, indicates the release of a "LeMans Ride Option for GTO". It was to include LeMans V-8 springs, shocks, and stabilizer bar. The purpose was "for the owner who desires a GTO with its looks and performance but with LeMans type ride."

- An engineering drawing dated 8-23-65 shows the cast iron styled wheel/brake for the 1966 Tempest. It shows eight lug nuts. It had 24 cooling fins versus 16 on the aluminum version. This wheel never went into production due to high weight and distortion.

- What became the 1966 230 cid OHC6 was originally to have been 215 cid.

- Pontiac Engineering Bulletin 66-20 indicates that the OHC6 was to have black painted ribs on the cam cover and timing belt cover. Red paint was to be on the "Overhead Cam" letters, the "PMD" letters, and the ribs that framed the PMD letters.

- Pontiac developed a rear mounted transmission, the EX-724, which was used in five experimental independent rear suspension transaxle cars.

- Pontiac designed an independent rear suspension with inboard disc brakes. A number of experimental cars were built.

- Pontiac designed a variable venturi carburetor. The design had no throttle blades. Rochester Products took the work over.

- Pontiac Engineering Bulletin 66-16 indicates that an electrically heated front seat and seat back was to have been a special order option on the 1966 Bonneville Brougham only.

- Pontiac developed (starting around 1967) a X-4 engine. It was an aluminum, two cycle, four-cylinder, air cooled, fuel injected engine.

- As late as 7-15-66, the 1967 Firebird was called the "PF" car. What appears to be the "Banshee" name is hazy on the drawings. What became the Firebird 400 was originally to be the "TT" with a different hood and emblems than finally used. TT stood for "Tourist Trophy". Some data indicates the TT was also to have the four-barrel OHC 6 available.

- The original 1967 Firebird option list shows "D35 - Bullet outside rearview mirror".

- Some 1969 development projects on the Pontiac 303 cid Trans-Am engine included center feed crankshaft oiling and gravity feed camshaft oiling.

- In 1969, Pontiac proposed an aluminum 297 cid V-8. Experimental 250 cid versions were built.

- In 1969, Pontiac built a 230 OHC 6 "Hemi". It had 325 gross hp.

- What became the 1969 Tempest Custom S was originally to be called the "Pontiac TC".

- Around 1969, Pontiac Engineering installed a 318 cid Plymouth V-8 in a Catalina for a performance and economy study.

- The 1970-1/2 Firebird came close to having a production Bendix Fuel Injection System (TBI type).

- In 1981, Pontiac proposed a "Safari" pickup based on the Sunbird. Production would have been in 1985 or 1986. The Norwood plant recently built one on its own.

- The 1982 Firebird was designed to contain the Pontiac manufactured V-8. The Turbo 301 required engine repackaging to make it fit.

- Alcoa made an "all-aluminum" Pontiac. It was a 1942 two-door streamliner and had its engine and other parts made of aluminum.

- In 1943, Pontiac designed a one-quarter-ton 4X4 truck proposed for build by Chevrolet.

- Some non-military work started again at Pontiac Engineering in 1943.

- Work was started on a five-inch Rocket Bomb in 1944. Pontiac also started making a 155mm shell.

- GM Coaches were worked on at Pontiac in 1944.

- There was almost no road testing due to restrictions on manpower and fuel in 1944.

- An experimental Pontiac 6 with a supercharger was built in 1945.

- An experimental Pontiac 6 with an aluminum intake manifold dual carburetor set-up was built in 1945.

- Postwar Pontiac V-8 projects included:
    — 269 cid Flathead (8:1 compression ratio) - two designs
    — 268 cid OHV
    — 272 cid OHV using an Oldsmobile block
    — 287 cid that became the 1955 production V-8. It was apparently related to the 268 cid above.

- In 1947, Pontiac demonstrated a car with the 269 cid flathead V-8 to GM management.

- 272 cid OHV V-8 - first Pontiac engines made in 1948.

- A 265 cid OHV Pontiac 6 was designed in 1948.

- 269 cid flathead V-8 work was dropped in May 1949 by Pontiac as not suitable for high compression.

• Pontiac built one 1200 OHV V-6, 251 cid for GM use in late 1949.

• Pontiac 268 cid OHV V-8s were made in 1950.

• A 248 cid OHV 6 was proposed to replace the 239 cid flathead six. It used the GMC Truck 248 cid block and crankshaft.

• A two-barrel, high output 239 cid flathead six was developed. Work stopped in 1950.

• A 239 cid F-head (not flathead) six was designed in 1950.

• There were plans for a longer wheelbase 1950 Pontiac.

• The 1951 Pontiac was originally planned to have a new "A" body to be shared with Chevrolet and Oldsmobile, with considerable interchangeability.

• What became the 1953 Pontiac was originally intended to be the 1952 model.

• Prior to the development of the 1977 151 cid four-cylinder (which started in 1974), four-cylinder proposals using V-8 tooling (like the old 195 cid version) were looked at. Possibly the most unusual was a S-4. This engine used the most forward cylinder on one side, then the two inner cylinders on the other side, and an end cylinder on the same side as the first. A prototype was built using a V-8 block and bob weights. It had unacceptable vibrations, later analyzed mathematically.

1928 Pontiac Model 6-28 coupe. (OCW)

1955 Pontiac Star Chief Custom Catalina two-door hardtop. (OCW)

1940 Pontiac Torpedo Eight four-door sedan. (AA)

• There was a serious production design to use the 1.8 liter, four-cylinder, non-turbo engine in the 1984 Fiero. The intent was to provide even higher levels of fuel economy.

• People have expressed interest in whether or not any high performance items existed for Pontiacs before 1955 before the V-8 engine. They are as follows:

• People did run pre-1955 Pontiacs in NASCAR. However, little else is known about this. (it's suspected they weren't too successful!)

• Special rear springs were offered in 1951 for Taxicabs, Police Cars, and Special Order Export. They were different from the Station Wagon and Sedan Delivery springs.

• In 1950 there was a "City Police" generator. It was used in conjunction with a 19 plate battery and a special voltage regulator. It was specifically not heavy-duty. It was for cars operated at low speeds with heavy electrical loads. It was not intended for use over 60 mph except for short periods.

• In 1954 a heavy-duty Hydra-Matic conversion package was available. It has an external transmission oil cooler, larger annular pistons, a modified engine water pump, and some other parts. It was intended for police cars, taxis, and road mail carriers. it could not be used on air conditioned cars. The cooler mounted on the transmission.

• 1954 air conditioned cars used a six bladed fan, 13 pound radiator cap, special equipment generator and battery, and heavy-duty fuel pump. Non-A/C cars used a seven pound cap. Eventually, special water temperature gauges were used in A/C cars because of this difference.

• It's believed that approximately 100 1971-1/2 GT-37s were built. Evidence of cars built at Fremont, as well as Pontiac, was uncovered. After a lot of searching in various records, no announcement was found that the 1971-1/2 existed although the stripes did find their way into the parts catalog.

• For those that wonder: Yes, the candy apple green color on the 1971 evaporative emissions line clip near the canister is correct!

• 1229 1986-1/2 Grand Prix 2 + 2s were made. Despite original plans, no 1987s were made. There were also four 1986-1/2 prototypes (including a black one and a maroon one). Beware, some people have already made additional ones by buying parts from Pontiac. All production ones were silver fastbacks.

1963 Pontiac Grand Prix. (OCW)

1998 Pontiac Sunfire SE four-door sedan. (PGMC)

OAKLAND/PONTIAC CARS BUILT DATA THROUGH 1972

The following information was compiled from the car building tags in the Past Records Department, together with some data received from the Material Record Department. In one instance the first car built does not carry the first serial number due to various delays of the #1 car in production.

The total cars built include the assembly plants and export.

The serial numbers are for Pontiac production.

In the case of Linden and California the numbers start with 1001 but have the prefix "C" for California and "L" for Linden, instead of "P" for Pontiac (through 1942)

Canadian production is included in totals in cases where our serial numbers were used by them.

YEAR	MAKE	MODEL	NAME	WHEELBASE	CAR SERIAL NUMBERS	STARTED PRODUCTION	FINISHED PROD. PRODUCTION	CARS BUILT	TOTAL BUILT
1918	Oak. 6	34-B			30001-34 to 116440	Sept. 1917	6-1-20	86,439	86,439
1919									
1920	Oak. 6	34-C			11701-34 to 152356	Jan. 1920	1-6-21	35,356	35,356
1921	Oak. 6	34-C			152357-34 to 159700	Jan. 1921	7-27-21	5,444	5,444
1922	Oak. 6	34-C			159701-34 to 167550	Aug. 1921	Approx. 12-31-21	7,849	7,849
1922	Oak. 6	6-44			1-44 to 41152	Jan. 1922	Approx. 6-15-23	41,152	41,152
1923									
1924	Oak. 6	6-54A			1054 to 37080	Aug. 1923	7-29-24	37,080	37,080
1925	Oak. 6	6-54B			37110-54 to 64523	7-17-24	5-29-25	27,423	27,423
1926	Oak. 6	6-54C	0/6		64601-54 to 120714	7-2-25	6-17-26	58,827	58,827
1927	Oak. 6	6-54D	CO/6	113"	120801-54 to 167943	6-7-26	5-24-27	44,658	44,658
1926	Pont. 6	6-27		110"	P-1 to 202100	12-28-25	10-31-27	204,553	204,553

Start of "Pontiac" Car 1926. Built were 6-27 1st Edition. 1927 Built were 6-27 2nd Edition

YEAR	MAKE	MODEL	NAME	WHEELBASE	CAR SERIAL NUMBERS	STARTED PRODUCTION	FINISHED PROD. PRODUCTION	CARS BUILT	TOTAL BUILT
1928	Oak. 6	6-212	AA6	117"	170001-AAS to 226438	6-2-27	6-25-28	60,121	284,905

212 Cu. In. Engine - All American 6, 1st Edition

| 1928 | Pont. 6 | 6-28 | | 110" | P-204001 to 408894 | 12-7-27 | 11-3-28 | 224,784 | |
| 1929 | Oak. 6 | 6-212 | AA6 | 117" | 227001-AAS to 272642 | 9-24-28 | 10-9-29 | 50,693 | 251,196 |

228 Cu. In. Engine - All American 6, 2nd Edition

1929	Pont. 6	6-29		110"	P-410101 to 590498	12-28-28	10-31-29	200,503	
1930	Oak. V-8	101	V-8	117"	273501 to 295245	11-23-29	9-25-30	21,943	84,831
1930	Pont. 6	6-30		110"	P-591501 to 648004	12-14-29	9-26-30	62,888	
1931	Oak. V-8	301	V-8	117"	296001 to 309415	12-15-30	10-8-31	13,408	98,116

Last Model with "Oakland" Name

| 1931 | Pont. 6 | 401 | | 112" | P-649001 to 728006 | 11-9-30 | 10-9-31 | 84,708 | |

Engine with Tapered Valve Guides

| 1932 | Pont. V-8 | 302 | V-8 | 117" | P8-310001 to 316282 | 12-22-31 | 3-22-32 | 6,281 | 45,340 |

Free Wheeling and Ride Control

| 1932 | Pont. 6 | 402 | | 114" | P6-729001 to 763983 | 12-8-31 | 8-23-32 | 39,059 | |
| 1933 | Pont. 8 | 601 | Str. 8 | 115" | P8-770001 to 838455 | 12-7-32 | 10-6-33 | 90,198 | 90,198 |

Torque Tube Drive - Built In Trunk - Chevrolet Brakes - Dash Starter Button

| 1934 | Pont. 8 | 603 | Str. 8 | 117-1/4" | P8-838501 to 908952 | 12-21-33 | 9-11-34 | 78,859 | 78,959 |

Dubonnet Front Susp. - Bendix Brakes - Accel. Pedal Starter Switch

| 1935 | Pont. 6 | 701-A | Deluxe 6 | 112" | P6AA-1001 to 32187 | 11-28-34 | 7-31-35 | 36,032 | 129,463 |

Dubonnet Front Susp. on 701A & 605, I-Beam Front Susp. on 7013 - Spare Wheel & Tire in Rear Compartment - Hydraulic Brakes, Dual W/S Wiper. Front door hinged at center pillar.

Standard Catalog of ® Pontiac, 2nd Edition

YEAR	MAKE	MODEL	NAME	WHEELBASE	CAR SERIAL NUMBERS	STARTED PRODUCTION	FINISHED PRODUCTION	CARS BUILT	TOTAL BUILT
1935	Pont. 6	701B	Master 6	112"	P6AB-1001 to 46572	1-2-35	7-31-35	49,302	129,463
1935	Pont. 8	605	Deluxe 8	116-5/8"	P8AA-1001 to 42561	11-30-34	7-31-35	44,134	
1936	Pont. 6	36-26A	Deluxe 6	112"	P6BA-1001 to 41352	9-16-35	8-4-36	44,040	176,270
			I-Beam Front Susp.						
1936	Pont. 6	36-26B	Master 6	112"	P6BB-1001 to 91362	9-13-35	8-4-36	93,475	
			Dubonnet Front Susp.						
1936	Pont. 8	36-28	Deluxe 8	116-5/8"	P8BA-1001 to 38371	9-11-35	7-31-36	36,755	
1937	Pont. 6	37-26	Deluxe 6	117"	P6CA-1001 to 154827	9-28-36	8-17-37	179,244	236,189
			SLA Front Susp. - Two Prop. Shafts - Direct Acting Rear Shocks						
1937	Pont. 8	37-28	Deluxe 8	122"	P8CA-1001 to 49442	10-8-36	8-20-37	56,945	97,139
1938	Pont. 6	38-26	Deluxe 6	117"	P6DA-1001 to 60416	9-8-37	7-15-38	77,713	
			SLA Front Susp. - Strg. Column Gearshift Spec. Eqpt.						
1938	Pont. 8	38-28	Deluxe 8	122"	P8DA-1001 to 15729	9-15-37	7-15-38	19,426	144,340
1939	Pont. 6	39-25	Quality 6	114-11/16"	P6EA-1001 to 43679	9-19-38	6-20-39	55,736	
			SLA Front Susp. - Strg. Column Gearshift Standard. Hypoid Axle - No Plain Back Sedans - Body Splash Apron instead of R/S available on 26 & 28. Spare tire upright in rear compartment on all-(Dual Taillamps, Dual Horns, Ashtray, Cigar Lighter are Std. on 28)						
1939	Pont. 6	39-26	Deluxe 6	120-1/4"	P6EB-1001 to 41263	9-8-38	6-20-39	53,830	
1939	Pont. 8	39-28	Deluxe 8	120-1/4"	P8EA-1001 to 27627	9-14-38	6-20-39	34,774	217,001
1940	Pont. 6	40-25	Spec. 6	116-1/2"	P6HA-1001 to 84545	10-9-39	7-3-40	106,892	
			Dual Carb. on 49-29. Built in Radio Speaker Grille in instrument panel. Sealed Beam Head Lamps. Dual Horns & Taillamps on all. Dual Carb. avail. on 49-29. Underseat Heater. Dual Sun Visors, Ashtray.						
1940	Pont. 6	40-26	Deluxe 6	120-1/4"	P6HB-1001 to 44296	8-21-39	7-3-40	58,452	
1940	Pont. 8	40-28	Deluxe 8	120-1/4"	P8HA-1001 to 16817	8-21-39	7-3-40	20,433	
1940	Pont. 8	40-29	Torpedo 8	121-1/2"	P8HB-1001 to 24376	9-15-39	7-3-40	31,224	330,061
1941	Pont. 6	41-24	Custom 6	"C" Body 122"	P6JC-1001 to 6345	8-6-40	7-30-40	8,257	
			Dual Carb. Std. on all 8-Cyl. "B" Series also have super streamliner models. "A" & "C" Models still have hump on deck door. "B" Models are plain back. Built in splash apron between bumper & Chassis - All cars less runningboard except in Opt. on "C" Series built in oil cleaner standard-cigar lighter.						
1941	Pont. 6	41-25	Deluxe 6	"A" Body 118-13/16"	P6JA-1001 to 80460	9-9-40	7-30-41	117,976	
1941	Pont. 6	41-26	Streamliner 6	"B" Body 122"	P6JB-1001 to 62545	8-1-40	7-30-41	82,527	
1941	Pont. 8	41-27	Deluxe 8	"A" Body 118-13/16"	P8JA-1001 to 27215	9-10-40	7-30-41	37,823	
1941	Pont. 8	41-28	Streamliner 8	"B" Body 122"	P8JB-1001 to 52428	8-1-40	7-30-41	66,287	
1941	Pont. 8	41-29	Custom 8	"C" Body 122"	P8JC-1001 to 12572	8-6-40	7-30-41	17,191	83,555
1942	Pont. 6	42-25	Torpedo 6	"A" Body 188-13/16"	P6KA-1001 to 25802	8-25-41	2-2-42	29,886	
			(About same as 1941)"B" Series had Chieftain Model until Dec. 15, 1941, when chrome & stainless were changed to paint on most all parts due to material shortage during World War II. All car production was discontinued in February 1942, for the duration of the war.						
1942	Pont. 6	42-26	Streamliner 6	"B" Body 122"	P6KB-1001 to 11115	8-25-41	2-10-42	*12,742	
1942	Pont. 8	42-27	Torpedo 8	"A" Body 118-13/16"	P8KA-1001 to 13146	8-25-41	2-2-42	14,421	
1942	Pont. 8	42-28	Streamliner 8	"B" Body 122"	P8KB-1001 to 22928	9-25-41	2-2-42	**26,506	

*Includes 2,458 Chieftains

**Includes 11,041 Chieftains

Due to World War II production was not resumed until 1946 model.

*Cars built at B O P Assembly Plants have serial numbers starting with 1001 same as at Pontiac Plant except the letter "P" changes to "C" South Gate, California, "L" Linden, New Jersey, "W" Wilmington, Delaware, "K" Kansas City, Kansas, "A" Doraville, Georgia, "F" Framingham, Massachusetts.

1946 – 1947 ("A" Body / "B" Body)

YEAR	MAKE	MODEL	NAME	WHEEL BASE	CAR SERIAL NUMBER PREFIX #1001 Up	STARTED PRODUCTION	FINISHED PONTIAC	TOTAL BUILT	GRAND TOTAL BUILT
1946	Pont. 6	46-25	Torpedo 6	118-13/16" "A" Body	P6LA-1001 up	6-10-46	12-30-46	26,636	137,640
1946	Pont. 8	46-27	Torpedo 8	118-13/16" "A" Body	P8LA-1001 up	6-10-46	12-30-46	18,273	
1946	Pont. 6	46-26	Streamliner 6	122" "B" Body	P6LB-1001 up	9-13-45	12-30-46	43,430	
1946	Pont. 8	46-28	Streamliner 8	122" "B" Body	P8LB-1001 up	9-13-45	12-30-46	49,301	

First Model after World War II, same general lines as 1942 - Grille redesigned, chrome moldings on "B" fenders.

1947	Pont. 6	47-25	Torpedo 6	118-13/16"	P6MA-1001 up	12-30-46	12-30-46	67,125	230,600
1947	Pont. 8	47-27	Torpedo 8	118-13/16"	P8MA-1001 up	12-19-46	1-9-48	34,815	
1947	Pont. 6	47-26	Streamliner 6	122"	P6MB-1001 up	12-30-46	1-9-48	42,336	
1947	Pont. 8	47-28	Streamliner 8	122"	P8MB-1001 up	12-26-46	1-9-48	86,324	

Same general lines as 1946 - no chrome moldings on fenders - Grille has horizontal bars only.

1948 – 1954

YEAR	MAKE	MODEL	NAME	WHEEL BASE	*CAR SERIAL NUMBER PREFIX #1001 Up SMT	HMT	STARTED PRODUCTION	FINISHED PONTIAC	PROD. PLANT	CARS BUILT SMT	HMT	TOTAL BUILT
1948	Pont. 6	48-25	Torpedo 6	118-13/16"	P6PA	P6PA	12-29-47	12-22-48	13,937	25,325	49,262	245,419
1948	Pont. 6	48-26	Streamliner 6	122	P6PB	P6PB	1-9-48	12-22-48	13,834	23,858	37,742	
1948	Pont. 8	48-27	Torpedo 8	118-13/16"	P8PA	P8PA	1-6-48	12-22-48	11,006	24,294	35,360	
1948	Pont. 8	48-28	Streamliner 8	122	P8PB	P8PB	12-22-47		98,469	29,515	69,654	

"A" Body Same General lines as 1947 - No beads on fenders - Deluxe Models with chrome molding on front fenders introduced - Hydra Matic Trans. - Brown Dinoc Interior.

"B" Body

"A" Body

| 1949 | Pont. 6 | 49-25 | Chieftain and Streamliner | 120 | P6RS | P6RH | 1-12-49 | 11-10-49 | 40,139 | 174,449 | 235,165 | 304,819 |
| 1949 | Pont. 8 | 49-27 | Chieftain and Streamliner | 120 | P8RS | P8RH | 11-10-49 | 11-10-49 | 40,716 | 24,930 | 115,542 | |

"A" Body New Model - Push Button Starter - Rear Fenders part of body - Metal Sta. Wgn. - Air Ride Tires - Body Air Ducts - Direct Acting Front Shocks - Low Water Pump.

"A" Body

| 1950 | Pont. 6 | 50-25 | Chieftain and Streamliner | 120 | P6TS | P6TH | 11-10-49 | 11-17-50 | 90,412 | 263,188 | 330,887 | 446,429 |
| 1950 | Pont. 8 | 50-27 | Chieftain and Streamliner | 120 | P8TS | P8TH | 11-19-49 | 11-17-50 | 67,699 | 10,195 | 53,748 | |

Catalina Body introduced - 8 Cylinder Bore increased - 1949 Body with revisions - Comb. Fuel and Vacuum Pump made Standard on 6 Cylinder - Dash Type Heater added - Carbon Core ignition wires.

| 1951 | Pont. 6 | 51-25 | Chieftain and Streamliner | 120 | P6US | P6UH | 11-27-50 | 11-19-51 | 43,553 | 251,987 | 316,411 | 370,159 |
| 1951 | Pont. 8 | 51-27 | Chieftain | 120 | P8US | P8UH | 11-2-51 | 11-7-52 | 64,424 | 4,227 | 19,809 | |

Same General Lines as 1950 - 6 Cylinder timing chain bumper - Rochester Carburetor - Generator from 35 to 40 amps - Speedo. Driven Gear integral with main shaft on HM Trans. - 7-lb. Radiator Cap - Chrome with clear paint - End of Streamliners May 1951.

| 1952 | Pont. 6 | 52-25 | Chieftain | 120 | P6WS | P6WH | 11-27-50 | 11-19-51 | 15,582 | 218,564 | 271,373 | |
| 1952 | Pont. 8 | 52-27 | Chieftain | 120 | P8WS | P8WH | 11-2-51 | 11-7-52 | 32,962 | 4,507@702 | 38,914 | |

Same General Lines as 1951 - Deluxe Models trimmed in three colors - Dual Range HMT - High Comp. Heads for HMT - one-piece die-cast hood ornament - Piston Pin Lock Rings - Nylon Speedometer Gears.

| 1953 | Pont. 6 | 53-25 | Chieftain | 122 | P6XS | P6XH | 11-17-52 | 11-20-53 | 33,705 | 293,343@17,797 | 379,705 | 418,619 |
| 1953 | Pont. 8 | 53-27 | Chieftain | 122 | P8XS | P8XH | 11-17-52 | 11-20-53 | 68,565 | 3,004 | 22,670 | |

New Model - 6 and 8 Cyl. Dip Stick moved back - 6 Cyl. Fuel Pump moved back - Concentric Gearshifts - Serial # Plates welded - Wraparound back window - one-piece curved W/S - Starter switch integral with Ign. Lock - Power Steering and Autronic Eye Spec. Eqpt.

| 1954 | Pont. 6 | 54-25 | Chieftain | 122 | P6ZS | P6ZH | 11-20-53 | 9-3-54 | 19,666 | | | 287,744 |

Same General Lines as 1953. 124" Wheelbase

(11" extended deck; 28 Model introduced. Nickel Chrome reinstated. Power Brakes and Air Conditioner Special Equipment.

*CAR SERIAL NUMBER PREFIX #1001 Up

YEAR	MAKE	MODEL	NAME	WHEEL BASE	SERIAL SMT	SERIAL HMT	STARTED PRODUCTION	FINISHED PROD. PONTIAC PLANT	CARS BUILT SMT	CARS BUILT HMT	TOTAL BUILT	GRAND TOTAL BUILT
1954	Pont. 8	54-27	Chieftain	122	P8ZS	P8ZH	12-1-53	9-3-54	29,906	120,000	149,986	
	Pont. 8	54-28	Star Chief	124	P8ZC	P8ZA	12-1-53	9-3-54	571	114,517	115,088	
1955	Pont. V-6	55-27	(Chieftain)	122	P755S	P755H	10-4-54	9-16-55	57,730	296,736	354,466	(554,090)
	Pont. V-8	55-28	Star Chief	124	P855S	P855H			1,156	198,468	199,624	
1956	Pont. V-6	56-27	Chieftain	122	P756S	P756H	10-3-55	10-3-56	24,117	160,115	184,232	405,730
	Pont. V-8	56-27	Super Chief	122	P756S	P756H			3,289	90,563	93,872	
	Pont. V-8	56-27	Star Chief Station Wag.	122	P756S	P756H			10	4,032	4,042	
	Pont. V-8	56-28	Star Chief	124	P856S	P856H			440	123,144	123,584	
1957	Pont. V-6	57-27	Chieftain	122	P7575S	P757H	10-17-56	9-13-57	12,267	149,708	162,574	334,041
	Pont. V-8	57-27	Super Chief	122	P757S	P7575H			1,063	(64,692)		
	Pont. V-8	57-27	Star Chief Station Wag.	122	P757S	P757H			4	3,186		
	Pont. V-8	57-27	Star Chief	124	P857S	P857H			309	103,279	103,588	
1958	Pont. V-6	58-25	Chieftain	122	P558S	P558H	10-14-57	7-31-58	210	19,389	19,599	217,303
		58-25	Bonneville	122	P558S	P558H						
		58-27	Chieftain	122	P758S	P758H			6,943	117,742	124,685	
			Star Chief Station Wagon	122	P758S	P758H						
		58-28	Super Chief	124	P858S	P858H			258	72,761	73,019	
		58-28	Star Chief	124	P858S	P858H						
1959	Pont. V-6	59-21	Catalina	122	159P		9-1-58	8-18-59	9,939	221,622	231,561	383,320
	Pont. V-6	59-24	Star Chief	124	459P				333	68,482	68,815	
	Pont. V-8	59-27	Bonneville	122	759P				16	4,657	4,673	
	Pont. V-8	59-28	Bonneville	124	859P				675	77,596	78,271	
1960	Pont. V-6	60-21	Catalina	122	160P		8-31-59	8-12-60	10,831	200,101	210,934	396,716
	Pont. V-8	60-23	Ventura	122	360P				2,301	53,896	56,277	
	Pont. V-8	60-24	Star Chief	124	460P				166	43,525	43,691	
	Pont. V-8	60-27	Bonneville	122	760P				12	5,151	5,163	
	Pont. V-8	60-28	Bonneville	124	860P				1,111	79,540	80,651	

Interspersed notes (in document order):

@ Cars equipped with Powerglide Transmission due to fire at Detroit Transmission Division.

*Prefix shown is for cars built at Pontiac Plat - B O P Assembly Plant cars are the same except the letter "P" is changed to: C - South Gate, California, W - Wilmington Delaware, A- Doraville, Georgia, T- Arlington, Texas, L - Lincoln, New Jersey, K - Kansas City, Kansas, F - Framingham, Massachusetts.

(1955) New Model - V-8 Engine - No Silver Streak on Deck Lid. - No Spring Covers - 12-Volt Electrical System - Wraparound Windshield.

(1956) Same General Lines as 1955 - New C/C HMT, four-door Catalina Sedan introduced on all three Series. Electric W/S Wiper Spec. Eqpt. - Extra Horsepower Engine.

(1957) New Look. Removed Hood Center Grilles - First Fuel Injection - Dual Exhaust Openings in Dumper Spec. Eqpt. - 347 Cu. In. Engine. Last Year for U/S Heater - Last Year for RHD.

(1958) Rubber Harmonic Balancer Weight. 370 Cu. In. Engine. Four Head Lamps & four Taillamps - suspended Brake & Clutch Pedals - Coil Springs Front & Rear - "X" Frame - Recessed Floor - No Fins. Air Suspension - Special Eqpt. Borg Warner SM Trans. Spec. Eqpt. Locking Differential Spec. Eqpt.

(1959) 389 Cu. In. Engine. Flexible Brake Shoes, Acrylic Lacquer All Jobs. V Tailfins, Fuel Filler Door in Rear - Discontinued Air Suspension. Wide Track Wheels. Overlap W/S Wipers. Heater Floor Ducts. Economy Engine. Flex Coupling Steering Cast for Power Steering.

(1960) Ventura Added. Custom 16-1/2" Dia. Strg. Wheel with Hand Grips. Lower Front Floor Tunnel. Wide Track Wheels Continued. Four-Speed SMT Special Order. Perm. Antifreeze Replaced Methanol.

*Prefix shown is for cars built at Pontiac Plant - B O P Assembly Plant cars are the same except the letter "P" is changed. Transmission type not identified after 1958 (S for SMT and H for HMT after the 8).

*CAR SERIAL NUMBER PREFIX #1001 Up

YEAR	MAKE	MODEL	NAME	WHEEL BASE	SMT	HMT	STARTED PRODUCTION	FINISHED PROD. PONTIAC PLANT	CARS BUILT SMT	CARS BUILT HMT	TOTAL BUILT	GRAND TOTAL BUILT
1961	Pont. V-8	61-23	Catalina	119	361P		9-1-60	7-23-61	6,337	107,017	113,354	340,635

Wide Track Tread reduced 1-1/2" - Ventura Series discontinued at end of model - Small tailfins added.

YEAR	MAKE	MODEL	NAME	WHEEL BASE	SMT	HMT	STARTED PRODUCTION	FINISHED PROD. PONTIAC PLANT	CARS BUILT SMT	CARS BUILT HMT	TOTAL BUILT	GRAND TOTAL BUILT
		61-25	Ventura	119	561P				1,940	25,269	27,209	
		61-26	Star Chief	123	661P				130	29,451	29,581	
		61-27	Bonneville (Sta.Wgn.)	119		761P				18	3,305	3,323
		61-28	Bonneville	123	861P				1,480	64,905	66,385	
			PONTIAC TOTAL						9,905	229,947	239,852	
	Tempest 195-(L-4)	61-21	Tempest	112	161P					26,737	72,042	*98,779

New Series - Tempest added 4-Cyl. Eng. Std. & Buick Aluminum V-8 Optional, Body & Frame Integral - Trans. mounted to Differential - Completely new bodies - coordinated with Buick, Oldsmobile & Chevrolet.

YEAR	MAKE	MODEL	NAME	WHEEL BASE	SMT	HMT	STARTED PRODUCTION	FINISHED PROD. PONTIAC PLANT	CARS BUILT SMT	CARS BUILT HMT	TOTAL BUILT	GRAND TOTAL BUILT
	**215 (V-8)		Tempest	112	161P				3	2,001	*2,004	
			TEMPEST TOTAL							26,740	74,043	100,783

** Aluminum Engine made by Buick
* Includes K.D. Export 480 SMT & 240 Automatic.

YEAR	MAKE	MODEL	NAME	WHEEL BASE	SERIAL NUMBER	STARTED PRODUCTION	FINISHED PROD. PONTIAC PLANT	CARS BUILT SMT	CARS BUILT AUTO.	TOTAL BUILT	GRAND TOTAL BUILT
1962	Pont. V-8	62-23	Catalina	120	362P	8-15-61	8-10-62	13,104	191,550	204,654	521,933

Grand Prix Series added with Bucket Seats Std. & Special Decor treatment.

YEAR	MAKE	MODEL	NAME	WHEEL BASE	SERIAL NUMBER	STARTED PRODUCTION	FINISHED PROD. PONTIAC PLANT	CARS BUILT SMT	CARS BUILT AUTO.	TOTAL BUILT	GRAND TOTAL BUILT
		62-26	Star Chief	123	662P			196	41,446	41,642	
		62-27	Bonneville (Sta.Wgn.)	120	762P			35	4,492	4,527	
		62-28	Bonneville	123	862P			1,874	95,848	97,722	
		62-29	Grand Prix	120	962P			3,639	26,556	30,195	
			PONTIAC TOTAL					18,848	359,892	378,740	
	195-(L4)	62-21	Tempest	112	162P			28,867	112,668	141,335	

LeMans Custom Option added. 4-Cyl Engine standard. 8-Cyl. Alum. Engine (Buick) Optional.

YEAR	MAKE	MODEL	NAME	WHEEL BASE	SERIAL NUMBER	STARTED PRODUCTION	FINISHED PROD. PONTIAC PLANT	CARS BUILT SMT	CARS BUILT AUTO.	TOTAL BUILT	GRAND TOTAL BUILT
	**215 (V-8)	62-21	Tempest	112	162P			86	1,572	1,658	
			TEMPEST TOTAL					28,953	114,240	***143,193	

** Aluminum Engine made by Buick.
*** Includes K.D. Export 48-L4 Automatic, SMT, 72-V-8 Automatic.

YEAR	MAKE	MODEL	NAME	WHEEL BASE	SERIAL NUMBER	STARTED PRODUCTION	FINISHED PROD. PONTIAC PLANT	CARS BUILT SMT	CARS BUILT AUTO.	TOTAL BUILT	GRAND TOTAL BUILT
1963	Pont. V-8	63-23	Catalina (Exc. sta. wag.)	120	361P	9-4-62	8-4-63	16,811	217,738	234,549	590,071

Wide Track increased from 61.1 to 64 - Self adjusting Brakes. Two year Coolant Option. Generator changed to Alternator.

YEAR	MAKE	MODEL	NAME	WHEEL BASE	SERIAL NUMBER	STARTED PRODUCTION	FINISHED PROD. PONTIAC PLANT	CARS BUILT SMT	CARS BUILT AUTO.	TOTAL BUILT	GRAND TOTAL BUILT
			Catalina Sta.Wgn.	119							
		63-26	Star Chief	123	661P			175	40,582	40,757	
		63-28	Bonneville	123	861P			1,819	108,497	*110,316	
		63-29	Grand Prix	120	961P			5,157	67,802	72,959	
			PONTIAC TOTAL					23,962	434,619	458,581	

YEAR	MAKE	MODEL	NAME	WHEEL BASE	SERIAL NUMBER	STARTED PRODUCTION	FINISHED PROD. PONTIAC PLANT	CARS BUILT SMT	CARS BUILT AUTO.	TOTAL BUILT	GRAND TOTAL BUILT
	Tempest	63-21	Tempest	112	161T			16,657	53,174	69,831	

Power Brakes added. 326 V-8 Engine introduced. 4-Cyl Engine Std. last year with Trans. Axle.

		63-22	LeMans	112	261T			18,034	43,625	61,659	
								34,691	96,799	*131,490	
							TEMPEST TOTAL				

* 5,156 were Station Wagons (119" Wheelbase).

** 195-(L4) Engine Standard for 81,280 cars.

326 (V-8) Engine Option for 50,210 cars.

| 1964 | Pont. V-8 | 64-23 | Catalina | 120 | 834P | 9-3-63 | 8-2-64 | 15,194 | 242,574 | 257,768 | 715,261 |

Major Face Lift

			(Exc. sta. wag.)								
			Catalina Sta. Wgn.	119							
		64-26	Star Chief	123	864P			132	37,521	37,653	
		64-28	Bonneville	123	884P			1,470	113,590	115,060	
			Bonneville Sta.Wgn.	119				42	5,802	5,844	
		64-29	Grand Prix	120	894P			3,124	60,686	63,810	
							PONTIAC TOTAL	19,962	460,173	480,135	
	Tempest	64-20	Tempest	115	04T			15,029	32,997	48,026	

Completely new (Still coordinated with Buick, Chevrolet & Oldsmobile.) - Frame separate with conventional rear axle & suspension & trans. Chevy-type 6-Cyl. engine standard exc. W62 GTO Option has 389 (Pont.) engine standard.

		64-21	Custom	115	14T			11,663	62,801	*74,464	
		64-22	LeMans	115	24T			43,313	69,323	112,636	
							TEMPEST TOTAL	70,005	165,121	*235,126	

* Includes 480 CKD Units for 64-21.

** Engine Breakdown for Tempest - 215 (6-Cyl) 98,778
326 (V-8) 103,898
389 (V-8 GTO) 32,450
Tempest Engine Total 235,126

* Digit 6 or 8 precedes Car Serial Number to denote 6 or 8 cylinder (8 cylinder is an RPO).

****VEHICLE

1965	Pont. V-8	65-52	Catalina	121	252	8-24-65	8-19-65	14,817	256,241	*271,058	802,000
			Catalina Sta. Wgn.	121							
		65-56	Star Chief	124	256			97	31,218	31,315	
		65-62	Bonneville	124	262			1,449	133,214	134,663	
			Bonneville Sta.Wgn.	121							
		65-66	Grand Prix	121	266			1,973	55,908	57,881	
							PONTIAC TOTAL	18,336	476,581	494,917	

Pontiac wheelbase increased 1" except Sta.Wgn. up 2". Articulated overlap W/S Wipers standard.

| | Tempest | 65-33 | Standard | 115 | 233 | | | 9,255 | 30,270 | 39,525 | |

* Includes 11,521 WS1 (2 + 2) Option - 5,316 Manual & 6,205 Automatic.

Tempest Face Lift with vertical head lamps added. Two-door HT Cpe. & Four-door Sedan added.

		65-35	Custom	115	235			10,630	74,023	84,653	
		65-37	LeMans	115	237			75,756	107,149	**182,905	
							TEMPEST TOTAL	95,641	211,442	307,083	

** Includes W62 GTO Option - 56,378 Manual & 18,974 Automatic = 75,342.

YEAR	MAKE	MODEL	NAME	WHEEL BASE	SERIAL NUMBER	STARTED PRODUCTION	FINISHED PROD. PONTIAC PLANT	CARS BUILT SMT	CARS BUILT AUTO.	TOTAL BUILT	GRAND TOTAL BUILT
1966	Pontiac	66-52	Catalina	121	252	9-13-65	8-3-66	5,003	242,924	247,927	831,331

768 KD Export, included in totals, (35 Series = 648, 37 Series = 120)

Pontiac has full plastic floating grille. An industry first. Sta.Wgn. with Wood Grain appearance to side added to Executive. Conv. added to Grand Prix.

YEAR	MAKE	MODEL	NAME	WHEEL BASE	SERIAL NUMBER	STARTED PRODUCTION	FINISHED PROD. PONTIAC PLANT	SMT	AUTO.	TOTAL BUILT	GRAND TOTAL BUILT
			Catalina Sta.Wgn.	119							
		66-54	2 + 2	121	254			2,208	4,175	6,383	
		66-56	Star Chief Executive	124	256			134	45,078	45,212	
		66-62	Bonneville	124	262			729	135,225	135,954	
		66-66	Grand Prix	121	266			917	35,840	36,757	
			PONTIAC TOTAL					8,991	463,242	472,233	
	Tempest	66-33	Standard	115	233			10,610	33,143	43,753	

Tempest rear tread up 1" to 59". Face lift. Wood appearance on side of Station Wagon added as a body style.

YEAR	MAKE	MODEL	NAME	WHEEL BASE	SERIAL NUMBER	STARTED PRODUCTION	FINISHED PROD. PONTIAC PLANT	SMT	AUTO.	TOTAL BUILT	GRAND TOTAL BUILT
		66-35	Custom	115	235			13,566	83,093	*96,659	
		66-37	LeMans	115	237			22,862	98,878	*121,740	
		66-42	GTO	115	242			61,279	35,667	96,946	
			TEMPEST TOTAL 108,317	250,781				359,098			

* Includes 624 KD Export (35 Series 240, 37 Series 384).

** Body Style Code # and year added to VIN for complete identification.

YEAR	MAKE	MODEL	NAME	WHEEL BASE	SERIAL NUMBER	STARTED PRODUCTION	FINISHED PROD. PONTIAC PLANT	SMT	AUTO.	TOTAL BUILT	GRAND TOTAL BUILT
1967	Pontiac V-8	67-52	Catalina	121	252	8-29-66	7-30-67	3,653	207,752	211,405	817,826

Pontiac first in 1967. Recessed Park W/S Wiper Blades. Star Chief renamed "Executive". Wood Grained Sta. Wgns. added. Grand Prix has concealed head lamps. 389 & 421 Cu. In. Engines increased to 400 & 428 Cu. In. Cornering Lamps introduced.

YEAR	MAKE	MODEL	NAME	WHEEL BASE	SERIAL NUMBER	STARTED PRODUCTION	FINISHED PROD. PONTIAC PLANT	SMT	AUTO.	TOTAL BUILT	GRAND TOTAL BUILT
		67-56	Catalina Sta. Wgn.	121	423			8,922	29,345	35,491	
		67-6	Executive	124	256			84	35,407	35,491	
		67-66	2Bonneville	124	262			278	96,430	96,708	
		67-66	Grand Prix	121	266			760	42,221	42,981	
		67-56	Executive Sta.Wgn.	121	256			38	11,458	11,496	
		67-56	Bonneville Sta.Wgn.	121	262			29	6,742	6,771	
			PONTIAC TOTAL					5,265	428,932	434,197	
	Tempest	67-33	Standard	115	233			7,154	27,455	34,609	

New Safari Wagon with Wood Grain Exterior. GT 400 Engine on GTO. New styling for improved appearance. New Options include Capacitor Discharge System & Cruise Control located in Turn Signal Lever.

YEAR	MAKE	MODEL	NAME	WHEEL BASE	SERIAL NUMBER	STARTED PRODUCTION	FINISHED PROD. PONTIAC PLANT	SMT	AUTO.	TOTAL BUILT	GRAND TOTAL BUILT
		67-35	Custom	115	235			8,302	67,023	75,325	
		67-37	LeMans	115	237			14,770	90,132	104,902	
		67-39	Safari	115	239			129	4,382	4,511	
		67-42	GTO	115	242			39,128	42,594	81,722	
			TEMPEST TOTAL					69,483	231,586	301,069	
	Firebird	67-23	Std. 6 Cyl.	108	223			5,258	5,597	10,855	

New Series, 6 Cyl. Standard. 8 Cylinder & Deluxe models merchandised as an R.P.O.

YEAR	MAKE	MODEL	NAME	WHEEL BASE	SERIAL NUMBER	STARTED PRODUCTION	FINISHED PROD. PONTIAC PLANT	SMT	AUTO.	TOTAL BUILT	GRAND TOTAL BUILT
		67-24	Std.8 Cyl.	108	223			8,224	15,301	23,525	
		67-25	Dlx.6 Cyl.	108	223			2,963	3,846	6,809	
		67-26	Dlx.8 Cyl.	108	113			11,526	29,845	41,371	
			FIREBIRD TOTAL				**8-5-68	27,971	54,589	82,560	
1968	Pontiac V-8	68-52	Catalina	121	252	**8-21-67		2,257	238,714	240,971	

First year for MVSS. Energy Absorbing Steering Column and Inst. Panel, All Series. Electric Side Marker Lamp. Uniform Shift Quadrant (A.T.) Anti-Theft Features - Ignition Key Buzzer Reminder - Visible V.I. Plate. Concealed Head Lamps Std. on G.P.

1968 Pontiac / Tempest

YEAR	MAKE	MODEL	NAME	WHEEL BASE	SERIAL NUMBER	STARTED PRODUCTION	FINISHED PROD. PONTIAC PLANT	CARS BUILT		TOTAL BUILT	GRAND TOTAL BUILT
								SMT	HMT		
			Catalina Sta.Wgn.	121	289			34,922	35,211		
		68-56	Executive	124	256			47	32,550	32,597	
		68-62	Bonneville	124	262			208	97,797	98,005	
		68-66	Grand Prix	121	266			306	31,405	31,711	
		68-56	Executive Sta.Wgn.	121	256			23	12,015	12,038	
		68-62	Bonneville Sta.Wgn.	121	262			9	6,917	6,926	
			PONTIAC TOTAL					3,139	454,320	457,459	
	Tempest	68-33	Standard	*	233			5,876	25,705	31,581	

Concealed W/S Wipers added on Tempest. Concealed Head Lamp Opt. on GTO. Many added safety features. GTO Industry First, Endura Bumper.

YEAR	MAKE	MODEL	NAME	WHEEL BASE	SERIAL NUMBER	STARTED PRODUCTION	FINISHED PROD. PONTIAC PLANT	CARS BUILT		TOTAL BUILT	GRAND TOTAL BUILT
								SMT	HMT		
		68-35	Custom	*	235			6,141	80,289	86,430	
		68-37	LeMans	*	237			12,223	124,074	136,297	
		68-39	Safari	*	239			122	4,292	4,414	
		68-42	GTO	112	242			36,299	51,385	87,684	
			TEMPEST TOTAL					60,661	285,745	346,406	

1968 Firebird

YEAR	MAKE	MODEL	NAME	WHEEL BASE	SERIAL NUMBER	STARTED PRODUCTION	FINISHED PROD. PONTIAC PLANT	CARS BUILT		TOTAL BUILT	GRAND TOTAL BUILT
								SMT	HMT		
	Firebird	68-23	Std. 6 Cyl.	108	223			7,528	8,441	15,969	

Front door vent windows eliminated. New Mon-Jet Carb. Auto. Hood adjustment on closing. New Upper Level Ventilation.

YEAR	MAKE	MODEL	NAME	WHEEL BASE	SERIAL NUMBER	STARTED PRODUCTION	FINISHED PROD. PONTIAC PLANT	CARS BUILT		TOTAL BUILT	GRAND TOTAL BUILT
								SMT	HMT		
		68-24	Std. 8 Cyl.	108	224			16,632	39,250	55,882	
		68-25	Dlx.6 Cyl.	108	225			7,534	25,202	32,736	
			FIREBIRD TOTAL					32,910	74,202	107,112	910,977

* Two-door Coupes Wheelbase 112", Four-door Sedans & Station Wagons 116".

** Assembly Plants (Plant #8 at Pontiac - Started 8-22-67 - Finished 7-26-68)

Percent Pontiac Series Manual Trans. 0.686

Percent Tempest Series Manual Trans. 17.51

Percent Firebird Series Manual Trans. 30.72

1969 Pontiac / Tempest

YEAR	MAKE	MODEL	NAME	WHEEL BASE	SERIAL NUMBER	STARTED PRODUCTION	FINISHED PROD. PONTIAC PLANT	CARS BUILT		TOTAL BUILT	GRAND TOTAL BUILT
								MANUAL	AUTO.		
1969	Pontiac V-8	69-52	Catalina	121	252	8-26-68	7-16-69	837	212,014	212,851	

Head Restraints Standard on all Series - Split Front Bumper with Endura Center Section - Column Mounted Ignition Lock - Upper Level Ventilation - Dual Hinged Tailgate.

YEAR	MAKE	MODEL	NAME	WHEEL BASE	SERIAL NUMBER	STARTED PRODUCTION	FINISHED PROD. PONTIAC PLANT	CARS BUILT		TOTAL BUILT	GRAND TOTAL BUILT
								MANUAL	AUTO.		
			Catalina Sta.Wgn.	121	170			33,575	33,745		
		69-56	Executive	124	256			25	25,820	25,845	
		69-62	Bonneville	124	262			44	89,290	89,334	
		69-56	Executive Sta.Wgn.	121	256			14	13,202	13,216	
		69-62	Bonneville Sta.Wgn.	121	262			7	7,421	7,428	
			PONTIAC TOTAL					1,097	381,322	382,419	
	Tempest	69-33	Standard	*	233			4,450	22,472	26,922	
		69-35	Custom	*	235			4,045	80,545	84,590	
		69-37	LeMans	*	237			6,303	93,698	100,001	
		69-39	Safari	*	239			86	4,029	4,115	
		69-42	GTO	112	242			31,433	40,854	72,287	
		69-76	Grand Prix	118	276			1,014	111,472	112,486	

GRAND TOTAL

Vent Windows removed on Coupes and Conv. - Dual Hinged Tailgate.

Grand Prix - Industry First, W/S Imbedded Radio Antenna - Wheelbase changed from 121" to 118" to give a personal car look - Recessed inside Door Releases a General Motors exclusive.

YEAR	MAKE	MODEL	NAME	WHEEL BASE	SERIAL NUMBER	STARTED PRODUCTION	FINISHED PROD. PONTIAC PLANT	CARS BUILT MANUAL	CARS BUILT AUTO.	TOTAL BUILT	GRAND TOTAL BUILT
	Firebird	69-23	Standard	108	223						870,528
							TEMPEST TOTAL	47,331	353,070	400,401	
							FIREBIRD TOTAL	20,840	66,868	87,708	
							GRAND TOTAL				

Merchandised as Firebird, Firebird Sprint, Firebird 350, and Firebird 400.

* Two-door Coupes Wheelbase 112", Four-door Sedans & Station Wagons 116".

Percent Pontiac Series Manual Trans. 0.286
Percent Tempest Series Manual Trans. 11.820
Percent Firebird Series Manual Trans. 23.760

YEAR	MAKE	MODEL	NAME	WHEEL BASE	SERIAL NUMBER	STARTED PRODUCTION	FINISHED PROD. PONTIAC PLANT	CARS BUILT MANUAL	CARS BUILT AUTO.	TOTAL BUILT	GRAND TOTAL BUILT
1970	Pontiac V-8	70-52	Catalina	121	252	8-11-69	7-16-70	579	193,407	193,986	

W/S imbedded antenna added to all series as standard. Fiberglass Belted Tires Standard on all lines. Headlamp Delay, Rotary I.P. Glovebox Lock on all lines.

MODEL	NAME	WHEEL BASE	SERIAL NUMBER	MANUAL	AUTO.	TOTAL BUILT
	Catalina Sta.Wgn.	121	113	29,281	29,394	
70-56	Executive	124	256	6	21,930	21,936
70-62	Bonneville	124	262	28	75,320	75,348
70-56	Executive Sta.Wgn.	121	256	8	10,482	10,490
70-62	Bonneville Sta.Wgn.	121	262	6	7,027	7,033
	PONTIAC TOTAL			740	337,447	338,187

MODEL	NAME	WHEEL BASE	SERIAL NUMBER	MANUAL	AUTO.	TOTAL BUILT
Tempest 70-33	Standard	*	233	5,148	36,899	42,047

Side Markers with Reflectors added to all lines as standard. Electrically Operated Power Door Locks. Silent Rear Window Defroster. Body Colored O/S Rear View Mirror.

MODEL	NAME	WHEEL BASE	SERIAL NUMBER	MANUAL	AUTO.	TOTAL BUILT
70-35	Custom	*	235	2,315	81,937	84,252
70-37	LeMans	*	237	3,413	68,766	72,179
70-42	GTO	112	242	16,033	24,116	40,149
70-76	Grand Prix	118	276	500	65,250	65,750
	TEMPEST TOTAL			27,409	276,968	304,377

MODEL	NAME	WHEEL BASE	SERIAL NUMBER	MANUAL	AUTO.	TOTAL BUILT
Firebird 70-23	Firebird	108	223	2,899	15,975	18,874

Flush Design O/S Door Handles and "Lock and Slam" Type Door Locks added standard. 250 Engine made standard. Merchandised as Models but designed as 223 with Optional Engines.

MODEL	NAME	WHEEL BASE	SERIAL NUMBER	MANUAL	AUTO.	TOTAL BUILT
70-24	Esprit	108	224	2,104	16,857	18,961
70-26	Formula	108	226	2,777	4,931	7,708
70-28	Trans Am	108	228	1,828	1,368	3,196
	FIREBIRD TOTAL			9,608	39,131	48,739
	GRAND TOTAL					691,303

* Two-door coupes Wheelbase 112", four-door Sedans & Station Wagons 116".

Percent Pontiac Series Manual Trans. 0.218
Percent Tempest Series Manual Trans. 9.005
Percent Firebird Series Manual Trans. 19.713

YEAR	MAKE	MODEL	NAME	WHEEL BASE	SERIAL NUMBER	STARTED PRODUCTION	FINISHED PROD. PONTIAC PLANT	CARS BUILT MANUAL	CARS BUILT AUTO.	TOTAL BUILT	GRAND TOTAL BUILT
1971	Pontiac	71-52	Catalina	124	252	8-10-70	7-20-71	** 144	129,839	129,983	

Ventura Option replaced by the Catalina Brougham. The Executive Series dropped. Bonneville offered at a new lower price and the Convertible dropped. Grand Ville Series added in three body styles, Catalina & Bonneville Station Wagons now known as Safari and Grand Safari.

MODEL	NAME	WHEEL BASE	SERIAL NUMBER	MANUAL	AUTO.	TOTAL BUILT	GRAND TOTAL BUILT
71-58	Safari Sta.Wgn.	127		30	19,586	19,616	
	Catalina Brougham		124	258	6	23,886	23,892
71-62	Bonneville	126	252	** 4	31,875	31,879	
	Grand Safari Sta.Wgn.	127	0	9,585	9,585		
71-68	Grand Ville	126	268	2	46,328	46,330	
	PONTIAC TOTAL			** 186	261,099	261,285	

350

Standard Catalog of ® Pontiac, 2nd Edition

YEAR	MAKE	MODEL	NAME	WHEEL BASE	SERIAL NUMBER	STARTED PRODUCTION	FINISHED PROD. PONTIAC PLANT	CARS BUILT MANUAL	AUTO.	TOTAL BUILT	GRAND TOTAL BUILT
	LeMans	71-33	T-37	*	233			5,525	39,461	44,986	40,941

The T-37 carried over from 1970-1/2. LeMans Station Wagon gets dual action tailgate standard. LeMans Sport Wagon dropped. Wood siding available on LeMans Station Wagon.

YEAR	MAKE	MODEL	NAME	WHEEL BASE	SERIAL NUMBER	STARTED PRODUCTION	FINISHED PROD. PONTIAC PLANT	CARS BUILT MANUAL	AUTO.	TOTAL BUILT	GRAND TOTAL BUILT
		71-35	LeMans	*	235			1,231	67,948	69,179	
		71-37	LeMans Sport	*	*			237	1,229	39,712	
		71-42	GTO	112	242			2,587	7,945	10,532	
							LEMANS TOTAL	10,688	213,274	223,962	
	Firebird	71-23	Firebird	108	223			2,778	20,244	23,022	

Introduced as a 1970-1/2 carry-over with minor changes. Seat construction revised. Front Fender Extractors added.

YEAR	MAKE	MODEL	NAME	WHEEL BASE	SERIAL NUMBER	STARTED PRODUCTION	FINISHED PROD. PONTIAC PLANT	CARS BUILT MANUAL	AUTO.	TOTAL BUILT	GRAND TOTAL BUILT
		71-24	Esprit	108	224			947	19,238	20,185	
		71-26	Formula	108	226			1,860	5,942	7,802	
		71-28	Trans Am	108	228	2-1-71		885	1,231	2,116	
							FIREBIRD TOTAL	6,470	46,655	53,125	
	Ventura II	71-21	Ventura II (6 Cyl.)	111	213		7-24-71	6,439	19,365	25,804	

New series introduced in two body styles. Released and built by Chevrolet.

YEAR	MAKE	MODEL	NAME	WHEEL BASE	SERIAL NUMBER	STARTED PRODUCTION	FINISHED PROD. PONTIAC PLANT	CARS BUILT MANUAL	AUTO.	TOTAL BUILT	GRAND TOTAL BUILT
		71-21	Ventura II (8 Cyl.)	214	2,103	20,577	22,680				
							VENTURA II TOTAL	8,542	39,942	48,484	

* Two-door Coupes Wheelbase 112", four-door Sedans & Station Wagons 116".

Percent Pontiac Series Manual Trans. 0.07
Percent LeMans Series Manual Trans. 4.77
Percent Firebird Series M.T. 12.20
Percent Ventura II M.T. 17.61

YEAR	MAKE	MODEL	NAME	WHEEL BASE	SERIAL NUMBER	STARTED PRODUCTION	FINISHED PROD. PONTIAC PLANT	CARS BUILT MANUAL	AUTO.	TOTAL BUILT	GRAND TOTAL BUILT
1972	Pontiac	72-52	Catalina	124	252	8-12-71	6-30-72	173,661	173,661		

New Single Position Hood Latch. Rear Bumpers will withstand 2-1/2 mph impact.

YEAR	MAKE	MODEL	NAME	WHEEL BASE	SERIAL NUMBER	STARTED PRODUCTION	FINISHED PROD. PONTIAC PLANT	CARS BUILT MANUAL	AUTO.	TOTAL BUILT	GRAND TOTAL BUILT
			Safari Sta. Wgn.	127	252			27,306	27,306		
		72-58	Catalina Brougham	124	258			27,316	27,316		
		72-62	Bonneville	126	262			36,084	36,084		
			Grand Safari Sta.Wgn.	127	262			14,541	14,541		
		72-68	Grand Ville	126	126			268	63,417	63,417	
							PONTIAC TOTAL	342,325	342,325		
	LeMans	72-35	LeMans	*	235			9,601	110,698	120,299	

GTO Std. engine changed to 400 four-barrel. T37 Series canceled. Luxury LeMans offered new with distinctive features.

YEAR	MAKE	MODEL	NAME	WHEEL BASE	SERIAL NUMBER	STARTED PRODUCTION	FINISHED PROD. PONTIAC PLANT	CARS BUILT MANUAL	AUTO.	TOTAL BUILT	GRAND TOTAL BUILT
		72-67	LeMans Sport	112	238			317	3,121	3,438	
		72-44	LeMans Luxury	*	244			269	45,987	46,256	
		72-76	Grand Prix	116	276				91,961		
							LEMANS TOTAL	10,187	251,767	261,954	
	Firebird	72-23	Firebird	108	223			1,263	10,738	12,001	

Six month strike at Lordstown Plant curtailed production.

YEAR	MAKE	MODEL	NAME	WHEEL BASE	SERIAL NUMBER	STARTED PRODUCTION	FINISHED PROD. PONTIAC PLANT	CARS BUILT MANUAL	AUTO.	TOTAL BUILT	GRAND TOTAL BUILT
		72-24	Esprit	108	224			504	10,911	11,415	
		72-26	Formula	108	226			1,082	4,167	5,249	
		72-28	Trans Am	108	228			458	828	1,286	
							FIREBIRD TOTAL	3,307	26,644	29,951	
	Ventura II	72-21	Ventura II	111	213		VENTURA TOTAL	6,421	66,366	72,787	
							GRAND TOTAL				** 586,856

YEAR	MAKE	MODEL	NAME	WHEEL BASE	SERIAL NUMBER	STARTED PRODUCTION	FINISHED PROD. PONTIAC PLANT	CARS BUILT MANUAL	AUTO.	TOTAL BUILT	GRAND TOTAL BUILT
											707,017

V-8 offered as option.

* Two-door Coupes Wheelbase 112", Four-door Sedans & Station Wagons 116"

Percent LeMans Series Manual Trans. 3.88
Percent Firebird Series Manual Trans. 11.00
Percent Ventura II Manual Trans. 9.6

GRAND TOTAL

Standard Catalog of ® Pontiac, 2nd Edition

VEHICLE CONDITIONS

Excellent

1. EXCELLENT: Restored to current maxiumum professional standards of quality in every area, or perfect original with components operating and appearing as new. A 95-plus point show car that is not driven.

Fine

2. FINE: Well-restored, or a combination of superior restoration and excellent original. Also, an *extremely* well-maintained original showing very minimal wear.

Very Good

3. VERY GOOD: Completely operable original or "older restoration" showing wear. Also, a good amateur restoration, all presentable and serviceable inside and out. Plus, combinations of well-done restoration and good operable components or a partially restored car with all parts necessary to complete and/or valuable NOS parts.

Good

4. GOOD: A driveable vehicle needing no or only minor work to be functional. Also, a deteriorated restoration or a very poor amateur restoration. All components may need restoration to be "excellent," but the car is mostly useable "as is."

Restorable

5. RESTORABLE: Needs complete restoration of body, chassis and interior. May or may not be running, but isn't weatered, wrecked or stripped to the point of being useful only for parts.

Parts Car

6. PARTS CAR: May or may not be running, but is weathered, wrecked and/or stripped to the point of being useful primarily for parts.

PONTIAC

<table>
<tr><th></th><th>1</th><th>2</th><th>3</th><th>4</th><th>5</th><th>6</th></tr>
<tr><td colspan="7">1926 Model 6-27, 6-cyl.</td></tr>
<tr><td>2d Cpe</td><td>740</td><td>2,220</td><td>3,700</td><td>7,400</td><td>12,950</td><td>18,500</td></tr>
<tr><td>2d Sed</td><td>700</td><td>2,100</td><td>3,500</td><td>7,000</td><td>12,250</td><td>17,500</td></tr>
<tr><td colspan="7">1927 Model 6-27, 6-cyl.</td></tr>
<tr><td>2d Spt Rds</td><td>880</td><td>2,640</td><td>4,400</td><td>8,800</td><td>15,400</td><td>22,000</td></tr>
<tr><td>2d Spt Cabr</td><td>840</td><td>2,520</td><td>4,200</td><td>8,400</td><td>14,700</td><td>21,000</td></tr>
<tr><td>2d Cpe</td><td>680</td><td>2,040</td><td>3,400</td><td>6,800</td><td>11,900</td><td>17,000</td></tr>
<tr><td>2d DeL Cpe</td><td>700</td><td>2,100</td><td>3,500</td><td>7,000</td><td>12,250</td><td>17,500</td></tr>
<tr><td>2d Sed</td><td>640</td><td>1,920</td><td>3,200</td><td>6,400</td><td>11,200</td><td>16,000</td></tr>
<tr><td>4d Lan Sed</td><td>680</td><td>2,040</td><td>3,400</td><td>6,800</td><td>11,900</td><td>17,000</td></tr>
<tr><td colspan="7">1928 Model 6-28, 6-cyl.</td></tr>
<tr><td>2d Rds</td><td>880</td><td>2,640</td><td>4,400</td><td>8,800</td><td>15,400</td><td>22,000</td></tr>
<tr><td>2d Cabr</td><td>840</td><td>2,520</td><td>4,200</td><td>8,400</td><td>14,700</td><td>21,000</td></tr>
<tr><td>4d Phae</td><td>840</td><td>2,520</td><td>4,200</td><td>8,400</td><td>14,700</td><td>21,000</td></tr>
<tr><td>2d Sed</td><td>600</td><td>1,800</td><td>3,000</td><td>6,000</td><td>10,500</td><td>15,000</td></tr>
<tr><td>4d Sed</td><td>580</td><td>1,740</td><td>2,900</td><td>5,800</td><td>10,150</td><td>14,500</td></tr>
<tr><td>4d Trs</td><td>620</td><td>1,860</td><td>3,100</td><td>6,200</td><td>10,850</td><td>15,500</td></tr>
<tr><td>2d Cpe</td><td>660</td><td>1,980</td><td>3,300</td><td>6,600</td><td>11,550</td><td>16,500</td></tr>
<tr><td>2d Spt Cpe</td><td>700</td><td>2,100</td><td>3,500</td><td>7,000</td><td>12,250</td><td>17,500</td></tr>
<tr><td>4d Lan Sed</td><td>720</td><td>2,160</td><td>3,600</td><td>7,200</td><td>12,600</td><td>18,000</td></tr>
<tr><td colspan="7">1929 Model 6-29A, 6-cyl.</td></tr>
<tr><td>2d Rds</td><td>1,000</td><td>3,000</td><td>5,000</td><td>10,000</td><td>17,500</td><td>25,000</td></tr>
<tr><td>4d Phae</td><td>980</td><td>2,940</td><td>4,900</td><td>9,800</td><td>17,150</td><td>24,500</td></tr>
<tr><td>2d Conv</td><td>640</td><td>1,920</td><td>3,200</td><td>6,400</td><td>11,200</td><td>16,000</td></tr>
<tr><td>2d Cpe</td><td>660</td><td>1,980</td><td>3,300</td><td>6,600</td><td>11,550</td><td>16,500</td></tr>
<tr><td>2d Sed</td><td>600</td><td>1,800</td><td>3,000</td><td>6,000</td><td>10,500</td><td>15,000</td></tr>
<tr><td>4d Sed</td><td>600</td><td>1,800</td><td>3,000</td><td>6,000</td><td>10,500</td><td>15,000</td></tr>
<tr><td>4d Spt Lan Sed</td><td>620</td><td>1,860</td><td>3,100</td><td>6,200</td><td>10,850</td><td>15,500</td></tr>
</table>

NOTE: Add 5 percent for horizontal louvers on early year cars.

<table>
<tr><td colspan="7">1930 Model 6-30B, 6-cyl.</td></tr>
<tr><td>2d Spt Rds</td><td>960</td><td>2,880</td><td>4,800</td><td>9,600</td><td>16,800</td><td>24,000</td></tr>
<tr><td>4d Phae</td><td>940</td><td>2,820</td><td>4,700</td><td>9,400</td><td>16,450</td><td>23,500</td></tr>
<tr><td>2d Cpe</td><td>600</td><td>1,800</td><td>3,000</td><td>6,000</td><td>10,500</td><td>15,000</td></tr>
<tr><td>2d Spt Cpe</td><td>620</td><td>1,860</td><td>3,100</td><td>6,200</td><td>10,850</td><td>15,500</td></tr>
<tr><td>2d Sed</td><td>560</td><td>1,680</td><td>2,800</td><td>5,600</td><td>9,800</td><td>14,000</td></tr>
<tr><td>4d Sed</td><td>560</td><td>1,680</td><td>2,800</td><td>5,600</td><td>9,800</td><td>14,000</td></tr>
<tr><td>4d Cus Sed</td><td>580</td><td>1,740</td><td>2,900</td><td>5,800</td><td>10,150</td><td>14,500</td></tr>
<tr><td colspan="7">1931 Model 401, 6-cyl.</td></tr>
<tr><td>2d Conv</td><td>1,000</td><td>3,000</td><td>5,000</td><td>10,000</td><td>17,500</td><td>25,000</td></tr>
<tr><td>2P Cpe</td><td>700</td><td>2,100</td><td>3,500</td><td>7,000</td><td>12,250</td><td>17,500</td></tr>
<tr><td>2d Spt Cpe</td><td>720</td><td>2,160</td><td>3,600</td><td>7,200</td><td>12,600</td><td>18,000</td></tr>
<tr><td>2d Sed</td><td>608</td><td>1,824</td><td>3,040</td><td>6,080</td><td>10,640</td><td>15,200</td></tr>
<tr><td>4d Sed</td><td>620</td><td>1,860</td><td>3,100</td><td>6,200</td><td>10,850</td><td>15,500</td></tr>
<tr><td>4d Cus Sed</td><td>640</td><td>1,920</td><td>3,200</td><td>6,400</td><td>11,200</td><td>16,000</td></tr>
<tr><td colspan="7">1932 Model 402, 6-cyl.</td></tr>
<tr><td>2d Conv</td><td>1,160</td><td>3,480</td><td>5,800</td><td>11,600</td><td>20,300</td><td>29,000</td></tr>
<tr><td>2d Cpe</td><td>740</td><td>2,220</td><td>3,700</td><td>7,400</td><td>12,950</td><td>18,500</td></tr>
<tr><td>2d RS Cpe</td><td>760</td><td>2,280</td><td>3,800</td><td>7,600</td><td>13,300</td><td>19,000</td></tr>
<tr><td>2d Sed</td><td>620</td><td>1,860</td><td>3,100</td><td>6,200</td><td>10,850</td><td>15,500</td></tr>
<tr><td>4d Cus Sed</td><td>640</td><td>1,920</td><td>3,200</td><td>6,400</td><td>11,200</td><td>16,000</td></tr>
<tr><td colspan="7">1932 Model 302, V-8</td></tr>
<tr><td>2d Conv</td><td>1,280</td><td>3,840</td><td>6,400</td><td>12,800</td><td>22,400</td><td>32,000</td></tr>
<tr><td>2d Cpe</td><td>820</td><td>2,460</td><td>4,100</td><td>8,200</td><td>14,350</td><td>20,500</td></tr>
<tr><td>2d Spt Cpe</td><td>840</td><td>2,520</td><td>4,200</td><td>8,400</td><td>14,700</td><td>21,000</td></tr>
<tr><td>2d Sed</td><td>660</td><td>1,980</td><td>3,300</td><td>6,600</td><td>11,550</td><td>16,500</td></tr>
<tr><td>4d Sed</td><td>680</td><td>2,040</td><td>3,400</td><td>6,800</td><td>11,900</td><td>17,000</td></tr>
<tr><td>4d Cus Sed</td><td>720</td><td>2,160</td><td>3,600</td><td>7,200</td><td>12,600</td><td>18,000</td></tr>
<tr><td colspan="7">1933 Model 601, 8-cyl.</td></tr>
<tr><td>2d Rds</td><td>1,080</td><td>3,240</td><td>5,400</td><td>10,800</td><td>18,900</td><td>27,000</td></tr>
<tr><td>2d Conv</td><td>1,000</td><td>3,000</td><td>5,000</td><td>10,000</td><td>17,500</td><td>25,000</td></tr>
<tr><td>2d Cpe</td><td>720</td><td>2,160</td><td>3,600</td><td>7,200</td><td>12,600</td><td>18,000</td></tr>
<tr><td>2d Spt Cpe</td><td>760</td><td>2,280</td><td>3,800</td><td>7,600</td><td>13,300</td><td>19,000</td></tr>
<tr><td>2d Sed</td><td>620</td><td>1,860</td><td>3,100</td><td>6,200</td><td>10,850</td><td>15,500</td></tr>
<tr><td>2d Trg Sed</td><td>628</td><td>1,884</td><td>3,140</td><td>6,280</td><td>10,990</td><td>15,700</td></tr>
<tr><td>4d Sed</td><td>640</td><td>1,920</td><td>3,200</td><td>6,400</td><td>11,200</td><td>16,000</td></tr>
<tr><td colspan="7">1934 Model 603, 8-cyl.</td></tr>
<tr><td>2d Conv</td><td>960</td><td>2,880</td><td>4,800</td><td>9,600</td><td>16,800</td><td>24,000</td></tr>
<tr><td>2d Cpe</td><td>760</td><td>2,280</td><td>3,800</td><td>7,600</td><td>13,300</td><td>19,000</td></tr>
<tr><td>2d Spt Cpe</td><td>780</td><td>2,340</td><td>3,900</td><td>7,800</td><td>13,650</td><td>19,500</td></tr>
<tr><td>2d Sed</td><td>580</td><td>1,740</td><td>2,900</td><td>5,800</td><td>10,150</td><td>14,500</td></tr>
<tr><td>2d Trg Sed</td><td>600</td><td>1,800</td><td>3,000</td><td>6,000</td><td>10,500</td><td>15,000</td></tr>
<tr><td>4d Sed</td><td>596</td><td>1,788</td><td>2,980</td><td>5,960</td><td>10,430</td><td>14,900</td></tr>
<tr><td>4d Trg Sed</td><td>600</td><td>1,800</td><td>3,000</td><td>6,000</td><td>10,500</td><td>15,000</td></tr>
<tr><td colspan="7">1935 Master Series 701, 6-cyl.</td></tr>
<tr><td>2d Cpe</td><td>640</td><td>1,920</td><td>3,200</td><td>6,400</td><td>11,200</td><td>16,000</td></tr>
<tr><td>2d Sed</td><td>536</td><td>1,608</td><td>2,680</td><td>5,360</td><td>9,380</td><td>13,400</td></tr>
<tr><td>2d Trg Sed</td><td>540</td><td>1,620</td><td>2,700</td><td>5,400</td><td>9,450</td><td>13,500</td></tr>
<tr><td>4d Sed</td><td>560</td><td>1,680</td><td>2,800</td><td>5,600</td><td>9,800</td><td>14,000</td></tr>
<tr><td>4d Trg Sed</td><td>580</td><td>1,740</td><td>2,900</td><td>5,800</td><td>10,150</td><td>14,500</td></tr>
</table>

<table>
<tr><th></th><th>1</th><th>2</th><th>3</th><th>4</th><th>5</th><th>6</th></tr>
<tr><td colspan="7">1935 DeLuxe Series 701, 6-cyl.</td></tr>
<tr><td>2d Cpe</td><td>660</td><td>1,980</td><td>3,300</td><td>6,600</td><td>11,550</td><td>16,500</td></tr>
<tr><td>2d Spt Cpe</td><td>680</td><td>2,040</td><td>3,400</td><td>6,800</td><td>11,900</td><td>17,000</td></tr>
<tr><td>2d Cabr</td><td>800</td><td>2,400</td><td>4,000</td><td>8,000</td><td>14,000</td><td>20,000</td></tr>
<tr><td>2d Sed</td><td>540</td><td>1,620</td><td>2,700</td><td>5,400</td><td>9,450</td><td>13,500</td></tr>
<tr><td>2d Trg Sed</td><td>544</td><td>1,632</td><td>2,720</td><td>5,440</td><td>9,520</td><td>13,600</td></tr>
<tr><td>4d Sed</td><td>548</td><td>1,644</td><td>2,740</td><td>5,480</td><td>9,590</td><td>13,700</td></tr>
<tr><td>4d Trg Sed</td><td>560</td><td>1,680</td><td>2,800</td><td>5,600</td><td>9,800</td><td>14,000</td></tr>
<tr><td colspan="7">1935 Series 605, 8-cyl.</td></tr>
<tr><td>2d Cpe</td><td>680</td><td>2,040</td><td>3,400</td><td>6,800</td><td>11,900</td><td>17,000</td></tr>
<tr><td>2d Spt Cpe</td><td>700</td><td>2,100</td><td>3,500</td><td>7,000</td><td>12,250</td><td>17,500</td></tr>
<tr><td>2d Cabr</td><td>960</td><td>2,880</td><td>4,800</td><td>9,600</td><td>16,800</td><td>24,000</td></tr>
<tr><td>2d Sed</td><td>544</td><td>1,632</td><td>2,720</td><td>5,440</td><td>9,520</td><td>13,600</td></tr>
<tr><td>2d Trg Sed</td><td>560</td><td>1,680</td><td>2,800</td><td>5,600</td><td>9,800</td><td>14,000</td></tr>
<tr><td>4d Sed</td><td>600</td><td>1,800</td><td>3,000</td><td>6,000</td><td>10,500</td><td>15,000</td></tr>
<tr><td>4d Trg Sed</td><td>620</td><td>1,860</td><td>3,100</td><td>6,200</td><td>10,850</td><td>15,500</td></tr>
<tr><td colspan="7">1936 DeLuxe Series Silver Streak, 6-cyl.</td></tr>
<tr><td>2d Cpe</td><td>700</td><td>2,100</td><td>3,500</td><td>7,000</td><td>12,250</td><td>17,500</td></tr>
<tr><td>2d Spt Cpe</td><td>720</td><td>2,160</td><td>3,600</td><td>7,200</td><td>12,600</td><td>18,000</td></tr>
<tr><td>2d Cabr</td><td>1,000</td><td>3,000</td><td>5,000</td><td>10,000</td><td>17,500</td><td>25,000</td></tr>
<tr><td>2d Sed</td><td>536</td><td>1,608</td><td>2,680</td><td>5,360</td><td>9,380</td><td>13,400</td></tr>
<tr><td>2d Trg Sed</td><td>544</td><td>1,632</td><td>2,720</td><td>5,440</td><td>9,520</td><td>13,600</td></tr>
<tr><td>4d Sed</td><td>548</td><td>1,644</td><td>2,740</td><td>5,480</td><td>9,590</td><td>13,700</td></tr>
<tr><td>4d Trg Sed</td><td>560</td><td>1,680</td><td>2,800</td><td>5,600</td><td>9,800</td><td>14,000</td></tr>
<tr><td colspan="7">1936 DeLuxe Series Silver Streak, 8-cyl.</td></tr>
<tr><td>2d Cpe</td><td>720</td><td>2,160</td><td>3,600</td><td>7,200</td><td>12,600</td><td>18,000</td></tr>
<tr><td>2d Spt Cpe</td><td>740</td><td>2,220</td><td>3,700</td><td>7,400</td><td>12,950</td><td>18,500</td></tr>
<tr><td>2d Cabr</td><td>920</td><td>2,760</td><td>4,600</td><td>9,200</td><td>16,100</td><td>23,000</td></tr>
<tr><td>2d Sed</td><td>560</td><td>1,680</td><td>2,800</td><td>5,600</td><td>9,800</td><td>14,000</td></tr>
<tr><td>2d Trg Sed</td><td>568</td><td>1,704</td><td>2,840</td><td>5,680</td><td>9,940</td><td>14,200</td></tr>
<tr><td>4d Sed</td><td>564</td><td>1,692</td><td>2,820</td><td>5,640</td><td>9,870</td><td>14,100</td></tr>
<tr><td>4d Trg Sed</td><td>572</td><td>1,716</td><td>2,860</td><td>5,720</td><td>10,010</td><td>14,300</td></tr>
<tr><td colspan="7">1937-1938 DeLuxe Model 6DA, 6-cyl.</td></tr>
<tr><td>2d Conv</td><td>1,240</td><td>3,720</td><td>6,200</td><td>12,400</td><td>21,700</td><td>31,000</td></tr>
<tr><td>4d Conv Sed</td><td>1,280</td><td>3,840</td><td>6,400</td><td>12,800</td><td>22,400</td><td>32,000</td></tr>
<tr><td>2d Bus Cpe</td><td>680</td><td>2,040</td><td>3,400</td><td>6,800</td><td>11,900</td><td>17,000</td></tr>
<tr><td>2d Spt Cpe</td><td>720</td><td>2,160</td><td>3,600</td><td>7,200</td><td>12,600</td><td>18,000</td></tr>
<tr><td>2d Sed</td><td>536</td><td>1,608</td><td>2,680</td><td>5,360</td><td>9,380</td><td>13,400</td></tr>
<tr><td>2d Trg Sed</td><td>540</td><td>1,620</td><td>2,700</td><td>5,400</td><td>9,450</td><td>13,500</td></tr>
<tr><td>4d Sed</td><td>560</td><td>1,680</td><td>2,800</td><td>5,600</td><td>9,800</td><td>14,000</td></tr>
<tr><td>4d Trg Sed</td><td>564</td><td>1,692</td><td>2,820</td><td>5,640</td><td>9,870</td><td>14,100</td></tr>
<tr><td>4d Sta Wag</td><td>1,280</td><td>3,840</td><td>6,400</td><td>12,800</td><td>22,400</td><td>32,000</td></tr>
<tr><td colspan="7">1937-1938 DeLuxe Model 8DA, 8-cyl.</td></tr>
<tr><td>2d Conv</td><td>1,320</td><td>3,960</td><td>6,600</td><td>13,200</td><td>23,100</td><td>33,000</td></tr>
<tr><td>4d Conv Sed</td><td>1,360</td><td>4,080</td><td>6,800</td><td>13,600</td><td>23,800</td><td>34,000</td></tr>
<tr><td>2d Bus Cpe</td><td>740</td><td>2,220</td><td>3,700</td><td>7,400</td><td>12,950</td><td>18,500</td></tr>
<tr><td>2d Spt Cpe</td><td>760</td><td>2,280</td><td>3,800</td><td>7,600</td><td>13,300</td><td>19,000</td></tr>
<tr><td>2d Sed</td><td>580</td><td>1,740</td><td>2,900</td><td>5,800</td><td>10,150</td><td>14,500</td></tr>
<tr><td>2d Trg Sed</td><td>584</td><td>1,752</td><td>2,920</td><td>5,840</td><td>10,220</td><td>14,600</td></tr>
<tr><td>4d Sed</td><td>584</td><td>1,752</td><td>2,920</td><td>5,840</td><td>10,220</td><td>14,600</td></tr>
<tr><td>4d Trg Sed</td><td>588</td><td>1,764</td><td>2,940</td><td>5,880</td><td>10,290</td><td>14,700</td></tr>
<tr><td colspan="7">1939 Special Series 25, 6-cyl.</td></tr>
<tr><td>2d Bus Cpe</td><td>680</td><td>2,040</td><td>3,400</td><td>6,800</td><td>11,900</td><td>17,000</td></tr>
<tr><td>2d Spt Cpe</td><td>720</td><td>2,160</td><td>3,600</td><td>7,200</td><td>12,600</td><td>18,000</td></tr>
<tr><td>2d Trg Sed</td><td>600</td><td>1,800</td><td>3,000</td><td>6,000</td><td>10,500</td><td>15,000</td></tr>
<tr><td>4d Trg Sed</td><td>600</td><td>1,800</td><td>3,000</td><td>6,000</td><td>10,500</td><td>15,000</td></tr>
<tr><td>4d Sta Wag</td><td>1,280</td><td>3,840</td><td>6,400</td><td>12,800</td><td>22,400</td><td>32,000</td></tr>
<tr><td colspan="7">1939 DeLuxe Series 26, 6-cyl.</td></tr>
<tr><td>2d Conv</td><td>1,160</td><td>3,480</td><td>5,800</td><td>11,600</td><td>20,300</td><td>29,000</td></tr>
<tr><td>2d Bus Cpe</td><td>700</td><td>2,100</td><td>3,500</td><td>7,000</td><td>12,250</td><td>17,500</td></tr>
<tr><td>2d Spt Cpe</td><td>740</td><td>2,220</td><td>3,700</td><td>7,400</td><td>12,950</td><td>18,500</td></tr>
<tr><td>2d Sed</td><td>600</td><td>1,800</td><td>3,000</td><td>6,000</td><td>10,500</td><td>15,000</td></tr>
<tr><td>4d Sed</td><td>604</td><td>1,812</td><td>3,020</td><td>6,040</td><td>10,570</td><td>15,100</td></tr>
<tr><td colspan="7">1939 DeLuxe Series 28, 8-cyl.</td></tr>
<tr><td>2d Conv</td><td>1,240</td><td>3,720</td><td>6,200</td><td>12,400</td><td>21,700</td><td>31,000</td></tr>
<tr><td>2d Bus Cpe</td><td>720</td><td>2,160</td><td>3,600</td><td>7,200</td><td>12,600</td><td>18,000</td></tr>
<tr><td>2d Spt Cpe</td><td>760</td><td>2,280</td><td>3,800</td><td>7,600</td><td>13,300</td><td>19,000</td></tr>
<tr><td>2d Sed</td><td>620</td><td>1,860</td><td>3,100</td><td>6,200</td><td>10,850</td><td>15,500</td></tr>
<tr><td>4d Trg Sed</td><td>624</td><td>1,872</td><td>3,120</td><td>6,240</td><td>10,920</td><td>15,600</td></tr>
<tr><td colspan="7">1940 Special Series 25, 6-cyl., 117" wb</td></tr>
<tr><td>2d Bus Cpe</td><td>680</td><td>2,040</td><td>3,400</td><td>6,800</td><td>11,900</td><td>17,000</td></tr>
<tr><td>2d Spt Cpe</td><td>720</td><td>2,160</td><td>3,600</td><td>7,200</td><td>12,600</td><td>18,000</td></tr>
<tr><td>2d Sed</td><td>576</td><td>1,728</td><td>2,880</td><td>5,760</td><td>10,080</td><td>14,400</td></tr>
<tr><td>4d Sed</td><td>580</td><td>1,740</td><td>2,900</td><td>5,800</td><td>10,150</td><td>14,500</td></tr>
<tr><td>4d Sta Wag</td><td>1,200</td><td>3,600</td><td>6,000</td><td>12,000</td><td>21,000</td><td>30,000</td></tr>
<tr><td colspan="7">1940 DeLuxe Series 26, 6-cyl., 120" wb</td></tr>
<tr><td>2d Conv</td><td>1,200</td><td>3,600</td><td>6,000</td><td>12,000</td><td>21,000</td><td>30,000</td></tr>
<tr><td>2d Bus Cpe</td><td>700</td><td>2,100</td><td>3,500</td><td>7,000</td><td>12,250</td><td>17,500</td></tr>
<tr><td>2d Spt Cpe</td><td>740</td><td>2,220</td><td>3,700</td><td>7,400</td><td>12,950</td><td>18,500</td></tr>
</table>

	1	2	3	4	5	6
2d Sed	560	1,680	2,800	5,600	9,800	14,000
4d Sed	588	1,764	2,940	5,880	10,290	14,700

1940 DeLuxe Series 28, 8-cyl., 120" wb

	1	2	3	4	5	6
2d Conv	1,240	3,720	6,200	12,400	21,700	31,000
2d Bus Cpe	720	2,160	3,600	7,200	12,600	18,000
2d Spt Cpe	760	2,280	3,800	7,600	13,300	19,000
2d Sed	588	1,764	2,940	5,880	10,290	14,700
4d Sed	592	1,776	2,960	5,920	10,360	14,800

1940 Torpedo Series 29, 8-cyl., 122" wb

	1	2	3	4	5	6
2d Spt Cpe	780	2,340	3,900	7,800	13,650	19,500
4d Sed	700	2,100	3,500	7,000	12,250	17,500

1941 DeLuxe Torpedo, 8-cyl.

	1	2	3	4	5	6
2d Bus Cpe	660	1,980	3,300	6,600	11,550	16,500
2d Spt Cpe	680	2,040	3,400	6,800	11,900	17,000
2d Conv	1,240	3,720	6,200	12,400	21,700	31,000
2d Sed	576	1,728	2,880	5,760	10,080	14,400
4d 4W Sed	584	1,752	2,920	5,840	10,220	14,600
4d 6W Sed	580	1,740	2,900	5,800	10,150	14,500

1941 Streamliner, 8-cyl.

	1	2	3	4	5	6
2d Cpe	700	2,100	3,500	7,000	12,250	17,500
4d Sed	640	1,920	3,200	6,400	11,200	16,000

1941 Super Streamliner, 8-cyl.

	1	2	3	4	5	6
2d Cpe	760	2,280	3,800	7,600	13,300	19,000
4d Sed	700	2,100	3,500	7,000	12,250	17,500

1941 Custom, 8-cyl.

	1	2	3	4	5	6
2d Spt Cpe	840	2,520	4,200	8,400	14,700	21,000
4d Sed	780	2,340	3,900	7,800	13,650	19,500
4d Sta Wag	1,280	3,840	6,400	12,800	22,400	32,000
4d DeL Sta Wag	1,320	3,960	6,600	13,200	23,100	33,000

NOTE: Deduct 10 percent for 6-cyl. models.

1942 Torpedo, 8-cyl.

	1	2	3	4	5	6
2d Conv	1,200	3,600	6,000	12,000	21,000	30,000
2d Bus Cpe	640	1,920	3,200	6,400	11,200	16,000
2d Spt Cpe	660	1,980	3,300	6,600	11,550	16,500
2d 5P Cpe	680	2,040	3,400	6,800	11,900	17,000
2d Sed	580	1,740	2,900	5,800	10,150	14,500
4d Sed	576	1,728	2,880	5,760	10,080	14,400
4d Metro Sed	592	1,776	2,960	5,920	10,360	14,800

1942 Streamliner, 8-cyl.

	1	2	3	4	5	6
2d Cpe	680	2,040	3,400	6,800	11,900	17,000
4d Sed	620	1,860	3,100	6,200	10,850	15,500
4d Sta Wag	1,200	3,600	6,000	12,000	21,000	30,000

1942 Chieftain, 8-cyl.

	1	2	3	4	5	6
2d Cpe	700	2,100	3,500	7,000	12,250	17,500
4d Sed	628	1,884	3,140	6,280	10,990	15,700
4d Sta Wag	1,240	3,720	6,200	12,400	21,700	31,000

NOTE: Deduct 10 percent for 6-cyl. models.

1946 Torpedo, 8-cyl.

	1	2	3	4	5	6
2d Conv	1,160	3,480	5,800	11,600	20,300	29,000
2d Bus Cpe	680	2,040	3,400	6,800	11,900	17,000
2d Spt Cpe	700	2,100	3,500	7,000	12,250	17,500
2d 5P Cpe	720	2,160	3,600	7,200	12,600	18,000
2d Sed	620	1,860	3,100	6,200	10,850	15,500
4d Sed	624	1,872	3,120	6,240	10,920	15,600

1946 Streamliner, 8-cyl.

	1	2	3	4	5	6
5P Cpe	760	2,280	3,800	7,600	13,300	19,000
4d Sed	632	1,896	3,160	6,320	11,060	15,800
4d Sta Wag	1,240	3,720	6,200	12,400	21,700	31,000
4d DeL Sta Wag	1,280	3,840	6,400	12,800	22,400	32,000

NOTE: Deduct 5 percent for 6-cyl. models.

1947 Torpedo, 8-cyl.

	1	2	3	4	5	6
2d Conv	1,200	3,600	6,000	12,000	21,000	30,000
2d DeL Conv	1,220	3,660	6,100	12,200	21,350	30,500
2d Bus Cpe	720	2,160	3,600	7,200	12,600	18,000
2d Spt Cpe	740	2,220	3,700	7,400	12,950	18,500
2d 5P Cpe	740	2,220	3,700	7,400	12,950	18,500
2d Sed	620	1,860	3,100	6,200	10,850	15,500
4d Sed	664	1,992	3,320	6,640	11,620	16,600

1947 Streamliner, 8-cyl.

	1	2	3	4	5	6
2d Cpe	760	2,280	3,800	7,600	13,300	19,000
4d Sed	680	2,040	3,400	6,800	11,900	17,000
4d Sta Wag	1,240	3,720	6,200	12,400	21,700	31,000
4d DeL Sta Wag	1,280	3,840	6,400	12,800	22,400	32,000

NOTE: Deduct 5 percent for 6-cyl. models.

1948 Torpedo, 8-cyl.

	1	2	3	4	5	6
2d Bus Cpe	700	2,100	3,500	7,000	12,250	17,500
2d Spt Cpe	720	2,160	3,600	7,200	12,600	18,000
2d 5P Cpe	740	2,220	3,700	7,400	12,950	18,500
2d Sed	620	1,860	3,100	6,200	10,850	15,500
4d Sed	600	1,800	3,000	6,000	10,500	15,000

1948 DeLuxe Torpedo, 8-cyl.

	1	2	3	4	5	6
2d Conv	1,200	3,600	6,000	12,000	21,000	30,000
2d Spt Cpe	740	2,220	3,700	7,400	12,950	18,500
2d 5P Cpe	760	2,280	3,800	7,600	13,300	19,000
4d Sed	668	2,004	3,340	6,680	11,690	16,700

1948 DeLuxe Streamliner, 8-cyl.

	1	2	3	4	5	6
2d Cpe	760	2,280	3,800	7,600	13,300	19,000
4d Sed	680	2,040	3,400	6,800	11,900	17,000
4d Sta Wag	1,280	3,840	6,400	12,800	22,400	32,000

NOTE: Deduct 5 percent for 6-cyl. models.

1949-1950 Streamliner, 8-cyl.

	1	2	3	4	5	6
2d Cpe Sed	568	1,704	2,840	5,680	9,940	14,200
4d Sed	564	1,692	2,820	5,640	9,870	14,100
4d Sta Wag	620	1,860	3,100	6,200	10,850	15,500
4d Wood Sta Wag ('49 only)	720	2,160	3,600	7,200	12,600	18,000

1949-1950 Streamliner DeLuxe, 8-cyl.

	1	2	3	4	5	6
4d Sed	572	1,716	2,860	5,720	10,010	14,300
2d Cpe Sed	576	1,728	2,880	5,760	10,080	14,400
4d Stl Sta Wag	600	1,800	3,000	6,000	10,500	15,000
4d Woodie (1949 only)	800	2,400	4,000	8,000	14,000	20,000
2d Sed Dely	720	2,160	3,600	7,200	12,600	18,000

1949-1950 Chieftain, 8-cyl.

	1	2	3	4	5	6
4d Sed	576	1,728	2,880	5,760	10,080	14,400
2d Sed	568	1,704	2,840	5,680	9,940	14,200
2d Cpe Sed	584	1,752	2,920	5,840	10,220	14,600
2d Bus Cpe	620	1,860	3,100	6,200	10,850	15,500

1949-1950 Chieftain DeLuxe, 8-cyl.

	1	2	3	4	5	6
4d Sed	580	1,740	2,900	5,800	10,150	14,500
2d Sed	572	1,716	2,860	5,720	10,010	14,300
2d Bus Cpe (1949 only)	650	2,000	3,300	6,600	11,600	16,500
2d HT (1950 only)	780	2,340	3,900	7,800	13,650	19,500
2d Cpe Sed	588	1,764	2,940	5,880	10,290	14,700
2d Sup HT (1950 only)	850	2,500	4,200	8,400	14,700	21,000
2d Conv	1,180	3,540	5,900	11,800	20,650	29,500

NOTE: Deduct 5 percent for 6-cyl. models.

1951-1952 Streamliner, 8-cyl. (1951 only)

	1	2	3	4	5	6
2d Cpe Sed	572	1,716	2,860	5,720	10,010	14,300
4d Sta Wag	620	1,860	3,100	6,200	10,850	15,500

1951-1952 Streamliner DeLuxe, 8-cyl. (1951 only)

	1	2	3	4	5	6
2d Cpe Sed	580	1,740	2,900	5,800	10,150	14,500
4d Sta Wag	640	1,920	3,200	6,400	11,200	16,000
2d Sed Dely	700	2,100	3,500	7,000	12,250	17,500

1951-1952 Chieftain, 8-cyl.

	1	2	3	4	5	6
4d Sed	580	1,740	2,900	5,800	10,150	14,500
2d Sed	572	1,716	2,860	5,720	10,010	14,300
2d Cpe Sed	584	1,752	2,920	5,840	10,220	14,600
2d Bus Cpe	620	1,860	3,100	6,200	10,850	15,500

1951-1952 Chieftain DeLuxe, 8-cyl.

	1	2	3	4	5	6
4d Sed	584	1,752	2,920	5,840	10,220	14,600
2d Sed	580	1,740	2,900	5,800	10,150	14,500
2d Cpe Sed	600	1,800	3,000	6,000	10,500	15,000
2d HT	860	2,580	4,300	8,600	15,050	21,500
2d HT Sup	900	2,700	4,500	9,000	15,750	22,500
2d Conv	1,200	3,600	6,000	12,000	21,000	30,000

NOTE: Deduct 5 percent for 6-cyl. models.

1953 Chieftain, 8-cyl., 122" wb

	1	2	3	4	5	6
4d Sed	584	1,752	2,920	5,840	10,220	14,600
2d Sed	580	1,740	2,900	5,800	10,150	14,500
4d Paint Sta Wag	620	1,860	3,100	6,200	10,850	15,500
4d Woodgrain Sta Wag	650	1,900	3,200	6,400	11,200	16,000
2d Sed Dely	800	2,400	4,000	8,000	14,000	20,000

1953 Chieftain DeLuxe, 8-cyl.

	1	2	3	4	5	6
4d Sed	588	1,764	2,940	5,880	10,290	14,700
2d Sed	584	1,752	2,920	5,840	10,220	14,600
2d HT	840	2,520	4,200	8,400	14,700	21,000
2d Conv	1,160	3,480	5,800	11,600	20,300	29,000
4d Mtl Sta Wag	600	1,800	3,000	6,000	10,500	15,000
4d Sim W Sta Wag	640	1,920	3,200	6,400	11,200	16,000

1953 Custom Catalina, 8-cyl.

	1	2	3	4	5	6
2d HT	860	2,580	4,300	8,600	15,050	21,500

NOTE: Deduct 5 percent for 6-cyl. models.

1954 Chieftain, 8-cyl., 122" wb

	1	2	3	4	5	6
4d Sed	592	1,776	2,960	5,920	10,360	14,800
2d Sed	588	1,764	2,940	5,880	10,290	14,700
4d Sta Wag	640	1,920	3,200	6,400	11,200	16,000

1954 Chieftain DeLuxe, 8-cyl.

	1	2	3	4	5	6
4d Sed	600	1,800	3,000	6,000	10,500	15,000
2d Sed	592	1,776	2,960	5,920	10,360	14,800
2d HT	840	2,520	4,200	8,400	14,700	21,000
4d Sta Wag	660	1,980	3,300	6,600	11,550	16,500

	1	2	3	4	5	6
1954 Custom Catalina, 8-cyl.						
2d HT	920	2,760	4,600	9,200	16,100	23,000
1954 Star Chief DeLuxe, 8-cyl.						
4d Sed	640	1,920	3,200	6,400	11,200	16,000
2d Conv	1,180	3,540	5,900	11,800	20,650	29,500
1954 Star Custom Chief, 8-cyl.						
4d Sed	680	2,040	3,400	6,800	11,900	17,000
1954 Star Chief Custom Catalina						
2d HT	960	2,880	4,800	9,600	16,800	24,000
NOTE: Deduct 5 percent for 6-cyl. models.						
1955 Chieftain 860, V-8						
4d Sed	560	1,680	2,800	5,600	9,800	14,000
2d Sed	564	1,692	2,820	5,640	9,870	14,100
2d Sta Wag	640	1,920	3,200	6,400	11,200	16,000
4d Sta Wag	620	1,860	3,100	6,200	10,850	15,500
1955 Chieftain 870, V-8, 122" wb						
4d Sed	580	1,740	2,900	5,800	10,150	14,500
2d Sed	584	1,752	2,920	5,840	10,220	14,600
2d HT	1,000	3,000	5,000	10,000	17,500	25,000
4d Sta Wag	640	1,920	3,200	6,400	11,200	16,000
1955 Star Chief Custom Safari, 122" wb						
2d Sta Wag	1,000	3,000	5,000	10,000	17,500	25,000
1955 Star Chief, V-8, 124" wb						
4d Sed	620	1,860	3,100	6,200	10,850	15,500
2d Conv	1,440	4,320	7,200	14,400	25,200	36,000
1955 Star Chief Custom, V-8, 124" wb						
4d Sed	660	1,980	3,300	6,600	11,550	16,500
1955 Custom Catalina						
2d HT	1,080	3,240	5,400	10,800	18,900	27,000
1956 Chieftain 860, V-8, 122" wb						
4d Sed	560	1,680	2,800	5,600	9,800	14,000
4d HT	600	1,800	3,000	6,000	10,500	15,000
2d Sed	560	1,680	2,800	5,600	9,800	14,000
2d HT	1,000	3,000	5,000	10,000	17,500	25,000
2d Sta Wag	680	2,040	3,400	6,800	11,900	17,000
4d Sta Wag	660	1,980	3,300	6,600	11,550	16,500
1956 Chieftain 870, V-8, 122" wb						
4d Sed	572	1,716	2,860	5,720	10,010	14,300
4d HT	640	1,920	3,200	6,400	11,200	16,000
2d HT	920	2,760	4,600	9,200	16,100	23,000
4d Sta Wag	1,040	3,120	5,200	10,400	18,200	26,000
1956 Star Chief Custom Safari, V-8, 122" wb						
2d Sta Wag	1,040	3,120	5,200	10,400	18,200	26,000
1956 Star Chief, V-8, 124" wb						
4d Sed	600	1,800	3,000	6,000	10,500	15,000
2d Conv	1,560	4,680	7,800	15,600	27,300	39,000
1956 Star Chief Custom Catalina, V-8, 124" wb						
4d HT	720	2,160	3,600	7,200	12,600	18,000
2d HT	1,160	3,480	5,800	11,600	20,300	29,000
1957 Chieftain, V-8, 122" wb						
4d Sed	560	1,680	2,800	5,600	9,800	14,000
4d HT	600	1,800	3,000	6,000	10,500	15,000
2d Sed	588	1,764	2,940	5,880	10,290	14,700
2d HT	1,040	3,120	5,200	10,400	18,200	26,000
4d Sta Wag	640	1,920	3,200	6,400	11,200	16,000
2d Sta Wag	660	1,980	3,300	6,600	11,550	16,500
1957 Super Chief, V-8, 122" wb						
4d Sed	600	1,800	3,000	6,000	10,500	15,000
4d HT	680	2,040	3,400	6,800	11,900	17,000
2d HT	1,120	3,360	5,600	11,200	19,600	28,000
4d Sta Wag	680	2,040	3,400	6,800	11,900	17,000
1957 Star Chief Custom Safari, V-8, 122" wb						
4d Sta Wag	960	2,880	4,800	9,600	16,800	24,000
2d Sta Wag	1,080	3,240	5,400	10,800	18,900	27,000
1957 Star Chief, V-8, 124" wb						
4d Sed	640	1,920	3,200	6,400	11,200	16,000
2d Conv	1,480	4,440	7,400	14,800	25,900	37,000
2d Bonneville Conv*	2,550	7,700	12,800	25,600	44,800	64,000
1957 Star Chief Custom, V-8, 124" wb						
4d Sed	660	1,980	3,300	6,600	11,550	16,500
4d HT	800	2,400	4,000	8,000	14,000	20,000
2d HT	1,200	3,600	6,000	12,000	21,000	30,000
*Available on one-to-a-dealer basis.						
1958 Chieftain, V-8, 122" wb						
4d Sed	324	972	1,620	3,240	5,670	8,100
4d HT	580	1,740	2,900	5,800	10,150	14,500
2d Sed	520	1,560	2,600	5,200	9,100	13,000
2d HT	760	2,280	3,800	7,600	13,300	19,000
2d Conv	1,240	3,720	6,200	12,400	21,700	31,000
4d 9P Safari	600	1,800	3,000	6,000	10,500	15,000
1958 Super-Chief, V-8, 122" wb						
4d Sed	344	1,032	1,720	3,440	6,020	8,600
4d HT	640	1,920	3,200	6,400	11,200	16,000
2d HT	800	2,400	4,000	8,000	14,000	20,000
1958 Star Chief, V-8, 124" wb						
4d Cus Sed	520	1,560	2,600	5,200	9,100	13,000
4d HT	680	2,040	3,400	6,800	11,900	17,000
2d HT	920	2,760	4,600	9,200	16,100	23,000
4d Cus Safari	720	2,160	3,600	7,200	12,600	18,000
1958 Bonneville, V-8, 122" wb						
2d HT	1,360	4,080	6,800	13,600	23,800	34,000
2d Conv	2,160	6,480	10,800	21,600	37,800	54,000
NOTE: Add 20 percent for fuel-injection Bonneville.						
1959 Catalina, V-8, 122" wb						
4d Sed	320	960	1,600	3,200	5,600	8,000
4d HT	520	1,560	2,600	5,200	9,100	13,000
2d Sed	300	900	1,500	3,000	5,250	7,500
2d HT	720	2,160	3,600	7,200	12,600	18,000
2d Conv	1,040	3,120	5,200	10,400	18,200	26,000
1959 Safari, V-8, 124" wb						
4d 6P Sta Wag	560	1,680	2,800	5,600	9,800	14,000
4d 9P Sta Wag	568	1,704	2,840	5,680	9,940	14,200
1959 Star Chief, V-8, 124" wb						
4d Sed	520	1,560	2,600	5,200	9,100	13,000
4d HT	600	1,800	3,000	6,000	10,500	15,000
2d Sed	540	1,620	2,700	5,400	9,450	13,500
1959 Bonneville, V-8, 124" wb						
4d HT	640	1,920	3,200	6,400	11,200	16,000
2d HT	840	2,520	4,200	8,400	14,700	21,000
2d Conv	1,280	3,840	6,400	12,800	22,400	32,000
1959 Custom Safari, V-8, 122" wb						
4d Sta Wag	660	1,980	3,300	6,600	11,550	16,500
1960 Catalina, V-8, 122" wb						
4d Sed	304	912	1,520	3,040	5,320	7,600
4d HT	520	1,560	2,600	5,200	9,100	13,000
2d Sed	320	960	1,600	3,200	5,600	8,000
2d HT	720	2,160	3,600	7,200	12,600	18,000
2d Conv	1,080	3,240	5,400	10,800	18,900	27,000
1960 Safari, V-8, 122" wb						
4d Sta Wag	600	1,800	3,000	6,000	10,500	15,000
4d 6P Sta Wag	620	1,860	3,100	6,200	10,850	15,500
1960 Ventura, V-8, 122" wb						
4d HT	560	1,680	2,800	5,600	9,800	14,000
2d HT	760	2,280	3,800	7,600	13,300	19,000
1960 Star Chief, V-8, 124" wb						
4d Sed	540	1,620	2,700	5,400	9,450	13,500
4d HT	600	1,800	3,000	6,000	10,500	15,000
2d Sed	560	1,680	2,800	5,600	9,800	14,000
1960 Bonneville, V-8, 124" wb						
4d HT	640	1,920	3,200	6,400	11,200	16,000
2d HT	880	2,640	4,400	8,800	15,400	22,000
2d Conv	1,240	3,720	6,200	12,400	21,700	31,000
1960 Bonneville Safari, V-8, 122" wb						
4d Sta Wag	680	2,040	3,400	6,800	11,900	17,000
1961 Tempest Compact, 4-cyl.						
4d Sed	308	924	1,540	3,080	5,390	7,700
2d Cpe	312	936	1,560	3,120	5,460	7,800
2d Cus Cpe	360	1,080	1,800	3,600	6,300	9,000
4d Safari Wag	360	1,080	1,800	3,600	6,300	9,000
NOTE: Add 20 percent for Tempest V-8.						
1961 Catalina, V-8, 119" wb						
4d Sed	380	1,140	1,900	3,800	6,650	9,500
4d HT	420	1,260	2,100	4,200	7,350	10,500
2d Sed	384	1,152	1,920	3,840	6,720	9,600
2d HT	640	1,920	3,200	6,400	11,200	16,000
2d Conv	840	2,520	4,200	8,400	14,700	21,000
4d Safari Wag	560	1,680	2,800	5,600	9,800	14,000
1961 Ventura, V-8, 119" wb						
4d HT	540	1,620	2,700	5,400	9,450	13,500
2d HT	720	2,160	3,600	7,200	12,600	18,000
1961 Star Chief, V-8, 123" wb						
4d Sed	420	1,260	2,100	4,200	7,350	10,500
4d HT	560	1,680	2,800	5,600	9,800	14,000
1961 Bonneville, V-8, 123" wb						
4d HT	580	1,740	2,900	5,800	10,150	14,500
2d HT	720	2,160	3,600	7,200	12,600	18,000
2d Conv	1,040	3,120	5,200	10,400	18,200	26,000
1961 Bonneville Safari, V-8, 119" wb						
4d Sta Wag	600	1,800	3,000	6,000	10,500	15,000

	1	2	3	4	5	6
1962 Tempest, 4-cyl., 122" wb						
4d Sed	268	804	1,340	2,680	4,690	6,700
2d Cpe	272	816	1,360	2,720	4,760	6,800
2d HT	520	1,560	2,600	5,200	9,100	13,000
2d Conv	640	1,920	3,200	6,400	11,200	16,000
4d Safari	360	1,080	1,800	3,600	6,300	9,000

NOTE: Add 20 percent for Tempest V-8.

	1	2	3	4	5	6
1962 Catalina, V-8, 120" wb						
4d Sed	380	1,140	1,900	3,800	6,650	9,500
4d HT	420	1,260	2,100	4,200	7,350	10,500
2d Sed	384	1,152	1,920	3,840	6,720	9,600
2d HT	640	1,920	3,200	6,400	11,200	16,000
2d Conv	800	2,400	4,000	8,000	14,000	20,000
4d Sta Wag	540	1,620	2,700	5,400	9,450	13,500
2d HT (421/405)	2,240	6,720	11,200	22,400	39,200	56,000
2d Sed (421/405)	2,240	6,720	11,200	22,400	39,200	56,000
1962 Star Chief, V-8, 123" wb						
4d Sed	400	1,200	2,000	4,000	7,000	10,000
4d HT	540	1,620	2,700	5,400	9,450	13,500
1962 Bonneville, V-8, 123" wb, Sta Wag 119" wb						
4d HT	560	1,680	2,800	5,600	9,800	14,000
2d HT	720	2,160	3,600	7,200	12,600	18,000
2d Conv	960	2,880	4,800	9,600	16,800	24,000
4d Sta Wag	580	1,740	2,900	5,800	10,150	14,500
1962 Grand Prix, V-8, 120" wb						
2d HT	720	2,160	3,600	7,200	12,600	18,000

NOTE: Add 30 percent for 421. Add 30 percent for "421" S-D models.

	1	2	3	4	5	6
1963 Tempest (Compact), 4-cyl., 112" wb						
4d Sed	260	780	1,300	2,600	4,550	6,500
2d Cpe	360	1,080	1,800	3,600	6,300	9,000
2d HT	420	1,260	2,100	4,200	7,350	10,500
2d Conv	640	1,920	3,200	6,400	11,200	16,000
4d Sta Wag	360	1,080	1,800	3,600	6,300	9,000

NOTE: Add 20 percent for Tempest V-8.

	1	2	3	4	5	6
1963 LeMans, V-8, 112" wb						
2d HT	560	1,680	2,800	5,600	9,800	14,000
2d Conv	680	2,040	3,400	6,800	11,900	17,000
1963 Catalina, V-8, 119" wb						
4d Sed	364	1,092	1,820	3,640	6,370	9,100
4d HT	424	1,272	2,120	4,240	7,420	10,600
2d Sed	384	1,152	1,920	3,840	6,720	9,600
2d HT	680	2,040	3,400	6,800	11,900	17,000
2d Conv	760	2,280	3,800	7,600	13,300	19,000
4d Sta Wag	560	1,680	2,800	5,600	9,800	14,000
1963 Catalina Super-Duty						
2d HT (421/405)	2,160	6,480	10,800	21,600	37,800	54,000
2d HT (421/410)	2,240	6,720	11,200	22,400	39,200	56,000
2d Sed (421/405)	2,160	6,480	10,800	21,600	37,800	54,000
2d Sed (421/410)	2,160	6,480	10,800	21,600	37,800	54,000

NOTE: Add 5 percent for 4-speed.

	1	2	3	4	5	6
1963 Star Chief, V-8, 123" wb						
4d Sed	380	1,140	1,900	3,800	6,650	9,500
4d HT	540	1,620	2,700	5,400	9,450	13,500
1963 Bonneville, V-8, 123" wb						
2d HT	720	2,160	3,600	7,200	12,600	18,000
4d HT	580	1,740	2,900	5,800	10,150	14,500
2d Conv	920	2,760	4,600	9,200	16,100	23,000
4d Sta Wag	580	1,740	2,900	5,800	10,150	14,500
1963 Grand Prix, V-8, 120" wb						
2d HT	760	2,280	3,800	7,600	13,300	19,000

NOTE: Add 5 percent for Catalina Ventura. Add 30 percent for "421" engine option.

	1	2	3	4	5	6
1964 Tempest Custom 21, V-8, 115" wb						
4d Sed	268	804	1,340	2,680	4,690	6,700
2d HT	420	1,260	2,100	4,200	7,350	10,500
2d Conv	640	1,920	3,200	6,400	11,200	16,000
4d Sta Wag	360	1,080	1,800	3,600	6,300	9,000

NOTE: Deduct 10 percent for 6-cyl. where available.

	1	2	3	4	5	6
1964 LeMans, V-8, 115" wb						
2d HT	640	1,920	3,200	6,400	11,200	16,000
2d Cpe	580	1,740	2,900	5,800	10,150	14,500
2d Conv	680	2,040	3,400	6,800	11,900	17,000
2d GTO Cpe	800	2,400	4,000	8,000	14,000	20,000
2d GTO Conv	1,040	3,120	5,200	10,400	18,200	26,000
2d GTO HT	880	2,640	4,400	8,800	15,400	22,000

NOTE: Deduct 20 percent for Tempest 6-cyl.

	1	2	3	4	5	6
1964 Catalina, V-8, 120" wb						
4d Sed	380	1,140	1,900	3,800	6,650	9,500
4d HT	420	1,260	2,100	4,200	7,350	10,500
2d Sed	380	1,140	1,900	3,800	6,650	9,500
2d HT	640	1,920	3,200	6,400	11,200	16,000
2d Conv	760	2,280	3,800	7,600	13,300	19,000
4d Sta Wag	520	1,560	2,600	5,200	9,100	13,000

	1	2	3	4	5	6
1964 Star Chief, V-8, 123" wb						
4d Sed	380	1,140	1,900	3,800	6,650	9,500
4d HT	540	1,620	2,700	5,400	9,450	13,500
1964 Bonneville, V-8, 123" wb						
4d HT	580	1,740	2,900	5,800	10,150	14,500
2d HT	680	2,040	3,400	6,800	11,900	17,000
2d Conv	880	2,640	4,400	8,800	15,400	22,000
4d Sta Wag	580	1,740	2,900	5,800	10,150	14,500
1964 Grand Prix, V-8, 120" wb						
2d HT	720	2,160	3,600	7,200	12,600	18,000

NOTE: Add 30 percent for tri power. Add 5 percent for Catalina-Ventura option. Add 10 percent for 2 plus 2.

	1	2	3	4	5	6
1965 Tempest, V-8, 115" wb						
4d Sed	304	912	1,520	3,040	5,320	7,600
2d Spt Cpe	364	1,092	1,820	3,640	6,370	9,100
2d HT	420	1,260	2,100	4,200	7,350	10,500
2d Conv	560	1,680	2,800	5,600	9,800	14,000
4d Sta Wag	360	1,080	1,800	3,600	6,300	9,000

NOTE: Add 20 percent for V-8.

	1	2	3	4	5	6
1965 LeMans, V-8, 115" wb						
4d Sed	360	1,080	1,800	3,600	6,300	9,000
2d Cpe	420	1,260	2,100	4,200	7,350	10,500
2d HT	580	1,740	2,900	5,800	10,150	14,500
2d Conv	760	2,280	3,800	7,600	13,300	19,000
2d GTO Conv	1,120	3,360	5,600	11,200	19,600	28,000
2d GTO HT	960	2,880	4,800	9,600	16,800	24,000
2d GTO Cpe	880	2,640	4,400	8,800	15,400	22,000

NOTE: Deduct 20 percent for 6-cyl. where available. Add 5 percent for 4-speed.

	1	2	3	4	5	6
1965 Catalina, V-8, 121" wb						
4d Sed	312	936	1,560	3,120	5,460	7,800
4d HT	400	1,200	2,000	4,000	7,000	10,000
2d Sed	380	1,140	1,900	3,800	6,650	9,500
2d HT	580	1,740	2,900	5,800	10,150	14,500
2d Conv	680	2,040	3,400	6,800	11,900	17,000
4d Sta Wag	580	1,740	2,900	5,800	10,150	14,500
1965 Star Chief, V-8, 123" wb						
4d Sed	360	1,080	1,800	3,600	6,300	9,000
4d HT	420	1,260	2,100	4,200	7,350	10,500
1965 Bonneville, V-8, 123" wb						
4d HT	540	1,620	2,700	5,400	9,450	13,500
2d HT	640	1,920	3,200	6,400	11,200	16,000
2d Conv	840	2,520	4,200	8,400	14,700	21,000
4d 2S Sta Wag	580	1,740	2,900	5,800	10,150	14,500
1965 Grand Prix, 120" wb						
2d HT	640	1,920	3,200	6,400	11,200	16,000

NOTE: Add 30 percent for "421" H.O. tri power V-8. Add 30 percent for tri power. Add 10 percent for 2 plus 2. Add 10 percent for Catalina-Ventura option. Add 10 percent for Ram Air.

	1	2	3	4	5	6
1966 Tempest Custom, OHC-6, 115" wb						
4d Sed	304	912	1,520	3,040	5,320	7,600
4d HT	308	924	1,540	3,080	5,390	7,700
2d HT	532	1,596	2,660	5,320	9,310	13,300
2d Cpe	400	1,200	2,000	4,000	7,000	10,000
2d Conv	560	1,680	2,800	5,600	9,800	14,000
4d Sta Wag	300	900	1,500	3,000	5,250	7,500

NOTE: Add 20 percent for V-8.

	1	2	3	4	5	6
1966 Lemans, OHC-6, 115" wb						
4d HT	316	948	1,580	3,160	5,530	7,900
2d Cpe	392	1,176	1,960	3,920	6,860	9,800
2d HT	560	1,680	2,800	5,600	9,800	14,000
2d Conv	620	1,860	3,100	6,200	10,850	15,500

NOTE: Add 20 percent for V-8.

	1	2	3	4	5	6
1966 GTO, V-8, 115" wb						
2d HT	840	2,520	4,200	8,400	14,700	21,000
2d Cpe	760	2,280	3,800	7,600	13,300	19,000
2d Conv	1,050	3,100	5,200	10,400	18,200	26,000

NOTE: Add 5 percent for 4-speed. Add 20 percent for tri power option.

	1	2	3	4	5	6
1966 Catalina, V-8, 121" wb						
4d Sed	308	924	1,540	3,080	5,390	7,700
4d HT	400	1,200	2,000	4,000	7,000	10,000
2d Sed	380	1,140	1,900	3,800	6,650	9,500
2d HT	620	1,860	3,100	6,200	10,850	15,500
2d Conv	800	2,400	4,000	8,000	14,000	20,000
4d Sta Wag	560	1,680	2,800	5,600	9,800	14,000
1966 2 Plus 2, V-8, 121" wb						
2d HT	660	1,980	3,300	6,600	11,550	16,500
2d Conv	760	2,280	3,800	7,600	13,300	19,000
1966 Executive, V-8, 124" wb						
4d Sed	380	1,140	1,900	3,800	6,650	9,500
4d HT	420	1,260	2,100	4,200	7,350	10,500
2d HT	620	1,860	3,100	6,200	10,850	15,500

Standard Catalog of ® Pontiac, 2nd Edition

	1	2	3	4	5	6

1966 Bonneville, V-8, 124" wb

	1	2	3	4	5	6
4d HT	540	1,620	2,700	5,400	9,450	13,500
2d HT	660	1,980	3,300	6,600	11,550	16,500
2d Conv	880	2,640	4,400	8,800	15,400	22,000
4d Sta Wag	600	1,750	2,900	5,800	10,200	14,500

1966 Grand Prix, V-8, 121" wb

	1	2	3	4	5	6
2d HT	680	2,040	3,400	6,800	11,900	17,000

NOTE: Add 30 percent for 421. Add 20 percent for Ram Air. Add 30 percent for tri power. Add 10 percent for Ventura Custom trim option.

1967 Tempest, 6-cyl., 115" wb

	1	2	3	4	5	6
4d Sed	300	900	1,500	3,000	5,250	7,500
2d Cpe	360	1,080	1,800	3,600	6,300	9,000
4d Sta Wag	384	1,152	1,920	3,840	6,720	9,600

NOTE: Add 20 percent for V-8.

1967 Tempest Custom, 6-cyl., 115" wb

	1	2	3	4	5	6
2d Cpe	364	1,092	1,820	3,640	6,370	9,100
2d HT	424	1,272	2,120	4,240	7,420	10,600
2d Conv	560	1,680	2,800	5,600	9,800	14,000
4d HT	368	1,104	1,840	3,680	6,440	9,200
4d Sed	304	912	1,520	3,040	5,320	7,600
4d Sta Wag	360	1,080	1,800	3,600	6,300	9,000

NOTE: Add 20 percent for V-8.

1967 Lemans, 6-cyl., 115" wb

	1	2	3	4	5	6
4d HT	360	1,080	1,800	3,600	6,300	9,000
2d Cpe	368	1,104	1,840	3,680	6,440	9,200
2d HT	520	1,560	2,600	5,200	9,100	13,000
2d Conv	620	1,860	3,100	6,200	10,850	15,500

NOTE: Add 20 percent for V-8.

1967 Tempest Safari, 6-cyl., 115" wb

	1	2	3	4	5	6
4d Sta Wag	360	1,080	1,800	3,600	6,300	9,000

NOTE: Add 20 percent for V-8.

1967 GTO, V-8, 115" wb

	1	2	3	4	5	6
2d Cpe	680	2,040	3,400	6,800	11,900	17,000
2d HT	800	2,400	4,000	8,000	14,000	20,000
2d Conv	920	2,760	4,600	9,200	16,100	23,000

1967 Catalina, V-8, 121" wb

	1	2	3	4	5	6
4d Sed	308	924	1,540	3,080	5,390	7,700
4d HT	400	1,200	2,000	4,000	7,000	10,000
2d Sed	384	1,152	1,920	3,840	6,720	9,600
2d HT	580	1,740	2,900	5,800	10,150	14,500
2d Conv	640	1,920	3,200	6,400	11,200	16,000

1967 2 Plus 2, V-8, 121" Wb

	1	2	3	4	5	6
2d HT	660	1,980	3,300	6,600	11,550	16,500
2d Conv	880	2,640	4,400	8,800	15,400	22,000
4d 3S Sta Wag	520	1,560	2,600	5,200	9,100	13,000

1967 Executive, V-8, 124" wb, Sta Wag 121" wb

	1	2	3	4	5	6
4d Sed	360	1,080	1,800	3,600	6,300	9,000
4d HT	420	1,260	2,100	4,200	7,350	10,500
2d HT	620	1,860	3,100	6,200	10,850	15,500
4d 3S Sta Wag	560	1,680	2,800	5,600	9,800	14,000

1967 Bonneville, V-8, 124" wb

	1	2	3	4	5	6
4d HT	520	1,560	2,600	5,200	9,100	13,000
2d HT	620	1,860	3,100	6,200	10,850	15,500
2d Conv	760	2,280	3,800	7,600	13,300	19,000
4d Sta Wag	560	1,680	2,800	5,600	9,800	14,000

1967 Grand Prix, V-8, 121" wb

	1	2	3	4	5	6
2d HT	640	1,920	3,200	6,400	11,200	16,000
Conv	840	2,520	4,200	8,400	14,700	21,000

NOTE: Add 30 percent for 428. Add 10 percent for Sprint option. Add 15 percent for 2 plus 2 option. Add 10 percent for Ventura Custom trim option.

1967 Firebird, V-8, 108" wb

	1	2	3	4	5	6
2d Cpe	720	2,160	3,600	7,200	12,600	18,000
2d Conv	880	2,640	4,400	8,800	15,400	22,000

NOTE: Deduct 25 percent for 6-cyl. Add 15 percent for 350 HO. Add 10 percent for 4-speed. Add 30 percent for the Ram Air 400 Firebird.

1968 Tempest, 6-cyl., 112" wb

	1	2	3	4	5	6
2d Spt Cpe	360	1,080	1,800	3,600	6,300	9,000
2d Cus "S" Cpe	380	1,140	1,900	3,800	6,650	9,500
2d Cus "S" HT	520	1,560	2,600	5,200	9,100	13,000
2d Cus "S" Conv	560	1,680	2,800	5,600	9,800	14,000
2d LeMans	360	1,080	1,800	3,600	6,300	9,000
2d LeMans Spt Cpe	400	1,200	2,000	4,000	7,000	10,000
2d LeMans Conv	720	2,160	3,600	7,200	12,600	18,000

NOTE: Add 20 percent for V-8.

1968 GTO, V-8, 112" wb

	1	2	3	4	5	6
2d HT	760	2,280	3,800	7,600	13,300	19,000
2d Conv	920	2,760	4,600	9,200	16,100	23,000

NOTE: Add 25 percent for Ram Air I, 40 percent for Ram Air II.

1968 Catalina, V-8, 122" wb

	1	2	3	4	5	6
4d Sed	300	900	1,500	3,000	5,250	7,500
4d HT	360	1,080	1,800	3,600	6,300	9,000
2d Sed	388	1,164	1,940	3,880	6,790	9,700
2d HT	520	1,560	2,600	5,200	9,100	13,000
2d Conv	600	1,800	3,000	6,000	10,500	15,000
4d Sta Wag	520	1,560	2,600	5,200	9,100	13,000

1968 Executive, V-8, 124" wb, Sta Wag 121" wb

	1	2	3	4	5	6
4d Sed	380	1,140	1,900	3,800	6,650	9,500
4d HT	400	1,200	2,000	4,000	7,000	10,000
2d HT	580	1,740	2,900	5,800	10,150	14,500
4d 3S Sta Wag	560	1,680	2,800	5,600	9,800	14,000

1968 Bonneville, V-8, 125" wb

	1	2	3	4	5	6
4d Sed	388	1,164	1,940	3,880	6,790	9,700
4d HT	420	1,260	2,100	4,200	7,350	10,500
2d HT	600	1,800	3,000	6,000	10,500	15,000
2d Conv	680	2,040	3,400	6,800	11,900	17,000
4d Sta Wag	580	1,740	2,900	5,800	10,150	14,500

1968 Grand Prix, V-8, 118" wb

	1	2	3	4	5	6
2d HT	640	1,920	3,200	6,400	11,200	16,000

NOTE: Add 10 percent for Sprint option. Add 30 percent for 428. Add 25 percent for Ram Air I, 40 percent for Ram Air II. Add 10 percent for Ventura Custom trim option.

1968 Firebird, V-8, 108" wb

	1	2	3	4	5	6
2d Cpe	720	2,160	3,600	7,200	12,600	18,000
2d Conv	880	2,640	4,400	8,800	15,400	22,000

NOTE: Deduct 25 percent for 6-cyl. Add 10 percent for 350 HO. Add 10 percent for 4-speed. Add 25 percent for the Ram Air 400 Firebird.

1969 Tempest, 6-cyl., 116" wb, 2d 112" wb

	1	2	3	4	5	6
4d Sed	284	852	1,420	2,840	4,970	7,100
2d Cpe	288	864	1,440	2,880	5,040	7,200

NOTE: Add 20 percent for V-8.

1969 Tempest "S" Custom, 6-cyl., 116" wb, 2d 112" wb

	1	2	3	4	5	6
4d Sed	300	850	1,450	2,900	5,050	7,200
4d HT	300	900	1,500	2,950	5,200	7,400
2d Cpe	300	900	1,450	2,900	5,100	7,300
2d HT	400	1,200	2,000	4,000	7,000	10,000
2d Conv	500	1,550	2,600	5,200	9,100	13,000
4d Sta Wag	300	900	1,500	3,000	5,250	7,500

NOTE: Add 20 percent for V-8.

1969 Tempest Lemans, 6-cyl., 116" wb, 2d 112" wb

	1	2	3	4	5	6
4d HT	300	900	1,500	3,000	5,250	7,500
2d Cpe	300	900	1,500	3,000	5,250	7,500
2d HT	420	1,260	2,100	4,200	7,350	10,500
2d Conv	580	1,740	2,900	5,800	10,150	14,500

NOTE: Add 20 percent for V-8.

1969 Tempest Safari, 6-cyl., 116" wb

	1	2	3	4	5	6
4d Sta Wag	308	924	1,540	3,080	5,390	7,700

NOTE: Add 20 percent for V-8.

1969 GTO, V-8, 112" wb

	1	2	3	4	5	6
2d HT	840	2,520	4,200	8,400	14,700	21,000
2d Conv	1,000	3,000	5,000	10,000	17,500	25,000

1969 Catalina, V-8, 122" wb

	1	2	3	4	5	6
4d Sed	300	900	1,500	3,000	5,250	7,500
4d HT	308	924	1,540	3,080	5,390	7,700
2d HT	420	1,260	2,100	4,200	7,350	10,500
2d Conv	580	1,740	2,900	5,800	10,150	14,500
4d 3S Sta Wag	400	1,200	2,000	4,000	7,000	10,000

1969 Executive, V-8, 125" wb, Sta Wag 122" wb

	1	2	3	4	5	6
4d Sed	304	912	1,520	3,040	5,320	7,600
4d HT	312	936	1,560	3,120	5,460	7,800
2d HT	520	1,560	2,600	5,200	9,100	13,000
4d 3S Sta Wag	408	1,224	2,040	4,080	7,140	10,200

1969 Bonneville, V-8, 125" wb

	1	2	3	4	5	6
4d Sed	304	912	1,520	3,040	5,320	7,600
4d HT	360	1,080	1,800	3,600	6,300	9,000
2d HT	540	1,620	2,700	5,400	9,450	13,500
2d Conv	620	1,860	3,100	6,200	10,850	15,500
4d Sta Wag	420	1,260	2,100	4,200	7,350	10,500

1969 Grand Prix, V-8, 118" wb

	1	2	3	4	5	6
2d HT	560	1,680	2,800	5,600	9,800	14,000

NOTE: Add 10 percent for LeMans Rally E Pkg. Add 30 percent for 428 cid V-8. Add 25 percent for Ram Air III. Add 40 percent for Ram Air IV. Add 40 percent for GTO Judge option. Add 25 percent for Ram

1969 Firebird, V-8, 108" wb

	1	2	3	4	5	6
2d Cpe	720	2,160	3,600	7,200	12,600	18,000
2d Conv	880	2,640	4,400	8,800	15,400	22,000
2d Trans Am Cpe	760	2,280	3,800	7,600	13,300	19,000
2d Trans Am Conv	1,040	3,120	5,200	10,400	18,200	26,000

NOTE: Deduct 25 percent for 6-cyl. Add 15 percent for "HO" 400 Firebird. Add 10 percent for 4-speed. Add 20 percent for Ram Air IV Firebird. Add 50 percent for '303' V-8 SCCA race engine.

1970 Tempest, 6-cyl., 116" wb, 2d 112" wb

	1	2	3	4	5	6
4d Sed	292	876	1,460	2,920	5,110	7,300
2d HT	400	1,200	2,000	4,000	7,000	10,000
2d Cpe	300	900	1,500	3,000	5,250	7,500

NOTE: Add 20 percent for V-8.

	1	2	3	4	5	6

1970 LeMans, 6 cyl., 116" wb, 2d 112" wb

	1	2	3	4	5	6
4d Sed	296	888	1,480	2,960	5,180	7,400
4d HT	360	1,080	1,800	3,600	6,300	9,000
2d Cpe	304	912	1,520	3,040	5,320	7,600
2d HT	420	1,260	2,100	4,200	7,350	10,500
4d Sta Wag	312	936	1,560	3,120	5,460	7,800

NOTE: Add 20 percent for V-8.

1970 LeMans Sport, 6-cyl., 116" wb, 2d 112" wb

	1	2	3	4	5	6
4d HT	368	1,104	1,840	3,680	6,440	9,200
2d Cpe	380	1,140	1,900	3,800	6,650	9,500
2d HT	520	1,560	2,600	5,200	9,100	13,000
2d Conv	540	1,620	2,700	5,400	9,450	13,500
4d Sta Wag	360	1,080	1,800	3,600	6,300	9,000

NOTE: Add 20 percent for V-8.

1970 LeMans GT 37, V-8, 112" wb

	1	2	3	4	5	6
2d Cpe	520	1,560	2,600	5,200	9,100	13,000
2d HT	580	1,740	2,900	5,800	10,150	14,500

1970 GTO, V-8, 112" wb

	1	2	3	4	5	6
2d HT	880	2,640	4,400	8,800	15,400	22,000
2d Conv	1,040	3,120	5,200	10,400	18,200	26,000

1970 Catalina, V-8, 122" wb

	1	2	3	4	5	6
4d Sed	300	900	1,500	3,000	5,250	7,500
4d HT	380	1,140	1,900	3,800	6,650	9,500
2d HT	520	1,560	2,600	5,200	9,100	13,000
2d Conv	560	1,680	2,800	5,600	9,800	14,000
4d 3S Sta Wag	400	1,200	2,000	4,000	7,000	10,000

1970 Executive, V-8, 125" wb, Sta Wag 122" wb

	1	2	3	4	5	6
4d Sed	304	912	1,520	3,040	5,320	7,600
4d HT	400	1,200	2,000	4,000	7,000	10,000
2d HT	540	1,620	2,700	5,400	9,450	13,500
4d 3S Sta Wag	408	1,224	2,040	4,080	7,140	10,200

1970 Bonneville, V-8, 125" wb, Sta Wag 122" wb

	1	2	3	4	5	6
4d Sed	360	1,080	1,800	3,600	6,300	9,000
4d HT	420	1,260	2,100	4,200	7,350	10,500
2d HT	560	1,680	2,800	5,600	9,800	14,000
2d Conv	620	1,860	3,100	6,200	10,850	15,500
4d 3S Sta Wag	420	1,260	2,100	4,200	7,350	10,500

1970 Grand Prix, V-8, 118" wb

	1	2	3	4	5	6
2d Hurst "SSJ" HT	620	1,860	3,100	6,200	10,850	15,500
2d HT	580	1,740	2,900	5,800	10,150	14,500

NOTE: Add 10 percent for V-8 LeMans Rally Pkg. Add 40 percent for GTO Judge. Add 40 percent for 455 HO V-8. Add 10 percent for Grand Prix S.J. Add 25 percent for Ram Air III. Add 40 percent for Ram Ai

1970 Firebird, V-8, 108" wb

	1	2	3	4	5	6
2d Firebird	600	1,800	3,000	6,000	10,500	15,000
2d Esprit	620	1,860	3,100	6,200	10,850	15,500
2d Formula 400	640	1,920	3,200	6,400	11,200	16,000
2d Trans Am	760	2,280	3,800	7,600	13,300	19,000

NOTE: Deduct 25 percent for 6-cyl. Add 10 percent for Trans Am with 4-speed. Add 25 percent for Ram Air IV Firebird.

1971 Ventura II, 6-cyl., 111" wb

	1	2	3	4	5	6
2d Cpe	304	912	1,520	3,040	5,320	7,600
4d Sed	288	864	1,440	2,880	5,040	7,200

1971 Ventura II, V-8, 111" wb

	1	2	3	4	5	6
2d Cpe	304	912	1,520	3,040	5,320	7,600
4d Sed	312	936	1,560	3,120	5,460	7,800

1971 LeMans T37, 6-cyl., 116" wb, 2d 112" wb

	1	2	3	4	5	6
2d Sed	300	900	1,500	3,000	5,250	7,500
4d Sed	280	840	1,400	2,800	4,900	7,000
2d HT	400	1,200	2,000	4,000	7,000	10,000

1971 LeMans, 6-cyl., 116" wb, 2d 112" wb

	1	2	3	4	5	6
2d Sed	280	840	1,400	2,800	4,900	7,000
4d Sed	284	852	1,420	2,840	4,970	7,100
4d HT	296	888	1,480	2,960	5,180	7,400
2d HT	520	1,560	2,600	5,200	9,100	13,000
4d 3S Sta Wag	280	840	1,400	2,800	4,900	7,000

1971 LeMans Sport, 6-cyl., 116" wb, 2d 112" wb

	1	2	3	4	5	6
4d HT	292	876	1,460	2,920	5,110	7,300
2d HT	540	1,620	2,700	5,400	9,450	13,500
2d Conv	600	1,800	3,000	6,000	10,500	15,000

NOTE: Add 20 percent for V-8.

1971 LeMans GT 37, V-8, 112" wb

	1	2	3	4	5	6
2d HT	600	1,800	3,000	6,000	10,500	15,000

1971 GTO

	1	2	3	4	5	6
2d HT	800	2,400	4,000	8,000	14,000	20,000
2d Conv	1,100	3,350	5,600	11,200	19,600	28,000

NOTE: Add 40 percent for GTO Judge option.

1971 Catalina

	1	2	3	4	5	6
4d	304	912	1,520	3,040	5,320	7,600
4d HT	308	924	1,540	3,080	5,390	7,700
2d HT	380	1,140	1,900	3,800	6,650	9,500
2d Conv	560	1,680	2,800	5,600	9,800	14,000

1971 Safari, V-8, 127" wb

	1	2	3	4	5	6
4d 2S Sta Wag	308	924	1,540	3,080	5,390	7,700
4d 3S Sta Wag	312	936	1,560	3,120	5,460	7,800

1971 Catalina Brougham, V-8, 123" wb

	1	2	3	4	5	6
4d Sed	312	936	1,560	3,120	5,460	7,800
4d HT	316	948	1,580	3,160	5,530	7,900
2d HT	388	1,164	1,940	3,880	6,790	9,700

1971 Grand Safari, V-8, 127" wb

	1	2	3	4	5	6
4d 2S Sta Wag	280	840	1,400	2,800	4,900	7,000
4d 3S Sta Wag	284	852	1,420	2,840	4,970	7,100

1971 Bonneville

	1	2	3	4	5	6
4d Sed	316	948	1,580	3,160	5,530	7,900
4d HT	360	1,080	1,800	3,600	6,300	9,000
2d HT	400	1,200	2,000	4,000	7,000	10,000

1971 Grandville

	1	2	3	4	5	6
4d HT	360	1,080	1,800	3,600	6,300	9,000
2d HT	408	1,224	2,040	4,080	7,140	10,200
2d Conv	680	2,040	3,400	6,800	11,900	17,000

1971 Grand Prix

	1	2	3	4	5	6
2d HT	600	1,800	3,000	6,000	10,500	15,000
2d Hurst "SSJ" Cpe	660	1,980	3,300	6,600	11,550	16,500

1971 Firebird, V-8, 108" wb

	1	2	3	4	5	6
2d Firebird	620	1,860	3,100	6,200	10,850	15,500
2d Esprit	600	1,800	3,000	6,000	10,500	15,000
2d Formula	640	1,920	3,200	6,400	11,200	16,000
2d Trans Am	760	2,280	3,800	7,600	13,300	19,000

NOTE: Add 25 percent for Formula 455. Deduct 25 percent for 6-cyl. Add 40 percent for 455 HO V-8. Add 10 percent for 4-speed. (Formula Series - 350, 400, 455).

1972 Ventura, 6-cyl., 111" wb

	1	2	3	4	5	6
4d Sed	268	804	1,340	2,680	4,690	6,700
2d Cpe	260	780	1,300	2,600	4,550	6,500

NOTE: Add 20 percent for V-8.

1972 LeMans, 6-cyl., 116" wb, 2d 112" wb

	1	2	3	4	5	6
2d Cpe	280	840	1,400	2,800	4,900	7,000
4d Sed	272	816	1,360	2,720	4,760	6,800
2d HT	540	1,620	2,700	5,400	9,450	13,500
2d Conv	600	1,800	3,000	6,000	10,500	15,000
4d 3S Sta Wag	280	840	1,400	2,800	4,900	7,000

1972 GTO

	1	2	3	4	5	6
2d HT	680	2,040	3,400	6,800	11,900	17,000
2d Sed	560	1,680	2,800	5,600	9,800	14,000

1972 Luxury LeMans, V-8

	1	2	3	4	5	6
4d HT	288	864	1,440	2,880	5,040	7,200
2d HT	560	1,680	2,800	5,600	9,800	14,000

NOTE: Add 10 percent for Endura option on LeMans models. Add 20 percent for V-8.

1972 Catalina, V-8, 123" wb

	1	2	3	4	5	6
4d Sed	260	780	1,300	2,600	4,550	6,500
4d HT	268	804	1,340	2,680	4,690	6,700
2d HT	380	1,140	1,900	3,800	6,650	9,500
2d Conv	580	1,740	2,900	5,800	10,150	14,500

1972 Catalina Brougham, V-8, 123" wb

	1	2	3	4	5	6
4d Sed	264	792	1,320	2,640	4,620	6,600
4d HT	280	840	1,400	2,800	4,900	7,000
2d HT	400	1,200	2,000	4,000	7,000	10,000

1972 Bonneville

	1	2	3	4	5	6
4d Sed	268	804	1,340	2,680	4,690	6,700
4d HT	300	900	1,500	3,000	5,250	7,500
2d HT	420	1,260	2,100	4,200	7,350	10,500

1972 Grandville

	1	2	3	4	5	6
4d HT	300	900	1,500	3,000	5,250	7,500
2d HT	428	1,284	2,140	4,280	7,490	10,700
2d Conv	640	1,920	3,200	6,400	11,200	16,000

1972 Safari, V-8, 127" wb

	1	2	3	4	5	6
4d 2S Sta Wag	264	792	1,320	2,640	4,620	6,600
4d 3S Sta Wag	268	804	1,340	2,680	4,690	6,700

1972 Grand Safari, V-8, 127" wb

	1	2	3	4	5	6
4d 2S Sta Wag	272	816	1,360	2,720	4,760	6,800
4d 3S Sta Wag	276	828	1,380	2,760	4,830	6,900

1972 Grand Prix

	1	2	3	4	5	6
2d HT	568	1,704	2,840	5,680	9,940	14,200
2d Hurst "SSJ" HT	620	1,860	3,100	6,200	10,850	15,500

1972 Firebird, V-8, 108" wb

	1	2	3	4	5	6
2d Firebird	580	1,740	2,900	5,800	10,150	14,500
2d Esprit	560	1,680	2,800	5,600	9,800	14,000
2d Formula	600	1,800	3,000	6,000	10,500	15,000
2d Trans Am	720	2,160	3,600	7,200	12,600	18,000

NOTE: Add 10 percent for Trans Am with 4-speed. Deduct 25 percent for 6-cyl. Add 40 percent for 455 HO V-8.

	1	2	3	4	5	6
1973 Ventura						
4d Sed	248	744	1,240	2,480	4,340	6,200
2d Cpe	236	708	1,180	2,360	4,130	5,900
2d HBk Cpe	252	756	1,260	2,520	4,410	6,300
1973 Ventura Custom						
4d Sed	252	756	1,260	2,520	4,410	6,300
2d Cpe	256	768	1,280	2,560	4,480	6,400
2d HBk Cpe	244	732	1,220	2,440	4,270	6,100
NOTE: Deduct 5 percent for 6-cyl. Deduct 5 percent for 6-cyl.						
1973 LeMans						
4d Sed	260	780	1,300	2,600	4,550	6,500
2d HT	308	924	1,540	3,080	5,390	7,700
1973 LeMans Spt						
2d Cpe	280	840	1,400	2,800	4,900	7,000
1973 Luxury LeMans						
2d Cpe	288	864	1,440	2,880	5,040	7,200
4d HT	280	840	1,400	2,800	4,900	7,000
1973 LeMans Safari, V-8, 116" wb						
4d 2S Sta Wag	260	780	1,300	2,600	4,550	6,500
4d 3S Sta Wag	260	780	1,300	2,600	4,550	6,500
1973 Grand AM						
2d HT	520	1,560	2,600	5,200	9,100	13,000
4d HT	300	900	1,500	3,000	5,250	7,500
2d GTO Spt Cpe	520	1,560	2,600	5,200	9,100	13,000
NOTE: Deduct 5 percent for 6-cyl.						
1973 Catalina						
4d HT	244	732	1,220	2,440	4,270	6,100
2d HT	300	900	1,500	3,000	5,250	7,500
1973 Bonneville						
4d Sed	248	744	1,240	2,480	4,340	6,200
4d HT	260	780	1,300	2,600	4,550	6,500
2d HT	316	948	1,580	3,160	5,530	7,900
1973 Safari, V-8, 127" wb						
4d 2S Sta Wag	260	780	1,300	2,600	4,550	6,500
4d 3S Sta Wag	264	792	1,320	2,640	4,620	6,600
1973 Grand Safari, V-8, 127" wb						
4d 2S Sta Wag	268	804	1,340	2,680	4,690	6,700
4d 3S Sta Wag	272	816	1,360	2,720	4,760	6,800
1973 Grandville						
4d HT	268	804	1,340	2,680	4,690	6,700
2d HT	324	972	1,620	3,240	5,670	8,100
2d Conv	640	1,920	3,200	6,400	11,200	16,000
1973 Grand Prix						
2d HT	540	1,620	2,700	5,400	9,450	13,500
2d "SJ" HT	550	1,650	2,750	5,500	9,600	13,700
1973 Firebird, V-8, 108" wb						
2d Cpe	560	1,680	2,800	5,600	9,800	14,000
2d Esprit	580	1,740	2,900	5,800	10,150	14,500
2d Formula	600	1,800	3,000	6,000	10,500	15,000
2d Trans Am	620	1,860	3,100	6,200	10,850	15,500
NOTE: Add 50 percent for 455 SD V-8 (Formula & Trans Am only). Deduct 25 percent for 6-cyl. Add 10 percent for 4-speed.						
1974 Ventura						
4d Sed	188	564	940	1,880	3,290	4,700
2d Cpe	176	528	880	1,760	3,080	4,400
2d HBk	192	576	960	1,920	3,360	4,800
1974 Ventura Custom						
4d Sed	192	576	960	1,920	3,360	4,800
2d Cpe	180	540	900	1,800	3,150	4,500
2d HBk	196	588	980	1,960	3,430	4,900
2d GTO	260	780	1,300	2,600	4,550	6,500
NOTE: Deduct 4 percent for 6-cyl.						
1974 LeMans						
4d HT	168	504	840	1,680	2,940	4,200
2d HT	228	684	1,140	2,280	3,990	5,700
4d Sta Wag	180	540	900	1,800	3,150	4,500
1974 LeMans Sport						
2d Cpe	200	600	1,000	2,000	3,500	5,000
1974 Luxury LeMans						
4d HT	192	576	960	1,920	3,360	4,800
2d HT	248	744	1,240	2,480	4,340	6,200
4d Safari	200	600	1,000	2,000	3,500	5,000
NOTE: Add 10 percent for GT option.						
1974 Grand AM						
2d HT	320	960	1,600	3,200	5,600	8,000
4d HT	232	696	1,160	2,320	4,060	5,800
1974 Catalina						
4d HT	192	576	960	1,920	3,360	4,800
2d HT	240	720	1,200	2,400	4,200	6,000
4d Sed	160	480	800	1,600	2,800	4,000
4d Safari	192	576	960	1,920	3,360	4,800

	1	2	3	4	5	6
1974 Bonneville						
4d Sed	168	504	840	1,680	2,940	4,200
4d HT	200	600	1,000	2,000	3,500	5,000
2d HT	256	768	1,280	2,560	4,480	6,400
1974 Grandville						
4d HT	204	612	1,020	2,040	3,570	5,100
2d HT	260	780	1,300	2,600	4,550	6,500
2d Conv	600	1,800	3,000	6,000	10,500	15,000
1974 Grand Prix						
2d HT	520	1,560	2,600	5,200	9,100	13,000
2d "SJ" Cpe	550	1,600	2,650	5,300	9,250	13,200
1974 Firebird, V-8, 108" wb						
2d Firebird	340	1,020	1,700	3,400	5,950	8,500
2d Esprit	520	1,560	2,600	5,200	9,100	13,000
2d Formula	580	1,740	2,900	5,800	10,150	14,500
2d Trans Am	600	1,800	3,000	6,000	10,500	15,000
NOTE: Add 40 percent for 455-SD V-8 (Formula & Trans Am only). Deduct 25 percent for 6-cyl. Add 10 percent for 4-speed.						
1975 Astre S						
2d Cpe	172	516	860	1,720	3,010	4,300
2d HBk	176	528	880	1,760	3,080	4,400
4d Safari	180	540	900	1,800	3,150	4,500
1975 Astre						
2d HBk	176	528	880	1,760	3,080	4,400
4d Safari	180	540	900	1,800	3,150	4,500
NOTE: Add 10 percent for Astre 'SJ'.						
1975 Ventura						
4d Sed	176	528	880	1,760	3,080	4,400
2d Cpe	180	540	900	1,800	3,150	4,500
2d HBk	184	552	920	1,840	3,220	4,600
NOTE: Deduct 5 percent for Ventura 'S'. Add 15 percent for Ventura 'SJ'. Add 5 percent for Ventura Custom.						
1975 LeMans						
4d HT	180	540	900	1,800	3,150	4,500
2d HT	220	660	1,100	2,200	3,850	5,500
4d Safari	184	552	920	1,840	3,220	4,600
NOTE: Add 10 percent for Grand LeMans.						
1975 LeMans Sport						
2d HT Cpe	228	684	1,140	2,280	3,990	5,700
1975 Grand AM						
4d HT	184	552	920	1,840	3,220	4,600
2d HT	240	720	1,200	2,400	4,200	6,000
NOTE: Add 5 percent for 4-speed. Add 20 percent for 455 HO V-8.						
1975 Catalina						
4d Sed	164	492	820	1,640	2,870	4,100
2d Cpe	180	540	900	1,800	3,150	4,500
4d Safari	160	480	800	1,600	2,800	4,000
1975 Bonneville						
4d HT	172	516	860	1,720	3,010	4,300
2d Cpe	184	552	920	1,840	3,220	4,600
4d Gr Safari	176	528	880	1,760	3,080	4,400
1975 Grand Ville Brougham						
4d HT	176	528	880	1,760	3,080	4,400
2d Cpe	192	576	960	1,920	3,360	4,800
2d Conv	680	2,040	3,400	6,800	11,900	17,000
NOTE: Add 20 percent for 455 V-8.						
1975 Grand Prix						
2d Cpe	300	900	1,500	3,000	5,250	7,500
2d "LJ" Cpe	300	900	1,500	3,050	5,300	7,600
2d "SJ" Cpe	300	900	1,550	3,100	5,400	7,700
NOTE: Add 12 percent for 455 V-8.						
1975 Firebird, V-8, 108" wb						
2d Cpe	300	900	1,500	3,000	5,250	7,500
2d Esprit	340	1,020	1,700	3,400	5,950	8,500
2d Formula	340	1,020	1,700	3,400	5,950	8,500
Trans Am	540	1,620	2,700	5,400	9,450	13,500
NOTE: Add 18 percent for 455 HO V-8. Deduct 25 percent for 6-cyl. Add 10 percent for 4-speed. Add $150 for Honeycomb wheels.						
1976 Astre, 4-cyl.						
2d Cpe	144	432	720	1,440	2,520	3,600
2d HBk	148	444	740	1,480	2,590	3,700
4d Sta Wag	152	456	760	1,520	2,660	3,800
1976 Sunbird, 4-cyl.						
2d Cpe	192	576	960	1,920	3,360	4,800
1976 Ventura, V-8						
4d Sed	184	552	920	1,840	3,220	4,600
2d Cpe	188	564	940	1,880	3,290	4,700
2d HBk	192	576	960	1,920	3,360	4,800
1976 Ventura SJ, V-8						
4d Sed	188	564	940	1,880	3,290	4,700
2d Cpe	192	576	960	1,920	3,360	4,800
2d HBk	196	588	980	1,960	3,430	4,900

	1	2	3	4	5	6

1976 LeMans, V-8

	1	2	3	4	5	6
4d Sed	192	576	960	1,920	3,360	4,800
2d Cpe	196	588	980	1,960	3,430	4,900
4d 2S Safari Wag	184	552	920	1,840	3,220	4,600
4d 3S Safari Wag	188	564	940	1,880	3,290	4,700

1976 LeMans Sport Cpe, V-8

	1	2	3	4	5	6
2d Cpe	208	624	1,040	2,080	3,640	5,200

1976 Grand LeMans, V-8

	1	2	3	4	5	6
4d Sed	196	588	980	1,960	3,430	4,900
2d Sed	200	600	1,000	2,000	3,500	5,000
4d 2S Safari Wag	192	576	960	1,920	3,360	4,800
4d 3S Safari Wag	196	588	980	1,960	3,430	4,900

1976 Catalina, V-8

	1	2	3	4	5	6
4d Sed	188	564	940	1,880	3,290	4,700
2d Cpe	192	576	960	1,920	3,360	4,800
2S Safari Wag	204	612	1,020	2,040	3,570	5,100
4d 3S Safari Wag	188	564	940	1,880	3,290	4,700

1976 Bonneville, V-8

	1	2	3	4	5	6
4d Sed	196	588	980	1,960	3,430	4,900
2d Cpe	200	600	1,000	2,000	3,500	5,000

1976 Bonneville Brougham, V-8

	1	2	3	4	5	6
4d Sed	204	612	1,020	2,040	3,570	5,100
2d Cpe	212	636	1,060	2,120	3,710	5,300

1976 Grand Safari, V-8

	1	2	3	4	5	6
4d 2S Sta Wag	192	576	960	1,920	3,360	4,800
4d 3S Sta Wag	196	588	980	1,960	3,430	4,900

1976 Grand Prix, V-8

	1	2	3	4	5	6
2d Cpe	300	900	1,500	3,000	5,250	7,500
2d Cpe SJ	308	924	1,540	3,080	5,390	7,700
2d Cpe LJ	328	984	1,640	3,280	5,740	8,200

NOTE: Add 10 percent for T-tops & Anniversary model.

1976 Firebird, V-8

	1	2	3	4	5	6
2d Cpe	248	744	1,240	2,480	4,340	6,200
2d Esprit Cpe	260	780	1,300	2,600	4,550	6,500
2d Formula Cpe	268	804	1,340	2,680	4,690	6,700
2d Trans Am Cpe	276	828	1,380	2,760	4,830	6,900

NOTE: Add 20 percent for 455 HO V-8. Deduct 25 percent for 6-cyl. Add 10 percent for 4-speed. Add $150 for Honeycomb wheels. Add 20 percent for Limited Edition.

1977 Astre, 4-cyl.

	1	2	3	4	5	6
2d Cpe	112	336	560	1,120	1,960	2,800
2d HBk	116	348	580	1,160	2,030	2,900
4d Sta Wag	120	360	600	1,200	2,100	3,000

1977 Sunbird, 4-cyl.

	1	2	3	4	5	6
2d Cpe	160	480	800	1,600	2,800	4,000
2d HBk	164	492	820	1,640	2,870	4,100

1977 Phoenix, V-8

	1	2	3	4	5	6
4d Sed	156	468	780	1,560	2,730	3,900
2d Cpe	160	480	800	1,600	2,800	4,000

1977 Ventura, V-8

	1	2	3	4	5	6
4d Sed	156	468	780	1,560	2,730	3,900
2d Cpe	160	480	800	1,600	2,800	4,000
2d HBk	164	492	820	1,640	2,870	4,100

1977 Ventura SJ, V-8

	1	2	3	4	5	6
4d Sed	160	480	800	1,600	2,800	4,000
2d Cpe	164	492	820	1,640	2,870	4,100
2d HBk	168	504	840	1,680	2,940	4,200

1977 LeMans, V-8

	1	2	3	4	5	6
4d Sed	160	480	800	1,600	2,800	4,000
2d Cpe	164	492	820	1,640	2,870	4,100
4d 2S Sta Wag	156	468	780	1,560	2,730	3,900
4d 3S Sta Wag	160	480	800	1,600	2,800	4,000

1977 LeMans Sport Cpe, V-8

	1	2	3	4	5	6
2d Cpe	208	624	1,040	2,080	3,640	5,200

NOTE: Add 20 percent for Can Am option.

1977 Grand LeMans, V-8

	1	2	3	4	5	6
4d Sed	164	492	820	1,640	2,870	4,100
2d Cpe	168	504	840	1,680	2,940	4,200
4d 2S Sta Wag	160	480	800	1,600	2,800	4,000
4d 3S Sta Wag	164	492	820	1,640	2,870	4,100

1977 Catalina, V-8

	1	2	3	4	5	6
4d Sed	156	468	780	1,560	2,730	3,900
2d Cpe	160	480	800	1,600	2,800	4,000
4d 2S Safari Wag	152	456	760	1,520	2,660	3,800
4d 3S Safari Wag	156	468	780	1,560	2,730	3,900

1977 Bonneville, V-8

	1	2	3	4	5	6
4d Sed	164	492	820	1,640	2,870	4,100
2d Cpe	168	504	840	1,680	2,940	4,200

1977 Bonneville Brougham, V-8

	1	2	3	4	5	6
4d Sed	172	516	860	1,720	3,010	4,300
2d Cpe	180	540	900	1,800	3,150	4,500

1977 Grand Safari

	1	2	3	4	5	6
4d 2S Sta Wag	168	504	840	1,680	2,940	4,200
4d 3S Sta Wag	172	516	860	1,720	3,010	4,300

1977 Grand Prix, V-8

	1	2	3	4	5	6
2d Cpe	268	804	1,340	2,680	4,690	6,700
2d Cpe LJ	280	840	1,400	2,800	4,900	7,000
2d Cpe SJ	320	960	1,600	3,200	5,600	8,000

1977 Firebird, V-8

	1	2	3	4	5	6
2d Cpe	232	696	1,160	2,320	4,060	5,800
2d Esprit Cpe	240	720	1,200	2,400	4,200	6,000
2d Formula Cpe	252	756	1,260	2,520	4,410	6,300
2d Trans Am Cpe	260	780	1,300	2,600	4,550	6,500

NOTE: Add 10 percent for 4-speed.

1978 Sunbird

	1	2	3	4	5	6
2d Cpe	116	348	580	1,160	2,030	2,900
2d Spt Cpe	120	360	600	1,200	2,100	3,000
2d Spt HBk	124	372	620	1,240	2,170	3,100
4d Spt Wag	120	360	600	1,200	2,100	3,000

1978 Phoenix

	1	2	3	4	5	6
4d Sed	120	360	600	1,200	2,100	3,000
2d Cpe	132	396	660	1,320	2,310	3,300
2d HBk	124	372	620	1,240	2,170	3,100

1978 Phoenix LJ

	1	2	3	4	5	6
4d Sed	124	372	620	1,240	2,170	3,100
2d Cpe	140	420	700	1,400	2,450	3,500

1978 LeMans

	1	2	3	4	5	6
4d Sed	160	480	800	1,600	2,800	4,000
2d Cpe	168	504	840	1,680	2,940	4,200
4d 2S Sta Wag	160	480	800	1,600	2,800	4,000

1978 Grand LeMans

	1	2	3	4	5	6
4d Sed	164	492	820	1,640	2,870	4,100
2d Cpe	172	516	860	1,720	3,010	4,300
4d 2S Sta Wag	164	492	820	1,640	2,870	4,100

1978 Grand Am

	1	2	3	4	5	6
4d Sed	168	504	840	1,680	2,940	4,200
2d Cpe	180	540	900	1,800	3,150	4,500

1978 Catalina

	1	2	3	4	5	6
4d Sed	160	480	800	1,600	2,800	4,000
2d Cpe	164	492	820	1,640	2,870	4,100
4d 2S Sta Wag	168	504	840	1,680	2,940	4,200

1978 Bonneville

	1	2	3	4	5	6
4d Sed	172	516	860	1,720	3,010	4,300
2d Cpe	180	540	900	1,800	3,150	4,500
4d 2S Sta Wag	180	540	900	1,800	3,150	4,500

1978 Bonneville Brougham

	1	2	3	4	5	6
4d Sed	180	540	900	1,800	3,150	4,500
2d Cpe	188	564	940	1,880	3,290	4,700

1978 Grand Prix

	1	2	3	4	5	6
2d Cpe	236	708	1,180	2,360	4,130	5,900
2d Cpe LJ	240	720	1,200	2,400	4,200	6,000
2d Cpe SJ	248	744	1,240	2,480	4,340	6,200

1978 Firebird, V-8, 108" wb

	1	2	3	4	5	6
2d Cpe	232	696	1,160	2,320	4,060	5,800
2d Esprit Cpe	240	720	1,200	2,400	4,200	6,000
2d Formula Cpe	252	756	1,260	2,520	4,410	6,300
2d Trans Am Cpe	260	780	1,300	2,600	4,550	6,500

NOTE: Add 10 percent for 4-speed.

1979 Sunbird

	1	2	3	4	5	6
2d Cpe	120	360	600	1,200	2,100	3,000
2d Spt Cpe	124	372	620	1,240	2,170	3,100
2d HBk	124	372	620	1,240	2,170	3,100
4d Sta Wag	128	384	640	1,280	2,240	3,200

1979 Phoenix

	1	2	3	4	5	6
2d Sed	124	372	620	1,240	2,170	3,100
2d Cpe	132	396	660	1,320	2,310	3,300
2d HBk	128	384	640	1,280	2,240	3,200

1979 Phoenix LJ

	1	2	3	4	5	6
4d Sed	128	384	640	1,280	2,240	3,200
2d Cpe	136	408	680	1,360	2,380	3,400

1979 LeMans

	1	2	3	4	5	6
4d Sed	164	492	820	1,640	2,870	4,100
2d Cpe	172	516	860	1,720	3,010	4,300
4d Sta Wag	164	492	820	1,640	2,870	4,100

1979 Grand LeMans

	1	2	3	4	5	6
4d Sed	168	504	840	1,680	2,940	4,200
2d Cpe	180	540	900	1,800	3,150	4,500
4d Sta Wag	168	504	840	1,680	2,940	4,200

1979 Grand Am

	1	2	3	4	5	6
4d Sed	180	540	900	1,800	3,150	4,500
2d Cpe	188	564	940	1,880	3,290	4,700

	1	2	3	4	5	6

1979 Catalina

	1	2	3	4	5	6
4d Sed	164	492	820	1,640	2,870	4,100
2d Cpe	168	504	840	1,680	2,940	4,200
4d Sta Wag	164	492	820	1,640	2,870	4,100

1979 Bonneville

	1	2	3	4	5	6
4d Sed	176	528	880	1,760	3,080	4,400
2d Cpe	180	540	900	1,800	3,150	4,500
4d Sta Wag	176	528	880	1,760	3,080	4,400

1979 Bonneville Brougham

	1	2	3	4	5	6
4d Sed	184	552	920	1,840	3,220	4,600
2d Cpe	192	576	960	1,920	3,360	4,800

1979 Grand Prix

	1	2	3	4	5	6
2d Cpe	200	600	1,000	2,000	3,500	5,000
2d LJ Cpe	208	624	1,040	2,080	3,640	5,200
2d SJ Cpe	216	648	1,080	2,160	3,780	5,400

1979 Firebird, V-8, 108" wb

	1	2	3	4	5	6
2d Cpe	248	744	1,240	2,480	4,340	6,200
2d Esprit Cpe	256	768	1,280	2,560	4,480	6,400
2d Formula Cpe	264	792	1,320	2,640	4,620	6,600
2d Trans Am Cpe	320	960	1,600	3,200	5,600	8,000

NOTE: Add 15 percent for 10th Anniversary Edition. Add 10 percent for 4-speed.

1980 Sunbird, V-6

	1	2	3	4	5	6
2d Cpe	140	420	700	1,400	2,450	3,500
2d HBk	144	432	720	1,440	2,520	3,600
2d Spt Cpe	144	432	720	1,440	2,520	3,600
2d Cpe HBk	148	444	740	1,480	2,590	3,700

NOTE: Deduct 10 percent for 4-cyl.

1980 Phoenix, V-6

	1	2	3	4	5	6
2d Cpe	148	444	740	1,480	2,590	3,700
4d Sed HBk	144	432	720	1,440	2,520	3,600

NOTE: Deduct 10 percent for 4-cyl.

1980 Phoenix LJ, V-6

	1	2	3	4	5	6
2d Cpe	152	456	760	1,520	2,660	3,800
4d Sed HBk	148	444	740	1,480	2,590	3,700

NOTE: Deduct 10 percent for 4-cyl.

1980 LeMans, V-8

	1	2	3	4	5	6
4d Sed	148	444	740	1,480	2,590	3,700
2d Cpe	156	468	780	1,560	2,730	3,900
4d Sta Wag	152	456	760	1,520	2,660	3,800

NOTE: Deduct 10 percent for V-6.

1980 Grand LeMans, V-8

	1	2	3	4	5	6
4d Sed	152	456	760	1,520	2,660	3,800
2d Cpe	160	480	800	1,600	2,800	4,000
4d Sta Wag	156	468	780	1,560	2,730	3,900

NOTE: Deduct 10 percent for V-6.

1980 Grand Am, V-8

	1	2	3	4	5	6
2d Cpe	164	492	820	1,640	2,870	4,100

1980 Firebird, V-8

	1	2	3	4	5	6
2d Cpe	236	708	1,180	2,360	4,130	5,900
2d Cpe Esprit	240	720	1,200	2,400	4,200	6,000
2d Cpe Formula	244	732	1,220	2,440	4,270	6,100
2d Cpe Trans Am	252	756	1,260	2,520	4,410	6,300

NOTE: Deduct 15 percent for V-6. Add 10 percent for Indy Pace Car.

1980 Catalina, V-8

	1	2	3	4	5	6
4d Sed	152	456	760	1,520	2,660	3,800
2d Cpe	156	468	780	1,560	2,730	3,900
4d 2S Sta Wag	156	468	780	1,560	2,730	3,900
4d 3S Sta Wag	160	480	800	1,600	2,800	4,000

NOTE: Deduct 10 percent for V-6.

1980 Bonneville, V-8

	1	2	3	4	5	6
4d Sed	156	468	780	1,560	2,730	3,900
2d Cpe	160	480	800	1,600	2,800	4,000
4d 2S Sta Wag	160	480	800	1,600	2,800	4,000
4d 3S Sta Wag	164	492	820	1,640	2,870	4,100

NOTE: Deduct 10 percent for V-6.

1980 Bonneville Brougham, V-8

	1	2	3	4	5	6
4d Sed	164	492	820	1,640	2,870	4,100
2d Cpe	172	516	860	1,720	3,010	4,300

NOTE: Deduct 10 percent for V-6.

1980 Grand Prix, V-8

	1	2	3	4	5	6
2d Cpe	216	648	1,080	2,160	3,780	5,400
2d Cpe LJ	220	660	1,100	2,200	3,850	5,500
2d Cpe SJ	224	672	1,120	2,240	3,920	5,600

NOTE: Deduct 10 percent for V-6.

1981 T1000, 4-cyl.

	1	2	3	4	5	6
2d Sed HBk	140	420	700	1,400	2,450	3,500
4d Sed HBk	144	432	720	1,440	2,520	3,600

1981 Phoenix, V-6

	1	2	3	4	5	6
2d Cpe	148	444	740	1,480	2,590	3,700
4d Sed HBk	144	432	720	1,440	2,520	3,600

NOTE: Deduct 10 percent for 4-cyl.

1981 Phoenix LJ, V-6

	1	2	3	4	5	6
2d Cpe	152	456	760	1,520	2,660	3,800
4d Sed HBk	148	444	740	1,480	2,590	3,700

NOTE: Deduct 10 percent for 4-cyl.

1981 LeMans, V-8

	1	2	3	4	5	6
4d Sed	156	468	780	1,560	2,730	3,900
4d Sed LJ	160	480	800	1,600	2,800	4,000
2d Cpe	160	480	800	1,600	2,800	4,000
4d Sta Wag	160	480	800	1,600	2,800	4,000

NOTE: Deduct 10 percent for V-6.

1981 Grand LeMans, V-8

	1	2	3	4	5	6
4d Sed	184	552	920	1,840	3,220	4,600
2d Cpe	168	504	840	1,680	2,940	4,200
4d Sta Wag	168	504	840	1,680	2,940	4,200

NOTE: Deduct 10 percent for V-6.

1981 Firebird, V-8

	1	2	3	4	5	6
2d Cpe	240	720	1,200	2,400	4,200	6,000
2d Cpe Esprit	244	732	1,220	2,440	4,270	6,100
2d Cpe Formula	248	744	1,240	2,480	4,340	6,200
2d Cpe Trans Am	260	780	1,300	2,600	4,550	6,500
2d Cpe Trans Am SE	250	800	1,350	2,700	4,750	6,800

NOTE: Deduct 15 percent for V-6.

1981 Catalina, V-8

	1	2	3	4	5	6
4d Sed	168	504	840	1,680	2,940	4,200
2d Cpe	172	516	860	1,720	3,010	4,300
4d 2S Sta Wag	172	516	860	1,720	3,010	4,300
4d 3S Sta Wag	176	528	880	1,760	3,080	4,400

NOTE: Deduct 10 percent for V-6.

1981 Bonneville, V-8

	1	2	3	4	5	6
4d Sed	172	516	860	1,720	3,010	4,300
2d Cpe	176	528	880	1,760	3,080	4,400
4d 2S Sta Wag	176	528	880	1,760	3,080	4,400
4d 3S Sta Wag	180	540	900	1,800	3,150	4,500

NOTE: Deduct 10 percent for V-6.

1981 Bonneville Brougham, V-8

	1	2	3	4	5	6
4d Sed	180	540	900	1,800	3,150	4,500
2d Cpe	184	552	920	1,840	3,220	4,600

1981 Grand Prix, V-8

	1	2	3	4	5	6
2d Cpe	216	648	1,080	2,160	3,780	5,400
2d Cpe LJ	220	660	1,100	2,200	3,850	5,500
2d Cpe Brgm	224	672	1,120	2,240	3,920	5,600

NOTE: Deduct 10 percent for V-6.

1982 T1000, 4-cyl.

	1	2	3	4	5	6
4d Sed HBk	148	444	740	1,480	2,590	3,700
2d Cpe HBk	144	432	720	1,440	2,520	3,600

1982 J2000 S, 4-cyl.

	1	2	3	4	5	6
4d Sed	156	468	780	1,560	2,730	3,900
2d Cpe	160	480	800	1,600	2,800	4,000
4d Sta Wag	160	480	800	1,600	2,800	4,000

1982 J2000, 4-cyl.

	1	2	3	4	5	6
4d Sed	160	480	800	1,600	2,800	4,000
2d Cpe	164	492	820	1,640	2,870	4,100
2d Cpe HBk	168	504	840	1,680	2,940	4,200
4d Sta Wag	168	504	840	1,680	2,940	4,200

1982 J2000 LE, 4-cyl.

	1	2	3	4	5	6
4d Sed	164	492	820	1,640	2,870	4,100
2d Cpe	168	504	840	1,680	2,940	4,200

1982 J2000 SE, 4-cyl.

	1	2	3	4	5	6
2d Cpe HBk	176	528	880	1,760	3,080	4,400

1982 Phoenix, V-6

	1	2	3	4	5	6
4d Sed HBk	152	456	760	1,520	2,660	3,800
2d Cpe	156	468	780	1,560	2,730	3,900

NOTE: Deduct 10 percent for 4-cyl.

1982 Phoenix LJ, V-6

	1	2	3	4	5	6
4d Sed HBk	156	468	780	1,560	2,730	3,900
2d Cpe	160	480	800	1,600	2,800	4,000

NOTE: Deduct 10 percent for 4-cyl.

1982 Phoenix SJ, V-6

	1	2	3	4	5	6
4d Sed HBk	160	480	800	1,600	2,800	4,000
2d Cpe	164	492	820	1,640	2,870	4,100

1982 6000, V-6

	1	2	3	4	5	6
4d Sed	168	504	840	1,680	2,940	4,200
2d Cpe	172	516	860	1,720	3,010	4,300

NOTE: Deduct 10 percent for 4-cyl.

1982 6000 LE, V-6

	1	2	3	4	5	6
4d Sed	172	516	860	1,720	3,010	4,300
2d Cpe	176	528	880	1,760	3,080	4,400

NOTE: Deduct 10 percent for 4-cyl.

1982 Firebird, V-8

	1	2	3	4	5	6
2d Cpe	252	756	1,260	2,520	4,410	6,300
2d Cpe SE	264	792	1,320	2,640	4,620	6,600

Standard Catalog of ® Pontiac, 2nd Edition

	1	2	3	4	5	6
2d Cpe Trans Am	276	828	1,380	2,760	4,830	6,900

NOTE: Deduct 15 percent for V-6.

1982 Bonneville, V-6

	1	2	3	4	5	6
4d Sed	180	540	900	1,800	3,150	4,500
4d Sta Wag	180	540	900	1,800	3,150	4,500

1982 Bonneville Brougham

	1	2	3	4	5	6
4d Sed	188	564	940	1,880	3,290	4,700

1982 Grand Prix, V-6

	1	2	3	4	5	6
2d Cpe	236	708	1,180	2,360	4,130	5,900
2d Cpe LJ	244	732	1,220	2,440	4,270	6,100
2d Cpe Brgm	248	744	1,240	2,480	4,340	6,200

1983 1000, 4-cyl.

	1	2	3	4	5	6
4d Sed HBk	152	456	760	1,520	2,660	3,800
2d Cpe	148	444	740	1,480	2,590	3,700

1983 2000, 4-cyl.

	1	2	3	4	5	6
4d Sed	160	480	800	1,600	2,800	4,000
2d Cpe	164	492	820	1,640	2,870	4,100
2d Cpe HBk	168	504	840	1,680	2,940	4,200
4d Sta Wag	168	504	840	1,680	2,940	4,200

1983 2000 LE, 4-cyl.

	1	2	3	4	5	6
4d Sed	168	504	840	1,680	2,940	4,200
2d Cpe	172	516	860	1,720	3,010	4,300
4d Sta Wag	172	516	860	1,720	3,010	4,300

1983 2000 SE, 4-cyl.

	1	2	3	4	5	6
2d Cpe HBk	176	528	880	1,760	3,080	4,400

1983 Sunbird, 4-cyl.

	1	2	3	4	5	6
2d Conv	340	1,020	1,700	3,400	5,950	8,500

1983 Phoenix, V-6

	1	2	3	4	5	6
4d Sed HBk	156	468	780	1,560	2,730	3,900
2d Cpe	160	480	800	1,600	2,800	4,000

NOTE: Deduct 10 percent for 4-cyl.

1983 Phoenix LJ, V-6

	1	2	3	4	5	6
4d Sed HBk	160	480	800	1,600	2,800	4,000
2d Cpe	164	492	820	1,640	2,870	4,100

NOTE: Deduct 10 percent for 4-cyl.

1983 Phoenix SJ, V-6

	1	2	3	4	5	6
4d Sed HBk	164	492	820	1,640	2,870	4,100
2d Cpe	168	504	840	1,680	2,940	4,200

1983 6000, V-6

	1	2	3	4	5	6
4d Sed	172	516	860	1,720	3,010	4,300
2d Cpe	176	528	880	1,760	3,080	4,400

NOTE: Deduct 10 percent for 4-cyl.

1983 6000 LE, V-6

	1	2	3	4	5	6
4d Sed	176	528	880	1,760	3,080	4,400
2d Cpe	180	540	900	1,800	3,150	4,500

NOTE: Deduct 10 percent for 4-cyl.

1983 6000 STE, V-6

	1	2	3	4	5	6
4d Sed	188	564	940	1,880	3,290	4,700

1983 Firebird, V-8

	1	2	3	4	5	6
2d Cpe	252	756	1,260	2,520	4,410	6,300
2d Cpe SE	256	768	1,280	2,560	4,480	6,400
2d Cpe Trans Am	264	792	1,320	2,640	4,620	6,600

NOTE: Deduct 15 percent for V-6.

1983 Bonneville, V-8

	1	2	3	4	5	6
4d Sed	192	576	960	1,920	3,360	4,800
4d Brgm	196	588	980	1,960	3,430	4,900
4d Sta Wag	196	588	980	1,960	3,430	4,900

NOTE: Deduct 10 percent for V-6.

1983 Grand Prix, V-8

	1	2	3	4	5	6
2d Cpe	220	660	1,100	2,200	3,850	5,500
2d Cpe LJ	228	684	1,140	2,280	3,990	5,700
2d Cpe Brgm	232	696	1,160	2,320	4,060	5,800

1984 1000, 4-cyl.

	1	2	3	4	5	6
4d HBk	152	456	760	1,520	2,660	3,800
2d HBk	148	444	740	1,480	2,590	3,700

1984 Sunbird 2000, 4-cyl.

	1	2	3	4	5	6
4d Sed LE	164	492	820	1,640	2,870	4,100
2d Cpe LE	160	480	800	1,600	2,800	4,000
2d Conv LE	340	1,020	1,700	3,400	5,950	8,500
4d Sta Wag LE	168	504	840	1,680	2,940	4,200
4d Sed SE	168	504	840	1,680	2,940	4,200
2d Cpe SE	164	492	820	1,640	2,870	4,100
2d HBk SE	172	516	860	1,720	3,010	4,300

NOTE: Deduct 5 percent for lesser models. Add 10 percent for turbo where available.

1984 Phoenix, 4-cyl.

	1	2	3	4	5	6
2d Sed	156	468	780	1,560	2,730	3,900
4d HBk	160	480	800	1,600	2,800	4,000
2d Sed LE	160	480	800	1,600	2,800	4,000
4d HBk LE	164	492	820	1,640	2,870	4,100

1984 Phoenix, V-6

	1	2	3	4	5	6
2d Sed	164	492	820	1,640	2,870	4,100
4d HBk	168	504	840	1,680	2,940	4,200
2d Sed LE	168	504	840	1,680	2,940	4,200
4d HBk LE	172	516	860	1,720	3,010	4,300
2d Sed SE	176	528	880	1,760	3,080	4,400

1984 6000, 4-cyl.

	1	2	3	4	5	6
4d Sed LE	180	540	900	1,800	3,150	4,500
2d Sed LE	184	552	920	1,840	3,220	4,600
4d Sta Wag LE	188	564	940	1,880	3,290	4,700

NOTE: Deduct 5 percent for lesser models.

1984 6000, V-6

	1	2	3	4	5	6
4d Sed LE	184	552	920	1,840	3,220	4,600
2d Sed LE	188	564	940	1,880	3,290	4,700
4d Sta Wag LE	192	576	960	1,920	3,360	4,800
4d Sed STE	196	588	980	1,960	3,430	4,900

NOTE: Deduct 5 percent for lesser models.

1984 Fiero, 4-cyl.

	1	2	3	4	5	6
2d Cpe	232	696	1,160	2,320	4,060	5,800
2d Cpe Spt	236	708	1,180	2,360	4,130	5,900
2d Cpe SE	240	720	1,200	2,400	4,200	6,000

NOTE: Add 40 percent for Indy Pace Car.

1984 Firebird, V-6

	1	2	3	4	5	6
2d Cpe	244	732	1,220	2,440	4,270	6,100
2d Cpe SE	252	756	1,260	2,520	4,410	6,300

1984 Firebird, V-8

	1	2	3	4	5	6
2d Cpe	264	792	1,320	2,640	4,620	6,600
2d Cpe SE	268	804	1,340	2,680	4,690	6,700
2d Cpe TA	272	816	1,360	2,720	4,760	6,800

1984 Bonneville, V-6

	1	2	3	4	5	6
4d Sed	184	552	920	1,840	3,220	4,600
4d Sed LE	188	564	940	1,880	3,290	4,700
4d Sed Brgm	192	576	960	1,920	3,360	4,800

1984 Bonneville, V-8

	1	2	3	4	5	6
4d Sed	192	576	960	1,920	3,360	4,800
4d Sed LE	196	588	980	1,960	3,430	4,900
4d Sed Brgm	200	600	1,000	2,000	3,500	5,000

1984 Grand Prix, V-6

	1	2	3	4	5	6
2d Cpe	220	660	1,100	2,200	3,850	5,500
2d Cpe LE	228	684	1,140	2,280	3,990	5,700
2d Cpe Brgm	236	708	1,180	2,360	4,130	5,900

1984 Grand Prix, V-8

	1	2	3	4	5	6
2d Cpe	232	696	1,160	2,320	4,060	5,800
2d Cpe LE	240	720	1,200	2,400	4,200	6,000
2d Cpe Brgm	256	768	1,280	2,560	4,480	6,400

1984 Parisienne, V-6

	1	2	3	4	5	6
4d Sed	180	540	900	1,800	3,150	4,500
4d Sed Brgm	184	552	920	1,840	3,220	4,600

1984 Parisienne, V-8

	1	2	3	4	5	6
4d Sed	188	564	940	1,880	3,290	4,700
4d Sed Brgm	192	576	960	1,920	3,360	4,800
4d Sta Wag	196	588	980	1,960	3,430	4,900

1985 1000, 4-cyl.

	1	2	3	4	5	6
4d Sed	152	456	760	1,520	2,660	3,800
2d Sed	148	444	740	1,480	2,590	3,700
2d HBk	156	468	780	1,560	2,730	3,900
4d Sta Wag	160	480	800	1,600	2,800	4,000

1985 Sunbird, 4-cyl.

	1	2	3	4	5	6
4d Sed	164	492	820	1,640	2,870	4,100
2d Cpe	160	480	800	1,600	2,800	4,000
Conv	340	1,020	1,700	3,400	5,950	8,500
4d Sta Wag	168	504	840	1,680	2,940	4,200
4d Sed SE	168	504	840	1,680	2,940	4,200
2d Cpe SE	164	492	820	1,640	2,870	4,100
2d HBk SE	172	516	860	1,720	3,010	4,300

NOTE: Add 20 percent for turbo.

1985 Grand AM, V-6

	1	2	3	4	5	6
2d Cpe	180	540	900	1,800	3,150	4,500
2d Cpe LE	184	552	920	1,840	3,220	4,600

NOTE: Deduct 15 percent for 4-cyl.

1985 6000, V-6

	1	2	3	4	5	6
4d Sed LE	184	552	920	1,840	3,220	4,600
2d Sed LE	188	564	940	1,880	3,290	4,700
4d Sta Wag LE	192	576	960	1,920	3,360	4,800
4d Sed STE	196	588	980	1,960	3,430	4,900

NOTE: Deduct 20 percent for 4-cyl. where available. Deduct 5 percent for lesser models.

1985 Fiero, V-6

	1	2	3	4	5	6
2d Cpe	240	720	1,200	2,400	4,200	6,000
2d Cpe Spt	244	732	1,220	2,440	4,270	6,100
2d Cpe SE	248	744	1,240	2,480	4,340	6,200
2d Cpe GT	252	756	1,260	2,520	4,410	6,300

NOTE: Deduct 20 percent for 4-cyl. where available.

	1	2	3	4	5	6
1985 Firebird, V-8						
2d Cpe	264	792	1,320	2,640	4,620	6,600
2d Cpe SE	268	804	1,340	2,680	4,690	6,700
2d Cpe Trans AM	272	816	1,360	2,720	4,760	6,800

NOTE: Deduct 30 percent for V-6 where available.

	1	2	3	4	5	6
1985 Bonneville, V-8						
4d Sed	184	552	920	1,840	3,220	4,600
4d Sed LE	188	564	940	1,880	3,290	4,700
4d Sed Brgm	192	576	960	1,920	3,360	4,800

NOTE: Deduct 25 percent for V-6.

	1	2	3	4	5	6
1985 Grand Prix, V-8						
2d Cpe	220	660	1,100	2,200	3,850	5,500
2d Cpe LE	228	684	1,140	2,280	3,990	5,700
2d Cpe Brgm	236	708	1,180	2,360	4,130	5,900

NOTE: Deduct 25 percent for V-6.

	1	2	3	4	5	6
1985 Parisienne, V-8						
4d Sed	188	564	940	1,880	3,290	4,700
4d Sed Brgm	192	576	960	1,920	3,360	4,800
4d Sta Wag	196	588	980	1,960	3,430	4,900

NOTE: Deduct 20 percent for V-6 where available. Deduct 30 percent for diesel.

	1	2	3	4	5	6
1986 Fiero, V-6						
2d Cpe Spt	240	720	1,200	2,400	4,200	6,000
2d Cpe SE	244	732	1,220	2,440	4,270	6,100
2d Cpe GT	252	756	1,260	2,520	4,410	6,300

NOTE: Deduct 20 percent for 4-cyl. where available.

	1	2	3	4	5	6
2d HBk	152	456	760	1,520	2,660	3,800
4d HBk	156	468	780	1,560	2,730	3,900
1986 Sunbird						
2d Cpe	160	480	800	1,600	2,800	4,000
2d HBk	164	492	820	1,640	2,870	4,100
2d Conv	344	1,032	1,720	3,440	6,020	8,600
4d GT Sed	164	492	820	1,640	2,870	4,100
2d GT Conv	352	1,056	1,760	3,520	6,160	8,800
1986 Grand Am						
2d Cpe	188	564	940	1,880	3,290	4,700
4d Sed	184	552	920	1,840	3,220	4,600
1986 Firebird						
2d Cpe	264	792	1,320	2,640	4,620	6,600
2d SE V-8 Cpe	268	804	1,340	2,680	4,690	6,700
Trans Am Cpe	276	828	1,380	2,760	4,830	6,900
1986 6000						
2d Cpe	192	576	960	1,920	3,360	4,800
4d Sed	188	564	940	1,880	3,290	4,700
4d Sta Wag	192	576	960	1,920	3,360	4,800
4d STE Sed	200	600	1,000	2,000	3,500	5,000
1986 Grand Prix						
2d Cpe	228	684	1,140	2,280	3,990	5,700
1986 Bonneville						
4d Sed	192	576	960	1,920	3,360	4,800
1986 Parisienne						
4d Sed	196	588	980	1,960	3,430	4,900
4d Sta Wag	232	696	1,160	2,320	4,060	5,800
4d Brgm Sed	200	600	1,000	2,000	3,500	5,000

NOTE: Add 10 percent for deluxe models.

	1	2	3	4	5	6
1986-1/2 Grand Prix 2 plus 2						
2d Aero Cpe	560	1,680	2,800	5,600	9,800	14,000

NOTE: Deduct 5 percent for smaller engines.

	1	2	3	4	5	6
1987 1000, 4-cyl.						
2d HBk	152	456	760	1,520	2,660	3,800
4d HBk	156	468	780	1,560	2,730	3,900
1987 Sunbird, 4-cyl.						
4d Sed	156	468	780	1,560	2,730	3,900
4d Sta Wag	160	480	800	1,600	2,800	4,000
2d SE Cpe	164	492	820	1,640	2,870	4,100
2d SE HBk	168	504	840	1,680	2,940	4,200
2d SE Conv	520	1,560	2,600	5,200	9,100	13,000
4d GT Turbo Sed	172	516	860	1,720	3,010	4,300
2d GT Turbo Cpe	168	504	840	1,680	2,940	4,200
2d GT Turbo HBk	172	516	860	1,720	3,010	4,300
2d GT Turbo Conv	560	1,680	2,800	5,600	9,800	14,000

NOTE: Add 5 percent for Turbo on all models except GT.

	1	2	3	4	5	6
1987 Grand Am, 4-cyl.						
4d Sed	192	576	960	1,920	3,360	4,800
2d Cpe	196	588	980	1,960	3,430	4,900
4d LE Sed	196	588	980	1,960	3,430	4,900
2d LE Cpe	200	600	1,000	2,000	3,500	5,000
4d SE Sed	204	612	1,020	2,040	3,570	5,100
2d SE Cpe	208	624	1,040	2,080	3,640	5,200
1987 Grand Am, V-6						
4d Sed	196	588	980	1,960	3,430	4,900
2d Cpe	200	600	1,000	2,000	3,500	5,000

	1	2	3	4	5	6
4d LE Sed	200	600	1,000	2,000	3,500	5,000
2d LE Cpe	204	612	1,020	2,040	3,570	5,100
4d SE Sed	212	636	1,060	2,120	3,710	5,300
2d SE Cpe	216	648	1,080	2,160	3,780	5,400
1987 6000, 4-cyl.						
4d Sed	200	600	1,000	2,000	3,500	5,000
2d Cpe	196	588	980	1,960	3,430	4,900
4d Sta Wag	204	612	1,020	2,040	3,570	5,100
4d LE Sed	204	612	1,020	2,040	3,570	5,100
4d LE Sta Wag	208	624	1,040	2,080	3,640	5,200
1987 6000, V-6						
4d Sed	204	612	1,020	2,040	3,570	5,100
2d Cpe	200	600	1,000	2,000	3,500	5,000
4d Sta Wag	208	624	1,040	2,080	3,640	5,200
4d LE Sed	208	624	1,040	2,080	3,640	5,200
4d LE Sta Wag	212	636	1,060	2,120	3,710	5,300
4d SE Sed	212	636	1,060	2,120	3,710	5,300
4d SE Sta Wag	216	648	1,080	2,160	3,780	5,400
4d STE Sed	216	648	1,080	2,160	3,780	5,400
1987 Fiero, V-6						
2d Cpe	244	732	1,220	2,440	4,270	6,100
2d Spt Cpe	248	744	1,240	2,480	4,340	6,200
2d SE Cpe	252	756	1,260	2,520	4,410	6,300

NOTE: Deduct 20 percent for 4-cyl.

	1	2	3	4	5	6
2d GT Cpe	260	780	1,300	2,600	4,550	6,500
1987 Firebird, V-6						
2d Cpe	268	804	1,340	2,680	4,690	6,700
1987 Firebird, V-8						
2d Cpe	276	828	1,380	2,760	4,830	6,900
2d Cpe Formula	280	840	1,400	2,800	4,900	7,000
2d Cpe Trans Am	288	864	1,440	2,880	5,040	7,200
2d Cpe GTA	296	888	1,480	2,960	5,180	7,400

NOTE: Add 10 percent for 5.7 liter V-8 where available.

	1	2	3	4	5	6
1987 Bonneville, V-6						
4d Sed	200	600	1,000	2,000	3,500	5,000
4d LE Sed	208	624	1,040	2,080	3,640	5,200
1987 Grand Prix, V-6						
2d Cpe	232	696	1,160	2,320	4,060	5,800
2d LE Cpe	236	708	1,180	2,360	4,130	5,900
2d Brgm Cpe	240	720	1,200	2,400	4,200	6,000
1987 Grand Prix, V-8						
2d Cpe	240	720	1,200	2,400	4,200	6,000
2d LE Cpe	244	732	1,220	2,440	4,270	6,100
2d Brgm Cpe	248	744	1,240	2,480	4,340	6,200
1987 Safari, V-8						
4d Sta Wag	208	624	1,040	2,080	3,640	5,200
1988 LeMans, 4-cyl.						
3d HBk	100	300	500	1,000	1,750	2,500
4d Sed	112	336	560	1,120	1,960	2,800
4d SE Sed	120	360	600	1,200	2,100	3,000
1988 Sunbird, 4-cyl.						
4d Sed	136	408	680	1,360	2,380	3,400
2d SE Cpe	144	432	720	1,440	2,520	3,600
4d SE Sed	148	444	740	1,480	2,590	3,700
4d Sta Wag	152	456	760	1,520	2,660	3,800
2d GT Cpe	200	600	1,000	2,000	3,500	5,000
2d GT Conv	340	1,020	1,700	3,400	5,950	8,500
1988 Grand Am, 4-cyl.						
2d Cpe	180	540	900	1,800	3,150	4,500
4d Sed	184	552	920	1,840	3,220	4,600
2d LE Cpe	192	576	960	1,920	3,360	4,800
4d Sed LE	196	588	980	1,960	3,430	4,900
2d SE Turbo Cpe	224	672	1,120	2,240	3,920	5,600
4d SE Turbo Sed	228	684	1,140	2,280	3,990	5,700
1988 6000, 4-cyl.						
4d Sed	156	468	780	1,560	2,730	3,900
4d Sta Wag	160	480	800	1,600	2,800	4,000
4d LE Sed	160	480	800	1,600	2,800	4,000
4d LE Sta Wag	168	504	840	1,680	2,940	4,200
1988 6000, V-6						
4d Sed	168	504	840	1,680	2,940	4,200
4d Sta Wag	180	540	900	1,800	3,150	4,500
4d Sed LE	200	600	1,000	2,000	3,500	5,000
4d LE Sta Wag	200	600	1,000	2,000	3,500	5,000
4d SE Sed	208	624	1,040	2,080	3,640	5,200
4d SE Sta Wag	220	660	1,100	2,200	3,850	5,500
4d STE Sed	288	864	1,440	2,880	5,040	7,200
1988 Fiero, V-6						
2d Cpe III	240	720	1,200	2,400	4,200	6,000
2d Formula Cpe	260	780	1,300	2,600	4,550	6,500
2d GT Cpe	272	816	1,360	2,720	4,760	6,800
1988 Firebird, V-6						
2d Cpe	240	720	1,200	2,400	4,200	6,000

	1	2	3	4	5	6
1988 Firebird, V-8						
2d Cpe	280	840	1,400	2,800	4,900	7,000
2d Formula Cpe	320	960	1,600	3,200	5,600	8,000
2d Cpe Trans Am	520	1,560	2,600	5,200	9,100	13,000
2d Cpe GTA	600	1,800	3,000	6,000	10,500	15,000
1988 Bonneville, V-6						
4d LE Sed	240	720	1,200	2,400	4,200	6,000
4d SE Sed	300	900	1,500	3,000	5,250	7,500
4d SSE Sed	520	1,560	2,600	5,200	9,100	13,000
1988 Grand Prix, V-6						
2d Cpe	260	780	1,300	2,600	4,550	6,500
2d LE Cpe	280	840	1,400	2,800	4,900	7,000
2d SE Cpe	320	960	1,600	3,200	5,600	8,000
1989 LeMans, 4-cyl.						
2d HBk	108	324	540	1,080	1,890	2,700
2d LE HBk	116	348	580	1,160	2,030	2,900
2d GSE HBk	136	408	680	1,360	2,380	3,400
4d LE Sed	132	396	660	1,320	2,310	3,300
4d SE Sed	140	420	700	1,400	2,450	3,500
1989 Sunbird, 4-cyl.						
4d LE Sed		184	552	920	1,840	3,220 4,600
2d LE Cpe		180	540	900	1,800	3,150 4,500
2d SE Cpe	188	564	940	1,880	3,290	4,700
2d GT Turbo Cpe	268	804	1,340	2,680	4,690	6,700
2d GT Turbo Conv	540	1,620	2,700	5,400	9,450	13,500
1989 Grand Am, 4-cyl.						
4d LE Sed	224	672	1,120	2,240	3,920	5,600
2d LE Cpe	220	660	1,100	2,200	3,850	5,500
4d SE Sed	252	756	1,260	2,520	4,410	6,300
2d SE Cpe	248	744	1,240	2,480	4,340	6,200
1989 6000, 4-cyl.						
4d Sed LE	228	684	1,140	2,280	3,990	5,700
1989 6000, V-6						
4d LE Sed	244	732	1,220	2,440	4,270	6,100
4d LE Sta Wag	256	768	1,280	2,560	4,480	6,400
4d STE Sed	320	960	1,600	3,200	5,600	8,000
1989 Firebird, V-6						
2d Cpe	260	780	1,300	2,600	4,550	6,500
1989 Firebird, V-8						
2d Cpe	280	840	1,400	2,800	4,900	7,000
2d Formula Cpe	300	900	1,500	3,000	5,250	7,500
2d Trans Am Cpe	560	1,680	2,800	5,600	9,800	14,000
1989 V-6						
2d Trans Am Cpe	550	1,700	2,800	5,600	9,800	14,000
2d GTA Cpe	600	1,800	3,000	6,000	10,500	15,000
NOTE: Add 10 percent for turbo pace car edition.						
1989 Bonneville, V-6						
4d LE Sed	272	816	1,360	2,720	4,760	6,800
4d SE Sed	312	936	1,560	3,120	5,460	7,800
4d SSE Sed	352	1,056	1,760	3,520	6,160	8,800
1989 Grand Prix, V-6						
2d Cpe	280	840	1,400	2,800	4,900	7,000
2d LE Cpe	300	900	1,500	3,000	5,250	7,500
2d SE Cpe	320	960	1,600	3,200	5,600	8,000
NOTE: Add 40 percent for McLaren Turbo Cpe.						
1989 Safari, V-8						
4d Sta Wag	288	864	1,440	2,880	5,040	7,200
1989-1/2 Firebird Trans Am Pace Car, V-6 Turbo						
Cpe	760	2,280	3,800	7,600	13,300	19,000
1990 LeMans, 4-cyl.						
2d Cpe	112	336	560	1,120	1,960	2,800
2d LE Cpe	128	384	640	1,280	2,240	3,200
2d GSE Cpe	144	432	720	1,440	2,520	3,600
4d LE Sed	128	384	640	1,280	2,240	3,200
1990 Sunbird, 4-cyl.						
2d VL Cpe	160	480	800	1,600	2,800	4,000
4d VL Sed	164	492	820	1,640	2,870	4,100
2d LE Cpe	168	504	840	1,680	2,940	4,200
2d LE Conv	300	900	1,500	3,000	5,250	7,500
4d LE Sed	172	516	860	1,720	3,010	4,300
2d SE Cpe	200	600	1,000	2,000	3,500	5,000
2d GT Turbo Cpe	240	720	1,200	2,400	4,200	6,000
1990 Grand Am, 4-cyl.						
2d LE Cpe	228	684	1,140	2,280	3,990	5,700
4d LE Cpe	240	720	1,200	2,400	4,200	6,000
2d SE Quad Cpe	260	780	1,300	2,600	4,550	6,500
4d SE Quad Sed	264	792	1,320	2,640	4,620	6,600
1990 6000, 4-cyl.						
4d LE Sed	180	540	900	1,800	3,150	4,500

	1	2	3	4	5	6
1990 6000, V-6						
4d LE Sed	200	600	1,000	2,000	3,500	5,000
4d LE Sta Wag	220	660	1,100	2,200	3,850	5,500
4d SE Sed	220	660	1,100	2,200	3,850	5,500
4d SE Sta Wag	240	720	1,200	2,400	4,200	6,000
1990 Firebird, V-6						
2d Cpe	260	780	1,300	2,600	4,550	6,500
1990 Firebird, V-8						
2d Cpe	300	900	1,500	3,000	5,250	7,500
2d Formula Cpe	320	960	1,600	3,200	5,600	8,000
2d Trans Am Cpe	520	1,560	2,600	5,200	9,100	13,000
2d GTA Cpe	600	1,800	3,000	6,000	10,500	15,000
1990 Bonneville, V-6						
4d LE Sed	280	840	1,400	2,800	4,900	7,000
4d SE Sed	300	900	1,500	3,000	5,250	7,500
4d SSE Sed	340	1,020	1,700	3,400	5,950	8,500
1990 Grand Prix, 4-cyl.						
2d LE Cpe	240	720	1,200	2,400	4,200	6,000
4d LE Sed	244	732	1,220	2,440	4,270	6,100
1990 Grand Prix, V-6						
2d LE Cpe	252	756	1,260	2,520	4,410	6,300
4d LE Sed	256	768	1,280	2,560	4,480	6,400
2d SE Cpe	320	960	1,600	3,200	5,600	8,000
4d STE Sed	340	1,020	1,700	3,400	5,950	8,500
1991 LeMans, 4-cyl.						
2d Aero Cpe	128	384	640	1,280	2,240	3,200
2d Aero LE Cpe	152	456	760	1,520	2,660	3,800
4d LE Sed	140	420	700	1,400	2,450	3,500
1991 Sunbird, 4-cyl.						
2d Cpe	152	456	760	1,520	2,660	3,800
4d Sed	152	456	760	1,520	2,660	3,800
2d LE Cpe	160	480	800	1,600	2,800	4,000
4d LE Cpe	160	480	800	1,600	2,800	4,000
2d LE Conv	320	960	1,600	3,200	5,600	8,000
2d SE Cpe	200	600	1,000	2,000	3,500	5,000
1991 Sunbird, V-6						
2d GT Cpe	260	780	1,300	2,600	4,550	6,500
1991 Grand Am, 4-cyl.						
2d Cpe	200	600	1,000	2,000	3,500	5,000
4d Sed	200	600	1,000	2,000	3,500	5,000
2d LE Cpe	208	624	1,040	2,080	3,640	5,200
4d LE Sed	208	624	1,040	2,080	3,640	5,200
2d SE Quad 4 Cpe	232	696	1,160	2,320	4,060	5,800
4d SE Quad 4 Sed	232	696	1,160	2,320	4,060	5,800
1991 6000, 4-cyl.						
4d LE Sed	180	540	900	1,800	3,150	4,500
1991 6000, V-6						
4d LE Sed	200	600	1,000	2,000	3,500	5,000
4d LE Sta Wag	220	660	1,100	2,200	3,850	5,500
4d SE Sed	216	648	1,080	2,160	3,780	5,400
1991 Firebird, V-6						
2d Cpe	260	780	1,300	2,600	4,550	6,500
2d Conv	560	1,680	2,800	5,600	9,800	14,000
1991 Firebird, V-8						
2d Cpe	300	900	1,500	3,000	5,250	7,500
2d Conv	600	1,800	3,000	6,000	10,500	15,000
2d Formula Cpe	320	960	1,600	3,200	5,600	8,000
2d Trans Am Cpe	520	1,560	2,600	5,200	9,100	13,000
2d Trans Am Conv	660	1,980	3,300	6,600	11,550	16,500
2d GTA Cpe	600	1,800	3,000	6,000	10,500	15,000
1991 Bonneville, V-6						
4d LE Sed	260	780	1,300	2,600	4,550	6,500
4d SE Sed	300	900	1,500	3,000	5,250	7,500
4d SSE Sed	320	960	1,600	3,200	5,600	8,000
1991 Grand Prix, Quad 4						
2d SE Cpe	220	660	1,100	2,200	3,850	5,500
4d LE Sed	220	660	1,100	2,200	3,850	5,500
4d SE Sed	232	696	1,160	2,320	4,060	5,800
1991 Grand Prix, V-6						
4d SE Cpe	240	720	1,200	2,400	4,200	6,000
2d GT Cpe	256	768	1,280	2,560	4,480	6,400
4d LE Sed	240	720	1,200	2,400	4,200	6,000
4d SE Sed	256	768	1,280	2,560	4,480	6,400
4d STE Sed	280	840	1,400	2,800	4,900	7,000
1992 LeMans, 4-cyl.						
2d Aero Cpe HBk	152	456	760	1,520	2,660	3,800
2d SE Aero Cpe HBk	156	468	780	1,560	2,730	3,900
4d SE Sed	160	480	800	1,600	2,800	4,000
1992 Sunbird, 4-cyl.						
4d LE Sed	160	480	800	1,600	2,800	4,000
2d LE Cpe	164	492	820	1,640	2,870	4,100

	1	2	3	4	5	6
4d SE Sed	168	504	840	1,680	2,940	4,200
2d SE Cpe	172	516	860	1,720	3,010	4,300
2d SE Conv	260	780	1,300	2,600	4,550	6,500
2d GT Cpe V-6	180	540	900	1,800	3,150	4,500

1992 Grand Am, 4-cyl.

	1	2	3	4	5	6
4d SE Sed	200	600	1,000	2,000	3,500	5,000
2d SE Cpe	220	660	1,100	2,200	3,850	5,500
4d GT Sed	240	720	1,200	2,400	4,200	6,000
2d GT Cpe	260	780	1,300	2,600	4,550	6,500

NOTE: Add 10 percent for V-6.

1992 Firebird, V-8

	1	2	3	4	5	6
2d Cpe	320	960	1,600	3,200	5,600	8,000
2d Conv	600	1,800	3,000	6,000	10,500	15,000
2d Formula Cpe	340	1,020	1,700	3,400	5,950	8,500
2d Trans Am Cpe	540	1,620	2,700	5,400	9,450	13,500
2d Trans Am Conv	620	1,860	3,100	6,200	10,850	15,500
2d GTA Cpe	580	1,740	2,900	5,800	10,150	14,500

NOTE: Deduct 10 percent for V-6.

1992 Bonneville, V-6

	1	2	3	4	5	6
4d SE Sed	260	780	1,300	2,600	4,550	6,500
4d SSE Sed	300	900	1,500	3,000	5,250	7,500
4d SSEi Sed	520	1,560	2,600	5,200	9,100	13,000

1992 Grand Prix, V-6

	1	2	3	4	5	6
4d LE Sed	220	660	1,100	2,200	3,850	5,500
4d SE Sed	240	720	1,200	2,400	4,200	6,000
2d SE Cpe	260	780	1,300	2,600	4,550	6,500
4d STE Sed	320	960	1,600	3,200	5,600	8,000
2d GT Cpe	340	1,020	1,700	3,400	5,950	8,500

1993 LeMans

	1	2	3	4	5	6
2d Aero Cpe	156	468	780	1,560	2,730	3,900
2d SE Aero Cpe	160	480	800	1,600	2,800	4,000
4d SE Sed	156	468	780	1,560	2,730	3,900

1993 Sunbird

	1	2	3	4	5	6
2d LE Cpe	168	504	840	1,680	2,940	4,200
4d LE Sed	170	510	850	1,700	2,975	4,250
2d SE Cpe	172	516	860	1,720	3,010	4,300
4d SE Sed	174	522	870	1,740	3,045	4,350
2d GT Cpe, V-6	180	540	900	1,800	3,150	4,500
2d SE Conv	188	564	940	1,880	3,290	4,700

1993 Grand Am, 4-cyl.

	1	2	3	4	5	6
2d SE Cpe	220	660	1,100	2,200	3,850	5,500
4d SE Sed	220	660	1,100	2,200	3,850	5,500
2d GT Cpe	224	672	1,120	2,240	3,920	5,600
4d GT Sed	224	672	1,120	2,240	3,920	5,600

1993 Grand Am, V-6

	1	2	3	4	5	6
2d SE Cpe	224	672	1,120	2,240	3,920	5,600
4d SE Sed	224	672	1,120	2,240	3,920	5,600
2d GT Cpe	228	684	1,140	2,280	3,990	5,700
4d GT Sed	228	684	1,140	2,280	3,990	5,700

1993 Firebird

	1	2	3	4	5	6
2d Cpe, V-6	320	960	1,600	3,200	5,600	8,000
2d Formula Cpe, V-8	500	1,550	2,600	5,200	9,100	13,000
2d Trans Am Cpe, V-8	550	1,600	2,700	5,400	9,450	13,500

1993 Bonneville, V-6

	1	2	3	4	5	6
4d SE Sed	320	960	1,600	3,200	5,600	8,000
4d SSE Sed	340	1,020	1,700	3,400	5,950	8,500
4d SSEi Sed	520	1,560	2,600	5,200	9,100	13,000

1993 Grand Prix

	1	2	3	4	5	6
2d SE Cpe	240	720	1,200	2,400	4,200	6,000

	1	2	3	4	5	6
2d GT Cpe	248	744	1,240	2,480	4,340	6,200
4d LE Sed	240	720	1,200	2,400	4,200	6,000
4d SE Sed	248	744	1,240	2,480	4,340	6,200
4d STE Sed	256	768	1,280	2,560	4,480	6,400

1994 Sunbird

	1	2	3	4	5	6
2d LE Cpe, 4-cyl.	220	660	1,100	2,200	3,850	5,500
4d LE Sed, 4-cyl.	224	672	1,120	2,240	3,920	5,600
2d LE Conv, 4-cyl.	300	900	1,500	3,000	5,250	7,500
2d SE Cpe, V-6	260	780	1,300	2,600	4,550	6,500

1994 Grand Am

	1	2	3	4	5	6
2d SE Cpe, 4-cyl.	244	732	1,220	2,440	4,270	6,100
4d SE Sed, 4-cyl.	248	744	1,240	2,480	4,340	6,200
4d GT Sed, 4-cyl.	260	780	1,300	2,600	4,550	6,500
2d SE Cpe, V-6	252	756	1,260	2,520	4,410	6,300
2d GT Cpe, V-6	256	768	1,280	2,560	4,480	6,400
4d SE Sed, V-6	256	768	1,280	2,560	4,480	6,400
4d GT Sed, V-6	260	780	1,300	2,600	4,550	6,500

1994 Firebird

	1	2	3	4	5	6
2d Cpe, V-6	420	1,260	2,100	4,200	7,350	10,500
2d Conv, V-6	540	1,620	2,700	5,400	9,450	13,500
2d Formula Cpe, V-8	500	1,450	2,400	4,800	8,400	12,000
2d Formula Conv, V-8	600	1,750	2,900	5,800	10,200	14,500
2d Trans Am Cpe, V-8	550	1,600	2,700	5,400	9,450	13,500
2d Trans Am GT Cpe, V-8	580	1,740	2,900	5,800	10,150	14,500
2d Trans Am GT Conv, V-8	620	1,860	3,100	6,200	10,850	15,500

1994 Bonneville, V-6

	1	2	3	4	5	6
4d SE Sed	340	1,020	1,700	3,400	5,950	8,500
4d SSE Sed	440	1,320	2,200	4,400	7,700	11,000

1994 Grand Prix

	1	2	3	4	5	6
2d SE Cpe	340	1,020	1,700	3,400	5,950	8,500
4d SE Sed	344	1,032	1,720	3,440	6,020	8,600

1995 Sunbird, 4-cyl.

	1	2	3	4	5	6
2d SE Cpe	200	650	1,100	2,200	3,850	5,500
4d SE Sed	200	650	1,100	2,250	3,900	5,600
2d SE Conv	300	900	1,500	3,000	5,250	7,500
2d GT Cpe	300	850	1,400	2,800	4,900	7,000

1995 Grand Am, 4-cyl. & V-6

	1	2	3	4	5	6
2d SE Cpe	250	750	1,200	2,450	4,250	6,100
4d SE Sed	250	750	1,250	2,500	4,350	6,200
2d GT Cpe	250	750	1,300	2,550	4,500	6,400
4d GT Sed	250	800	1,300	2,600	4,550	6,500

1995 Firebird, V-6 & V-8

	1	2	3	4	5	6
2d Cpe, V-6	400	1,250	2,100	4,200	7,350	10,500
2d Conv, V-6	550	1,600	2,700	5,400	9,450	13,500
2d Formula Cpe, V-8	500	1,450	2,400	4,800	8,400	12,000
2d Formula Conv, V-8	600	1,750	2,900	5,800	10,200	14,500
2d Trans Am Cpe, V-8	550	1,600	2,700	5,400	9,450	13,500
2d Trans Am Conv, V-8	600	1,850	3,100	6,200	10,900	15,500

1995 Bonneville, V-6

	1	2	3	4	5	6
4d SE Sed	350	1,000	1,700	3,400	5,950	8,500
4d SSE Sed	450	1,300	2,200	4,400	7,700	11,000
4d SSEi Sed	500	1,500	2,500	5,000	8,750	12,500

1995 Grand Prix, V-6

	1	2	3	4	5	6
2d SE Cpe	350	1,000	1,700	3,400	5,950	8,500
4d SE Sed	350	1,050	1,700	3,450	6,000	8,600

OAKLAND

	1	2	3	4	5	6
1907 Model A, 4-cyl., 96" wb - 100" sb						
All Body Styles	1,480	4,440	7,400	14,800	25,900	37,000
1909 Model 20, 2-cyl., 112" wb						
All Body Styles	1,360	4,080	6,800	13,600	23,800	34,000
1909 Model 40, 4-cyl., 112" wb						
All Body Styles	1,280	3,840	6,400	12,800	22,400	32,000
1910-1911 Model 24, 4-cyl., 96" wb						
Rds	1,040	3,120	5,200	10,400	18,200	26,000
1910-1911 Model 25, 4-cyl., 100" wb						
Tr	960	2,880	4,800	9,600	16,800	24,000
1910-1911 Model 33, 4-cyl., 106" wb						
Tr	1,120	3,360	5,600	11,200	19,600	28,000
1910-1911 Model K, 4-cyl., 102" wb						
Tr	1,200	3,600	6,000	12,000	21,000	30,000

	1	2	3	4	5	6
1910-1911 Model M, 4-cyl., 112" wb						
Rds	1,240	3,720	6,200	12,400	21,700	31,000
NOTE: Model 33 1911 only.						
1912 Model 30, 4-cyl., 106" wb						
5P Tr	760	2,280	3,800	7,600	13,300	19,000
Rbt	780	2,340	3,900	7,800	13,650	19,500
1912 Model 40, 4-cyl., 112" wb						
5P Tr	760	2,280	3,800	7,600	13,300	19,000
Cpe	600	1,800	3,000	6,000	10,500	15,000
Rds	800	2,400	4,000	8,000	14,000	20,000
1912 Model 45, 4-cyl., 120" wb						
7P Tr	1,000	3,000	5,000	10,000	17,500	25,000
4P Tr	1,040	3,120	5,200	10,400	18,200	26,000
Limo	960	2,880	4,800	9,600	16,800	24,000
1913 Greyhound 6-60, 6-cyl., 130" wb						
4P Tr	1,120	3,360	5,600	11,200	19,600	28,000

	1	2	3	4	5	6
7P Tr	1,080	3,240	5,400	10,800	18,900	27,000
Rbt	920	2,760	4,600	9,200	16,100	23,000

1913 Model 42, 4-cyl., 116" wb

	1	2	3	4	5	6
5P Tr	880	2,640	4,400	8,800	15,400	22,000
3P Rds	840	2,520	4,200	8,400	14,700	21,000
4P Cpe	600	1,800	3,000	6,000	10,500	15,000

1913 Model 35, 4-cyl., 112" wb

	1	2	3	4	5	6
5P Tr	800	2,400	4,000	8,000	14,000	20,000
3P Rds	800	2,400	4,000	8,000	14,000	20,000

1913 Model 40, 4-cyl., 114" wb

	1	2	3	4	5	6
5P Tr	840	2,520	4,200	8,400	14,700	21,000

1913 Model 45, 4-cyl., 120" wb

	1	2	3	4	5	6
7P Limo	760	2,280	3,800	7,600	13,300	19,000

1914 Model 6-60, 6-cyl., 130" wb

	1	2	3	4	5	6
Rbt	840	2,520	4,200	8,400	14,700	21,000
Rds	1,000	3,000	5,000	10,000	17,500	25,000
Cl Cpl	800	2,400	4,000	8,000	14,000	20,000
Tr	1,080	3,240	5,400	10,800	18,900	27,000

1914 Model 6-48, 6-cyl., 130" wb

	1	2	3	4	5	6
Spt	640	1,920	3,200	6,400	11,200	16,000
Rds	920	2,760	4,600	9,200	16,100	23,000
Tr	960	2,880	4,800	9,600	16,800	24,000

1914 Model 43, 4-cyl., 116" wb

	1	2	3	4	5	6
5P Tr	800	2,400	4,000	8,000	14,000	20,000
Cpe	560	1,680	2,800	5,600	9,800	14,000
Sed	540	1,620	2,700	5,400	9,450	13,500

1914 Model 36, 4-cyl., 112" wb

	1	2	3	4	5	6
5P Tr	760	2,280	3,800	7,600	13,300	19,000
Cabr	740	2,220	3,700	7,400	12,950	18,500

1914 Model 35, 4-cyl., 112" wb

	1	2	3	4	5	6
Rds	720	2,160	3,600	7,200	12,600	18,000
5P Tr	740	2,220	3,700	7,400	12,950	18,500

1915-1916 Model 37 - Model 38, 4-cyl., 112" wb

	1	2	3	4	5	6
Tr	720	2,160	3,600	7,200	12,600	18,000
Rds	680	2,040	3,400	6,800	11,900	17,000
Spd	660	1,980	3,300	6,600	11,550	16,500

1915-1916 Model 49 - Model 32, 6-cyl., 110"-123.5" wb

	1	2	3	4	5	6
Tr	800	2,400	4,000	8,000	14,000	20,000
Rds	780	2,340	3,900	7,800	13,650	19,500

1915-1916 Model 50, 8-cyl., 127" wb

	1	2	3	4	5	6
7P Tr	920	2,760	4,600	9,200	16,100	23,000

NOTE: Model 37 and Model 49 are 1915 models.

1917 Model 34, 6-cyl., 112" wb

	1	2	3	4	5	6
Rds	640	1,920	3,200	6,400	11,200	16,000
5P Tr	660	1,980	3,300	6,600	11,550	16,500
Cpe	540	1,620	2,700	5,400	9,450	13,500
Sed	520	1,560	2,600	5,200	9,100	13,000

1917 Model 50, 8-cyl., 127" wb

	1	2	3	4	5	6
7P Tr	920	2,760	4,600	9,200	16,100	23,000

1918 Model 34-B, 6-cyl., 112" wb

	1	2	3	4	5	6
5P Tr	640	1,920	3,200	6,400	11,200	16,000
Rds	620	1,860	3,100	6,200	10,850	15,500
Rds Cpe	540	1,620	2,700	5,400	9,450	13,500
Tr Sed	520	1,560	2,600	5,200	9,100	13,000
4P Cpe	340	1,020	1,700	3,400	5,950	8,500
Sed	320	960	1,600	3,200	5,600	8,000

1919 Model 34-B, 6-cyl., 112" wb

	1	2	3	4	5	6
5P Tr	640	1,920	3,200	6,400	11,200	16,000
Rds	620	1,860	3,100	6,200	10,850	15,500
Rds Cpe	540	1,620	2,700	5,400	9,450	13,500
Cpe	340	1,020	1,700	3,400	5,950	8,500
Sed	320	960	1,600	3,200	5,600	8,000

1920 Model 34-C, 6-cyl., 112" wb

	1	2	3	4	5	6
Tr	640	1,920	3,200	6,400	11,200	16,000
Rds	620	1,860	3,100	6,200	10,850	15,500
Sed	420	1,260	2,100	4,200	7,350	10,500
Cpe	520	1,560	2,600	5,200	9,100	13,000

1921-22 Model 34-C, 6-cyl., 115" wb

	1	2	3	4	5	6
Tr	680	2,040	3,400	6,800	11,900	17,000
Rds	660	1,980	3,300	6,600	11,550	16,500
Sed	420	1,260	2,100	4,200	7,350	10,500
Cpe	520	1,560	2,600	5,200	9,100	13,000

1923 Model 6-44, 6-cyl., 115" wb

	1	2	3	4	5	6
Rds	680	2,040	3,400	6,800	11,900	17,000
Tr	700	2,100	3,500	7,000	12,250	17,500
Spt Rds	700	2,100	3,500	7,000	12,250	17,500
Spt Tr	720	2,160	3,600	7,200	12,600	18,000
2P Cpe	380	1,140	1,900	3,800	6,650	9,500
4P Cpe	376	1,128	1,880	3,760	6,580	9,400
Sed	300	900	1,500	3,000	5,250	7,500

1924-25 Model 6-54, 6-cyl., 113" wb

	1	2	3	4	5	6
5P Tr	760	2,280	3,800	7,600	13,300	19,000
Spl Tr	780	2,340	3,900	7,800	13,650	19,500
Rds	740	2,220	3,700	7,400	12,950	18,500
Spl Rds	760	2,280	3,800	7,600	13,300	19,000
4P Cpe	540	1,620	2,700	5,400	9,450	13,500
Lan Cpe	540	1,620	2,700	5,400	9,450	13,500
Sed	400	1,200	2,000	4,000	7,000	10,000
Lan Sed	420	1,260	2,100	4,200	7,350	10,500
2d Sed	380	1,140	1,900	3,800	6,650	9,500
2d Lan Sed	400	1,200	2,000	4,000	7,000	10,000

1926-27 Greater Six, 6-cyl., 113" wb

	1	2	3	4	5	6
Tr	780	2,340	3,900	7,800	13,650	19,500
Spt Phae	800	2,400	4,000	8,000	14,000	20,000
Rds	760	2,280	3,800	7,600	13,300	19,000
Spt Rds	780	2,340	3,900	7,800	13,650	19,500
Lan Cpe	580	1,740	2,900	5,800	10,150	14,500
2d Sed	520	1,560	2,600	5,200	9,100	13,000
Sed	420	1,260	2,100	4,200	7,350	10,500
Lan Sed	520	1,560	2,600	5,200	9,100	13,000

1928 Model 212, All-American, 6-cyl., 117" wb

	1	2	3	4	5	6
Spt Rds	820	2,460	4,100	8,200	14,350	20,500
Phae	840	2,520	4,200	8,400	14,700	21,000
Lan Cpe	600	1,800	3,000	6,000	10,500	15,000
Cabr	760	2,280	3,800	7,600	13,300	19,000
2d Sed	560	1,680	2,800	5,600	9,800	14,000
Sed	540	1,620	2,700	5,400	9,450	13,500
Lan Sed	560	1,680	2,800	5,600	9,800	14,000

1929 Model 212, All-American, 6-cyl., 117" wb

	1	2	3	4	5	6
Spt Rds	1,120	3,360	5,600	11,200	19,600	28,000
Spt Phae	1,160	3,480	5,800	11,600	20,300	29,000
Cpe	600	1,800	3,000	6,000	10,500	15,000
Conv	1,040	3,120	5,200	10,400	18,200	26,000
2d Sed	560	1,680	2,800	5,600	9,800	14,000
Brgm	600	1,800	3,000	6,000	10,500	15,000
Sed	540	1,620	2,700	5,400	9,450	13,500
Spl Sed	560	1,680	2,800	5,600	9,800	14,000
Lan Sed	580	1,740	2,900	5,800	10,150	14,500

1930 Model 101, V-8, 117" wb

	1	2	3	4	5	6
Spt Rds	1,120	3,360	5,600	11,200	19,600	28,000
Phae	1,160	3,480	5,800	11,600	20,300	29,000
Cpe	720	2,160	3,600	7,200	12,600	18,000
Spt Cpe	760	2,280	3,800	7,600	13,300	19,000
2d Sed	600	1,800	3,000	6,000	10,500	15,000
Sed	580	1,740	2,900	5,800	10,150	14,500
Cus Sed	592	1,776	2,960	5,920	10,360	14,800

1931 Model 301, V-8, 117" wb

	1	2	3	4	5	6
Cpe	760	2,280	3,800	7,600	13,300	19,000
Spt Cpe	800	2,400	4,000	8,000	14,000	20,000
Conv	1,160	3,480	5,800	11,600	20,300	29,000
2d Sed	580	1,740	2,900	5,800	10,150	14,500
Sed	592	1,776	2,960	5,920	10,360	14,800
Cus Sed	600	1,800	3,000	6,000	10,500	15,000

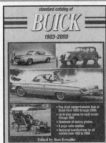

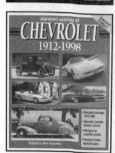

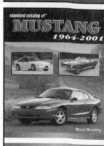